Accounting and Finance for Managers

Claud Pitts III

George K. Sharghi

Larry Gonzales

University of Phoenix

SIMON & SCHUSTER
CUSTOM PUBLISHING

Cover Art: "Discombobulated," by Marcie Wolf-Hubbard
Cover Design: Marika Alzadon

Excerpts taken from:

Introduction to Management Accounting, Tenth Edition,
by Charles T. Horngren, Gary L. Sundem, and William O. Stratton
Copyright © 1996, 1993, 1990, 1987, 1984, 1981, 1978, 1974, 1970, 1965 by Prentice-Hall, Inc.
Simon & Schuster Company / A Viacom Company
Upper Saddle River, New Jersey 07458

Foundations of Finance, by Arthur J. Keown, David F. Scott, Jr.,
John D. Martin, and J. William Petty
Copyright © 1994 by Prentice-Hall, Inc.
Simon & Schuster Company / A Viacom Company
Upper Saddle River, New Jersey 07458

Introduction to Financial Accounting, Sixth Edition
by Charles T. Horngren, Gary L. Sundem, and John A. Elliott
Copyright © 1996, 1993, 1990, 1988, 1987, 1984, 1981 by Prentice-Hall, Inc.
Simon & Schuster Company / A Viacom Company
Upper Saddle River, New Jersey 07458

Essentials of Finance: An Integrated Approach,
by George W. Gallinger and Jerry B. Poe
Copyright © 1995 by Prentice-Hall, Inc.
Simon & Schuster Company / A Viacom Company
Upper Saddle River, New Jersey 07458

Fundamentals of Financial Management, Ninth Edition,
by James C. Van Horne and John M. Wachowicz, Jr.
Copyright © 1995 by Prentice-Hall, Inc.
Simon & Schuster Company / A Viacom Company
Upper Saddle River, New Jersey 07458

Basic Financial Management, Seventh Edition, by Arthur J. Keown,
David F. Scott, Jr., John D. Martin, and J. William Petty
Copyright © 1996 by Prentice-Hall, Inc.
Simon & Schuster Company / A Viacom Company
Jpper Saddle River, New Jersey 07458

special edition published in cooperation with
ı & Schuster Custom Publishing

in the United States of America

8   7   6   5   4   3   2   1

6-59911-4

'ON & SCHUSTER CUSTOM PUBLISHING
ould Street/Needham Heights, MA 02194
ı & Schuster Education Group

CONTENTS

CHAPTER 6   Analyzing Cost Behavior   165

SECTION 3   Cost Management Systems   193

CHAPTER 7   Introduction to Cost Management Systems   195

CHAPTER 8   Relevant Accounting Information Used to Make Marketing Decisions   227

CHAPTER 9   Relevant Accounting Information Used to Make Production Decisions   261

SECTION 4   Financial Planning and Forecasting   281

CHAPTER 10   The Formal Budgeting Process   283

CHAPTER 11   Flexible Budgets and Standard Cost Systems   311

CHAPTER 20   Introduction to Capital Budgeting   581

CHAPTER 21   Capital Budgeting Decisions and Depreciation   619

SECTION 9   Capital Structure, Leasing, and Debt Financing   639

CHAPTER 22   Introduction to Cost of Capital   641

CHAPTER 23   Term Loans and Leasing Financing   681

CHAPTER 24   Valuing Long-Term Debt   707

SECTION 10   Equity Financing and Business Restructuring   729

CHAPTER 25   Valuing Preferred and Common Stock   731

CHAPTER 26   Business Restructuring and Failure   751

APPENDICES   773

ACCOUNTING GLOSSARY   787

FINANCE GLOSSARY   797

TOPIC INDEX   811

COMPANY INDEX   821

The Accounting Environment

CHAPTER 1

Introduction to Accounting

Accounting information can help managers in all types of organizations answer vital questions. Consider the following broad range of problems that demand solutions:

- Boeing engineers have prepared manufacturing specifications for a new airplane, the 7X7. There are three possible ways to organize the assembly of the plane. Which is the most cost-effective approach?
- A product manager at Kellogg's is designing a new marketing plan for Frosted Flakes. Market research predicts that distributing free samples in the mail will increase annual sales by 4%. How will the cost of the free samples (including the cost of distributing them) compare with the profits from the added sales?
- University National Bank offers free checking to customers who keep a minimum balance of $300 in their account. How much does it cost the bank to provide this free service?
- Kitsap County Special Olympics holds a series of athletic events for disabled youth. How much money must be raised in the group's annual fund drive to support its planned activities?
- Chez Bonaparte is a dinner-only restaurant located in a middle-class neighborhood. The proprietor is considering opening for lunch. To be competitive, the average lunch must be priced about $7, and about 40 patrons can be served. Can the restaurant produce a lunch that meets its quality standards at an average cost of less than $7?
- The Monroe County School District is negotiating with the teacher's union. Among the issues are teachers' salaries, class size, and number of extracurricular activities offered. The union and the district have each made several proposals. How much will each of the various proposals cost? If class size were to increase by one student per class, what would be the added cost, and would these costs differ for elementary, junior high, and high school levels?

In answering these and a wide variety of other questions, managers turn to accounting for information. In this chapter, we consider the purposes and roles of accounting and accountants in different types of organizations as well as some of the trends and challenges faced by accountants today.

PURPOSES OF ACCOUNTING

Ultimately, all accounting information is accumulated to help someone make decisions. That someone may be a company president, a production manager, a hospital or school administrator, a sales manager, a shareholder, a small-business owner, a politician—the list is almost infinite. Almost all managers in every organization are better equipped to perform their duties when they have a reasonable grasp of accounting data. For example, a knowledge of accounting is crucial for decisions by government agencies regarding research contracts, defense contracts, and loan guarantees. The U.S. government continually makes decisions about loan guarantees to tiny businesses (for instance, through the Small Business Administration) and large corporations (such as Chrysler) as well as to banks and savings and loan companies. In fact, a survey of managers ranked accounting as the most important business course for future managers.

Users of Accounting Information

In general, users of accounting information fall into three categories.

1. Internal managers who use the information for short-term planning and controlling routine operations.
2. Internal managers who use the information for making nonroutine decisions (e.g., investing in equipment, pricing products and services, choosing which products to emphasize or de-emphasize) and formulating overall policies and long-range plans.
3. External parties, such as investors and government authorities, who use the information for making decisions about the company.

Both internal parties (managers) and external parties share an interest in accounting information, but their uses differ. Therefore, the types of accounting information they demand may also differ. *Management accounting* refers to accounting information developed for managers within an organization. In other words, **management accounting** is the process of identifying, measuring, accumulating, analyzing, preparing, interpreting, and communicating information that helps managers fulfill organizational objectives. In contrast, **financial accounting** refers to accounting information developed for the use of external parties such as stockholders, suppliers, banks, and government regulatory agencies.[1] The major distinctions between management accounting and financial accounting are listed in Figure 1-1.

The Need for Accounting Systems

Despite these differences, most organizations prefer a general-purpose accounting system that can supply appropriate information to all three types of users. An **accounting system** is a formal mechanism for gathering, organizing, and communicating information about an organization's activities. A good accounting system helps

---

[1]For a book-length presentation of the subject, see Charles T. Horngren, Gary L. Sundem, and John A. Elliott, *Introduction to Financial Accounting* (Englewood Cliffs, NJ: Prentice Hall, 1996).

FIGURE 1-1   Distinctions Between Management Accounting and Financial Accounting

	Management Accounting	Financial Accounting
Primary users	Organization managers at various levels.	Outside parties such as investors and government agencies but also organization managers.
Freedom of choice	No constraints other than costs in relation to benefits of improved management decisions.	Constrained by generally accepted accounting principles (GAAP).
Behavioral implications	Concern about how measurements and reports will influence managers' daily behavior.	Concern about how to measure and communicate economic phenomena. Behavioral considerations are secondary, although executive compensation based on reported results may have behavioral impacts.
Time focus	Future orientation: formal use of budgets as well as historical records. Example: 19X6 budget versus 19X6 actual performance.	Past orientation: historical evaluation. Example: 19X6 actual performance versus 19X5 actual performance
Time span	Flexible, varying from hourly to 10 to 15 years.	Less flexible; usually 1 year or 1 quarter.
Reports	Detailed reports: concern about details of parts of the entity, products, departments, territories, etc.	Summary reports: concern primarily with entity as a whole.
Delineation of activities	Field is less sharply defined. Heavier use of economics, decision sciences, and behavioral sciences.	Field is more sharply defined. Lighter use of related disciplines.

---

an organization achieve its goals and objectives by helping to answer three types of questions.

1. *Scorecard questions:* Am I doing well or poorly? **Scorekeeping** is the accumulation and classification of data. This aspect of accounting enables both internal and external parties to evaluate organizational performance. The collection, classification, and reporting of scorekeeping information is the task that dominates day-to-day accounting.
2. *Attention-directing questions:* Which problems should I look into? **Attention directing** means reporting and interpreting information that helps managers to

focus on operating problems, imperfections, inefficiencies, and opportunities. This aspect of accounting helps managers to concentrate on important areas of operations promptly enough for effective action. Attention directing is commonly associated with current planning and control, and with the analysis and investigation of recurring *routine* internal accounting reports.

3. *Problem-solving questions:* Of the several ways of doing a job, which is the best? The **problem-solving** aspect of accounting quantifies the likely results of possible courses of action and often recommends the best course to follow. Problem solving is commonly associated with nonrecurring decisions, situations that require special accounting analyses or reports.

The scorecard and attention-directing uses of information are closely related. The same information may serve a scorecard function for a manager and an attention-directing function for the manager's superior. For example, many accounting systems provide performance reports in which actual results of decisions and activities are compared with previously determined plans. By pinpointing where actual results differ from plans, such performance reports can show managers how they are doing and show the managers' superiors where to take action. In addition, the actual results help answer scorecard questions of financial accounting, which is chiefly concerned with reporting the results of the organization's activities to external parties.

In contrast, problem-solving information may be used in long-range planning and in making special, nonrecurring decisions, such as whether to make or buy parts, replace equipment, or add or drop a product. These decisions often require expert advice from specialists such as industrial engineers, budgetary accountants, and statisticians.

Sometimes all three facets of accounting overlap, making it difficult to classify a particular accounting task as a scorekeeping, attention-directing, or problem-solving task. Nevertheless, attempts to make these distinctions provide insight into the objectives and tasks of both accountants and managers. Figure 1-2 summarizes the relationships among the types of accounting information and their uses. Remember, however, that accounting systems are worthwhile only if they lead to better decisions.

Internal Versus External Accounting Systems

Using one accounting system for both financial and management purposes sometimes creates problems. External forces (for example, income tax authorities and regulatory bodies such as the U.S. Securities and Exchange Commission and the California Health Facility Commission) often limit management's choices of accounting methods for external reports. Many organizations develop systems primarily to satisfy legal requirements imposed by external parties. These systems often neglect the needs of internal users.

Consider the annual financial reports by public corporations. These reports must adhere to a set of standards known as **generally accepted accounting principles (GAAP)**. GAAP includes broad concepts or guidelines and detailed practices, including all conventions, rules, and procedures, that together make up accepted accounting practice at a given time. However, internal accounting reports need not be restricted by GAAP. For instance, GAAP requires that organizations account for their assets (economic resources) according to their historical cost. For its own manage-

Type of Accounting Information	Major Uses: Helping Decisions
Problem-Solving Information	1. Managers for Long-Range Planning and Special Decisions
Scorekeeping Information Attention-Directing Information Problem-Solving Information	2. Managers for Planning and Controlling Routine Operations
Scorekeeping Information	3. Outsiders (Investors, Tax Collectors, Regulators, and Others) for Various Decisions

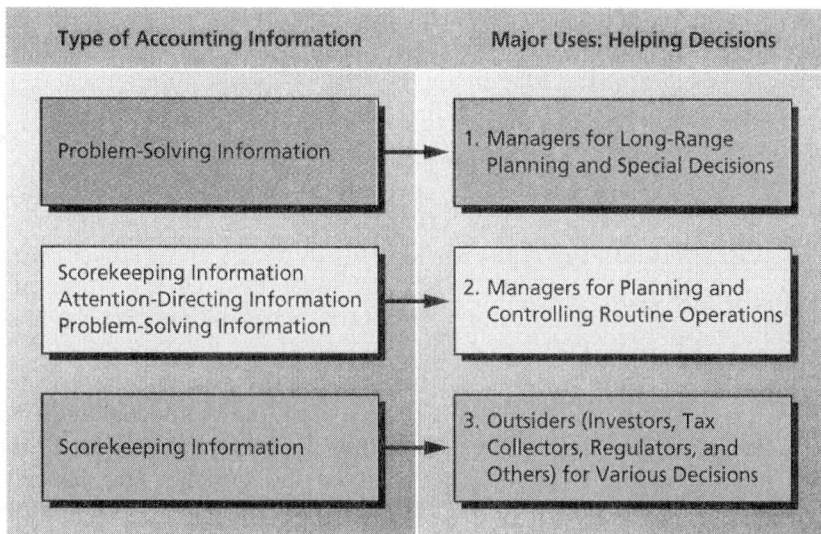

FIGURE 1-2
Uses of Accounting Information

ment purpose, however, an organization can account for its economic resources on the basis of their *current values*, as measured by estimates of replacement costs. No outside agency can prohibit such accounting. Managers can create whatever kind of internal accounting system they want—provided they are willing to pay the cost of developing and operating the system.

Of course, satisfying internal demands for information (as well as external demands) means that organizations may have to keep more than one set of records. At least in the United States, there is nothing immoral or unethical about having simultaneous sets of books—but they are expensive. Because external financial reports are required by authorities, many organizations do not choose to invest in a separate system for internal management purposes. Managers are forced to use information designed to meet external users' needs instead of information designed for their specific decisions.

Effects of Government Regulation

Even when management is willing to pay for a separate internal accounting system, that system may be affected by government regulation. The reason is that government agencies have legal power to order into evidence any internal document that they deem necessary.

Universities and defense contractors, for example, must allocate costs to government contracts in specified ways or risk government's refusal to pay. For example, in a widely publicized case in the early 1990s, Stanford University and several other prominent universities were denied reimbursement for certain costs that the government deemed inappropriate.

The **Foreign Corrupt Practices Act** is a U.S. law forbidding bribery and other corrupt practices. This law also requires that accounting records be maintained in reasonable detail and accuracy, and that an appropriate system of internal accounting controls be maintained. The title is misleading because the act's provisions apply to all publicly held companies, even if they conduct no business outside the United States.

The greatest impact of the act on accounting systems stems from the requirement that management must document the adequacy of internal accounting controls. As a result, many companies have greatly increased their internal auditing staffs and have elevated the status of such staffs. Often the internal audit staff reports directly to the president, sometimes even to the board of directors.

Internal auditors help review and evaluate systems to help minimize errors, fraud, and waste. More important, many internal auditing staffs have a primary responsibility for conducting management audits. A **management audit** is a review to determine whether the policies and procedures specified by top management have been implemented. Management audits are not confined to profit-seeking organizations. The General Accounting Office (GAO) of the U.S. government conducts these audits on a massive scale. Most states also have audit agencies that audit departments of the state government. Some also audit municipalities and other local government organizations.

The overall impact of government regulation is very controversial. Many managers insist that the extra costs of compliance far exceed any possible benefits. One benefit, however, is that operating managers, now more than ever, must become more intimately familiar with their accounting systems. The resulting changes in the systems sometimes provide stronger controls and more informative reports.

MANAGEMENT ACCOUNTING IN SERVICE AND NONPROFIT ORGANIZATIONS

The basic ideas of management accounting were developed in manufacturing organizations. These ideas, however, have evolved so that they are applicable to all types of organizations including service organizations. Service organizations, for our purposes, are all organizations other than manufacturers, wholesalers, and retailers. That is, they are organizations that do not make or sell tangible goods. Public accounting firms, law firms, management consultants, real estate firms, transportation companies, banks, insurance companies, and hotels are profit-seeking service organizations.

Almost all nonprofit organizations, such as hospitals, schools, libraries, museums, and government agencies, are also service organizations. Managers and accountants in nonprofit organizations have much in common with their counterparts in profit-seeking organizations. There is money to be raised and spent. There are budgets to be prepared and control systems to be designed and implemented. There is an obligation to use resources wisely. If used intelligently, accounting contributes to efficient operations and helps nonprofit organizations achieve their objectives.

The characteristics of both profit-seeking and nonprofit service organizations include the following:

1. *Labor is intensive:* The highest expenses in schools and law firms are wages, salaries, and payroll-related costs, not the costs relating to the use of machinery, equipment, and physical facilities.

2. *Output is usually difficult to define:* The output of a university might be defined as the number of degrees granted, but many critics would maintain that the real output is "what is contained in the students' brains." Therefore, measuring output is often considered impossible.

3. *Major inputs and outputs cannot be stored:* An empty airline seat cannot be saved for a later flight, and a hotel's available labor force and rooms are either used or unused as each day occurs.

In this book, references are made to service industry and nonprofit organization applications as the various management accounting techniques are discussed. A major generalization is worth mentioning at the outset. Simplicity is the watchword for installation of systems in service industries and nonprofit organizations. In fact, many professionals such as physicians, professors, or government officials resist even filling out a time card. In fact, simplicity is a fine watchword for the design of any accounting system. Complexity tends to generate costs of gathering and interpreting data that often exceed prospective benefits. Concern for simplicity is sometimes expressed as KISS (which means "keep it simple, stupid").

COST-BENEFIT AND BEHAVIORAL CONSIDERATIONS

In addition to simplicity, two major themes should guide the design of all accounting systems: (1) cost-benefit balances and (2) behavioral implications. Both will be described briefly now. Because of their importance, both will also be mentioned often in succeeding chapters.

The **cost-benefit balance**—weighing estimated costs against probable benefits—is the primary consideration in choosing among accounting systems and methods. The need to balance costs and benefits dominates management accounting and will dominate this book. Systems and methods are economic goods available at various costs. Which system does a manager want to buy? A simple file drawer for amassing receipts and canceled checks? An elaborate budgeting system based on computerized descriptive models of the organization and its subunits? Or something in between?

The answer depends on the buyer's perceptions of the expected benefits in relation to the costs. For example, a hospital administrator may contemplate the installation of a Technicon computerized system for controlling hospital operations. Users of such a system need only enter a piece of information once. The system automatically incorporates that datum into financial records, medical records, costs by departments, nurse staffing requirements, drug administration, billings for patients, revenue generated by physicians, and so forth. Such a system is highly efficient and is subject to few errors. The system costs $14 million, however. Thus the system is neither a "good buy" nor a "bad buy" in itself. Rather, it must meet the test of the economics of information—its value must exceed its cost.

The value of a loaf of bread may exceed a cost of 50¢ a loaf, but it may not exceed a cost of $5 per loaf. Similarly, a particular accounting system may be a wise investment if its cost is sufficiently small. Like a consumer who switches from bread to potatoes if the cost of bread is too high, managers seek other sources of information if accounting systems are too expensive. In many organizations it may be more economical to gather some kinds of data by one-shot special efforts than by a ponderous system that repetitively gathers rarely used data.

The need to balance costs and benefits appeals to both the hard-headed manager and the theoretician. Managers have been using the cost-benefit test for years, even though they may refer to it as "just being practical."

In addition to the costs and benefits of an accounting system, the buyer of such a system should also consider **behavioral implications**, that is, the system's effect on the behavior (decisions) of managers. The system must provide accurate, timely budgets and performance reports in a form useful to managers. If managers do not use accounting reports, the reports create no benefits.

Management accounting reports affect employees' feelings and behavior. Consider a performance report that is used to evaluate the operations under the responsibility of a particular manager. If the report unfairly attributes excessive costs to the operation, the manager may lose confidence in the system and not let it influence future decisions. In contrast, a system that managers believe in and trust can be a major influence on their decisions and actions.

In a nutshell, management accounting can best be understood as a balance between costs and benefits coupled with an awareness of the importance of behavioral effects. Even more than financial accounting, management accounting spills over into related disciplines, such as economics, the decision sciences, and the behavioral sciences.

THE MANAGEMENT PROCESS AND ACCOUNTING

Regardless of the type of organization, managers benefit when accounting provides information that helps them plan and control the organization's operations.

The Nature of Planning and Controlling

The management process is a series of activities in a cycle of planning and control. **Decision making**—the purposeful choice from among a set of alternative courses of action designed to achieve some objective—is the core of the management process. Decisions range from the routine (making daily production schedules) to the nonroutine (launching a new product line).

Decisions within an organization are often divided into two types: (1) planning decisions and (2) control decisions. In practice, planning and control are so intertwined that it seems artificial to separate them. In studying management, however, it is useful to concentrate on either the planning phase or the control phase to simplify the analysis.

The left side of Figure 1-3 demonstrates the planning and control cycle of current operations. *Planning* (the top box) refers to setting objectives and outlining how they will be attained. Thus planning provides the answers to two questions: What is desired? When and how is it to be accomplished? In contrast, *controlling* (the two boxes labeled "Action" and "Evaluation") refers to *implementing* plans and *using feedback* to attain objectives. Feedback is crucial to the cycle of planning and control. Planning determines action, action generates feedback, and feedback influences further planning. Timely, systematic reports provided by the internal accounting system are the chief source of useful feedback.

Management by Exception

The right side of Figure 1-3 shows that accounting formalizes *plans* by expressing them as budgets. A **budget** is a quantitative expression of a plan of action; it is also an aid to coordinating and implementing the plan. Budgets are the chief devices for compelling and disciplining management planning. Without budgets, planning may not get the front-and-center focus that it usually deserves.

Accounting formalizes control as **performance reports** (the last box), which provide feedback by comparing results with plans and by highlighting **variances**, which are deviations from plans. The accounting system records, measures, and classifies actions in order to produce performance reports.

Figure 1-4 shows a simple performance report for a law firm. Performance reports are used to judge decisions and the productivity of organizational units and managers. By comparing actual results to budgets, performance reports motivate managers to achieve the budgeted objectives.

Performance reports spur investigation of exceptions—items for which actual amounts differ significantly from budgeted amounts. Operations are then brought into conformity with the plans, or the plans are revised. This is often called **management by exception**, which means concentrating on areas that deviate from the plan and ignoring areas that are presumed to be running smoothly. Thus the management-by-exception approach frees managers from needless concern with those phases of operations that are adhering to plans. However, well-conceived plans should incorporate enough discretion or flexibility so that the manager may feel free to pursue

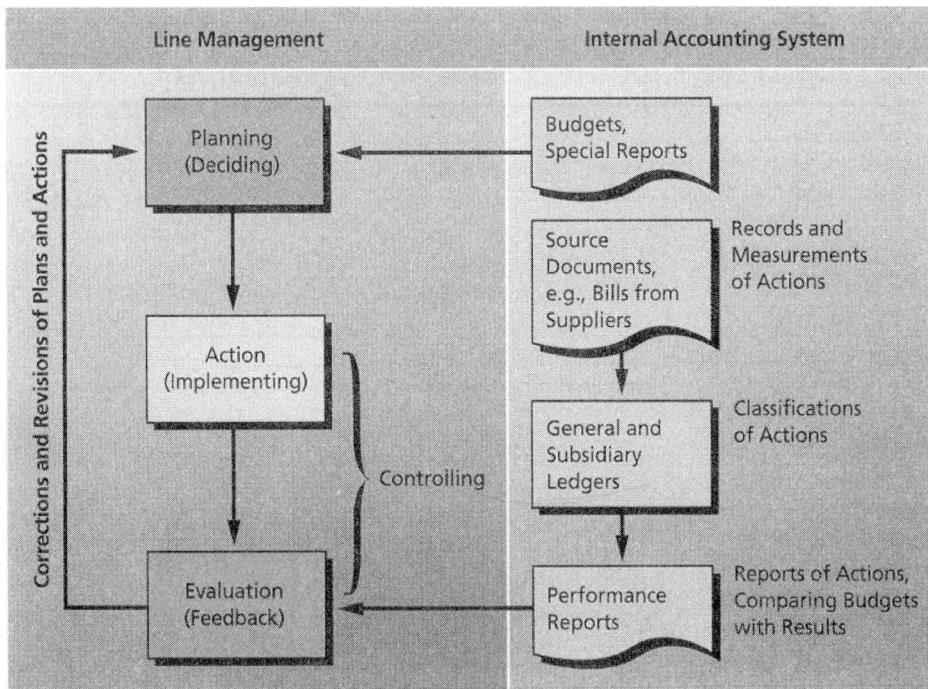

FIGURE 1-3
Accounting Framework for Planning and Control

any unforeseen opportunities. In other words, control should not be a straightjacket. When unfolding events call for actions not specifically authorized in the plan, managers should be able to take these actions.

FIGURE 1-4   Performance Report

	Budgeted Amounts	Actual Amounts	Deviations or Variances	Explanation
Revenue from fees	XXX	XXX	XX	—
Various expenses	XXX	XXX	XX	—
Net income	**XXX**	**XXX**	**XX**	—

Illustration of Budgets and Performance Reports

Suppose the Casaverde Company manufactures electric fans. Consider the department that assembles the fans. Workers assemble the parts and install the motor largely by hand. They then inspect each fan before transferring it to the packaging and shipping department. The present sales forecast has led managers to plan a production schedule of 10,000 fans for the coming month. The assembly department budget in Figure 1-5 shows cost classifications.

FIGURE 1-5   Casaverde Company
Assembly Department Budget for the Month Ended March 31, 19X1

Production activity	10,000 fans
Material (detailed by type: metal stampings, motors, etc.)	$ 68,000
Assembly labor (detailed by job classification, number of workers, etc.)	43,000
Other labor (managers, inspectors)	12,000
Utilities, maintenance, etc.	7,500
Supplies (small tools, lubricants, etc.)	2,500
Total	**$133,000**

The operating plan for the department, in the form of a department budget for the coming month, is prepared in conferences attended by the department manager, the manager's supervisor, and an accountant. They scrutinize each of the costs subject to the manager's control. They often use the average amount of the cost for the past few months as a guide, especially if past performance has been good. However, the budget is a *forecast* of costs for the projected level of production activity. Hence, conference members must predict each cost in light of trends, price changes, alterations in product mix and characteristics, production methods, and changes in the level of production activity from month to month. Only then can they formulate the budget that becomes the manager's target for the month.

As actual factory costs are incurred, Casaverde's accounting system collects them and classifies them by department. At the end of the month (or weekly, or even daily, for such key items as materials or assembly labor), the accounting department prepares an assembly department performance report. Figure 1-6 is a simplified report. In practice, this report may be very detailed and contain explanations of variances from the budget.

Department heads and their superiors use the performance report to help appraise how effectively and efficiently the department is operating. Their focus is on the variances—the deviations from the budget. Casaverde's assembly department performance report (Figure 1-6) shows that although the department produced 140 fewer fans than planned, material costs were $1,000 over budget, and assembly labor was $1,300 over budget. By investigating such variances managers may find better ways of doing things.

FIGURE 1-6	Casaverde Company			
	Assembly Department Performance Report for the Month Ended March 31, 19X1			
		Budget	Actual	Variance
Production activity in units		10,000	9,860	140 U
Material (detailed by type: metal stampings, motors, etc.)		$ 68,000	$ 69,000	$1,000 U
Assembly labor (detailed by job classification, number of workers, etc.)		43,000	44,300	1,300 U
Other labor (managers, inspectors)		12,000	11,200	800 F
Utilities, maintenance, etc.		7,500	7,400	100 F
Supplies (small tools, lubricants, etc.)		2,500	2,600	100 U
Total		$133,000	$134,500	$1,500 U

U = Unfavorable; actual exceeds budget
F = Favorable; actual is less than budget

Notice that although budgets aid planning and performance reports aid control, it is not accountants but other managers and their subordinates who evaluate accounting reports and actually plan and control operations. Accounting *assists* the managerial planning and control function by providing prompt measurements of actions and by systematically pinpointing trouble spots.

PLANNING AND CONTROL FOR PRODUCT LIFE CYCLES

Many management decisions relate to a single good or service, or to a group of related products. To effectively plan for and control production of such goods or services, accountants and other managers must consider the product's life cycle. **Product life cycle** refers to the various stages through which a product passes, from conception and development through introduction into the market through maturation and, finally, withdrawal from the market. At each stage, managers face differing costs and potential returns. Figure 1-7 shows a typical product life cycle.

FIGURE 1-7   Typical Product Life Cycle

No Sales	Sales Growth	Stable Sales Level	Low Sales → No Sales
Product Development	Introduction to Market	Mature Market	Phase-out of Product

---

Product life cycles range from a few months (for fashion clothing or faddish toys) to many years (for automobiles or refrigerators). Some products, such as many computer software packages, have long development stages and relatively short market lives. Others, such as Boeing 727 airplanes, have market lives many times longer than their development stage.

In the planning process, managers must recognize revenues and costs over the entire life cycle—however long or short. Accounting needs to track actual costs and revenues throughout the life cycle, too. Periodic comparisons between *planned* costs and revenues and *actual* costs and revenues allow managers to assess the current profitability of a product, determine its current product life-cycle stage, and make any needed changes in strategy.

For example, suppose a pharmaceutical company is developing a new drug to reduce high blood pressure. The budget for the product should plan for costs without revenues in the product development stage. Most of the revenues come in the introduction and mature-market stages, and a pricing strategy should recognize the need for revenues to cover both development and phase-out costs as well as the direct costs of producing the drug. During phase-out, costs of producing the drug must be balanced with both the revenue generated and the need to keep the drug on the market for those who have come to rely on it.

ACCOUNTING'S POSITION IN THE ORGANIZATION

To assist other managers in the decision making vital to an organization's success, most companies (and many nonprofit organizations and government agencies) employ a variety of accounting personnel with various types of authority and responsibility.

Line and Staff Authority

The organization chart in Figure 1-8 shows how a typical manufacturing company divides responsibilities. Notice the distinction between line and staff authority. **Line authority** is authority exerted downward over subordinates. **Staff authority** is authority to advise but not command. It may be exerted downward, laterally, or upward.

Most organizations specify certain activities as their basic mission. Most missions involve the production and sale of goods or services. All subunits of the organization that are directly responsible for conducting these basic activities are called line departments. The others are called staff departments because their principal task is to support or service the line departments. Thus staff activities are indirectly related to the basic activities of the organization. Figure 1-8 shows a series of factory service departments that perform staff functions supporting the line functions carried on by the production departments.

The top accounting officer of an organization is often called the **controller** or, especially in a government organization, a **comptroller**. This executive, like virtually everyone in an accounting function, fills a staff role, whereas sales and production executives and their subordinates fill line roles. The accounting department does not exercise direct authority over line departments. Rather, the accounting department provides other managers with specialized service including advice and help in budgeting, analyzing variances, pricing, and making special decisions.

Figure 1-9 shows how a controller's department may be organized. In particular, note the distinctions among the scorekeeping, attention-directing, and problem-solving roles of various personnel. Unless some internal accountants are given the last two roles as their primary responsibilities, the score-keeping tasks tend to dominate and the system becomes less responsive to management's decision making.

The Controller

The controller position varies in stature and duties from company to company. In some firms the controller is confined to compiling data, primarily for external reporting purposes. In others, such as General Electric, the controller is a key executive who aids managerial planning and control throughout the company's subdivisions. In most firms controllers have a status somewhere between these two extremes. For example, their opinions on the tax implications of certain management decisions may be carefully weighed, yet their opinions on other aspects of these decisions may not be sought.

Although controllers (or comptrollers) have a staff role, they are generally empowered by the firm's president to approve, install, and oversee the organization's accounting system to ensure uniform accounting and reporting methods. In theory, the controller proposes these systems and methods to the president, who approves and orders compliance with them on the part of line personnel (thus preserving the "staff" advisory role of accounting). In practice, however, controllers usually directly specify how production records should be kept or how time records should be completed. The controller holds delegated authority from top-line management over such matters.

In theory, then, controllers have no line authority except over the accounting department. Yet, by reporting and interpreting relevant data, controllers do exert a force or influence that leads management toward logical decisions that are consistent with the organization's objectives.

Distinctions Between Controller and Treasurer

Many people confuse the offices of controller and treasurer. The Financial Executives Institute, an association of corporate treasurers and controllers, distinguishes their functions as follows:

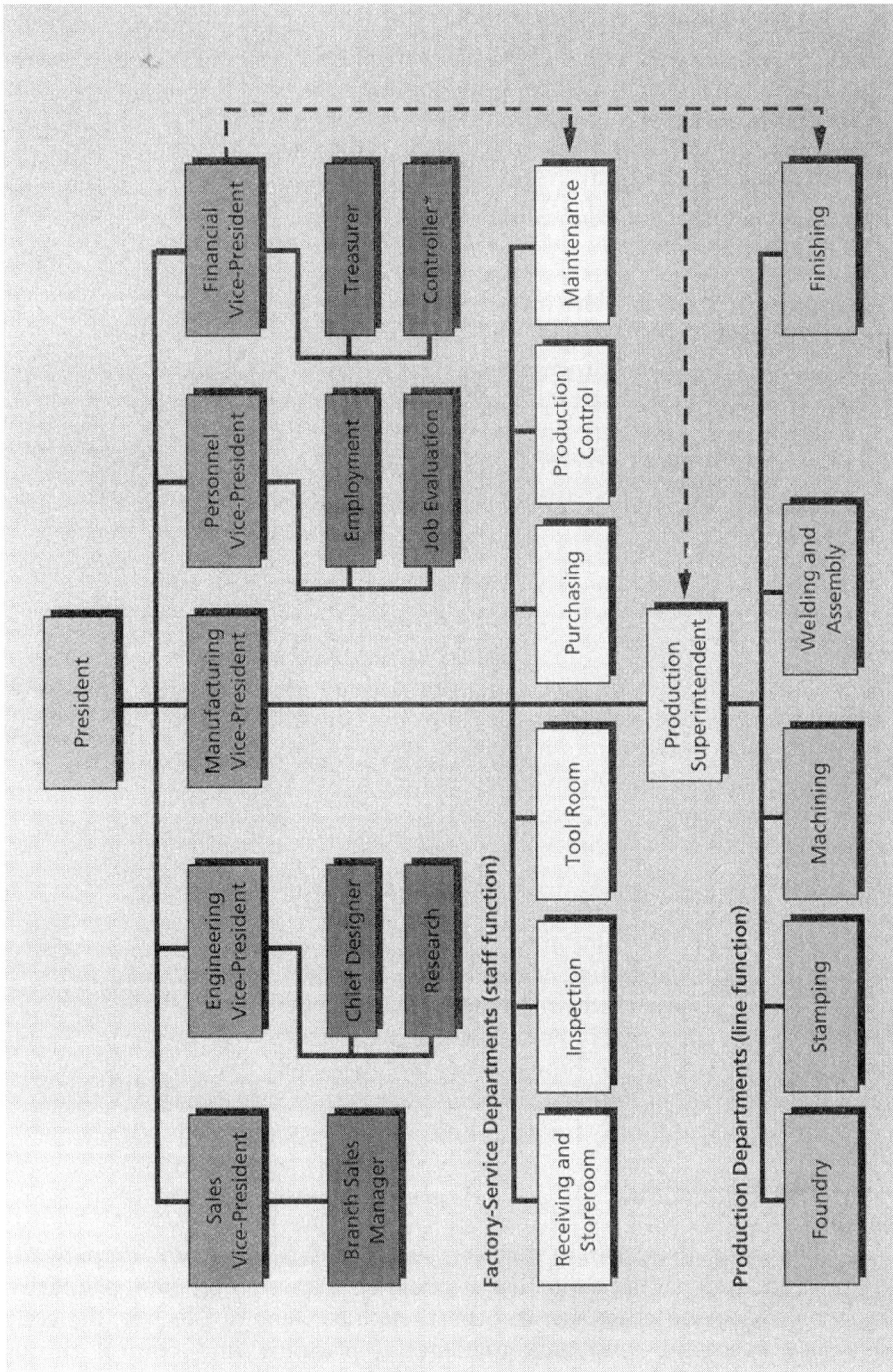

FIGURE 1-8
Partial Organization Chart of a Manufacturing Company

*For detailed organization of a controller's department, see Figure 1-9. Dashed line represents staff authority of the finance staff to advise those in manufacturing operations.

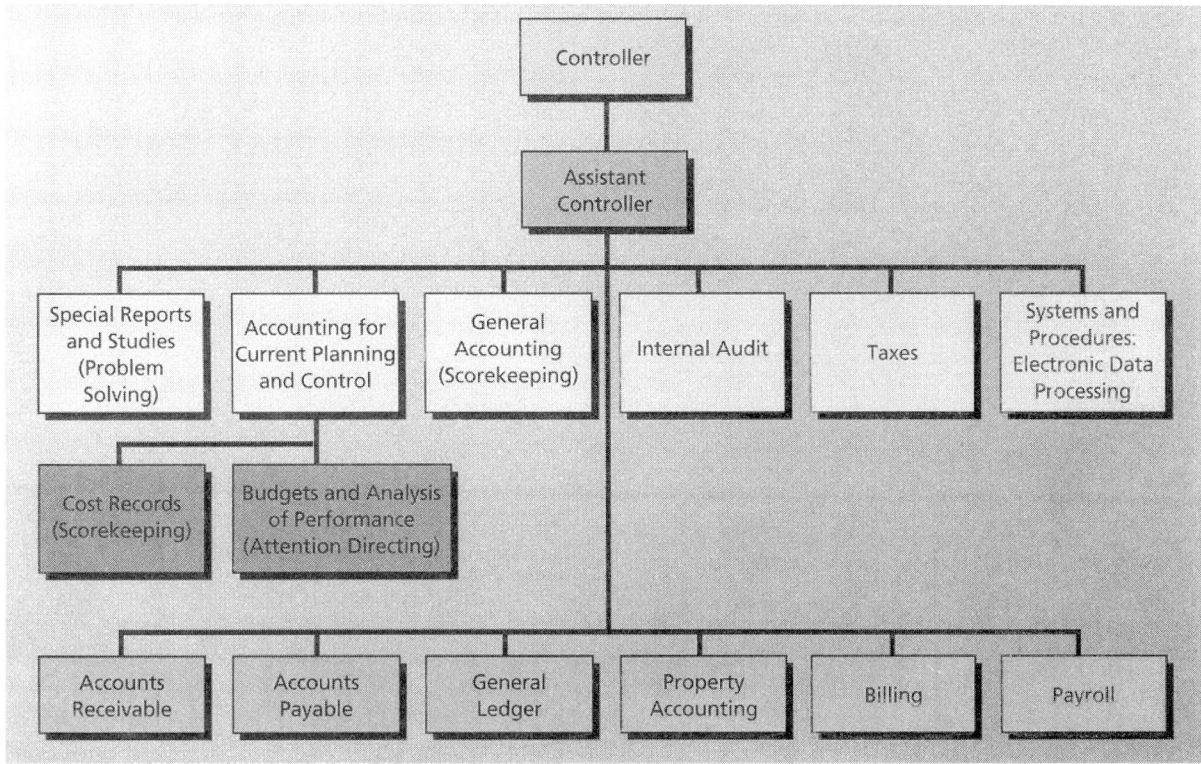

FIGURE 1-9
Organization Chart of a Controller's Department

CONTROLLERSHIP

1. Planning for control
2. Reporting and interpreting
3. Evaluating and consulting
4. Tax administration
5. Government reporting
6. Protection of assets
7. Economic appraisal

TREASURERSHIP

1. Provision of capital
2. Investor relations
3. Short-term financing
4. Banking and custody
5. Credits and collections
6. Investments
7. Risk management (insurance)

Management accounting is the primary means of implementing the first three functions of controllership.

The treasurer is concerned mainly with the company's financial matters, the controller with operating matters. The exact division of accounting and financial duties varies from company to company. In a small organization, the same person might be both treasurer and controller.

The controller has been compared with a ship's navigator. The navigator uses specialized training to assist the captain. Without the navigator, the ship may founder on reefs or miss its destination entirely. The navigator guides and informs the captain as to how well the ship is being steered, but the captain exerts the right to command. This navigator role is especially evident in the first three functions listed for controllership.

CAREER OPPORTUNITIES IN MANAGEMENT ACCOUNTING

The many types and levels of accounting personnel found in the typical organization mean that there are broad opportunities awaiting those who master the accounting discipline.

Certified Management Accountant

When accounting is mentioned, most people think first of independent auditors who reassure the public about the reliability of the financial information supplied by company managers. These external auditors are called certified public accountants in the United States and chartered accountants in many other English-speaking nations. In the United States, an accountant earns the designation of **Certified Public Accountant (CPA)** by a combination of education, qualifying experience, and the passing of a two-day written national examination. The major U.S. professional association in the private sector that regulates the quality of outside auditors is the American Institute of Certified Public Accountants (AICPA).

In recent years, increased interest in and demand for management accounting has led to development of the **Certified Management Accountant (CMA)** designation, the internal accountant's counterpart to the CPA. The **Institute of Management Accountants (IMA),** formerly called the National Association of Accountants, is the largest U.S. professional organization of accountants whose major interest is management accounting. The IMA oversees the CMA program, which has three main objectives:

1. To establish management accounting as a recognized profession by identifying the role of the management accountant and the underlying body of knowledge and by outlining a course of study by which such knowledge can be acquired
2. To foster higher educational standards in the field of management accounting
3. To establish an objective measure of an individual's knowledge and competence in the field of management accounting

The highlight of the CMA program is a two-day qualifying examination in four parts: (1) economics, finance, and management; (2) financial accounting and reporting; (3) management reporting, analysis, and behavioral issues; and (4) decision analysis and information systems.[2] The CMA designation is gaining increased stature in the management community as a credential parallel to the CPA.

Training for Top Management Positions

In addition to preparing you for a position in an accounting department, studying accounting—and working as a management accountant—can prepare you for the

[2]Information can be obtained from the IMA, 10 Paragon Drive, Montvale, NJ 07645-1759.

very highest levels of management. Accounting deals with all facets of an organization, no matter how complex, so it provides an excellent opportunity to gain broad knowledge. Accounting must embrace all management functions, including purchasing, manufacturing, wholesaling, retailing, and a variety of marketing and transportation activities. Senior accountants or controllers in a corporation are sometimes picked as production or marketing executives. Why? Because they may have impressed other executives as having acquired general management skills. A number of recent surveys have indicated that more chief executive officers began their careers in an accounting position than in any other area, including marketing, production, and engineering.

Former controllers have risen to the top of such mammoth companies as Pepsico and Pfizer. According to *Business Week,* controllers

> are now getting involved with the operating side of the company, where they give advice and influence production, marketing, and investment decisions as well as corporate planning. Moreover, many controllers who have not made it to the top have won ready access to top management. . . . Probably the main reason the controller is getting the ear of top management these days is that he or she is virtually the only person familiar with all the working parts of the company.

ADAPTATION TO CHANGE

The growing interest in management accounting also stems from its ability to help managers adapt to change. Indeed, the one constant in the world of business is change. Today's economic decisions differ from those of 10 years ago. As decisions change, demands for information change. *Accountants must adapt their systems to the changes in management practices and technology.* A system that produces valuable information in one setting may be valueless in another.

Accountants have not always been responsive to the need to change. A decade ago many managers complained about the irrelevance of accounting information. Why? Because their decision environment had changed but accounting systems had not. However, most progressive companies have now changed their accounting systems to recognize the realities of today's complex, technical, and global business environment. Instead of being irrelevant, accountants in such companies are adding more value than ever. For example, *Management Accounting* (September 1994) reported on a Champion International Corporation paper mill that made major changes in its accounting system. By working with managers to produce the information considered relevant for their decisions, accountants became regarded as "business partners." Previously, managers had considered accountants to be a "financial police department." Instead of merely pointing out problems, the accountants became part of the solution.

Current Trends

Three major factors are causing changes in management accounting today:

1. Shift from a manufacturing-based to a service-based economy
2. Increased global competition
3. Advances in technology

Each of these factors will affect your study of management accounting.

The service sector now accounts for almost 80% of the employment in the United States. Service industries are becoming increasingly competitive, and their use of accounting information is growing. Basic accounting principles are applied to service organizations throughout this book.

Global competition has increased in recent years as many international barriers to trade, such as tariffs and duties, have been lowered. In addition, there has been a worldwide trend toward deregulation. The result has been a shift in the balance of economic power in the world. Nowhere has this been more evident than in the United States. To regain their competitive edge, many U.S. companies are redesigning their accounting systems to provide more accurate and timely information about the cost of activities, products, or services. To be competitive, managers must understand the effects of their decisions on costs, and accountants must help managers predict such effects.

By far the most dominant influence on management accounting over the past decade has been technological change. This change has affected both the production and the use of accounting information. The increasing capabilities and decreasing cost of computers, especially personal computers (PCs), has changed how accountants gather, store, manipulate, and report data. Most accounting systems, even small ones, are automated. In addition, computers enable managers to access data directly and to generate their own reports and analyses in many cases. By using spreadsheet software and graphics packages, managers can use accounting information directly in their decision process. Thus, all managers need a better understanding of accounting information now than they may have needed in the past. In addition, accountants need to create databases that can be readily understood by managers.

Technological change has also dramatically changed the manufacturing environment for many companies, causing changes in how accounting information is used. Manufacturing processes are increasingly automated. Automated manufacturing processes make extensive use of robots and other computer-controlled equipment and less use of human labor for direct production activities. Many early accounting systems were designed primarily to measure and report the cost of labor. Why? Because human labor was the largest cost in the production of many products and services. Clearly, such systems are not appropriate in automated environments. Accountants in such settings have had to change their systems to produce information for decisions about how to acquire and use materials and automated equipment efficiently.

Just-in-Time Philosophy and Computer-Integrated Manufacturing

Accompanying technological change has been a change in management philosophy. The most important recent change leading to increased efficiency in American factories has been the adoption of a **just-in-time (JIT) philosophy**. The essence of the philosophy is to eliminate waste. Managers try to (1) reduce the time that products spend in the production process and (2) eliminate the time that products spend on activities that do not add value (such as inspection and waiting time).

Process time can be reduced by redesigning and simplifying the production process. Companies can use **computer-aided design (CAD)** to design products that can be manufactured efficiently. Even small changes in design often lead to large manu-facturing cost savings. Companies can also use **computer-aided manufacturing (CAM),** in which computers direct and control production equipment. CAM often leads to a smoother, more efficient flow of production with fewer delays.

Systems that use CAD and CAM together with robots and computer-controlled machines are called **computer-integrated manufacturing (CIM) systems.** Compa-nies that install a full CIM system use very little labor. Robots and computer-con-trolled machines perform the routine jobs that were previously done by assembly-line workers. In addition, well-designed systems provide great flexibility because design changes require alterations only in computer programs, not retraining of an entire work force.

Time spent on activities that do not add value to the product can be eliminated or reduced by focusing on quality, improving plant layout, and cross-training workers. Achieving zero production defects ("doing it right the first time") reduces inspection time and eliminates rework time. One midwestern factory saved production time by redesigning its plant layout so that the distance products traveled from one opera-tion to the next during production was reduced from 1,384 feet to 350 feet. Another company reduced setup time on a machine from 45 minutes to 1 minute by storing the required tools nearby and training the machine operator to do the setup. A Brit-ish company reduced the time to manufacture a vacuum pump from 3 weeks to 6 minutes by switching from long assembly lines to manufacturing cells that accom-plish the entire process in quick succession.

Originally, JIT referred only to an inventory system that minimized inventories by arranging for materials and subcomponents to arrive just as they were needed and for goods to be made just in time to be shipped to customers—no sooner and no later. But JIT has become the cornerstone of a broad management philosophy. It origi-nated in Japanese companies such as Toyota and Kawasaki, and now has been adopted by many large U.S. companies including Hewlett-Packard and Xerox. Many small firms have also embraced JIT.

Implications for the Study of Management Accounting

As you read the remainder of this book, remember that accounting systems change as the world changes. The techniques presented in this book are being applied in real organizations today. Tomorrow may be different, however. *To adapt to changes, you must understand why the techniques are being used, not just how they are used. We urge you to resist the temptation simply to memorize rules and techniques.* Instead, develop your understanding of the underlying concepts and principles. These will continue to be useful in developing and understanding new techniques for changing environments.

IMPORTANCE OF ETHICAL CONDUCT

Although accounting systems may change, the need for accountants to adhere to high ethical standards of professional conduct has never been greater.

Standards of Ethical Conduct

Public opinion surveys consistently rank accountants high in terms of their professional ethics. CPAs and CMAs adhere to codes of conduct regarding competence, confidentiality, integrity, and objectivity. Figure 1-10 contains the **Standards of Ethical Conduct for Management Accountants** developed by the IMA. Professional accounting organizations have procedures for reviewing alleged behavior not consistent with the standards.

Preparing objective, accurate external and internal financial reports is primarily the responsibility of line managers. However, management accountants are also responsible for the reports. Ensuring that accounting systems, procedures, and compilations are reliable and free of manipulation is ultimately the responsibility of every accountant.

Ethical Dilemmas

What makes an action by an accountant unethical? An unethical act is one that violates the ethical standards of the profession. The standards, however, leave much room for individual interpretation and judgment.

When one action is clearly unethical and another alternative is clearly ethical, managers and accountants should have no difficulty choosing between them. Unfortunately, most ethical dilemmas are not that clear-cut. The most difficult situations arise when there is strong pressure to take an action that is borderline or when two ethical standards conflict.

Suppose you are an accountant who has been asked to supply the company's banker with a profit forecast for the coming year. A badly needed bank loan rides on the prediction. The company president is absolutely convinced that profits will be at least $500,000. Anything less than that and the loan is not likely to be approved.

Your analysis shows that if the planned introduction of a new product goes extraordinarily well, profits will exceed $500,000. The most likely outcome, however, is for a modestly successful introduction and a $100,000 profit. If the product fails, the company stands to lose $600,000. Without the loan, the new product cannot be taken to the market, and there is no way the company can avoid a loss for the year. Bankruptcy is even a possibility.

What forecast would you make? There is no easy answer. A forecast of less than $500,000 seems to guarantee financial problems, perhaps even bankruptcy. Stockholders, management, employees, suppliers, and customers may all be hurt. But a forecast of $500,000 may not be fair and objective. The bank may be misled by it. Still, the president apparently thinks a $500,000 forecast is reasonable, and you know that there is some chance it will be achieved. Perhaps the potential benefit to the company of an overly optimistic forecast is greater than the possible cost to the bank.

There is no right answer to this dilemma. The important point is to recognize the ethical dimensions and weigh them when forming your judgment.

The tone set by top management can have a great influence on managers' ethics. Complete integrity and outspoken support for ethical standards by senior managers is the single greatest motivator of ethical behavior throughout an organization. In

FIGURE 1-10   Standards of Ethical Conduct for Management Accountants

Management accountants have an obligation to the organizations they serve, their profession, the public, and themselves to maintain the highest standards of ethical conduct. In recognition of this obligation, the Institute of Management Accountants has adopted the following standards of ethical conduct for management accountants. Adherence to these standards is integral to achieving the objectives of management accounting. Management accountants shall not commit acts contrary to these standards nor shall they condone the commission of such acts by others within their organizations.

Competence

Management accountants have a responsibility to
- Maintain an appropriate level of professional competence by ongoing development of their knowledge and skills.
- Perform their professional duties in accordance with relevant laws, regulations, and technical standards.
- Prepare complete and clear reports and recommendations after appropriate analyses of relevant and reliable information.

Confidentiality

Management accountants have a responsibility to
- Refrain from disclosing confidential information acquired in the course of their work except when authorized, unless legally obligated to do so.
- Inform subordinates as appropriate regarding the confidentiality of information acquired in the course of their work and monitor their activities to assure the maintenance of that confidentiality.
- Refrain from using or appearing to use confidential information acquired in the course of their work for unethical or illegal advantage either personally or through third parties.

Integrity

Management accountants have a responsibility to
- Avoid actual or apparent conflicts of interest and advise all appropriate parties of any potential conflict.
- Refrain from engaging in any activity that would prejudice their ability to carry out their duties ethically.
- Refuse any gift, favor, or hospitality that would influence or would appear to influence their actions.
- Refrain from either actively or passively subverting the attainment of the organization's legitimate and ethical objectives.
- Recognize and communicate professional limitations or other constraints that would preclude responsible judgment or successful performance of an activity.
- Communicate unfavorable as well as favorable information and professional judgments or opinions.
- Refrain from engaging in or supporting any activity that would discredit the profession.

Objectivity

Management accountants have a responsibility to
- Communicate information fairly and objectively.
- Disclose fully all relevant information that could reasonably be expected to influence an intended user's understanding of the reports, comments, and recommendations presented.

Ethics at General Motors

The importance of ethics to management accountants was emphasized when *Management Accounting,* the journal of the Institute of Management Accountants, put out a special issue on ethics in June 1990. Two thrusts run through the articles in the issue: (1) business schools must make students aware of the ethical dimension of the decisions they will face in the business world, and (2) business firms must recognize that establishing standards of ethical conduct for their employees is important to financial success. As a follow-up, *Management Accounting* instituted a regular column on ethics. A recent column presented a case on the ethics of planned obsolescence of products. Many readers submitted solutions to the case, some of which were published in *Management Accounting,* showing that ethical dilemmas generate a great deal of interest.

Roger B. Smith, former chairman and chief executive officer of General Motors, stated that "ethical practice is, quite simply, good business." Since 1977 GM has had a policy on personal integrity. But GM recognizes that making ethical decisions is not always easy. Because the world is complex, there are often competing obligations to share-holders, customers, suppliers, fellow managers, society, and self and family. As Smith says, "It is easy to do what is right; it is hard to know what is right." A basic rule used by GM is that employees "should never do anything [they] would be ashamed to explain to [their] families or be afraid to see on the front page of the local newspaper."

General Motors is not alone in promoting ethical conduct. Over half of the large companies in the United States have a "Corporate Code of Conduct." These codes provide support to employees who feel pressured to make decisions they believe to be unethical. They also provide training in the types of behavior expected of employees.

Sources: From Roger B. Smith, "Ethics in Business: An Essential Element of Success," Management Accounting, *Special Issue on Ethics in Corporate America (June 1990), p. 50; Robert B. Sweeney and Howard L. Siers, "Ethics in America,"* Management Accounting, *Special Issue on Ethics in Corporate America (June 1990), pp. 34–40; and James A. Healy and Roy L. Nersesian, "The Case of Planned Obsolescence,"* Management Accounting *(February 1994), pp. 67–68.*

the final analysis, however, ethical standards are personal and depend on the values of the individual.

SUMMARY

Accounting information is useful to internal managers for making short-term planning and control decisions, for making nonroutine decisions, and for formulating overall policies and long-range plans. The accounting information answers scorekeeping, attention-directing, and problem-solving questions. Management accounting focuses on information for internal decision makers (managers), and financial accounting focuses on information for external parties.

Many management accounting techniques were developed in profit-seeking manufacturing companies because such companies often had a greater need for sophisticated accounting information. However, there is increasing application of management accounting in service and nonprofit organizations.

Management accounting systems exist for the benefit of managers. Systems should be judged by a cost-benefit criterion—the benefits of better decisions should exceed the cost of the system. The benefit of a system will be affected by behavioral factors—how the system affects managers and their decisions.

An essential tool for performance evaluation is a budget. A performance report compares actual results to the budget. To interpret accounting information about a particular product appropriately, it is often important to recognize the product's position in its product life cycle.

Accountants are staff employees who provide information and advice for line managers. The head of accounting is often called the controller. Unlike the treasurer, who is concerned primarily with financial matters, the controller measures and reports on operating performance.

The future worth of an accounting system will be affected by how easily and well the system can adapt to change. A changing business environment may require the accounting system to collect and report new data and discontinue reporting information that is no longer needed. Changes affecting accounting systems include growth in the service sector of the economy, increased global competition, and advances in technology. Information needs of organizations that adopt a just-in-time philosophy or use computer-aided design and manufacturing systems differ from those of more traditional firms.

Finally, both external and internal accountants are expected to adhere to standards of ethical conduct. Many ethical dilemmas, however, require value judgments, not the simple application of standards.

SELF-CORRECTION PROBLEMS

Try to solve these problems before examining the solutions that follow.

1. The scorekeeping, attention-directing, and problem-solving duties of the accountant have been described in this chapter. The accountant's usefulness to management is said to be directly influenced by how good an attention director and problem solver he or she is.

    Evaluate this contention by specifically relating the accountant's duties to the duties of operating management.

2. Using the organization charts in this chapter (Figures 1-8 and 1-9), answer the following questions:

    a. Which of the following have line authority over the machining manager: maintenance manager, manufacturing vice-president, production superintendent, purchasing agent, scorekeeper, personnel vice-president, president, chief budgetary accountant, chief internal auditor?

    b. What is the general role of service departments in an organization? How are they distinguished from operating or production departments?

    c. Does the controller have line or staff authority over the cost accountants? The accounts receivable clerks?

    d. What is probably the *major duty* (scorekeeping, attention directing, or problem solving) of the following?

Payroll clerk	Cost analyst
Accounts receivable clerk	Head of internal auditing
Cost record clerk	Head of special reports and studies
Head of general accounting	Head of accounting for planning
Head of taxes	and control
Budgetary accountant	Controller

3. Yang Electronics Company (YEC) developed a high-speed, low-cost copying machine. It marketed the machine primarily for home use. However, as YEC customers learned how easy and inexpensive it was to make copies with the YEC machine, its use by small businesses grew. Sales soared as some businesses ordered large numbers of the copiers. However, the heavier use by these companies caused breakdowns in a certain component of the equipment. The copiers were warrantied for two years, regardless of the amount of usage. Consequently, YEC experienced high costs for replacing the damaged components.

　　As the quarterly meeting of the Board of Directors of YEC approached, Mark Chua, assistant controller, was asked to prepare a report on the situation. Unfortunately, it was hard to predict the exact effects. However, it seemed that many business customers were starting to switch to more expensive copiers sold by competitors. And it was clear that the increased maintenance costs would significantly affect YEC's profitability. Mark summarized the situation as best he could for the Board.

　　Alice Martinez, the controller of YEC, was concerned about the impact of the report on the Board. She does not disagree with the analysis, but thinks it makes management look bad and might even lead the Board to discontinue the product. She is convinced from conversations with the head of engineering that the copier can be slightly redesigned to meet the needs of higher-volume users, so discontinuing it may pass up a potentially profitable opportunity.

　　Martinez called Chua into her office and asked him to delete the part of his report dealing with the component failures. She said it was all right to mention this orally to the Board, noting that engineering is nearing a solution to the problem. However, Chua feels strongly that such a revision in his report would mislead the Board about a potentially significant negative impact on the company's earnings.

Explain why Martinez's request to Chua is unethical. How should Chua resolve this situation?

SOLUTIONS TO SELF-CORRECTION PROBLEMS

1. Operating managers may have to be good scorekeepers, but their major duties are to concentrate on the day-to-day problems that most need attention, to make longer-range plans, and to arrive at special decisions. Accordingly, because managers are concerned mainly with attention directing and problem solving, they will obtain the most benefit from the alert internal accountant who is a useful attention director and problem solver.

2. a. The only executives having line authority over the machining manager are the president, the manufacturing vice-president, and the production superintendent.
   b. A typical company's major purpose is to produce and sell goods or services. Unless a department is directly concerned with producing or selling, it is called a service or staff department. Service departments exist only to help the production and sales departments with their major tasks: the efficient production and sale of goods or services.

c. The controller has line authority over all members of his or her own department, all those shown in the controller's organization chart (Figure 1-9).

d. The major duty of the first five—through the head of taxes—is typically scorekeeping. Attention directing is probably the major duty of the next three. Problem solving is probably the primary duty of the head of special reports and studies. The head of accounting for planning and control and the controller should be concerned with all three duties: scorekeeping, attention directing, and problem solving. However, there is a perpetual danger that day-to-day pressures will emphasize scorekeeping. Therefore accountants and managers should constantly see that attention directing and problem solving are also stressed. Otherwise the major management benefits of an accounting system may be lost.

3. According to the Standards of Ethical Conduct for Management Accountants in Figure 1-10, Martinez's request violates requirements for competence, integrity, and objectivity. It violates competence because she is asking Chua to prepare a report that is not complete and clear, one that omits potentially relevant information. Therefore, the Board will not have all the information it should to make a decision about the component failure problem.

The request violates the integrity requirement because the revised report may subvert the attainment of the organization's objectives in order to achieve Martinez's objectives. Management accountants are specifically responsible for communicating unfavorable as well as favorable information.

Finally, the revised report would not be objective. It would not disclose all relevant information that could be expected to influence the Board's understanding of operations and therefore their decisions.

Chua's responsibility is to discuss this issue with increasingly higher levels of authority within YEC. First, he should let Martinez know about his misgivings. Possibly the issue can be resolved by her withdrawing the request. If not, he should inform her that he intends to take up the matter with her superior and then continue up to higher levels of authority, even to the Board, if necessary, until the issue is resolved. So that Chua does not violate the standard of confidentiality, he should not discuss the matter with persons outside of YEC.

QUESTIONS

1. Why does an organization invest resources in an accounting system?
2. Distinguish among scorekeeping, attention directing, and problem solving.
3. "The emphases of financial accounting and management accounting differ." Explain.
4. "The field is less sharply defined. There is heavier use of economics, decision sciences, and behavioral sciences." Identify the branch of accounting described in the quotation.
5. "Additional government regulation assists the development of management accounting systems." Do you agree? Explain.
6. "The Foreign Corrupt Practices Act applies to bribes paid outside the United States." Do you agree? Explain.

7. Give three examples of service organizations. What distinguishes them from other types of organizations?
8. What two major considerations affect all accounting systems? Explain each.
9. "The accounting system is intertwined with operating management. Business operations would be a hopeless tangle without the paperwork that is so often regarded with disdain." Do you agree? Explain, giving examples.
10. Distinguish among a budget, a performance report, and a variance.
11. "Management by exception means abdicating management responsibility for planning and control." Do you agree? Explain.
12. "Good accounting provides automatic control of operations." Do you agree? Explain.
13. Why are accountants concerned about the product life cycle?
14. Distinguish between line and staff authority.
15. "The controller does control in a special sense." Explain.
16. "Planning is much more vital than control." Do you agree? Explain.
17. Describe the contents of the qualifying examination for becoming a CMA.
18. How are changes in technology affecting management accounting?
19. What is the essence of the JIT philosophy?
20. Standards of ethical conduct for management accountants have been divided into four major responsibilities. Describe each of the four in 20 words or less.
21. "Why are there ethical dilemmas? I thought accountants had standards that specified what is ethical behavior." Discuss.

PROBLEMS

1. **Scorekeeping, Attention Directing, and Problem Solving.**   For each of the activities listed below, identify the function that the accountant is performing—scorekeeping, attention directing, or problem solving. Also state whether the departments mentioned are production or service departments.

   a. Analyzing, for a Ford production superintendent, the impact on costs of some new drill presses.
   b. Preparing a scrap report for the finishing department of a Honda parts factory.
   c. Preparing the budget for the maintenance department of St. Jude's Hospital.
   d. Interpreting why a Springfield foundry did not adhere to its production schedule.
   e. Explaining the stamping department's performance report.
   f. Preparing a monthly statement of European sales for the Ford marketing vice-president.
   g. Preparing, for the manager of production control of an Inland Steel plant, a cost comparison of two computerized manufacturing control systems.
   h. Interpreting variances on the Yale University purchasing department's performance report.
   i. Analyzing, for a Honda international manufacturing manager, the desirability of having some auto parts made in Korea.
   j. Preparing a schedule of depreciation for forklift trucks in the receiving department of a General Electric factory in Scotland.

2. **Management by Exception.** The Gamma-Omega fraternity held a homecoming party. The fraternity expected attendance of 80 persons and prepared the following budget:

Room rental	$ 150
Food	800
Entertainment	600
Decorations	220
Total	**$1,770**

After all bills for the party were paid, the total cost came to $1,948, or $178 over budget. Details are $150 for room rental; $1,008 for food; $600 for entertainment; and $190 for decorations. Ninety-five persons attended the party.

a. Prepare a performance report for the party that shows how actual costs differed from the budget. That is, include in your report the budget amounts, actual amounts, and variances.
b. Suppose the fraternity uses a management-by-exception rule. Which costs deserve further examination? Why?

3. **Accounting's Position in the Organization: Line and Staff Functions.**

a. Of the following, who has line authority over a cost record clerk: budgetary accountant, head of accounting for current planning and control, head of general accounting, controller, storekeeper, production superintendent, manufacturing vice-president, president, production control chief?
b. Of the following, who has line authority over an assembler: stamping manager, assembly manager, production superintendent, production control chief, storekeeper, manufacturing vice-president, engineering vice-president, president, controller, budgetary accountant, cost record clerk?

4. **Scorekeeping, Attention Directing, and Problem Solving.** For each of the activities listed below identify the function the accountant is performing—scorekeeping, attention directing, or problem solving. Also state whether the departments for which the tasks are performed are production or service departments. If a department is neither of these, name the department and indicate whether it is staff or line.

a. Daily recording of material purchase vouchers.
b. Analyzing the costs of acquiring and using each of two alternate types of welding equipment.
c. Preparing a report of overtime labor costs by production departments.
d. Posting daily cash collections to customers' accounts.
e. Estimating the costs of moving corporate headquarters to another city.
f. Interpreting increases in nursing costs per patient-day in a hospital.
g. Analyzing deviations from the budget of the factory maintenance department.
h. Assisting in a study by the manufacturing vice-president to determine whether to buy certain parts needed in large quantities for manufacturing products or to acquire facilities for manufacturing these parts.
i. Allocating factory service department costs to production departments.
j. Recording overtime hours of the product finishing department.

k. Compiling data for a report showing the ratio of advertising expenses to sales for each branch store.

l. Investigating reasons for increased returns and allowances for drugs purchased by a hospital.

m. Preparing a schedule of fuel costs by months and government departments.

n. Estimating the operating costs and outputs that could be expected for each of two large metal-stamping machines offered for sale by different manufacturers. Only one of these machines is to be acquired by your company.

o. Computing and recording end-of-year adjustments for expired fire insurance on the factory warehouse for materials.

5. **Management by Exception.** The Lummi Indian Tribe sells fireworks for the 4 weeks preceding July 4. The tribe's stand at the corner of Highway 104 and Acorn Road was the largest, with budgeted sales for 19X5. of $70,000. Expected expenses were as follows:

Cost of fireworks	$30,000
Labor cost	15,000
Other costs	8 000
Total costs	**$53,000**

Actual sales were $69,860, almost equal to the budget. The tribe spent $34,000 for fireworks, $13,000 for labor, and $8,020 for other costs.

a. Compute budgeted profit and actual profit.

b. Prepare a performance report to help identify those costs that were significantly different from the budget.

c. Suppose the tribe uses a management-by-exception rule. What costs deserve further explanation? Why?

6. **Accounting's Position in Organization: Controller and Treasurer.** For each of the following activities, indicate whether it is most likely to be performed by the controller (C) or treasurer (T):

a. Prepare credit checks on customers.

b. Help managers prepare budgets.

c. Advise which alternative action is least costly.

d. Prepare divisional financial statements.

e. Arrange short-term financing.

f. Prepare tax returns.

g. Arrange insurance coverage.

h. Meet with financial analysts from Wall Street.

Accounting Concepts, Techniques, and Conventions

Accounting is often called the language of business. It has a special vocabulary aimed at conveying the financial story of organizations. To understand corporate annual reports, you must learn at least the fundamentals of the language. This chapter introduces the basic words and ideas used by accountants and other managers when discussing financial matters. It also introduces financial statements—what they say and, equally important, what they do not say.

You will explore the essence of profit-making activities and how accountants portray them. The more technical processes (e.g., ledger accounts) and language (e.g., debit and credit) are left for the chapter appendices. As we examine what accountants do, we introduce the relevant concepts and conventions. Although our focus will be on profit-seeking organizations, the main ideas also apply to nonprofit organizations.

THE NEED FOR ACCOUNTING

Most people think of accountants as scorekeepers who determine whether a business is making money (and how much, if any). In fact, all kinds of organizations (sometimes called *entities*)—government agencies, nonprofit organizations, and others—rely on accounting to gauge their progress.

Managers, investors, and other interest groups usually want the answers to two important questions about an organization: How well did the organization perform for a given period? Where does the organization stand at a given point? Accountants answer these questions with two major financial statements: an *income statement* and a *balance sheet*. To obtain these statements, accountants continually record the history of an organization. Through the financial accounting process, the accountant accumulates, analyzes, quantifies, classifies, summarizes, and reports events and their effects on the organization.

The accounting process focuses on transactions. A **transaction** is any event that affects the financial position of an organization and requires recording. Through the years, many concepts, conventions, and rules have been developed regarding what events are to be recorded as *accounting transactions* and how their financial impact is measured. These concepts will be introduced gradually over the remaining chapters.

FINANCIAL STATEMENTS

Financial statements are summarized reports of accounting transactions. They can apply to any point in time and to any span of time.

An efficient way to learn about accounting is to study a specific illustration. Suppose King Hardware Company began business as a corporation on March 1. An opening *balance sheet* follows:

King Hardware Company
Balance Sheet (Statement of Financial Position) As of March 1, 19X1

Assets		Equities	
Cash	$100,000	Paid-in capital	$100,000

The **balance sheet** (more accurately called **statement of financial position** or **statement of financial condition**) is a snapshot of financial status at an instant of time. It has two counterbalancing sections—assets and equities. **Assets** are economic resources that are expected to benefit future activities. **Equities** are the claims against, or interests in, the assets.

The accountant conceives of the balance sheet as an equation:

$$\text{assets} = \text{equities}$$

The equities side of this fundamental equation is often divided as follows:

$$\text{assets} = \text{liabilities} + \text{owners' equity}$$

Liabilities are the entity's economic obligations to nonowners. **Owners' equity** is the excess of the assets over the liabilities. For a **corporation**—a business organized as a separate legal entity and owned by its stockholders—the owners' equity is called **stockholders' equity**. In turn, the stockholders' equity is composed of the ownership claim against, or interest in, the total assets arising from any paid-in investment (**paid-in capital**), plus the ownership claim arising as a result of profitable operations (**retained income** or **retained earnings**):

$$\begin{aligned} \text{assets} \ &= \ \text{liabilities} + \text{stockholders' equity} \\ &= \ \text{liabilities} + (\text{paid-in capital} + \text{retained earnings}) \end{aligned}$$

Consider a summary of King Hardware's *transactions* in March:

1. Initial investment by owners, $100,000 cash.
2. Acquisition of inventory for $75,000 cash.
3. Acquisition of inventory for $35,000 on open account. A purchase (or a sale) on open account is an agreement whereby the buyer pays cash some time after the date of sale, often in 30 days. Amounts owed on open accounts are usually called **accounts payable**, liabilities of the purchasing entity.
4. Merchandise carried in inventory at a cost of $100,000 was sold on open account for $120,000. These open customer accounts are called **accounts receivable**, assets of the selling entity.
5. Cash collections of accounts receivable, $30,000.
6. Cash payments of accounts payable, $10,000.
7. On March 1, $3,000 cash was disbursed for store rent for March, April, and May. Rent is $1,000 per month, payable quarterly in advance, beginning March 1.

Note that these are indeed *summarized* transactions. For example, all the sales did not occur at once, nor did all purchases of inventory, collections from customers, or disbursements to suppliers. Many repetitive transactions occur in practice, and specialized data collection techniques are used to measure their effects on the organization.

The foregoing transactions can be analyzed using the balance sheet equation, as shown in Figure 2-1.

Transaction 1, the initial investment by owners, increases assets and increases equities. That is, cash increases and so does paid-in capital—the claim arising from the owners' total initial investment in the corporation.

Transactions 2 and 3, the purchases of inventory, are steps toward the ultimate goal—the earning of a profit. But stockholders' equity is unaffected. That is, no profit is recorded until a sale is made.

Transaction 4 is the sale of $100,000 of inventory for $120,000. Two things happened simultaneously: a new asset, Accounts Receivable, is acquired (4a) in exchange for the giving up of Inventory (4b), and Stockholders' Equity is increased by the amount of the asset received ($120,000) and decreased by the amount of the asset given up ($100,000). The increase in Stockholders' Equity is called *revenue* or *sales*, and the decrease is an *expense* called *cost of goods sold*.

Transaction 5, cash collection of accounts receivable, is an example of an event that has no impact on stockholders' equity. Collections are merely the transformation of one asset (Accounts Receivable) into another (Cash).

Transaction 6, cash payment of accounts payable, also does not affect stockholders' equity—it affects assets and liabilities only. In general, collections from customers and payments to suppliers have no direct impact on stockholders' equity, unless part of the payment represents *interest expense*.

Transaction 7, the cash disbursement for rent, is made to acquire the right to use store facilities for the next 3 months. On March 1, the $3,000 measured the future benefit from these services, so the asset *Prepaid Rent* was created (7a). Prepaid rent is an asset even though you cannot see or touch it as you can such assets as cash or inventory. Assets also include legal rights to future services such as the use of facilities.

Transaction 7b recognizes that one-third of the rental services has expired during March, so the asset is reduced and stockholders' equity is also reduced by $1,000 as rent *expense* for March. This recognition of rent expense means that $1,000 of the asset Prepaid Rent has been "used up" (or has flowed out of the entity) in the conduct of operations during March.

For simplicity, we have assumed no expenses other than *cost of goods sold* and *rent*. Based on this information, King's accountant can prepare at least two financial statements—the balance sheet and the income statement—as follows:

King Hardware Co.
Income Statement for the Month Ended March 31, 19X1

Sales (revenue)		$120,000
Expenses		
Cost of goods sold	$100,000	
Rent	1,000	
Total expenses		101,000
Net income		$ 19,000

King Hardware Co.
Balance Sheet as of March 31, 19X1

Assets		Liabilities and Stockholders' Equity		
Cash	$ 42,000	Liabilities: accounts payable		$ 25,000
Accounts receivable	90,000	Stockholders' equity		
Inventory	10,000	Paid-in capital	$100,000	
Prepaid rent	2,000	Retained income	19,000	119,000
Total	$144,000	Total		$144,000

Relationship of Balance Sheet and Income Statement

The **income statement** measures the performance of an organization by matching its accomplishments (revenue from customers, which is usually called *sales*)[1] and its efforts (*cost of goods sold* and other expenses). The balance sheet shows the organization's financial position at an instant of time, but the income statement measures performance for a span of time, whether it be a month, a quarter, or longer. Thus, the income statement is the major link between balance sheets.

Examine the changes in retained income in Figure 2-1. The accountant records *revenue* and *expense* to indicate increases (revenues) and decreases (expenses) in the owners' claims. At the end of a given period, these items are summarized in the form of an income statement. The heading of a balance sheet indicates a *single date*. The heading of an income statement indicates a specific *period*. A balance sheet is a destination; an income statement is a journey.

---

[1]Income statements for British companies use "turnover" instead of "sales." Other countries' financial statements use the same basic approach as U.S. statements, but terminology and specific measurement rules may differ.

FIGURE 2-1   King Hardware Co.
Analysis of Transactions (in Dollars) for March 19X1

| | Assets | | | | Liabilities + | Equities | |
| | | | | | | Stockholders' Equity | |
Transactions	Cash +	Accounts Receivable +	Inventory +	Prepaid Rent	Accounts = Payable +	Paid-in Capital +	Retained Income
1. Initial investment	+100,000				=	+100,000	
2. Acquire inventory for cash	−75,000		+75,000		=		
3. Acquire inventory for credit			+35,000		= +35,000		
4a. Sales on credit		+120,000			=		+120,000 (revenue)
4b. Cost of inventory sold			−100,000		=		−100,000 (expense)
5. Collect from customers	+30,000	−30,000			=		
6. Pay accounts of suppliers	−10,000				= −10,000		
7a. Pay rent in advance	−3,000			+3,000	=		
7b. Recognize expiration of rental services				−1,000	=		− 1,000 (expense)
Balance, 3/31/X1	+42,000	+ 90,000	+ 10,000	+2,000	=+ 25,000	+ 100,000	+ 19,000

144,000   144,000

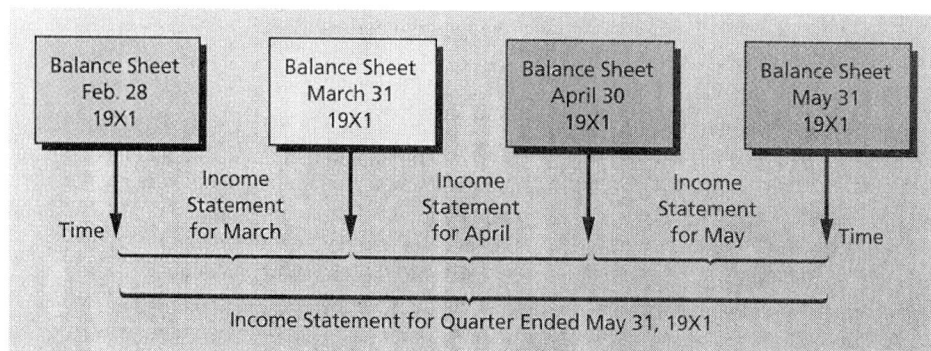

Each item in a financial statement is frequently called an **account**. In the preceding example, the outflows of assets are represented by decreases in the inventory and prepaid rent accounts and corresponding decreases in stockholders' equity in the form of cost of goods sold and rent expense. Expense accounts are basically negative elements of stockholders' equity. Similarly, the sales (revenue) account is a positive element of stockholders' equity.

Revenues and Expenses

Return to Figure 2-1, and review transaction 4. Notice that this transaction has two phases, a revenue phase (4a) and an expense phase (4b) (dollar signs omitted):

Description of Transactions	Assets		=	Equities	
Balances after transaction 3 in Figure 2-1		135,000*	=		135,000*
4a. Sales on credit (inflow)	Accounts receivable	+120,000	=	Stockholders' equity	+120,000
4b. Cost of inventory sold (outflow)	Inventory	−100,000	=	Stockholders' equity	−100,000
Balances, after transaction 4		155,000	=		155,000

*Cash of $100,000 − $75,000	=	$ 25,000	Accounts payable	$ 35,000
Inventory of $75,000 + $35,000	=	110,000	Paid-in capital	100,000
		$135,000		$135,000

Transaction 4a illustrates the recognition of revenue. **Revenues** generally arise from gross increases in assets from delivering goods or services. To be recognized (i.e., formally recorded in the accounting records as revenue during the current period), revenue must ordinarily meet two tests. First, revenues must be *earned*. That is, the goods must be delivered or services must be fully rendered to customers. Second, revenues must be *realized*. That is, an exchange of resources evidenced by a market transaction must occur (e.g., the buyer pays or promises to pay cash and the seller delivers merchandise). If cash is not received directly, the collectibility of the asset (e.g., an account receivable) must be reasonably assured.

Transaction 4b illustrates the incurrence of an expense. **Expenses** generally arise from gross decreases in assets from delivering goods or services.

Transactions 4a and 4b also illustrate the fundamental meaning of **profits** or **earnings** or **income**, which is the excess of revenues over expenses.

As the Retained Income column in Figure 2-1 shows, increases in revenues also increase stockholders' equity. In contrast, increases in expenses decrease stockholders' equity.

Transactions 2 and 3 were purchases of merchandise inventory. They were steps toward the ultimate goal—the earning of a profit. But by themselves purchases earn no profit; remember that stockholders' equity was unaffected by the inventory acquisitions in transactions 2 and 3. That is, no profit is recognized until a sale is actually made to customers.

Transaction 4 is the $120,000 sale on open account of inventory that had cost $100,000. Two things happen simultaneously: a $120,000 inflow of assets in the form of accounts receivable (4a) in exchange for a $100,000 outflow of assets in the form of inventory (4b). Liabilities are completely unaffected, so owners' equity increases by $120,000 – $100,000, or $20,000.

Users of financial statements desire an answer to the question: How well did the organization perform for a given period? The income statement helps answer this question. King Hardware Co. has a positive change in stockholders' equity attributable solely to operations. This change is measured by the revenue and expenses that constitute income for the specific period.

For an example of a real company, consider Childrobics, Inc., the company that owns and operates "Play Centers" for children and families in the New York City metropolitan area. The company was incorporated in 1993, and at the end of its first year (on February 28, 1994) it reported:

Revenues	$250,393
Expenses	247,877
Net income	$ 2,516

The company paid no dividends, so its retained earnings increased from $0 to $2,516 during the year.

The Analytical Power of the Balance Sheet Equation

The balance sheet equation can highlight the link between the income statement and balance sheet. Indeed, the entire accounting system is based on the simple balance sheet equation:

$$\text{assets (A)} = \text{liabilities (L)} + \text{stockholders' equity (SE)} \tag{1}$$

SE equals the original ownership claim plus the increase in ownership claim because of profitable operations. That is, SE equals the claim arising from paid-in capital plus the claim arising from retained income. Therefore:

$$A = L + \text{paid-in capital} + \text{retained income} \qquad (2)$$

Then, because retained income equals revenue minus expenses (see Figure 2-1):

$$A = L + \text{paid-in capital} + \text{revenue} - \text{expenses} \qquad (3)$$

Revenue and *expense accounts* are nothing more than subdivisions of stockholders' equity—temporary stockholders' equity accounts. Their purpose is to summarize the volume of sales and the various expenses, so that management is kept informed of the reasons for the continual increases and decreases in stockholders' equity in the course of ordinary operations. In this way, managers can make comparisons, set standards or goals, and exercise better control.

Notice in Figure 2-1 that, for each transaction, the equation is *always* kept in balance. If the items affected are confined to one side of the equation, you will find the total amount added equal to the total amount subtracted on that side. If the items affected are on both sides, then equal amounts are simultaneously added or subtracted on each side.

The striking feature of the balance sheet equation is its universal applicability. No transaction has ever been conceived, no matter how simple or complex, that cannot be analyzed via the equation. The top technical partners in the world's largest professional accounting firms, when confronted with the most intricate transactions of multinational companies, will inevitably discuss and think about their analyses in terms of the balance sheet equation. They focus on its major components: assets, liabilities, and owners' equity (including the explanations of changes in owners' equity that most often take the form of revenues and expenses in an income statement).

ACCRUAL BASIS AND CASH BASIS

Measurements of income and financial position are anchored to the accrual basis of accounting, as distinguished from the cash basis. The **accrual basis** recognizes the impact of transactions on the financial statements in the periods when revenues and expenses occur instead of when cash is received or disbursed. That is, revenue is recorded as it is earned, and expenses are recorded as they are incurred—not necessarily when cash changes hands.

Transaction 4a in Figure 2-1, shows an example of the accrual basis. Revenue is recognized when sales are made on credit, not when cash is received. Similarly, transactions 4b and 7b (for cost of goods sold and rent) show that expenses are recorded as efforts are expended or services are used to obtain the revenue (regardless of when cash is disbursed). Therefore income is often affected by measurements of noncash resources and obligations. The accrual basis is the principal conceptual framework for relating accomplishments (revenues) with efforts (expenses).

More than 95% of all business is conducted on a credit basis; cash receipts and disbursements are not the critical transactions as far as the recognition of revenue and expense is concerned. Thus the accrual basis evolved in response to a desire for a more complete, and therefore more accurate, report of the financial impact of various events.

If the **cash basis** of accounting were used instead of the accrual basis, revenue and expense recognition would occur when cash is received and disbursed. In March, King Hardware would show $30,000 of revenue, the amount of cash collected from customers. Similarly, cost of goods sold would be the $10,000 cash payment for the purchase of inventory, and rent expense would be $3,000 (the cash disbursed for rent) rather than the $1,000 rent applicable to March. A cash measurement of net income or net loss is obviously ridiculous in this case, and it could mislead those unacquainted with the fundamentals of accounting.

Ponder the rent example. Under the cash basis, March must bear expenses for the entire quarter's rent of $3,000 merely because cash outflows occurred then. In contrast, the accrual basis measures performance more sharply by allocating the rental expenses to the operations of each of the 3 months that benefited from the use of the facilities. In this way, the economic performance of each month will be comparable. Most accountants maintain that it is nonsense to say that March's rent expense was $3,000 and April's and May's was zero.

The major deficiency of the cash basis of accounting is that it is incomplete. It fails to match efforts and accomplishments (expenses and revenues) in a manner that properly measures economic performance and financial position. Moreover, it omits key assets (such as accounts receivable and prepaid rent) and key liabilities (such as accounts payable) from balance sheets.

Nonprofit Organizations

The examples in this chapter are focused on profit-seeking organizations, but balance sheets and income statements are also used by nonprofit organizations. For example, hospitals and universities have income statements, although they are called *statements of revenue and expense.* The "bottom line" is frequently called "excess of revenue over expense" rather than "net income."

The basic concepts of assets, liabilities, revenues, and expenses are applicable to all organizations, whether they be utilities, symphony orchestras, private, public, American, Asian, and so forth. However, some nonprofit organizations have been slow to adopt several ideas that are widespread in progressive companies. For example, many government organizations still use the cash basis of accounting. The lack of accrual-based financial statements has hampered the evaluation of the performance of such organizations.

ADJUSTMENTS TO THE ACCOUNTS

To measure income under the accrual basis, accountants use adjustments at the end of each reporting period. **Adjustments** record *implicit transactions,* in contrast to the *explicit transactions* that trigger nearly all day-to-day routine entries.

Earlier we defined a *transaction* as any economic event that should be recorded by the accountant. Note that this definition is not confined to market transactions, which are actual exchanges of goods and services between the entity and another party. For instance, the losses of assets from fire or theft are also transactions even though no market exchange occurs.

To illustrate, entries for explicit transactions such as credit sales, credit purchases, cash received on account, and cash disbursed on account are, supported by explicit evidence, is usually in the form of **source documents** (e.g., sales slips, purchase invoices, employee time records). On the other hand, adjustments for implicit transactions, such as unpaid wages, prepaid rent, interest owed, and the like, are prepared from special schedules or memorandums that recognize events (such as the passage of time) that are temporarily ignored in day-to-day recording procedures. Adjustments refine the accountant's accuracy and provide a more complete and significant measure of efforts, accomplishments, and financial position. Hence, they are an essential part of accrual accounting. They are generally made when the financial statements are about to be prepared.

The principal adjustments may be classified into four types:

1. Expiration of Unexpired Costs
2. Recognition (Earning) of Unearned Revenues
3. Accrual of Unrecorded Expenses
4. Accrual of Unrecorded Revenues

ADJUSTMENT TYPE I: EXPIRATION OF UNEXPIRED COSTS

Assets frequently expire because of the passage of time. This first type of adjustment was illustrated in Figure 2-1 by the recognition of rent expense in transaction 7b.

Assets may be viewed as bundles of economic services awaiting future use or expiration. It is helpful to think of assets, other than cash and receivables, as prepaid or stored costs that are carried forward to future periods rather than immediately charged against revenue:

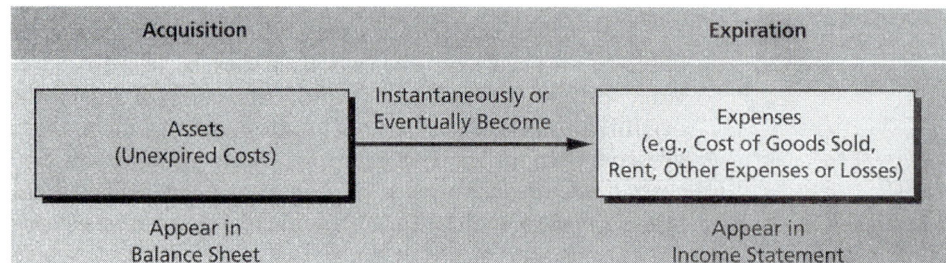

Expenses are used-up assets. An **unexpired cost** is any asset that ordinarily becomes an expense in future periods. Examples in our King Hardware Co. illustration are inventory and prepaid rent. Other examples are equipment and various prepaid expenses such as prepaid insurance and prepaid property taxes. When costs expire, accountants often say they are *written off* to expenses.

The analysis of the inventory and rent transactions in Figure 2-1 maintains this distinction of acquisition and expiration. The unexpired costs of inventory and prepaid rent are assets until they are used up and become expenses.

Timing of Asset Expiration

Sometimes services are acquired and used almost instantaneously. Examples are advertising services, interest services (the cost of money, which is a service), miscellaneous supplies, and sales salaries and commissions. Conceptually, these costs should, at least momentarily, be viewed as assets on acquisition before being written off as expenses. For example, suppose there was an eighth transaction in Figure 2-1, whereby newspaper advertising was acquired for $1,000 cash. To abide by the acquisition-expiration sequence, the transaction might be analyzed in two phases:

	Assets			= Liabilities +	Stockholders' Equity	
Transaction	Cash +	Other Assets +	Unexpired Advertising =		Paid-in Capital +	Retained Income
8a. Acquire advertising services	−1,000		+1,000 =			
8b. Use advertising services			−1,000 =			−1,000 (expense)

However, services are often acquired and used up so quickly that accountants do not bother recording an asset such as Unexpired Advertising or Prepaid Rent for them. Instead, they take a shortcut:

Transaction	Cash +	Other Assets	=	Liabilities +	Paid-in Capital +	Retained income
8 (a) and (b) together	−1,000		=			−1,000 (expense)

Making the entry in two steps instead of one may seem cumbersome, and it is—from a practical bookkeeping viewpoint. But our purpose is not to teach you to be efficient bookkeepers. We want you to develop an orderly way of thinking about what the manager does. The manager acquires goods and services, not expenses per se. These goods and services become expenses as they are used in obtaining revenue.

When does an asset expire and become an expense? Sometimes this question is not easily answered. For example, some accountants believe that research and development costs should be accounted for as assets (listed on balance sheets as "Deferred Research and Development Costs") and written off (charged as an expense) in some systematic manner over a period of years. But the regulators of financial accounting in the United States have ruled that such costs have vague future benefits that are difficult to measure reliably. Thus research costs must be written off as expenses immediately. In cases like this, research costs are not found in balance sheets. This is not always the case, however. Outside the United States, many countries, such as Japan and France, allow research and development to be recorded as an asset.

Depreciation

To keep the expense-adjustment illustration simple, until now we have deliberately ignored the accounting for long-lived assets such as equipment. Suppose King Hardware Co. had acquired some store equipment for $14,000 on March 1. Equipment is really a bundle of future services that will have a limited useful life. Accountants usually (1) predict the length of the useful life, (2) predict the ultimate **residual value** (the predicted sales value of a long-lived asset at the end of its useful life), and (3) allocate the cost of the equipment to the years of its useful life in some systematic way. This process is called the recording of depreciation expense; it applies to physical assets such as buildings, equipment, furniture, and fixtures owned by the entity. (Land is not subject to depreciation.)

The most popular depreciation method for financial reporting is the *straight-line method,* which depreciates an asset by the same amount each year. Suppose the predicted life of the equipment is 10 years, and the estimated residual value is $2,000:

$$\text{straight-line depreciation} = \frac{\text{original cost} - \text{estimated residual value}}{\text{years of useful life}}$$

$$= \frac{\$14,000 - \$2,000}{10}$$

$$= \$1,200 \text{ per year, or } \$100 \text{ per month}$$

We discuss depreciation in more detail in subsequent chapters. But the essence of the general concept of expense should be clear by now. The purchases and uses of goods and services (e.g., inventories, rent, equipment) ordinarily consist of two basic steps: (1) the *acquisition* of the *assets* (transactions 2, 3, and 7a) and (2) the *expiration* of the assets as *expenses* (transactions 4b and 7b). When these assets expire, the total assets and owners' equity are decreased.

ADJUSTMENT TYPE II: RECOGNITION (EARNING) OF UNEARNED REVENUES

Transaction 6 in Figure 2-2 is $3,000 collected in advance from customers for merchandise they ordered. This transaction is an example of **unearned revenue**, sometimes called **deferred revenue**. It is a liability because the retailer is obligated to deliver the goods ordered or to refund the money if the goods are not delivered. Some companies call this account *advances from customers* or *customer deposits*, but it is an unearned revenue account no matter what its label. That is, it is revenue collected in advance that has not yet been earned. Advance collections of rent and magazine subscriptions are other examples.

FIGURE 2-2   King Hardware Co.
Analysis of Transactions (in Dollars) for April 19X1

Transaction	Assets				=	Liabilities			+	Stockholders' Equity	
	Cash +	Accounts Receivable +	Inventory +	Prepaid Rent	=	Accounts Payable +	Accrued Wages Payable +	Unearned Sales Revenue	+	Paid-in Capital +	Retained Income
Bal. 3/31/X1	+42,000	+90,000	+10,000	+2,000	=	+25,000				+100,000	+ 19,000
1.	+88,000	−88,000			=						
2.	−24,000				=	−24,000					
3.			+80,000		=	+80,000					
4a.		+85,000			=						+ 85,000 (revenue)
4b.			−70,000		=						− 70,000 (expense)
5.				−1,000	=						− 1,000 (expense)
6.	+3,000				=			+3,000*			
7.	−6,000				=						− 6,000 (expense)
8.					=		+600				− 600 (expense)
9.	−18,000				=						− 18,000 (dividend)
4/30/X1	+85,000	+87,000	+20,000	+1,000	=	+81,000	+600	+3 000		+100,000	+ 8,400
	193,000				=	193,000					

*Some accountants would call this account "Customer Deposits," "Advances from Customers," "Deferred Sales Revenue," or "Unrealized Sales Revenue."

FIGURE 2-3   King Hardware Company
Balance Sheet as of April 30, 19X1

Assets		Liabilities and Stockholders' Equity		
Cash	$ 85,000	Liabilities		
Accounts receivable	87,000	Accounts payable	$ 81,000	
Inventory	20,000	Accrued wages payable	600	
Prepaid rent	1,000	Unearned sales revenue	3,000	$ 84,600
		Stockholders' equity		
		Paid-in capital	$100,000	
		Retained income	8,400	108,400
Total assets	**$193,000**	Total equities		**$193,000**

FIGURE 2-4   King Hardware Company
Income Statement (Multiple-Step)* for the Month Ended April 30, 19X1

Sales		$85,000
Cost of goods sold		70,000
Gross profit		$15,000
Operating expenses		
Rent	$1,000	
Wages	6,600	7,600
Net income		**$ 7,400**

*A "single-step" statement would not draw the gross profit figure but would merely list all the expenses—including cost of goods sold—and deduct the total from sales. *Gross profit* is defined as the excess of sales over the cost of the inventory that was sold. It is sometimes called *gross margin.*

FIGURE 2-5   King Hardware Company
Statement of Retained Income for the Month Ended April 30, 19X1

Retained income, March 31, 19X1	$19,000
Net income for April	7,400
Total	$26,400
Dividends	18,000
Retained income, April 30, 19X1	**$ 8,400**

Sometimes it is easier to see how accountants analyze transactions by visualizing the financial positions of both parties to a contract. For instance, consider the rent transaction of March 1. Compare the financial impact on King Hardware Co. with the impact on the landlord who received the rental payment:

	Owner of Property (Landlord, Lessor)			King Hardware Co. (Tenant, Lessee)		
	A	= L	+ SE	A	= L	+ SE
		Unearned				
		Rent	Rent		Prepaid	Rent
	Cash	Revenue	Revenue	Cash	Rent	Expense
(a) Explicit transaction (advance payment of three months' rent)	+3,000	= +3,000		−3,000 +3,000		=
(b) March adjustment (for one month's rent)		= −1,000	+1,000		−1,000	= −1,000
(c) April adjustment (for one month's rent)		= −1,000	+1,000		−1,000	= −1,000
(d) May adjustment (for one month's rent)		= −1,000	+1,000		−1,000	= −1,000

You are already familiar with the King Hardware analysis. The $1,000 monthly entries for King Hardware are examples of the first type of adjustments, the expiration of unexpired costs.

Now study the transactions from the viewpoint of the owner of the rental property. The first transaction recognizes *unearned revenue*, which is a *liability* because the lessor is obligated to deliver the rental services (or to refund the money if the services are not delivered).

As you can see from the preceding table, adjustments for the expiration of unexpired costs (Type I) and for the realization of unearned revenues (Type II) are really mirror images of each other. If one party to a contract has a prepaid expense, the other has unearned revenue. A similar analysis could be conducted for, say, a 3-year fire insurance policy or a 3-year magazine subscription. The buyer recognizes a prepaid expense (asset) and uses adjustments to spread the initial cost to expense over the life of the services. In turn, the seller, such as a magazine publisher, must initially recognize its liability, unearned subscription revenue. The *unearned* revenue is then systematically recognized as *earned* revenue as magazines are delivered throughout the life of the subscription.

You have now seen how two types of adjustments might occur: (1) expiration of unexpired costs and (2) recognition (earning) of unearned revenues. Next we consider the third type of adjustment: accrual of unrecorded expenses, as illustrated by wages.

ADJUSTMENT TYPE III: ACCRUAL OF UNRECORDED EXPENSES

Accrue means to accumulate a receivable or payable during a given period even though no explicit transaction occurs. Examples of accruals are the wages of employees for partial payroll periods and the interest on borrowed money before the interest payment date. The receivables or payables grow as the clock ticks or as some services are continuously acquired and used, so they are said to accrue (accumulate).

Computerized accounting systems can make weekly, daily, or even "real-time" recordings in the accounts for many accruals. However, such frequent entries are often costly and unnecessary. Usually, adjustments are made to bring each expense (and corresponding liability) account up to date just before the formal financial statements are prepared.

Accounting for Payment of Wages

Consider wages. Most companies pay their employees at predetermined times. Here is a sample calendar for April:

Suppose King Hardware Co. pays its employees each Friday for services rendered during that week. For example, wages paid on April 26 would be compensation for the week ended April 26. The cumulative total wages paid on the Fridays during April were $6,000. Although day-to-day and week-to-week procedures may differ from entity to entity, a popular way to account for wages expense is the shortcut procedure described earlier for goods and services that are routinely consumed in the period of their purchase:

	Assets (A) = Liabilities (L) + Stockholders' Equity (SE)		
	Cash		Wages Expense
7. Routine entry for explicit transactions	−6,000	=	−6,000

Accounting for Accrual of Wages

King Hardware Co.'s wages are $300 per day. In addition to the $6,000 already paid, King Hardware owes $600 for employee services rendered during the last 2 days of April. The employees will not be paid for these services until the next regular weekly payday, May 3, so an accrual is necessary. No matter how simple or complex a set of accounting procedures may be in a particular entity, periodic adjustments ensure that the financial statements adhere to accrual accounting. The tabulation that follows repeats entry 7 for convenience and then adds entry 8:

	A	=	L	+	SE
			Accrued Wages		Wages
	Cash		Payable		Expense
7. Routine entry for explicit transactions	−6,000	=			−6,000
8. Adjustment for implicit transaction, the accrual of unrecorded wages		=	+600		− 600
Total effects	**−6,000**	=	**+600**		**−6,600**

Conceptually, entries 7 and 8 could each be subdivided into the asset acquisition-asset expiration sequence, but this two-step sequence is not generally used in practice for such expenses that represent the immediate consumption of services.

Accrued expenses arise when payment *follows* the rendering of services; prepaid expenses arise when payment *precedes* the services. Other examples of accrued expenses include sales commissions, property taxes, income taxes, and interest on borrowed money. Interest is rent paid for the use of money, just as rent is paid for the use of buildings or automobiles. The interest accumulates (accrues) as time unfolds, regardless of when the actual cash for interest is paid.

ADJUSTMENT TYPE IV: ACCRUAL OF UNRECORDED REVENUES

The final type of adjustment, the realization of revenues that have been earned but not yet recorded as such in the accounts, is not illustrated in the "Summary Problem for Your Review." It is the mirror image of the accrual of unrecorded expenses. Suppose Security State Bank lends cash to King Hardware Co. on a 3-month promissory note for $50,000 with interest at 1% per month payable at maturity. The following tabulation shows the mirror-image effect of the adjustment for interest at the end of the first month ($.01 \times \$50,000 = \$500$):

Security State Bank (Lender)					King Hardware Co. (Borrower)				
A	=	L	+	SE		A	=	L	+	SE
Accrued Interest Receivable			Interest Revenue			Accrued Interest Payable			Interest Expense
+500	=		+500	=		+500			−500

To recapitulate, Figure 2-6 summarizes the four major types of adjustments needed to implement the accrual basis of accounting.

DIVIDENDS AND RETAINED INCOME

Figure 2-2 shows how revenues increase and expenses decrease the retained income portion of stockholders' equity. Transaction 9 shows another type of transaction that affects retained income—payment of dividends.

Dividends Are Not Expenses

Dividends are distributions of assets to stockholders that reduce retained income. (Cash dividends are distributions of *cash* rather than some other asset.) Dividends are not expenses like rent and wages. They should not be deducted from revenues because dividends are not directly related to the generation of sales or the conduct of operations.

The ability to pay dividends is fundamentally caused by profitable operations. Retained income increases as profits accumulate and decreases as dividends occur.

The entire right-hand side of the balance sheet equation can be thought of as claims against the total assets. The liabilities are the claims of creditors. The stockholders' equity represents the claims of owners arising out of their initial investment (paid-in capital) and subsequent profitable operations (retained income). As a company grows, the retained income account can soar enormously if dividends are not paid. Retained income is frequently the largest stockholders' equity account. For example, H.J. Heinz, the food products company, had retained income of $3,633 million in 1994 compared to paid-in capital of only $242 million.

FIGURE 2-6   Four Major Types of Accounting Adjustments Before Preparation of Financial Statements

		Expense		Revenue
Payment Precedes Recognition of Expense or Revenue	I	Expiration of unexpired costs. *Illustration:* The write-off of prepaid rent as rent expense (Figure 2-2, entry 5)	II	Recognition (earning) of unearned revenues. *Illustration:* The mirror image of Type I, whereby the landlord recognizes rent revenue and decreases unearned rent revenue (rent collected in advance)
Recognition of Expense or Revenue Precedes Payment	III	Accrual of unrecorded expenses. *Illustration:* wage expense for wages earned by employees but not yet paid (Figure 2-2, entry 8)	IV	Accrual of unrecorded revenues. *Illustration:* Interest revenue earned but not yet collected by a financial institution

Retained Income Is Not Cash

Although retained income is a result of profitable operations, it is not a pot of cash awaiting distribution to stockholders. Consider the following illustration:

Step 1. Assume an opening balance sheet of:

Cash	$100	Paid-in capital	$100

Step 2. Purchase inventory for $50 cash. The balance sheet now reads:

Cash	$ 50	Paid-in capital	$100
Inventory	50		
	$100		

Steps 1 and 2 demonstrate a fundamental point. Ownership equity (paid-in capital, here) is an undivided claim against the total assets (in the aggregate). For example, half the shareholders do not have a specific claim on cash, and the other half do not have a specific claim on inventory. Instead, all the shareholders have an undivided claim against (or, if you prefer, an undivided interest in) all the assets.

Step 3. Now sell the inventory for $80, which produces a retained income of $80 − $50 = $30:

Cash	$130	Paid-in capital	$100
		Retained income	30
		Total equities	$130

At this stage, the retained income might be related to a $30 increase in cash. But the $30 in retained income connotes only a *general* claim against *total* assets. This may be clarified by the transaction that follows.

Step 4. Purchase equipment and inventory, in the amounts of $70 and $50, respectively. Now cash is $130 − $70 − $50 = $10:

Cash	$ 10	Paid-in capital	$100
Inventory	50	Retained income	30
Equipment	70		
Total assets	$130	Total equities	$130

To what assets is the $30 in retained income related? Is it linked to Cash, to Inventory, or to Equipment? The answer is all three. This example helps to explain the nature of the Retained Income account. It is a claim, not a pot of gold. You cannot buy a loaf of bread with retained income.

Retained income is increased by profitable operations, but the cash inflow from sales is an increment in assets (see step 3). When the cash inflow takes place, management will use the cash, most often to buy more inventory or equipment (step 4). Retained income (and also paid-in capital) is a general claim against, or undivided interest in, total assets, not a specific claim against cash or against any other particular asset. Do not confuse the assets themselves with the claims against the assets.

Nature of Dividends

As stated earlier, dividends are distributions of assets that reduce ownership claims. The cash assets that are disbursed typically arose from profitable operations. Thus dividends or withdrawals are often spoken of as "distributions of profits" or "distributions of retained income." Dividends are often erroneously described as being "paid *out* of retained income." In reality, cash dividends are distributions of assets that liquidate a portion of the ownership claim. The distribution is made possible by profitable operations.

The amount of cash dividends declared by the board of directors of a company depends on many factors, the least important of which is usually the balance in retained income. Although profitable operations are generally essential, dividend policy is also influenced by the company's cash position and future needs for cash to pay debts or to purchase additional assets. It is also influenced by whether the company is committed to a stable dividend policy or to a policy that normally ties dividends to fluctuations in net income. Under a stable policy, dividends may be paid consistently even if a company encounters a few years of little or no net income.

SOLE PROPRIETORSHIPS AND PARTNERSHIPS

This chapter has focused on the accounting for a corporation, King Hardware Co. However, the basic accounting concepts that underlie the owners' equity are unchanged regardless of whether ownership takes the form of a corporation, a **sole proprietorship**—a business entity with a single owner, or a **partnership**—an organization that joins two or more individuals together as co-owners. However, in proprietorships and partnerships, distinctions between paid-in capital (i.e., the investments by owners) and retained income are rarely made. Compare the possibilities for King Hardware Co. as of April 30:

Owners' Equity for a Corporation

Stockholders' equity		
Capital stock (paid-in capital)	$100,000	
Retained income	8,400	
Total stockholders' equity		**$108,400**

Owners' Equity for a Sole Proprietorship

Alice Walsh, capital	**$ 108,400**

Owners' Equity for a Partnership

Susan Zingler, capital	$ 54,200
John Martin, capital	54,200
Total partners' equity	**$108,400**

In contrast to corporations, sole proprietorships and partnerships are not legally required to account separately for paid-in capital (i.e., proceeds from issuances of capital stock) and for retained income. Instead, they typically accumulate a single amount for each owner's original investments, subsequent investments, share of net income, and withdrawals. In the case of a sole proprietorship, then, the owner's equity will consist of a lone capital account.

Note that, although owners' equity is sometimes called **net worth,** owners' equity is not a measure of the "current value" of the business to an outside buyer. The selling price of a business depends on future profit projections that may have little relationship to the existing assets or equities of the entity as measured by its accounting records.

GENERALLY ACCEPTED ACCOUNTING PRINCIPLES

Accounting is more an art than a science. It is based on a set of principles on which there is general agreement, not on rules that can be "proved."

Auditor's Independent Opinion

The financial statements of publicly held corporations and many other corporations are subject to an *independent audit* that forms the basis for a professional accounting firm's opinion, typically including the following key phrasing:

> In our opinion, such financial statements present fairly, in all material respects, the financial position of Microsoft Corporation and subsidiaries as of June 30, 1993 and 1994, and the results of their operations and their cash flows for each of the 3 years in the period ended June 30, 1994, in conformity with generally accepted accounting principles.

An accounting firm must conduct an audit before it can render the foregoing opinion. An **audit** is an "examination" or in-depth inspection that is made in accordance with generally accepted auditing standards, which have been developed primarily by the American Institute of Certified Public Accountants (AICPA), the leading organization of auditors. An audit includes tests of the accounting records, internal control systems, and other procedures as deemed necessary. After auditing a company, an accountant issues an *independent opinion*—the accountant's testimony that *management's* financial statements are in conformity with generally accepted accounting principles.

The auditor's opinion usually appears at the end of annual reports prepared for the stockholders and other external users. Investors often mistakenly rely on the opinion as an infallible guarantee of financial truth. Somehow accounting is thought to be an exact science, perhaps because of the aura of precision that financial statements possess. But, as noted earlier, accounting is more art than science. The financial reports may appear accurate because of their neatly integrated numbers, but they are the result of a complex measurement process that rests on a huge bundle of assumptions and conventions.

The conventions, rules, and procedures that together make up accepted accounting practice at any given time are called generally accepted accounting principles (GAAP). Accounting principles become "generally accepted" by agreement. Such agreement is not influenced solely by formal logical analysis. Experience, custom, usage, and practical necessity contribute to the set of principles. Accordingly, it might be better to call them *conventions*, because principles suggest that they are the product of airtight logic.

FASB and SEC

American GAAP is largely the work of the **Financial Accounting Standards Board (FASB).** The FASB, consisting of seven full-time members, is an independent creation of the private sector. It is financially supported by various companies and professional accounting associations.

By federal law, the **Securities and Exchange Commission (SEC),** a government agency, has the ultimate responsibility for specifying GAAP for U.S. companies whose stock is held by the general investing public. However, the SEC has informally delegated much rule-making power to the FASB. This public-sector—private-sector relationship may be sketched as follows:

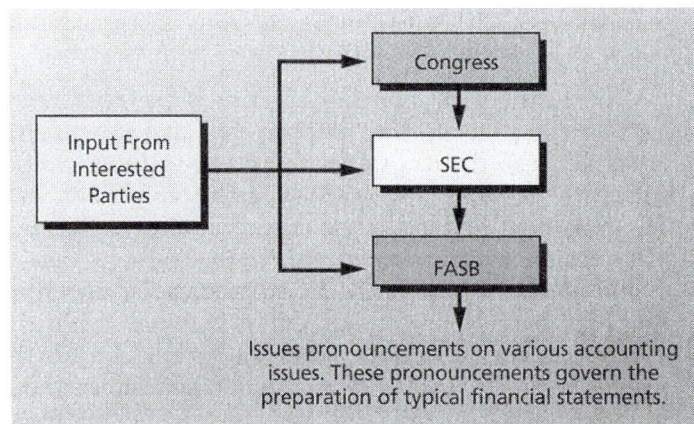

The FASB issues pronouncements on various accounting issues. These pronouncements govern the preparation of typical financial statements.

Consider this three-tiered structure. Note that Congress can overrule both the SEC and FASB, and the SEC can overrule the FASB. Such undermining of the FASB occurs rarely, but pressure is exerted on all three tiers by corporations and other interested parties if they think an impending pronouncement is "wrong." Hence the setting of accounting principles is a complex process involving heavy interactions among the affected parties: public regulators (Congress and the SEC), private regulators (FASB), companies, the public accounting profession, representatives of investors, and other interested groups.

THREE MEASUREMENT CONVENTIONS

Three broad measurement or valuation conventions (principles) underlie accrual accounting: *recognition* (when to record revenue), *matching* and *cost recovery* (when to record expense), and the *stable monetary unit* (what unit of measure to use).

Recognition

The first broad measurement or valuation convention, *recognition,* was discussed earlier in this chapter in the section "Revenues and Expenses." In general, revenue is recognized when the goods or services in question are delivered to customers.

Matching and Cost Recovery

You may often encounter a favorite buzzword in accounting: **matching.** Matching is the relating of accomplishments or revenues (as measured by the selling prices of goods and services delivered) and efforts or expenses (as measured by the cost of goods and services used) to a *particular period* for which a measurement of income is desired. In short, matching is a short description of the accrual basis for measuring income.

Accountants apply matching as follows:

1. Identify the revenue recognized during the period.
2. Link the expenses to the recognized revenue directly (e.g., sales commissions or costs of inventories sold to customers) or indirectly (e.g., wages of janitors and supplies used). The latter expenses are costs of operations during a specific time period that have no measurable benefit for a *future* period.

The heart of recognizing expense is the **cost recovery** concept. That is, assets such as inventories, prepayments, and equipment are carried forward as assets because their costs are expected to be recovered in the form of cash inflows (or reduced cash outflows) in future periods. At the end of each period, the accountant (especially the outside auditor at the end of each year) carefully examines the evidence to be assured that these assets—these unexpired costs—should not be written off as an expense of the current period. For instance, in our chapter example, prepaid rent of $2,000 was carried forward as an asset as of March 31 because the accountant is virtually certain that it represents a future benefit. Why? Because without the prepayment, cash outflows of $2,000 would have to be made for April and May. So the presence of the prepayment is a benefit in the sense that future cash outflows will be reduced by $2,000. Furthermore, future revenue (sales) will be high enough to ensure the recovery of the $2,000.

Stable Monetary Unit

The monetary unit (e.g., the dollar) is the principal means for measuring assets and equities. It is the common denominator for quantifying the effects of a wide variety of transactions. While companies in the United States, Canada, Australia, and New Zealand use the dollar as the monetary unit, in other countries they use the franc, pound, mark, yen, or some other monetary unit.

Such measurement assumes that the monetary unit—the dollar, for example—is an unchanging yardstick. Yet we all know that a 1997 dollar does not have the same purchasing power as a 1987 or 1977 dollar. Therefore users of accounting statements that include dollars from different years must recognize the limitations of the basic measurement unit.

Accountants have been extensively criticized for not making explicit and formal adjustments to remedy the defects of their measuring unit. In the face of this, some accountants maintain that price-level adjustments would lessen objectivity and would add to the general confusion. They claim that the price-level problem has been exaggerated, and that the adjustments would not significantly affect the vast bulk of corporate statements because most accounts are in current or nearly current dollars.

On the other hand, inflation has been steady and its effects are sometimes surprisingly pervasive. Several countries, including Brazil and Argentina, routinely adjust their accounting numbers for the effects of inflation. The most troublesome aspect, however, is how to interpret the results after they are measured. Investors and managers in the United States are accustomed to the conventional statements. The intelligent interpretation of statements adjusted for changes in the price level will require extensive changes in the habits of users.

The body of generally accepted accounting principles contains more than the measurement conventions just discussed. Other major concepts include going concern, objectivity, materiality, and cost benefit. These are discussed in Addendum 2A.

SUMMARY

An underlying structure of concepts, techniques, and conventions provides a basis for accounting practice. Two basic financial statements, the balance sheet (or statement of financial position) and income statement, are presented in this chapter. Their main elements are assets, liabilities, owners' equity, revenues, and expenses. Income statements and balance sheets are linked because the revenues and expenses appearing on income statements are components of stockholders' equity. Revenues increase stockholders' equity; expenses decrease stockholders' equity.

The accrual basis is the heart of accounting. Under accrual accounting revenues are recognized as earned and expenses as incurred rather than as related cash is received or disbursed. Expense should not be confused with the term *cash disbursement*, and revenue should not be confused with the term *cash receipt.*

The balance sheet equation provides a framework for recording accounting transactions. At the end of each accounting period, adjustments must be made so that financial statements may be presented on a full-fledged accrual basis. The major adjustments are for (1) expiration of unexpired costs, (2) recognition (earning) of unearned revenues, (3) accrual of unrecorded expenses, and (4) accrual of unrecorded revenues. After transactions are recorded and adjustments are made, the data can be compiled into financial statements.

Dividends are not expenses; they are distributions of assets that reduce ownership claims. Similarly, retained income is not cash; it is a claim against total assets.

Entities can be organized as corporations, partnerships, or sole proprietorships. The type of organization does not affect most accounting entries. Only the owners' equity section will differ among organizational types.

Three major conventions that affect accounting are recognition, matching and cost recovery, and stable monetary unit. Recognition affects when revenues will be recorded in the income statement, matching and cost recovery specify when expenses will be recorded, and stable monetary units justify use of a unit of currency (the dollar in the United States) to measure accounting transactions.

SELF-CORRECTION PROBLEMS

1. The King Hardware Co. transactions for March were analyzed in Figure 2-1. The balance sheet showed the following balances as of March 31, 19X1:

	Assets	Equities
Cash	$ 42,000	
Accounts receivable	90,000	
Inventory	10,000	
Prepaid rent	2,000	
Accounts payable		$ 25,000
Paid-in capital		100,000
Retained income		19,000
	$144,000	**$144,000**

The following is a summary of the transactions that occurred during the next month, April:

1. Cash collections of accounts receivable, $88,000.
2. Cash payments of accounts payable, $24,000.
3. Acquisitions of inventory on open account, $80,000.
4. Merchandise carried in inventory at a cost of $70,000 was sold on open account for $85,000
5. Adjustment for recognition of rent expense for April.
6. Some customers paid $3,000 in advance for merchandise that they ordered but did not expect in inventory until mid-May. (What asset must rise? Does this transaction increase liabilities or stockholders' equity?)
7. Total wages of $6,000 (which were ignored for simplicity in March) were paid on four Fridays in April. These payments for employee services were recognized by increasing Wages Expense and decreasing Cash.
8. Wages of $600 were incurred near the end of April, but the employees had not been paid as of April 30. Accordingly, the accountant increased Wages Expense and increased a liability, Accrued Wages Payable.
9. Cash dividends declared by the board of directors and disbursed to stockholders on April 29 equaled $18,000. (What account besides Cash is affected?) As will be explained on page 657, Cash and Retained Income are each decreased by $18,000.

a. Using the *accrual basis* of accounting, prepare an analysis of transactions, employing the equation approach demonstrated in Figure 2-1. Be sure to leave plenty of columns for new accounts.
b. Prepare a balance sheet as of April 30, 19X1, and an income statement for the month of April.
c. Prepare a new report, the Statement of Retained Income, which should show the beginning balance in the Retained Income account, followed by a description of any major changes, and end with the balance as of April 30, 19X1.

Note: Entries 6 through 9 and the statement of retained income have not been explained. However, as a learning step, try to respond to the requirements here anyway. Explanations follow almost immediately.

2. The following interpretations and remarks are sometimes encountered regarding financial statements. Do you agree or disagree? Explain fully.

     a. "If I purchase 100 shares of the outstanding common stock of General Motors Corporation (or King Hardware Co.), I invest my money directly in that corporation. General Motors must record that transaction."

     b. "Sales show the cash coming in from customers and the various expenses show the cash going out for goods and services. The difference is net income."

     c. Consider the following recent accounts of Walgreens, the largest U.S. drugstore chain:

Paid-in capital	$ 76,919,000
Retained earnings	1,496,721,000
Total stockholders' equity	**$1,573,640,000**

     A shareholder commented, "Why can't that big drugstore pay higher wages and dividends too? It can use its hundreds of millions of dollars of retained earnings to do so."

     d. "The total Walgreens stockholders' equity measures the amount that the shareholders would get today if the corporation were liquidated."

SOLUTIONS TO SELF-CORRECTION PROBLEMS

1. a. **Analysis of transactions.** The answer is in Figure 2-2. The first five transactions are straightforward extensions or repetitions of the March transactions, but the rest of the transactions are new. They are discussed in the sections that follow the solution to the second part of this problem.

     b., c. **Preparation of financial statements.** See Figures 2-3, 2-4, and 2-5. The first two of these exhibits show financial statements already described in this chapter: the balance sheet and the income statement. Figure 2-5 presents a new statement, the *statement of retained income,* which is merely a formal presentation of the changes in retained income during the reporting period. It starts with the beginning balance, adds net income for the period in question, and deducts cash dividends to arrive at the ending balance. Frequently, this statement is tacked on to the bottom of an income statement. If so, the result is a *combined* statement of income and statement of retained income.

2. a. Money is invested directly in a corporation only upon original issuance of the stock by the corporation. For example, 100,000 shares of stock may be issued at $80 per share, bringing in $8 million to the corporation. This is a transaction between the corporation and the stockholders. It affects the corporate financial position:

Cash	$8,000,000	Stockholders' equity	$8,000,000

     In turn, 100 shares of that stock may be sold by an original stockholder (A) to another individual (B) for $92 per share. This is a private transaction; no cash comes to the corporation. Of course, the corporation records the fact that 100 shares originally owned by A are now owned by B, but the corporate financial position is unchanged. Accounting focuses on the business entity; the private dealings of the owners have no direct effect on the financial position of the entity and hence are unrecorded except for detailed records of the owners' identifies.

b. Cash receipts and disbursements are not the fundamental basis for the accounting recognition of revenues and expenses. Credit, not cash, lubricates the economy. Therefore, if services or goods have been rendered to a customer, a collectible claim to cash in the form of a receivable is deemed sufficient justification for recognizing revenue; similarly, if services or goods have been used up, an obligation in the form of a payable is justification for recognizing expense.

   This approach to the measurement of net income is known as the accrual basis. Revenue is recognized as it is earned and realized. Expenses or losses are recognized when goods or services are used up in the obtaining of revenue (or when such goods or services cannot justifiably be carried forward as an asset because they have no potential future benefit). The expenses and losses are deducted from the revenue, and the result of this matching process is net income, the net increase in stockholders' equity from the conduct of operations.

c. As the chapter indicated, retained earnings is not cash. It is a stockholders' equity account that represents the accumulated increase in ownership claims because of profitable operations. This claim or interest may be partially liquidated by the payment of cash dividends, but a growing company will reinvest cash in sustaining the added investments in receivables, inventories, plant, equipment, and other assets so necessary for expansion. As a result, the ownership claims reflected by retained earnings may become "permanent" in the sense that, as a practical matter, they will never be liquidated as long as the company remains in business.

   This linking of retained earnings and cash is only one example of erroneous interpretation. As a general rule, there is no direct relationship between the individual items on the two sides of the balance sheet. For example, Walgreens had cash of less than $78 million on the above balance sheet date when its retained earnings were nearly $1.5 billion.

d. Stockholders' equity is a difference, the excess of assets over liabilities. If the assets were carried in the accounting records at their liquidating value today, and the liabilities were carried at the exact amounts needed for their extinguishment, the remark would be true. But such valuations would be coincidental because assets are customarily carried at historical cost expressed in an unchanging monetary unit. Intervening changes in markets and general price levels in inflationary times may mean that the assets are woefully understated. Investors may make a critical error if they think that balance sheets indicate current values.

   Furthermore, the "market values" for publicly owned shares are usually determined by daily trading conducted in the financial marketplaces such as the New York Stock Exchange. These values are affected by numerous factors including the *expectations* of (a) price appreciation and (b) cash flows in the form of dividends. The focus is on the future; the present and the past are examined only as clues to what may be forthcoming. Therefore the present stockholders' equity is usually of only incidental concern.

For example, stockholders' equity for Walgreens was $1,573,640,000 ÷ 123,070,536 shares, or $13 per share, while the company's market price per common share fluctuated between $34 and $43.

QUESTIONS

1. What types of questions are answered by the income statement and balance sheet?
2. Criticize: "Assets are things of value owned by an organization."
3. How are the income statement and balance sheet related?
4. Criticize: "Net income is the difference in the ownership capital account balances at two points in time."
5. Distinguish between the accrual basis and the cash basis.
6. How do adjusting entries differ from routine entries?
7. Explain why advertising should be viewed as an asset on acquisition.
8. Why is it better to refer to the *costs*, rather than *values*, of assets such as plant or inventories?
9. "Depreciation is cost allocation, not valuation." Do you agree? Explain.
10. Criticize: "As a stockholder, I have a right to more dividends. You have millions stashed away in retained earnings. It's about time that you let the true owners get their hands on that pot of gold."
11. Criticize: "Dividends are distributions of profits."
12. Explain the relationship between the FASB and the SEC.
13. What is the major criticism of the dollar as the principal accounting measure?
14. What does the accountant mean by *going concern*?
15. What does the accountant mean by *objectivity*?
16. What is the role of cost-benefit (economic feasibility) in the development of accounting principles?

PROBLEMS

1. **Balance Sheet Equation.**   For each of the following independent cases, compute the amounts (in thousands) for the items indicated by letters, and show your supporting computations:

	Case		
	a	b	c
Revenues	$140	$K	$300
Expenses	110	170	270
Dividends declared	–0–	5	Q
Additional investment			
by stockholders	–0–	30	35
Net income	E	20	P
Retained income			
Beginning of year	40	60	100
End of year	D	J	110
Paid-in capital			
Beginning of year	15	10	N
End of year	C	H	85
Total assets			
Beginning of year	85	F	L
End of year	95	275	M
Total liabilities			
Beginning of year	A	90	105
End of year	B	G	95

2. **Analysis of Transactions, Preparation of Statements.**   The Ekern Company was incorporated on April 1, 19X5. Ekern had ten holders of common stock. Elke Ekern, who was the president and chief executive officer, held 51% of the shares. The company rented space in chain discount stores and specialized in selling ladles' shoes. Ekern's first location was in a store of Nordic Market Centers, Inc.

The following events occurred during April:

1. The company was incorporated. Common stockholders invested $90,000 cash.
2. Purchased merchandise inventory for cash, $35,000.
3. Purchased merchandise inventory on open account, $25,000.
4. Merchandise carried in inventory at a cost of $37,000 was sold for cash for $25,000 and on open account for $65,000, a grand total of $90,000. Ekern (not Nordic) carries and collects these accounts receivable.
5. Collection of the above accounts receivable, $15,000.
6. Payments of accounts payable, $18,000. See transaction 3.
7. Special display equipment and fixtures were acquired on April 1 for $36,000. Their expected useful life was 36 months with no terminal scrap value. Straight-line depreciation was adopted. This equipment was removable. Ekern paid $12,000 as a down payment and signed a promissory note for $24,000.
8. On April 1, Ekern signed a rental agreement with Nordic. The agreement called for a flat $2,000 per month, payable quarterly in advance. Therefore Ekern paid $6,000 cash on April 1.
9. The rental agreement also called for a payment of 10% of all sales. This payment was in addition to the flat $2,000 per month. In this way, Nordic would share in any success of the venture and be compensated for

general services such as cleaning and utilities. This payment was to be made in cash on the last day of each month as soon as the sales for the month were tabulated. Therefore Ekern made the payment on April 30.

10. Wages, salaries, and sales commissions were all paid in cash for all earnings by employees. The amount was $38,000.
11. Depreciation expense was recognized. See transaction 7.
12. The expiration of an appropriate amount of prepaid rental services was recognized. See transaction 8.

a. Prepare an analysis of Ekern Company's transactions, employing the equation approach demonstrated in Figure 2-1. Two additional columns will be needed: Equipment and Fixtures and Note Payable. Show all amounts in thousands.

b. Prepare a balance sheet as of April 30, 19X5, and an income statement for the month of April. Ignore income taxes.

c. Given these sparse facts, analyze Ekern's performance for April and its financial position as of April 30, 19X5.

3. **Cash Basis Versus Accrual Basis.** Refer to the preceding problem. If Ekern Company measured income on the cash basis, what revenue would be reported for April? Which basis (accrual or cash) provides a better measure of revenue? Why?

4. **Balance Sheet Equation.** Micron Technology is one of the leading producers of semiconductor components. Its net income grew from $7 million in 1985 to more than $1.6 billion in 1994. The company's actual data (in millions of dollars) follow for its fiscal year ended September 1, 1994:

Assets, beginning of period	$ 965.7
Assets, end of period	E
Liabilities, beginning of period	A
Liabilities, end of period	480.4
Paid-in capital, beginning of period	357.0
Paid-in capital, end of period	D
Retained earnings, beginning of period	282.5
Retained earnings, end of period	C
Revenues	1,628.6
Costs and expenses	B
Net income	400.5
Dividends	12.2
Additional investments by stockholders	21.5

Find the unknowns (in millions), showing computations to support your answers.

5. **Analysis of Transactions, Preparation of Statements.**   Hino Motors has maintained its top position in the sales of medium- and heavy-duty diesel trucks in Japan since 1973. The company's actual condensed balance sheet data, March 31, 1994, follows (in billions of Japanese yen):

Assets		Equities	
Cash	¥ 52	Accounts payable	¥ 84
Accounts receivable	64	Other liabilities	86
Inventories	27		
Prepaid expenses and other assets	60	Paid-in capital	44
Property, plant, and equipment	160	Retained earnings	149
Total	¥ 363	Total	¥ 363

The following summarizes some major transactions during April 1994 (in billions of yen):

1. Trucks carried in inventory at a cost of ¥30 were sold for cash of ¥20 and on open account of ¥50, a grand total of ¥70.
2. Acquired inventory on account, ¥50.
3. Collected receivables, ¥30.
4. On April 2, used ¥25 cash to prepay some rent and insurance for 1995.
5. Payments on accounts payable (for inventories), ¥45.
6. Paid selling and administrative expenses in cash, ¥10.
7. A total of ¥9 of prepaid expenses for rent and insurance expired in April 1994.
8. Depreciation expense of ¥18 was recognized for April.

a. Prepare an analysis of the Hino Motors transactions, employing the equation approach demonstrated in Figure 2-1. Show all amounts in billions of yen. (For simplicity, only a few major transactions are illustrated here.)
b. Prepare a statement of earnings for the month ended April 30, 1994, and a balance sheet as of April 30, 1994. Ignore income taxes.

6. **Cash Basis Versus Accrual Basis.**   Refer to the preceding problem. If Hino Motors measured income on the cash basis, what revenue would be reported for April? Which basis (accrual or cash) provides a better measure of revenue? Why?

ADDENDUM 2A: ADDITIONAL ACCOUNTING CONCEPTS

This addendum describes several concepts that are prominent parts of the body of generally accepted accounting principles: continuity or going concern, objectivity or verifiability, materiality, conservatism, and cost-benefit.

The Continuity or Going Concern Convention

The **continuity** or **going concern convention** is the assumption that in all ordinary situations an entity persists indefinitely. This notion implies that existing *resources,* such as plant assets, *will be used* to fulfill the general purposes of a continuing entity *rather than sold* in tomorrow's real estate or equipment markets. It also implies that existing liabilities will be paid at maturity in an orderly manner.

Suppose some old specialized equipment has a depreciated cost (i.e., original cost less accumulated depreciation) of $10,000, a replacement cost of $12,000, and a realizable value of $7,000 on the used-equipment market. The continuity convention is often cited as the justification for adhering to acquisition cost (or acquisition cost less depreciation, $10,000 in this example) as the primary basis for valuing assets such as inventories, land, buildings, and equipment. Some critics of these accounting practices believe that such valuations are not as informative as their replacement cost ($12,000) or their realizable values on sale ($7,000). Defenders of using $10,000 as an appropriate asset valuation argue that a going concern will generally use the asset as originally intended. Therefore the recorded cost (the acquisition cost less depreciation) is the preferable basis for accountability and evaluation of performance. Hence other values are not germane because replacement or disposal will not occur en masse as of the balance sheet date.

The opposite view to this going concern or continuity convention is an immediate-liquidation assumption whereby all items on a balance sheet are valued at the amounts appropriate if the entity's assets were to be sold and its liabilities paid in piecemeal fashion within a few days or months. This liquidation approach to valuation is usually used only when the entity is in severe, near-bankrupt straits.

Objectivity or Verifiability

Users want assurance that the numbers in the financial statements are not fabricated by management or by accountants to mislead or falsify the firm's financial position and performance. Consequently, accountants seek and prize **objectivity** (or **verifiability**) as one of their principal strengths and regard it as an essential characteristic of measurement. A financial statement item is *objective or verifiable* if there would be a high extent of consensus among independent measures of the item. For example, the amount paid for assets is usually highly verifiable, but the predicted cost to replace assets often is not.

Many critics of existing accounting practices want to trade objectivity (accuracy) for what they conceive as more relevant or valid information. For example, the accounting literature is peppered with suggestions that accounting should attempt to measure "economic income," even though objectivity may be lessened. This particular suggestion often involves introducing asset valuations at replacement costs when these are higher than historical costs. The accounting profession has generally rejected these suggestions, even when reliable replacement price quotations are available, because no evidence short of a bona fide sale is regarded as sufficient to justify income recognition.

Materiality

Because accounting is a practical art, the practitioner often tempers accounting reports by applying judgments about **materiality**. A financial statement item is not *material* if it is sufficiently small that its omission or misstatement would not mislead a user of the financial statements. Many outlays that should theoretically be recorded as assets are immediately written off as expenses because of their lack of significance. For example, many corporations have a rule that requires the immediate write-off to expense of all outlays under a specified minimum of, say, $100, regardless of the useful life of the asset acquired. In such a case, coat hangers may be acquired that may last indefinitely but may never appear in the balance sheet as assets. The resulting $100 understatement of assets and stockholders' equity would be too trivial to worry about.

When is an item material? There will probably never be a universal clear-cut answer. What is trivial to IBM may be material to Joe's Computer Repair Service. A working rule is that an item is material if its proper accounting would probably affect the decision of a knowledgeable user. In sum, although materiality is an important convention, it is difficult to use anything other than prudent judgment to tell whether an item is material.

The Conservatism Convention

Conservatism has been a hallmark of accounting. In a technical sense, the **conservatism convention** means selecting the method of measurement that yields the gloomiest immediate results. This attitude is reflected in such working rules as "Anticipate no gains, but provide for all possible losses," and "If in doubt, write it off."

Accountants have traditionally regarded the historical costs of acquiring an asset as the ceiling for its valuation. Assets may be written up only upon an exchange, but they may be written down without an exchange. For example, consider *lower-of-cost-or-market* procedures in which inventories are written down when replacement costs decline, but they are never written up when replacement costs increase.

Conservatism has been criticized as being inherently inconsistent. If replacement market prices are sufficiently objective and verifiable to justify write-downs, why aren't they just as valid for write-ups? Furthermore, the critics maintain, conservatism is not a fundamental concept. Accounting reports should try to present the most accurate picture feasible—neither too high nor too low. Accountants defend their attitude by saying that erring in the direction of conservatism would usually have less severe economic consequences than erring in the direction of overstating assets and net income.

Conservatism that leads to understating net income in one period also creates an overstatement of net income in a future period. For example, if a $100 inventory is written down to $80, net income is reduced by $20 in the period of the write-down but *increased* by $20 in the period the inventory is sold.

Cost-Benefit

Accounting systems vary in complexity from the minimum crude records kept to satisfy government authorities to the sophisticated budgeting and feedback schemes that are at the heart of management planning and controlling. As a system is changed, its potential benefits should exceed its additional costs. Often the benefits are difficult to measure, but this **cost-benefit criterion** at least implicitly underlies the decisions about the design of accounting systems. Sometimes the reluctance to adopt suggestions for new ways of measuring financial position and performance is because of inertia. More often, it is because the apparent benefits do not exceed the obvious costs of gathering and interpreting the information.

Room for Judgment

Accounting is commonly misunderstood as being a precise discipline that produces exact measurements of a company's financial position and performance. As a result, many individuals regard accountants as little more than mechanical tabulators who grind out financial reports after processing an imposing amount of detail in accordance with stringent predetermined rules. Although accountants take methodical steps with masses of data, their rules of measurement allow much room for judgment. Managers and accountants who exercise this judgment have more influence on financial reporting than is commonly believed. These judgments are guided by the basic concepts, techniques, and conventions called GAAP. Examples of the latter include the basic concepts just discussed. Their meaning will become clearer as these concepts are applied in future chapters.

ADDENDUM 2B: USING LEDGER ACCOUNTS

Chapter 2 focused on the balance sheet equation, the general framework used by accountants to record economic transactions. This appendix focuses on some of the main techniques that accountants use to record the transactions illustrated in the chapter.

The Account

To begin, consider how the accountant would record the King Hardware Co. transactions that were introduced in the chapter. Figure 2-1 showed their effects on the elements of the balance sheet equation:

	A		=	L	+	SE
	Cash	Inventory		Accounts Payable		Paid-in Capital
1. Initial investment by owners	+100,000		=			+100,000
2. Acquire inventory for cash	− 75,000	+75,000	=			
3. Acquire inventory on credit		+35,000	=	+35,000		

This balance sheet equation approach emphasizes the concepts, but it can obviously become unwieldy if many transactions occur. You can readily see that changes in the balance sheet equation can occur many times daily. In large businesses, such as in a department store, hundreds or thousands of repetitive transactions occur hourly. In practice, **ledger accounts** must be used to keep track of how these multitudes of transactions affect each particular asset, liability, revenue, expense, and so forth. These accounts used here are simplified versions of those used in practice. These are called T-accounts because they take the form of the capital letter *T*. The preceding transactions would be shown in T-accounts as follows:

Assets		=	Liabilities+ Stockholders' Equity	

Cash

Increases		Decreases	
(1)	100,000	(2)	75,000
Bal.	25,000		

Accounts Payable

Decreases	Increases	
	(3)	35,000

Inventory

Increases		Decreases
(2)	75,000	
(3)	35,000	
Bal.	110,000	

Paid-in Capital

Decreases	Increases	
	(1)	100,000

The entries were made in accordance with the rules of a **double-entry system,** whereby each transaction affects at least two accounts. Asset accounts have left side balances. They are increased by entries on the left side and decreased by entries on the right side.

Liabilities and stockholders' equity accounts have right-side balances. They are increased by entries on the right side and decreased by entries on the left side.

The format of the T-account eliminates the use of negative numbers. Any entry that reduces an account balance is *added* to the side of the account that *decreases* the account balance.

Each T-account summarizes the changes in a particular asset or equity. Each transaction is keyed in some way, such as by the numbering used in this illustration or by date or both. This keying facilitates the rechecking (auditing) process by aiding the tracing of transactions to original sources. A balance of an account is computed by totaling each side of an account and deducting the smaller total amount from the larger. Accounts exist to keep an up-to-date summary of the changes in specific assets and equities.

A balance sheet can be prepared at any time if the accounts are up to date. The necessary information is tabulated in the accounts. For example, the balance sheet after the first three transactions would contain:

Assets		Liabilities and Stockholders' Equity	
Cash	$ 25,000	Liabilities	
Inventory	110,000	Accounts payable	$ 35,000
		Stockholders' equity	
		Paid-in capital	100,000
Total assets	**$135,000**	Total equities	**$135,000**

General Ledger

Figure 2-7 is the *general ledger* of King Hardware Co. The **general ledger** is defined as a collection of the group of accounts that supports the items shown in the major financial statements.[2] Figure 2-7 is merely a recasting of the facts that were analyzed in Figure 2-1. Study Figure 2-7 by comparing its analysis of each transaction against its corresponding analysis in Figure 2-1.

Debits and Credits

The balance sheet equation has been mentioned often in this chapter. Recall:

A= L + owner's equity   (1)
A = L + paid-in capital + retained income   (2)
A = L + paid-in capital + revenue – expenses   (3)

[2]The general ledger is usually supported by various *subsidiary ledgers,* which provide details for accounts in the general ledger. For instance, an accounts receivable subsidiary ledger would contain a separate account for each credit customer. The accounts receivable balance that appears in the Sears balance sheet is in a single account in the Sears general ledger. However, that single balance is buttressed by detailed individual accounts receivable with millions of credit customers. You can readily visualize how some accounts in general ledgers might have subsidiary ledgers supported by sub-subsidiary ledgers, and so on. Thus a subsidiary accounts receivable ledger might be subdivided alphabetically into Customers A-D, E-H, and so forth.

FIGURE 2-7   General Ledger of King Hardware Co.

1. Initial investment
2. Acquire inventory for cash
3. Acquire inventory on credit
4a. Sales on credit
4b. Cost of inventory sold
5. Collect from customers
6. Pay accounts of suppliers
7a. Payrent in advance
7b. Recognize expiration of rental services

Assets
(Increases on Left,
Decreases on Right)

Cash

(1)	100,000	(2)	75,000
(5)	30,000	(6)	10,000
		(7a)	3,000
3/31 Bal.	42,000		

Accounts Receivable

| (4a) | 120,000 | (5) | 30,000 |
| 3/31 Bal. | 90,000 | | |

Inventory

(2)	75,000	(4b)	100,000
(3)	35,000		
3/31 Bal.	10,000		

Prepaid Rent

| (7a) | 3,000 | (7b) | 1,000 |
| 3/31 Bal. | 2,000 | | |

Liabilities and Stockholders' Equity
(Decreases on Left,
Increases on Right)

Accounts Payable

| (6) | 10,000 | (3) | 35,000 |
| | | 3/31 Bal. | 25,000 |

Paid-In Capital

| | | (1) | 100,000 |
| | | 3/31 Bal. | 100,000 |

Retained Income

| | | 3/31 Bal. | 19,000* |

Expense and Revenue Accounts

Cost of Goods Sold

| (4b) | 100,000 | | |

Rent Expense

| (7b) | 1,000 | | |

Sales

| | | (4a) | 120,000 |

* The details of the revenue and expense accounts appear in the income statement. Their net effect is then transferred to a single account, Retained Income, in the balance sheet.

The accountant often talks about entries in a technical way:

Transposing,

$$A + \text{expenses} = L + \text{paid-in capital} + \text{revenue} \tag{4}$$

Finally,

$$\text{left side} = \text{right side} \tag{5}$$
$$\text{debit} = \text{credit}$$

Debit means one thing and one thing only—"left side of an account" (not "bad," "something coming," etc.). **Credit** means one thing and one thing only—"right side of an account" (not "good," "something owed," etc.). The word *charge* is often used instead of *debit,* but no single word is used as a synonym for *credit.*

For example, if you asked an accountant what entry to make for Transaction 4b, the answer would be: "I would debit (or charge) Cost of Goods Sold for $100,000; and I would credit Inventory for $100,000." Note that the total dollar amounts of the debits (entries on the left side of the account[s] affected) will *always* equal the total dollar amount of credits (entries on the right side of the account[s] affected) because the whole accounting system is based on an equation. The symmetry and power of this analytical debit-credit technique is indeed impressive.

The words *debit* and *credit* have a Latin origin. They were used centuries ago when double-entry bookkeeping was introduced by Pacioli, an Italian monk. Even though *left* and *right* are more descriptive words, *debit* and *credit* are too deeply entrenched to avoid.

Debit and credit are used as verbs, adjectives, or nouns. That is, "debit $1,000 to cash and credit $1,000 to accounts receivable" are examples of uses as verbs, meaning that $1,000 should be placed on the left side of the cash account and on the right side of the accounts receivable account. Similarly, if "a debit is made to cash" or "cash has a debit balance of $12,000," then *debit* is a noun or adjective that describes the status of a particular account.

In our everyday conversation we sometimes use the words *debits* and *credits* in a general sense that may completely diverge from their technical accounting uses. For instance, we may give praise by saying "She deserves plenty of credit for her good deed" or "That misplay is a debit on his ledger." When you study accounting, forget these general uses and misuses of the words. Merely think right side or left side.

Assets are traditionally carried as left-side balances. Why do assets and expenses both carry debit balances? They carry left-side balances for different reasons. *Expenses* are temporary stockholders' equity accounts. Decreases in stockholders' equity are entered on the left side of the accounts because they offset the normal (i.e., right-side) stockholders' equity balances. Because expenses decrease stockholders' equity, they are carried as left-side balances.

To recapitulate:

Assets		=	Liabilities		+	Stockholders' Equity	
Increase	Decrease		Decrease	Increase		Decrease	Increase
+	−		−	+		−	+
debit	credit		debit	credit		debit	credit
left	right		left	right		left	right

Because revenues increase stockholders' equity, they are recorded as credits. Because expenses decrease stockholders' equity, they are recorded as debits.

CHAPTER 3

Legal Forms of Business Organization and Federal Income Taxation

Financial management is concerned with the maintenance and creation of wealth. Consequently, this book focuses on decision making with an eye to creating wealth. In introducing decision-making techniques we will emphasize the logic behind those techniques, thereby ensuring that you don't lose sight of the concepts when dealing with the calculations.

To lay a foundation, we will begin by introducing the goal of the firm—maximization of shareholder wealth—which we will use as a guide in developing rules for decision making. Several alternative business forms, focusing on the corporate form and the tax environment in which the corporation exists, will be introduced. In discussing the tax environment, we will concentrate only on that portion of the tax code that affects business decisions.

LEGAL FORMS OF BUSINESS ORGANIZATION

In the chapters ahead we will focus on financial decisions for corporations. Although the corporation is not the only legal form of business available, it is the most logical choice for a firm that is large or growing. It is also the dominant business form in terms of sales in this country. In this section we will explain why this is so. This will in turn allow us to simplify the remainder of the text, as we will assume that the proper tax code to follow is the corporate tax code, rather than examine different tax codes for different legal forms of businesses. Keep in mind that our primary purpose is to develop an understanding of the logic of financial decision making. Taxes will become important only when they affect our decisions, and our discussion of the choice of the legal form of the business is directed at understanding why we will limit our discussion of taxes to the corporate form.

Legal forms of business organization are diverse and numerous. However, there are three categories: the sole proprietorship, the partnership, and the corporation. To understand the basic differences between each form, we need to define each form and understand its advantages and disadvantages. As we will see, as the firm grows, the advantages of the corporation begin to dominate. As a result, most large firms take on the corporate form.

Sole Proprietorship

The **sole proprietorship** is a business owned by a single individual. The owner maintains title to the assets and is personally responsible, generally without limitation, for the liabilities incurred. The proprietor is entitled to the profits from the business but must also absorb any losses. This form of business is initiated by the mere act of beginning the business operations. Typically, no legal requirement must be met in starting the operation, particularly if the proprietor is conducting the business in his or her own name. If a special name is used, an assumed-name certificate should be filed, requiring a small registration fee. Termination occurs on the owner's death or by the owner's choice. Briefly stated, the sole proprietorship is for all practical purposes the absence of any formal *legal* business structure.

Partnership

The primary difference between a **partnership** and a sole proprietorship is that the partnership has more than one owner. A partnership is an association of two or more persons coming together as co-owners for the purpose of operating a business for profit. Partnerships fall into two types: (1) general partnerships and (2) limited partnerships.

General partnership.   In a general partnership each partner is fully responsible for the liabilities incurred by the partnership. Also, any partner's ill conduct even having the appearance of relating to the firm's business renders the remaining partners liable as well. The relationship among partners is dictated entirely by the partnership agreement, which may be an oral commitment or a formal document.

Limited partnership.   In addition to the general partnership, in which all partners are jointly liable without limitation, many states provide for a limited partnership. The state statutes permit one or more of the partners to have limited liability, restricted to the amount of capital invested in the partnership. Several conditions must be met to qualify as a limited partner. First, at least one general partner must remain in the association for whom the privilege of limited liability does not apply. Second, the names of the limited partners may not appear in the name of the firm. Third, the limited partners may not participate in the management of the business. If one of these restrictions is violated, all partners forfeit their right to limited liability. In essence, the intent of the statutes creating the limited partnership is to provide limited liability for a person whose interest in the partnership is purely as an investor. That individual may not assume a management function within the organization.

Corporation

The **corporation** has been a significant factor in the economic development of the United States. As early as 1819 Chief Justice John Marshall set forth the legal definition of a corporation as "an artificial being, invisible, intangible, and existing only in the contemplation of law."[1] This entity *legally* functions separate and apart from its owners. As such, the corporation can individually sue and be sued, and purchase, sell, or own property; and its personnel are subject to criminal punishment for crimes. However, despite this legal separation, the corporation is composed of owners who dictate its direction and policies. The owners elect a board of directors, whose members in turn select individuals to serve as corporate officers, including president, vice-president, secretary, and treasurer. Ownership is reflected in common stock certificates, designating the number of shares owned by its holder. The number of shares owned relative to the total number of shares outstanding determines the stockholder's proportionate ownership in the business. Because the shares are transferable, ownership in a corporation may be changed by a shareholder simply remitting the shares to a new shareholder. The investor's liability is confined to the amount of the investment in the company, thereby preventing creditors from confiscating stockholders' personal assets in settlement of unresolved claims. Finally, the life of a corporation is not dependent on the status of the investors. The death or withdrawal of an investor does not affect the continuity of the corporation. The management continues to run the corporation when stock is sold or when it is passed on through inheritance.

Comparison of Organizational Forms

Owners of new businesses have some important decisions to make in choosing an organizational form. Whereas each business form seems to have some advantages over the others, we will see that as the firm grows and needs access to the capital markets to raise funds, the advantages of the corporation begin to dominate.

Why large and growing firms choose the corporate form: Ease in raising capital. Because of the limited liability, the ease of transferring ownership through the sale of common shares, and the flexibility in dividing the shares, the corporation is the ideal business entity in terms of attracting new capital. In contrast, the unlimited liabilities of the sole proprietorship and the general partnership are deterrents to raising equity capital. Between the extremes, the limited partnership does provide limited liability for limited partners, which has a tendency to attract wealthy investors. However, the impracticality of having a large number of partners and the restricted marketability of an interest in a partnership prevent this form of organization from competing effectively with the corporation. Therefore, when developing our decision models we will assume we are dealing with the corporate form. The taxes incorporated in these models will deal only with the corporate tax codes. Because our goal is to develop an understanding of the management, measurement, and creation of wealth, and not to become tax experts, we will only focus on those characteristics of the corporate tax code that will affect our financial decisions.

---

[1]The Trustees of Dartmouth College v. Woodard, 4 Wheaton 636 (1819).

FEDERAL INCOME TAXATION

Before presenting the nine axioms of finance that will provide the conceptual under-pinnings for what will follow, we will examine those tax features that will affect our decisions. We will describe the environment and set up the ground rules under which financial decisions are made. As the nation's politics change, so does the tax system. The purpose of looking at the current tax structure is not to become tax experts, but rather to gain an understanding of taxes and how they affect business decisions. There is a good chance that corporate tax rates may change significantly before you enter the work force. However, although rates may change, taxes will continue to remain a cash outflow and therefore something to avoid. Thus, we will pay close attention to which expenses are and are not deductible for tax purposes, and in do-ing so focus on how taxes affect business decisions.

Objectives of Income Taxation

Originally, the sole objective of the federal government in taxing income was to gen-erate financing for government expenditures. Although this purpose continues to be important, social and economic objectives have been added. For instance, a company may receive possible reductions in taxes if (1) it undertakes certain technological research, (2) it pays wages to certain economically disadvantaged groups, or (3) if it locates in certain economically depressed areas. Other socially oriented stipulations in the tax laws include exemptions for dependents, old age, and blindness and a reduction in taxes on retirement income. In addition, the government uses tax legis-lation to stabilize the economy. In recessionary periods taxes may be reduced, giving the public more discretionary income in the hope that this income will be spent to increase the demand for products and thereby generate new jobs.

In short, three objectives may be given for the taxation of revenues: (1) the provi-sion of revenues for government expenditures, (2) the achievement of socially desir-able goals, and (3) economic stabilization.

Types of Taxpayers

To understand the tax system, we must first ask, "Who is the taxpayer?" For the most part, there are three basic types of taxable entities: individuals, corporations, and fiduciaries. Individuals include company employees, self-employed persons own-ing their own businesses, and members of a partnership. Income is reported by these individuals in their personal tax returns.[2] The corporation, as a separate legal entity, reports its income and pays any taxes related to these profits. The owners (stock-holders) of the corporation need not report these earnings in their personal tax re-turns, except when all or a part of the profits are distributed in the form of dividends. Finally, fiduciaries, such as estates and trusts, file a tax return and pay taxes on the income generated by the estate or trust which isn't distributed to (and included in the taxable income of) a beneficiary.

---

[2]Partnerships report only the income from the partnership. The income is then reported again by each partner, who pays any taxes owed.

Although taxation of individual and fiduciary income is an important source of income to the government, neither is especially relevant to the financial manager. Since most firms of any size are corporations, we will restrict our discussion to the corporation. A caveat is necessary, however. Tax legislation can be quite complex, with numerous exceptions to most general rules. The laws can also change quickly, and certain details discussed here may no longer apply in the near future. It sometimes is true that "a little knowledge is a dangerous thing."

Computing Taxable Income

The taxable income for a corporation is based on the gross income from all sources, except for allowable exclusions, less any tax-deductible expenses. *Gross income* equals the firm's dollar sales from its product less the cost of producing or acquiring the product. Tax-deductible expenses include any operating expenses, such as marketing expenses and administrative expenses. Also, *interest expense* paid on the firm's outstanding debt is a tax-deductible expense. However, dividends paid to the firm's stockholders are *not* deductible expenses but rather distributions of income. Other taxable income includes interest income and dividend income.

To demonstrate how to compute a corporation's taxable income, consider the J and S Corporation, a manufacturer of home accessories. The firm, originally established by Kelly Stites, had sales of $50,000,000 for the year. The cost of producing the accessories totaled $23,000,000. Operating expenses were $10,000,000. The corporation has $12,500,000 in debt outstanding, with an 8% interest rate, which resulted in $1,000,000 interest expense ($12,500,000 × .08 = $1,000,000). Management paid $1,000,000 in dividends to the firm's common stockholders. No other income, such as interest or dividend income, was received. The taxable income for the J and S Corporation would be $16,000,000, as shown in Figure 3-1.

Once we know the J and S Corporation's taxable income, we can next determine the amount of taxes the firm will owe.

Computing the Taxes Owed

The taxes to be paid by the corporation on its taxable income are based on the corporate tax rate structure. The specific rates effective for the corporation, as of 1994, are given in Figure 3-2. Under the Revenue Reconciliation Act of 1993 a new top marginal corporate tax rate of 35% was added for taxable income in excess of $ 10,000,000. Also, a surtax of 3% was imposed on taxable income between $15,000,000 and $18,333,333. This, in combination with the previously existing 5% surtax on taxable income between $100,000 and $335,000, recaptures the benefits of the lower marginal rates and as a result both the average and marginal tax rate on taxable income above $18,333,333 becomes 35%.

For example, the tax liability for the J and S Corporation, which had $16,000,000 in taxable earnings, would be $5,530,000, calculated as follows:

FIGURE 3-1   J and S Corporation Taxable Income

Sales		$50,000,000
Cost of goods sold		23,000,000
Gross profit		$27,000,000
Operating expenses		
Administrative expenses	$4,000,000	
Depreciation expenses	1,500,000	
Marketing expenses	4,500,000	
Total operating expenses		10,000,000
Operating income (earnings before		
interest and taxes)		$17,000,000
Other income		0
Interest expense		1,000,000
Taxable income		**$16,000,000**

Dividends paid to common stockholders ($1,000,000) are not tax-deductible expenses.

Earnings	×	Marginal Tax Rate	=	Taxes
$ 50,000	×	15%	=	$ 7,500
25,000	×	25%	=	6,250
9,925,000	×	34%	=	3,374,500
6,000,000	×	35%	=	2,100,000
				$5,488,250

Additional Surtaxes:
- Add 5% surtax on income between
  $100,000 and $335,000
  (5% × [$335,000 − $100,000])   11,750
- Add 3% surtax on income between
  $15,000,000 and $18,333,333
  (3% × [$16,000,000 − $15,000,000])   30,000

| Total Tax Liability | | | | **$5,530,000** |

The tax rates shown in Figure 3-2 are defined as the *marginal* tax rates, or rates applicable to the next dollar of income. For instance, if a firm has earnings of $60,000 and is contemplating an investment that would yield $10,000 in additional profits, the tax rate to be used in calculating the taxes on this added income is 25%; that is, the marginal tax rate is 25%. However, if the corporation already expects $20,000,000 without the new investment, the extra $10,000 in earnings would be taxed at 35%, the marginal tax rate. In the example, where the J and S Corporation has taxable income of $16,000,000, its marginal tax rate is 38% (this is because $16,000,000 falls into the 35% tax bracket *with* a 3% surtax); that is, any additional income from new investments will be taxed at a rate of 38%. However, after taxable income exceeds $18,333,333, the marginal tax rate declines to 35%, when the 3% surtax no longer applies.

FIGURE 3-2   Corporate Tax Rates

15%	$ 0–$50,000
25%	$ 50,001–$75,000
34%	$ 75,001–$10,000,000
35%	over $10,000,000

Additional surtax:
- 5% on income between $100,000 and $335,000.
- 3% on income between $15,000,000 and $18,333,333.

For financial decision making, it's the *marginal tax rate* rather than the average tax rate that we will be concerned with. As will become increasingly clear throughout the text, we always want to consider the tax consequences of any financial decision. The appropriate rate to be used in the analysis is the marginal tax rate, because it is this rate that will be applicable for any changes in earnings as a result of the decision being made. Thus, when making financial decisions involving taxes, always use the marginal tax rate in your calculations.[3]

The tax rate structure used in computing the J and S Corporation's taxes assumes that the income occurs in the United States. Given the globalization of the economy, it may well be that some of the income originates in a foreign country. If so, the tax rates, and the method of taxing the firm, frequently vary. Figure 3-3 sheds some light on the basic differences in tax rates in several industrialized countries. As financial manager, you would minimize the firm's taxes by reporting as much income as possible in the low-tax-rate countries and as little as possible in the high-tax-rate countries. Of course, other factors, such as political risk, may discourage your efforts to minimize taxes across national borders.

Other Tax Considerations

In addition to the fundamental computation of taxes, several other aspects of the existing tax legislation have relevance for the financial manager. These are (1) the dividend income exclusion for corporations, (2) the effects of depreciation on the firm's taxes, (3) the tax treatment of operating losses, and (4) the recognition of capital gains and losses. We also need to consider any additional taxes that may be imposed on a firm for the "excessive accumulation" of profits within the business in an effort to avoid double taxation. Finally, we should be familiar with the tax provision that allows a corporation to be taxed as a partnership, which became increasingly important with the Tax Reform Act of 1986. Let's look at each of these tax provisions in turn.

---

[3]On taxable income between $335,000 and $10,000,000, both the marginal and average tax rates equal 34%, owing to the imposition of the 5% surtax that applies to taxable income between $100,000 and $335,000. After the company's taxable income exceeds $18,333,333, both the marginal and average tax rate equal 35%, because the 3% surtax on income between $15,000,000 and $18,333,333 eliminates the benefits of having the first $10,000,000 of income taxed at 34 rather than 35%.

FIGURE 3-3   Comparison of Foreign Taxes

Country	Income Tax Rates	Value-Added Tax	Other Taxes
France	42%	5.5% on food items; up to 33.3% on luxury items	
Japan	42% on income not distributed to stockholders; 32% if distributed		Excise taxes on consumer goods; 13.2% local taxes
Korea	20%–33%	10% on goods and services	
United Kingdom	25%–35%	15% on goods and services	
West Germany	56% on income not distributed to stockholders; 36% if distributed	14% on goods and services	

Source: *International Tax Summaries*, Coopers & Lybrand International Tax Network (New York: Wiley, 1989).

Dividend exclusion.   A corporation may normally exclude 70% of any dividends received from another corporation. For instance, if corporation A owns common stock in corporation B and receives dividends of $1,000 in a given year, only $300 will be subject to tax, and the remaining $700 (70% of $1,000) will be tax exempt. If the corporation receiving the dividend income is in a 34% tax bracket, only $102 in taxes (34% of $300) will result.[4]

Depreciation.   Essentially, there are three methods for computing depreciation expenses: (1) straight-line depreciation, (2) the double-declining balance method, and (3) the modified accelerated cost recovery system. Any one of the three methods results in the same depreciation expense over the life of the asset; however, the last two approaches allow the firm to take the depreciation earlier as opposed to later, which in turn defers taxes until later. Assuming a time value of money, there is an advantage to using the accelerated techniques. Also, management may use straight-line depreciation for reporting income to the shareholders while still using an accelerated method for calculating taxable income.

Net operating loss deduction.   If a corporation has an operating loss (which is simply a loss from operating a business), that loss may be applied against income in other years. The tax laws provide for a **net operating loss carryback and carryforward.** A carryback permits the taxpayer to apply the loss against the profits for the three prior years. If the loss has not been completely absorbed by the profits in these three

---

[4]If corporation A owns at least 20% of corporation B, but less than 80%, 80% of any dividends received may be excluded from taxable income. If 80% or more is owned, all the dividends received may be excluded.

years, the loss may be carried forward to each of the fifteen following years (carryforward). At that time, any loss still remaining may no longer be used as a tax deduction. To illustrate, a 1994 operating loss may be used to recover, in whole or in part, the taxes paid during 1991, 1992, and 1993. If any part of the loss still remains, this amount may be used to reduce taxable income, if any, during the fifteen-year period of 1995 through 2009. A complete example of the net operating loss deduction is provided in Figure 3-4.

Capital gains and losses.   An important tax consideration prior to 1987 was the preferential tax treatment for capital gains; that is, gains from the sale of assets not bought or sold in the ordinary course of business. The Tax Reform Act of 1986 repealed any special treatment of capital gains and while the Revenue Reconciliation Act of 1993 reinstituted preferential treatment in certain unique circumstances, in general, capital gains are taxed at the same rates as ordinary income. However, if a corporation has capital losses that exceed capital gains in any year, these net capital losses may not be deducted from ordinary income. The net losses may, however, be carried back and applied against net capital gains in each of the three years before the current year. If the loss is not completely used in the three prior years, any remaining loss may be carried forward and applied against any net gains in each of the next five years. For example, if a corporation has an $80,000 net capital loss in 1993, it may apply this loss against any net gains in 1990, 1991, and 1992. If any loss remains, it may be carried forward and applied against any gains through 1998.

As an example of the net operating loss carryback and carryforward, assume the Sang Lee Corporation, a trucking operation, has had the following profits and losses reported from 1987 through 1994:

1987	$ 52,000
1988	76,000
1989	100,000
1990	(152,000)
1991	100,000
1992	(194,000)
1993	12,000
1994	94,000

In 1990 and 1992 the corporation incurred operating losses, which may be applied to reduce taxable income and taxes in other years. The tax payments and tax refunds for each year are calculated in Figure 3-4.

Accumulated Earnings Tax

The earnings generated by a corporation are subject to "double taxation," first at the corporate level and then at the stockholder level as the firm's profits are distributed in the form of dividends. If the shareholders have no immediate need for dividend income, the corporation could retain its profits and perhaps even employ the funds for the personal benefit of the company's owners. For example, management could

---

FIGURE 3-4   Sang Lee Corporation Tax Payments and Refunds

Year	Taxable Income	Tax Consequence
1987	$ 52,000	TAX PAYMENT OF $8,000 15% of $50,000 plus 25% of $2,000.
1988	$ 76,000	TAX PAYMENT OF $14,090 15% of $50,000 plus 25% of $25,000 plus 34% of $1,000.
1989	100,000	TAX PAYMENT OF $22,250 15% of $50,000 plus 25% of $25,000 plus 34% of $25,000.
1990	(152,000)	TAX REFUND OF $30,250 $52,000 of the $152,000 loss is applied against 1987 income for a refund of $8000; $76,000 of the loss is applied against 1988 income for a refund of $14,090, leaving $24,000 to be applied against 1989 income of $100,000 for a refund of $8,160—34% of $24,000.
1991	100,000	TAX PAYMENT OF $22,250 Same computation as 1989.
1992	(194,000)	TAX REFUND OF $36,340 AND $18,000 CARRYFORWARD $76,000 of the loss is applied against 1989 income ($24,000 had already been used in 1990) for a refund of $14,090; $100,000 of the loss is applied against 1991 income for a refund of $22,250. The remaining $18,000 loss ($194,000 – $176,000) is to be carried to future years.
1993	12,000	NO TAX PAYMENT OR REFUND; $6000 CARRYFORWARD The $18,000 carryforward from 1992 is used to avoid having to pay any tax, leaving $6000 carryforward ($18,000 – $12,000) for future years.
1994	94,000	TAX PAYMENT OF $18,170 Tax is calculated on $88,000 income ($94,000 income less the $6000 carryforward originating in 1992): 15% of $50,000 plus 25% of $25,000 plus 34% of $13,000.

---

retain the corporate profits but make a personal loan to the stockholders. Also, if the profits were accumulated within the firm, the price of the common stock should rise. Until the stock is sold, the investor would not be required to pay any tax.

To prevent such stratagems, a 28% surtax in addition to the regular income tax is assessed at the corporate level on any accumulation of earnings by a corporation for the purpose of avoiding taxes on its shareholders. The tax does not apply to the retention of profits for *reasonable business* needs. Nor must the money be reinvested immediately as long as there is evidence that future needs require the current accumulation of earnings. Although it is difficult to state exactly when the accumulation of profits is thought to be reasonable, examples would include (1) providing for the replacement of plant and equipment, (2) retiring debt created in connection with the corporation's business, (3) extending more credit to customers, and (4) financing the acquisition of a new business.

Subchapter S Corporation

In deciding between the sole proprietorship or partnership and the corporation, tax considerations are important. Owners attempt to select the form of business organization that maximizes their after-tax returns. To minimize the tax influence on the decision, Congress established the Subchapter S Corporation, which enables a corporation to be taxed as a partnership. This provision eliminates the "double taxation" effect on the corporation. The Subchapter S Corporation files a tax return for information purposes only and pays no taxes. The taxes from the business are paid by the stockholders, whether or not the earnings are distributed. However, to qualify as a Subchapter S Corporation, the following requirements must be met:

1. The firm must be a domestic corporation.
2. There may be no more than 35 shareholders at the beginning of the corporation's life. These shareholders must be individuals, estates, or certain trusts.
3. The corporation cannot be a member of an affiliated group eligible to file a consolidated tax return with another corporation.
4. There may be only one class of stock.
5. A nonresident alien cannot be a stockholder.

Only small to moderate-sized firms typically can satisfy the Subchapter S Corporation requirements. However, if the qualifications can be met, the company may potentially receive the benefits of a corporation while being taxed as a partnership.

Corporate Taxes: An Example

To illustrate certain portions of the tax laws for a corporation, assume that the Griggs Corporation had sales during the past year of $5 million; its cost of goods sold was $3 million; and it incurred operating expenses of $1 million. In addition, it received $185,000 in interest income and $100,000 in dividend income from another corporation. In turn, it paid $40,000 in interest and $75,000 in dividends. Also, it sold old machinery, which had originally cost $350,000, for $200,000. The equipment, purchased five years ago, was being depreciated (straight-line) over a 10-year life and had a book value of $175,000. Finally, the company sold a piece of land for $100,000 that had cost $50,000 six years ago. Given this information, the firm's taxable income is $1,250,000, as computed in the top part of Figure 3-5.

Based on the tax rates from Figure 3-2, Griggs's tax liability is $425,000, as shown at the bottom of Figure 3-5. Note that the $75,000 Griggs paid in dividends is not tax deductible. Also, since the firm's taxable income exceeds $335,000, and the 5% surtax no longer applies, the marginal tax rate and the average tax rate both equal 34%; that is, we could have computed Griggs's tax liability as 34% of $1,250,000, or $425,000.

FIGURE 3-5   Griggs Corporation Tax Computations

Sales			$5,000,000
Cost of goods sold			(3,000,000)
Gross profit			$2,000,000
Operating expenses			(1,000,000)
Operating Income			$1,000,000
Other taxable income and			
expenses:			
Interest income		$185,000	
Dividend income	$100,000		
Less 70% exclusion	70,000	30,000	
Interest expense		(40,000)	175,000
Gain on sale of equipment:			
Selling price		$200,000	
Book value		175,000	25,000
Gain on land sale:			
Selling price		$100,000	
Cost		(50,000)	$ 50,000
Total taxable income			**$1,250,000**
Tax computation:			
15% x $ 50,000 = $ 7,500			
25% x 25,000 = 6,250			
34% x 1,175,000 = 399,500			
$ 1,250,000			
Add 5% surtax for income			
between $100,000 and			
$335,000	$ 11,750		
Tax liability	**$ 425,000**		

SUMMARY

The legal forms of business are then examined. The sole proprietorship is a business operation owned and managed by a single individual. Initiating this form of business is simple and generally does not involve any substantial organizational costs. The proprietor has complete control of the firm but must be willing to assume full responsibility for its outcomes.

The general partnership, which is simply a coming together of two or more individuals, is similar to the sole proprietorship. The limited partnership is another form of partnership sanctioned by states to permit all but one of the partners to have limited liability if this is agreeable to all partners.

The corporation increases the flow of capital from public investors to the business community. Although larger organizational costs and regulations are imposed on this legal entity, the corporation is more conducive to raising large amounts of capital. Limited liability, continuity of life, and ease of transfer in ownership, which increase the marketability of the investment, have contributed greatly in attracting large numbers of investors to the corporate environment. The formal control of the corporation is vested in the parties who own the greatest number of shares. However, day-to-day operations are managed by the corporate officers, who theoretically serve on behalf of the common stockholders.

The tax environment is also presented. In introducing taxes we focus on taxes that affect our business decisions. Three taxable entities exist: the individual, including partnerships; the corporation; and the fiduciary. Only information on the corporate tax environment is given here.

For the most part, taxable income for the corporation is equal to the firm's operating income plus capital gains less any interest expense. The corporation is allowed an income exclusion of 70% of the dividends received from another corporation. Also, if the Internal Revenue Service considers the corporation to be retaining unreasonable amounts of earnings within the business, an accumulated earnings tax may be imposed. To minimize the tax influence in selecting the form of legal organization, a corporation may choose to be a Subchapter S Corporation and be taxed as a partnership, provided certain qualifications can be satisfied.

Tax consequences have a direct bearing on the decisions of the financial manager. The relationships are grounded in the taxability of investment income and the difference in tax treatment for interest expense and dividend payments. Also, shareholders' tax status may influence their preference between gains from stock sale and dividends, which in turn may influence corporate dividend policy.

SELF-CORRECTION PROBLEMS

1. **Corporate Income Tax.**   The Dana Flatt Corporation had sales of $2 million this past year. Its cost of goods sold was $1.2 million, and its operating expenses were $400,000. Interest expenses on outstanding debts were $100,000, and the company paid $40,000 in preferred stock dividends. The corporation received $10,000 in preferred stock dividends and interest income of $12,000. The firm sold stock that had been owned for two years for $40,000; the original cost of the stock was $30,000. Determine the corporation's taxable income and its tax liability.

2. **Carryback-Carryforward.**   Stocking, Inc., has a chain of fast-food restaurants. The firm has been operating for eight years, during which the profits have fluctuated significantly. The taxable income for the past eight years is shown below. Compute the tax payments and refunds for each year.

1986	$ (50,000)	1990	$ 50,000
1987	25,000	1991	150,000
1988	150,000	1992	200,000
1989	(225,000)	1993	(50,000)

SOLUTIONS TO SELF-CORRECTION PROBLEMS

1.

Sales		$2,000,000
Cost of goods sold		1,200,000
Gross profit		800,000
Tax-deductible expenses:		
Operating expenses	$ 400,000	
Interest expenses	100,000	500,000
		$ 300,000
Other income:		
Interest income		12,000
Preferred dividend income	$ 10,000	
Less 70% exclusion	7,000	3,000
Taxable ordinary income		$ 315,000
Gain on sale:		
Selling price	$ 40,000	
Cost	30,000	10,000
Taxable income		**$ 325,000**

Tax liability

.15	×	$ 50,000	= $ 7,500
.25	×	25,000	= 6,250
.34	×	250,000	= 85,000
5% surtax			11,250
			$ 110,000

2.

Year	Taxable Income	Tax Payments	Carryback	Carryforward	Tax Refunds
1986	$ (50,000)				
1987	25,000			$25,000 from 1986	
1988	150,000	$32,000[a]	$125,000 from 1989	25,000 from 1986	
1989	(225,000)				$32,000[b]
1990	50,000			50,000 from 1989	
1991	150,000	22,250[c]	50,000 from 1993	50,000 from 1989	
1992	200,000	61,250			
1993	(50,000)				14,750[d]

[a]Taxes are based on $125,000 ($150,000 taxable income – $25,000 carryforward from 1986).
[b]The tax refund results from a $125,000 carryback to 1988 to recoup the taxes paid in 1988.
[c]Taxes are based on $100,000 ($150,000 taxable income – $50,000 carryforward).
[d]The tax refund results from a $50,000 carryback to 1991. The taxes in 1991 were originally $22,250 based on $100,000 income. With the $50,000 carryback from 1993, the taxes for 1991 are recomputed on $50,000, or $7,500. The difference between the amount originally paid in 1991, or $22,250, and the recalculated $7,500 in taxes is $14,750.

QUESTIONS

1. Define (a) sole proprietorship, (b) partnership, and (c) corporation.
2. Identify the primary characteristics of each form of legal organization.
3. Using the following criteria, specify the legal form of business that is favored: (a) organizational requirements and costs, (b) liability of the owners, (c) continuity of business, (d) transferability of ownership, (e) management control and regulations, (f) ability to raise capital, and (g) income taxes.
4. Does a partnership pay taxes on its income? Explain.
5. When a corporation receives a dividend from another corporation, how is it taxed?
6. What is the purpose of the net operating loss deduction?
7. What is the rationale for an accumulated earnings tax?
8. What is the purpose of the Subchapter S Corporation? In general, what type of firm would qualify as a Subchapter S Corporation?

PROBLEMS

1. The William B. Waugh Corporation is a regional Toyota dealer. The firm sells new and used trucks and is actively involved in the parts business. During the most recent year the company generated sales of $3 million. The combined cost of goods sold and the operating expenses were $2.1 million. Also, $400,000 in interest expense was paid during the year. The firm received $6,000 during the year in dividend income from 1,000 shares of common stock that had been purchased three years previously. However, the stock was sold toward the end of the year for $100 per share; its initial cost was $80 per share. The company also sold land that had been recently purchased and had been held for only four months. The selling price was $50,000; the cost was $45,000. Calculate the corporation's tax liability.

2. Sales for L. B. Menielle, Inc., during the past year amounted to $5 million. The firm provides parts and supplies for oil field service companies. Gross profits for the year were $3 million. Operating expenses totaled $1 million. The interest and dividend income from securities owned were $20,000 and $25,000, respectively. The firm's interest expense was $100,000. The firm sold securities on two occasions during the year, receiving a gain of $40,000 on the first sale but losing $50,000 on the second. The stock sold first had been owned for four years; the stock sold second had been purchased three months prior to the sale. Compute the corporation's tax liability.

3. Sandersen, Inc., sells minicomputers. During the past year the company's sales were $3 million. The cost of its merchandise sold came to $2 million, and cash operating expenses were $400,000; depreciation expense was $100,000, and the firm paid $150,000 in interest on bank loans. Also, the corporation received $50,000 in dividend income but paid $25,000 in the form of dividends to its own common stockholders. Calculate the corporation's tax liability.

Financial Statements Analysis

CHAPTER 4

The Basic Financial Statements

Investors often use financial statements to assess a company's position and prospects. Consider the financial statements of Microsoft, the world's largest computer software company. The company's income statements show a growth in net income from $279 million in 1990 to $1,146 million in 1994, based on an increase in revenues from $1.2 billion to $4.6 billion. Balance sheets show that total assets grew from $1.1 billion in 1990 to $5.4 billion in 1994, whereas liabilities increased from $.2 billion to $.9 billion. During this 4-year period, optimistic investors bid its price up from under $10 per share to more than $50.

This chapter focuses on what investors and other decision makers can learn from financial statements. It extends the discussion of balance sheets and income statements and introduces another major financial statement, the statement of cash flows.

Accounting is commonly misunderstood as being a precise discipline that produces exact measurements of a company's financial position and performance. As a result, many individuals regard accountants as little more than mechanical tabulators who grind out financial reports after processing an imposing amount of detail in accordance with stringent predetermined rules. Although accountants do take methodical steps with masses of data, their rules of measurement allow room for judgment. Managers and accountants who exercise this judgment have more influence on financial reporting than is commonly believed. To understand financial statements fully, you must recognize the judgments that go into their construction.

CLASSIFIED BALANCE SHEET

Figure 4-1 shows the 1993 and 1994 classified balance sheets for Nike, Inc., maker of athletic footwear. They classify assets and equities into five main sections: current assets, noncurrent assets, current liabilities, noncurrent liabilities, and shareholders' equity. Be sure to locate each of these items in the exhibit when you read the description of the item in the following pages.

Current Assets

Current assets include cash and all other assets that are reasonably expected to be converted to cash or sold or consumed during the normal operating cycle. An **operating cycle** is the time span during which cash is spent to acquire goods and services that are used to produce the organization's output, which in turn is sold to customers, who in turn pay for their purchases with cash. Consider a retail business. Its operating cycle is illustrated in the following diagram (figures are hypothetical):

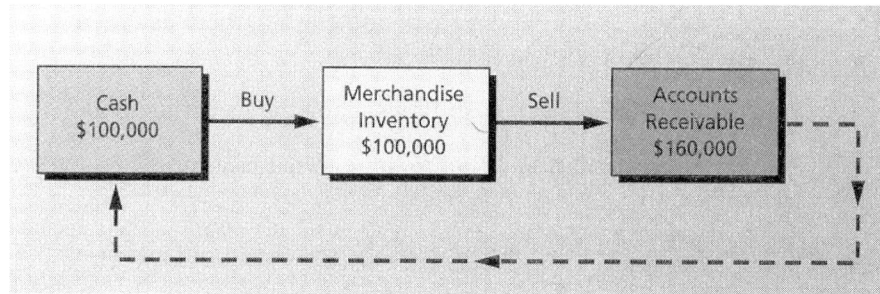

The box for Accounts Receivable (amounts owed to the business by customers) is larger than the other two boxes because the objective of a business is to sell goods at a price higher than acquisition cost. The total amount of profit a firm earns during a particular period depends on how much its selling prices exceed its costs of producing or purchasing the products and additional expenses incurred during the period.

Accountants sometimes assume that an operating cycle is 1 year. But some businesses have several operating cycles during 1 year. Others—such as the distillery, tobacco, and lumber industries—need more than 1 year to complete a single cycle. Inventories in such industries are nevertheless regarded as current assets. Similarly, installment accounts and notes receivable are typically classified as current assets even though they will not be fully collected within 1 year.

As Figure 4-1 shows, current assets fall into several broad categories, such as cash and cash equivalents, accounts receivable, inventories, prepaid expenses, and other current assets. *Cash* consists of bank deposits in checking accounts plus money on hand. **Cash equivalents** are short-term investments that can easily be converted into cash with little delay.[1] Examples include money market funds and Treasury bills. They represent an investment of excess cash not needed immediately. These securities are usually shown at cost or market price, whichever is lower. The market price is disclosed parenthetically if it is above cost. In 1994, Nike had $518,816,000 in cash and cash equivalents.

---

[1]Short-term investments are frequently called *marketable securities*, but this is a misnomer. Strictly speaking, marketable securities may be held for either a short-term or a long-term purpose. Short-term investments should be distinguished from *long-term investments* in the capital stock or bonds of other companies. The latter are noncurrent assets.

FIGURE 4-1   Nike, Inc. Balance Sheet

	May 31	
(in thousands)	1994	1993
ASSETS		
Current assets		
Cash and equivalents	$ 518,816	$ 291,284
Accounts receivable, less allowance for		
doubtful accounts of 28,291 and 19,447	703,682	667,547
Inventories	470,023	592,986
Prepaid expenses	40,307	42,452
Other current assets	37,603	23,499
Total current assets	**1,770,431**	**1,617,768**
Noncurrent assets		
Property, plant, and equipment		
At cost	639,085	571,032
Less: accumulated depreciation	233,240	193,037
Net property, plant, and equipment	405,845	377,995
Goodwill	157,187	159,579
Other assets	40,352	30,927
Total noncurrent assets	603,384	568,501
Total Assets	**$2,373,815**	**$2,186,269**
LIABILITIES AND SHAREHOLDERS' EQUITY		
Current liabilities		
Notes payable	$ 127,378	$ 108,165
Accounts payable	210,576	135,701
Accrued liabilities	181,889	138,563
Income taxes payable	38,287	17,150
Current portion of long-term debt	3,857	52,985
Total current liabilities	**561,987**	**452,564**
Noncurrent liabilities		
Long-term debt	12,364	15,033
Deferred income taxes	18,228	31,978
Other noncurrent liabilities	39,987	43,575
Total noncurrent liabilities	70,579	90,586
Total liabilities	**632,566**	**543,150**
Shareholders' equity		
Redeemable preferred stock	300	300
Common stock at stated value	2,863	2,879
Capital in excess of stated value	108,284	108,451
Retained earnings	1,644,925	1,539,279
Foreign currency translation adjustment	(15,123)	(7,790)
Total shareholders' equity	1,741,249	1,643,119
Total liabilities and shareholders' equity	**$2,373,815**	**$2,186,269**

Accounts receivable is the total amount owed to the company by its customers. Because some customers ultimately will not pay their bill, the total is reduced by an allowance or provision for doubtful accounts (i.e., possible "bad debts"). The difference represents the net amount that the company will probably collect. At the end of the 1994 fiscal year[2] Nike had gross accounts receivable of $731,973,000, but after deducting $28,291,000 for doubtful accounts, the company expects to collect $703,682,000 from its accounts receivable.

Inventories consist of merchandise, finished products of manufacturers, goods in the process of being manufactured, and raw materials. Accountants state inventories at their cost or market price (defined as replacement cost), whichever is lower. Cost of manufactured products normally is composed of raw material cost plus the costs of converting it into a finished product (direct labor and manufacturing overhead). Nike's 1994 inventories stood at $470,023,000.

Determining the cost of inventories is not always as easy as it may seem at first glance. When the total cost of goods purchased or produced by a company is measured, how should it be allocated between the goods sold (an expense) and the goods still on hand (an asset)? Allocation is easy if each unit of the product is readily identifiable, like the cars of an automobile dealer or the expensive merchandise of a jewelry store. Advanced data processing systems have made such specific identification possible for more and more organizations. But it is still expensive to have an elaborate identification system for goods that are purchased and sold in vast numbers and variety.

Prepaid expenses are advance payments to suppliers. They are usually unimportant in relation to other assets. Examples are prepayment of rent and insurance premiums for coverage over the coming operating cycle. They belong in current assets because, if they were not present, more cash would be needed to conduct current operations. In 1994, Nike shows $40,307,000 of prepaid expenses, which is only 2.3% of total current assets.

Other current assets are miscellaneous current assets that do not fit into the listed categories. They might include *notes receivable* and *short-term investments* that are not cash equivalents. For Nike, such assets amounted to $37,603,000 in 1994.

Property, Plant, and Equipment

Property, plant, and equipment are sometimes called **fixed assets** or plant assets. Because they are physical items that can be seen and touched, they are also called **tangible assets**. Details about property, plant, and equipment are usually found in a footnote to the financial statements such as the one for Nike shown in Figure 4-2. Footnotes are an integral part of financial statements. They contain explanations for the summary figures that appear in the statements.

Land is typically accounted for as a separate item and is carried indefinitely at its original cost.

Buildings and *machinery* and *equipment* are initially recorded at cost: the invoice amount, plus freight and installation, less cash discounts. The major difficulties of measurement center on the choice of *depreciation* method—the allocation of the origi-

---

[2]A *fiscal year* is defined as the year established for accounting purposes for the preparation of annual reports. Nike's fiscal year is June 1 through May 31.

FIGURE 4-2   Nike, Inc. Footnote 5 to the 1994 Financial Statements

Note 5. Property, Plant, and Equipment (thousands)

	1994	1993
Land	$ 59,761	$ 50,851
Buildings	154,731	152,368
Machinery and equipment	317,782	296,680
Leasehold improvements	54,383	46,611
Construction-in-progress	52,428	24,522
	$639,085	$571,032
Less: accumulated depreciation	233,240	193,037
Net property, plant, and equipment	**$405,845**	**$377,995**

nal cost to the particular periods or products that benefit from the use of the assets. Remember that depreciation only means allocating the original cost of plant and equipment, not valuing them in the ordinary sense of the term. Balance sheets typically do *not* show replacement cost, resale value, or the price changes since acquisition.

The amount of original cost to be allocated over the total useful life of the asset as depreciation is the difference between the total acquisition cost and the estimated *residual value*. The residual value is the amount expected to be received when selling the asset at the end of its economic life. The depreciation allocation to each year may be made on the basis of time or service. The estimate of useful life, which is an important factor in determining the yearly allocation of depreciation, is influenced by estimates of physical wear and tear, technological change, and economic obsolescence. Thus the useful life is usually less than the physical life.

There are three general methods of depreciation: *straight line, accelerated,* and *units of production.* The straight-line method allocates the same cost to each year of an asset's useful life. Accelerated methods allocate more of the cost to the early years and less to the later years. The units-of-production method allocates cost based on the amount of production rather than the passage of time.

Which method is best? It depends on the firm's goal, the asset involved, and the type of financial statement being prepared. The straight-line method is most popular. More than 90% of all firms use it for at least some assets when preparing financial statements for reporting to the public. In contrast, most U.S. firms use accelerated depreciation when preparing financial statements for the IRS.

Suppose a business spends $42,000 to buy equipment with an estimated useful life of 4 years and an estimated residual value of $2,000. Using the straight-line method of depreciation, the annual depreciation expense in each of the 4 years would be:

$$\frac{\text{original cost} - \text{estimated residual value}}{\text{years of useful life}}$$

$$= \frac{(\$42,000 - \$2,000)}{4}$$

$$= \$10,000 \text{ per year}$$

Figure 4-3 shows how the asset would be displayed in the balance sheet.

FIGURE 4-3   Straight-line Depreciation (figures assumed)

	Balances at End of Year			
	1	2	3	4
Plant and equipment (at original acquisition cost)	$42,000	$42,000	$42,000	$42,000
Less: accumulated depreciation (the portion of original cost that has already been charged to operations as expense)	10,000	20,000	30,000	40,000
Net book value (the portion of original cost not yet charged as expense)	$32,000	$22,000	$12,000	$ 2,000

In Figures 4-1 and 4-2 the original cost of fixed assets on Nike's 1994 balance sheet is $639,085,000. There is *accumulated depreciation* of $233,240,000, the portion of the original cost of the asset that was previously charged as depreciation expense, so the net property, plant, and equipment at May 31, 1994 is $639,085,000 – $233,240,000 = $405,845,000.

Depreciation is the part of an asset that has been used up. It is gone. It is not a pool of cash set aside to replace the asset. If a company decides to accumulate specific cash to replace assets, such cash should be specifically labeled as a cash *fund* for replacement and expansion. Holiday Inns, Inc., has used such a fund, calling it a *capital construction fund.* Such funds are quite rare because most companies can earn better returns by investing any available cash in ordinary operations rather than in special funds. Typically, companies use or acquire cash for the replacement and expansion of plant assets only as specific needs arise.

Leasehold improvements are investments made by a lessee (tenant) in items such as painting, decorating, fixtures, and air-conditioning equipment that cannot be removed from the premises when a lease expires. The costs of leasehold improvements are written off in the same manner as depreciation, but their periodic write-off is called *amortization.*

Construction in progress is shown separately from other assets because the assets are not yet ready for use. It represents assets that will be part of buildings or machinery and equipment when completed.

Natural resources such as mineral deposits are not illustrated here, but they are typically grouped with plant assets. Their original cost is written off in the form of *depletion* as the resources are used. For example, a coal mine may cost $10 million and originally contain an estimated 5 million tons. The depletion rate would be $2 per ton. If 500,000 tons were mined during the first year, depletion would be $1 million for that year; if 300,000 tons were mined the second year, depletion would be $600,000; and so forth until the entire $10 million has been charged as depletion expense.

Long-term investments are also noncurrent assets. They include long-term holdings of securities of other firms. Nike does not have any long-term investments, unless they are combined with other small, miscellaneous noncurrent assets in the $40,352,000 of *other assets* shown in Figure 4-1.

Intangible Assets

Tangible assets such as cash or equipment can be physically observed. In contrast, **intangible assets** are a class of *long-lived assets* that are not physical in nature. They are rights to expected future benefits deriving from their acquisition and continued possession. Examples are goodwill, franchises, patents, trademarks, and copyrights. In Figure 4-1 goodwill of $157,187,000 at May 31, 1994, is Nike's only intangible asset.

Goodwill is the excess of the cost of an acquired company over the sum of the fair market values of its identifiable individual assets less its liabilities. For example, Nike acquired Cole Haan for $95 million. It could assign only $13 million to various identifiable assets such as receivables, plant, and patents less liabilities assumed by Nike; the remainder, $82 million, was recorded as goodwill.

The accounting for goodwill illustrates how an exchange transaction is a basic concept of accounting. After all, many owners could obtain a premium price if they sold their companies. But such goodwill is never recorded. Only the goodwill arising from an *actual acquisition* should be shown as an asset on the purchaser's records.

For shareholder-reporting purposes, goodwill must be amortized (depreciated), generally in a straight-line manner, over the periods benefited. In the United States, the longest allowed amortization period is 40 years; in Japan and France, for example, it is 5 years. Nike is amortizing its $82 million of goodwill from the Cole Haan purchase at the rate of $82,000,000 \div 40 = $2,050,000 per year. The shortest amortization period is not specified, but a lump-sum write-off on acquisition is forbidden for U.S. firms.

Many managers and accountants insist that some intangible assets have unlimited lives. Nevertheless, the attitude of the regulatory bodies toward accounting for intangible assets has become increasingly conservative. For example, before 1970, the amortization of goodwill, trademarks, and franchises with indefinite useful lives was not mandatory in the U.S. But in 1970 the regulators ruled that the values of all intangible assets eventually disappear, thus making amortization mandatory.

Companies in many countries regard research and development costs as assets. They assume that research costs are incurred to purchase an asset that would benefit future operations and thus amortize research costs over the years of expected benefit, usually 3 to 6 years. In the U.S., however, the FASB has banned deferral and required write-off of these costs as incurred. The FASB admits that research and development costs may generate many long-term benefits, but the general high degree of uncertainty about the extent and measurement of future benefits has led to conservative accounting in the form of immediate write-off.

Liabilities

Assets are, of course, only part of the picture of any organization's financial health. Its *liabilities*, both current and noncurrent, are equally important.

Current liabilities are an organization's debts that fall due within the coming year or within the normal operating cycle if longer than a year. Turn again to Figure 4-1. *Notes payable* are short-term debt backed by formal promissory notes held by a bank or business creditors. *Accounts payable* are amounts owed to suppliers who extended credit for purchases on open account. *Accrued liabilities* or *accrued expenses payable* are recognized for wages, salaries, interest, and similar items. The accountant recognizes expenses as they occur—regardless of when they are paid for in cash. *Income taxes payable* is a special accrued expense of enough magnitude to warrant a separate classification. The *current portion of long-term debt* shows the payments due within the next year on bonds and other long-term debt.

Some companies also list *unearned revenue,* also called deferred revenue. Such revenue occurs when cash is received before the related goods or services are delivered. For example, *Newsweek* magazine has such an account because it is obligated to send magazines to subscribers with prepaid subscriptions. Nike had no unearned revenue in 1994, but it did have current liabilities totaling $561,987,000.

Noncurrent liabilities, also called **long-term liabilities,** are an organization's debts that fall due beyond one year. Figure 4-1 shows Nike's noncurrent liabilities for 1994 as $70,579,000, making its total liabilities $632,566,000. Nike has two noncurrent liabilities, long-term debt (which we will discuss in more depth in a moment) and *deferred income taxes.* The latter rather technical and controversial item arises because the financial statements used for reporting to shareholders differ legitimately from those used for reporting to the income tax authorities. Addendum 4 provides more details about deferred taxes.

Figure 4-4 is a footnote from the financial statements that further breaks down Nike's long-term debts. Note especially the next to last line in this exhibit, "Less: current maturities." This item refers to payments due in the next year. The $3,857,000 noted on this line is subtracted from long-term debt because it has already been included in current liabilities. The remaining $12,364,000 is shown as "Long-term debt" in Figure 4-1.

Long-term debt may be secured or unsecured. *Secured debt* provides debt-holders with first claim on specified assets. Mortgage bonds are an example of secured debt. If the company is unable to meet its regular obligations on the bonds, the specified assets may be sold and the proceeds used to pay off the firm's obligations to its bondholders, in which case secured debt holders have first claim. Nike's obligation for the capital warehouse lease is like a secured debt. If Nike cannot make the installment payments, the warehouse will be returned to the lessor.

Unsecured debt consists of **debentures** (e.g., bonds, notes, or loans), which are formal certificates of indebtedness that are accompanied by a promise to pay interest at a specified annual rate. Unsecured debt holders are general creditors who have a

---

FIGURE 4-4   Nike, Inc. Footnote 8 to the 1994 Financial Statements

Note 8. Long-Term Debt (Thousands)

	May 31	
	1994	1993
8.45% unsecured term loan, due July 1993	—	$25,000
7.90% unsecured term loan, due June 1993	—	25,000
9.43% capital warehouse lease, payable in quarterly installments through 2007	$ 9,098	9,628
Other	7,123	8,390
	$16,221	$68,018
Less: Current maturities	3,857	52,985
TOTAL	**$12,364**	**$15,033**

general claim against total assets rather than a specific claim against particular assets. Most of Nike's long-term debt is unsecured. Holders of **subordinated** *bonds* or *debentures* are junior to the other creditors in exercising claims against assets.

The following simplified example should clarify these ideas. Suppose a corporation is liquidated. **Liquidation** means converting assets to cash and using the cash to pay off outside claims. The company had a single asset, a building, that was sold for $120,000 cash:

Assets		Liabilities and Stockholders' Equity	
Cash	$120,000	Accounts payable	$ 60,000
		First-mortgage bonds payable	80,000
		Subordinated debentures payable	40,000
		Total liabilities	$180,000
		Stockholders' equity (negative)	(60,000)
Total assets	**$120,000**	Total liab. and stk. eq.	**$120,000**

The mortgage (secured) bondholders would be paid in full ($80,000). Trade creditors such as suppliers would be paid the remaining $40,000 for their $60,000 claim ($.67 on the dollar). Other claimants would get nothing. If the debentures were *unsubordinated,* the $40,000 of cash remaining after paying $80,000 to the mortgage holders would be used to settle the $100,000 claims of the unsecured creditors as follows:

To trade creditors	6/10 × $40,000 = $24,000
To debenture holders	4/10 × $40,000 = 16,000
Total cash distributed	**$40,000**

To increase the appeal of their bonds, many corporations issue debt that is *convertible* into common stock. Convertibility allows bondholders to participate in a company's success without the risk of holding common stock. Suppose convertible bonds are issued for $1,000 when the stock price is $22, with a provision that each bond can be converted into 40 common shares. If the stock price increases by 50% to $33 a share, the bondholder could exchange the $1,000 bond for 40 shares worth 40 × $33 = $1,320. If the stock price falls (or does not increase beyond $25 a share), the bondholder can keep the bond and receive $1,000 at maturity.

Stockholders' Equity

The final element of a balance sheet is *stockholders' equity* (also called *shareholders' equity* or *owners' equity* or *capital* or *net worth*), the total residual interest in the business. It is the excess of total assets over total liabilities. The main elements of stockholders' equity arise from two sources: (1) contributed or paid-in capital and (2) retained income.

Paid-in capital typically comes from owners who invest in the business in exchange for stock certificates, which are issued as evidence of stockholder rights. Capital stock can be divided into two major classes: *common stock* and *preferred stock*. Some companies have several categories of each, all with a variety of different attributes.

All corporations have **common stock**. Such stock has no predetermined rate of dividends and is the last to obtain a share in the assets when the corporation is dissolved. Common shares usually have voting power in the management of the corporation. Common stock is usually the riskiest investment in a corporation, being unattractive in dire times but attractive in prosperous times because, unlike other stocks, there is no limit to the stockholder's potential participation in earnings.

Figure 4-1 shows that Nike has preferred stock, in addition to common stock. About 40% of the major companies in the United States issue **preferred stock.** It typically has some priority over other shares regarding dividends or the distribution of assets on liquidation. For example, Nike pays an annual preferred stock dividend of $.10 per share, or $30,000 in total. These dividends must be paid in full before any dividends are paid to any other classes of stock. Preferred shareholders in Nike, as in most companies with preferred stock, do not have voting privileges regarding the management of the corporation.

Stock frequently has a designated **par** or **legal** or **stated value** that is printed on the face of the certificate. For preferred stock (and bonds), par is a basis for designating the amount of dividends or interest. Many preferred stocks have $100 par values. That is, a 9%, $100 par preferred stock would carry a $9 annual dividend. Similarly, an 8% *bond* usually means that the investor is entitled to annual interest of $80 because most bonds have par values of $1,000.

In contrast, par value has no practical importance for common stock. Historically, the par amount of common stock was intended only to measure the maximum legal liability of the stockholder in case the corporation could not pay its debts. (Shareholders typically have **limited liability,** which means that creditors cannot seek payment from them as individuals if the corporation itself cannot pay its debts.) Currently, par is set at a nominal amount (e.g., $1) in relation to the market value of the stock on issuance (e.g., $70). It is generally illegal for a corporation to sell an original issue of its common stock below par.

Capital in excess of stated value is the excess received over the stated, par, or legal value of the shares issued. Common shares are almost always issued at a price substantially greater than par. Suppose all outstanding common shares of Nike had been issued for cash. The cumulative balance sheet effect at May 31, 1994, would be:

Cash	$111,147,000	Common stock, at stated value	$ 2,863,000
		Capital in excess of stated value	108,284,000
		Total paid-in capital	$111,147,000

Retained earnings, called *retained income,* is the increase in stockholders' equity caused by profitable operations. Retained earnings is the dominant item of stockholders' equity for most companies. For instance, as of May 31, 1994, Nike had common stockholders' equity of $1,741,249,000, of which $1,644,925,000 was retained income.

The final item in Figure 4-1, *foreign currency translation adjustment,* exists only for companies with foreign operations. It arises from changes in the exchange rate between the dollar and foreign currencies. Further details are beyond the scope of this book.

Many companies have **treasury stock,** which is a corporation's own stock that has been issued and subsequently repurchased by the company and is being held for a specific purpose. Such repurchase is a decrease in ownership claims. It should therefore appear on a balance sheet as a deduction from total stockholders' equity. The stock is not retired; it is only held temporarily "in the treasury" to be distributed later, possibly as a part of an employee stock purchase plan or as an executive bonus or for use in acquiring another company. Cash dividends are not paid on shares held in the treasury, but are distributed only to the outstanding shares (those in the hands of stockholders). Treasury stock is usually of minor significance in the financial picture of a corporation. Nike had no treasury stock in 1994.

INCOME STATEMENT

Most investors are vitally concerned about a company's ability to produce long-run earnings and dividends. In this regard, income statements are more important than balance sheets. Revenue is shown first; this represents the total sales value of products delivered and services rendered to customers. Expenses are then listed and deducted.

Use of Subtotals

An income statement can take one of two major forms: single step or multiple step. A single-step statement merely lists all expenses without drawing subtotals, whereas a multiple-step statement contains one or more subtotals. Subtotals highlight significant relationships. As explained in the preceding chapter, sometimes cost of goods sold is deducted from sales to show gross profit or gross margin. The size of the margin above merchandise costs is an important statistic for many managers and analysts.

Figure 4-5 illustrates the two most common subtotals: *gross profit* and *income from operations* (also called *operating income*).

Depreciation expense, selling expenses, and administrative expenses are often grouped as "operating expenses" and deducted from the gross profit to obtain operating income, which is also called *operating profit.* (Of course, cost of goods sold is also an operating expense. Why? Because it is also deducted from sales revenue to obtain "operating income.") In 1994, Nike had a gross profit of $1,488,245,000 and operating income of $514,146,000.

Operating and Financial Management

Operating income is a popular subtotal because of the often made distinction between operating management and financial management. *Operating management* is mainly concerned with the major day-to-day activities that generate sales revenue.

FIGURE 4-5   Nike, Inc. Statement of Income (thousands except per share data)

	Year Ended May 31	
	1994	1993
Revenues	$3,789,668	$3,930,984
Cost of sales	2,301,423	2,386,993
Gross profit	$1,488,245	$1,543,991
Selling and administrative expenses	974,099	922,261
Income from operations	$ 514,146	$ 621,730
Other expense (income)		
Interest expense	$ 15,282	$ 25,739
Miscellaneous expense	8,270	1,475
Total other expense	$ 23,552	$ 27,214
Income before provision for income taxes	$ 490,594	$ 594,516
Provision for income taxes	191,800	229,500
Net income	$ 298,794	$ 365,016
Earnings per share*	$ 3.96	$ 4.74

*Computation of earnings per share:

	1994	1993
Net income	$298,794,000	$365,016,000
Divided by average common shares outstanding	75,456,000	77,063,000
Earnings per share	$ 3.96	$ 4.74

In contrast, *financial management* is mainly concerned with where to get cash and how to use cash for the benefit of the organization. That is, financial management attempts to answer such questions as: How much cash should be held in checking accounts? Should we pay a dividend? Should we borrow or issue common stock? The best managers are superb at both operating management and financial management. However, many managers are better operating managers than financial managers, or vice versa.

Because interest income and expense are usually a result of financial rather than operating decisions, they often appear as separate items after operating income. This approach facilitates comparisons of operating income between years and between companies. Some companies make heavy use of debt, which causes high interest expense, whereas other companies incur little debt and interest expense. Other nonoperating items might include gains or losses from foreign exchange transactions or from disposals of fixed assets.

Income, Earnings, and Profits

Although this book tends to use *income* most often, the terms *income, earnings,* and *profits* are often used as synonyms. The income statement is also called the *statement of earnings, the statement of profit and loss,* and the *P & L statement.* Most companies still use net *income* on their income statements, but the term "earnings" is becoming increasingly popular because it has a preferable image. Nike's 1994 net income was $298,794,000.

FIGURE 4-6   Nike, Inc. Statement of Retained Earnings for the Year Ended May 31, 1990 (thousands of dollars)

Retained earnings, May 31, 1993		$1,539,279
Net income (Figure 4-5)		298,794
Total		1,838,073
Deduct:	dividends on common stock	59,485
	dividends on preferred stock	30
	repurchase of common stock	133,633
Retained earnings, May 31, 1994		**$1,644,925**

The term **net income** is the popular "bottom line"—the residual after deducting *all* expenses including income taxes. The term *net* is seldom used for any subtotals that precede the calculation of *net income.* Instead, the subtotals are called *income.* Thus the appropriate term is *operating income* or *income from operations,* not *net operating income.*

Income taxes are often a prominent expense and are not merely listed with operating expenses. Instead, income taxes are usually deducted as a separate item immediately before net income. This expense is often called "provision for income taxes," as in Figure 4-5.

Income statements conclude with disclosure of **earnings per share.** Figure 4-5 illustrates this as the net income divided by the average number of common shares outstanding during the year. Nike earned $3.96 per share in 1994.

STATEMENT OF RETAINED EARNINGS

Using the net income figure from the income statement enables accountants to analyze the changes in retained earnings. This analysis is frequently placed in a separate statement, the **statement of retained earnings** (also called **statement of retained income**). As Figure 4-6 demonstrates, the major reasons for changes in retained earnings are dividends and net income. Note especially that dividends are *not* expenses; they are not deductions in computing net income. Nike also reduced retained earnings by repurchasing some of its own common stock. The retained earnings associated with the repurchased shares is deducted because those shares are no longer outstanding.

Dividends, you will recall, are distributions of assets to stockholders that reduce retained income.

STATEMENT OF CASH FLOWS

Many decision makers focus primarily on two financial statements, the income statement and the balance sheet. However, another statement, the *statement of cash flows,* is also required as a basic financial statement. The statement has the following purposes:

1. It shows the relationship of net income to changes in cash balances. Cash balances can decline despite positive net income and vice versa.
2. It reports past cash flows as an aid to
    a. Predicting future cash flows
    b. Evaluating management's generation and use of cash
    c. Determining a company's ability to pay interest and dividends, and to pay debts when they are due
3. It reveals commitments to assets that may restrict or expand future courses of action.

Basic Concepts

A **statement of cash flows** reports the cash receipts and cash payments of an organization during a particular period. Note that balance sheets show the status of an entity at a day in time. In contrast, statements of cash flows, income statements, and statements of retained income cover periods. They provide the explanations of why the balance sheet items have changed by providing information about operating, investing, and financing activities. This linkage is depicted in the accompanying diagram:

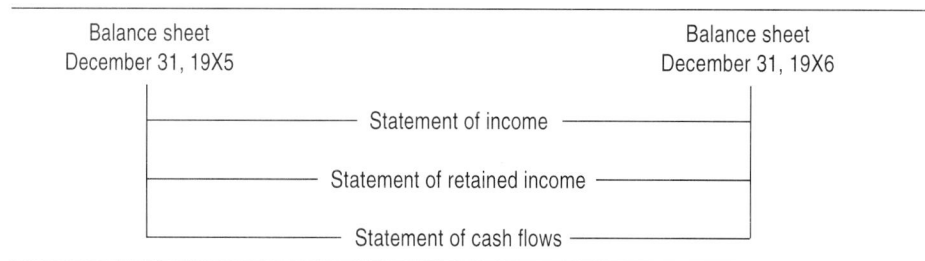

Balance sheet		Balance sheet
December 31, 19X5		December 31, 19X6
	Statement of income	
	Statement of retained income	
	Statement of cash flows	

The statement of cash flows explains where cash came from during a period and where it was spent.

One reason for the popularity of cash flow statements is that they show information that readers of financial reports could otherwise obtain only by makeshift analysis and interpretation of published balance sheets and statements of income and retained income.

The statement of cash flows usually explains changes in cash and cash equivalents, both of which can quickly be used to meet obligations. *Cash equivalents,* as noted earlier in this chapter, are highly liquid short-term investments that can easily be converted into cash with little delay. Hereafter, when we refer to cash, we mean both cash and cash equivalents.

Typical Activities Affecting Cash

The fundamental approach to the statement of cash flows is simple: (1) list the activities that increased cash (i.e., cash inflows) and those that decreased cash (cash outflows), and (2) place each cash inflow and outflow into one of three categories according to the type of activity that caused it: *operating activities, investing activities,* and *financing activities.*

The following activities are those found most often in statements of cash flows:

Operating Activities

Cash Inflows
Collections from customers
Interest and dividends collected
Other operating receipts

Cash Outflows
Cash payments to suppliers
Cash payments to employees
Interest paid
Taxes paid
Other operating cash payments

Investing Activities

Cash Inflows
Sale of property, plant, and
  equipment
Sale of securities that are not cash
  equivalents
Receipt of loan repayments

Cash Outflows
Purchase of property, plant, and
  equipment
Purchase of securities that are not
  cash equivalents
Making loans

Financing Activities

Cash Inflows
Borrowing cash from creditors
Issuing equity securities

Cash Outflows
Repayment of amounts borrowed
Repurchase of equity shares
  (including the purchase of
  treasury stock)
Payment of dividends

As the lists of activities indicate, cash flows from operating activities are generally the effects of transactions that affect the income statement (e.g., sales and wages). Investing activities include (1) lending and collecting on loans and (2) acquiring and selling long-term assets. Financing activities include obtaining resources from creditors and owners and providing them with returns *of* their investments and owners with returns *on* their investments in the form of cash dividends.

Perhaps the most troublesome classifications are the receipts and payments of interest and the receipts of dividends. After all, these items are associated with investment and financing activities. After much debate, the FASB decided to include these items with cash flows from operating activities. Why? Mainly because they affect the computation of income. In contrast, payments of cash dividends are financing activities because they do not affect income.

Focus of a Statement of Cash Flows

The basic ideas underlying the statement of cash flows are straightforward. Consider the illustration of the hypothetical Balmer Company. Figure 4-7 shows the company's condensed balance sheets and income statement. (We will look at the more complex, real statement for Nike at the end of this chapter.)

Because the statement of cash flows explains the *causes* for the change in cash, the first step is to compute the amount of the change (which represents the net *effect*):

**FIGURE 4-7   Balmer Company Statement of Income for the Year Ended December 31, 19X2
(in thousands)**

Sales		$200
Costs and expenses		
Cost of goods sold	$100	
Wages and salaries	36	
Depreciation	17	
Interest	4	
Total costs and expenses		157
Income before income taxes		43
Income taxes		20
Net income		**$ 23**

Balmer Company
Balance Sheet as of December 31 (in thousands)

Assets				Liabilities and Stockholders' Equity			
	19X2	19X1	Increase (Decrease)		19X2	19X1	Increase (Decrease)
Current assets				Current liabilities			
Cash	$ 16	$ 25	$ (9)	Accounts payable	$ 74	$ 6	$ 68
Accounts receivable	45	25	20	Wages and salaries			
Inventory	100	60	40	payable	25	4	21
Total current assets	161	110	51	Total current liabilities	99	10	89
Fixed assets, gross	581	330	251	Long-term debt	125	5	120
Less accum. depreciation	(101)	(110)	9	Stockholders' equity	417	315	102
Net fixed assets	480	220	260	Total liabilities and			
Total assets	$641	$330	$311	stockholders' equity	$641	$330	$311

Cash, December 31, 19X1	$25,000
Cash, December 31, 19X2	16,000
Net decrease in cash	**$ 9,000**

Figure 4-8 illustrates how this information is often shown at the bottom of a statement of cash flows. The beginning cash balance is added to the net change to compute the ending cash balance. Another common practice is to place the beginning cash balance at the top of the statement and the ending cash balance at the bottom. However, there is no requirement that beginning and ending cash balances be shown explicitly in the statement of cash flows. Showing only the net change is sufficient.

When business expansion occurs, as in this case, and where there is a strong cash position at the outset, cash often declines. Why? Because cash is usually needed for investment in various business assets required for expansion, including investment in accounts receivable and inventories.

FIGURE 4-8   **Balmer Company Statement of Cash Flows for the Year Ended December 31, 19X2 (in thousands)**

Cash Flows from Operating Activities

Cash collections from customers		$180
Cash payments		
To suppliers	$72	
To employees	15	
For interest	4	
For taxes	20	
Total cash payments		(111)
Net cash provided by operating activities		$ 69

Cash Flows from Investing Activities

Purchases of fixed assets	$(287)	
Proceeds from sale of fixed assets	10	
Net cash used in investing activities		(277)

Cash Flows from Financing Activities

Proceeds from issue of long-term debt	$120	
Proceeds from issue of common stock	98	
Dividends paid	(19)	
Net cash provided by financing activities		199
Net decrease in cash		$ (9)
Cash, December 31, 19X1		25
Cash, December 31, 19X2		**$ 16**

The statement in Figure 4-8 gives a direct picture of where cash came from and where it went. In this instance, the excess of cash outflows over cash inflows reduced cash by $9,000. Without the statement of cash flows, the readers of the annual report would have to conduct their own analyses of the beginning and ending balance sheets, the income statement, and the statement of retained income to get a grasp of the impact of financial management decisions.

Most important, this illustration demonstrates how a firm may simultaneously (1) have a significant amount of net income, as computed by accountants on the accrual basis, and yet (2) have a decline in cash that could become severe. Indeed, many growing businesses are desperate for cash even though reported net income zooms upward.

PREPARATION OF A STATEMENT OF CASH FLOWS: THE DIRECT METHOD

Now that you know why statements of cash flow are important, we can consider the preparation of such statements. The first major section in the statement of cash flows in Figure 4-8 is **cash flows from operating activities.** The section might also be called *cash flow from operations, cash provided by operations,* or, if operating activities decrease cash, *cash used for operations.*

Collections from sales to customers are almost always the major operating activity that increases cash. Correspondingly, disbursements for purchases of goods to be sold and operating expenses are almost always the major operating cash outflows. The excess of collections over disbursements is the net cash provided by operating activities. There are two ways to compute this amount: the *direct method* and the *indirect method.*

Because it is easier to understand, the FASB favors the *direct method.* It is used in Figure 4-8: collections minus operating disbursements equals net cash provided by operating activities—$180,000 – $111,000 = $69,000. The *indirect method* is explained later in this chapter.

The second and third major sections of the statement present examples of cash flows from investing activities ($277,000 outflow) and financing activities ($199,000 inflow), respectively.

Working from Income Statement Amounts to Cash Amounts

Many accountants build the statement of cash flows from the *changes* in balance sheet items, a few additional facts, and their familiarity with the typical causes of changes in cash. For instance, for convenience we used $180,000 as the amount of cash collections from Balmer Company customers for 19X2. However, most accounting systems do not provide such a balance. Therefore accountants often compute the collections by beginning with the sales in the income statement (an amount calculated using the accrual basis) and adding (or deducting) the *change* in the accounts receivable balance. A detailed analysis of collections and other operating items follows.

a. Balmer Company recognized $200,000 of revenue in 19X2, but because accounts receivable increased by $20,000, Balmer collected only $180,000 from customers:

	Sales	$200,000
+	Beginning accounts receivable	25,000
	Potential collections	$225,000
–	Ending accounts receivable	45,000
	Cash collections from customers	**$180,000**

Instead of adding the beginning accounts receivable balance and then deducting the ending accounts receivable, we could add the decrease in accounts receivable (or deduct the increase):

Sales	$200,000
Decrease (increase) in accounts receivable	(20,000)
Cash collections from customers	**$180,000**

b. The difference between the $100,000 cost of goods sold and the $72,000 cash payment to suppliers is accounted for by changes in inventory *and* accounts payable. The $40,000 increase in inventory indicates that purchases exceeded the cost of goods sold by $40,000:

	Ending inventory	$100,000
+	Cost of goods sold	100,000
	Inventory to account for	$200,000
−	Beginning inventory	(60,000)
	Purchases of inventory	**$140,000**

Although purchases were $140,000, payments to suppliers were only $72,000. Why? Because trade accounts payable increased by $68,000, from $6,000 to $74,000:

	Beginning trade accounts payable	$ 6,000
+	Purchases	140,000
	Total amount to be paid	$146,000
−	Ending trade accounts payable	(74,000)
	Accounts paid in cash	**$ 72,000**

The effects of inventory and trade accounts payable can be combined as follows:

Cost of goods sold	$100,000
Increase (decrease) in inventory	40,000
Decrease (increase) in trade accounts payable	(68,000)
Payments to suppliers	**$ 72,000**

c. Cash payments to employees were only $15,000 because the wages and salaries expense of $36,000 was offset by a $21,000 increase in wages and salaries payable:

	Beginning wages and salaries payable	$ 4,000
+	Wages and salaries expense	36,000
	Total to be paid	$40,000
−	Ending wages and salaries payable	(25,000)
	Cash payments to employees	**$15,000**

or

Wages and salaries expense	$36,000
Decrease (increase) in wages and salaries payable	(21,000)
Cash payments to employees	**$15,000**

d. Note that both interest payable and income taxes payable were zero at the beginning and at the end of 19X2. Therefore the entire $4,000 interest expense and the $20,000 income tax expense were paid in cash in 19X2.

Figure 4-9 summarizes the differences between Balmer Company's net income of $23,000 and net cash provided by operating activities of $69,000 in 19X2. Examine Figure 4-8 and confirm that the $69,000 cash inflow from operating activities is shown in the first section of the statement of cash flows.

FIGURE 4-9   Comparison of Net Income and Net Cash Provided by Operating Activities

	Income Statement	Adjustments	Cash Flows Statement
Sales	$200,000		
Increase in accounts receivable		$(20,000)	
Cash collections from customers			$180,000
Cost of goods sold	(100,000)		
Increase in inventory		(40,000)	
Increase in accounts payable		68,000	
Cash payments to suppliers			(72,000)
Wages and salaries expense	(36,000)		
Increase in wages and salaries payable		21,000	
Cash paid to employees			(15,000)
Interest: expense equals cash flow	(4,000)		(4,000)
Income taxes: expense equals cash flow	(20,000)		(20,000)
Depreciation: deducted in computing net income but not a cash outflow	(17,000)	17,000	
Net income	$ 23,000		
Total additions (deductions)		$ 46,000	
Net cash provided by operating activities			$ 69,000

Investing and Financing Cash Flows

If the necessary information regarding investing and financing cash flows is not directly available, accountants analyze *changes* in all balance sheet items *except* cash. The following rules pertain:

- *Increases in cash (cash inflows)* are from:
  Increases in liabilities or stockholders' equity
  Decreases in noncash assets

- *Decreases in cash (cash outflows)* are from:
  Decreases in liabilities or stockholders' equity
  Increases in noncash assets

Consider Balmer Company's balance sheet (Figure 4-7). All noncash *current* assets and *current* liabilities of Balmer Company were affected only by operating activities, which we just discussed. Now let's look at three *noncurrent* accounts: fixed assets, long-term debt, and stockholders' equity.

a. Fixed assets increased by $260,000 in 19X2. Three items usually explain changes in net fixed assets: (1) asset acquisitions, (2) asset dispositions, and (3) depreciation expense for the period. Therefore:

increase in net plant assets = acquisitions – disposals – depreciation expense

If we had no information about Balmer Company's asset disposals, we could compute the book value of disposals from the above equation and get:

$$\$260,000 \; = \; \$287,000 - \text{disposals} - \$17,000$$
$$\text{disposals} \; = \; \$287,000 - \$17,000 - \$260,000$$
$$\text{disposals} \; = \; \$10,000$$

Balmer Company received exactly the book value for the assets sold. (We discuss disposals for other than book value later in this chapter.) If we know the amount of disposals, but either acquisitions or depreciation expense were unknown, we could determine the missing item by applying this same equation. Both asset acquisitions and asset disposals are *investing activities* that affect cash.

b. Long-term debt increased by $125,000 – $5,000 = $120,000. Long-term debt was issued, which is a *financing activity* that increased cash.

c. The $102,000 increase in stockholders' equity can be explained by three factors: (1) issuance (or repurchase) of capital stock, (2) net income (or loss), and (3) dividends. Therefore:

increase in stockholders' equity = new issuance + net income – dividends

Suppose data about the issuance of new capital stock has not been provided:

$$\$102,000 \; = \; \text{new issuance} + \$23,000 - \$19,000$$
$$\text{new issuance} \; = \; \$102,000 - \$23,000 + \$19,000$$
$$\text{new issuance} \; = \; \$98,000, \text{an inflow of cash}$$

Both the issuance of new shares and the payment of cash dividends are *financing activities* that affect cash.

Reexamine Figure 4-8. The asset acquisitions and disposals from paragraph **a** are listed with cash flows from investing activities, and the effects of debt and equity issues and dividend payments from paragraphs **b** and **c** are shown with cash flows from financing activities.

Noncash Investing and Financing Activities

Major investment and financing activities that do not affect cash must be reported in a schedule that accompanies the statement of cash flows. For example, consider the acquisition of a $120,000 warehouse in exchange for the issuance of capital stock. The transaction would not be included in the body of the statement of cash flows. Why? Because cash was unaffected. But the transaction is almost identical to one in which capital stock is issued for cash of $120,000, which is immediately used to purchase the warehouse. Therefore such a transaction should be disclosed to readers of a statement of cash flows. Disclosure is made in a schedule that follows directly after the statement. Balmer Company did not have such a transaction in 19X2.

Cash Flow and Earnings

A focal point of the statement of cash flows is the net cash flow from operating activities. Frequently, this is called simply **cash flow**. The importance of cash flow has been stressed by Harold Williams, the former chairman of the SEC, quoted in *Forbes:* "If I had to make a forced choice between having earnings information and having cash flow information, today I would take cash flow information." Fortunately, we do not have to make a choice. Cash flow and income both convey useful information about an entity.

Some companies used to stress a cash-flow-per-share figure and provide it in addition to the required earnings-per-share figure. But cash-flow-per-share ignores noncash expenses that are just as important as cash expenses for judging overall company performance. Moreover, a reported cash-flow-per-share says nothing about the cash needed for replacement and expansion of facilities. Thus the entire per-share cash flow from operations may not be available for cash dividends. Because it gives an incomplete picture, a cash-flow-per-share figure can be quite misleading. Accordingly, the FASB has specifically prohibited the reporting of cash-flow-per-share amounts.

Both cash flow and accrual earnings data are useful. As Professor Loyd Heath said, "Asking which one is better, cash flow or earnings, is like asking which shoe is more useful, your right or your left."

PREPARATION OF A STATEMENT OF CASH FLOWS: THE INDIRECT METHOD

Instead of using the direct method of preparing statements of cash flows, accountants often find it convenient to compute cash flows from operating activities by the **indirect method.** The indirect method reconciles net income to the net cash provided by operating activities. It also shows the link between the income statement and the statement of cash flows.

Reconciliation of Net Income to Net Cash Provided by Operations

The reconciliation begins with net income. Accountants then make additions or deductions for items that affect net income and net cash flow differently. Using the numbers in our Balmer Company example, Figure 4-10 shows the reconciliation. Net cash provided by operating activities exceeds net income by $46,000.

Consider the logic applied in the reconciliation in Figure 4-10:

1. Depreciation is added back to net income because it was deducted in the computation of net income. If the purpose is to calculate cash provided by operations, the depreciation of $17,000 should not have been subtracted. Why? Because it was not a cash expense this period. Since it was subtracted, it must now be added back to income to get cash from operations. The addback simply cancels the earlier deduction.
2. Increases in noncash current assets such as receivables and inventory result in less cash flow from operations. For instance, suppose the $20,000 increase in receivables resulted from credit sales made near the end of the year. The $20,000 sales figure would be included in the computation of net income, but the $20,000 would not have increased cash flow from operations. Therefore the reconciliation deducts the $20,000 from the net income to help pinpoint the effects on cash.
3. Increases in current liabilities such as accounts payable and wages payable result in more cash flow from operations. For instance, suppose the $21,000 increase in

---

FIGURE 4-10 Supporting Schedule to Statement of Cash Flows Reconciliation of Net Income to Net Cash Provided by Operating Activities (in thousands)

Net income		$23
Adjustments to reconcile net income		
to net cash provided by operating activities		
Depreciation	$17	
Net increase in accounts receivable	(20)	
Net increase in inventory	(40)	
Net increase in accounts payable	68	
Net increase in wages and salaries payable	21	
Total additions and deductions		46
Net cash provided by operating activities		**$69**

---

wages payable was attributable to wages earned near the end of the year, but not yet paid in cash. The $21,000 wages expense would be deducted in computing net income, but the $21,000 would not have decreased cash flow from operations. Therefore the reconciliation adds the $21,000 to net income to offset the deduction and thereby shows the effect on cash.

The reconciliation's most common additions or deductions from net income are:

- Add decreases (or deduct increases) in accounts receivable
- Add decreases (or deduct increases) in inventories
- Add increases (or deduct decreases) in accounts payable
- Add increases (or deduct decreases) in wages and salaries payable
- Add increases (or deduct decreases) in unearned revenue

The general rules for reconciling for these items are:

- Deduct increases in noncash current assets
- Add decreases in noncash current assets
- Add increases in current liabilities
- Deduct decreases in current liabilities

A final step is to reconcile for amounts that are included in net income but represent investing or financing activities (in contrast to operating activities). Examples include:

- Add loss (or deduct gain) from sale of fixed assets
- Add loss (or deduct gain) on extinguishment of debt

In our earlier example, Balmer Company had no losses or gains that were a result of investing or financing activities. However, suppose Balmer Company sold another asset for $12,000 cash. The asset had a book value of $8,000, so a gain of $4,000 would be part of pretax income:

Proceeds from sale of fixed asset	$12,000
Book value of asset sold	8,000
Gain on sale of asset	**$ 4,000**

For simplicity, assume that this sale did not affect income taxes. Therefore Balmer Company's net income would be $23,000 (from Figure 4-7) *plus* the gain of $4,000, or a total of $27,000.

The sale of the asset is an investing activity, so the entire cash inflow should be listed under investing activities in the statement of cash flows:

Proceeds from sale of fixed asset	$12,000

The section "cash flows from operating activities" should not be affected by this sale. But net income includes the $4,000 gain. In a reconciliation schedule that begins with net income (as in Figure 4-10), the gain must be subtracted:

Net income ($23,000 from Figure 4-8 plus $4,000 gain)	$27,000
Plus adjustments in Figure 4-10	46,000
Less gain on disposal of fixed assets	(4,000)
Net cash provided by operating activities	**$69,000**

Note that the sale of the asset affected net income because of the gain, but it did not affect net cash provided by operating activities.

Reconciliation Schedule under Direct and Indirect Methods

The FASB requires all preparers of a statement of cash flows to use either the direct or the indirect method. Furthermore, the reconciliation schedule must be included in some fashion under either the direct or the indirect method:

- *Direct Method* (favored by FASB)
  Figure 4-8 as the body. Include Figure 4-10 as a supporting schedule.

- *Indirect Method* (permitted by FASB)
  Alternative Format 1:
  Figure 4-8 as the body. However, replace the first section with a one-line item, net cash provided by operating activities. Include Figure 4-10 as a supporting schedule.
  Alternative Format 2:
  Figure 4-8, except use Figure 4-10 in the body as the first section, cash flows from operating activities. Figure 4-11 illustrates this widely used method.

Role of Depreciation

The most crucial aspect of a statement of cash flows is how depreciation and other expenses that do not require cash relate to the flow of cash. There is widespread misunderstanding of the role of depreciation in financial reporting, so let us examine this point in detail.

Accountants view depreciation as an allocation of historical cost to expense. Therefore, depreciation expense does not entail a current outflow of cash. Consider again the comparison of Balmer Company's net income and cash flows. Why is the $17,000 of depreciation added to net income to compute cash flow? Simply to cancel its deduction in calculating net income. Unfortunately, use of the indirect method may at first glance create an erroneous impression that depreciation is added because it, by itself, is a source of cash. If that were really true, a corporation could merely double or triple its bookkeeping entry for depreciation expense when cash was badly needed! What would happen? Income would decline, but cash provided by operations would be unaffected. Suppose depreciation for Balmer Company were doubled:

	With Depreciation of $17,000	With Depreciation of $34,000
Sales	$200,000	$200,000
All expenses except depreciation (including income taxes)*	(160,000)	(160,000)
Depreciation	(17,000)	(34,000)
Net income	$ 23,000	$ 6,000
Nondepreciation adjustments†	29,000	29,000
Add depreciation	17,000	34,000
Net cash provided by operating activities	$ 69,000	$ 69,000

* $100,000 + $36,000 + $4,000 + $20,000 = $160,000
† $(20,000) + (40,000) + $68,000 + $21,000 = $29,000

The doubling would affect depreciation and net income, but have no direct influence on cash provided by operations, which would still amount to $69,000.

Statement of Cash Flows for Nike, Inc.

Figure 4-11 contains the 1994 statement of cash flows for Nike, Inc. Other publicly held corporations may include more details, but the general format of the statement of cash flows is similar to that shown. Note that Nike uses the indirect method in the body of the statement of cash flows to report the cash flows from operating activities. Most companies use this format.

Most of the items in Figure 4-11 have been discussed earlier in the chapter, but three deserve mention here. First, deferred income taxes are added back to net income. These taxes are charged as expense but are not currently payable. Therefore they are a noncash expense, similar to depreciation. Second, proceeds from the exercise of options are *cash received* from issuance of shares to executives as part of a stock option compensation plan. Third, the effect of changes in the exchange rate on cash shows the impact of changes in the relative prices of foreign currencies on multinational operations. It is beyond the scope of this text.

FIGURE 4-11   Nike, Inc. Statement of Cash Flows for the Year Ended May 31, 1994 (thousands)

Cash provided (used) by operations	
Net income	$298,794
Income charges (credits) not affecting cash	
Depreciation	64,531
Deferred income taxes	(23,876)
Other, including amortization	4,479
Changes in certain working capital components	
Decrease in inventory	160,823
Decrease in accounts receivable	23,979
Decrease in other current assets	6,888
Increase in accounts payable, accrued	
liabilities, and income taxes payable	40 845
Cash provided by operations	576 463
Cash provided (used) by investing activities	
Additions to property, plant, and equipment	(95,266)
Disposals of property, plant, and equipment	12,650
Acquisition of subsidiaries	(3,552)
Additions to other assets	(5,450)
Cash used by investing activities	(91,618)
Cash provided (used) by financing activities	
Additions to long-term debt	6,044
Reductions in long-term debt including current portion	(56,986)
Decrease in notes payable	(2,939)
Proceeds from exercise of options	4,288
Repurchase of stock	(140,104)
Dividends—common and preferred	(60,282)
Cash used by financing activities	(249,979)
Effect of exchange rate changes on cash	(7,334)
Net increase in cash and equivalents	227,532
Cash and equivalents, beginning of year	291,284
Cash and equivalents, end of year	**$518,816**

You might also notice that changes in account balances cannot be computed directly from the balance sheets in Figure 4-1. This is a result of factors beyond the scope of this text, primarily the incorporation of the accounts of companies acquired by Nike during fiscal 1994.

SUMMARY

This chapter explains the meanings of the account titles most often found in the major financial statements. In the balance sheet, assets and liabilities are divided into current and noncurrent items. Stockholders' equity is the residual interest in the business, part arising from paid-in capital and part from retained income. The income statement summarizes performance over a period including operating and financial management.

Statements of cash flows report the cash receipts and cash payments during a period, classified according to the activities that caused the cash flow. Operating activities are the major source of cash inflows for most companies. The largest inflow usually is collections from customers. The largest outflows are generally for purchases of goods to be sold and operating expenses. Investment activities usually create a net cash outflow. These activities include purchases and disposals of land and equipment and long-term investments in other companies. Financing activities are often an important source of cash. Increases in debt and issuance of equity securities for cash provide cash inflows. Retirement of debt or equity and payment of dividends are cash outflows.

The FASB favors use of the direct method for the statement of cash flows, but the indirect method is also acceptable. Whichever form is used, a reconciliation of net income to net cash provided by operations must be included. It is especially important to understand the relationship of depreciation to cash. Depreciation is added back to net income when reconciling net income and net cash provided by operations because depreciation is a noncash expense—*not* because depreciation is a source of cash.

SELF-CORRECTION PROBLEMS

1. "The book value of plant assets is the amount that would be spent today for their replacement." Do you agree? Explain.

2. On December 31, 19X1, a magazine publishing company receives $150,000 in cash for 3-year subscriptions. This sum is regarded as unearned revenue. Show the balances in that account at December 31, 19X2, 19X3, and 19X4. How much revenue would be earned in each of those 3 years?

3. The Buretta Company has prepared the data in Figure 4-12. In December 19X1, Buretta paid $54 million cash for a new building acquired to accommodate an expansion of operations. This was financed partly by a new issue of long-term debt for $40 million cash. During 19X1. the company also sold fixed assets for $5 million cash, which was equal to their book value. All sales and purchases of merchandise were on credit.

    Because the net income of $4 million was the highest in the company's history, Mr. Buretta, the chairman of the board, was perplexed by the company's extremely low cash balance.

    a. Prepare a statement of cash flows. Ignore income taxes. You may wish to use Figure 4-8 as a guide. Use the direct method for reporting cash flows from operating activities.
    b. Prepare a supporting schedule that reconciles net income to net cash provided by operating activities.
    c. What is revealed by the statement of cash flows? Does it help you reduce Mr. Buretta's puzzlement? Why?

FIGURE 4-12   Buretta Co. Income Statement and Statement of Retained Earnings for the Year Ended December 31, 19X1 (millions)

Sales		$100
Less cost of goods sold		
Inventory, December 31, 19X0	$ 15	
Purchases	104	
Cost of goods available for sale	$119	
Inventory, December 31, 19X1	46	73
Gross profit		$ 27
Less other expenses		
General expenses	$ 8	
Depreciation	8	
Property taxes	4	
Interest expense	3	23
Net income		$ 4
Retained earnings, December 31, 19X0		7
Total		$ 11
Dividends		1
Retained earnings, December 31, 19X1		$ 10

Balance Sheets as of December 31 (millions)

Assets	19X1	19X0	Increase (Decrease)
Cash	$ 1	$20	$ (19)
Accounts receivable	20	5	15
Inventory	46	15	31
Prepaid general expenses	4	2	2
Fixed assets, net	91	50	41
	$162	$92	$ 70

Equities			
Accounts payable for merchandise	$ 39	$14	$25
Accrued property tax payable	3	1	2
Long-term debt	40	—	40
Capital stock	70	70	—
Retained earnings	10	7	3
	$162	$92	$70

SOLUTIONS TO SELF-CORRECTION PROBLEMS

1. Net book value of the plant assets is the result of deducting accumulated depreciation from original cost. This process does not attempt to capture all the technological and economic events that may affect replacement value. Consequently, there is little likelihood that net book value will approximate replacement cost.

2. The balance in unearned revenue would decline at the rate of $50,000 yearly; $50,000 would be recognized as earned revenue in each of the 3 years.

	December 31			
	19X1	19X2	19X3	19X4
Unearned revenue	$150,000	$100,000	$50,000	$ 0

3. a. See Figure 4-13. Cash flows from operating activities were computed as follows (in millions):

Sales	$100
Less increase in accounts receivable	(15)
Cash collections from customers	**$ 85**
Cost of goods sold	$ 73
Plus increase in inventory	31
Purchases	$104
Less increase in accounts payable	(25)
Cash paid to suppliers	**$ 79**
General expenses	$ 8
Plus increase in prepaid general expenses	2
Cash payment for general expenses	**$ 10**
Property taxes	$ 4
Less increase in accrued property tax payable	(2)
Cash paid for properly taxes	**$ 2**
Cash paid for interest	**$ 3**

FIGURE 4-13 Buretta Company Statement of Cash Flows for the Year Ended December 31, 19X1 (in millions)

Cash Flows from Operating Activities

Cash collections from customers		$85
Cash payments		
Cash paid to suppliers	$(79)	
General expenses	(10)	
Interest paid	(3)	
Property taxes	(2)	(94)
Net cash used by operating activities		$ (9)

Cash Flows from Investing Activities

Purchase of fixed assets (building)	$(54)	
Proceeds from sale of fixed assets	5	
Net cash used by investing activities		(49)

Cash Flows from Financing Activities

Long-term debt issued	$40	
Dividends paid	(1)	
Net cash provided by financing activities		39
Net decrease in cash		$(19)
Cash balance, December 31, 19X1		20
Cash balance, December 31, 19X2		$ 1

FIGURE 4-14   Buretta Company Reconciliation of Net Income to Net Cash Provided by Operating Activities for the Year Ended December 31, 19X1 (Millions)

Supporting Schedule to Statement of Cash Flows

Net income (from income statement)	$ 4
Adjustments to reconcile net income to net cash provided by operating activities	
Add: depreciation, which was deducted in the computation of net income but does not decrease cash	8
Deduct: increase in accounts receivable	(15)
Deduct: increase in inventory	(31)
Deduct: increase in prepaid general expenses	(2)
Add: increase in accounts payable	25
Add: increase in accrued property tax payable	2
Net cash provided by operating activities	$ (9)

b. Figure 4-14 reconciles net income to net cash provided by operating activities.

c. The statement of cash flows shows where cash has come from and where it has gone. Operations used $9 million of cash. Why? Figure 4-14 shows that large increases in accounts receivable ($15 million) and inventory ($31 million), plus a $2 million increase in prepaid expenses, used $48 million of cash. In contrast, only $39 million (that is, $4 + $8 + $25 + $2 million) was generated. Figure 4-13 explains the $9 million use of cash slightly differently; the $85 million of cash receipts and $94 million in disbursements are shown directly. Investing activities also consumed cash because $54 million was invested in a building, and only $5 million was received from sales of fixed assets. Financing activities generated $39 million cash, which was $19 million less than the $58 million used by operating and investing activities.

Mr. Buretta should no longer be puzzled. The statement of cash flows shows clearly that cash payments exceeded receipts by $19 million. However, he may still be concerned about the depletion of cash. Either operations must be changed so that they do not require so much cash, or investment must be curtailed, or more long-term debt or ownership equity must be raised. Otherwise Buretta Company will soon run out of cash.

QUESTIONS

1. "The operating cycle for a company is one year." Do you agree? Why?
2. Why is the term *marketable securities* a misnomer?
3. Why should short-term prepaid expenses be classified as current assets?
4. Enumerate the items most commonly classified as current assets.
5. "Sometimes 100 shares of stock should be classified as current assets and sometimes not." Explain.
6. "Accumulated depreciation is the cumulative amount charged as expense." Explain.

7. "Accumulated depreciation is a sum of cash being accumulated for the replacement of fixed assets." Do you agree? Explain.
8. "Most companies use straight-line depreciation, but they should use accelerated depreciation." Criticize this quote.
9. Criticize: "Depreciation is the loss in value of a fixed asset over a given span of time."
10. What factors influence the estimate of useful life in depreciation accounting?
11. "Accountants sometimes are too concerned with physical objects or contractual rights." Explain.
12. "Goodwill may have nothing to do with the personality of the manager or employees." Do you agree? Explain.
13. Why are intangible assets and deferred charges usually swiftly amortized?
14. What is a subordinated debenture?
15. What is the role of the par value of stock or bonds?
16. "Common shareholders have limited liability." Explain.
17. "Treasury stock; is negative stockholders' equity." Do you agree? Explain.
18. "The statement of cash flows is an optional statement included by most companies in their annual reports." Do you agree? Explain.
19. What are the purposes of a statement of cash flows?
20. What three types of activities are summarized in the statement of cash flows?
21. Name four major operating activities included in a statement of cash flows.
22. Name three major investing activities included in a statement of cash flows.
23. Name three major financing activities included in a statement of cash flows.
24. Where does interest received or paid appear on the statement of cash flows?
25. Why is there usually a difference between the cash collections from customers and sales revenue in a period's financial statements?
26. What are the two major ways of computing net cash provided by operating activities?
27. The indirect method for reporting cash flows from operating activities can create an erroneous impression about noncash expenses (such as depreciation). What is the impression and why is it erroneous?
28. An investor's newsletter had the following item: "The company expects increased cash flow in 1997 because depreciation charges will be substantially greater than they were in 1996." Comment.
29. "Net losses mean drains on cash." Do you agree? Explain.
30. "Depreciation is an integral part of a statement of cash flows." Do you agree? Explain.
31. "Cash flow per share can be downright misleading." Why?
32. XYZ Company's only transaction in 19X5 was the sale of a fixed asset for cash of $20,000. The income statement included only "Gain on sale of fixed asset, $4,000." Correct the following statement of cash flows:

Cash flows from operating activities	
Gain on sale of fixed asset	$ 4,000
Cash flows from investing activities	
Proceeds from sale of fixed asset	20,000
Total increase in cash	$24,000

33. Why are noncash investing and financing activities listed on a separate schedule accompanying the statement of cash flows?

34. The Lawrence Company sold fixed assets with a book value of $5,000 and recorded a $3,000 gain. How should this be reported on a statement of cash flows?

35. "The presence of a deferred tax liability on the balance sheet means that cumulative tax payments have exceeded the cumulative tax expense charged on financial reports to shareholders." Do you agree? Explain.

PROBLEMS

1. **Balance Sheet and Income Statement.**   The Storski Company had the following items on its December 31, 19X0, balance sheet and 19X0 income statement (in dollars except for number of shares outstanding):

Cash and equivalents	$ 39,000
Notes payable	40,000
Revenues	800,000
Long-term debt, excluding current portion	210,000
Accounts receivable, net	63,000
Provision for income taxes	55,000
Other long-term assets	110,000
Interest expense	55,000
Deferred income tax liability	44,000
Retained earnings	202,000
Income taxes payable	37,000
Cost of sales	460,000
Inventories	31,000
Prepaid expenses	15,000
Common stock (50,000 shares outstanding)	25,000
Property, plant, and equipment, at cost	580,000
Accounts payable	49,000
Interest income	20,000
Goodwill, patents, and trademarks	75,000
Current portion of long-term debt	15,000
Less: accumulated depreciation	170,000
Selling and administrative expenses	150,000
Additional paid-in capital	?

   Prepare in proper form the December 31, 19X0, balance sheet and the 19X0 income statement for Storski Company. Include the proper amount for *additional paid-in capital*.

2. **Prepare a Statement of Cash Flows, Direct Method.**   The Outdoor Comfort Clothing Stores chain had a cash balance on December 31, 19X5, of $48 thousand. Its net income for 19X6 was $464 thousand. Its 19X6 transactions affecting income or cash were (in thousands):

   a. Sales of $1,700, all on credit. Cash collections from customers, $1,450.

   b. The cost of items sold, $850. Purchases of inventory totaled $900; inventory and accounts payable were affected accordingly.

   c. Cash payments on trade accounts payable, $775.

d. Salaries and wages: accrued, $190; paid in cash, $200.

e. Depreciation, $45.

f. Interest expense, all paid in cash, $11.

g. Other expenses, all paid in cash, $100.

h. Income taxes accrued, $40; income taxes paid in cash, $35.

i. Bought plant and facilities for $435 cash.

j. Issued debt for $120 cash.

k. Paid cash dividends of $39.

Prepare a statement of cash flows using the direct method for reporting cash flows from operating activities. Omit supporting schedules.

3. **Reconciliation of Net Income and Net Cash Provided by Operating Activities.** Refer to Problem 2. Prepare a supporting schedule that reconciles net income to net cash provided by operating activities.

4. **Depreciation and Cash Flows.**   O'Neill Company had sales of $820,000, all received in cash. Total operating expenses were $620,000. All except depreciation were paid in cash. Depreciation of $90,000 was included in the $620,000 of operating expenses. Ignore income taxes.

a. Compute net income and net cash provided by operating activities.

b. Assume that depreciation is tripled. Compute net income and net cash provided by operating activities.

5. **Balance Sheet Format.**   Georgia-Pacific Corporation, one of the world's largest forest products companies, lists the following balance sheet items for January 1, 1994 (in millions):

Property, plant, and equipment, at cost	$10,986
Common stock	71
Cash	41
Commercial paper and other short-term notes payable	650
Receivables	377
Prepaid expenses and other current assets	26
Accumulated depreciation	(5,538)
Accounts payable	582
Other long-term liabilities	827
Additional paid-in capital	1,202
Inventories	1,202
Other assets	2,070
Current portion of long-term debt	57
Accrued compensation, interest, and other payables	602
Timber and timberlands, net	1,381
Deferred income tax liability	1,095
Short-term bank loans	173
Long-term debt, excluding current portion	4,157
Retained earnings	?

Prepare a balance sheet in proper form for Georgia-Pacific. Include the proper amount for retained earnings.

6. **Preparation of Statement of Cash Flows.**   Walgreen's Co., the largest drugstore chain in the United States, had the following items in its financial statements for the fiscal year ended August 31, 1994 (in thousands):

Net sales	$1,496,721
Net earnings	281,929
Additions to property and equipment	(289,976)
Depreciation and amortization	118,118
Cash dividends paid	(81,226)
Other non-cash expenses	7,880
Increases in inventories	(169,365)
Investment in corporate-owned life insurance	(6,445)
Increases in trade accounts payable	105,631
Increases in other current assets	(3,910)
Payments of long-term obligations	(5,760)
Net proceeds from employee stock plans	948
Increases in accrued expenses and other liabilities	59,507
Net purchases of marketable securities	(815)
Increases in accounts receivable, net	(50,692)
Other investments	444
Retained earnings	1,496,721
Deferred income taxes	5,653
Increases in income taxes payable	693
Proceeds from disposition of property and equipment	13,704
Total assets	2,908,749
Cash and cash equivalents at end of year	77,915
Net decrease in cash and cash equivalents	(13,682)

Select the items from this list that would appear in Walgreen's' statement of cash flows and prepare the statement in proper form. Use the indirect method for reporting cash flows from operating activities. (Note: Deferred income taxes is a noncash expense.)

7. **Cash Provided by Operations.**   PepsiCo., Inc., maker of snack foods (for example, Fritos) as well as soft drinks, had net income of $1,784.0 million in 1993. Additional information follows (in millions):

	1993	
Depreciation and amortization	$1,576.5	
Other noncash charges	$ 324.2	
Interest expense	$ 645.0	
Provision for income taxes	$ 880.4	
Changes in noncash working capital accounts		
Accounts and notes receivable	$ 111.8	Increase
Inventories	$ 101.6	Increase
Prepaid expenses	$ 1.2	Decrease
Accounts payable	$ 30.4	Increase
Income taxes payable	$ 54.4	Increase
Other current liabilities	$ 158.7	Increase

Compute the net cash provided by operating activities.

ADDENDUM 4: SHAREHOLDER REPORTING, INCOME TAX REPORTING, AND DEFERRED TAXES

In the United States, reports to stockholders must abide by "generally accepted accounting principles (GAAP)." In contrast, reports to income tax authorities must abide by the income tax rules and regulations. These rules comply with GAAP in many respects, but they frequently diverge. Therefore there is nothing immoral or unethical about "keeping two sets of records." In fact, it is necessary.

Keep in mind that the income tax laws are patchworks that often are designed to give taxpayers special incentives for making investments. For example, tax authorities in some countries have permitted taxpayers to write off the full cost of new equipment as expense in the year acquired. Although such a total write-off may be permitted for income tax purposes, it is not permitted for shareholder reporting purposes.

Major differences between U.S. GAAP and the U.S. tax laws are found in accounting for amortization and depreciation. For example, consider how the accounting for perpetual franchises, trademarks, and goodwill differs. Their acquisition costs must be amortized for shareholder reporting. However, the IRS will not allow amortization because such assets have indefinite useful lives. Tax reporting and shareholder reporting are *required* to differ.

Depreciation causes the largest differences between tax and shareholder reporting in the United States. Most companies use straight-line depreciation for reporting to shareholders. Why? Managers believe that it best matches expenses with revenues. But companies use accelerated depreciation for tax reporting because it postpones (or defers) tax payments. Congress provided this deferral opportunity to motivate companies to increase their investment.

For reporting to shareholders, accountants must match income tax expense with the revenues and expenses that cause the taxes. When revenues and expenses on the statement to tax authorities differ from the revenues and expenses on the shareholders' report, deferred taxes can arise. Most often deferred taxes arise when tax expenses exceed book expenses. The result is a deferred tax *liability*.

FIGURE 4-15   Illustration of Deferred Taxes

	19X0	19X1	Total
Income statement for tax purposes			
Revenue	$100,000	$100,000	$200,000
Expenses, except depreciation	80,000	80,000	160,000
Depreciation	20,000	0	20,000
Operating income			
(or taxable income)	$ 0	$ 20,000	$ 20,000
Taxes payable @ 40%	0	8,000	8,000
Net income	$ 0	$ 12,000	$ 12,000
Income statement for shareholder reporting			
Revenue	$100,000	$100,000	$200,000
Expenses, except depreciation	80,000	80,000	160,000
Depreciation	10 000	10 000	20 000
Operating income	$ 10,000	$ 10,000	$ 20,000
Less income taxes			
Paid or payable almost immediately	0	8,000	8,000
Deferred	4,000	(4,000)	0
Net income	$ 6,000	$ 6,000	$ 12,000

	December 31	
	19X0	19X1
Balance sheet effect		
Liability: Deferred income taxes	$4,000	$0

Consider a simple example. The total depreciation on a company's only asset over a 2-year period, 19X0-19X1, was $20,000. Revenue was $100,000 each year, expenses (other than depreciation) were $80,000, and the combined federal and state income tax rate was 40%. For tax purposes, the entire $20,000 of depreciation was charged as an expense in 19X0; for shareholder reporting, $10,000 was charged each year. Such differences in timing of expenses are completely legitimate.

Figure 4-15 illustrates tax deferral. Total operating income over the two years was $20,000, and total taxes were $8,000. According to U.S. tax law, all $20,000 of operating income and $8,000 of taxes applied to 19X1. In contrast, for financial reporting, half of the operating income was recognized each year, so half of the taxes should be recognized each year. Although $4,000 of taxes was related to 19X0 revenues and expenses, the *payment* was postponed *(deferred)* to 19X1. A $4,000 *expense* for deferred taxes was included on the 19X0 financial reporting income statement, and the obligation for future payment of the tax became a liability on the balance sheet. In 19X1 $4,000 of tax *expense* was again related to the revenues and expenses of the period. However, the tax *payment* was $8,000. The payment covers the $4,000 expense for 19X1 and pays off the $4,000 of taxes deferred from 19X0.

CHAPTER 5

Analysis of Financial Statements

This chapter focuses on **financial statement analysis,** which means using financial statement data to assess a company's performance. Sources of information about companies, the objectives of financial statement analysis, and methods for evaluating financial statements are covered. The majority of the chapter deals with ratios and how to understand the financial statements as prepared under GAAP. A few additional steps in producing the financial statements are presented, including calculating earnings per share and preparing segmental disclosures of the parts of the business.

Disclosure practices in the United States have evolved with the specific purpose of providing information to investors, creditors, managers, suppliers, customers—anyone who wants to know about a company's financial position or prospects. The preceding chapters concentrated on how information is collected, aggregated, and disclosed. We have frequently provided examples of ratios and other tools of analysis and have demonstrated how the information might aid in making decisions. In this chapter we integrate prior material and discuss additional tools for analyzing and evaluating the company's financial position.

Internationally, financial statement analysis is significantly complicated by a variety of factors. Throughout the text we have considered differences in accounting methods used. In addition we should stress the obvious but easily forgotten differences in the language of reporting and the currency of measurement. For example, most U.S. analysts cannot read financial statements in Japanese and do not readily "have a feel for" the value of yen versus dollars. Last, but not least, is the fact that different structures for security markets, different tax laws, and different preferences among citizens of different countries all affect the relative value of financial assets.

SOURCES OF INFORMATION ABOUT COMPANIES

Financial statement analysis focuses on techniques used by analysts external to the organization being analyzed, although managers use many of the same methods. These analysts rely on publicly available information.

Publicly available information refers primarily to published information and analysis that is broadly available to analysts and investors. Companies provide periodic press releases, which provide the financial community with news about company developments, including the following:

1. Changes in personnel.
2. Changes in dividends.
3. Issuance or retirement of debt.
4. Acquisition or sale of assets or business units.
5. New products.
6. New orders.
7. Changes in production plans.
8. Financial results.

Members of the financial press decide which information in press releases will be interesting and important. When a small company announces that thirty people will be laid off, the *Wall Street Journal* may ignore the event, while it will be front page news in the company's home town where many citizens are affected. Similarly, in certain regions, an industry focus determines what news is carried. The *Tulsa World* is a newspaper in Oklahoma that publishes significant details about oil exploration and production; for example, oil rigs in use, newly discovered oil or gas deposits, and changes in management of petroleum companies. The *Washington Post* in Washington, D.C., would not cover these issues but does provide up-to-date news on some thirty prominent firms that have a substantial employment or sales base in the nation's capital. The national business daily, the *Wall Street Journal,* does not publish as much detail in these specific areas as either the *Tulsa World* or the *Washington Post.*

A major source of information about an individual firm is the company's annual report. In addition to the financial statements (income statement, balance sheet, statement of cash flows, and statement of stockholders' equity), annual reports usually contain:

1. Footnotes to the financial statements.
2. A summary of the accounting principles used.
3. Management's discussion and analysis of the financial results.
4. The auditor's report.
5. Comparative financial data for a series of years.
6. Narrative information about the company.

To be useful, the financial statements and their accompanying footnotes and other disclosures must provide all significant or *material* information. Although analysts can learn much from the various parts of an annual report, we will focus most of our attention on the financial statements themselves.

Companies also prepare reports for the Securities and Exchange Commission (SEC). Form 10-K presents financial statement data in a standard format and is generally more comprehensive than the financial statements published in annual reports. Form 10-Q includes quarterly financial statements, so it provides more timely information than the annual reports, although the reports are less complete. Other SEC reports are required for certain specified events and for issuance of common shares or debt.

Both annual reports and SEC reports are issued well after the events being reported have occurred. More timely information is often available from company press releases and articles in the business press. The *Wall Street Journal, Business Week, Forbes, Fortune,* and *Barron's* are among the more popular publications. Services such as *Value Line,* Moody's Investors Services, and Standard and Poor's Industrial Surveys also provide useful information. In addition, stockbrokers prepare company analyses for their clients, and private investment services and newsletters supply information to their subscribers.

Heavy financial commitments, whether by investors purchasing many shares of the common stock of a company or by banks making large loans to a new customer, are preceded by thorough investigations. These investigations use information from many sources. When the amounts being invested are significant, investors and creditors often ask for a set of projected financial statements. Such a **pro forma statement** is a carefully formulated expression of predicted results. Major creditors expect the projections to include a schedule of the amounts and timings of cash repayments.

Most investors and creditors are not able to request specific information from companies. For example, the typical trade creditor cannot afford the time or resources for an exhaustive investigation of every customer. Instead, such creditors rely on published information and reports from credit agencies such as Dun & Bradstreet.

Because of the wide range of information available, this chapter on financial statement analysis covers only the most common methods used by financial analysts. Nevertheless, the techniques presented in this chapter constitute an important step in gaining a thorough understanding of a company's position and prospects.

OBJECTIVES OF FINANCIAL STATEMENT ANALYSIS

Investors purchase capital stock expecting to receive dividends and an increase in the value of the stock. Creditors make loans with the expectation of receiving interest and eventual repayment. However, both investors and creditors bear the risk that they will not receive their expected returns. They use financial statement analysis to (1) predict the amount of expected returns and (2) assess the risks associated with those returns.

Because creditors generally have specific fixed amounts to be received and have the first claim on assets, they are most concerned with assessing short-term liquidity and long-term solvency. **Short-term liquidity** is an organization's ability to meet current payments as they become due. **Long-term solvency** is the ability to generate enough cash to repay long-term debts as they mature.

In contrast, equity investors are more concerned with profitability, dividends, and future security prices. Why? Because dividend payments depend on profitable operations, and stock price appreciation depends on the market's assessment of the company's prospects. However, creditors also assess profitability. Why? Because profitable operations are the prime source of cash to repay loans.

How can financial statement analysis help creditors and investors? After all, financial statements report on past results and current position, but creditors and investors want to predict future returns and their risks. Financial statement analysis is useful because past performance is often a good indicator of future performance, and current position is the base on which future performance must be built. For example, trends in past sales, operating expenses, and net income may continue. Furthermore, evaluation of management's past performance gives clues to its ability to generate future returns. Finally, the assets a company owns, the liabilities it must pay, its levels of receivables and inventories, its cash balance, and other indicators of current position all provide clues to its future prospects.

EVALUATING TRENDS AND COMPONENTS OF THE BUSINESS

This section discusses methods used to analyze financial statement data. These methods focus on trend analysis and assessing the components of the business. Trend analysis examines changes over time. Component analysis can mean several things. One application concentrates on the components of the financial statements themselves, the relative size of current assets, the level of investment in fixed assets, the gross margin percentage, and so on. At another level, component analysis means sorting out the parts of the company's business. The company can be separated into different business units or kinds of businesses, different geographic areas of production or marketing, or different customer groups such as private versus government.

Trend Analysis

Financial statements contain both the current year's and the previous year's amounts. In addition, annual reports must include the amounts of key financial items for at least the last five years. Many companies include ten years of data. Using these data, financial analysts can examine in detail the changes in the past year and can examine longer-term trends in several important items.

Consider the balance sheets and income statements of Oxley Company (a retailer of lawn and garden products) in Figures 5-1 and 5-2. The third column shows the amount of the change in each item from 19X1 to 19X2. The fourth shows the percentage change, computed as follows:

$$\text{Percentage change 19X1 to 19X2} = \frac{\text{Amount of change}}{\text{19X1 amount}} \times 100$$

The percentage change shows the percentage by which the current-year amount exceeds or falls short of the base-year amount, 19X1 in this case. For example, Oxley's accounts receivables increased from $70,000 at the end of 19X1 to $95,000 at the end of 19X2, an increase of 35.7%:

$$\text{Percentage change} = \frac{\$95,000 - \$70,000}{\$70,000} \times 100 = 35.7\%$$

FIGURE 5-1   Oxley Company Statement of Income (in thousands except earnings per share)

	For the Year Ended December 31, 19X2	For the Year Ended December 31, 19X1	Increase (Decrease) Amount	Percentage
Sales	$999	$800	$199	24.9%
Cost of goods sold	399	336	63	18.8
Gross profit (or gross margin)	$600	$464	$136	29.3
Operating expenses:				
Wages	$214	$150	$ 64	42.7
Rent	120	120	0	0.0
Miscellaneous	100	50	50	100.0
Depreciation	40	40	0	0.0
Total operating expenses	$474	$360	$ 114	31.7
Operating income (or operating profit)	$126	$104	$ 22	21.2
Other revenue and expense:				
Interest revenue	36	36	0	0.0
Deduct: Interest expense	(12)	(12)	0	0.0
Income before income taxes	$150	$128	$ 22	17.2
Income tax expense	60	48	12	25.0
Net income	$ 90	$ 80	$ 10	12.5
Earnings per common share*	$.45	$.40	$.05	12.5%

*Dividends per share, $.40 and $.20, respectively. For publicly held companies, there is a requirement to show earnings per share on the face of the income statement, but it is not necessary to show dividends per share. Calculation of earnings per share: $90,000 ÷ 200,000 = $.45, and $80,000 ÷ 200,000 = $.40.

Notice that each percentage change is independent of the others. Unlike the amounts of change, the percentage changes cannot be added or subtracted to obtain subtotals.

Changes must be interpreted carefully. Both the amount and the percentage changes should be examined. For example, the amount of the sales increase, $199,000, seems much larger than the increase in operating income, $22,000. But the base for sales is much larger, so the percentage increase is only slightly larger, 24.9% to 21.2%. Examination of percentage changes alone can also be misleading. For instance, the 140% increase in accrued wages payable seems to dominate the percentage increases. But the increase is only $14,000, a relatively small amount in the overall picture.

What would an analyst conclude from Oxley Company's changes from 19X1 to 19X2? Consider Figure 5-1, the income statement. The sales increase, 24.9%, is larger than the increase in cost of goods sold, 18.8%, causing a 29.3% increase in gross profit. That is the good news. The bad news is that operating expenses increased by 31.7%. This would be of special concern because huge increases in only two items, wages and miscellaneous expenses, caused the entire increase. In addition, income tax expense increased by a larger percentage than pretax income (25.0% to 17.2%), meaning that the effective tax rate must have increased. In total, the nearly 25% increase in sales led to only a 12.5% increase in net income.

Changes in dollar amount and percentage terms are used to identify patterns. This procedure focuses the analysts' attention and encourages questions that probe for underlying causes. Examination of the balance sheet changes in Figure 5-2 might

(Place a clip on this page for easy reference.)

FIGURE 5-2   Oxley Company Balance Sheet (in thousands)

	December 31		Increase (Decrease)	
	19X2	19X1	Amount	Percentage
ASSETS				
Current assets:				
Cash	$150	$ 57	$ 93	163.2%
Accounts receivable	95	70	25	35.7
Accrued interest receivable	15	15	0	0.0
Inventory of merchandise	20	60	(40)	(66.7)
Prepaid rent	10	—	10	*
Total current assets	$290	$202	$ 88	43.6
Long-term assets:				
Long-term note receivable	288	288	0	0.0
Equipment, less accumulated depreciation				
of $120 and $80	80	120	(40)	(33.3)
Total assets	$658	$610	$ 48	7.9%
LIABILITIES AND STOCKHOLDERS' EQUITY				
Current liabilities:				
Accounts payable	$ 90	$ 65	$ 25	38.5%
Accrued wages payable	24	10	14	140.0
Accrued income taxes payable	16	12	4	33.3
Accrued interest payable	9	9	0	0.0
Unearned sales revenue	—	5	(5)	(100.0)
Note payable—current portion	80	—	80	*
Total current liabilities	$219	$101	$118	116.8
Long-term note payable	40	120	(80)	(66.7)
Total liabilities	$259	$221	$ 38	17.2
Stockholders' equity:				
Paid-in capital†	$102	$102	$ 0	0.0
Retained income	297	287	10	3.5
Total stockholders' equity	$399	$389	$ 10	2.6
Total liabilities and stockholders' equity	$658	$610	$ 48	7.9%

*When the base-year amount is zero, no percentage change can be computed.

†Details are often shown in a supplementary statement or in footnotes. In this case, there are 200,000 common shares outstanding, $.25 par per share, or 200,000 × $.25 = $50,000. Additional paid-in capital is $52,000.

lead the analysts to question why the composition of the assets changed so considerably, with current assets increasing by 43.6% while equipment decreased by 33.3%. Within the current assets, cash and accounts receivable had substantial increases, and inventories plummeted. Total liabilities increased by 17.2%, but most significant is the 116.8% increase in current liabilities and 66.7% decrease in long-term liabilities. This change is attributable primarily to $80,000 of the note payable becoming due within the next year, thereby qualifying as a current liability.

The large percentage fluctuations can now be understood. Cash is being accumulated to pay an imminent debt obligation and the equipment is depreciating quickly. A plan for replacement of the equipment should be considered.

FIGURE 5-3 Oxley Company Five-Year Financial Summary
(in thousands, except per share amounts)

| | For the Year Ended December 31 | | | | |
	19X2	19X1	19X0	19Y9	19Y8
Income Statement Data:					
Sales	$999	$800	$765	$790	$694
Gross profit	600	464	448	460	410
Operating income	126	104	85	91	78
Net income	90	80	62	66	56
Earnings per share.	.45	.40	.31	.33	.28
Dividends per share	.40	.20	.20	.20	.15
Balance Sheet Data (as of December 31):					
Total assets	$658	$610	$590	$585	$566
Total liabilities	259	221	241	258	265
Stockholders' equity	399	389	349	327	301

Financial analysts often examine changes over a series of years, not just the current year's changes. Figure 5-3 shows a five-year summary of key items for Oxley Company. Percentage changes could be computed for each year, using the earlier year as the base year. For example, percentage changes in sales are:

19X2

19X1

$$\left(\frac{\$999 - \$800}{\$800}\right) \times 100 = 24.9\% \qquad \left(\frac{\$800 - \$765}{\$765}\right) \times 100 = 4.6\%$$

$$\left(\frac{\$765 - \$790}{\$790}\right) \times 100 = (3.2\%) \qquad \left(\frac{\$790 - \$694}{\$694}\right) \times 100 = 13.8\%$$

Sales growth rates are highly variable. In this business, weather might be one factor. Rates of new home construction might also play a role. Awareness of this variability may aid the analyst in determining the core economic factors that drive the business. We might learn that Oxley's sales decline in 19X0 was associated with a recession, or that the significant increase in 19X2 involved a new product.

Common-Size Statements

To aid comparisons with a company's previous years and especially to aid the comparison of several companies that differ in size, income statements and balance sheets are often analyzed by percentage relationships, called **component percentages.** The resulting statements, in which the components are assigned a relative percentage, are called **common-size statements.** Consider Oxley Company's common-size statements in Figure 5-4. It is difficult to compare Oxley's $290,000 of current assets with a larger company's $480,000. But suppose the other company has total assets of $1 million. Oxley's 44% current asset *percentage* (shown in Figure 5-4) can be directly compared with the other company's $480,000 ÷ $1,000,000 = 48%.

The income statement percentages are usually based on sales = 100%. Oxley seems very profitable, but such percentages have more meaning when comparing the budgeted performance with another competitor's values, or with the industry average. Our concern that high margins attract price competition might be reduced if we learned that high margins were characteristic of the industry.

The behavior of each expense in relation to changes in total revenue is often revealing. That is, which expenses go up or down as sales fluctuate? For example, during these two years, rent, depreciation, and interest have been fixed in total but have decreased in relation to sales. In contrast, the wages have increased in total and as a percentage of sales. The latter is not a welcome sign. Figure 5-4 indicates that wages

FIGURE 5-4 Oxley Company Common-Size Statements (in thousands except percentages)

	For the Year Ended December 31			
	19X2		19X1	
Statement of Income				
Sales	$999*	100%	$800	100%
Cost of goods sold	399	40	336	42
Gross profit (or gross margin)	$600*	60%	$464	58%
Wages	$214	21 %	$150	19%
Rent	120	12	120	15
Miscellaneous	100	10	50	6
Depreciation	40	4	40	5
Operating expenses	$474	47%	$360	45%
Operating income	$126	13%	$104	13%
Other revenue and expense	24	2	24	3
Pretax income	$150	15%	$128	16%
Income tax expense	60	6	48	6
Net income	$ 90	9%	$ 80	10%

	December 31			
	19X2		19X1	
Balance Sheet				
Current assets	$290	44%	$202	33%
Long-term note receivable	288	44	288	47
Equipment, net	80	12	120	20
Total assets	$658	100%	$610	100%
Current liabilities	$219	33%	$101	16%
Long-term note	40	6	120	20
Total liabilities	$259	39%	$221	36%
Stockholders' equity	399	61	389	64
Total liab. and stk. eq.	$658	100%	$610	100%
Working capital	$ 71		$101	

*Note the use of dollar signs in columns of numbers. Frequently, they are used at the top and bottom only and not for every subtotal. Their use by companies depends on the preference of management.

in 19X1 were $150 ÷ $800 = 19% of sales, whereas wages in 19X2 were $214 ÷ $999 = 21% of sales.

The balance sheet percentages are usually based on total assets = 100%. See Figure 5-4. The most notable feature of the balance sheet percentages is that both current assets and current liabilities are more prominent at the end of 19X2. This arises from the $80,000 debt coming due, which was also highlighted in our review of percentage changes.

Management's Discussion and Analysis

Both trends and component percentages are generally discussed in a required section of annual reports called **management's discussion and analysis** (often called **MD&A**). The MD&A section explains the major changes in the income statement and the major changes in liquidity and capital resources. The space most companies devote to the section in annual reports has increased dramatically in recent years.

The Truth, the Whole Truth, . . .

The Securities Exchange Commission is serious about full disclosure. You might characterize the SEC approach as a *no surprises* concept. Management should share *material* information with investors as it becomes known. "Management's Discussion and Analysis" is one place where information is shared. A recent enforcement action against Caterpillar, Inc., manufacturer of heavy equipment, illustrates both the concept of timely disclosure and the concept of material facts. A few months after the 1989 annual report and the first quarter 1990 report were issued, Caterpillar announced that 1990 earnings were expected to be *well below* earlier projections. The majority of the decrease was associated with an earnings decline in its Brazilian subsidiary. The stock price fell sharply on this news. The SEC believed that Caterpillar's disclosure about the negative Brazilian events constituted a case of too little information too late.

Ultimately, the problem was that Caterpillar's segment reporting did not identify the fact that 23% of its 1989 profit of $497 million was generated in Brazil. In December 1989 Brazil elected a new president, whose administration adopted severe programs to curb Brazil's hyperinflation. The subsequent decline in economic activity in Brazil substantially affected 1990 earnings of many multinationals, including Ford and GM. Yet, Caterpillar's *1989 Annual Report* observed only a potential decline in sales due to "post election politics" in Bra-

zil. Worse yet, the first quarter 1990 report indicated increased demand worldwide while barely mentioning uncertain economic conditions in Brazil, in spite of disclosures by management to Caterpillar's board of directors in February 1990 that the economic conditions in Brazil would have major negative effects on 1990 results.

The action against Caterpillar stresses the SEC's commitment to increase disclosure. As James Lyons noted in a 1992 *Forbes* article, ". . . if management is worried about something, it should say so."

Segment reporting is the area of greatest concern to analysts. In order to assess the entity's performance to date and to predict future earnings, analysts want to know how the parts of the company are doing. In the Caterpillar case, the issue was geographic: How is the Brazilian business doing? In the chapter, the Pepsico information includes reference to future uncertainty regarding the consequences of the devaluation of the Mexican peso during 1994 to 1995. It is also important to know how different lines of business are performing. An analyst following Ford might want to separate the automobile business from the truck business and the financing business in order to refine his or her forecasts. An analyst following Pepsico might want to separate restaurants like Kentucky Fried Chicken (KFC) and Taco Bell from the soft drink business. As this text is being written, FASB is developing new rules to guide the nature and extent of segment data to be required.
Source: Forbes *(May 25, 1992).* Pepsico 1994 Annual Report.

For example, a recent McDonald's Corporation annual report has a twelve-page MD&A section.

Figure 5-5 contains excerpts from the chairman's letter and management's discussion and analysis in the annual report of Pepsico. The annual report is fifty-two pages long. About half is discussion and analysis and half is financial statements and the related notes. The cover shows a picture of Cindy Crawford reading the annual

---

FIGURE 5-5   Pepsico 1994 Excerpts from Chairman's Letter and Management Discussion and Analyisis

---

Chairman's Letter

As I was telling Cindy, Pepsico had a strong year in 1994—for the most part. Sales, earnings and dividends hit all-time highs. Particularly strong were domestic soft drinks and domestic snack foods, our two most profitable businesses.

Our international beverage and snack businesses also had a big year. And across all of our international businesses, sales grew to more that $8 billion. That's bigger than all of Pepsico was just nine years ago.

On the other hand, our restaurant segment slowed down in 1994. While sales grew a respectable 12% and earnings were nearly three-quarters of a billion dollars, that was still a good bit shy of the remarkable 17% average annual growth our restaurants had posted for well over a decade. In response, we've already realigned and strengthened management and created some promising new programs. . . .

Measuring the Business

I'd like to share with you—and with Cindy—a little about the basic health of Pepsico. How we measure the business. How we gauge our progress. What we look at to determine if we're on the right track. . . .

Four of Our Yardsticks

There are different ways to look at different businesses. Because Pepsico is a very large, multi-line, growth-oriented consumer products company, we look primarily at four measurements:

- Volume growth
- Operating profit growth
- Cash growth
- Investment returns

Here's how I think about them.

Volume Growth

Other than acquisitions, the only unassailable, completely healthy way for consumer business to grow year in and year out is to sell more products. In our case this means selling lots more bottles of Pepsi, bags of chips, buckets of chicken. Volume growth is probably the single best gauge of a consumer products company because it tells us whether we're satisfying consumers and how we're doing against our competitors. In 1994, volume was up at nearly all our businesses, especially in beverages and snack foods. . . . So in terms of volume growth, most of our businesses are doing just fine.

Operating Profit Growth

Now obviously volume has to grow in a way that's profitable. And when you combine our strong volume growth with good profit margins, you're headed for the kind of operating profits that would make any investor smile. Over the last five years, our operating profit margin has been fairly steady, averaging 11%. As a result, our operating profits have grown at a compounded annual rate of 13%. So based on operating profit growth, Pepsico is also in excellent shape.

Cash Growth

One of my favorite measures of financial strength, and one that says an awful lot about Pepsico, is cash. I'm talking about what's left after we pay for things like labor and raw materials.

(continued)

All three of our business segments generate operating cash and plenty of it—totaling nearly $5 billion in 1994. And that's been growing steadily. Our segment operating cash grew at 9% in 1994 and at a compounded annual rate of 13% over the past five years.

Over the last five years with our strong cash flow we've been able to invest over $8 billion in existing businesses, invest nearly $4 billion in new ones, pay $2 billion in dividends, and repurchase more that $1 billion worth of Pepsico stock.

Investment Returns

Of course when you're investing $3 billion a year, as we did in 1994, it's important to be smart about it. That's where our fourth measurement comes in. We look for our individual investments to produce returns well over our 11% cost of capital. And the higher those returns are, the more value we create for our shareholders.

If you look at our investment in Pepsico overall, measured by our return on equity, the results are excellent. In 1994 our return on equity was 27%, nearly our best in a decade. And over the last five years it's averaged about 25%.

Putting It All Together

So, as I pointed out to Cindy, these four ways we measure and manage our business-volume growth, operating profit growth, cash growth, and investment returns—tell me Pepsico is thriving. I hope you get the same feeling.

Wayne Calloway

Chairman of the Board and Chief Executive Officer.

MANAGEMENT DISCUSSION AND ANALYSIS

Marketplace Actions

Pepsico's domestic and international businesses operate in markets that are highly competitive and subject to global and local economic conditions including inflation, commodity price, and currency fluctuations, and governmental actions. In Mexico, for example, our businesses have benefited in past years from improving conditions. Conversely, the significant devaluation of the Mexican peso at the end of 1994 and continuing into 1995 will not only negatively impact reported earnings from Mexico due to translation, but is expected to create a much less favorable economic climate in the country. Pepsico's operating and investing strategies are designed, where possible, to mitigate these factors through aggressive actions on several fronts including: (a) enhancing the appeal and value of its products through brand promotion, product innovation, quality improvement and prudent pricing actions; (b) providing better service to customers; (c) increasing world-wide availability of its products; (d) acquiring businesses and forming alliances to increase market presence and utilize resources more efficiently; and (e) containing costs through efficient and effective purchasing, manufacturing, distribution and administrative processes.

Restructurings

Restructuring actions realign resources for more efficient and effective execution of operating strategies. As a result, Pepsico continually considers and executes restructuring actions that vary in size and impact, for example from a minor sales force reorganization at a local facility to a significant organizational and process redesign affecting an entire operating division. The resulting cost savings or profits from increased sales are reinvested in the business to increase Pepsico's shareholder value.

Currency Exchange Effects

In 1994, 1993 and 1992, international businesses represented 18.6%, 18.0% and 17.7%, respectively, of Pepsico's total segment operating profits. The following paragraphs describe the effects of currency exchange rate movements on Pepsico's reported results. See Other Factors Expected to Impact 1995 Results. . . .

Translation of the income statements of international businesses into U.S. dollars affects year-over-year comparability of operating results. In 1994 and 1993, sales and operating profit growth rates for our consolidated international businesses were not materially impacted.

Changes in currency exchange rates also result in reported foreign exchange gains and losses. Pepsico reported a net foreign exchange gain of $4.5 million and $ 17.4 million in 1993 and 1992, respectively.

report, and the report begins "To humanize the facts, figures, and financial data of our annual report, we decided to aim it at a real live person—a typical investor next door. We chose Cindy Crawford. So sit back, pop open a Pepsi, and, along with Cindy read about your company." The discussions compare 1992, 1993, and 1994. The edited version in Figure 5-5 captures the essence. Percentage comparisons are a common part of the discussion. Management then augments observed changes with examples of underlying causes.

Management's Analysis—Results of Operations

Net Sales rose $3.5 billion or 14% in 1994 of which $215 million or 1 point was contributed by net acquisitions. The balance of the increase reflected volume gains of $2.2 billion and $934 million due to additional restaurant units.

Cost of sales as a percentage of Net Sales was 48.2%, 47.7% and 48.3% in 1994, 1993 and 1992, respectively. The decline in the 1994 gross margin reflected a mix shift to lower-margin businesses in international beverages and worldwide restaurants, and lower net pricing in domestic beverages, partially offset by a mix shift to higher-margin packages and products in international snack foods and manufacturing efficiencies in domestic snack foods.

Selling, general and administrative expenses rose 14% in 1994 and 13% in 1993, reflecting base business growth.

Operating Profit increased 10% in 1994 and 23% in 1993. Excluding the Unusual Items, operating profit increased $262 million or 9% in 1994 and $342 million or 13% in 1993, driven by combined segment operating profit growth of 7% in 1994 and 14% in 1993. The 1994 increase reflected $850 million from higher volumes and $73 million from additional restaurant units, partially offset by higher operating expenses.

Interest expense, net of Interest income, increased 15% in 1994 and 2% in 1993. The 1994 increase reflected higher average borrowings partially offset by higher interest rates on investment balances.

Provision for Income Taxes as a percentage of pretax income was 33.0%, 34.5% and 31.4% in 1994, 1993 and 1992, respectively.

Income and Income Per Share before Cumulative Effect of Accounting Changes. "Income" and "income per share" in 1994 increased 12% to $1.8 billion and 13% to $2.22, respectively, and in 1993 increased 22% to $1.6 billion and 22% to $ 1.96, respectively. Excluding the Unusual Items, income and income per share rose 8% and 9%, respectively, in 1994 and 13% and 12%, respectively, in 1993. Growth in income per share was depressed by estimated dilution from acquisitions of $0.03 or 1 point in 1994 and $0.05 or 3 points in 1993, primarily due to international beverage acquisitions in both years.

The Mexican peso devaluation may unfavorably impact Net Sales and Net Income in 1995: however, due to many uncertainties in Mexico, we are unable to quantify the impacts.

Segment Reporting

The Pepsico management discussion in Figure 5-5 includes a comparison of domestic and international performance. Such detailed disclosure is part of the gradual evolution toward fuller disclosure during the 1980s and 1990s. The financial statements become thicker and more complex and are impressively adorned with detailed footnotes and supplementary information. Among the more controversial requirements was the issuance by the FASB in 1976 of *Statement No. 14*, "Financial Reporting for Segments of a Business Enterprise." Corporations must now disclose data about their operations in different industries and in foreign countries, their export sales, and their major customers. Almost twenty years later, the FASB is considering changes to these rules to help investors better understand the parts of the enterprise.

The purpose of consolidated financial statements is to provide an overall view of an economic entity. However, consolidated data can hide some of the details that might be useful in predicting profitability, risk, and growth. The purpose of segment disclosures is to facilitate such prediction.

Figure 5-6 lists the four types of disclosures required by *Statement No. 14*. An *industry segment* is a product or service or a group of related products or services. Management has much discretion in defining industry segments. The nature of the product, the nature of the production process, and the markets or marketing methods should be considered in identifying a company's segments. Examples of industry segments include the following:

- American Express Company: travel-related services; international banking services; investment services; IDS financial services; insurance services
- Alcoa: aluminum processing; finished products

If an industry segment meets any one of the three criteria for disclosure in Figure 5-6, the segment's revenue, profit, assets, depreciation, and capital expenditures must be reported.

FIGURE 5-6   Main Provisions of FASB Statement No. 14

Type of Disclosure	Criteria Disclosure	Items to Be Disclosed
1. Industry segment	a. Revenue at least 10% of company revenue, b. Profit at least 10% of company profit, or c. Assets at least 10% of company assets.	a. Segment revenue b. Segment profit c. Segment assets d. Other (e.g., segment depreciation and capital expenditures)
2. Geographic segment	a. Foreign operations contribute at least 10% of company's revenue, or b. Foreign operations use more than 10% of the company's assets	a. Segment revenue b. Segment profit c. Segment assets
3. Export disclosures	At least 10% of revenues from export sales	Export sales by geographic area
4. Major customers	Any customer providing more than 10% of company's revenue	Customer identity and amount of revenue

Companies with significant operations in foreign countries must separately disclose the results of operations by geographic area. For example, American Express Company reports revenue, profits, and assets for the United States, Europe, and Asia/Pacific. Even companies without foreign operations must disclose foreign *sales* by geographic area if such export sales are 10% or more of total revenues.

Finally, companies must report aggregate sales to any customer accounting for more than 10% of revenues. For example, Ball Corporation, maker of packaging materials, including metal beverage containers for brewers and soft drink companies, reports that 23% of its sales were to Anheuser-Busch and 20% were to various agencies of the United States government. Figure 5-7 shows the industry and geographic segment information from Pepsico's 1994 annual report.

FINANCIAL RATIOS

The cornerstone of financial statement analysis is the computation and interpretation of ratios. Figure 5-8 groups some of the most popular ratios into four categories. (A dash in the column means that the ratio is being introduced in this chapter for the first time.)

Evaluating Financial Ratios

Evaluation of a financial ratio requires a comparison. There are three main types of comparisons: (1) with a company's own historical ratios (called **time-series comparisons**), (2) with general *rules of thumb* or **bench marks**, and (3) with ratios of other companies or with industry averages (called **cross-sectional comparisons**).

Much can be learned by examining the *time-series trend* of a company's ratios. That is why annual reports typically contain a table of comparative statistics for five or ten years. For example, some of the items listed in the 1994 annual report of Pepsico are:

	1994	1993	1992	1991	1990
Income per share	$ (2.18)	$ 1.96	$ .46	$ 1.35	$ 1.35
Debt as a percentage of total capitalization	49%	50%	49%	51%	51%
Return on common stockholders' equity	(27.0)%	27.2%	23.9%	20.7%	24.8%

Broad *rules of thumb* often serve as bench marks for comparison. Historically, the most quoted bench mark is a current ratio of 2 to 1. Recently, changes in management practices have reduced cash and inventory levels, and average current ratios are moving toward 1 to 1. Other bench marks are described in *Industry Norms and Key Business Ratios* by Dun & Bradstreet, the financial services firm.

Bench marks are general guides. More specific comparisons come from cross-sectional comparisons; that is, by examining ratios of similar companies or from in-

FIGURE 5-7   Pepsico 1994 Segment and Geographic Disclosures

	Growth Rate 1989-1994	1994		Growth Rate 1989-1994	1994
Net Sales			**Operating Profits**		
Beverages:					
Domestic	7.2%	$ 6,541.2	Domestic	12.1%	$1,022.3
International	22.2%	3,146.3	International	20.0%	194.7
	10.9%	**9,687.5**		13.2%	**1,217.0**
Snack Foods:					
Domestic	9.3%	5,011.3	Domestic	8.9%	1,025.1
International	32.0%	3,253.1	International	27.1 %	351.8
	15.5%	**8,264.4**		12.2%	**1,376.9**
Restaurants:					
Domestic	13.2%	8,693.9	Domestic	12.2%	658.8
International	26.4%	1,826.6	International	4.3%	71.5
	14.9%	**10,520.5**		11.3%	**730.3**
Combined Segments					
Domestic	10.1%	20,246.4	Domestic	11.1%	2,706.2
International	26.6%	8,226.0	International	20.6%	618.0
	13.6%	**$28,472.4**		12.3%	**3,324.2**

Geographic Areas	Net Sales	Segment Operating Profits	Identifiable Assets
	1994	1994	1994
United States	$20,246.4	$2,706.2	$14,218.4
Europe	2,177.1	16.7	3,062.0
Mexico	2,022.8	261.4	994.7
Canada	1,244.3	81.6	1,342.1
Other	2,781.8	258.3	2,195.6
Combined Segments	**$28,472.4**	**$3,324.2**	21,812.8
Corporate			2,979.2
			$24,792.0

	Depreciation Expense		Amortization of Intangible Assets	
	Growth Rate 1989–1994	1994	Growth Rate 1989–1994	1994
Beverages	14.9%	$ 385.4	7.6%	$164.8
Snack Foods	11.7%	297.0	17.8%	42.0
Restaurants	17.5%	538.8	28.9%	105.4
Corporate		7.0		
	15.0%	**$1,228.2**	14.0%	**$312.2**

	Identifiable Assets		Capital Spending	
	Growth Rate 1989–1994	1994	Growth Rate 1989–1994	1994
Beverages	9.1 %	$ 9,566.0	20.4%	$ 677.1
Snack Foods	8.8%	5,043.9	15.6%	532.1
Restaurants	18.6%	7,202.9	20.3%	1,072.0
Corporate		2,979.2		7.2
	10.4%	**$24,792.0**	19.0%	**$2,288.4**

FIGURE 5-8   Some Typical Financial Ratios

Typical Name of Ratio	Numerator	Denominator	Using Appropriate Oxley Numbers Applied to December 31 of Year	
	TOP	_BOTTOM_	19X2	19X1
Short-term liquidity ratios:				
Current ratio	Current assets	Current liabilities	$290 \div 219 = 1.3$	$202 \div 101 = 2.0$
Quick ratio	Cash + marketable securities + receivables	Current liabilities	$(150 + 0 + 95) \div 219 = 1.1$	$(57 + 0 + 70) \div 101 = 1.3$
Average collection period in days	Average accounts receivable $\times$ 365	Sales	$[1/2(95 + 70) \times 365] \div 999 = 30^{\dagger}$	Unknown*
Inventory turnover	Cost of goods sold	Average inventory at cost	$399 \div 1/2(20 + 60) = 10$	Unknown*
Long-term solvency ratios:				
Total debt to total assets	Total liabilities	Total assets	$259 \div 658 = 39.4\%$	$221 \div 610 = 36.2\%$
Total debt to equity	Total liabilities	Stockholders' equity	$259 \div 399 = 64.9\%$	$221 \div 389 = 56.8\%$
Interest coverage	Income before interest end taxes	Interest expense	$(150 + 12) \div 12 = 13.5$	$(128 + 12) \div 12 = 11.7$
Profitability ratios:				
Return on stockholders' equity	Net income _Net Income / stockholdersequity_	Average stock-holders' equity	$90 \div 1/2(399 + 389) = 22.8\%$	Unknown* _Higher is better_
Gross profit rate or percentage	Gross profit or gross margin	Sales	$600 \div 999 = 60\%$	$464 \div 800 = 58\%$
Return on sales	Net income	Sales	$90 \div 999 = 9\%$	$80 \div 800 = 10\%$
Asset turnover _NET PROFIT_ _NET profit% / sales_	Sales	Average total assets available	$999 \div 1/2(658 + 610) = 1.6$	Unknown* _Higher_
Pretax return on operating assets	Operating income	Average total assets available	$126 \div 1/2(658 + 610) = 19.9\%$	Unknown*
Earnings per share	Net income less dividends on preferred stock, if any	Average common shares outstanding _(Shares out there)_	$90 \div 200 = \$.45$	$80 \div 200 = \$.40$
Market price and dividend ratios:				
Price-earnings	Market price of common share (assume $4 and $3)	Earnings per share	$4 \div .45 = 8.9$	$3 \div .40 = 7.5$
Dividend-yield	Dividends per common share	Market price of common share (assume $4 and $3)	$.40 \div 4 = 10.0\%$	$.20 \div 3 = 6.7\%$
Dividend-payout	Dividends per common share	Earnings per share	$.40 \div .45 = 89\%$	$.20 \div .40 = 50\%$

*Insufficient data available because the _beginning_ balance sheet balances for 19X1 are not provided. Without them, the average investment in receivables, inventory, total assets, or stockholders' equity during 19X1 cannot be computed.

†This may be easier to see as follows: Average receivables = 1/2(95 + 70) = 82.5. Average receivables as a percentage of annual sales = 82.5 ÷ 999 = 8.25%. Average collection period = 8.25% × 365 days = 30 days.

dustry averages. Dun & Bradstreet informs its subscribers of the creditworthiness of thousands of individual companies. In addition, the firm regularly compiles many ratios of the companies it monitors. Compare the ratios for Oxley Company in Figure 5-8 to some of the Dun & Bradstreet ratios for 1,712 retail nurseries and garden stores:

Dun & Bradstreet Ratios	Current Ratio	Quick Ratio	Average Collection Period (Days)	Total Debt to Stockholders' Equity (Percent)	Net Income on Sales (Percent)	Net Income on Stockholders' Equity (Percent)
1,712 companies:						
Upper quartile	4.2	1.5	5.5	32.3	6.1	30.2
Median	2.0	0.5	11.3	92.8	2.5	12.6
Lower quartile	1.3	0.2	23.0	230.7	0.5	2.6
Oxley*	1.3	1.1	30.0	64.9	9.0	22.8

*Ratios are from Figure 5-8. Please consult that exhibit for an explanation of the components of each ratio.

The individual ratios are ranked from best to worst. The ratio ranked in the middle is the *median.* The upper quartile is the ratio ranked halfway between the median and the best value. The lower quartile is the ratio ranked halfway between the median and the worst value. The concept of best and worst must be considered carefully. Different constituencies may adopt different points of view. For example, a short-term creditor would think that a very high current ratio was good, because it means the assets are there to repay the debt. From management's perspective, however, it is possible that current assets are excessive.

Short-Term Liquidity Ratios

Questions concerning liquidity focus on whether there are sufficient current assets to satisfy current liabilities as they become due. The most commonly used liquidity ratio is the current ratio. The higher the current ratio, the more assurance the short-term creditor usually has about being paid in full and on time. As Figure 5-8 shows, Oxley's current ratio of 1.3 has declined from 2.0 and is unimpressive in relation to the industry median of 2.0, which is shown in the previous section.

The quick ratio measures shorter-term liquidity. The numerator includes only those current assets that can quickly be turned into cash: cash, marketable securities, and accounts receivable. Oxley's quick ratio has also declined in 19X2, from 1.3 to 1.1, but is still greater than the industry median of 0.5.

Liquidity is also affected by how soon accounts receivable will be collected and how soon inventory will be sold. The average collection period and inventory turnover are closely watched signals. Deteriorations through time in these ratios can help alert investors and creditors to problem areas. For example, a decrease in inventory turnover may suggest slower-moving (or even unsalable) merchandise or a worsening coordination of the buying and selling functions. An increase in the average collection period of receivables may indicate increasing acceptance of poor credit risks or less-energetic collection efforts. Whether the inventory turnover of 10 and the average collection period of 30 days are "fast" or "slow" depends on past performance and the performance of similar companies. Inventory turnover is not available from Dun & Bradstreet on an industry-comparable basis. The average collection period for Oxley is nearly three times as long as the industry median of 11.3 days.

Many analysts use sales *on account* in the denominator of the average collection period. This ratio focuses attention on how long it takes to collect credit accounts, in contrast to how long it takes to receive payment on sales in general. A company with many cash sales may have a short average collection period for total sales, even though there may be long delays in receiving payments for items sold on credit. Suppose half of Oxley's sales were for cash (including bank cards) and only half on open credit. The average collection period for *credit sales* would be

$$\frac{(1/2)\,(95 + 70) \times 365}{(1/2)\,(999)} = 60\,\text{day}$$

To be compared with industry averages, the averages must also be adjusted for credit sales. Suppose only one-fourth of the sales in retail nurseries are on credit. The industry median collection period for credit accounts would be $10.2 \div (1/4) = 40.8$ days.

Long-Term Solvency Ratios

Ratios of debt to assets and debt to equity are used for solvency evaluation. Although the focus is on the ability to repay long-term creditors, both creditors and shareholders watch these ratios to judge the degree of risk of insolvency and the stability of profits. Typically, companies with heavy debt in relation to ownership capital are in greater danger of suffering net losses or even insolvency when business conditions sour. Why? Because revenues and many expenses decline, but interest expenses and maturity dates do not change. Oxley's debt-to-equity ratio of 64.9% is below the industry median of 92.8%, reflecting less-than-average uncertainty concerning the company's ability to pay its debts on time.

Another solvency measure is the interest coverage ratio. It shows how much danger there is that operations will not generate operating income (before interest expense) at least as large as the company's interest expense. A common rule of thumb is that the interest coverage ratio should be at least five. Oxley's ratio of 13.5 comfortably exceeds this bench mark.

Profitability Ratios

Earnings per share (EPS) is the best known of all financial ratios. It measures the "bottom line," earnings available to the holder of a share of common stock. Extended discussion appears later in this chapter, where we examine some issues that arise for more complex companies than Oxley.

The primary profitability measure is return on stockholders' equity. Abbreviated ROE, this ratio relates an accounting measure of income to the level of ownership capital used to generate the income. The ratio is:

$$ROE = \text{Net income} / \text{Average shareholders' equity}$$

Oxley's return of 22.8% is above the 1994 industry median of 12.6%. What explains Oxley's superior performance? Two additional profitability ratios help explain it. Figure 5-8 shows that the return on sales has fallen from 10% to 9%. But the 9% level, which indicates that 9 cents of every dollar of sales is profit, places Oxley well above the 75th percentile of nurseries and garden stores according to Dun & Bradstreet. The second key to assessing Oxley's superior ROE is the efficiency with which Oxley uses its asset structure to generate sales. To accomplish this, we now examine some distinctions between operating performance and financial performance.

OPERATING PERFORMANCE AND FINANCIAL PERFORMANCE

ROE, discussed above, is affected by financing choices. *Financial management* is concerned with where to get cash and how to use that cash to benefit the entity. Borrowed funds create interest costs and affect net income, the numerator of the ratio. *Operating management* is concerned with the day-to-day activities that generate revenues and expenses. Ratios to assess operating efficiency should not be affected by financial considerations.

Market Price and Dividend Ratios

Investors are particularly concerned with the market price of common shares. Both earnings and dividends are related to share price. The price-earnings (P/E) ratio shows how market participants value $1 of a company's earnings. Generally, high P/E means that investors expect earnings to grow faster than average, and a low P/E indicates small expected earnings growth. In 1995, the average economy-wide P/E ratio was 16, but some companies such as Microsoft, the computer software company, had P/E ratios over 35. In contrast, IBM had a P/E of 15 and McDonald's 21. Oxley's P/E of 8.9 is above last year's 7.5, but it is below the economy-wide average. Apparently, investors think Oxley has below-average growth potential.

Oxley doubled its dividend per share in 19X2, increasing the dividend yield to 10.0%. Therefore an investor who buys $1,000 of Oxley common stock will receive annual cash dividends of 10% × $1,000 = $100 if dividend rates do not change. Oxley is paying out 89% of earnings, as shown by the dividend-payout ratio. The high payout ratio may be one reason for the low projected growth; Oxley is not reinvesting much of its earnings.

Operating Performance

In general, we evaluate the overall success of an investment by comparing what the investment returns to us with the investment we initially made. In general, the rate of return on investment can be defined as:

$$\text{Rate of return on investment} = \frac{\text{Income}}{\text{Invested capital}} \qquad (1)$$

In various settings, we find it useful to define *income* differently, sometimes as net earnings and sometimes as either pretax income from operations or earnings before interest and taxes (**EBIT**). We also define *invested capital* differently, sometimes as the stockholders' equity and other times as the total capital provided by both debt and equity sources. These choices are determined by the purpose of the analysis.

The measurement of *operating* performance (that is, how profitably assets are employed) should not be influenced by the management's *financial* decisions (that is, how assets are financed). Operating performance is best measured by **pretax operating rate of return on total assets:**

$$\frac{\text{Pretax operating rate}}{\text{of return on total assets}} = \frac{\text{Operating income}}{\text{Average total assets available}} \tag{2}$$

The right side of Equation 2 consists, in turn, of two important ratios:

$$\frac{\text{Operating income}}{\text{Average total assets available}} = \frac{\text{Operating income}}{\text{Sales}} \times \frac{\text{Sales}}{\text{Average total assets available}} \tag{3}$$

Using Figures 5-1 and 5-2, we can compute the following 19X2 results for Oxley Company:

$$\frac{\$126}{1/2\,(\$658 + \$610)} = \frac{\$126}{\$999} \times \frac{\$999}{\$634} = 19.9\%$$

These relationships are displayed in a boxed format in Figure 5-9.

The right-side terms in Equation 3 are often called the **operating income percentage on sales** and the **total asset turnover (asset turnover),** respectively. Equation 3 may be reexpressed:

$$\frac{\text{Pretax operating rate}}{\text{of return on total assets}} = \text{Operating income percentage on sales} \times \text{Total asset turnover}$$

$$\tag{4}$$

$$19.9\% = 12.6\% \times 1.576\,\text{times}$$

If ratios are used to evaluate operating performance, they should exclude extraordinary items that are regarded as nonrecurring items that do not reflect normal performance.

Equation 4 highlights two basic factors in profit making: operating margin percentage and turnover. An improvement in either will, by itself, increase the rate of return on total assets.

The ratios could be computed on the basis of figures after taxes, and often are. However, the peculiarities of the income tax laws may sometimes distort results—for example, the tax rate may change, or losses carried back or forward might eliminate the tax in certain years.

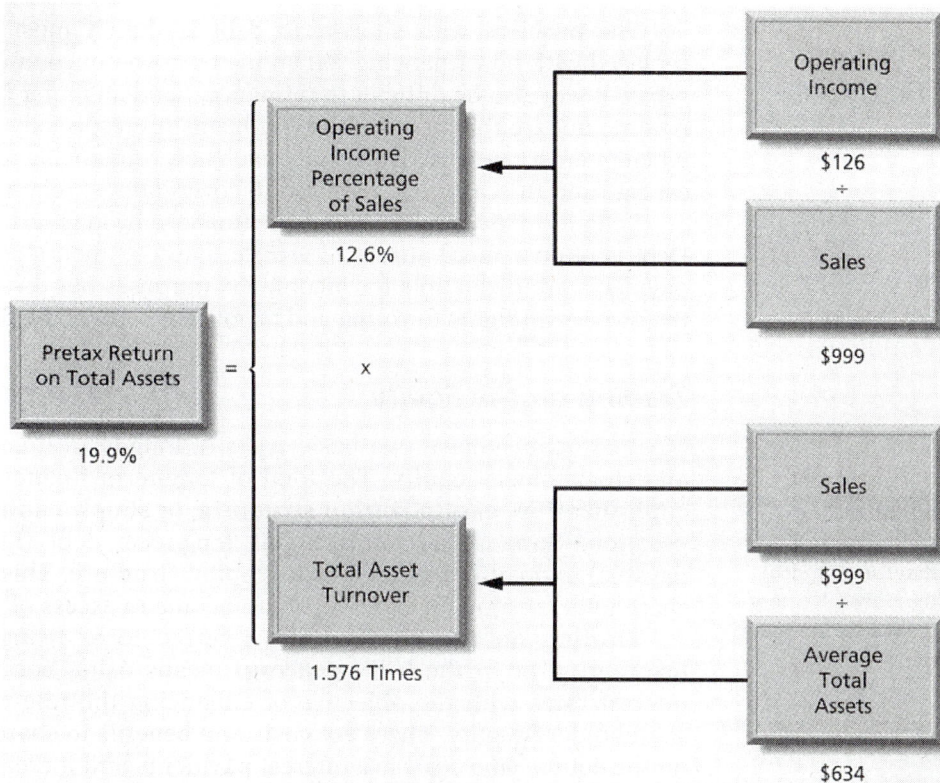

FIGURE 5-9
Major Ingredients of Return on Total Assets

Financial Performance

A major aspect of financial performance is achieving an appropriate balance of debt and equity financing. Debt surrounds us. Governments issue debt securities of all kinds for many purposes. Businesses do likewise. Individuals have small loans (on refrigerators) and big loans (on homes).

In addition to a decision about how much debt is appropriate, a firm must choose how much to borrow short-term (e.g., accounts payable and some bank debt) and how much to borrow by issuing bonds or other longer-term debt. Short-term financing should ordinarily be for investments in current assets. Some entities have edged into deep financial water by using short-term debt for long-term investments (for example, plant and equipment). A notable example is the city of New York, which was unable to pay its debt during the 1970s.

The problem with short-term debt is that it must be quickly repaid or replaced with new financing. When the borrower encounters trouble and cannot repay, it will also be difficult to refinance. Lenders prefer healthy, profitable borrowers, not troubled ones. Such problems are especially severe during periods when interest rates are rising, since each new refinancing occurs at a higher interest rate and the cash flow required to cover interest requirements rises steadily.

Long-term investments should be financed by long-term capital: debt or stock. Debt is often a more attractive vehicle than common stock because (1) interest payments are deductible for income tax purposes but dividends are not, and (2) the ownership rights to voting and profits are kept by the present shareholders.

Trading on the Equity

Most companies have two basic types of long-term financing: long-term debt and stockholders' equity. The total of long-term financing is often called the **capitalization, capitalization structure,** or simply **capital structure** of a corporation. Suppose a company has long-term debt (in the form of bonds payable) and common stock as its capital structure. This means that common shareholders enjoy the benefits of all income in excess of interest on the bonds.

Trading on the equity (also referred to as using **financial leverage, leveraging,** or in the U.K., **gearing**) means using borrowed money at fixed interest rates with the objective of enhancing the rate of return on common shareholders' equity. There are costs and benefits to shareholders from trading on the equity. The costs are interest payments and increased risk, and the benefits are the larger returns to the common shareholders—as long as overall income is sufficiently large.

Consider three companies, A, B, and C, each in the same industry with $80,000 of average assets and with the same rate of return on total assets (ROA) in any year. However, the ROA varies: In Year 1 it is 20%, in Year 2 it is 10%, and in Year 3 it is 5%. The three companies have chosen very different capital structures. Company A has no debt, company B has $30,000 in debt, and Company C has $60,000 in debt. Company B pays 10% interest, while the more heavily indebted Company C must pay 12%. How do the shareholders fare in these three companies in different years? The results are summarized in Figure 5-10.

The first column of Figure 5-10 gives the income before interest expense. To clearly focus on leverage, this example ignores taxes. Recall that the return on assets is calculated as

$$\text{Rate of return on total assets} = \frac{\text{Income before interest expense}}{\text{Average total assets}}$$

Therefore, income before interest expense equals rate of **return on total assets (ROA)** times average total assets. In this instance we assume a given ROA for each year and therefore can calculate income by multiplying ROA times the constant asset level of $80,000. The values are the same for all three companies within a year but vary from year to year. The interest expense is different for each company because each has a different level of debt. Our primary interest is the effect of leverage on the level of the **rate of return on common stockholders' equity (ROE)** defined as:

$$\text{Rate of return on stockholders' equity} = \frac{\text{Net income}}{\text{Average stockholders' equity}}$$

FIGURE 5-10   Trading on the Equity-Effects of Debt on Rates of Return

	(1) Income before Interest	(2) Interest Expense	(3) Net Income	(4) Stockholders' Equity	(5) Return on Equity
	(ROA × Assets)*	(Debt × Interest Rate)†	(1) – (2)		(3) ÷ (4)
Year 1: 20% ROA					
Company A	$16,000	$ 0	$16,000	$80,000	20%
Company B	16,000	3,000	13,000	50,000	26%
Company C	16,000	7,200	8,800	20,000	44%
Year 2: 10% ROA					
Company A	$ 8,000	$ 0	$ 8,000	$80,000	10%
Company B	8,000	3,000	5,000	50,000	10%
Company C	8,000	7,200	800	20,000	4%
Year 3: 5% ROA					
Company A	$ 4,000	$ 0	$ 4,000	$80,000	5%
Company B	4,000	3,000	1,000	50,000	2%
Company C	4,000	7,200	(3,200)	20,000	(16%)

*All three companies have $80,000 in assets.
†Company A, no debt; Company B. $30,000 in debt at 10%; Company C, $60,000 in debt at 12%.

What do we learn from Figure 5-10? First, a debt-free, or *unlevered*, company has identical ROA and ROE. Note that Company A's ROE and ROA are identical in each year: 20%, 10%, and 5%. Second, when a company has an ROA greater than its interest rate, ROE exceeds ROA. This is called favorable financial leverage and describes both companies B and C in Year 1. They earn 20% on their assets and pay either 10% or 12% on their debt. The earnings in excess of the interest cost increase earnings available to shareholders. Year 2 is interesting because Company B has an ROA of 10%, which equals its interest rate. Thus, like Company A, Company B has an ROE of 10%. In contrast Company C experiences *unfavorable* financial leverage. Since its 10% ROA is less than the 12% interest cost, its ROE falls sharply to 4%.

Year 3 further stresses the effects of leverage in poor years. When ROA falls noticeably below the firm's interest cost, ROE falls sharply as well. Company B falls to an ROE of 2%, while the more highly leveraged Company C faces a loss year and negative ROE.

When a company is unable to earn at least the interest rate on the money borrowed, the return on equity will be lower than for the debt-free company. If earnings are low enough that the interest and principal payments on debt cannot be made, a company may be forced into bankruptcy. The possibility of bankruptcy increases the risk to the common stockholders even more than to debtholders.

Obviously, the more stable the income, the less dangerous it is to trade on the equity. Therefore regulated utilities such as electric, gas, and telephone companies tend to have a much heavier proportion of debt than manufacturers of computers or steel. The *prudent* use of debt is part of intelligent financial management.

Income Tax Effects

Because interest payments are deductible as an expense for income tax purposes but dividends are not, if all other things are equal, the use of debt is less costly to the corporation than equity. Suppose additional capital of $10 million is going to be raised by a company either through long-term debt or through preferred stock. The typical preferred stock is a part of shareholders' equity, and the dividend thereon is not deductible for income tax purposes. Moreover, the rate of preferred dividends is usually higher than the rate of interest because the preferred stockholders have a greater risk due to their lower-priority claim on the total assets of a company. Assume that an interest rate of 10% for debt and a preferred dividend rate of 11% are applicable. The income tax rate is 40%. Compare the effects of obtaining additional capital by these two methods shown in the accompanying table.

	$10 Million Long-Term Debt	$10 Million Preferred Stock
Income before interest expense (assumed)	$5,000,000	$5,000,000
Interest expense at 10% of long-term debt	1,000,000	—
Income before income taxes	$4,000,000	$5,000,000
Income tax expense at 40%	1,600,000	2,000,000
Net income	$2,400,000	$3,000,000
Dividends to preferred shareholders at 11%	—	1,100,000
Net income less dividends	$2,400,000	$1,900,000
Pretax cost of capital raised	10%	11%
After-tax cost of capital raised:		
$600,000* ÷ $10,000,000	6%	
$1,100,000 ÷ $10,000,000		11%

*Interest expense	$1,000,000
Income tax savings because of interest deduction:	
.40 × $1,000,000	400,000
Interest expense after tax savings	$ 600,000

Three points deserve emphasis:

1. Interest is tax deductible, so its after-tax cost can be considerably less than dividends on preferred stock. In other words, *net income attributable to common shareholders* can be substantially higher if debt is used.
2. Interest is an expense, whereas preferred dividends are not. Therefore *net income* is higher if preferred shares are used. Note that trading on the equity can benefit the common stockholders by the issuance of either long-term debt securities or preferred stock, provided that there are sufficient earnings on the additional assets acquired.
3. Failure to pay interest is an act of bankruptcy, which gives creditors rights to control or liquidate the company. Failure to pay dividends is not.

Measuring Safety

Investors in debt securities want assurance that future operations will easily provide cash sufficient to make the scheduled payments of interest and principal. Corporate borrowers have a natural concern for the degree of risk they assume by borrowing. Thus lenders and borrowers have a mutual aversion to excessive risks from debt, although lenders understandably have the stronger aversion.

Debt securities often have protective provisions, such as mortgage liens on real estate or restrictions on dividend payments to holders of common stock. However, these provisions are of minor importance compared with prospective earnings. Bondholders would like to avoid the trouble, costs, and inconvenience of foreclosure or bankruptcy litigation; they would rather receive a steady stream of interest and repayments of principal.

Debt-to-equity ratios are popular measures of risk. But they do not focus on the major concern of the holders of long-term debt: the ability to meet debt obligations on schedule. A ratio that focuses on interest-paying ability is **interest coverage** (sometimes called **times interest earned**). For example, interest coverage is:

$$\text{Interest coverage} = \frac{\text{Income before interest expense and income taxes}}{\text{Interest expense}}$$

$$= \frac{\$5,000,000}{\$1,000,000} = 5.0 \text{ times}$$

The equation is self-explanatory. A rule of thumb for adequate safety of an industrial bond is that all interest charges should be earned at least five times in the poorest year in a span of seven to ten years that might be under review. The numerator does not deduct income taxes because interest expense is deductible for income tax purposes. In effect, income taxes, as a periodic "claim" on earnings, have a lower priority than interest. For instance, if the numerator were only $1 million, interest would be paid, leaving a net taxable income of zero. This tax-deductibility feature is a major reason why bonds are used much more widely than preferred stock.

PROMINENCE OF EARNINGS PER SHARE

Throughout this text we have viewed earnings per share (EPS) as a basic reporting element in the financial statements. However, we have generally expressed it in the context of a simple owners' equity structure consisting solely of common stock. Three issues that might complicate matters are discussed below: preferred stock, stock issues and redemptions, and the possibility of exercise of options or various convertible securities. If common stock is issued during the year, the weighted average number of shares must be calculated. If preferred stocks exist, the priority claims of those shareholders must be considered. Finally, if there are exchange privileges outstanding such as stock options or convertible securities, their potential effect must be considered.

Weighted Average Shares and Preferred Stock

When the capital structure is relatively simple, computations of EPS are straightforward. For example, consider the following calculation (figures assumed):

$$\begin{array}{l} \text{Earnings per share} \\ \text{of common stock} \end{array} = \frac{\text{Net income}}{\begin{array}{c} \text{Weighted–average number of shares} \\ \text{outstanding during the period} \end{array}}$$

$$= \frac{\$1,000,000}{800,000} = \$1.25$$

Computations of EPS are based on the weighted-average number of shares outstanding during a period. For example, suppose 750,000 shares were outstanding at the beginning of a calendar year, and 200,000 of additional shares were issued on October 1 (three months before the end of the year). The weighted average is based on the number of months that the shares were outstanding during the year. The basic computation can be accomplished in two different ways:

750,000 × weighting of 12/12 = 750,000		750,000 × 9/12 = 562,500	
200,000 × weighting of 3/12 = 50,000	*or*	950,000 × 3/12 = 237,500	
Weighted average shares = **800,000**		= **800,000**	

In addition, if the capital structure includes preferred stock that is nonconvertible, the dividends on preferred stock applicable to the current period, whether or not paid, should be deducted in calculating earnings applicable to common stock (figures assumed):

$$\begin{array}{l} \text{Earnings per share} \\ \text{of common stock} \end{array} = \frac{\text{Net income} - \text{Preferred dividends}}{\begin{array}{c} \text{Weighted} - \text{average number of shares} \\ \text{outstanding during the period} \end{array}}$$

$$= \frac{\$1,000,000 - \$200,000}{800,000} = \$1.00$$

Historical summaries of EPS must be made comparable by adjusting for changes in capitalization structure (for example, stock splits and stock dividends).

Primary and Fully Diluted EPS

Accounting Principles Board *Opinion No. 15*, "Earnings per Share," stresses that the foregoing simple computations are inadequate when companies have convertible securities, stock options, or other financial instruments that can be exchanged for or converted to common shares. For example, suppose a firm has some convertible preferred stock in its capital structure:

5% convertible preferred stock; $100 par, each share convertible into 2 common shares	100,000 shares
Common stock	1,000,000 shares

The simple EPS computation follows:

Computation of earnings per share:	
Net income	$ 10,500,000
Preferred dividends	500,000
Net income to common stock	**$10,000,000**
Earnings per share of common stock:	
$10,000,000 ÷ 1,000,000 shares	**$ 10.00**

However, note how EPS would be affected if the preferred stock were converted, that is, exchanged for common stock. *Dilution,* a reduction in EPS, will occur. EPS can be calculated *as if* conversion had occurred at the beginning of the fiscal year:

Net income	$10,500,000
Preferred dividends	0
Net income to common stock	**$10,500,000**
Earnings per share of common stock—assuming conversion:	
$10,500,000 ÷ 1,200,000 shares	**$ 8.75**

The potential earnings dilution of common stock is $10.00 − $8.75 = $1.25 per share.

APB *Opinion No. 15* requires companies to divide securities that could cause dilution into two categories: (1) common stock equivalents and (2) other sources of dilution. Common stock equivalents are securities whose major value is attributable to their being exchangeable for or convertible to common stock. There are complex rules, beyond the scope of this text, for identifying common stock equivalents. **Primary EPS** is the EPS calculated as if *common stock equivalents* that dilute EPS were converted. **Fully diluted EPS** is an EPS that includes assumed conversion of *all* potentially dilutive securities. Primary EPS is reported on the income statement. If primary and fully diluted EPS differ by more than 3%, both must be reported.

Assume that the convertible preferred stock in our example is not a common stock equivalent. EPS would be presented as follows:

Primary earnings per common share (Note A)	$10.00
Fully diluted earnings per common share (Note B)	$ 8.75

Note A: Per share data are based on the average number of common shares outstanding during each year, after recognition of the dividend requirements on the 5% preferred stock.

Note B: Per share data based on the assumption that the outstanding preferred stock is converted into common shares at the beginning of the year, reflecting the 200,000 shares issuable on conversion and eliminating the preferred dividend requirements.

DISCLOSURE OF NONRECURRING ITEMS

Security analysts evaluate the prospects of the firm relative to the future. Therefore it is very important to distinguish the elements of the current financial statements that reflect recurring aspects of the firm from those that represent one-time events or items that will not continue. These items fall into three major categories: special items, extraordinary items, and discontinued operations. Each category is explained briefly.

Special Items

Special items, which are large and somewhat unusual, represent a category of event that may recur with some frequency. During the 1980s and into the 1990s, the most common special item has been restructuring charges. A restructuring occurs when a firm decides to substantially change the size or scope or location of a part of the business. It often involves relocation, plant closings, and reductions in personnel. The costs will typically be incurred over an extended period of time, often several years, but GAAP requires that the total costs be estimated and recorded when the plan is made. In 1994 the FASB and the SEC acted to assure that restructuring changes did not include costs that will benefit future periods. Specifically they cannot include relocation and training costs for people who will continue to work for the firm. These are properly matched to future revenues. Disclosure occurs by reporting the cost as a separate line item among operating expenses, with discussion of the plan in the footnotes. The following example is condensed from the AT&T 1991 annual report:

AT&T and Subsidiaries Consolidated Statements of Income Year Ended December 31 (dollars in millions)

	1991
Sales and revenues	$63,089
Costs	38,825
Gross margin	24,264
Operating expenses	
Selling, general, and administrative expenses	16,220
Research and development expenses	3,114
Provision for business restructuring (D)	**3,572**
Total operating expenses	22,906
Operating income	1,358
Other income—net	977
Income before income taxes	883
Provision for income taxes	361
Net income	$ 522

(D) Business Restructuring and Other Charges

The 1991 charges were recorded as a $3,572 provision for business restructuring, $501 of selling, general and administrative expenses, $123 as cost of products and systems, and the remainder as other costs and expenses, including other income—net. The provision for business restructuring includes the estimated costs associated with force reductions and relocations, facility consolidations, contractual obligations, including lease buyouts, and other restructuring activities.

How would an analyst use this information to project future earnings? Since a restructuring of such magnitude is rare, the analyst might argue that the expense of $3,572 is nonrecurring. We should, then, adjust net earnings for the special item to make predictions and to better evaluate trends. However, the special item decreased the income tax provision. If we assume a 40% tax rate, the special item reduced taxable income by $3,572 and therefore reduced the tax provision by 40% of $3,572, or $1,429. The special item's after-tax effect would be $3,572 − (.40 × 3,572) = $2,143 million. In estimating future net income the analyst would add back $2,143 million to reported net income of $522 million and estimate the sustainable level at approximately $2,665 million. This proposed adjustment proved reasonable, even conservative. AT&T did not record additional special items in the next three years and net income reached $4,710 million in 1994.

Notice that because special items are reported with other expenses, they are reported before tax. Taxable income is thus reduced and income tax expense is affected. The next two segregated items discussed in this chapter, extraordinary items and discontinued operations, are more explicitly segregated in the financial statements. They are reported below income from continuing operations, and their income tax effects are calculated separately and reported separately, either parenthetically or in the footnotes. Figure 5-11 provides an example.

Extraordinary Items

The FASB and SEC insist that, with three exceptions, all items of revenue, expense, gain, and loss recognized during the period be shown in the current income statement. The three exceptions are: (1) correction of errors, such as the failure to recognize depreciation in a previous period, (2) tax effects of preacquisition loss carryforwards of purchased subsidiaries, and (3) specified foreign currency translation adjustments. In contrast, in earlier years, many special or *extraordinary items* were shown in the Statement of Retained Income and never appeared as a part of the computation of net income or EPS for any year. Today they are listed in a special section of the income statement and are included in net income.

Only the following items are *excluded* from the determination of net income:

a. Charges or credits resulting from transactions in the company's own capital stock.
b. Transfers to and from accounts properly designated as appropriated retained earnings (such as general purpose contingency reserves or provisions for replacement costs of fixed assets).

Extraordinary items that affect net income are segregated and reported net of tax, as in Figure 5-11.

Through the years, the definition of extraordinary items has been narrowed considerably. Accounting Principles Board *Opinion No. 30* concluded that an event or transaction should be presumed to be an ordinary and usual activity of the reporting entity, and hence includable in income before extraordinary items, unless the evidence clearly supports its classification as an extraordinary item as defined in *Opinion No. 30*. **Extraordinary items** result from events that must have both an *unusual nature* and an *infrequency of occurrence*. Therefore writedowns of receivables and inventories are ordinary items, as are gains or losses on the sale or abandonment of

---

FIGURE 5-11   Illustrated Partial Income Statement (in millions, data assumed)

Income from continuing operations before income taxes		$ 50
Deduct applicable income taxes		20
Income from continuing operations		$ 30
Discontinued operations (Note _____):		
Income from operations of discontinued Division ×		
(less applicable income taxes of $4)	$ 6	
Loss on disposal of Division X, including provision of		
$3 for operating losses during phase-out period		
(less applicable income taxes of $6)	(9)	(3)
Income before extraordinary items		$ 27
Add extraordinary items:		
Loss from earthquake (less applicable income taxes of $2)	(3)	
Gain from early extinguishment of debt		
(less applicable income taxes of $8)	12	9
Net income		**$ 36**
Per share amounts (in dollars), assuming 4 million shares		
of common stock outstanding:		
Income from continuing operations		$7.50
Loss on discontinued operations		(.75)
Income before extraordinary items		$6.75
Extraordinary items		2.25
Net income		**$9.00**

---

fixed assets. The effects of a strike and many foreign currency revaluations are also ordinary items. *Opinion No. 30* specifically states that casualties such as an earthquake or government expropriation or prohibition are examples of events that are likely to qualify as extraordinary items.

In an average year, fewer than 10% of major U.S. companies report an extraordinary item; fewer than 5% have an extraordinary item greater than 10% of their net income. Most of the extraordinary items arise from extinguishment of debt as shown in the following extract from the 1994 income statement of Spectrum Control, Inc. (in thousands).

Income before extraordinary item	$ 982
Gain on extinguishment of debt, net of applicable income taxes	4,012
Net income	**$4,994**

A tragic illustration of an extraordinary charge was caused by criminal tampering with Tylenol capsules. The manufacturer, Johnson & Johnson, reported the following on its income statement (in millions):

Earnings before extraordinary charge	$146.5
Extraordinary charge—costs associated with the withdrawal	
of TYLENOL capsules (less applicable tax relief of $50.0)	50.0
Net earnings	**$ 96.5**

Discontinued Operations

Discontinued operations involve the termination of a segment of the business, not just a single plant or location. *Opinion No. 30* states that the results of continuing operations should be reported separately from *discontinued operations,* although both must be reported on the income statement. Moreover, any gain or loss from the disposal of a segment of a business should be reported in conjunction with the related results of discontinued operations and not as an extraordinary item, as Figure 5-11 illustrates.

Amounts of applicable income taxes should be disclosed on the face of the income statement or in related notes. Revenues applicable to the discontinued operations should be disclosed separately in the related notes.

In a comparative income statement, the income or loss of the discontinued segment's operations should be condensed and reclassified from continuing operations to discontinued operations for both years. In this way, the income from continuing operations is placed on a comparable basis.

The CSX income statement for 1990, 1992, and 1994 below combines segment disclosures and a restructuring charge. Discontinued operations are shown separately, net of tax.

Financial presentations such as those in Figure 5-11 and the CSX Corporation example are often criticized as being unnecessarily complex. However, the financial results of an entity are often produced by a variety of complicated forces. Consequently, the simplifying of innately complex data is not easy. Indeed, too much condensation and summarization may be undesirable.

EFFICIENT MARKETS AND INVESTOR DECISIONS

Much recent research in accounting and finance has concentrated on whether the stock markets are "efficient." An **efficient capital market** is one in which market prices "fully reflect" all information available to the public. Therefore searching for "underpriced" securities in such a market would be fruitless unless an investor has information that is not generally available. If the real-world markets are indeed efficient, a relatively inactive approach would be an appropriate investment strategy for most investors. The hallmarks of this approach are risk control, high diversification, and low turnover of securities. The role of accounting information would mainly be in identifying the different degrees of risk among various stocks so that investors can maintain desired levels of risk and diversification.

Research in finance and accounting during the past twenty years has reinforced the idea that financial ratios and other data such as reported earnings provide inputs to predictions of such economic phenomena as financial failure or earnings growth. Furthermore, many ratios are used simultaneously rather than one at a time for such predictions. Above all, the research has shown that accounting reports are only one source of information and that in the aggregate the market is not fooled by companies that choose the least conservative accounting policies. In sum, the market as a whole sees through attempts by companies to gain favor through the choice of accounting policies that tend to boost immediate income. Thus there is evidence that the stock markets may indeed be relatively "efficient," at least in their reflection of most accounting data. However, the stock market crash of October 1987 and other reported "anomalies" prevent unqualified endorsement of stock market efficiency.

Suppose you are the chief executive officer of Company A. Reported earnings are $4 per share and the stock price is $40. You are contemplating changing your method of depreciation for investor-reporting purposes from accelerated to straight-line. Your competitors use straight-line. You think the Company A stock price unjustifiably suffers in comparison with other companies in the same industry.

CSX Corporation and Subsidiaries Consolidated Statement of Earnings
(millions of dollars, except per share amounts)

	Years Ended December 31,		
	1994	1992	1990
Operating Revenue			
Transportation	$ 9,410	$ 8,550	$ 7,947
Non-Transportation	198	184	258
Total	9,608	8,734	8,205
Operating Expense			
Transportation	8,232	7,644	7,195
Non-Transportation	144	125	142
Productivity/Restructuring Charge	—	699	53
Total	8,376	8,468	7,390
Earnings (Loss)			
Operating Income	1,232	266	815
Other Income	55	3	41
Interest Expense	281	276	319
Earnings (Loss) from Continuing Operations before Income Taxes	1,006	(7)	537
Income Tax Expense	354	(27)	172
Earnings from Continuing Operations	652	20	365
Discontinued Operations, Net of Income Taxes:			
Earnings (Loss) from Energy Segment			(1)
Gain on Disposition of Energy Segment Assets			52
Net Earnings	$ 652	$ 20	$ 416
Per Common Share			
Earnings Per Share:			
From Continuing Operations	$ 6.23	$ .19	$ 3.63
From Discontinued Operations:			
Earnings (Loss) from Energy Segment			(.01)
Gain on Disposition of Energy Segment Assets			.53
Earnings Per Share	$ 6.23	$ .19	$ 4.15
Average Common Shares Outstanding (thousands)	104,652	102,907	98,252
Cash Dividends Paid Per Common Share	$ 1.76	$ 1.52	$ 1.40

If straight-line depreciation is adopted by Company A, reported earnings will be $5 instead of $4 per share. Would the stock price rise accordingly from $40 to $50? No, the empirical research on these issues indicates that the stock price would remain at $40 (all other things equal).

Remember that the market is efficient only with respect to *publicly available* information. Therefore accounting issues that deal with the disclosure of new information are important, but concerns about the format for reporting already available data are less important. William Beaver has commented on the implications of market efficiency for accounting regulators:

> Many reporting issues are trivial and do not warrant an expenditure of FASB resources. The properties of such issues are twofold: (1) There is essentially no difference in cost to the firm of reporting either method. (2) There is essentially no cost to statement users in adjusting from one method to the other. In such cases, there is a simple solution. Report one method, with sufficient footnote disclosure to permit adjustment to the other, and let the market interpret implications of the data for security prices.
>
> The FASB should shift its resources to those controversies where there is nontrivial additional cost to the firms or to investors in order to obtain certain types of information (for example, replacement cost accounting for depreciable assets). Whether such information should be a required part of reporting standards is a substantive issue.[1]

Be aware also that accounting statements are not the only source of financial information about companies. Some alternative sources were listed at the beginning of the chapter. However, financial statement information may be more directly related to the item of interest, and it may be more reliable, lower-cost, or more timely than information from alternative sources.

The research described above concentrates on the effects of accounting on investors in the aggregate. Individual investors must either incur the costs of conducting careful analyses or delegate that chore to professional analysts. In any event, intelligent analysis cannot be accomplished without an understanding of the assumptions and limitations of financial statements, including the presence of various alternative accounting methods.

FOREIGN-CURRENCY ISSUES

Today, companies conduct business in various countries and so must learn to do business using different currencies. Two problems arise. One problem is accounting for day-to-day transactions that occur in foreign currencies. Another problem is consolidating a subsidiary that exists in another country and does its own accounting in the currency of that country.

These issues are important because of fluctuating **foreign-currency exchange rates.** The foreign-currency exchange rate specifies how many units of one currency are required to obtain one unit of another currency. Recently, the conversion rate of Japanese yen into U.S. dollars has been approximately $.0111. This means that one yen buys 1.11 cents. The relation could be expressed as the conversion rate of U.S. dollars into Japanese yen, which would be ¥90. If conversion rates were constant, no accounting problems would arise, but the rates often change significantly. Forty years ago, the conversion rate of dollars into yen was ¥360. In the spring of 1991 it was around ¥138, and in the spring of 1995 around ¥90. During this time the value of the yen increased relative to the value of the dollar.

[1] William H. Beaver, "What Should Be the FASB's Objectives?" *Journal of Accountancy,* Vol. 136, p. 52.

Accounting for Transactions in Foreign Currencies

If a U.S. firm exports an automobile to Japan for $10,000, the sale will often be on credit and *denominated* in yen. The customer owes ¥900,000 (because the conversion rate at the time of the sale was ¥90). The U.S. firm will record the sale in dollars, and the receivable would be $10,000 on its books. After one month, the buyer remits ¥900,000 to the seller. Suppose the yen has fallen (or weakened) against the dollar, and the new exchange rate is ¥92. When the yen is converted to dollars the seller ends up with only $9,782.61 (¥900,000 / ¥92). The transaction has given rise to a loss of $217.39, which would be recorded as follows:

Cash	$9,782.61	
Loss on currency fluctuation	217.39	
Accounts receivable		$10,000.00

Not surprisingly, the currency exchange rate could move in the other direction and give rise to a gain. Many companies use sophisticated financial transactions to eliminate the effect of currency fluctuations, but these hedging transactions and their accounting are covered in more advanced courses.

Consolidating International Subsidiaries

The previous section dealt with a company in one country doing business with a company in another country. A more complex problem arises in an international parent-subsidiary relationship. Suppose a U.S. company (parent) owns a Japanese company (subsidiary, or sub) doing business in Japan in yen. At the end of the year the parent must consolidate the sub's financial data with its own and create a single set of statements. What exchange rate should be used?

GAAP requires that different exchange rates be used for different elements of the financial statements. Assets and liabilities of the sub are translated at the year-end exchange rate. The common stock account is translated at the historic rate existing when the sub was created. The average exchange rate during the year is used to account for the transactions in the income statement. These translated net income figures annually increase the retained earnings of the parent. Over time, the parent's retained earnings reflect yen translations at different exchange rates. The problem is apparent. If the assets of the sub equal its liabilities plus its owners' equity in yen, and different rates are used to translate assets, liabilities, and equity, then the consolidated balance sheet is forced out of balance. To bring it back in balance a **translation adjustment** is created, which is reported as part of shareholders' equity. Details of computing this translation adjustment are beyond the scope of this text.

The stockholders' equity sections of most multinational firms include foreign-currency translation adjustments. The title and amount of the translation adjustment and total stockholders' equity for some international companies follow:

Company	Account Name	Amount	Total SE
Quaker Oats	Cumulative translation adjustment	(75.4)	446
Kellogg	Currency translation adjustment	(159)	1,808
McDonald's	Foreign currency translation adjustment	(115)	6,885

SUMMARY

Financial and operating information is available from many sources, including daily newspapers. Various regulations in the United States require the issuance of annual reports and govern their content. In addition, publicly traded companies must disclose particular information by filing 10-K, 8-K, and other forms with the SEC on a periodic basis.

Financial information is provided to aid investors in assessing the risk and return of a potential investment. Investors in debt are particularly concerned about the solvency and liquidity of the issuer, while equity investors are more interested in profitability.

Trend analysis is a form of financial statement analysis that concentrates on changes in the financial statements through time. It involves comparing relationships for a period of years or quarters. Common-size financial statements are constructed by expressing the elements of the balance sheet as a percentage of total assets and the elements of the income statement as a percentage of total revenue. They enhance the ability to compare one company with another or to conduct a trend analysis over time.

The basic financial ratios allow us to put numbers in perspective. By relating one part of the financial statements to another they facilitate questions such as "Given the change in revenues, was the change in accounts receivable reasonable?" and "Is the company's inventory level, given its size, comparable to industry norms?"

Liquidity ratios deal with the immediate ability to make payments. Solvency ratios deal with the longer-term ability to meet obligations. Both are often incorporated into debt covenants to ensure lenders' rights. Profitability ratios are used to assess operating efficiency performance.

Return on equity (ROE) is the most fundamental profitability ratio because it relates income to the shareholder's investment. Return on assets is one of several related elements that focuses on the profitable use of all assets. It can be further divided into the return on sales and the total asset turnover.

Earnings per share (EPS) is a fundamental measure of performance. In this chapter three complexities in calculating this measure were identified and incorporated into the calculation. Since preferred shares receive preference to dividends, their dividends are deducted from earnings in the numerator. Since shares outstanding may change during the year, the denominator is calculated as a weighted average over the year. The presence of options and convertible securities creates a potential to issue new shares as a result of the actions of others. Therefore, EPS is calculated on both a primary and a fully diluted basis.

Special items, extraordinary items, and discontinued operations are three categories of unusual and possibly nonrecurring items. Separately disclosing these allows analysts to refine forecasts of future performance based on current operations. Special items are included with other expenses but identified separately. Extraordinary items and discontinued items are shown separately below earnings from operations and net of their individual tax effects.

Efficient markets refer to the probability that the actions of analysts to carefully evaluate disclosures lead to their incorporating all available information into the market price for securities. Evidence suggests this is substantially, but not totally, true. This fact means that complete disclosure is more important than the form of the disclosure. For example, investors are unlikely to be confused in their efforts to price securities by differences in the methods of depreciation or inventory accounting in use.

Multinational companies do business in more than one country. Sometimes they export products produced in the home country to other markets. In this case, transactions with foreign customers are often in the customer's currency, although they are accounted for in the home currency. Exchange-rate fluctuations between the sale date and the collection date give rise to gains or losses, which appear in the seller's earnings statement and affect net earnings. In other cases, foreign subsidiaries manufacture and sell outside the home country. Foreign subsidiaries hold assets, conduct business, and account for it in their own currency. Translation problems arise when the subsidiary's financial statements are translated into the parent's currency for consolidation. In the United States such translations for consolidation give rise to translation adjustments recorded in stockholders' equity with no effect on consolidated net earnings.

SELF-CORRECTION PROBLEMS

Figure 5-12 contains a condensed income statement and balance sheet for Gannett Company, Inc., the nation's largest newspaper group with eighty dailies, including *USA Today.*

1. Compute the following ratios: (a) current ratio, (b) quick ratio, (c) average collection period, (d) total debt to stockholders' equity, (e) return on sales, and (f) return on stockholders' equity.

2. Using the 1994 Gannett values provided below and the following Dun & Bradstreet 1994–95 ratios for 503 newspaper companies, assess Gannett's liquidity, solvency, and profitability.

	Current Ratio	Quick Ratio	Average Collection Period	Total Debt to Stockholders' Equity	Net Income on Sales	Net Income on Stockholders' Equity
Upper quartile	5.5	4.0	28.1	18.0	9.0	27.4
Median	2.2	1.7	37.6	47.0	4.2	11.8
Lower quartile	1.3	0.9	46.5	151.4	1.0	3.4

Using only the ratios in #1 above, assess Gannett Company's liquidity, solvency, and profitability.

SOLUTIONS TO SELF-CORRECTION PROBLEMS

Gannett's 1994 ratios are also provided for comparison, although data for their calculation are not provided in the problem.

1.

		1991	1994
a. Current ratio =	$\dfrac{636,101}{443,835}$ =	1.4	1.2
b. Quick ratio =	$\dfrac{70,673 + 444,568}{443,835}$ =	1.2	1.1
c. Average collection period =	$\dfrac{(1/2)(444,568 + 469,701) \times 365}{3,382,035}$ =	49.3	44.7
d. Total debt to stockholders' equity =	$\dfrac{2,144,593}{1,539,487}$ =	139.3%	103.0%
e. Return on sales =	$\dfrac{301,649}{3,382,035}$ =	8.9%	12.2%
f. Return on stockholders' equity =	$\dfrac{301,649}{(1/2)(1,539,487 + 2,063,077)}$ =	16.8%	25.0%

FIGURE 5-12   Gannett Company, Inc. (in thousands)

Income Statement	For the Year Ended *December 29, 1991*
Revenues	$3,382,035
Operating expenses	(2,823,088)
Operating income	558,947
Interest expense	(71,057)
Interest and other income	14,859
Income before income taxes	502,749
Provision for income taxes	(201,100)
Net income	$ 301,649

	For the Year Ended	
Balance Sheets	*December 29, 1991*	*December 30, 1990*
Assets		
Current assets:		
Cash and marketable securities	$ 70,673	$ 56,238
Receivables	444,568	469,071
Inventories	51,380	66,525
Prepaid expenses	69,480	76,856
Total current assets	636,101	668,690
Property, plant, and equipment, net	1,484,910	1,472,123
Intangible and other assets	1,563,069	1,685,332
Total assets	$3,684,080	$3,826,145
Liabilities and Shareholders' Equity		
Total current liabilities	$ 443,835	$ 500,203
Long-term liabilities	1,700,758	1,262,865
Total liabilities	2,144,593	1,763,068
Total shareholders' equity	1,539,487	2,063,077
Total liabilities and shareholders' equity	$3,684,080	$3,826,145

2. The measures of profitability improved significantly from 1991 to 1994. In 1994 Gannett continued to manage current assets aggressively while reducing the level of debt in the capital structure. The increased profitability in 1994 was caused by a number of factors including the increased popularity of *USA Today,* "the nation's newspaper." In 1994, Gannett was below the median on liquidity measures and more leveraged than the median. However, profitability was very high.

QUESTIONS

1. Why do decision makers use financial statement analysis?
2. In addition to the basic financial statements, what information is usually presented in a company's annual report?
3. Give three sources of information for investors besides accounting information.

4. "Financial statements report on *history*. Therefore they are not useful to creditors and investors who want to predict *future* returns and risk." Do you agree? Explain.

5. How do common-size statements aid comparisons with other companies?

6. What information is presented in the "management's discussion and analysis" (MD&A) section of annual reports?

7. Name three types of comparisons that are useful in evaluating financial ratios.

8. "Ratios are mechanical and incomplete." Explain.

9. Ratios are open grouped into four categories. What are the categories?

10. What two measures of operating performance are combined to give the pretax operating return on total assets?

11. "Trading on the equity means exchanging bonds for stock." Do you agree? Explain.

12. "Borrowing is a two-edged sword." Do you agree? Explain.

13. Why are companies with heavy debt in relation to ownership capital in greater danger when business conditions sour?

14. "The tax law discriminates against preferred stock and in favor of debt." Explain.

15. "An efficient capital market is one where securities are traded through stockbrokers." Do you agree? Explain.

16. Suppose the president of your company wanted to switch depreciation methods to increase reported net income: "Our stock is 10% below what I think it should be; changing the depreciation method will increase income by 10%, thus getting our share price up to its proper level." How would you respond?

17. Evaluate the following quotation from *Forbes:* "If IBM had been forced to expense [the software development cost of] $785 million, its earnings would have been cut by 72 cents a share. With IBM selling at 14 times earnings, expensing the costs might have knocked over $10 off IBM's share price."

18. Suppose you wanted to compare the financial statements of Colgate-Palmolive and Procter and Gamble. What concerns might you have in comparing their various ratios?

19. Suppose you wanted to evaluate the financial performance of IBM over the last ten years. What factors might affect the comparability of a firm's financial ratios over such a long period of time?

20. Suppose you worked for a small manufacturing company and the president said that you must improve your current ratio. Would you interpret this to mean that you should increase it or decrease it? How might you do so?

21. Suppose you work for a small local department store that manages its own accounts receivable with a private charge card. Your boss has told you to improve the accounts receivable turnover from 4 to 5 times. How would you go about this? What are the risks in your proposal that might affect the company negatively?

22. Would you expect the return on equity to be greater than or less than the return on assets? Explain.

23. Suppose the current ratio for your company changed from 2 to 1 to become 1.8 to 1. Would you expect the level of working capital to increase or to decrease? Why?

24. Suppose you compared the financial statements of an airline and a grocery store. Which would you expect to have the higher values for the following ratios: debt-to-equity ratio, current ratio, inventory turnover ratio, accounts receivable turnover ratio, and return on equity? Explain.

25. As the chief financial officer you have just been presented with a set of comparative ratios for your firm. Which of the following facts would you be likely to view as good news? Why? Consider each one as an independent case. Assume all else is unchanged.
    a. Increase in current ratio.
    b. Decrease in inventory turnover.
    c. Decrease in interest-coverage.
    d. Increase in return on sales.
    e. Increase in the price/earnings ratio.
26. Describe a circumstance under which each of the following independent events would be viewed as good news. Explain why. You may take the approach of management or of an investor.
    a. Interest rates have risen.
    b. The company reduced its accounts receivable turnover.
    c. The company created a stock option plan.
    d. The company increased its dividend.
    e. The company increased its inventory turnover.
    When might the view of management and of an investor be different?

CHAPTER 6

Analyzing Cost Behavior

How do the costs and revenues of a hospital change as one more patient is admitted for a 4-day stay? How are the costs and revenues of an airline affected when one more passenger is boarded at the last moment, or when one more flight is added to the schedule? How should the budget request by the Arizona Department of Motor Vehicles be affected by the predicted increase in the state's population? These questions introduce one common question: What will happen to financial results if a specified level of activity or volume fluctuates? Answering this question is the first step in analyzing **cost behavior**—how the activities of an organization affect its costs. A knowledge of the patterns of cost behavior offers valuable insights in planning and controlling short- and long-run operations. While this lesson is emphasized throughout this book, in this introductory chapter, our goal is to provide perspective rather than to impart an intimate knowledge of the complexities of cost behavior.

COST DRIVERS

Activities that affect costs are often called **cost drivers.** An organization may have many cost drivers. Consider the costs of running a warehouse that receives and stores material and supplies. The costs of operating the warehouse may be driven by the total dollar value of items handled, the weight of the items handled, the number of different orders received, the number of different items handled, the number of different suppliers, the fragility of the items handled, and possibly several other cost drivers. A major task in specifying cost behavior is to identify the cost drivers—that is, to determine the activities that cause costs to be incurred.

To examine cost behavior without undue complexity, this chapter focuses on *volume-related cost drivers.* Later chapters will introduce cost drivers that are not related to volume. Volume-related cost drivers include the number of orders processed, the number of items billed in a billing department, the number of admissions to a theater, the number of pounds handled in a warehouse, the hours of labor worked in an assembly department, the number of rides in an amusement park, the seat-miles on an airline, and the dollar sales in a retail business. All of these cost drivers can serve either directly or indirectly as a measure of the volume of output of goods or services. Of course, when only one product is being produced, the units of production is the most obvious volume-related cost driver for production-related costs.

COMPARISON OF VARIABLE AND FIXED COSTS

A key to understanding cost behavior is distinguishing *variable costs* from *fixed costs.* Costs are classified as variable or fixed depending on how much they change as the level of a particular cost driver changes. A **variable cost** is a cost that changes in direct proportion to changes in the cost driver. In contrast, a **fixed cost** is not immediately affected by changes in the cost driver. Suppose units of production is the cost driver of interest. A 10% increase in the units of production would produce a 10% increase in variable costs. However, the fixed costs would remain unchanged.

Some examples may clarify the differences between fixed and variable costs. The costs of most merchandise, materials, parts, supplies, commissions, and many types of labor are generally variable with respect to most volume-related cost drivers. Real estate taxes, real estate insurance, many executive salaries, and space rentals tend to be fixed with respect to any volume-related cost driver.

Consider some variable costs. Suppose Watkins Products pays its door-to-door sales personnel a 40% straight commission on sales. The total cost of sales commissions to Watkins is 40% of sales dollars—a variable cost with respect to sales revenues. Or suppose Dan's Bait Shop buys bags of fish bait for $2 each. The total cost of fish bait is $2 times the number of bags purchased—a variable cost with respect to units (number of bags) purchased. Notice that variable costs are uniform *per unit,* but that the *total* fluctuates in direct proportion to the cost-driver activity. Figure 6-1 depicts these relationships between cost and cost-driver activity graphically.

Now consider a fixed cost. Suppose Sony rents a factory to produce picture tubes for color television sets for $500,000 per year. The *total cost* of $500,000 is not affected

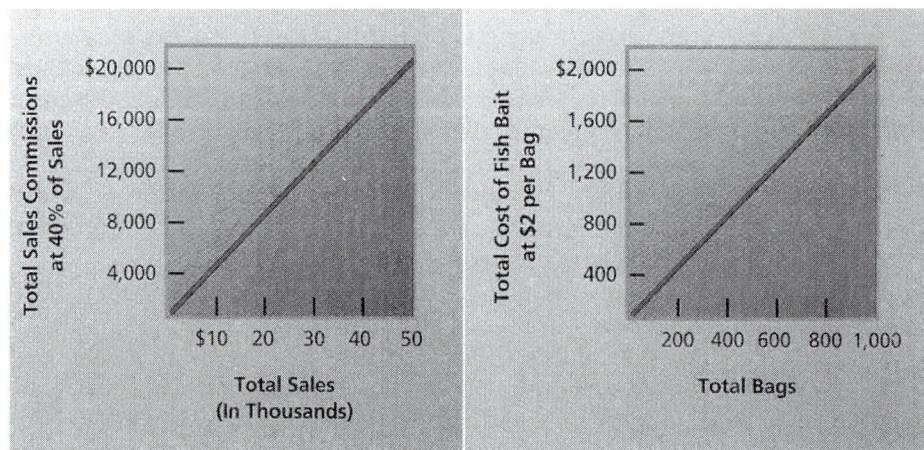

FIGURE 6-1
Variable-Cost Behavior

by the number of picture tubes produced. The *unit cost* of rent applicable to each tube, however, does depend on the total number of tubes produced. If 100,000 tubes are produced, the unit cost will be $500,000 ÷ 100,000 = $5. If 50,000 tubes are produced, the unit cost will be $500,000 ÷ 50,000 = $10. Therefore, a fixed cost does not change *in total*, but it becomes progressively smaller on a *per-unit* basis as the volume increases.

Note carefully from these examples that the "variable" or "fixed" characteristic of a cost relates to its *total dollar amount* and not to its per-unit amount. The following table summarizes these relationships.

Type of Cost	If Cost-Driver Activity Level Increases (or Decreases):	
	Total Cost	*Cost Per Unit**
Fixed costs	No change	Decrease (or increase)
Variable costs	Increase (or decrease)	No change

*Per unit of activity volume, for example, product units, passenger-miles, sales dollars.

When predicting costs, two rules of thumb are useful:

1. Think of fixed costs as a *total*. Total fixed costs remain unchanged regardless of changes in cost-driver activity.
2. Think of variable costs on a *per-unit* basis. The *per-unit* variable cost remains unchanged regardless of changes in cost-driver activity.

Relevant Range

Although we have just described fixed costs as unchanging regardless of cost-driver activity, this rule of thumb holds true only within reasonable limits. For example, rent costs will rise if increased production requires a larger or additional building— or if the landlord just decides to raise the rent. Conversely, rent costs may go down if decreased production causes the company to move to a smaller plant. The **relevant range** is the limit of cost-driver activity within which a specific relationship between costs and the cost driver is valid. In addition, remember that even within the relevant range, a fixed cost remains fixed only over a given period of time—usually the budget period. Fixed costs may change from budget year to budget year solely because of changes in insurance and property tax rates, executive salary levels, or rent levels. But these items are unlikely to change within a given year.

For example, suppose that a General Electric plant has a relevant range of between 40,000 and 85,000 cases of light bulbs per month and that total monthly fixed costs within the relevant range are $100,000. Within the relevant range, fixed costs will remain the same. If production falls below 40,000 cases, changes in personnel and salaries would slash fixed costs to $60,000. If operations rise above 85,000 cases, increases in personnel and salaries would boost fixed costs to $115,000.

These assumptions—a given period and a given activity range—are shown graphically at the top of Figure 6-2. It is highly unusual, however, for monthly opera-

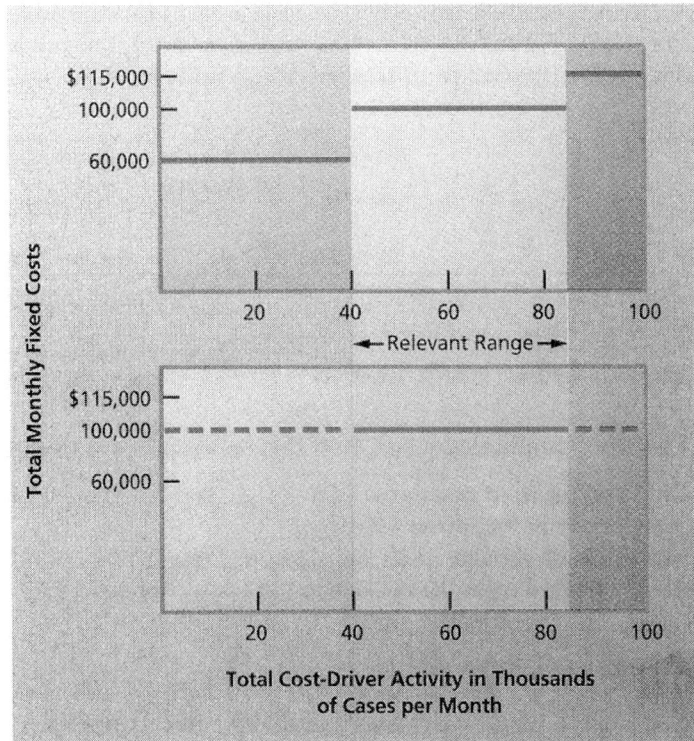

FIGURE 6-2
Fixed Costs and Relevant Range

tions to be outside the relevant range. Therefore, the three-level refinement at the top of Figure 6-2 is usually not graphed. Instead, a single horizontal line is typically extended through the plotted activity levels, as at the bottom of the exhibit. Often a dashed line is used outside the relevant range.

The basic idea of a relevant range also applies to variable costs. That is, outside a relevant range, some variable costs, such as fuel consumed, may behave differently per unit of cost-driver activity. For example, the efficiency of motors is affected if they are used too much or too little.

Differences in Classifying Costs

As you may suspect, it is often difficult to classify a cost as exactly variable or exactly fixed. Many complications arise including the possibility of costs behaving in some nonlinear way (not producing a straight line graph). For example, as tax preparers learn to process the new year's tax forms, their productivity rises. This means that total costs may actually behave as in Panel A that follows, not as in Panel B.

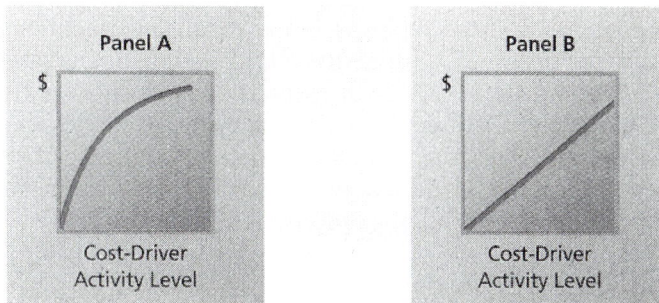

Moreover, costs may simultaneously be affected by more than one cost driver. For example, the costs of shipping labor may be affected by *both* the weight and the number of units handled. We shall investigate various facets of this problem in succeeding chapters; for now, we shall assume that any cost may be classified as either variable or fixed. We assume also that a given variable cost is associated with *only one* volume-related cost driver, and that relationship is *linear.*

Finally, in the real world, classifying costs as fixed or variable depends on the decision situation. More costs are fixed and fewer are variable when decisions involve very short time spans and very small changes in activity level. Suppose a United Airlines plane with several empty seats will depart from its gate in 2 minutes. A potential passenger is running down a corridor bearing a transferable ticket from a competing airline. Unless the airplane is held for an extra 30 seconds, the passenger will miss the departure and will not switch to United for the planned trip. What are the variable costs to United of delaying the departure and placing one more passenger in an otherwise empty seat? Variable costs (for example, one more meal) are negligible. Virtually all the costs in that decision situation are fixed. Now in contrast, suppose United's decision is whether to add another flight, acquire another gate, add another city to its routes, or acquire another airplane. Many more costs would be regarded as variable and fewer as fixed.

These examples underscore the importance of how the decision affects the analysis of cost behavior. Whether costs are really "fixed" depends heavily on the relevant range, the length of the planning period in question, and the specific decision situation.

COST-VOLUME-PROFIT ANALYSIS

Managers often classify costs as fixed or variable when making decisions that affect the volume of output. The managers want to know how such decisions will affect costs and revenues. They realize that many factors in addition to the volume of output will affect costs. Yet, a useful starting point in their decision process is to specify the relationship between the volume of output and costs and revenues.

The managers of profit-seeking organizations usually study the effects of output volume on revenue (sales), expenses (costs), and net income (net profit). This study is commonly called **cost-volume-profit (CVP) analysis.** The managers of nonprofit organizations also benefit from the study of CVP relationships. Why? No organization has unlimited resources, and knowledge of how costs fluctuate as volume changes helps managers to understand how to control costs. For example, administrators of nonprofit hospitals are constantly concerned about the behavior of costs as the volume of patients fluctuates.

To apply CVP analysis, managers usually resort to some simplifying assumptions. The major simplification is to classify costs as either variable or fixed with respect to a single measure of the volume of output activity. This chapter focuses on such a simplified relationship.

CVP Scenario

Amy Winston, the manager of food services for Middletown Community College, is trying to decide whether to rent a line of food vending machines. Although individual snack items have various acquisition costs and selling prices, Winston has decided that an average selling price of 50¢ per unit and an average acquisition cost of 40¢ per unit will suffice for purposes of this analysis. She predicts the following revenue and expense relationships.

	Per Unit	Percentage of Sales
Selling price	$ .50	100%
Variable cost of each item	.40	80
Selling price less variable cost	$ .10	20%
Monthly fixed expenses		
Rent	$1,000	
Wages for replenishing and servicing	4,500	
Other fixed expenses	500	
Total fixed expenses per month	$6,000	

We will next use these data to illustrate several applications of CVP analysis.

Break-even Point—Contribution Margin and Equation Techniques

The most basic CVP analysis computes the monthly break-even point in number of units and in dollar sales. The **break-even point** is the level of sales at which revenue equals expenses and net income is zero. The business press frequently refers to break-even points. For example, a news story on hotel occupancy rates in San Francisco in 1994 stated that "seventy% [occupancy] is considered a break-even for hoteliers." Another news story stated that "the Big Three auto makers have slashed their sales break-even point in North America from 12.2 million cars and trucks to only 9.1 million this year." Finally, an article on Outboard Marine Corporation reported that, as a result of restructuring, the company's "break-even point will be $250 million lower than it was in 1993."

The study of cost-volume-profit relationships is often called *break-even analysis.* This term is misleading, because finding the break-even point is often just the first step in a planning decision. Managers usually concentrate on how the decision will affect sales, costs, and net income.

One direct use of the break-even point, however, is to assess possible risks. By comparing planned sales with the break-even point, managers can determine a **margin of safety:**

margin of safety = planned unit sales − break-even unit sales

The margin of safety shows how far sales can fall below the planned level before losses occur.

We next explore two basic techniques for computing a break-even point: contribution margin and equation.

Contribution-margin technique.   Consider the following commonsense arithmetic approach. Every unit sold generates a **contribution margin** or **marginal income,** which is the sales price minus the variable cost per unit. For the vending machine snack items, the contribution margin per unit is $.10:

Unit sales price	$.50
Unit variable cost	.40
Unit contribution margin to fixed costs and net income	**$.10**

When is the break-even point reached? When enough units have been sold to generate a *total* contribution margin (total number of units sold × contribution margin per unit) equal to the total fixed costs. Divide the $6,000 in fixed costs by the $.10 unit contribution margin. The number of units that must be sold to break even is $6,000 ÷ $.10 = 60,000 units. The sales revenue at the break-even point is 60,000 units × $.50 per unit, or $30,000.

Think about the contribution margin of the snack items. Each unit purchased and sold generates *extra* revenue of $.50 and *extra* cost of $.40. Fixed costs are unaffected. If zero units were sold, a loss equal to the fixed cost of $6,000 would be incurred. Each unit reduces the loss by $.10 until sales reach the break-even point of 60,000 units. After that point, each unit adds (or *contributes*) $.10 to profit.

The condensed income statement at the break-even point is

	Total	Per Unit	Percentage
Units	60,000		
Sales	$30,000	$.50	100%
Variable costs	24,000	.40	80
Contribution margin*	$ 6,000	**$.10**	**20%**
Fixed costs	6,000		
Net income	$ 0		

*Sales less variable costs.

Sometimes the unit price and unit variable costs are not known. This situation is common at companies that sell more than one product because no single price or variable cost applies to all products. For example, a grocery store sells hundreds of products at many different prices. A break-even point *in units* would not be meaningful. In such cases, you can use total sales and total variable costs to calculate variable costs as a *percentage of each sales dollar.*

Consider our vending machine example:

Sales price	100%
Variable expenses as a percentage of dollar sales	80
Contribution-margin percentage	**20%**

Therefore, 20% of each sales dollar is available for the recovery of fixed expenses and the making of net income: $6,000 ÷ .20 = $30,000 sales are needed to break even. The contribution-margin percentage is based on dollar sales and is often expressed as a ratio (.20 instead of 20%). Using the contribution-margin percentage, you can compute the break-even volume in dollar sales without determining the break-even point in units.

Equation technique. The equation technique is the most general form of analysis, the one that may be adapted to any conceivable cost-volume-profit situation. You are familiar with a typical income statement. Any income statement can be expressed in equation form, or as a *mathematical model,* as follows:

$$\text{sales} - \text{variable expenses} - \text{fixed expenses} = \text{net income} \tag{1}$$

That is,

$$\left(\begin{array}{c}\text{unit} \\ \text{sales} \times \\ \text{price}\end{array}\begin{array}{c}\text{number} \\ \text{of} \\ \text{units}\end{array}\right) - \left(\begin{array}{c}\text{unit} \\ \text{variable} \times \\ \text{cost}\end{array}\begin{array}{c}\text{number} \\ \text{of} \\ \text{units}\end{array}\right) - \begin{array}{c}\text{fixed} \\ \text{expenses}\end{array} = \begin{array}{c}\text{net} \\ \text{income}\end{array}$$

At the break-even point net income is zero:

$$\text{sales} - \text{variable expenses} - \text{fixed expenses} = 0$$

Let N = number of units to be sold to break even. Then, for the vending machine example,

$$
\begin{aligned}
\$.50N - \$.40N - \$6,000 &= 0 \\
\$.10N &= \$6,000 \\
N &= \$6,000 \div \$.10 \\
N &= 60,000 \text{ units}
\end{aligned}
$$

Total sales in the equation is a price-times-quantity relationship, which was expressed in our example as $.50N. To find the *dollar* sales, multiply 60,000 *units* by $.50, which would yield the break-even dollar sales of $30,000.

You can also solve the equation for sales dollars without computing the unit break-even point by using the relationship of variable costs and profits as a *percentage* of sales:

$$\text{variable–cost ratio or percentage} = \frac{\text{variable cost per unit}}{\text{sales price per unit}}$$

$$= \frac{\$.40}{\$.50}$$

$$= .80 \text{ or } 80\%$$

Let S = sales in dollars needed to break even. Then

$$S - .80S - \$6,000 = 0$$

$$.20S = \$60,000$$

$$S = \$6,000 \div .20$$

$$S = \$30,000$$

Relationship between the two techniques.   You may have noticed that the contribution-margin technique is merely a shortcut version of the equation technique. Look at the last three lines in the two solutions given for equation 1. They read

Break-even Volume	
Units	**Dollars**
$.10N = \$6,000$	$.20S = \$6,000$
$N = \dfrac{\$6,000}{\$.10}$	$S = \dfrac{\$6,000}{.20}$
$N = 60,000$ units	$S = \$30,000$

From these equations, we can derive the following general shortcut formulas:

$$\frac{\text{break–even volume}}{\text{in units}} = \frac{\text{fixed expenses}}{\text{contribution margin per unit}} \tag{2}$$

$$\frac{\text{break–even volume}}{\text{in dollars}} = \frac{\text{fixed expenses}}{\text{contribution–margin ratio}} \tag{3}$$

Which should you use, the equation or the contribution-margin technique? Use either. The choice is a matter of personal preference or convenience within a particular case.

Break-even point—graphical techniques.   Figure 6-3 is a graph of the cost-volume-profit relationship in our vending machine example. Study the graph as you read the procedure for constructing it.

1. Draw the axes. The horizontal axis is the sales volume, and the vertical axis is dollars of cost and revenue.
2. Plot sales volume. Select a convenient sales volume, say, 100,000 units, and plot point A for total sales dollars at that volume: 100,000 × $.50 = $50,000. Draw the revenue (i.e., sales) line from point A to the origin, point 0.
3. Plot fixed expenses. Draw the line showing the $6,000 fixed portion of expenses. It should be a horizontal line intersecting the vertical axis at $6,000, point B.
4. Plot variable expenses. Determine the variable portion of expenses at a convenient level of activity: 100,000 units × $.40 = $40,000. Add this to the fixed expenses: $40,000 + $6,000 = $46,000. Plot point C for 100,000 units and $46,000. Then draw a line between this point and point B. This is the total expenses line.
5. Locate the break-even point. The break-even point is where the total expenses line crosses the sales line, 60,000 units or $30,000, namely, where total sales revenues exactly equal total costs, point D.

The break-even point is only one facet of this cost-volume-profit graph. More generally, the graph shows the profit or loss at *any* rate of activity. At any given volume, the vertical distance between the sales line and the total expenses line measures the net income or net loss.

Managers often use break-even graphs because they show potential profits over a wide range of volume more easily than numerical exhibits. Whether graphs or other types of exhibits are used depends largely on management's preference.

Note that the concept of relevant range is applicable to the entire break-even graph. Almost all break-even graphs show revenue and cost lines extending back to the vertical axis as shown in Figure 6-4(A). This approach is misleading because the

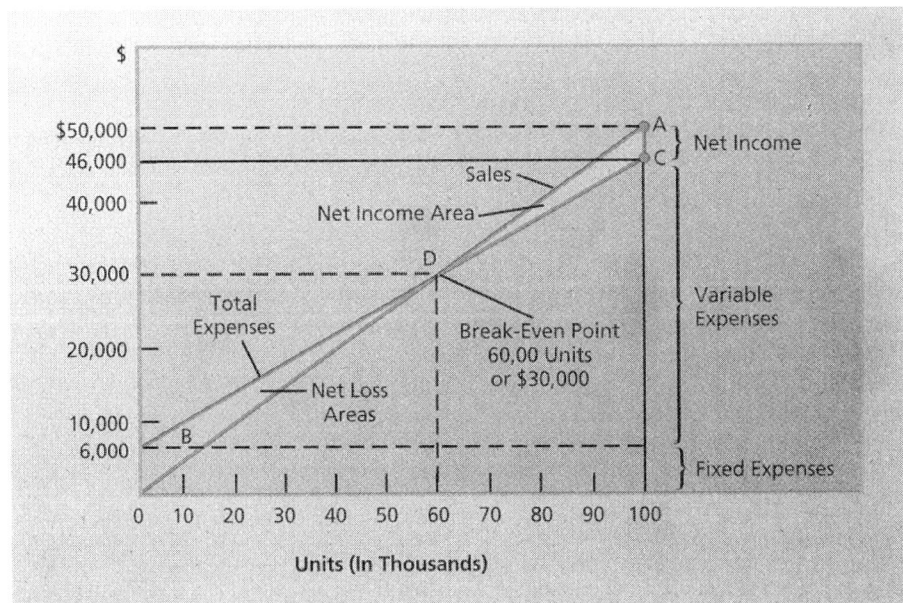

FIGURE 6-3
Cost-Volume-Profit Graph

relationships depicted in such graphs are valid only within the relevant range that underlies the construction of the graph. Figure 6-4(B), a modification of the conventional break-even graph, partially demonstrates the multitude of assumptions that must be made in constructing the typical break-even graph. Some of these assumptions follow:

1. Expenses may be classified into variable and fixed categories. Total variable expenses vary directly with activity level. Total fixed expenses do not change with activity level.
2. The behavior of revenues and expenses is accurately portrayed and is linear over the relevant range. The principal differences between the accountant's break-even chart and the economist's are that (1) the accountant's sales line is drawn on the assumption that selling prices do not change with production or sales, and the economist assumes that reduced selling prices are normally associated with increased sales volume; and (2) the accountant usually assumes a constant variable expense per unit, and the economist assumes that variable expense per unit changes with production levels. Within the relevant range, the accountant's and the economist's sales and expense lines are usually close to one another, although the lines may diverge greatly outside the range.
3. Efficiency and productivity will be unchanged.
4. Sales mix will be constant. The **sales mix** is the relative proportions or combinations of quantities of products that constitute total sales. (See Addendum 6A for more on sales mixes.)
5. The difference in inventory level at the beginning and at the end of a period is insignificant.

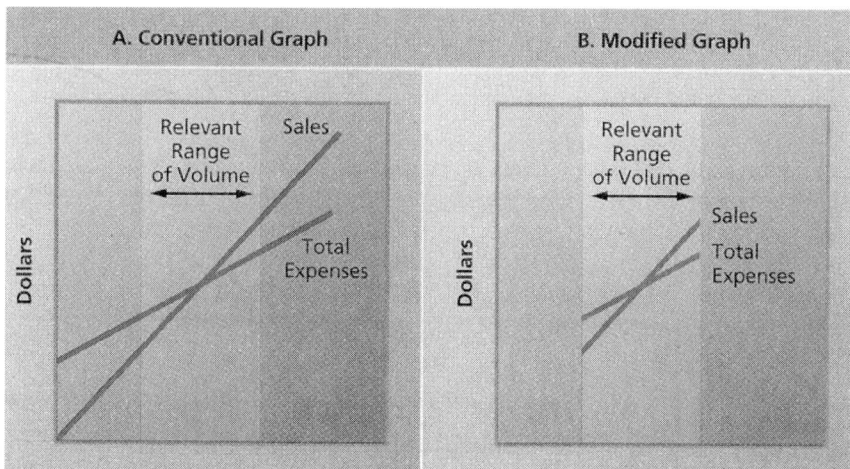

FIGURE 6-4
Conventional and Modified Break-even Graphs

Changes in Fixed Expenses

Changes in fixed expenses cause changes in the break-even point. For example, if the $1,000 monthly rent of the vending machines were doubled, what would be the monthly break-even point in number of units and dollar sales?

The fixed expenses would increase from $6,000 to $7,000, so

$$\frac{\text{break–even volume}}{\text{in units}} = \frac{\text{fixed expenses}}{\text{contribution margin per unit}} = \frac{\$7,000}{\$.10} = 70,000\,\text{units} \qquad (2)$$

$$\frac{\text{break–even volume}}{\text{in dollars}} = \frac{\text{fixed expenses}}{\text{contribution–margin ratio}} = \frac{\$7,000}{\$.20} = \$35,000 \qquad (3)$$

Note that a one-sixth increase in fixed expenses altered the break-even point by one-sixth: from 60,000 to 70,000 units and from $30,000 to $35,000. This type of relationship always exists if everything else remains constant.

Companies frequently lower their break-even points by reducing their total fixed costs. For example, closing or selling factories decreases property taxes, insurance, depreciation, and managers' salaries.

Changes in Contribution Margin per Unit

Changes in variable costs also cause the break-even point to shift. Companies can reduce their break-even points by increasing their contribution margins per unit of product through either increases in sales prices or decreases in unit variable costs, or both.

For example, assume that the fixed rent is still $1,000. (1) If the owner is paid 1¢ rental per unit sold in addition to the fixed rent, find the monthly break-even point in number of units and in dollar sales. (2) If the selling price falls from 50¢ to 45¢ per unit, and the original variable expenses per unit are unchanged, find the monthly break-even point in number of units and in dollar sales.

Here's what happens to the break-even point:

1. The variable expenses would increase from 40¢ to 41¢, the unit contribution margin would decline from 10¢ to 9¢, and the contribution-margin ratio would become .18 ($.09 ÷ $.50).

   The original fixed expenses of $6,000 would be unaffected, but the denominators would change from those previously used. Thus,

$$\text{break–even point in units} = \frac{\$6,000}{\$.09} = 66,667\,\text{units} \qquad (2)$$

$$\text{break–even points in dollars} = \frac{\$6,000}{.18} = \$33,333 \qquad (3)$$

2. If the selling price fell from 50¢ to 45¢, and the original variable expenses were unchanged, the unit contribution would be reduced from 10¢ to 5¢ (i.e., 45¢ − 40¢), and the break-even point would soar to 120,000 units ($6,000 ÷ $.05). The break-even point in dollars would also change because the selling price and contribution-margin ratio change. The contribution-margin ratio would be .1111 ($.05 ÷ $.45). The break-even point, in dollars, would be $54,000 (120,000 units × $.45) or, using the formula:

$$\text{break–even points in dollars} = \frac{\$6,000}{.1111} = \$54,00 \qquad (3)$$

Target Net Profit and an Incremental Approach

Managers can also use CVP analysis to determine the total sales, in units and dollars, needed to reach a target profit. For example, in our snack-vending example, suppose Winston considers $480 per month the minimum acceptable net income. How many units will have to be sold to justify the adoption of the vending machine plan? How does this figure "translate" into dollar sales?

The method for computing desired or target sales volume in units and the desired or target net income is the same as was used in our earlier break-even computations. Now the targets, however, are expressed in the equations:

$$\text{target sales – variable expenses – fixed expenses} = \text{target net income} \qquad (4)$$

or

$$\text{target sales volume in units} = \frac{\text{fixed expenses} + \text{target net income}}{\text{contribution margin per unit}} \qquad (5)$$

$$= \frac{\$6,000 + \$480}{\$.10} = 64,800 \text{ units}$$

Another way of getting the same answer is to use your knowledge of the break-even point and adopt an incremental approach. The term **incremental** is widely used in accounting. It refers to the *change* in total results (such as revenue, expenses, or income) under a new condition in comparison with some given or known condition.

In this instance, the given condition is assumed to be the 60,000-unit break-even point. All expenses would be recovered at that volume. Therefore the *change* or *increment* in net income for every unit *beyond* 60,000 would be equal to the contribution margin of $.50 – $.40 = $.10. If $480 were the target net profit, $480 ÷ $.10 would show that the target volume must exceed the break-even volume by 4,800 units; it would therefore be 60,000 + 4,800 = 64,800 units.

To find the answer in terms of *dollar* sales, multiply 64,800 units by $.50 or use the formula:

$$\text{target sales volume in dollars} = \frac{\text{fixed expenses} + \text{target net income}}{\text{contribution margin per unit}} \qquad (6)$$

$$= \frac{\$6,000 + \$480}{.20} = \$32,400$$

To solve directly for sales dollars with the alternative incremental approach, the break-even point, in dollar sales of $30,000, becomes the frame of reference. Every sales dollar beyond that point contributes $.20 to net profit. Divide $480 by .20. Dollar sales must exceed the break-even volume by $2,400 to produce a net profit of $480; thus the total dollar sales would be $30,000 + $2,400 = $32,400.

The following table summarizes these computations:

	Break-even Point	Increment	New Condition
Volume in units	60,000	4,800	64,800
Sales	$30,000	$2,400	$32,400
Variable expenses	24,000	1,920	25,920
Contribution margin	$ 6,000	$ 480	$ 6,480
Fixed expenses	6,000	—	6,000
Net income	$0	$ 480	$ 480

Multiple Changes in Key Factors

In the real world, managers often must make decisions about the probable effects of multiple factor changes. For instance, suppose that after the vending machines have been in place a while, Winston is considering locking them from 6:00 P.M. to 6:00 A.M., which she estimates will save $820 in wages monthly. The cutback from 24-hour service would hurt volume substantially because many nighttime employees use the machines. Employees could find food elsewhere, however, so not too many complaints are expected.[1] Should the machines remain available 24 hours per day? Assume that monthly sales would decline by 10,000 units from current sales of (1) 62,000 units and (2) 90,000 units. Consider two approaches. One approach is to construct and solve equations for conditions that prevail under each alternative and select the volume level that yields the highest net income.

Regardless of the current volume level, be it 62,000 or 90,000 units, if we accept the prediction that sales will decline by 10,000 units as accurate, the closing from 6:00 P.M. to 6:00 A.M. will decrease net income by $180.

	Decline from 62,000 to 52,000 Units		Decline from 90,000 to 80,000 Units	
Units	62,000	52,000	90,000	80,000
Sales	$31,000	$26,000	$45,000	$40,000
Variable expenses	24,800	20,800	36,000	32,000
Contribution margin	$ 6,200	$ 5,200	$ 9,000	$ 8,000
Fixed expenses	6,000	5,180	6,000	5,180
Net income	$ 200	$ 20	$ 3,000	$ 2,820
Change in net income	($180)		($180)	

A second approach—an incremental approach—is quicker and simpler. Simplicity is important to managers because it keeps the analysis from being cluttered by irrelevant and potentially confusing data.

What does the insightful manager see in this situation? First, whether 62,000 or 90,000 units are being sold is irrelevant to the decision at hand. The issue is the de-

[1]The quality of overall working conditions might affect these decisions, even though such factors are difficult to quantify. In particular, if costs or profits do not differ much between alternatives, the nonquantifiable, subjective aspects may be the deciding factors.

cline in volume, which would be 10,000 units in either case. The essence of this decision is whether the prospective savings in cost exceed the prospective loss in total contribution-margin dollars.

Lost total contribution margin, 10,000 units @.10	$1,000
Savings in fixed expenses	$ 820
Prospective decline in net income	$ 180

Locking the vending machines from 6:00 P.M. to 6:00 A.M. would cause a $180 decrease in monthly net income. Whichever way you analyze it, locking the machines is not a sound financial decision.

CVP Analysis in the Computer Age

As we have seen, cost-volume-profit analysis is based on a mathematical model, the equation

$$\text{sales} - \text{variable expenses} - \text{fixed expenses} = \text{net income}$$

The CVP model is widely used as a *planning model.* Managers in a variety of organizations use a personal computer and a CVP modeling program to study combinations of changes in selling prices, unit variable costs, fixed costs, and desired profits. Many nonprofit organizations also use computerized CVP modeling. For example, some private universities have models that help measure how decisions such as raising tuition, adding programs, and closing dormitories during winter holidays will affect financial results. The computer quickly calculates the results of changes and can display them both numerically and graphically.

Figure 6-5 is a sample spreadsheet that shows what the sales level would have to be at three different fixed expense levels and three different variable expense levels to reach three different income levels. The computer calculates the 27 different sales levels rapidly and without error. Managers can insert any numbers they want for fixed expenses (column A), variable expense percentage (column B), target net income (row 3 of columns C, D, and E), or combinations thereof, and the computer will compute the required sales level.

In addition to speed and convenience, computers allow a more sophisticated approach to CVP analysis than the one illustrated in this chapter. The assumptions listed above are necessary to simplify the analysis enough for most managers to construct a CVP model by hand. Computer analysts, however, can construct a model that does not require all the simplifications. Computer models can include multiple cost drivers, nonlinear relationships between costs and cost drivers, varying sales mixes, and analyses that need not be restricted to a relevant range.

Use of computer models is a cost-benefit issue. Sometimes the costs of modeling are exceeded by the value of better decisions made using the models. However, the reliability of these models depends on the accuracy of their underlying assumptions about how revenues and costs will actually be affected. Moreover, in small organizations, simplified CVP models often are accurate enough that more sophisticated modeling is unwarranted.

FIGURE 6-5   Spreadsheet Analysis of CVP Relationships

	A	B	C	D	E
1			Sales Required to Earn		
2	Fixed	Variable	Annual Net Income of		
3	Expenses	Expense %	$2,000	$4,000	$6,000
4					
5	$4,000	0.40	$10,000*	$13,333	$16,667
6	$4,000	0.44	$10,714*	$14,286	$17,857
7	$4,000	0.48	$11,538*	$15,385	$19,231
8	$6,000	0.40	$13,333	$16,667	$20,000
9	$6,000	0.44	$14,286	$17,857	$21,429
10	$6,000	0.48	$15,385	$19,231	$23,077
11	$8,000	0.40	$16,667	$20,000	$23,333
12	$8,000	0.44	$17,857	$21,429	$25,000
13	$8,000	0.48	$19,231	$23,077	$26,923
15					
16	*(A5 + C3)/(1 − B5) = ($4,000 + $2,000)/(1 − $.40)				
17	(A6 + C3)/(1 − B6) = ($4,000 + $2,000)/(1 − $.44)				
18	(A7 + C3)/(1 − B7) = ($4,000 + $2,000)/(1 − $.48)				
19					

ADDITIONAL USES OF COST-VOLUME ANALYSIS

Best Combination of Factors

The analysis of cost-volume-profit relationships is an important management responsibility. Managers usually try to obtain the most profitable combination of variable- and fixed-cost factors. For example, purchasing automated machinery may raise fixed costs but reduce labor cost per unit. Conversely, it may be wise to reduce fixed costs to obtain a more favorable combination. Thus, direct selling by a salaried sales force (a fixed cost) may be supplanted by the use of manufacturer's agents who are compensated via sales commissions (variable costs).

Generally, companies that spend heavily for advertising are willing to do so because they have high contribution-margin percentages (airlines, cigarette and cosmetic companies). Conversely, companies with low contribution-margin percentages usually spend less for advertising and promotion (manufacturers of industrial equipment). Obviously, two companies with the same unit sales volumes at the same unit prices could have different attitudes toward risking an advertising outlay. Assume the following:

	Perfume Company	Janitorial Service Company
Unit sales volume	100,000 bottles	100,000 square feet
Dollar sales at $20 per unit	$2,000,000	$2,000,000
Variable costs	200,000	1,700,000
Contribution margin	$1,800,000	$ 300,000
Contribution-margin percentage	90%	15%

Suppose each company wants to increase sales volume by 10%:

	Perfume Company	Janitorial Service Company
Increase in sales volume, 10,000 × $20	$200,000	$200,000
Increase in contribution margin, 90%, 15%	180,000	30,000

The perfume company would be inclined to increase advertising considerably to boost the contribution margin by $180,000. In contrast, the janitorial service company would be foolhardy to spend large amounts to increase the contribution margin by $30,000.

Note that when the contribution-margin percentage of sales is low, great increases in volume are necessary before significant increases in net profits can occur. As sales exceed the break-even point, a high contribution-margin percentage increases profits faster than does a small contribution-margin percentage.

Operating Leverage

In addition to weighing the varied effects of changes in fixed and variable costs, managers need to consider their firm's ratio of fixed to variable costs, called **operating leverage.** In highly leveraged companies—those with high fixed costs and low variable costs—small changes in sales volume result in large changes in net income. Companies with less leverage (that is, lower fixed costs and higher variable costs) are not affected as much by changes in sales volume.

Figure 6-6 shows cost behavior relationships at two firms, one highly leveraged and one with low leverage. The firm with higher leverage has fixed costs of $14,000 and variable cost per unit of $.10. The firm with lower leverage has fixed costs of only $2,000 but variable costs of $.25 per unit. Expected sales at both companies are 80,000 units at $.30 per unit. At this sales level, both alternatives would have net incomes of $2,000. If sales fall short of 80,000 units, profits *drop* most sharply for the

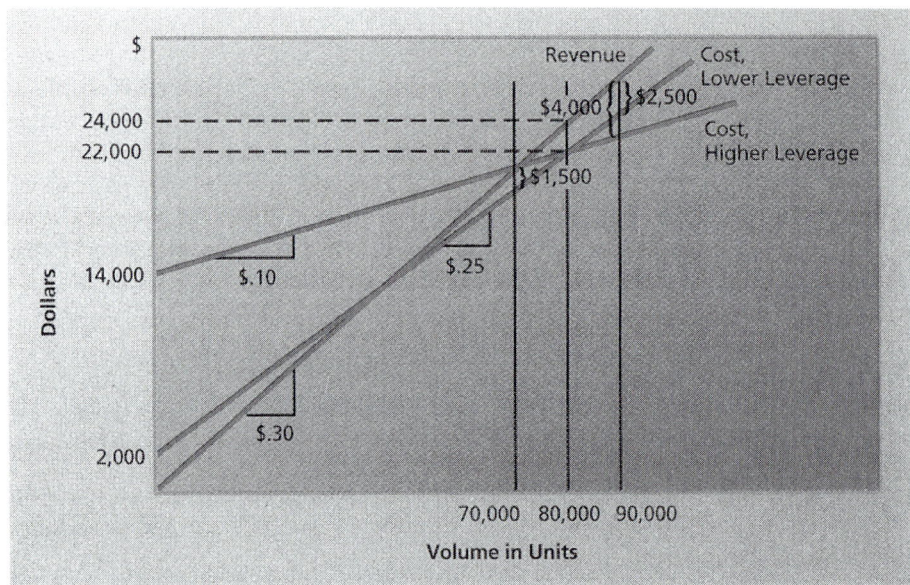

FIGURE 6-6
High Versus Low Leverage

highly leveraged business. If sales exceed 80,000 units, however, profits *increase* most sharply for the highly leveraged concern.

The highly leveraged alternative is more risky. Why? Because it provides the highest possible net income and the highest possible losses. In other words, net income is highly variable, depending on the actual level of sales. The low-leverage alternative is less risky because variations in sales lead to only small variability in net income. At sales of 90,000 units, net income is $4,000 for the higher-leveraged firm but only $2,500 for the lower-leveraged firm. At sales of 70,000 units, however, the higher-leveraged firm has zero profits, compared to $1,500 for the lower-leveraged firm.

Contribution Margin and Gross Margin

Contribution margin may be expressed as a *total* absolute amount, a *unit* absolute amount, a *ratio*, and a *percentage*. The **variable-cost ratio** or **variable-cost percentage** is defined as all variable costs divided by sales. Thus a contribution-margin ratio of 20% means that the variable-cost ratio is 80%.

Too often people confuse the terms *contribution margin* and *gross margin*. **Gross margin** (which is also called **gross profit**) is the excess of sales over the **cost of goods sold** (that is, the cost of the merchandise that is acquired or manufactured and then sold). It is a widely used concept, particularly in the retailing industry.
Compare the gross margin with the contribution margin:

gross margin = sales price − cost of goods sold
contribution margin = sales price − all variable expenses

The following comparisons from our vending machine illustration show the similarities and differences between the contribution margin and the gross margin in a retail store:

Sales	$.50
Variable costs: acquisition cost of unit sold	.40
Contribution margin and gross margin are equal	**$.10**

Thus the original data resulted in no difference between the measure of contribution margin and gross margin. There *would* be a difference between the two, however, if the firm had to pay additional rent of 1¢ per unit sold:

	Contribution Margin	Gross Margin
Sales	$.50	$.50
Acquisition cost of unit sold	$.40	.40
Variable rent	.01	
Total variable expense	.41	
Contribution margin	**$.09**	
Gross margin		**$.10**

As the preceding tabulation indicates, contribution margin and gross margin are not the same concepts. Contribution margin focuses on sales in relation to *all variable costs*, whereas gross margin focuses on sales in relation to cost of goods sold. For example, consider MascoTech, a Detroit-based auto parts supplier. A newspaper article reported that MascoTech's "gross profit margin on sales is about 21% today, but for each additional sales dollar the contribution margin is more like 30%."

NONPROFIT APPLICATION

Consider how cost-volume-profit relationships apply to nonprofit organizations. Suppose a city has a $100,000 lump-sum budget appropriation for a government agency to conduct a counseling program for drug addicts. The variable costs for drug prescriptions are $400 per patient per year. Fixed costs are $60,000 in the relevant range of 50 to 150 patients. If all of the budget appropriation is spent, how many patients can be served in a year?

Let N be the number of patients.

$$\text{revenue} - \text{variable expenses} - \text{fixed expenses} = 0 \text{ if budget is completely spent}$$
$$\$100,000 \text{ lump sum} - \$400N - \$60,000 = 0$$
$$\$400N = \$100,000 - \$60,000$$
$$N = \$40,000 \div 400$$
$$N = 100 \text{ patients}$$

Suppose the total budget appropriation for the following year is cut by 10%. Fixed costs will be unaffected, but service will decline:

$$
\begin{aligned}
\text{revenue} - \text{variable expenses} - \text{fixed expenses} &= 0 \\
\$90,000 - \$400N - \$60,000 &= 0 \\
\$400N &= \$90,000 - \$60,000 \\
N &= \$30,000 \div \$400 \\
N &= 75 \text{ patients}
\end{aligned}
$$

The reduction in service is more than the 10% reduction in the budget. Without restructuring operations, the service volume must be reduced 25% (from 100 to 75 patients) to stay within budget. Note that lump-sum revenue is a horizontal line on the graph:

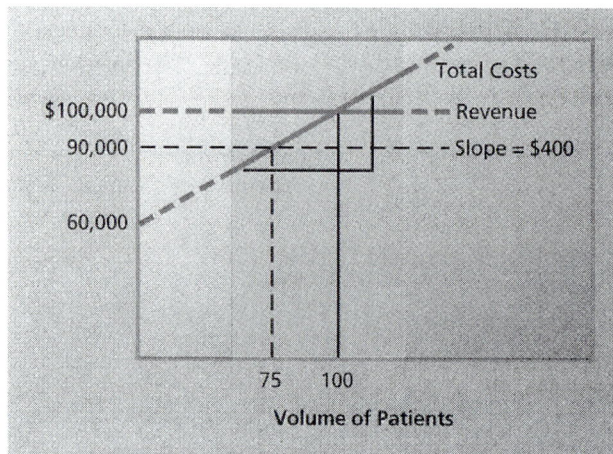

SUMMARY

Understanding cost behavior patterns and cost-volume-profit (CVP) relationships can help guide a manager's decisions. The first step in assessing cost behavior is to identify cost drivers. Variable costs and fixed costs have contrasting behavior patterns with respect to a particular cost driver—variable costs change in proportion to changes in the cost driver, whereas fixed costs are unaffected by cost-driver activity.

CVP analysis (sometimes called break-even analysis) can be approached graphically or with equations. Managers use CVP analysis to compute a break-even point, to compute a target net income, or to examine the effects on income of changes in factors such as fixed costs, variable costs, or volume. CVP analysis is used in non-profit organizations as well as in profit-seeking companies.

Be sure to recognize the limitations of CVP analysis. Most important, it relies on the ability to separate costs into fixed and variable categories. Therefore, it is applicable only over a relevant range of activity. In addition, it assumes constant efficiency, sales mix, and inventory levels.

The contribution margin—the difference between sales price and variable costs—is an important concept. Do not confuse it with gross margin, the difference between sales price and cost of goods sold.

SELF-CORRECTION PROBLEM

1. The budgeted income statement of Port Williams Gift Shop is summarized as follows:

Net revenue	$800,000
Less: expenses, including $400,000 of fixed expenses	880,000
Net loss	$(80,000)

The manager believes that an increase of $200,000 on advertising outlays will increase sales substantially.

a. At what sales volume will the store break even after spending $200,000 on advertising?
b. What sales volume will result in a net profit of $40,000?

SOLUTION TO SELF-CORRECTION PROBLEM

1. a. Note that all data are expressed in dollars. No unit data are given. Most companies have many products, so the overall break-even analysis deals with dollar sales, not units. The variable expenses are $880,000 – $400,000, or $480,000. The variable-expense ratio is $480,000 ÷ $800,000, or .60. Therefore the contribution-margin ratio is .40. Let S = break-even sales in dollars. Then

$$S - \text{variable expenses} - \text{fixed expenses} = \text{net profit}$$

$$S - .60S - (\$400,000 + \$200,00) = 0$$

$$.40S = \$600,000$$

$$S = \frac{\$600,000}{.40} = \frac{\text{fixed expenses}}{\text{contribution–margin ratio}}$$

$$S = \$1,500,000$$

b.

$$\text{required sales} = \frac{\text{fixed expenses} + \text{target net profit}}{\text{contribution–margin ratio}}$$

$$\text{required sales} = \frac{\$600,000 + \$40,000}{.40} = \frac{\$640,000}{.40}$$

$$\text{required sales} = \$1,600,000$$

Alternatively, we can use an incremental approach and reason that all dollar sales beyond the $1.5 million break-even point will result in a 40% contribution to net profit. Divide $40,000 by .40. Sales must therefore be $100,000 beyond the $1.5 million break-even point to produce a net profit of $40,000.

QUESTIONS

1. "Cost behavior is simply identification of cost drivers and their relationships to costs." Comment.
2. Give three examples of variable costs and of fixed costs.
3. "Fixed costs decline as volume increases." Do you agree? Explain.
4. "It is confusing to think of fixed costs on a per-unit basis." Do you agree? Why or why not?
5. "The relevant range pertains to fixed costs, not variable costs." Do you agree? Explain.
6. Identify two simplifying assumptions that underlie CVP analysis.
7. "Classification of costs into variable and fixed categories depends on the decision situation." Explain.
8. "Contribution margin is the excess of sales over fixed costs." Do you agree? Explain.
9. Why is "break-even analysis" a misnomer?
10. "Companies in the same industry generally have about the same break-even point." Do you agree? Explain.
11. Distinguish between the equation technique of CVP analysis and the unit contribution-margin technique.
12. Describe three ways of lowering a break-even point.
13. "Incremental analysis is quicker, but it has no other advantage over an analysis of all costs and revenues associated with each alternative." Do you agree? Why or why not?
14. Explain operating leverage and why a highly leveraged company is risky.
15. "CVP analysis is a common management use of personal computers." Do you agree? Explain.
16. "The contribution margin and gross margin are always equal." Do you agree? Explain.
17. "CVP relationships are unimportant in nonprofit organizations." Do you agree? Explain.
18. "Two products were sold. Total budgeted and actual total sales in number of units were identical to the units budgeted. Actual unit variable costs and sales prices were the same as budgeted. Actual contribution margin was lower than budgeted." What could be the reason for the lower contribution margin?
19. Present the CVP formula for computing the target income before income taxes.
20. Present the CVP formula for computing the effects of a change in volume on after-tax income.

PROBLEMS

1. **Cost-Volume-Profits and Vending Machines.**   Delgado Food Services Company operates and services snack vending machines located in restaurants, gas stations, factories, etc., in four Midwestern states. The machines are rented from the manufacturer. In addition, Delgado must rent the space occupied by its machines. The following expense and revenue relationships pertain to a contemplated expansion program of 20 machines.

Fixed monthly expenses follow:

Machine rental: 20 machines @ $21.75	$ 435
Space rental: 20 locations @ $14.40	288
Part-time wages to service the additional 20 machines	727
Other fixed costs	50
Total monthly fixed costs	**$1,500**

Other data follow:

	Per Unit	Per $100 of Sales
Selling price	$.50	100%
Cost of snack	.40	80
Contribution margin	$.10	20%

These questions relate to the above data unless otherwise noted. **Consider each question independently.**

a. What is the monthly break-even point in number of units? In dollar sales?

b. If 18,000 units were sold, what would be the company's net income?

c. If the space rental cost were doubled, what would be the monthly break-even point in number of units? In dollar sales?

d. If, in addition to the fixed rent, Delgado Food Services Company paid the vending machine manufacturer 1¢ per unit sold, what would be the monthly break-even point in number of units? In dollar sales? Refer to the original data.

e. If, in addition to the fixed rent, Delgado paid the machine manufacturer 2¢ for each unit sold in excess of the break-even point, what would the new net income be if 18,000 units were sold? Refer to the original data.

2. **Exercises in Cost-Volume-Profit Relationships.** The MacKenzie-Hawkins Transportation Company specializes in hauling heavy goods over long distances. The company's revenues and expenses depend on revenue miles, a measure that combines both weights and mileage. Summarized budget data for next year are based on predicted total revenue miles of 800,000.

	Per Revenue Mile
Average selling price (revenue)	$1.50
Average variable expenses	1.30
Fixed expenses, $110,000	

a. Compute the budgeted net income. Ignore income taxes.

b. Management is trying to decide how various possible conditions or decisions might affect net income. Compute the new net income for each of the following changes. Consider each case independently.

(1) A 10% increase in revenue miles
(2) A 10% increase in sales price
(3) A 10% increase in variable expenses
(4) A 10% increase in fixed expenses
(5) An average decrease in selling price of 3¢ per mile and a 5% increase in revenue miles. Refer to the original data
(6) An average increase in selling price of 5% and a 10% decrease in revenue miles
(7) A 10% increase in fixed expenses in the form of more advertising and a 5% increase in revenue miles

3. **Basic CVP Exercises.**   Each problem is *unrelated* to the others.

a. Given: Selling price per unit, $20; total fixed expenses, $5,000; variable expenses per unit, $15. Find break-even sales in units.
b. Given: Sales, $40,000; variable expenses, $30,000; fixed expenses, $7,500; net income, $2,500. Find break-even sales.
c. Given: Selling price per unit, $30; total fixed expenses, $33,000; variable expenses per unit, $14. Find total sales in units to achieve a profit of $7,000, assuming no change in selling price.
d. Given: Sales, $50,000; variable expenses, $20,000; fixed expenses, $20,000; net income, $10,000. Assume no change in selling price; find net income if activity volume increases 10%.
e. Given: Selling price per unit, $40; total fixed expenses, $80,000; variable expenses per unit, $30. Assume that variable expenses are reduced by 20% per unit, and the total fixed expenses are increased by 10%. Find the sales in units to achieve a profit of $20,000, assuming no change in selling price.

4. **Basic CPV Analysis.**   Peter Landis opened his own small day care facility, Toys 'N Tots (TNT), just over 2 years ago. After a rocky start, TNT has been thriving. Peter is now preparing a budget for November 19X6.
   Monthly fixed costs for TNT are

Rent	$ 800
Salaries	1,400
Other fixed costs	100
Total fixed costs	**$2,300**

The salary is for Lynn McGraw, the only employee, who works with Peter in caring for the children. Peter does not pay himself a salary, but he receives the excess of revenues over costs each month.
   The cost driver for variable costs is "child-days." One child-day is one day in day care for one child, and the variable cost is $10 per child-day. The facility is open 6:00 A.M. to 6:00 P.M. weekdays (i.e., Monday through Friday), and there are 22 weekdays in November 19X6. An average day has 8 children attending TNT. State law prohibits TNT from having more than 14 children, a limit it has never reached. Peter charges $30 per day per child, regardless of how long the child is at TNT.

a. Suppose attendance for November 19X6 is equal to the average, resulting in $22 \times 8 = 176$ child-days. What amount will Peter have left after paying all his expenses?

b. Suppose both costs and attendance are difficult to predict. Compute the amount Peter will have left after paying all his expenses for each of the following situations. Consider each case independently.

(1) Average attendance is 9 children per day instead of 8, generating 198 child-days.
(2) Variable costs increase to $11 per child-day.
(3) Rent is increased by $200 per month.
(4) Peter spends $300 on advertising (a fixed cost) in November, which increases average daily attendance to 9.5 children.
(5) Peter begins charging $33 per day on November 1, and average daily attendance slips to 7 children.

ADDENDUM 6A: SALES-MIX ANALYSIS

To emphasize fundamental ideas, the cost-volume-profit analysis in this chapter has focused on a single product. Nearly all companies, however, sell more than one product. *Sales mix* is defined as the relative proportions or combinations of quantities of products that comprise total sales. If the proportions of the mix change, the cost-volume-profit relationships also change.

Suppose Ramos Company has two products, wallets (W) and key cases (K). The income budget follows:

	Wallets (W)	Key Cases (K)	Total
Sales in units	300,000	75,000	375,000
Sales @ $8 and $5	$2,400,000	$375,000	$2,775,000
Variable expenses @ $7 and $3	2,100,000	225,000	2,325,000
Contribution margins @ $1 and $2	$300,000	$150,000	$ 450,000
Fixed expenses			180,000
Net income			$ 270,000

For simplicity, ignore income taxes. What would be the break-even point? The typical answer assumes a constant mix of 4 units of W for every unit of K. Therefore, let K = number of units of product K to break even, and 4K = number of units of product W to break even:

$$\text{sales} - \text{variable expenses} - \text{fixed expenses} = \text{zero net income}$$
$$\$8(4K) + \$5(K) - \$7(4K) - \$3(K) - \$180,000 = 0$$
$$\$32K + \$5K - \$28K - \$3K - \$180,000 = 0$$
$$\$6K = \$180,000$$
$$K = 30,000$$
$$4K = 120,000 = W$$

The break-even point is 30,000K + 120,000W = 150,000 units.

This is the only break-even point for a sales mix of four wallets for every key case. Clearly, however, there are other break-even points for other sales mixes. For instance, suppose only key cases were sold, fixed expenses being unchanged:

$$\text{break--even point} = \frac{\text{fixed expenses}}{\text{contribution margin per unit}}$$

$$= \frac{\$180,000}{\$2}$$

$$= 90,000 \text{ key cases}$$

If only wallets were sold:

$$\text{break--even point} = \frac{180,000}{\$1}$$

$$= 180,000 \text{ wallets}$$

Managers are not primarily interested in the break-even point for its own sake. Instead, they want to know how changes in a planned sales mix will affect net income. When the sales mix changes, the break-even point and the expected net income at various sales levels are altered. For example, suppose overall actual total sales were equal to the budget of 375,000 units. However, only 50,000 key cases were sold:

	Wallets (W)	Key Cases (K)	Total
Sales in units	325,000	50,000	375,000
Sales @ $8 and $5	$2,600,000	$250,000	$2,850,000
Variable expenses @ $7 and $3	2,275,000	150,000	2,425,000
Contribution margins @ $1 and $2	$ 325,000	$100,000	$ 425,000
Fixed expenses			180,000
Net income			$ 245,000

The change in sales mix has resulted in a $245,000 actual net income rather than the $270,000 budgeted net income, an unfavorable difference of $25,000. The budgeted and actual sales in number of units were identical, but the proportion of the product bearing the higher unit contribution margin declined.

Different advertising strategies may also affect the sales mix. Clearly, if a sales budget is not actually attained, the budgeted net income will be affected by the individual sales volume of each product. The fewer the units sold, the lower the profit, and vice versa. All other factors being equal, the higher the proportion of the more profitable products, the higher the profit. For example, Reynolds Industries sells highly profitable cigarettes (such as the Winston brand) and less profitable canned goods (such as the Del Monte brand). For any given level of total sales, the greater the proportion of the cigarettes, the greater the total profit.

Managers usually want to maximize the sales of all their products. Faced with limited resources and time, however, executives prefer to generate the most profitable sales mix achievable. For example, consider a recent annual report of Deere & Co., a manufacturer of farm equipment: "The increase in the ratio of cost of goods sold to net sales resulted from higher production costs [and] a less favorable mix of products sold."

Profitability of a given product helps guide executives who must decide to emphasize or de-emphasize particular products. For example, given limited production facilities or limited time of sales personnel, should we emphasize wallets or key cases? These decisions may be affected by other factors beyond the contribution margin per unit of product.

ADDENDUM 6B: IMPACT OF INCOME TAXES

Thus far we have (as so many people would like to) ignored income taxes. In most nations, however, private enterprises are subject to income taxes. Reconsider the vending machine example in the chapter. As part of our CVP analysis, we discussed the sales necessary to achieve a target income before income taxes of $480. If an income tax were levied at 40%, the new result would be

Income before income tax	$480	100%
Income tax	192	40
Net income	**$288**	**60%**

Note that

$$\text{net income} = \text{income before income taxes} - .40 \text{ (income before income taxes)}$$

$$\text{net income} = .60 \text{ (income before income taxes)}$$

$$\text{income before income taxes} = \frac{\text{net income}}{.60}$$

or

$$\text{target income before income taxes} = \frac{\text{target after–tax net income}}{1 - \text{tax rate}}$$

$$\text{target income before income taxes} = \frac{\$288}{1 - .40} = \frac{\$288}{.60} = \$480$$

Suppose the target net income after taxes was $288. The only change in the general equation approach would be on the right-hand side of the following equation:

$$\text{target sales} - \text{variable expenses} - \text{fixed expenses} = \frac{\text{target after–tax net income}}{1 - \text{tax rate}}$$

Thus, letting N be the number of units to be sold at $.50 each with a variable cost of $.40 each and total fixed costs of $6,000,

$$\$.50N - \$.40N - \$6,000 = \frac{\$288}{1 - .4}$$

$$\$.10N = \$6,000 + \frac{\$288}{.6}$$

$$\$.06N = \$3,600 + \$288 = 3,888$$

$$N = \$3,888 \div \$.06 = 64,800 \text{ units}$$

Sales of 64,800 units produce an *after-tax* profit of $288 as shown here and a *before-tax* profit of $480 as shown in the chapter.

Suppose the target net income after taxes was $480. The volume needed would rise to 68,000 units, as follows:

$$\$.50N - \$.40N - \$6,000 = \frac{\$480}{1-.4}$$

$$\$.10N = \$6,000 + \frac{\$480}{.6}$$

$$\$.06N = \$3,600 + \$480 = \$4,080$$

$$N = \$4,080 \div \$.06 = 68,000 \text{ units}$$

As a shortcut to computing the effects of volume on the change in after-tax income, use the formula

$$\begin{array}{c}\text{change}\\ \text{in net}\\ \text{income}\end{array} = \left(\begin{array}{c}\text{change in volume}\\ \text{in units}\end{array}\right) \times \left(\begin{array}{c}\text{contribution margin}\\ \text{per unit}\end{array}\right) \times (1 - \text{tax rate})$$

In our example, suppose operations were at a level of 64,800 units and $288 after-tax net income. The manager is wondering how much after-tax net income would increase if sales become 68,000 units.

$$\begin{aligned}\text{change in net income} &= (68,000 - 64,800) \times \$.10 \times (1 - .4)\\ &= 3,200 \times \$.10 \times .60 = 3,200 \times \$.06\\ &= \$192\end{aligned}$$

In brief, each unit beyond the break-even point adds to after-tax net profit at the unit contribution margin multiplied by (1 – income tax rate).

Throughout our illustration, the break-even point itself does not change. Why? Because there is *no income tax at a level of zero profits*.

Cost Management Systems

CHAPTER 7

Introduction to Cost Management Systems

Managers rely on accountants to measure the cost of the goods and services the company produces. Consider the following commentaries on the modern role of management accountants:

> We (cost accountants) had to understand what the numbers mean, relate the numbers to business activity, and recommend alternative courses of action. Finally, we had to evaluate alternatives and make decisions to maximize business efficiency.
>
> —South Central Bell

> Because the ABC (Activity-Based Costing) system now mirrors the manufacturing process, the engineers and production staff believe the cost data produced by the accounting system. Engineering and production regularly ask accounting to help find the product design combination that will optimize costs. . . . The accountants now participate in product design decisions. They help engineering and production understand how costs behave. . . . The ABC system makes the professional lives of the accountants more rewarding.
>
> —Hewlett-Packard Company

As you can see, all kinds of organizations—manufacturing firms, service companies, and nonprofit organizations—need some form of **cost accounting,** that part of the accounting system that measures costs for the purposes of management decision making and financial reporting. Because it is the most general case, embracing production, marketing, and general administration functions, we will focus on cost accounting in a manufacturing setting. Remember, though, that you can apply this framework to any organization.

In this chapter we introduce the concepts of cost and management accounting appropriate to any manufacturing company. We also consider recent changes that have led to what is called the *new manufacturing environment.* Manufacturing companies are in the midst of great changes. The need to compete in global markets has changed the types of information useful to managers. At the same time technology has changed both the manufacturing processes and information-processing capabilities. Although the basic *concepts* of management accounting have not changed, their *application* is significantly different in many companies than it was a decade ago. Management accountants today must be able to develop systems to support globally oriented, technology-intensive companies, often called *world-class manufacturing companies.*

In addition, we discuss how cost accounting affects and is affected by financial reporting, and how the need to use costs for reported income statements and balance sheets influences the way cost accounting systems are structured.

CLASSIFICATIONS OF COSTS

Costs may be classified in many ways—far too many to be covered in a single chapter. This chapter concentrates on the big picture of how manufacturing costs are accumulated and classified

Cost Accumulation and Cost Objectives

A **cost** may be defined as a sacrifice or giving up of resources for a particular purpose. Costs are frequently measured by the monetary units (for example, dollars or francs) that must be paid for goods and services. Costs are initially recorded in elementary form (for example, repairs or advertising). Then these costs are grouped in different ways to help managers make decisions, such as evaluating subordinates and subunits of the organization, expanding or deleting products or territories, and replacing equipment.

To aid decisions, managers want to know the cost of something. This "something" is called a **cost objective** or **cost object,** defined as *any activity or resource for which a separate measurement of costs is desired.* Examples of cost objectives include departments, products, territories, miles driven, bricks laid, patients seen, tax bills sent, checks processed, student hours taught, and library books shelved.

The cost accounting system typically includes two processes:

1. **Cost accumulation:** Collecting costs by some "natural" classification such as materials or labor.
2. **Cost allocation:** Tracing and reassigning costs to one or more cost objectives such as departments, customers, or products.

Figure 7-1 illustrates these processes. First, the costs of all raw materials are *accumulated.* Then they are *allocated* to the departments that use them and further to the specific items made by these departments. The total raw materials cost of a particular product is the sum of the raw materials costs allocated to it in the various departments.

To make intelligent decisions, managers want reliable measurements. An extremely large U.S. grocery chain, A&P, ran into profit difficulties. It began retrenching by closing many stores. Management's lack of adequate cost information about

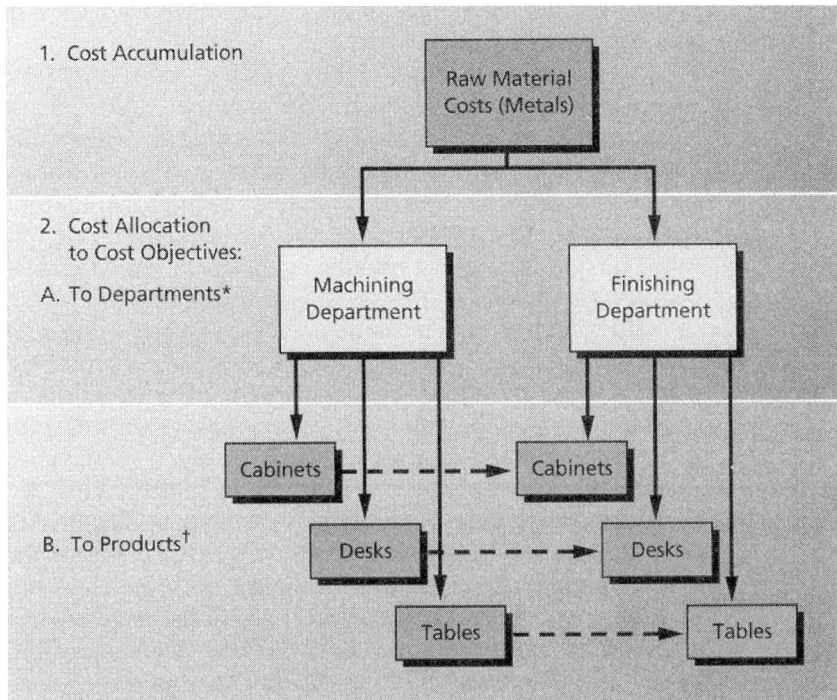

1. Cost Accumulation
   - Raw Material Costs (Metals)

2. Cost Allocation to Cost Objectives:
   A. To Departments*
      - Machining Department
      - Finishing Department
   B. To Products†
      - Cabinets → Cabinets
      - Desks → Desks
      - Tables → Tables

*Purpose: to evaluate performance of manufacturing departments.
†Purpose: to obtain costs of various products for valuing inventory, determining income, and judging product profitability.

FIGURE 7-1
Cost Accumulation and Allocation

individual store operations made the closing program a hit-or-miss affair. A news story reported the following:

> Because of the absence of detailed profit-and-loss statements, and a cost-allocation system that did not reflect true costs, A&P's strategists could not be sure whether an individual store was really unprofitable. For example, distribution costs were shared equally among all the stores in a marketing area without regard to such factors as a store's distance from the warehouse. Says one close observer of the company: "When they wanted to close a store, they had to wing it. They could not make rational decisions, because they did not have a fact basis."

Direct and Indirect Costs

A major feature of costs in both manufacturing and nonmanufacturing activities is whether the costs have a direct or an indirect relationship to a particular cost objective. **Direct costs** can be identified specifically and exclusively with a given cost objective in an economically feasible way. In contrast, **indirect costs** cannot be identified specifically and exclusively with a given cost objective in an economically feasible way.

Whenever it is "economically feasible," managers prefer to classify costs as direct rather than indirect. In this way, managers have greater confidence in the reported costs of products and services. "Economically feasible" means "cost effective," in the sense that managers do not want cost accounting to be too expensive in relation to expected benefits. For example, it may be economically feasible to trace the exact cost of steel and fabric (direct cost) to a specific lot of desk chairs, but it may be economically infeasible to trace the exact cost of rivets or thread (indirect costs) to the chairs.

Other factors also influence whether a cost is considered direct or indirect. The key is the particular cost objective. For example, consider a supervisor's salary in the maintenance department of a telephone company. If the cost objective is the department, the supervisor's salary is a direct cost. In contrast, if the cost objective is a service (the "product" of the company) such as a telephone call, the supervisor's salary is an indirect cost. In general, many more costs are direct when a department is the cost objective than when a service (a telephone call) or a physical product (a razor blade) is the cost objective.

Frequently managers want to know both the costs of running departments and the costs of products, services, activities, or resources. Costs are inevitably allocated to more than one cost objective. Thus a particular cost may simultaneously be direct and indirect. As you have just seen, a supervisor's salary can be both direct (with respect to his or her department) and indirect (with respect to the department's individual products or services).

Categories of Manufacturing Costs

Any raw material, labor, or other input used by any organization could, in theory, be identified as a direct or indirect cost, depending on the cost objective. In manufacturing operations, which transform materials into other goods through the use of labor and factory facilities, products are frequently the cost objective. As a result, manufacturing costs are most often divided into three major categories: (1) direct materials, (2) direct labor, and (3) factory overhead.

1. **Direct-material costs** include the acquisition costs of all materials that are physically identified as a part of the manufactured goods and that may be traced to the manufactured goods in an economically feasible way. Examples are iron castings, lumber, aluminum sheets, and subassemblies. Direct materials often do not include minor items such as tacks or glue because the costs of tracing these items are greater than the possible benefits of having more precise product costs. Such items are usually called *supplies* or *indirect materials,* which are classified as a part of the factory overhead described in this list.
2. **Direct-labor costs** include the wages of all labor that can be traced specifically and exclusively to the manufactured goods in an economically feasible way. Examples are the wages of machine operators and assemblers. Much labor, such as that of janitors, forklift truck operators, plant guards, and storeroom clerks, is considered to be *indirect labor* because it is impossible or economically infeasible to trace such activity to specific products. Such indirect labor is classified as a part of factory overhead. In highly automated factories, there may be no direct labor costs. Why? Because it may be economically infeasible to physically trace any labor cost directly to specific products.

3. **Factory-overhead costs** include all costs associated with the manufacturing process that are not classified as direct material or direct labor. Other terms used to describe this category are **factory burden** and **manufacturing overhead.** Examples are power, supplies, indirect labor, supervisory salaries, property taxes, rent, insurance, and depreciation.

In traditional accounting systems, all manufacturing overhead costs are considered to be indirect. However, computers have allowed modern systems to physically trace many overhead costs to products in an economically feasible manner. For example, meters wired to computers can monitor the electricity used to produce each product, and costs of setting up a batch production run can be traced to the items produced in the run. In general, the more overhead costs that can be traced directly to products, the more accurate the product cost.

Prime Costs, Conversion Costs, and Direct-Labor Costs

Figure 7-2 shows that direct labor is sometimes combined with one of the other types of manufacturing costs. The combined categories are **prime costs**—direct labor plus direct materials—or **conversion costs**—direct labor plus factory overhead.

The twofold categorization, direct materials and conversion costs, has replaced the threefold categorization, direct materials, direct labor, and factory overhead, in many modern, automated manufacturing companies. Why? Because direct labor in such a company is a small part of costs and not worth tracing directly to the products. In fact, some companies call their two categories direct materials and factory overhead, and simply include direct labor costs in the factory overhead category.

Why so many different systems? As mentioned earlier, accountants and managers weigh the costs and benefits of additional categories when they design their cost accounting systems. When the costs of any single category or item become relatively insignificant, separate tracking may no longer be desirable. For example, in highly automated factories direct labor is often less than 5% of total manufacturing costs. In such cases, it may make economic sense to combine direct-labor costs with one of the

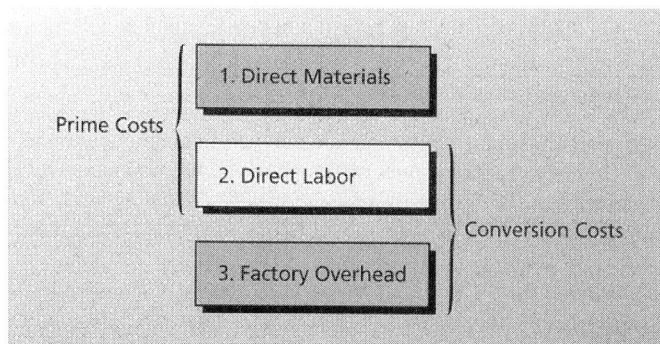

FIGURE 7-2
Relationships of Key Categories of Manufacturing Costs for
Product-Costing Purposes

other major cost categories. Such is the case at several Hewlett-Packard plants, which collect direct labor as just another subpart of factory overhead.

To recap, the three major categories for manufacturing product costs are direct material, direct labor, and factory overhead. Some companies, however, have only two categories: direct materials and conversion costs. As information technology improves, some companies may have four or more. For instance, a company might have direct materials, direct labor, other direct costs (such as specifically metered power), and factory overhead.

In addition to direct-material, direct-labor, and factory-overhead costs, all manufacturing companies also incur selling and administrative costs. These costs are accumulated by departments such as advertising and sales departments. However, as you will see later in this chapter, most firm's *financial statements* do not allocate these costs to the physical units produced. In short, these costs do not become a part of the reported inventory cost of the manufactured products. To aid in decisions, however, managers often want to know the selling and administrative costs associated with each product. Therefore, *management reports* often include such costs as product costs.

COST ACCOUNTING FOR FINANCIAL REPORTING

Regardless of the type of cost accounting system used, the resulting costs are used in a company's financial statements. This section discusses how financial reporting requirements influence the design of cost accounting systems.

Costs are reported on both the income statement, as cost of goods sold, and the balance sheet, as inventory amounts.

Product Costs and Period Costs

When preparing both income statements and balance sheets, accountants frequently distinguish between *product costs* and *period costs*. **Product costs** are costs identified with goods produced or purchased for resale. Product costs are initially identified as part of the inventory on hand. These product costs (inventoriable costs) become expenses (in the form of *cost of goods sold*) only when the inventory is sold. In contrast, **period costs** are costs that are deducted as expenses during the current period without going through an inventory stage.

For example, look at the top half of Figure 7-3. A merchandising company (retailer or wholesaler) acquires goods for resale without changing their basic form. The only product cost is the purchase cost of the merchandise. Unsold goods are held as merchandise inventory cost and are shown as an asset on a balance sheet. As the goods are sold, their costs become expenses in the form of "cost of goods sold."

A merchandising company also has a variety of selling and administrative expenses. These costs are period costs because they are deducted from revenue as expenses without ever being regarded as a part of inventory.

The bottom half of Figure 7-3 illustrates product and period costs in a manufacturing firm. Note that direct materials are transformed into salable form with the help of direct labor and factory overhead. All these costs are product costs because they are allocated to inventory until the goods are sold. As in merchandising ac-

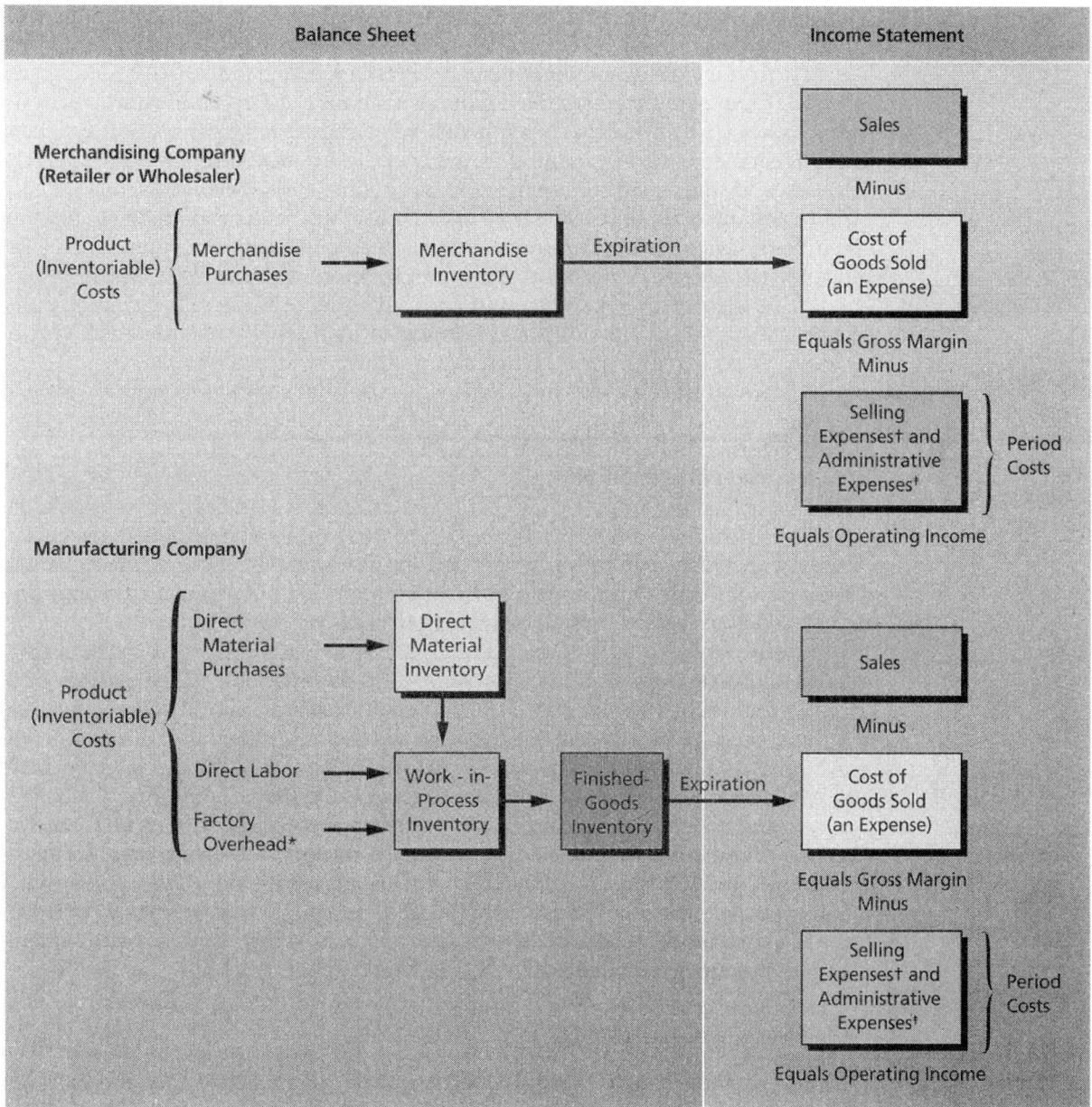

*Examples: indirect labor, factory supplies, insurance, and depreciation on plant.
†Examples: insurance on salespersons' cars, depreciation on salespersons' cars, salespersons' salaries.
‡Examples: insurance on corporate headquarters building, depreciation on office equipment, clerical salaries.
Note particularly that when insurance and depreciation relate to the manufacturing function, they are inventoriable, but when they relate to selling and administration, they are not inventoriable.

FIGURE 7-3
Relationships of Product Costs and Period Costs

counting, the selling and administrative expenses are not regarded as product costs but are treated as period costs.[1]

Be sure you are clear on the differences between merchandising accounting and manufacturing accounting for such costs as insurance, depreciation, and wages. In merchandising accounting, all such items are period costs (expenses of the current period). In manufacturing accounting, many of these items are related to production activities and thus, as factory overhead, are product costs (become expenses in the form of cost of goods sold as the inventory is sold).

In both merchandising and manufacturing accounting, selling and general administrative costs are period costs. Thus the inventory cost of a manufactured product *excludes* sales salaries, sales commissions, advertising, legal, public relations, and the president's salary. *Manufacturing overhead* is traditionally regarded as a part of finished-goods inventory cost, whereas *selling* expenses and *general administrative* expenses are not.

Balance Sheet Presentation

Examining both halves of Figure 7-3 together, you can see that the balance sheets of manufacturers and merchandisers differ with respect to inventories. The merchandiser's "inventory account" is supplanted in a manufacturing concern by three inventory classes that help managers trace all product costs through the production process to the time of sales.

These classes are:

- *Direct-materials inventory:* Materials on hand and awaiting use in the production process.
- *Work-in-process inventory:* Goods undergoing the production process but not yet fully completed. Costs include appropriate amounts of the three major manufacturing costs (direct material, direct labor, and factory overhead).
- *Finished-goods inventory:* Goods fully completed but not yet sold.

The only essential difference between the structure of the balance sheet of a manufacturer and that of a retailer or wholesaler would appear in their respective current asset sections:

---

[1] This distinction between product and period costs has a long tradition for both internal and external reporting. During the late 1980s new U.S. income tax requirements forced companies to treat many selling and administrative costs as product instead of period costs. These special requirements, however, are confined to reporting to income tax authorities only.

Current Asset Sections of Balance Sheets

Manufacturer			Retailer or Wholesaler	
Cash		$ 4,000	Cash	$ 4,000
Receivables		25,000	Receivables	25,000
Finished goods	$32,000			
Work in process	22,000			
Direct material	23,000			
Total inventories		77,000	Merchandise inventories	77,000
Other current assets		1,000	Other current assets	1,000
Total current assets		**$107,000**	Total current asset	**$107,000**

Unit Costs for Product Costing

Reporting cost of goods sold or inventory values requires costs to be assigned to units of product. Assume the following:

Total cost of goods manufactured	**$40,000,000**
Total units manufactured	**10,000,000**
Unit cost of product for inventory purposes ($40,000,000 ÷ 10,000,000)	$ 4

If some of the 10 million units manufactured are still unsold at the end of the period, a part of the $40 million cost of goods manufactured will be "held back" as a cost of the ending inventory of finished goods (and shown as an asset on a balance sheet). The remainder becomes "cost of goods sold" for the current period and is shown as an expense on the income statement.

Costs and Income Statements

In income statements, the detailed reporting of selling and administrative expenses is typically the same for manufacturing and merchandising organizations, but the cost of goods sold is different:

Manufacturer
Manufacturing cost of goods produced and then sold, usually composed of the three major categories of cost: direct materials, direct labor, and factory overhead.

Retailer or Wholesaler
Merchandise cost of goods sold, usually composed of the purchase cost of items, including freight in, that are acquired and then resold.

Consider the additional details as they are presented in the model income statement of a manufacturing company in Figure 7-4. The $40 million cost of goods manu-

---

FIGURE 7-4   Model Income Statement, Manufacturing Company

Sales (8,000,000 units @ $10)			$80,000,000
Cost of goods manufactured and sold			
Beginning finished-goods inventory			$ –0–
Cost of goods manufactured			
Direct materials used	$20,000,000		
Direct labor	12,000,000		
Factory overhead	8,000,000	40,000,000	
Cost of goods available for sale		$40,000,000	
Ending finished-goods inventory,			
2,000,000 units @ $4		8,000,000	
Cost of goods sold (an expense)			32,000,000
Gross margin or gross profit			$48,000,000
Less: other expenses			
Selling costs (an expense)		$30,000,000	
General and administrative costs			
(an expense)		8,000,000	38,000,000
Operating income*			**$10,000,000**

*Also net income in this example because other expenses such as interest and income taxes are ignored here for simplicity.

---

factured is subdivided into the major components of direct materials, direct labor, and factory overhead. In contrast, a wholesale or retail company would replace the entire "cost-of-goods-manufactured" section with a single line, "cost of goods purchased."

The terms "costs" and "expenses" are often used loosely by accountants and managers. "Expenses" denotes all costs deducted from (matched against) revenue in a given period. On the other hand, "costs" is a much broader term and is used to describe both an asset (the cost of inventory) and an expense (the cost of goods sold). Thus manufacturing costs are funneled into an income statement as an expense (in the form of cost of goods sold) via the multistep inventory procedure shown earlier in Figure 7-3. In contrast, selling and general administrative costs are commonly deemed expenses immediately as they are incurred.

Transactions Affecting Inventories

The three manufacturing inventory accounts are affected by the following transactions:

- Direct Materials Inventory
    Increased by purchases of direct materials
    Decreased by use of direct materials
- Work-in-Process Inventory
    Increased by use of direct materials, direct labor, or factory overhead
    Decreased by transfer of completed goods to finished-goods inventory
- Finished-Goods Inventory
    Increased by transfers of completed goods from work-in-process inventory
    Decreased by the amount of cost of goods sold at time of sale

Direct labor and factory overhead are used at the same time they are acquired. Therefore, they are entered directly into work-in-process inventory and have no separate inventory account. In contrast, direct materials are often purchased in advance of their use and held in inventory for some time.

Figure 7-5 traces the effects of each transaction. It uses the dollar amounts from Figure 7-4, with one exception. Purchases of direct materials totaled $30 million, with $20 million used in production (as shown in Figure 7-4) and $10 million left in inventory at the end of the period. As the bottom of Figure 7-5 indicates, the ending balance sheet amounts would be:

Direct-material inventory	$10,000,000
Work-in-process inventory	0
Finished-goods inventory	8,000,000
Total inventories	**$18,000,000**

COST BEHAVIOR AND INCOME STATEMENTS

In addition to differences between manufacturing and merchandising firms, manufacturers differ among themselves in accounting for costs on income statements, with some favoring an *absorption* approach and others using a *contribution* approach. To highlight the different effects of these approaches, we will assume that in 19X2 the Samson Company has direct-material costs of $7 million and direct-labor costs of $4 million. Assume also that the company incurred the factory overhead illustrated in Figure 7-6 and the selling and administrative expenses illustrated in Figure 7-7. Total sales were $20 million. Finally, assume that the units produced are equal to the units sold. That is, there is no change in inventory levels.

Note that Figures 7-6 and 7-7 subdivide costs as variable or fixed. Many companies do not make such subdivisions in their income statements. Furthermore, when such subdivisions are made, sometimes arbitrary decisions are necessary as to whether a given cost is variable, fixed, or partially fixed (for example, repairs). Nevertheless, to aid decision making, many companies are attempting to report the extent to which their costs are approximately variable or fixed.

FIGURE 7-5   Inventory Transactions (in millions)

Inventory	Direct Materials Transaction	Work-in-Process Inventory	Finished-Goods Inventory
Beginning balance	$ 0	$ 0	$ 0
Purchase direct materials	+30	—	—
Use direct materials	−20	+20	—
Acquire and use direct labor	—	+12	—
Acquire and use factory overhead	—	+8	—
Complete production	—	−40	+40
Sell goods and record cost of goods sold	—	—	$−32
Ending balance	$ 10	$ 0	$ 8

**FIGURE 7-6   Samson Company Schedules of Factory Overhead (Product Costs)
for the Year Ended December 31, 19X2 (thousands of dollars)**

Schedule 1: Variable Costs

Supplies (lubricants, expendable tools, coolants, sandpaper)	$ 150	
Material-handling labor (forklift operators)	700	
Repairs	100	
Power	50	$1,000

Schedule 2: Fixed Costs

Managers' salaries	$ 200	
Employee training	90	
Factory picnic and holiday party	10	
Supervisory salaries	700	
Depreciation, plant and equipment	1,800	
Property taxes	150	
Insurance	50	3,000
Total manufacturing overhead		**$4,000**

**FIGURE 7-7   Samson Company Schedules of Selling and Administrative Expenses
(Period Costs) for the Year Ended December 31, 19X2 (thousands of dollars)**

Schedule 3: Selling Expenses

Variable		
Sales commissions	$ 700	
Shipping expenses for products sold	300	$1,000
Fixed		
Advertising	$ 700	
Sales salaries	1,000	
Other	300	2,000
Total selling expenses		**$3,000**

Schedule 4: Administrative Expenses

Variable		
Some clerical wages	$ 80	
Computer time rented	20	$ 100
Fixed		
Office salaries	$ 100	
Other salaries	200	
Depreciation on office facilities	100	
Public-accounting fees	40	
Legal fees	100	
Other	360	900
Total administrative expenses		**$1,000**

Absorption Approach

Figure 7-8 presents Samson's income statement using the **absorption approach** (*absorption costing*), the approach used by most companies. Firms that take this approach consider all factory overhead (both variable and fixed) to be product (inventoriable) costs that become an expense in the form of manufacturing cost of goods sold only as sales occur.

Note in Figure 7-8 that gross profit or gross margin is the difference between sales and the *manufacturing* cost of goods sold. Note too that the *primary classifications* of costs on the income statement are by three major management *functions:* manufacturing, selling, and administrative.

Contribution Approach

In contrast, Figure 7-9 presents Samson's income statement using the **contribution approach** (*variable costing* or *direct costing*). The contribution approach is not allowed for external financial reporting. However, many companies use this approach for internal (management accounting) purposes and an absorption format for external purposes, because they expect the benefits of making better decisions to exceed the extra costs of using different reporting systems simultaneously.

For decision purposes, the major difference between the contribution approach and the absorption approach is that the former emphasizes the distinction between variable and fixed costs. Its primary classifications of costs are by variable and fixed *cost behavior patterns,* not by *business functions.*

The contribution income statement provides a *contribution margin,* which is computed after deducting from revenue all variable costs including variable selling and administrative costs. This approach makes it easier to understand the impact of changes in sales demand on operating income.

The contribution approach stresses the lump-sum amount of fixed costs to be recouped before net income emerges. This highlighting of total fixed costs focuses management attention on fixed-cost behavior and control in making both short-run

---

FIGURE 7-8   Samson Company Absorption Income Statement for the Year Ended December 31, 19X2 (thousands of dollars)

Sales		$20,000
Less: manufacturing costs of goods sold		
Direct material	$7,000	
Direct labor	4,000	
Factory overhead (Schedules 1 plus 2)*	4,000	15,000
Gross margin or gross profit		$ 5,000
Selling expenses (Schedule 3)	$3,000	
Administrative expenses (Schedule 4)	1,000	
Total selling and administrative expenses		4,000
Operating income		**$ 1,000**

*Note: Schedules 1 and 2 are in Figure 7-6. Schedules 3 and 4 are in Figure 7-7.

FIGURE 7-9   Samson Company Contribution Income Statement for the Year Ended December 31, 19X2 (thousands of dollars)

Sales		$20,000
Less: variable expenses		
Direct material	$ 7,000	
Direct labor	4,000	
Variable indirect manufacturing costs (Schedule 1)'	1,000	
Total variable manufacturing cost of goods sold	$12,000	
Variable selling expenses (Schedule 3)	1,000	
Variable administrative expenses (Schedule 4)	100	
Total variable expenses		13,100
Contribution margin		$ 6,900
Less: fixed expenses		
Manufacturing (Schedule 2)	$ 3,000	
Selling (Schedule 3)	2,000	
Administrative (Schedule 4)	900	5,900
Operating income		**$ 1,000**

'Note: Schedules 1 and 2 are in Figure 7-6. Schedules 3 and 4 are in Figure 7-7.

---

and long-run plans. Remember that advocates of the contribution approach do not maintain that fixed costs are unimportant or irrelevant. They do stress, however, that the distinctions between behaviors of variable and fixed costs are crucial for certain decisions.

The difference between the gross margin (from the absorption approach) and the contribution margin (from the contribution approach) is striking in manufacturing companies. Why? Because fixed manufacturing costs are regarded as a part of cost of goods sold, and these fixed costs reduce the gross margin accordingly. However, *fixed* manufacturing costs do not reduce the contribution margin, which is affected solely by revenues and *variable* costs.

The implications of the *absorption approach* and the *contribution approach* for decision making are discussed in the next chapter.

ACTIVITY-BASED ACCOUNTING, VALUE-ADDED COSTING, AND JUST-IN-TIME PRODUCTION

In the past decade, many companies in the United States, struggling to keep up with competitors from Japan, Germany, and other countries, adopted new management philosophies and developed new production technologies. In many cases, these changes prompted corresponding changes in accounting systems.

For example, Borg-Warner's Automotive Chain Systems Operation transformed its manufacturing operation to a just-in-time manufacturing system with work cells. This change in the way manufacturing was done made the traditional accounting system obsolete. A new cost accounting system coupled with the new production systems "improved the overall reporting, controls, and efficiency dramatically."[2]

---

[2]A. Phillips and Don Collins, "How Borg-Warner Made the Transition From Pile Accounting to JIT," *Management accounting,* October 1990, pp. 32–35.

Activity-Based Accounting

The primary focus of the changes in operations and accounting has been an increased attention to the cost of the *activities* undertaken to design, produce, sell, and deliver a company's products or services. **Activity-based accounting (ABA)** or **activity-based costing (ABC)** systems first accumulate overhead costs for each of the *activities* of an organization, and then assign the costs of activities to the products, services, or other cost objects that caused that activity.

Consider the Salem manufacturing plant of a major appliance producer. Figure 7-10 contrasts the traditional costing system with an ABC system. In the traditional cost system, the portion of *total overhead* allocated to a product depends on the proportion of *total direct-labor-hours* consumed in making the product. In the ABC system, significant overhead activities (machining, assembly, quality inspection, etc.) and related resources are separately identified and traced to products using cost drivers—machine hours, number of parts, number of inspections, etc. In the ABC system, the amount of overhead costs allocated to a product depends on the proportion of total machine hours, total parts, total inspections, and so on, consumed in making the product. One large overhead cost pool has been broken into several pools, each associated with a key activity. We now consider a more in-depth illustration of the design of an ABC system.

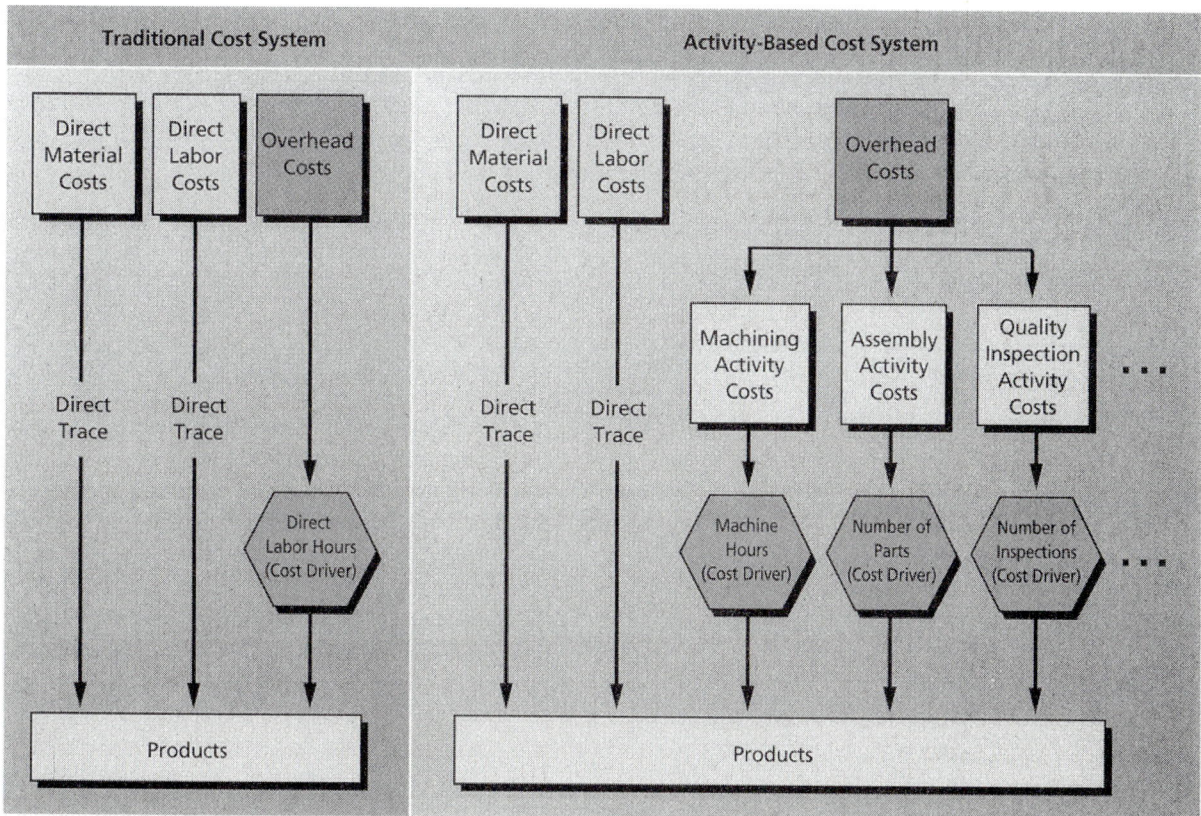

FIGURE 7-10
Traditional and Activity-Based Cost Systems

Illustration of Activity-Based Costing[3]

Consider the Billing Department at Portland Power Company (PPC), an electric utility. The Billing Department (BD) at PPC provides account inquiry and bill printing services for two major classes of customers—residential and commercial. Currently, the BD services 120,000 residential and 20,000 commercial customer accounts.

Two factors are having a significant impact on PPC's profitability. First, deregulation of the power industry has led to increased competition and lower rates, so PPC must find ways of reducing its operating costs. Second, the demand for power in PPC's area will increase due to the addition of a large housing development and a shopping center. The marketing department estimates that residential demand will increase by almost 50% and commercial demand will increase by 10% during the next year. Since the BD is currently operating at full capacity, it needs to find ways to create capacity to service the expected increase in demand. A local service bureau has offered to take over the BD functions at an attractive lower cost (compared to the current cost). The service bureau's proposal is to provide all the functions of the BD at $3.50 per account regardless of the type of account.

Figure 7-11 depicts the residential and commercial customer classes (cost objects) and the resources used to support the BD. The costs associated with the BD are all indirect—they cannot be identified specifically and exclusively with either customer class in an economically feasible way. The BD used a traditional costing system that allocated all support costs based on the number of account inquiries of the two customer classes. Figure 7-11 shows that the cost of the resources used in the BD last month was $565,340. BD received 23,000 account inquiries during the month, so the cost per inquiry was $565,340 ÷ 23,000 = $24.58. There were 18,000 residential account inquiries, 78.26% of the total. Thus residential accounts were charged with 78.26% of the support costs while commercial accounts were charged with 21.74%. The resulting cost per account is $3.69 and $6.15 for residential and commercial accounts, respectively.

Management believed that the actual consumption of support resources was much greater than 22% for commercial accounts because of their complexity. For example, commercial accounts average 50 lines per bill compared with only 12 for residential accounts. Management was also concerned about activities such as correspondence (and supporting labor) resulting from customer inquiries because these activities are costly but do not add value to PPC's services from the customer's perspective. However, management wanted a more thorough understanding of key BD activities and their interrelationships before making important decisions that would impact PPC's profitability. The company decided to perform a study of the BD using activity-based costing. The following is a description of the study and its results.

The activity-based-costing study was performed by a team of managers from the BD and the chief financial officer from PPC. The team followed a four-step procedure to conduct the study.

Step 1: Determine cost objectives, key activities centers, resources, and related cost drivers. Management had set the objective for the study—determine the BD cost per account for each customer class. The team identified the following activities, and related cost drivers for the BD through interviews with appropriate personnel.

---

[3]Much of the discussion in this section is based on an illustration used in "Implementing Activity-Based Costing—The Modeling Approach," a workshop sponsored by the Institute of Management Accountants and Sapling Corporation.

Current Costing Based on One Overall Rate – Total Cost $565,340

Telecommunications
$58,520

Computer
$178,000

Supervisors
$33,600

Paper
$7,320

Occupancy
$47,000

Account Inquiry Labor
$118,400

Printing Machines
$55,000

Billing Labor
$67,500

Number of Inquiries = 23,000

18,000 (78.26%)   5,000 (21.74%)

Residential Accounts
$442,440

Commercial Accounts
$122,900

	Cost/Inquiry $565,340/23,000 (1)	# Inquiries (2)	Total Cost (1) x (2)	# Accounts (3)	Cost/Account (1)x(2)÷(3)
Residential	$24.58	18,000	442,440	120,000	$3.69
Commercial	$24.58	5,000	122,900	20,000	$6.15

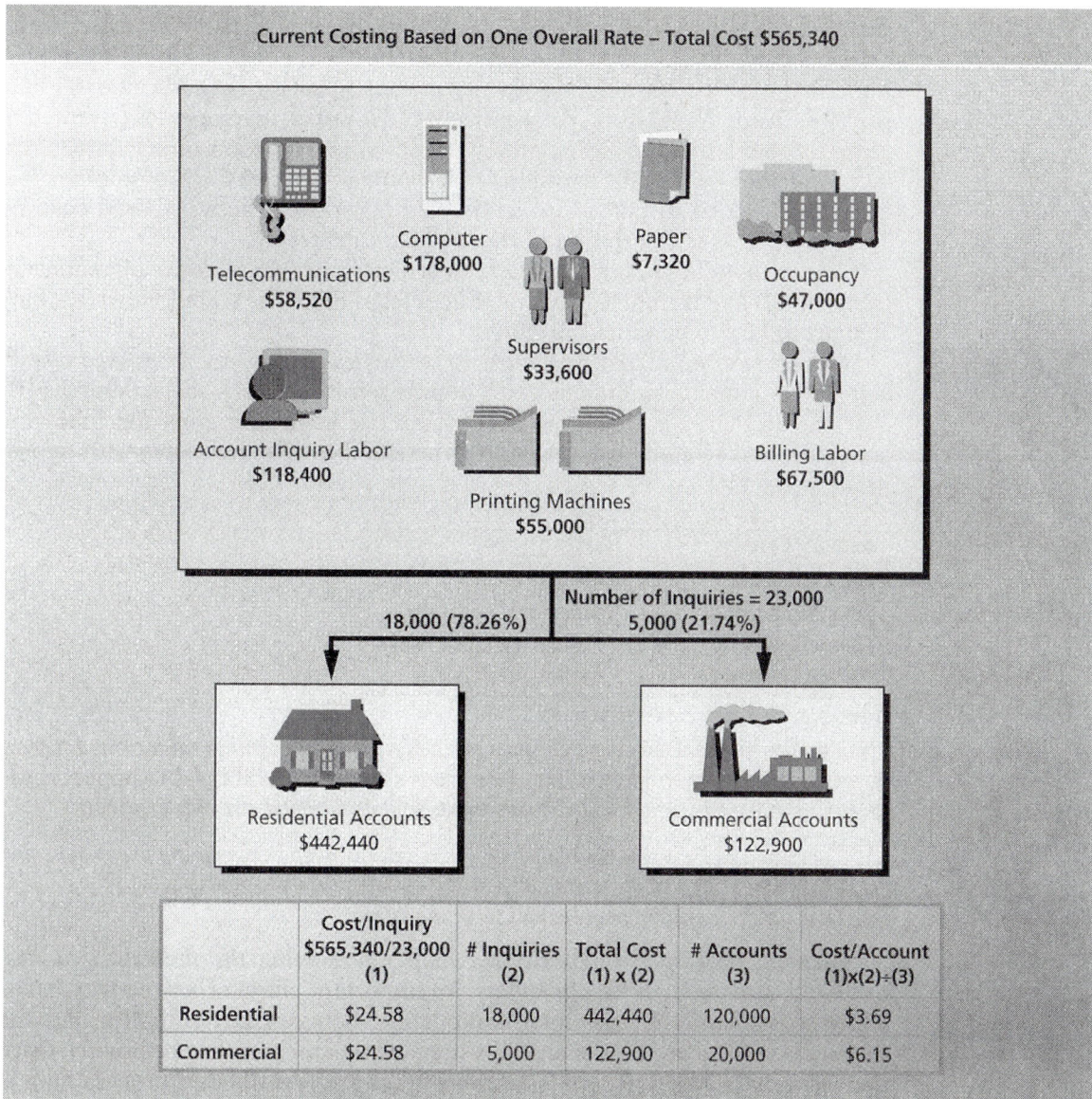

FIGURE 7-11
Current (Traditional) Costing System: Portland Power Company—Billing Department

Activity Centers	Cost Drivers
Account billing	Number of lines
Bill verification	Number of accounts
Account inquiry	Number of labor hours
Correspondence	Number of letters

The four key BD activity centers are *account billing, bill verification, account inquiry,* and *correspondence.* The resources shown in Figure 7-11 support these major activity centers. Cost drivers were selected based on two criteria:

1. There had to be a reasonable cause-effect relationship between the driver unit and the consumption of resources and/or the occurrence of supporting activities.
2. Data on the cost-driver units had to be available.

Step 2: Develop a process-based map representing the flow of activities, resources, and their interrelationships. An important phase of any activity-based analysis is identifying the interrelationships between key activities and the resources consumed. This is typically done by interviewing key personnel. Once the linkages between activities and resources are identified, a process map is drawn that provides a visual representation of the operations of the BD.

Figure 7-12 is a process map that depicts the flow of activities and resources at the BD.[4] Note that there are no costs on Figure 7-12. The management team first focused on understanding business processes. Costs were not considered until Step 3, after the key interrelationships of the business were understood.

Consider residential accounts. Three key activities support these accounts: account inquiry, correspondence, and account billing. Account inquiry activity consumes account inquiry labor time. Account inquiry laborers, in turn, use telecommunication and computer resources, occupy space, and are supervised. Correspondence is sometimes necessary as a result of inquiries. This activity requires account inquiry laborers who are supervised. The account billing activity is performed by billing laborers using printing machines. The printing machines occupy space and require paper and computer resources. Billing laborers also occupy space, use telecommunications, and are supervised. The costs of each of the resources consumed were determined during Step 3—data collection.

Step 3: Collect relevant data concerning costs and the physical flow of the cost-driver units among resources and activities. Using the process map as a guide, BD accountants collected the required cost and operational data by further interviews with relevant personnel. Sources of data include the accounting records, special studies, and sometimes "best estimates of managers."

Figure 7-13 is a graphical representation of the data collected for the four activity centers identified in Step 1. For each activity center, data collected included traceable costs and the physical flow of cost-driver units. For example, Figure 7-13 shows traceable costs of $235,777 for the account billing activity. Traceable costs include the costs of the printing machines ($55,000 from Figure 7-11) plus portions of the costs of all other resources that support the billing activity (paper, occupancy, computer, and billing labor). Notice that the total traceable costs of $205,332 + $35,384 + $235,777 + $88,847 = $565,340 in Figure 7-13 equals the total indirect costs in Figure 7-11. Next, the physical flow of cost-driver units was determined for each activity or cost object. For each activity center, the traceable costs were divided by the sum of the physical flows to establish a cost per cost-driver unit.

---

[4]This example illustrates the process-based modeling approach to activity-based costing. For a more detailed description of the process modeling approach see Raef A. Lawson, "Beyond ABC: Process-Based Costing," *Journal of Cost Management*, Vol. 8, No. 3 (Fall 1994), pp. 33–43. Also, for a discussion of how one major firm used process-based costing to implement ABC in its billing center, see T. Hobdy, J. Thomson, and P. Sharman, "Activity-Based Management at AT&T," *Management Accounting* (April 1994), pp. 35–39.

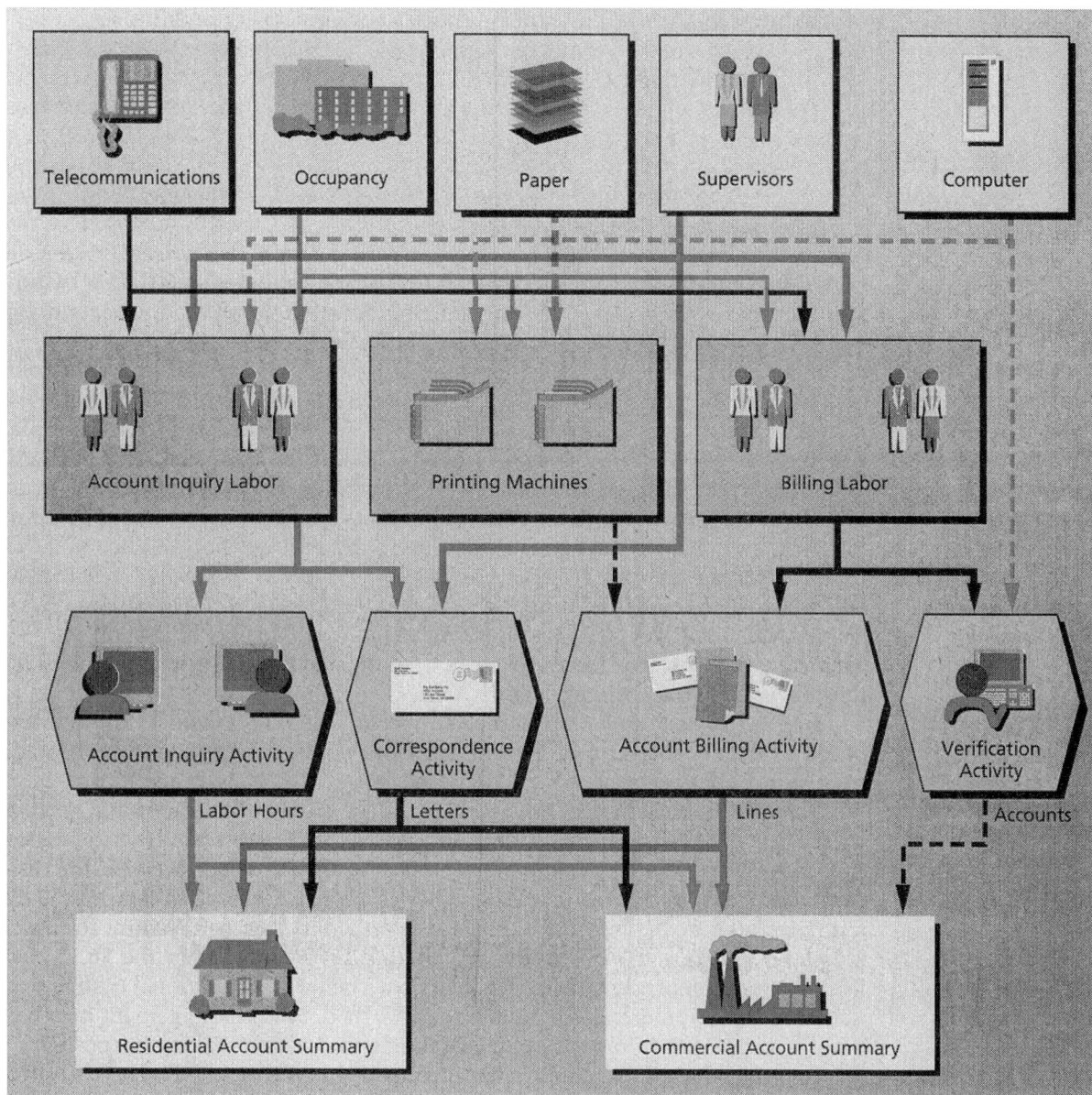

FIGURE 7-12
Process Map of Billing Department Activities

Step 4: Calculate and interpret the new activity-based information.   The activity-based cost per account for each customer class can be determined from the data in Step 3. Figure 7-14 shows the computations.

Examine the last two items in Figure 7-14. Notice that traditional costing overcosted the high-volume residential accounts and substantially undercosted the low-volume, complex commercial accounts. The cost per account for residential accounts using ABC is $2.28, which is $1.41 (or 38%) less than the $3.69 cost generated

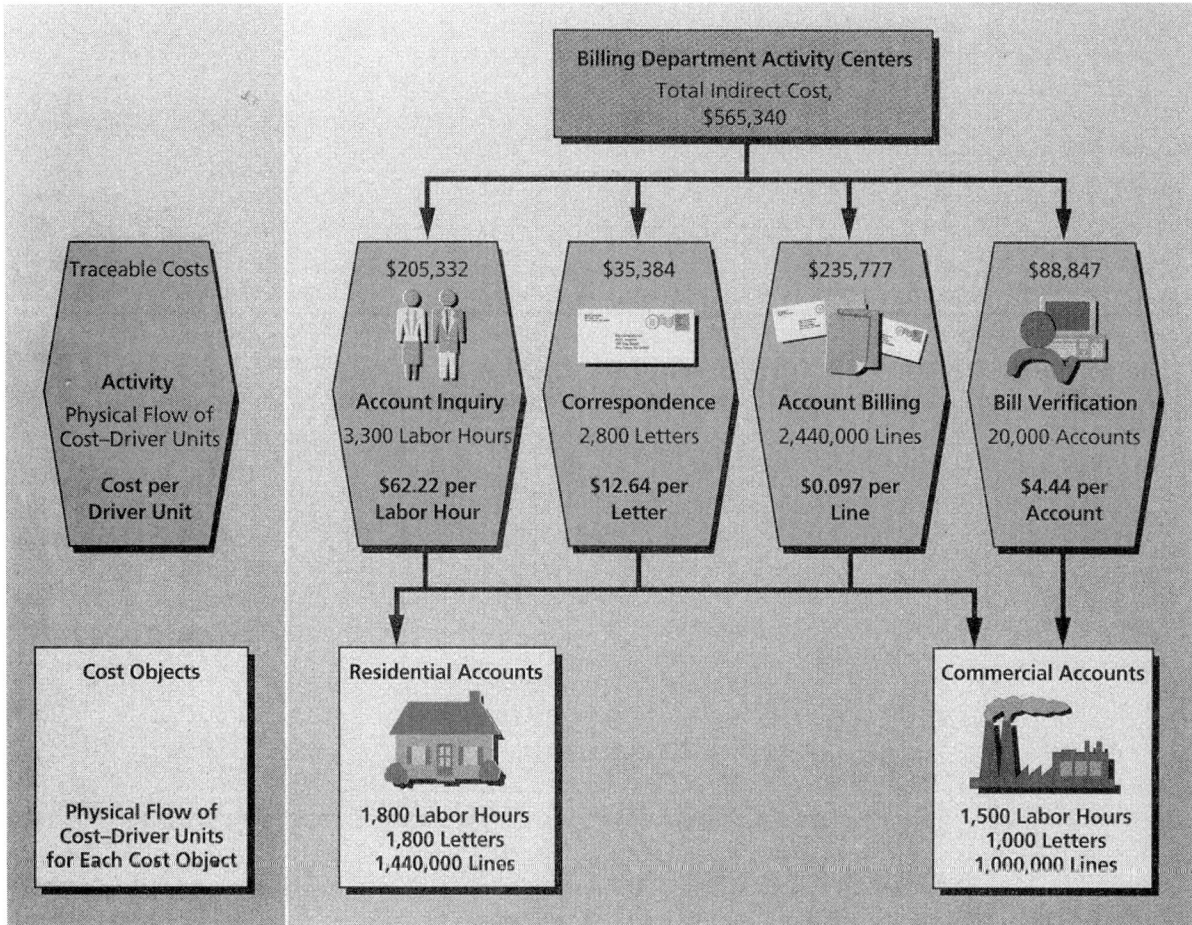

FIGURE 7-13
ABC System: Portland Power Company—Billing Department

by the traditional costing system. The cost per account for commercial accounts is $14.57, which is $8.42 (or 137%) more than the $6.15 cost from the traditional cost system. Management's belief that traditional costing was undercoating commercial accounts was confirmed. PPC's management now has more accurate cost information for planning and decision-making purposes.

These results are common when companies perform activity-based-costing studies—high volume cost objects with simple processes are overcosted when only one volume-based cost driver is used. In the BD, this volume-based cost-driver was the number of inquiries. Which system makes more sense—the existing allocation system that "spreads" all support costs to customer classes based solely on the number of inquiries, or the activity-based-costing system that identifies key activities and assigns costs based on the consumption of units of cost drivers chosen for each key activity? For PPC, the probable benefits of the new activity-based-costing system appear to outweigh the costs of implementing and maintaining the new cost system. However, the cost-benefit balance must be assessed on a case-by-case basis.

FIGURE 7-14   Key Results of Activity-Based-Costing Study

Driver Costs

Activity/Resource (Driver Units)	Traceable Costs (From Figure 7-13) (1)	Total Physical Flow of Driver Units (From Figure 7-13) (2)	Cost per Driver Unit (1)÷(2)
Account inquiry (labor hours)	$205,332	3,300 Hours	$62.2218
Correspondence (letters)	35,384	2,800 Letters	12.6371
Account billing (lines)	235,777	2,440,000 Lines	0.09663
Bill verification (accounts)	88,847	20,000 Accounts	4.44235

Cost per Customer Class

		Residential		Commercial	
	Cost per Driver Unit	Physical Flow of Driver Units	Cost	Physical Flow of Driver Units	Cost
Account inquiry	$62.2218	1,800 Hrs.	$111,999	1,500 Hrs.	$ 93,333
Correspondence	$12.6371	1,800 Ltrs.	22,747	1,000 Ltrs.	12,637
Account billing	$0.09663	1,440,000 Lines	139,147	1,000,000 Lines	96,630
Bill verification	$4.44235	0	0	20,000 Accts.	88,847
Total cost			$273,893		$291,447
Number of accounts			120,000		20,000
Cost per account			$ 2.28		$ 14.57
Cost per account, traditional system from Figure 7-11			$ 3.69		$ 6.15

Summary of Activity-Based Costing

Activity-based accounting systems can turn many indirect manufacturing overhead costs into direct costs, costs identified specifically with given cost objectives. Appropriate selection of activities and cost drivers allows managers to trace many manufacturing overhead costs to cost objectives just as specifically as they have traced direct-material and direct-labor costs. Because activity-based accounting systems classify more costs as direct than do traditional systems, managers have greater confidence in the accuracy of the costs of products and services reported by activity-based systems.

Activity-based accounting systems are more complex and costly than traditional systems, so not all companies use them. But more and more organizations in both manufacturing and nonmanufacturing industries are adopting activity-based systems for a variety of reasons:

- Fierce competitive pressure has resulted in shrinking profit margins. Companies may know their overall margin, but they often do not believe in the accuracy of the margins for *individual* products or services. Some are winners and some are losers—but which ones? Accurate costs are essential for answering this question.

- Business complexity has increased, which results in greater diversity in the types of products and services as well as customer classes. Therefore, the consumption of a company's shared resources also varies substantially across products and customers.
- New production techniques have increased the proportion of indirect costs—that is, indirect costs are far more important in today's world-class manufacturing environment. In many industries direct labor is being replaced by automated equipment. Indirect costs are sometimes over 50% of total cost.
- The rapid pace of technological change has shortened product life cycles. Hence, companies do not have time to make price or cost adjustments once costing errors are discovered.
- The costs associated with bad decisions that result from inaccurate cost determinations are substantial (bids lost due to overcosted products, hidden losses from undercosted products, failure to detect activities that are not cost effective, etc.). Companies with accurate costs have a huge advantage over those with inaccurate costs.
- Computer technology has reduced the costs of developing and operating cost systems that track many activities.

Cost-Management Systems and Value-Added Costing

To support managers' decisions better, accountants go beyond simply determining the cost of products and services. They develop cost-management systems. A **cost-management system** identifies how management's decisions affect costs. To do so, it first measures the resources used in performing the organization's activities and then assesses the effects on costs of changes in those activities.

The cornerstone of cost management is distinguishing between value-added costs and non-value-added costs. A **value-added cost** is the cost of an activity that cannot be eliminated without affecting a product's value to the customer. Value-added costs are necessary (as long as the activity that drives such costs is performed efficiently). In contrast, companies try to minimize **non-value-added costs,** costs that *can* be eliminated without affecting a product's value to the customer. Activities such as handling and storing inventories, transporting partly finished products from one part of the plant to another, and changing the setup of production-line operations to produce a different model of the product are all non-value-adding activities that can be reduced, if not eliminated, by careful redesign of the plant layout and the production process. Often accounting is regarded as a non-value-adding activity. Although it cannot be eliminated, organizations should be sure that the benefits derived from accounting information exceed the costs.

JIT Systems

Attempts to minimize non-value-added costs have led many organizations to adopt JIT systems to eliminate waste and improve quality. In a **just-in-time (JIT) production system,** an organization purchases materials and parts and produces components *just* when they are needed in the production process. Goods are not produced until it is time for them to be shipped to a customer. The goal is to have zero inventory, because holding inventory is a non-value-added activity.

JIT companies are customer-oriented because customer orders drive the production process. An order triggers the immediate delivery of materials, followed by production and delivery of the goods. Instead of producing inventory and hoping an order will come, a JIT system produces products directly for received orders. Several factors are crucial to the success of JIT systems:

1. *Focus on quality:* JIT companies try to involve all employees in controlling quality. Although any system can seek quality improvements, JIT systems emphasize *total quality control (TQC)* and *continuous improvement in quality.* Having all employees striving for zero defects minimizes non-value-added activities such as inspection and rework for defective items.

2. *Short* **production cycle times,** *the time from initiating production to delivering the goods to the customer:* Keeping production cycle times short allows timely response to customer orders and reduces the level of inventories. Many JIT companies have achieved remarkable reductions in production cycle times. For example, applying JIT methods in one AT&T division cut production cycle time by a factor of 12.

3. *Smooth flow of production:* Fluctuations in production rates inevitably lead to delays in delivery to customers and excess inventories. To achieve smooth production flow, JIT companies simplify the production process to reduce the possibilities of delay, develop close relationships with suppliers to assure timely delivery and high quality of purchased materials, and perform routine maintenance on equipment to prevent costly breakdowns.

   Many companies help achieve these objectives by improving the physical layout of their plants. In conventional manufacturing, similar machines (lathes, molding machines, drilling machines, etc.) are grouped together. Workers specialize in only one machine operation (operating either the molding or the drilling machine). There are at least two negative effects of such a layout. First, products must be moved from one area of the plant to another for required processing. This increases material handling costs and results in work-in-process inventories that can be substantial. These are non-value-added activities and costs. Second, the specialized labor resource is often idle—waiting for work-in-process. This wasted resource—labor time—is also non-value-added.

   In a JIT production system, machines are often organized in cells according to the specific requirements of a product family. This is called **cellular manufacturing.** Only the machines that are needed for the product family are in the cell, and these machines are located as close to each other as possible. Workers are trained to use all the cellular machines. Each cell (often shaped in the form of a "U") is a mini-factory or focused factory. Many problems associated with the conventional production layout are eliminated in cellular manufacturing. Work-in-process inventories are reduced or eliminated because there is no need for moving and storing inventory. Idle time is reduced or eliminated because workers are capable of moving from idle machine activity to needed activities. As a result, cycle times are reduced.

4. *Flexible production operations:* Two dimensions are important: facilities flexibility and employee flexibility. Facilities should be able to produce a variety of components and products to provide extra capacity when a particular product is in high demand and to avoid shut-down when a unique facility breaks down. Facilities should also require short setup times, the time it takes to switch from producing one product to another. Cross-training employees—training employ-

ees to do a variety of jobs—provides further flexibility. Multiskilled workers can fill in when a particular operation is overloaded and can reduce setup time. One company reported a reduction in setup time from 45 minutes to 1 minute by training production workers to perform the setup operations.

Accounting for a JIT system is often simpler than for other systems. Most cost accounting systems focus on determining product costs for inventory valuation. But JIT systems have minimal inventories, so there is less benefit from an elaborate inventory costing system. In true JIT systems, material, labor, and overhead costs can be charged directly to cost of goods sold because inventories are small enough to be ignored. All costs of production are assumed to apply to products that have already been sold.

SUMMARY

Many new terms were introduced in this chapter. Review those in bold print to make sure you know their exact meaning. Basic terms, such as cost, cost objective, cost accumulation, and cost allocation are especially important.

A major feature of costs for both manufacturing and nonmanufacturing organizations is whether the costs have a direct or an indirect relationship to cost objectives such as a department or product. Manufacturing costs (direct material, direct labor, and factory overhead) are traditionally regarded as product costs (inventoriable costs). In contrast, selling and administrative costs are period costs; hence they are typically deducted from revenue as expenses in the period incurred.

Financial statements for manufacturers differ from those of merchandisers. Costs such as utilities, wages, and depreciation, which are treated as period costs by a merchandising company, are product costs (part of factory overhead) for a manufacturing company if they are related to the manufacturing process. Balance sheets of manufacturers may include three inventory accounts: direct materials, work in process, and finished goods.

The contribution approach to preparing an income statement emphasizes the distinction between fixed and variable costs, and is a natural extension of the CVP analysis used in decisions. In contrast, the absorption approach emphasizes the distinction between manufacturing costs and selling and administrative costs.

Activity-based costing (ABC) and just-in-time (JIT) production systems are two approaches used by modern companies to improve their competitiveness. The focus of activity-based costing is on more accurate product or service costing. Management can then use ABC information to manage costs better. To manage costs, they try to eliminate non-value-added activities. The JIT approach focuses on improving operating efficiencies by reducing waste. JIT and ABC can be used separately or together—many modern companies use both.

SELF-CORRECTION PROBLEMS

1. Review the illustrations in Figures 7-6 through 7-9. Suppose that all variable costs fluctuate in direct proportion to units produced and sold, and that all fixed costs are unaffected over a wide range of production and sales. What would operating income have been if sales (at normal selling prices) had been $20.9 million instead of $20.0 million? Which statement, the absorption income statement or the contribution income statement, did you use as a framework for your answer? Why?

2. Suppose employee training (Figure 7-6) was regarded as a variable rather than a fixed cost at a rate of $90,000 ÷ 1,000,000 units, or $.09 per unit. How would your answer in question 1 change?

SOLUTIONS TO SELF-CORRECTION PROBLEMS

1. Operating income would increase from $1,000,000 to $1,310,500, computed as follows:

Increase in revenue	$ 900,000
Increase in total contribution margin:	
Contribution-margin ratio in contribution income statement	
(Figure 7-9) is $6,900,000 ÷ $20,000,000 = .345	
Ratio times revenue increase is .345 × $900,000	$ 310,500
Increase in fixed expenses	–0–
Operating income before increase	1,000,000
New operating income	$1,310,500

Computations are easily made by using data from the contribution income statement. In contrast, the traditional absorption costing income statement must be analyzed and divided into variable and fixed categories before the effect on operating income can be estimated.

2. The original contribution-margin ratio would be lower because the variable costs would be higher by $.09 per unit: ($6,900,000 − $90,000) ÷ $20,000,000 = .3405.

	Given Level	Higher Level	Difference
Revenue	$20,000,000	$20,900,000	$900,000
Variable expense ($13,100,000 + $90,000)	13,190,000	13,783,550	593,550
Contribution margin at .3405	$ 6,810,000	$ 7,116,450	$306,450
Fixed expenses ($5,900,000 − $90,000)	5,810,000	5,810,000	—
Operating income	$ 1,000,000	$1,306,450	$306,450

QUESTIONS

1. Name four cost objectives or cost objects.
2. "Departments are not cost objects or objects of costing." Do you agree? Explain.
3. What is the major purpose of detailed cost-accounting systems?
4. "The same cost can be direct and indirect." Do you agree? Explain.
5. "Economic feasibility is an important guideline in designing cost-accounting systems." Do you agree? Explain.
6. How does the idea of economic feasibility relate to the distinction between direct and indirect costs?
7. "The typical accounting system does not allocate selling and administrative costs to units produced." Do you agree? Explain.
8. Distinguish between prime costs and conversion costs.
9. "For a furniture manufacturer, glue or tacks become an integral part of the finished product, so they would be direct material." Do you agree? Explain.
10. Many cost-accounting systems have a twofold instead of a threefold category of manufacturing costs. What are the items in the twofold category?
11. "Depreciation is an expense for financial statement purposes." Do you agree? Explain.
12. Distinguish between "costs" and "expenses."
13. "Unexpired costs are always inventory costs." Do you agree? Explain.
14. "Advertising is noninventoriable." Explain.
15. Why is there no direct-labor inventory account on a manufacturing company's balance sheet?
16. What is the advantage of the contribution approach as compared with the absorption approach?
17. Distinguish between manufacturing and merchandising companies.
18. "The primary classifications of costs are by variable- and fixed-cost behavior patterns, not by business functions." Name three commonly used terms that describe this type of income statement.
19. Name 4 steps in the design and implementation of an activity-based-costing system.
20. Refer to the Portland Power Company illustration in Figure 7-11. Which BD resource costs depicted in Figure 7-11 would have variable cost behavior?
21. Why are more and more organizations adopting activity-based-costing systems?
22. Why do managers want to distinguish between value-added activities and non-value-added activities?
23. Name four factors crucial to the success of JIT production systems.
24. "ABC and JIT are alternative techniques for achieving competitiveness." Do you agree?

PROBLEMS

1. **Straightforward Income Statement.**   The Goldsmith Company had the following manufacturing data for the year 19X6 (in thousands of dollars):

Beginning and ending inventories	None
Direct material used	$425
Direct labor	350
Supplies	20
Utilities—variable portion	45
Utilities—fixed portion	15
Indirect labor—variable portion	100
Indirect labor—fixed portion	50
Depreciation	110
Property taxes	20
Supervisory salaries	50

Selling expenses were $325,000 (including $70,000 that were variable) and general administrative expenses were $148,000 (including $24,000 that were variable). Sales were $1.9 million.

Direct labor and supplies are regarded as variable costs.

a. Prepare two income statements, one using the contribution approach and one using the absorption approach.
b. Suppose that all variable costs fluctuate directly in proportion to sales, and that fixed costs are unaffected over a very wide range of sales. What would operating income have been if sales had been $2.2 million instead of $1.9 million? Which income statement did you use to help obtain your answer? Why?

2. **Meaning of Technical Terms.**   Refer to the absorption income statement of your solution to the preceding problem. Give the amounts of the following: (a) prime cost, (b) conversion cost, (c) factory burden, (d) factory overhead, and (e) manufacturing overhead.

3. **Activity-Based Costing.**   Quality Machining Products (QMP) is an automotive component supplier. QMP has been approached by General Motors to consider expanding its production of part G108 to a total annual quantity of 2,000 units. This part is a low-volume, complex product with a high gross margin that is based on a proposed (quoted) unit sales price of $7.50. QMP uses a traditional costing system that allocates factory-overhead costs based on direct-labor costs. The rate currently used to allocate factory-overhead costs is 400% of direct-labor cost. This rate is based on the $3,300,000 annual factory overhead divided by $825,000 annual direct-labor cost. To produce 2,000 units of G108 requires $5,000 of direct materials and $1,000 of direct labor. The unit cost and gross margin percentage for Part G108 based on the traditional cost system are computed as follows:

	Total	Per Unit (÷ 2,000)
Direct material	$5,000	$2.50
Direct labor	1,000	.50
Factory overhead:		
[400% × direct labor]	4,000	2.00
Total cost	$10,000	$5.00
Sales price quoted		7.50
Gross margin		$2.50
Gross margin percentage		33.3%

The management of QMP decided to examine the effectiveness of their traditional costing system versus an activity-based-costing system. The following data have been collected by a team consisting of accounting and engineering analysts:

Activity Center	Traceable Factory Overhead Costs (Annual)
Quality	$ 800,000
Production scheduling	50,000
Setup	600,000
Shipping	300,000
Shipping administration	50,000
Production	1,500,000
Total factory overhead cost	$3,300,000

Activity Center: Cost Drivers	Annual Cost-Driver Quantity
Quality: number of pieces scrapped	10,000
Production scheduling and setup:	
number of setups	500
Shipping: number of containers shipped	60,000
Shipping administration: number of shipments	1,000
Production: number of machine hours	10,000

The accounting and engineering team has performed activity analysis and provides the following estimates for the total quantity of cost drivers to be used to produce 2,000 units of part G108:

Cost Driver	Cost-Driver Consumption
Pieces scrapped	120
Setups	4
Containers shipped	10
Shipments	5
Machine hours	15

a. Prepare a schedule calculating the unit cost and gross margin of Part G108 using the activity-based-costing approach.

b. Based on the ABC results, which course of action would you recommend regarding the proposal by General Motors? List the benefits and costs associated with implementing an activity-based-costing system at QMP.

4. **Contribution and Absorption Income Statements.** The following information is taken from the records of the Queensland Company for the year ending December 31, 19X5. There were no beginning or ending inventories.

Sales	$11,000,000	Long-term rent, factory	$ 110,000
Sales commissions	550,000	Factory superintendent's	
Advertising	225,000	salary	32,000
Shipping expenses	310,000	Supervisors' salaries	105,000
Administrative executive		Direct material used	4,100,000
salaries	100,000	Direct labor	2,200,000
Administrative clerical		Cutting bits used	60,000
salaries (variable)	450,000	Factory methods research	40,000
Fire insurance on		Abrasives for machining	100,000
factory equipment	2,000	Indirect labor	810,000
Property taxes on		Depreciation on	
factory equipment	10,000	equipment	300,000

a. Prepare a contribution income statement and an absorption income statement. If you are in doubt about any cost behavior pattern, decide on the basis of whether the total cost in question will fluctuate substantially over a wide range of volume. Prepare a separate supporting schedule of indirect manufacturing costs subdivided between variable and fixed costs.

b. Suppose that all variable costs fluctuate directly in proportion to sales, and that fixed costs are unaffected over a wide range of sales. What would operating income have been if sales had been $12.5 million instead of $11 million? Which income statement did you use to help get your answer? Why?

5. **JIT and Non-value-Added Activities.** A motorcycle manufacturer was concerned with declining market share because of foreign competition. To become more efficient, the company was considering changing to a JIT production system. As a first step in analyzing the feasibility of the change, the company identified its major activities. Among the 120 activities were the following:

Materials receiving and inspection
Production scheduling
Production setup
Rear-wheel assembly
Movement of engine from fabrication to assembly building
Assembly of handlebars
Paint inspection
Reworking of defective brake assemblies
Installation of speedometer
Placement of completed motorcycle in finished goods storage

a. From the preceding list of 10 activities, prepare two lists: one of value-added activities and one of non-value-added activities.
b. For each non-value-added activity, explain how a JIT production system might eliminate, or at least reduce, the cost of the activity.

6. **Activity-Based Costing.** The cordless phone manufacturing division of a consumer electronics company uses activity-based accounting. For simplicity, assume that its accountants have identified only the following three activities and related cost drivers for manufacturing overhead:

Activity	Cost Driver
Materials handling	Direct materials cost
Engineering	Engineering change notices
Power	Kilowatt hours

Three types of cordless phones are produced: CL3, CL5, and CL9. Direct costs and cost-driver activity for each product for a recent month are as follows:

	CL3	CL5	CL9
Direct materials cost	$25,000	$ 50,000	$125,000
Direct labor cost	$4,000	$1,000	$3,000
Kilowatt hours	50,000	200,000	150,000
Engineering change notices	13	5	2

Manufacturing overhead for the month was:

Materials handling	$10,000
Engineering	30,000
Power	24,000
Total manufacturing overhead	**$64,000**

a. Compute the manufacturing overhead allocated to each product with the activity-based accounting system.
b. Suppose all manufacturing overhead costs had been allocated to products in proportion to their direct-labor costs. Compute the manufacturing overhead allocated to each product.
c. In which product costs, those in part a or those in part b, do you have the most confidence? Why?

ADDENDUM 7: MORE ON LABOR COSTS

Classifications of Labor Costs

The terms used to classify labor costs are often confusing. Each organization seems to develop its own interpretation of various labor-cost classifications. We begin by considering some commonly encountered labor-cost terms:

- Direct labor (already defined)
- Factory overhead (examples of prominent labor components of these indirect manufacturing costs follow)
    - Indirect labor (wages)
        - Forklift truck operators (internal handling of materials)
        - Maintenance (to set up for production runs)
        - Janitors
        - Expediting (overseeing special orders, usually on a rush basis)
        - Plant guards
        - Rework labor (time spent by direct laborers redoing defective work)
        - Overtime premium paid to all factory workers
        - Idle time
    - Managers' salaries
    - Payroll fringe costs (for example, health care premiums, pension costs)

All factory labor wages, other than those for direct labor and manager salaries, are usually classified as **indirect labor** costs, a major component of factory overhead. The term *indirect labor* is usually divided into many subsidiary classifications. The wages of forklift truck operators are generally not commingled with janitors' salaries, for example, although both are regarded as indirect labor.

Costs are classified in a detailed fashion primarily to associate a specific cost with its specific cost driver. Two classes of indirect labor deserve special mention: overtime premium and idle time.

Overtime premium paid to all factory workers is usually considered a part of overhead. If a lathe operator earns $8 per hour for straight time and time and one-half for overtime, the premium is $4 per overtime hour. If the operator works 44 hours, including 4 overtime hours, in 1 week, the gross earnings are classified as follows:

Direct labor: 44 hours × $8	$352
Overtime premium (factory overhead): 4 hours × $4	16
Total earnings for 44 hours	**$368**

Why is overtime premium considered an indirect cost rather than direct? After all, it can usually be traced to specific batches of work. It is usually not considered a direct charge because the scheduling of production jobs is generally random. Suppose that at 8:00 A.M. you bring your automobile to a shop for repair. Through random scheduling, your auto is repaired between 5:00 and 6:00 P.M., when technicians receive overtime pay. Then, when you come to get your car, you learn that all the overtime premium had been added to your bill. You probably would not be overjoyed.

Thus, in most companies, the overtime premium is not allocated to any specific job. Instead, the overtime premium is considered to be attributable to the heavy overall volume of work, and its cost is thus regarded as part of the indirect manufacturing costs (factory overhead). The latter approach does not penalize a particular batch of work solely because it happened to be worked on during the overtime hours.

Another subsidiary classification of indirect-labor costs is **idle time.** This cost typically represents wages paid for unproductive time caused by machine breakdowns, material shortages, sloppy production scheduling, and the like. For example, if the same lathe operator's machine broke down for 3 hours during the week, the operator's earnings would be classified as follows:

Direct labor: 41 hours × $8	$328
Overtime premium (factory overhead): 4 hours × $4	16
Idle time (factory overhead): 3 hours × $8	24
Total earnings for 44 hours	**$368**

Manager salaries usually are not classified as a part of indirect labor. Instead, the compensation of supervisors, department heads, and all others who are regarded as part of manufacturing management are placed in a separate classification of factory overhead.

Payroll Fringe Costs

A type of labor cost that is growing in importance is **payroll fringe costs** such as employer contributions to employee benefits such as social security, life insurance, health insurance, and pensions. Most companies classify these as factory overhead. In some companies, however, fringe benefits related to direct labor are charged as an additional direct-labor cost. For instance, a direct laborer, such as a lathe operator or an auto mechanic, whose gross wages are computed on the basis of $10 an hour, may enjoy fringe benefits totaling $4 per hour. Most companies classify the $10 as direct-labor cost and the $4 as factory overhead. Other companies classify the entire $14 as direct-labor cost. The latter approach is conceptually preferable because these costs are a fundamental part of acquiring labor services.

Accountants and managers need to pinpoint exactly what direct labor includes and excludes. Such clarity may avoid disputes regarding cost reimbursement contracts, income tax payments, and labor union matters. For example, some countries offer substantial income tax savings to companies that locate factories there. To qualify, these companies' "direct labor" in that country must equal at least a specified percentage of the total manufacturing costs of their products. Disputes have arisen regarding how to calculate the direct-labor percentage for qualifying for such tax relief. Are payroll fringe benefits on direct labor an integral part of direct labor, or are they a part of factory overhead? Depending on how companies classify costs, you can readily see that the two identical firms may show different percentages of total manufacturing costs. Consider a company with $10,000 of payroll fringe costs:

Classification A			Classification B		
Direct materials	$ 80,000	40%	Direct materials	$ 80,000	40%
Direct labor	40,000	20	Direct labor	50,000	25
Factory overhead	80,000	40	Factory overhead	70,000	35
Total manufacturing costs	**$200,000**	**100%**	Total manufacturing costs	**$200,000**	**100%**

Classification A assumes that payroll fringe costs are part of factory overhead. In contrast, Classification B assumes that payroll fringe costs are part of direct labor.

CHAPTER 8

Relevant Accounting Information Used to Make Marketing Decisions

What price should a Safeway store charge for a pound of hamburger? What should Boeing charge for a 757 airplane? Should a clothing manufacturer accept a special order from Wal-Mart at a price lower than that generally charged? Should an appliance manufacturer add a new product, say an automatic bread maker, to its product line? Or should an existing product be dropped? Which product makes best use of a particular limited resource? All these questions relate to the marketing strategy of a firm, in which accounting information plays an important role.

At the start of this book, we emphasized that the purpose of management accounting is to provide information that enables managers to make sound decisions. In this chapter and the next we focus on identifying *relevant information* for particular management decisions, with this chapter focusing primarily on marketing decisions. Although the word "relevant" has been much overworked in recent years, the ability to separate relevant from irrelevant information is often the difference between success and failure in modern business.

MEANING OF RELEVANCE: THE MAJOR CONCEPTUAL LESSON

What information is relevant depends on the decision being made. Decision making is essentially choosing among several courses of action. The available actions are determined by an often time-consuming formal or informal search and screening process, perhaps carried on by a company team that includes engineers, accountants, and operating executives. Accountants have an important role in the decision-making process, not as decision makers but as collectors and reporters of relevant information. (Although many managers want the accountant to recommend the proper decision, the final choice always rests with the operating executive.) The accountant's role in decision making is primarily that of a technical expert on financial analysis who helps managers focus on relevant data, information that will lead to the best decision.

Relevance Defined

In the final stages of the decision-making process, managers compare two or more alternative courses of action. The decision is based on the predicted difference in future performance under each alternative. The key question is: What difference will the choice make? **Relevant information** is the predicted future costs and revenues that will differ among the alternatives.

Note that relevant information is a prediction of the future, not a summary of the past. Historical (past) data have no *direct* bearing on a decision. Such data can have an *indirect* bearing on a decision because they may help in predicting the future. But past figures, in themselves, are irrelevant to the decision itself. Why? Because the decision cannot affect past data. Decisions affect the future. Nothing can alter what has already happened.

Of the expected future data, only those that will differ from alternative to alternative are relevant to the decision. Any item that will remain the same regardless of the alternative selected is irrelevant. For instance, if a department manager's salary will be the same regardless of the products stocked, the salary is irrelevant to the selection of products.

Accuracy and Relevance

In the best of all possible worlds, information used for decision making would be perfectly relevant *and* accurate. However, in reality, the cost of such information often exceeds its benefit. Accountants often trade relevance for accuracy. Of course, relevant information must be reasonably accurate but not precisely so.

Precise but irrelevant information is worthless for decision making. For example, a university president's salary may be $140,000 per year, to the penny, but may have no bearing on the question of whether to buy or rent data processing equipment. On the other hand, imprecise but relevant information can be useful. For example, sales predictions for a new product may be subject to great error, but they still are helpful to the decision of whether to manufacture the product.

The degree to which information is relevant or precise often depends on the degree to which it is *qualitative* or *quantitative*. Qualitative aspects are those for which measurement in dollars and cents is difficult and imprecise; quantitative aspects are those for which measurement is easy and precise. Accountants, statisticians, and mathematicians try to express as many decision factors as feasible in quantitative terms, because this approach reduces the number of qualitative factors to be judged. Just as we noted that relevance is more crucial than precision in decision making, so a qualitative aspect may easily carry more weight than a measurable (quantitative) financial impact in many decisions. For example, the opposition of a militant union to new labor-saving machinery may cause a manager to defer or even reject completely the contemplated installation even if it would save money. Alternatively, to avoid a long-run dependence on a particular supplier, a company may pass up the opportunity to purchase a component from the supplier at a price below the cost of producing it themselves.

On the other hand, managers sometimes introduce new technology (e.g., advanced computer systems or automated equipment) even though the expected quantitative results seem unattractive. Managers defend such decisions on the grounds that failure to keep abreast of new technology will surely bring unfavorable financial results sooner or later.

Examples of Relevance

The following examples will help you clarify the sharp distinctions needed to discriminate between relevant and irrelevant information.

Suppose you always buy gasoline from either of two nearby gasoline stations. Yesterday you noticed that one station was selling gasoline at $1.50 per gallon; the other, at $1.40. Your automobile needs gasoline, and in making your choice of stations, you *assume* that these prices have not changed. The relevant costs are $1.50 and $1.40, the expected future costs that will differ between the alternatives. You use your past experience (i.e., what you observed yesterday) for predicting today's price. Note that the relevant cost is not what you paid in the past, or what you observed yesterday, but what you *expect to pay* when you drive in to get gasoline. This cost meets our two criteria: (1) it is the expected future cost, and (2) it differs between the alternatives.

You may also plan to have your car lubricated. The recent price at each station was $12, and this is what you anticipate paying. This expected future cost is irrelevant because it will be the same under either alternative. It does not meet our second criterion.

On a business level, consider the following decision. A manufacturer is thinking of using aluminum instead of copper in a line of ashtrays. The cost of direct material will decrease from 30¢ to 20¢ per ashtray. The analysis in a nutshell is as follows:

	Aluminum	Copper	Difference
Direct material	$.20	$.30	$.10

The cost of copper used for this comparison probably came from historical cost records on the amount paid most recently for copper, but the *relevant* cost in the foregoing analysis is the expected future cost of copper compared with the expected future cost of aluminum.

The direct-labor cost will continue to be 70¢ per unit regardless of the material used. It is irrelevant because our second criterion—an element of difference between the alternatives—is not met.

	Aluminum	Copper	Difference
Direct material	$.20	$.30	$.10
Direct labor	.70	.70	—

Therefore we can safely exclude direct labor from the comparison of alternatives. There is no harm in including irrelevant items in a formal analysis, provided that they are included properly. However, confining the reports to the relevant items provides greater clarity and time savings for busy managers.

Figure 8-1 provides a more elaborate view of this decision than is necessary for this simple decision, but it serves to show the appropriate framework for more complex decisions. Box 1(A) represents historical data from the accounting system. Box 1(B) represents other data, such as price indices or industry statistics, gathered from outside the accounting system. Regardless of their source, the data in step 1 help the formulation of *predictions* in step 2. (Remember that although historical data may act as a guide to predicting, they are irrelevant to the decision itself.)

In step 3 these predictions become inputs to the *decision model.* A **decision model** is defined as any method for making a choice. Such models often require elaborate quantitative procedures, such as a petroleum refinery's mathematical method for choosing what products to manufacture for any given day or week. A decision model, however, may also be simple. It may be confined to a single comparison of costs for choosing between two materials. In this instance our decision model is: Compare the predicted unit costs and select the alternative with the lesser cost.

We will be referring back to Figure 8-1 frequently because it displays the major conceptual lesson in this chapter. Above all, note the commonality of the relevant-information approach to the various special decisions explored in this chapter. In all decisions managers should focus on predictions of future outcomes, not dwell on past outcomes. The major difficulty is predicting how revenues and costs will be affected under each alternative. No matter what the decision situation, the key question to ask is: What difference will it make?

THE SPECIAL SALES ORDER

The first decision for which we examine relevant information is the special sales order.

Illustrative Example

Figure 8-2 illustrates the primary data from Figures 7-8 and 7-9, two very important general exhibits. As you can see, the two income statements differ somewhat in format. The difference in format may be unimportant if the accompanying cost analysis leads to the same set of decisions. However, these two approaches sometimes lead to different *unit* costs that must be interpreted warily.

In our illustration, suppose 1 million units of product, such as some automobile replacement part, were made and sold. Under the absorption-costing approach, the unit manufacturing cost of the product would be $15,000,000 ÷ 1,000,000, or $15 per

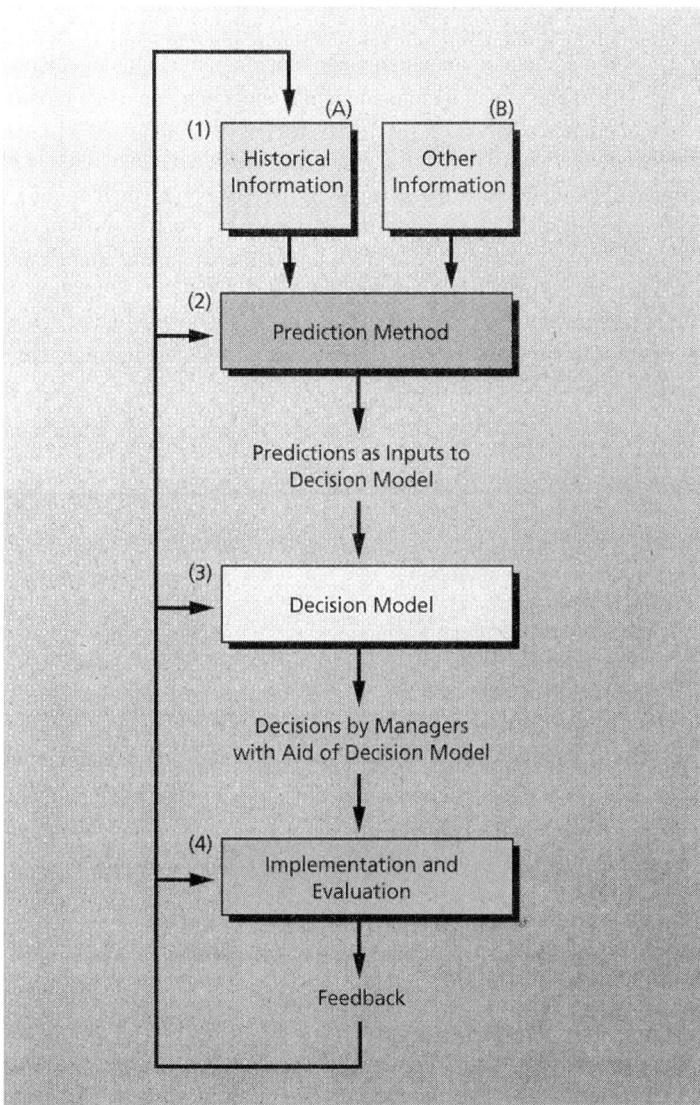

FIGURE 8-1
Decision Process and Role of Information

unit. Suppose a mail-order house near year-end offered Samson $13 per unit for a 100,000-unit special order that (1) would not affect Samson's regular business in any way, (2) would not raise any antitrust issues concerning price discrimination, (3) would not affect total fixed costs, (4) would not require any additional variable selling and administrative expenses, and (5) would use some otherwise idle manufacturing capacity. Should Samson accept the order? Perhaps the question should be stated more sharply: What is the difference in the short-run financial results between not accepting and accepting? As usual, the key question is: What difference will it make?

FIGURE 8-2   Absorption and Contribution Forms of the Income Statement
Samson Company Income Statement for the Year Ended December 31, 19X2
(thousands of dollars)

Absorption Form		Contribution Form		
Sales	$20,000	Sales		$20,000
Less: manufacturing cost		Less: variable expenses		
of goods sold	15,000	Manufacturing	$12,000	
Gross margin or gross profit	$ 5,000	Selling and		
Less: selling and admin-		administrative	1,100	13,100
istrative expenses	4,000	Contribution margin		$ 6,900
Operating income	$ 1,000	Less: fixed expenses		
		Manufacturing	$ 3,000	
		Selling and		
		administrative	2,900	5,900
		Operating income		$ 1,000

Correct Analysis

The correct analysis employs the contribution approach and concentrates on the final *overall* results. As Figure 8-3 shows, only variable manufacturing costs are affected by the particular order, at a rate of $12 per unit. All other variable costs and all fixed costs are unaffected, so a manager may safely ignore them in making this special-order decision. Note how the contribution approach's distinction between variable- and fixed-cost behavior patterns aids the necessary cost analysis. Total short-run income will increase by $100,000 if the order is accepted—despite the fact that the unit selling price of $13 is less than the absorption manufacturing cost of $15.

FIGURE 8-3   Comparative Predicted Income Statements, Contribution Approach
Samson Company for Year Ended December 31, 19X2

	Without Special Order, 1,000,000 units	Effect of Special Order 100,000 units		With Special Order, 1,100,000 Units
		Total	Per Unit	
Sales	$20,000,000	$1,300,000	$13	$21,300,000
Less: variable expenses				
Manufacturing	$12,000,000	$1,200,000	$12	$13,200,000
Selling and administrative	1,100,000	—	—	1,100,000
Total variable expenses	$13,100,000	$1,200,000	$12	$14,300,000
Contribution margin	$ 6,900,000	$ 100,000	$ 1	$ 7,000,000
Less: fixed expenses				
Manufacturing	$ 3,000,000	—	—	$ 3,000,000
Selling and administrative	2,900,000	—	—	2,900,000
Total fixed expenses	$ 5,900,000	—	—	$ 5,900,000
Operating income	$ 1,000,000	$ 100,000	$ 1	$ 1,100,000

Figure 8-3 shows total fixed expenses in the first and last columns. There is no harm in including such irrelevant items in an analysis as long as they are included under every alternative at hand.

A fixed-cost element of an identical amount that is common among all alternatives is essentially irrelevant. Whether irrelevant items should be included in an analysis is a matter of taste, not a matter of right or wrong. However, if irrelevant items are included in an analysis, they should be inserted in a correct manner.

Incorrect Analysis

Faulty cost analysis sometimes occurs because of misinterpreting unit fixed costs. For instance, managers might erroneously use the $15 absorption manufacturing cost per unit to make the following prediction for the year:

Incorrect Analysis	Without Special Order	Incorrect Effect of Special Order	With Special Order
	1,000,000 Units	100,000 Units	1,100,000 Units
Sales	$20,000,000	$1,300,000	$21,300,000
Less: manufacturing cost of goods sold @ $15	15,000,000	1,500,000	16,500,000
Gross margin	5,000,000	(200,000)	4,800,000
Selling and administrative expenses	4,000,000	—	4,000,000
Operating income	$ 1,000,000	$ (200,000)	$ 800,000

The incorrect prediction of a $1.5 million increase in costs results from multiplying 100,000 units by $15. Of course, the fallacy in this approach is that it treats a fixed cost (fixed manufacturing cost) as if it were variable. Avoid the assumption that unit costs may be used indiscriminately as a basis for predicting how total costs will behave. Unit costs are useful for predicting variable costs but often misleading when used to predict fixed costs.

Confusion of Variable and Fixed Costs

Consider the relationship between total fixed manufacturing costs and a fixed manufacturing cost per unit of product:

$$\text{fixed cost per unit of product} = \frac{\text{total fixed manufacturing costs}}{\text{some selected volume level used as the denominator}}$$

$$= \frac{\$3,000,000}{1,000,000 \text{ units}} = \$3 \text{ per unit}$$

The typical cost accounting system serves two purposes simultaneously: *planning and control* and *product costing*. The total fixed cost for *budgetary planning and control purposes* can be graphed as a lump sum:

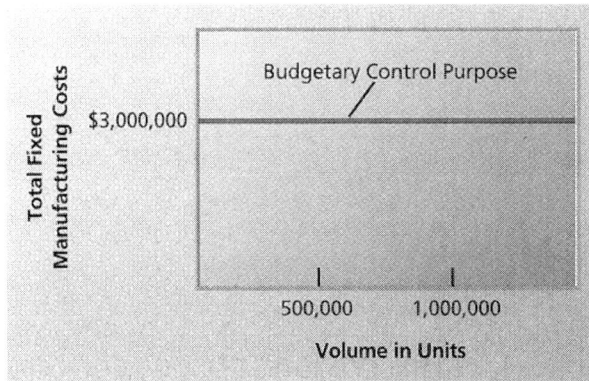

For *product-costing purposes,* however, the absorption-costing approach implies that these *fixed* costs have a *variable*-cost behavior pattern:

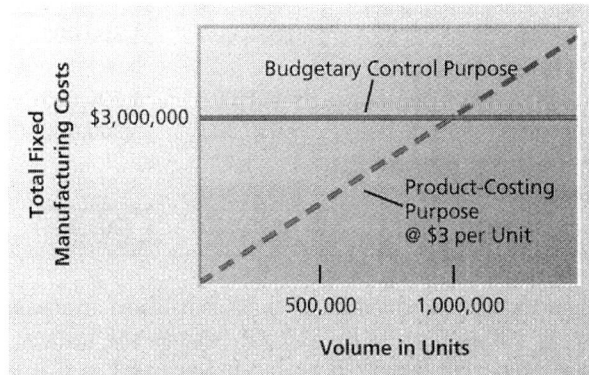

The addition of 100,000 units will not add any *total* fixed costs as long as total output is within the relevant range. The incorrect analysis, however, includes 100,000 × $3 = $300,000 of fixed cost in the predictions of increases in total costs.

In short, the increase in manufacturing costs should be computed by multiplying 1,000,000 units by $12, not by $15. The $15 includes a $3 component that will not affect the total manufacturing costs as volume changes.

Spreading Fixed Costs

As you have just seen, the distinction between unit cost and total cost can become particularly troublesome when analyzing fixed-cost behavior. Assume the same facts concerning the special order as before, except that the order was for 250,000 units at a selling price of $11.50. Then, to avoid the analytical pitfalls of unit-cost analysis, use the contribution approach and concentrate on *totals* instead of units (in thousands of dollars):

	Without Special Order	Effect of Special Order	With Special Order
	1,000,000 Units	250,000 Units	1,250,000 Units
Sales	20,000	2,875*	22,875
Variable manufacturing costs	12,000	3,000†	15,000
Other variable costs	1,100	—	1,100
Total variable costs	13,100	3,000	16,100
Contribution margin	6,900	(125)‡	6,775

*250,000 × $11.50 selling price of special order.
†250,000 × $12.00 variable manufacturing cost per unit of special order.
‡250,000 × $.50 negative contribution margin per unit of special order.

Short-run income will fall by $125,000 (that is, 250,000 units × $.50) if the special order is accepted. No matter how the fixed manufacturing costs are "unitized" and "spread" over the units produced, their total of $3 million will be *unchanged* by the special order (in thousands of dollars):

	Without Special Order	Effect of Special Order	With Special Order
	1,000,000 Units	250,000 Units	1,250,000 Units
Contribution margin (as above)	6,900	(125)	6,775
Total fixed costs			
At an average rate of $3.00*:			
1,000,000 × $3 00	3,000		
At an average rate of $2.40†:			
1,250,000 × $2.40	—	—	3,000
Contribution to other fixed			
costs and operating income	3,900	(125)	3,775

*$3,000,000 ÷ 1,000,000.
†$3,000,000 ÷ 1,250,000.

Notice that no matter how fixed costs are spread for *unit* product-costing purposes, *total* fixed costs are unchanged, even though fixed costs *per unit* fall from $3.00 to $2.40.

The lesson here is important. Do not be deceived. Follow what was called Robert McNamara's First Law of Analysis when he was U.S. Secretary of Defense: "Always start by looking at the grand total. Whatever problem you are studying, back off and look at it in the large." In this context, that law means, "Beware of unit costs. When in doubt, convert all unit costs into the total costs under each alternative to get the big picture." In particular, beware of unit costs when analyzing fixed costs. Think in terms of totals instead.

Multiple-Cost Drivers and Special Orders

To identify costs affected by a special order (or by other special decisions), more and more firms are going a step beyond simply identifying fixed and variable costs. Many different cost drivers may cause companies to incur costs. Businesses that have identified all their significant cost drivers can predict the effects of special orders more accurately.

Suppose Samson Company examined its $12 million of variable costs very closely and identified two significant cost drivers: $9 million that varies directly with *units produced* at a rate of $9 per unit and $3 million that varies with the *number of production setups*. Normally, for production of 1,000,000 units, Samson has 500 setups at a cost of $6,000 per setup, with an average of 2,000 units produced for each setup. Additional sales generally require a proportional increase in the number of setups.

Now suppose the special order is for 100,000 units that vary only slightly in production specifications. Instead of the normal 50 setups, Samson will need only 5 setups, and producing 100,000 units will take only $930,000 of additional variable cost:

Additional unit-based variable cost, 100,000 × $9	$900,000
Additional setup-based variable cost, 5 × $6,000	30,000
Total additional variable cost	**$930,000**

Instead of the original estimate of 100,000 × $12 = $1,200,000 additional variable cost, the special order will cost only $930,000, or $270,000 less than the original estimate. Therefore, the special order is $270,000 more profitable than predicted from the simple, unit-based assessment of variable cost.

A special order may also be more costly than predicted by a simple fixed- and variable-cost analysis. Suppose the 100,000-unit special order called for a variety of models and colors delivered at various times, so that 100 setups are required. The variable cost of the special order would be $1.5 million.

Additional unit-based variable cost, 100,000 × $9	$ 900,000
Additional setup-based variable cost, 100 × $6,000	600,000
Total additional variable cost	**$1,500,000**

DELETION OR ADDITION OF PRODUCTS OR DEPARTMENTS

The same principles of relevance applied to special orders apply—albeit in slightly different ways—to decisions about adding or deleting products or departments.

Avoidable and Unavoidable Costs

Consider a discount department store that has three major departments: groceries, general merchandise, and drugs. Management is considering dropping groceries, which have consistently shown a net loss. The following table reports the present annual net income (in thousands of dollars).

| | | Departments | | |
	Total	Groceries	General Merchandise	Drugs
Sales	$1,900	$1,000	$800	$100
Variable cost of goods sold and expenses*	1,420	800	560	60
Contribution margin	$ 480 (25%)	$ 200 (20%)	$240 (30%)	$ 40 (40%)
Fixed expenses (salaries, depreciation, insurance, property taxes, etc.):				
Avoidable	$ 265	$ 150	$100	$ 15
Unavoidable	180	60	100	20
Total fixed expenses	$ 445	$ 210	$200	$ 35
Operating income	$ 35	$ (10)	$ 40	$ 5

*Examples of variable expenses include paper bags and sales commissions.

Notice that the fixed expenses are divided into two categories, *avoidable* and *unavoidable*. **Avoidable costs**—costs that will *not* continue if an ongoing operation is changed or deleted—are relevant. Avoidable costs include department salaries and other costs that could be eliminated by not operating the specific department. **Unavoidable costs**—costs that continue even if an operation is halted—are not relevant because they are not affected by a decision to delete the department. Unavoidable costs include many **common costs,** which are defined as those costs of facilities and services that are shared by users. Examples are store depreciation, heating, air conditioning, and general management expenses.[1]

Assume first that the only alternatives to be considered are dropping or continuing the grocery department, which shows a loss of $10,000. Assume further that the total assets invested would be unaffected by the decision. The vacated space would be idle, and the unavoidable costs would continue. Which alternative would you recommend? An analysis (in thousands of dollars) follows:

---

[1]The concept of avoidable cost is used by government regulators as well as business executives. For example, Amtrak divides its costs into avoidable—costs that "would cease if the route were eliminated"—and fixed—costs that would "remain relatively constant if a single route were discontinued." The U.S. Interstate Commerce Commission then considers the avoidable costs when considering approval of a railroad's request to abandon a route. Similarly, the Canadian government looks at the avoidable cost when determining the amount of subsidy to give to the country's passenger-rail system. The Montreal *Gazette* reported that in 1993 revenues covered only 35% of the "$7 million in avoidable costs (costs that wouldn't exist if the train disappeared tomorrow—things like staff salaries, food, fuel, and upkeep of train stations)."

Income Statements	Store as a Whole		
	Total Before Change (a)	Effect of Dropping Groceries (b)	Total After Change (a) – (b)
Sales	$1,900	$1,000	$900
Variable expenses	1,420	800	620
Contribution margin	$ 480	$ 200	$280
Avoidable fixed expenses	265	150	115
Profit contribution to common space and other unavoidable costs	$ 215	$ 50	$165
Common space and other unavoidable costs	180	—	180
Operating income	$ 35	$ 50	$(15)

The preceding analysis shows that matters would be worse, rather than better, if groceries were dropped and the vacated facilities left idle. In short, as the income statement shows, groceries bring in a contribution margin of $200,000, which is $50,000 more than the $150,000 fixed expenses that would be saved by closing the grocery department. The grocery department showed a loss in the first income statement because of the unavoidable fixed costs charged to it.

Assume now that the space made available by the dropping of groceries could be used to expand the general merchandise department. The space would be occupied by merchandise that would increase sales by $500,000, generate a 30% contribution-margin percentage, and have avoidable fixed costs of $70,000. The $80,000 increase in operating income of general merchandise more than offsets the $50,000 decline from eliminating groceries, providing an overall increase in operating income of $65,000 – $35,000 = $30,000.

(In thousands of dollars)	Effects of Changes			
	Total Before Change (a)	Drop Groceries (b)	Expand General Merchandise (c)	Total After Changes (a) – (b) + (c)
Sales	$1,900	$1,000	$500	$1,400
Variable expenses	1,420	800	350	970
Contribution margin	$ 480	$ 200	$150	$ 430
Avoidable fixed expenses	265	150	70	185
Contribution to common space and other unavoidable costs	$ 215	$ 50	$ 80	$ 245
Common space and other unavoidable costs*	180	—	—	180
Operating income	$ 35	$ 50	$ 80	$ 65

*Includes the $60,000 of former grocery fixed costs, which were allocations of unavoidable common costs that will continue regardless of how the space is occupied.

As the following summary analysis demonstrates, the objective is to obtain, from a given amount of space or capacity, the maximum contribution to the payment of those unavoidable costs that remain unaffected by the nature of the product sold (in thousands of dollars):

	Groceries	**Expansion of General Merchandise**	**Difference**
		Profit Contribution of Given Space	
Sales	$1,000	$500	$500U
Variable expenses	800	350	450F
Contribution margin	$ 200	$150	$ 50U
Avoidable fixed expenses	150	70	80F
Contribution to common space and other unavoidable costs	$ 50	$ 80	30F

F = Favorable difference resulting from replacing groceries with general merchandise.
U = Unfavorable difference.

In this case, the general merchandise will not achieve the dollar sales volume that groceries will, but the higher contribution margin percentage and the lower wage costs (mostly because of the diminished need for stocking and checkout clerks) will bring more favorable net results.

This illustration contains another lesson. Avoid the idea that relevant-cost analysis merely says, "Consider all variable costs, and ignore all fixed costs." In this case, *some* fixed costs are relevant because they differ under each alternative.

OPTIMAL USE OF LIMITED RESOURCES

When a multiproduct plant is being operated at capacity, managers often must decide which orders to accept. The contribution approach also applies here, because the product to be emphasized or the order to be accepted is the one that makes the biggest *total* profit contribution per unit of the limiting factor. A **limiting factor** or **scarce resource** restricts or constrains the production or sale of a product or service. Limiting factors include labor-hours and machine-hours that limit production and hence sales in manufacturing firms, and square feet of floor space or cubic meters of display space that limit sales in department stores.

The contribution approach must be used wisely, however. Managers sometimes mistakenly favor those products with the biggest contribution margin or gross margin per sales dollar, without regard to scarce resources.

Assume that a company has two products: a plain portable heater and a fancier heater with many special features. Unit data follow:

	Plain Heater	Fancy Heater
Selling price	$20	$30
Variable costs	16	21
Contribution margin	$ 4	$ 9
Contribution-margin ratio	20%	30%

Which product is more profitable? On which should the firm spend its resources? The correct answer is: It depends. If sales are restricted by demand for only a limited *number* of heaters, fancy heaters are more profitable. Why? Because sale of a plain heater adds $4 to profit; sale of a fancy heater adds $9. If the limiting factor is *units* of sales, the more profitable product is the one with the higher contribution *per unit*.

Now suppose annual demand for heaters of both types is more than the company can produce in the next year. Productive capacity is the limiting factor. If 10,000 hours of capacity are available, and three plain heaters can be produced per hour in contrast to one fancy heater, the plain heater is more profitable. Why? Because it contributes more profit *per hour* of capacity:

	Plain Heater	Fancy Heater
1. Units per hour	3	1
2. Contribution margin per unit	$4	$9
Contribution margin per hour (1) x (2)	$12	$9
Total contribution for 10,000 hours	$120,000	$90,000

The criterion for maximizing profits when one factor limits sales is to obtain the greatest possible contribution to profit for each unit of the limiting or scarce factor. The product that is most profitable when one particular factor limits sales may be the least profitable if a different factor restricts sales.

When there are capacity limitations, the conventional contribution-margin or gross-margin-per-sales-dollar ratios provide an insufficient clue to profitability. Consider an example of two department stores. The conventional gross profit percentage (gross profit ÷ selling price) is an insufficient clue to profitability because profits also depend on the space occupied and the **inventory turnover** (number of times the average inventory is sold per year). Discount department stores such as Wal-Mart, Target, and K-Mart have succeeded while using lower markups than traditional department stores because they have been able to increase turnover and thus increase the contribution to profit per unit of space. Figure 8-4 illustrates the same product, taking up the same amount of space, in each of two stores. The contribution margins per unit and per sales dollar are less in the discount store, but faster turnover makes the same product a more profitable use of space in the discount store. In general, companies seek faster inventory turnover. A survey of retail shoe stores showed that those with above-average financial performance had an inventory turnover of 2.6 compared to an industry average of 2.0.

FIGURE 8-4   **Effect of Turnover on Profit**

	Regular Department Store	Discount Department Store
Retail price	$4.00	$3.50
Cost of merchandise and other variable costs	3.00	3.00
Contribution to profit per unit	$1.00 (25%)	$ .50 (14%)
Units sold per year	10,000	22,000
Total contribution to profit, assuming the same space allotment in both stores	$10,000	$11,000

Notice that throughout this discussion fixed costs have been correctly ignored. They are irrelevant unless their total is affected by the choices.

ROLE OF COSTS IN PRICING DECISIONS

One of the major decisions managers face is pricing. Actually, pricing can take many forms. Among the many pricing decisions to be made are:

1. Setting the price of a new product
2. Setting the price of products sold under private labels
3. Responding to a new price of a competitor
4. Pricing bids in both sealed and open bidding situations

The pricing decision is extensively covered in the literature of economics and marketing. Our purpose here is not to provide a comprehensive review of that literature, but simply to highlight a few important points that help define the role of costs in pricing.

Economic Theory and Pricing

Pricing decisions depend on the characteristics of the market a firm faces. In **perfect competition**, a firm can sell as much of a product as it can produce, all at a single market price. If it charges more, no customer will buy. If it charges less, it sacrifices profits. Therefore, every firm in such a market will charge the market price, and the only decision for managers is how much to produce.

Although costs do not directly influence prices in perfect competition, they affect the production decision. Consider the *marginal cost curve* in Figure 8-5. The **marginal cost** is the additional cost resulting from producing and selling one additional unit. The marginal cost often decreases as production increases up to a point because efficiencies are possible with larger production amounts. At some point, however,

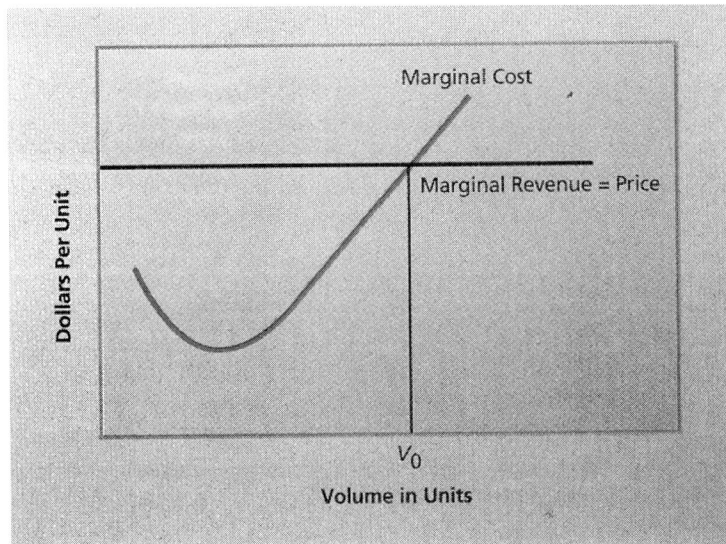

FIGURE 8-5
Marginal Revenue and Cost in Perfect Competition

marginal costs begin to rise with increases in production because facilities begin to be overcrowded, resulting in inefficiencies.

Figure 8-5 also includes a *marginal revenue curve*. The **marginal revenue** is the additional revenue resulting from the sale of an additional unit. In perfect competition, the marginal revenue curve is a horizontal line equal to the price per unit at all volumes of sales.

As long as the marginal cost is less than the price, additional production and sales are profitable. When marginal cost exceeds price, however, the firm loses money on each additional unit. Therefore, the profit-maximizing volume is the quantity at which marginal cost equals price. In Figure 8-5, the firm should produce V_0 units. Producing fewer units passes up profitable opportunities; producing more units reduces profit because each additional unit costs more to produce than it generates in revenue.

In **imperfect competition,** a firm's price will influence the quantity it sells. At some point, price reductions are necessary to generate additional sales. Figure 8-6 contains a demand curve (also called the average revenue curve) for imperfect competition that shows the volume of sales at each possible price. To sell additional units, the price of *all units sold* must be reduced. Therefore, the marginal revenue curve, also shown in Figure 8-6, is below the demand curve. That is, the marginal revenue for selling one additional unit is less than the price at which it is sold because the price of all other units falls as well. For example, suppose 10 units can be sold for $50 per unit. The price must be dropped to $49 per unit to sell 11 units, to $48 to sell 12 units, and to $47 to sell 13 units. The fourth column of Figure 8-7 shows the marginal revenue for units 11 through 13. Notice that the marginal revenue decreases as volume increases.

To estimate marginal revenue, managers must predict the effect of price changes on sales volume, which is called **price elasticity.** If small price increases cause large

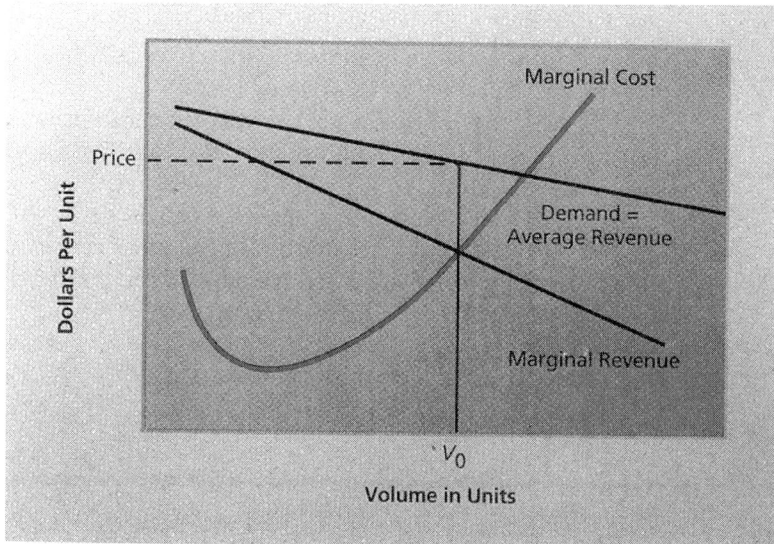

FIGURE 8-6
Marginal Revenue and Cost in Imperfect Competition

volume declines, demand is highly *elastic*. If prices have little or no effect on volume, demand is highly *inelastic*.

Now suppose the marginal cost of the units is as shown in the fifth column of Figure 8-7. The optimal production and sales level would be 12 units. The last column illustrates that the 11th unit adds $4 to profit, the 12th adds $1, but production and sale of the 13th unit would *decrease* profit by $2. In general, firms should produce and sell units until the marginal revenue equals the marginal cost, represented by volume V_0 in Figure 8-6. The optimal price charged will be the amount that creates a demand for V_0 units.

Notice that in economic theory the *marginal cost* is relevant for pricing decisions. The accountant's approximation to marginal cost is *variable cost*. What is the major difference between the economist's marginal cost and the accountant's variable cost? Variable cost is assumed to be constant within a relevant range of volume, whereas marginal cost may change with each unit produced. Within large ranges of produc-

FIGURE 8-7   Profit Maximization in Imperfect Competition

Units Sold	Price per Unit	Total Revenue	Marginal Revenue	Marginal Cost	Profit from Production and Sale of Additional Unit
10	$50	10 × $50 = $500			
11	49	11 × 49 = 539	$539 − $500 = $39	$35	$39 − $35 = $4
12	48	12 × 48 = 576	576 − 539 = 37	36	37 − 36 = 1
13	47	13 × 47 = 611	611 − 576 = 35	37	35 − 37 = (2)

tion volume, however, changes in marginal cost are often small. Therefore, using variable cost can be a reasonable approximation to marginal cost in many situations.

Maximization of Total Contribution

Managers seldom compute marginal revenue curves and marginal cost curves. Instead, they use estimates based on judgment to predict the effects of additional production and sales on profits. In addition, they examine selected volumes, not the whole range of possible volumes. Such simplifications are justified because the cost of a more sophisticated analysis would exceed the benefits.

Consider a division of General Electric (GE) that makes microwave ovens. Suppose market researchers estimate that 700,000 ovens can be sold if priced at $200 per unit, but 1,000,000 could be sold at $180. The variable cost of production is $130 per unit at production levels of both 700,000 and 1,000,000. Both volumes are also within the relevant range so that fixed costs are unaffected by the changes in volume. Which price should be charged?

The GE manager could compute the additional revenue and additional costs of the 300,000 additional units of sales at the $180 price:

Additional revenue: $(1,000,000 \times \$180) - (700,000 \times \$200)$ =	$ 40,000,000
– Additional costs: $300,000 \times \$130$ =	39,000,000
Additional profit:	$ 1,000,000

Alternatively, the manager could compare the total contribution for each alternative:

Contribution at $180: $(\$180 - \$130) \times 1,000,000$ =	$50,000,000
Contribution at $200: $(\$200 - \$130) \times 700,000$ =	49,000,000
Difference:	$ 1,000,000

Notice that comparing the total contributions is essentially the same as computing the additional revenues and costs. Further, both approaches correctly ignore fixed costs, which are unaffected by this pricing decision.

INFLUENCES ON PRICING IN PRACTICE

Several factors interact to shape the environment in which managers make pricing decisions. Legal requirements, competitors' actions, costs, and customer demands all influence pricing.

Legal Requirements

Pricing decisions must be made within constraints imposed by U.S. and international laws. In addition to prohibiting out-and-out collusion in setting prices, these laws generally prohibit prices that are *predatory* or *discriminatory*.

Predatory pricing is establishing prices so low that competitors are driven out of the market so that the predatory pricer then has no significant competition and can raise prices dramatically. For example, Wal-Mart has been accused of predatory pricing—selling at low cost to drive out local competitors. U.S. courts have generally ruled that pricing is predatory only if companies set prices below average variable cost.

Discriminatory pricing is charging different prices to different customers for the same product or service. For example, a large group of neighborhood pharmacies sued several large drug companies, alleging that their practice of allowing discounts to mail-order drug companies, health maintenance organizations, and other managed-care entities constitutes discriminatory pricing. However, pricing is not discriminatory if it reflects a cost differential incurred in providing the good or service.

Businesses can defend themselves against charges of either predatory or discriminatory pricing by citing their costs as a basis for their prices. Therefore, a good understanding of the cost of a product or service, especially the activities that cause additional costs to be incurred, is useful in avoiding legal pitfalls. Our discussion here assumes that pricing practices do not violate legal constraints.

Competitors' Actions

Competitors usually react to the price changes of their rivals. Many companies will gather information regarding a rival's capacity, technology, and operating policies. In this way, managers make more informed predictions of competitors' reactions to a company's prices. The study of game theory, for which two economists won the 1994 Nobel Prize, focuses on predicting and reacting to competitors' actions.

Tinkering with prices is often most heavily affected by the price setter's expectations of competitors' reactions and of the overall effects on the total industry demand for the good or service in question. For example, an airline might cut prices even if it expects price cuts from its rivals, hoping that total customer demand for the tickets of all airlines will increase sufficiently to offset the reduction in the price per ticket.

Competition is becoming increasingly international. Overcapacity in some countries often causes aggressive pricing policies, particularly for a company's exported goods.

Costs

Costs influence the deliberate setting of prices in some industries, but not in others. Frequently, the market price is regarded as a given. Examples include the prices of metals and agricultural commodities. Consider gold. A mining company sells at the established market prices. Whether profits or losses are forthcoming depends on how well the company controls its costs and volume. Here cost data help managers decide on the level and mix of outputs.

The influence of costs on the setting of prices is often overstated. Nevertheless, many managers say that their prices are set by cost-plus pricing. For example, consider the construction and automobile industries. Their executives describe the procedure as computing an average unit cost and then adding a "reasonable" **markup** (i.e., the amount by which price exceeds cost) that will generate a target return on investment. The key, however, is the "plus" in cost plus. It is rarely an unalterable markup. Its magnitude depends on the behavior of competitors and customers.

Prices are most directly related to costs in industries where revenue is based on cost reimbursement. A prime example is defense contracting. Cost-reimbursement contracts generally specify how costs should be measured and what costs are allowable. For example, only coach-class (not first-class) fares are reimbursable for business air travel on government projects.

Ultimately, though, the market sets prices after all. Why? Because the price as set by a cost-plus formula is inevitably adjusted "in light of market conditions." The maximum price that may be charged is the one that does not drive the customer away. The minimum price might be considered to be zero (e.g., companies may give out free samples to gain entry into a market). A more practical guide is that, in the short run, the minimum price to be quoted, *subject to consideration of long-run effects,* should be equal to the costs that may be avoided by not landing the order—often all variable costs of producing, selling, and distributing the good or service. In the long run, the price must be high enough to cover all costs including fixed costs.

Customer Demands and Target Costing

More than ever before, managers are recognizing the needs of customers. Pricing is no exception. If customers believe a price is too high, they may turn to other sources for the product or service, substitute a different product, or decide to produce the item themselves.

Most companies have traditionally started with costs and added a markup to get prices. However, a growing number of companies are turning the equation around and developing costs based on prices. Companies that use **target costing** first determine the price at which they can sell a new product or service and then design a product or service that can be produced at a low enough cost to provide an adequate profit margin. Product designers thus become aware of the cost impacts of the design of both the product itself and the process used to produce it.

For example, market research may indicate that Toyota could sell 100,000 units of one model of a sports car annually at a list price of $35,000. The engineers who design the product might consider several different combinations of features bearing different costs. If the total product cost is sufficiently low, the product may be launched. Conversely, if the total product cost is too high, the product may be unjustified. Of course, the point here is that the customer helps determine the price. The product designers and the management accountants work together to see if a product can be developed at a target cost that will provide room for an attractive profit.

Target costing originated in Japan, but now it is used by many companies worldwide, including Chrysler, Mercedes-Benz, Procter & Gamble, and Caterpillar. Even some hospitals use target costing.

Whether a company sets prices based on costs or costs based on prices, it is inevitable that prices and costs interact. If the focus is on prices that are influenced primarily by market forces, managers must make sure that all costs can be covered in the long run. If prices are based on a markup of costs, managers must examine the actions of customers and competitors to ensure that products or services can be sold at the determined prices.

FIGURE 8-8   Variety of Cost Terms

	Cost per Unit of Product		
Variable manufacturing cost	$12.00	$12.00	$12.00
Variable selling and administrative cost	1.10		1.10
Total variable cost	**$13.10**		
Fixed manufacturing cost		3.00*	3.00
Absorption cost		**$15.00†**	
Fixed selling and administrative cost			2.90*
Full cost (often called fully allocated cost)			**$19.00**

*Fixed manufacturing costs, $3,000,000 ÷ 1,000 000 = $3.00.
Fixed selling and administrative costs, $2,900,000 ÷ 1,000,000 units = $2.90.
†This amount must be used by U.S. companies for inventory valuation in reports to shareholders.

Choice of Cost Words and Terms

Earlier chapters have alerted you to the meanings of various accounting terms. Each organization has its own cost vocabulary, which often contains cost definitions that clash with their meanings in management accounting literature. In a specific situation, be sure to obtain the exact meaning of the terms used.

Figure 8-8 displays how the costs of products and services are usually described. Note particularly that **full cost** or **fully allocated cost** means the total of all manufacturing costs plus the total of all selling and administrative costs.

Target Pricing

Cost plus is often the basis for target prices. The size of the "plus" depends on target (desired) operating incomes, which, in turn, frequently depend on the target return on investment for a division, a product line, or a product.

Target prices can be based on a host of different markups based on a host of different definitions of cost. Thus, there are many ways to arrive at the *same target price.* They simply reflect different arrangements of the components of the same income statement.

Figure 8-9 displays the relationships of costs to target selling prices, assuming a target operating income of $1 million. The percentages there represent four popular markup formulas for pricing: (1) as a percentage of variable manufacturing costs, (2) as a percentage of total variable costs, (3) as a percentage of full costs, and (4) as a percentage of absorption costs.

Of course, the percentages differ. For instance, the markup on variable manufacturing costs is 66.67%, and on absorption costs it is 33.33%. Regardless of the formula used, the pricing decision maker will be led toward the *same* target price. For a volume of 1 million units, assume that the target selling price is $20 per unit. If the decision maker is unable to obtain such a price consistently, the company will not achieve its $1 million operating income objective.

FIGURE 8-9   Relationships of Costs to Same Target Selling Prices

		Alternative Markup Percentages to Achieve Same Target Sales Prices
Target sales price	$20.00	
Variable costs		
(1) Manufacturing	$12.00*	($20.00 – $12.00) ÷ $12.00 = 66.67%
Selling and administrative	1.10	
(2) Unit variable costs	$13.10	($20.00 – $13.10) ÷ $13.10 = 52.67%
Fixed costs		
Manufacturing	$ 3.00*	
Selling and administrative	2.90	
Unit fixed costs	$ 5.90	
(3) Full costs	$19.00	($20.00 – $19.00) ÷ $19.00 = 5.26%
Target operating income	$ 1.00	

*(4) A frequently used formula is based on absorption costs:
[$20.00 – ($12.00 + $3.00)] ÷ $15.00 = 33.33%.

ADVANTAGES OF VARIOUS APPROACHES TO PRICING DECISIONS

We have seen that prices can be based on various types of cost information, from variable costs to absorption costs to full costs. Each approach has advantages and disadvantages.

Contribution Approach Provides Detailed Information

Prices based on variable costs represent a contribution approach to pricing. When used intelligently, the contribution approach has some advantages over the absorption-costing and full-cost approaches, because the latter often fail to highlight different cost behavior patterns.

Obviously, the contribution approach offers more detailed information because it displays variable- and fixed-cost behavior patterns separately. Because the contribution approach is sensitive to cost-volume-profit relationships, it is a helpful basis for developing pricing formulas. Consequently, this approach makes it easier for managers to prepare price schedules at different volume levels.

The correct analysis in Figure 8-10 shows how changes in volume affect operating income. The contribution approach helps managers with pricing decisions because it readily displays the interrelationships among variable costs, fixed costs, and potential changes in selling prices.

In contrast, target pricing with absorption costing or full costing presumes a given volume level. When volume changes, the unit cost used at the original planned volume may mislead managers. As our "incorrect cost analysis" above showed, managers sometimes erroneously assume that the change in total costs may be computed by multiplying any change in volume by the full unit cost.

The incorrect analysis in Figure 8-10 shows how managers may be misled if the $19 full cost per unit is used to predict effects of volume changes on operating in-

FIGURE 8-10   Analyses of Effects of Changes in Volume on Operating Income

	Correct Analysis			Incorrect Analysis		
Volume in units	900,000	1,000,000	1,100,000	900,000	1,000,000	1,100,000
Sales @ $20.00	$18,000,000	$20,000,000	$22,000,000	$18,000,000	$20,000,000	$22,000,000
Total variable						
costs @ $13.10*	11,790,000	13,100,000	14,410,000			
Contribution margin	6,210,000	6,900,000	7,590,000			
Fixed costs[†]	5,900,000	5,900,000	5,900,000			
Full costs @ $19.00*				17,100,000	19,000,000	20,900,000
Operating income	$ 310,000	$1,000,000	$ 1,690,000	$ 900,000	$ 1,000,000	$ 1,100,000

*From Figure 8-8.

[†]Fixed manufacturing costs	$3,000,000
Fixed selling and administrative costs	2,900,000
Total fixed costs	**$5,900,000**

come. Suppose a manager uses the $19 figure to predict an operating income of $900,000 if the company sells 900,000 instead of 1,000,000 units. If actual operating income is $310,000 instead, as the correct analysis predicts, that manager may be stunned—and possibly looking for a new job.

Other Advantages of Contribution Approach

Two other advantages of the contribution approach deserve mention. First, a normal or target-pricing formula can be developed as easily by the contribution approach as by absorption-costing or full-costing approaches, as Figure 8-9 showed.

Second, the contribution approach offers insight into the short-run versus long-run effects of cutting prices on special orders. For example, assume the same cost behavior patterns as at the Samson Co. (Figure 8-3). The 100,000-unit order added $100,000 to operating income at a selling price of $13, which was $7 below the target selling price of $20 and $2 below the absorption manufacturing cost of $15. Given all the stated assumptions, accepting the order appeared to be the better choice. No general answer can be given, but the relevant information was more easily generated by the contribution approach. Consider the contribution and absorption-costing approaches:

	Contribution Approach	Absorption-Costing Approach
Sales, 100,000 units @ $13	$1,300,000	$1,300,000
Variable manufacturing costs @ $12	1,200,000	
Absorption manufacturing costs @ $15		1,500,000
Apparent change in operating income	$ 100,000	($ 200,000)

Under the absorption approach, the decision maker has no direct knowledge of cost-volume-profit relationships. The decision maker must make the decision by hunch. On the surface, the offer is definitely unattractive because the price of $13 is $2 below absorption costs.

Under the contribution approach, the decision maker sees a short-run advantage of $100,000 from accepting the offer. Fixed costs will be unaffected by whatever decision is made and operating income will increase by $100,000. Still, there often are long-run effects to consider. Will acceptance of the offer undermine the long-run price structure? In other words, is the short-run advantage of $100,000 more than offset by highly probable long-run financial disadvantages? The decision maker may think so and may reject the offer. But—and this is important—by doing so the decision maker is, in effect, forgoing $100,000 now to protect certain long-run market advantages. Generally, the decision maker can assess problems of this sort by asking whether the probability of long-run benefits is worth an "investment" equal to the forgone contribution margin ($100,000 in this case). Under absorption approaches, the decision maker must ordinarily conduct a special study to find the immediate effects. Under the contribution approach, the manager has a system that will routinely and more surely provide such information.

Advantages of Absorption-Cost or Full-Cost Approaches

Our general theme of focusing on relevant information also extends into the area of pricing. To say that either a contribution approach or an absorption-cost approach or a full-cost approach provides the "best" guide to pricing decisions is a dangerous oversimplification of one of the most perplexing problems in business. Lack of understanding and judgment can lead to unprofitable pricing regardless of the kind of cost data available or cost accounting system used.

Frequently, managers do not employ a contribution approach because they fear that variable costs will be substituted indiscriminately for full costs and will therefore lead to suicidal price cutting. This problem should *not* arise if the data are used wisely. However, if top managers perceive a pronounced danger of underpricing when variable-cost data are revealed, they may justifiably prefer an absorption-costing approach or a full-cost approach for guiding pricing decisions.

Cost-plus pricing based on absorption costs or full costs entails circular reasoning. That is, price, which influences sales volume, is often based on an average absorption cost per unit, which in turn is partly determined by the underlying volume of sales.

Despite the criticism, absorption costs or full costs are far more widely used in practice than is the contribution approach. Why? In addition to the reasons already mentioned, the following have been offered:

1. In the long run, all costs must be recovered to stay in business. Sooner or later fixed costs do indeed fluctuate as volume changes. Therefore it is prudent to assume that all costs are variable (even if some are fixed in the short run).
2. Computing target prices based on cost plus may indicate what competitors might charge, especially if they have approximately the same level of efficiency as you and also aim at recovering all costs in the long run.
3. Absorption-cost or full-cost formula pricing meets the cost-benefit test. It is too expensive to conduct individual cost-volume tests for the many products (sometimes thousands) that a company offers.

4. There is much uncertainty about the shape of the demand curves and the correct price-output decisions. Absorption-cost or full-cost pricing copes with this uncertainty by not encouraging managers to take too much marginal business.
5. Absorption-cost or full-cost pricing tends to promote price stability. Managers prefer price stability because it eases their professional lives, primarily because planning is more dependable.
6. Absorption-cost pricing or full-cost pricing provides the most defensible basis for justifying prices to all interested parties including government antitrust investigators.
7. Absorption-cost or full-cost pricing provides convenient reference (target) points to simplify hundreds or thousands of pricing decisions.

No single method of pricing is always best. An interview study of executives reported use of *both* full-cost and variable-cost information in pricing decisions: "The full-vs.-variable-cost pricing controversy is not one of either black or white. The companies we studied used both approaches."[2]

The history of accounting reveals that most companies' systems have gathered costs via some form of full-manufacturing-cost system because this is what is required for financial reporting. In recent years, when systems are changed, variable costs and fixed costs are often identified. But managers have regarded this change as an addition to the existing full-manufacturing-cost system. That is, many managers insist on having information regarding both variable costs per unit and the allocated fixed costs per unit before setting selling prices. If the accounting system routinely gathers data regarding both variable and fixed costs, such data can readily be provided. However, most absorption-costing systems in practice do not organize their data collection so as to distinguish between variable and fixed costs. As a result, special studies or special guessing must be used to designate costs as variable or fixed.

Managers are especially reluctant to focus on variable costs and ignore allocated fixed costs when their performance evaluations, and possibly their bonuses, are based on income shown in published financial statements. Why? Because such statements are based on absorption costing and thus are affected by allocations of fixed costs.

Format for Pricing

Figure 8-9 showed how to compute alternative general markup percentages that would produce the same selling prices if used day after day. In practice, the format and arithmetic of quote sheets, job proposals, or similar records vary considerably.

Figure 8-11 is from an actual quote sheet used by the manager of a small job shop that bids on welding machinery orders in a highly competitive industry. The Figure 8-11 approach is a tool for informed pricing decisions. Notice that the *maximum* price is not a matter of cost at all; it is what you think you can obtain. The *minimum* price is the total variable cost.

Of course, the manager will rarely bid the minimum price. To do so regularly would virtually ensure eventual bankruptcy. Still, the manager wants to know the

---

[2]T. Bruegelmann, G. Haessly, C. Wolfangel, and M. Schiff, "How Variable Costing Is Used in Pricing Decisions," *Management Accounting*, Vol. 65, no. 10, p. 65.

FIGURE 8-11   Quote Sheet for Pricing

Direct materials, at cost	$25,000
Direct labor and variable manufacturing overhead, 600 direct- labor-hours × $30	18,000
Sales commission (varies with job)	2,000
Total variable costs—minimum price*	45,000
Add fixed costs allocated to job, 600 direct-labor-hours × $20	12,000
Total costs	57,000
Add desired markup	30,000
Selling price—maximum price that you think you can obtain*	**$87,000**

*This sheet shows two prices, maximum and minimum. Any amount you can get above the minimum price is a contribution margin.

effect of a job on the company's total variable costs. Occasionally, a bid near that minimum price may be justified because of idle capacity or the desire to establish a presence in new markets or with a new customer.

Note that Figure 8-11 classifies costs especially for the pricing task. Pricing decisions may be made by more than one person. The accountant's responsibility is to prepare an understandable format that involves a minimum of computations. Figure 8-11 combines direct labor and variable manufacturing overhead. All fixed costs, whether manufacturing, selling, or administrative, are lumped together and applied to the job using a single fixed-overhead rate per direct-labor-hour. Obviously, if more accuracy is desired, many more detailed cost items and overhead rates could be formulated. To obtain the desired accuracy, many companies are turning to activity-based costing.

Some managers, particularly in construction and service industries such as auto repair, compile separate categories of costs of (1) direct materials, parts, and supplies and (2) direct labor. These managers then use different markup rates for each category. These rates are developed to provide revenue for both related overhead costs and operating profit. For example, an automobile repair shop might have the following format for each job:

	Billed to Customers
Auto parts ($200 cost plus 40% markup)	$280

Direct labor (Cost is $20 per hour. Bill at 300% to recover
    overhead and provide for operating profit. Billing rate is
    $20 × 300% = $60 per hour. Total billed for 10 hours
    is $60 × 10 = $600)
	600

Total billed to customer	**$880**

Another example is an Italian printing company in Milan that wants to price its jobs so that each one generates a margin of 28% of revenues—14% to cover selling and administrative expenses and 14% for profit. To achieve this, the manager uses a pricing formula of 140% times predicted materials cost plus 25,000 Italian Lira (abbreviated Lit.) per hour of production time. The latter covers labor and overhead costs of Lit.18,000 per hour. For a product with Lit.400,000 of materials cost and 30 hours of production time, the price would be Lit.1,310,000:

	Cost	Price	Profit
Materials	Lit.400,000	Lit. 560,000	Lit.160,000
Labor and overhead	540,000	750,000	210,000
Total	**Lit.940,000**	**Lit.1,310,000**	**Lit.370,000**

The profit of Lit.370,000 is approximately 40% of the cost of Lit.940,000 and 28% of the price of Lit.1,310,000.

Thus there are numerous ways to compute selling prices. However, some general words of caution are appropriate here. Managers are better able to understand their options and the effects of their decisions on profits if they know their costs. That is, it is more informative to pinpoint costs first, before adding markups, than to have a variety of markups already embedded in the "costs" used as guides for setting selling prices. For example, if materials cost $1,000, they should be shown on a price quotation guide at $1,000, not at, say, a marked-up $1,400 because that is what the seller hopes to get.

SUMMARY

The accountant's role in decision making is primarily that of a technical expert on financial analysis. The accountant's responsibility is to help the manager use relevant data as guidance for decisions. Accountants and managers must have a penetrating understanding of relevant information, especially costs.

To be relevant to a particular decision, a cost must meet two criteria: (1) it must be an expected *future* cost, and (2) it must have an element of *difference* among the alternatives. All *past* (*historical* or *sunk*) costs are in themselves irrelevant to any *decision* about the future, although they often provide the best available basis for the *prediction* of expected future data.

The combination of the relevant-costing and contribution approaches provides a commonality of approach, a fundamental framework, based on economic analysis, that applies to a vast range of problems. The following generalizations apply to a variety of decisions:

1. Whenever feasible, think in terms of total costs rather than unit costs. Too often, unit costs are regarded as an adequate basis for predicting changes in total costs. This assumption is satisfactory when analyzing variable costs but it is frequently misleading when analyzing fixed costs.
2. A common error is to regard all unit costs indiscriminately, as if all costs were variable costs. In the short run, changes in volume will affect *total* variable costs but not *total* fixed costs. The danger then is to predict total costs assuming that all unit costs are variable. The correct relationships are:

	Behavior as Volume Fluctuates	
	Variable Cost	*Fixed Cost*
Cost per unit	No change	Change
Total cost	Change	No change

Decisions to accept or reject a special sales order should focus on the *additional* revenues and *additional* costs of the order. Decisions on whether to delete a department or a product require analysis of the revenues forgone and the costs saved from the deletion. The key to obtaining the maximum profit from a given capacity is to obtain the greatest possible contribution to profit per unit of the limiting or scarce factor.

Pricing decisions are influenced by economics, the law, customers, competitors, and costs. Profit markups can be added to a variety of cost bases including variable manufacturing costs, all variable costs, absorption (full manufacturing) cost, or all costs. The contribution approach to pricing has the advantage of providing detailed information that is consistent with cost-volume-profit analysis.

SELF-CORRECTION PROBLEMS

1. a. Return to the basic illustration in Figure 8-3. Suppose Samson Co. received a special order like that described in conjunction with Figure 8-3 that had the following terms: selling price would be $13.50 instead of $13.00, but a manufacturer's agent who had obtained the potential order would have to be paid a flat fee of $40,000 if the order were accepted. What would be the new special-order difference in operating income if the order were accepted?

   b. Assume the original facts concerning the special order, except that the order was for 250,000 units at a selling price of $11.50. Some managers have been known to argue for acceptance of such an order as follows: "Of course, we will lose $.50 each on the variable manufacturing costs, but we will gain $.60 per unit by spreading our fixed manufacturing costs over 1.25 million units instead of 1 million units. Consequently, we should take the offer because it represents an advantage of $.10 per unit."

Old fixed manufacturing cost per unit, $3,000,000 ÷ 1,000,000	$3.00
New fixed manufacturing cost per unit, $3,000,000 ÷ 1,250,000	2.40
"Saving" in fixed manufacturing cost per unit	$ .60
Loss on variable manufacturing cost per unit, $11.50 − $12.00	.50
Net saving per unit in manufacturing cost	$ .10

Explain why this is faulty thinking.

2. Custom Graphics is a Chicago printing company that bids on a wide variety of design and printing jobs. The owner of the company, Janet Solomon, prepares the bids for most jobs. Her cost budget for 19X6 follows.

Materials		$ 350,000
Labor		250,000
Overhead		
Variable	$300,000	
Fixed	150,000	450,000
Total production cost of jobs		1,050,000
Selling and administrative expenses		
Variable	$ 75,000	
Fixed	125,000	200,000
Total costs		**$1,250,000**

Solomon has a target profit of $250,000 for 19X6.

Compute the average target markup percentage for setting prices as a percentage of:

  a. Prime costs (materials plus labor)
  b. Variable production cost of jobs
  c. Total production cost of jobs
  d. All variable costs
  e. All costs

SOLUTIONS TO SELF-CORRECTION PROBLEMS

1. a. Focus on the *differences* in revenues and costs. In this problem, in addition to the difference in variable costs, there is a difference in fixed costs between the two alternatives.

Additional revenue, 100,000 units @ $13.50 per unit	$1,350,000
Less additional costs	
Variable costs, 100,000 units @ $12 per unit	1,200,000
Fixed costs, agent's fee	40,000
Increase in operating income from special order	**$ 110,000**

  b. The faulty thinking comes from attributing a "savings" to the decrease in unit fixed costs. Regardless of how the fixed manufacturing costs are "unitized" or "spread" over the units produced, their *total* of $3 million will be *unchanged* by the special order. As the tabulation indicates, short-run income will fall by 250,000 units × ($12.00 − $11.50) = $125,000 if the second special order is accepted.

2. The purpose of this problem is to emphasize that many different approaches to pricing might be used that, properly employed, would achieve the *same* target selling prices. To achieve $250,000 of profit, the desired revenue for 19X6 is $1,250,000 + $250,000 = $1,500,000. The target markup percentages are

a. Percent of prime cost $= \dfrac{(\$1,500,000 - \$600,000)}{(\$600,000)} = 150\%$

b. Percent of variable production cost of jobs $= \dfrac{(\$1,500,000 - \$900,00)}{(\$900,000)} = 66.7\%$

c. Percent of total production cost of jobs $= \dfrac{(\$1,500,000 - \$1,050,000)}{(\$1,050,000)} = 42.9\%$

d. Percent of all variables costs $= \dfrac{(\$1,500,000 - \$975,000)}{(\$975,000)} = 53.8\%$

e. Percent of all costs $= \dfrac{(\$1,500,000 - \$1,250,000)}{(\$1,250,000)} = 20\%$

QUESTIONS

1. "The distinction between precision and relevance should be kept in mind." Explain.
2. Distinguish between the quantitative and qualitative aspects of decisions.
3. Describe the accountant's role in decision making.
4. "Any future cost is relevant." Do you agree? Explain.
5. Why are historical or past data irrelevant to special decisions?
6. Describe the role of past or historical costs in the decision process. That is, how do these costs relate to the prediction method and the decision model?
7. "There is a commonality of approach to various special decisions." Explain.
8. "No matter what the decision situation, the key question to ask is: What difference does it make?" Explain the nature of the difference.
9. "In relevant-cost analysis, beware of unit costs." Explain.
10. "Increasing sales will decrease fixed costs because it spreads them over more units." Do you agree? Explain.
11. "The key to decisions to delete a product or department is identifying avoidable costs." Do you agree? Explain.
12. "Avoidable costs are variable costs." Do you agree? Explain.
13. Give four examples of limiting or scarce factors.
14. Compare and contrast *marginal cost* and *variable cost*.
15. Describe four major factors that influence pricing decisions.
16. Why are customers one of the factors influencing price decisions?
17. "Basing pricing on only the variable costs of a job results in suicidal underpricing." Do you agree? Why?
18. Provide three examples of pricing decisions other than the special order.
19. List four popular markup formulas for pricing.
20. Describe two long-run effects that may lead to managers rejecting opportunities to cut prices and obtain increases in short-run profits.
21. Give two reasons why full costs are far more widely used than variable costs for guiding pricing.
22. Why do most executives use both full-cost and variable-cost information for pricing decisions?
23. "Target costing is the opposite of target pricing." Do you agree? Explain.

PROBLEMS

1. **Special Order.**   Consider the following details of the income statement of the Moinpour Pen Company for the year ended December 31, 19X6:

Sales	$10,000,000
Less manufacturing cost of goods sold	6,000,000
Gross margin or gross profit	$ 4,000,000
Less selling and administrative expenses	3,300,000
Operating income	$ 700,000

Moinpour's fixed manufacturing costs were $2.4 million and its fixed selling and administrative costs were $2.5 million. Sales commissions of 3% of sales are included in selling and administrative expenses.

The company had sold 2 million pens. Near the end of the year, Pizza Hut Corporation offered to buy 150,000 pens on a special order. To fill the order, a special clip bearing the Pizza Hut emblem would have had to be made for each pen. Pizza Hut intended to use the pens in special promotions in an eastern city during early 19X7.

Even though Moinpour had some idle plant capacity, the president rejected the Pizza Hut offer of $660,000 for the 150,000 pens. He said:

> The Pizza Hut offer is too low. We'd avoid paying sales commissions, but we'd have to incur an extra cost of $.20 per clip for the emblem and its assembly with the pens. If Moinpour sells below its regular selling prices, it will begin a chain reaction of competitors' price cutting and of customers wanting special deals. I believe in pricing at no lower than 8% above our full costs of $9,300,000 2,000,000 units = $4.65 per unit plus the extra $.20 per clip less the savings in commissions.

   a. Using the contribution approach, prepare an analysis similar to that in Figure 8-3. Use four columns: without the special order, the effect of the special order (total and per unit), and totals with the special order.
   b. By what percentage would operating income increase or decrease if the order had been accepted? Do you agree with the president's decision? Why?

2. **Choice of Products.**   The Skill-Craft Company has two products: a plain electric mixer and a fancy electric mixer. The plain mixer sells for $64 and has a variable cost of $48. The fancy mixer sells for $100 and has a variable cost of $70.

   a. Compute contribution margins and contribution-margin ratios for plain and fancy mixers.
   b. The demand is for more units than the company can produce. There are only 20,000 machine-hours of manufacturing capacity available. Two plain mixers can be produced in the same average time (1 hour) needed to produce one fancy mixer. Compute the total contribution margin for 20,000 hours for plain mixers only and for fancy mixers only.
   c. Use two or three sentences to state the major lesson of this problem.

3. **Formulas for Pricing.**   Zeke Podolsky, a building contractor, constructs houses in tracts, often building as many as 20 homes simultaneously. Podolsky has budgeted costs for an expected number of houses in 19X7 as shown next.

Direct materials	$3,500,000
Direct labor	1,000,000
Job construction overhead	1,500,000
Cost of jobs	$6,000,000
Selling and administrative costs	1,500,000
Total costs	**$7,500,000**

The job construction overhead includes approximately $600,000 of fixed costs, such as the salaries of supervisors and depreciation on equipment. The selling and administrative costs include $300,000 of variable costs, such as sales commissions and bonuses that depend fundamentally on overall profitability.

Podolsky wants an operating income of $1.5 million for 19X7.

Compute the average target markup percentage for setting prices as a percentage of

a. Prime costs (direct materials plus direct labor)
b. The full "cost of jobs"
c. The variable "cost of jobs"
d. The full "cost of jobs" plus selling and administrative costs
e. The variable "cost of jobs" plus variable selling and administrative costs

4. **Terminology and Straightforward Interpretations of Unit Costs.**   Following is the income statement of a manufacturer of blue jeans:

DANUBE COMPANY
Income Statement for the Year Ended December 31, 19X4

	Total	Per Unit
Sales	$40,000,000	$20.00
Less manufacturing cost of goods sold	24,000,000	12.00
Gross margin	$16,000,000	$ 8.00
Less selling and administrative expenses	15,000,000	7.50
Operating income	$ 1,000,000	$ .50

Danube had manufactured 2 million pairs of jeans, which had been sold to various clothing wholesalers and department stores. At the start of 19X5, the president, Rosemary Munoz, died from a stroke. Her son, Hector, became the new president. Hector had worked for 15 years in the marketing phases of the business. He knew very little about accounting and manufacturing, which were his mother's strengths. Hector has several questions for you including inquiries regarding the pricing of special orders.

a. To prepare better answers, you decide to recast the income statement in contribution form. Variable manufacturing cost was $19 million. Variable selling and administrative expenses, which were mostly sales commissions, shipping expenses, and advertising allowances paid to customers based on units sold, were $9 million.

b. Hector asks, "I can't understand financial statements until I know the meaning of various terms. In scanning my mother's assorted notes, I found the following pertaining to both total and unit costs: *absorption cost, full manufacturing cost, variable cost, full cost, fully allocated cost, gross margin, contribution margin.* Using our data for 19X4, please give me a list of these costs, their total amounts, and their per-unit amounts."

c. "Near the end of 19X4 I brought in a special order from Sears for 100,000 jeans at $17 each. I said I'd accept a flat $20,000 sales commission instead of the usual 6% of selling price, but my mother refused the order. She usually upheld a relatively rigid pricing policy, saying that it was bad business to accept orders that did not at least generate full manufacturing cost plus 80% of full manufacturing cost.

   "That policy bothered me. We had idle capacity. The way I figured, our manufacturing costs would go up by $100,000 \times \$12 = \$1,200,000$, but our selling and administrative expenses would go up by only $20,000. That would mean additional operating income of $100,000 \times (\$17 - \$12)$ minus $20,000, or $500,000 minus $20,000, or $480,000. That's too much money to give up just to maintain a general pricing policy. Was my analysis of the impact on operating income correct? If not, please show me the correct additional operating income."

d. After receiving the explanations offered in parts a and b, Hector said: "Forget that I had the Sears order. I had an even bigger order from J. C. Penney. It was for 500,000 units and would have filled the plant completely. I told my mother I'd settle for no commission. There would have been no selling and administrative costs whatsoever because J. C. Penney would pay for the shipping and would not get any advertising allowances.

   "J. C. Penney offered $9.20 per unit. Our fixed manufacturing costs would have been spread over 2.5 million instead of 2 million units. Wouldn't it have been advantageous to accept the offer? Our old fixed manufacturing costs were $2.50 per unit. The added volume would reduce that cost more than our loss on our variable costs per unit.

   "Am I correct? What would have been the impact on total operating income if we had accepted the order?"

5. **Unit Costs and Capacity.**   (CMA, adapted.) Moorhead Manufacturing Company produces two industrial solvents for which the following data have been tabulated. Fixed manufacturing cost is applied to products at a rate of $1.00 per machine-hour.

Per Unit	XY-7	BD-4
Selling price	$6.00	$4.00
Variable manufacturing costs	3.00	1.50
Fixed manufacturing cost	.80	.20
Variable selling cost	2.00	2.00

The sales manager has had a $160,000 increase in her budget allotment for advertising and wants to apply the money on the most profitable product. The solvents are not substitutes for one another in the eyes of the company's customers.

a. How many machine-hours does it take to produce one XY-7? To produce one BD-4? (*Hint:* Focus on applied fixed manufacturing cost.)

b. Suppose Moorhead has only 100,000 machine-hours that can be made available to produce XY-7 and BD-4. If the potential increase in sales units for either product resulting from advertising is far in excess of these production capabilities, which product should be produced and advertised and what is the estimated increase in contribution margin earned?

6. **Dropping a Product Line.**   Hambley's Toy Store is on Regent Street in London. It has a magic department near the main door. Suppose that management is considering dropping the magic department, which has consistently shown an operating loss. The predicted income statements, in thousands of pounds (£), follow (for ease of analysis, only three product lines are shown):

	Total	General Merchandise	Electronic Products	Magic Department
Sales	£6,000	£5,000	£400	£600
Variable expenses	4,090	3,500	200	390
Contribution margin	£1,910 (32%)	£1,500 (30%)	£200 (50%)	£210 (35%)
Fixed expenses (compensation, depreciation, property taxes, insurance, etc.)	1,110	750	50	310
Operating income	£ 800	£ 750	£150	£(100)

The £310,000 of magic department fixed expenses include the compensation of employees of £100,000. These employees will be released if the magic department is abandoned. All equipment is fully depreciated, so none of the £310,000 pertains to such items. Furthermore, disposal values of equipment will be exactly offset by the costs of removal and remodeling.

If the magic department is dropped, the manager will use the vacated space for either more general merchandise or more electronic products. The expansion of general merchandise would not entail hiring any additional salaried help, but more electronic products would require an additional person at an annual cost of £25,000. The manager thinks that sales of general merchandise would increase by £300,000; electronic products, by £200,000. The manager's modest predictions are partially based on the fact that she thinks the magic department has helped lure customers to the store and thus improved overall sales. If the magic department is closed, that lure would be gone.

Should the magic department be closed? Explain, showing computations.

CHAPTER 9

Relevant Accounting Information Used to Make Production Decisions

Should Chrysler make the tires it mounts on its cars, or should it buy them from suppliers? Should General Mills sell the flour it mills, or should it use the flour to make more breakfast cereal? Should American Airlines add routes to use idle airplanes, or should it sell the planes? Successful managers can discriminate between relevant and irrelevant information in making decisions such as these. In the preceding chapter we provided a framework for identifying relevant costs and applied the framework to various marketing decisions. In this chapter we extend the analysis by introducing the concepts of opportunity cost and differential costs and by examining some production decisions: make or buy, sell or process further, and replace or keep equipment.

This chapter and the preceding one illustrate relevant costs for many types of decisions. Does this mean that each decision requires a different approach to identifying relevant costs? No. *The fundamental principle in all decision situations is that relevant costs are future costs that differ among alternatives.* The principle is simple, but its application is not always straightforward. Because it is so important to be able to apply this principle, we present multiple examples.

OPPORTUNITY, OUTLAY, AND DIFFERENTIAL COSTS

The concept of opportunity cost is often used by decision makers. An **opportunity cost** is the maximum available contribution to profit forgone (or passed up) by using limited resources for a particular purpose. This definition indicates that opportunity cost is not the usual outlay cost recorded in accounting. An **outlay cost,** which requires a cash disbursement sooner or later, is the typical cost recorded by accountants.

An example of an opportunity cost is the salary forgone by a person who quits a job to start a business. Consider Maria Morales, a certified public accountant employed by a large accounting firm at $60,000 per year. She is yearning to have her own independent practice.

Maria's alternatives may be framed in more than one way. A straightforward comparison follows:

| | Alternatives Under Consideration | | |
	Remain as Employee	Open an Independent Practice	Difference
Revenues	$60,000	$200,000	$140,000
Outlay costs (operating expenses)	—	120,000	120,000
Income effects per year	$60,000	$ 80,000	$ 20,000

The annual difference of $20,000 favors Maria's choosing independent practice.

This tabulation is sometimes called a *differential analysis.* The *differential revenue* is $140,000, the *differential cost* is $120,000, and the *differential income* is $20,000. Each amount is the difference between the corresponding items under each alternative being considered. **Differential cost** and **incremental cost** are widely used synonyms. They are defined as the difference in total cost between two alternatives. For instance, the differential costs or incremental costs of increasing production from 1,000 automobiles to 1,200 automobiles per week would be the additional costs of producing the additional 200 automobiles each week. In the reverse situation, the decline in costs caused by reducing production from 1,200 to 1,000 automobiles per week would often be called *differential* or *incremental savings.*

Returning to Maria Morales, focus on the meaning of opportunity cost. What is the contribution to profit of the best of the rejected alternatives? Independent practice has an opportunity cost of $60,000, the forgone annual salary.

These same facts may also be presented as follows:

		Alternative Chosen: Independent Practice
Revenue		$200,000
Expenses		
Outlay costs (operating expenses)	$120,000	
Opportunity cost of employee salary	60,000	180,000
Income effects per year		$ 20,000

Ponder the two preceding tabulations. Each produces the correct key difference between alternatives, $20,000. The first tabulation does not mention opportunity cost because the economic impacts (in the form of revenues and outlay costs) are individually measured for each of the alternatives (two in this case). Neither alternative has been excluded from consideration. The second tabulation mentions opportunity cost because the $60,000 annual economic impact of the *best excluded* alternative is included as a cost of the chosen alternative. The failure to recognize opportunity cost in the second tabulation will misstate the difference between alternatives.

Suppose Morales prefers less risk and chooses to stay as an employee:

		Alternative Chosen: Remain as Employee
Revenue		$ 60,000
Expenses		
Outlay costs	$ 0	
Opportunity cost of		
independent practice	80,000	80,000
Decrease in income per year		$(20,000)

If the employee alternative is selected, the key difference in favor of independent practice is again $20,000. The opportunity cost is $80,000, the annual operating income forgone by rejecting the best excluded alternative. Morales is sacrificing $20,000 annually to avoid the risks of an independent practice. In sum, the opportunity cost is the contribution of the best alternative that is excluded from consideration.

The major message here is straightforward: Do not overlook opportunity costs. Consider a homeowner who has made the final payment on the mortgage. While celebrating, the owner says, "It's a wonderful feeling to know that future occupancy is free of any interest cost!" Many owners have similar thoughts. Why? Because no future outlay costs for interest are required. Nevertheless, there is an opportunity cost of continuing to live in the home. After all, an alternative would be to sell the home, place the proceeds in some other investment, and rent an apartment. The owner forgoes the interest in the other investment, so this forgone interest income becomes an opportunity cost of home ownership.

MAKE-OR-BUY DECISIONS

Companies often must decide whether to produce a product or service within the firm or purchase it from an outside supplier. They apply relevant cost analysis to a variety of such make-or-buy decisions, including:

- Boeing's decision whether to buy or make many of the tools used in assembling 747 airplanes.
- IBM's decision whether to develop its own operating system for a new computer or to buy it from a software vendor.
- A local school district's decision whether to use its own personnel or hire a consulting firm to design and implement a new computerized accounting system.

Make-or-Buy and Idle Facilities

To focus on basic principles, we examine relatively straightforward make-or-buy decisions. Consider manufacturers who must often decide whether to make or buy a product. For example, should a firm manufacture its own parts and subassemblies or buy them from vendors? Sometimes qualitative factors dominate quantitative assessments of costs. Some manufacturers always make parts because they want to control quality, others because they possess special know-how, usually skilled labor or rare materials needed in production. Alternatively, some companies always purchase parts to protect mutually advantageous long-run relationships with their suppliers. These companies may deliberately buy from vendors even during slack times to avoid difficulties in obtaining needed parts during boom times, when there may well be shortages of materials and workers, but no shortage of sales orders.

What quantitative factors are relevant to the decision of whether to make or buy? The answer, again, depends on the situation. A key factor is whether there are idle facilities. Many companies make parts only when their facilities cannot be used to better advantage.

Assume that the following costs are reported:

General Electric Company Cost of Making Part No. 900		
	Total Cost for 20,000 Units	Cost per Unit
Direct material	$ 20,000	$ 1
Direct labor	80,000	4
Variable factory overhead	40,000	2
Fixed factory overhead	80,000	4
Total costs	$220,000	$11

Another manufacturer offers to sell General Electric (GE) the same part for $10. Should GE make or buy the part?

Although the $11 unit cost shown seemingly indicates that the company should buy, the answer is rarely so obvious. The essential question is the difference in expected future costs between the alternatives. If the $4 fixed overhead per unit consists of costs that will continue regardless of the decision, the entire $4 becomes irrelevant. Examples of such costs include depreciation, property taxes, insurance, and allocated executive salaries.

Again, are only the variable costs relevant? No. Perhaps $20,000 of the fixed costs will be eliminated if the parts are bought instead of made. For example, a supervisor with a $20,000 salary might be released. In other words, fixed costs that may be avoided in the future are relevant.

For the moment, suppose the capacity now used to make parts will become idle if the parts are purchased and the $20,000 supervisor's salary is the only fixed cost that would be eliminated. The relevant computations follow:

	Make		Buy	
	Total	*Per Unit*	*Total*	*Per Unit*
Purchase cost			$200,000	$10
Direct material	$ 20,000	$1		
Direct labor	80,000	4		
Variable factory overhead	40,000	2		
Fixed factory overhead that can be avoided by not making (supervisor's salary)	20,000˙	1˙		
Total relevant costs	$160,000	$8	$200,000	$10
Difference in favor of making	$ 40,000	$2		

˙Note that unavoidable fixed costs of $80,000 – $20,000 = $60,000 are irrelevant. Thus the irrelevant costs per unit are $4 – $1 = $3.

The key to make-or-buy decisions is identifying the *additional* costs for making (or the *costs avoided* by buying) a part or subcomponent. Activity analysis helps identify these costs. Production of a product requires a set of activities. A company with accurate measurements of the costs of its various activities can better estimate the additional costs incurred to produce an item. GE's activities for production of part number 900 were measured by two cost drivers, units of production of $8 per unit and supervision at a $20,000 fixed cost. Sometimes identification and measurement of additional cost drivers, especially non-volume-related cost drivers, can improve the predictions of the additional cost to produce a part or subcomponent.

Essence of Make or Buy: Use of Facilities

The choice in our example is not only whether to make or buy; it is how best to use available facilities. Although the data indicate that making the part is the better choice, the figures are not conclusive—primarily because we have no idea of what can be done with the manufacturing facilities if the component is bought. Only if the released facilities will otherwise remain idle are the preceding figures valid.

Suppose the released facilities can be used advantageously in some other manufacturing activity (to produce a contribution to profits of, say, $55,000) or can be rented out (say, for $35,000). These alternatives merit consideration. The two courses of action now become four (figures are in thousands):

	Make	**Buy and Leave Facilities Idle**	**Buy and Rent out Facilities**	**Buy and Use Facilities for Other Products**
Rent revenue	$ —	$ —	$ 35	$ —
Contribution from other products	—	—	—	55
Obtaining of parts	(160)	(200)	(200)	(200)
Net relevant costs	$(160)	$(200)	$(165)	$(145)

The final column indicates that buying the parts and using the vacated facilities for the production of other products would yield the lowest net costs in this case.

In sum, the make-or-buy decision should focus on relevant costs in a particular decision situation. In all cases, companies should relate make-or-buy decisions to the long-run policies for the use of capacity:

> One company does subcontract work for *other* manufacturers during periods when sales of its own products do not fully use the plant, but such work could not be carried on regularly without expansion of its plant. The profit margin on subcontracts would not be large enough to cover the additional costs of operating an expanded plant, and hence work is accepted only when other business is lacking. The same company sometimes meets a period of high volume by *purchasing* parts or having them made by subcontractors. Although the cost of such parts is usually higher than the cost to make them in the company's own plant, the additional cost is less than it would be if they were made on equipment which could be used only part of the time.[1]

JOINT PRODUCT COSTS

Nature of Joint Products

When two or more manufactured products (1) have relatively significant sales values and (2) are not separately identifiable as individual products until their split-off point, they are called **joint products.** The **split-off point** is that juncture of manufacturing where the joint products become individually identifiable. Any costs beyond that stage are called **separable costs** because they are not part of the joint process and can be exclusively identified with individual products. The costs of manufacturing joint products before the split-off point are called **joint costs.** Examples of joint products include chemicals, lumber, flour, and the products of petroleum refining and meat packing. A meat-packing company cannot kill a sirloin steak; it has to slaughter a steer, which supplies various cuts of dressed meat, hides, and trimmings.

Sell or Process Further

Management frequently faces decisions of whether to sell joint products at split-off or to process some or all products further. Suppose the 500,000 liters of Y can be processed further and sold to the plastics industry as product YA, an ingredient for plastic sheeting. The additional processing cost would be $.08 per liter for manufacturing and distribution, a total of $40,000 for 500,000 liters. The net sales price of YA would be $.16 per liter, a total of $80,000.

Product X will be sold at the split-off point, but management is undecided about Product Y. Should Y be sold or should it be processed into YA? The joint costs must be incurred to reach the split-off point: They do not differ between alternatives and are completely irrelevant to the question of whether to sell or process further. The only approach that will yield valid results is to concentrate on the separable costs and revenue *beyond* split-off, as shown in Figure 9-1.

---

[1]*The Analysis of Cost-Profit Relationships,* National Association of Accountants, Research Series No. 17, p. 552.

FIGURE 9-1   Illustration of Sell or Process Further

	Sell at Split-Off as Y	Process Further and Sell as YA	Difference
Revenues	$30,000	$80,000	$50,000
Separable costs beyond split-off @ $.08	—	40,000	40,000
Income effects	$30,000	$40,000	$10,000

This analysis shows that it would be $10,000 more profitable to process Y beyond split-off than to sell Y at split-off. Briefly, it is profitable to extend processing or to incur additional distribution costs on a joint product *if* the additional revenue exceeds the additional expenses.

Figure 9-2 illustrates another way to compare the alternatives of (1) selling Y at the split-off point and (2) processing Y beyond split-off. It includes the joint costs, which are the same for each alternative and therefore do not affect the difference.

Earlier discussions in this and the preceding chapter have emphasized the desirability of concentrating on totals and being wary of unit costs and allocations of fixed costs. Similarly, the allocation of joint product costs to units of product is fraught with analytical perils.

The allocation of joint costs would not affect the decision, as Figure 9-2 demonstrates. The joint costs are not allocated in the exhibit, but no matter how they might be allocated, the total income effects would be unchanged.

IRRELEVANCE OF PAST COSTS

The ability to recognize and thereby ignore irrelevant costs is sometimes just as important to decision makers as identifying relevant costs. How do we know that past costs, although sometimes predictors, are irrelevant in decision making? Consider such past costs as obsolete inventory and the book value of old equipment to see why they are irrelevant to decisions.

FIGURE 9-2   Sell or Process Further Analysis-Firm as Whole

	(1) Alternative One			(2) Alternative Two			(3) Differential Effects
	X	Y	Total	X	YA	Total	
Revenues	$90,000	$30,000	$120,000	$90,000	$80,000	$170,000	$50,000
Joint costs			$100,000			$100,000	—
Separable costs			—		40,000	40,000	40,000
Total costs			$100,000			$140,000	$40,000
Income effects			$ 20,000			$ 30,000	$10,000

Obsolete Inventory

Suppose General Dynamics has 100 obsolete aircraft parts in its inventory at a manu-facturing cost of $100,000. General Dynamics can (1) remachine the parts for $30,000 and then sell them for $50,000 or (2) scrap them for $5,000. Which should it do?

This is an unfortunate situation, yet the $100,000 past cost is irrelevant to the decision to remachine or scrap. The only relevant factors are the expected future revenues and costs:

	Remachine	Scrap	Difference
Expected future revenue	$ 50,000	$ 5,000	$45,000
Expected future costs	30,000	—	30,000
Relevant excess of revenue over costs	$ 20,000	$ 5,000	$15,000
Accumulated historical inventory cost*	100,000	100,000	—
Net overall loss on project	$(80,000)	$(95,000)	$15,000

*Irrelevant because it is unaffected by the decision.

We can completely ignore the $100,000 historical cost and still arrive at the $15,000 difference, the key figure in the analysis.

Book Value of Old Equipment

Like obsolete parts, the book value of equipment is not a relevant consideration in deciding whether to replace such equipment. When equipment is purchased, its cost is spread over (or charged to) the future periods in which the equipment is expected to be used. This periodic cost is called **depreciation.** The equipment's **book value** (or **net book value**) is the original cost less *accumulated depreciation,* which is the summa-tion of depreciation charged to past periods. For example, suppose a $10,000 ma-chine with a 10-year life has depreciation of $1,000 per year. At the end of 6 years, accumulated depreciation is $6 \times \$1,000 = \$6,000$, and the book value is $\$10,000 - \$6,000 = \$4,000$.

Consider the following data for a decision whether to replace an old machine:

	Old Machine	Replacement Machine
Original cost	$10,000	$8,000
Useful life in years	10	4
Current age in years	6	0
Useful life remaining in years	4	4
Accumulated depreciation	$ 6,000	0
Book value	$ 4,000	Not acquired yet
Disposal value (in cash) now	$ 2,500	Not acquired yet
Disposal value in 4 years	0	0
Annual cash operating costs (maintenance, power, repairs, coolants, etc.)	$ 5,000	$3,000

We have been asked to prepare a comparative analysis of the two alternatives. Before proceeding, consider some important concepts. The most widely misunderstood facet of replacement decision making is the role of the book value of the old equipment in the decision. The book value, in this context, is sometimes called a **sunk cost,** which is really just another term for *historical* or *past cost,* a cost that has already been incurred and, therefore, is irrelevant to the decision-making process. At one time or another, we all try to soothe the wounded pride arising from having made a bad purchase decision by using an item instead of replacing it. It is a serious mistake to think, however, that a current or future action can influence the long-run impact of a past outlay. All past costs are down the drain. Nothing can change what has already happened.

The irrelevance of past costs for decisions does not mean that knowledge of past costs is useless. Often managers use past costs to help predict future costs. In addition, past costs affect future payments for income taxes. However, the past cost *itself* is not relevant. The only relevant cost is the predicted future cost.

In deciding whether to replace or keep existing equipment, four commonly encountered items differ in relevance:[2]

- *Book value of old equipment:* Irrelevant, because it is a past (historical) cost. Therefore, depreciation on old equipment is irrelevant.
- *Disposal value of old equipment:* Relevant (ordinarily), because it is an expected future inflow that usually differs among alternatives.
- *Gain or loss on disposal:* This is the algebraic difference between book value and disposal value. It is therefore a meaningless combination of irrelevant and relevant items. The combination form, *loss* (or *gain*) *on disposal,* blurs the distinction between the irrelevant book value and the relevant disposal value. Consequently, it is best to think of each separately.
- *Cost of new equipment:* Relevant, because it is an expected future outflow that will differ among alternatives. Therefore depreciation on new equipment is relevant.

Figure 9-3 should clarify the foregoing assertions. It deserves close study. Book value of old equipment is irrelevant regardless of the decision-making technique used. The "difference" column in Figure 9-3 shows that the $4,000 book value of the *old* equipment is not an element of difference between alternatives. It should be completely ignored for decision-making purposes. The difference is merely one of timing. The amount written off is still $4,000, regardless of any available alternative. The $4,000 appears on the income statement either as a $4,000 deduction from the $2,500 cash proceeds received to obtain a $1,500 loss on disposal in the first year or as $1,000 of depreciation in each of 4 years. But how it appears is irrelevant to the replacement decision. In contrast, the $2,000 annual depreciation on the new equipment is relevant because the total $8,000 depreciation is a future cost that may be avoided by not replacing. The three relevant items, operating costs, disposal value, and acquisition cost give replacement a net advantage of $2,500.

---

[2]For simplicity, we ignore income tax considerations and the effects of the interest value of money in this chapter. Book value is irrelevant even if income taxes are considered, however, because the relevant item is then the tax cash flow, not the book value. The book value is essential information for predicting the amount and timing of future tax cash flows, but, by itself, the book value is irrelevant.

Examination of Alternatives Over the Long Run

Figure 9-3 is the first example that looks beyond one year. Examining the alternatives over the entire lives ensures that peculiar nonrecurring items (such as loss on disposal) will not obstruct the long-run view vital to many managerial decisions.

Figure 9-4 concentrates on relevant items only: the cash operating costs, the disposal value of the old equipment, and the depreciation on the new equipment. To demonstrate that the amount of the old equipment's book value will not affect the answer, suppose the book value of the old equipment is $500,000 rather than $4,000. Your final answer will not change. The cumulative advantage of replacement is still $2,500. (If you are in doubt, rework this example, using $500,000 as the book value.)

IRRELEVANCE OF FUTURE COSTS THAT WILL NOT DIFFER

In addition to past costs, some *future* costs may be irrelevant because they will be the same under all feasible alternatives. These, too, may be safely ignored for a particular decision. The salaries of many members of top management are examples of expected future costs that will be unaffected by the decision at hand.

Other irrelevant future costs include fixed costs that will be unchanged by such considerations as whether machine X or machine Y is selected. However, it is not merely a case of saying that fixed costs are irrelevant and variable costs are relevant. Variable costs can be irrelevant, and fixed costs can be relevant. For instance, sales commissions might be paid on an order regardless of whether the order was filled from plant G or plant H. Variable costs are irrelevant whenever they do not differ among the alternatives at hand, and fixed costs are relevant whenever they differ under the alternatives at hand.

FIGURE 9-3   Cost Comparison—Replacement of Equipment Including Relevant and Irrelevant Items

	Four Years Together		
	Keep	*Replace*	*Difference*
Cash operating costs	$20,000	$12,000	$8,000
Old equipment (book value)			
Periodic write-off as depreciation	4,000	—	
or			—
Lump-sum write-off		4,000*	
Disposal value	—	−2,500*	2,500
New machine			
Acquisition			
Cost	—	8,000†	−8,000
Total costs	**$24,000**	**$21,500**	**$2,500**

The advantage of replacement is $2,500 for the four years together.

*In a formal income statement, these two items would be combined as "loss on disposal" of $4,000 − $2,500 = $1,500.
†In a formal income statement, written off as straight-line depreciation of $8,000 ÷ 4 = $2,000 for each of 4 years.

FIGURE 9-4   Cost Comparison—Replacement of Equipment, Relevant Items Only

	Four Years Together		
	Keep	Replace	Difference
Cash operating costs	$20,000	$12,000	$8,000
Disposal value of old machine	—	–2,500	2,500
New machine acquisition cost	—	8,000	–8,000
Total relevant costs	$20,000	$17,500	$2,500

BEWARE OF UNIT COSTS

Because unit costs should be analyzed with care in decision making, there are two major ways to go wrong: (1) the inclusion of irrelevant costs, such as the $3 allocation of unavoidable fixed costs in the make-or-buy example that would result in a unit cost of $11 instead of the relevant unit cost of $8, and (2) comparisons of unit costs not computed on the same volume basis, as the following example demonstrates. Generally, be wary of unit fixed costs. Use total costs rather than unit costs. Then, if desired, the totals may be unitized. Machinery sales personnel, for example, often brag about the low unit costs of using the new machines. Sometimes they neglect to point out that the unit costs are based on outputs far in excess of the volume of activity of their prospective customer.

Assume that a new $100,000 machine with a five-year life can produce 100,000 units a year at a variable cost of $1 per unit, as opposed to a variable cost per unit of $1.50 with an old machine. A sales representative claims that the new machine will reduce cost by $.30 per unit. Is the new machine a worthwhile acquisition?

The new machine is attractive at first glance. If the customer's expected volume is 100,000 units, unit-cost comparisons are valid, provided that new depreciation is also considered. Assume that the disposal value of the old equipment is zero. Because depreciation is an allocation of *historical* cost, the depreciation on the old machine is irrelevant. In contrast, the depreciation on the new machine is relevant because the new machine entails a *future* cost that can be avoided by not acquiring it:

	Old Machine	New Machine
Units	100,000	100,000
Variable costs	$150,000	$100,000
Straight-line depreciation	—	20,000
Total relevant costs	$150,000	$120,000
Unit relevant costs	$ 1.50	$ 1.20

Apparently, the sales representative is correct. However, if the customer's expected volume is only 30,000 units per year, the unit costs change in favor of the old machine:

	Old Machine	New Machine
Units	30,000	30,000
Variable costs	$45,000	$30,000
Straight-line depreciation	—	20,000
Total relevant costs	$45,000	$50,000
Unit relevant costs	$ 1.50	$1.6667

CONFLICTS BETWEEN DECISION MAKING AND PERFORMANCE EVALUATION

We have focused on using relevant information in decision making. To motivate people to make optimal decisions, methods of evaluating the performance of managers should be consistent with the decision analysis.

Consider the replacement decision shown in Figure 9-4, where replacing the machine had a $2,500 advantage over keeping it. To motivate managers to make the right choice, the method used to evaluate performance should be consistent with the decision model—that is, it should show better performance when managers replace the machine than when they keep it. Because performance is often measured by accounting income, consider the accounting income in the first year after replacement compared with that in years 2, 3, and 4.

	Year 1		Years 2, 3, and 4	
	Keep	Replace	Keep	Replace
Cash operating costs	$5,000	$3,000	$5,000	$3,000
Depreciation	1,000	2,000	1,000	2,000
Loss on disposal ($4,000 – $2,500)	—	$1,500	—	—
Total charges against revenue	$6,000	$6,500	$6,000	$5,000

If the machine is kept rather than replaced, first-year costs will be $6,500 – $6,000 = $500 lower, and first-year income will be $500 higher. Because managers naturally want to make decisions that maximize the measure of their performance, they may be inclined to keep the machine. This is an example of a conflict between the analysis for decision making and the method used to evaluate performance.

The conflict is especially severe if managers are transferred often from one position to another. Why? Because the $500 first-year advantage for keeping will be offset by a $1,000 annual advantage of replacing in years 2 to 4. (Note that the net difference of $2,500 in favor of replacement over the 4 years together is the same as in Figure 9-4.) A manager who moves to a new position after the first year, however, bears the entire loss on disposal without reaping the benefits of lower operating costs in years 2 to 4.

The decision to replace a machine earlier than planned also reveals that the original decision to purchase the machine may have been flawed. The old machine was bought 6 years ago for $10,000; its expected life was 10 years. However, if a better machine is now available, then the useful life of the old machine was really 6 years, not 10. This feedback on the actual life of the old machine has two possible effects, the first good and the second bad. First, managers might learn from the earlier mistake. If the useful life of the old machine was overestimated, how believable is the prediction that the new machine will have a 4-year life? Feedback can help avoid repeating past mistakes. Second, another mistake might be made to cover up the earlier one. A "loss on disposal" could alert superiors to the incorrect economic-life prediction used in the earlier decision. By avoiding replacement, the $4,000 remaining book value is spread over the future as "depreciation," a more appealing term than "loss on disposal." The superiors may never find out about the incorrect prediction of economic life. The accounting income approach to performance evaluation mixes the financial effects of various decisions, hiding both the earlier misestimation of useful life and the current failure to replace.

The conflict between decision making and performance evaluation is a widespread problem in practice. Unfortunately, there are no easy solutions. In theory, accountants could evaluate performance in a manner consistent with decision making. In our equipment example, this would mean predicting year-by-year income effects over the planning horizon for 4 years, noting that the first year would be poor, and evaluating actual performance against the predictions.

The trouble is that evaluating performance, decision by decision, is a costly procedure. Therefore aggregate measures are used. For example, an income statement shows the results of many decisions, not just the single decision of buying a machine. Consequently, in many cases like our equipment example, managers may be most heavily influenced by the first-year effects on the income statement. Thus managers refrain from taking the longer view that their superiors prefer.

SUMMARY

The previous chapters have focused on identifying relevant information for a variety of decisions. Relevant costs are future costs that differ among alternatives. Past costs are not relevant, but they might help predict future costs.

Sometimes the notion of an opportunity cost is helpful in cost analysis. An opportunity cost is the maximum sacrifice in rejecting an alternative; it is the maximum earnings that might have been obtained if the productive good, service, or capacity had been applied to some alternative use. The opportunity-cost approach does not affect the important final differences between the courses of action, but the format of the analysis differs. This chapter also introduces differential costs or incremental costs, which are the differences in the total costs under each alternative.

Some generalizations about the decisions in this chapter follow:

- Make-or-buy decisions are, fundamentally, examples of obtaining the most profitable use of given facilities.
- Joint product costs are irrelevant in decisions about whether to sell at split-off or process further.
- The book value of old equipment is always irrelevant in replacement decisions. This cost is often called a sunk cost. Disposal value, however, is generally relevant.

Also, be aware that managers are often motivated to reject desirable economic decisions because of a conflict between the measures used in decision making and those used in performance evaluation.

SELF-CORRECTION PROBLEM

1. Figure 9-5 contains data for the Block Company for the year just ended. The company makes industrial power drills. Figure 9-5 shows the costs of the plastic housing separately from the costs of the electrical and mechanical components.

   a. During the year, a prospective customer in an unrelated market offered $82,000 for 1,000 drills. The latter would be in addition to the 100,000 units sold. The regular sales commission rate would have been paid. The president rejected the order because "it was below our costs of $97 per unit." What would operating income have been if the order had been accepted?

   b. A supplier offered to manufacture the year's supply of 100,000 plastic housings for $13.50 each. What would be the effect on operating income if the Block Company purchased rather than made the housings? Assume that $350,000 of the separable fixed costs assigned to housings would have been avoided if the housings were purchased.

   c. The company could have purchased the housings for $13.50 each and used the vacated space for the manufacture of a deluxe version of its drill. Assume that 20,000 deluxe units could have been made (and sold in addition to the 100,000 regular units) at a unit variable cost of $90, exclusive of housings and exclusive of the 10% sales commission. The 20,000 extra plastic housings could also be purchased for $13.50 each. The sales price would have been $130. All the fixed costs pertaining to the plastic housings would have continued, because these costs related primarily to the manufacturing facilities used. What would operating income have been if Block had bought the housings and made and sold the deluxe units?

FIGURE 9-5   Block Company Cost of Industrial Drills

	A	B	A+B
	Electrical and Mechanical Components'	Plastic Housing	Industrial Drills
Sales: 100,000 units, @ $100			$10,000,000
Variable costs			
Direct material	$4,400,000	$ 500,000	$ 4,900,000
Direct labor	400,000	300,000	700,000
Variable factory overhead	100,000	200,000	300,000
Other variable costs	100,000	—	100,000
Sales commissions, @ 10% of sales	1,000,000	—	1,000,000
Total variable costs	$6,000,000	$1,000,000	$ 7,000,000
Contribution margin			$ 3,000,000
Separable fixed costs	$1,900,000	$ 400,000	$ 2,300,000
Common fixed costs	320,000	80,000	400,000
Total fixed costs	$2,220,000	$ 480,000	$ 2,700,000
Operating income			$ 300,000

'Not including the costs of plastic housing (column B).

SOLUTION TO SELF-CORRECTION PROBLEM

1. a. The costs of filling the special order follow:

Direct material	$49,000
Direct labor	7,000
Variable factory overhead	3,000
Other variable costs	1,000
Sales commission @ 10% of $82,000	8,200
Total variable costs	$68,200
Selling price	82,000
Contribution margin	**$13,800**

Operating income would have been $300,000 + $13,800, or $313,800, if the order had been accepted. In a sense, the decision to reject the offer implies that the Block Company is willing to invest $13,800 in immediate gains forgone (an opportunity cost) in order to preserve the long-run selling-price structure.

b. Assuming that $350,000 of the fixed costs could have been avoided by not making the housings and that the other fixed costs would have been continued, the alternatives can be summarized as follows:

	Make	**Buy**
Purchase cost		$1,350,000
Variable costs	$1,000,000	
Avoidable fixed costs	350,000	
Total relevant costs	**$1,350,000**	**$1,350,000**

If the facilities used for plastic housings became idle, the Block Company would be indifferent as to whether to make or buy. Operating income would be unaffected.

c. The effect of purchasing the plastic housings and using the vacated facilities for the manufacture of a deluxe version of its drill is:

Sales would increase by 20,000 units, @ $130		$2,600,000
Variable costs exclusive of parts would increase by		
20,000 units, @ $90	$1,800,000	
Plus: sales commission, 10% of $2,600,000	260,000	2,060,000
Contribution margin on 20,000 units		$ 540,000
Housings: 120,000 rather than 100,000 would be		
needed		
Buy 120,000 @ $13.50	$1,620,000	
Make 100,000 @ $10 (only the variable costs		
are relevant)	1,000,000	
Excess cost of outside purchase		620,000
Fixed costs, unchanged		—
Disadvantage of making deluxe units		$ 80,000

Operating income would decline to $220,000 ($300,000 – $80,000). The deluxe units bring in a contribution margin of $540,000, but the additional costs of buying rather than making housings is $620,000, leading to a net disadvantage of $80,000.

QUESTIONS

1. "Qualitative factors generally favor making over buying a component." Do you agree? Explain.
2. "Choices are often mislabeled as *make* or *buy*." Do you agree? Explain.
3. Distinguish between an opportunity cost and an outlay cost.
4. "I had a chance to rent my summer home for two weeks for $800. But I chose to have it idle. I didn't want strangers living in my summer house." What term in this chapter describes the $800? Why?
5. "Accountants do not ordinarily record opportunity costs in the formal accounting records." Why?
6. Distinguish between an incremental cost and a differential cost.
7. "Incremental cost is the addition to costs from the manufacture of one unit." Do you agree? Explain.
8. "The differential costs or incremental costs of increasing production from 1,000 automobiles to 1,200 automobiles per week would be the additional costs of producing the additional 200 automobiles." If production were reduced from 1,200 to 1,000 automobiles per week, what would the decline in costs be called?
9. "No technique used to assign the joint cost to individual products should be used for management decisions regarding whether a product should be sold at the split-off point or processed further." Do you agree? Explain.
10. "Past costs are indeed relevant in most instances because they provide the point of departure for the entire decision process." Do you agree? Why?
11. Which of the following items are relevant to replacement decisions? Explain.
    a. Book value of old equipment
    b. Disposal value of old equipment
    c. Cost of new equipment
12. Give an example of a situation in which the performance evaluation model is not consistent with the decision model.
13. "Evaluating performance, decision by decision, is costly. Aggregate measures, like the income statement, are frequently used." How might the wide use of income statements affect managers' decisions about buying equipment?
14. Explain the one-year-at-a-time approach for acquiring equipment in not-for-profit organizations.
15. "The financial consequences of Decision A regarding the acquisition of equipment should be separated from similar Decision B consequences made at a later date." Why?
16. "Some expected future costs may be irrelevant." Do you agree? Explain.
17. "Variable costs are irrelevant whenever they do not differ among the alternatives at hand." Do you agree? Explain.
18. There are two major reasons why unit costs should be analyzed with care in decision making. What are they?
19. "Machinery sales personnel sometimes erroneously brag about the low unit costs of using their machines." Identify one source of an error concerning the estimation of unit costs.

PROBLEMS

1. **Replacing Old Equipment.**   Consider these data regarding Chippewa County's photocopying requirements:

	Old Equipment	Proposed Replacement Equipment
Useful life, in years	5	3
Current age, in years	2	0
Useful life remaining, in years	3	3
Original cost	$25,000	$15,000
Accumulated depreciation	10,000	0
Book value	15,000	Not acquired yet
Disposal value (in cash) now	3,000	Not acquired yet
Disposal value in 2 years	0	0
Annual cash operating costs for power, maintenance, toner, and supplies	14,000	7,500

The county administrator is trying to decide whether to replace the old equipment. Because of rapid changes in technology, she expects the replacement equipment to have only a three-year useful life. Ignore the effects of taxes.

   a. Tabulate a cost comparison that includes both relevant and irrelevant items for the next three years together. (*Hint:* See Figure 9-3.)
   b. Tabulate a cost comparison of all relevant items for the next three years together. Which tabulation is clearer, this one or the one in question 1? (*Hint:* See Figure 9-4.)
   c. Prepare a simple "shortcut" or direct analysis to support your choice of alternatives.

2. **Decision and Performance Model.**   Refer to the preceding problem.

   a. Suppose the "decision model" favored by top management consisted of a comparison of a three-year accumulation of cash under each alternative. As the manager of office operations, which alternative would you choose? Why?
   b. Suppose the "performance evaluation model" emphasized the minimization of overall costs of photocopying operations for the first year. Which alternative would you choose?

3. **Hospital Opportunity Cost.**   An administrator at University Hospital is considering how to use some space made available when the Family Medical Center moved to a new building. She has narrowed her choices as follows:

   a. Use the space to expand laboratory testing. Expected future annual revenue would be $300,000; future costs, $270,000.
   b. Use the space to expand the eye clinic. Expected future annual revenue would be $500,000; future costs, $480,000.
   c. The gift shop is rented by an independent retailer who wants to expand into the vacated space. The retailer has offered a $9,000 yearly rental for the space. All operating expenses will be borne by the retailer.

The administrator's planning horizon is unsettled. However, she has decided that the yearly data given will suffice for guiding her decision.

Tabulate the total relevant data regarding the decision alternatives. Omit the concept of opportunity cost in one tabulation, but use the concept in a second tabulation. As the administrator, which tabulation would you prefer to get if you could receive only one?

4. **Joint Products: Sell or Process Further.** The Visqual Chemical Company produced three joint products at a joint cost of $105,000. These products were processed further and sold as follows:

Chemical Product	Sales	Additional Processing Costs
A	$260,000	$220,000
B	330,000	300,000
C	175,000	100,000

The company has had an opportunity to sell at split-off directly to other processors. If that alternative had been selected, sales would have been: A, $56,000; B. $28,000; and C, $54,000.

The company expects to operate at the same level of production and sales in the forthcoming year.

Consider all the available information, and assume that all costs incurred after split-off are variable.

a. Could the company increase operating income by altering its processing decisions? If so, what would be the expected overall operating income?
b. Which products should be processed further and which should be sold at split-off?

5. **Role of Old Equipment Replacement.** On January 2, 19X1, the K. Sung Company installed a brand-new $84,000 special molding machine for producing a new product. The product and the machine have an expected life of three years. The machine's expected disposal value at the end of 3 years is zero.

On January 3, 19X1, Jill Swain, a star salesperson for a machine tool manufacturer, tells Mr. Sung: "I wish I had known earlier of your purchase plans. I can supply you with a technically superior machine for $99,000. The machine you just purchased can be sold for $16,000. I guarantee that our machine will save $35,000 per year in cash operating costs, although it too will have no disposal value at the end of three years."

Sung examines some technical data. Although he has confidence in Swain's claims, Sung contends: "I'm locked in now. My alternatives are clear: (a) disposal will result in a loss, (b) keeping and using the 'old' equipment avoids such a loss. I have brains enough to avoid a loss when my other alternative is recognizing a loss. We've got to use that equipment until we get our money out of it."

The annual operating costs of the old machine are expected to be $60,000, exclusive of depreciation. Sales, all in cash, will be $850,000 per year. Other annual cash expenses will be $750,000 regardless of this decision. Assume that the equipment in question is the company's only fixed asset.

Ignore income taxes and the time value of money.

a. Prepare statements of cash receipts and disbursements as they would appear in each of the next 3 years under both alternatives. What is the total cumulative increase or decrease in cash for the 3 years?
b. Prepare income statements as they would appear in each of the next 3 years under both alternatives. Assume straight-line depreciation. What is the cumulative increase or decrease in net income for the 3 years?
c. Assume that the cost of the "old" equipment was $1 million rather than $84,000. Would the net difference computed in parts a and b change? Explain.
d. As Jill Swain, reply to Mr. Sung's contentions.
e. What are the irrelevant items in each of your presentations for parts a and b? Why are they irrelevant?

6. **Make or Buy.**   A Volkswagen executive in Germany is trying to decide whether the company should continue to manufacture an engine component or purchase it from Hanover Corporation for 50 deutsche marks (DM) each. Demand for the coming year is expected to be the same as for the current year, 200,000 units. Data for the current year follow:

Direct material	DM5,000,000
Direct labor	2,000,000
Factory overhead, variable	1,000,000
Factory overhead, fixed	2,500,000
Total costs	**DM10,500,000**

   If Volkswagen makes the components, the unit costs of direct material will increase 10%.

   If Volkswagen buys the components, 40% of the fixed costs will be avoided. The other 60% will continue regardless of whether the components are manufactured or purchased. Assume that variable overhead varies with output volume.

a. Tabulate a comparison of the make-or-buy alternatives. Show totals and amounts per unit. Compute the numerical difference between making and buying. Assume that the capacity now used to make the components will become idle if the components are purchased.
b. Assume also that the Volkswagen capacity in question can be rented to a local electronics firm for DM1,250,000 for the coming year. Tabulate a comparison of the net relevant costs of the three alternatives: make, buy and leave capacity idle, buy and rent. Which is the most favorable alternative? By how much in total?

7. **Sell or Process Further.**   ConAgra, Inc. produces meat products with brand names such as Swift, Armour, and Butterball. Suppose one of the company's plants processes beef cattle into various products. For simplicity, assume that there are only three products: steak, hamburger, and hides, and that the average steer costs $500. The three products emerge from a process that costs $100 per cow to run, and output from one steer can be sold for the following net amounts:

Steak (100 pounds)	$300
Hamburger (500 pounds)	500
Hides (120 pounds)	100
Total	**$900**

Assume that each of these three products can be sold immediately or processed further in another ConAgra plant. The steak can be the main course in frozen dinners sold under the Healthy Choice label. The vegetables and desserts in the 400 dinners produced from the 100 pounds of steak would cost $120, and production, sales, and other costs for the 400 meals would total $350. Each meal would be sold wholesale for $1.90.

The hamburger could be made into frozen Salisbury Steak patties sold under the Armour label. The only additional cost would be a $200 processing cost for the 500 pounds of hamburger. Frozen Salisbury Steaks sell wholesale for $1.50 per pound.

The hides can be sold before or after tanning. The cost of tanning one hide is $80, and a tanned hide can be sold for $175.

a. Compute the total profit if all three products are sold at the split-off point.
b. Compute the total profit if all three products are processed further before being sold.
c. Which products should be sold at the split-off point? Which should be processed further?
d. Compute the total profit if your plan in part c is followed.

Financial Planning and Forecasting

CHAPTER 10

The Formal Budgeting Process

Planning is the key to good management. This is true for individuals, small family-owned companies, new high-technology companies, large corporations, government agencies, and nonprofit organizations. For example, most successful students who earn good grades, finance their education, and finish their degrees in a reasonable amount of time do so because they plan their time, their work, and their recreation. These students are *budgeting* their scarce resources to make the best use of their time, money, and energy. Likewise, owners of successful small companies who survive and grow even in difficult economic times carefully plan or budget their inventory purchases and their expansion of facilities so that they do not overextend themselves financially but are still able to meet customers' needs.

High-technology firms are often started by highly intelligent scientists and engineers who have valuable product ideas, but the high-technology firms that thrive are those whose managers also have superior planning and budgeting skills. Coordinating the use of scarce resources in a large, diverse corporation is an extremely complex and vital activity. Budgeting in these large corporations usually is ongoing throughout the year. Taxpayers demand that governments plan for the effective use of their hard-earned dollars, so government budgeting is especially important in difficult economic times, when tax dollars could otherwise have been spent for private purposes. Nonprofit organizations must develop more effective plans to achieve their objectives as they compete for scarce donations or grant monies. Not only are budgets critical to good planning in any endeavor, budgets are necessary for evaluation of performance. Keeping score is an American tradition, whether on the football field or in the boardroom. A *budget*—a formal, quantitative expression of plans (whether for an individual, business, or other organization)—provides a benchmark against which to measure actual performance.

As you will see in this chapter, a budget can be much more than a limit on expenditures. Although government agencies too often use a budget merely as a limit on their spending, businesses and other organizations generally use budgets to focus on operating or financial problems early, so that managers can take steps to avoid or remedy the problems. Thus a budget is a tool that helps managers both *plan* and *control* operations.

Surveys of company practices indicate the importance of budgeting. For example, in a recent survey of manufacturing companies, the top ranked technique for cost reduction and control was budgetary planning and control. Advocates of budgeting maintain that the process of budgeting *forces a manager to become a better administrator and puts planning in the forefront of the manager's mind.* Indeed, failure to draw up, monitor, and adjust budgets to changing conditions is one of the primary reasons behind the collapse of many businesses.

In this chapter we will look at the uses and benefits of budgets and consider the construction of the master budget.

BUDGETS: WHAT THEY ARE AND HOW THEY BENEFIT THE ORGANIZATION

Another way to describe a budget is as a condensed business plan for the forthcoming year (or less). Few investors or bank loan officers today will provide funds for the would-be entrepreneur without a credible business plan. Similarly, within a firm, managers need budgets to guide them in allocating resources and maintaining control and to enable them to measure and reward progress.

Budgeting over Time

The planning horizon for budgeting may vary from one day to many years, depending on the organization's objectives and the uncertainties involved. The most forward-looking budget is the **strategic plan,** which sets the overall goals and objectives of the organization. (Note, though, that some business analysts do not call a strategic plan a budget because it covers no specific period and does not produce forecasted financial statements.)

Long-range planning produces forecasted financial statements for 5- or 10-year periods. Decisions made during long-range planning include addition or deletion of product lines, design and location of new plants, acquisitions of buildings and equipment, and other long-term commitments. Long-range plans are coordinated with **capital budgets,** which detail the planned expenditures for facilities, equipment, new products, and other long-term investments.

A master budget is essentially a more extensive analysis of the first year of the long-range plan. A *budget* is a formal, quantitative expression of management plans. A **master budget** summarizes the planned activities of all subunits of an organization—sales, production, distribution, and finance. The master budget quantifies targets for sales, cost-driver activity, purchases, production, net income, cash position, and any other objective that management specifies. *Thus, the master budget is a periodic business plan that includes a coordinated set of detailed operating schedules and financial statements.* It includes forecasts of sales, expenses, cash receipts and disbursements, and balance sheets. Master budgets are also called **pro forma statements,** another term for forecasted financial statements. Management might prepare monthly budgets for the year or perhaps monthly budgets for only the first quarter and quarterly budgets for the three remaining quarters. The master budget is the most detailed budget that is coordinated across the whole organization, but individual managers may also prepare daily or weekly *task-oriented* budgets to help them carry out their particular functions and meet operating and financial goals.

Continuous budgets or **rolling budgets** are a very common form of master budgets that add a month in the future as the month just ended is dropped. Continuous budgets compel mangers to think specifically about the forthcoming 12 months and thus maintain a stable planning horizon. As they add a new 12th month to a continuous budget, managers may update the other 11 months as well. Then they can compare actual monthly results with both the original plan and the most recently revised plan.

Components of Master Budget

The terms used to describe assorted budget schedules vary from organization to organization; however, most master budgets have common elements. The usual master budget for a nonmanufacturing company has the following components:

A. Operating budget
   1. Sales budget (and other cost-driver budgets as necessary)
   2. Purchases budget
   3. Cost-of-goods-sold budget
   4. Operating expenses budget
   5. Budgeted income statement
B. Financial budget
   1. Capital budget
   2. Cash budget
   3. Budgeted balance sheet

Figure 10-1 presents a condensed diagram of the relationships among the various parts of a master budget for a nonmanufacturing company. In addition to these categories, manufacturing companies that maintain physical product inventories prepare ending inventory budgets and additional budgets for each type of resource activity (such as labor, materials, and factory overhead).

The two major parts of a master budget are the operating budget and the financial budget. The **operating budget** focuses on the income statement and its supporting schedules. Though sometimes called the **profit plan,** an operating budget may show a budgeted *loss,* or even be used to budget expenses in an organization or agency with no sales revenues. In contrast, the **financial budget** focuses on the effects that the operating budget and other plans (such as capital budgets and repayments of debt) will have on cash.

In addition to the master budget, there are countless forms of special budgets and related reports. For example, a report might detail goals and objectives for improvements in quality or customer satisfaction during the budget period.

Advantages of Budgets

All managers do some kind of planning or budgeting. Sometimes plans and budgets are unwritten, especially in small organizations. This might work in a small organi-

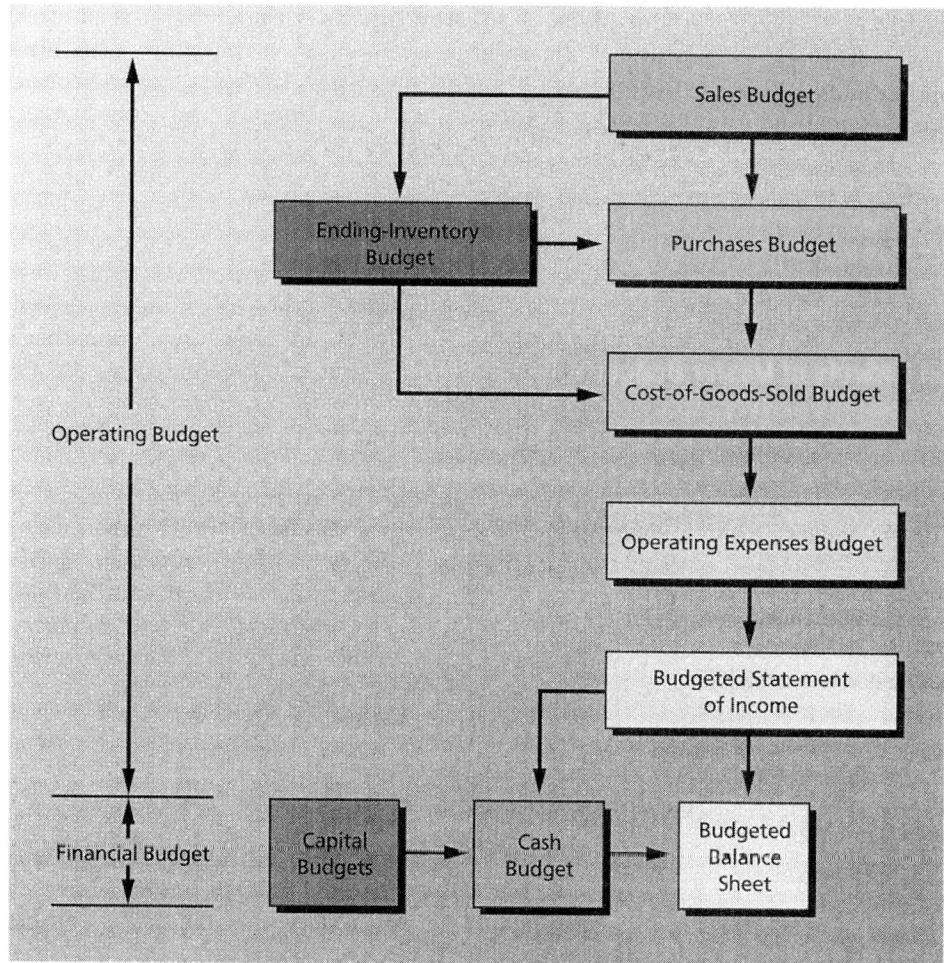

FIGURE 10-1
Preparation of Master Budget for Nonmanufacturing Company

zation, but as an organization grows, informal, seat-of-the-pants planning is not enough. A more formal budgetary system becomes more than an attractive alternative—it is a necessity.

Skeptical managers have claimed, "I face too many uncertainties and complications to make budgeting worthwhile for me." Be wary of such claims. Planning and budgeting are especially important in uncertain environments. A budget allows *systematic rather than chaotic reaction to change.* For example, the Natural Resources Group of W. R. Grace & Co. greatly reduced a planned expansion in reaction to a worldwide abundance of oil and gas. A top executive, quoted in the company's annual report, stated that "management used the business planning process to adjust to changes in operating conditions."

Three major benefits of budgeting are as follows:

1. Budgeting compels managers to think ahead by formalizing their responsibilities for planning.
2. Budgeting provides definite expectations that are the best framework for judging subsequent performance.
3. Budgeting aids managers in coordinating their efforts, so that the objectives of the organization as a whole match the objectives of its parts.

Let's look more closely at each of these benefits.

Formalization of planning.   Budgeting forces managers to think ahead—to anticipate and prepare for changing conditions. The budgeting process makes planning an *explicit* management responsibility. Too often, managers operate from day to day, extinguishing one business brush fire after another. They simply have "no time" for any tough-minded thinking beyond the next day's problems. Planning takes a back seat to or is actually obliterated by daily pressures.

The trouble with the day-to-day approach to managing an organization is that objectives are never crystallized. Managers react to current events rather than plan for the future. To prepare a budget, a manager should set goals and objectives, and establish policies to aid their achievement. The objectives are the destination points, and budgets are the road maps guiding us to those destinations. Without goals and objectives, company operations lack direction; problems are not foreseen; and results are difficult to interpret afterward.

Expectations: framework for judging performance.   Budgeted goals and performance are generally a better basis for judging actual results than is past performance. The news that a company had sales of $100 million this year, as compared with $80 million the previous year, may or may not indicate that the company has been effective and has met company objectives. Perhaps sales should have been $110 million this year. The major drawback of using historical results for judging current performance is that inefficiencies may be concealed in the past performance. Intervening changes in economic conditions, technology, maneuvers by competitors, personnel, and so forth also limit the usefulness of comparisons with the past.

Communication and coordination.   Another benefit of budgeting is that personnel are informed of what is expected of them. Nobody likes to drift along, not knowing what "the boss" expects or hopes to achieve. A good budget process communicates both from the top down and from the bottom up. Top management makes clear the goals and objectives of the organization in its budgetary directives to middle- and lower-level managers, and increasingly to all employees. Employees and lower-level managers then inform higher-level managers how they plan to achieve the goals and objectives.

Budgets also help managers coordinate objectives. For example, a budget forces purchasing personnel to integrate their plans with production requirements, while production managers use the sales budget and delivery schedule to help them anticipate and plan for the employees and physical facilities they will require. Similarly, financial officers use the sales budget, purchasing requirements, and so forth to anticipate the company's need for cash. Thus the budgetary process forces managers to visualize the relationship of their department's activities to other departments and to the company as a whole.

ILLUSTRATION OF PREPARATION OF MASTER BUDGET

Now that you know what budgets are and why they are important, we can return to Figure 10-1 and trace the preparation of the master budget components. *Do not rush; follow each step carefully and completely.* Although the process may seem largely mechanical, remember that the master-budgeting process generates key decisions regarding pricing, product lines, capital expenditures, research and development, personnel assignments, and so forth. Therefore, the first draft of the budget leads to decisions that prompt subsequent drafts before a final budget is chosen. Because budget preparation is somewhat mechanical, many organizations use powerful spreadsheet or modeling software to prepare and modify budget drafts. Addendum 10 discusses using personal computer spreadsheets for budgeting.

Description of Problem

To illustrate the budgeting process we will use as an example the Cooking Hut Company (CHC), a local retailer of a wide variety of kitchen and dining room items. The company rents a retail store in a midsized community near a large metropolitan area. CHC's management prepares a continuous budget to aid financial and operating decisions. For simplicity in this illustration, the planning horizon is only 4 months, April through July. In the past, sales have increased during this season. Collections lag behind sales, and cash is needed for purchases, wages, and other operating outlays. In the past, the company has met this cash squeeze with the help of short-term loans from a local bank and will continue to do so, repaying those loans as cash is available.

Figure 10-2 is the closing balance sheet for the fiscal year just ended. Sales in March were $40,000. Monthly sales are forecasted as follows:

April	$50,000
May	$80,000
June	$60,000
July	$50,000
August	$40,000

Management expects future sales collections to follow past experience: 60% of the sales should be in cash and 40% on credit. All credit accounts are collected in the month following the sales. The $16,000 of accounts receivable on March 31 represents credit sales made in March (40% of $40,000). Uncollectable accounts are negligible and are to be ignored. Also ignore all local, state, and federal taxes for this illustration.

Because deliveries from suppliers and customer demands are uncertain, at the end of each month, CHC wants to have on hand a basic inventory of items valued at $20,000 plus 80% of the expected cost of goods sold for the following month. The cost of merchandise sold averages 70% of sales. Therefore, the inventory on March 31 is $20,000 + .7(.8 × April sales of $50,000) = $20,000 + $28,000 = $48,000. The purchase terms available to CHC are net, 30 days. CHC pays for each month's purchases as follows: 50% during that month and 50% during the next month. Therefore, the ac-

---

FIGURE 10-2 **The Cooking Hut Company**
                        Balance Sheet March 31, 19X1

Assets

Current assets		
Cash	$10,000	
Accounts receivable, net (.4 × March sales of		
$40,000)	16,000	
Merchandise inventory, $20,000 + .7 (.8 × April		
sales of $50,000)	48,000	
Unexpired insurance	1,800	$ 75,800
Plant assets		
Equipment, fixtures, and other	$37,000	
Accumulated depreciation	12,800	24,200
Total assets		**$100,000**

Liabilities and Owners' Equity

Current liabilities		
Accounts payable (.5 × March purchases		
of $33,600)	$16,800	
Accrued wages and commissions payable		
($1,250 + $3,000)	4,250	$ 21,050
Owners' equity		78,950
Total liabilities and owners' equity		**$100,000**

---

counts payable balance on March 31 is 50% of March's purchases, or $33,600 × .5 = $16,800.

CHC pays wages and commissions semimonthly, half a month after they are earned. They are divided into two portions: monthly fixed wages of $2,500 and commissions, equal to 15% of sales, which we will assume are uniform throughout each month. Therefore, the March 31 balance of accrued wages and commissions payable is (.5 × $2,500) + .5(.15 × $40,000) = $1,250 + $3,000 = $4,250. CHC will pay this $4,250 on April 15.

In addition to buying new fixtures for $3,000 cash in April, CHC's other monthly expenses are as follows:

Miscellaneous expenses	5% of sales, paid as incurred
Rent	$2,000, paid as incurred
Insurance	$200 expiration per month
Depreciation, including new fixtures	$500 per month

The company wants a minimum of $10,000 as a cash balance at the end of each month. To keep this simple, we will assume that CHC can borrow or repay loans in multiples of $1,000. Management plans to borrow no more cash than necessary and to repay as promptly as possible. Assume that borrowing occurs at the beginning and repayment at the end of the months in question. Interest is paid, under the terms of this credit arrangement, when the related loan is repaid. The interest rate is 18% per year.

Steps in Preparation of Master Budget

The principal steps in preparing the master budget are:

Operating Budget

1. Using the data given, prepare the following detailed schedules for each of the months of the planning horizon:
   a. Sales budget
   b. Cash collections from customers
   c. Purchases budget
   d. Disbursements for purchases
   e. Operating expense budget
   f. Disbursements for operating expenses
2. Using these schedules, prepare a budgeted income statement for the 4 months ending July 31, 19X1 (Figure 10-3).

Financial Budget

3. Using the data given and the supporting schedules, prepare the following forecasted financial statements:
   a. Cash budget including details of borrowings, repayments, and interest for each month of the planning horizon (Figure 10-4)
   b. Budgeted balance sheet as of July 31, 19X1 (Figure 10-5)

You will need schedules 1a, 1c, and 1e to prepare the budgeted income statement (Figure 10-3), and schedules 1b, 1d, and 1f to prepare the cash budget (Figure 10-4).

Organizations with effective budget systems have specific guidelines for the steps and timing of budget preparation. Although the details differ, the guidelines invariably include the preceding steps. As we follow these steps to examine the schedules of this illustrative problem, *be sure that you understand the source of each figure in each schedule and budget.* The logic of this manual example is identical to the logic used to prepare computerized budgeting models and systems (see the addendum).

Step 1: Preparation of Operating Budget

You should now be ready to trace the budgeting process.

Step 1a: Sales budget.   The sales budget (schedule a in the table below) is the starting point for budgeting because inventory levels, purchases, and operating expenses are geared to the rate of sales activities (and other cost drivers that are not present in this example). Accurate sales and cost-driver activity forecasting is essential to effective budgeting; sales forecasting is considered in a later section of this chapter. March sales are included in schedule a because they affect cash collections in April. Trace the final column in schedule a to the first row of Figure 10-3. In nonprofit organizations, forecasts of revenue or some level of services are also the focal points for budgeting. Examples are patient revenues and government reimbursement expected by hospitals and donations expected by churches. If no revenues are generated, as in the case of municipal fire protection, a desired level of service is predetermined.

Step 1b: Cash collections.   It is easiest to prepare schedule b, cash collections, at the same time as preparing the sales budget. Cash collections include the current month's cash sales plus the previous month's credit sales. We will use total collections in preparing the cash budget—see Figure 10-4.

	March	April	May	June	July	April-July Total
Schedule a: Sales Budget						
Credit sales, 40%	$16,000	$20,000	$32,000	$24,000	$20,000	
Plus cash sales, 60%	24,000	30,000	48,000	36,000	30,000	
Total sales	$40,000	$50,000	$80,000	$60,000	$50,000	$240,000
Schedule b: Cash Collections						
Cash safes this month		$30,000	$48,000	$36,000	$30,000	
Plus 100% of last month's						
credit sales		16,000	20,000	32,000	24,000	
Total collections		$46,000	$68,000	$68,000	$54,000	

	March	April	May	June	July	April-July Total
Schedule c: Purchases Budget						
Desired ending inventory	$48,000˙	$64,800	$ 53,600	$48,000	$42,400	
Plus cost of goods sold[†]	28,000	35,000	56,000	42,000	35,000	$168,000
Total needed	$76,000	$99,800	$109,600	$90,000	$77,400	
Less beginning inventory	42,400[‡]	48,000	64,800	53,600	48,000	
Purchases	$33,600	$51,800	$ 44,800	$36,400	$29,400	
Schedule d: Disbursements for Purchases						
50% of last month's purchases		$16,800	$ 25,900	$22,400	$18,200	
Plus 50% of this month's purchases		25,900	. 22,400	18,200	14,700	
Disbursements for purchases		$42,700	$ 48,300	$40,600	$32,900	

˙$20,000 + (.8 × April cost of goods sold) = $20,000 + .8($35,000) = $48,000.
[†].7 × March sales of $40,000 = $28,000; .7 × April sales of $50,000 = $35,000, and so on.
[‡]$20,000 + (.8 × March cost of goods sold of $28,000) = $20,000 + $22,400 = $42,400.

Step 1c: Purchases budget.   After sales are budgeted, prepare the purchases budget (schedule c). The total merchandise needed will be the sum of the desired ending inventory plus the amount needed to fulfill budgeted sales demand. The total need will be partially met by the beginning inventory; the remainder must come from planned purchases. These purchases are computed as follows:

budgeted purchases = desired ending inventory + cost of goods sold − beginning inventory

Trace the total purchases figure in the final column of schedule c to the second row of Figure 10-3.

Step 1d: Disbursements for purchases. Schedule d, disbursements for purchases, is based on the purchases budget. Disbursements include 50% of the current month's purchases and 50% of the previous month's purchases. We will use total disbursements in preparing the cash budget, Figure 10-4, for the financial budget.

Step 1e: Operating expense budget. The budgeting of operating expenses depends on various factors. Month-to-month fluctuations in sales volume and other cost-driver activities directly influence many operating expenses. Examples of expenses driven by sales volume include sales commissions and many delivery expenses. Other expenses are not influenced by sales or other cost-driver activity (such as rent, insurance, depreciation, and salaries) within appropriate relevant ranges and are regarded as fixed. Trace the total operating expenses in the final column of schedule e, which summarizes these expenses, to the budgeted income statement, Figure 10-3.

	March	April	May	June	July	April-July Total
Schedule e: Operating Expense Budget						
Wages (fixed)	$2,500	$ 2,500	$ 2,500	$ 2,500	$ 2,500	
Commissions (15% of current month's sales)	6,000	7,500	12,000	9,000	7,500	
Total wages and commissions	**$8,500**	$10,000	$14,500	$11,500	$10,000	$46,000
Miscellaneous expenses (5% of current sales)		2,500	4,000	3,000	2,500	12,000
Rent (fixed)		2,000	2,000	2,000	2,000	8,000
Insurance (fixed)		200	200	200	200	800
Depreciation (fixed)		500	500	500	500	2,000
Total operating expenses		**$15,200**	**$21,200**	**$17,200**	**$15,200**	**$68,800**

FIGURE 10-3   The Cooking Hut Company Budgeted Income Statement for 4 Months Ending July 31, 19X1

	Data	Source of Data
Sales	$240,000	Schedule a
Cost of goods sold	168,000	Schedule c
Gross margin	$ 72,000	
Operating expenses:		
Wages and commissions	$46,000	Schedule e
Rent	8,000	Schedule e
Miscellaneous	12,000	Schedule e
Insurance	800	Schedule e
Depreciation	2,000 68,800	Schedule e
Income from operations	$ 3,200	
Interest expense	675	Figure 10-4
Net income	$ 2,525	

FIGURE 10-4   The Cooking Hut Company
Cash Budget for 4 Months Ending July 31, 19X1

	April	May	June	July
Beginning cash balance	$ 10,000	$10,550	$10,970	$ 10,965
Cash receipts				
Collections from customers (schedule b)	46,000	68,000	68,000	54,000
Total cash available, before financing **(w)**	$ 56,000	$78,550	$78,970	$ 64,965
Cash disbursements				
Merchandise (schedule d)	42,700	48,300	40,600	32,900
Operating expenses (schedule f)	13,750	18,250	18,000	15,250
Purchase of new fixtures (given)	3,000	—	—	—
Total disbursements **(x)**	$ 59,450	$66,550	$58,600	$ 48,150
Minimum cash balance desired **(y)**	10,000	10,000	10,000	10,000
Total cash needed	$ 69,450	$76,550	$68,600	$ 58,150
Excess (deficiency) of total cash available over total cash needed before financing **(w − x − y)**	$(13,450)	$ 2,000	$10,370	$ 6,815
Financing				
Borrowing (at beginning of month)	$ 14,000†			
Repayments (at end of month)	—	$ (1,000)	$ (9,000)	$ (4,000)
Interest (at 18% per year)‡	—	(30)	(405)	(240)
Total cash increase (decrease) from financing **(z)**	$ 14,000	$ (1,030)	$ (9,405)	$ (4,240)
Ending cash balance **(w − x + z)**	$ 10,550	$10,970	$10,965	$ 12,575

*Letters are keyed to the explanation in the text.
†Borrowing and repayment of principal are made in multiples of $1,000, at an interest rate of 18% per year.
‡Interest computations: .18 × $1,000 × 2/12; .18 × $9,000 × 3/12; .18 × $4,000 × 4/12.

Step 1f: Operating expense disbursements.   Disbursements for operating expenses are based on the operating expense budget. Disbursements include 50% of last month's and this month's wages and commissions, and miscellaneous and rent expenses. We will use the total of these disbursements in preparing the cash budget, Figure 10-4.

	March	April	May	June	July	April-July Total
Schedule f: Disbursements for Operating Expenses						
Wages and commission						
50% of last month's expenses		$ 4,250	$ 5,000	$ 7,250	$ 5,750	
50% of this month's expenses		5,000	7,250	5,750	5,000	
Total wages and commissions		$ 9,250	$12,250	$13,000	$10,750	
Miscellaneous expenses		2,500	4,000	3,000	2,500	
Rent		2,000	2,000	2,000	2,000	
Total disbursements		**$13,750**	**$18,250**	**$18,000**	**$15,250**	

Step 2: Preparation of Budgeted Income Statement

Steps 1a through 1f provide enough information to construct a budgeted income statement *from operations* (Figure 10-3). The income statement will be complete after addition of the interest expense, which is computed after the cash budget has been prepared. Budgeted income from operations is often a benchmark for judging management performance.

Step 3: Preparation of Financial Budget

The second major part of the master budget is the financial budget, which consists of the capital budget, cash budget, and ending balance sheet. This chapter focuses on the cash budget and the ending balance sheet. In our illustration, the $3,000 purchase of new fixtures would be included in the capital budget.

Step 3a: Cash budget.   The **cash budget** is a statement of planned cash receipts and disbursements. The cash budget is heavily affected by the level of operations summarized in the budgeted income statement. The cash budget has the following major sections, where the letters **w, x, y,** and **z** refer to the lines in Figure 10-4 that summarize the effects of that section.

The *total cash available before financing* **(w)** equals the beginning cash balance plus cash receipts. Cash receipts depend on collections from customers' accounts receivable and cash sales and on other operating income sources. Trace total collections from schedule b to Figure 10-4.

Cash disbursements **(x)** for

1. Purchases depend on the credit terms extended by suppliers and the bill-paying habits of the buyer (disbursements for merchandise from schedule d should be traced to Figure 10-4).
2. Payroll depends on wage, salary, and commission terms and on payroll dates (wages and commissions from schedule f should be traced to Figure 10-4).
3. Some costs and expenses depend on contractual terms for installment payments, mortgage payments, rents, leases, and miscellaneous items (miscellaneous and rent from schedule f should be traced to Figure 10-4).
4. Other disbursements include outlays for fixed assets, long-term investments, dividends, and the like (the $3,000 expenditure for new fixtures).

Management determines the *minimum cash balance desired* **(y)** depending on the nature of the business and credit arrangements.

Financing requirements **(z)** depend on how the *total cash available,* **w** in Figure 10-4, compares with the *total cash needed.* Needs include the disbursements, **x,** plus the desired ending cash balance, **y.** If the total cash available is less than the cash needed, borrowing is necessary—Figure 10-4 shows that CHC will borrow $14,000 in April to cover the planned *deficiency.* If there is an *excess,* loans may be repaid—$1,000, $9,000, and $4,000 are repaid in May, June, and July, respectively. The pertinent outlays for interest expenses are usually contained in this section of the cash budget. Trace the calculated interest expense to Figure 10-3, which then will be complete.

The *ending cash balance is* $\mathbf{w} - \mathbf{x} + \mathbf{z}$. Financing, **z,** has either a positive (borrowing) or a negative (repayment) effect on the cash balance. The illustrative cash budget shows the pattern of short-term, "self-liquidating" financing. Seasonal peaks often result in heavy drains on cash—for merchandise purchases and operating expenses— before the sales are made and cash is collected from customers. The resulting loan is "self-liquidating"—that is, the borrowed money is used to acquire merchandise for sale, and the proceeds from sales are used to repay the loan. This "working capital cycle" moves from cash to inventory to receivables and back to cash.

Cash budgets help management to avoid having unnecessary idle cash, on the one hand, and unnecessary cash deficiencies, on the other. A well-managed financing program keeps cash balances from becoming too large or too small.

Step 3b: Budgeted balance sheet.   The final step in preparing the master budget is to construct the budgeted balance sheet (Figure 10-5) that projects each balance sheet item in accordance with the business plan as expressed in the previous schedules. Specifically, the beginning balances at March 31 would be increased or decreased in light of the expected cash receipts and cash disbursements in Figure 10-4 and in light of the effects of noncash items appearing on the income statement in Figure 10-3. For example, unexpired insurance would decrease from its balance of $1,800 on March 31 to $1,000 on July 31, even though it is a noncash item.

When the complete master budget is formulated, management can consider all the major financial statements as a basis for changing the course of events. For example, the initial formulation may prompt management to try new sales strategies to generate more demand. Alternatively, management may explore the effects of various adjustments in the timing of receipts and disbursements. The large cash deficiency in April, for example, may lead to an emphasis on cash sales or an attempt to speed up collection of accounts receivable. In any event, the first draft of the master budget is rarely the final draft. As it is reworked, the budgeting process becomes an integral part of the management process itself—budgeting is planning and communicating.

CAUTION: DIFFICULTIES OF SALES FORECASTING

As you have seen in the foregoing illustration, the sales budget is the foundation of the entire master budget. The accuracy of estimated purchases budgets, production schedules, and costs depends on the detail and accuracy (in dollars, units, and mix) of the budgeted sales.

Sales forecasting is a key to preparing the sales budget, but a forecast and a budget are not necessarily identical. A **sales forecast** is a *prediction* of sales under a given set of conditions. A **sales budget** is the result of *decisions* to create the conditions that will generate a *desired* level of sales. For example, you may have forecasts of sales at various levels of advertising. The forecast for the one level you decide to implement becomes the budget.

Sales forecasts are usually prepared under the direction of the top sales executive. Important factors considered by sales forecasters include the following:

FIGURE 10-5   The Cooking Hut Company
Budgeted Balance Sheet July 31, 19X1

Assets

Current assets		
Cash (Figure 10-4)	$12,575	
Accounts receivable, net (.4 × July sales of $50,000,		
schedule a)	20,000	
Merchandise inventory (schedule c)	42,400	
Unexpired insurance ($1,800 − $800)	1,000	$ 75,975
Plant assets		
Equipment, fixtures, and other ($37,000 + $3,000		
fixtures)	$40,000	
Accumulated depreciation ($12,800 + $2,000		
depreciation expense)	(14,800)	25,200
Total assets		**$101,175**

Liabilities and Owners' Equity

Current liabilities		
Accounts payable (.5 × July purchases of		
$29,400, schedule c)	$14,700	
Accrued wages and commissions payable (.5 x		
$10,000, schedule e)	5,000	$ 19,700
Owners' equity ($78,950 + $2,525 net income)		81,475
Total liabilities and owners' equity		**$101,175**

Note: Beginning balances are used as a start for the computations of unexpired insurance, plant, and owners' equity.

1. *Past patterns of sales:* Past experience combined with detailed past sales by product line, geographical region, and type of customer can help predict future sales.
2. *Estimates made by the sales force:* A company's sales force is often the best source of information about the desires and plans of customers.
3. *General economic conditions:* Predictions for many economic indicators, such as gross domestic product and industrial production indexes (local and foreign), are published regularly. Knowledge of how sales relate to these indicators can aid sales forecasting.
4. *Competitors' actions:* Sales depend on the strength and actions of competitors. To forecast sales, a company should consider the likely strategies and reactions of competitors, such as changes in their prices, product quality, or services.
5. *Changes in the firm's prices:* Sales can be increased by decreasing prices and vice versa. A company should consider the effects of price changes on customer demand.
6. *Changes in product mix:* Changing the mix of products often can affect not only sales levels but also overall contribution margin. Identifying the most profitable products and devising methods to increase their sales is a key part of successful management.
7. *Market research studies:* Some companies hire market experts to gather information about market conditions and customer preferences. Such information is useful to managers making sales forecasts and product mix decisions.

8. *Advertising and sales promotion plans:* Advertising and other promotional costs affect sales levels. A sales forecast should be based on anticipated effects of promotional activities.

Sales forecasting usually combines various techniques. In addition to the opinions of the sales staff, statistical analysis of correlations between sales and economic indicators (prepared by economists and members of the market research staff) provide valuable help. The opinions of line management also heavily influence the final sales forecasts. Ultimately, no matter how many technical experts are used in forecasting, the *sales budget* is the responsibility of line management.

Sales forecasting is still somewhat mystical, but its procedures are becoming more formalized and are being reviewed more seriously because of the intensity of global competitive pressures. Although this book does not include a detailed discussion of the preparation of the sales budget, the importance of an accurate sales forecast cannot be overstressed.

Governments and other nonprofit organizations also face a problem similar to sales forecasting. For example, the budget for city revenues may depend on a variety of factors, such as predicted property taxes, traffic fines, parking fees, license fees, and city income taxes. In turn, property taxes depend on the extent of new construction and, in most localities, general increases in real estate values. Thus, a municipal budget may require forecasting that is just as sophisticated as that required by a private firm.

PROCESS OF MAKING A BUDGET WORK: ANTICIPATING HUMAN BEHAVIOR

No matter how accurate sales forecasts are, if budgets are to benefit an organization, they need the support of all the firm's employees. Lower-level workers and managers' attitudes toward budgets will be heavily influenced by the attitude of top management. Even with the support of top management, however, budgets—and the managers who implement them—can run into opposition.

Managers often compare actual results with budgets in evaluating subordinates. Few individuals are immediately ecstatic about techniques used to check their performance. Lower-level managers sometimes regard budgets as embodiments of restrictive, negative top-management attitudes. Accountants reinforce this view if they use a budget only to point out managers' failings. Such negative attitudes are even greater when the budget's primary purpose is to limit spending. For example, budgets are generally unpopular in government agencies where their only use is to request and authorize funding. To avoid negative attitudes toward budgets, accountants and top management must demonstrate how budgets can *help each manager and employee* achieve better results. Only then will the budgets become a positive aid in motivating employees at all levels to work toward goals, set objectives, measure results accurately, and direct attention to the areas that need investigation.

Another serious human relations problem, which may preclude some of these benefits of budgeting, can result if budgets stress one set of performance goals, but employees and managers are rewarded for performance on other dimensions. For example, a budget may concentrate on current costs of production, but managers and employees may be rewarded on quality of production and on timely delivery of products to customers. These dimensions of performance could be in direct conflict.

The overriding importance of the human aspects of budgeting cannot be overemphasized. Too often, top management and accountants are overly concerned with the mechanics of budgets, ignoring the fact that the effectiveness of any budgeting system depends directly on whether the affected managers and employees understand and accept the budget. Budgets formulated with the active participation of all affected employees are generally more effective than budgets imposed on subordinates. This involvement is usually called **participative budgeting.**

FINANCIAL PLANNING MODELS

Properly constructed and implemented, the master budget is the best practical approximation to a formal *model* of the total organization: its objectives, inputs, constraints, and outputs. Managers try to predict how various decisions will affect the master budget. This is a step-by-step process whereby tentative plans are revised as managers exchange views on various aspects of expected activities.

Today, most large companies have developed **financial planning models,** mathematical models of the master budget that can react to any set of assumptions about sales, costs, product mix, and so on. For instance, Dow Chemical's model uses 140 separate, constantly revised cost inputs that are based on several different cost drivers.

By mathematically describing the relationships among all the operating and financial activities and among the other major internal and external factors that can affect the results of management decisions, financial planning models allow managers to assess the predicted impacts of various alternatives before final decisions are selected. For example, a manager might want to predict the consequences of changing the mix of products offered for sale to emphasize several products with the highest prospects for growth. A financial planning model would provide operational and financial budgets well into the future under alternative assumptions about the product mix, sales levels, production constraints, quality levels, scheduling, and so on. Most important, managers can get answers to "what if" questions, such as "What if sales are 10% below forecasts? What if material prices increase 8% instead of 4% as expected? What if the new union contract grants a 6% raise in consideration for productivity improvements?" Building models that can help answer "what if" questions is the subject of Addendum 10.

Financial planning models have shortened managers' reaction times dramatically. A revised plan for a large company that took many accountants many days to prepare by hand can be prepared in minutes. Public Service Electric & Gas, a New Jersey utility, can run its total master budget several times a day, if necessary.

Warning: The use of spreadsheet software on personal computers has put financial planning models within reach of even the smallest organizations. The ready access to powerful modeling, however, does not guarantee plausible or reliable results. Financial planning models are only as good as the assumptions and the inputs used to build and manipulate them—what computer specialists call GIGO (garbage in, garbage out). Nearly every chief financial officer has a horror story to tell about following bad advice from a faulty financial planning model.

SUMMARY

A budget outlines an organization's objectives and possible steps for achieving them. The budgetary process compels managers to think and to prepare for changing conditions. Budgets are aids in planning, communicating, setting standards of performance, motivating personnel toward goals, measuring results, and directing attention to the areas that need investigation.

Master budgets typically cover relatively short periods—usually 1 month to 1 year. Long-range plans, however, may extend over a much longer time horizon, up to 10 years ahead. Because the future is uncertain, long-range plans focus on strategic considerations. The master budget is more detailed and offers specific guidance over the immediate budget period. Within the master budget are operating budgets, which detail resource requirements, and financial budgets, which are forecasted financial plans. The steps involved in preparing a master budget vary across organizations but follow the general outline given above. Invariably, the first step is to forecast sales or service levels, which can be quite difficult. The next step should be to forecast cost-driver activity levels, given expected sales and service. From these forecasts and knowledge of cost behavior, collection patterns, and so on, the operating and financing budgets can be prepared.

One of the most crucial determinants of successful budgeting is how the organization includes and considers the people who are directly affected by the budget. Negative attitudes toward budgets usually prevent realization of many of the benefits of budgeting. Such attitudes are usually caused by managers who use budgets to force behavior or to punish substandard performance. Budgets generally are more useful when they are formulated with the willing participation of all affected parties.

Financial planning models are mathematical representations of the organization's master budget. Most large companies use financial planning models, and many small companies are beginning to use them. These models usually are prepared with computer spreadsheet software that allows powerful budget analysis and flexible planning (see Addendum 10).

SELF-CORRECTION PROBLEM

Do not attempt to solve this problem until you understand the *step-by-step* illustration in this chapter.

1. The Country Store is a retail outlet for a variety of hardware and homewares. The owner of the Country Store is anxious to prepare a budget for the next quarter, which is typically quite busy. She is most concerned with her cash position because she expects that she will have to borrow to finance purchases in anticipation of sales. She has gathered all the data necessary to prepare a simplified budget. Figure 10-6 shows these data in tabular form. In addition, equipment will be purchased in April for $19,750 cash, and dividends of $4,000 will be paid in June. Review the structure of the example in the chapter and then prepare the Country Store's master budget for the months of April, May, and June. The solu-

---

FIGURE 10-6   The Country Store
Budget Data Balance Sheet as of March 31, 19X4

Assets		Budgeted Sales	
Cash	$ 9,000	March (actual)	$60,000
Accounts receivable	48,000	April	70,000
Inventory	12,600	May	85,000
Plant and equipment (net)	200,000	June	90,000
Total assets	**$269,600**	July	50,000
Liabilities and equities		Required minimum cash balance	$ 8,000
Interest payable	0	Sales mix, cash/credit:	
Note payable	0	Cash sales	20%
Accounts payable	18,300	Credit sales (collected the following	
Capital stock	180,000	month)	80%
Retained earnings	71,300	Gross profit rate	40%
Total liabilities and equities	**$269,600**	Loan interest rate (interest paid in cash	
Budgeted expenses (per month)		monthly)	12%
Wages and salaries	$ 7,500	Inventory paid for in:	
Freight out as a % of sales	6%	Month purchased	50%
Advertising	$ 6,000	Month after purchase	50%
Depreciation	$ 2,000		
Other expense as a % of sales	4%		
Minimum inventory policy as a %			
of next month's cost of goods sold	30%		

---

tion follows after the budget data. Note that there are a few minor differences between this example and the one in the chapter. These are identified in Figure 10-6 and in the solution. The primary difference is in the payment of interest on borrowing. Borrowing occurs at the end of a month when cash is needed. Repayments (if appropriate) occur at the end of a month when cash is available. Interest also is paid in cash at the end of the month at an annual rate of 12% on the amount of note payable outstanding during that month.

SOLUTION TO SELF-CORRECTION PROBLEM

Schedule a: Sales budget

	April	May	June	Total
Credit sales, 80%	$56,000	$68,000	$72,000	$196,000
Cash sales, 20%	14,000	17,000	18,000	49,000
Total sales	**$70,000**	**$85,000**	**$90,000**	**$245,000**

Schedule b: Cash collections

	April	May	June	Total
Cash sales	$14,000	$17,000	$18,000	$ 49,000
Collections from prior month	48,000	56,000	68,000	172,000
Total collections	**$62,000**	**$73,000**	**$86,000**	**$221,000**

Schedule c: Purchases budget

	April	May	June	Total
Desired ending inventory	$15,300	$16,200	$ 9,000	$ 40,500
Plus cost of goods sold	42,000	51,000	54,000	147,000
Total needed	$57,300	$67,200	$ 63,000	$187,500
Less beginning inventory	12,600	15,300	16,200	44,100
Total purchases	**$44,700**	**$51,900**	**$46,800**	**$143,400**

Schedule d: Cash disbursements for purchases

	April	May	June	Total
For March*	$18,300			$ 18,300
For April	22,350	$22,350		44,700
For May		25,950	$25,950	51,900
For June			23,400	23,400
Total disbursements	**$40,650**	**$48,300**	**$49,350**	**$138,300**

*The amount payable from the previous month.

Schedules e and f: Operating expenses and disbursements for expenses (except interest)

	April	May	June	Total
Cash expenses				
Salaries & wages	$ 7,500	$ 7,500	$ 7,500	$22,500
Freight-out	4,200	5,100	5,400	14,700
Advertising	6,000	6,000	6,000	18,000
Other expenses	2,800	3,400	3,600	9,800
Total disbursements for				
expenses	$20,500	$22,000	$22,500	$65,000
Noncash expenses				
Depreciation	2,000	2,000	2,000	6,000
Total expenses	**$22,500**	**$24,000**	**$24,500**	**$71,000**

The Country Store Cash Budget April-June, 19X4

	April	May	June
Beginning cash balance	$ 9,000	$ 8,000	$ 8,000
Cash collections	62,000	73,000	86,000
Total cash available	71,000	81,000	94,000
Cash disbursements			
Inventory purchases	40,650	48,300	49,350
Operating expenses	20,500	22,000	22,500
Equipment purchases	19,750	0	0
Dividends	0	0	1,000
Interest*	0	179	154
Total disbursements	80,900	70,479	76,004
Minimum cash balance	8,000	8,000	8,000
Total cash needed	**$ 88,900**	**$78,479**	**$84,004**
Cash excess (deficit)	**$(17,900)**	**$ 2,521**	**$ 9,996**
Financing			
Borrowing†	17,900	0	0
Repayments	0	(2,521)	(9,996)
Total cash from financing	17,900	(2,521)	(9,996)
Ending cash balance	**$ 8,000**	**$ 8,000**	**$ 8,000**

*In this example interest is paid on the loan amounts outstanding during the month; May: (0.12 ÷ 12) × ($17,900) = $179; June: (0.12 ÷ 12) × ($17,900 − $2,521) = $154.

†In this example, borrowings are at the end of the month in the amounts needed. Repayments also are made at the end of the month as excess cash permits.

The Country Store Budgeted Income Statement April-June, 19X4

	April	May	June	April-June Total
Sales	$70,000	$85,000	$90,000	$245,000
Cost of goods sold	42,000	51,000	54,000	147,000
Gross margin	28,000	34,000	36,000	98,000
Operating expenses				
Salaries and wages	7,500	7,500	7,500	22,500
Freight-out	4,200	5,100	5,400	14,700
Advertising	6,000	6,000	6,000	18,000
Other	2,800	3,400	3,600	9,800
Interest*	—	179	154	333
Depreciation	2,000	2,000	2,000	6,000
Total expense	$22,500	$24,179	$24,654	$71,333
Net operating income	$ 5,500	$ 9,821	$11,346	$26,667

*Note that interest expense is the monthly interest rate times the borrowed amount held for the month: May $(0.12 \div 12) \times \$17,900 = \$179$; June: $(0.12 \div 12) \times \$15,379 = \$154$.

The Country Store Budgeted Balance Sheets as of the Ends of April-June, 19X4

Assets	April	May	June*
Current assets			
Cash	$ 8,000	$ 8,000	$ 8,000
Accounts receivable	56,000	68,000	72,000
Inventory	15,300	16,200	9,000
Total current assets	79,300	92,200	89,000
Plant, less accumulated			
depreciation†	217,750	215,750	213,750
Total assets	$297,050	$307,950	$302,750
Liabilities and Equities			
Liabilities			
Accounts payable	$ 22,350	$ 25,950	$ 23,400
Notes payable	17,900	15,379	5,383
Total liabilities	40,250	41,329	28,783
Stockholders equity			
Capital stock	180,000	180,000	180,000
Retained earnings	76,800	86,621	93,967
Total equities	256,800	266,621	273,967
Total liabilities & equities	$297,050	$307,950	$302,750

*The June 30, 19X4 balance sheet is the ending balance sheet for the entire three-month period.
†$200,000 + \$19,750 - \$2,000 = \$217,750$.

QUESTIONS

1. Is budgeting used primarily for scorekeeping, attention directing, or problem solving?
2. "Budgets are okay in relatively certain environments. But everything changes so quickly in the electronics industry that budgeting is a waste of time." Comment on this statement.
3. What are the major benefits of budgeting?
4. Why is budgeted performance better than past performance as a basis for judging actual results?
5. What is the major technical difference between historical and budgeted financial statements?
6. "Budgets are primarily a tool used to limit expenditures." Do you agree? Explain.
7. How do strategic planning, long-range planning, and budgeting differ?
8. "Capital budgets are plans for managing long-term debt and common stock." Do you agree? Explain.
9. "I oppose continuous budgets because they provide a moving target. Managers never know what to aim at." Discuss.
10. "Pro forma statements are those statements prepared in conjunction with continuous budgets." Do you agree? Explain.
11. Differentiate between an operating budget and a financial budget.
12. Why is the sales forecast the starting point for budgeting?
13. What is the principal objective of a cash budget?
14. Differentiate between a sales forecast and a sales budget.
15. What factors influence the sales forecast?
16. "Education and salesmanship are key features of budgeting." Explain.
17. What are financial planning models?
18. "Budgeting for a manufacturing firm is fundamentally different from budgeting for a retail firm." Do you agree? Explain.
19. "I cannot be bothered with setting up my monthly budget on a spreadsheet. It just takes too long to be worth the effort." Comment.
20. Explain the importance of understanding cost behavior to preparing the master budget.
21. Explain the relationship between the sales (or service) forecast and cost-driver activity.

PROBLEMS

1. **Prepare Master Budget.**   A wholesaling subsidiary of Paul Lamb Industries has a strong belief in using highly decentralized management. You are the new manager of one of its small "Apex" stores (Store No. 82). You know much about how to buy, how to display, how to sell, and how to reduce shoplifting. You know little about accounting and finance, however.

   Top management is convinced that training for higher management should include the active participation of store managers in the budgeting process. You have been asked to prepare a complete master budget for your store for June, July, and August. You are responsible for its actual full preparation. All accounting is done centrally, so you have no expert help on the premises. In addition, tomorrow the branch manager and the assistant controller will be here to examine your work; at that time they will assist you in formulating the final budget document. The idea is to have you prepare the budget a few times so that you gain more confidence about accounting matters. You want to make a favorable impression on your superiors, so you gather the following data as of May 31, 19X6:

		Recent and Projected Sales	
Cash	$ 29,000		
Inventory	420,000	April	$300,000
Accounts receivable	369,000	May	350,000
Net furniture and fixtures	168,000	June	700,000
Total assets	**$986,000**	July	400,000
Accounts payable	$475,000	August	400,000
Owners' equity	511,000	September	300,000
Total liabilities and owners' equities	**$986,000**		

Credit sales are 90% of total sales. Credit accounts are collected 80% in the month following the sale and 20% in the following month. Assume that bad debts are negligible and can be ignored. The accounts receivable on May 31 are the result of the credit sales for April and May: $(.20 \times .90 \times \$300,000 = \$54,000) + (1.00 \times .90 \times \$350,000 = \$315,000) = \$369,000$. The average gross profit on sales is 40%.

The policy is to acquire enough inventory each month to equal the following month's projected sales. All purchases are paid for in the month following purchase.

Salaries, wages, and commissions average 20% of sales; all other variable expenses are 4% of sales. Fixed expenses for rent, property taxes, and miscellaneous payroll and other items are $55,000 monthly. Assume that these variable and fixed expenses require cash disbursements each month. Depreciation is $2,500 monthly.

In June, $55,000 is going to be disbursed for fixtures acquired in May. The May 31 balance of accounts payable includes this amount.

Assume that a minimum cash balance of $25,000 is to be maintained. Also assume that all borrowings are effective at the beginning of the month and all repayments are made at the end of the month of repayment. Interest is paid only at the time of repaying principal. The interest rate is 12% per annum; round interest computations to the nearest ten dollars. All loans and repayments of principal must be made in multiples of a thousand dollars.

a. Prepare a budgeted income statement for the coming quarter, a budgeted statement of monthly cash receipts and disbursements (for the next 3 months), and a budgeted balance sheet for August 30, 19X6. All operations are evaluated on a before-income tax basis. Also, because income taxes are disbursed from corporate headquarters, they may be ignored here.

b. Explain why there is a need for a bank loan and what operating sources supply cash for repaying the bank loan.

2. **Prepare Master Budget.** The Little Teddy Company wants a master budget for the next 3 months, beginning January 1, 19X7. It desires an ending minimum cash balance of $5,000 each month. Sales are forecasted at an average selling price of $4 per miniature teddy bear. In January, Little Teddy is beginning JIT deliveries from suppliers, which means that purchases equal expected sales. On January 1, purchases will cease until inventory reaches $6,000, after which time purchases will equal sales. Merchandise costs are $2 per bear. Purchases during any given month are paid in full during the following month. All sales are on credit, payable within 30 days, but experience has shown that 60% of current sales is collected in the current month, 30% in the next month, and 10% in the month thereafter. Bad debts are negligible.

Monthly operating expenses are as follows:

Wages and salaries	$15,000
Insurance expired	125
Depreciation	250
Miscellaneous	2,500
Rent	250/month + 10% of quarterly sales over $10,000

Cash dividends of $1,500 are to be paid quarterly, beginning January 15, and are declared on the 15th of the previous month. All operating expenses are paid as incurred, except insurance, depreciation, and rent. Rent of $250 is paid at the beginning of each month, and the additional 10% of sales is paid quarterly on the 10th of the month following the end of the quarter. The next settlement is due January 10.

The company plans to buy some new fixtures for $3,000 cash in March.

Money can be borrowed and repaid in multiples of $500 at an interest rate of 12% per annum. Management wants to minimize borrowing and repay rapidly. Interest is computed and paid when the principal is repaid. Assume that borrowing occurs at the beginning, and repayments at the end, of the months in question. Money is never borrowed at the beginning and repaid at the end of the *same* month. Compute interest to the nearest dollar.

Assets as of December 31, 19X6		Liabilities as of December 31, 19X6	
Cash	$ 5,000	Accounts payable	
Accounts receivable	12,500	(merchandise)	$35,550
Inventory*	39,050	Dividends payable	1,500
Unexpired insurance	1,500	Rent payable	7,800
Fixed assets, net	12,500		$44,850
	$70,550		

*November 30 inventory balance = $16,000

Recent and forecasted sales:

| October | $38,000 | December | $25,000 | February | $75,000 | April | $45,000 |
| November | 25,000 | January | 62,000 | March | 38,000 | | |

a. Prepare a master budget including a budgeted income statement, balance sheet, statement of cash receipts and disbursements, and supporting schedules for the months January through March 19X7.
b. Explain why there is a need for a bank loan and what operating sources provide the cash for the repayment of the bank loan.

ADDENDUM 10: USE OF SPREADSHEETS FOR BUDGETING

Spreadsheet software for personal computers is an extremely powerful and flexible tool for budgeting. An obvious advantage of the spreadsheet is that arithmetic errors are virtually nonexistent. The real value of spreadsheets, however, is that they can be used to make a mathematical model (a financial planning model) of the organization. This model can be used repeatedly at a very low cost and can be altered to reflect possible changes in expected sales, cost drivers, cost functions, and so on. The objective of this appendix is to illustrate *sensitivity analysis,* one aspect of the power and flexibility of spreadsheet software that has made this software an indispensable budgeting tool.

Recall the chapter's master budgeting example. Suppose CHC has preparer its master budget using spreadsheet software. To simplify making changes to the budget, the relevant forecasts and other budgeting details have been placer in Figure 10-7. Note that for simplification, only the data necessary for the purchases budget have been shown here; the full master budget would require larger table with all the data given in the chapter. Each part of the table can be identified by its column and row intersection or "cell address." For example, the beginning inventory for the budget period can be located with the cell address "D4," which is shown as $48,000.

By referencing the budget data's cell addresses, you can generate the purchases budget (Figure 10-8) within the same spreadsheet by entering *formulas* instead of numbers into the schedule. Consider Figure 10-8. Instead of typing $48,000 as April's beginning inventory in the purchases budget at cell D17, type a "formula" with the cell address for the beginning inventory from the preceding *table,* + D4 (the cell address preceded by a "+" sign—a spreadsheet rule to identify a formula; some spreadsheets use "=" to indicate a formula). Likewise, all the cells of the purchases budget will be composed of formulas containing cell addresses instead of numbers. The *total needed* in April (D16) is + D13 + D14, and *purchases* in April (D19) are budgeted to be + D16 – D17. The figures for May, June, and July are computed similarly within the respective columns. This approach gives the spreadsheet the most flexibility, because you could change any number in the budget data in Figure 10-7 (e.g., a sales forecast), and the software automatically recalculates the numbers in the entire purchases budget. Figure 10-8 shows the formulas used for the purchases budget. Figure 10-9 is the purchases budget displaying the numbers generated by the formulas in Figure 10-8.

Now, what if sales could be 10% higher than initially forecasted during April through August? What effect will this alternative forecast have on budgeted purchases? Even to revise this simple purchases budget would require a considerable number of manual recalculations. Merely changing the sales forecasts in spreadsheet

FIGURE 10-7 The Cooking Hut Company
Budget Data (Column and row labels are given by the spreadsheet)

	A	B	C	D	E	F	6
1	Budget data						
2	Sales forecasts		Other information				
3							
4	March (actual)	$40,000	Beginning inventory	$48,000			
5	April	50,000	Desired ending inventory: Base amount	$20,000			
6	May	80,000	Plus percent of next				
7	June	60,000	month's cost of				
8	July	50,000	goods sold	80%			
9	August	40,000	Cost of goods sold				
10			as percent of sales	70%			

FIGURE 10-8 The Cooking Hut Company
Purchases Budget Formulas

	A	B	C	D	E	F	G
11	Schedule c						
12	Purchases budget			April	May	June	July
13	Desired ending inventory			+D5+D8 D10*B6	+D5+D8 D10*B7	+D5+D8 D10*B8	+D5+D8 D10*B9
14	Plus cost of goods sold			+D10*B5	+D10*B6	+D10*B7	+D10*B8
15							
16	Total needed			+D13+ D14	+E13+E14	+F13+F14	+G13+G14
17	Less beginning inventory			+D4	+D13	+E13	+F13
18							
19	Purchases			+D16–D17	+E16–E17	+F16–F17	+G16–G17
20							

Figure 10-7, however, results in a nearly instantaneous revision of the purchases budget. Figure 10-10 shows the alternative sales forecasts (in colored type) and other unchanged data along with the revised purchases budget. We could alter every piece of budget data in the table, and easily view or print out the effects on purchases. This sort of analysis, assessing the effects of varying one of the budget inputs, up or down, is called *sensitivity analysis*. **Sensitivity analysis** for budgeting is the systematic varying of budget data input to determine the effects of each change on the budget. This type of "what if" analysis is one of the most powerful uses of spreadsheets for financial planning models. Note, though, that it is not generally a good idea to vary more than one of the types of budget inputs at a time, unless they are obviously related, because doing so makes it difficult to isolate the effect of each change.

Every schedule, operating budget, and financial budget of the master budget can be prepared on the spreadsheet. Each schedule would be linked by the appropriate cell addresses just as the budget input data (Figure 10-7) are linked to the purchases budget (Figures 10-8 and 10-9). As in the purchases budget, ideally all cells in the master budget are formulas, not numbers. That way, every budget input can be the subject of sensitivity analysis, if desired, by simply changing the budget data in Figure 10-7.

Preparing the master budget on a spreadsheet is time-consuming—the first time. After that, the time savings and planning capabilities through sensitivity analysis are enormous compared with a manual approach. A problem can occur, however, if the master budget model is not well documented when a person other than the author attempts to modify the spreadsheet model. Any assumptions that are made should be described either within the spreadsheet or in a separate budget preparation document.

**FIGURE 10-9   The Cooking Hut Company
                Purchases Budget**

	A	B	C	D	E	F	G
11	Schedule c						
12	Purchases budget			April	May	June	July
13	Desired ending inventory			$64,800	$53,600	$48,000	$42,400
14	Plus cost of goods sold			35,000	56,000	42,000	35,000
15							
16	Total needed			99,800	109,600	90,000	77,400
17	Less beginning inventory			48,000	64,800	53,600	48,000
18							
19	Purchases			$51,800	$44,800	$36,400	$29,400
20							

FIGURE 10-10   The Cooking Hut Company
Purchases Budget

	A	B	C	D	E	F	G
1	Budgeted data						
2	Sales forecasts		Other information				
3							
4	March (actual)	$40,000	Beginning inventory	$48,000			
5	April	55,000	Desired ending inventory: Base amount	$20,000			
6	May	88,000	Plus percent of next				
7	June	66,000	month's cost of				
8	July	55,000	goods sold	80%			
9	August	44,000	Cost of goods sold				
10			as percent of sales	70%			
11	Schedule c						
12	Purchases budget			April	May	June	July
13	Desired ending inventory			$69,280	$56,960	$50,800	$44,640
14	Plus cost of goods sold			38,500	61,600	46,200	38,500
15							
16	Total needed			107,780	118,560	97,000	83,140
17	Beginning inventory			48,000	69,280	56,960	50,800
18							
19	Purchases			59,780	49,280	$40,040	$32,340
20							

CHAPTER 11

Flexible Budgets and Standard Cost Systems

Formal budgeting procedures result in comprehensive operational and financial plans for future periods. These budgets guide managers and employees as they make their daily decisions and as they try to anticipate future problems and opportunities. As the budget period unfolds, it is only natural that employees and managers want to know, "How did we do?" Employees and their supervisors at the shop floor or at the customer service desk should know how they are doing in meeting their nonfinancial objectives (such as making on-time deliveries and resolving customer problems). Upper-level managers also want to know how the organization is meeting its financial objectives as spelled out in the master budget. Managers obtain feedback on how effectively economic conditions were forecast and how well plans were executed by comparing budgets to actual results. Knowing what went right and what went wrong should help managers plan and manage more effectively in future periods. The accounting system in most organizations is designed to record transactions continuously and report actual financial results at designated intervals. The way budgets and actual results are compared, however, determines the value of financial feedback.

This chapter introduces flexible budgets, which are budgets designed to direct management to areas of actual financial performance that deserve attention. (Managers can apply this same basic process to control of other important areas of performance such as quality or customer service.) After discussing flexible budgets and basic budget variances that are applicable to all organizations, we take a detailed look at variances for traditional manufacturing inputs such as material, labor, and overhead.

FLEXIBLE BUDGETS: BRIDGE BETWEEN STATIC BUDGETS AND ACTUAL RESULTS

Static Budgets

All *master budgets* are *static* or inflexible, because even though they may be easily revised, the budgets as accepted assume fixed levels of future activity. A master budget is prepared for only one level of activity (for example, one volume of sales activity). To illustrate, a typical master budget is a plan tailored to a single target sales level of, say, 9,000 units. The terms *static budget* and *master budget* are usually regarded as synonyms.

All *actual* results could be compared with the original plan, regardless of changes in ensuing conditions—even though, for example, sales volume turned out to be only 7,000 units instead of the originally planned 9,000 units. Suppose the Dominion Company, a one-department firm in Toronto, manufactures and sells a wheeled, collapsible suitcase carrier that is popular with airline flight crews. Manufacture of this suitcase carrier requires several manual and machine operations. The product has some variations, but may be viewed for our purposes essentially as a single product bearing one selling price.

The master (static) budget for June 19X4 included the condensed income statement shown in Figure 11-1, column 2. The actual results for June 19X4 are in column 1. Differences or variances between actual results and the master budget are in column 3. The master budget called for production and sales of 9,000 units, but only 7,000 units were actually produced and sold. There were no beginning or ending inventories, so the units made in June were sold in June.

The master budget was based on carefully forecasted sales and operations. The performance report in Figure 11-1 compares the actual results with the master budget. *Performance report* is a generic term that usually means a comparison of actual results with some budget. A helpful performance report will include *variances* that direct upper management's attention to significant deviations from expected results, allowing *management by exception.* Recall that a *variance* is a deviation of an actual amount from the expected or budgeted amount. Figure 11-1 shows variances of actual results from the master budget; these are called **master (static) budget variances.** Actual revenues that exceed expected revenues result in favorable revenue variances; when actual revenues are below expected revenues, variances are unfavorable. Similarly, actual expenses that exceed budgeted expenses result in **unfavorable expense variances;** actual expenses that are less than budgeted expenses, result in **favorable expense variances.** Each significant variance should cause a manager to ask "Why?" By explaining why a variance occurs, managers are forced to recognize changes that have affected costs and that might affect future decisions.

Suppose the president of Dominion Company asks you to explain *why* there was an operating loss of $11,570 when a profit of $12,800 was budgeted. Clearly, sales were below expectations, but the favorable variances for the variable costs are misleading. Considering the lower-than-projected level of sales activity, was cost control really satisfactory? The comparison of actual results with a master budget does not give much help in answering that question. Master budget variances are not very useful for management by exception.

FIGURE 11-1   Dominion Company
                  Performance Report Using Master Budget For the Month Ended June 30, 19X3

	Actual (1)	Master Budget (2)	Master Budget Variances (3)
Units	7,000	9,000	2,000
Sales	$217,000	$279,000	$62,000 U
Variable expenses			
Variable manufacturing expenses	$151,270	$189,000	$37,730 F
Shipping expenses (selling)	5,000	5,400	400 F
Administrative expenses	2,000	1,800	200 U
Total variable expenses	$158,270	$196,200	$37,930 F
Contribution margin	$ 58,730	$ 82,800	$24,070 U
Fixed expenses			
Fixed manufacturing expenses	$ 37,300	$ 37,000	$300 U
Fixed selling and administrative expenses	33,000	33,000	—
Total fixed expenses	$ 70,300	$ 70,000	$ 300 U
Operating income (loss)	$ (11,570)	$ 12,800	$24,370 U

U = **Unfavorable expense variances** occur when actual expenses are more than budgeted expenses.
F = **Favorable expense variances** occur when actual expenses are less than budgeted expenses.

Flexible Budgets

In contrast to the performance report based only on comparing the master budget to actual results, a more helpful benchmark for analysis is the *flexible budget*. A **flexible budget** (sometimes called **variable budget**) is a budget that adjusts for changes in sales volume and other cost-driver activities. The flexible budget is identical to the master budget in format, but managers may prepare it for any level of activity. For performance evaluation, the flexible budget would be prepared at the actual levels of activity achieved. In contrast, the master budget is kept fixed or static to serve as the primary benchmark for evaluating performance. It shows revenues and costs at only the originally *planned* levels of activity.

    To reiterate, flexible budgets have the following distinguishing features: (1) they may be prepared for a range of activity (as shown in Addendum 10, this is a natural use of financial planning software), and (2) they provide a dynamic basis for comparison with the actual results because they are automatically matched to changes in activities.

    The flexible-budget approach says, "Give me any activity level you choose, and I'll provide a budget tailored to that particular level." Many companies routinely "flex" their budgets to help evaluate recent financial performance. For example, Procter & Gamble evaluates monthly financial performance of all its business units by comparing actual results to new, flexible budgets that are prepared for actual levels of activity.

Flexible-Budget Formulas

The flexible budget is based on the same assumptions of revenue and cost behavior (within the relevant range) as the master budget. It is based on knowledge of cost behavior regarding appropriate cost drivers—*cost functions* or *flexible-budget formulas.* Cost functions can be used as flexible-budget formulas. Recall that these cost functions had units of volume as the single cost driver. The flexible budget incorporates effects on each cost and revenue caused by changes in activity. Figures 11-2 and 11-3 show Dominion Company's simple flexible budget, which has a single cost driver, units of output. Dominion Company's cost functions or flexible budget formulas are believed to be valid within the relevant range of 7,000 to 9,000 units. Be sure that you understand that each column of Figure 11-2 (7,000, 8,000, and 9,000 units, respectively) is prepared using the same flexible-budget formulas—and any activity level within this range could be used, as shown in the graph in Figure 11-3. Note that fixed costs are expected to be constant across this range of activity.

Evaluation of Financial Performance Using Flexible Budgets

Comparing the flexible budget to actual results accomplishes an important performance evaluation purpose. There are basically two reasons why actual results might not have conformed to the master budget. One is that sales and other cost-driver activities were not the same as originally forecasted. The second is that revenues or variable costs per unit of activity and fixed costs per period were not as expected. Though these reasons may not be completely independent (for example, higher sales

---

FIGURE 11-2   Dominion Company Flexible Budgets

		Flexible Budgets for Various Levels of Sales/Production Activity		
BUDGET FORMULA PER UNIT				
Units		7,000	8,000	9,000
Sales	$31.00	$217,000	$248,000	$279,000
Variable costs/expense				
Variable manufacturing costs	$21.00	$147,000	$168,000	$189,000
Shipping expenses (selling)	.60	4,200	4,800	5,400
Administrative	.20	1,400	1,600	1,800
Total variable costs/expenses	$21.80	$152,600	$174,400	$196,200
Contribution margin	$ 9.20	$ 64,400	$ 73,600	$ 82,800
BUDGET FORMULA PER MONTH				
Fixed costs				
Fixed manufacturing costs	$37,000	$37,000	$37,000	$37,000
Fixed selling and administrative costs	33,000	33,000	33,000	33,000
Total fixed costs	$70,000	$70,000	$70,000	$70,000
Operating income (loss)		$ (5,600)	$ 3,600	$12,800

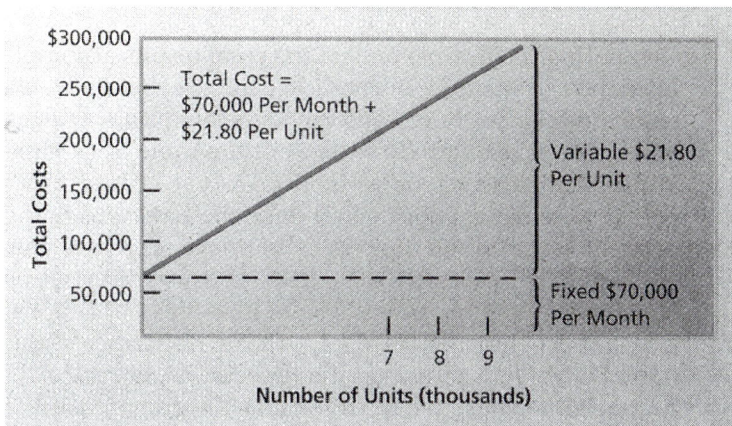

FIGURE 11-3
Dominion Company: Graph of Flexible Budget of Costs

prices may have caused lower sales levels), it is useful to separate these effects because different people may be responsible for them and because different management actions may be indicated. The intent of using the flexible budget for performance evaluation is to isolate unexpected effects on actual results that can be cor-
rected if adverse or enhanced if beneficial. Because the flexible budget is prepared at
the actual levels of activity (in our example, sales volume), any variances between
the flexible budget and actual results cannot be due to activity levels (again, assuming cost and revenue functions are valid). These *variances between the flexible budget
and actual results* are called **flexible-budget variances** and must be due to *departures
of actual costs or revenues from flexible-budget formula amounts*—because of pricing or
cost control. In contrast, any differences or *variances between the master budget and the
flexible budget are due to activity levels,* not cost control. These latter differences between the master budget amounts and the amounts in the flexible budget are called
activity-level variances.

Consider Figure 11-4. The flexible budget (column 3) taken from Figure 11-2 (and
simplified) provides an explanatory bridge between the master budget (column 5)
and the actual results (column 1). The variances for operating income are summarized at the bottom of Figure 11-4. Note that the sum of the activity-level variances
(here sales-activity variances because sales is the only activity used as a cost driver)
and the flexible-budget variances equals the total of the master budget variances.
The difference between actual results and the original master budget has two components: the sales-activity variances and the flexible-budget variances.

ISOLATION OF BUDGET VARIANCES AND THEIR CAUSES

Managers use comparisons between actual results, master budgets, and flexible budgets to evaluate organizational performance. When evaluating performance, it is useful
to distinguish between **effectiveness**—the degree to which a goal, objective, or target is met—and **efficiency**—the degree to which inputs are used in relation to a given
level of outputs.

Performance may be effective, efficient, both, or neither. For example, Dominion Company set a master budget objective of manufacturing and selling 9,000 units. Only 7,000 units were actually made and sold, however. Performance, as measured by sales-activity variances, was ineffective because the sales objective was not met.

Was Dominion's performance efficient? Managers judge the degree of efficiency by comparing actual outputs achieved (7,000 units) with actual inputs (such as the costs of direct materials and direct labor). *The less input used to produce a given output, the more efficient the operation.* As indicated by the flexible-budget variances, Dominion was inefficient in its use of a number of inputs. Later in this chapter we consider in detail direct material, direct labor, and variable overhead flexible-budget variances.

Flexible-Budget Variances

Flexible budget variances measure the efficiency of operations at the actual level of activity. The first three columns of Figure 11-4 compare the actual results with the flexible-budget amounts. The flexible-budget variances are the differences between columns 1 and 3, which total $5,970 unfavorable because:

$$\text{total flexible-budget variance} = \text{total actual results} - \text{total flexible budget, planned results}$$
$$= (-\$11{,}570) - (-\$5{,}600)$$
$$= \$-5{,}970, \text{ or } \$5{,}970 \text{ unfavorable}[1]$$

FIGURE 11-4   Dominion Company
Summary of Performance for the Month Ended June 30, 19X4

	Actual Results at Actual Activity Level[*] (1)	Flexible-Budget Variances[†] (2) = (1) − (3)	Flexible-Budget for Actual Sales Activity[‡] (3)	Sales-Activity Variances (4) = (3) − (5)	Master Budget (5)
Units	7,000	—	7,000	2,000 U	9,000
Sales	$217,000	—	$217,000	$62,000 U	$279,000
Variable costs	158,270	5,670 U	152,600	43,600 F	196,200
Contribution margin	$ 58,730	$5,670 U	$ 64,400	$18,400 U	$ 82,800
Fixed costs	70,300	300 U	70,000	—	70,000
Operating income	$ (11,570)	$5,970 U	$ (5,600)	$18,400 U	$ 12,800

Total flexible-budget variances, $5,970 U   Total sales-activity variances, $18,400 U

Total master budget variances, $24,370 U

U = Unfavorable. F = Favorable.
[*]Figures are from Figure 11-1.
[†]Figures are shown in more detail in Figure 11-5.
[‡]Figures are from the 7,000-unit column in Figure 11-2.

[1]What if the total flexible budget results were positive—say, $4,000? The total flexible-budget variance would be (−$11,570) − ($4,000) = $−15,570, or $15,570 unfavorable.

The total flexible-budget variance arises from sales prices received and the variable and fixed costs incurred. Dominion Company had no difference between actual sales price and the flexible-budgeted sales price, so the focus is on the differences between actual costs and flexible-budgeted costs at the actual 7,000-unit level of activity. Without the flexible budget in column 3, we cannot separate the effects of differences in cost behavior from the effects of changes in sales activity. The flexible-budget variances indicate whether operations were efficient or not, and may form the basis for periodic performance evaluation. Operations managers are in the best position to explain flexible-budget variances.

Companies that use variances primarily to fix blame, however, often find that managers resort to cheating and subversion to beat the system. Managers of operations usually have more information about those operations than higher-level managers. If that information is used against them, lower-level managers can be expected to withhold or misstate valuable information for their own protection. For example, one manufacturing firm actually *reduced* the next period's departmental budget by the amount of the department's unfavorable variances in the current period. If a division had a $50,000 expense budget and experienced a $2,000 unfavorable variance, the following period's budget would be set at $48,000. This system led managers to cheat and to falsify reports to avoid unfavorable variances. We can criticize departmental managers' ethics, but the system was as much at fault as the managers.

Figure 11-5 gives an expanded, line-by-line computation of variances for all master budget items at Dominion. Note how most of the costs that had seemingly favorable variances when a master budget was used as a basis for comparison have, in reality, unfavorable variances. Do not conclude automatically that favorable flexible-budget variances are good and unfavorable flexible-budget variances are bad. Instead, *interpret all variances as signals that actual operations have not occurred exactly as anticipated* when the flexible-budget formulas were set. Any cost that differs significantly from the flexible budget deserves an explanation. The last column of Figure 11-5 gives possible explanations for Dominion Company's variances.

Sales-Activity Variances

Sales-activity variances measure how effective managers have been in meeting the planned sales objective. In Dominion Company, sales activity fell 2,000 units short of the planned level. The final three columns of Figure 11-4 clearly show how the sales-activity variances (totaling $18,400 U) are unaffected by any changes in unit prices or variable costs. Why? Because the same budgeted unit prices and variable costs are used in constructing both the flexible and master budgets. Therefore, all unit prices and variable costs are held constant in columns 3 through 5.

The total of the sales-activity variances informs the manager that falling short of the sales target by 2,000 units caused operating income to be $18,400 lower than initially budgeted (a $5,600 loss instead of a $12,800 profit). In summary, the shortfall of sales by 2,000 units caused Dominion Company to incur a total sales activity variance of 2,000 units at a contribution margin of $9.20 per unit (from the first column of Figure 11-2).

FIGURE 11-5   Dominion Company
Cost-Control Performance Report for the Month Ended June 30, 19X4

	Actual Costs Incurred	Flexible Budget*	Flexible Budget Variances†	Explanation
Units	7,000	7,000	—	
Variable costs				
Direct material	$ 69,920	$ 70,000	$ 80 F	Lower prices but higher usage
Direct labor	61,500	56,000	5,500 U	Higher wage rates and higher usage
Indirect labor	9,100	11,900	2,800 F	Decreased setup time
Idle time	3,550	2,800	750 U	Excessive machine breakdowns
Cleanup time	2,500	2,100	400 U	Cleanup of spilled solvent
Supplies	4,700	4,200	500 U	Higher prices and higher usage
Variable manufacturing costs	$151,270	$147,000	$4,270 U	
Shipping	5,000	4,200	800 U	Use of air freight to meet delivery
Administration	2,000	1,400	600 U	Excessive copying and long distance calls
Total variable costs	$158,270	$152,600	$5,670 U	
Fixed costs				
Factory supervision	$ 14,700	$ 14,400	$ 300 U	Salary increase
Factory rent	5,000	5,000	—	
Equipment depreciation	15,000	15,000	—	
Other fixed factory costs	2,600	2,600	—	
Fixed manufacturing costs	$ 37,300	$ 37,000	$ 300 U	
Fixed selling and administrative costs	33,000	33,000	—	
Total fixed costs	$ 70,300	$ 70,000	$ 300 U	
Total variable and fixed costs	**$228,570**	**$222,600**	**$5,970 U**	

*From 7,000-unit column of Figure 11-2.
†This is a line-by-line breakout of the variances in column 2 of Figure 11-4.

$$\begin{pmatrix} \text{total sales-activity} \\ \text{variance} \end{pmatrix} = \begin{pmatrix} \text{actual sales units} - \\ \text{master budget sales units} \end{pmatrix} \times \begin{pmatrix} \text{budgeted contribution} \\ \text{margin per unit} \end{pmatrix}$$

$$= (9,000 - 7,000) \times \$9.20$$

$$= \$18,400 \, \text{Unfavorable}$$

Who has responsibility for the sales-activity variance? Marketing managers usually have the primary responsibility for reaching the sales level specified in the static budget. Of course variations in sales may be attributable to many factors.[2] Nevertheless, marketing managers are typically in the best position to explain why sales activities attained differed from plans.

[2]For example, sales-activity variances can be subdivided into sales quantity, sales mix, market size, and market share variances. This more advanced treatment of sales activity variances is covered in Charles T. Horngren, George Foster, and Srikant M. Datar, *Cost Accounting: A Managerial Emphasis* (Englewood Cliffs, NJ: Prentice Hall, 1994), pp. 758–763. These sales activity variances might result from changes in the product, changes in customer demand, effective advertising, and so on.

Expectations, Standard Costs, and Standard Cost Systems

Expectations or *standard costs* are the building blocks of a planning and control system. An **expected cost** is the cost that is most likely to be attained. A **standard cost** is a carefully developed cost per unit that *should* be attained. It is often synonymous with the expected cost, but some companies intentionally set standards above or below expected costs to create desired incentives. Do not confuse having expectations or standards with having a *standard cost system*. **Standard cost systems** value products according to standard costs only.[3] These inventory valuation systems simplify financial reporting, but in most companies they are expensive to install and to maintain. Therefore, standard costs may not be revised often enough to be useful for management decision making regarding specific products or services. (Ideally, only one cost system should be necessary in any organization, but in practice many organizations have developed multiple cost systems.) The expected costs used in flexible budgets also may be called standards because they are benchmarks or objectives to be attained. The fact that they are called standards does not imply that the organization also must have a *standard cost system* for inventory valuation or that it must use the standard cost system for planning and control.

Current Attainability: Most Widely Used Standard

What standard of expected performance should be used in flexible budgets? Should it be so strict that it is rarely, if ever, attained? Should it be attainable 50% of the time? 90%? 20%? Individuals who have worked a lifetime setting and evaluating standards for performance disagree, so there are no universal answers to this question.

Perfection standards (also called **ideal standards**) are expressions of the most efficient performance possible under the best conceivable conditions, using existing specifications and equipment. No provision is made for waste, spoilage, machine breakdowns, and the like. Those who favor using perfection standards maintain that the resulting unfavorable variances will constantly remind personnel of the continuous need for improvement in all phases of operations. Though concern for continuous improvement is widespread, these standards are not widely used because they have an adverse effect on employee motivation. Employees tend to ignore unreasonable goals, especially if they would not share the gains from meeting imposed perfection standards. Organizations that apply the JIT philosophy attempt to achieve continuous improvement from "the bottom up," not by prescribing what should be achieved via perfection standards.

Currently attainable standards are levels of performance that can be achieved by realistic levels of effort. Allowances are made for normal detectives, spoilage, waste, and nonproductive time. There are at least two popular interpretations of the meaning of currently attainable standards. The first interpretation has standards set just tightly enough that employees regard their attainment as highly probable if normal effort and diligence are exercised. That is, variances should be random and negligible. Hence, the standards are predictions of what will indeed occur, anticipating

---

[3]Details of standard cost systems for financial reporting are covered in Charles T. Horngren, George Foster, and Srikant M. Datar, *Cost Accounting: A Managerial Emphasis* (Upper Saddle River, NJ: Prentice Hall, 1994), Chapters 7 and 8, pp. 225–296.

some inefficiencies. Managers accept the standards as being reasonable goals. The major reasons for "reasonable" standards, then, are:

1. The resulting standards serve multiple purposes. For example, the same cost can be used for financial budgeting, inventory valuation, and budgeting departmental performance. In contrast, perfection standards cannot be used for inventory valuation or financial budgeting, because the costs are known to be inaccurate.
2. Reasonable standards have a desirable motivational impact on employees, especially when combined with incentives for continuous improvement. The standard represents reasonable future performance, not fanciful goals. Therefore, unfavorable variances direct attention to performance that is not meeting reasonable expectations.

A second interpretation of currently attainable standards is that standards are set tightly. That is, employees regard their fulfillment as possible, though unlikely. Standards can be achieved only by very efficient operations. Variances tend to be unfavorable; nevertheless, employees accept the standards as being tough but not unreasonable goals. Is it possible to achieve continuous improvement using currently attainable standards? Yes, but expectations must reflect improved productivity and must be tied to incentive systems that reward continuous improvement.

Trade-offs Among Variances

Because the operations of organizations are linked, the level of performance in one area of operations will affect performance in other areas. Nearly any combination of effects is possible: Improvements in one area could lead to improvements in others and vice versa. Likewise, substandard performance in one area may be balanced by superior performance in others. For example, a service organization may generate favorable labor variances by hiring less-skilled customer representatives, but this favorable variance may lead to unfavorable customer satisfaction and future unfavorable sales-activity variances. In another situation, a manufacturer may experience unfavorable materials variances by purchasing higher-quality materials at a higher than planned price, but this variance may be more than offset by the favorable variances caused by lower inventory handling costs (e.g., inspections) and higher-quality products (such as favorable scrap and rework variances).

Because of the many interdependencies among activities, an "unfavorable" or "favorable" label should not lead the manager to jump to conclusions. By themselves, such labels merely raise questions and provide clues to the causes of performance. *They are attention directors, not problem solvers.* Furthermore, the cause of variances might be faulty expectations rather than the execution of plans by managers. One of the first questions a manager should consider when explaining a large variance is whether expectations were valid.

When to Investigate Variances

When should variances be investigated? Frequently the answer is based on subjective judgments, hunches, guesses, and rules of thumb that have proved to be useful. The most troublesome aspect of using the feedback from flexible budgeting is deciding when a variance is large enough to warrant management's attention. The master and flexible budgets imply that the standard cost is the only permissible outcome. Practically speaking, the accountant (and everybody else) realizes that the standard is one of the many possible acceptable cost outcomes. Consequently, the accountant expects variances to fluctuate randomly within some normal limits. Of course, an activity that allows wildly fluctuating variances as "normal" may be a poorly designed activity. A random variance from a well-designed activity, by definition, is not caused by controllable actions and calls for no corrective action. In short, a random variance is attributable to chance rather than to management's implementation of plans. Consequently, the more a variance randomly fluctuates, the larger the variance required to make investigation worthwhile. There are two questions: First, what is a large versus a small variance? Second, is a large variance random or controllable? Usually, the second question is answered only after an investigation, so answering the first question is critical.

Managers recognize that, even if everything operates as planned, variances are unlikely to be exactly zero. They predict a range of "normal" variances; this range may be based on economic criteria (i.e., how big a variance must be before investigation could be worth the effort) or on statistical criteria. For some critical items, any deviation may prompt a follow-up. For most items, a minimum dollar or percentage deviation from budget may be necessary before investigations are expected to be worthwhile. For example, a 4% variance in a $1 million material cost may deserve more attention than a 20% variance in a $10,000 repair cost. Because knowing exactly when to investigate is difficult, many organizations have developed such rules of thumb as, "Investigate all variances exceeding $5,000 or 25% of expected cost, whichever is lower."

Comparisons with Prior Period's Results

Some organizations compare the most recent budget period's actual results with last year's results for the same period rather than use flexible budget benchmarks. For example, an organization might compare June 19X4's actual results to June 19X3's actual results. In general these comparisons are not as useful for evaluating performance of an organization as comparisons of actual outcomes with planned results for the same period. Why? Because many changes probably have occurred in the environment and in the organization that make a comparison across years invalid. Very few organizations and environments are so stable that the only difference between now and a year ago is merely the passage of time. Even comparisons with last month's actual results may not be as useful as comparisons with flexible budgets. Comparisons over time may be useful for analyzing *trends* in such key variables as sales volume, market share, and product mix, but they do not help answer questions such as "Why did we have a loss of $11,570 in June, when we expected a profit of $12,800?"

FLEXIBLE-BUDGET VARIANCES IN DETAIL

The rest of this chapter probes the analysis of variances in detail. The emphasis is on subdividing labor, material, and overhead cost variances into usage and price or spending components. Note that in companies where direct-labor costs are small in relation to total costs (that is, in highly automated companies) direct-labor costs may be treated as an overhead-cost item, so separate labor standards, budgets, or variances need not be analyzed.

Variances from Material and Labor Standards

Consider Dominion Company's $10 standard cost of direct materials and $8 standard cost of direct labor. These standards per unit are derived from two components: a standard quantity of an input and a standard price for the input.

	Standards		
	Standard Inputs Expected per Unit of Output	*Standard Price Expected per Unit of Input*	*Standard Cost Expected per Unit of Output*
Direct material	5 pounds	$2	$10
Direct labor	1/2 hour	16	8

Once standards are set and actual results are observed, we can measure variances from the flexible budget. To show how the analysis of variances can be pursued more fully, we will reconsider Dominion's direct-material and direct-labor costs, as shown in Figure 11-5, and assume that the following actually occurred for the production of 7,000 units of output:

- *Direct material:* 36,800 pounds of material were purchased and *used* at an actual unit *price* of $1.90 for a total actual cost of $69,920.
- *Direct labor:* 3,750 hours of labor were *used* at an actual hourly *price* (rate) of $16.40, for a total cost of $61,500.

Note that the flexible-budget variances for direct labor and direct material can be attributed to (1) using more or less of the resource than planned and (2) spending more or less for the resource than planned at the actual level of output achieved. These additional data enable us to subdivide the flexible-budget variances (column 3) from Figure 11-5 into the separate *usage* and *price* components, which are shown below in columns 4 and 5.

	(1) Actual Costs	(2) Flexible-Budget	(3) Flexible-Budget Variance	(4) Price Variance*	(5) Usage Variance*
Direct material	$69,920	$70,000	$ 80 F	$3,680 F	$3,600 U
Direct labor	61,500	56,000	5,500 U	1,500 U	4,000 U

*Computations to be explained shortly.

The flexible-budget totals for direct materials and direct labor are the amounts that would have been spent with expected efficiency. They are often labeled total *standard costs allowed*, computed as follows:

$$\begin{array}{c}\text{flexible} \\ \text{budget or} \\ \text{total standard} \\ \text{cost allowed}\end{array} = \begin{array}{c}\text{units of good} \\ \text{output} \\ \text{achieved}\end{array} \times \begin{array}{c}\text{input allowed} \\ \text{per unit of} \\ \text{output}\end{array} \times \begin{array}{c}\text{standard unit} \\ \text{price of input}\end{array}$$

$$\begin{array}{c}\text{standard direct–materials} \\ \text{cost allowed}\end{array} = 7{,}000 \text{ units} \times 5 \text{ pounds} \times \$2.00 \text{ per pound} = \$70{,}000$$

$$\begin{array}{c}\text{standard direct–labor cost} \\ \text{allowed}\end{array} = 7{,}000 \text{ units} \times 1/2 \text{ hour} \times \$16.00 \text{ per hour} = \$56{,}000$$

Before reading on, note particularly that the flexible-budget amounts (i.e., the standard costs allowed) are tied to an initial question: What was the output achieved? Always ask yourself: What was the good output? Then proceed with your computations of the total standard cost allowed for the good output achieved.

Price and Usage Variances

As noted earlier, we computed the flexible-budget amounts using the flexible-budget formulas, or currently attainable standards. Flexible-budget variances measure the relative efficiency of achieving the actual output. Price and usage variances subdivide each flexible-budget variance into the following:

1. **Price variance**—difference between actual input prices and standard input prices multiplied by the actual quantity of inputs used.
2. **Usage variance**—difference between the quantity of inputs actually used and the quantity of inputs that should have been used to achieve the actual quantity of output multiplied by the expected price of the input (also called a **quantity variance** or **efficiency variance**).

When feasible, you should separate the variances that are subject to a manager's direct influence from those that are not. This aids scorekeeping, attention directing, and problem solving. The usual approach is to separate price factors from usage factors. Price factors are less subject to immediate control than are usage factors, principally because of external forces, such as general economic conditions, that can influence prices. Even when price factors are regarded as being outside management control, isolating them helps to focus on the efficient usage of inputs. For example, the commodity prices of wheat, oats, corn, and rice are outside the control of General Mills. By separating price variances from usage variances, the breakfast cereal maker can focus on whether grain was used efficiently.

Price and usage variances are helpful because they provide feedback to those responsible for inputs. These variances should not be the only information used for decision making, control, or evaluation, however. Exclusive focus on material price variances by purchasing agents or buyers, for example, can work against an organization's JIT and total quality management goals. A buyer may be motivated to earn favorable material price variances by buying in large quantities and by buying low-quality material. The result could then be excessive inventory-handling and opportunity costs and increased manufacturing defects owing to faulty material. Similarly, exclusive focus on labor price and usage variances could motivate supervisors to use lower-skilled workers or to rush workers through critical tasks, both of which could impair quality of products and services.

Price and Usage Variance Computations

We now consider the detailed calculation of price and usage variances. The objective of these variance calculations is to hold either price or usage constant so that the effect of the other can be isolated. When calculating the price variance, you hold use of inputs constant at the actual level of usage. When calculating the usage variance, you hold price constant at the standard price. For Dominion Company the price variances are:

Direct-material price variance
$$= \text{(actual price} - \text{standard price)} \times \text{actual quantity}$$
$$= (\$1.90 - \$2.00) \text{ per pound} \times 36{,}800 \text{ pounds}$$
$$= \$3{,}680 \text{ favorable}$$

Direct-labor price variance
$$= \text{(actual price} - \text{standard price)} \times \text{actual quantity}$$
$$= (\$16.40 - \$16.00) \text{ per hour} \times 3{,}750 \text{ hours}$$
$$= \$1{,}500 \text{ unfavorable}$$

The usage variances are:

Direct-material usage variance
$$= \text{(actual quantity used} - \text{standard quantity allowed)}$$
$$\quad \times \text{standard price}$$
$$= [36{,}800 - (7{,}000 \times 5)] \text{ pounds} \times \$2.00 \text{ per pound}$$
$$= (36{,}800 - 35{,}000) \times \$2$$
$$= \$3{,}600 \text{ unfavorable}$$

Direct-labor usage variance
$$= \text{(actual quantity used} - \text{standard quantity allowed)} \times \text{standard price}$$
$$= [3{,}750 - (7{,}000 \times 1/2)] \text{ hours} \times \$16 \text{ per hour}$$
$$= (3{,}750 - 3{,}500) \times \$16$$
$$= \$4{,}000 \text{ unfavorable}$$

To determine whether a variance is favorable or unfavorable, use logic rather than memorizing a formula. A price variance is favorable if the actual price is less than the standard. A usage variance is favorable if the actual quantity used is less than the standard quantity allowed. The opposite relationships imply unfavorable variances.

Note that the sum of the direct-labor price and usage variances equals the direct labor flexible-budget variance. Furthermore, the sum of the direct-material price and usage variances equals the total direct-material flexible-budget variance.

Direct-materials flexible-budget variance = $80 favorable = $3,680 favorable + $3,600 unfavorable
Direct-labor flexible-budget variance= $5,500 unfavorable = $1,500 unfavorable + $4,000 unfavorable

Variances themselves do not show why the budgeted operating income was not achieved. They raise questions, provide clues, and direct attention, however. For instance, one possible explanation for this set of variances is that a manager might have made a trade-off—the manager might have purchased at a favorable price some materials that were substandard quality, saving $3,680 (the materials price variance). Excessive waste might have nearly offset this savings, as indicated by the $3,600 unfavorable material usage variance and net flexible-budget variance of $80 favorable. The material waste also might have caused at least part of the excess use of direct labor. Suppose more than $80 of the $4,000 unfavorable direct-labor usage variance was caused by reworking units with defective materials. Then the manager's trade-off was not successful. The cost inefficiencies caused by using substandard materials exceeded the savings from the favorable price.

Figure 11-6 shows the price and usage variance computations for labor graphically. The standard cost (or flexible budget) is the standard quantity multiplied by the standard price—the square shaded light blue. The price variance is the difference between the unit prices, actual and standard, multiplied by actual quantity used—the rectangle shaded dark blue. The usage variance is the standard price multiplied by the difference between the actual quantity used and the standard quantity allowed for the good output achieved—the area of the shaded rectangle on the lower right. (Note that for clarity the graph portrays only unfavorable variances.)

Effects of Inventories

Analysis of Dominion Company was simplified because (1) there were no finished goods inventories—any units produced were sold in the same period—and (2) there was no direct-material inventory—the materials were purchased and used in the same period.

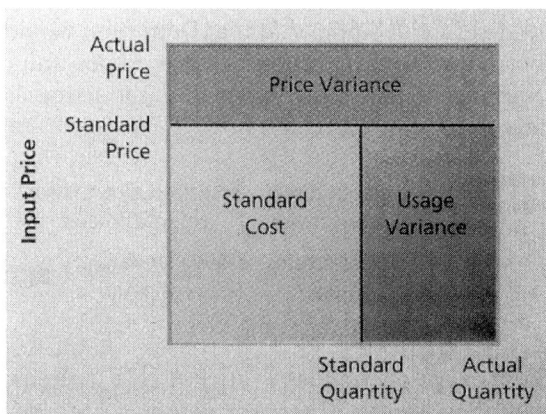

FIGURE 11-6
Graphical Representation of Price and Usage Variances for Labor

What if production does not equal sales? The sales-activity variance then is the difference between the static budget and the flexible budget for the number of units *sold*. In contrast, the flexible-budget cost variances compare actual costs with flexible-budgeted costs for the number of units *produced*.

Generally managers vacant quick feedback and want variances to be identified as early as is practical. In the case of direct materials, that time is when the materials are purchased rather than when they are used, which may be much later. Therefore, the material price variance is usually based on the quantity purchased, measured at the time of purchase. The material usage variance remains based on the quantity used. Suppose Dominion Company purchased 40,000 pounds of material (rather than the 36,800 pounds used) at $1.90 per pound. The material price variance would be (actual price – standard price) × material *purchased* = ($1.90 – $2.00) per pound × 40,000 pounds = $4,000 favorable. The material usage variance would remain at $3,600 unfavorable because it is based on the material *used*.

OVERHEAD VARIANCES

Direct-material and direct-labor variances are often subdivided into price and usage components. In contrast, many organizations believe that it is not worthwhile to monitor individual overhead items to the same extent. Therefore, overhead variances often are not subdivided beyond the flexible-budget variances—the complexity of the analysis may not be worth the effort.

But in some cases, it may be worthwhile to subdivide the flexible-budget overhead variances, especially those for variable overhead. Part of the variable overhead flexible-budget variance is related to control of the cost driver and part to the control of overhead spending itself. When actual cost-driver activity differs from the standard amount allowed for the actual output achieved, a **variable-overhead efficiency variance** will occur. Suppose that Dominion Company's cost of supplies, a variable-overhead cost, is driven by direct-labor hours. A variable-overhead cost rate of $.60 per unit at Dominion would be equivalent to $1.20 per direct-labor hour (because 1/2 hour is allowed per unit of output). Of the $500 unfavorable variance, $300 unfavorable is due to using 3,750 direct-labor hours rather than the 3,500 allowed by the flexible budget, as calculated below:

$$\begin{array}{l} \text{Variable-overhead} \\ \text{efficiency variance} \\ \text{for supplies} \end{array} = \left(\begin{array}{l}\text{actual direct} \\ \text{labor hours}\end{array} - \begin{array}{l}\text{standard direct labor} \\ \text{hours allowed}\end{array}\right) \times \begin{array}{l}\text{standard} \\ \text{variable-overhead} \\ \text{rate per hour}\end{array}$$

$$= \left(\begin{array}{l}\text{3,750 actual} \\ \text{hours}\end{array} - \begin{array}{l}\text{3,500 standard} \\ \text{hours allowed}\end{array}\right) \times \text{\$1.20 per hour}$$

$$= \text{\$300 unfavorable}$$

This $300 excess usage of supplies is attributable to inefficient use of cost-driver activity, direct-labor hours. Whenever actual cost-driver activity exceeds that allowed for the actual output achieved, overhead efficiency variances will be unfavorable and vice versa. In essence this efficiency variance tells management the cost of *not* controlling the use of cost-driver activity. The remainder of the flexible-budget variance measures control of overhead spending itself, given actual cost-driver activity.

$$\text{Variable–overhead spending} \atop \text{variance for supplies} = {\text{actual variable} \atop \text{overhead}} - \left({\text{expected variable} \atop \text{overhead rate}} \times {\text{actual direct} \atop \text{labor hours used}} \right)$$

$$= 4{,}700 - (\$1.20 \times 3{,}750 \text{ hours})$$

$$\text{rs} = \$4{,}700 - \$4{,}500$$

$$= \$200 \text{ unfavorable}$$

That is, the **variable-overhead spending variance** is the difference between the actual variable overhead and the amount of variable overhead budgeted for the actual level of cost-driver activity.

Like other variances, the overhead variances by themselves cannot identify causes for results that differ from the static and flexible budgets. The only way for management to discover why overhead performance did not agree with the budget is to investigate possible causes. The distinction between spending and usage variances provides a springboard for more investigation, however.

GENERAL APPROACH

Figure 11-7 presents the analysis of direct material and direct labor in a format that deserves close study. The general approach is at the top of the figure; the specific applications then follow. Even though the figure may seem unnecessarily complex at first, its repeated use will solidify your understanding of variance analysis. Of course, the other flexible-budget variances in Figure 11-5 could be further analyzed in the same manner in which direct labor and direct material are analyzed in Figure 11-7. Such a detailed investigation depends on the manager's perception of whether the extra benefits will exceed the extra costs of the analysis.

Column A of Figure 11-7 contains the actual costs incurred for the inputs during the budget period being evaluated. Column B is the flexible-budgeted costs for the inputs *given the actual inputs used,* using expected prices but actual usage. Column C is the flexible budget amount using both expected prices and expected usage for the outputs actually achieved. (This is the flexible budget amount from Figure 11-5 for 7,000 units.) Column B is inserted between A and C by using *expected* prices and *actual* usage. The difference between columns A and B is attributed to changing prices because usage is held constant between A and B at actual levels. The difference between columns B and C is attributed to changing usage because price is held constant between B and C at expected levels.

Actual output achieved in Column C is measured in units of product. However, most organizations manufacture a variety of products. When the variety of units are added together, the sum is frequently a nonsensical number (such as apples and oranges). Therefore, all units of output are often expressed in terms of the standard inputs allowed for their production, such as pounds of fruit. Labor hours may also become the common denominator for measuring total output volume. Thus production, instead of being expressed as 12,000 chairs and 3,000 sofas, could be expressed as 20,000 standard hours allowed (or more accurately as *standard hours of input allowed for outputs achieved*). Remember that *standard hours allowed* is a measure of actual *output* achieved. A key idea illustrated in Figure 11-7 is the versatility of the flexible budget. A flexible budget is geared to activity volume, and Figure 11-7 shows

FIGURE 11-7   General Approach to Analysis of Direct Labor and Direct Material Variances

	A	B	C
	Actual Cost Incurred: Actual Inputs × Actual Prices	Flexible Budget Based on Actual Inputs × Expected Prices	Flexible Budget Based on Standard Inputs Allowed for Actual Outputs Achieved × Expected Prices
In general	$xxx	$xxx	$xxx

In general:
Price variance (A − B)   Usage variance (B − C)
Flexible budget variance (A − C)

Direct material:

| | 36,800 lb × $1.90/lb = $69,920 | 36,800 lb × $2.00/lb = $73,600 | 7,000 units × 5 × $2.00 = $70,000 |

Price variance (A − B) = $69,920 − $73,600 = $3,680 F

Usage variance (B − C) = $73,600 − $70,000 = $3,600 U

Flexible budget variance (A − C) $69,920 − $70,000 = $80 F

Direct labor:

| | 3,750 hr × $16.40/hr = $61,500 | 3,750 hr × $16.00/hr = $60,000 | 7,000 units × .5 × $16.00 = $56,000 |

Price variance (A − B) = $61,500 − $60,000 = $1,500 U

Usage variance (B − C) = $60,000 − $56,000 = $4,000 U

Flexible-budget variance (A − C) $61,500 − $56,000 = $5,500 U

that activity volume can be measured in terms of either *actual inputs used* (columns A and B) or *standard inputs allowed for actual outputs achieved* (column C).

Figure 11-8 summarizes the general approach to overhead variances. The flexible-budget variances for fixed-overhead items are not subdivided here. Note that the sales activity variance for fixed overhead is zero, because as long as activities remain within relevant ranges, the fixed-overhead budget is the same at both planned and actual levels of activity.

SUMMARY

Flexible budgets are geared to changing levels of activity rather than to the single, static level of the master budget. Flexible budgets may be tailored to particular levels

FIGURE 11-8   General Approach to Analysis of Overhead Variances

	A	B	C
	Actual Overhead Costs Incurred	**Flexible Budget Based on Actual Inputs × Expected Prices**	**Flexible Budget Based on Standard Inputs Allowed for Actual Outputs Achieved × Expected Prices**
Supplies (and other similar variable overhead items)	$4,700 (given)	3,750 hr × $1.20/hr = $4,500	3,500 hr × $1.20/hr = $4,200

Spending variance (A − B)
$4,700 − $4,500 = $200 U

Efficiency variance (B − C)
$4,500 − $4,200 = $300 U

Flexible-budget variance (A − C)
$4,700 − $4,200 = $500 U

| Factory supervision (and other similar fixed overhead items) | $14,700 | | $14,400 |

Flexible-budget variance (A − C)
$14,700 − $14,400 = $300 U

of sales or cost-driver activity—before or after the fact. They tell how much revenue and cost to expect for any level of activity.

Cost functions, or flexible-budget formulas, reflect fixed- and variable-cost behavior and allow managers to compute budgets for any desired output or cost-driver activity level. The flexible budget amounts are computed by multiplying the variable cost per unit of activity times the level of activity expected for the actual outputs achieved.

The evaluation of performance is aided by feedback that compares actual results with budgeted expectations. The flexible-budget approach helps managers explain why the master budget was not achieved. Master budget variances are divided into (sales) activity and flexible-budget variances. Activity variances reflect the organization's effectiveness in meeting financial plans. Flexible-budget variances reflect the organization's efficiency at actual levels of activity.

Expectations form the basis for budgeting and performance evaluation. Expectations may be formalized as standard costs and may be incorporated into standard cost systems, but only expectations (which may be called standards) are required for master and flexible budgets. The most commonly used standards are considered to be attainable with reasonable effort.

Flexible-budget variances for variable inputs can be further broken down into price (or spending) and usage (or efficiency) variances. Price variances reflect the effects of changing input prices, holding usage of inputs constant at actual use. Usage variances reflect the effects of different levels of input usage, holding prices constant at expected prices.

SELF-CORRECTION PROBLEMS

1. Refer to the data contained in Figures 11-1 and 11-2. Suppose actual production and sales were 8,500 units instead of 7,000 units; actual variable costs were $188,800; and actual fixed costs were $71,200. The selling price remained at $31 per unit.

   a. Compute the master budget variance. What does this tell you about the efficiency of operations? The effectiveness of operations?
   b. Compute the sales-activity variance. Is the performance of the marketing function the sole explanation for this variance? Why?
   c. Using a flexible budget at the actual activity level, compute the budgeted contribution margin, budgeted operating income, and flexible-budget variance. What do you learn from this variance?

2. The following questions are based on the data contained in the Dominion Company illustration used in this chapter.

   - Direct materials: standard, 5 pounds per unit @ $2 per pound
   - Direct labor: standard, 1/2 hour @ $16 per hour

   Suppose the following were the actual results for production of 8,500 units:

   - Direct material: 46,000 pounds purchased and used at an actual unit price of $1.85 per pound, for an actual total cost of $85,100
   - Direct labor: 4,125 hours of labor used at an actual hourly rate of $16.80, for a total actual cost of $69,300

   a. Compute the flexible-budget variance and the price and usage variances for direct labor and direct material.
   b. Suppose the company is organized so that the purchasing manager bears the primary responsibility for purchasing materials, and the production manager is responsible for the use of materials. Assume the same facts as in question 1 except that the purchasing manager bought 60,000 pounds of material. This means that there is an ending inventory of 14,000 pounds of material. Recompute the materials variances.

SOLUTIONS TO SELF-CORRECTION PROBLEMS

1. a.

$$\text{actual operating income} = (8{,}500 \times \$31) - \$188{,}800 - \$71{,}200 = \$3{,}500$$
$$\text{master budget operating income} = \$12{,}800 \text{ (from Figure 11-1)}$$
$$\text{master budget variance} = \$12{,}800 - \$3{,}500 = \$9{,}300 \text{ U}$$

Three factors affect the master budget variance: sales activity, efficiency, and price changes. There is no way to tell from the master budget variance alone how much of the $9,300 U was caused by any of these factors alone.

   b.

$$\text{sales-activity variance} = \text{budgeted unit contribution margin} \times \text{difference between the master budget unit sales and the actual unit sales}$$
$$= \$9.20 \text{ per unit CM} \times (9{,}000 - 8{,}500)$$
$$= \$4{,}600 \text{ U}$$

This variance is labeled as a sales-activity variance because it quantifies the impact on operating income of the deviation from an original sales target while holding price and efficiency factors constant. This is a measure of the effectiveness of the operations—Dominion was ineffective in meeting its sales objective. Of course, the failure to reach target sales may be traceable to several causes beyond the control of marketing personnel including material shortages, factory breakdowns, and so on.

c. The budget formulas in Figure 11-2 are the basis for the following answers:

$$
\begin{aligned}
\text{flexible-budget contribution margin} &= \$9.20 \times 8,500 = \$78,200 \\
\text{flexible-budget operating income} &= \$78,200 - \$70,000 \text{ fixed costs} = \$8,200 \\
\text{actual operating income} &= \$3,500 \text{ (from requirement 1)} \\
\text{flexible-budget variance} &= \$8,200 - \$3,500 = \$4,700 \text{ U}
\end{aligned}
$$

The flexible-budget variance shows that the company spent $4,700 more to produce and sell the 8,500 units than it should have if operations had been efficient and unit costs had not changed. Note that this variance plus the $4,600 U sales-activity variance total to the $9,300 U master budget variance.

2. a. The variances are:

	A	B	C
	Actual Cost Incurred: Actual Inputs × Actual Prices	**Flexible Budget Based on Actual Inputs × Expected Prices**	**Flexible Budget Based on Standard Inputs Allowed for Actual Outputs Achieved × Expected Prices**
Direct material	46,000 lb × $1.85/lb = $85,100	46,000 lb × $2.00/lb = $92,000	8,500 units × 5 lb × $2.00/lb = $85,000

Price variance (A − B) =
$85,100 − $92,000
$6,900 F

Usage variance (B − C) =
$92,000 − $85,000 =
$7,000 U

Flexible budget variance (A − C)
$85,100 − 85,000 =
$100 U

	A	B	C
Direct labor	4,125 hr × $16.80/hr = $69,300	4,125 hr × $16.00/hr = $66,000	8,500 units × .5 hr × $16.00/h = $68,000

Price variance (A − B) =
$69,300 − $66,000
$3,300 U

Usage variance (B − C) =
$66,000 − $68,000 =
$2,000 F

Flexible budget variance (A − C)
$69,300 − $68,000 =
$1,300 U

b. Price variances are isolated at the most logical control point—time of purchase rather than time of use. In turn, the operating departments that later use the materials are generally charged at some predetermined budget, expected or standard price rather than at actual prices. This represents a slight modification of the approach in part a as shown below.

Note that this favorable price variance on balance may not be a good outcome—Dominion Company may not desire the extra inventory in excess of its immediate needs, and the favorable price variance may reflect that quality of the material is lower than planned. Note also that the usage variance is the same in parts a and b. Typically, the price and usage variances for materials now would be reported separately and not added together because they are based on different measures of volume. The price variance is based on inputs *purchased*, but the usage variance is based on inputs *used*.

Control point for direct materials	A Actual Cost Incurred: Actual Inputs × Actual Price	B Flexible Budget Based on Actual Inputs × Expected Price	C Flexible Budget Based on Standard Inputs Allowed for Actual Outputs Achieved × Expected Price
Purchasing	60,000 lb × $1.85/lb = $111,000	60,000 lb × $2.00/lb = $120,000	
		Price variance (A – B) = $111,000 – $120,000 = $9,000 F	
Using		46,000 lb × $2.00/lb = $92,000	42,500 lb × $2.00/lb = $85,000
			Usage variance (B – C) = $92,000 – $85,000 = $7,000 U

QUESTIONS

1. "The flex in the flexible budget relates solely to variable costs." Do you agree? Explain.
2. "We want a flexible budget because costs are difficult to predict. We need the flexibility to change budgeted costs as input prices change." Does a flexible budget serve this purpose? Explain.
3. "Effectiveness and efficiency go hand in hand. You can't have one without the other." Do you agree? Explain.
4. Differentiate between a master-budget variance and a flexible-budget variance.
5. Why do some companies classify direct-labor costs as part of factory overhead?
6. Differentiate between perfection standards and currently attainable standards.
7. What are two possible interpretations of "currently attainable standards"?
8. Why should a budgeted cost not be merely an extension of past experience?
9. "Price variances should be computed even if prices are regarded as being outside of company control." Do you agree? Explain.

10. Are direct-material price variances generally recognized when the materials are purchased or when they are used? Why?

11. Explain the role of understanding cost behavior and cost-driver activities for flexible budgeting.

12. Why do the techniques for controlling overhead differ from those for controlling direct materials?

13. How does the variable-overhead spending variance differ from the direct-labor price variance?

14. "Failure to meet price standards is the responsibility of the purchasing officer." Do you agree? Explain.

15. "A standard is one point in a band or range of acceptable outcomes." Evaluate this statement.

16. "A good control system places the blame for every unfavorable variance on someone in the organization. Without affixing blame, no one will take responsibility for cost control." Do you agree? Explain.

17. What are the key questions in the analysis and follow-up of variances?

18. What are some common causes of usage variances?

19. When should managers investigate variances?

PROBLEMS

1. **Flexible and Static Budgets.** RDC Transportation Company's manager has had trouble interpreting operating performance for several years. The company has used a budget based on detailed expectations for the forthcoming quarter. For example, the condensed performance report for a recent quarter is shown at the top of the next page.

   Although the manager was upset about not obtaining enough revenue, she was happy that her cost performance was favorable; otherwise her net operating income would be even worse.

   The president was totally unhappy and remarked: "I can see some merit in comparing actual performance with budgeted performance because we can see whether actual revenue coincided with our best guess for budget purposes. But I can't see how this performance report helps me evaluate cost control performance."

   a. Prepare a columnar flexible budget for RDC at revenue levels of $7,000,000, $8,000,000 and $9,000,000. Use the format of the last three columns of Figure 11-2. Assume that the prices and mix of products sold are equal to the budgeted prices and mix.

   b. Express the flexible budget for costs in formula form.

   c. Prepare a condensed table showing the static (master) budget variance, the sales activity variance, and the flexible-budget variance. Use the format of Figure 11-4.

2. **Direct-Material and Direct-Labor Variances.** The Handy Dandy Company manufactures metal giftware that is hand-shaped and hand-finished. The following standards were developed for a line of vases:

	Budget	Actual	Variance
Net revenue	$8,000,000	$7,600,000	$400,000 U
Fuel	$ 160,000	$ 157,000	$ 3,000 F
Repairs and maintenance	80,000	78,000	2,000 F
Supplies and miscellaneous	800,000	788,000	12,000 F
Variable payroll	5,360,000	5,200,000	160,000 F
Total variable costs*	$6,400,000	$6,223,000	$177,000 F
Supervision	$ 160,000	$ 160,000	—
Rent	160,000	160,000	—
Depreciation	480,000	480,000	—
Other fixed costs	160,000	160,000	—
Total fixed costs	$ 960,000	$ 960,000	—
Total costs charged against revenue	$7,360,000	$7,183,000	$177,000 F
Operating income	$ 640,000	$ 417,000	$223,000 U

U = Unfavorable. F = Favorable.

*For purposes of this analysis, assume that all these costs are totally variable with respect to sales revenue. In practice, many are mixed and have to be subdivided into variable and fixed components before a meaningful analysis can be made. Also assume that the prices and mix of services sold remain unchanged.

	Standard Inputs Expected for Each Unit of Output Achieved	Standard Price per Unit of Input
Direct materials	10 pounds	$ 6 per pound
Direct labor	5 hours	$ 25 per hour

During April, 550 vases were scheduled for production. However, only 525 were actually produced.

Direct materials purchased and used amounted to 5,500 pounds at a unit price of $5.25 per pound. Direct labor was actually paid $26.00 per hour, and 2,850 hours were used.

a. Compute the standard cost per vase for direct materials and direct labor.
b. Compute the price variances and usage variances for direct materials and direct labor.
c. Based on these sketchy data, what clues for investigation are provided by the variances?

3. **Activity Level Variances.** DataTech Company provides information systems services to local businesses. The costs of these services are driven by customer demand. One important cost is the cost of systems consultants who design data collecting, encoding, and reporting systems to fit customers' special needs. An overall cost driver is believed to be the number of these requests made to the systems consulting department. The expected variable cost of handling a request for June 19X7 was $60, and the number of requests expected was 75. Monthly fixed costs for the department (salaries, equipment depreciation, space costs) were budgeted at $7,000.

The actual number of requests serviced by systems consulting in June 19X7 was 90, and the total costs incurred by the department was $12,300. Of that amount, $7,800 was for fixed costs.

Compute the master (static) budget variances and the flexible-budget variances for the systems consulting department for June 19X7.

4. **Summary Performance Reports.** Consider the following data for Monarch Escrow Company:

   - Master budget data: sales, 2,500 clients at $35 each; variable costs, $25 per client; fixed costs, $15,000.
   - Actual results at actual prices: sales, 3,000 clients at $36 per client; variable costs, $80,000; fixed costs, $15,750.

   a. Prepare a summary performance report similar to Figure 11-4.
   b. Fill in the blanks:

Master budget operating income		$ —
Variances		
Sales-activity variances	$ —	
Flexible-budget variances	——	
Actual operating income		$ —

5. **Material and Labor Variances.** Consider the following data:

	Direct Material	Direct Labor
Actual price per unit of input (lb and hr)	$ 18	$ 12
Standard price per unit of input	$ 14	$ 13
Standard inputs allowed per unit of output	5	2
Actual units of input	56,000	30,000
Actual units of output (product)	14,400	14,400

   a. Compute the price, usage, and flexible-budget variances for direct material and direct labor. Use U or F to indicate whether the variances are unfavorable or favorable.
   b. Prepare a plausible explanation for the performance.

6. **Variable-Overhead Variances.** You have been asked to prepare an analysis of the overhead costs in the billing department of a hospital. As an initial step, you prepare a summary of some events that bear on overhead for the most recent period. The variable-overhead flexible-budget variance was $5,000 unfavorable. The standard variable-overhead price per billing was $.06. Ten bills per hour is regarded as standard productivity per clerk. The total overhead incurred was $202,200, of which $134,500 was fixed. There were no variances for fixed overhead. The variable-overhead spending variance was $2,500 favorable.

Find the following:

a. Variable-overhead efficiency variance
b. Actual hours of input
c. Standard hours allowed for output achieved

Management Control Systems

CHAPTER 12

Introduction to Management Control Systems

The previous chapters have presented many important tools of management accounting. Tools such as activity-based costing, relevant costing, budgeting, and variance analysis are each useful by themselves. They are most useful, however, when they are parts of an integrated *system*—an orderly, logical plan to coordinate and evaluate all the activities of the organization, from the long-range planning of the chief executive officer, to the individual responses to customer or client inquiries, to the maintenance of physical assets. Managers of most organizations today, for example, realize that long-run success depends on focusing on cost, quality, and service—three components of the competitive edge. This chapter considers how management accounting tools combined into a management control system focus resources and talents of the individuals in an organization on such goals as cost, quality, and service. As you will see, no single system is inherently superior to another. The "best" system is the one that consistently leads to decisions that meet the organization's goals and objectives.

This chapter builds on previous ones to present how the individual tools of management accounting are blended systematically to help achieve organizational goals. The chapter discusses a rough sequence of steps to follow to design a successful management control *system:*

- Specify organizational goals, subgoals, and objectives.
- Identify responsibility centers.
- Develop measures of performance for motivation and goal congruence.
- Measure and report financial performance.
- Measure and report nonfinancial performance.

The chapter also discusses management control in service, government, and nonprofit organizations.

MANAGEMENT CONTROL SYSTEMS AND ORGANIZATIONAL GOALS

The foundation of control is the planning process. The outcome of planning, whether it be a mission statement, long-range objectives, or operating budgets, provides the basis for control. A **management control system** is a logical integration of management accounting tools to gather and report data and to evaluate performance. A well-designed management control system aids and coordinates the process of making decisions and motivates individuals throughout the organization to act in concert. A management control system coordinates forecasting sales and cost-driver activity levels, budgeting, measuring and evaluating performance, and motivating employees. Indeed, explicit coordination of individuals' activities, actions, and choices is the hallmark of the management control system.

Information to support the management control system often comes primarily from the organization's financial accounting system. Yet, too often, financial accounting systems focus on technical details of data processing or external financial reporting, or emphasize compliance with legal requirements or detection of fraud, but give little consideration to employee motivation, performance evaluation, or management decision making. For example, most financial accounting systems do not distinguish between fixed- and variable-cost behavior and are not concerned with using appropriate cost drivers, both of which may be critical for management decision making. Thus, some organizations maintain multiple accounting systems—one for financial reporting and one to support management control. Whether it is part of one large system or a separate system, however, the *management control system* should be designed to improve decision making within an organization. The management control system is distinguished from a financial accounting system by its focus on organizational goals and objectives, internal management decision making, and motivation and evaluation of performance consistent with the organization's goals.

Organizational Goals

The first step in designing a management control system is to specify the organization's goals. Every organization exists because some individuals, acting alone or collectively, seek to achieve some *purpose* over the long run. These individuals are called stakeholders. In open organizations, stakeholders include a variety of groups—shareholders, employees, customers, suppliers, and community organizations. All of these groups have interests in the organization's activities, and each provides input to the planning process. The goals of the organization should reflect the interests of these groups. For example, UNICEF's long-run purpose and goal is to improve the condition of children throughout the world, especially in developing and underdeveloped countries. For another example, the long-run goal of profit-seeking firms (such as IBM) in a market economy is to generate competitive levels of profit. Organizations' goals vary across individuals, ownership, cultures, political systems, and time, to mention just a few factors.

Organizational Subgoals and Objectives

Broad goals, such as achieving competitive profits, usually are too vague to provide guidance for individuals who manage and work in the organizations. Consequently, the top managers of most successful organizations (those that meet their overriding goal) specify *subgoals* and *objectives,* and develop means of motivating and evaluating performance in achieving them *as a means of achieving the organization's overall goal.*

An organization's *subgoals* are usually called other names, such as *critical success factors, key variables, critical variables,* or *key result areas.* Top management judges these subgoals to be more specific than the dominant, overall goal, such as long-run, competitive profitability. Surveys indicate that many executives believe that to be successful in the 1990s, businesses need to focus on the following five critical success factors:

1. Customer responsiveness
2. Profitability
3. Quality
4. Innovation
5. Flexibility

Although subgoals give members of an organization more focus than an overall goal, they still do not give lower-level managers and employees the direction they need to guide their daily actions. Objectives—*specific tangible achievements* that can be observed on a short-term basis—provide this direction. For example, consider AMP Incorporated (1994 annual sales of over $4 billion and over 30,000 employees), producer of electronic connection devices and related tools and machines. To achieve its subgoal of "industry leadership in quality, delivery, service, and innovation," AMP launched a broad system (its "Plan for Excellence") for continuous improvement in the areas of quality, delivery, and service. This program counts on employee-generated, "bottom-up" improvements in such specific *objectives* as scrap rates, response times, and on-time deliveries. Progress is monitored and compared with the performance of companies noted for their "worldclass" success in those areas. By meeting such objectives as on-time delivery, AMP Incorporated expects to attain industry leadership in customer deliveries and service, and, in turn, its overriding goal of competitive profitability.

Balance of Goals, Subgoals, and Objectives

While working toward subgoals and objectives is critical in any organization, be aware of their *short-run* nature. Overemphasis on any single subgoal or objective can easily create a focus on the short run, to the detriment of the long-run organizational goals. For example, some critics insist that many U.S. companies overstress short-run profits in contrast to successful Japanese and European companies. Although not all U.S. firms are short-run oriented, examples of a short-run focus abound. According to a former chief executive of ITT: "Every CEO says he plans for the long term. But every CEO lies. He's always temporizing with quarterly earnings. If he doesn't hack it quarter to quarter, he doesn't survive." In one study, the average holding period of stock of U.S. companies went from 7 years to less than 2 years during 1960–1990. Thus, key stakeholders have a short-run focus that often is reflected in management's actions.

Pressure for short-term profits can come from inside and outside a business. CEOs worry about how stock analysts will respond if profits drop even briefly. They and other top managers feel the pull of compensation plans that are based on short-term profit measures. Lower-level managers feel pressure to demonstrate that they deserve promotion, so they too have incentives to work for short-term profits that may not be beneficial in the long run. We may deplore these decisions, but our criticism should be aimed at the objectives and the management control systems as much as at the individuals involved. The objectives and systems were misspecified—they emphasized short-run performance at the expense of long-run performance. Design of a management control system that emphasizes short-run objectives that are congruent with long-run goals is both a challenging and vital task.

To encourage a longer-term view, for example, many companies are changing the way they pay bonuses. In 1992 AT&T changed from paying bonuses in cash or stock to paying them in AT&T stock *options* that require increases in stock prices before they can be exercised (a stock option is the right to purchase a share of a firm at a stated price) to shift the strategic orientation of AT&T's senior management to a more long-term view. Many companies also have instituted Employee Stock Ownership Plans (ESOPs) in part to promote a long-run focus for all employees.

Balancing the various subgoals and objectives is a critical part of management control. Sometimes the management control system ignores key success factors or inadvertently emphasizes the wrong factors. Managers often face trade-off decisions. For example, a manager can increase market share, at least in the short run, by cutting prices, but this may also mean cutting profits. Making wise trade-offs or finding other, innovative solutions to the trade-offs often makes the difference between success and failure of managers and the organizations they oversee.

DESIGNING MANAGEMENT CONTROL SYSTEMS

To create a management control system that meets the organization's needs, designers need to recognize existing constraints, identify responsibility centers, weigh costs and benefits, provide motivations to achieve goal congruence and managerial effort, and install internal controls.

Process of Working Within Constraints

Every management control system needs to fit the organization's goals. In addition, a management control system must fit into the organization's structure. Some firms are organized primarily by *functions* such as manufacturing, sales, and service. Others are organized by *divisions* that bear profit responsibility along product or geographical lines. Still others may be organized by some hybrid arrangement, as in the case of Barleycorn, Inc., a retail grocery company with the basic organizational structure shown in Figure 12-1.

Most of the time, changes in control systems are piecemeal improvements rather than complete replacements. Occasionally, however, the management control system designer is able to persuade top management to change the organization structure before redesigning the system. Large companies may use an autonomous division to experiment with changes in organization structure and management control systems before implementing wholesale changes throughout the organization. For example, Champion International Corporation's mill in Hamilton, Ohio, which produces products for the premium paper market, changed its organizational structure when it implemented flexible manufacturing and just-in-time production. Newly adopted goals such as reduced cycle time and first-pass yield (the percentage of product flowing directly without rework to its intended destination) resulted in new demands on the accounting function. Accountants now include nonfinancial perfor-

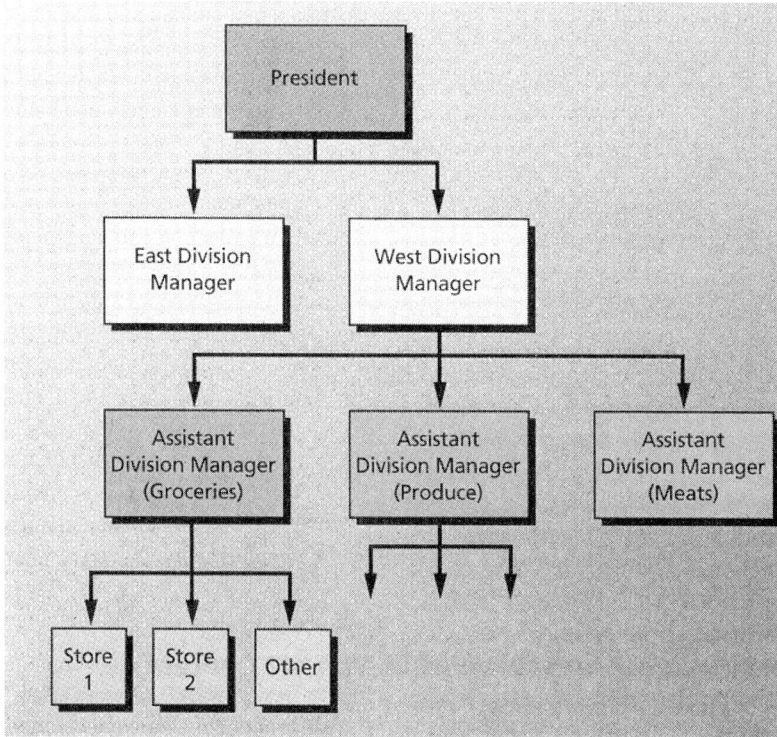

FIGURE 12-1
Organization Chart of Barleycorn, Inc.

mance measures along with financial results and work with production management as "business partners."

Identification of Responsibility Centers

In addition to organizational structures, designers of management control systems
must consider the desired *responsibility centers* in an organization. A **responsibility
center** is defined as a set of activities assigned to a manager, a group of managers, or
other employees. A set of machines and machining tasks, for example, may be a
responsibility center for a production supervisor; the full production department may
be a responsibility center for the department head; and the entire organization may
be a responsibility center for the president. In some organizations, management responsibility is shared by groups of employees to create wide "ownership" of management decisions, allow creative decision making, and prevent one person's concern (or lack of concern) for risks of failure to dominate decisions.

An effective management control system gives each lower-level manager responsibility for a group of activities and objectives and then reports on (1) the results of
the activities, (2) the manager's influence on those results, and (3) effects of uncontrollable events. Such a system has innate appeal for most top managers because it
helps them delegate decision making and frees them to plan and control. Lower-
level managers appreciate the autonomy of decision making they inherit. Thus system designers apply **responsibility accounting** to identify what parts of the organi-

zation have primary responsibility for each objective, develop measures of achievement of objectives, and create reports of these measures by organization subunit or responsibility center. Responsibility centers usually have multiple objectives (e.g., cost and quality) that the management control system monitors. Responsibility centers usually are classified according to their *financial* responsibility as cost centers, profit centers, or investment centers.

Cost, Profit, and Investment Centers

A **cost center** is a responsibility center for which costs are accumulated. Its financial responsibilities are to control and report costs only. An entire department may be considered a single cost center, or a department may contain several cost centers. For example, although an assembly department may be supervised by one manager, it may contain several assembly lines and regard each assembly line as a separate cost center. Likewise, within each line, separate machines or test equipment may be regarded as separate cost centers. The determination of the number of cost centers depends on cost-benefit considerations—do the benefits of smaller cost centers (for planning, control, and evaluation) exceed the higher costs of reporting?

Unlike cost centers, **profit centers** have responsibility for controlling revenues as well as costs (or expenses)—that is, profitability. Despite the name, a profit center can exist in nonprofit organizations (though it might not be referred to as such) when a responsibility center receives revenues for its services. For example, the Western Area Power Authority (WAPA) is charged with recovering its costs of operations through sales of power to electric utilities in the western United States. WAPA essentially is a profit center with the objective of breaking even. All profit center managers are responsible for both revenues and costs, but they may not be expected to maximize profits.

An **investment center** goes a step further. Its success is measured not only by its income but also by relating that income to its invested capital, as in a ratio of income to the value of the capital employed. In practice, the term investment center is not widely used. Instead, the term profit center is used indiscriminately to describe centers that are always assigned responsibility for revenues and expenses, but may or may not be assigned responsibility for the capital investment.

Weighing of Costs and Benefits

The designer of the management control system must also weigh the costs and benefits of various alternatives, given the circumstances of the specific organization. No system is perfect, but one system may be better than another if it can improve operating decisions at a reasonable cost.

Both benefits and costs of management control systems are often difficult to measure, and both may become apparent only after experimentation or use. For example, the director of accounting policy of Citicorp has stated that, after several years of experience with a very detailed management control system, the system has proved to be too costly to administer relative to the perceived benefits. Accordingly, Citicorp planned to return to a simpler, less costly—though less precise—management control system.

Motivation of Employees to Achieve Goal Congruence and Exert Managerial Effort

To achieve maximum benefits at minimum cost, a management control system must foster *goal congruence* and *managerial effort*. **Goal congruence** exists when individuals and groups aim at the same organizational goals. Goal congruence is achieved when employees, working in their own perceived best interests, make decisions that help meet the overall goals of the organization. **Managerial effort** is defined as exertion toward a goal or objective. Effort here means not merely working faster but also working *better*. Effort includes all conscious actions (such as supervising, planning, and thinking) that result in more efficiency and effectiveness. Effort is a matter of degree—it is optimized when individuals and groups *strive* for their objectives.

Goal congruence can exist with little accompanying effort, and vice versa, but *incentives* are necessary for both to be achieved. The challenge of management control system design is to specify objectives and rewards that induce (or at least do not discourage) employee decisions that would achieve organizational goals. For example, an organization may specify one of its subgoals to be continuous improvement in employee efficiency and effectiveness. Employees, however, might perceive that continuous improvements will result in tighter standards, faster pace of work, and loss of jobs. Even though they may agree with management that continuous improvements are competitively necessary, they should not be expected to exert effort for continuous improvements unless incentives are in place to make this effort in their own best interests. You may be pleasantly surprised that some individuals will act selflessly, but management control systems should be designed to take advantage of more typical human behavior. Be aware that self-interest may be perceived differently in different cultures.

As another example, students may enroll in a college course because their goal is to learn about management accounting. The faculty and the students share the same goal, but goal congruence is not enough. Faculty also introduce incentives in the form of a grading system to spur student effort. Grading is a form of *performance evaluation,* as is use of management control reports for raises, promotions, and other forms of rewards in other settings. Performance evaluation is a widely used means of improving congruence and effort because most individuals tend to perform better when they receive feedback that is tied to their own self-interest. Thus Allen-Bradley Co., Corning, and other manufacturers who set quality improvements as critical subgoals put quality objectives into the bonus plans of top managers. Corning has quality incentives for factory workers as well.

To achieve goal congruence and managerial effort, designers of management control systems focus on *motivating* employees. **Motivation** has been defined as a drive toward some selected goal that creates effort and action toward that goal. Yet employees differ widely in their motivations. The system designer's task is more complex, ill structured, and more affected by human behavior than many people believe at first. The system designer must align individuals' self-interest with the goals of the organization. Thus the designer must focus on the different motivational impact—how each system will cause people to respond—of one management control system versus another.

To see how failure to anticipate motivational impact can cause problems, consider that some years ago in Russia, managers of the Moscow Cable Company decided to reduce copper wastage and actually slashed it by 60% that year. As a result they had only $40,000 worth of scrap instead of the $100,000 originally budgeted.

Top management in the central government then fined the plant $45,000 for not meeting its scrap budget. What do you think this did to the cable company managers' motivation to control waste?

Responsibility accounting, budgets, variances, and the entire inventory of management control tools should constructively influence behavior. They may, however, be misused as negative weapons to punish, place blame, or find fault. Viewed positively, they assist employees to improve decisions. Used negatively, they pose a threat to employees, who will resist and undermine the use of such techniques.

Design of Internal Controls

One of the few external constraints on management control systems in the United States was imposed by the Foreign Corrupt Practices Act, passed in 1977. Despite its title, it requires *all* publicly owned U.S. companies to maintain accurate and detailed accounting records and a documented system of *internal control.* Both managers and accountants are responsible for developing, maintaining, and evaluating internal control systems. An **internal control system** consists of methods and procedures to:

1. Prevent errors and irregularities by a system of authorization for transactions, accurate recording of transactions, and safeguarding of assets
2. Detect errors and irregularities by reconciling accounting records with independently kept records and physical counts and reviewing accounts for possible reductions of values
3. Promote operating efficiency by examining policies and procedures for possible improvements

A management control system encompasses *administrative controls* (such as budgets for planning, controlling, and evaluating operations) and *accounting controls* (such as the common internal control procedure of separating the duties of the person who counts cash from the duties of the person who has access to the accounts receivable records). This text concentrates on the administrative control aspects of the management control system.

Occasional breakdowns in systems, controls, and communication at the top of an organization may not be completely preventable because of human errors. John Teets, chairman, president, and chief executive officer of Dial Corp. (consumer products, services, and passenger buses), recalled in *Institutional Investor* (July 1991) that one such breakdown occurred because an engineering manager in charge of redesigning a bus for a large customer let the redesign proceed far beyond the original scope of the contract. The manager thought the customer and his top management would interpret his checking with his managers to be a sign of weakness. The redesign changes would cost Dial upward of $25 million and resulted in legal actions, strained customer relations, and, likely, difficulties for the engineering manager involved.

Development of Measures of Performance

Because most responsibility centers have multiple objectives, only some of these objectives are expressed in financial terms, such as operations budgets, profit targets, or required return on investment, depending on the financial classification of the center. Other objectives, which are to be achieved concurrently, are nonfinancial in nature. The well-designed management control system functions alike for both financial and nonfinancial objectives to develop and report measures of performance. Good performance measures will:

1. Relate to the goals of the organization
2. Balance long-term and short-term concerns
3. Reflect the management of key activities
4. Be affected by actions of employees
5. Be readily understood by employees
6. Be used in evaluating and rewarding employees
7. Be reasonably objective and easily measured
8. Be used consistently and regularly

Both financial and nonfinancial performance measures are important. Sometimes accountants and managers focus too much on financial measures such as profit or cost variances because they are readily available from the accounting system. Managers, however, can improve operational control by also considering nonfinancial measures of performance. Such measures may be more timely and more closely affected by employees at lower levels of the organization, where the product is made or the service is rendered. Nonfinancial measures are often easier to quantify and understand. Hence, employees can be easily motivated toward achieving performance goals. For example, AT&T Universal Card Services, which was awarded the prestigious Baldridge National Quality Award (presented by the U.S. Department of Commerce), uses 18 performance measures for its customer inquiries process. These measures include average speed of answer, abandon rate, and application processing time (3 days compared to the industry average of 34 days).

Often the effects of poor nonfinancial performance (quality, productivity, and customer satisfaction) do not show up in the financial measures until considerable ground has been lost. As a result, many companies now stress management of the *activities* that drive revenues and costs rather than waiting to explain the revenues or costs themselves after the activities have occurred. Superior financial performance usually follows from superior nonfinancial performance.

In the rest of this chapter, we consider both financial and nonfinancial measures of performance used in many management control systems.

CONTROLLABILITY AND MEASUREMENT OF FINANCIAL PERFORMANCE

Management control systems often distinguish between controllable and uncontrollable events and between controllable and uncontrollable costs. Usually, responsibility center managers are in the best position to explain their center's results even if the managers had little influence over them. For example, an importer of grapes from Chile to the United States suffered a sudden loss of sales several years ago after a few of the grapes were found to contain poisonous cyanide. The tampering was beyond the importer's control, so the importer's management control system compared actual profits to flexible-budgeted profits, given that actual sales were unusually depressed. This separated effects of activity volume—sales levels—from effects of efficiency, and reported the importer's profitability *given* the uncontrollable drop in sales.

An **uncontrollable cost** is any cost that cannot be affected by the management of a responsibility center within a given time span. For example, a mail-order supervisor may be responsible only for costs of labor, shipping costs, ordering errors and adjustments, and customer satisfaction. The supervisor would not be responsible for costs of the supporting information system because the supervisor cannot control that cost.

Controllable costs should include all costs that are *influenced* by a manager's decision and actions. For example, the costs of the mail-order information system, though uncontrollable by the mail-order supervisor, are controllable by the manager in charge of information systems.

In a sense, the term "controllable" is a misnomer because no cost is completely under the control of a manager. The term is widely used, however, to refer to any cost that is affected by a manager's decisions, even if not totally "controlled." Thus the cost of operating the mail-order information system may be affected by equipment or software failures that are not completely—but are partially—under the control of the manager of information systems, who would be held responsible for all of the costs of the information system, even the costs of downtime.

The distinction between controllable and uncontrollable costs serves an information purpose. Costs that are completely uncontrollable tell nothing about a manager's decisions and actions because, by definition, nothing the manager does will affect the costs. Such costs should be ignored in evaluating the responsibility center manager's performance. In contrast, reporting controllable costs provides evidence about a manager's performance.

Because responsibility for costs may be widespread, systems designers must depend on understanding cost behavior to help identify controllable costs. This understanding is increasingly gained through activity-based costing. Both Procter & Gamble and Upjohn, Inc., for example, are experimenting with activity-based costing systems in some divisions. Procter & Gamble credits its experimental activity-based management control system for identifying controllable costs in one of its detergent divisions, which led to major strategic changes.

Contribution Margin

Many organizations combine the contribution approach to measuring income with responsibility accounting—that is, they report by cost behavior as well as by degrees of controllability.

Figure 12-2 displays the contribution approach to measuring the financial performance of the various organizational units of Barleycorn, Inc., which we encountered earlier in Figure 12-1. Study this figure carefully. It provides perspective on how a management control system can be designed to stress cost behavior, controllability, manager performance, and responsibility center performance simultaneously.

Line a in Figure 12-2 shows the contribution margin, sales revenues less all variable expenses. The contribution margin is especially helpful for predicting the impact on income of short-run changes in activity volume. Managers may quickly calculate any expected changes in income by multiplying increases in dollar sales by the contribution margin ratio. The contribution margin ratio for meats in the West Division is $180 ÷ $900 = .20. Thus a $1,000 increase in sales of meats in the West Division should produce a $200 increase in income (.20 x $1,000 = $200) if there are no changes in selling prices, operating expenses, or mix of sales between stores 1 and 2.

Contribution Controllable by Segment Managers

Lines b and c in Figure 12-2 separate the contribution that is controllable by segment managers (b) and the overall segment contribution (c). Responsibility also defines *segments*. **Segments** are responsibility centers for which a separate measure of revenues and costs is obtained. Designers of management control systems distinguish between the *segment* as an economic investment and the *manager* as a professional decision maker. For instance, an extended period of drought coupled with an aging population may adversely affect the desirability of continued economic investment in a ski resort, but the resort manager may be doing an excellent job under the circumstances.

The manager of store 1 may have influence over some local advertising but not other advertising, some fixed salaries but not other salaries, and so forth. Moreover, the meat manager at both the division and store levels may have zero influence over store depreciation or the president's salary. Therefore, Figure 12-2 separates costs by controllability. Managers on all levels are asked to explain the total segment contribution but are held responsible only for the controllable contribution.

Note that fixed costs controllable by the segment managers are deducted from the contribution margin to obtain the *contribution* controllable by segment managers. These controllable costs are usually discretionary fixed costs such as local advertising and some salaries, but not the manager's own salary. Other, noncontrollable, fixed costs (shown between lines a and b) are not allocated in the breakdown because they are not considered controllable this far down in the organization. That is, of the $160,000 fixed cost that is controllable by the manager of the West Division, $140,000 is also controllable by subordinates (grocery, produce, and meat managers), but $20,000 is not. The latter is controllable by the West Division manager but not by lower managers. Similarly, the $30,000 in that same line are costs that are attributable to the meat department of the West Division but not to individual stores.

In many organizations, managers have latitude to trade off some variable costs for fixed costs. To save variable material and labor costs, managers might make heavier outlays for automation, quality management and employee training programs, and so on. Moreover, decisions on advertising, research, and sales promotion have effects on sales activity and hence on contribution margins. The controllable contribution includes these expenses and attempts to capture the results of these trade-offs.

The distinctions in Figure 12-2 among which items belong in what cost classification are inevitably not clear-cut. For example, determining controllability is always a problem when service department costs are allocated to other departments. Should the store manager bear a part of the division headquarters costs? If so, how much and on what basis? How much, if any, store depreciation or lease rentals should be deducted in computing the controllable contribution? There are no easy answers to these questions. Each organization picks ways that benefit it most with the lowest relative cost (unlike the situation in external financial accounting systems, which must follow strict regulations).

Contribution by Segments

The *contribution by segments,* line c in Figure 12-2, is an attempt to approximate the financial performance of the *segment,* as distinguished from the financial performance

FIGURE 12-2　Barleycorn, Inc.
Contribution Approach: Model Income Statement, by Segments* (Thousands of Dollars)

	Company as a Whole	Company Breakdown into Two Divisions		Breakdown of West Division Only				Breakdown of West Division, Meats Only		
		East Division	West Division	Not Allocated†	Groceries	Produce	Meats	Not Allocated†	Store 1	Store 2
Net sales	$4,000	$1,500	$2,500	—	$1,300	$300	$900	—	$600	$300
Variable costs										
Cost of merchandise sold	$3,000	$1,100	$1,900	—	$1,000	$230	$670	—	$450	$220
Variable operating expenses‡	260	100	160	—	100	10	50	—	35	15
Total variable costs	$3,260	$1,200	$2,060	—	$1,100	$240	$720	—	$485	$235
(a) Contribution margin	$ 740	$ 300	$ 440	—	$ 200	$ 60	$180	—	$115	$ 65
Less: fixed costs controllable by segment managers§	260	100	160	$ 20	40	10	90	$ 30	35	25
(b) Contribution controllable by segment managers	$ 480	$ 200	$ 280	$ (20)	$ 160	$ 50	$ 90	$ (30)	$ 80	$ 40
Less: fixed costs controllable by others¶	200	90	110	20	40	10	40	10	22	8
(c) Contribution by segments	$ 280	$ 110	$ 170	$ (40)	$ 120	$ 40	$ 50	$ (40)	$ 58	$ 32
Less: unallocated costs‖	100									
(d) Income before income taxes	$ 180									

*Three different types of segments are illustrated here: divisions, product lines, and stores. As you read across, note that the focus becomes narrower from East and West divisions to West Division only, to meats in West Division only.

†Only those costs clearly identifiable to a product line should be allocated.

‡Principally wages and payroll-related costs.

§Examples are certain advertising, sales promotion, salespersons' salaries, management consulting, training and supervision costs.

¶Examples are depreciation, property taxes, insurance, and perhaps the segment manager's salary.

‖These costs are not clearly or practically allocable to any segment except by some highly questionable allocation base.

of its *manager,* which is measured in line b. The "fixed costs controllable by others" typically include committed costs (such as depreciation and property taxes) and discretionary costs (such as the segment manager's salary). These costs are attributable to the segment but primarily are controllable only at higher levels of management.

Unallocated Costs

Figure 12-2 shows "unallocated costs" immediately before line d. They might include central corporate costs such as the costs of top management and some corporate-level services (e.g., legal and taxation). When a persuasive cause and effect or activity-based justification for allocating such costs cannot be found, many organizations favor not allocating them to segments.

The contribution approach highlights the relative objectivity of various means of measuring financial performance. The contribution margin itself tends to be the most objective. As you read downward in the report, the allocations become more subjective, and the resulting measures of contributions or income become more subject to dispute. Though such disputes may be unproductive uses of management time, the allocations do direct managers' attention to the costs of the entire organization and lead to organizational cost control.

NONFINANCIAL MEASURES OF PERFORMANCE

For many years organizations have monitored their nonfinancial performance. Sales organizations have followed up on customers to ensure their satisfaction. Manufacturers have tracked manufacturing defects and product performance. Government health organizations have kept meticulous statistics on disease incidence and reduction, which indicate the effectiveness of disease control efforts such as education, sanitation, and inoculation. In recent years, most organizations have developed a new awareness of the importance of controlling such nonfinancial performance as quality, cycle time, and productivity.

Quality control is the effort to ensure that products and services perform to customer requirements. Organizations around the globe have adopted formal quality management programs. It has also become apparent that improvements in quality (from inception of the product to delivery and after-sales service) lead to reduced cycle time and increased productivity.

Because these factors are closely related, it is not coincidental that all types of organizations are concerned about quality, cycle time, and productivity. They are key subgoals that lead to long-term profitability for privately owned companies and are increasingly important in nonprofit and government organizations, where tighter appropriations and increasing demands for services are facts of life.

Control of Quality

In essence, customers or clients define quality by comparing their needs to the attributes of the product or service. For example, buyers judge the quality of an automobile based on reliability, performance, styling, safety, and image relative to their needs, budget, and the alternatives. Defining quality in terms of customer requirements is only half the battle. There remains the problem of reaching and maintaining the desired level of quality. There are many approaches to controlling quality. The traditional approach in the United States was to inspect products after they were completed, and reject or rework those that failed the inspections. Because testing is expensive, often only a sample of products were inspected. The process was judged to be in control as long as the number of defective products did not exceed an *acceptable quality level*. This meant that some defective products could still make their way to customers.

In recent years, however, U.S. companies, confronted with the success of Japanese products, have learned that this is a very costly way to control quality. All the resources consumed to make a defective product and to detect it are wasted, or considerable rework may be necessary to correct the defects. In addition, it is very costly to repair products in use by a customer or to win back a dissatisfied customer. IBM's Chief Executive Officer John Akers was quoted in the *Wall Street Journal* as saying, "I am sick and tired of visiting plants to hear nothing but great things about quality and cycle time—and then to visit customers who tell me of problems."[1] The high costs of achieving quality by "inspecting it in" are evident in a **cost of quality report,** which displays the financial impact of quality. The quality cost report shown in Figure 12-3 measures four categories of quality costs:

1. Prevention—costs incurred to prevent the production of defective products or delivery of substandard services including engineering analyses to improve product design for better manufacturing, improvements in production processes, increased quality of material inputs, and programs to train personnel
2. Appraisal—costs incurred to identify defective products or services including inspection and testing
3. Internal failure—costs of defective components and final products or services that are scrapped or reworked; also costs of delays caused by defective products or services
4. External failure—costs caused by delivery of defective products or services to customers, such as field repairs, returns, and warranty expenses

This report shows that most of the costs incurred by Eastside Manufacturing Company are due to internal or external failures. These costs almost certainly are understated, however. Poor quality can result in large opportunity costs because of internal delays and lost sales. For example, quality problems in American-built automobiles in the 1970s and 1980s probably caused forgone sales that were significantly more costly than the tangible costs measured in any quality cost report.

In recent years, more and more U.S. companies have been rethinking this approach to quality control. Instead, they have adopted an approach first espoused by an American, W. Edwards Deming, and embraced by Japanese companies decades ago: *total quality management* (TQM). Following the old adage, "an ounce of prevention is worth a pound of cure," it focuses on *prevention* of defects and on customer satisfaction. The TQM approach is based on the assumption that the cost of quality is minimized when a firm achieves high quality levels. **Total quality management** is the application of quality principles to *all* of the organization's endeavors to satisfy customers. The U.S. Department of Commerce presents the Baldridge Award to com-

[1]Quoted in Graham Sharman, "When Quality Control Gets in the Way of Quality," *Wall Street Journal*, February 24, 1992, p. A14.

FIGURE 12-3   Eastside Manufacturing Company Quality Cost Report* (Thousands of Dollars)

Month			Quality Cost Area	Year to Date		
Actual	Plan	Variance		Actual	Plan	Variance
			1. Prevention Cost			
3	2	1	A. Quality—administration	5	4	1
16	18	(2)	B. Quality—engineering	37	38	(1)
7	6	1	C. Quality—planning by others	14	12	2
5	7	(2)	D. Supplier assurance	13	14	(1)
31	33	(2)	Total prevention cost	69	68	1
5.5%	6.1%		% of Total quality cost	6.2%	6.3%	
			2. Appraisal cost			
31	26	5	A. Inspection	55	52	3
12	14	(2)	B. Test	24	28	(4)
7	6	1	C. Insp. & test of purchased mat.	15	12	3
11	11	0	D. Product quality audits	23	22	1
3	2	1	E. Maint. of insp. & test equip.	4	4	0
2	2	0	F. Mat. consumed in insp. & test	5	4	1
66	61	5	Total appraisal cost	126	122	4
11.8%	11.3%		% of Total quality cost	11.4%	11.3%	
			3. Internal failure cost			
144	140	4	A. Scrap & rework—manuf.	295	280	15
55	53	2	B. Scrap & rework—engineering	103	106	(3)
28	30	(2)	C. Scrap & rework—supplier	55	60	(5)
21	22	(1)	D. Failure investigation	44	44	0
248	245	3	Total internal failure cost	497	490	7
44.3%	45.4%		% of Total quality cost	44.9%	45.3%	
345	339	6	Total internal quality cost (1 + 2 + 3)	692	680	12
61.6%	62.8%		% of Total quality cost	62.6%	62.8%	
			4. External failure quality cost			
75	66	9	A. Warranty exp.—manuf.	141	132	9
41	40	1	B. Warranty exp.—engineering	84	80	4
35	35	0	C. Warranty exp.—sales	69	70	(1)
46	40	6	D. Field warranty cost	83	80	3
18	20	(2)	E. Failure investigation	37	40	(3)
215	201	14	Total external failure cost	414	402	12
38.4%	37.2%		% of Total quality cost	37.4%	37.2%	
560	540	20	Total quality cost	1,106	1,082	24
9,872	9,800		Total product cost	20,170	19,600	
5.7%	5.5%		%Tot. qual. cost to tot. prod. cost	5.5%	5.5%	

*Adapted from Allen H. Seed III, *Adapting Management Accounting Practice to an Advanced Manufacturing Environment* (National Association of Accountants, 1988). Table 5–2, p. 76.

panies that excel in quality, based on their customer-oriented quality achievements. TQM has significant implications for organization goals, structure, and management control systems. A complete discussion of TQM is beyond the scope of this text, but it includes delegating responsibility for many management functions to employees. For TQM to work, though, employees must be very well trained in the process, the product or service, and the use of quality-control information.

To implement TQM, employees are trained to prepare, interpret, and act on *quality-control charts,* such as that shown in Figure 12-4. The **quality-control chart** is a statistical plot of measures of various product dimensions or attributes. This plot helps detect process deviations before the process generates defects. These plots also identify excessive variation in product dimensions or attributes that should be addressed by process or design engineers. The chart in Figure 12-4 shows that the Eastside Manufacturing Company generally is not meeting its defects objective of .5% defects (which is a relatively high defect rate). Corrective action is indicated.

Control of Cycle Time

One key to improving quality is to reduce *cycle time.* **Cycle time,** or throughput time, is the time taken to complete a product or service, or any of the components of a product or service. It is a summary measure of manufacturing or service efficiency and effectiveness, and an important cost driver. The longer a product or service is in process, the more costs are consumed. Low cycle time means quick completion of a product or service (without defects). Lowering cycle time requires smooth-running processes and high quality, and also creates increased flexibility and quicker reactions to customer needs. As cycle time is decreased, quality problems become apparent throughout the process and must be solved if quality is to be improved. Decreasing cycle time also results in bringing products or services more quickly to customers, a product or service characteristic customers value.

Firms measure cycle time for the important stages of a process and for the process as a whole. An effective means of measuring cycle time is to use *barcoding,* where a barcode (similar to symbols on most grocery products) is attached to each component or product, and read at the end of each stage of completion. Cycle time is measured for each stage as the time between readings of barcodes. Barcoding also permits effective tracking of materials and products for inventories, scheduling, and delivery.

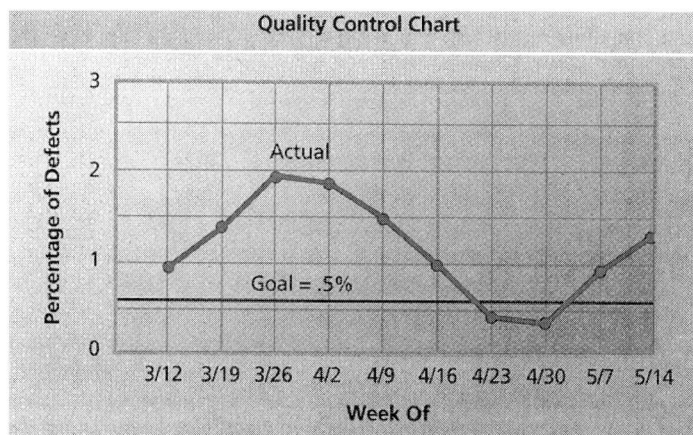

FIGURE 12-4
Eastside Manufacturing Company Quality Control Chart

Figure 12-5 shows a sample cycle-time report. (Cycle time can also be displayed on a control chart.) This report shows that Eastside Manufacturing Company is meeting its cycle-time objectives at two of its five production process stages. Explanations of the variances indicate that poor quality materials and poor design led to extensive rework and retesting.

Control of Productivity

More than half the companies in the United States manage productivity as part of the effort to improve their competitiveness. In concept, defining productivity is simple. **Productivity** is a measure of outputs divided by inputs. The fewer inputs needed to produce a given output, the more productive the organization. This simple definition, however, raises difficult measurement questions. How should outputs and inputs be measured? Specific management control problems usually determine the most appropriate measures of inputs and outputs. Labor-intensive (especially service) organizations are concerned with increasing the productivity of labor, so labor-based measures are appropriate. Highly automated companies are concerned with machine use and productivity of capital investments, so capacity-based measures, such as the percentage of time machines are available, may be most important to them. Manufacturing companies in general are concerned with the efficient use of materials, and so for them measures of material *yield* (a ratio of material outputs over material inputs) may be useful indicators of productivity. In all cases of productivity ratios, a measure of the resource that management wishes to control is in the denominator (the input) and some measure of the objective of using the resource is in the numerator (the output).

Figure 12-6 shows 12 possible productivity measures. As you can see, they vary widely according to the type of resource with which management is concerned.

Choice of productivity measures. Which productivity measures should a company choose to manage? The choice depends on the behaviors desired. Managers generally concentrate on achieving the performance levels desired by their superiors. Thus, if top management evaluates subordinates' performance based on direct-labor productivity, lower-level managers will focus on improving that specific measure.

The challenge in choosing productivity measures is that a manager may be able to improve a single measure but hurt performance elsewhere in the organization. For example, long production runs may improve machine productivity but result in excessive inventories. Alternatively, improved labor productivity in the short run may be accompanied by a high rate of product defects.

Use of a single measure of productivity is unlikely to result in overall improvements in performance. As before, choice of management controls requires balancing trade-offs that employees can be expected to make to improve their performance evaluations. Many organizations focus management control on more fundamental activities, such as control of quality and service, and use productivity measures to monitor the actual benefits of improvements in these activities.

Caveat. Be careful with comparing productivity measures over time. Changes in the process or in the rate of inflation can prove misleading. For example, consider labor productivity at Ameritech Corporation (the Midwest U.S. telecommunications company). One measure of productivity tracked by Ameritech is *sales revenue per employee*.

FIGURE 12-5   Eastside Manufacturing Company
Cycle Time Report for the Second Week of May, 19X3

Process Stage	Actual Cycle Time*	Standard Cycle Time	Variance	Explanation
Materials processing	2.1	2.5	0.4 F	
Circuit board assembly	44.7	28.8	15.9 U	Poor quality materials caused rework
Power unit assembly	59.6	36.2	23.4 U	Engineering change required rebuilding all power units
Product assembly	14.6	14.7	0.1 F	
Functional and environmental test	53.3	32.0	21.3 U	Software failure in test procedures required retesting

F = Favorable.
U = Unfavorable.
*Average time per stage over the week.

	1990	1985	Percent Change
Total revenue (millions)	$ 4,788.8	$ 4,364.7	9.7%
Employees	75,780	74,883	1.2%
Revenue per employee (unadjusted for inflation)	$63,193	$58,287	8.4%

By this measure, Ameritech appears to have achieved an 8.4% increase in the productivity of labor. Total revenue has not been adjusted for the effects of inflation, however. Because of inflation, each 1985 dollar was equivalent to 1.207 1990 dollars. Therefore, Ameritech's 1985 sales revenue, expressed in 1990 dollars (to be equivalent with 1990 sales revenue) is $4,364.7 x 1.207 = $5,268.19. The adjusted 1985 sales revenue per employee is as follows:

	1990	1985 (Adjusted)	Percent Change
Total revenue ($millions)	$ 4,788.8	$ 5,268.2	− 9.1%
Employees	75,780	74,883	+ 1.2%
Revenue per employee (adjusted for inflation)	$63,193	$70,352	− 10.2%

Adjusting for the effects of inflation reveals that Ameritech's labor productivity has dropped dramatically rather than improved. This is a signal to management that corrective action should be taken to reverse this slide—such as raising prices or reducing the number of employees. This slide in productivity in the United States may

FIGURE 12-6   Measures of Productivity

Resource	Possible Outputs (Numerator)		Possible Inputs (Denominator)
Labor	Standard direct labor hours allowed for good output	÷	Actual direct labor hours used
	Sales revenue	÷	Number of employees
	Sales revenue	÷	Direct labor cost
	Bank deposit/loan activity (by a bank)	÷	Number of employees
	Service calls	÷	Number of employees
	Customer orders	÷	Number of employees
Materials	Weight of output	÷	Weight of input
	Number of good units	÷	Total number of units
Equipment, capital, physical capacity	Time (e.g., hours) used	÷	Time available for use
	Time available for use	÷	Time (e.g., 24 hours per day)
	Expected machine hours for good output	÷	Actual machine hours
	Sales revenue	÷	Direct labor cost

explain why Ameritech purchased an *unregulated* New Zealand telephone company, where prices and lines of business may be managed more freely and where there is greater potential for higher productivity (i.e., increases in the numerator, revenue).

The Balanced Scorecard

A world-class company today requires a state-of-the-art performance measurement system that monitors the vital signs (critical success factors) of the company. One newly evolving approach to the design of a performance measurement system is the balanced scorecard. A **balanced scorecard** is a performance measurement system that strikes a balance between financial and operating measures, links performance to rewards, and gives explicit recognition to the diversity of stakeholder interests. Companies such as Champion International (see above) and Apple Computer use the balanced scorecard to focus management's attention on items subject to action on a month-by-month and day-by-day basis. One key advantage of this approach is that line managers can understand the numbers presented due to the use of nonfinancial measures.

MANAGEMENT CONTROL SYSTEMS IN SERVICE, GOVERNMENT, AND NONPROFIT ORGANIZATIONS

Most service, government, and nonprofit organizations have more difficulty implementing management control systems than do manufacturing firms. The main problem is that the outputs of service and nonprofit organizations are more difficult to measure than the cars or computers that are produced by manufacturers. As a result, it may be more difficult to know whether the service provided is, for example, of top quality until (long) after the service has already been delivered.

The key to successful management control in any organization is proper training and motivation of employees to achieve goal congruence and effort, followed by consistent monitoring of objectives set in accordance with critical subgoals, but it is even more important in service-oriented organizations. For example, MBNA America, a large issuer of bank credit cards, identifies customer retention as its primary subgoal. MBNA trains its customer representatives carefully, each day measures and reports performance on 14 objectives consistent with customer retention (such as answering every call by the second ring, keeping the computer up 100% of the time, processing credit-line requests within 1 hour), and rewards every employee based on those 14 objectives. Employees have earned bonuses as high as 20% of their annual salaries by meeting those objectives.

Nonprofit and government organizations have additional problems designing and implementing an objective that is analogous to the financial "bottom line" that so often serves as a powerful incentive in private industry. Furthermore, many people seek positions in nonprofit organizations primarily for other than monetary rewards. For example, volunteers in the Peace Corps receive very little pay but derive much satisfaction from helping to improve conditions in underdeveloped countries. Thus monetary incentives are generally less effective in nonprofit organizations. Control systems in nonprofit organizations probably will never be as highly developed as in profit-seeking firms because:

1. Organizational goals and objectives are less clear. Moreover, they are often multiple, requiring difficult trade-offs.
2. Professionals (for example, teachers, attorneys, physicians, scientists, economists) tend to dominate nonprofit organizations. Because of their perceived professional status, they have been less receptive to the installation or improvement of formal control systems.
3. Measurements are more difficult because
   a. There is no profit measure.
   b. There are heavy amounts of discretionary fixed costs, which makes the relationships of inputs to outputs difficult to specify and measure.
4. There is less competitive pressure from other organizations or "owners" to improve management control systems. As a result, for example, many cities in the United States are "privatizing" some essential services such as sanitation by contracting with private firms.
5. The role of budgeting is often more a matter of playing bargaining games with sources of funding to get the largest possible authorization than it is rigorous planning.
6. Motivations and incentives of individuals may differ from those in for-profit organizations.

FUTURE OF MANAGEMENT CONTROL SYSTEMS

As organizations mature and as environments change, managers cope with their responsibilities by expanding and refining their management control tools. The management control techniques that were quite satisfactory 10 or 20 years ago may not be adequate for many organizations today. One often hears accounting systems criticized for being especially slow to adapt to organizational change.

A changing environment often means that organizations must set different subgoals or critical success factors. Different subgoals create different objectives to be used as targets and create different benchmarks for evaluating performance. Obviously, the management control system must evolve, too, or the organization may not manage its resources effectively or efficiently. Thus the management control tools presented in this text may not be adequate even a short time from now.

Does this mean that the time spent studying this material has been wasted? No. Certain management control principles that will always be important and that can guide the redesign of systems to meet new management needs follow:

1. Always expect that individuals will be pulled in the direction of their own self-interest. You may be pleasantly surprised that some individuals will act selflessly, but management control systems should be designed to take advantage of more typical human behavior. Be aware that self-interest may be perceived differently in different cultures.

2. Design incentives so that individuals who pursue their own self-interest are also achieving the organization's objectives. If there are multiple objectives (as is usually the case), then multiple incentives are appropriate. Do not underestimate the difficulty of balancing these incentives—some experimentation may be necessary to achieve multiple objectives.

3. Evaluate actual performance based on expected or planned performance, revised, if possible, for actual output achieved. The concept of flexible budgeting can be applied to most subgoals and objectives, both financial and nonfinancial.

4. Consider nonfinancial performance to be just as important as financial performance. In the short run, a manager may be able to generate good financial performance while neglecting nonfinancial performance, but it is not likely over a longer haul.

5. Array performance measures across the entire value chain of the company. The **value chain** is the sequence of functions that adds value to the company's products or services. These functions include research and development, product process design, production, marketing, distribution, and customer service. This ensures that all activities that are critical to the long-run success of the company are integrated into the management control system.

6. Periodically review the success of the management control system. Are objectives being met? Does meeting the objectives mean that subgoals and goals are being met, too? Do individuals have, understand, and use the management control information effectively?

7. Learn from the management control successes (and failures) of competitors around the world. Despite cultural differences, human behavior is remarkably similar. Successful applications of new technology and management controls may be observed in the performance of others.

SUMMARY

The starting point for designing and evaluating a management control system is the identification goals, subgoals, and objectives as specified by top management. Systems are typically designed within the constraints of a given set of goals and a given organizational structure.

The evolutionary design of management control systems depends on criteria of cost benefit, goal congruence, and employee effort. The design should be the one that is expected to produce the best decisions at a reasonable cost.

The way performance is measured and evaluated affects individuals' behavior. Measuring performance in areas such as quality and productivity causes employees to direct attention to those areas. The more rewards are tied to performance measures, the more incentive there is to improve the measures.

Measures of performance must be carefully thought out for their behavioral effects. Improving the measures should improve organizational performance toward achieving its goals. Poorly designed or balanced measures may actually work against the organization's goals.

Responsibility accounting assigns particular revenue or cost objectives to the management of the subunit that has the greatest influence over them. Responsibility accounting classifies organizational subunits as cost, profit, or investment centers according to their financial responsibilities. The contribution approach to measuring income aids performance evaluation by separating a segment's costs into those controllable by the segment management and those beyond management's control.

Nonfinancial performance is as important as financial performance. In fact, nonfinancial performance usually leads to financial performance in time. Many companies focus on short-term nonfinancial performance measures, knowing that financial results will follow.

Management control in service, government, and nonprofit organizations is difficult because of a number of factors, chief of which is a relative lack of clearly observable outcomes. Systems designers in these organizations must contend with particularly difficult trade-offs among objectives.

Management control systems must evolve with changing economic and organizational conditions if the systems are to continue to assist managers in their decision making, controlling, and evaluation tasks.

SELF-CORRECTION PROBLEM

1. The Book & Game Company has two bookstores: Auntie's and Merlin's. Each store has a manager who has a great deal of decision authority over the individual stores. Advertising, market research, acquisition of books, legal services, and other staff functions, however, are handled by a central office. The Book & Game Company's current accounting system allocates all costs to the stores. Results for 19X6 were

Item	Total Company	Auntie's	Merlin's
Sales revenue	$700,000	$350,000	$350,000
Cost of merchandise sold	450,000	225,000	225,000
Gross margin	250,000	125,000	125,000
Operating expenses			
Salaries and wages	63,000	30,000	33,000
Supplies	45,000	22,500	22,500
Rent and utilities	60,000	40,000	20,000
Depreciation	15,000	7,000	8,000
Allocated staff costs	60,000	30,000	30,000
Total operating expenses	243,000	129,500	113,500
Operating income (loss)	$ 7,000	$ (4,500)	$ 11,500

Each bookstore manager makes decisions that affect salaries and wages, supplies, and depreciation. In contrast, rent and utilities are beyond the managers' control because the managers did not choose the location or the size of the store.

Supplies are variable costs. Variable salaries and wages are equal to 8% of the cost of merchandise sold; the remainder of salaries and wages is a fixed cost. Rent, utilities, and depreciation also are fixed costs. Allocated staff costs are unaffected by any events at the bookstores, but they are allocated as a proportion of sales revenue.

a. Using the contribution approach, prepare a performance report that distinguishes the performance of each bookstore from that of the bookstore manager.
b. Evaluate the financial performance of each bookstore.
c. Evaluate the financial performance of each manager.

SOLUTION TO SELF-CORRECTION PROBLEM

1. a.

Item	Total Company	Auntie's	Merlin's
Sales revenue	$700,000	$350,000	$350,000
Variable costs			
Cost of merchandise sold	450,000	225,000	225,000
Salaries and wages	36,000	18,000	18,000
Supplies	45,000	22,500	22,500
Total variable costs	531,000	265,500	265,500
Contribution margin by bookstore	169,000	84,500	84,500
Less: fixed costs controllable by bookstore managers			
Salaries and wages	27,000	12,000	15,000
Depreciation	15,000	7,000	8,000
Total controllable fixed costs	42,000	19,000	23,000
Contribution controllable by managers	127,000	65,500	61,500
Less: fixed costs controllable by others			
Rent and utilities	60,000	40,000	20,000
Contribution by bookstore	67,000	$ 25,500	$ 41,500
Unallocated costs	60,000		
Operating income	$ 7,000		

b. The financial performances of the bookstores (i.e., segments of the company) are best evaluated by the line "contribution by bookstores." Merlin's has a substantially higher contribution, despite equal levels of sales revenues in the two stores. The major reason for this advantage is the lower rent and utilities paid by Merlin's.
c. The financial performance by managers is best judged by the line "contribution controllable by managers." By this measure, the performance of Auntie's manager is better than that of Merlin's. The contribution margin is the same for each store, but Merlin's manager paid $4,000 more in controllable fixed costs than did Auntie's manager. Of course, this decision could be beneficial

in the long run. What is missing from each of these segment reports is the year's master budget and a flexible budget, which would be the best benchmark for evaluating both bookstore and bookstore manager.

QUESTIONS

1. What are stakeholder groups? Which stakeholder groups are most important? Why?
2. "There are corporate objectives other than profit." Name three.
3. Give three examples of how managers may improve short-run performance to the detriment of long-run results.
4. "Performance evaluation seeks to achieve *goal congruence* and *managerial effort*." Describe what is meant by this statement.
5. "Control systems in nonprofit organizations will never be as highly developed as in profit-seeking organizations." Do you agree? Explain.
6. "We evaluate the performance of managers using accounting reports based on whatever rules are required for financial reporting." Is this a desirable policy? Explain.
7. The head of the public library in a major city said, "Budgeting is a necessary evil for us. We would rather spend the time providing help to library users, but we have to prepare a budget to get city funding." Discuss this statement.
8. "Variable costs are controllable and fixed costs are uncontrollable." Do you agree? Explain.
9. "Managers of profit centers should be held responsible for the center's entire profit. They are responsible for profit even if they cannot control all factors affecting it." Discuss.
10. Name two major factors that influence controllability.
11. What is the most controversial aspect of the contribution approach to responsibility accounting?
12. Give four examples of segments.
13. "Always try to distinguish between the performance of a segment and its manager." Why?
14. "The contribution margin is the best measure of short-run performance." Do you agree? Explain.
15. What is the most important criterion in judging the effectiveness of a measure of performance?
16. What does the Foreign Corrupt Practices Act have to do with accounting?
17. Identify the three goals of an internal control system.
18. What are four nonfinancial measures of performance that managers find useful?
19. There are four categories of cost in the quality cost report; explain them.
20. Why are companies increasing their quality control emphasis on the prevention of defects?
21. Discuss how quality, cycle time, and productivity are related.
22. "Nonfinancial measures of performance can be controlled just like financial measures." Do you agree? Explain.
23. Identify three measures of labor productivity, one using all physical measures, one using all financial measures, and one that mixes physical and financial measures.
24. Discuss the difficulties of comparing productivity measures over time.

PROBLEMS

1. **Responsibility of Purchasing Agent.**   Acme Electronics Company, a privately held enterprise, has a subcontract from a large aerospace company on the West Coast. Although Acme was a low bidder, the aerospace company was reluctant to award the business to Acme, a newcomer to this kind of activity. Consequently, Acme assured the aerospace company of its financial strength by submitting its audited financial statements. Moreover, Acme agreed to a penalty clause of $2,000 per day to be paid by Acme for each day of late delivery for whatever cause.

   Jean Lou, the Acme purchasing agent, is responsible for acquiring materials and parts in time to meet production schedules. She placed an order with an Acme supplier for a critical manufactured component. The supplier, who had a reliable record for meeting schedules, gave Lou an acceptable delivery date. Lou checked up several times and was assured that the component would arrive at Acme on schedule.

   On the date specified by the supplier for shipment to Acme, Lou was informed that the component had been damaged during final inspection. It was delivered 10 days late. Lou had allowed 4 extra days for possible delays, but Acme was 6 days late in delivering to the aerospace company and so had to pay a penalty of $12,000.

   What department should bear the penalty? Why?

2. **Contribution Approach to Responsibility Accounting.**   George McBee owns a small chain of specialty toy stores in Denver and Kansas City. The company's organization chart follows:

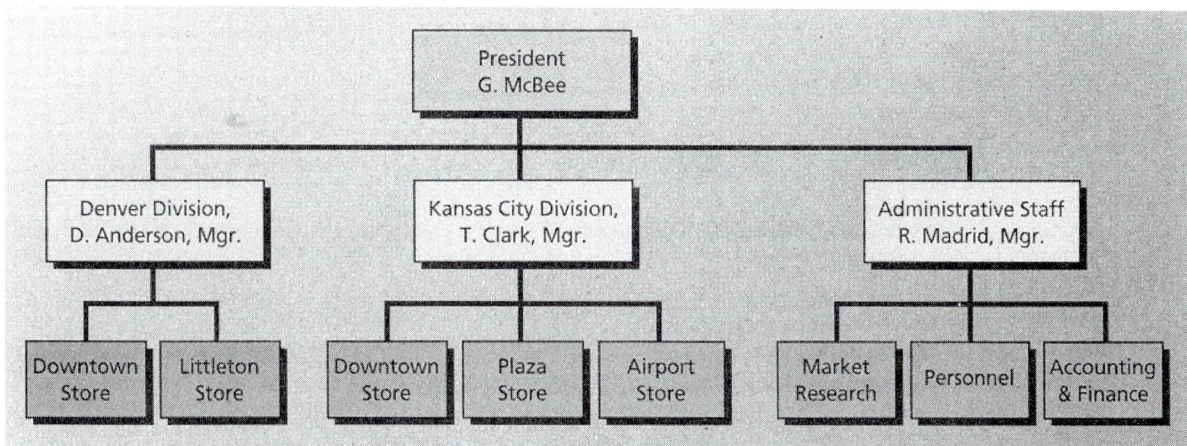

Financial results for 19X7 were

Sales revenue	**$8,000,000**
Cost of merchandise sold	5,000,000
Gross margin	3,000,000
Operating expenses	2,200,000
Income before income taxes	$ 800,000

The following data about 19X7 operations were also available:

a. All five stores used the same pricing formula; therefore all had the same gross margin percentage.
b. Sales were largest in the two Downtown stores, with 30% of the total sales volume in each. The Plaza and Airport stores each provided 15% of total sales volume, and the Littleton store provided 10%.
c. Variable operating costs at the stores were 10% of revenue for the Downtown stores. The other stores had lower variable and higher fixed costs. Their variable operating costs were only 5% of sales revenue.
d. The fixed costs over which the store managers had control were $125,000 in each of the Downtown stores, $160,000 at Plaza and Airport, and $80,000 at Littleton.
e. The remaining $910,000 of operating costs consisted of

   (1) $180,000 controllable by the Kansas City division manager, but not by individual stores
   (2) $130,000 controllable by the Denver division manager, but not by individual stores
   (3) $600,000 controllable by the administrative staff

f. Of the $600,000 spent by the administrative staff, $350,000 directly supported the Kansas City division, with 20% for the Downtown store, 30% for each of the Plaza and Airport stores, and 20% for Kansas City operations in general. Another $150,000 supported the Denver division, 50% for the Downtown store, 25% for the Littleton store, and 25% supporting Denver operations in general. The other $100,000 was for general corporate expenses.

Prepare an income statement by segments using the contribution approach to responsibility accounting. Use the format of Figure 12-2. Column headings should be

	Breakdown into Two Divisions		Breakdown of Denver Division			Breakdown of Kansas City Division			
Company as a Whole	Denver	Kansas City	Not allocated	Downtown	Littleton	Not allocated	Downtown	Plaza	Airport

3. **Comparison of Productivity.** World Comm and Intertel are communications companies. Comparative data for 1989 and 1995 are

		World Comm	Intertel
Sales revenue	1989	$5,824,000,000	$7,658,000,000
	1995	$6,764,000,000	$9,667,000,000
Number of employees	1989	56,600	75,900
	1995	54,800	76,200

Assume that each 1989 dollar is equivalent to 1.2 1995 dollars, owing to inflation.

a. Compute 1989 and 1995 productivity measures in terms of revenues per employee for World Comm and Intertel.

b. Compare the change in productivity between 1989 and 1995 for World Comm with that for Intertel.

4. **Responsibility Accounting.** (CMA, adapted.) The Filler Company operates a standard cost system, calculates standard cost variances for each department, and reports them to department managers. Managers are supposed to use the information to improve their operations. Superiors use the same information to evaluate managers' performance.

Sharon Keller was recently appointed manager of the assembly department of the company. She has complained that the system as designed is disadvantageous to her department. Included among the variances charged to the departments is one for rejected units. The inspection occurs at the end of the assembly department. The inspectors attempt to identify the cause of the rejection so that the department where the error occurred can be charged with it. Not all errors can easily be identified with a department, however. The nonidentified units are totaled and apportioned to the departments according to the number of identified errors. The variance for rejected units in each department is a combination of the errors caused by the department plus a portion of the unidentified causes of rejects.

a. Is Keller's complaint valid? Explain the reason(s) for your answer.

b. What would you recommend that the company do to solve its problem with Keller and her complaint?

5. **Divisional Contribution, Performance' and Segment Margins.** The president of the Northwest Railroad wants to obtain an overview of his operations, particularly with respect to comparing freight and passenger business. He has heard about "contribution" approaches to cost allocations that emphasize cost behavior patterns and *contribution margins, contributions controllable by segment managers,* and *contributions by segments.* Pertinent data for the year ended December 31, 19X6, follow.

Total revenue was $80 million, of which $72 million was freight traffic and $8 million was passenger traffic. Fifty percent of the latter was generated by Division 1; 40% by Division 2; and 10% by Division 3.

Total variable costs were $45 million, of which $36 million was freight traffic. Of the $9 million allocable to passenger traffic, $3.3, $2.8, and $2.9 million could be allocated to Divisions 1, 2, and 3, respectively.

Total separable discretionary fixed costs were $8 million, of which $7.6 million applied to freight traffic.. Of the remainder, $80,000 could not be allocated to specific divisions, although it was clearly traceable to passenger traffic in general. Divisions 1, 2, and 3 should be allocated $240,000, $60,000, and $20,000, respectively.

Total separable committed costs, which were not regarded as being controllable by segment managers, were $25 million, of which 90% was allocable to freight traffic. Of the 10% traceable to passenger traffic, Divisions 1, 2, and 3 should be allocated $1.5 million, $350,000, and $150,000, respectively; the balance was unallocable to a specific division.

The common fixed costs not clearly allocable to any part of the company amounted to $800,000.

a. The president asks you to prepare statements, dividing the data for the company as a whole between the freight and passenger traffic and then subdividing the passenger traffic into three divisions.

b. Some competing railroads actively promote a series of one-day sightseeing tours on summer weekends. Most often, these tours are timed so that the cars with the tourists are hitched on with regularly scheduled passenger trains. What costs are relevant for making decisions to run such tours? Other railroads, facing the same general cost picture, refuse to conduct such sightseeing tours. Why?

c. For purposes of this analysis, even though the numbers may be unrealistic, suppose that Division 2's figures represented a specific run for a train instead of a division. Suppose further that the railroad has petitioned government authorities for permission to drop Division 2. What would be the effect on overall company net income for 19X7, assuming that the figures are accurate and that 19X7 operations are in all other respects a duplication of 19X6 operations?

6. **Quality Cost Report.** The manufacturing division of Green River, Inc., makes a variety of home furnishings. In 19X4 the company installed a system to report on quality costs. At the end of 19X6, Amy Green, the division general manager, wanted an assessment of whether quality costs in 19X6 differed from those in 19X4. Each month the actual costs had been compared with the plan, but at this time Green wanted to see only total annual numbers for 19X6 compared with 19X4. The production supervisor prepared the report shown in Figure 12-7.

a. For each of the four quality cost areas, explain what types of costs are included and how those costs have changed between 19X4 and 19X6.

b. Assess overall quality performance in 19X6 compared with 19X4. What do you suppose has caused the changes observed in quality costs?

FIGURE 12-7 Green River
Quality Cost Report (thousands of dollars)

Quality Cost Area	19X4 Cost	19X6 Cost
1. Prevention cost	45	107
% of Total quality cost	3.3%	12.4%
2. Appraisal cost	124	132
% of Total quality cost	9.1%	15.2%
3. Internal failure cost	503	368
% of Total quality cost	36.9%	42.5%
Total internal quality cost (1 + 2 + 3)	672	607
% of Total quality cost	49.3%	70.1%
4. External failure cost	691	259
% of Total quality cost	50.7%	29.9%
Total quality cost	1,363	866
Total product cost	22,168	23,462

CHAPTER 13

Valuing Inventories and the Cost of Goods Sold

This chapter introduces the details involved in assigning value to inventories and calculating the cost of goods sold. These important measures are used to determine a firm's gross profits. Since a firm's goal is profitable sales, we need effective accounting techniques to measure profitability. This chapter covers the methods and procedures for valuing inventory on the balance sheet and for recording costs of goods sold on the income statement. As in prior chapters, the chapter also presents ratios to assess the profitability of the firm and the effective management of inventory levels.

This chapter continues to link the preparation of the income statement and the balance sheet. When inventory is acquired it initially appears on the balance sheet as an asset. Under the matching principle, when revenue is recognized, the cost of the sale is also recognized. Thus, when a sale occurs the costs of the inventory become an expense, cost of goods sold, in the income statement. The chapter also explains how different inventory valuation techniques affect financial statements.

The accounting procedures discussed in this chapter are responses to a reporting need encountered in every nation of the world. While the dominant practices differ slightly from country to country, the issues remain. Even within a country, many different procedures are encountered. Thus, the reader of financial statements must understand alternative practices in order to intelligently compare the economic performance of different firms.

GROSS PROFIT AND COST OF GOODS SOLD

For firms that purchase and resell merchandise, a beginning guide to assessing profitability is *gross profit* (also called *profit margin* or *gross margin*), which is defined as the difference between sales revenues and the costs of the goods sold. These calculations rely on the value of the firms' inventories, which are goods that are being held for resale.

Sales revenue must cover the cost of goods sold and provide a gross profit sufficient to cover all other costs, including research and development, selling and marketing, administration, and so on. As illustrated in Figure 13-1, prior to sale, items held for sale are reported as inventory, a current asset in the balance sheet. When the goods are sold, the costs of the inventory become an expense, Cost of Goods Sold, in the income statement. This expense is deducted from Net Sales to determine Gross Profit, and additional expenses are deducted from Gross Profit to determine Net Income.

The Basic Concept of Inventory Accounting

The key to calculating the cost of goods sold is accounting for inventory. Conceptually, the process is very simple. Suppose Christina sells T-shirts. Periodically, she orders many shirts of various sizes and colors. They sell, she orders more, and her business operating cycle continues. After a year, to evaluate her success, Christina prepares financial statements. To calculate the value of inventory on hand, she obtains a *physical count* of inventory items remaining at year end. She then develops a **cost valuation,** which assigns a specific value from the historical cost records to each item in ending inventory. With 100 shirts remaining at a cost of $5.00 each, Christina's

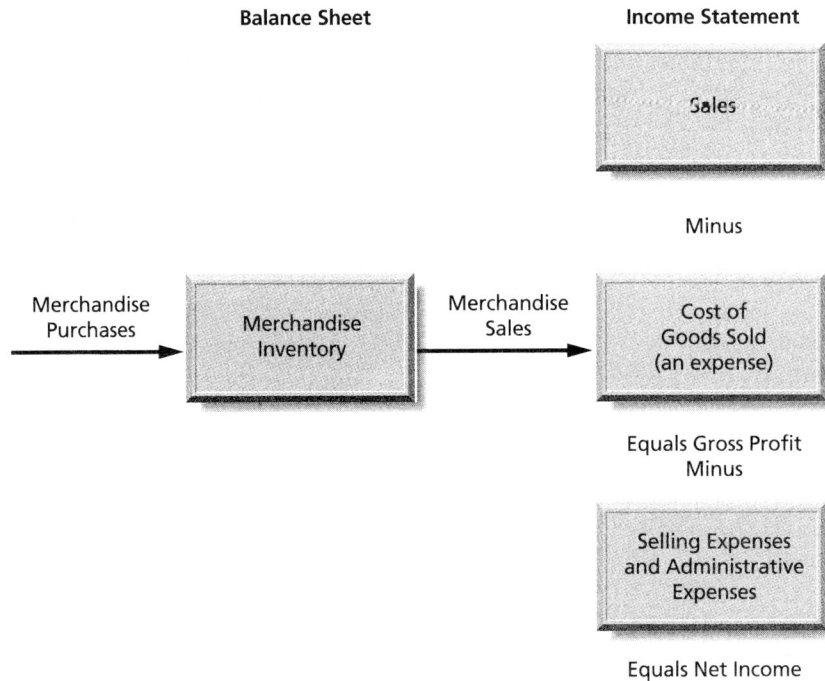

FIGURE 13-1
Merchandising Company (Retailer or Wholesaler)

total ending inventory is $500. Suppose she had no shirts at the beginning of the year, and total purchases for the year were $26,000. Her cost of goods sold is $25,500 ($26,000 of available shirts minus $500 of unsold shirts).

In practice, the process is not this simple. Complexity arises from many sources. The following sections describe alternate techniques for measuring inventories and how they differ.

PERPETUAL AND PERIODIC INVENTORY SYSTEMS

There are two fundamental ways of keeping inventory records for merchandise: perpetual and periodic. The **perpetual inventory system** (which has been assumed in previous chapters) keeps a running, continuous record that tracks inventories and the cost of goods sold on a day-to-day basis. Such a record helps managers control inventory levels and prepare interim financial statements. Nonetheless, physical inventory counts should be taken at least once a year to check on the accuracy of the clerical records.

Previous chapters have described the inventory cycle as follows:

		A	=	L	+	SE
a.	Purchase	+ Increase Merchandise Inventory	=	+ Increase Accounts Payable		
b.	Sale	+ Increase Accounts Receivable	=		+	Increase Sales Revenue
	Cost of inventory sold	− Decrease Inventory	=		−	Increase Cost of Goods Sold

In the perpetual inventory system, the journal entries are:

a. When inventory is purchased:
Merchandise inventory xxx
    Accounts payable xxx
b. When inventory is sold:
Accounts receivable (or cash) xxx
    Sales revenue xxx
Cost of goods sold xxx
    inventory xxx

Thus, in the perpetual inventory system, the sale and the inventory reduction are recorded simultaneously.

The **periodic inventory system,** conversely, does *not* involve a day-to-day record of inventories or of the cost of goods sold. Instead the cost of goods sold and an updated inventory balance are computed only at the end of an accounting period, when a physical count of inventory is taken. The cost of the goods purchased is accumulated by recording the individual purchase transactions throughout any given reporting period, such as a year. The accountant computes the cost of goods sold by subtracting the ending inventories (determined by physical count) from the sum of the opening inventory and purchases. Christina applied the periodic inventory method to her T-shirt business.

While the cost of goods sold under the perpetual system is computed instantaneously as goods are sold, under the periodic system, the computation is delayed:

$$\frac{\text{Beginning inventory} + \text{Purchases} - \text{Ending inventory} = \text{Cost of goods sold}}{\text{Goods available for sales} - \text{Inventory left over} = \text{Cost of goods sold}}$$

The periodic system computes cost of goods sold as a *residual amount.* First, the beginning inventory is added to the purchases to obtain the total **cost of goods available for sale.** Then the ending inventory is counted, and its cost is deducted from the cost of goods available for sale to obtain the cost of goods sold.

Comparison of Systems

Figure 13-2 compares the perpetual and periodic inventory systems. For annual financial statements, the two methods give equivalent results. Historically, the perpetual system has been used for low-volume, high-value items. The periodic system has been preferred for high-volume, low-value, and mixed-value inventory operations. The more expensive and cumbersome perpetual system was typically implemented when it gave significant managerial information to aid in pricing or ordering. Sometimes it improved control over loss and theft of inventory. Computerized inventory systems and optical scanning equipment at checkout counters have made implementation of perpetual inventory systems less costly.

The perpetual system does not eliminate the need for a physical count and valuation of the inventory. While the perpetual system captures information about goods

---

FIGURE 13-2   Inventory Systems

Periodic System		Perpetual System
Beginning inventories		Cost of goods sold (kept on a
(by physical count)	xxx	day-to-day basis rather than
Add: Purchases	xxx	being determined periodically)*
xxx		
Cost of goods available for sale	xxx	
Less: Ending inventories		
(by physical count)	xxx	
Cost of goods sold	**xxx**	

*Such a condensed figure does not preclude the presentation of a supplementary schedule similar to that on the left.

purchased and sold, the physical inventory allows management to delete from inventory goods that are damaged or obsolete. It also reveals disagreements between perpetual records and the physical count that may arise from **inventory shrinkage.** Inventory shrinkage refers to theft, breakage, and loss, which are substantial factors in some businesses.

If the physical count differs from the perpetual inventory amount, the following result might be obtained:

Perpetual inventory record:	Part 1F68X	142 units @ $20	$2,840
Physical count:	Part 1F68X	125 units @ $20	$2,500

Seventeen units (142 units – 125 units) have disappeared without being charged as cost of goods sold. The journal entry to adjust inventory from $2,840 to $2,500 is:

Inventory shrinkage	340	
Merchandise inventory		340
To adjust the ending inventory to its balance per physical count.		

In summary, the perpetual system is more accurate in providing timely information, but it is more costly. The periodic system is less accurate, especially for monthly or quarterly statements. It is less costly because there is no day-to-day processing regarding cost of goods sold. However, if theft or the accumulation of obsolete merchandise is likely, periodic systems often prove to be more expensive in the long run.

Physical Inventory

Good inventory control procedures require a **physical count** of each item being held in inventory at least annually in both periodic and perpetual inventory systems. The physical count is an imposing, time-consuming, and expensive process. You may have seen "closed for inventory" signs. To simplify counting and valuation, firms often choose fiscal accounting periods so that the year ends when inventories are low. For example, Kmart and JC Penney have late January year ends, which follow the holiday season.

The physical inventory is so important to income determination that external auditors usually observe the client's physical count and confirm the accuracy of the subsequent valuation. Some audit firms hire outside experts to assist them. For example, assessing a jeweler's inventory might require an expert to test the color, size, clarity, and imperfections in the diamonds on hand. Similarly, the client and auditor might rely on an engineer to measure the physical dimensions of an electric utility's coal pile so the volume and weight could be estimated without actually weighing the coal itself.

COST OF MERCHANDISE ACQUIRED

Measuring Cost of Merchandise Acquired

Some of the complexity in inventory accounting stems from the question of what constitutes the cost of the merchandise. To be more specific, does cost include all or part of the following: invoice price, transportation charges, trade and cash discounts, cost of handling and placing in stock, storage, purchasing department, receiving department, and other indirect charges? In practice, accountants usually consider the cost of merchandise to include only the invoice price plus the directly identifiable transportation charges less any offsetting discounts. The costs of the purchasing and receiving departments are treated as period costs and appear on the income statement as they are incurred.

The accounting for *purchase* returns, *purchase* allowances, and cash discounts on *purchases* is just the opposite of their sales counterparts. Using the periodic inventory system, suppose gross purchases are $960,000 and purchase returns and allowances are $75,000. The summary journal entries are:

Purchases	960,000	
Accounts payable		960,000
Accounts payable	75,000	
Purchase returns and allowances		75,000

Suppose also that cash discounts of $5,000 are taken upon payment of the remaining $960,000 − $75,000 = $885,000 of payables. The summary journal entry is:

Accounts payable	885,000	
Cash discounts on purchases		5,000
Cash		880,000

The accounts Cash Discounts on Purchases and Purchase Returns and Allowances are deducted from Purchases in calculating cost of goods sold.

Car dealers sometimes sell cars "below cost" or "$100 below invoice." Do dealers lose money on such sales? Probably not, because gross invoice cost to the dealer and final cost of goods sold may differ. Dealers receive incentives from the manufacturers such as volume discounts or special discounts to push particular models. The dealer's invoice shows the list price before discounts and allowances, not the final net dealer cost.

Inward Transportation

The major cost of transporting merchandise is typically the freight charges from the shipping point of the seller to the receiving point of the buyer. When the seller bears this cost, the terms are stated on the sales invoice as **F.O.B.** (free on board) **destination.** When the buyer bears this cost, the terms are stated as **F.O.B. shipping point.**

In theory, any transportation costs borne by the buyer should be added to the cost of the inventory acquired. In practice, several different items are typically ordered and shipped simultaneously. Therefore it is often difficult to allocate freight costs among the items. In addition, management may want to compile freight costs separately to see how they compare with regard to periods and modes of transportation. Consequently, accountants frequently use a separate transportation cost account, labeled as Freight In, Transportation In, Inbound Transportation, or Inward Transportation.

Freight in (or **inward transportation**) appears in the purchases section of an income statement as an additional cost of the goods acquired during the period. On the other hand, **freight out** represents the costs borne by the *seller* and is shown as a "shipping expense," which is a form of selling expense. Thus Freight In affects the gross profit section of an income statement for the buyer, but Freight Out does not and therefore appears below the gross profit line on the seller's income statement. A detailed gross profit section is often arranged as follows (figures in thousands are assumed):

Gross sales				$1,740
Deduct: Sales returns and allowances			$ 70	
Cash discounts on sales			100	170
Net sales				$1,570
Deduct: Cost of goods sold:				
Merchandise inventory, December 31, 19X1			$ 100	
Purchases (gross)		$960		
Deduct: Purchase returns and allowances	$75			
Cash discounts on purchases	5	80		
Net purchases		$880		
Add: Freight in		30		
Total cost of merchandise acquired			910	
Cost of goods available for sale			$1,010	
Deduct: Merchandise inventory,				
December 31, 19X2			140	
Cost of goods sold				870
Gross profit				$ **700**

While management may find such detail valuable, summary information is much more common in the annual report to shareholders:

Net Sales	$1,570
Cost of Goods Sold	870
Gross Profit	$ **700**

COMPARING ACCOUNTING PROCEDURES FOR PERIODIC AND PERPETUAL INVENTORY SYSTEMS

A Detailed Example

GoodEarth Products, Inc., has a balance of $100,000 in merchandise inventory at the beginning of 19X2 (December 31, 19X1). A summary of transactions for 19X2 follows:

a. Purchases	$990,000
b. Purchase returns and allowances	80,000

Net purchases were therefore $990,000 less $80,000, or $910,000. The physical count of the ending inventory for 19X2 led to a cost valuation of $140,000. Note how these figures can be used to compute the $870,000 cost of goods sold:

$$\underset{\text{inventory}}{\text{Beginning}} + \text{Net purchases} - \underset{\text{inventory}}{\text{Ending}} = \underset{\text{goods sold}}{\text{Cost of}}$$

$$\$100,000 + \$910,000 \qquad - \$140,000 \qquad = \$870,000$$

$$\underset{\text{for sale}}{\text{Cost of goods}} - \underset{\text{left over}}{\text{Cost of goods}} = \underset{\text{goods sold}}{\text{Cost of}}$$

$$\$1,010,000 \qquad - \$140,000 \qquad = \$870,000$$

The periodic and perpetual procedures would record these transactions differently. As Figure 13-3 shows, the perpetual system entails directly increasing the Inventory account by the $990,000 purchases (entry *a*) and decreasing it by the $80,000 in returns and allowances (entry *b*) and the $870,000 cost of goods sold (entry *c*). The Cost of Goods Sold account would be increased daily as sales are made. In a nutshell, these entries should be familiar. The only new aspect here is the purchase returns and allowances, which directly reduce the Inventory account. Although no purchase (cash) discounts are illustrated, their treatment would parallel purchase returns and allowances.

Before proceeding, reflect on how the perpetual system in Figure 13-3 creates the ending inventory of $140,000.

GoodEarth Products, Inc.
General Ledger at December 31, 19X2 (amounts in thousands)
Perpetual Inventory

Inventory				Cost of Goods Sold			
Balance 12/31/X1	100	(b)	80	(c)	870	(d3)	870
(a)	990	(c)	870				
Balance 12/31/X2	140						

The periodic system is called "periodic" because neither the Cost of Goods Sold account nor the Inventory account is computed on a daily basis. Moreover, Purchases and Purchase Returns and Allowances are accounted for in a separate account, as entries *a* and *b* indicate. Entries *d1* and *d2* at the bottom of Figure 13-3 show the eventual periodic calculation of cost of goods sold in the Cost of Goods Sold Account.

Entry *d1* transfers the beginning inventory balance, purchases, and purchase returns and allowances, totaling $1,010,000, to cost of goods sold. This provides the cost of goods available for sale, the first step in calculating cost of goods sold.

Next, the ending inventory is physically counted and its cost is computed. Entry *d2* recognizes the $140,000 ending inventory and reduces the $1,010,000 cost of goods available for sale by $140,000 to obtain a final cost of goods sold of $870,000. All of these details can be shown in the cost of goods sold section of the income statement.

FIGURE 13-3   Comparison of Perpetual and Periodic Inventory Entries (amounts in thousands)

Perpetual Records			Periodic Records		

a. Gross
purchases:
	Inventory 990
	   Accounts payable ......
		990	Purchases 990
			   Accounts payable ....
				990	

b. Returns and
allowances:
	Accounts payable 80
	   Inventory ....
		80	Accounts payable 80
			   .... Purchase returns
			    and allowances ....
				80	

c. As goods are sold:	Cost of goods sold .... 870 Inventory	870	No entry		

d. At the end
of the
accounting
period:
	d1. & d2. No entry		d1. Cost of goods sold 1,010
			   Purchase returns
			    and allowances 80
			    Purchases ....
			    Inventory ....
			
			d2. Inventory 140
			   Cost of goods sold ....
				990
				100
				
				140	

	d3. Income summary 870
	   Cost of goods sold.
		870	d3. Income summary 870
			   Cost of goods sold ....
				870	

However, published income statements usually include only a single cost of goods sold number.

The periodic system may seem awkward when compared with the perpetual system. The beginning inventory and cost of goods sold accounts are untouched until the end of the period. However, the periodic system avoids the costly process of calculating the cost of goods sold for each sale.

GoodEarth Products, Inc.
General Ledger at December 31, 19X2 (amounts in thousands)
Periodic Inventory

Inventory				Cost of Goods Sold			
Balance 12/31/X1	100	(d1)	100	(d1)	1,010	(d2)	140
(d2)	140					(d3)	870
Balance 12/31/X2	140						

As shown in entry *d3,* the cost of goods sold is closed to Income Summary under either method.

Note that the periodic method produces the same final balances in Inventory and Income Summary as the perpetual method. However, as entries *d1* and *d2* demonstrate, the cost of goods sold is computed at the end of the year; consequently, the related journal entries and postings are made then.

Note that in the perpetual system, the Inventory and Cost of Goods Sold account balances are always up to date, without special action by the accountant. In contrast, under the periodic system, more accounts are in use and information is simply being accumulated. No balance appears in the Cost of Goods Sold account until the company prepares financial statements and uses an adjusting journal entry to properly state inventory balances and cost of goods sold.

PRINCIPAL INVENTORY VALUATION METHODS

Each period, accountants must divide the cost of beginning inventory and merchandise acquired between cost of goods sold and cost of items remaining in ending inventory. Under a perpetual system, a cost must be assigned to each item sold. Under a periodic system, the costs of the items remaining in ending inventory must be measured. Regardless of the inventory system, costs of individual items must be determined by some inventory valuation method. Four principal inventory valuation methods have been generally accepted in the United States: specific identification, FIFO, LIFO, and weighted-average. Each will be explained and compared in this section.

If unit prices and costs did not fluctuate, all inventory methods would show identical results. But prices change, and these changes raise central issues regarding cost of goods sold (income measurement) and inventories (asset measurement). As a simple example of the valuation method choices facing management, consider Emilio, a new vendor of a cola drink at the fairgrounds, who begins the week with no inventory. He buys one can on Monday for 30 cents; a second can on Tuesday for 40 cents; and a third can on Wednesday for 56 cents. He then sells one can on Thursday for 90 cents. What is his gross profit? His ending inventory? Answer these questions in your own mind before reading on.

Four Major Methods

Panel I of Figure 13-4 provides a first glimpse of the nature of the four generally accepted methods for inventory valuation. As the figure shows, Emilio's choice of an inventory method can significantly affect the amount reported as cost of goods sold (and hence gross profit and net income) and ending inventory. Note, for example, that three different gross profit margins may occur under the specific identification method. FIFO yields a 60 cent profit, while LIFO yields only a 34 cent profit.

1. **Specific identification method.** This method concentrates on the *physical* linking of the *particular* items sold. Suppose Emilio could tell which can of cola was purchased on each day. If he reached for the Monday can instead of the Wednesday can, the *specific identification* method would show different results. Thus Panel I of Figure 13-4 indicates that gross profit for operations of Monday through Thursday could be 60 cents, 50 cents, or 34 cents, depending on the particular can handed to the customer. Emilio could choose which can to sell and affect reported results by doing so.

2. **First-in, first-out (FIFO).** This method assumes that the stock acquired earliest is sold (used up) first. It does not track the physical flow of individual items except

by coincidence. Thus the Monday can of cola is deemed to have been sold regardless of the actual can delivered. In times of rising prices, FIFO usually shows the *largest* gross profit (60 cents in Panel I of Figure 13-4).

3. **Last-in, first-out (LIFO).**   This method assumes that the stock acquired most recently is sold (used up) first. Thus the Wednesday can of cola is deemed to have been sold regardless of the actual can delivered. In times of rising prices, LIFO generally shows the lowest gross profit (34 cents in Panel I of Figure 13-4).

4. **Weighted-average cost.**   This method computes a unit cost by dividing the total acquisition cost of all items available for sale by the number of units available for sale. Figure 13-4 shows the calculations Emilio would make. The weighted-average method usually produces a gross profit somewhere between that obtained under FIFO and that under LIFO (48 cents as compared with 60 cents and 34 cents in Panel I of Figure 13-4).

Inventory Methods and the Matching Principle

Under the matching principle, we must link the cost of goods sold with the sales revenue generated when the product is delivered to a customer. What is challenging is to *measure* cost of goods sold. Panel I of Figure 13-4 identifies four measurement methods—specific identification, FIFO, LIFO, and weighted-average cost—each with both strengths and weaknesses.

Think of these methods as expressions of how Emilio might physically store and sell his cola. He could mark each can with its cost and record that cost as cost of goods sold when the can was handed to a customer. Specific identification captures this procedure. He could put each new can, as it is acquired, into the top of a cooler. At each customer purchase, the top can is the one sold. LIFO reflects this procedure. In contrast, each new can could be placed at the back of the cooler to chill and the oldest, coldest can sold first. FIFO captures this physical flow. If the cans are mixed together, the weighted-average method is a rough approximation of what Emilio knows about the cost of each can sold.

Because the physical flow of products has little importance to the financial success of most businesses, the accounting profession has concluded that companies may choose any of the four methods to record cost of goods sold. Since the method is not linked to the physical flow of merchandise, inventory methods are often referred to as *cost flow assumptions.* For example, when we decide that the cost of the first inventory item purchased will be matched with the sales revenue from the first item sold to calculate the gross profit from the sale, we are adopting the FIFO cost flow assumption.

Suppose Emilio sells his remaining inventory on Friday and enters a more attractive business. Panel II of Figure 13-4 shows Friday's gross profit. Panel III of Figure 13-4 shows that the *cumulative* gross profit over the life of Emilio's business would be the same $1.44 under any of the inventory methods. What makes the choice of method important is our having to match particular costs to particular periods *dur-*

FIGURE 13-4   Emilio's Cola Sales Comparison of Inventory Methods
(all monetary amounts are in cents)

	(1) Specific Identification			(2) FIFO	(3) LIFO	(4) Weighted Average
	(1A)	(1B)	(1C)			
Panel I						
Income Statement for the Period Monday through Thursday						
Sales	90	90	90	90	90	90
Deduct cost of goods sold:						
1 30¢ (Monday) unit	30	30				
1 40¢ (Tuesday) unit		40				
1 56¢ (Wednesday) unit			56		56	
1 weighted-average unit [(30 + 40 + 56) ÷ 3 = 42]	—	—	—	—	—	42
Gross profit for Monday through Thursday	60	50	34	60	34	43
Thursdays ending inventory, 2 units:						
Monday unit @ 30¢		30	30		30	
Tuesday unit @ 40¢	40		40	40	40	
Wednesday unit @ 56¢	56	56		56		
Weighted-average units @ 42¢	—	—	—	—	—	84
Total ending inventory on Thursday	96	86	70	96	70	84
Panel II						
Income Statement for Friday						
Sales, 2 units @ 90¢	180	180	180	180	180	180
Cost of goods sold (Thursday ending inventory from above)	96	86	70	96	70	84
Gross profit, Friday only	84	94	110	84	110	96
Panel III						
Gross profit for full week						
Monday through Thursday (Panel I)	60	50	34	60	34	48
Friday (Panel II)	84	94	110	84	110	96
Total gross profit	144	144	144	144	144	144

ing the life of the business in order to prepare financial statements and evaluate performance.

The Consistency Convention

While companies have broad latitude in choosing their inventory cost flow assumption, they are expected to use the chosen method consistently over time. The FASB has referred to **consistency** as "conformity from period to period with unchanging policies and procedures." Interpreting financial performance over time involves comparing the results of different periods. If accounting methods for inventory were changed often, meaningful comparisons over time would be impossible. Figure 13-4 illustrates the extreme difference that the choice of inventory method produces for Emilio's reported gross profits in different periods.

Occasionally a change in market conditions or other circumstances may justify a change in inventory method. With its auditor's approval, a firm may change method.

But the firm is required to note the change in its financial statements, and the auditor will also refer to the change in the audit opinion so that financial statement readers are alerted to the possible effects of the change on their analysis.

CHOOSING AND USING INVENTORY METHODS

The four inventory methods have different benefits and drawbacks. Among the issues facing management when choosing a method are such questions as: Which method provides the highest reported net income? Which method provides management the most flexibility to affect reported earnings? How do the methods affect income tax obligations? Which methods are inexpensive to apply? Which method provides an inventory valuation that approximates the actual value of the inventory?

Consider the link between cost of goods sold and the valuation of ending inventory. Emilio's three cola cans had a total cost of goods available for sale of $1.26. At the end of the period, this $1.26 must be allocated either to cans sold or to cans in ending inventory. The higher the cost of goods sold, the lower the ending inventory. Figure 13-5 illustrates that interdependence. At one extreme, FIFO treats the 30 cent cost of the first can acquired as cost of goods sold and 96 cents as ending inventory. At the other extreme, LIFO treats the 56 cent cost of the last can acquired as cost of goods sold and 70 cents as ending inventory.

Before considering each method in detail, one other general relation is worth studying. Note from columns 2 and 3 of Figure 13-4 that during this period of rising prices, FIFO yields higher inventory *and* higher gross profit than LIFO. This result is consistent with the accounting equation that requires that A = L + SE. If inventory is higher under FIFO (higher assets) and the equation is to balance, either liabilities or stockholders' equity must also be higher. Higher gross profit under FIFO implies

FIGURE 13-5   Emilio's Cola Sales
Diagram of Inventory Methods (data are from Panel I, Figure 13-4; monetary amounts are in cents)

Beginning inventory	+	Merchandise purchases	=	Cost of goods available for sale
0	+	126	=	126
Cost of goods available for sale	−	Cost of goods sold	=	Ending inventory

126 (1 @ 30, 1 @ 40, 1 @ 56)	−	30 or 40 or 56	=	96 or 86 or 70	Specific identification
126	−	30	=	96	FIFO
126	−	56	=	70	LIFO
126	−	42	=	84	Weighted average

higher net income and higher stockholder's equity (SE in the equation). Note that nothing in our choice of methods would affect accounts payable. We record each new inventory purchase at its cost and recognize a liability in that amount in the same way under all of these methods.

Specific Identification

The specific identification method, which uses physical observation or the labeling of items in stock with individual numbers or codes, is easy and economically justifiable for relatively expensive low-volume merchandise like custom artwork, diamond jewelry, and automobiles. However, most organizations have vast segments of inventories that are too numerous and insufficiently valuable per unit to warrant such individualized attention. Since the cost of goods sold is determined by the specific item handed to the customer, this method permits managers to manipulate income and inventory values by filling a sales order from a number of physically equivalent items with different historical costs.

FIFO

FIFO is sometimes referred to as LISH (Last In, Still Here). When the first costs represent goods sold, the last costs represent goods still on hand. By using the latest costs to measure the ending inventory, FIFO tends to provide inventory valuations that closely approximate the actual market value of the inventory at the balance sheet date. In addition, in periods of rising prices, FIFO leads to higher net income. Higher reported incomes may favorably affect investor attitudes toward the company. Similarly, higher reported incomes may lead to higher salaries, higher bonuses, or higher status for the management of the company. Unlike specific identification, FIFO specifies the order in which acquisition costs will become cost of goods sold, so management cannot affect income by choosing to sell one identical item rather than another.

LIFO

While FIFO associates the most recent costs with inventories, LIFO treats the most recent costs as costs of goods sold. LIFO provides an income statement perspective in the sense that net income measured using LIFO combines current sales prices and current acquisition costs. *In a period of rising prices and constant or grooving inventories, LIFO yields lower net income.* Why is lower net income such an important feature of LIFO? Because in the United States LIFO is an acceptable inventory accounting method for income tax purposes. When lower income is reported to the tax authorities, lower taxes are paid, so it is not surprising that almost two-thirds of U.S. corporations use LIFO for at least some of their inventories. The Internal Revenue Code requires that if LIFO is used for tax purposes, it must also be used for financial reporting purposes.

During a recent period of higher inflation, the *Wall Street Journal* reported that many small firms changed from FIFO to LIFO. As an example, Chicago Heights Steel Co. "boosted cash by 5% to 10% by lowering income taxes when it switched to LIFO."

When Becton, Dickinson and Company changed to LIFO, its annual report stated that its "change to the LIFO method . . . for both financial reporting and income tax purposes resulted in improved cash flow due to lower income taxes paid." Indeed, some observers maintain that executives are guilty of serious mismanagement by not adopting LIFO when FIFO produces significantly higher taxable income.

LIFO does permit management to influence reported income by the *timing of purchases* of inventory items. Consider Emilio's case. Suppose that acquisition prices increase from 56 cents on Wednesday to 68 cents on Thursday, the day of the sale of the one unit. How is net income affected if one more unit is acquired on Thursday? Under LIFO, cost of goods sold would change to 68 cents, and profit would fall by 12 cents. In contrast, FIFO cost of goods sold and gross profit would be unchanged.

	LIFO		FIFO	
	As in Figure 13-4	*If One More Unit Acquired*	*As in Figure 13-4*	*If One More Unit Acquired*
Sales	90¢	90¢	90¢	90¢
Cost of goods sold	<u>56¢</u>	<u>68¢</u>	<u>30¢</u>	<u>30¢</u>
Gross profit	**34¢**	**22¢**	**60¢**	**60¢**
Ending inventory:				
First layer, Monday	30¢	30¢		
Second layer, Tuesday	<u>40¢</u>	40¢	40¢	40¢
Third layer, Wednesday		<u>56¢</u>	<u>56¢</u>	56¢
Fourth layer, Thursday				<u>68¢</u>
	70¢	**126¢**	**96¢**	**164¢**

Weighted Average

Figure 13-4 illustrates that the weighted average costing method produces less extreme results than either LIFO or FIFO relative to both the income statement and the balance sheet. The weighted average is also subject to minimal manipulation by management action. The term *weighted* average can be better understood by assuming Emilio bought two cans rather than one on Monday at 30 cents each. To get the weighted average, we must consider not only the price paid, but also the number purchased as follows:

$$\text{Weighted average} = \text{Cost of goods available for sale} \div \text{Units available for sale}$$
$$\text{Weighted average} = [(2 \times 30¢) + (1 \times 40¢) + (1 \times 56¢)] \div 4$$
$$= 156¢ \div 4$$
$$= 39¢$$

Summarizing the Four Methods

LIFO is the most popular inventory method for large U.S. companies. As we said, about two-thirds of the companies use LIFO for at least *some* of their inventories. Over 60% use FIFO, and 40% use weighted average for a *portion* of their inventories.

Less than 10% use any other method, including specific identification. Over half the companies use more than one inventory method.

In a study by the American Institute of Certified Accountants, fewer than 25% of the respondents in the following industries used LIFO: electronics, business equipment, ship building, and railway equipment. If tax benefits are so important, why doesn't everyone use LIFO? Recall that LIFO yields lower net income and lower taxes *in a period of rising prices and constant or growing inventories.* One answer is that some industries don't face rising prices. For such industries, FIFO yields lower net income and lower taxes. In electronics, for example, technology has consistently driven prices down. Think back to two decades of constant reductions in prices for radios, stereo systems, clocks, and watches. The situation is similar for business equipment such as word processors and computers. With ship building and railway equipment, specific identification is an appropriate method since each unit is large and expensive.

CHARACTERISTICS AND CONSEQUENCES OF LIFO

Given the dominant role that LIFO has in inventory accounting in the United States, this section addresses some of the peculiarities of the LIFO inventory method. But remember that LIFO's dominant role is more a result of an inflationary world and tax benefits than any theoretical dominance over other methods. Internationally, LIFO is not common. In many countries—for example, in Brazil and Australia—it is not permitted at all. In Canada it is disallowed for tax purposes. LIFO is a minority practice in many countries. The predominant choice worldwide is an average cost method, and the next most common choice is FIFO.

Holding Gains and Inventory Profits

LIFO's income statement orientation provides a reasonable economic interpretation of operating performance in inflationary periods. Consider Emilio. For him to be as well off after selling the can of cola as he was before, he must be able to replace it with the proceeds from his sale. If he must spend 56 cents to replace the can that was sold, we might call 56 cents the **replacement cost** of the inventory. The 26 cent difference between the historical cost of, say, 30 cents (the Monday can) and 56 cents (the Wednesday replacement cost) is called a **holding gain.** This holding gain is sometimes called an **inventory profit.** Because LIFO matches recent acquisition costs with sales revenue, LIFO cost of goods sold typically offers a close approximation to replacement cost, and reported net income rarely contains significant holding gains. The LIFO profit is 90 – 56 = 34 cents. In contrast, recall that using FIFO Emilio reports a profit of 60 cents (90 cents – 30 cents). This profit contains two parts, the economic profit of 34 cents calculated as sales price less replacement costs, plus the inventory profit or holding gain of 26 cents that arose because the value of the inventory item rose with the passage of time.

In commenting on inventory profits, a *Newsweek* article said:

> In an inflationary world, parts acquired for inventory tend to appreciate in value by the time they are used in the manufacturing process. The company then reflects the difference in its selling price—and takes an "inventory profit." It must restock at the new,

higher cost, of course, but as long as the inflation continues, so does the inventory-profit process.

LIFO Layers

The ending inventory under LIFO may contain prices from many different periods. With Emilio, the ending inventory contained two cans, one acquired on Monday at 30 cents and one acquired on Tuesday for 40 cents. Each distinct element of inventory might be called a **LIFO layer** (also called **LIFO increment**), an identifiable addition to inventory. As a company grows, the LIFO layers tend to pile on top of one another over the years. Suppose Emilio's business grew for years, ending each year with two more cans in inventory than the year before. Each year would have an identifiable LIFO layer, much like the rings that grow on a tree each year. After five years of inventory growth and rising prices, his ending inventory might be structured as follows:

Year 1	layer 1—1 can @.30	
	layer 2—1 can @.40	.70
Year 2	layer 3—2 cans @.45	.90
Year 3	layer 4—2 cans @.50	1.00
Year 4	layer 5—2 cans @.55	1.10
Total inventory		**$3.70**

Many LIFO companies show inventories that have ancient layers going back as far as 1940, when LIFO was first used. Reported LIFO inventory values may therefore be far below what the true market value or current replacement value of the inventory might be.

LIFO Inventory Liquidations

The existence of old LIFO layers can cause problems if inventory decreases. Examine Figure 13-6. Suppose Harbor Electronics bought an inventory of 100 units at $10 per unit on December 31, 19X0. The company bought and sold 100 units each year, 19X1 through 19X4, at the purchase and selling prices shown. The example assumes replacement costs and sales prices rise in tandem with a difference per unit of $3. In 19X5 100 units were sold but none were purchased.

Compare the gross profit each year under LIFO with that under FIFO in Figure 13-6. LIFO gross profit is generally less than FIFO gross profit because prices were rising. But what happened in 19X5? The old 19X0 inventory became the cost of goods sold under LIFO because inventory was depleted. Consequently, gross profit under LIFO soared to $1,300, well above the FIFO gross profit, which was stable at $500. In general, when the physical amount of inventory decreases, LIFO charges the cost of old LIFO layers as cost of goods sold, beginning with the most recent layers. This treatment can create a very low cost of goods sold and high gross profit. In a sense a LIFO liquidation means that the cumulative inventory profit from years of increasing prices is reflected in the income statement in one year.

FIGURE 13-6   Harbor Electronics

Effect of Inventory Liquidations under LIFO (Purchases and sales of 100 units in 19X1–19X4. Purchases but no sales in 19X0; sales but no purchases in 19X5.)

Year	Purchase Price Per Unit	Selling Price Per Unit	Revenue	FIFO Cost of Goods Sold	FIFO Gross Profit	FIFO Ending Inventory	LIFO Cost of Goods Sold	LIFO Gross Profit	LIFO Ending Inventory
19X0	$10	—	—	—	—	$1,000	—	—	$1,000
19X1	12	$15	$1,500	$1,000	$ 500	1,200	$1,200	$ 300	1,000
19X2	14	17	1,700	1,200	500	1,400	1,400	300	1,000
19X3	16	19	1,900	1,400	500	1,600	1,600	300	1,000
19X4	18	21	2,100	1,600	500	1,800	1,800	300	1,000
19X5		23	2,300	1,800	500	0	1,000	1,300	0
Total			$9,500	$7,000	$2,500		$7,000	$2,500	

In general, prices have been rising throughout the world for many years. Companies that have been on LIFO for a number of years typically have many LIFO layers, some at unit prices that are relatively old and low. Occasionally, circumstances (such as a prolonged strike or the discontinuance of a segment of the business) call for the liquidation of some or all of the LIFO layers. This decrease in the physical levels of inventories would cause unusually low cost of goods sold, high income, and high income tax expense in comparison with FIFO. For example, LIFO inventory liquidations by Amoco, an international oil company, increased its 1993 net income by $50 million, about 3% of its $1.8 billion income before tax.

A company's **LIFO reserve,** which is generally defined as the difference between inventories valued at LIFO and what they would be under FIFO, measures the potential effects of inventory liquidations. Refer to Figure 13-6. What is Harbor Electronics' LIFO reserve at the end of 19X1? It is $1,200 – $1,000 = $200, the difference in the LIFO and FIFO ending inventories. Note that it is the same as the difference in gross profit of $200. What about year 19X2? The LIFO reserve is $400 (FIFO ending inventory of $1,400 less LIFO ending inventory of $1,000). This difference represents the cumulative effect on earnings (or gross profit) over the first two years the company was in business. The specific effect on earnings *during* 19X2 is the *change* in the LIFO reserve, or $200. Figure 13-7 summarizes these effects.

From Figure 13-7 note that the *annual* difference between gross profit using FIFO and that using LIFO is the yearly *change* in the LIFO reserve. Finally, when all of the inventory is sold in 19X5, the liquidation of the LIFO inventory leads to recognition of higher earnings than under FIFO by the amount of the LIFO reserve. LIFO recognizes inventory profits when inventory levels are reduced. The LIFO reserve indicates the *cumulative* gross profit effect over all prior years due to LIFO.

How significant are the effects of LIFO? Ford Motor Company reported 1994 inventory of $6.5 billion. LIFO was used for the U.S. inventories. If FIFO had been used for all inventories, the total inventory would have been $1.4 billion higher (over a 20% difference). This means that over time, Ford has reported lower income on its

FIGURE 13-7   Harbor Electronics
                Annual and Cumulative Effects of LIFO Reserve

| | Ending Inventory | | | | Gross Profit Effect | |
Year	FIFO	LIFO	LIFO Reserve	Change in Reserve	*Current*	*Cumulative*
X0	$1,000	$1,000	$ 0	$ 0	$ 0	$ 0
X1	1,200	1,000	200	200	200	200
X2	1,400	1,000	400	200	200	400
X3	1,600	1,000	600	200	200	600
X4	1,800	1,000	800	200	200	800
X5	0	0	0	(800)	(800)	0

tax returns and paid lower taxes of approximately $560 million ($ 1.4 billion times approximately a 40% tax rate) as a result of its decision to use LIFO rather than FIFO.

LOWER-OF-COST-OR-MARKET METHOD

Under the **lower-of-cost-or-market method (LCM),** a market-price test is run on an inventory costing method. The *current market price* is compared with *historical cost* derived under one of the four primary methods: specific identification, FIFO, LIFO, or average. The lower of the two—current market value or historical cost—is conservatively selected as the basis for the valuation of goods at a specific inventory date. When market value is lower and is used for valuing the ending inventory, the effect is to increase the amount reported as cost of goods sold.

LCM is an example of conservatism. **Conservatism** means selecting methods of measurement that yield lower net income, lower assets, and lower stockholders' equity in the early years. Conservatism was illustrated in accounts receivable with the use of an allowance for bad debts. We estimated and recorded losses on uncollectible accounts before they were certain. With inventories, conservatism dictates the use of the LCM method.

Conservatism has been criticized as being inherently inconsistent. If replacement market prices are sufficiently objective and verifiable to substitute for cost when market prices are declining, why are they not sufficient to use when market values are rising? Accountants reply by saying that erring in the direction of conservatism usually has less severe economic consequences than erring in the direction of overstating assets and net income. The accountant's conservatism balances management's optimism. Management prepares the financial statements. The conservatism principle moderates management's human tendency to hope for, and expect, the best.

Role of Replacement Cost

Under GAAP, the definition of *market* is complex. For our purposes we will think of it as the *replacement cost* of the inventory item—that is, the cost that would be incurred to buy the inventory item today. Implicit in the method is the assumption that when replacement costs decline in the wholesale market, so do the retail selling prices. Consider the following example. The Ripley Company has 100 units in its ending FIFO inventory on December 31, 19X1. Its gross profit for 19X1 has been tentatively computed as follows:

Sales	$2,180
Cost of goods available for sale	$1,980
Ending inventory of 100 units, at cost	$ 790
Cost of goods sold	$1,190
Gross profit	$ 990

Assume a sudden decline in market prices during the final week of December from $7.90 per unit to $4 per unit. If the lower market price is indicative of lower ultimate sales prices, an inventory **write-down** of ($7.90 – $4.00) x 100 units, or $390, is in order. A write-down is a reduction in carrying value to below cost in response to a decline in value. The required journal entry is:

Loss on write-down of inventory (or cost of goods sold)	390	
Inventory		390
To write down inventory from $790 cost to $400 market value.		

The write-down of inventories increases cost of goods sold by $390. Therefore reported income for 19X1 would be lowered by $390:

	Before $390 Write-Down	After $390 Write-Down	Difference
Sales	$2,180	$2,180	
Cost of goods available	$1,980	$1,980	
Ending inventory	790	400	– $390
Cost of goods sold	$1,190	$1,580	+ $390
Gross profit	$ 990	$ 600	– $390

The theory states that of the $790 historical cost, $390 is considered to have expired during 19X1 because the cost cannot be justifiably carried forward to the future as an asset. Furthermore, the decision to purchase was made during 19X1, and the fluctuation in the replacement market price occurred during the same period. This decline in price caused the inventory to lose some value, some revenue-producing power, because the decline in replacement cost generally corresponds to a decline in selling price.

If *selling prices* are not likely to fall, the revenue-producing power of the inventory will be maintained and no write-down would be justified. In sum, if predicted selling prices will be *unaffected* by the fact that current replacement costs are below the carrying cost of the inventory, do nothing. If predicted selling prices will be lower, use replacement cost.

If a write-down occurs, the new $4 per unit replacement cost valuation becomes, for accounting purposes, the unexpired cost of the inventory. Thus, if replacement prices subsequently rise to $8 per unit in January 19X2, no restoration of the December write-down will be permitted. In short, the lower-of-cost-or-market method would regard the December 31 $4 cost as the "new historical cost" of the inventory. Historical cost is the ceiling for valuation under generally accepted accounting principles.

Conservatism in Action

Compared with a pure cost method, the lower-of-cost-or-market method reports less net income in the period of decline in market value of the inventory and more net income in the period of sale. More generally, cumulative net income (the sum of all net income amounts from the inception of the firm to the present date) is never lower and is usually higher under the strict cost method. The lower-of-cost-or-market method affects how much income is reported in each year but not the total income over the company's life. Figure 13-8 underscores this point. Suppose the Ripley Company goes out of business in early 19X2. That is, no more units are acquired. There are no sales in 19X2 except for the disposal of the inventory in question at $8 per unit (100 x $8 = $800). Neither combined gross profit nor combined net income for the two periods will be affected by the LCM method, as the bottom of Figure 13-8 reveals.

This example shows that conservatism can be a double-edged sword in the sense that net income in a current year will be hurt by a write-down of inventory (or any asset), and net income in a future year will be helped by the amount of the write-down. As Figure 13-8 illustrates, 19X2 income is $390 higher because of the $390 write-down of 19X1.

A full-blown lower-of-cost-or-market method is rarely encountered in practice. Why? Because it is expensive to get the correct replacement costs of hundreds or

---

FIGURE 13-8   The Ripley Company Effects of Lower-of-Cost-or-Market

	Cost Method		Lower-of Cost-or- Market Method	
	19X1	19X2	19X1	19X2
Sales	$2,180	$800	$2,180	$800
Cost of goods available	$1,980	$790	$1,980	$400
Ending inventory	790	—	400*	—
Cost of goods sold	$1,190	$790	$1,580	$400
Gross profit	$ 990	$ 10	$ 600	$400
Combined gross profit for two years:				
Cost method: $990 + $10 = $1,000				
Lower-of-cost-or-market method: $600 + $400 = $1,000				

*The inventory is shown here after being written down by $390, from $790 to $400. For internal purposes, many accountants prefer to show the write-down separately, presenting a gross profit before write-down of inventory, the write-down, and a gross profit after write-down.

thousands of different products in inventory. Still, auditors definitely feel that the costs of inventories should be fully recoverable from future revenues. Therefore auditors inevitably make market-price tests of a representative sample of the ending inventories. In particular, auditors want to write down the subclasses of inventory that are obsolete, shopworn, or otherwise of only nominal value.

EFFECTS OF INVENTORY ERRORS

Inventory errors can arise from many sources. Examples are wrong physical counts (possibly because goods that are in receiving or shipping areas instead of the inventory stockroom were omitted when physical counts were made) and clerical errors.

An undiscovered inventory error usually affects two reporting periods. It is counterbalanced by the ordinary accounting process in the next period. That is, the error affects income by identical offsetting amounts. An undiscovered inventory error affects the balance sheet at the end of the first period but not at the end of the second. For example, suppose ending inventory in 19X7 is understated by $10,000 because of errors in the physical count. The year's cost of goods sold would be overstated, pretax income understated, assets understated, and retained income understated.

These effects are easier to understand when a complete illustration is studied. Consider the following income statements (all numbers are in thousands), which assume ending 19X7 inventory is reported to be $10 too low.

19X7	Correct Reporting		Incorrect Reporting*		Effects of Errors
Sales		$980		$980	
Deduct: Cost of goods sold:					
Beginning inventory	$100		$100		
Purchases	500		500		
Cost of goods available for sale	$600		$600		
Deduct: Ending inventory	70		60		Understated by $10
Cost of goods sold		530		540	Overstated by $10
Gross profit		$450		$440	Understated by $10
Other expenses		250		250	
Income before income taxes		$200		$190	Understated by $10
Income tax expense at 40%		80		76	Understated by $4
Net income		**$120**		**$114**	Understated by $6
Ending balance sheet items:					
Inventory		$ 70		$ 60	Understated by $10
Retained income includes					
current net income of		120		114	Understated by $6
Income tax liability[†]		80		76	Understated by $4

*Because of error in ending inventory.
[†]For simplicity, assume that the entire income tax expense for the year will not be paid until the succeeding year. Therefore the ending liability will equal the income tax expense.

Think about the effects of the uncorrected error on the following year, 19X8. The beginning inventory will be $60,000 rather than the correct $70,000. Therefore *all* the errors in 19X7 will be offset by counterbalancing errors in 19X8. Thus the retained income at the end of 19X8 would show a cumulative effect of zero. This is because the net income in 19X7 would be understated by $6,000, but the net income in 19X8 would be overstated by $6,000.

The point to stress is that the ending inventory of one period is also the beginning inventory of the succeeding period. Assume that the operations during 19X8 are a duplication of those of 19X7 except that the ending inventory is correctly counted as $40,000. Note the role of the error in the beginning inventory.

19X8	Correct Reporting		Incorrect Reporting*		Effects of Errors
Sales		$980		$980	
Deduct: Cost of goods sold:					
Beginning inventory	$ 70		$ 60		Understated by $10
Purchases	500		500		
Cost of goods available for sale	$570		$560		Understated by $10
Deduct: Ending inventory	40		40		
Cost of goods sold		530		520	Understated by $10
Gross profit		$450		$460	Overstated by $10
Other expenses		250		250	
Income before income taxes		$200		$210	Overstated by $10
Income tax expense at 40%		80		84	Overstated by $4
Net income		**$120**		**$126**	Overstated by $6
Ending balance sheet items:					
Inventory		$ 40		$ 40	Correct
Retained income includes:					
Net income of previous year		120		114	Counterbalanced and
Net income of current year		120		126	thus now correct in total
Two-year total		**240**		**240**	
Income tax liability:					
End of previous year		80		76	Counterbalanced and
End of current year		80		84	thus now correct in total[†]
Two-year total		**160**		**160**	

*Because of error in beginning inventory.
[†]The $84 really consists of the $4 that pertains to income of the previous year plus $80 that pertains to income of the current year.

The complete illustration shows the full detail of the inventory error, but we can use the accounting equation to develop our intuition. A useful generalization is: If ending inventory is understated, retained income is understated. If ending inventory is overstated, retained income is overstated. These relations are clear from the accounting equation. The presence of taxes means only that the effects need to be considered in two parts. Understated inventory implies overstated cost of goods sold and therefore lower current-year income and lower taxes. The shortcut analysis follows:

	A	=	L	+	SE
	Inventory		Income Tax Liability		Retained Income
Effects of error	$10,000 understated = $4,000 understated + $6,000 understated˙				

˙Cost of goods overstated	**$10,000**
Pretax income understated	**$10,000**
Income taxes understated	4,000
Net income, which is included in ending retained income, understated	**$ 6,000**

THE IMPORTANCE OF GROSS PROFITS

As we have seen, gross profits are the result of sales revenue less the cost of goods sold as determined by one of the accounting methods for inventory valuation. Management and investors are intensely interested in gross profit and its changes. Will gross profits be large enough to cover operating expenses and produce a net income?

Gross Profit Percentage

Gross profit is often expressed as a percentage of sales. Consider the following information on a past year for a typical Safeway grocery store:

	Amount	Percentage
Sales	$10,000,000	100%
Net cost of goods sold	7,500,000	75%
Gross profit	$ 2,500,000	25%

The *gross profit percentage*—gross profit divided by sales—here is 25%. The following illustrates the extent to which gross profit percentages vary among industries.

Industry	Gross Profit (%)
Auto retailers	12.3
Auto manufacturers	17.6
Jewelry retailers	47.6
Grocery retailers	22.6
Grocery wholesalers	16.1
Drug manufacturers	40.8

Source: Robert Morris Associates, *Financial Statement Studies for 1994.*

The gross profit percentages range from a low of 12.3% to a high of 47.6%. Several patterns are evident. **Wholesalers** sell in larger quantity and incur fewer selling costs because they sell to other companies rather than individuals. As a result of competition and high volumes, they have smaller gross profit percentages than **retailers.** Retailers sell directly to individuals. Among retailers, jewelers have twice the gross profits of grocers because of expensive inventory and extensive personal selling. High gross profit percentages for drug manufacturers derive from patent protection and the need for substantial research and development outlays (up to 15% of sales). In contrast, auto manufacturers face more direct competition and earn lower gross profit percentages.

Estimating Intraperiod Gross Profit and Inventory

Exact ending inventory balances are not usually available for monthly or quarterly reports. The physical count required for an exact inventory count and accurate cost of goods sold calculation is too costly to obtain other than for year-end annual statements and reports. Interim reports thus use estimates derived from percentage or ratio methods. When the actual ending inventory is unavailable for monthly and quarterly financial statements, the gross profit percentage is often used to estimate the amount.

For example, assume that past sales of Tip Top Variety Store have usually resulted in a gross profit percentage of 25%. (Unless otherwise stated, any gross profit percentage given is based on net sales, not cost.) The accountant would estimate gross profit to be 25% of sales. If the monthly sales are $800,000, the cost of goods sold can be estimated as follows:

$$\text{Sales} - \text{Cost of goods sold} = \text{Gross profit}$$
$$S - CGS = GP$$
$$\$800,000 - CGS = 0.25 \times \$800,000 = \$200,000$$
$$CGS = \$600,000$$

If we know Tip Top's beginning inventory is $30,000 and purchases are $605,000, we can estimate ending inventory to be $35,000 as follows:

$$\text{Beginning inventory} + \text{Purchases} - \text{Ending inventory} = CGS$$
$$BI + P - EI = CGS$$
$$\$30,000 + \$605,000 - EI = \$600,000$$
$$EI = \$35,000$$

In retailing, profit margins may be expressed as "markups" on cost. When an item costing $60 is sold for $80 it is a 25% profit margin as defined in this accounting text, but marketing professionals might call it a 33 1/3% markup on cost ($20 markup ÷ $60 cost).

Gross Profit Percentage and Turnover

Retailers often attempt to increase total profits by increasing sales levels. They lower prices and hope to increase their gross profits by selling their inventories more quickly, replenishing, selling again, and so forth. Managers speak of improving their **inven-**

tory turnover, which is defined as cost of goods sold divided by the average inventory held during a given period. Average inventory is usually the sum of beginning inventory and ending inventory divided by 2. For the Tip Top Variety Store, the average inventory is ($30,000 + $35,000) ÷ 2 = $32,500. The inventory turnover is computed as follows:

$$\text{Turnover} = \text{Cost of goods sold} \div \text{Average inventory}$$
$$= \$600,000 \div \$32,500 = 18.5$$

Suppose the inventory sells twice as quickly if prices are lowered. With a 5% reduction in sales price, sales revenue on the current level of business drops from $800,000 to (0.95 × $800,000), or $760,000. But twice as many units are sold, so total revenue becomes 2 × $760,000, or $1,520,000. How profitable is Tip Top? Cost of goods sold doubles from $600,000 to $1,200,000. Total gross profit is $320,000. The inventory turnover doubles: $1,200,000 divided by $32,500 (the unchanged average inventory) is 36.9. However, the gross profit percentage falls from 25% to 21% ($320,000 divided by $1,520,000).

Is the company better off? Maybe. Certainly, in the current month gross profit has risen. However, strategic questions remain. *Is this new sales level maintainable?* For some products, when prices fall, consumers sharply increase purchases and stockpile the extras for later consumption. There is little increase in underlying demand, just a shift of future purchases to the present.

Another strategic question is, *What will competition do?* If Tip Top's increased sales came at a competitor's expense, the competitor's response may be a similar decrease in prices. The competition might recover most of its old customers, with each buying a little more at the new price than at the old. But the whole market would see, not a doubling of sales, but perhaps a 20% sales growth. Tip Top would be worse off in the aggregate; the 20% growth would not cover the 5% price reduction.

Figure 13-9 illustrates two principles. Panel A shows that if a firm can increase inventory turnover while maintaining a constant gross profit percentage, it should do so. However, as shown in panel B. if the increased inventory turnover results from a decrease in sales price, the gross margin percentage may fall. The desirability of the change depends on whether the sales gain could offset the decreased margin. In the Tip Top Variety Store example, when a 5% price reduction produces a 20% increase in units sold, the new gross margin of $192,000 is still less than the initial $200,000. Dropping the price is not justified even though the inventory turnover rises to 22.2 from 18.5. However, at a 50% increase in sales volume, the new gross margin of $240,000 exceeds the original $200,000.

The industry variability in gross margin percentages referred to earlier is also reflected in inventory turnover percentages.

Industry	Gross Profit (%)	Inventory Turnover
Grocery wholesalers	16.1	14.7
Grocery retailers	22.6	16.9
Drug manufacturers	40.8	3.3
Jewelry retailers	47.6	1.4

Source: Robert Morris Associates, *Financial Statement Studies for 1994.*

FIGURE 13-9   **Tip Top Variety Store**
              Effects of Increased Inventory Turnover (in thousands)

| Panel A | Original | Unit Sales Increase | | |
		20%	50%	100%
No change in sales price				
Sales	$800	$960	$1,200	$1,600
Cost of goods sold (75%)	600	720	900	1,200
Gross margin (25%)	**$200**	**$240**	**$ 300**	**$ 400**
Inventory turnover	18.5	22.2	27.7	36.9
Panel B				
5% reduction in sales price				
Sales (95% of above)	$760	$912	$1,140	$1,520
Cost of goods sold (as above)	600	720	900	1,200
Gross margin (21% of sales)	**$160**	**$192**	**$ 240**	**$ 320**
Inventory turnover (as above)	18.5	22.2	27.7	36.9

The data are ordered from lowest gross profit percentage to highest for the industries displayed. There is a tendency for the inventory turnovers to move in the opposite direction.

When ratios are being calculated it is important to keep the accounting methods in mind. Consider the following data for Ford Motor Company:

Ford Motor Company ($ in millions)

| | 1994 Inventory | | | Cost of Goods Sold |
	Beginning	Ending	Average	
LIFO	$5,538	$6,487	$6,012.5	$96,180
LIFO Reserve	1,342	1,383	1,362.5	
FIFO	**$6,880**	**$7,870**	**$7,375.0**	$96,139

Using reported LIFO results for Ford Motor Company, we can calculate the inventory turnover and gross profit percentages (sales of $ 107,137 million) to be:

LIFO
Gross profit percentage: (107,137 − 96,180) ÷ 107,137 = 10.23%
Inventory turnover: 96,180 ÷ 6,012.5 = 16.00
FIFO
Gross profit percentage: (107,137 − 96,139) ÷ 107,137 = 10.27%
Inventory turnover: 96,139 ÷ 7,375.0 = 13.04

LIFO tends to *decrease* the gross profit percentage and to *increase* the inventory turnover relative to FIFO. Why? Because, under LIFO, cost of goods sold is usually greater and inventory values are lower.

Adjusting from LIFO to FIFO

Ford Motor Company uses LIFO and therefore reports higher cost of goods sold and lower inventory levels than it would if FIFO were used. Ford reports the LIFO *reserve* to aid analysts in understanding this difference. The LIFO reserve concept was illustrated above for Harbor Electronics. Here we use the Ford data to extend our understanding. Note that Ford's LIFO reserve increased from $1,342 million to $1,383 million during the year. This increase of $41 million in the LIFO reserve is exactly the amount by which the cost of goods sold for the year under LIFO exceeds the cost of goods sold under FIFO ($96,180 million − $96,139 million = $41 million, see above).

Why is the LIFO cost of goods sold higher? Because costs are rising and under LIFO the new higher costs flow directly to the cost of goods sold reported in the earnings statement. In contrast, under FIFO the new higher costs flow into ending inventory, while older lower costs are used to calculate cost of goods sold. Cumulatively, this process has happened year after year for Ford. We can use the LIFO reserve to answer two questions. The *change* in the LIFO reserve from one year to the next answers the question "How much did this year's LIFO cost of goods sold differ from what the cost of goods sold would have been if FIFO were used?" In contrast, the end of year *level* of the LIFO reserve is the answer to the question "During the years that Ford has used LIFO, what has the total, cumulative effect been on cost of goods sold over all those years?" To see this, do the mental experiment of having Ford sell all of its 1994 year-end inventory for $10,000 million. This complete *liquidation* would produce *higher* profits under LIFO. These higher profits in the final liquidation year are equal to the cumulative amount by which gross profits were lower under LIFO in past years. The hypothetical liquidation of Ford inventories would show:

	LIFO	FIFO	Difference
Sales	$10,000	$10,000	—
Cost of goods sold	6,487	7,870	(1,383)
Gross profit	$ 3,513	$ 2,130	1,383

Gross Profit Tests

Auditors, including those from the Internal Revenue Service (IRS), use the gross profit percentage to help satisfy themselves about the accuracy of records. For example, the IRS compiles gross profit percentages by types of retail establishment. If a company shows an unusually low percentage compared with similar companies, IRS auditors may suspect that the taxpayer has failed to record all cash sales. Similarly, managers watch changes in gross profit percentages to judge operating profitability and to monitor how well employee theft and shoplifting are being controlled.

Suppose an internal revenue agent, a manager, or an outside auditor had gathered the following data for a particular jewelry company for the past three years (in millions):

	19X3	19X2	19X1
Net sales	$350	$300	$300
Cost of goods sold	210	150	150
Gross profit	$140	$150	$150
Gross profit percentage	40%	50%	50%

These data illustrate a **gross profit test** whereby the gross profit percentages are compared to detect any phenomenon worth investigating. Obviously, the decline in the percentage might be attributable to many factors. Possible explanations include the following:

1. Competition has intensified, resulting in intensive price wars that reduced selling prices.
2. The mix of goods sold has shifted so that, for instance, the $350 million of sales in 19X3 is composed of relatively more products bearing lower gross margins (e.g., more costume jewelry bearing low margins and less diamond jewelry bearing high margins).
3. Shoplifting or embezzling has soared out of control. For example, a manager may be pocketing and not recording cash sales of $70 million. After all, sales in 19X3 would have been $210 × 2 = $420 million if the past 50% margin had been maintained.

Reports to Shareholders

The importance of gross profits to investors is demonstrated in the following example based on a quarterly report to shareholders of Superscope, Inc., a real-life manufacturer and distributor of stereophonic equipment that encountered rocky times. The following condensed income statement was presented for a three-month period (in thousands):

	Current Year	Previous Year
Net sales	$40,000	$40,200
Cost and expenses:		
Cost of sales	33,100	28,200
Selling, general, and administrative	11,200	9,900
Interest	2,000	1,200
Total costs and expenses	46,300	39,300
Income (loss) before income tax		
provision (benefit)	(6,300)	900
Income tax provision (benefit)	(3,000)	200
Net income (loss)	$ (3,300)	$ 700

Although the statement does not show the amount of gross profit, the gross profit percentages can readily be computed as ($40,000 − $33,100) ÷ $40,000 = 17% and ($40,200 − $28,200) ÷ $40,200 = 30%. To show how seriously these percentages are considered, the chairman's letter to shareholders began as follows:

I shall attempt herein to provide you with a candid analysis of the Company's present condition, the steps we have instituted to overcome current adversities, and the potential which we believe can, in due course, be realized by the Company's realistic positive determination to regain profitability.

In the second quarter the Company's gross profit margins decreased to 17% compared to 30% in the corresponding quarter of a year ago. For the first six months gross profit margins were 22%, down from 31% for the corresponding period of a year ago.

Essentially, the gross profits and consequential operating losses in the second quarter, as reflected in the condensed financial statements appearing in this report, resulted from lower than anticipated sales volume and from the following second quarter factors: liquidation of our entire citizens band inventory; increases in dealer cash discounts and sales incentive expenses; gross margin reductions resulting from sales of slow moving models at less than normal prices; and markdown of slow moving inventory on hand to a realistic net realizable market value.

SUMMARY

Inventory accounting involves allocating the cost of goods available for sale between cost of goods sold and ending inventory as of the balance sheet date. Under the *perpetual* system, this allocation occurs continually; cost of goods sold is recorded for each sale. Under the *periodic* system, the allocation occurs via an adjusting entry at year end. A physical inventory is conducted under either system. The goods on hand are counted, and a cost is calculated for each item from purchase records. The cost of an item of inventory includes not only the purchase price but also inward transportation costs.

Under the *periodic* system the physical inventory is the basis for the year-end adjusting entry to recognize cost of goods sold. Under the perpetual system the physical inventory is used to confirm the accounting records. Differences, if any, lead to adjustments to cost of goods sold and ending inventory. Adjustments reflect inventory shrinkage due to theft, spoilage, damage, and so on, or to accounting errors in the perpetual records.

Valuation of inventories involves the assignment of specific historical costs of acquisition either to units sold or to units on hand. Four major inventory valuation methods are in use: specific identification, weighted average, FIFO, and LIFO. When prices are rising and inventories are constant or growing, less income is shown by LIFO than by FIFO. LIFO liquidation refers to the relatively higher profits generated under LIFO when reductions in inventory levels cause older, lower inventory costs to be used in calculating cost of goods sold. Notice that even with declining inventories, with rising costs the *cumulative* taxable income is always less under LIFO than FIFO because the inventory valuation is less and the cumulative cost of goods sold is higher.

LIFO is popular in the United States among companies who face rising prices, for whom lower profits under LIFO mean lower taxes. The U.S. tax law contains a conformity requirement that allows LIFO for tax purposes only if it is used also for financial reporting purposes.

Conservatism leads to the lower-of-cost-or-market method, which treats cost as the maximum value of inventory. Inventory is reduced to replacement cost (with a corresponding increase in cost of goods sold) when acquisition prices fall below historical cost levels.

The nature of accrual accounting for inventories creates a self-correcting quality about errors in counting or valuing the ending inventory. This occurs because the ending inventory in one period becomes the beginning inventory of the subsequent period.

Financial analysts and managers use gross profit percentages as a measure of profitability and inventory turnover as a measure of efficient asset use. These measures are compared with prior levels to examine trends and with current levels of other industry members to assess relative performance.

SELF-CORRECTION PROBLEMS

1. Examine Figure 13-10. The company uses the periodic inventory system. Using these facts, prepare a columnar comparison of income statements for the year ended December 31, 19X2. Compare the FIFO, LIFO, and weighted-average inventory methods. Assume that other expenses are $1,000. The income tax rate is 40%.

2. "When prices are rising, FIFO results in fool's profits because more resources are needed to maintain operations than previously." Do you agree? Explain.

FIGURE 13-10 Facts for Problem One

	Purchases	Sales	Inventory
December 31, 19X1			200 @ $5 = $1,000
January 25	170 @ $6 = $1,020		
January 29		150*	
May 28	190 @ $7 = $1,330		
June 7		230*	
November 20	150 @ $8 = $1,200		
December 15		100*	
Total	510 $3,550	480*	
December 31, 19X2			230 @ ?

*Selling prices were $9, $11, and $13, respectively, providing total sales of:

		Summary of costs:	
150 @ $ 9 = $1,350		Beginning inventory	$1,000
230 @ $11 = $2,530		Purchases	$3,550
100 @ $13 = $1,300		Cost of goods available	
Total sales 480 $5,180		for sale	$4,550

---

3. Fay's Incorporated operates about 260 super drugstores in the Northeast and 321 stores in total, including a chain of discount auto supply stores and 29 Paper Cutter stores. Some results for fiscal 1994 were (in thousands):

Sales	$919,719
Cost of merchandise sold	649,078
Net earnings	5,223
Beginning merchandise inventory	137,896
Ending merchandise inventory	153,627

    a. Calculate the 1994 gross profit and gross profit percentage for Fay's Incorporated.

    b. Calculate the inventory turnover ratio.

    c. What gross profit would have been reported if inventory turnover in 1994 had been 7, the gross profit percentage calculated in question a. had been achieved, and the level of inventory was unchanged?

4. At the end of 19X1, a $1,000 error was made in the physical inventory so the inventory value was understated. The error went undetected. The subsequent inventory at the end of 19X2 was done correctly. Assess the effect of this error on income before tax, taxes, net income, and retained earnings for 19X1 and 19X2, assuming a 40% tax rate.

SOLUTIONS TO SELF-CORRECTION PROBLEMS

1. See Figure 13-11.

2. The merit of this position depends on the concept of income favored. LIFO gives a better measure of "distributable" income than FIFO. Recall the Emilio's Cola Sales example in the chapter (Figure 13-4). The gross profit under FIFO was 60 cents, and under LIFO it was 34 cents. The 60¢ − 34¢ = 26¢ difference is a fool's profit because it must be reinvested to maintain the same inventory level as previously. It arises from a profit on holding inventory as prices change rather than from buying at wholesale and selling at retail. Therefore the 26 cents cannot be distributed as a cash dividend without reducing the current level of operations.

3. a.   Gross profit = Sales − Cost of merchandise sold
                  = $919,719 − $649,078
                  = $270,641
   Gross profit percentage = Gross profit ÷ Sales
                        = $270,641 ÷ $919,719
                        = 29.4%

   b.   Inventory turnover = Cost of merchandise sold ÷ Average
                        merchandise inventory
                  = $649,078 ÷ [($137,896 + $153,627) ÷ 2]
                  = $649,078 ÷ $145,762
                  = 4.45

   c. Cost of merchandise sold = Inventory turnover x Average
                           merchandise inventory
                      = 7 × $145,762
                      = $1,020,334
   Gross profit percentage = (Sales − Cost of merchandise sold) ÷ Sales
             29.4% = (S − $1,020,334) ÷ S
         0.294 × S = S − $1,020,334
      S − (0.294 × S) = $1,020,334
      S × (1 − 0.294) = $1,020,334
                S = $1,020,334 ÷ (1 − 0.294)
                S = $1,445,232

FIGURE 13-11 Comparison of Inventory Methods for the Year Ended December 31, 19X2

	FIFO		LIFO		Weighted Average	
Sales, 480 units		$5,180		$5,180		$5,180
Deduct cost of goods sold:						
Beginning inventory, 200 @ $5	$1,000		$1,000		$1,000	
Purchases, 510 units (from Figure 13-10)*	3,550		3,550		3,550	
Available for sale, 710 units†	$4,550		$4,550		$4,550	
Ending inventory, 230 units‡						
150 @ $8	$1,200					
80 @ $7	560	1,760				
or						
200 @ $5			$1,000			
30 @ $6			180	1,180		
or						
230 @ $6.408					1,474	
Cost of goods sold, 480 units	———	2,790	———	3,370		3,076
Gross profit		$2,390		$1,810		$2,104
Other expenses		1,000		1,000		1,000
Income before income taxes		$1,390		$ 810		$1,104
Income taxes at 40%		556		324		442
Net income		$ 834		$ 486		$ 662

*Always equal across all three methods.

†These amounts will not be equal in general across the three methods because beginning inventories will generally be different. They are equal here only because beginning inventories were assumed to be equal.

‡Under FIFO, the ending inventory is composed of the last purchases plus the second-last purchases, and so forth, until the costs of 230 units are compiled. Under LIFO, the ending inventory is composed of the beginning inventory plus the earliest purchases of the current year until the costs of 230 units are compiled. Under weighted average, the ending inventory and cost of goods sold are accumulations based on a unit cost. The latter is the cost of goods available for sale divided by the number of units available for sale: $4,550 ÷ 710 = $6.408.

$$\text{Gross profit} = \text{Sales} - \text{Cost of merchandise sold}$$
$$= \$1,44S,232 - \$1,020,334$$
$$= \$424,898$$

The increase in inventory turnover from 4.45 to 7.0 would raise gross profit from $270,641 to $424,898.

4. First calculate the effect on Cost of Goods Sold.

	19X1	19X2
Beginning Inventory	ok	too low
Purchases	ok	ok
Goods available for sale	ok	too low
Ending Inventory	too low	ok
Cost of goods sold	too high	too low

Note that 19X1 Ending Inventory becomes 19X2 Beginning Inventory, reversing the effects on Cost of Goods Sold.

The 19X1 Cost of Goods Sold being too high causes 19X1 income before tax to be too low by $1,000. Therefore taxes will be too low by .40 × $1,000 = $400 and net income will be too low by $600, causing retained income to be too low by $600 also.

In 19X2 the effects reverse and by year's end retained income is correctly stated.

QUESTIONS

1. "There are two major steps in accounting for inventories at year end." What are they?
2. Distinguish between *F.O.B. destination* and *F.O.B. shipping point.*
3. "Freight out should be classified as a direct offset to sales, not as an expense." Do you agree? Explain.
4. What are the two phases of accounting for a sales transaction?
5. Distinguish between the *perpetual* and *periodic* inventory systems.
6. "An advantage of the perpetual inventor system is that a physical count of inventory is unnecessary. The periodic method requires a physical count to compute cost of goods sold." Do you agree? Explain.
7. Name the four inventory cost flow assumptions or valuation methods that are generally accepted in the United States. Give a brief phrase describing each.
8. What is *consistency,* and why is it an important accounting principle?
9. "An inventory profit is a fictitious profit." Do you agree? Explain.
10. LIFO produces absurd inventory valuations. Why?
11. "Purchases of inventory at the end of a fiscal period can have a direct effect on income under LIFO." Do you agree? Explain.
12. There is a single dominant reason who micro and more U.S. companies have adopted LIFO" What is the reason?
13. "Conservatism always results in lower reported profits." Do you agree? Explain.
14. Accountants have traditionally favored taking some losses but no gains before an asset is exchanged." What is this tradition or convention called?
15. What does *market* mean in inventory accounting?
16. "The lower-of-cost-or-market method is inherently inconsistent." Do you agree? Explain.
17. Express the cost of goods sold section of the income statement as an equation.
18. "Gross profit percentages help in the preparation of interim financial statements." Explain.
19. "Inventory errors are counterbalancing." Explain.
20. If a company uses a FIFO cost flow assumption, will it report the same cost of goods sold using the periodic inventory method that it reports using the perpetual method? Why or why not?
21. Assume that the physical level of inventory is constant at the beginning and end of year and that the cost of inventor items is rising. Which will produce a higher ending inventory value, LIFO or FIFO?
22. Will LIFO or FIFO produce higher cost of goods sold during a period of *falling* paces? Explain.

23. Which of the following items would a company be likely to account for using a perpetual inventory system and the specific identification inventory method?
    a. Corporate jet aircraft
    b. Large sailboats
    c. Pencils
    d. Diamond rings
    e. Timex watches
    f. Automobiles
    g. Books
    h. Compact discs

ADDENDUM 13: INVENTORY IN A MANUFACTURING ENVIRONMENT

In the chapter, inventory accounting is covered from the viewpoint of a wholesaler or retailer, companies that acquire their inventory by purchase from another company. When a company *manufactures* products, the cost of inventory is a combination of the acquisition cost of raw material, the wages paid to workers who combine the raw materials into finished products, and an allocation of the costs of space, energy, and equipment used by the workers as they transform the various elements into a finished product.

Consider how costs are accumulated in a manufacturing environment for Packit, a company that makes backpacks. The raw materials are heavy fabric, glue, and thread. The transformation occurs when workers use cutters to make the panels that other workers sew and glue together. The costs of manufacture include depreciation on the manufacturing building, depreciation on the sewing machines and cutters, and utilities to support the effort in the form of heat, power, and light. The finished goods are backpacks.

The accounting process is easiest to understand when calculating the cost of a complete year of production. In the example below, 100,000 backpacks are produced during Packit's first year at a total cost of $800,000, providing a cost per backpack of $8.00 each ($800,000 ÷ 100,000 units). At year end, if all have been sold, the financial statements would include $800,000 in cost of goods sold.

Calculation of cost of manufacturing for a year's production of 100,000 backpacks:

Beginning inventory	—
Fabric purchased and used	$200,000
Wages paid to workers	300,000
Thread and glue used	50,000
Depreciation on building and equipment	220,000
Utilities	30,000
Total Costs to Manufacture	$800,000
Cost per backpack ($800,000 ÷ 100,000)	$ 8.00

In the above example, all of the materials acquired during the year are transformed into finished products before year end and sold. In fact, if we take a snapshot of the typical backpack manufacturer at year end we would observe bolts of fabric, spools of thread and gallons of glue waiting to be put into production. We call these items held for use in the manufacturing of a product **raw material inventory.** In addition we would also observe fabric already cut but not assembled and some partially completed backpacks.

We refer to the material, labor and other costs accumulated for partially completed items as **work in process inventory.** When manufacture is complete and the goods are ready to deliver to customers, the inventory is called **finished goods inventory.** The accounting system for managing these costs is illustrated in Figure 13-12 for the second year of production of our backpack manufacturer. During this second year 120,000 backpacks are completed and 110,000 are sold. Some remain in the assembly process at year end, and unused fabric thread and glue are held in preparation for future production.

The schematic in Figure 13-12 captures the production process. You might think of each of the accounts as corresponding to a physical reality. The raw material is stored in a locked room, ready for use. The work-in-process is located in the production room and as it is finished it is physically transferred to a storage site. When goods are sold they are removed from that storage site and are given to the customer in exchange for cash or an account receivable. Raw materials, work-in-process, and finished goods are all forms of inventory and appear on the balance sheet as current assets. They are simply in different stages of completion. The act of sale converts the asset into an expense to be reported on the income statement. At year end, Packit will show total inventory on its year 2 balance sheet of $126,000, as follows:

Raw Materials Inventory	$ 25,000
Work in Process Inventory	22,000
Finished Goods Inventory	79,000
Total Inventory	**$126,000**

The summary journal entries to record these events for year 2 would be:

Purchase of raw material:		
Raw material inventory	335,000	
Accounts payable		335,000
Production activity:		
Workin process niventory	310,000	
Raw materialsinventory		310,000
Work in process inventory	660,000	
Wages payable		380,000
Accumulated depreciation		240,000
Utilities payable		40,000
Completion of production:		
Finished goods inventory	869,000	
Work in process inventory		869,000

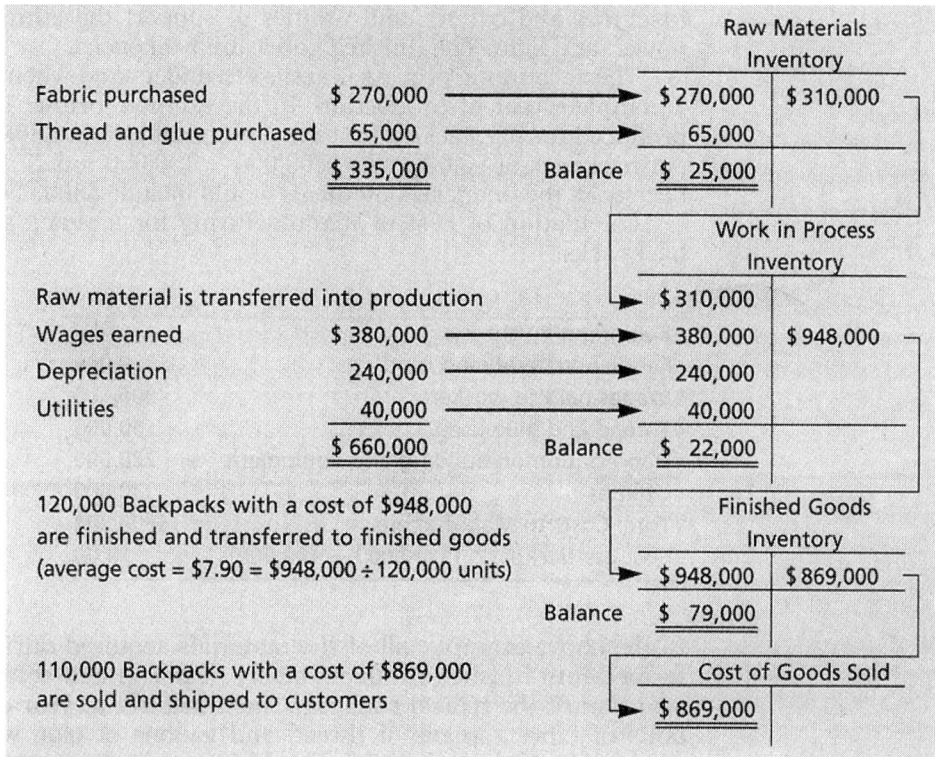

FIGURE 13-12
Packit Company Accounting for Manufacturing Costs

CHAPTER 14

Internal Management Control Systems

Internal control requirements were extended to managers in the public sector by the Federal Managers' Financial Integrity Act. Briefly, the act requires each executive agency to establish a system of internal accounting and administrative control that meets prescribed standards. They must also report annually, based on an evaluation conducted in accordance with established guidelines, to the president, Congress, and the public on the extent to which the agency's systems comply with the standards.

The documentation of internal control should systematically refer to (1) management's cost-benefit choices regarding the system and (2) management's evaluation of how well the internal control system is working. Documentation includes memos, minutes of meetings discussing internal control concepts with all affected individuals, written statements of compliance, flowcharts, procedures manuals, and the like. Moreover, there should be a written program for ongoing review and evaluation of the system. Finally, there should be letters from independent auditors stating that they found no material weaknesses in internal control during their audit, or that necessary improvements have been made.

THE AUDIT COMMITTEE

The first objective of internal accounting control is authorization; transactions should be executed in accordance with management's intentions. Moreover, management bears primary responsibility for the entity's financial statements. This authority and responsibility extends upward to the board of directors. Most boards have an **audit committee,** which oversees the internal accounting controls, financial statements, and financial affairs of the corporation. Indeed, such committees are required of companies whose shares are listed on the New York Stock Exchange.

Audit committees typically have three or more "outside" board members. Not everyday employees of the company, they are considered to be more independent than the "inside" directors—employees who serve as part of the corporation's management.[1] The committee provides contact and communication among the board, the external auditors, the internal auditors, the financial executives, and the operating executives. These relationships are depicted in Figure 14-1.

Figure 14-1 shows only one of many possible arrangements. Above all, note how the audit committee serves as the main pipeline to the board of directors, especially for individuals responsible for the accounting function. In Figure 14-1, the internal audit manager is directly responsible (solid line) through the controller on up to the board. The dashed lines indicate that the audit committee should communicate with and gather information directly from the internal auditors as well as the external auditors.

These relationships are evolving. For example, the internal auditing department sometimes is directly responsible to the executive vice-president. But increasingly the internal audit department is directly responsible to the audit committee itself and is totally independent of the financial officers.

The audit committee meets at least twice annually. The first meeting is typically to review the annual external audit plan; the second, to review the audited financial statements before their publication. Additional meetings may be held (1) to consider the retention or replacement of the independent external auditors; (2) to review the company's accounting system, particularly the internal controls; and (3) to review any special matters raised by internal audits. At least once a year, the committee should discuss with the independent auditors their evaluation of corporate management (without the presence of the latter). Similarly, the committee should obtain management's evaluation of the independent auditors.

Many companies include an audit committee report in their annual report. Merck & Co., the pharmaceutical firm, included the report shown in Figure 14-2.

CHECKLIST OF INTERNAL CONTROL

All good systems of internal control have certain features in common. These features can be summarized in a **checklist of internal control,** which may be used to appraise any specific procedures for cash, purchases, sales, payroll, and the like. This checklist is sometimes called **principles** or **rules** or **concepts** or **characteristics** or **features** or **elements.** The following checklist summarizes the guidance that is found in much of the systems and auditing literature.[2]

1. Reliable Personnel with Clear Responsibilities

The most important element of successful control is personnel. Incompetent or dishonest individuals can undermine a system, no matter how well it meets the other items on the checklist. Procedures to hire, train, motivate, and supervise employees are essential. Individuals must be given authority, responsibility, and duties commensurate with their abilities, interests, experience, and reliability. Yet many em-

---

[1]Mobil Corporation, the oil company, has a typical board composition. Of sixteen directors, six are also members of management and ten are "outside" directors. Five of the outside directors form the audit committee.
[2]For an expanded discussion, see A. Arens and J. Loebbecke, *Auditing,* 5th ed. (Upper Saddle River, NJ: Prentice Hall, 1991), Chap. 9.

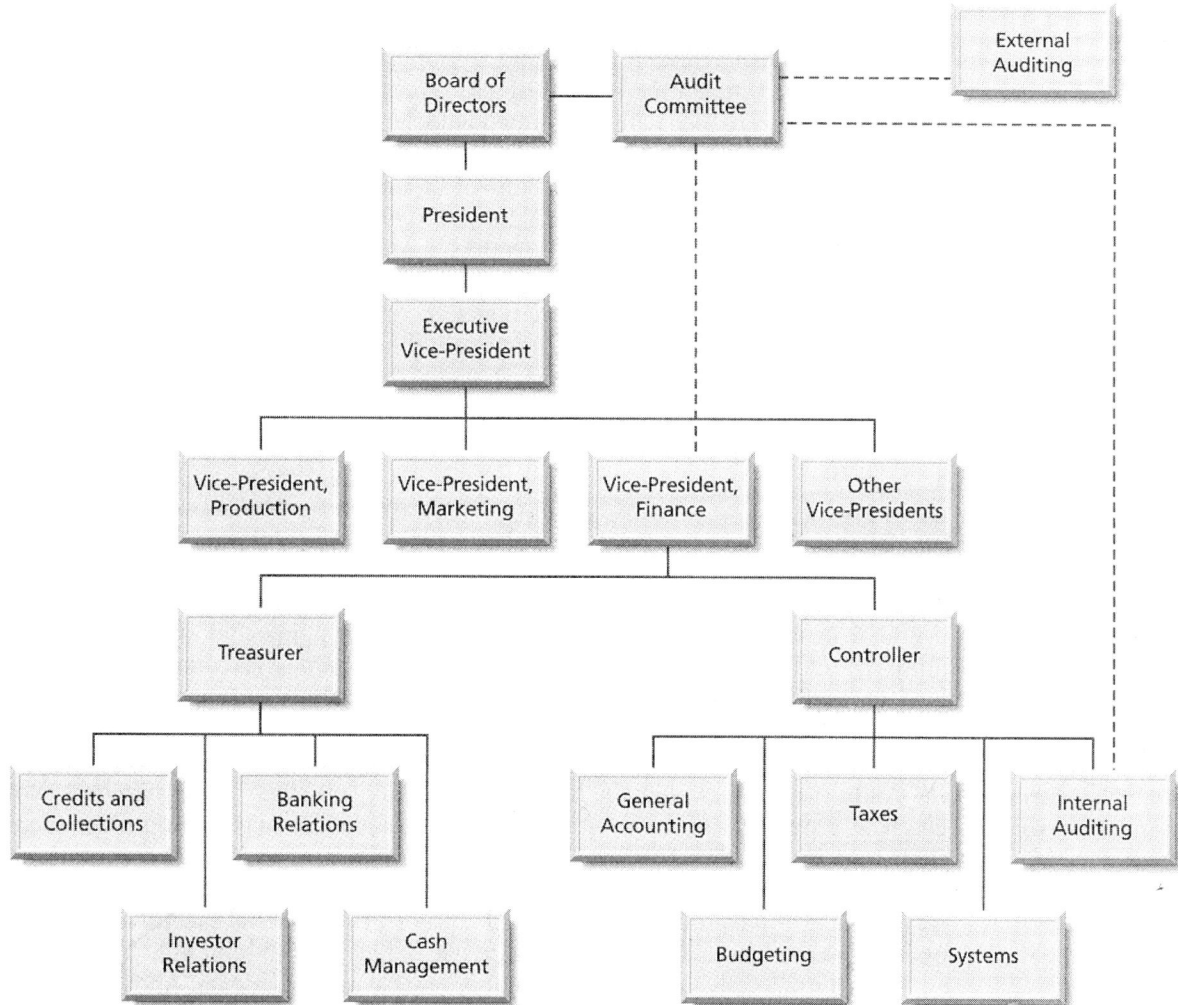

FIGURE 14-1
Organization Chart Showing Position of Audit Committee

ployers use low-cost talent that may prove exceedingly expensive in the long run, not only because of fraud but because of poor productivity.

Assessing responsibility means tracking actions as far down in the organization as is feasible, so that results can be related to individuals. It means having sales clerks sign sales slips, inspectors initial packing slips, and workers sign time cards and requisitions. Grocery stores often assign each cashier a separate money tray; therefore shortages can easily be traced to the person responsible. The psychological impact of fixing responsibility tends to promote care and efficiency. Employees often perform better when they must explain deviations from required procedures.

The possibility of employee theft is distasteful to most managers, but it must be taken seriously. The National Mass Retailing Institute estimates that retailers lose about 2% of sales to theft and mistakes. Shoplifting accounts for part of this, but employee theft causes much larger losses than shoplifting. The institute estimates

---

FIGURE 14-2   Merck & Co. Audit Committee's Report

The Audit Committee of the Board of Directors is comprised of five outside directors. The members of the Committee are Charles E. Exley, Jr., Chairman; Carolyn K. Davis, Ph.D., Vice Chair; Sir Derek Birkin; William N. Kelley, M.D.; and Dennis Weatherstone. The committee held three meetings during 1993.

The Audit Committee meets with the independent public accountants, management, and internal auditors to assure that all are carrying out their respective responsibilities. The Audit Committee reviews the performance and fees of the independent public accountants prior to recommending their appointment and meets with them, without management present, to discuss the scope and results of their audit work, including the adequacy of internal controls and the quality of financial reporting. Both the independent public accountants and the internal auditors have full access to the Audit Committee.

---

that an average retail store loses $10 per shift per clerk. Convenience stores and fast-food restaurants are especially vulnerable to employee theft. Such businesses need to be especially concerned with internal control systems.

2. Separation of Duties

The separation of duties not only helps ensure accurate compilation of data but also limits the chances for fraud that would require the collusion of two or more persons. This extremely important and often neglected element can be subdivided into four parts:

1. *Separation of operational responsibility from recordkeeping responsibility.* The entire accounting function should be divorced from operating departments. For example, product inspectors, not machine operators, should count units produced; inventory records clerks or computers, not material handlers, should keep perpetual inventory records. Why? Because those keeping the records should have nothing to gain by falsifying the records. A material handler should not be able to steal materials and cover up the theft by recording the issue of the materials to production.

2. *Separation of the custody of assets from accounting.* This practice reduces temptation and fraud. For example, the bookkeeper should not handle cash, and the cashier should not have access to ledger accounts such as the individual records of customers. A person with both accounting and cash-handling duties could pocket cash that is received and make a false entry in the accounting records.

    In a computer system, a person with custody of assets should not have access to programming or any input of records. In a classic example, a programmer in a bank rounded transactions to the next lower cent rather than the nearest cent and had the computer put the fraction of a cent into his account. For example, a customer amount of $10.057 became $10.05, and the programmer's account received $.007. With millions of transactions, the programmer's account became very large.

3. *Separation of the authorization of transactions from the custody of related assets.* To the extent feasible, persons who authorize transactions should not have control over the related asset. For instance, the same individual should not authorize the payment of a supplier's invoice and also sign the check in payment of the bill. Nor should an individual who handles cash receipts have the authority to indicate which accounts receivable should be written off as uncollectible.

The latter separation of powers prevents such embezzlement as the following: A bookkeeper opens the mail, removes a $1,000 check from a customer, and somehow cashes it. To hide the theft, the bookkeeper prepares the following journal entry:

Allowance for bad debts	1,000	
Accounts receivable		1,000
To write off an amount owed by a customer.		

4. *Separation of duties within the accounting function.* An employee should not be able to record a transaction from its origin to its ultimate posting in a ledger. Independent performance of various phases will help ensure control over errors. Even a small company should have some separation of duties. For example, if there is only one bookkeeper who writes checks and keeps the accounting records, the owner can at least sign the checks and reconcile the monthly bank statement.

A main goal of the separation of duties is to make sure that one person, acting alone, cannot defraud the company. It is more difficult, although not impossible, for two or more employees to collude in a fraud. This is why movie theaters have a cashier selling tickets and an usher taking them. The cashier takes in cash, the usher keeps the ticket stubs, and in an audit step performed by a third person, the cash is compared with the number of stubs. But suppose they do collude. The ticket seller pockets the cash and issues a fake ticket. The usher accepts the fake ticket and allows entry. Separation of duties alone will not prevent collusive theft.

3. Proper Authorization

The Foreign Corrupt Practices Act stresses proper authorization. Authorization can be either *general* or *specific.* General authorization is usually found in writing. It often sets definite limits on what price to pay (whether to fly economy or first class), on what price to receive (whether to offer a sales discount), on what credit limits to grant to customers, and so forth. There may also be complete prohibitions (against paying extra fees or bribes or overtime premiums).

Specific authorization usually means that a superior manager must permit (typically in writing) any particular deviations from the limits set by general authorization. For example, the plant manager, rather than the lathe supervisor, may have to approve any overtime. Another example is the need for approval from the board of directors regarding expenditures for capital assets in excess of a specific limit.

4. Adequate Documents

Documents and records vary considerably, from source documents such as sales invoices and purchase orders to journals and ledgers. Immediate, complete, and tamper-proof recording is the aim. It is encouraged by optical scanning of bar-coded data, by having all source documents prenumbered and accounted for, by using devices such as cash registers, and by designing forms for ease of recording.

Immediate recording is especially important for handling cash sales. Devices used to ensure immediate recording include "rewards" to customers if they are not offered a receipt at the time of sale and forcing clerks to make change by pricing items at $1.99, $2.99, and $3.99 rather than at $2, $3, and $4. (Historically, such pricing was originally adopted to force clerks to make change as well as for its psychological impact on potential customers.) The need to access the change drawer forces the clerk to ring up the sale so the drawer will open.

5. Proper Procedures

Most organizations have **procedures manuals,** which specify the flow of documents and provide information and instructions to facilitate adequate recordkeeping.

Routine and automatic checks are major ways of attaining proper procedures. In a phrase, this means doing things "by the numbers." Repetitive procedures may be prescribed for order taking, order filling, collating, and inspecting. The use of general routines permits specialization of effort, division of duties, and automatic checks on previous steps in the routine.

6. Physical Safeguards

Obviously, losses of cash, inventories, and records are minimized by safes, locks, guards, and limited access. For example, many companies (such as Boeing and Hewlett-Packard) require all *visitors* to sign a register and wear a name tag. Often *employees* will also wear name tags that are coded to show the facilities to which they have access. Doors to research areas or computer rooms often may be opened only with special keys or by use of a specific code.

Sometimes small businesses are especially vulnerable to theft of physical assets. For example, retail stores use alarm systems, guard dogs, security guards, special lighting, and many other safeguards to protect their property.

7. Bonding, Vacations, and Rotation of Duties

Key people may be subject to excessive temptation. Thus, top executives, branch managers, and individuals who handle cash or inventories should have understudies, be required to take vacations, and be bonded.

Rotating employees and requiring them to take vacations ensures that at least two employees know how to do each job so that an absence due to illness or a sudden resignation does not create major problems. Further, the practice of having another employee periodically perform their duties discourages employees from engaging in fraudulent activities that might be discovered when someone else has access to their records.

Rotation of duties is illustrated by the common practice of having employees such as receivables and payables clerks periodically exchange duties. Or a receivables clerk may handle accounts from A to C for three months and then be rotated to accounts M to P for three months, and so forth.

Incidentally, the act of **bonding**—that is, buying insurance against embezzlement—is not a substitute for vacations, rotation of duties, and similar precautions. Insurance companies will pay only when a loss is proved; establishing proof is often difficult and costly in itself.

8. Independent Check

All phases of the system should be subjected to periodic review by outsiders (for example, by independent public accountants) and by internal auditors. Auditors have a degree of objectivity that allows them to spot weaknesses overlooked by managers immersed in day-to-day operations. It is too costly for external auditors to examine all transactions, so they inspect a sample of the transactions. By first evaluating the system of internal control and testing the extent to which it is being followed, the auditor decides on the likelihood of undetected errors. If internal controls are weak, there is a greater probability of significant errors in the accounting records. Then the auditor must examine many transactions to provide reasonable assurance that existing errors will be found. If internal controls are strong, the auditor can use a smaller sample to develop confidence in the accuracy of the accounting records.

Internal auditors are company employees who help design control systems and assess the degree of compliance with the existing systems. Their main goal is to enhance efficiency of operations by promoting adherence to both administrative and accounting controls and to continuously improve the system.

The idea of an independent check extends beyond the work performed by professional auditors. For example, bank statements should be reconciled with book balances. The bank provides an independent record of cash. Furthermore, the monthly bank reconciliations should be conducted by some clerk other than the cash, receivables, or payables clerks. Other examples of independent checks include monthly statements sent to credit customers and physical counts of inventory to check against perpetual records.

9. Cost-Benefit Analysis

Highly complex systems tend to strangle people in red tape, impeding rather than promoting efficiency. Besides, the "cost of keeping the costs" sometimes gets out of hand. Investments in more costly systems must be compared with the expected benefits. Unfortunately, it is easier to relate new lathes or production methods to cost savings in manufacturing than to link a new computer to cost savings in inventory control. Yet efforts must be made. For example, the accounting firm of KPMG Peat Marwick completed a study of office automation for a client. After examining the jobs of 2,600 white-collar workers, KPMG Peat Marwick quantified a cost-benefit relationship: "A single investment of $10 million would result in a productivity savings equal to $8.4 million every year."

Although many companies implement more complex procedures to improve internal control, a few have taken a reverse course. They have decided that the increased costs of additional scrutiny are not worth the expected savings from catching mistakes or crooks. For example, an aerospace manufacturer routinely pays the invoice amounts without checking supporting documentation except on a random-sampling basis. An aluminum company sends out a blank check with its purchase orders, and then the supplier fills out the check and deposits it.

No framework for internal control is perfect in the sense that it can prevent some shrewd individual from "beating the system" either by outright embezzlement or by producing inaccurate records. The task is not total prevention of fraud, nor is it implementation of operating perfection; rather, the task is the designing of a *cost-effective* tool that will help achieve efficient operations and reduce temptation.

EFFECTS OF COMPUTERS ON INTERNAL CONTROL

The nine items in the preceding checklist apply to both computer and manual accounting systems. However, computers change the focus of internal control in two ways:

1. The computer can accomplish traditional internal control functions more efficiently.
2. But, additional controls must be put in place to ensure the accuracy and reliability of computer-processed data.

Computers Change the Control Environment

The computer has allowed relatively inexpensive processing of huge volumes of accounting data. However, internal control over computerized operations is essential. Consider an error that a human might make once a month. Such an error would be repeated thousands of times a day in a computer program for processing vast quantities of data. Further, errors that would be obvious by scanning journal entries could go undetected because data are "invisible," stored on tape or disks. Input and output data transmitted over phone lines may be vulnerable to unauthorized access. Thus the installation of internal control systems must accompany computerization.

Computers are amazingly accurate. The focus of internal control is not *computer* errors. Invariably, the computer has done exactly what it was told (or programmed) to do. Errors usually result because someone entered the wrong data, programmed the computer incorrectly, ran the wrong program, or asked for the wrong output.

Types of Control for Computer Systems

The greatest source of errors in computerized systems is the data input. Both the original recording (for example, a sales slip) and the transcription of the data to computer-readable form (for example, key-punching cards or direct entry from a remote terminal) are frequent sources of error. Other possible sources of errors are managed by processing, output, and general controls.

Input controls can help guard against the entry of false or erroneous data, especially those due to multiple steps in handling the data when human processing is involved. Such controls include using standardized forms and verifying data input. Accountants also program the computer to verify that all required data are included on each input document, identify key numbers outside a range of reasonableness, and conduct other such checks. Use of optical scanning equipment can also limit data-recording errors.

Processing controls start with the design and programming of the system, including complete documentation. They also include control of operations, including normal separation and rotation of duties. For example, programmers should not be allowed to operate the computers. A computer consultant commented that he had immense stealing opportunities when he ran computer operations for a large bank: "I alone designed the dividend-payment operation, wrote the program for it, and ran the job on the machine. The operation was so big that it had a mistake tolerance of nearly $100,000. I could have paid at least half that much to myself, in small checks, and the money wouldn't even have been missed."

Output controls check output against input, possibly by random manual processing of data. Output controls should also ensure that only authorized persons receive the reports. Computers often generate literally tons of printed output. A paper shredder can be an important control tool to safeguard privileged information.

General controls focus on the organization and operation of the data-processing activity. Good internal control requires well-defined procedures for developing, testing, and approving new systems and programs or changing old ones. Access to equipment and files should be restricted. But most important, as in any system, manual or computerized, are personnel controls. Hiring reliable personnel and keeping temptation from their doorsteps through common-sense controls are important goals of any internal control system.

EXAMPLES OF INTERNAL CONTROL

This section discusses specific internal control considerations for cash and inventories. Additional details are provided in Addenda 14A and 14B.

Internal Control of Cash

Cash is almost always the most enticing asset for potential thieves and embezzlers. Therefore, internal controls are far more elaborate for cash than for, say, the paper clips and desks on the premises. The following points are especially noteworthy:

1. As previously mentioned, the function of receiving cash should be separated from the function of disbursing cash. Moreover, individuals who handle cash or checks should not have access to the accounting records.
2. All receipts should be deposited intact daily. That is, none of the currency and checks received each day should be used directly for any other purposes. For example, sales in retail establishments are recorded in a cash register. A supervisor compares the locked cash register tape with the actual cash in the register drawer. Then the cash receipts are deposited, and the tape is forwarded to the accounting department as a basis for accounting entries. If cash from the till is sometimes used to pay suppliers, there is a serious internal control weakness.
3. All major disbursements should be made by serially numbered checks. Gaps should be investigated. The *Wall Street Journal* cited an example of good controls used poorly: "A bookkeeping assistant [was] under strict orders to note every missing number. . . . But no one checked to see how many were missing or why."
4. Bank accounts should be reconciled monthly. (This recommendation also applies to personal banking accounts.) A **bank reconciliation** is an analysis that explains any difference between the cash balance shown by the depositor and that shown by the bank. It is surprising how many businesses (some of substantial size) do not reconcile their bank accounts regularly.

Control of cash requires procedures for handling both checks and currency. To control checks, many organizations use check protectors that perforate or otherwise establish an unalterable amount on the face of each check. Dual signatures are frequently required on large checks.

Currency is probably the most alluring form of cash. Businesses that handle much currency, such as gambling establishments, restaurants, and bars, are particularly subject to theft and false reporting. For example, many owners of small retail outlets do not record all of their cash receipts, a procedure known as *skimming*. Why? To save income taxes.

A recent news story reported: "Federal undercover agents in New York City opened an attack on the underground economy, which spawns billions of dollars yearly in untaxed income through off-the-books transactions." According to the affidavits, the establishments searched by the agents grossed more than $5 million while reporting on their tax returns only $3.6 million.

Tax authorities often use known gross profit margins for an industry to assess the reasonableness of the profits based on reported revenues and costs of goods sold for a particular company. Measures such as industry average sales per square foot of store space allow assessment of the adequacy of reported revenue.

Comparing reported results with averages is not foolproof. An exclusive clothing store in San Francisco paid a percentage of sales for rent. Reported sales for a recent year were $11.2 million; an independent audit later disclosed actual sales of $20.5 million. The lessor always compared sales per square foot of floor space with those of similar stores. No clue to any impropriety arose. In fact, the lessor termed the reported sales per square foot "extraordinary" and the actual results as "unheard of."

Internal Control of Inventories

In many organizations, inventories are more easily accessible than cash. Therefore they become a favorite target for thieves.

Retail merchants must contend with inventory shrinkage, a polite term for shoplifting by customers and embezzling by employees. *Inventory shrinkage* is the difference between (1) the value of inventory that would occur if there were no pilferage, misclassifications, breakage, or clerical errors and (2) the value of inventory when it is physically counted. Consider the following footnote from a recent annual report of Associated Dry Goods, one of the largest operators of department and discount stores in the country: "Physical inventories are taken twice each year. Department store inventory shrinkage at retail, as a percent of retail sales, was 2.4% this year compared with 2.1% last year. Discount store inventory shrinkage as a percent of retail sales was 0.4% and 0.3%, respectively." Some department stores have suffered shrinkage losses of 4% to 5% of their sales volume. Compare this with the typical net profit margin of 5% to 6%.

A management consulting firm has demonstrated how widespread shoplifting has become. The firm concentrated on a midtown New York City department store. Five hundred shoppers, picked at random, were followed from the moment they entered the store to the time they departed. Forty-two shoppers, or one out of every twelve, took something. They stole $300 worth of merchandise, an average of $7.15 each. Similar experiments were conducted in Boston (1 of 20 shoplifted), Philadelphia (1 of 10), and again in New York (1 of 12).

Experts on controlling inventory shrinkage generally agree that the best deterrent is an alert employee at the point of sale. Retail stores use sensitized tags on merchandise; if not detached or neutralized by a salesclerk, these miniature transmitters trip an alarm as the culprit begins to leave the store. Many libraries use a similar system to safeguard their books. Macy's in New York has continuous surveillance with over fifty television cameras.

Retailers must also scrutinize their own personnel, because they account for at least 30% to 40% of inventory shortages. Some stores have actors pose as shoplifters, who are then subjected to fake arrests. If potential thieves see the arrests, they may be deterred. Such ploys have helped reduce thefts by employees at major retail chains.

The problem of stealing is not confined to profit-seeking entities. According to the student newspaper at Northwestern University, $14,000 worth of silverware, glasses, and china was stolen from the university dining halls annually. That amounts to $4.71 for every regular customer. Signs posted at the end of each school term requesting the return of "borrowed" goods have had little success. The food service director commented: "Two years ago, we put up really nice signs and set out boxes for returns. Kids saw the boxes and stole them for packing."

The imposing magnitude of retail inventory shrinkage demonstrates how management objectives may differ among industries. For example, consider the grocery business, where net income is about 1% of sales. You can readily see why a prime responsibility of the store manager is to control inventory shrinkage rather than boost gross sales volume. The trade-off is clear: If the operating profit is 2% of sales, to offset a $1,000 increase in shrinkage requires a $50,000 boost in gross sales.

Shrinkage in Perpetual and Periodic Inventory Systems

Measuring inventory shrinkage is straightforward for companies that use a perpetual inventory system. Shrinkage is simply the difference between the cost of inventory identified by a physical count and the clerical inventory balance. Consider the following example:

Sales	$100,000
Cost of goods sold (perpetual inventory system)	$ 80,000
Beginning inventory	$ 15,000
Purchases	$ 85,000
Ending inventory, per clerical records	$ 20,000
Ending inventory, per physical count	$ 18,000

Shrinkage is $20,000 – $18,000 = $2,000. The journal entries under a perpetual inventory system would be:

Inventory shrinkage	2,000	
Inventory		2,000
To adjust ending inventory to its balance per physical count.		
Cost of goods sold	2,000	
Inventory shrinkage		2,000
To close inventory shrinkage to cost of goods sold.		

The total cost of goods sold would be $80,000 + $2,000 = $82,000.

By definition, a periodic inventory system has no clerical balance of the inventory account. Inventory shrinkage is automatically included in cost of goods sold. Why? Because beginning inventory plus purchases less ending inventory measures all inventory that has flowed out, whether it went to customers, shoplifters, or embezzlers, or was simply lost or broken. Our example would show:

Beginning inventory	$ 15,000
Plus: Purchases	85,000
Goods available for sale	$100,000
Less: Ending inventory, per physical count	18,000
Cost of goods sold	**$ 82,000**

To assess shrinkage, we need some way to *estimate* what the ending inventory *should be.* The difference between this *estimate* and the physical count is inventory shrinkage. Addendum 14B describes how these estimates are made. No journal entries are necessary.

SUMMARY

It is tempting to delegate internal control decisions to accountants. However, managers at all levels have a major responsibility for the success of internal controls. In fact, in the United States there is a federal law that explicitly places the ultimate responsibility for the adequacy of internal controls of publicly held companies on top management. To help monitor internal control, boards of directors appoint audit committees, which oversee accounting controls, the financial statements, and general financial affairs of the company.

The following general characteristics form a checklist that can be used as a starting point for judging the effectiveness of internal control:

1. Reliable personnel with clear responsibilities
2. Separation of duties
3. Proper authorization
4. Adequate documents
5. Proper procedures
6. Physical safeguards
7. Bonding, vacations, and rotation of duties
8. Independent check
9. Cost-benefit analysis

Managers and accountants should recognize that the role of an internal control system is as much a positive one (enhancing efficiency) as a negative one (reducing errors and fraud).

The checklist of internal controls applies to both computerized and manual systems. However, computerized systems change the emphasis of internal controls. Although computers process data exactly as instructed, controls over programming and data input are especially important.

Control systems for cash and inventories are usually well developed because these assets are often the targets of theft or embezzlement.

SELF-CORRECTION PROBLEMS

1. Identify the internal control weaknesses in each of the following situations:

    a. Mike Reynolds performs all purchasing functions for Bayside Marine. He orders merchandise, oversees its delivery, and approves invoices for payment.

    b. The Winthrop Mudhens, a minor league baseball team, is struggling financially. To save costs, and because all seating is general admission, the team has eliminated ticket takers. The ticket seller simply lets fans go through the gate when they pay the admission fee.

    c. Cash and checks received by mail from customers who purchased items on open account are opened by an accounts receivable clerk, who deposits the cash and checks in the bank and prepares the appropriate accounting journal entry.

    d. Ruth Ann Kilstromis a trusted and dedicated employee. In fact, she is so dedicated that she has not taken a vacation in five years. Her boss appreciates her dedication because no one could do her job if she were gone.

    e. Employees in Wing Point Grocery do a variety of jobs. When business is slack, they stock shelves and perform other necessary tasks. When the checkout stands are busy, everyone is expected to help with checkouts by operating whatever cash register is available. Each employee works at an average of four different checkout stands in an average shift, and every checkout stand is manned by an average of six different persons each day.

2. A news story reported:

    A federal grand jury indicted seven former Cenco, Inc., officials, accusing them of an inventory overstatement scheme that led the concern to report about $25 million in false profits. The indictment charged that the overstatement was accomplished by increasing the number of products shown on inventory tabulating cards and making up new cards. The inflation of inventory lessened the reported cost of sales and thereby resulted in a greater reported profit figure.

    Given this description, were any assets stolen? What is the major feature in the chapter checklist of internal control that is aimed at preventing such dishonesty? Indicate how such dishonest acts could be accomplished and how the dishonest officials might have expected to benefit from those acts.

SOLUTIONS TO SELF-CORRECTION PROBLEMS

1. a. A single person should not perform all these functions. Reynolds could order fictitious merchandise, record its delivery, and authorize payment to his own (or a confederate's) account.

   b. There is no control against the ticket seller's letting friends in free or pocketing cash without issuing a ticket, by simply letting the fans go through the gate.

   c. The accounts receivable clerk performs too many functions. The clerk could keep cash (or forge an endorsement of a check) and make a false entry in the accounts, such as writing off the account as a bad debt.

   d. There are at least two problems with Kilstrom's dedication. First, because no one else could do her job, the company would be in dire straits if something happened to her or if she resigned suddenly. Second, she has too great an opportunity to perpetrate a fraud without anyone discovering it. If someone replaced her periodically, he or she might be in a position to discover any fraud.

   e. Responsibility is not well defined. If a shortage of cash occurs at any check-out stand, it will be impossible to identify the employee responsible.

2. Assets in the form of inventories were probably not stolen. Overstatement of ending inventory also causes overstatement of net income in the current period. Major motives were job security (by means of a display of higher net income) and greed (by means of management bonuses and raises in future salaries). Indeed, the manager who began the scheme was hired on a four-year contract with Cenco, giving him a modest annual base salary of $40,000 plus a bonus that added 1% to his salary for every 1% increase in the Cenco Medical Health (CMH) Group's net income. Net profits soared during the life of the manager's contract. The manager reaped total compensation far in excess of his base salary.

   Two subordinate managers had no incentive bonus plans, but they played along with the inventory scheme to please their boss. A variety of ways were used to overstate inventories. For example, three boxes of gauze pads would become twenty-three. The auditors were fooled with the help of fake invoices and lies. The scheme was uncovered when a subordinate informed the company treasurer. Three executives were given prison terms ranging from one to three years.

   The major feature that should prevent such dishonesty is *separation of duties.* Collusion makes dishonest acts harder to accomplish. Nevertheless, as the Cenco case illustrates, separation of duties is not enough to detect fictitious inventories when there is collusion.

   Reliable personnel with clear responsibilities is an additional feature on the checklist that is illustrated by this case. Personnel must be not only competent and honest but also adequately instructed and supervised. Immediate supervisors should know enough about underlying operations so that they can sense any significant unauthorized conduct. *Independent check* is another feature that helps. That is why outside auditors conduct their own counts and observe management's counts.

QUESTIONS

1. "The words *internal control* are commonly misunderstood to refer only to those facets of the accounting system that are supposed to help prevent embezzling." Comment.

2. Distinguish between *internal accounting control* and *internal administrative control.*

3. Into what four categories of transactions can the most repetitive, voluminous transactions in most organizations be divided?

4. "Business operations would be a hopeless tangle without the paperwork that is often regarded with disdain." Explain.

5. "The primary responsibility for internal controls rests with the outside auditors." Do you agree? Explain.

6. Give three examples of documentation of an internal accounting control system.

7. What is the primary responsibility of the audit committee?

8. "Internal control systems have both negative and positive objectives." Do you agree? Explain.

9. Prepare a checklist of important factors to consider in judging an internal control system.

10. "The most important element of successful control is personnel." Explain.

11. What is the essential idea of separation of duties?

12. Authorization can be general or specific. Give an example of each.

13. Internal control of a computerized system consists of applications controls and general controls. What are the three types of applications controls?

14. Briefly describe how a bottler of soda water might compile data regarding control of breakage of bottles at the plant, where normal breakage can be expected.

15. The branch manager of a national retail grocery chain has stated: "My managers are judged more heavily on the basis of their merchandise-shrinkage control than on their overall sales volume." Why? Explain.

16. "It is easy to be ethical. Just identify the ethical choice and then do it." Do you agree? Explain.

17. "Our managers know they are expected to meet budgeted profit targets. We do not take excuses. Good managers find a way to make budget." Discuss the possible consequences of this policy.

18. Pressure for profits extends beyond managers in profit-seeking companies. A news story reported: "The profit motive, even in nonprofit hospitals, is steadily eroding the traditional concern to provide care to the medically indigent." Why does the profit motive affect even nonprofit organizations?

ADDENDUM 14A: INTERNAL CONTROL OF CASH

This appendix describes how organizations control cash. Most cash is kept in bank accounts. Therefore the focus is on understanding bank statements and transactions.

The Bank Statement

Figure 14-3 displays a bank statement for account number 96848602, one of thousands of the bank's deposits. Together, these accounts form the subsidiary ledger that supports the bank's general ledger account *Deposits,* a liability.

The supporting documents for the detailed checks on the statement are canceled checks; for additional deposits, deposit slips. Notice that the minimum balance, $–33.39, is negative. This indicates an *overdraft,* which is a negative account balance arising from the bank's paying a check even though the depositor had insufficient funds available at the instant the check was presented.

Overdrafts are permitted as an occasional courtesy by the bank. However, the depositor is rarely given more than a day or two to eliminate the overdraft by making a deposit. Moreover, the bank may levy a fee (e.g. $10 or $30) for each overdraft.

Banks often provide (for a fee plus interest) "automatic" loan privileges, short-term loans (from ten to thirty days or more) to cover overdrafts. That is, when a depositor has insufficient funds, the bank increases the depositor's account with an "automatic" loan. The depositor avoids any embarrassment or risks of a bank's delaying payment of a check to await an additional deposit.

Bank Reconciliations

Figure 14-4 demonstrates how an independent check of cash balances works for any bank depositor (individual or business entity). First, note how parallel records are kept. The balance on December 31 is an asset (Cash) on the depositor's books and a liability (Deposits) on the bank's books. The terms *debit* and *credit* as used by banks may seem strange. Banks *credit* the depositor's account for additional deposits because the bank has a liability to the depositor. Banks *debit* the account for checks cleared and canceled (paid) by the bank. When the $2,000 check drawn by the depositor on January 5 is paid by the bank on January 8, the bank's journal entry would be:

Jan. 8 Deposits	$2,000	
Cash		$2,000
To decrease the depositor's account.		

A credit balance on the bank's books means that the bank owes money to the depositor.

A monthly *bank reconciliation* is conducted by the depositor to make sure that all cash receipts and disbursements are accounted for. Bank reconciliations take many forms, but the objective is unchanged: to explain all differences in the cash balances

FIGURE 14-3   An Actual Bank Statement

SEAFIRST BANK

University Branch
4701 University Way NE
Seattle WA 98145

		Account Number
Richard B. Sandstrom	777	96848602
2420 Highline Rd.		Statement Period
Redmond WA 98110		11-21-95 to 12-20-95

SUMMARY OF YOUR ACCOUNTS

CHECKING

First Choice Minimum Balance	96848602
Beginning Balance	368.56
Deposits	5,074.00
Withdrawals	3,232.92
Service Charges/Fees	16.00
Ending Balance	2,193.64
Minimum Balance on 12-9-95	**− 33.39**

CHECKING ACTIVITY

Deposits

Posted	Amount	Description
11-21	700.00	Deposit
11-25	1,810.00	Payroll Deposit
12-10	1,810.00	Payroll Deposit
12-16	754.00	Deposit

Withdrawals

Ck No	Paid	Amount
1606	12-02	1134.00
1607	11-28	561.00
1609*	12-09	12.00
1617*	12-05	7.00
1629*	11-26	10.00
1630	11-25	16.95
1639*	12-02	96.00
1641*	12-09	1025.00
1642	12-05	50.00
1643	12-15	236.25
1644	12-17	84.72

* = Gap in check sequence
Total number of checks = 10

FIGURE 14-4   Comparative Cash Balances, January 19X2

Depositor's Records

Cash in Bank
(receivable from bank)

1/1/X2 Bal.	11,000	1/5	2,000
		1/15	3,000
1/10	4,000		
		1/19	5,000
1/24	6,000		
1/31	7,000	1/29	10,000
	28,000		20,000
1/31/X2 Bal.	8,000		

Bank's Records

Deposits (payable)

1/8	2,000	1/1/X2 Bal.	11,000
1/20	3,000		
		1/11	4,000
1/28	5,000	1/26	6,000
1/31	20*		
	10,020		21,000
		1/31/X2 Bal.	10,980

*Service charge for printing checks.

Date	Depositor's General Journal	Debit	Credit
1/5	Accounts payable	2,000	
	Cash		2,000
	Check No. 1.		
1/10	Cash	4,000	
	Accounts receivable		4 000
	Deposit slip No. 1.		
1/15	Income taxes payable	3,000	
	Cash		3,000
	Check No. 2.		
1/19	Accounts payable	5,000	
	Cash		5,000
	Check No. 3.		
1/24	Cash	6,000	
	Accounts receivable		6,000
	Deposit No. 2.		
1/29	Accounts payable	10,000	
	Cash		10,000
	Check No. 4.		
1/31	Cash	7,000	
	Accounts receivable		7,000
	Deposit No. 3.		

shown on the bank statement and in the depositor's general ledger at a given date. Using the data in Figure 14-4:

Bank Reconciliation January 31, 19X2

Balance per books (also called *balance per check register, register balance*)	$ 8,000
Deduct: Bank service charges for January not recorded on the books (also include any other charges by the bank not yet deducted)*	20
Adjusted (corrected) balance per books	**$7,980**
Balance per bank (also called *bank statement balance, statement balance*)	$10,980
Add: Deposits not recorded by bank (also called *unrecorded deposits, deposits in transit*), deposit of 1/31	7,000
Total	$17,980
Deduct: Outstanding checks, check of 1/29	10,000
Adjusted (corrected) balance per bank	**$ 7,980**

---

*Note that new entries on the depositories books are required for all previously unrecorded additions and deductions made to achieve the adjusted balance per books.

As the bank reconciliation indicates, an adjustment is necessary on the books of the depositor:

Jan. 31 Bank service charge expense	20	
Cash		20
To record bank charges for printing checks.		

This popular format has two major sections. The first section begins with the balance per books (that is, the balance in the Cash T-account). Adjustments are made for items not entered on the books but already entered by the *bank,* such as deduction of the $20 service charge. No additions are shown in the illustrated section, but an illustrative addition would be the bank's collection of a customer receivable on behalf of the company. The second section begins with the balance per bank. Adjustments are made for items not entered by the *bank* but already entered in the books. After adjustments, each section should end with identical adjusted cash balances. This is the amount that should appear as cash in bank on the depositor's balance sheet.

Paperless Bank Transactions

Each passing year brings us closer to so-called paperless banking. For example, many employees never see their payroll checks. Instead the employer deposits the "checks" in the employees' bank accounts. This is an example of an "automatic" deposit. If the employee forgets to add the amount to his or her check register, the bank's books would show a higher balance than the depositor's books. Similarly, some 75% of transactions in "branch banking" offices occur at automatic teller machines (ATM). Many depositors may forget to record these, but will find them when they reconcile their bank statement with their books (check register).

Petty Cash

Every organization desires to minimize red tape—for example, avoiding unjustifiably complicated procedures for minor disbursements. Consequently, petty cash funds are usually created and accounted for on an **imprest basis.** An imprest petty cash fund is initiated with a fixed amount of currency and coins. As the currency is used, petty cash receipts or vouchers are prepared to show the purposes of the disbursements. When the balance of currency gets low, the fund is restored to its original level by drawing and cashing a single check for the exact amount of the needed cash replenishment. The following are typical journal entries:

Petty cash	100	
Cash in bank		100
To set up a fund for miscellaneous minor office disbursements. (A check is drawn, cashed, and proceeds placed with some responsible person.)		
Postage	10	
Freight in	40	
Miscellaneous office expenses	35	
Cash in bank		85
To replenish the petty cash fund and record expenses paid therefrom.		

Examples of petty cash outlays include special post-office charges for certifying or insuring mail, collections by delivery personnel, and dinner money given to an employee when working overtime.

Note that after inception, the petty cash account itself is never directly charged or credited unless the $100 initial amount of the fund is increased or decreased. Further, the cash on hand plus the receipts (or vouchers) should always equal the $100 amount of the petty cash fund.

ADDENDUM 14B: INVENTORY CONTROL VIA RETAIL METHOD, COST RATIOS, AND CUTOFFS

Retail Method of Inventory Control

A popular inventory costing method, known as the **retail inventory method,** or simply **retail method,** is often used as a control device. Its role in obtaining an inventory valuation (at cost) for financial statement purposes will be discussed in the next section; for now, concentrate on its internal control characteristics. Consider how a food store might use the retail method to control grocery inventories. Merchandise is accounted for at *retail prices* as follows:

		Retail Prices
	Inventory, January 5 (by surprise count by branch auditors)	$ 15,000
	Purchases (shipments to store from branch warehouse)	101,000
	Additional retail price changes:	
	Markups (from initial retail prices)	2,000
	Markdowns (from initial retail prices)	(5,000)
(1)	Total merchandise to account for	$113,000
	Sales (per cash-register records)	$100,000
	Allowable shrinkage (shoplifting, breakage, etc., usually a predetermined percentage of sales)	1,000
(2)	Total deductions	$101,000
(1) – (2)	Inventory, February 11 (should be)	$ 12,000
	Inventory, February 11 (by physical count)	11,100
	Excess shrinkage	$ 900

The total retail value of merchandise to account for is $113,000. What happens to it? Most is sold, some disappears as shrinkage, and some remains in ending inventory. Cash-register tabulations indicate sales of $100,000. If there were absolutely no shrinkage, the ending inventory at retail should be $113,000 – $100,000 = $13,000. But suppose "normal" shrinkage is 1% of sales, or $1,000. Therefore the expected inventory is $13,000 – $1,000 = $12,000. The actual physical count provides a retail valuation of $11,100. Thus the total shrinkage is $1,900, including $900 of excess shrinkage ($12,000 – $11,100 = $900). If the inventory shrinkage is not within predetermined limits, the manager usually bears prime responsibility.

Computerized checkout systems help to control inventory shrinkage. Such systems record each individual item that is sold, allowing a store to keep an item-by-item perpetual inventory. Pinpointing the items that are disappearing allows additional control measures to be applied to these items.

Role of Cost Ratios and Gross Profit Percentages

While retail inventory values provide a satisfactory basis for internal control, inventories in financial statements are reported at cost. Therefore the retail values of inventories must be converted to costs. This is accomplished using the ratio of cost to retail value. Consider the data in our prior illustration with a "cost" column added.

		Retail Prices	Cost
	Inventory, January 5 (by surprise count by branch auditors)	$ 15,000	$12,300
	Purchases (shipments to store from branch warehouse)	101,000	78,100
	Additional retail price changes:		
	Markups (from initial retail prices)	2,000	
	Markdowns (from initial retail prices)	(5,000)	
(1)	Total merchandise to account for	$113,000	$90,400
	Ratio of cost to retail value		80%
	Sales (per cash-register records)	$100,000	$80,000
	Allowable shrinkage (shoplifting, breakage, etc., usually a predetermined percentage of sales)	1,000	800
(2)	Total deductions	$101,000	$80,800
(1) – (2)	Inventory, February 11 (should be)	$ 12,000	$ 9,600
	Inventory, February 11 (by physical count)	11,100	8,880
	Excess shrinkage	$ 900	$ 720

The line denoted as (1) provides the basis for a ratio of cost to retail value:

$90,400 ÷ $113,000 = .80

This critical ratio[3] is then used to develop the key subsequent amounts at cost:

	Retail Prices	Average Ratio of Cost To Retail Value		Cost
Allowable shrinkage	$ 1,000	×	.80 =	$ 800
Inventory per physical count	11,100	×	.80 =	8,880
Excess shrinkage	900	×	.80 =	720

These amounts can be used in an income statement for a company with a periodic inventory system:

---

[3]Both markdowns and markups are included in this illustrative computation. Many retailers prefer to exclude markdowns because a lower cost ratio is developed:

$90,400 ÷ ($113,000 + $5,000 Markdowns) =.7661

This ratio would provide a "more conservative" ending inventory. Advocates of this approach say that it yields a better approximation of the lower-of-cost-or-market method.

Sales		$100,000
Cost of sales:		
Beginning inventory per physical count	$12,300	
Purchases	78,100	
Available for sale	$90,400	
Ending inventory per physical count	8,880	
Cost of sales (including $800 allowable		
shrinkage and $720 excess shrinkage)		81,520
Gross margin (after inventory shrinkage)		**$ 18,480**

This approach is used over and over again as periods unfold. The ending inventory of $8,880 becomes the beginning inventory of the next reporting period. Purchases are then added at cost, a new ratio of cost to retail value is developed, and shrinkage and ending inventory values are approximated:

1. Compute the goods available for sale at retail value and cost.
2. Compute the ratio of cost to retail value.
3. Count the ending inventory and value it at retail value.
4. Convert the retail value of the ending inventory to cost by using the ratio of cost to retail value.

The *cost* of shrinkage, which can be divided into normal and excess components, is approximated by using the ratio of cost to retail value.

Note that the ratio of cost to retail value is the complement of the gross profit ratio. In this illustration, the gross profit percentage is 100% − 80% = 20%. Thus the gross profit percentage or its related ratio of cost to retail value is a key element of internal control.

Cutoff Errors, Consignments, and Inventory Valuation

The accrual basis of accounting should include the physical counting and careful valuation of inventory at least once yearly. Auditors routinely search for **cutoff errors,** which are failures to record transactions in the correct time period. For example, assume a periodic inventory system. Suppose a physical inventory is conducted on December 31. Inventory purchases of $100,000 arrive in the receiving room during the afternoon of December 31. The acquisition is included in Purchases and Accounts Payable but excluded from the ending inventory valuation. Such an error would understate ending inventory, thereby overstating cost of goods sold and understating gross profit. On the other hand, if the acquisition were not recorded until January 2, the error would understate both the ending inventory and Accounts Payable as of December 31. However, cost of goods sold and gross profit would be correct because Purchases and the ending inventory would be understated by the same amount.

The general approach to recording purchases and sales is keyed to the legal transfer of ownership. Some major points follow:

1. Ownership typically changes hands when the goods are delivered by the seller to the purchaser. These terms are usually F.O.B. destination. If the terms are F.O.B.

shipping point, ownership passes to the purchaser when the goods are delivered to the transportation company.

2. Sometimes goods are shipped on **consignment.** These are goods shipped for future sale, title remaining with the shipper (consignor), for which the receiver (consignee), upon his or her acceptance, is accountable. Even though such goods are physically elsewhere, they are part of the consignor's inventory until sold. For example, a manufacturer of bicycles might ship 20 units on consignment to a new retailer. Under such terms, the bicycles are included in the manufacturer's inventory and excluded from the retailer's inventory.

Auditors are especially careful about cutoff tests because the pressure for profits sometimes causes managers to postpone the recording of bona fide purchases of goods and services. Similarly, the same managers may deliberately include sales *orders* near year end (rather than bona fide completed sales) in revenues. For example, consider the case of Datapoint, a maker of small computers and telecommunications equipment. A news story reported: "Datapoint's hard-pressed sales force was still logging orders that might not hold up after shipment." In the wake of an accounting scandal, Datapoint's president declared a three-week "amnesty period" during which scheduled shipments could be taken off the books, no questions asked.

A similar news story referred to difficulties at McCormick & Co., a firm known for its spices: "The investigation also found that improprieties included the company's accounting for sales. In a longstanding practice, the company recorded as sales, goods that had been selected and prepared for shipment rather than waiting until after they had been shipped as is the customary accounting practice."

The Financial Management Environment

CHAPTER 15

Introduction to Financial Management

Do you intend to make a career in marketing, purchasing, production, or human resources management? Possibly you want to be an economist, an attorney, a tax expert, a public relations specialist, or your goal is your own communications firm. No matter which field you choose, you will be involved with finance in one way or another. Let's look at a few of these careers to see how each may incorporate finance. Decisions by marketing managers influence growth in sales; as a result, there may be a need for increased funds to support further investment in plant and equipment. Purchasing managers must know whether sufficient funds exist to take advantage of volume discounts. Lower material costs increase profits, and increased profits may result in higher value of the firm. Public relations specialists must know about the financial strengths and weaknesses of the business so they can carry on informed discussions with inquiring reporters and investors. Attorneys are involved in corporate fund raising or in litigation in which the value of a company may be at stake. As an owner of a small business, an entrepreneur has complete financial responsibility and must closely manage money and credit.

An understanding of finance can do more than enhance your career. It can also sharpen your day-to-day grasp of current events and give you a better handle on your personal finances. How much of today's morning business broadcast or financial page of the newspaper did you understand? Chances are you found the glut of facts too much to absorb in one sitting. If you did make the effort to comprehend the material about "bulls and bears," the Dow Jones Industrial Average, interest rates, money supply, and so on, you possibly came away wondering how the information will affect you. If this describes your reaction, you are not unusual. Most people have difficulty applying the meaning of financial data to their own situations. For instance, they do not know:

- How actions of the Federal Reserve affect the level of interest rates.
- How interest rates affect investments.

- How to calculate effective interest rates charged on their credit cards.
- How to evaluate the risk of an investment.
- How bonds or stocks are valued, or how to buy them.
- How to read annual reports issued by companies.

And so people often make decisions about financial matters without really understanding what financial news means and how finance operates.

Let's begin the study of finance by discussing the origins of the finance discipline. The meaning of the word *finance* is derived from the Latin word *finis*. During Roman times, *finis* meant the completion of a contract between parties with either a transfer of money or barter (exchange) or a credit agreement. The word *finance* has much the same meaning today. However, we must conceptualize the discipline of finance in broader terms. **Finance** encompasses the analysis of, the issuance of, the distribution of, and the purchase of financial contracts written against **real assets.** Implicit in these activities is the determination of *value;* finance involves a process of deciding what something is worth.

The issuers, or suppliers, of financial contracts include individuals, business corporations, and government agencies located worldwide. The issuers must use the funds efficiently to provide satisfactory returns to investors who buy the contracts in financial markets. The efficient use of funds requires that the issuers administrate and manage investors' funds efficiently; they must practice sound financial decision making.

This brief introduction to finance suggests that it is a multifaceted discipline, international in scope, and bound together by contracts. It includes the areas of managerial finance, investments, and financial markets. These areas are closely related for a very simple reason: *the most widely accepted financial objective of a company is maximization of its market value.* Management's actions can influence the market value, but they are unable to determine the value completely. The simultaneous interplay of supply and demand for financial securities (ownership claims) in financial markets determines market value. Through the mechanism of these financial markets, other companies also participate as suppliers of securities, and a great number of investors participate as demanders for these securities. The study of finance provides an explanation of how securities are valued and how investors behave by taking into account the relationships among these investors' decisions. The interactions of the demands of all investors determine market values.

Finance in its broadest terms is an integrated body of knowledge built around the guiding principles of wealth maximization, time value of money, expected return versus risk, leverage, and diversification. You will see how they help to integrate the areas of managerial finance, investments, and financial markets.

When you have completed this chapter, you should understand:

- Some of the differences and similarities among managerial finance, investments, and financial markets.
- The dominant guiding principles of finance.
- Common elements of finance that cross all the subareas of the discipline.
- How finance is integrated with and depends on other areas of business.
- Ethical issues that are important to finance.

TRADITIONAL FINANCE AREAS

Finance and many other business disciplines were originally part of the field of economics. By the turn of the century, as a result of the growth of industry engendered by the Industrial Revolution, a greater need for study of detailed business problems and processes arose. About this time business schools began, and managerial finance, or corporate finance, as it was called more generally, was one of the first specialties to be taught separately from economics. The principal emphasis in economics first was on institutions and institutional arrangements. The economics of the individual firm had not yet been developed as a focal point of economic inquiry. Within this general context, the purpose of the newly defined area of managerial finance was to describe and document the rapidly evolving, complex nature of financial market institutions, instruments, and practices. Rather than correspond to managerial finance as we know it today, these studies precede the modern-day finance subareas of financial markets and investments. Thus, managerial finance began as a descriptive, legalistic, and institutional subject with little focus on financial decision making within the firm.

The study of finance changed little until the 1940s, when critics questioned the lack of interest in day-to-day problems of financial management such as those pertaining to cash, accounts receivable, and inventory. However, it was not until the late 1950s and early 1960s that finance began to evolve into the dynamic field of study called *financial economics.* Academicians in economics and mathematics, namely, Harry Markowitz, Merton Miller, Franco Modigliani, and William Sharpe, provided the impetus for this change. Each of these founders of modern finance has received the Nobel Prize in economics in recognition for their contributions. Their insights and research contributions are the basis for today's valuation concepts.

The areas of managerial finance, investments, and financial markets are used frequently to classify financial topics. Managerial finance deals with financial decisions in the business organization. It is usually the area that receives the most emphasis in the finance class required of all business students. The area of investments primarily relates to the valuation of financial securities and their grouping to satisfy an investor's objectives. Financial markets represent the channels for transferring funds from savings into investment. Taken together, a study of managerial finance, investments, and financial markets provides a strong understanding of the financial system.

Managerial Finance

Managerial finance has evolved from its early beginning as a descriptive, institutional subject to the dynamic study of decision making on financial issues pertaining to the firm. Specifically, **managerial finance** addresses the following issues:

- What investments should the firm make?
- What type of financing should be used to pay for the investments?
- How should daily financial activities be managed to satisfy cash requirements?

We can classify the first two issues, which pertain to investment and financing alternatives, as **strategic decisions.** These decisions select from among investment and financing alternatives that offer long-term opportunities for management to increase the value of the firm. An example is General Motors Corporation's decision in early 1993 to close several assembly plants in an effort to return to profitability. Another example is Ford Motor Company's decision of whether to build a new assembly plant or buy an existing plant that GM abandons. The third issue, concerning daily financial activities, such as management of cash, accounts receivable, inventories, and short-term liabilities, applies to **tactical decisions.** These decisions concern managing resources, including money, to ensure the firm meets customer demand.

The financial manager must worry about the interrelationships between strategic and tactical decisions and the effect these decisions may have on the value of the firm. For example, if Ford buys a plant from GM, can Ford generate enough cash from operations to pay back any debt borrowed to finance the acquisition?

There is little difference in most types of decisions domestic and international financial managers face. However, two significant financial problems confront firms competing in foreign markets. Managers cannot ignore two constant risks: currency risks and political risks. An unexpected currency devaluation or expropriation of the company's foreign facilities by an unfriendly government can wipe out profit margins on sales to foreign clients.

A major difference exists between financial management practices in developed countries and in developing countries. In the major developed countries, financial markets are very sophisticated and market participants usually engage in independent corporate financial decision making. However, even within the leading world economies, significant differences exist. For example, investment and financing decisions by German and Japanese firms often involve more communications between bankers and firms' managers than do similar decisions in Britain, Canada, or the United States. In less developed economies, the governments and financial institutions play a significant role in corporate financial decision making.

Investments

The financial area of **investments** includes investors' activities and decision rules about the selection and management of assets, such as stocks, bonds, gold, and real estate. When a group of assets is held by an investor, the collection is called a **portfolio.** The portfolio can be arranged to lessen total risk for a targeted expected return.

The *expected return versus risk concept* is central. An underlying assumption of this concept is the existence of **efficient financial markets;** that is, markets in which competition is as fierce and extreme as possible. Investors act quickly and efficiently to incorporate any new information in the determination of each asset's price. Because all investors respond in a similar manner, no investor can consistently earn **excess profits**—returns more than necessary to compensate for risk. In finance, we call such markets *informationally* efficient markets. Asset prices set in informationally efficient financial markets reflect the market's assessment of managerial performance. The broadest measure of a firm's achievements over time is the extent to which the firm develops its future earnings potential while controlling the risk.

Sometimes the amount and quality of information in financial markets can be a problem. Often there is a scarcity of information about young firms or foreign firms. Also, accounting philosophies vary among countries, and this can result in difficulty interpreting information about companies. Regulatory monitoring of financial markets also varies drastically from one country to another. The protection afforded investors in the United States does not exist in every financial market in the world.

Investment decisions involve asset selection and portfolio formation with respect to longer-term risk and return relationships. Another important aspect of investments is the art of *trading assets.* Trading is a complex activity separate from investing. **Trading** involves the implementation of investment decisions and buying and selling assets in an attempt to profit from weekly, daily, hourly, or shorter, price swings. The New York Stock Exchange (NYSE) is the most renowned securities marketplace in the world for trading shares of over 1800 companies from around the world.

Financial Markets

Financial markets consist of *money markets* and *capital markets.* If financial contracts are for one year or less, they have a short-term duration and trade in **money markets.** The most important money markets are in New York and London. Financial contracts with durations in excess of one year are long term and trade in **capital markets,** with the largest markets located in Tokyo and New York. Financial markets are the channels whereby savings are translated into investment—into accumulation of assets. There are three broad ways in which investment takes place:

- Households (individuals and families) buy assets.
- Firms buy assets and finance them by selling stocks and bonds to households.
- Firms buy assets and finance them by loans from *financial intermediaries,* who in turn take in households' savings.

Financial intermediaries are firms whose principal business is taking deposits, making loans, and buying securities. The best known type of financial intermediary is a commercial bank, such as Citibank. The financial markets for stocks and bonds coordinate the actions of households, firms, and financial intermediaries. **Stock markets,** like the New York Stock Exchange, are markets in which shares (commonly called *stocks*) representing ownership of firms, such as Home Shopping Network, Inc., trade. The **bond market** is the market in which debts issued by firms like CSX Corporation and local, state, or national governments trade.

GUIDING PRINCIPLES OF FINANCE

Managerial finance, investments, and financial markets are integrated under the broad heading of finance through shared principles. These important principles are: *maximization of wealth, time value of money, expected return versus risk trade-off, leverage,* and *diversification.* We will review each principle and how it affects financial decision making.

Maximization of Wealth

The most important guiding principle is *wealth maximization,* which is the creation of as much wealth as possible with the resources available. A wealth-maximizing goal looks beyond the short run and explicitly seeks to incorporate the entire future stream of cash flows that will be generated by the decision. Needless to say, the principle assumes that wealth is created lawfully and ethically.

Many people would temper a goal of wealth maximization to include a goal of social responsibility, which is generally defined as a consciousness for the good of all people in society and a respect for the environment on the part of the corporation. Social responsibility can extend as far as the role of corporations in funding social programs. While many individuals may see this as a noble goal to embrace, we must remember that we are dealing with the role of the business entity. Nobel laureate economist Milton Friedman argues that when investors bring a corporation into existence through buying stock, they do so on the condition that corporate managers will follow their wishes—usually, to make a profit.[1] A moral obligation is thus generated for managers, namely, to serve as agents for profit-seeking investors. It follows that using the investors' money otherwise is equivalent to stealing. Theodore Levitt states that if business were to become a protector of the welfare society, the result could be disastrous.[2] Levitt argues that because corporate officials are not democratically elected business should stick to business. It has no holy mission and it ought not become a new "church." Yet there are some business managers, such as those of Ben and Jerry's Ice Cream, who disagree with this position and take active roles to promote through financial incentives the opening of franchises in minority urban neighborhoods. We will come to see that there is room for much firm-specific decision making—on all levels—within the financial discipline.

The wealth-maximization goal has broad applicability to the areas of managerial finance, investments, and financial markets. For the financial manager, maximization of wealth means operating the firm with the goal of increasing shareholders' wealth. Financial management decisions, such as buying new equipment or extending credit to customers, are all subject to decision rules whose aim it is to **maximize shareholders' wealth,** that is, to maximize the long-run stock price.

From an investment perspective, it is clear that investors choose financial contracts expecting to increase wealth. The decision to invest in different types of assets or combinations of assets into a portfolio is a simple example. Deciding whether to invest in low-risk, low-expected-return assets versus high-risk, high-expected-return assets is another case.

Financial markets provide individuals and firms with the means to make wealth increasing decisions by efficiently transacting financial contracts. Efficient financial markets provide buyers and sellers with more opportunities to select securities that satisfy their needs.

Time Value of Money

The principle of *time value of money* is central to financial decision making. **Time value of money** means that funds have an opportunity cost because alternative uses for the funds exist. Should opportunity number one or opportunity number two be taken?

---

[1] Milton Friedman, "The Social Responsibility of Business Is to Increase Its Profits," *New York Times Magazine,* September 13, 1970, p. 33.
[2] Theodore Levitt, "The Dangers of Social Responsibility," *Harvard Business Review* (September–October 1958), p. 49.

Managers and investors evaluate potential wealth-increasing decisions using an interest rate called the *opportunity cost of money* to value *all* future cash flows.

A technique called **future value analysis** finds the value of funds to be received in the future. If the opportunity rate is 8%, $1 received two periods from now is worth $1 × (1 + 0.08) x (1 + 0.08) = $1.166. Because interest paid on money can itself earn interest, there is a multiplicative growth dimension to the future amount. The growth dimension is called **compounding.** As the interest rate increases, a dollar invested today appreciates faster to some future value. For example, if the Native Americans who sold Manhattan for $24 had invested this money at 6% compounded annually, it would have been worth about $74 billion at the end of 1994.

We can also use the opportunity rate to convert *future* cash flows into a *present* value to determine if the wealth-maximization goal is satisfied. More present value dollars are sought rather than fewer. The present value process is called **discounted cash flow analysis.** For example, $1 received one year from now is worth $0.926 today if the opportunity cost of money is 8%: $1 ÷ (1 + 0.08) = $0.926. If the opportunity cost of money is 10%, the value of that same $1 is about $0.909 today. Check this number. The present worth declines as the interest rate, or opportunity cost of money, increases.

Expected Return versus Risk Trade-off

The principle that ties finance together is the *expected return versus risk trade-off concept.* The **expected return-risk principle** states that if investments *A* and *B* have the same risk, the investment with the greater expected return, B. should be chosen. Or consider a firm that issues additional debt, which causes risk to increase. Investors' expected return must increase to compensate for the higher risk. Figure 15-1 shows these relationships.

The cornerstone of managerial finance and investments is the application of discounted cash flow analysis and expected return and risk concepts to the **valuation** (that is, finding the present value) of financial claims. The opportunity rate used to discount cash flows is the same rate we could have expected to earn from alternative investments of equal risk.

A necessary assumption of the expected return-risk principle is that market *equilibrium prices* exist in financial markets. A market **equilibrium price** is the price at which the quantity demanded of financial instruments equals the quantity supplied. At the equilibrium price, opposing forces exactly balance each other. Trust officers at Wells Fargo & Company, investment officers employed by Metropolitan Life Insurance Company, money managers hired by CalPERS to invest pension funds, specialized dealers on the floor of the stock exchange, individual investors, and thousands of other organizations constantly trade financial securities, thereby maintaining equality between demand and supply.

Leverage

Some costs are constant, or **fixed,** over a range of business activity. Other costs are **variable** and change in direct response to changes in business activity. The linkage,

Investment *B* is better than investment *A* because for equal risk, *B* offers higher return. When risk increases, the risk-return relationship moves to point *C*. The basic formulation states that a positive relationship exists between risk and expected return. Any additional expected return accompanies additional risk.

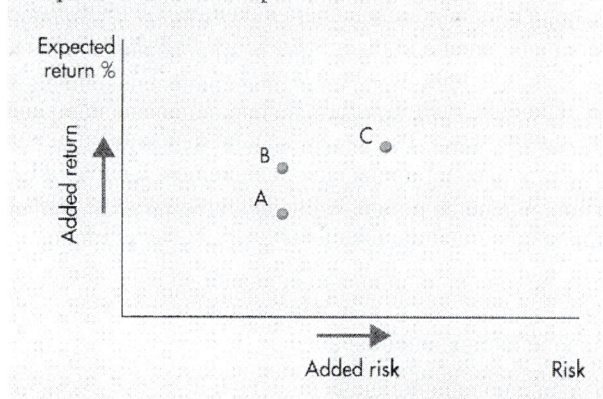

FIGURE 15-1
Expected Return-Risk Trade-Off

or *leverage,* between the fixed and variable costs offers significant financial gains or losses. There are two types of leverage: *operating* and *financial.*

The particular choice of fixed and variable *operating costs* existing within a firm is a result of the production technology chosen by management to compete in the industry. **Operating costs** are the necessary outlays incurred in producing the product or service. A business like Intel Corporation uses highly advanced technology to produce state-of-the-art computer chips. The result is relatively high fixed operating costs, which result in relatively high **operating leverage.** Operating leverage is favorable if sales (the activity) expand faster than additional fixed costs. Operating leverage is unfavorable if sales decline faster than any reduction in fixed costs.

Financial leverage is the use of debt financing to support income-earning investments. The commitment of the firm or investor to pay interest on borrowed funds (that is, the leverage portion) is not (usually) related to the amount of product or services produced by the assets financed. As business activity improves without any changes in fixed costs, financial leverage causes profits to increase. A change in the opposite direction causes losses. Profits improve if debt-financed investments earn more than the cost of debt. Conversely, losses increase if the cost of debt exceeds the return earned by the assets. The financial leverage relationship holds true for all participants in the financial system, whether they be managers, individuals, or financial institutions.

Diversification

The principle of diversification is based on the need for the firm or investor to reduce risk. **Diversification** means to introduce variety into the portfolio. The maxim stating "Don't put all your eggs in one basket" describes the concept of diversification.

Too much or too little of one type of investment can be detrimental at any time. For example, Artisoft, Inc. produces and sells local area networks (LANS). Artisoft's LANS may be very profitable when that product is in demand. However, if consumers stop buying LANS, Artisoft may become unprofitable eventually cease to exist. A similar result can happen if competitors take market share away from an undiversified firm selling a product or service that is similar to many other firms. Casualties in the airline industry in recent years provide an example. American West, Eastern, TWA, and Continental airlines filed bankruptcy. Likewise, if an investor's retirement income is dependent on a single financial security, say IBM stock, that person is more likely to find that not enough money exists in the retirement account upon reaching retirement age than if he or she invested in several securities. A prudent person invests in several different assets to diversify risk. The finance terminology is that the person seeks an efficient portfolio.

ELEMENTS COMMON TO THE THREE AREAS OF FINANCE

Common elements are woven throughout the areas of managerial finance, investments, and financial markets helping to integrate the discipline. These elements include: *investment decision rules, financial analysis, organizational form, taxes,* and *politics.* We examine each of these elements in the following sections.

Investment Decision Rules

Investment decision rules specify the desired standards of financial decision making. The most widely accepted investment decision standard is the maximization of wealth. From an investment perspective, the investor seeks to invest in and trade securities that result in the greatest appreciation in long-term value of the portfolio.

From a managerial finance perspective, shareholders are the owners of the firm and the investment rule states that a financial decision that adds to the net wealth position of shareholders is a good decision. An unwise decision is one that knowingly causes shareholders' wealth to deteriorate. If several actions increase shareholders' wealth, the more desirable action is the one that results in greater wealth with equal or less risk. Sales maximization, profit maximization, and firm size maximization, among others, are sometimes used as investment decision standards. These standards are inferior to maximization of shareholders' wealth; generally, they tend to make managers more happy than they do shareholders.

Financial Analysis

Managerial finance relies on economic and quantitative analysis to fulfill the goal of increasing wealth of shareholders. The financial manager must have the analytical skills and insights that reveal ways to reduce costs and increase revenues and thus lead to improved profitability for the company. In the areas of investments and financial markets, financial analysis helps investors by providing guidelines for evaluating the risk versus expected return trade-off.

Financial analysis takes its meaning from the study of the financial interrelationships that exist in a particular problem. You cannot assume that these relationships are constant from problem to problem. For example, common stock issued by BankAmerica Corporation, a financial institution, is more sensitive to interest rate changes than is common stock issued by Cincinnati Milacron Inc., a manufacturer. The reason is that financial institutions have significant investments in debt securities (financial assets) whose values move inversely to interest rates. Manufacturing firms invest heavily in physical, or real, assets such as plant and equipment. Values of investments in physical assets are less affected by changes in interest rates. Ignoring expected changes in interest rates when analyzing stock prices of financial institutions will result in questionable conclusions.

Techniques we use to explore financial interrelationships are the basic mathematical tools of financial analysis. The dominant analytical tools are financial ratio analysis, statistical models to analyze expected return versus risk, and operations research models to determine the acceptability of investments. Imagination and ability are proving the only limits to recently developed techniques for financial analysis.

Organizational Form

Economic organizations are entities through which people interact to reach individual and collective economic goals. The economic system consists of networks of people and organizations linked together. The highest-level organization is the economy as a whole. At the next level are entities more traditionally regarded as organizations: business organizations, labor unions, and government agencies. A key characteristic of an organization at this level is its legal identity. For example, consider the definition of a **business organization** in a broad context. It means the set of contracts between an entity, called the firm (for example, Club Med, Inc.), and its *stakeholders*. **Stakeholders** are those who have an interest in the welfare of the firm, including the firm's creditors, customers, employees, governments, managers, shareholders, and suppliers. Laws and legal remedies help to enforce the contracts between stakeholders.

Three primary forms of business organizations exist: the sole proprietorship, the partnership, and the corporation. Most firms operating in the world are proprietorships. However, most of the dollar value of sales is attributed to corporations like Exxon and The Home Depot. State governments charter corporations to do business. In chartering a corporation, the state grants to it certain rights and privileges and imposes certain duties and obligations. By demanding that corporations act responsibly and in a legal manner, states attempt, through the chartering process, to bring any corporate abuse under control. A problem arises if one state, Texas for example, decides to impose more stringent duties upon corporations chartered in its state. The corporations could move to a state where the laws are less demanding. Today, most of the major corporations are established in Delaware, a state with the least restrictive chartering laws.

The issue of ownership versus control is an important topic in finance. When ownership and control in the corporation are separate, a *principal-agent problem* exists. The important issue centers on whether corporate managers **(agents)** have the proper incentives for them to act in the interests of stakeholders **(principals).** The **principal-agent problem** assumes that managers, if left alone, will operate in their own interest, not in the interest of the stakeholders. Critics make the following claims:

- Managers invest a firm's earnings in low-value projects to expand their empires when the funds would be better distributed to the shareholders to invest for themselves.
- Managers supposedly hang on to badly performing operations when new managers could run them more profitably.
- Managers pay themselves exorbitantly and lavish expensive perquisites upon themselves.
- Managers resist attempts to force more profitable operations, especially by resisting takeovers that threaten their jobs.

All these alleged misdeeds serve the interests of the managers themselves, not the interests of the firm's owners. Agents' actions may be detrimental to the wealth of principals. For example, consider the actions of senior management of Pinnacle West Capital Corporation, a firm whose securities trade on the New York Stock Exchange. We have excerpted the following passage from pages 11 and 12 of the company's *Notice and Proxy Statement,* dated April 17, 1992:

> Effective January 1, 1992 the Company established a supplemental executive benefit plan to provide certain benefits to directors and officers of the Company and its subsidiaries upon the occurrence of certain events, which generally include **bankruptcy,** . . .

Management is protecting its own future even if its actions result in bankruptcy of the firm! Ask yourself: If I am a shareholder, a supplier, a creditor, or an employee, would I feel protected if Pinnacle West became bankrupt? As a shareholder your stock would lose much of its value, as a supplier or creditor you would likely not receive full value on your claims, and as an employee you could lose your job. The need for a sense of trust is an integral part of the business relationship. Ethical decisions (or unethical ones) affect the world of finance as much as they do any aspect of business. Hence, an awareness of the principal-agent problem should improve our study of finance.

Taxes

Tax rules legislated by governments affect the rates of return investments earn both before and after any taxes. Before-tax rates of return differ because domestic and foreign federal, state, and local taxing authorities are not consistent in their application of taxes. They tax returns to different types of investments differently. Different jurisdictions tax similar investments differently. We will also find that returns to similar investments within the same jurisdiction are taxed differently depending upon the organizational form; corporations are taxed differently than partnerships. Finally, returns to similar investments located in the same jurisdiction and owned by the same type of organization receive differential tax treatment if the operating histories of the organizations differ.

As an example of the problem managers face, consider the Italian federal corporate tax system. Italian tax authorities assume that no corporation operating in Italy would submit a tax return showing its true profits. The presumption is that firms understate actual profits 30 to 70%. They are essentially correct. Thus, about six months after the deadline for filing tax returns, the tax authorities issue an "invitation to discuss" the tax return to each corporation. At the meeting, the Italian revenue authorities state the amount of corporate income tax which it believes is due. The authorities and the corporation then proceed through several rounds of bargaining until they reach a settlement.

The area of taxes is a highly specialized topic and subjected to frequent changes by governmental attempts to raise revenues to fund government programs or stimulate the economy.

Politics

Most discussions about finance leave politics to the politicians. However, it can be said that politics is an inseparable facet of many financial decisions. Historically, times of business depression and social unrest have periodically given rise to attacks upon "big corporations" by those who hope to gain public support and political office. Yet surprisingly little has been done to inhibit the use of the corporate form of business. Many corporations maintain offices in a country's capital city not only to influence legislation, but also to help management predict changes in government policy.

Financial markets, via the buying and selling actions of investors, are constantly responding to either real or anticipated changes in legislation. The attitudes of government can seriously affect certain business segments. For instance:

- Expectations of decreased demand for defense contributed to General Dynamics Corporation, Northrop Corporation, and other American firms cutting back on making investment decisions in their defense businesses.
- The Tax Reform Act of 1986 reversed some incentives given to real estate investors a few years earlier. The new act greatly reduced the attractiveness of investing in real estate.

Politics and economic policy are more complex when we consider international financial markets. Actions of many governments become part of the decision-making process. Integrating political considerations into managerial finance is particularly appropriate in **multinational firms,** such as Pepsico, Inc., Motorola, Inc., and Caterpillar, Inc., which build facilities in both domestic and foreign markets. The development of multinational firms is partially a response to world conditions that do not allow free movement of labor, materials, goods, and services between countries. The reason for many of the barriers is understandable from a political perspective. For instance, international trade agreements between countries exist because of import restrictions and other politically motivated arguments.

RELATIONSHIP OF FINANCE TO OTHER DISCIPLINES

Finance incorporates information from the disciplines of economics, management, accounting, and quantitative methods. Figure 15-2 depicts the relationships. Economics provides the underlying theory for financial decision making, whereas accounting provides a form for much of the data used to analyze financial decisions through various quantitative techniques. The field of management provides an understanding of organizational psychology that enhances decision making.

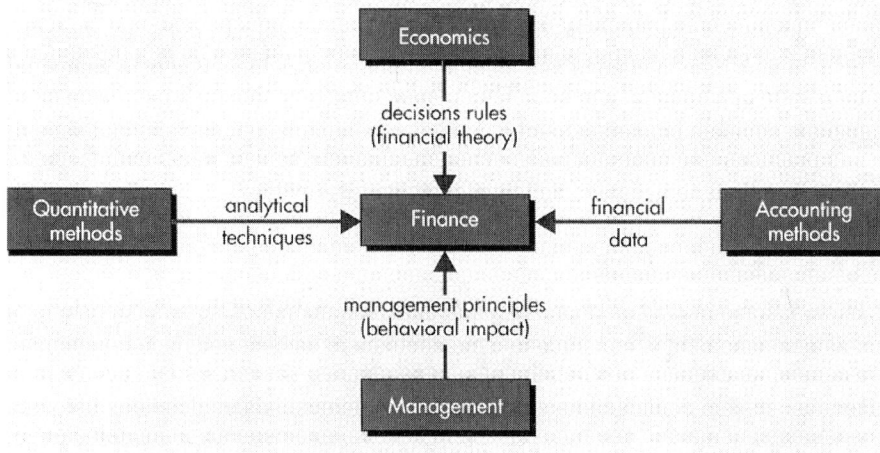

FIGURE 15-2
Relationship of Finance with Other Disciplines

Economics

Finance is said to represent applied microeconomics. For example, the rule a financial manager uses to decide to accept or reject a proposed project or investment is essentially the same as the economist's *marginal revenue versus marginal cost rule*. The financial decision rule says: Accept all projects whose expected rates of return are greater than the opportunity cost of capital; or simply, accept projects whose marginal revenues exceed marginal costs.

Another interplay between economics and finance has to do with the economic concept of an *efficient market*. The basis for modern financial theory is a belief in efficient financial markets, which is adapted from the economist's concept of perfect competition. As stated earlier, an efficient financial market is one in which investors cannot consistently earn excess returns because essentially everyone has access to the same information, which is reflected in security prices.

Management

In all areas of finance, decisions are unmistakably affected by behavioral issues, both on the parts of individuals and as a consequence of organizational form. A key element of managerial finance is *decision making*, and decisions are made by *people who are managers*. Financial managers oversee the efficient use of resources within the firm. A manager's understanding of organizational psychology can be an important factor in motivating employees to produce quality products and improving the firm's performance.

From an investor's perspective, knowledge of the psychology of behavior applied to an aggregation of investors can influence decisions about buying and selling securities. This knowledge may entail anything from a "sense" or "feel" some investors might have to large-scale predictions about behavior. For example, many professional investors take the position that when most investors see "good times" ahead, it is time to sell securities. The idea is that the euphoria about the financial market is likely wrong and securities soon may decline significantly in value.

Accounting

Good accounting data are necessary for both the financial manager and the investor to make informed financial decisions. Financial statements accompanied by complete notes explaining the accounting rules followed allow a better understanding of how management derived items like sales, profits, and assets. However, comparison of accounting information from one firm to another can often be difficult because generally accepted accounting principles (known as *GAAP* and pronounced *gap*) allow alternative methods for management to choose from to record transactions.

Institutions such as the American Institute of Certified Public Accountants and the United States Securities and Exchange Commission (SEC) provide guidance or legal monitoring of financial markets. These actions improve the quality of financial information available to investors in the United States. However, accounting philosophies and practices vary internationally. When the financial analyst works with foreign data, these variations sometimes lead to poor-quality information.

Quantitative Methods

Finance draws heavily on quantitative methods for analysis of financial decisions. Some decisions use fairly straightforward quantitative approaches such as ratio analysis. For example, we calculate profitability of sales by dividing net income by sales. Both numbers are readily available in a firm's income statement. Other decisions use complex mathematical models. For instance, a portfolio manager may use a quadratic programming model to decide on the allocation of funds among several securities to be included in a portfolio. In another case, a financial analyst for a manufacturing firm may use a linear programming model to recommend which of several projects to select, given future cash flows and a limited amount of money to invest.

ETHICS AND FINANCE

A theoretical discussion of finance implicitly assumes that participants conduct activities and relationships in an ethical manner. Unfortunately, this is not always the case. In 1980, *Fortune* magazine surveyed 1,043 large companies.[3] A total of 117 of the corporations satisfied *Fortune's* definition of law violation—conviction on criminal charges or consent decrees for bribery, criminal fraud, illegal political contributions, tax evasion, and criminal antitrust.

In some cases, it is easy to understand why corporate managers may act unethically. Consider a company on the brink of bankruptcy. Can the president be expected to reject an ethically objectionable but potentially lucrative last-minute gamble to save the company on the grounds that, because it is unethical, it will be

---

[3]"How Lawless Are Big Companies?" *Fortune,* December 1, 1980, p. 57.

unprofitable in the long run? The president may reason that unless the gamble is taken, there will be no long run.

Or consider the many activities of securities brokers. They execute transactions in financial markets for clients, examine the securities of various companies as possible investments, and recommend securities to individual clients. Financial institutions with brokerage offices may also be in the business of investment banking. **Investment bankers** help companies sell their financial securities to investors. As brokers try to perform all these functions, especially the provision of financial advice, there is room for serious questions of professional ethics. One legitimate ethics question involves the objectivity of research about a public company. Consider what can happen when an investment banking division of a large financial institution such Merrill Lynch & Company takes a firm public in an initial public offering of stock (called an IPO) and then passes its research on to the brokers. The investment banking division receives a large fee for taking the firm public. The brokers, in turn, try to convince investors to buy the public company's securities. Brokerages are typically reluctant to issue sell recommendations about stocks. What does this imply about the investment banking brokerage relationship?

Another question about ethics in securities markets addresses the distinction between investments, speculation, and gambling. Is the only distinction the degree of risk involved in a particular transaction? Stock exchange officials react in horror to the commonly voiced opinion that Wall Street is "the biggest casino in the world." Yet, some say, the grounds for distinction are not clear. There are relatively safe bets available to gamblers and extremely risky propositions in securities markets, such as the new issues of a young firm.

Of the many ethical issues surrounding financial markets, the most intriguing and publicized in recent years is *insider trading.* The common definition of **insider trading** is trading in which someone buys or sells securities using information that is not publicly available to all investors. Thus, instead of the financial markets being efficient in the sense that all investors have equal access to information, a significant market imperfection exists. *Asymmetric information* exists; information is known only to certain people. The presence of asymmetric information inhibits the accurate valuation of assets.

Insider trading is extremely difficult to define legally, however. Securities and Exchange Commission (SEC) officials have frequently refused to define the term. Former SEC Commissioner Irving Pollock said at a Congressional hearing: "I see it in the same way the Supreme Court Justice Stewart saw pornography. You can't define insider trading, but you know it when you see it."

Another very contentious issue is the responsibility that management has to shareholders of the company; this is the principal-agent problem that we discussed earlier. Managers have been known to use many tactics to protect their positions, including issuance of voting stock to friendly shareholders, the nomination of a slate of directors that is friendly to management, and the use of *golden parachutes,* or employment contracts that provide large severance pay if senior managers lose their jobs because of an unfriendly takeover by another firm. For instance, the chief executive officer of Pinnacle West Capital Corporation has a severance agreement calling for severance benefits of about three times his average annual compensation over the preceding five years if there is change of control of the company.

SUMMARY

Traditional Finance Areas

- The traditional finance areas are managerial finance, investments, and financial markets.
- Managerial finance addresses what investments to make, how these investments should be financed, and how daily financial activities should be managed.
- Investments relate to activities and decision rules about selecting, managing, and trading assets, such as stocks and bonds. The underlying theory is that assets trade in perfect markets so that investors earn profits consistent with their risk exposure.
- Financial markets—money and capital markets—are the channels which direct funds to their most profitable use. These markets determine the appropriate risk-adjusted rate to evaluate investments.

Guiding Principles of Finance

- Five guiding principles integrate the three areas of finance:
    1. Maximization of wealth
    2. Time value of money
    3. Expected return versus risk trade-off
    4. Leverage
    5. Diversification

- Maximization of wealth principle provides the necessary focus for evaluating decisions.
- The principles of time value of money and expected return versus risk tradeoff are critical for determining value and maximizing wealth.
- Leverage allows output or wealth to expand for a fixed input.
- The principle of diversification is investing in more than one asset to reduce risk.

Elements Common to the Three Areas of Finance

- The subject of finance uses the common elements of financial analysis, investment decision rules, organizational form, taxes, and politics.
- Finance, as a quantitative subject, relies on insightful analysis to make wealth maximization decisions.
- Organizational form influences these decisions. Proprietors, as owners, are responsible for creating their own wealth. At the other extreme, nonowner managers' decisions affect the wealth of the stakeholders of the business, including the shareholders, who are the real owners of the corporation. In this latter case, principal-agent problems can arise.
- Investors and managers make decisions based on both taxes and legal concerns.

Relationship of Finance to Other Disciplines

- The discipline of finance relies on economics, accounting, quantitative methods, and management.

- Economics provides theoretical foundations for assessing wealth-creating decisions.
- Accounting provides much of the data necessary to evaluate decisions.
- Quantitative methods offer several techniques for analyzing the data.
- The area of management provides skills for understanding people, as they behave in organizations, who ultimately carry out the wealth-creating decisions.

Ethics and Finance

- The role of ethics in finance is significant in several areas. Investment in securities is a major area of concern, and managers also can make decisions that are ethically objectionable.
- Insider stock trading clearly is unethical. There are several gray areas a student of finance must evaluate as well, such as corporate decisions that injure local economies in the interest of short-term profit and unrealistically high executive compensation or severance packages.

SELECTED REFERENCES

Donaldson, Gordon, *Managing Corporate Wealth: The Operation of a Comprehensive Financial Goals System,* New York: Praeger Publishers, 1984. This book furnishes an interesting real-world view of how senior managers think about their business and its financial challenges.

Mokhiber, Russell, *Corporate Crime and Violence: Big Business and the Abuse of the Public Trust,* San Francisco: Sierra Club Books, 1989. The book examines several case histories of companies valuing short-term economic profits above human lives, community safety, or long-term health of the environment.

Rappaport, Alfred, *Creating Shareholder Value: The New Standard for Business Performance,* New York: The Free Press, 1986. This book provides managers with a practical standard for measuring their efforts in strategic planning, competitiveness, asset control, and other areas.

Scholes, Myron S., and Mark A. Wolfson, *Taxes and Business Strategy: A Planning Approach,* Englewood Cliffs, NJ: Prentice Hall, 1992. The book renders a bridge between tax theory and practice.

Stewart, James B., *Den of Thieves,* New York: Simon & Schuster, 1991. This book reports in detail the full story of insider trading that nearly destroyed Wall Street.

CHAPTER 16

Financial Markets and Rates of Return

At times internally generated funds will not be sufficient to finance all of the firm's proposed expenditures. In these situations, the corporation may find it necessary to attract large amounts of financial capital externally.[1] This chapter focuses on the market environment in which long-term capital is raised. It also introduces and covers the logic behind the determination of interest rates and required rates of return in the capital markets. We will explore interest rate levels and risk differentials over recent time periods and will study several theories that attempt to explain the shape of the *term structure of interest rates*. Long-term funds are raised in the capital market. By the term *capital market*, we mean all institutions and procedures that facilitate transactions in long-term financial instruments (like common stocks and bonds).

THE MIX OF CORPORATE SECURITIES SOLD IN THE CAPITAL MARKET

When corporations decide to raise cash in the capital market, what type of financing vehicle is most favored? Many individual investors think that common stock is the answer to this question. This is understandable, given the coverage of the level of common stock prices by the popular news media. All the major television networks, for instance, quote the closing price of the Dow Jones Industrial Average on their nightly news broadcasts. Common stock, though, is not the financing method relied on most heavily by corporations. The answer to this question is **corporate bonds.** *The corporate debt markets clearly dominate the corporate equity markets when new funds are being raised.* This is a long-term relationship—it occurs year after year. Figure 16-1 bears this out.

---

[1]By *externally generated,* we mean that the funds are obtained by means other than through retentions or depreciation. Funds from these latter two sources are commonly called *internally generated* funds.

In Figure 16-1 we see the total volume (in millions of dollars) of domestic corporate securities sold for cash over the 1981–1991 period. The percentage breakdown among common stock, preferred stock, and bonds is also displayed. We will learn from our discussions of the cost of capital and planning the firm's financing mix that the U.S. tax system inherently favors debt as a means of raising capital. Quite simply, interest expense is deductible from other income when computing the firm's federal tax liability, whereas the dividends paid on both preferred and common stock are not.

Financial executives responsible for raising corporate cash know this. When they have a choice between marketing new bonds and marketing new preferred stock, the outcome is usually in favor of bonds. The after-tax cost of capital on the debt is less than that incurred on the preferred stock. Likewise, if the firm has unused debt capacity and the general level of equity prices is depressed, financial executives favor the issuance of debt securities over the issuance of new common stock. It is always good to keep some benchmark figures in your head. The average (unweighted) mix of corporate securities sold for cash over the 1981–1991 period follows. This *excludes* private debt placements or the bonds and notes categories would be a bit higher. Figure 16-2 illustrates this financing pattern.

Common stock	23.3%
Preferred stock	4.4
Bonds and notes	72.3
Total	**100.0%**

In this chapter we cover material that introduces the financial manager to the processes involved in raising funds in the nation's capital markets and also cover the logic that lies behind the determination of interest rates and required rates of return in those capital markets.

We will see that the United States has a highly developed, complex, and competitive system of financial markets that allows for the quick transfer of savings from

FIGURE 16-1   Corporate Securities Offered for Cash (Domestic Offerings)

Year	Total Volume ($ millions)	Percent Common Stock	Percent Preferred Stock	Percent Bonds and Notes
1991	$352,344	13.6%	4.9%	81.5%
1990	212,712	9.1	1.9	89.0
1989	213,617	12.2	2.9	84.9
1988	244,670	14.7	2.7	82.6
1987	262,725	16.4	3.9	79.7
1986	248,722	23.7	4.9	71.4
1985	133,460	27.5	5.3	67.2
1984	95,287	23.3	4.5	72.2
1983	103,355	43.9	7.7	48.4
1982	73,397	32.3	6.7	61.0
1981	64,500	39.5	2.6	57.9

Source: *Economic Report of the President*, January 1989, p. 415, and *Federal Reserve Bulletin*, February 1993, p. A33.

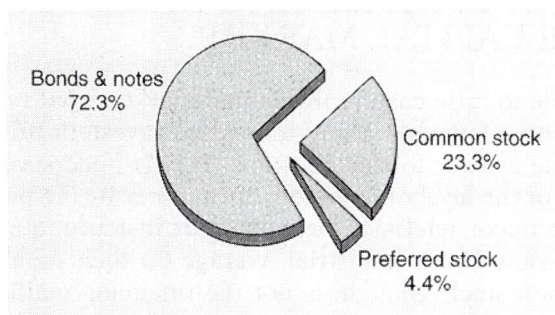

FIGURE 16-2
Corporate External Financing Patterns 1981–1991

those economic units with a surplus of savings to those economic units with a savings deficit. Such a system of highly developed financial markets allows great ideas (like the personal computer) to be financed and increases the overall wealth of the economy. Consider your wealth, for example, compared to that of the average family in Russia. Russia lacks a complex system of financial markets to facilitate transactions in financial claims (securities). As a result, real capital formation there has suffered.

WHY FINANCIAL MARKETS EXIST

Financial markets are institutions and procedures that facilitate transactions in all types of financial claims. The purchase of your home, the common stock you may own, and your life insurance policy all took place in some type of financial market. Why do financial markets exist? What would the economy lose if our complex system of financial markets were not developed? We will address these questions here.

Some *economic units,* such as households, firms, or governments, spend more during a given period than they earn. Other economic units spend *less* on current consumption than they earn. For example, business firms in the aggregate usually spend more during a specific period than they earn. Households in the aggregate spend less on current consumption than they earn. As a result, some mechanism is needed to facilitate the transfer of savings from those economic units with a surplus to those with a deficit. That is precisely the function of financial markets. Financial markets exist in order to allocate the supply of savings in the economy to the demanders of those savings. The central characteristic of a financial market is that it acts as the vehicle through which the forces of demand and supply for a specific type of financial claim (such as a corporate bond) are brought together.

Now, why would the economy suffer without a developed financial market system? The answer is that the wealth of the economy would be less without the financial markets. The rate of capital formation would not be as high if financial markets did not exist. This means that the net additions during a specific period to the stocks of (1) dwellings, (2) productive plant and equipment, (3) inventory, and (4) consumer durables would occur at lower rates. Figure 16-3 helps clarify the rationale behind this assertion. The abbreviated balance sheets in the figure refer to firms or any other type of economic units that operate in the private as opposed to governmental sec-

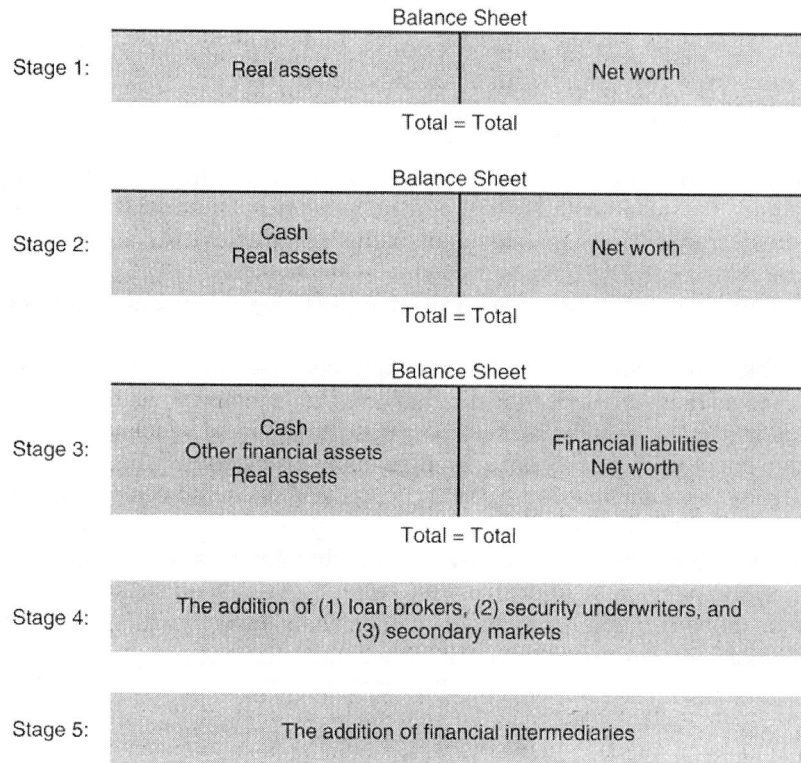

FIGURE 16-3
Development of a Financial Market System

tors of the economy. This means that such units cannot issue money to finance their own activities.

At stage 1 in Figure 16-3 only real assets exist in the hypothetical economy. **Real assets** are tangible assets like houses, equipment, and inventories. They are distinguished from **financial assets,** which represent claims for future payment on other economic units. Common and preferred stocks, bonds, bills, and notes all are types of financial assets. If only real assets exist, then savings for a given economic unit, such as a firm, must be accumulated in the form of real assets. If the firm has a great idea for a new product, that new product can be developed, produced, and distributed only out of company savings (retained earnings). Furthermore, all investment in the new product must occur simultaneously as the savings are generated. If you have the idea, and we have the savings, there is no mechanism to transfer our savings to you. This is not a good situation.

At stage 2 paper money (cash) comes into existence in the economy. Here, at least, you can *store* your own savings in the form of money. Thus, you can finance your great idea by drawing down your cash balances. This is an improvement over stage 1, but there is still no effective mechanism to transfer our savings to you. You see, we will not just hand you our dollar bills. We will want a receipt.

The concept of a receipt that represents the transfer of savings from one economic unit to another is a monumental advancement. The economic unit with excess savings can lend the savings to an economic unit that needs them. To the lending unit these receipts are identified as "other financial assets" in stage 3 of Figure 16-3. To the borrowing unit, the issuance of financial claims (receipts) shows up as "financial liabilities" on the stage 3 balance sheet. The economic unit with surplus savings will earn a rate of return on those funds. The borrowing unit will pay that rate of return, but it has been able to finance its great idea.

In stage 4 the financial market system moves further toward full development. Loan brokers come into existence. These brokers help locate pockets of excess savings and channel such savings to economic units needing the funds. Some economic units will actually purchase the financial claims of borrowing units and sell them at a higher price to other investors; this process is called **underwriting.** Underwriting will be discussed in more detail later in this chapter. In addition, **secondary markets** develop. Secondary markets simply represent trading in already existing financial claims. If you buy your brother's General Motors common stock, you have made a secondary market transaction. Secondary markets reduce the risk of investing in financial claims. Should you need cash, you can liquidate your claims in the secondary market. This induces savers to invest in securities.

The progression toward a developed and complex system of financial markets ends with stage 5. Here, financial intermediaries come into existence. You can think of financial intermediaries as the major financial institutions with which you are used to dealing. These include commercial banks, savings and loan associations, credit unions, life insurance companies, and mutual funds. Financial intermediaries share a common characteristic: They offer their own financial claims, called **indirect securities,** to economic units with excess savings. The proceeds from selling their indirect securities are then used to purchase the financial claims of other economic units. These latter claims can be called **direct securities.** Thus, a mutual fund might sell mutual fund shares (their indirect security) and purchase the common stocks (direct securities) of some major corporations. A life insurance company sells life insurance policies and purchases huge quantities of corporate bonds. Financial intermediaries thereby involve many small savers in the process of capital formation. This means there are more "good things" for everybody to buy.

A developed financial market system provides for a greater level of wealth in the economy. In the absence of financial markets, savings are not transferred to the economic units most in need of those funds. It is difficult, after all, for a household to build its own automobile. The financial market system makes it *easier* for the economy to build automobiles and all the other goods that economic units like to accumulate.

FINANCING OF BUSINESS: THE MOVEMENT OF FUNDS THROUGH THE ECONOMY

The Financing Process

We now understand the crucial role that financial markets play in a capitalist economy. At this point we will take a brief look at how funds flow across some selected sectors of the U.S. economy. In addition, we will focus a little more closely on the process of financial intermediation that was introduced in the preceding section. Some actual data are used to sharpen our knowledge of the financing process. We will see that financial institutions play a major role in bridging the gap between savers and borrowers in the economy. Nonfinancial corporations, we already know, are significant borrowers of financial capital.

Figure 16-4 shows how funds were supplied and raised by the major sectors of our economy in 1990. Households were the largest net supplier of funds to the financial markets. This is the case, by the way, year in and year out. In 1990, households made available $160.3 billion in funds to other sectors. That was the excess of their funds supplied over their funds raised in the markets. In the jargon of economics, the household sector is a *savings-surplus* sector.

Likewise in 1990, the nonfinancial business sector is a savings-surplus sector. In 1990 we see that nonfinancial corporations supplied $46.6 billion more in funds to the financial markets than they raised. This was due to extensive repurchases of their own common stock by firms the marketplace. In fact, during the 11-year period of 1980–90 corporations were *net buyers* (rather than issuers) of common stock on eight occasions. However, during longer periods, such as 20 to 30 years, the nonfinancial business sector is typically a *savings-deficit* sector. That is, this sector raises more financial capital in the markets than it supplies.

Next, it can also be seen that the U.S. government sector was a savings-deficit sector for 1990. In 1990 the federal government raised $217.3 billion in excess of the funds it supplied to the financial markets. This highlights a serious problem for the entire economy and for the financial manager. Persistent federal deficits have increased the role of the federal government in the market for borrowed funds. The last time the federal government posted a budget surplus was 1969; the last time prior to that was 1960. The federal government has thus become a "quasi-permanent" savings-deficit sector. Most financial economists agree that this tendency puts upward pressure on interest rates in the financial marketplace and thereby raises the general (overall) cost of capital to corporations. This phenomenon has become known as *crowding-out:* The private borrower is pushed out of the financial markets in favor of the government borrower.

Figure 16-4 further highlights how important *foreign* financial investment is to the activity of the U.S. economy. As the federal government has become more of a "confirmed" savings-deficit sector, the need for funds has been increasingly *supplied*

FIGURE 16-4   Sector View of Flow of Funds in U.S. Financial Markets for 1990 (Billions of Dollars)

Sector	[1] *Funds Raised*	[2] *Funds Supplied*	[2] – [1] *Net Funds Supplied*
Households[a]	$259.1	$419.4	$160.3
Nonfinancial corporate business	53.6	100.2	46.6
U.S. government	246.6	29.3	–217.3
State and local governments	20.3	–8.0	–28.3
Foreign	72.9	104.5	31.6

[a]Includes personal trusts and nonprofit organizations.

Source: *Flow of Funds Accounts, Second Quarter 1991,* Flow of Funds Section (Washington, DC: Board of Governors of the Federal Reserve System, September 1991).

by foreign interests. Thus, in 1990, the foreign sector *supplied* a net $31.6 billion to the domestic capital markets. As recently as 1982, the foreign sector *raised*—rather than supplied—$30.8 billion in the U.S. financial markets! This illustrates the dynamic nature of financial management.

Figure 16-4 demonstrates that the financial market system must exist to facilitate the orderly and efficient flow of savings from the surplus sectors to the deficit sectors of the economy. The result during long periods is that the nonfinancial business sector is *typically* dependent on the household sector to finance its investment needs. The governmental sectors—especially the federal government—are quite reliant on foreign financing.

As we noted in the preceding section, the financial market system includes a complex network of intermediaries that assist in the transfer of savings among economic units. Two intermediaries will be highlighted here: life insurance companies and pension funds. They are especially important participants in the capital market of the country.

Because of the nature of their business, life insurance firms can invest heavily in long-term financial instruments. This investment tendency arises for two key reasons: (1) life insurance policies usually include a *savings element* in them, and (2) their liabilities liquidate at a very predictable rate. Thus, life insurance companies invest in the "long end" of the securities markets. This means that they favor (1) mortgages and (2) corporate bonds as investment vehicles rather than shorter-term-to-maturity financial instruments like Treasury bills. To a lesser extent, they acquire corporate stocks for their portfolios.

Over recent years, about 47% of the financial assets of life insurance firms are represented by corporate stocks and bonds. We see that life insurance companies are an important financial intermediary. By issuing life insurance policies (indirect securities), they can acquire direct securities (corporate stocks and bonds) for their investment portfolios. Their preference, by far, is for bonds over stocks.

Let us now direct our attention to another financial intermediary, private pension funds. In comparison with life insurance companies, three factors are emphasized. First, since 1960, private pension funds have grown at a *much faster rate* than have the insurance companies. Second, a *greater proportion* of the financial asset mix of the pension funds is devoted to *corporate stocks* and bonds. Third, the pension funds *invest more heavily* in corporate stocks than they do in corporate bonds. Over recent years, about 62% of the financial assets of private pension funds have been tied up in corporate stocks and bonds. These financial institutions also are significant *sources* of business financing in this country. The pension funds play the same *intermediary* role as does the life insurance subsector of the economy.

Movement of Savings

Figure 16-5 provides a useful way to summarize our discussion of (1) why financial markets exist and (2) the movement of funds through the economy. It also serves as an introduction to the role of the investment banker—a subject discussed in detail later in this chapter.

We see that savings are ultimately transferred to the business firm in need of cash in three ways:

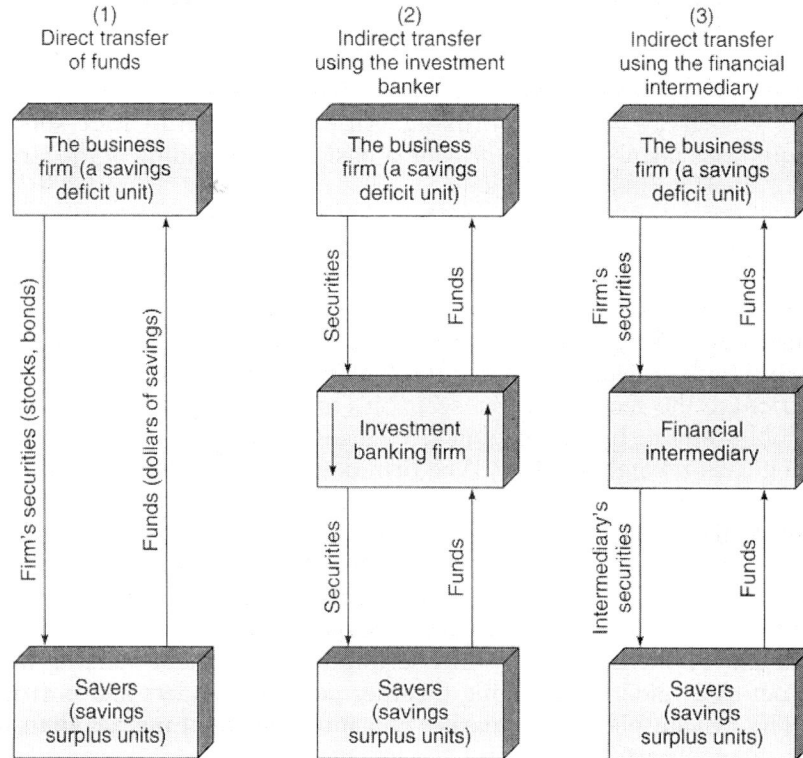

FIGURE 16-5
Three Ways to Transfer Financial Capital in the Economy

1. **The direct transfer of funds.** Here the firm seeking cash sells its securities directly to savers (investors) who are willing to purchase them in hopes of earning a reasonable rate of return. New business formation is a good example of this process at work. The new business may go directly to a saver or group of savers called venture capitalists. The venture capitalists will lend funds to the firm or take an equity position in the firm if they feel the product or service the new firm hopes to market will be successful.

2. **Indirect transfer using the investment banker.** In a common arrangement under this system, the managing investment banking house will form a syndicate of several investment bankers. The syndicate will buy the entire issue of securities from the firm that is in need of financial capital. The syndicate will then sell the securities at a higher price than it paid for them to the investing public (the savers). Merrill Lynch Capital Markets and The First Boston Corporation are examples of investment banking firms. They tend to be called "houses" by those who work in the financial community. Notice that under this second method of transferring savings, the securities being issued just pass through the investment banking firm. They are not transformed into a different type of security.

3. **Indirect transfer using the financial intermediary.** This is the type of system life insurance companies and pension funds operate within. The financial intermediary collects the savings of individuals and issues its own (indirect) securities in exchange for these savings. The intermediary then uses the funds collected from the individual savers to acquire the business firm's (direct) securities, such as stocks and bonds.

We all benefit from the three transfer mechanisms displayed in Figure 16-5. Capital formation and economic wealth are greater than they would be in the absence of this financial market system.

COMPONENTS OF THE U.S. FINANCIAL MARKET SYSTEM

Numerous approaches exist for classifying the securities markets. At times, the array can be confusing. An examination of four sets of dichotomous terms can help provide a basic understanding of the structure of the U.S. financial markets.

Public Offerings and Private Placements

When a corporation decides to raise external capital, those funds can be obtained by making a public offering or a private placement. In a **public offering** both individual and institutional investors have the opportunity to purchase the securities. The securities are usually made available to the public at large by a managing investment banking firm and its underwriting (risk-taking) syndicate. The firm does not meet the ultimate purchasers of the securities in the public offering. The public market is an impersonal market.

In a **private placement,** also called a **direct placement,** the securities are offered and sold to a limited number of investors. The firm will usually hammer out, on a face-to-face basis with the prospective buyers, the details of the offering. In this setting the investment banking firm may act as a finder by bringing together potential lenders and borrowers. The private placement market is a more personal market than its public counterpart.

Primary Markets and Secondary Markets

Primary markets are those in which securities are offered for the *first* time to potential investors. A new issue of common stock by AT&T is a primary market transaction. This type of transaction increases the total stock of financial assets outstanding in the economy.

As mentioned in our discussion of the development of the financial market system, **secondary markets** represent transactions in currently outstanding securities. If the first buyer of the AT&T stock subsequently sells it, he or she does so in the secondary market. All transactions after the initial purchase take place in the secondary market. The sales do *not* affect the total stock of financial assets that exist in the economy. Both the money market and the capital market, described next, have primary and secondary sides.

Money Market and Capital Market

Money market.   The key distinguishing feature between the money and capital markets is the maturity period of the securities traded in them. The **money market** refers to all institutions and procedures that provide for transactions in short-term debt instruments generally issued by borrowers with very high credit ratings. By financial convention, *short term* means maturity periods of one year or less. Notice that equity instruments, either common or preferred, are not traded in the money market. The major instruments issued and traded are U.S. Treasury bills, various federal agency securities, bankers' acceptances, negotiable certificates of deposit, and commercial paper. Keep in mind that the money market is an intangible market. You do not walk into a building on Wall Street that has the words "Money Market" etched in stone over its arches. Rather, the money market is primarily a telephone market.

Capital market.   The **capital market** refers to all institutions and procedures that provide for transactions in long-term financial instruments. *Long-term* here means having maturity periods that extend beyond one year. In the broad sense this encompasses term loans and financial leases, corporate equities, and bonds. The funds that comprise the firm's capital structure are raised in the capital market. Important elements of the capital market are the organized security exchanges and the over-the-counter markets.

Organized Security Exchanges and Over-the-Counter Markets

Organized security exchanges are tangible entities; they physically occupy space (such as a building or part of a building), and financial instruments are traded on their premises. The **over-the-counter markets** include all security markets *except* the organized exchanges. The money market, then, is an over-the-counter market. Because both markets are important to financial officers concerned with raising *long-term capital,* some additional discussion is warranted.

Organized security exchanges.   For practical purposes there are seven major security exchanges in the United States.[2] These are the (1) New York Stock Exchange, (2) American Stock Exchange, (3) Midwest Stock Exchange, (4) Pacific Stock Exchange, (5) Philadelphia Stock Exchange, (6) Boston Stock Exchange, and (7) Cincinnati Stock Exchange. The New York Stock Exchange (NYSE) and the American Stock Exchange (AMEX) are called *national* exchanges, whereas the others are loosely described as *regionals.* All of these seven active exchanges are registered with the Securities and Exchange Commission (SEC). Firms whose securities are traded on the registered exchanges must comply with reporting requirements of both the specific exchange and the SEC.

An indication of the importance of the NYSE to our financial market system is reflected in something known as "consolidated tape volume." The Consolidated Tape

[2]Others include (1) The Honolulu Stock Exchange, which is unregistered; (2) the Board of Trade of the City of Chicago, which does not now trade stocks; and (3) the Chicago Board Options Exchange, Inc., which deals in options rather than stocks. The cities of Colorado Springs, Salt Lake City, and Spokane also have small exchanges. From time to time you may hear of the New York Futures Exchange (NYFE). This subsidiary of the NYSE was incorporated on April 5, 1979. Trading on the NYFE is in futures contracts and options contracts.

prints all of the transactions on stocks that are listed on the NYSE and are traded on other organized markets. These markets include the exchanges mentioned earlier plus over-the-counter markets. In 1991, the NYSE accounted for 82.3% of consolidated volume.[3]

The business of an exchange, including securities transactions, is conducted by its **members.** Members are said to occupy "seats." There are 1,366 seats on the NYSE, a number that has remained constant since 1953. Major brokerage firms own seats on the exchanges. An officer of the firm is designated to be the member of the exchange, and this membership permits the brokerage house to use the facilities of the exchange to effect trades. During 1991 the prices of seats that were exchanged for cash ranged from a low of $345,000 to a high of $440,000.[4] The record price, by the way, was $1.15 million paid on September 21, 1987—just prior to the October 19 market debacle.

Both corporations and investors enjoy several benefits provided by the existence of organized security exchanges. These include:

1. **Providing a continuous market.** This may be the most important function of an organized security exchange. A continuous market provides a series of continuous security prices. Price changes from trade to trade tend to be smaller than they would be in the absence of organized markets. The reasons are that there is a relatively large sales volume in each security, trading orders are executed quickly, and the range between the price asked for a security and the offered price tends to be narrow. The result is that price volatility is reduced.

2. **Establishing and publicizing fair security prices.** An organized exchange permits security prices to be set by competitive forces. They are not set by negotiations off the floor of the exchange, where one party might have a bargaining advantage. The bidding process flows from the supply and demand underlying each security. This means the specific price of a security is determined in the manner of an auction. In addition, the security prices determined at each exchange are widely publicized.

3. **Helping business raise new capital.** Because a continuous secondary market exists where prices are competitively determined, it is easier for firms to float new security offerings successfully. This continuous pricing mechanism also facilitates the determination of the offering price of a new issue. This means that comparative values are easily observed.

To receive the benefits provided by an organized exchange, the firm must seek to have its securities listed on the exchange. An application for listing must be filed and a fee paid. The requirements for listing vary from exchange to exchange; those of the NYSE are the most stringent. The general criteria for listing fall into these categories: (1) profitability, (2) size, (3) market value, and (4) public ownership. To give you the flavor of an actual set of listing requirements, those set forth by the NYSE are displayed in Figure 16-6.[5]

Over-the-counter markets.   Many publicly held firms do not meet the listing requirements of major stock exchanges. Others may want to avoid the reporting re-

---

[3]New York Stock Exchange, *Fact Book* (New York, 1992), p. 24.
[4]New York Stock Exchange, *Fact Book* (New York, 1992), p. 74.
[5]New York Stock Exchange, *Fact Book* (New York, 1992), p. 32.

FIGURE 16-6   NYSE Listing Requirements

Profitability

Earnings before taxes (EBT) for the most recent year must be at least $2.5 million.
For the two years preceding that, EBT must be at least $2.0 million.

Size

Net tangible assets must be at least $18.0 million.

Market Values[a]

The market value of publicly held stock must be at least $18.0 million.

Public Ownership

There must be at least 1.1 million publicly held common shares. There must be at least 2000 holders of 100 shares or more.

---

[a]The market value is tied to the level of common stock prices prevailing in the marketplace at the time of the listing application From time to time the $18.0 million requirement noted above may be lessened. Under current regulations of the NYSE, the requirement can never be less than $9.0 million.

quirements and fees required to maintain listing. As an alternative their securities may trade in the over-the-counter markets. On the basis of sheer numbers (not dollar volume), more stocks are traded over-the-counter than on organized exchanges. As far as secondary trading in corporate bonds is concerned, the over-the-counter markets are where the action is. In a typical year, more than 90% of corporate bond business takes place over-the-counter.

Most over-the-counter transactions are done through a loose network of security traders who are known as broker-dealers and brokers. Brokers do not purchase securities for their own account, whereas dealers do. Broker-dealers stand ready to buy and sell specific securities at selected prices. They are said to "make a market" in those securities. Their profit is the spread or difference between the price they will pay for a security (bid price) and the price at which they will sell the security (asked price).

The availability of prices is not as continuous in the over-the-counter market as it is on an organized exchange. Since February 8, 1971, however, when a computerized network called NASDAQ came into existence, the availability of prices in this market has improved substantially. NASDAQ stands for National Association of Security Dealers Automated Quotation System. It is a telecommunications system that provides a national information link among the brokers and dealers operating in the over-the-counter markets. Subscribing traders have a terminal that allows them to obtain representative bids and ask prices for thousands of securities traded over-the-counter. NASDAQ is a quotation system, not a transactions system. The final trade is still consummated by direct negotiation between traders.

NASDAQ price quotes for many stocks are published daily in the *Wall Street Journal*. This same financial newspaper also publishes prices on hundreds of other stocks traded over-the-counter. Local papers supply prices on stocks of regional interest. Finally, the National Quotation Bureau publishes daily "pink sheets," which contain prices on about 8,000 securities; these sheets are available in the offices of most security dealers.

THE INVESTMENT BANKER

Most corporations do not raise long-term capital frequently. The activities of working-capital management go on daily, but attracting long-term capital is, by comparison, episodic. The sums involved can be huge, so these situations are considered of great importance to financial managers. Because most managers are unfamiliar with the subtleties of raising long-term funds, they enlist the help of an expert. That expert is an investment banker.

Definition

The **investment banker** is a financial specialist involved as an intermediary in the merchandising of securities. He or she acts as a "middle person" by facilitating the flow of savings from those economic units that want to invest to those units that want to raise funds. We use the term investment banker to refer both to a given individual and to the organization for which such a person works, variously known as an **investment banking firm** or an **investment banking house.** Although these firms are called investment bankers, they perform no depository or lending functions. The activities of commercial banking and investment banking as we know them today were separated by the Banking Act of 1933 (also known as the Glass-Steagall Act of 1933). Just what does this middleman role involve? That is most easily understood in terms of the basic functions of investment banking.

Functions

The investment banker performs three basic functions: (1) underwriting, (2) distributing, and (3) advising.

Underwriting.   The term **underwriting** is borrowed from the field of insurance. It means "assuming a risk." The investment banker assumes the risk of selling a security issue at a satisfactory price. A satisfactory price is one that will generate a profit for the investment banking house.

The procedure goes like this. The managing investment banker and its syndicate will buy the security issue from the corporation in need of funds. The **syndicate** is a group of other investment bankers who are invited to help buy and resell the issue. The managing house is the investment banking firm that originated the business because its corporate client decided to raise external funds. On a specific day, the firm that is raising capital is presented with a check in exchange for the securities being issued. At this point the investment banking syndicate owns the securities. The corporation has its cash and can proceed to use it. The firm is now immune from the possibility that the security markets might turn sour. If the price of the newly issued security falls below that paid to the firm by the syndicate, the syndicate will suffer a loss. The syndicate, of course, hopes that the opposite situation will result. Its objective is to sell the new issue to the investing public at a price per security greater than its cost.

Distributing.   Once the syndicate owns the new securities, it must get them into the hands of the ultimate investors. This is the distribution or selling function of investment banking. The investment banker may have branch offices across the United States, or it may have an informal arrangement with several security dealers who regularly buy a portion of each new offering for final sale. It is not unusual to have 300 to 400 dealers involved in the selling effort. The syndicate can properly be viewed as the security wholesaler, and the dealer organization can be viewed as the security retailer.

Advising.   The investment banker is an expert in the issuance and marketing of securities. A sound investment banking house will be aware of prevailing market conditions and can relate those conditions to the particular type of security that should be sold at a given time. Business conditions may be pointing to a future increase in interest rates. The investment banker might advise the firm to issue its bonds in a timely fashion to avoid the higher yields that are forthcoming. The banker can analyze the firm's capital structure and make recommendations as to what general source of capital should be issued. In many instances the firm will invite its investment banker to sit on the board of directors. This permits the banker to observe corporate activity and make recommendations on a regular basis.

Distribution Methods

Several methods are available to the corporation for placing new security offerings in the hands of final investors. The investment banker's role is different in each of these. Sometimes, in fact, it is possible to bypass the investment banker. These methods are described in this section. Private placements, because of their importance, are treated separately later in the chapter.

Negotiated purchase.   In a negotiated underwriting, the firm that needs funds makes contact with an investment banker, and deliberations concerning the new issue begin. If all goes well, a *method* is negotiated for determining the price the investment banker and the syndicate will pay for the securities. For example, the agreement might state that the syndicate will pay $2 less than the closing price of the firm's common stock on the day before the offering date of a new stock issue. The negotiated purchase is the most prevalent method of securities distribution in the private sector. It is generally thought to be the most profitable technique as far as investment bankers are concerned.

Competitive bid purchase.   The method by which the underwriting group is determined distinguishes the competitive bid purchase from the negotiated purchase. In a competitive underwriting, several underwriting groups bid for the right to purchase the new issue from the corporation that is raising funds. The firm does not directly select the investment banker. The investment banker that underwrites and distributes the issue is chosen by an auction process. The syndicate willing to pay the greatest dollar amount per new security will win the competitive bid.

Most competitive bid purchases are confined to three situations, compelled by legal regulations: (1) railroad issues, (2) public utility issues, and (3) state and municipal bond issues. The argument in favor of competitive bids is that any undue influence of the investment banker over the firm is mitigated and the price received by the firm for each security should be higher. Thus, we would intuitively suspect that the cost of capital in a competitive bid situation would be less than in a negotiated purchase situation. Evidence on this question, however, is mixed. One problem with the competitive bid purchase as far as the fundraising firm is concerned is that the benefits gained from the advisory function of the investment banker are lost. It may be necessary to use an investment banker for advisory purposes and then by law exclude the banker from the competitive bid process.

Commission or best-efforts basis. Here, the investment banker acts as an agent rather than as a principal in the distribution process. The securities are *not* underwritten. The investment banker attempts to sell the issue in return for a fixed commission on each security actually sold. Unsold securities are returned to the corporation. This arrangement is typically used for more speculative issues. The issuing firm may be smaller or less established than the investment banker would like. Because the underwriting risk is not passed on to the investment banker, this distribution method is less costly to the issuer than a negotiated or competitive bid purchase. On the other hand the investment banker only has to give it his or her "best effort." A successful sale is not guaranteed.

Privileged subscription. Occasionally, the firm may feel that a distinct market already exists for its new securities. When a new issue is marketed to a definite and select group of investors, it is called a **privileged subscription.** Three target markets are typically involved: (1) current stockholders, (2) employees, or (3) customers. Of these, distributions directed at current stockholders are the most prevalent. Such offerings are called **rights offerings.** In a privileged subscription the investment banker may act only as a selling agent. It is also possible that the issuing firm and the investment banker might sign a **standby agreement,** which would obligate the investment banker to underwrite the securities that are not accepted by the privileged investors.

Direct sale. In a **direct sale** the issuing firm sells the securities directly to the investing public without involving an investment banker. Even among established corporate giants this procedure is relatively rare. A variation of the direct sale, though, was used more frequently in the 1970s than in previous decades. This involves the private placement of a new issue by the fundraising corporation *without* the use of an investment banker as an intermediary. Texaco, Mobil Oil, and International Harvester (now Navistar) are examples of large firms that have followed this procedure.[6]

Industry leaders. All industries have their leaders, and investment banking is no exception. We have discussed investment bankers in general at some length in this chapter. Figure 16-7 gives us some idea who the major players are within the investment banking industry. It lists the top 10 houses in 1991 based on the dollar volume of security issues that were managed. The number of issues the house participated in as lead manager is also identified, along with its share of the market.

---

[6]See Wyndham Robertson, "Future Shock at Morgan Stanley," *Fortune 97* (February 27, 1978), pp. 88, 90.

FIGURE 16-7   Leading U.S. Investment Bankers, 1991

Firm	Underwriting Volume (Billions of Dollars)	Number of Issues	Percent of Market
1. Merrill Lynch	$100.0	1180	17.2%
2. Goldman, Sachs	72.7	1013	12.5
3. Lehman Brothers	67.6	1336	11.7
4. First Boston	56.8	944	9.8
5. Kidder, Peabody	50.0	1705	8.6
6. Morgan Stanley	48.0	564	8.3
7. Salomon Brothers	43.7	626	7.5
8. Bear, Stearns	33.9	1087	5.8
9. Prudential Securities	18.2	613	3.1
10. Donaldson, Lulkin & Jenrette	11.2	324	1.9

Source: IDD Information Services as reported in the *New York Times*, January 2, 1992, p. C6.

PRIVATE PLACEMENTS

Private placements are an alternative to the sale of securities to the public or to a restricted group of investors through a privileged subscription. Any type of security can be privately placed (directly placed). This market, however, is clearly dominated by debt issues. Thus, we restrict this discussion to debt securities. From year to year the volume of private placements will vary. Figure 16-8 shows, though, that the private placement market is always a significant portion of the U.S. capital market.

The major investors in private placements are large financial institutions. Based on the volume of securities purchased, the three most important investor groups are (1) life insurance companies, (2) state and local retirement funds, and (3) private pension funds.

In arranging a private placement the firm may (1) avoid the use of an investment banker and work directly with the investing institutions or (2) engage the services of an investment banker. If the firm does not use an investment banker, of course, it does not have to pay a fee. Conversely, investment bankers can provide valuable advice in the private placement process. They are usually in contact with several major institutional investors; thus, they will know if a firm is in a position to invest in its proposed offering, and they can help the firm evaluate the terms of the new issue.

Private placements have advantages and disadvantages compared with public offerings. The financial manager must carefully evaluate both sides of the question. The advantages associated with private placements are these:

1. **Speed.** The firm usually obtains funds more quickly through a private placement than a public offering. The major reason is that registration of the issue with the SEC is not required.
2. **Reduced flotation costs.** These savings result because the lengthy registration statement for the SEC does not have to be prepared, and the investment banking underwriting and distribution costs do not have to be absorbed.

FIGURE 16-8 Publicly and Privately Placed Corporate Debt Placed Domestically
(Gross Proceeds of All New U.S. Corporate Debt Issues)

Year	Total Volume ($ million)	Percent Publicly Placed	Percent Privately Placed
1991	$362,006	79.3%	20.7%
1990	276,259	68.5	31.5
1989	298,813	60.7	39.3
1988	329,919	61.3	38.7
1987	301,447	69.5	30.5
1986	313,502	74.2	25.8
1985	165,754	72.1	27.9
1984	109,903	66.9	33.1
1983	68,370	69.1	30.9
1982	53,636	81.7	18.3
1981	45,092	84.5	15.5

Source: *Federal Reserve Bulletin*, various issues.

3. **Financing flexibility.** In a private placement the firm deals on a face-to-face basis with a small number of investors. This means that the terms of the issue can be tailored to meet the specific needs of the company. For example, all of the funds need not be taken by the firm at once. In exchange for a commitment fee the firm can "draw down" against the established amount of credit with the investors. This provides some insurance against capital market uncertainties, and the firm does not have to borrow the funds if the need does not arise. There is also the possibility of renegotiation. The terms of the debt issue can be altered. The term to maturity, the interest rate, or any restrictive covenants can be discussed among the affected parties.

The following disadvantages of private placements must be evaluated:

1. **Interest costs.** It is generally conceded that interest costs on private placements exceed those of public issues. Whether this disadvantage is enough to offset the reduced flotation costs associated with a private placement is a determination the financial manager must make. There is some evidence that on smaller issues, say $500,000 as opposed to $30 million, the private placement alternative would be preferable.
2. **Restrictive covenants.** Dividend policy, working-capital levels, and the raising of additional debt capital may all be affected by provisions in the private-placement debt contract. That is not to say that such restrictions are always absent in public debt contracts. Rather, the financial officer must be alert to the tendency for these covenants to be especially burdensome in private contracts.
3. **The possibility of future SEC registration.** If the lender (investor) should decide to sell the issue to a public buyer before maturity, the issue must be registered with the SEC. Some lenders, then, require that the issuing firm agree to a future registration at their option.

FLOTATION COSTS

The firm raising long-term capital incurs two types of **flotation costs:** (1) the underwriter's spread and (2) issuing costs. Of these two costs, the underwriter's spread is the larger. The **underwriter's spread** is simply the difference between the gross and net proceeds from a given security issue expressed as a percent of the gross proceeds. The **issue costs** include (1) printing and engraving, (2) legal fees, (3) accounting fees, (4) trustee fees, and (5) several other miscellaneous components. The two most significant issue costs are printing and engraving and legal fees.

Data published by the SEC have consistently revealed two relationships about flotation costs. First, the costs associated with issuing common stock are notably greater than the costs associated with preferred stock offerings. In turn, preferred stock costs exceed those of bonds. Second, flotation costs (expressed as a percent of gross proceeds) decrease as the size of the security issue increases.

In the first instance, the stated relationship reflects the fact that issue costs are sensitive to the risks involved in successfully distributing a security issue. Common stock is riskier to own than corporate bonds. Underwriting risk is, therefore, greater with common stock than with bonds. Thus, flotation costs just mirror these risk relationships. In the second case, a portion of the issue costs is fixed. Legal fees and accounting costs are good examples. So, as the size of the security issue rises, the fixed component is spread over a larger gross proceeds base. As a consequence, average flotation costs vary inversely with the size of the issue.

REGULATION

Following the severe economic downturn of 1929–32, Congressional action was taken to provide for federal regulation of the securities markets. State statutes (blue sky laws) also govern the securities markets where applicable, but the federal regulations are clearly more pressing and important. The major federal regulations are reviewed here.

Primary Market Regulations

The new issues market is governed by the Securities Act of 1933. The intent of the act is important. It aims to provide potential investors with accurate, truthful disclosure about the firm and the new securities being offered to the public. This does *not* prevent firms from issuing highly speculative securities. The SEC says nothing whatsoever about the possible investment worth of a given offering. It is up to the investor to separate the junk from the jewels. The SEC does have the legal power and responsibility to enforce the 1933 act.

Full public disclosure is achieved by the requirement that the issuing firm file a registration statement with the SEC containing requisite information. The statement details particulars about the firm and the new security being issued. During a minimum 20-day waiting period, the SEC examines the submitted document. In numerous instances the 20-day wait has been extended by several weeks. The SEC can ask for additional information that was omitted in order to clarify the original document. The SEC can also order that the offering be stopped.

During the registration process a preliminary prospectus (the red herring) may be distributed to potential investors. When the registration is approved, the final prospectus must be made available to the prospective investors. The prospectus is actually a condensed version of the full registration statement. If, at a later date, the information in the registration statement and the prospectus is found to be lacking, purchasers of the new issue who incurred a loss can sue for damages. Officers of the issuing firm and others who took part in the registration and marketing of the issue may suffer both civil and criminal penalties.

Generally, the SEC defines public issues as those that are sold to more than 25 investors. Some public issues need not be registered. These include

1. Relatively small issues where the firm sells less than $1.5 million of new securities per year.
2. Issues that are sold entirely intrastate.
3. Issues that are basically short-term instruments. This translates into maturity periods of 270 days or less.
4. Issues that are already regulated or controlled by some other federal agency. Examples here are the Federal Power Commission (public utilities) and the Interstate Commerce Commission (railroads).

Secondary Market Regulations

Secondary market trading is regulated by the **Securities Exchange Act of 1934.** This act created the SEC to enforce federal securities laws. The Federal Trade Commission enforced the 1933 act for one year. The major aspects of the 1934 act can be best presented in outline form:

1. Major security exchanges must register with the SEC. This regulates the exchanges and places reporting requirements on the firms whose securities are listed on them.
2. Insider trading is regulated. Insiders can be officers, directors, employees, relatives, major investors, or anyone having information about the operation of the firm that is not public knowledge. If an investor purchases the security of the firm in which the investor is an insider, he or she must hold it for at least six months before disposing of it. Otherwise, profits made from trading the stock within a period of less than six months must be returned to the firm. Furthermore, insiders must file with the SEC a monthly statement of holdings and transactions in the stock of their corporation.[7]

[7]On November 14, 1986, the SEC announced that Ivan F. Boesky had admitted to illegal inside trading after an intensive investigation. Boesky at the time was a very well-known Wall Street investor, speculator, and arbitrageur. Boesky was an owner or part owner in several companies, including an arbitrage fund named Ivan F. Boesky & Co. L. P. Boesky agreed to pay the U.S. government $50 million, which represented a return of illegal profits, another $50 million in civil penalties; to withdraw permanently from the securities industry; and to plead guilty to criminal charges. The far-reaching investigation continued into 1987 and implicated several other prominent investment figures.

The chairman of the SEC during this period was John S. R. Shad. Shad suggested that security trades would be considered illegal if they were based on "material, nonpublic information." As you would expect, this insider trading case garnered a lot of attention in the popular business press and led to renewed discussions of ethics in business schools. See "Who'll Be the Next to Fall?" *Business Week,* December 1, 1986, pp. 28–30; "Wall Street Enters the Age of the Supergrass," *The Economist,* November 22–28, 1986, pp. 77–78; "Going After the Crooks," *Time,* December 1, 1986, pp. 48–51, and "The Decline and Fall of Business Ethics," *Fortune* 114, December 8, 1986, pp. 65–66, 68, 72.

3. Manipulative trading of securities by investors to affect stock prices is prohibited.
4. The SEC is given control over proxy procedures.
5. The Board of Governors of the Federal Reserve System is given responsibility for setting margin requirements. This affects the flow of credit into the securities markets. Buying securities on margin simply means using credit to acquire a portion of the subject financial instruments.

MORE RECENT REGULATORY DEVELOPMENTS

Securities Acts Amendments of 1975

The Securities Acts Amendments of 1975 touched on three important issues. First, Congress mandated the creation of a national market system (NMS). Only broad goals for this national exchange were identified by Congress. Implementation details were left to the SEC and, to a much lesser extent, the securities industry in general. Congress was really expressing its desire for (1) widespread application of auction market trading principles, (2) a high degree of competition across markets, and (3) the use of modern electronic communication systems to link the fragmented markets in the country into a true NMS. The NMS is still a goal toward which the SEC and the securities industry are moving. Agreement as to its final form and an implementation date have not occurred.

A second major alteration in the habits of the securities industry also took place in 1975. This was the elimination of fixed commissions (fixed brokerage rates) on public transactions in securities. This was closely tied to the desire for an NMS in that fixed brokerage fees provided no incentive for competition among brokers. A third consideration of the 1975 amendments focused on such financial institutions as commercial banks and insurance firms. These financial institutions were prohibited from acquiring membership on stock exchanges in order to reduce or save commissions on their own trades.

Shelf Registration

On March 16, 1982, the SEC began a new procedure for registering new issues of securities. Formally it is called SEC Rule 415; informally the process is known as a **shelf registration,** or a **shelf offering.** The essence of the process is rather simple. Rather than go through the lengthy, full registration process each time the firm plans an offering of securities, it can get a blanket order approved by the SEC. A master registration statement that covers the financing plans of the firm over the coming two years is filed with the SEC. On approval, the firm can market some or all of the securities over this two-year period. The securities are sold in a piecemeal fashion, or "off the shelf." Prior to each specific offering, a short statement about the issue is filed with the SEC.

Corporations raising funds approve of this new procedure. The tedious full registration process is avoided with each offering pulled off the shelf. This should result in a saving of fees paid to investment bankers. Moreover, an issue can more quickly be brought to the market. Also, if market conditions change, an issue can easily be redesigned to fit the specific conditions of the moment.

As is always the case, there is another side to the story. Recall that the reason for the registration process in the first place is to give investors useful information about the firm and the securities being offered. Under the shelf registration procedure some of the information about the issuing firm becomes old as the two-year horizon unfolds. Some investment bankers feel they do not have the proper amount of time to study the firm when a shelf offering takes place. This is one of those areas of finance where more observations are needed before any final conclusions can be made. Those observations will only come with the passage of time.

RATES OF RETURN IN THE FINANCIAL MARKETS

Earlier in this chapter in discussing "the financing process" we noted that net users of funds (saving-deficit economic units) must compete with one another for the funds supplied by net savers (savings-surplus economic units). Consequently, to obtain financing for projects that will benefit the firm's stockholders, that firm must offer the supplier (savings-surplus unit) a rate of return *competitive* with the next best investment alternative available to that saver (investor). This rate of return on the next best investment alternative to the saver is known as the supplier's **opportunity cost of funds.** The opportunity cost concept is crucial in financial management.

Rates of Return Over Long Periods

History can tell us a great deal about the returns that investors earn in the financial markets. A primary source for a historical perspective comes from Ibbotson and Sinquefield's *Stocks, Bonds, Bills, and Inflation,* which examines the realized rates of return for a wide variety of securities spanning the period from 1926 through 1990.[8] As part of their study, Ibbotson and Sinquefield calculated the average annual rates of return investors earned over the preceding 64 years, along with the average inflation rate for the same period.

Ibbotson and Sinquefield's results are summarized in Figure 16-9. These returns represent the average inflation rate and the average observed rates of return for different types of securities. The average inflation rate was 3.2% for the period covered by the study. We will refer to this rate as the "inflation-risk premium." The investor who earns only the rate of inflation has earned no "real return." That is, the *real return* is the return earned above the rate of increase in the general price level for goods and services in the economy, which is the inflation rate. In addition to the danger of not earning above the inflation rate, investors are concerned about the risk of the borrower defaulting or failing to repay the loan when due. Thus, we would expect a default-risk premium for long-term corporate bonds over long-term government bonds. We would also expect an even greater risk premium for common stocks visa-vis long-term corporate bonds, since the variability in average returns is greater for common stocks. The Ibbotson and Sinquefield study verifies such a risk premium. Finally, there is even a greater risk premium associated with the common stock of small firms when compared with all common stocks. This small-firm or "size" risk premium probably reflects the lack of information available for small firms.

---

[8]Roger G. Ibbotson and Rex A. Sinquefield, *Stocks, Bonds, Bills, and Inflation: Historical Returns* (Chicago: Dow Jones-Irwin, 1991).

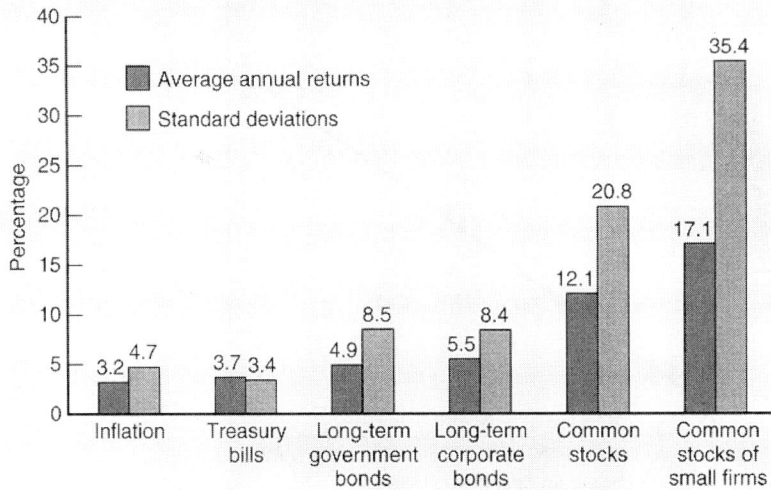

FIGURE 16-9
Average Annual Returns and Standard Deviations of Returns

Source: Roger G. Ibbotson and Rex A. Sinquefield, *Stocks, Bonds, Bills, and Inflation: Historical Returns* (Chicago: Dow Jones-Irwin, 1991. © Ibbotson Associates.)

Remember: the greater the risk, the greater will be the expected returns. Such a relationship is shown in Figure 16-10.

Interest Rate Levels over Recent Periods

The *nominal* interest rates on some key fixed-income securities are displayed within both Figure 16-11 and Figure 16-12 for the 1981–1992 time frame. The rate of inflation

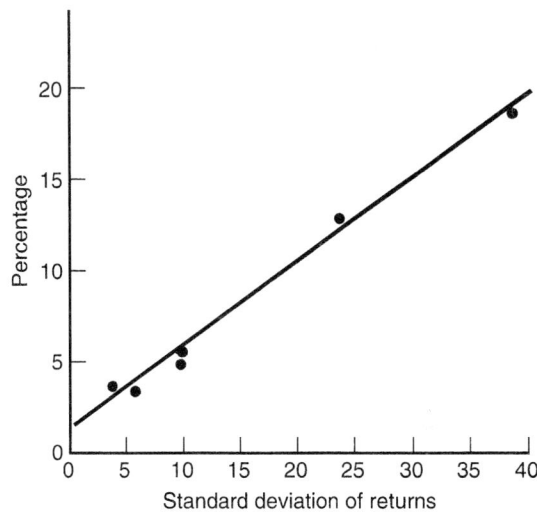

FIGURE 16-10
Rates of Return 1926–90

FIGURE 16-11 Interest Rate Levels and Inflation Rates 1981–1992

Year	3-Month Treasury Bills	30-Year Treasury Bonds	Aaa Rated Corporate Bonds	Inflation Rate
1981	14.08%	13.44%	14.17%	8.9%
1982	10.69	12.76	13.79	3.9
1983	8.63	11.18	12.04	3.8
1984	9.52	12.39	12.71	4.0
1985	7.49	10.79	11.37	3.8
1986	5.98	7.80	9.02	1.1
1987	5.82	8.58	9.38	4.4
1988	6.68	8.96	9.71	4.4
1989	8.12	8.45	9.26	4.6
1990	7.51	8.61	9.32	6.1
1991	5.42	8.14	8.77	3.1
1992	3.45	7.67	8.14	2.9
Mean	7.78%	9.90%	10.64%	4 25%

Source: *Federal Reserve Bulletin*, various issues, and *Federal Reserve Statistical Release* H.15 (519), various issues.

at the consumer level is also presented in those two exhibits. This allows us to observe quite easily several concepts that were mentioned in the section above. Specifically, we can observe (1) the inflation-risk premium, (2) the default-risk premium across the several instruments, and (3) the real return for each instrument. Looking at the mean (average) values for each security and the inflation rate at the bottom of Figure 16-11 will facilitate the discussion.

Notice that the average inflation rate over this more recent period is higher than reported in the longer period covered by the Ibbotson and Sinquefield analysis. According to the logic of the financial markets, investors will *require* a nominal rate of

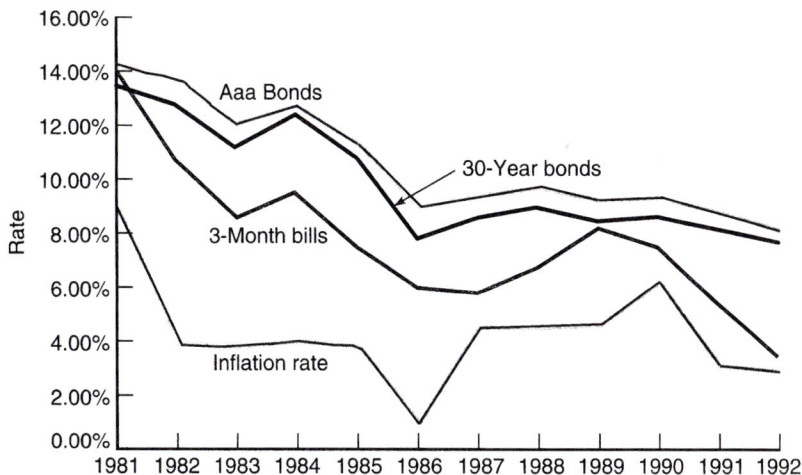

FIGURE 16-12
Interest Rate Levels and Inflation Rates 1981–1992

interest that exceeds the inflation rate or else their realized *real* return will be negative. Earning a negative return over long periods of time is not very smart.

Figure 16-11 indicates that investor rationality prevailed. For example, the average inflation-risk premium demanded on U.S. Treasury bills with a three-month maturity was 3.53% (or 353 basis points). That is, an average 7.78% yield on Treasury bills over the period *minus* the average inflation rate of 4.25% over the same period produces a premium of 3.53%.

The default-risk premium is also evident in Figure 16-11 and Figure 16-12. If we array the securities in these two exhibits from low risk to high risk the following tabulation results:

Security	Yield
3-month Treasury bills	7.78%
30-year Treasury bonds	9.90
Aaa Corporate bonds	10.64

Again, the basic rationale of the financial markets prevailed. The default-risk premium on high-rated (Aaa) corporate bonds relative to long-term Treasury bonds of 30-year maturity was 0.74%.

The array above can also be used to identify another factor that affects interest rate levels. It is referred to as the "maturity premium." This maturity premium arises even if securities possess equal (or approximately equal) odds of default. This is the case with Treasury bills and Treasury bonds, for instance, since the full faith and credit of the U.S. government stands behind these financial contracts. They are considered risk free (i.e., possessing no chance of default).

Notice that Treasury bonds with a 30-year maturity commanded a 2.12% yield differential over the shorter, three-month-to-maturity Treasury bonds. This provides an estimate of the maturity premium demanded by investors over this specific 1981–1992 period. More precisely, the *maturity premium* can be defined as: **The additional return required by investors in longer-term securities (bonds in this case) to compensate them for the greater risk of price fluctuations on those securities caused by interest rate changes.**

One other type of risk premium that helps determine interest rate levels needs to be identified and defined. It is known as the "liquidity premium." The *liquidity premium* is defined as: **The additional return required by investors in securities that cannot be quickly converted into cash at a reasonably predictable price.**

The secondary markets for small-bank stocks, especially community banks, provide a good example of the liquidity premium. A bank holding company that trades on the New York Stock Exchange, like Barnett Bank, will be more liquid to investors than, say, the common stock of Citizens National Bank of Leesburg, Florida. Such a liquidity premium will be reflected across the spectrum of financial assets, from bonds to stocks.

Back to the Fundamentals

Axiom 1: The Risk-Return Tradeoff—We Won't Take on Additional Risk Unless We Expect To Be Compensated with Additional Return established the fundamental risk-return tradeoffs that govern the financial markets. We are now trying to provide you with an understanding of the kinds of risks that are rewarded in the risk-return tradeoff presented in **Axiom 1.**

INTEREST RATE DETERMINANTS IN A NUTSHELL

Our review of rates of return and interest rate levels in the financial markets permits us to synthesize our introduction to the different types of risks that impact interest rates. We can, thereby, generate a simple equation with the **nominal** (i.e., observed) rate of interest being the output variable from the equation. The nominal interest rate is sometimes called the "quoted" rate. It is the rate that you would read about in the *Wall Street Journal* for a specific fixed-income security. That equation follows:

$$k = k^* + IRP + DRP + MP + LP \tag{1}$$

where: k = the nominal or observed rate of interest on a specific fixed-income security.

k^* = the real risk-free rate of interest; it is the required rate of interest on a fixed-income security that has no risk and in an economic environment of zero inflation. This can be reasonably thought of as the rate of interest demanded by investors in U.S. Treasury securities during periods of no inflation.

IRP = the inflation-risk premium.

DRP = the default-risk premium.

MP = the maturity premium.

LP = the liquidity premium.

Sometimes in analyzing interest rate relationships over time it is of use to focus on what is called the "nominal risk-free rate of interest." Again, by nominal we mean "observed." So let us designate the nominal risk-free interest rate as k_{rf}. Drawing, then, on our discussions and notation from above we can write this expression for k_{rf}:

$$k_{rf} = k^* + IRP \tag{2}$$

This equation just says that the nominal risk-free rate of interest is equal to the real risk-free interest rate plus the inflation-risk premium. It also provides a quick and *approximate* way of estimating the risk-free rate of interest, k^*, by solving directly for this rate. This basic relationship in equation (2) contains important information for the financial decision maker. It has also for years been the subject of fascinating and lengthy discussions among financial economists. We will look more at the substance of the real rate of interest in the next section. In this following section we will improve on equation (2) by making it more precise.

The Effects of Inflation on Rates of Return and the Fisher Effect

When a rate of interest is quoted, it is generally the nominal, or observed rate. The **real rate of interest,** on the other hand, represents the rate of increase in actual purchasing power, after adjusting for inflation. For example, if you have $100 today and loan it to someone for a year at a nominal rate of interest of 11.3%, you will get back $111.30 in one year. But if during the year prices of goods and services rise by 5%, it will take $105 at year end to purchase the same goods and services that $100 purchased at the beginning of the year. What was your increase in purchasing power over the year? The quick and dirty answer is found by subtracting the inflation rate from the nominal rate, 11.3% − 5% = 6.3%, but this is not exactly correct. To be more precise, let the nominal rate of interest be represented by k_{rf}, the anticipated rate of inflation by IRP, and the real rate of interest by k^*. Using these notations, we can express the relationship among the nominal interest rate, the rate of inflation, and the real rate of interest as follows:

$$1 + k_{rf} = (1 + k^*)(1 + IRP) \tag{3}$$

or

$$k_{rf} = k^* + IRP + (k^* \times IRP)$$

Consequently, the nominal rate of interest (k_{rf}) is equal to the sum of the real rate of interest (k^*), the inflation rate (IRP), and the product of the real rate and the inflation rate. This relationship among nominal rates, real rates, and the rate of inflation has come to be called the **Fisher effect.**[9] It means that the observed nominal rate of interest includes both the real rate and an *inflation premium* as noted in the previous section.

Substituting into equation (3) using a nominal rate of 11.3% and an inflation rate of 5%, we can calculate the real rate of interest, k^*, as follows:

$$k_{rf} = k^* + IRP + (k^* \times IRP)$$
$$.113 = k^* + .05 + .05k^*$$
$$k^* = .06 = 6\%$$

Thus, at the new higher prices, your purchasing power will have increased by only 6%, although you have $11.30 more than you had at the start of the year. To see why, let's assume that at the outset of the year one unit of the market basket of goods and services costs $1, so you could purchase 100 units with your $100. At the end of the year you have $11.30 more, but each unit now costs 1.05 (remember the 5% rate of inflation). How many units can you buy at the end of the year? The answer is $111.30 ÷ $1.05 = 106, which represents a 6% increase in real purchasing power.

THE TERM STRUCTURE OF INTEREST RATES

The relationship between a debt security's rate of return and the length of time until the debt matures is known as the **term structure of interest rates** or the **yield to maturity.** For the relationship to be meaningful to us, all the factors other than maturity, meaning factors such as the chance of the bond defaulting, must be held constant. Thus, the term structure reflects observed rates or yields on similar securities, except for the length of time until maturity, at a particular moment in time.

Figure 16-13 shows an example of the term structure of interest rates. The curve is upward sloping, indicating that longer terms to maturity command higher returns, or yields. In this hypothetical term structure, the rate of interest on a 5-year note or bond is 11.5%, whereas the comparable rate on a 20-year bond is 13%.

---

[9]This relationship was analyzed many years ago by Irving Fisher.

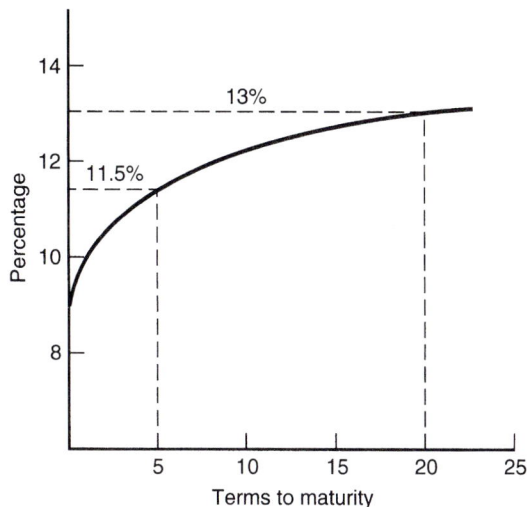

FIGURE 16-13
The Term Structure of Interest Rates

Observing Historical Term Structures of Interest Rates

As we might expect, the term structure of interest rates changes over time, depending on the environment. The particular term structure observed today may be quite different from the term structure a month ago and different still from the term structure one month from now. A perfect example of the changing term structure, or yield curve, was witnessed during the early days of the Persian Gulf crisis in August 1990. Figure 16-14 shows the yield curves one day prior to the Iraqi invasion of Kuwait and then again just three weeks later. The change is noticeable, particularly for long-term interest rates. Investors quickly developed new fears about the prospect of increased inflation to be caused by the crisis and consequently increased their required rates of return.

Although the upward sloping term structure curves in Figures 16-13 and 16-14 are the ones most commonly observed, yield curves can assume several shapes. Sometimes the term structure is downward sloping; at other times it rises and then falls (hump-backed); and at still other times it may be relatively flat. Figure 16-15 shows some yield curves at different points in time.

Trying to Explain the Shape of the Term Structure

A number of theories may explain the shape of the term structure of interest rates at any point. Three possible explanations are prominent: (1) the unbiased expectations theory, (2) the liquidity preference theory, and (3) the market segmentation theory.[10] Let's look at each in turn.

---

[10]See Richard Roll, *The Behavior of Interest Rates: An Application of the Efficient Market Model to U.S. Treasury Bills* (New York: Basic Books, 1970).

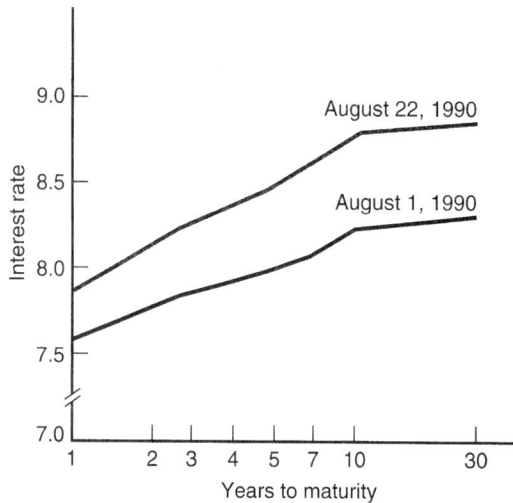

FIGURE 16-14
Changes in the Term Structure of Interest Rates for Government Securities at the Outbreak of the Persian Gulf Crisis

The Unbiased Expectations Theory

The **unbiased expectations theory** says that the term structure is determined by an investors expectations about future interest rates.[11] To see how this works, consider the following investment problem faced by Mary Maxell. Mary has $10,000 that she wants to invest for two years, at which time she plans to use her savings to make a down payment on a new home. Wanting not to take any risk of losing her savings, she decides to invest in U.S. government securities. She has two choices. First, she can purchase a government security that matures in two years, which offers her an interest rate of 9% per year. If she does this, she will have $11,881 in two years, calculated as follows:[12]

Principal amount	$10,000
Plus: Year 1 interest (.09 × $10,000)	900
Principal plus interest at the end of year 1	$10,900
Plus: Year 2 interest (.09 × $10,900)	981
Principal plus interest at the end of year 2	**$11,881**

Alternatively, Mary could buy a government security maturing in one year that pays an 8% rate of interest. She would then need to purchase another one-year secu-

---

[11]Irving Fisher thought of this idea in 1896. The theory was later refined by J. R. Hicks in *Value and Capital* (London: Oxford University Press, 1946) and F. A. Lutz and V. C. Lutz in *The Theory of Investment in the Firm* (Princeton, NJ: Princeton University Press, 1951).
[12]We could also calculate the principal plus interest for Mary's investment using the following compound interest equation: $10,000 (1 + 09)^2 = $11,881.

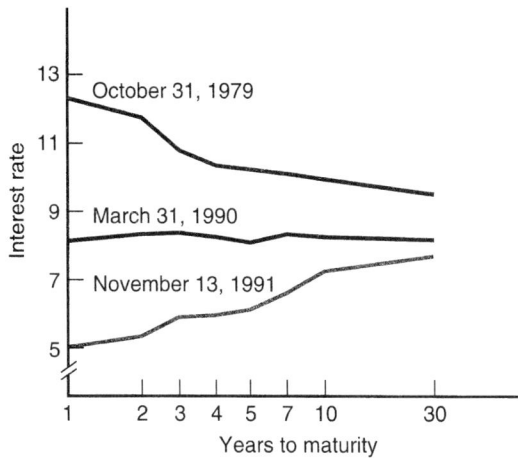

FIGURE 16-15
Historical Term Structures of Interest Rates for Government Securities

rity at the end of the first year. Which alternative Mary will prefer obviously depends in part on the rate of interest she expects to receive on the government security she will purchase a year from now. We cannot tell Mary what the interest rate will be in a year; however, we can at least calculate the rate that will give her the same two-year total savings she would get from her first choice, or $11,881. The interest rate can be calculated as follows:

Savings needed in two years	$11,881
Savings at the end of the first year	
$10,000 (1 + .08)	$10,000
Interest needed in year two	**$ 1,081**

For Mary to receive $1,081 in the second year, she would have to earn about 10% on her second-year investment, computed as follows:

$$\frac{\text{interest received in year 2}}{\text{investment made at beginning of year 2}} = \frac{\$1,081}{\$10,800} = 10\%$$

So the term structure of interest rates for our example consists of the one-year interest rate of 8% and the two-year rate of 9%, which is shown in Figure 16-16. This exercise also gives us information about the *expected* one-year rate for investments made one year hence. In a sense, the term structure contains implications about investor expectations of future interest rates; thus, this explains the unbiased expectations theory of the term structure of interest rates.

Although we can see a relationship between current interest rates with different maturities and the investor's expectations about future interest rates, is this the whole story? Are there influences other than the investor's expectations about future interest rates? Probably, so let's continue to think about Mary's dilemma.

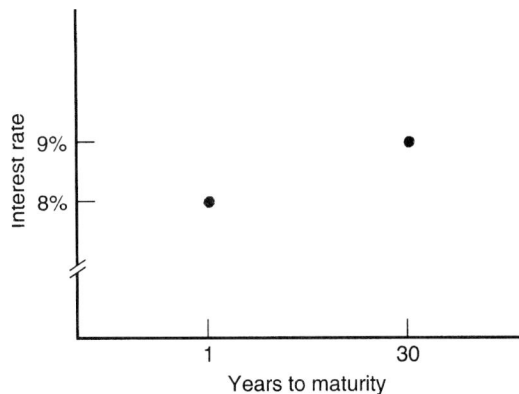

FIGURE 16-16
Term Structure of Interest Rates

Liquidity Preference Theory

In presenting Mary's choices, we have suggested that she would be indifferent to a choice between the two-year government security offering a 9% return and two consecutive one-year investments offering 8 and 10%, respectively. However, that would be so only if she is unconcerned about the risk associated with not knowing the rate of interest on the second security as of today. If Mary is risk averse (that is, she dislikes risk), she might not be satisfied with expectations of a 10% return on the second one-year government security. She might require some additional expected return to be truly indifferent. Mary might in fact decide that she will expose herself to the uncertainty of future interest rates only if she can reasonably *expect* to earn an additional .5% in interest, or 10.5%, on the second one-year investment. This *risk premium* (additional required interest rate) to compensate for the risk of changing future interest rates is nothing more than the maturity premium **(MP)** introduced earlier, and this concept underlies the liquidity preference theory of the term structure.[13] In the **liquidity preference theory,** investors require maturity premiums to compensate them for buying securities that expose them to the risks of fluctuating interest rates.

Market Segmentation Theory

The **market segmentation theory** is the third popular theory of the term structure of interest rates. This concept is built on the notion that legal restrictions and personal preferences limit choices for investors to certain ranges of maturities. For example, commercial banks prefer short- to medium-term maturities as a result of the short-term nature of their deposit liabilities. They prefer not to invest in long-term securities. Life insurance companies, on the other hand, have longer-term liabilities, so they prefer longer maturities in investments. At the extreme, the market segmenta-

---

[13]This theory was first presented by John R. Hicks in *Value and Capital* (London: Oxford University Press, 1946), pp. 141–145, with the risk premium referred to as the liquidity premium. For our purposes we will use the term **maturity premium (MP)** to describe this risk premium, thereby keeping our terminology consistent within this chapter.

tion theory implies that the rate of interest for a particular maturity is determined solely by demand and supply for a given maturity and that it is independent of the demand and supply for securities having different maturities. A more moderate version of the theory allows investors strong maturity preferences, but it also allows them to modify their feelings and preferences if significant yield inducements occur.

SUMMARY

This chapter centers on the market environment in which corporations raise long-term funds, including the structure of the U.S. financial markets, the institution of investment banking, and the various methods for distributing securities. It also discusses the role of interest rates in allocating savings to ultimate investment.

Mix of Corporate Securities Sold

When corporations go to the capital market for cash, the most favored financing method is debt. The corporate debt markets clearly dominate the equity markets when new funds are raised. The U.S. tax system inherently favors debt capital as a fundraising method. In an average year over the 1981–91 period, bonds and notes made up 72% of external cash that was raised.

Why Financial Markets Exist

The function of financial markets is to allocate savings efficiently in the economy to the ultimate demander (user) of the savings. In a financial market the forces of supply and demand for a specific financial instrument are brought together. The wealth of an economy would not be as great as it is without a fully developed financial market system.

Financing of Business

Every year households are a net supplier of funds to the financial markets. The nonfinancial business sector is always a net borrower of funds. Both life insurance companies and private pension funds are important buyers of corporate securities. Savings are ultimately transferred to the business firm seeking cash by means of (1) the direct transfer, (2) the indirect transfer using the investment banker, or (3) the indirect transfer using the financial intermediary.

Components of U.S. Financial Market System

Corporations can raise funds through public offerings or private placements. The public market is impersonal in that the security issuer does not meet the ultimate investors in the financial instruments. In a private placement, the securities are sold directly to a limited number of institutional investors.

The primary market is the market for new issues. The secondary market represents transactions in currently outstanding securities. Both the money and capital markets have primary and secondary sides. The money market refers to transactions in short-term debt instruments. The capital market, on the other hand, refers to transactions in long-term financial instruments. Trading in the money and capital markets can occur in either the organized security exchanges or the over-the-counter market. The money market is exclusively an over-the-counter market.

Investment Banker

The investment banker is a financial specialist involved as an intermediary in the merchandising of securities. He or she performs the functions of (1) underwriting, (2) distributing, and (3) advising. Major methods for the public distribution of securities include (1) the negotiated purchase, (2) the competitive bid purchase, (3) the commission or best-efforts basis, (4) privileged subscriptions, and (5) direct sales. The direct sale bypasses the use of an investment banker. The negotiated purchase is the most profitable distribution method to the investment banker. It also provides the greatest amount of investment banking services to the corporate client.

Private Placements

Privately placed debt provides an important market outlet for corporate bonds. Major investors in this market are (1) life insurance firms, (2) state and local retirement funds, and (3) private pension funds. Several advantages and disadvantages are associated with private placements. The financial officer must weigh these attributes and decide if a private placement is preferable to a public offering.

Flotation Costs

Flotation costs consist of the underwriter's spread and issuing costs. The flotation costs of common stock exceed those of preferred stock, which, in turn, exceed those of debt. Moreover, flotation costs as a percent of gross proceeds are inversely related to the size of the security issue.

Regulation

The new issues market is regulated at the federal level by the Securities Act of 1933. It provides for the registration of new issues with the SEC. Secondary market trading is regulated by the Securities Exchange Act of 1934. The Securities Acts Amendments of 1975 placed on the SEC the responsibility for devising a national market system. This concept is still being studied. The shelf registration procedure (SEC Rule 415) was initiated in March 1982. Under this regulation and with the proper filing of documents, firms that are selling new issues do not have to go through the old, lengthy registration process each time the firm plans an offering of securities.

The Logic of Rates of Return and Interest Rate Determination

The financial markets give managers an informed indication of investors' opportunity costs. The more efficient the market, the more informed the indication. This information is a useful input about the rates of return that investors require on financial claims. In turn, this will become useful to financial managers as they estimate the overall cost of capital used as a screening rate in the capital budgeting process.

Rates of return on various securities are based on the underlying supply of loanable funds (savings) and demand for those loanable funds. In addition to a risk-free return, investors will want to be compensated for the potential loss of purchasing power resulting from inflation. Moreover, investors require a greater return the greater the default-risk, maturity premium, and liquidity premium are on the securities being analyzed.

QUESTIONS

1. What are financial markets? What function do they perform? How would an economy be worse off without them?
2. Define in a technical sense what we mean by *financial intermediary.* Give an example of your definition.
3. Distinguish between the money and capital markets.
4. What major benefits do corporations and investors enjoy because of the existence of organized security exchanges?
5. What are the general categories examined by an organized exchange in determining whether an applicant firm's securities can be listed on it? (Specific numbers are not needed here, but rather areas of investigation.)
6. Why do you think most secondary market trading in bonds takes place over-the-counter?
7. What is an investment banker, and what major functions does he or she perform?
8. What is the major difference between a negotiated purchase and a competitive bid purchase?
9. Why is an investment banking syndicate formed?
10. Why might a large corporation want to raise long-term capital through a private placement rather than a public offering?
11. As a recent business school graduate, you work directly for the corporate treasurer. Your corporation is going to issue a new security and is concerned with the probable flotation costs. What tendencies about flotation costs can you relate to the treasurer?
12. When corporations raise funds, what type of financing vehicle (instrument or instruments) is most favored?
13. What is the major (most significant) savings-surplus sector in the U.S. economy?
14. Identify three distinct ways that savings are ultimately transferred to business firms in need of cash.
15. Explain the term opportunity cost with respect to cost of funds to the firm.
16. Compare and explain the historical rates of return for different types of securities.
17. Explain the impact of inflation on rates of return.

18. Define the term structure of interest rates.
19. Explain the popular theories for the rationale of the term structure of interest rates.

PROBLEMS

1. What would you expect the nominal rate of interest to be if the real rate is 4% and the expected inflation rate is 7%?

2. Assume the expected inflation rate to be 4%. If the current real rate of interest is 6%, what ought the nominal rate of interest be?

3. Assume the expected inflation rate to be 5%. If the current real rate of interest is 7%, what would you expect the nominal rate of interest to be?

ADDENDUM 16: READING THE BOND AND STOCK TABLES

KEEPING TABS ON CORPORATE BONDS

Many daily newspapers, such as *The Wall Street Journal*, report bond transactions that occur on the NYSE and AMEX. Although not stated in the newspapers, the par value of these bonds is $1,000. Figure 16-17 shows information about NYSE bonds traded April 20, 1994. *Volume* of $35,960,000 is the par value of bonds traded on this date. This number differs from the actual market value of the bonds traded, since bond prices vary from par value. The dollar volume reported is a small fraction—1 to 12%—of all the bonds traded on that day because most bonds trade in the OTC market or directly among market makers (brokerage houses) for institutional investors. Fred Zuckerman, treasurer of RJR Nabisco Holdings Corporation, which lists its debt on the NYSE, says: "You're not legally obligated to list your bonds, but you are morally obligated to. Institutional investors can take care of themselves but you owe a lot more to the individual investors."[14] Unfortunately, this view is not shared widely by many corporations.

Issues traded lists the number of different bonds sold on April 20 and on the previous trading day. *Advances* shows the number of bonds that traded at a price higher than on the previous day. *Declines* represents the number of bonds that traded at a price below the price of the previous trading day. *Unchanged* indicates the number of bonds with no price changes from the previous day. *New highs* lists the number of bonds trading at all-time highs. *New lows* shows the number of bonds trading at all-time lows. The *Dow Jones Bond Averages* are straight arithmetic summaries and averages of the prices of 20 selected utility and industrial bonds.

The highlighted Navistar Company *(Navstr)* bond has a coupon rate of 9% and the bond matures in the year 2004. This is shown by the coding *9s04.* The bond promises to pay the bearer $90 a year (that is, 9% ¥ $1000 par value) until it matures. The *s*

---

[14]See Leslie Scism, "Big Board Fights to Revive Bond Market," *The Wall Street Journal*, May 27, 1993, p. C1.

NEW YORK EXCHANGE BONDS

Quotations as of 4 p.m. Eastern Time
Wednesday, April 20, 1994

Volume $35,960,000

	Domestic		All Issues	
	Wed.	Tue.	Wed.	Tue.
Issues traded	352	393	360	398
Advances	106	115	107	116
Declines	162	209	168	213
Unchanged	84	69	85	69
New highs	1	0	1	0
New lows	86	100	91	103

SALES SINCE JANUARY 1
(000 omitted)

1994	1993	1992
$2,578,365	$3,533,852	$4,243,408

Dow Jones Bond Averages

—1993—		—1994—				---1994---			--1993--	
High	Low	High	Low			Close	Chg.	%Yld	Close	Chg.
109.77	103.49	105.61	98.49	20 Bonds		98.49	−0.10	7.33	107.00	+0.16
105.59	102.30	103.43	96.25	10 Utilities		96.30	+0.05	7.65	104.06	−0.07
114.51	104.58	107.93	100.68	10 Industrials		100.68	−0.25	7.02	109.95	+0.39

NASDAQ

Convertible Debentures

Wednesday, April 20, 1994

FIGURE 16-17
New York Stock Exchange Bonds

Source: *The Wall Street Journal*, April 21, 1994, p. C16.

appearing after the interest rate is not a meaningful symbol. It is used simply to separate the interest rate figures from the following figures. Usually *s* appears when the interest rate does not include a fraction and may be confused with the numbers following (see, for example, its exclusion in the quote for Harris 7 3/4 01). The *Cur Yld* column shows that the current yield is 9.2%, which is more than the 9% coupon rate.

We calculate the yield by dividing the annual coupon interest amount of $90 by the closing price of the bond listed under the *Close* column. We must multiply the closing price of 98 by 10 to obtain the true closing price of $980 (= 98 × 10). The newspaper simply quotes bond prices as a % of par value. Thus, the calculation of current yield is $90 ÷ $980 = 0.0918, or 9.2%. The *Vol* column says that $15,000 worth of face value Navistar 9s04 bonds traded on April 20. The last column labeled *Net Chg.* informs us that the closing price was down 1% of par value over the previous trading day, or down $10 (= $1000 × 0.01). The New England Telephone (NETel 6 7/8 23) rows below this one shows three dots (. . .) in the net change column. This coding informs us that the April 20 closing price was the same as the previous trading day.

Bonds trade on an accrued interest basis. This means that the buyer of the bond pays to the seller, in addition to the price of the bond, a sum representing the interest that the original owner has earned since the last interest payment. Normally, interest is paid on a bond every six months. If 30 days have passed since the last interest payment, the buyer pays 30 days of accrued interest. In the preceding example of the Navistar bond, accrued interest would amount to 9% × $1000 × 30 days ÷ 360 days, or a $7.50 additional payment.

KEEPING TABS ON STOCKS

Stock quotations represent a large portion of the financial pages. Figure 16-18 shows a sample of NYSE quotations for April 20, 1994. The table provides daily information on share prices, yields, and trading volume of both preferred and common stocks of many companies that trade on the exchange. Prices are in dollars and a dollar fraction. The fractions are in eighths, or "eighths of a point." Every eighth of a dollar has a value of 12.5 cents. The figure also provides some "explanatory notes."

Interpretation of the information in the table is straightforward. Assume you have an interest in Avon Products, the cosmetic company. It is shown in the table as *AvonPdts* in the second column under the heading *Stock.*[15] The company's symbol on the NYSE is *AVP*, as indicated in the column labeled *Sym*. The two columns to the left of the company's name labeled *52 Weeks/Hi Lo* show the price range of the stock over the preceding 52 weeks. At some point in the previous 12 months, Avon's stock traded as high as $61 1/4 per share and as low as $47 5/8 per share. On April 20, 1994, the stock closed the day at a price of $58 3/4, as shown under the *Close* column. The −1/8 entry under the *Net Chg* column means the stock closed $0.125 cents lower than the previous day's close. During the day the stock sold as high as $59 1/8 and as low as $58 1/2, as shown under columns *Hi* and *Lo*, respectively. The *Vol 100s* column indicates that 270,100 shares traded on April 20.

---

[15]If the company name is followed by the letters *pf*, this means the listing is for a preferred stock.

The figure under the *Div* column estimates the company's annual dividend to be $1.80 per share. The dividend amount represents the most recent quarterly payment to shareholders multiplied by 4 to obtain an annual dividend. The dividend yield, shown under the column *Yld %*, is found by dividing the dividend amount by the closing stock price: $1.80 ÷ $58.75 = .031 or 3.1%. Yield is one calculation used by investors to compare different companies.

The remaining item, listed under column *PE*, is the price-earnings ratio. The *PE ratio* measures the relationship between the current price of the stock and the company's annual earnings per share *(EPS)*. PE is the current price of the stock divided by the EPS. The latter figure is not shown in the table but is available from other investment sources. Based on Avon's closing price of $48.25 and its PE of 15, EPS must be $3.22 (= $48.25 ÷ 15). The price-earnings ratio helps investors judge how expensive or inexpensive a stock's price is relative to its reported earnings. A PE of 15 means 15 years of constant earnings of $3.22 are necessary to repay the investment if you buy the stock at a price of $48.25 (ignoring the time value of money). In general, "out-of-favor" companies have low price-earnings ratios and popular companies have high ratios. Growth prospects of the firm greatly affect its PE ratio.

Usually, companies smaller than those listed on the NYSE trade on either the American Stock Exchange (AMEX) or over the counter. *The Wall Street Journal's* AMEX report, called "American Stock Exchange Composite Transactions," is identical in form to "NYSE Composite Transactions." Over-the-counter (OTC) stocks, generally issued by even smaller or newer companies than those traded on the AMEX, do not trade at an exchange. For OTC stocks, brokers have established a market using a computerized network referred to as NASDAQ (National Association of Securities Dealers Automated Quotations).

We can follow the OTC market in *The Wall Street Journal* in the "NASDAQ National Market Issues," a section that lists the most actively traded OTC stocks. The listing is similar to the New York and American Exchange listings. The remainder of the OTC stocks is listed with last traded price under "NASDAQ Small-Cap Issues." About every six months, a committee of the National Association of Securities Dealers meets to determine what revisions are necessary in each of these NASDAQ listings. Some stocks are downgraded because of lack of trading volume, whereas others are promoted to the higher prestige category.

Foreign shares listed in the United States trade as **American depository receipts (ADRs).** There are about 700 foreign companies currently trading as ADRs. Examples of prominent companies include the Honda Motor Company Ltd., Sony Corporation, Telefonos de Mexico, S.A. de C.V., British Telecommunications plc, and Glaxo Holdings plc. An ADR is a negotiable receipt issued by an American banking institution, such as Morgan Guaranty Trust or Citibank, in lieu of the underlying shares it holds in custody outside the United States. The bank acts as an intermediary between the foreign company's stock transfer agent and the U.S. investor. A buyer of an ADR is entitled to the same dividends and gains or losses accruing to a shareholder purchasing shares on an exchange in the home country of the company. ADRs are denominated in dollars, so price quotes reflect the latest currency exchange rates.

ADRs are either *sponsored* or *unsponsored.* For a **sponsored ADR** the foreign issuer agrees to comply with all SEC reporting requirements and signs a contract with a single depository bank. Such ADRs trade on the exchanges and NASDAQ. **Unsponsored ADRs,** by contrast, usually have more than one bank acting as deposi-

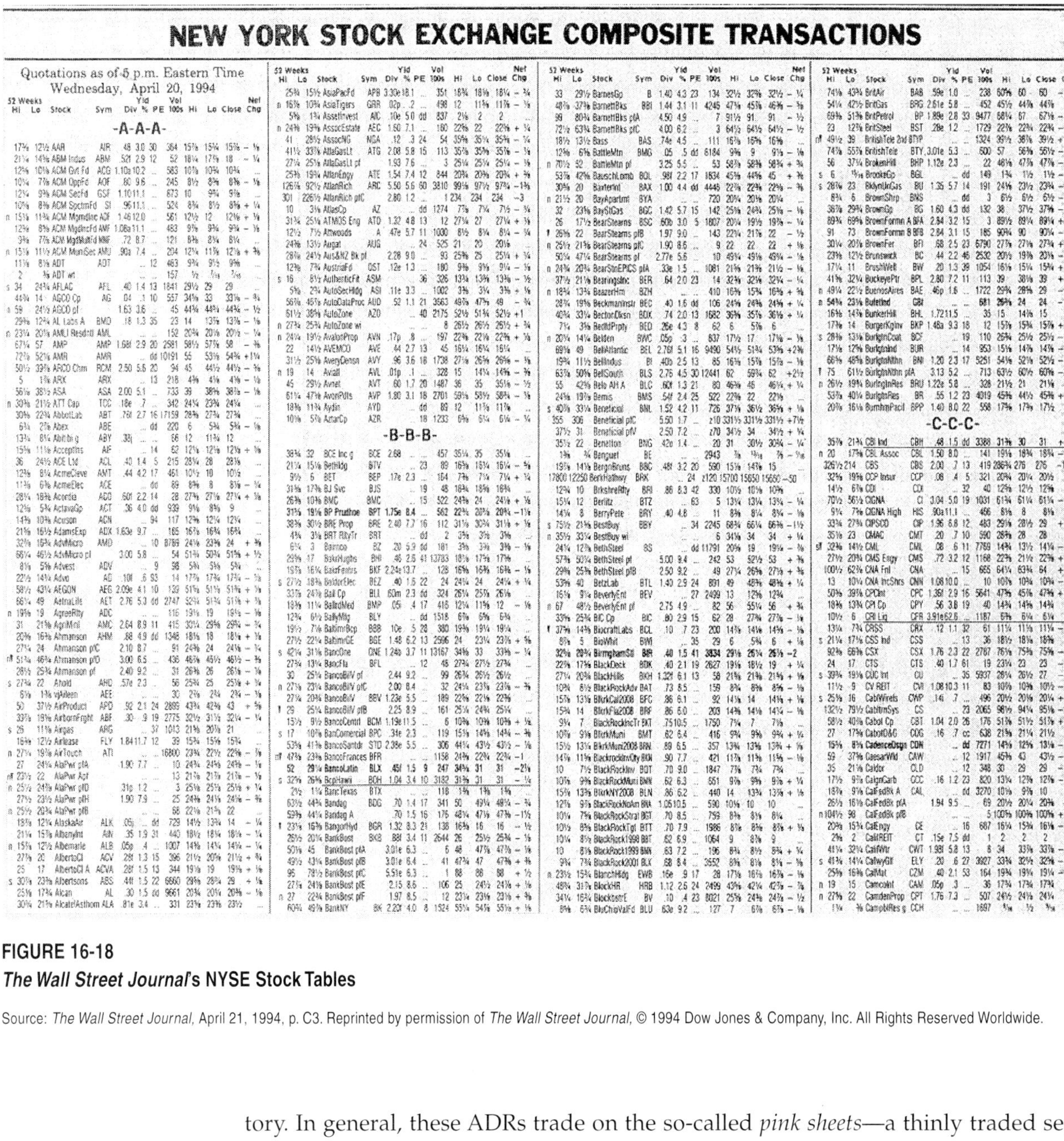
NEW YORK STOCK EXCHANGE COMPOSITE TRANSACTIONS
Quotations as of 5 p.m. Eastern Time
Wednesday, April 20, 1994
-A-A-A-
-B-B-B-
-C-C-C-

FIGURE 16-18

***The Wall Street Journal*'s NYSE Stock Tables**

Source: *The Wall Street Journal,* April 21, 1994, p. C3. Reprinted by permission of *The Wall Street Journal,* © 1994 Dow Jones & Company, Inc. All Rights Reserved Worldwide.

tory. In general, these ADRs trade on the so-called *pink sheets*—a thinly traded segment of the over-the-counter market. Although the bank registers the ADR with the SEC, less financial information is usually available for an unsponsored ADR than for a sponsored ADR.

FIGURE 16-18
(continued)

EXPLANATORY NOTES

The following explanations apply to New York and American exchange listed issues and the Nasdaq Stock Market. NYSE and Amex prices are composite quotations that include trades on the Chicago, Pacific, Philadelphia, Boston and Cincinnati exchanges and reported by the National Association of Securities Dealers.

Boldfaced quotations highlight those issues whose price changed by 5% or more if their previous closing price was $2 or higher.

Underlined quotations are those stocks with large changes in volume, per exchange, compared with the issue's average trading volume. The calculation includes common stocks of $5 a share or more with an average volume over 65 trading days of at least 5,000 shares. The underlined quotations are for the 40 largest volume percentage leaders on the NYSE and the Nasdaq National Market. It includes the 20 largest volume percentage gainers on the Amex.

The 52-week high and low columns show the highest and lowest price of the issue during the preceding 52 weeks plus the current week, but not the latest trading day. These ranges are adjusted to reflect stock payouts of 1% or more, and cash dividends or other distributions of 10% or more.

Dividend/Distribution rates, unless noted, are annual disbursements based on the last monthly, quarterly, semiannual, or annual declaration. Special or extra dividends or distributions, including return of capital, special situations or payments not designated as regular are identified by footnotes.

Yield is defined as the dividends or other distributions paid by a company on its securities, expressed as a percentage of price.

The P/E ratio is determined by dividing the closing market price by the company's primary per-share earnings for the most recent four quarters. Charges and other adjustments usually are excluded when they qualify as extraordinary items under generally accepted accounting rules.

Sales figures are the unofficial daily total of shares traded, quoted in hundreds (two zeros omitted).

Exchange ticker symbols are shown for all New York and American exchange common stocks, and Dow Jones News/Retrieval symbols are listed for Class A and Class B shares listed on both markets. Nasdaq symbols are listed for all Nasdaq NMS issues. A more detailed explanation of Nasdaq ticker symbols appears with the NMS listings.

FOOTNOTES: ▲-New 52-week high. ▼-New 52-week low. a-Extra dividend or extras in addition to the regular dividend. b-Indicates annual rate of the cash dividend and that a stock dividend was paid. c-Liquidating dividend. cc-P/E ratio is 100 or more. dd-Loss in the most recent four quarters. e-Indicates a dividend was declared in the preceding 12 months, but that there isn't a regular dividend rate. Amount shown may have been adjusted to reflect stock split, spinoff or other distribution. f-Annual rate, increased on latest declaration. g-Indicates the dividend and earnings are expressed in Canadian money. The stock trades in U.S. dollars. No yield or P/E ratio is shown. gg-Special sales condition; no regular way trading. h-Temporary exemption from Nasdaq requirements. i-Indicates amount declared or paid after a stock dividend or split. j-Indicates dividend was paid this year, and that at the last dividend meeting a dividend was omitted or deferred. k-Indicates dividend declared this year on cumulative issues with dividends in arrears. m-Annual rate, reduced on latest declaration. n -Newly issued in the past 52 weeks. The high-low range begins with the start of trading and doesn't cover the entire period. p-Initial dividend. pf-Preferred. pp-Holder owes installment(s) of purchase price. pr-Preference. r-Indicates a cash dividend declared in the preceding 12 months, plus a stock dividend. rt-Rights. s-Stock split or stock dividend amounting to 10% or more in the past 52 weeks. The high-low price is adjusted from the old stock. Dividend calculations begin with the date the split was paid or the stock dividend occurred. t-Paid in stock in the preceding 12 months, estimated cash value on ex-dividend or ex-distribution date, except some Nasdaq listings where payments are in stock. un-Units. v-Trading halted on primary market. vi-In bankruptcy or receivership or being reorganized under the Bankruptcy Code, or securities assumed by such companies. wd-When distributed. wi-When issued. wt-Warrants. ww-With warrants. x-Ex-dividend, ex-distribution, ex-rights or without warrants. z-Sales in full, not in 100s.

Working Capital Management

CHAPTER 17

Introduction to Working Capital Management

Traditionally, **working capital** has been defined as the firm's investment in current assets. **Current assets** comprise all assets that the firm expects to convert into cash within the year, including cash, marketable securities, accounts receivable, and inventories. Managing the firm's working capital, however, has come to mean more than simply managing the firm's investment in current assets. In fact, a more descriptive title for this chapter might be "Net Working-Capital Management," where **net working capital** refers to the difference in the firm's current assets and its current liabilities:

$$\text{net working capital} = \text{current assets} - \text{current liabilities} \tag{1}$$

Thus, in managing the firm's net working capital, we are concerned with *managing the firm's liquidity.* This entails managing two related aspects of the firm's operations:

1. Investment in current assets
2. Use of short-term or current liabilities

This chapter provides the basic principles underlying the analysis of each of these aspects.

In examining investment in current assets and the use of short-term liabilities, two major issues are involved: (1) How much short-term financing should the firm use? and (2) What specific sources of short-term financing should the firm select? We will first use the hedging principle of working-capital management to answer the first of these two questions. We will then answer the second of the questions above: How should the financial manager select sources of short-term credit? In general, three basic factors should be considered in selecting a source of short-term credit: (1) the effective cost of credit, (2) the availability of credit in the amount needed and for the period financing is required, and (3) the influence of the use of a particular credit source on the cost and availability of other sources of financing. We discuss the problem of estimating the cost of short-term credit before introducing the various sources of credit because the same procedure is used for all sources.

The importance of working-capital management cannot be overstated. As we will see, for many firms current assets represent over half of the total assets. Moreover, surveys of financial managers indicate that the majority of their time is taken by the management of the day-to-day operations of the firm. This is largely the management of current assets and liabilities. Finally, for smaller firms, working-capital management takes on even greater importance. For smaller firms, access to capital markets, and the long-term sources of financing they supply, is limited. As such, smaller firms are forced to rely more heavily on short-term sources of financing, such as trade credit, accounts receivable, and inventory loans.

MANAGING CURRENT ASSETS AND LIABILITIES

Other things remaining the same, the greater the firm's investment in current assets, the greater its liquidity. As a means of increasing its liquidity, the firm may choose to invest additional funds in cash or marketable securities. Such action involves a tradeoff, however, because such assets earn little or no return. The firm thus finds that it can reduce its risk of illiquidity only by reducing its overall return on invested funds, and vice versa.

Working-Capital Management and the Risk-Return Tradeoff

The **risk-return tradeoff** involved in managing the firm's working capital involves a tradeoff between the firm's liquidity and its profitability. By maintaining a large investment in current assets like cash and inventory the firm reduces the chance of production stoppages and lost sales from inventory shortages and the inability to pay bills on time, which might in turn result in credit rating problems. However, as the firm increases its investment in working capital there is not a corresponding increase in its returns. This means that the firm's return on investment drops because profits are unchanged while the investment in assets increases.

The firm's use of current versus long-term debt also involves a risk-return tradeoff. *Other things remaining the same, the greater the firm's reliance on short-term debt or current liabilities in financing its asset investments, the greater the risk of illiquidity.* On the other hand, the use of current liabilities offers some very real advantages in that they can be less costly than long-term financing and they provide the firm with a flexible means of financing its fluctuating needs for assets. However, if for some reason the firm has problems raising short-term funds or needs funds for longer than expected, there can be real trouble. Thus, a firm can reduce its risk of illiquidity through the use of long-term debt at the expense of a reduction in its return on invested funds. Once again we see that the risk-return tradeoff involves an increased risk of illiquidity versus increased profitability.

Advantages of Current Liabilities: The Return

Flexibility.   Current liabilities offer the firm a flexible source of financing. They can be used to match the timing of a firm's needs for short-term financing. If, for example, a firm needs funds for a three-month period during each year to finance a seasonal expansion in inventories, then a three-month loan can provide substantial cost savings over a long- term loan (even if the interest rate on short-term financing should be higher). The use of long-term debt in this situation involves borrowing for the entire year rather than for the period when the funds are needed, which increases the amount of interest the firm must pay. This brings us to the second advantage generally associated with the use of short-term financing.

Interest Cost.   In general, interest rates on short-term debt are lower than on long-term debt for a given borrower. This relationship is referred to as the term structure of interest rates. For a given firm, the term structure might appear as follows:

Loan Maturity	Interest Rate
3 months	4.00%
6 months	4.60
1 year	5.30
3 years	5.90
5 years	6.75
10 years	7.50
30 years	8.25

Note that this term structure reflects the rates of interest applicable to a given borrower at a particular time; it would not, for example, describe the rates of interest available to another borrower or even those applicable to the same borrower at a different time.

Disadvantages of Current Liabilities: The Risk

The use of current liabilities or short-term debt as opposed to long-term debt subjects the firm to a greater risk of illiquidity for two reasons. First, short-term debt, due to its very nature, must be repaid or rolled over more often, and so it increases the possibility that the firm's financial condition might deteriorate to a point where the needed funds might not be available.[1]

A second disadvantage of short-term debt is the uncertainty of interest costs from year to year. For example, a firm borrowing during a six-month period each year to finance a seasonal expansion in current assets might incur a different rate of interest each year. This rate reflects the current rate of interest at the time of the loan, as well as the lender's perception of the firm's riskiness. If fixed rate long-term debt were used, the interest cost would be known for the entire period of the loan agreement.

---

[1]The dangers of such a policy are readily apparent in the experiences of firms that have been forced into bankruptcy. Penn Central, for example, had $80 million in short-term debt that it was unable to refinance (roll over) when it became bankrupt.

APPROPRIATE LEVEL OF WORKING CAPITAL

Managing the firm's net working capital (its liquidity) has been shown to involve simultaneous and interrelated decisions regarding investment in current assets and use of current liabilities. Fortunately, a guiding principle exists that can be used as a benchmark for the firm's working-capital policies: the **hedging principle,** or **principle of self-liquidating debt.** This principle provides a guide to the maintenance of a level of liquidity sufficient for the firm to meet its maturing obligations on time.[2]

Hedging Principle

Very simply, the *hedging principle* involves *matching* the cash-flow-generating characteristics of an asset with the maturity of the source of financing used to finance its acquisition. For example, a seasonal expansion in inventories, according to the hedging principle, should be financed with a short-term loan or current liability. The rationale underlying the rule is straightforward. Funds are needed for a limited period, and when that time has passed, the cash needed to repay the loan will be generated by the sale of the extra inventory items. Obtaining the needed funds from a long-term source (longer than one year) would mean that the firm would still have the funds after the inventories they helped finance had been sold. In this case the firm would have "excess" liquidity, which it either holds in cash or invests in low-yield marketable securities until the seasonal increase in inventories occurs again and the funds are needed. The result of all this would be an overall lowering of firm profits.

Consider an example in which a firm purchases a new conveyor belt system, which is expected to produce cash savings to the firm by eliminating the need for two laborers and, consequently, their salaries. This amounts to an annual savings of $14,000, whereas the conveyor belt costs $150,000 to install and will last 20 years. If the firm chooses to finance this asset with a 1-year note, then it will not be able to repay the loan from the $14,000 cash flow generated by the asset. In accordance with the hedging principle, the firm should finance the asset with a source of financing that more nearly matches the expected life and cash-flow-generating characteristics of the asset. In this case, a 15- to 20-year loan would be more appropriate.

Permanent and Temporary Assets

The notion of *maturity matching* in the hedging principle can be most easily understood when we think in terms of the distinction between **permanent** and **temporary investments in assets** as opposed to the more traditional fixed and current asset categories. A permanent investment in an asset is an investment that the firm expects to hold for a period longer than one year. Note that we are referring to the period the firm plans to hold an investment, not the useful life of the asset. For example, perma-

---

[2]A value-maximizing approach to the management of the firm's liquidity involves assessing the value of the benefits derived from increasing the firm's investment in liquid assets and weighing them against the added costs to the firm's owners resulting from investing in low-yield current assets. Unfortunately the benefits derived from increased liquidity relate to the expected costs of bankruptcy to the firm's owners, and these costs are "unmeasurable" by existing technology. Thus, a "valuation" approach to liquidity management exists only in the theoretical realm.

nent investments are made in the firm's minimum level of current assets, as well as in its fixed assets. Temporary asset investments, on the other hand, are composed of current assets that will be liquidated and not replaced within the current year. Thus, some part of the firm's current assets is permanent and the remainder is temporary. For example, a seasonal increase in level of inventories is a temporary investment; the buildup in inventories will be eliminated when it is no longer needed.

Temporary, Permanent, and Spontaneous Sources of Financing

Since total assets must always equal the sum of temporary, permanent, and spontaneous sources of financing, the hedging approach provides the financial manager with the basis for determining the sources of financing to use at any point.

Now, what constitutes a temporary, permanent, or spontaneous source of financing? Temporary sources of financing consist of current liabilities. Short-term notes payable constitute the most common example of a temporary source of financing. Examples of notes payable include unsecured bank loans, commercial paper, and loans secured by accounts receivable and inventories. Permanent sources of financing include intermediate-term loans, long-term debt, preferred stock, and common equity.

Spontaneous sources of financing consist of trade credit and other accounts payable that arise *spontaneously* in the firm's day-to-day operations. For example, as the firm acquires materials for its inventories, trade credit is often made available spontaneously or on *demand* from the firm's suppliers. Trade credit appears on the firm's balance sheet as accounts payable, and the size of the accounts payable balance varies directly with the firm's purchases of inventory items. In turn, inventory purchases are related to anticipated sales. Thus, part of the financing needed by the firm is spontaneously provided in the form of trade credit.

In addition to trade credit, wages and salaries payable, accrued interest, and accrued taxes also provide valuable sources of spontaneous financing. These expenses accrue throughout the period until they are paid. For example, if a firm has a wage expense of $10,000 a week and pays its employees monthly, then its employees effectively provide financing equal to $10,000 by the end of the first week following a payday, $20,000 by the end of the second week, and so forth. Since these expenses generally arise in direct conjunction with the firm's ongoing operations, they too are referred to as *spontaneous*.

Hedging Principle: Graphic Illustration

The hedging principle can now be stated very succinctly: *Asset needs of the firm not financed by spontaneous sources should be financed in accordance with this rule: Permanent asset investments are financed with permanent sources, and temporary investments are financed with temporary sources.*

The hedging principle is depicted in Figure 17-1. Total assets are broken down into temporary and permanent asset investment categories. The firm's permanent investment in assets is financed by the use of permanent sources of financing (intermediate- and long-term debt, preferred stock, and common equity) or spontaneous sources (trade credit and other accounts payable). For illustration purposes sponta-

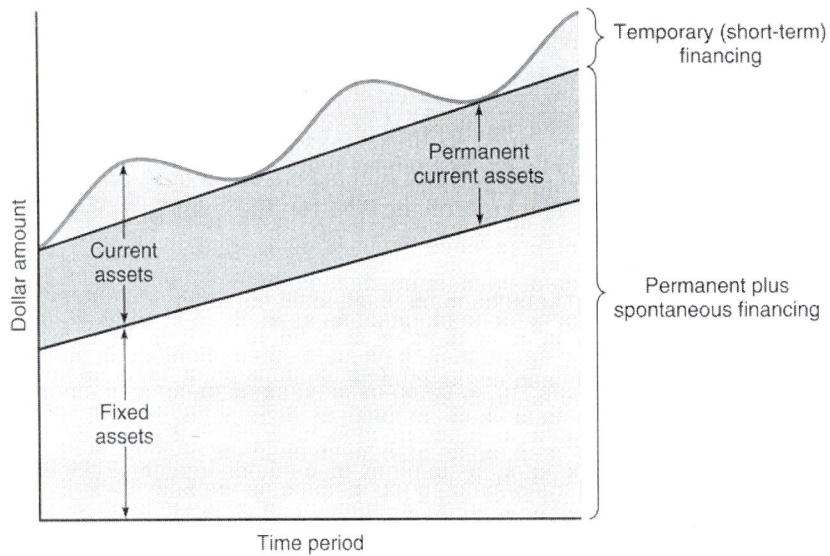

FIGURE 17-1
Hedging Financing Strategy

neous sources of financing are treated as if their amount were fixed. In practice, of course, spontaneous sources of financing fluctuate with the firm's purchases and its expenditures for wages, salaries, taxes, and other items that are paid on a delayed basis. Its temporary investment in assets is financed with temporary (short-term) debt.

ESTIMATION OF COST OF SHORT-TERM CREDIT

Approximate Cost-of-Credit Formula

The procedure for estimating the cost of short-term credit is a very simple one and relies on the basic interest equation:

$$\text{interest} = \text{principal} \times \text{rate} \times \text{time} \qquad (2)$$

where *interest* is the dollar amount of interest on a *principal* that is borrowed at some annual *rate* for a fraction of a year (represented by *time*). For example, a six-month loan for $1,000 at 8% interest would require an interest payment of $40:

$$\text{interest} = \$1,000 \times .08 \times 1/2 = \$40$$

We use this basic relationship to solve for the cost of a source of short-term financing or the annual percentage rate (APR) where the interest amount, the principal sum, and the time period for financing are known. Thus, solving the basic interest equation for APR produces[3]

$$APR = \frac{interest}{principal \times time} \qquad (3)$$

or

$$APR = \frac{interest}{principal} \times \frac{1}{time}$$

This equation, called the APR calculation, is clarified with the following example. The SKC Corporation plans to borrow $1,000 for a 90-day period. At maturity the firm will repay the $1,000 principal amount plus $30 interest. The effective annual rate of interest for the loan can be estimated using the ARP equation, as follows:

$$APR = \frac{\$30}{\$1,000} \times \frac{1}{90/360}$$

$$= .03 \times \frac{360}{90} = .12, or\ 12\%$$

The effective annual cost of funds provided by the loan is therefore 12%.

Annual Percentage Yield Formula

The simple APR calculation does not consider compound interest. To account for the influence of compounding, we can use the following equation:

$$APY = \left(1 + \frac{i}{m}\right)^m - 1 \qquad (4)$$

where APY is the annual percentage yield, i is the nominal rate of interest per year (12% in the above example), and m is the number of compounding periods within a year [m = 1/TIME = 1/(90/360) = 4 in the preceding example]. Thus, the effective rate of interest on the example problem, considering compounding, is

$$APY = \left(1 + \frac{.12}{4}\right)^4 - 1 = .126, or\ 12.6\%$$

Compounding effectively raises the cost of short-term credit. Because the differences between APR and APY are usually small, we use the simple interest version of APR to compute the cost of short-term credit.

SOURCES OF SHORT-TERM CREDIT

Short-term credit sources can be classified into two basic groups: unsecured and secured. **Unsecured** loans include all those sources that have as their security only the

---

[3]For ease of computation we will assume a 30-day month and 360-day year in this chapter.

lender's faith in the ability of the borrower to repay the funds when due. Major sources of unsecured short-term credit include accrued wages and taxes, trade credit, unsecured bank loans, and commercial paper. **Secured** loans involve the pledge of specific assets as collateral in the event the borrower defaults in payment of principal or interest. Commercial banks, finance companies, and factors are the primary suppliers of secured credit. The principal sources of collateral include accounts receivable and inventories.

Unsecured Sources: Accrued Wages and Taxes

Because most businesses pay their employees only periodically (weekly, biweekly, or monthly), firms accrue a wages payable account that is, in essence, a loan from their employees. For example, if the wage expense for the Appleton Manufacturing Company is $450,000 per week and it pays its employees monthly, then by the end of a four-week month the firm will owe its employees $1.8 million in wages for services they have already performed during the month. Consequently, the employees finance their own efforts through waiting a full month for payment.

Similarly, firms generally make quarterly income tax payments for their estimated quarterly tax liability. This means that the firm has the use of the tax monies it owes based on quarterly profits up through the end of the quarter. In addition, the firm pays sales taxes and withholding (income) taxes for its employees on a deferred basis. The longer the period that the firm holds the tax payments, the greater the amount of financing they provide.

Note that these sources of financing *rise and fall spontaneously* with the level of firm sales. That is, as the firm's sales increase so do its labor expense, sales taxes collected, and income tax. Consequently, these accrued expense items provide the firm with automatic or spontaneous sources of financing.

Unsecured Sources: Trade Credit

Trade credit provides one of the most flexible sources of short-term financing available to the firm. We previously noted that trade credit is a primary source of spontaneous, or on-demand, financing. That is, trade credit arises spontaneously with the firm's purchases. To arrange for credit the firm need only place an order with one of its suppliers. The supplier checks the firm's credit and, if it is good, sends the merchandise. The purchasing firm then pays for the goods in accordance with the supplier's credit terms.

Credit terms and cash discounts.   Very often the credit terms offered with trade credit involve a cash discount for early payment. For example, a supplier might offer terms of 2/10, net 30, which means that a 2% discount is offered for payment within 10 days or the full amount is due in 30 days. Thus, a 2% penalty is involved for not paying within 10 days or for delaying payment from the 10th to the 30th day (that is, for 20 days). The effective annual cost of not taking the cash discount can be quite severe. Using a $1 invoice amount, the effective cost of passing up the discount period using the preceding credit terms and our APR equation can be estimated.

FIGURE 17-2   Effective Rates of Interest on Selected Trade Credit Terms

Credit Terms	Effective Rate
2/10, net 60	14.69%
2/10, net 90	9.18%
3/20, net 60	27.84%
6/10, net 90	28.72%

$$\text{APY} = \frac{\$.02}{\$.98} \times \frac{1}{20/360} \quad .3673, \text{ or } 36.73\%$$

Note that the 2% cash discount is the *interest* cost of extending the payment period an *additional* 20 days. Note also that the principal amount of the credit is $.98. This amount constitutes the full principal amount as of the 10th day of the credit period, after which time the cash discount is lost. The effective cost of passing up the 2% discount for twenty days is quite expensive: 36.73%. Furthermore, once the discount period has passed, there is no reason to pay before the final due date (the 30th day). Figure 17-2 lists the effective annual cost of a number of alternative credit terms. Note that the cost of trade credit varies directly with the size of the cash discount and inversely with the length of time between the end of the discount period and the final due date.

Stretching of trade credit.   Some firms that use trade credit engage in a practice called *stretching* of trade accounts. This practice involves delaying payments beyond the prescribed credit period. For example, a firm might purchase materials under credit terms of 3/10, net 60; however, when faced with a shortage of cash, the firm might extend payment to the eightieth day. Continued violation of trade terms can eventually lead to a loss of credit. However, for short periods, and at infrequent intervals, stretching offers the firm an emergency source of short-term credit.

Advantages of trade credit.   As a source of short-term financing, trade credit has a number of advantages. First, trade credit is conveniently obtained as a normal part of the firm's operations. Second, no formal agreements are generally involved in extending credit. Furthermore, the amount of credit extended expands and contracts with the needs of the firm; this is why it is classified as a spontaneous, or on-demand, source of financing.

Unsecured Sources: Bank Credit

Commercial banks provide unsecured short-term credit in two basic forms: lines of credit and transaction loans (notes payable). Maturities of both types of loans are usually one year or less, with rates of interest depending on the creditworthiness of the borrower and the level of interest rates in the economy as a whole.

Line of credit.   A **line of credit** is generally an informal agreement or understanding between the borrower and the bank as to the maximum amount of credit that the bank will provide the borrower at any one time. Under this type of agreement there is no *legal* commitment on the part of the bank to provide the stated credit. In a **revolving credit agreement,** which is a variant of this form of financing, a legal obligation is involved. The line of credit agreement generally covers a period of one year corresponding to the borrower's *fiscal* year. Thus, if the borrower is on a July 31 fiscal year, its lines of credit will be based on the same annual period.

Lines of credit generally do not involve fixed rates of interest; instead they state that credit will be extended at *1/2% over prime* or some other spread over the bank's prime rate.[4] Furthermore, the agreement usually does not spell out the specific use that will be made of the funds beyond a general statement, such as *for working-capital purposes.*

Lines of credit usually require that the borrower maintain a minimum balance in the bank throughout the loan period, called a **compensating balance.** This required balance (which can be stated as a percent of the line of credit or the loan amount) increases the effective cost of the loan to the borrower, unless a deposit balance equal to or greater than this balance requirement is ordinarily maintained in the bank.

The effective cost of short-term bank credit can be estimated using the APR equation. Consider the following example: M & M Beverage Company has a $300,000 line of credit that requires a compensating balance equal to 10% of the loan amount. The rate paid on the loan is 12% per annum, $200,000 is borrowed for a six-month period, and the firm does not currently have a deposit with the lending bank. The dollar cost of the loan includes the interest expense and, in addition, the opportunity cost of maintaining an idle cash balance equal to the 10% compensating balance. To accommodate the cost of the compensating balance requirement, assume that the added funds will have to be borrowed and simply left idle in the firm's checking account. Thus, the amount actually borrowed (B) will be larger than the $200,000 needed. In fact, the needed $200,000 will constitute 90% of the total borrowed funds because of the 10% compensating balance requirement, hence $.90B = \$200,000$, such that $B = \$222,222$. Thus, interest is paid on a $222,222 loan ($222,222 \times .12 \times 1/2 = \$13,333.32$), of which only $200,000 is available for use by the firm.[5] The effective annual cost of credit therefore is

$$APR = \frac{\$13,333.32}{\$200,000} \times \frac{1}{180/360} = 13.33\%$$

In the M & M Beverage Company example the loan required the payment of principal ($222,222) plus interest ($13,333.32) at the end of the six-month loan period. Frequently, bank loans will be made on a discount basis. That is, the loan interest will be deducted from the loan amount before the funds are transferred to the borrower. Extending the M & M Beverage Company example to consider discounted interest involves reducing the loan proceeds ($200,000) in the previous example by the amount of interest for the full six months ($13,333.32). The effective rate of interest on the loan is now:

---

[4]The *prime rate of interest* is the rate that a bank charges its most creditworthy borrowers.
[5]The same answer would have been obtained by assuming a total loan of $200,000, of which only 90% or $180,000 was available for use by the firm; that is,

$$APR = \frac{\$12,000}{\$180,000} \times \frac{1}{180/360} = 13.33\%$$

Interest is now calculated on the $200,000 loan amount ($12,000 = \$200,000 \times .12 \times 1/2$).

$$APR = \frac{\$13,333.32}{\$200,000 - \$13,333.32} \times \frac{1}{180/360}$$

$$= .1429, \text{ or } 14.29\%$$

The effect of discounting interest was to raise the cost of the loan from 13.33% to 14.29%. This results from the fact that the firm pays interest on the same amount of funds as before ($222,222); however, this time it gets the use of $13,333.32 less, or $200,000 − $13,333.32 = $186,666.68.[6]

Transaction loans. Still another form of unsecured short-term bank credit can be obtained in the form of **transaction loans.** Here the loan is made for a specific purpose. This is the type of loan that most individuals associate with bank credit and is obtained by signing a promissory note.

Unsecured transaction loans are very similar to a line of credit regarding cost, term to maturity, and compensating balance requirements. In both instances commercial banks often require that the borrower *clean up* its short-term loans for a 30- to 45-day period during the year. This means, very simply, that the borrower must be free of any bank debt for the stated period. The purpose of such a requirement is to ensure that the borrower is not using short-term bank credit to finance a part of its permanent needs for funds.

Unsecured Sources: Commercial Paper

Only the largest and most creditworthy companies are able to use **commercial paper,** which is simply a short-term *promise to pay* that is sold in the market for short-term debt securities.

Credit terms. The maturity of this credit source is generally six months or less, although some issues carry 270-day maturities. The interest rate on commercial paper is generally slightly lower (.5% to 1%) than the prime rate on commercial bank loans. Also, interest is usually discounted, although sometimes interest-bearing commercial paper is available.

New issues of commercial paper are either placed directly (sold by the issuing firm directly to the investing public) or dealer placed. Dealer placement involves the

---

[6]If M&M needs the use of a full $200,000 then it will have to borrow more than $222,222 to cover both the compensating balance requirement and the discounted interest. In fact, the firm will have to borrow some amount *B* such that

$$B - .10B - (.12 \times 1/2)B = \$200,000$$

$$.84B = \$200,000$$

$$B = \frac{\$200,000}{.84} = \$238,095$$

The cost of credit remains the same at 14.29%, as we see below:

$$APR = \frac{\$14,285.70}{\$238,095 - \$23,810 - \$14,285.70} \times \frac{1}{180/360}$$

$$= .1429, \text{ or } 14.29\%$$

use of a commercial paper dealer, who sells the issue for the issuing firm. Many major finance companies, such as General Motors Acceptance Corporation, place their commercial paper directly. The volume of direct versus dealer placements is roughly 4 to 1 in favor of direct placements. Dealers are used primarily by industrial firms that either make only infrequent use of the commercial paper market or, owing to their small size, would have difficulty placing the issue without the help of a dealer.

Commercial paper as a source of short-term credit.   Several advantages accrue to the user of commercial paper:

1. **Interest rate.** Commercial paper rates are generally lower than rates on bank loans and comparable sources of short-term financing.
2. **Compensating balance requirement.** No minimum balance requirements are associated with commercial paper. However, issuing firms usually find it desirable to maintain lines of credit agreements sufficient to back up their short-term financing needs in the event that a new issue of commercial paper cannot be sold or an outstanding issue cannot be repaid when due.
3. **Amount of credit.** Commercial paper offers the firm with very large credit needs a single source for all its short-term financing. Because of loan restrictions placed on the banks by the regulatory authorities, obtaining the necessary funds from a commercial bank might require dealing with a number of institutions.[7]
4. **Prestige.** Because it is widely recognized that only the most creditworthy borrowers have access to the commercial paper market, its use signifies a firm's credit status.

Using commercial paper for short-term financing, however, involves a very important *risk*. That is, the commercial paper market is highly impersonal and denies even the most creditworthy borrower any flexibility in terms of repayment. When bank credit is used, the borrower has someone with whom he or she can work out any temporary difficulties that might be encountered in meeting a loan deadline. This flexibility simply does not exist for the user of commercial paper.

Estimation of the cost of commercial paper.   The cost of commercial paper can be estimated using the simple effective cost-of-credit equation (APR). The key points to remember are that commercial paper interest is usually discounted and that if a dealer is used to place the issue, a fee is charged. Even if a dealer is not used, the issuing firm will incur costs associated with preparing and placing the issue, and these costs must be included in estimating the cost of credit.

For example, EPG Mfg. Company uses commercial paper regularly to support its needs for short-term financing. The firm plans to sell $100 million in 270-day-maturity paper on which it expects to have to pay discounted interest at a rate of 12% per annum ($9,000,000). In addition, EPG expects to incur a cost of approximately $100,000 in dealer placement fees and other expenses of issuing the paper. The effective cost of credit to EPG can be calculated as follows:

---

[7]Member banks of the Federal Reserve System are limited to 10% of their total capital, surplus, and undivided profits when making loans to a single borrower. Thus, when a corporate borrower's needs for financing are very large it may have to deal with a group of participating banks to raise the needed funds.

$$\text{APR} = \frac{\$9,000,000 + \$100,000}{\$100,000,000 - \$100,000 - \$9,000,000} \times \frac{1}{270/360}$$

$$= .1335, \text{ or } 13.35\%$$

where the interest cost is calculated as $\$100,000,000 \times .12 \times [270/360] = \$9,000,000$ plus the $\$100,000$ dealer placement fee. Thus, the effective cost of credit to EPG is 13.35%.

Secured Sources: Accounts Receivable Loans

Secured sources of short-term credit have certain assets of the firm pledged as collateral to secure the loan. Upon default of the loan agreement, the lender has first claim to the pledged assets in addition to its claim as a general creditor of the firm. Hence, the secured credit agreement offers an added margin of safety to the lender.

Generally, a firm's receivables are among its most liquid assets. For this reason they are considered by many lenders to be prime collateral for a secured loan. Two basic procedures can be used in arranging for financing based on receivables: pledging and factoring.

Pledging accounts receivable.   Under the **pledging** arrangement the borrower simply pledges accounts receivable as collateral for a loan obtained from either a commercial bank or a finance company. The amount of the loan is stated as a percent of the face value of the receivables pledged. If the firm provides the lender with a *general line* on its receivables, then all of the borrower's accounts are pledged as security for the loan. This method of pledging is simple and inexpensive. However, because the lender has no control over the quality of the receivables being pledged, it will set the maximum loan at a relatively low percent of the total face value of the accounts, generally ranging downward from a maximum of around 75%.

Still another approach to pledging involves the borrower's presenting specific invoices to the lender as collateral for a loan. This method is somewhat more expensive in that the lender must assess the creditworthiness of each individual account pledged; however, given this added knowledge the lender will be willing to increase the loan as a percent of the face value of the invoices. In this case the loan might reach as high as 85% or 90% of the face value of the pledged receivables.

Accounts receivable loans generally carry an interest rate 2% to 5% higher than the bank's prime lending rate. Finance companies charge an even higher rate. In addition, the lender will usually charge a handling fee stated as a percent of the face value of the receivables processed, which may be as much as 1% to 2% of the face value. Consider the following example.

The A. B. Good Company sells electrical supplies to building contractors on terms of net 60. The firm's average monthly sales are $\$100,000$; thus, given the firm's two-month credit terms, its average receivables balance is $\$200,000$. The firm pledges all its receivables to a local bank, which in turn advances up to 70% of the face value of the receivables at 3% over prime and with a 1% processing charge on *all* receivables pledged. A. B. Good follows a practice of borrowing the maximum amount possible, and the current prime rate is 10%.

The APR of using this source of financing for a full year is computed as follows:

$$\text{APR} = \frac{\$18,200 + \$12,000}{\$140,000} \times \frac{1}{360/360} = .2157 \text{ or } 21.57\%$$

where the total dollar cost of the loan consists of both the annual interest expense (.13 × .70 × $200,000 = $18,200) and the annual processing fee (.01 × $100,000 × 12 months = $12,000). The amount of credit extended is .70 × $200,000 = $140,000. Note that the processing charge applies to *all* receivables pledged. Thus, the A. B. Good Company pledges $100,000 each month, or $1,200,000 during the year, on which a 1% fee must be paid, for a total annual charge of $12,000.

One more point: The lender, in addition to making advances or loans, may be providing certain credit services to the borrower. For example, the lender may provide billing and collection services. The value of these services should be considered in computing the cost of credit. In the preceding example, A. B. Good Company may *save* credit department expenses of $10,000 per year by pledging all its accounts and letting the lender provide those services. In this case, the cost of short-term credit is only

$$\text{APR} = \frac{\$18,200 + \$12,000 - \$10,000}{\$140,000} \times \frac{1}{360/360} = .1443 \text{ or } 14.43\%$$

The primary advantage of pledging as a source of short-term credit is the flexibility it provides the borrower. Financing is available on a continuous basis. The new accounts created through credit sales provide the collateral for the financing of new production. Furthermore, the lender may provide credit services that eliminate or at least reduce the need for similar services within the firm. The primary disadvantage associated with this method of financing is its cost, which can be relatively high compared with other sources of short- term credit, owing to the level of the interest rate charged on loans and the processing fee on pledged accounts.

Factoring accounts receivable.   **Factoring accounts receivable** involves the outright sale of a firm's accounts to a financial institution called a *factor*. A **factor** is a firm that acquires the receivables of other firms. The factoring institution may be a commercial finance company that engages solely in the factoring of receivables (known as an *old-line factor*) or it may be a commercial bank. The factor, in turn, bears the risk of collection and, for a fee, services the accounts. The fee is stated as a percent of the face value of all receivables factored (usually from 1% to 3%).

The factor firm typically does *not* make payment for factored accounts until the accounts have been collected or the credit terms have been met. Should the firm wish to receive immediate payment for its factored accounts, it can borrow from the factor, using the factored accounts as collateral. The maximum loan the firm can obtain is equal to the face value of its factored accounts less the factor's fee (1% to 3%) less a reserve (6% to 10%) less the interest on the loan. For example, if $100,000 in receivables is factored, carrying 60-day credit terms, a 2% factor's fee, a 6% reserve, and interest at 1% per month on advances, then the maximum loan or advance the firm can receive is computed as follows:

Face amount of receivables factored	$100,000
Less: Fee (.02 × $100,000)	(2,000)
Reserve (.06 × $100,000)	(6,000)
Interest (.01 × $92,000 × 2 months)	(1,840)
Maximum advance	$ 90,160

Note that interest is discounted and calculated based on a maximum amount of funds available for advance ($92,000 = $100,000 − $2000 − $6000). Thus, the effective cost of credit can be calculated as follows:

$$\text{APR} = \frac{\$1,840 + \$2,000}{\$90,160} \times \frac{1}{60/360}$$

$$= .2555 \text{ or } 25.55\%$$

Secured Sources: Inventory Loans

Inventory loans provide a second source of security for short-term secured credit. The amount of the loan that can be obtained depends on both the marketability and perishability of the inventory. Some items, such as raw materials (grains, oil, lumber, and chemicals), are excellent sources of collateral, because they can easily be liquidated. Other items, such as work-in-process inventories, provide very poor collateral because of their lack of marketability.

There are several methods by which inventory can be used to secure short-term financing. These include a *floating* or *blanket lien, chattel mortgage, field warehouse receipt,* and *terminal warehouse receipt.*

Under a **floating lien** agreement the borrower gives the lender a lien against all its inventories. This provides the simplest but least secure form of inventory collateral. The borrowing firm maintains full control of the inventories and continues to sell and replace them as it sees fit. Obviously, this lack of control over the collateral greatly dilutes the value of this type of security to the lender.

Under a **chattel mortgage agreement** the inventory is identified (by serial number or otherwise) in the security agreement and the borrower retains title to the inventory but cannot sell the items without the lender's consent.

Under a **field warehouse financing agreement,** inventories used as collateral are physically separated from the firm's other inventories and placed under the control of a third-party field warehousing firm.

The **terminal warehouse agreement** differs from the field warehouse agreement in only one respect. Here the inventories pledged as collateral are transported to a public warehouse that is physically removed from the borrower's premises. The lender has an added degree of safety or security because the inventory is totally removed from the borrower's control. Once again the cost of this type of arrangement is increased because the warehouse firm must be paid by the borrower; in addition, the inventory must be transported to and eventually from the public warehouse.

SUMMARY

Working capital management involves managing the firm's liquidity, which in turn involves managing (1) the firm's investment in current assets and (2) its use of current liabilities. Each of these problems involves risk—return tradeoffs. Investing in current assets reduces the firm's risk of illiquidity at the expense of lowering its overall rate of return on its investment in assets. Furthermore, the use of long-term sources of financing enhances the firm's liquidity while reducing its rate of return on assets.

The *hedging principle,* or *principle of self-liquidating debt,* is a benchmark for working-capital decisions. Basically, this principle involves matching the cash-flow-generating characteristics of an asset with the cash flow requirements of the source of funds used to finance its acquisition.

Three basic factors provide the key considerations in selecting a source of short-term financing: (1) the effective cost of credit, (2) the availability of financing in the amount and for the time needed, and (3) the effect of the use of credit from a particular source on the cost and availability of other sources of credit.

The various sources of short-term credit can be categorized into two groups: unsecured and secured. Unsecured credit offers no specific assets as security for the loan agreement. The primary sources include trade credit, lines of credit, unsecured transaction loans from commercial banks, and commercial paper. Secured credit is generally provided to business firms by commercial banks, finance companies, and factors. The most popular sources of security involve the use of accounts receivable and inventories. Loans secured by accounts receivable include pledging agreements, in which a firm pledges its receivables as security for a loan, and factoring agreements, in which the firm sells the receivables to a factor. A primary difference in these two arrangements relates to the ability of the lender to seek payment from the borrower in the event the accounts used as collateral become uncollectable. In a pledging arrangement the lender retains the right of recourse in the event of default, whereas in factoring, a lender is generally without recourse.

Loans secured by inventories can be made using one of several types of security arrangements. Among the most widely used are the floating lien, chattel mortgage, field warehouse agreement, and terminal warehouse agreement. The form of agreement used will depend on the type of inventories pledged as collateral and the degree of control the lender wishes to exercise over the loan collateral.

SELF-CORRECTION PROBLEMS

1. The Marilyn Sales Company is a wholesale machine tool broker that has gone through a recent expansion of its activities resulting in a doubling of its sales. The company has determined that it needs an additional $200 million in short-term funds to finance peals season sales during roughly six months of the year. Marilyn's treasurer has recommended that the firm use a commercial paper offering to raise the needed funds. Specifically, he has determined that a $200 million offering would require 10% interest (paid in advance or discounted) plus a $125,000 placement fee. The paper would carry a six-month (180-day) maturity. What is the effective cost of credit?

2. The treasurer of the Lights-a-Lot Mfg. Company is faced with three alternative bank loans. The firm wishes to select the one that minimizes its cost of credit on a $200,000 note that it plans to issue in the next 10 days. Relevant information for the three loan configurations is found below:

   a. An 18% rate of interest with interest paid at year-end and no compensating balance requirement.

b. A 16% rate of interest but carrying a 20% compensating balance requirement. This loan also calls for interest to be paid at year-end.

c. A 14% rate of interest that is discounted plus a 20% compensating balance requirement.

Analyze the cost of each of these alternatives. You may assume the firm would not normally maintain any bank balance that might be used to meet the 20% compensating balance requirements of alternatives (b) and (c).

SOLUTIONS TO SELF-CORRECTION PROBLEMS

1. The discounted interest cost of the commercial paper issue is calculated as follows:

$$\text{Interest expense} = .10 \times \$200,000,000 \times 180/360 = \$10,000,000$$

The effective cost of credit can now be calculated as follows:

$$\text{APR} = \frac{\$10,000,000 + \$125,000}{\$200,000,000 - \$125,000 - \$10,000,000} \times \frac{1}{180/360}$$

$$= .1066 \text{ or } 10.66\%$$

2. a.

$$\text{APR} = \frac{.18 \times \$200,000}{\$200,000,000} \times \frac{1}{1}$$

$$= .18, \text{ or } 18\%$$

   b.

$$\text{APR} = \frac{.16 \times \$200,000}{\$200,000 - (.20 \times \$200,000)} \times \frac{1}{1}$$

$$= .20 \text{ or } 20\%$$

   c.

$$\text{APR} = \frac{.14 \times \$200,000}{\$200,000 - (.14 \times \$200,000) - (.2 \times \$200,000)} \times \frac{1}{1}$$

$$= .2121 \text{ or } 21.21\%$$

Alternative (a) offers the lower-cost service of financing, although it carries the highest stated rate of interest. The reason for this is that there is no compensating balance requirement, nor is interest discounted for this alternative.

QUESTIONS

1. Define and contrast the terms *working capital* and *net working capital.*
2. Discuss the risk-return relationship involved in the firm's asset investment decisions as that relationship pertains to working-capital management.
3. What advantages and disadvantages are generally associated with the use of short-term debt? Discuss.
4. Explain what is meant by the statement "The use of current liabilities as opposed to long-term debt subjects the firm to a greater risk of illiquidity."
5. Define the hedging principle. How can this principle be used in the management of working capital?
6. Define the following term
   a. Permanent asset investments
   b. Temporary asset investments
   c. Permanent sources of financing
   d. Temporary sources of financing
   e. Spontaneous sources of financing
7. What distinguishes short-term, intermediate-term, and long-term debt?
8. What considerations should be used in selecting a source of short-term credit?
9. How can the formula "interest = principal × rate × time" be used to estimate the effective cost of short-term credit?
10. How can we accommodate the effects of compounding in our calculation of the effective cost of short-term credit?
11. There are three major sources of unsecured short-term credit other than accrued wages and taxes. List and discuss the distinguishing characteristics of each.
12. What is meant by the following trade credit terms: 2/10, net 30? 4/20, net 60? 3/15, net 45?
13. Define the following:
    a. Line of credit
    b. Commercial paper
    c. Compensating balance
    d. Prime rate
14. List and discuss four advantages of the use of commercial paper.
15. What risk is involved in the firm's use of commercial paper as a source of short-term credit? Discuss.
16. List and discuss the distinguishing features of the principal sources of secured credit based on accounts receivable.

PROBLEMS

1. **Estimating the Cost of Bank Credit.**   Paymaster Enterprises has arranged to finance its seasonal working-capital needs with a short-term bank loan. The loan will carry a rate of 12% per annum with interest paid in advance (discounted). In addition, Paymaster must maintain a minimum demand deposit with the bank of 10% of the loan balance throughout the term of the loan. If Paymaster plans to borrow $100,000 for a period of three months, what is the effective cost of the bank loan?

2. **Estimating the Cost of Commercial Paper.**   On February 3, 199X, the Burlington Western Company plans a commercial paper issue of $20 million. The firm has never used commercial paper before but has been assured by the firm placing the issue that it will have no difficulty raising the funds. The commercial paper will carry a 270-day maturity and will require interest based on a rate of 11% per annum. In addition, the firm will have to pay fees totaling $200,000 in order to bring the issue to market and place it. What is the effective cost of the commercial paper issue to Burlington Western?

3. **Cost of Trade Credit.**   Calculate the effective cost of the following trade credit terms where payment is made on the net due date.

   a. 2/10, net 30
   b. 3/15, net 30
   c. 3/15, net 45
   d. 2/15, net 60

4. **Annual Percentage Yield.**   Compute the cost of the trade credit terms in problem 3 using the compounding formula or annual percentage yield.

CHAPTER 18

Liquid Asset Management

In this chapter, we will explore in more depth management of the asset components of the working capital equation. Accordingly, we will focus on the alternatives available to managers for increasing shareholder wealth with respect to the most important types of current assets: (1) cash, (2) marketable securities, (3) accounts receivable and inventory. These are listed in order of declining liquidity.

Such alternatives will include (1) techniques available to management for favorably influencing cash receipts and disbursements patterns, (2) investments that allow a firm to employ excess cash balances productively, (3) critical decision formulas for determining the appropriate amount of investment in accounts receivable, and (4) methods, such as those pertaining to order quantity and order point issues, for evaluating most suitable levels of inventory.

These issues are important to the financial manager for several reasons. For example, judicious management of cash and near-cash assets allows the firm to hold the minimum amount of cash necessary to meet the firm's obligations in a timely manner. As a result, the firm is able to take advantage of the opportunity to earn a return on its liquid assets and increase its profitability.

Wise management of accounts receivable and inventory is important because these two classes of assets generally constitute a large portion of a firm's total assets; taking into consideration all industries in the United States, accounts receivable exceeds 26% and inventory approaches 5% of the average firm's assets. Any changes in assets of such magnitude to the firm almost certainly will affect its profitability. An increase in accounts receivable, for example, not only results in higher sales through extension of additional trade credit, but also increases the need for financing to support the additional investment. The costs of credit investigation and collection also are increased, as could be bad debt expense. Likewise, a larger investment in inventory, by allowing more efficient production and speedier delivery to customers, leads to increased sales. At the same time, additional financing is required to support the increased level of inventory and the concomitant handling and carrying costs.

With such significance in mind, we begin the study of current asset management by exploring the various aspects of the management of cash and marketable securities. Afterward, we will turn to an analysis of the important issues related to the management of accounts receivable and inventory.

Before proceeding to our discussion of cash management, it will be helpful to distinguish among several terms. **Cash** is the currency and coin the firm has on hand in petty cash drawers, in cash registers, or in checking accounts (i.e., demand deposit accounts) at the various commercial banks. **Marketable securities,** also called near cash or near-cash assets, are security investments that the firm can quickly convert into cash balances. Generally, firms hold marketable securities with very short maturity periods—less than one year. Together, cash and marketable securities constitute the most liquid assets of a firm.

WHY A COMPANY HOLDS CASH

A thorough understanding of why and how a firm holds cash requires an accurate conception of how cash flows into and through the enterprise. Figure 18-1 depicts the process of cash generation and disposition in a typical manufacturing setting. The arrows designate the direction of the flow—that is, whether the cash balance increases or decreases.

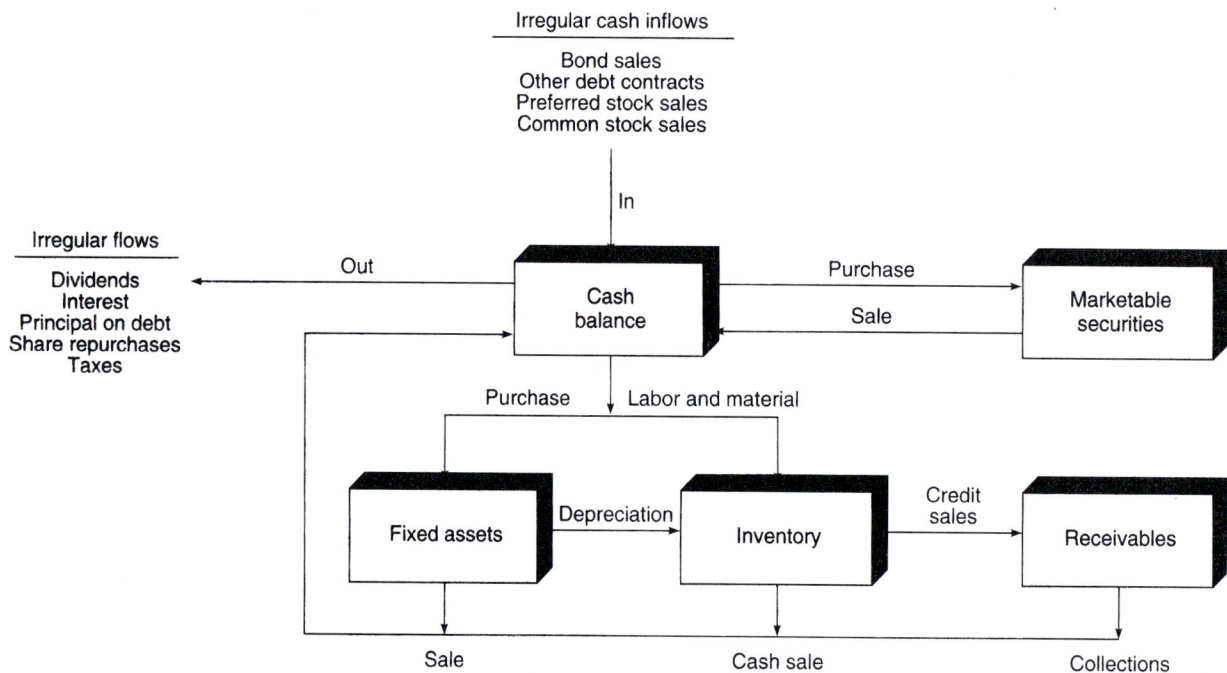

FIGURE 18-1
The Cash Generation and Disposition Process

Cash Flow Process

The irregular increases in the firm's cash holdings can come from several external sources. Funds can be obtained in the financial markets from the sale of securities, such as bonds, preferred stock, and common stock, or the firm can enter into nonmarketable debt contracts with lenders such as commercial banks. These irregular cash inflows do not occur on a daily basis. The reason is that external financing contracts or arrangements usually involve huge sums of money stemming from a major need identified by the company's management, and these needs do not occur every day. For example, a new product might be in the launching process, or a plant expansion might be required to provide added productive capacity.

In most organizations the financial officer responsible for cash management also controls the transactions that affect the firm's investment in marketable securities. As excess cash becomes temporarily available, marketable securities are purchased. When cash is in short supply, a portion of the marketable securities portfolio is liquidated.

Whereas the irregular cash inflows are from external sources, the other main sources of cash arise from internal operations and occur on a more regular basis. Over long periods, the largest receipts come from accounts receivable collections and to a lesser extent from direct cash sales of finished goods. Many manufacturing concerns also generate cash on a regular basis through the liquidation of scrap or obsolete inventory. At various times fixed assets may also be sold, thereby generating some cash inflow.

Apart from the investment of excess cash in near-cash assets, the cash balance experiences reductions for three key reasons. First, on an irregular basis, withdrawals are made to (1) pay cash dividends on preferred and common stock shares, (2) meet interest requirements on debt contracts, (3) repay the principal borrowed from creditors, (4) buy the firm's own shares in the financial markets for use in executive compensation plans or as an alternative to paying a cash dividend, and (5) pay tax bills. Again, by an *irregular basis* we mean items *not* occurring on a daily or frequent schedule. Second, the company's capital expenditure program designates that fixed assets be acquired at various intervals. Third, inventories are purchased on a regular basis to ensure a steady flow of finished goods off the production line. Note that the arrow linking the investment in fixed assets with the inventory account is labeled *depreciation*. This indicates that a portion of the cost of fixed assets is charged against the products coming off the assembly line. This cost is subsequently recovered through the sale of the finished goods inventory, since the product selling price will be set by management to cover all the costs of production, including depreciation.

Motives for Holding Cash

The influences described above that affect the firm's cash balance can be classified in terms of the three motives put forth by John Maynard Keynes: (1) the transactions motive, (2) the precautionary motive, and (3) the speculative motive.[1]

---

[1]John Maynard Keynes, *The General Theory of Employment, Interest, and Money* (New York: Harcourt Brace Jovanovich, 1936).

The transactions motive.   Balances held for transactions purposes allow the firm to meet cash needs that arise in the ordinary course of doing business. In Figure 18-1, transactions balances would be used to meet the irregular outflows as well as the planned acquisition of fixed assets and inventories.

The relative amount of cash needed to satisfy transactions requirements is affected by a number of factors, such as the industry in which the firm operates. It is well known that utilities can forecast cash receipts quite accurately, because of stable demand for their services. Computer software firms, however, have a more difficult time predicting their cash flows. New products are brought to market at a rapid pace, thereby making it difficult project cash flows and balances precisely.

The precautionary motive.   Precautionary balances are a buffer stock of liquid assets. This motive for holding cash relates to the maintenance of balances to be used to satisfy possible, but as yet indefinite, needs.

Cash flow predictability also has a material influence on the firm's demand for cash through this precautionary motive. The airline industry provides a typical illustration. Air passenger carriers are plagued with a high degree of cash flow uncertainty. The weather, rising fuel costs, and continual strikes by operating personnel make cash forecasting difficult for any airline. The upshot of this problem is that because of all the things that *might* happen, the minimum cash balances desired by the management of the air carriers tend to be large.

In actual business practice, the precautionary motive is met to a large extent by the holding of a portfolio of *liquid assets,* not just cash. Notice in Figure 18-1 the two-way flow of funds between the company's holdings of cash and marketable securities. In large corporate organizations, funds may flow either into or out of the marketable securities portfolio on a daily basis.

The speculative motive.   Cash is held for speculative purposes in order to take advantage of potential profit-making situations. Construction firms that build private dwellings will at times accumulate cash in anticipation of a significant drop in lumber costs. If the price of building supplies does drop, the companies that built up their cash balances stand to profit by purchasing materials in large quantities. This will reduce their cost of goods sold and increase their net profit margin. Generally, the speculative motive is the least important component of a firm's preference for liquidity. The transactions and precautionary motives account for most of the reasons why a company holds cash balances.

CASH MANAGEMENT OBJECTIVES AND DECISIONS

The Risk-Return Tradeoff

A companywide cash management program must be concerned with minimizing the firm's risk of insolvency. In the context of cash management, the term **insolvency** describes the situation where the firm is unable to meet its maturing liabilities on time. In such a case the company is **technically insolvent** in that it lacks the necessary liquidity to make prompt payment on its current debt obligations. A firm could avoid this problem by carrying large cash balances to pay the bills that come due.

The financial manager must strike an acceptable balance between holding too much cash and too little cash. This is the focal point of the risk-return tradeoff. A large cash investment minimizes the chances of insolvency, but penalizes company profitability. A small cash investment frees excess balances for investment in both marketable securities and longer-lived assets; this enhances company profitability and the value of the firm's common shares, but increases the chances of running out of cash.

The Objectives

The risk-return tradeoff can be reduced to two prime objectives for the firm's cash-management system:

1. Enough cash must be on hand to meet the disbursal needs that arise in the course of doing business.
2. Investment in idle cash balances must be reduced to a minimum.

Evaluation of these operational objectives, and a conscious attempt on the part of management to meet them, gives rise to the need for some typical cash-management decisions.

The Decisions

Two conditions or ideals would allow the firm to operate for extended periods with cash balances near or at a level of zero: (1) a completely accurate forecast of net cash flows over the planning horizon and (2) perfect synchronization of cash receipts and disbursements.

Cash flow forecasting is the initial step in any effective cash-management program. Given that the firm will, as a matter of necessity, invest in some cash balances, certain types of decisions related to the size of those balances dominate the cash-management process. These include decisions that answer the following questions:

1. What can be done to speed up cash collections and slow down or better control cash outflows?
2. What should be the composition of a marketable securities portfolio?

The remainder of this chapter dwells on these two questions.

COLLECTION AND DISBURSEMENT PROCEDURES

The efficiency of the firm's cash-management program can be enhanced by knowledge and use of various procedures aimed at (1) accelerating cash receipts and (2) improving the methods used to disburse cash. We will see that greater opportunity for corporate profit improvement lies with the cash receipts side of the funds flow process, although it would be unwise to ignore opportunities for favorably affecting cash-disbursement practices.

Managing the Cash Inflow

The reduction of float lies at the center of the many approaches employed to speed up cash receipts. **Float** (or total float) has four elements:

1. **Mail float** is caused by the time lapse from the moment a customer mails a remittance check until the firm begins to process it.
2. **Processing float** is caused by the time required for the firm to process remittance checks before they can be deposited in the bank.
3. **Transit float** is caused by the time necessary for a deposited check to clear through the commercial banking system and become usable funds to the company. Credit is deferred for a maximum of two business days on checks that are cleared through the Federal Reserve System.
4. **Disbursing float** derives from the fact that funds are available in the company's bank account until its payment check has cleared through the banking system.

We will use the term *float* refer to the total of its four elements just described. Float reduction can yield considerable benefits in terms of usable funds that are released for company use and returns produced on such freed-up balances. As an example, for 1991 IBM reported total revenues of $64.8 billion. The amount of usable funds that would be released if IBM could achieve a one-day reduction in float can be approximated by dividing annual revenues (sales) by the number of days in a year. In this case one day's freed-up balances would be

$$\frac{\text{annual revenues}}{\text{days in years}} = \frac{\$64,800,000,000}{365} = \$177,534,247$$

If these released funds, which represent one day's sales, of approximately $177.5 million could be invested to return 6% a year, then the annual value of the one-day float reduction would be

$$(\text{sales per day}) \times (\text{assumed yield}) = \$177,534,247 \times .06 = \$10,652,055$$

It is clear that effective cash management can yield impressive opportunities for profit improvement. Let us look now at specific techniques for reducing float.

The lock-box arrangement. The lock-box system is the most widely used commercial banking service for expediting cash gathering. Banks have offered this service since 1946. Such a system speeds up the conversion of receipts into usable funds by reducing both mail and processing float. In addition, it is possible to reduce transit float if lock boxes are located near Federal Reserve Banks and their branches. For large corporations that receive checks from all parts of the country, float reductions of two to four days are not unusual.

Figure 18-2 illustrates an elementary, but typical, cash collection system for a hypothetical firm. It also shows the origin of mail float, processing float, and transit float. In this system the customer places his or her remittance check in the U.S. mail, which is then delivered to the firm's headquarters. This causes the mail float. On the check's arrival at the firm's headquarters (or local collection center), general accounting personnel must go through the bookkeeping procedures needed to prepare them for local deposit. The checks are then deposited. This causes the processing float. The

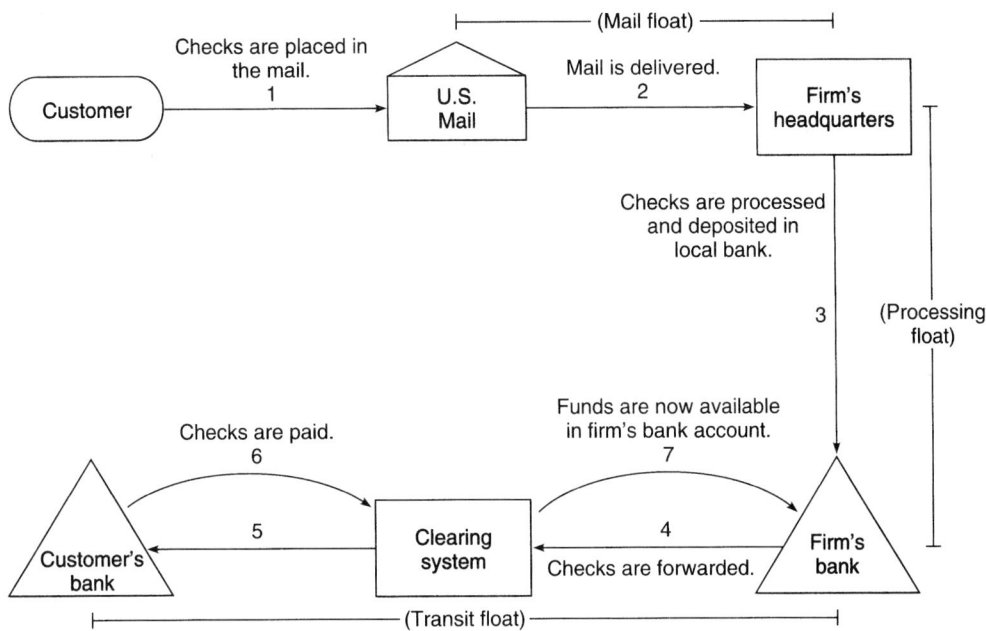

FIGURE 18-2
Ordinary Cash-Gathering System

checks are then forwarded for payment through the commercial bank clearing mechanism. The checks will be charged against the customer's own bank account. At this point the checks are said to be "paid" and become "good" funds available for use by the company that received them. This bank clearing procedure represents transit float and, as we said earlier, can amount to a delay of up to two business days.

The lock-box arrangement shown in Figure 18-3 is based on a simple procedure. The firm's customers are instructed to mail their remittance checks not to company headquarters or regional offices, but to a numbered Post Office box. The bank that is providing the lock-box service is authorized to open the box, collect the mail, process the checks, and deposit the checks directly into the company's account.

Typically a large bank will collect payments from the lock box at one- to two-hour intervals, 365 days of the year. During peak business hours, the bank may pick up mail every 30 minutes.

Once the mail is received at the bank, the checks will be examined, totaled, photocopied, and microfilmed. A deposit form is then prepared by the bank, and each batch of processed checks is forwarded to the collection department for clearance. Funds deposited in this manner are usually available for company use in one business day or less.

The bank can notify the firm via some type of telecommunications system the same day deposits are made as to their amount. At the conclusion of each day all check photocopies, invoices, deposit slips, and any other documents included with the remittances are mailed to the firm.

Note that the firm that receives checks from all over the country will have to use several lock boxes to take full advantage of a reduction in mail float. The firm's major

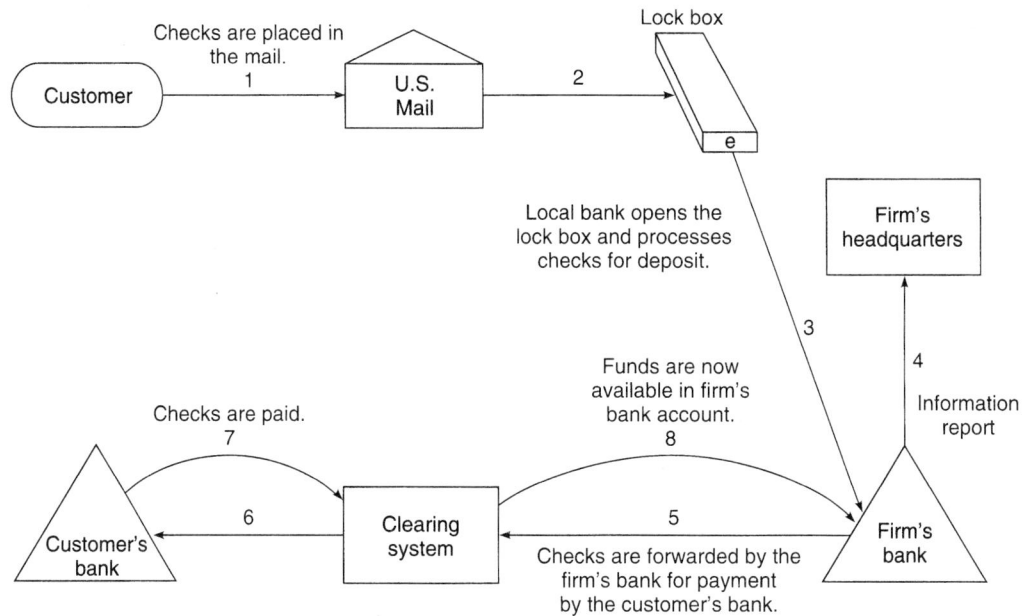

FIGURE 18-3
Simple Lock-Box System

bank should be able to offer as a service a detailed lock-box study, analyzing the company's receipt patterns to determine the proper number and location of lock-box receiving points.

The two systems described by Figures 18-2 and 18-3 are summarized in Figure 18-4. There, the step numbers refer to those shown in Figure 18-2 (the ordinary system). Furthermore, Figure 18-4 assumes that the customer and the firm's headquarters or its collection center are located in different cities. This causes the lag of two working days before the firm actually receives the remittance check. We notice at the bottom of Figure 18-4 that the installation of the lock-box system can result in funds being credited to the firm's bank account a full *four* working days *faster* than is possible under the ordinary collection system.

Previously in this chapter we calculated the 1991 sales per day for IBM to be $177.5 million and assumed the firm could invest its excess cash in marketable securities to yield 6% annually. If IBM could speed up its cash collections by four days, as the hypothetical firm did in Figure 18-4, the results would be startling. The gross annual savings to IBM (apart from operating the lock-box system) would amount to $42.6 million, as follows:

$$\text{(sales per day)} \times \text{(days of float reduction)} \times \text{(assumed yield)}$$
$$= \$177,534,247 \times (4) \times .06 = \$42,608,219$$

As you might guess, the prospects for generating revenues of this magnitude are important not only to the firms involved, but also to commercial banks that offer lock-box services.

Step Numbers	Ordinary System and Time		Advantage of Lock Box
1	Customer writes check and places it in the mail	1 Day	
2	Mail is delivered to firm's headquarters	2 Days	Mail will not have to travel as far. Result: save 1 day
3	Accounting personnel process the checks and deposit them in the firm's local bank	2 Days	Bank personnel prepare checks for deposit. Result: save 2 days
4 and 5	Checks are forwarded for payment through the clearing mechanism	1 Day	As the lock boxes are located near Federal Reserve Banks or branches, transit float can be reduced.
6 and 7	The firm receives notice from its bank that the checks have cleared and the funds are now "good"	1 Day	Result: save 1 day
	Total working days	7	Overall result: Save 4 working days

FIGURE 18-4
Comparison of Ordinary Cash-Gathering System with Simple Lock-Box System

In summary, the benefits of a lock-box arrangement are these:

1. **Increased working cash.** The time required for converting receivables into available funds is reduced. This frees up cash for use elsewhere in the enterprise.
2. **Elimination of clerical functions.** The bank takes over the tasks of receiving, endorsing, totaling, and depositing checks. With less handling of receipts by employees, better audit control is achieved and the chance of documents becoming lost is reduced.
3. **Early knowledge of dishonored checks.** Should a customer's check be uncollectible because of lack of funds, it is returned, usually by special handling, to the firm.

These benefits are not free. Usually, the bank levies a charge for each check processed through the system. The benefits derived from the acceleration of receipts must exceed the incremental costs of the lock-box system, or the firm would be better off without it. Later in this chapter a straightforward method for assessing the desirability of a specific cash-management service, such as the lock-box arrangement, will be illustrated.

Preauthorized checks (PACs).   Whereas the lock-box arrangement can often reduce total float by two to four days, for some firms the use of PACs can be an even more effective way of converting receipts into working cash. A PAC resembles the ordinary check, but it does not contain nor require the signature of the person on whose account it is being drawn. A PAC is created only with the individual's legal authorization.

The PAC system is advantageous when the firm regularly receives a large volume of payments of a fixed amount from the same customers. This type of cash-management service has proved useful to insurance companies, savings and loan associations, consumer credit firms, leasing enterprises, and charitable and religious organizations. The objective of this system is to reduce both mail and processing float. Notice, in relation to either the typical cash-gathering system (Figure 18-2) or the lock-box system (Figure 18-3), that the customer no longer (1) physically writes his or her own check or (2) deposits such check in the mail.

The operation of a PAC system is illustrated in Figure 18-5. It involves the following sequence of events:

1. The firm's customers authorize it to draw checks on their respective demand deposit accounts.
2. Indemnification agreements are signed by the customers and forwarded to the banks where they maintain their demand deposit accounts. These agreements authorize the banks to honor the PACs when they are presented for payment through the commercial bank clearing system.
3. The firm prepares a magnetic tape that contains all appropriate information about the regular payments.
4. At each processing cycle (monthly, weekly, semimonthly) the corporation retains a hard copy listing of all tape data for control purposes. Usually, the checks that are about to be printed will be deposited in the firm's demand deposit account, so a deposit ticket will also be forwarded to the bank.
5. Upon receipt of the tape the bank will produce the PACs, deposit them to the firm's account, forward them for clearing through the commercial banking system, and return a control report to the firm.

For firms that can take advantage of a PAC system, the benefits include the following:

1. **Highly predictable cash flows.**
2. **Reduced expenses.** Billing and postage costs are eliminated, and the clerical processing of customer payments is significantly reduced.
3. **Customer preference.** Many customers prefer not to be bothered with a regular billing. With a PAC system the check is actually written for the customer and the payment made even if he or she is on vacation or otherwise out of town.
4. **Increased working cash.** Mail float and processing float can be dramatically reduced in comparison with other payment processing systems.

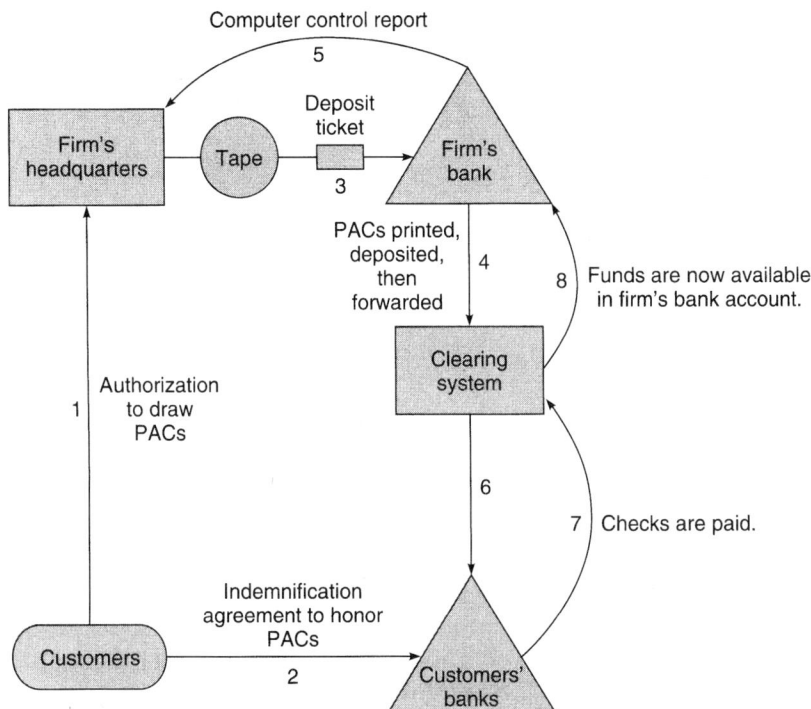

FIGURE 18-5
Preauthorized Check System (PAC)

Depository transfer checks.   Both depository transfer checks and wire transfers are used in conjunction with what is known as *concentration banking.* A concentration bank is one where the firm maintains a major disbursing account.

In an effort to accelerate collections, many companies have established multiple collection centers. Regional lock-box networks are one type of approach to strategically located collection points. Even without lock boxes, firms may have numerous sales outlets throughout the country and collect cash over the counter. This requires many local bank accounts to handle daily deposits. Rather than have funds sitting in these multiple bank accounts in different geographic regions of the country, most firms will regularly transfer the surplus balances to one or more concentration banks. Centralizing the firm's pool of cash provides the following benefits:

1. **Lower levels of excess cash.** Desired cash balance target levels are set for each regional bank. These target levels consider both compensating balance requirements and necessary working levels of cash. Cash in excess of the target levels can be transferred regularly to concentration banks for deployment by the firm's top-level management.
2. **Better control.** With more cash held in fewer accounts, stricter control over available cash is achieved. Quite simply, there are fewer problems. The concentration banks can prepare sophisticated reports that detail corporatewide movements of funds into and out of the central cash pool.

3. **More efficient investments in near-cash assets.** The coupling of information from the firm's cash forecast with data on available funds supplied by the concentration banks allows the firm quickly to transfer cash to the marketable securities portfolio.

Depository transfer checks provide a means for moving funds from local bank accounts to concentration accounts. The depository transfer check itself is an unsigned, nonnegotiable instrument. It is payable only to the bank of deposit (the concentration bank) for credit to the firm's specific account. The firm files an authorization form with each bank from which it might withdraw funds. This form instructs the bank to pay the depository transfer checks without any signature. The movement of cash through the use of depository transfer checks can operate with a conventional mail system or an automated system.

When the mail system is used, a company employee deposits the day's receipts in a local bank and fills out a preprinted depository transfer check for the exact amount of the deposit. The company then mails the depository transfer check to the firm's concentration bank. While this document is traveling in the mails, the checks just deposited at the local bank are being cleared. As soon as the concentration bank receives the depository transfer check, the firm's account is credited for the designated amount. The funds credited to the concentration account are not available for the firm's use, of course, until the document has been cleared with the local depository bank for payment.

If the firm's depository banks are geographically dispersed so that the mail will take several days in reaching the concentration bank, then *no* float reduction might be achieved through this system. In an attempt to reduce the mail float associated with conventional depository transfer check systems, some banks have initiated a type of special mail handling of these instruments that can cut as much as one full day off regular mail delivery schedules.

An innovation in speeding cash into concentration accounts is the **automated depository transfer check system.** In this system the mail float involved in moving the transfer document from the local bank to the concentration bank is *eliminated.* Here is how it works.

The local company employee makes the daily deposit as usual. This employee does *not,* however, manually fill out the preprinted depository transfer check; instead, he or she telephones the deposit information to a regional data collection center. Usually, the center is operated for a fee by a firm, such as National Data Corporation. Various data collection centers will accumulate information throughout the day on the firm's regional deposits. Then, at specified cutoff times the deposit information from all local offices is transmitted to the concentration bank.

At this point the concentration bank prepares the depository transfer check and credits it to the company's account. The transfer checks are placed into the commercial bank check-clearing process and presented to the firm's local bank for payment. When paid by the local bank, the funds become available in the concentration account for company use. Major banks claim that funds transferred by use of the automated depository transfer check system can become available for company use in one business day or less. This system is depicted in Figure 18-6.

Wire Transfers. The fastest way to move cash between banks is by use of **wire transfers,** which eliminate transit float. Funds moved in this manner, then, immediately

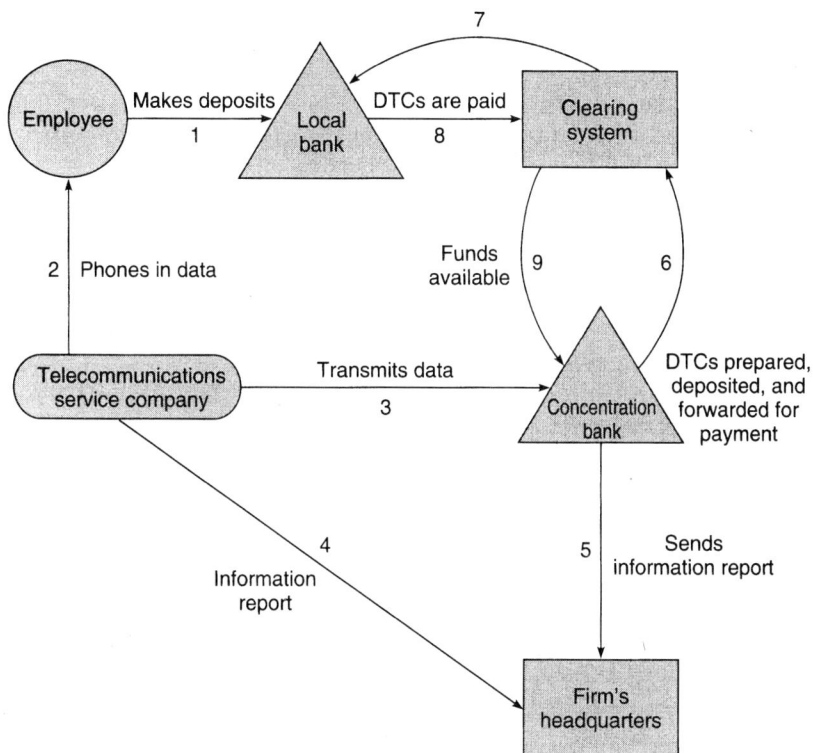

FIGURE 18-6
Automated Depository Transfer Check System (DTC)

become usable funds or "good funds" to the firm at the receiving bank. The following two major communication facilities are used to accommodate wire transfers:

1. **Bank Wire.** Bank Wire is a private wire service used and supported by approximately 250 banks in the United States for transferring funds, exchanging credit information, or effecting securities transactions.
2. **Federal Reserve Wire System.** The Fed Wire is directly accessible to commercial banks that are members of the Federal Reserve System. A commercial bank that is not on the Bank Wire or is not a member of the Federal Reserve System can use the wire transfer through its correspondent bank.

Wire transfers are often initiated on a standing-order basis. By means of a written authorization from company headquarters, a local depository bank might be instructed to transfer funds regularly to the firm's concentration bank.

As might be expected, wire transfers are a relatively expensive method of marshaling funds through a firm's money management system. Generally, the movement of small amounts does not justify the use of wire transfers.

Management of Cash Outflow

Significant techniques and systems for improving the firm's management of cash disbursements include (1) zero balance accounts, (2) payable-through drafts, and (3) remote disbursing. The first two offer markedly better control over companywide payments, and as a secondary benefit they *may* increase disbursement float. The last technique, remote disbursing, aims solely to increase disbursement float.

Zero balance accounts. Large corporations that operate multiple branches, divisions, or subsidiaries often maintain numerous bank accounts (in different banks) for the purpose of making timely operating disbursements. It does make good business sense for payments for purchased parts that go into, say, an automobile transmission to be made by the Transmission and Chassis Division of the auto manufacturer rather than its central office. The Transmission and Chassis Division originates such purchase orders, receives and inspects the shipment when it arrives at the plant, authorizes payment, and writes the appropriate check. To have the central office involved in these matters would be a waste of company time.

What tends to happen, however, is that with several divisions utilizing their own disbursal accounts, excess cash balances build up in outlying banks and rob the firm of earning assets. Zero balance accounts are used to alleviate this problem. The objectives of a zero balance account system are (1) for the firm to achieve better control over its cash payments, (2) to reduce excess cash balances held in regional banks for disbursing purposes, and (3) to increase disbursing float.

Zero balance accounts permit centralized control (at the headquarters level) over cash outflows while maintaining divisional disbursing authority. Under this system the firm's authorized employees, representing their various divisions, continue to write checks on their individual accounts. Note that the numerous individual disbursing accounts are now *all* located in the same concentration bank. Actually, these separate accounts contain no funds at all, thus their appropriate label, "zero balance." These accounts have all the characteristics of regular demand deposit accounts including separate titles, numbers, and statements.

Figure 18-7 presents a schematic of a zero balance account (ZBA) disbursing system. The firm is assumed to have three operating divisions, each with its own ZBA. The system works as follows. The firm's authorized agents write their payment checks as usual against their specific accounts (Step 1). These checks clear through the banking system in the usual way. On a daily basis checks will be presented to the firm's concentration bank (the drawee bank) for payment. As the checks are paid by the bank, negative (debit) balances will build in the proper disbursing accounts (Step 2). At the end of each day the negative balances will be restored to a zero level by means of credits to the zero balance accounts (Step 3); a corresponding reduction in funds is made against the firm's concentration (master) demand deposit account (also Step 3). Each morning a report is electronically forwarded to corporate headquarters reflecting the balance in the master account as well as the previous day's activity in each zero balance account (Step 4). Using the report, the financial officer in charge of near-cash investments is ready to initiate appropriate transactions.

Managing the cash outflow through use of a ZBA system offers the following benefits to the firm with many operating units:

1. Centralized control over disbursements is achieved, even though payment authority continues to rest with operating units.
2. Management time spent on superficial cash-management activities is reduced. Exercises such as observing the balances held in numerous bank accounts, transferring funds to those accounts short of cash, and reconciling the accounts demand less attention.
3. Excess balances held in outlying accounts can be reduced.
4. The costs of cash management can be reduced, as wire transfers to build up funds in outlying disbursement accounts are eliminated.
5. Funds may be made available for company use through an increase in disbursement float. When local bank accounts are used to pay nearby suppliers, the checks clear rapidly. The same checks, if drawn on a ZBA located in a more distant concentration bank, will take more time to clear against the disbursing firm's account.

Payable-through drafts. **Payable-through drafts** are legal instruments that have the physical appearance of ordinary checks but are *not* drawn on a bank. Instead,

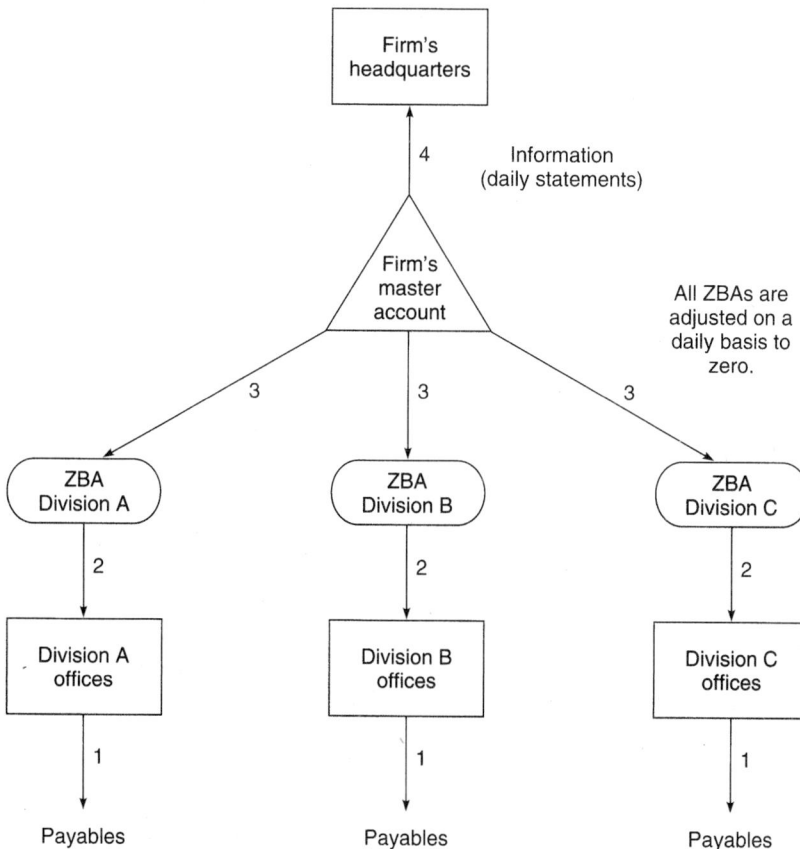

FIGURE 18-7
Zero Balance Account Cash Disbursement System (ZBA)

payable-through drafts are drawn on and payment is authorized by the issuing firm against its demand deposit account. Like checks, the drafts are cleared through the banking system and are presented to the issuing firm's bank. The bank serves as a collection point and passes the drafts on to the firm. The corporate issuer usually has to return by the following business day all drafts it does not wish to cover (pay). Those documents not returned to the bank are automatically paid. The firm inspects the drafts for validity by checking signatures, amounts, and dates. Stop-payment orders can be initiated by the company on any drafts considered inappropriate.

The main purpose of using a payable-through draft system is *to provide for effective control over field payments.* Central office control over payments begun by regional units is provided as the drafts are reviewed in advance of final payment. Payable-through drafts, for example, are used extensively in the insurance industry. The claims agent does not typically have check-signing authority against a corporate disbursement account. This agent can issue a draft, however, for quick settlement of a claim.

The Federal Reserve System requires transfer of available or "good" funds upon presentation of drafts to the payable-through bank. The payable-through bank will cover drafts but will be reluctant to absorb the float that would occur until the issuing firm authorized payment the next business day. Therefore, the drafts that are presented for payment will usually be charged *in total* against the corporate master demand deposit account. This is for purposes of measuring usable funds available to the firm on that day. Legal payment of the *individual drafts* will still take place after their review and approval by the firm. Figure 18-8 illustrates a payable-through draft system.

Remote disbursing.   A few banks will provide the corporate customer with a cash-management service specifically designed to extend disbursing float. The firm's concentration bank may have a correspondent relationship with a smaller bank located in a distant city. In that remote city the Federal Reserve System is unable to maintain frequent clearings of checks drawn on local banks. For example, a firm that is located in Dallas and maintains its master account there may open an account with a bank situated in, say, Amarillo, Texas. The firm will write the bulk of its payment checks against the account in the Amarillo bank. The checks will probably take at least one business day longer to clear, so the firm can "play the float" to its advantage.

A firm must use this technique of remote disbursing with extreme care. If a key supplier of raw materials located in Dallas has to wait the extra day for funds drawn on the Amarillo account, the possibility of incurring ill will might outweigh the apparent gain from an increase in the disbursing float. The impact on the firm's reputation of using remote disbursing should be explicitly evaluated. The practice of remote disbursing is discouraged by the Federal Reserve System.

EVALUATION OF COSTS OF CASH-MANAGEMENT SERVICES

A form of breakeven analysis can help the financial officer decide whether a particular collection or disbursement service will provide an economic benefit to the firm. The evaluation process involves a very basic relationship in microeconomics:

$$\text{added costs} = \text{added benefits} \tag{1}$$

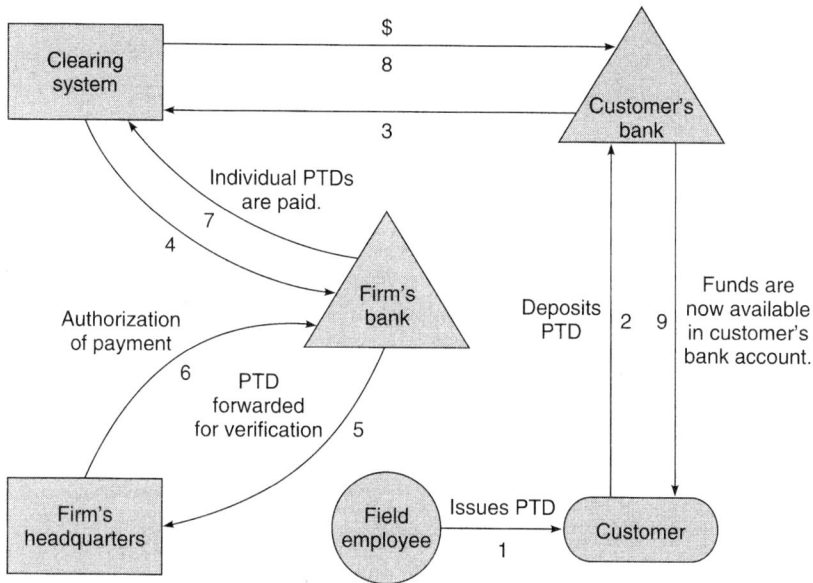

FIGURE 18-8
Payable-Through Draft Cash Disbursement System (PTD)

If equation (1) holds exactly, then the firm is no better or worse off for having adopted the given service. We will illustrate this procedure in terms of the desirability of installing an additional lock box. Equation (1) can be restated on a per-unit basis as follows:

$$P = (D)(S)(i) \tag{2}$$

where P = increases in per-check processing cost if the new system is adopted
       D = days saved in the collection process (float reduction)
       S = average check size in dollars
       i = the daily, before-tax opportunity cost (rate of return) of carrying cash

Assume now that check processing cost, P, will rise by $.18 a check if the lock box is used. The firm has determined that the average check size, S, that will be mailed to the lock-box location will be $900. If funds are freed by use of the lock box, they will be invested in marketable securities to yield an *annual* before-tax return of 6%. With these data it is possible to determine the reduction in check collection time, D, that is required to justify use of the lock box. That level of D is found to be

$$\$.18 = (D)(\$900)\left(\frac{.06}{365}\right)$$

$$1.217\,\text{days} = D$$

Thus, the lock box is justified if the firm can speed up its collections by *more* than 1.217 days. This same style of analysis can be adapted to analyze the other tools of cash management.

Before moving on to a discussion of the firm's marketable securities portfolio, it will be helpful to draw together the preceding material. Figure 18-9 summarizes the salient features of the cash-collection and disbursal techniques we have considered here.

COMPOSITION OF MARKETABLE SECURITIES PORTFOLIO

Once the design of the firm's cash receipts and payments system has been determined, the financial manager faces the task of selecting appropriate financial assets for inclusion in the firm's marketable securities portfolio.

General Selection Criteria

Certain criteria can provide the financial manager with a useful framework for selecting a proper marketable securities mix. These considerations include evaluation of the (1) financial risk, (2) interest rate risk, (3) liquidity, (4) taxability, and (5) yields among different financial assets. We will briefly delineate these criteria from the investor's viewpoint.

Financial risk.   *Financial risk* here refers to the uncertainty of expected returns from a security attributable to possible changes in the financial capacity of the security issuer to make future payments to the security owner. If the chance of default on the terms of the instrument is high (low), then the financial risk is said to be high (low).

In both financial practice and research, when estimates of riskfree returns are desired, the yields available on Treasury securities are consulted and the safety of other financial instruments is weighed against them.

Interest rate risk.   **Interest rate risk** refers to the uncertainty of expected returns from a financial instrument attributable to changes in interest rates. Of particular concern to the corporate treasurer is the price volatility associated with instruments that have long, as opposed to short, terms to maturity. An illustration can help clarify this point.

Suppose the financial officer is weighing the merits of investing temporarily available corporate cash in a new offering of U.S. Treasury obligations that will mature in either (1) three years or (2) 20 years from the date of issue. The purchase price of the three-year notes or 20-year bonds is at their par value of $1,000 per security. The maturity value of either class of security is equal to par, $1,000, and the coupon rate (stated interest rate) is set at 7%, compounded annually.

If after one year from the date of purchase prevailing interest rates rise to 9%, the market prices of these currently outstanding Treasury securities will fall to bring their yields to maturity in line with what investors could obtain by buying a new issue of a given instrument. The market prices of *both* the 3-year and 20-year obligations will decline. The price of the 20-year instrument will decline by a greater dollar amount, however, than that of the three-year instrument.

One year from the date of issue the price obtainable in the marketplace for the original 20-year instrument, which now has 19 years to go to maturity, can be found by computing P as follows:

FIGURE 18-9   Features of Selected Cash-Collection and Disbursal Techniques: A Summary

Technique	Objective	How Accomplished
Cash-Collection Techniques		
1. Lock-box system	Reduce (1) mail float, (2) processing float, and (3) transit float.	Strategic location of lock boxes to reduce mail float and transit float. Firm's commercial bank has access to lock box to reduce processing float.
2. Preauthorized checks	Reduce (1) mail float and (2) processing float.	The firm writes the checks (the PACs) *for* its customers to be charged against their demand deposit accounts.
3. (Ordinary) Depository transfer checks	Eliminate excess funds in regional banks.	Used in conjunction with concentration banking whereby the firm maintains several collection centers. The transfer check authorizes movement of funds from a local bank to the concentration bank.
4. Automated depository transfer checks	Eliminate the mail float associated with the ordinary transfer check.	Telecommunications company transmits deposit data to the firm's concentration bank.
5. Wire transfers	Move funds immediately between banks. This eliminates transit float in that only "good funds" are transferred.	Use of Bank Wire or the Federal Reserve Wire System.
Cash-Disbursal Techniques		
1. Zero balance accounts	(1) Achieve better control over cash payments, (2) reduce excess cash balances held in regional banks, and (3) possibly increase disbursing float.	Establish zero balance accounts for all of the firm's disbursing units. These accounts are all in the same concentration bank. Checks are drawn against these accounts, with the balance in each account never exceeding $0. Divisional disbursing authority is thereby maintained at the local level of management.
2. Payable-through drafts	Achieve effective central office control over field-authorized payments.	Field office issues drafts rather than checks to settle up payables.
3. Remote disbursing	Extend disbursing float.	Write checks against demand deposit accounts held in distant banks.

$$P = \sum_{t=1}^{19} \frac{\$70}{(1+.09)^t} + \frac{\$1,000}{(1+.09)^{19}} = \$821.01$$

In the previous expression (1) T is the year in which the particular return, either interest or principal amount, is received; (2) $70 is the annual interest payment; and (3) $1,000 is the contractual maturity value of the bond. The rise in interest rates has forced the market price of the bond down to $821.01.

FIGURE 18-10 Market Price Effect of Rise in Interest Rates

Item	Three-year Instrument	Twenty-year Instrument
Original price	$1,000.00	$1,000.00
Price after one year	964.84	821.01
Decline in price	$ 35.16	$ 178.99

Now, what will happen to the price of the note that has two years remaining to maturity? In a similar manner, we can compute its price, P:

$$P = \sum_{t=1}^{2} \frac{\$70}{(1+.09)^t} + \frac{\$1,000}{(1+.09)^2} = \$964.84$$

The market price of the shorter-term note will decline to $964.84. Figure 18-10 shows that the market value of the shorter-term security was penalized much less by the given rise in the general level of interest rates.

If we extended the illustration, we would see that, in terms of market price, a one-year security would be affected less than a two-year security, a 91-day security less than a 182-day security, and so on. Equity securities would exhibit the largest price changes because of their infinite maturity periods. To hedge against the price volatility caused by interest rate risk, the firm's marketable securities portfolio will tend to be composed of instruments that mature over short periods.

Liquidity.   In the present context of managing the marketable securities portfolio, **liquidity** refers to the ability to transform a security into cash. Should an unforeseen event require that a significant amount of cash be immediately available, then a sizable portion of the portfolio might have to be sold. The financial manager will want the cash *quickly* and will not want to accept a large *price concession* in order to convert the securities. Thus, in the formulation of preferences for the inclusion of particular instruments in the portfolio, the manager must consider (1) the period needed to sell the security and (2) the likelihood that the security can be sold at or near its prevailing market price.

Taxability.   The tax treatment of the income a firm receives from its security investments does not affect the ultimate mix of the marketable securities portfolio as much as the criteria mentioned earlier. This is because the interest income from most instruments suitable for inclusion in the portfolio is taxable at the federal level. Still, some corporate treasurers seriously evaluate the taxability of interest income and capital gains.

The interest income from only one class of securities escapes the federal income tax. That class of securities is generally referred to as **municipal obligations,** or more simply as **municipals.** Because of the tax-exempt feature of interest income from state and local government securities, municipals sell at lower yields to maturity in the market than do securities that pay taxable interest. The after-tax yield on a municipal obligation, however, could be higher than the yield from a non-tax-exempt security. This would depend mainly on the purchasing firm's tax situation.

Consider Figure 18-11. A firm is assumed to be analyzing whether to invest in a one-year tax-free debt issue yielding 6% on a $1,000 outlay or a one-year taxable issue that yields 8% on a $1,000 outlay. The firm pays federal taxes at the rate of 34%. The yields quoted in the financial press and in the prospectuses that describe debt issues are *before-tax* returns. The actual *after-tax* return enjoyed by the investor depends on his or her tax bracket. Notice that the actual after-tax yield received by the firm is only 5.28% on the taxable issue versus 6% on the tax-exempt obligation. The lower portion of Figure 18-11 shows that the fully taxed bond must yield 9.091% to make it comparable with the tax-exempt issue.

Yields. The final selection criterion that we mention is a significant one—the yields that are available on the different financial assets suitable for inclusion in the near-cash portfolio. By now it is probably obvious that the factors of (1) financial risk, (2) interest rate risk, (3) liquidity, and (4) taxability all influence the available yields on financial instruments. The yield criterion involves an evaluation of the risks and benefits inherent in all of these factors. If a given risk is assumed, such as lack of liquidity, a higher yield may be expected on the non-liquid instrument.

Figure 18-12 summarizes our framework for designing the firm's marketable securities portfolio. The four basic considerations are shown to influence the yields available on securities. The financial manager must focus on the risk-return tradeoffs identified through analysis. Coming to grips with these tradeoffs will enable the financial manager to determine the proper marketable securities mix for the company. Let us look now at the marketable securities prominent in firms' near-cash portfolios.

FIGURE 18-11 Comparison of After-Tax Yields

	Tax-exempt Debt Issue (6% Coupon)	Taxable Debt Issue (8% Coupon)
Interest income	$ 60.00	$ 80.00
Income tax (.34)	0.00	27.20
After-tax interest income	$ 60.00	$ 52.80
After-tax yield	$ 60.00 = 6%	$ 52.80 = 5.28%
	$1,000.00	$1,000.00

Derivation of equivalent before-tax yield on a taxable debt issue:

$$r = \frac{r^*}{1-I} = \frac{.06}{1-.34} = 9.901\%$$

where r = equivalent before-tax yield,
   r* = after-tax yield on tax-exempt security,
   T = firm's marginal income tax rate.

Proof: Interest income [$1,000 × .09091]	= $90.91
Income tax (.34)	30.91
After-tax interest income	**$60.00**

Marketable Security Alternatives

U.S. Treasury bills.   *U.S. Treasury bills* are the best-known and most popular short-term investment outlet among firms. A Treasury bill is a direct obligation of the United States government sold on a regular basis by the U.S. Treasury. New Treasury bills are issued in denominations of $10,000, $15,000, $50,000, $100,000, $500,000, and $1,000,000. In effect, therefore, one can buy bills in multiples of $5,000 above the smallest purchase price of $10,000 by combining $10,000 bills and $15,000 bills to reach the desired sum.

Bills currently are regularly offered with maturities of 91, 182, and 365 days. The three-month and six-month bills are auctioned weekly by the Treasury, and the one-year bills are offered every four weeks. Bids (orders to purchase) are accepted by the various Federal Reserve Banks and their branches, which perform the role of agents for the Treasury. Each Monday, bids are received until 1:30 P.M.; after that time they are opened, tabulated, and forwarded to the Treasury for allocation (filling the purchase orders).

Treasury bills are sold on a discount basis; for that reason the investor does not receive an actual interest payment. The return is the difference between the purchase price and the face (par) value of the bill.

The bills are marketed by the Treasury only in *bearer* form. They are purchased, therefore, without the investor's name on them. This attribute makes them easily transferable from one investor to the next. Of prime importance to the corporate treasurer is the fact that a very active secondary market exists for bills. After a bill has been acquired by the firm, should the need arise to turn it into cash, a group of securities dealers stand ready to purchase it. This highly developed secondary market for bills not only makes them extremely liquid, but also allows the firm to buy bills with maturities of a week or even less.

As bills have the full financial backing of the United States government, they are, for all practical purposes, risk free. This negligible financial risk and high degree of liquidity makes the yields lower than those obtainable on other marketable securities. The income from Treasury bills is subject to federal income taxes, but *not* to state and local government income taxes.

Federal agency securities.   **Federal agency securities** are debt obligations of corporations and agencies that have been created to effect the various lending programs of the United States government. Five such government-sponsored corporations account for the majority of outstanding agency debt. The "big five" agencies are

1. The Federal National Mortgage Association (FNMA)
2. The Federal Home Loan Banks (FHLB)

FIGURE 18-12 Designing the Marketable Securities Portfolio

Considerations	→	Influence	→	Focus Upon	→	Determine
Financial risk Interest rate risk Liquidity Taxability		Yields		Risk vs. return preferences		Marketable securities mix

---

3. The Federal Land Banks
4. The Federal Intermediate Credit Banks
5. The Banks for Cooperatives

It is not true that the "big five" federally sponsored agencies are owned by the United States government and that the securities they issue are fully guaranteed by the government. The "big five" agencies are now entirely owned by their member associations or the general public. In addition, the issuing agency stands behind its promises to pay, not the federal government.

These agencies sell their securities in a variety of denominations. The entry barrier caused by the absolute dollar size of the smallest available Treasury bill—$10,000— is not as severe in the market for agencies. A wide range of maturities is also available. Obligations can at times be purchased with maturities as short as 30 days or as long as 15 years.

Agency debt usually sells on a coupon basis and pays interest to the owner on a semiannual schedule, although there are exceptions. Some issues have been sold on a discount basis, and some have paid interest only once a year.

The income from agency debt that the investor receives is subject to taxation at the federal level. Of the "big five" agencies, only the income from FNMA issues is taxed at the state and local level.

The yields available on agency obligations will always exceed those of Treasury securities of similar maturity. This yield differential is attributable to lesser marketability and greater default risk. The financial officer might keep in mind, however, that none of these agency issues has ever gone into default.

Bankers' acceptances.   **Bankers' acceptances** are one of the least understood instruments suitable for inclusion in the firm's marketable securities portfolio. Their part in U.S. commerce today is largely concentrated in the financing of foreign transactions. Generally, an acceptance is a draft (order to pay) drawn on a specific bank by an exporter in order to obtain payment for goods shipped to a customer, who maintains an account with that specific bank.

Because acceptances are used to finance the acquisition of goods by one party, the document is not "issued" in specialized denominations; its dollar size is determined by the cost of the goods being purchased. Usual sizes, however, range from $25,000 to $1 million. The maturities on acceptances run from 30 to 180 days, although longer periods are available from time to time. The most common period is 90 days.

Acceptances, like Treasury bills, are sold on a discount basis and are payable to the bearer of the paper. A secondary market for the acceptances of large banks does exist.

The income generated from investing in acceptances is fully taxable at the federal, state, and local levels. Because of their greater financial risk and lesser liquidity, acceptances provide investors a yield advantage over Treasury bills and agency obligations. In fact, the acceptances of major banks are a very safe investment, making the yield advantage over Treasuries worth looking at from the firm's vantage point.

Negotiable certificates of deposit.   A **negotiable certificate of deposit, CD,** is a marketable receipt for funds that have been deposited in a bank for a fixed period. The deposited funds earn a fixed rate of interest. These are not to be confused with ordinary passbook savings accounts or nonmarketable time deposits offered by all commercial banks. CDs are offered by major money-center banks. We are talking here about "corporate" CDs—not those offered to individuals.

CDs are offered by key banks in a variety of denominations running from $25,000 to $10,000,000. The popular sizes are $100,000, $500,000, and $1,000,000. The original maturities on CDs can range from 1 to 18 months.

CDs are offered by banks on a basis differing from Treasury bills; that is, they are not sold at a discount. Rather, when the certificate matures, the owner receives the full amount deposited plus the earned interest.

A secondary market for CDs does exist, the heart of which is found in New York City. Whereas CDs may be issued in registered or bearer form, the latter facilitates transactions in the secondary market and thus is the more common.

Even though the secondary market for CDs of large banks is well organized, it does not operate as smoothly as the aftermarket in Treasuries. CDs are more heterogeneous than Treasury bills. Treasury bills have similar rates, maturity periods, and denominations; more variety is found in CDs. This makes it harder to liquidate large blocks of CDs, because a more specialized investor must be found. The securities dealers who "make" the secondary market in CDs mainly trade in $1 million units. Smaller denominations can be traded but will bring a relatively lower price.

The income received from an investment in CDs is subject to taxation at all government levels. In recent years CD yields have been above those available on barkers' acceptances.

Commercial paper. **Commercial paper** refers to short-term, unsecured promissory notes sold by large businesses to raise cash. These are sometimes described in the popular financial press as short-term corporate IOUs. Because they are unsecured, the issuing side of the market is dominated by large corporations, which typically maintain sound credit ratings. The issuing (borrowing) firm can sell the paper to a dealer who will in turn sell it to the investing public; if the firm's reputation is solid, the paper can be sold directly to the ultimate investor.

The denominations in which commercial paper can be bought vary over a wide range. At times paper can be obtained in sizes from $5,000 to $5 million, or even more.

Commercial paper can be purchased with maturities that range from 3 to 270 days. Notes with maturities exceeding 270 days are very rare, because they would have to be registered with the Securities and Exchange Commission—a task firms avoid, when possible, because it is time consuming and costly.

These notes are *generally* sold on a discount basis in bearer form, although sometimes paper that is interest bearing and can be made payable to the order of the investor is available.

The next point is of considerable interest to the financial officer responsible for management of the firm's near-cash portfolio. For practical purposes, there is *no* active trading in a secondary market for commercial paper. This distinguishes commercial paper from all the previously discussed short-term investment vehicles. On occasion, a dealer or finance company (the borrower) will redeem a note prior to its contract maturity date, but this is not a regular procedure. Thus, when the corporation evaluates commercial paper for possible inclusion in its marketable securities portfolio, it should plan to hold it to maturity.

The return on commercial paper is fully taxable to the investor at all levels of government. Because of its lack of marketability, commercial paper in past years consistently provided a yield advantage over other near-cash assets of comparable maturity. The lifting of interest rate ceilings in 1973 by the Federal Reserve Board on certain large CDs, however, allowed commercial banks to make CD rates fully competitive in the attempt to attract funds. Over any time period, then, CD yields *may* be slightly above the rates available on commercial paper.

Repurchase agreements. **Repurchase agreements (repos)** are legal contracts that involve the actual sale of securities by a *borrower* to the *lender,* with a commitment on the part of the borrower to *repurchase* the securities at the contract price plus a stated interest charge. The securities sold to the lender are U.S. government issues or other instruments of the money market such as those described above. The borrower is either a major financial institution—most important, a commercial bank—or a dealer in U.S. government securities.

Why might the corporation with excess cash prefer to buy repurchase agreements rather than a given marketable security? There are two major reasons. First, the original maturities of the instruments being sold can, in effect, be adjusted to suit the particular needs of the investing corporation. Funds available for very short periods, such as one or two days, can be productively employed. The second reason is closely related to the first. The firm could, of course, buy a Treasury bill and then resell it in the market in a few days when cash was required. The drawback here would be the risk involved in liquidating the bill at a price equal to its earlier cost to the firm. The purchase of a repo removes this risk. The contract price of the securities that make up the arrangement is *fixed* for the duration of the transaction. The corporation that buys a repurchase agreement, then, is protected against market price fluctuations throughout the contract period. This makes it a sound alternative investment for funds that are freed up for only very short periods.

These agreements are usually executed in sizes of $1 million or more. The maturities may be for a specified time period or may have no fixed maturity date. In the latter case either lender or borrower may terminate the contract without advance notice.

The returns the lender receives on repurchase agreements are taxed at all governmental levels. Because the interest rates are set by direct negotiation between lender and borrower, no regular published series of yields is available for direct comparison with the other short-term investments. The rates available on repurchase agreements, however, are closely related to, but generally *less* than, Treasury bill rates of comparable maturities.

Money market mutual funds. The money market funds sell their shares to raise cash, and by pooling the funds of large numbers of small savers, they can build their liquid-asset portfolios. Many of these funds allow the investor to start an account with as little as $1,000. This small initial investment, coupled with the fact that some liquid-asset funds permit subsequent investments in amounts as small as $100, makes this type of outlet for excess cash suited to the small firm and even the individual. Furthermore, the management of a small enterprise may not be highly versed in the details of short-term investments. By purchasing shares in a liquid-asset fund, the investor is also buying managerial expertise.

Money market funds typically invest in a diversified portfolio of short-term, high-grade debt instruments such as those described above. Some such funds, however, will accept more interest rate risk in their portfolios and acquire some corporate bonds and notes. Money market mutual funds offer the investing firm a high degree of liquidity. By redeeming (selling) shares, the investor can obtain cash quickly. Procedures for liquidation vary among the funds, but shares can usually be redeemed by means of (1) special redemption checks supplied by the fund, (2) telephone instructions, (3) wire instructions, or (4) a letter. When liquidation is ordered by telephone or wire, the mutual fund can remit to the investor by the next business day.

The returns earned from owning shares in a money market fund are taxable at all governmental levels. The yields follow the returns the investor could receive by purchasing the marketable securities directly.

The Yield Structure of Marketable Securities

What type of return can the financial manager expect on a marketable securities portfolio? This is a reasonable question. Some insight can be obtained by looking at the past, although we must realize that future returns are not guided by past experience. It is also useful to have some understanding of how the returns on one type of instrument stack up against another. The behavior of yields on short-term debt instruments over the 1980-1992 period is shown in Figure 18-13.

The discussion in this chapter on designing the firm's marketable securities portfolio touched on the essential elements of several near cash assets. At times it is difficult to sort out the distinguishing features among these short-term investments. To alleviate that problem, Figure 18-14 draws together their principal characteristics.

FIGURE 18-13 Annual Yields (Percent) on Selected Three-Month Marketable Securities

Year	T-Bills	Agencies	Acceptances	Commercial Paper	CDs
1980	11.51	12.09	12.72	12.66	13.07
1981	14.03	15.28	15.32	15.32	15.91
1982	10.69	11.68	11.89	11.89	12.27
1983	8.61	8.95	8.90	8.88	9.07
1984	9.52	10.13	10.14	10.10	10.37
1985	7.48	8.00	7.92	7.95	8.05
1986	5.98	6.49	6.38	6.49	6.51
1987	5.82	6.47	6.75	6.82	6.87
1988	6.68	7.60	7.56	7.66	7.73
1989	8.12	8.75	8.87	8.99	9.09
1990	7.51	7.99	7.93	8.06	8.15
1991	5.42	5.81	5.70	5.87	5.83
1992	3.45	n.a.	3.62	3.75	3.68

Source: *Federal Reserve Bulletin*, various issues. Note: n.a. means not available.

FIGURE 18-14 Features of Selected Money Market Instruments

Instrument	Denominations	Maturities	Basis	Form	Liquidity	Taxability
U.S. Treasury bills—direct obligations of the U.S. government	$10,000 15,000 50,000 100,000 500,000 1,000,000	91 days 182 days 365 days 9-month not presently issued	Discount	Bearer	Excellent secondary market	Exempt from state and local income
Federal agency securities—obligations of corporations and agencies created to effect the federal government's lending programs	Wide variation; from $1,000 to $1 million	5 days (Farm Credit consolidated system-wide discount notes) to more than 10 years	Discount or coupon; usually on coupon	Bearer or registered	Good for issues of "big five" agencies	Generally exempt at local level; FNMA issues are *not*
Bankers' acceptances—drafts accepted for future payment by commercial banks	No set size; typically range from $25,000 to $1 million	Predominantly from 30 to 180 days	Discount	Bearer	Good for acceptances of large "money market" banks	Taxed at all levels of government
Negotiable certificates of deposit—marketable receipts for funds deposited in a bank for a fixed time period	$25,000 to $10 million	1 to 18 months	Accrued interest	Bearer or registered; bearer is preferable from liquidity standpoint	Fair to good	Taxed at all levels of government
Commercial paper—short-term unsecured promissory notes	$5,000 to $5 million; $1,000 and $5,000 multiples above the initial offering size are sometimes available	3 to 270 days	Discount	Bearer	Poor; no active secondary market in usual sense	Taxed at all levels of government
Repurchase agreements—legal contracts between a borrower (security seller) and lender (security buyer). The borrower will repurchase at the contract price plus an interest charge.	Typical sizes are $500,000 or more	According to terms of contract	Not applicable	Not applicable	Fixed by the agreement; that is, borrower will repurchase	Taxed at all levels of government
Money market mutual funds—holders of diversified portfolios of short-term, high-grade debt instruments	Some require an initial investment as small as $1,000	Your shares can be sold at any time	Net asset value	Registered	Good; provided by the fund itself	Taxed at all levels of government

ACCOUNTS RECEIVABLE MANAGEMENT

We now turn from the most liquid of the firm's current assets (cash and marketable securities) to those which are less liquid—accounts receivable and inventories. All firms by their very nature are involved in selling either goods or services. Although some of these sales will be for cash, a large portion will involve credit. Whenever a sale is made on credit, it increases the firm's accounts receivable. Thus, the importance of how a firm manages its accounts receivable depends on the degree to which the firm sells on credit.

Accounts receivable typically comprise over 25% of a firm's assets. In effect, when we discuss management of accounts receivable, we are discussing the management of one-quarter of the firm's assets. Moreover, because cash flows from a sale cannot be invested until the account is collected, control of receivables takes on added importance; efficient collection determines both profitability and liquidity of the firm.

Size of Investment in Accounts Receivable

The size of the investment in accounts receivable is determined by several factors. First, the percentage of credit sales to total sales affects the level of accounts receivable held. Although this factor certainly plays a major role in determining a firm's investment in accounts receivable, it generally is not within the control of the financial manager. The nature of the business tends to determine the blend between credit sales and cash sales. A large grocery store tends to sell exclusively on a cash basis, whereas most construction-lumber supply firms make their sales primarily with credit.

The level of sales is also a factor in determining the size of the investment in accounts receivable. Very simply, the more sales, the greater accounts receivable. It is not a decision variable for the financial manager, however.

The final determinants of the level of investment in accounts receivable are the credit and collection policies—more specifically, the *terms of sale,* the *quality of customer,* and *collection efforts.* These policies *are* under the control of the financial manager. The terms of sale specify both the time period during which the customer must pay and the terms, such as penalties for late payments or discounts for early payments. The type of customer or credit policy also affects the level of investment in accounts receivable. For example, the acceptance of poorer credit risks and their subsequent delinquent payments may lead to an increase in accounts receivable. The strength and timing of the collection efforts can affect the period for which past-due accounts remain delinquent, which in turn affects the level of accounts receivable. Collection and credit policy decisions may further affect the level of investment in accounts receivable by causing changes in the sales level and the ratio of credit sales to total sales. The factors that determine the level of investment in accounts receivable are displayed in Figure 18-15.

Terms of Sale—Decision Variable

The **terms of sale** identify the possible discount for early payment, the discount period, and the total credit period. They are generally stated in the form a/b net c, indicating that the customer can deduct a percent if the account is paid within b days;

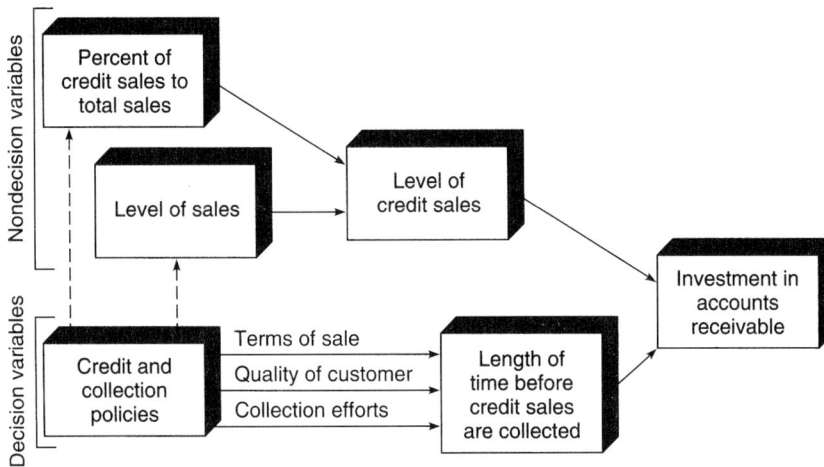

FIGURE 18-15
Determinants of Investment in Accounts Receivable

otherwise, the account must be paid within c days. Thus, for example, trade credit terms of 2/10, net 30 indicate that a 2% discount can be taken if the account is paid within 10 days; otherwise it must be paid within 30 days. Failure to take the discount represents a cost to the customer. For instance, if the terms are 2/10, net 30, the annualized opportunity cost of passing up this 2% discount in order to withhold payment for an additional 20 days is 36.73%. This is determined as follows:

$$\left(\begin{array}{c} \text{annualized opportunity cost} \\ \text{of forgoing the discount} \end{array}\right) = \frac{a}{1-a} \times \frac{360}{c-b} \tag{3}$$

Substituting the values from the example, we get

$$36.73\% = \frac{.02}{1-.02} \times \frac{360}{30-10} \tag{4}$$

In industry the typical discount ranges anywhere from one-half percent to 10%, whereas the discount period is generally 10 days and the total credit period varies from 30 to 90 days. Although the terms of credit vary radically from industry to industry, they tend to remain relatively uniform within any particular industry. Moreover, the terms tend to remain relatively constant over time, and they do not appear to be used frequently as a decision variable.

Type of Customer—Decision Variable

A second decision variable involves determining the *type of customer* who is to qualify for trade credit. Several costs always are associated with extending credit to less creditworthy customers. First, as the probability of default increases, it becomes more important to identify which of the possible new customers would be a poor risk. When more time is spent investigating the less credit-worthy customer, the costs of credit investigation increase.

Default costs also vary directly with the quality of the customer. As the customer's credit rating declines, the chance that the account will not be paid on time increases. In the extreme case, payment never occurs. Thus, taking on less credit-worthy customers results in increases in default costs.

Collection costs also increase as the quality of the customer declines. More delinquent accounts force the firm to spend more time and money collecting them. Overall, the decline in customer quality results in increased costs of credit investigation, collection, and default.

In determining whether to grant credit to an individual customer, we are primarily interested in the customer's short-run welfare. Thus, liquidity ratios, other obligations, and the overall profitability of the firm become the focal point in this analysis. Credit-rating services, such as Dun & Bradstreet, provide information on the financial status, operations, and payment history for most firms. Other possible sources of information would include credit bureaus, trade associations, Chambers of Commerce, competitors, bank references, public financial statements, and, of course, the firm's past relationship with the customer.

One way in which both individuals and firms are often evaluated as credit risks is through the use of credit scoring. **Credit scoring** involves the numerical evaluation of each applicant. An applicant receives a score based on his or her answers to a simple set of questions. This score is then evaluated according to a predetermined standard, its level relative to the standard determining whether credit should be extended. The major advantage of credit scoring is that it is inexpensive and easy to perform. For example, once the standards are set, a computer or clerical worker without any specialized training could easily evaluate any applicant.

The techniques used for constructing credit-scoring indexes range from the simple approach of adding up default rates associated with the answers given to each question, to sophisticated evaluations using multiple discriminate analysis (MDA). MDA is a statistical technique for calculating the appropriate importance to assign each question used in evaluating the applicant.

Another model that could be used for credit scoring has been provided by Edward Altman, who used multiple discriminant analysis to identify businesses that might go bankrupt. In his landmark study Altman used financial ratios to predict which firms would go bankrupt over the period 1946 to 1965. Using multiple discriminant analysis, Altman came up with the following index:

$$Z = 3.3 \left(\frac{EBIT}{total\ assets} \right) + 1.0 \left(\frac{sales}{total\ assets} \right) + 0.6 \left(\frac{market\ value\ of\ equity}{book\ value\ of\ debt} \right)$$

$$+ 1.4 \left(\frac{retained\ earnings}{total\ assets} \right) + 1.2 \left(\frac{working\ capital}{total\ assets} \right)$$

(5)

Altman found that of the firms that event bankrupt over this time period, 94% had Z scores of less than 2.7 one year prior to bankruptcy and only 6% had scores above 2.7%. Conversely, of those firms that did not go bankrupt, only 3% had Z scores below 2.7 and 97% had scores above 2.7.

Collection Efforts—Decision Variable

The key to maintaining control over collection of accounts receivable is the fact that the probability of default increases with the age of the account. Thus, control of accounts receivable focuses on the control and elimination of past-due receivables. One common way of evaluating the current situation is **ratio analysis**. The financial manager can determine whether accounts receivables are under control by examining the average collection period, the ratio of receivables to assets, the ratio of credit sales to receivables (called the accounts receivable turnover ratio), and the amount of bad debts relative to sales over time. In addition, the manager can perform what is called an aging of accounts receivable to provide a breakdown in both dollars and in percentages of the proportion of receivables that are past due. Comparing the current aging of receivables with past data offers even more control.

Once the delinquent accounts have been identified, the firm's accounts receivable group makes an effort to collect them. For example, a past-due letter, called a *dunning letter,* is sent if payment is not received on time, followed by an additional dunning letter in a more serious tone if the account becomes 3 weeks past due, followed after 6 weeks by a telephone call. Finally, if the account becomes 12 weeks past due, it might be turned over to a collection agency. Again, a direct tradeoff exists between collection expenses and lost goodwill on one hand and noncollection of accounts on the other, and this tradeoff is always part of making the decision.

INVENTORY MANAGEMENT

Inventory management involves the control of the assets that are produced to be sold in the normal course of the firm's operations. The general categories of inventory include raw materials inventory, work-in-process inventory, and finished goods inventory. The importance of inventory management to the firm depends on the extent of the inventory investment. For an average firm, approximately 4.88% of all assets are in the form of inventory. However, the percentage varies widely from industry to industry. Thus the importance of inventory management and control varies from industry to industry also. For example, it is much more important in the automotive dealer and service station trade, where inventories make up 49.72% of total assets, than in the hotel business, where the average investment in inventory is only 1.56% of total assets.

Purposes and Types of Inventory

The purpose of carrying inventories is to uncouple the operations of the firm—that is, to make each function of the business independent of each other function—so that delays or shutdowns in one area do not affect the production and sale of the final product. Because production shutdowns result in increased costs, and because delays in delivery can lose customers, the management and control of inventory are important duties of the financial manager.

Decision making in investment in inventory involves a basic tradeoff between risk and return. The risk is that if the level of inventory is too low, the various functions of business do not operate independently, and delays in production and customer delivery can result. The return results because reduced inventory investment saves money. As the size of inventory increases, storage and handling costs as well as the required return on capital invested in inventory rise. Therefore, as the inventory a firm holds is increased, the risk of running out of inventory is lessened, but inventory expenses rise.

Raw Materials Inventory

Raw materials inventory consists of basic materials purchased from other firms to be used in the firm's production operations. These goods may include steel, lumber, petroleum, or manufactured items such as wire, ball bearings, or tires that the firm does not produce itself. Regardless of the specific form of the raw materials inventory, all manufacturing firms by definition maintain a raw materials inventory. Its purpose is to uncouple the production function from the purchasing function—that is, to make these two functions independent of each other, so that delays in shipment of raw materials do not cause production delays. In the event of a delay in shipment, the firm can satisfy its need for raw materials by liquidating its inventory.

Work-in-Process Inventory

Work-in-process inventory consists of partially finished goods requiring additional work before they become finished goods. The more complex and lengthy the production process, the larger the investment in work-in-process inventory. The purpose of work-in-process inventory is to uncouple the various operations in the production process so that machine failures and work stoppages in one operation will not affect the other operations. Assume, for example, there are 10 different production operations, each one involving the piece of work produced in the previous operation. If the machine performing the first production operation breaks down, a firm with no work-in-process inventory will have to shut down all 10 production operations. Yet if a firm has such inventory, the remaining 9 operations can continue by drawing the input for the second operation from inventory.

Finished-Goods Inventory

Finished-goods inventory consists of goods on which production has been completed but that are not yet sold. The purpose of a finished-goods inventory is to uncouple the production and sales functions so that it is not necessary to produce the good before a sale can occur— sales can be made directly out of inventory. In the auto industry, for example, people would not buy from a dealer who made them wait weeks or months when another dealer could fill the order immediately.

Stock of Cash

Although we have already discussed cash management at some length, it is worthwhile to mention cash again in the light of inventory management. This is because the *stock of cash* carried by a firm is simply a special type of inventory. In terms of uncoupling the various operations of the firm, the purpose of holding a stock of cash is to make the payment of bills independent of the collection of accounts due. When cash is kept on hand, bills can be paid without prior collection of accounts.

Inventory-Management Techniques

The importance of effective inventory management is directly related to the size of the investment in inventory. Effective management of these assets is essential to the goal of shareholder wealth maximization. To control the investment in inventory, management must solve two problems: the order quantity problem and the order point problem.

Order Quantity Problem

The *order quantity problem* involves determining the optimal order size for an inventory item given its expected usage, carrying costs, and ordering costs.

The economic order quantity (EOQ) model attempts to determine the order size that will minimize total inventory costs. It assumes that

$$\frac{\text{total}}{\text{inventory costs}} = \frac{\text{total}}{\text{carrying costs}} + \frac{\text{total}}{\text{ordering costs}} \tag{6}$$

Assuming that inventory is allowed to fall to zero and then is immediately replenished (this assumption will be lifted when we discuss the order point problem), the average inventory becomes $Q/2$, where Q is inventory order size in units. This can be seen graphically in Figure 18-16.

If the average inventory is $Q/2$ and the carrying cost per unit is C, then carrying costs become:

$$\frac{\text{total}}{\text{carrying costs}} = \left(\frac{\text{average}}{\text{inventory}}\right)\left(\frac{\text{carrying cost}}{\text{per unit}}\right) \tag{7}$$

$$= \left(\frac{Q}{2}\right) C \tag{8}$$

$$\begin{aligned} \text{where } Q &= \text{the inventory order size in units} \\ C &= \text{carrying costs per unit} \end{aligned}$$

The carrying costs on inventory include the required rate of return on investment in inventory, in addition to warehouse or storage costs, wages for those who operate the warehouse, and costs associated with inventory shrinkage. Thus, carrying costs include both real cash flows and opportunity costs associated with having funds tied up in inventory.

The ordering costs incurred are equal to the ordering costs per order times the number of orders. If we assume total demand over the planning period is S and we order in lot sizes of Q, then S/Q represents the number of orders over the planning period. If the ordering cost per order is O, then

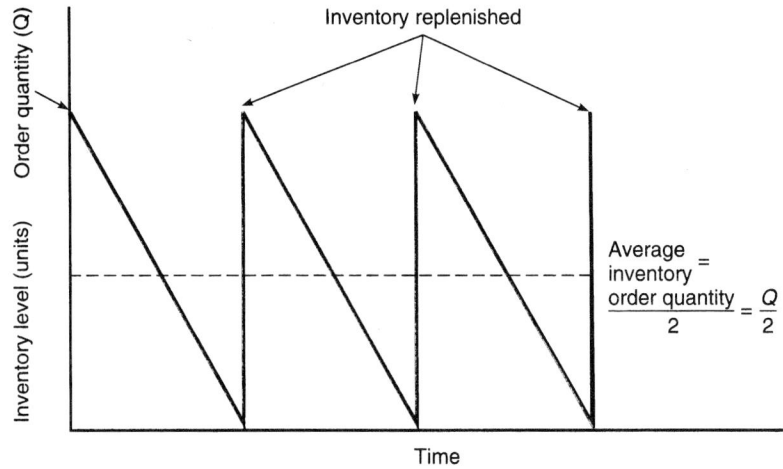

FIGURE 18-16   Inventory Level and the Replenishment Cycle

$$\begin{array}{c} \text{total} \\ \text{ordering costs} \end{array} = \left(\begin{array}{c} \text{number} \\ \text{of orders} \end{array} \right) \left(\begin{array}{c} \text{ordering cost} \\ \text{per order} \end{array} \right) \tag{9}$$

$$= \left(\frac{S}{Q} \right) O \tag{10}$$

where S = total demand in units over the planning period
O = ordering cost per order

Thus, total costs in equation (6) become

$$\text{total costs} = \left(\frac{Q}{2} \right) C + \left(\frac{S}{Q} \right) O \tag{11}$$

Figure 18-17 illustrates this equation graphically.

What we are looking for is the ordering size, Q^*, which provides the minimum total costs. By manipulating equation (11), we find that the optimal value of Q—that is, the economic ordering quantity (EOQ)—is

$$Q^* = \sqrt{\frac{2SO}{C}} \tag{12}$$

The use of the EOQ model can best be illustrated through an example. Suppose a firm expects total demand (S) for its product over the planning period to be 5,000 units, whereas the ordering cost per order (O) is $200 and the carrying cost per unit (C) is $2. Substituting these values into equation (12) yields

$$Q^* = \sqrt{\frac{2 \cdot 5000 \cdot 200}{2}} = \sqrt{1,000,000} = 1,000 \text{ units}$$

Thus, if this firm orders in 1,000-unit lot sizes, it will minimize its total inventory costs.

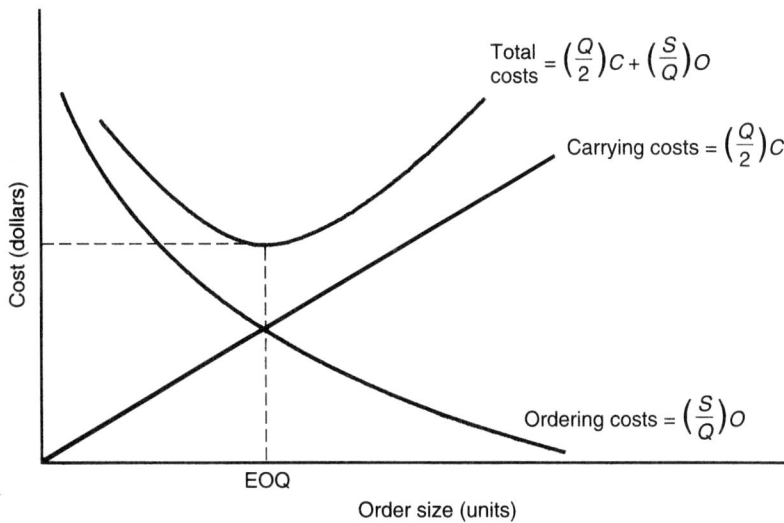

$$\text{Total costs} = \left(\frac{Q}{2}\right)C + \left(\frac{S}{Q}\right)O$$

$$\text{Carrying costs} = \left(\frac{Q}{2}\right)C$$

$$\text{Ordering costs} = \left(\frac{S}{Q}\right)O$$

FIGURE 18-17   Total Cost and EOQ Determination

Examination of EOQ Assumptions

Despite the fact that the EOQ model tends to yield quite good results, there are weaknesses in the EOQ model associated with several of its assumptions. When its assumptions have been dramatically violated, the EOQ model can generally be modified to accommodate the situation. The model's assumptions are as follows:

1. **Constant or uniform demand.** Although the EOQ model assumes constant demand, demand may vary from day to day. If demand is stochastic—that is, not known in advance—the model must be modified through the inclusion of a safety stock.
2. **Constant unit price.** The inclusion of variable prices resulting from quantity discounts can be handled quite easily through a modification of the original EOQ model, redefining total costs and solving for the optimum order quantity.
3. **Constant carrying costs.** Unit carrying costs may vary substantially as the size of the inventory rises, perhaps decreasing because of economies of scale or storage efficiency or increasing as storage space runs out and new warehouses have to be rented. This situation can be handled through a modification in the original model similar to the one used for variable unit price.
4. **Constant ordering costs.** Although this assumption is generally valid, its violation can be accommodated by modifying the original EOQ model in a manner similar to the one used for variable unit price.
5. **Instantaneous delivery.** If delivery is not instantaneous, which is generally the case, the original EOQ model must be modified through the inclusion of a safety stock, that is, the inventory held to accommodate any unusually large and unexpected usage during the delivery time.
6. **Independent orders.** If multiple orders result in cost savings by reducing paperwork and transportation cost, the original EOQ model must be further modified.

Although this modification is somewhat complicated, special EOQ models have been developed to deal with it.

These assumptions illustrate the limitations of the basic EOQ model and the ways in which it can be modified to compensate for them. An understanding of the limitations and assumptions of the EOQ model provides the financial manager with more of a base for making inventory decisions.

Order Point Problem

The two most limiting assumptions—those of constant or uniform demand and instantaneous delivery—are dealt with through the inclusion of **safety stock,** which is the inventory held to accommodate any unusually large and unexpected usage during delivery time. The decision on how much safety stock to hold is generally referred to as the **order point problem;** that is, how low should inventory be depleted before it is reordered?

Two factors go into the determination of the appropriate order point: (1) the procurement or delivery-time stock and (2) the safety stock desired. Figure 18-18 graphs the process involved in order point determination. We observe that the order point problem can be decomposed into its two components, the **delivery-time stock**—that is, the inventory needed between the order date and the receipt of the inventory ordered—and the safety stock. Thus, the order point is reached when inventory falls to a level equal to the delivery-time stock plus the safety stock.

$$\begin{matrix} \text{inventory order point} \\ \text{[order new inventory} \\ \text{when the level of inventory} \\ \text{falls to this level]} \end{matrix} = \begin{pmatrix} \text{delivery-time} \\ \text{stock} \end{pmatrix} + \begin{pmatrix} \text{safety} \\ \text{stock} \end{pmatrix} \tag{13}$$

As a result of constantly carrying safety stock, the average level of inventory increases. Whereas before the inclusion of safety stock the average level of inventory was equal to EOQ/2, now it will be

$$\text{average inventory} = \frac{\text{EOQ}}{2} + \text{safety stock} \tag{14}$$

In general, several factors simultaneously determine how much delivery-time stock and safety stock should be held. First, the efficiency of the replenishment system affects how much delivery-time stock is needed. Because the delivery-time stock is the expected inventory usage between ordering and receiving inventory, efficient replenishment of inventory would reduce the need for delivery-time stock.

The uncertainty surrounding both the delivery time and the demand for the product affects the level of safety stock needed. The more certain the patterns of these inflows and outflows from the inventory, the less safety stock required. In effect, if these inflows and outflows are highly predictable, then there is little chance of any stock-out occurring. However, if they are unpredictable, it becomes necessary to carry additional safety stock to prevent unexpected stock-outs.

The safety margin desired also affects the level of safety stock held. If it is a costly experience to run out of inventory, the safety stock held will be larger than it would be otherwise. If running out of inventory and the subsequent delay in supplying

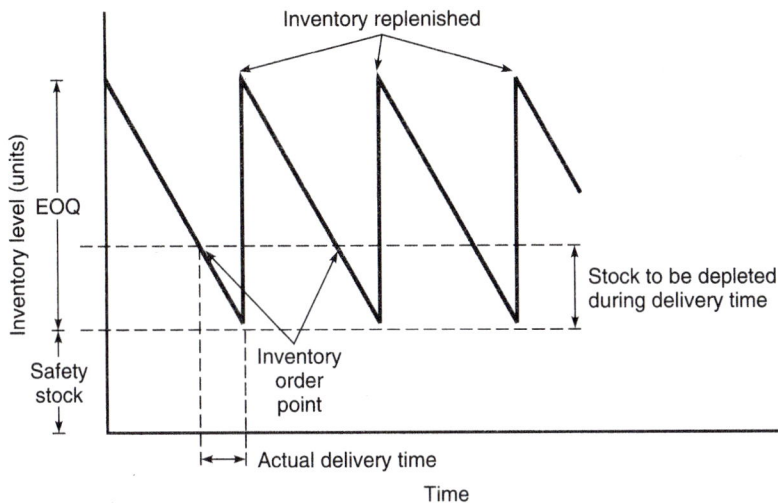

FIGURE 18-18   Order Point Determination

customers result in strong customer dissatisfaction and the possibility of lost future sales, then additional safety stock is necessary. A final determinant is the cost of carrying additional inventory, in terms of both the handling and storage costs and the opportunity cost associated with the investment in additional inventory. Very simply, the greater the costs, the smaller the safety stock.

Inflation and EOQ

Inflation affects the EOQ model in two major ways. First, although the EOQ model can be modified to assume constant price increases, often major price increases occur only once or twice a year and are announced ahead of time. If this is the case, the EOQ model may lose its applicability and may be replaced with **anticipatory buying**—that is, buying in anticipation of a price increase to secure the goods at a lower cost. Of course, as with most decisions, there are tradeoffs. The costs are the added carrying costs associated with the inventory. The benefits, of course, come from buying at a lower price. The second way inflation affects the EOQ model is through increased carrying costs. As inflation pushes interest rates up, the cost of carrying inventory increases. In our EOQ model this means that C increases, which results in a decline in Q*, the optimal economic order quantity:

$$\downarrow Q^* = \sqrt{\frac{2SO}{C\uparrow}} \tag{15}$$

JUST-IN-TIME INVENTORY CONTROL

The **just-in-time inventory control system** is more than just an inventory control system, it is a production and management system. Not only is inventory cut down to a minimum, but the time and physical distance between the various production operations are also reduced. In addition, management is willing to trade off costs to develop close relationships with suppliers and promote speedy replenishment of inventory in return for the ability to hold less safety stock.

The just-in-time inventory control system was originally developed in Japan by Taiichi Okno, a vice-president of Toyota. The idea behind the system is that the firm should keep a minimum level of inventory on hand, relying on suppliers to furnish parts "just in time" for them to be assembled. This is in direct contrast to the traditional inventory philosophy of U.S. firms, which is sometimes referred to as a "just-in-case" system, which keeps healthy levels of safety stocks to ensure that production will not be interrupted. Although large inventories may not be a bad idea when interest rates are low, when interest rates are high they become very costly.

Although the just-in-time inventory system is intuitively appealing, it has not proved easy to implement. Long distances from suppliers and plants constructed with too much space for storage and not enough access (doors and loading docks) to receive inventory have limited successful implementation. But many firms' relationships with their suppliers have been forced to change. Because firms rely on suppliers to deliver high-quality parts and materials immediately, they must have a close long-term relationship with them. Despite the difficulties of implementation, many U.S. firms are committed to moving toward a just-in-time system. In fact, between 1977 and 1986 the average level of inventory relative to total assets for all American corporations fell by 46.04%.

Although the just-in-time system does not at first appear to bear much of a relationship to the EOQ model, it simply alters some of the assumptions of the model with respect to delivery time and ordering costs, and draws out the implications. Actually, it is just a new approach to the EOQ model that tries to produce the lowest average level of inventory possible. If we look at the average level of inventory as defined by the EOQ model, we find it to be

$$\text{average inventory} = \frac{\sqrt{\dfrac{2SO\downarrow}{C}}}{2} + \text{safety stock}\downarrow$$

The just-in-time system attacks this equation in two places. First, by locating inventory supplies in convenient locations, laying out plants in such a way that it is inexpensive and easy to unload new inventory shipments, and computerizing the inventory order system, the cost of ordering new inventory, O, is reduced. Second, by developing a strong relationship with suppliers located in the same geographical area and setting up restocking strategies that cut time, the safety stock is also reduced. The philosophy behind the just-in-time inventory system is that the benefits associated with reducing inventory and delivery time to a bare minimum through adjustment in the EOQ model will more than offset the costs associated with the increased possibility of stock-outs.

SUMMARY

In this chapter, we have developed many of the tools that a financial manager needs to manage the firm's cash and other current assets with the overall objective of ensuring that the firm has an appropriate level of liquidity or net working capital to carry out the goal of maximizing shareholder wealth.

The firm experiences both regular and irregular cash flows. Once cash is obtained, the firm will have three motives for holding cash rather than investing it: to satisfy transactions, precautionary and speculative liquidity needs. To a certain extent, such needs can be satisfied by holding readily marketable securities rather than cash. A significant challenge of cash management, then, is dealing with the tradeoff between the firm's need to have cash on hand to pay liabilities that arise in the course of doing business and the objective of maximizing wealth by reducing to a minimum idle cash balances that earn no return.

Various procedures exist to improve the efficiency of a firm's cash management. Such procedures focus not only (although primarily) on accelerating the firm's cash receipts, but also on improving the methods for disbursing cash. Generally, at the heart of attempts to accelerate cash receipts is a significant effort to reduce the mail, processing and transit elements of the float. Often used in conjunction with concentration banking and a lock-box arrangement are depository transfer checks and wire transfers.

On the cash disbursements side, firms try to prolong the time cash stays in their own accounts by increasing the disbursement float through the use of zero balance accounts, payable-through drafts, and, especially, remote disbursing. The first two of these methods also offer much better central-office control over disbursements. Before any collection or disbursement procedure is introduced, however, a careful analysis should be performed to ensure that expected benefits outweigh the expected costs of such procedures.

Because idle cash earns no return, a financial manager will look for opportunities to invest such cash until it is required in the operations of the company. A variety of different readily marketable securities, which are described in the chapter, are available in the market today. The yields on such securities vary depending on four factors: the (1) financial risk, (2) interest rate risk, (3) liquidity, and (4) taxability of the security. By simultaneously taking into account these factors and the desired rate of return, the financial manager is able to determine the most suitable mix of cash and marketable securities for the firm.

When we consider that accounts receivable constitute approximately 25% of total assets for the typical firm, the importance of accounts receivable management becomes even more apparent. The size of a firm's investment in accounts receivable depends on three factors: the percentage of credit sales to total sales, the level of sales, and the credit and collection policies of the firm. The financial manager, however, generally only has control over the terms of sale, the quality of customer, and the collection efforts.

Although the level of investment in inventories by the typical firm is less than the investment in accounts receivable, inventory management and control remains an important function of the financial manager because inventories play a significant role in the operations of the firm. The purpose of holding inventory is to make each function of the business independent of the other functions. The primary issues related to inventory management are: How much inventory should be ordered and when the order should be placed. The EOQ model is used to answer the first of these questions. The order-point model, which depends on the desired levels of delivery-time stock and safety stock, is applied to answer the second question. The relatively new just-in-time approach to inventory control is growing in popularity as an attempt to obtain additional cost savings by reducing the level of inventory a firm needs to have on hand. Instead of depending solely on its own inventories, the firm relies on its vendors to furnish supplies "just in time" to satisfy the firm's production requirements.

SELF-CORRECTION PROBLEMS

1. Mountaineer Outfitters has $2 million in excess cash that it might invest in marketable securities. To buy and sell the securities, however, the firm must pay a transactions fee of $45,000.

   a. Would you recommend purchasing the securities if they yield 12% annually and are held for

      (1) One month?
      (2) Two months?
      (3) Three months?
      (4) Six months?
      (5) One year?

   b. What minimum required yield would the securities have to return for the firm to hold them for three months? (What is the breakeven yield for a three-month holding period?)

2. Consider the following inventory information and relationships for the F. Beamer Corporation:

   - Orders can be placed only in multiples of 100 units.
   - Annual unit usage is 300,000. (Assume a 50-week year in your calculations.)
   - The carrying cost is 30% of the purchase price of the goods.
   - The purchase price is $10 per unit.
   - The ordering cost is $50 per order.
   - The desired safety stock is 1,000 units. (This does not include delivery-time stock.)
   - Delivery time is two weeks.

   Given this information

   a. What is the optimal EOQ level?
   b. How many orders will be placed annually?
   c. At what inventory level should a reorder be made?

SOLUTIONS TO SELF-CORRECTION PROBLEMS

1. a. Here we must calculate the dollar value of the estimated return for each holding period and compare it with the transactions fee to determine if a gain can be made by investing in the securities. Those calculations and the resultant recommendations follow:

		Recommendation
(1) $2,000,000 (.12) (1/12)	= $ 20,000 < $45,000	No
(2) $2,000,000 (.12) (2/12)	= $ 40,000 < $45,000	No
(3) $2,000,000 (.12) (3/12)	= $ 60,000 > $45,000	Yes
(4) $2,000,000 (.12) (6/12)	= $120,000 > $45,000	Yes
(5) $2,000,000 (.12) (12/12)	= $240,000 > $45,000	Yes

b. Let (%) be the required yield. With $2 million to invest for three months we have

$2,000,000 (%) (3/12)   = $ 45,000
$2,000,000 (%)   = $180,000
                        = $180,000/2,000,000 = 9%

The breakeven yield, therefore, is 9%.

2. a.

$$EOQ = \sqrt{\frac{2SO}{C}}$$

$$= \sqrt{\frac{2(300,000)(50)}{3}}$$

= 3,162 units, but because orders must be placed in 100 unit lots, the effective EOQ becomes 3,200 units.

b.

$$\frac{\text{Total usage}}{\text{EOQ}} = \frac{300,000}{3,200} = 93.75 \text{ orders per year}$$

c.

Inventory order point = delivery time + safety stock

$$= \frac{2}{50} \times 300,000 + 1,000$$

$$= 12,000 + 1,000$$

$$= 13,000 \text{ units}$$

QUESTIONS

1. What is meant by the cash flow process?
2. Identify the principal motives for holding cash and near-cash assets. Explain the purpose of each motive.
3. What is concentration banking and how may it be of value to the firm?
4. What are the two major objectives of the firm's cash-management system?
5. What three decisions dominate the cash-management process?
6. Within the context of cash management, what are the key elements of (total) float? Briefly define each element.

7. Distinguish between financial risk and interest rate risk as these terms are commonly used in discussions of cash management.

8. Your firm invests in only three different classes of marketable securities: commercial paper, Treasury bills, and federal agency securities. Recently, yields on these money market instruments of three months' maturity were quoted at 6.10, 6.25, and 5.90%. Match the available yields with the types of instruments your firm purchases.

9. What key factors might induce a firm to invest in repurchase agreements rather than a specific security of the money market?

10. What factors determine the size of the investment a firm makes in accounts receivable? Which of these factors are under the control of the financial manager?

11. If a credit manager experienced no bad debt losses over the past year, would this be an indication of proper credit management? Why or why not?

12. What are the risk-return tradeoffs associated with adopting a more liberal trade credit policy?

13. What is the purpose of holding inventory? Name several types of inventory and describe their purpose.

14. Can cash be considered a special type of inventory? If so, what functions does it attempt to uncouple?

15. What are the major assumptions made by the EOQ model?

16. How might inflation affect the EOQ model?

PROBLEMS

1. **Concentration Banking.**   Byron Sporting Goods operates in Miami, Florida. The firm produces and distributes a full line of athletic equipment on a nationwide basis. The firm currently uses a centralized billing system. Byron Sporting Goods has annual credit sales of $362 million. Austin National Bank has presented an offer to operate a concentration banking system for the company. Byron already has an established line of credit with Austin. Austin says it will operate the system on a flat-fee basis of $175,000 per year. The analysis done by the bank's cash-management services division suggests that three days in mail float and one day in processing float can be eliminated.

    Because Byron borrows almost continuously from Austin National, the value of the float reduction would be applied against the line of credit. The borrowing rate on the line of credit is set at an annual rate of 7%. Furthermore, because of the reduction in clerical help, the new system will save the firm $57,500 in processing costs. Byron uses a 365-day year in analyses of this sort. Should Byron accept the bank's offer to install the new system?

2. **Buying and Selling Marketable Securities.**   Miami Dice & Card Company has generated $800,000 in excess cash that it could invest in marketable securities. In order to buy and sell the securities, the firm will pay total transactions fees of $20,000.

    a. Would you recommend purchasing the securities if they yield 10.5% annually and are held for

(1) One month?
(2) Two months?
(3) Three months?
(4) Six months?
(5) One year?

b. What minimum required yield would the securities have to return for the firm to hold them for two months? (What is the breakeven yield for a two-month holding period?)

3. **Costs of Services.** Mustang Ski-Wear, Inc., is investigating the possibility of adopting a lock-box system as a cash receipts acceleration device. In a typical year this firm receives remittances totaling $12 million by check. The firm will record and process 6,000 checks over this same period. The Colorado Springs Second National Bank has informed the management of Mustang that it will expedite checks and associated documents through the lock-box system for a unit cost of $.20 per check. Mustang's financial manager has projected that cash freed by adoption of the system can be invested in a portfolio of near-cash assets that will yield an annual before-tax return of 7%. Mustang financial analysts use a 365-day year in their procedures.

a. What reduction in check collection time is necessary for Mustang to be neither better nor worse off for having adopted the proposed system?
b. How would your solution to (a) be affected if Mustang could invest the freed balances only at an expected annual return of 4.5%?
c. What is the logical explanation for the difference in your answers to (a) and (b)?

4. **Lock-Box System.** Penn Steelworks is a distributor of cold-rolled steel products to the automobile industry. All its sales are on a credit basis, net 30 days. Sales are evenly distributed over its 10 sales regions throughout the United States. Delinquent accounts are no problem. The company has recently undertaken an analysis aimed at improving its cash-management procedures. Penn determined that it takes an average of 3.2 days for customers' payments to reach the head office in Pittsburgh from the time they are mailed. It takes another full day in processing time prior to depositing the checks with a local bank. Annual sales average $4,800,000 for each regional office. Reasonable investment opportunities can be found yielding 7% per year. To alleviate the float problem confronting the firm, the use of a lock-box system in each of the 10 regions is being considered. This would reduce mail float by 1.2 days. One day in processing float would also be eliminated, plus a full day in transit float. The lock-box arrangement would cost each region $250 per month.

a. What is the opportunity cost to Penn Steelworks of the funds tied up in mailing and processing? Use a 365-day year.
b. What would the net cost or savings be from use of the proposed cash-acceleration technique? Should Penn adopt the system?

5. **Cash Receipts Acceleration System.** Peggy Pierce Designs, Inc., is a vertically integrated, national manufacturer and retailer of women's clothing. Currently, the firm has no coordinated cash-management system. A proposal, however, from

the First Pennsylvania Bank aimed at speeding up cash collections is being examined by several of Pierce's corporate executives.

The firm currently uses a centralized billing procedure, which requires that all checks be mailed to the Philadelphia head office for processing and eventual deposit. Under this arrangement all the customers' remittance checks take an average of five business days to reach the head office. Once in Philadelphia another two days are required to process the checks for ultimate deposit at the First Pennsylvania Bank.

The firm's daily remittances average $1 million. The average check size is $2,000. Pierce Designs currently earns 6% annually on its marketable securities portfolio.

The cash acceleration plan proposed by officers of First Pennsylvania involves both a lock-box system and concentration banking. First Pennsylvania would be the firm's only concentration bank. Lock boxes would be established in (1) San Francisco, (2) Dallas, (3) Chicago, and (4) Philadelphia. This would reduce funds tied up by mail float to three days, and processing float will be eliminated. Funds would then be transferred twice each business day by means of automated depository transfer checks from local banks in San Francisco, Dallas, and Chicago to the First Pennsylvania Bank. Each ADTC costs $15. These transfers will occur all 270 business days of the year. Each check processed through the lock-box system will cost $.18.

a. What amount of cash balances will be freed if Pierce Designs, Inc., adopts the system suggested by First Pennsylvania?
b. What is the opportunity cost of maintaining the current banking setup?
c. What is the projected annual cost of operating the proposed system?
d. Should Pierce adopt the new system? Compute the net annual gain or loss associated with adopting the system.

Time Value of Money and Capital Budgeting

CHAPTER 19

The Time Value of Money

We now focus on determining the value of the firm and the desirability of investment proposals. A key concept that underlies this material is the *time value of money;* that is, a dollar today is worth more than a dollar received a year from now. Intuitively this idea is easy to understand. We are all familiar with the concept of interest. This concept illustrates what economists call an opportunity cost of passing up the earning potential of a dollar today. This *opportunity* cost is the time value of money.

In evaluating and comparing investment proposals, we need to examine how dollar values might accrue from accepting these proposals. To do this, all dollar values must first be comparable; since a dollar received today is worth more than a dollar received in the future, we must move all dollar flows back to the present or out to a common future date. An understanding of the time value of money is essential, therefore, to an understanding of financial management, whether basic or advanced.

COMPOUND INTEREST

Most of us encounter the concept of compound interest at an early age. Anyone who has ever had a savings account or purchased a government savings bond has received compound interest. **Compound interest** occurs when interest paid on the investment during the first period is added to the principal and then, during the second period, interest is earned on this new sum.

For example, suppose we place $100 in a savings account that pays 6% interest, compounded annually. How will our savings grovel? At the end of the first year we have earned 6%, or $6 on our initial deposit of $100, giving us a total of $106 in our savings account. The mathematical formula illustrating this phenomenon is

$$FV_1 = PV(1 + i) \tag{1}$$

where
- FV_1 = the future value of the investment at the end of one year
- i = the annual interest (or discount) rate
- PV = the present value, or original amount invested at the beginning of the first year

In our example

$$
\begin{aligned}
FV_1 &= PV(1 + i) \\
&= \$100(1 + .06) \\
&= \$100(1.06) \\
&= \$106
\end{aligned}
\tag{1}
$$

Carrying these calculations one period further, we find that we now earn the 6% interest on a principal of $106, which means we earn $6.36 in interest during the second year. Why do we earn more interest during the second year than we did during the first? Simply because we now earn interest on the sum of the original principal, or present value, and the interest we earned in the first year. In effect we are now earning interest on interest; this is the concept of compound interest. Examining the mathematical formula illustrating the earning of interest in the second year, we find

$$FV_2 = FV_1(1 + i) \tag{2}$$

which, for our example, gives

$$
\begin{aligned}
FV_2 &= \$106(1.06) \\
&= \$112.36
\end{aligned}
$$

Looking back at equation (1), we can see that FV_1, or $106, is actually equal to $PV(1 + i)$, or $100 (1 + .06)$. If we substitute these values into equation (2), we get

$$
\begin{aligned}
FV_2 &= PV(1 + i)(1 + i) \\
&= PV(1 + i)^2
\end{aligned}
\tag{3}
$$

Carrying this forward into the third year, we find that we enter the year with $112.36 and we earn 6%, or $6.74 in interest, giving us a total of $119.10 in our savings account. Expressing this mathematically:

$$
\begin{aligned}
FV_3 &= FV_2(1 + i) \\
&= \$112.36(1.06) \\
&= \$119.10
\end{aligned}
\tag{4}
$$

If we substitute the value in equation (3) for FV_2 into equation (4), we find

$$
\begin{aligned}
FV_3 &= PV(1 + i)(1 + i)(1 + i) \\
&= PV(1 + i)^3
\end{aligned}
\tag{5}
$$

By now a pattern is beginning to be evident. We can generalize this formula to illustrate the value of our investment if it is compounded annually at a rate of i for n years to be

$$FV_n = PV(1 + i)^n \tag{6}$$

where FV_n = the future value of the investment at the end of n years

              n = the number of years during which the compounding occurs

              i = the annual interest (or discount) rate

           PV = the present value or original amount invested at the beginning of the first year

Figure 19-1 illustrates how this investment of $100 would continue to grow for the first 10 years at a compound interest rate of 6%. Notice how the amount of interest earned annually increases each year. Again, the reason is that each year interest is received on the sum of the original investment plus any interest earned in the past.

When we examine the relationship between the number of years an initial investment is compounded for and its future value graphically, as shown in Figure 19-2, we see that we can increase the future value of an investment by either increasing the number of years for which we let it compound or by compounding it at a higher interest rate. We can also see this from equation (6), since an increase in either i or n while PV is held constant will result in an increase in FV_n.

For example, if we place $1,000 in a savings account paying 5% interest compounded annually, how much will our account accrue to in 10 years? Substituting $PV = \$1000$, $i = 5\%$, and $n = 10$ years into equation (6), we get

$$
\begin{aligned}
FV_n &= PV(1 + i)^n \tag{6}\\
&= \$1,000(1 + .05)^{10}\\
&= \$1,000(1.62889)\\
&= \$1,628.89
\end{aligned}
$$

Thus at the end of 10 years we will have $1,628.89 in our savings account.

As the determination of future value can be quite time consuming when an investment is held for a number of years, the **future-value interest factor** for i and n ($FVIF_{i,n}$), defined as $(1 + i)^n$, has been compiled for various values of i and n. An abbreviated compound interest or future-value interest factor table appears in Figure 19-3, with a more comprehensive version of this appearing in Appendix B. Alternatively, the $FVIF_{i,n}$ values could easily be determined using a calculator. Note that

---

Figure 19-1   Illustration of Compound Interest Calculations

Year	Beginning Value	Interest Earned	Ending Value
1	$100.00	$ 6.00	$106.00
2	106.00	6.36	112.36
3	112.36	6.74	119.10
4	119.10	7.15	126.25
5	126.25	7.57	133.82
6	133.82	8.03	141.85
7	141.85	8.51	150.36
8	150.36	9.02	159.38
9	159.38	9.57	168.95
10	168.95	10.13	179.08

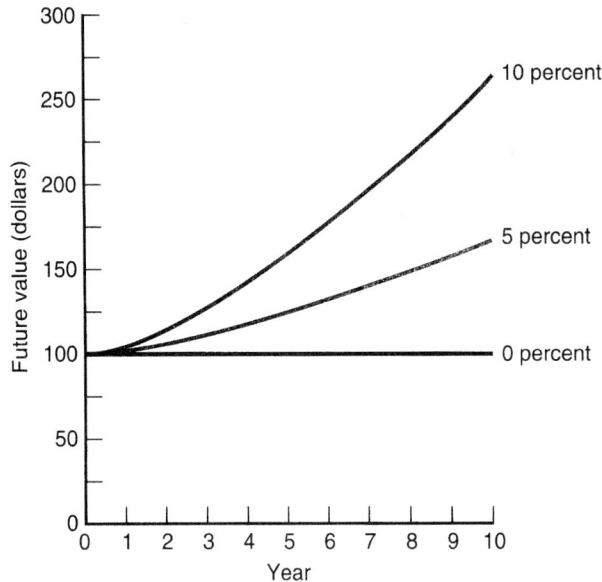

FIGURE 19-2
Future Value of $100 Initially Deposited and Compounded at 0, 5, and 10%

the compounding factors given in these tables represent the value of $1 compounded at rate i at the *end* of the nth year. Thus, to calculate the future value of an initial investment we need only determine the $FVIF_{i,n}$ using a calculator or the appendices and multiply this times the initial investment. In effect, we can rewrite equation (6) as follows:

$$FV_n = PV(FVIF_{i,n}) \tag{6a}$$

As an example, if we invest $500 in a bank where it will earn 8% compounded annually, how much will it be worth at the end of seven years? Looking at Figure 19-3 in the row $n = 7$ and column $i = 8\%$, we find that $FVIF_{8\%, 7\,yr}$ has a value of 1.714. Substituting this in equation (6a), we find

$$\begin{aligned} FV_n &= PV\,(FVIF_{8\%, 7\,yr}) \\ &= \$500(1.714) \\ &= \$857 \end{aligned} \tag{6a}$$

Thus, we will have $857 at the end of seven years.

In the future we will find several uses for equation (6); not only will we find the future value of an investment, but we can also solve for PV, i, or n. In any case, we will be given three of the four variables and will have to solve for the fourth.

For instance, how many years will it take for an initial investment of $300 to grow to $774 if it is invested at 9% compounded annually? In this problem we know the initial investment, $PV = \$300$; the future value, $FV_n = \$774$; the compound growth rate, $i = 9\%$; and we are solving for the number of years it must compound for, $n = ?$ Substituting the known values in equation (6), we find

FIGURE 19-3 $FVIF_{i,n}$ or the Compound Sum of $1

n	1%	2%	3%	4%	5%	6%	7%	8%	9%	10%
1	1.010	1.020	1.030	1.040	1.050	1.060	1.070	1.080	1.090	1.100
2	1.020	1.040	1.061	1.082	1.102	1.124	1.145	1.166	1.188	1.210
3	1.030	1.061	1.093	1.125	1.158	1.191	1.225	1.260	1.295	1.331
4	1.041	1.082	1.126	1.170	1.216	1.262	1.311	1.360	1.412	1.464
5	1.051	1.104	1.159	1.217	1.276	1.338	1.403	1.469	1.539	1.611
6	1.062	1.126	1.194	1.265	1.340	1.419	1.501	1.587	1.677	1.772
7	1.072	1.149	1.230	1.316	1.407	1.504	1.606	1.714	1.828	1.949
8	1.083	1.172	1.267	1.369	1.477	1.594	1.718	1.851	1.993	2.144
9	1.094	1.195	1.305	1.423	1.551	1.689	1.838	1.999	2.172	2.358
10	1.105	1.219	1.344	1.480	1.629	1.791	1.967	2.159	2.367	2.594
11	1.116	1.243	1.384	1.539	1.710	1.898	2.105	2.332	2.580	2.853
12	1.127	1.268	1.426	1.601	1.796	2.012	2.252	2.518	2.813	3.138
13	1.138	1.294	1.469	1.665	1.886	2.133	2.410	2.720	3.066	3.452
14	1.149	1.319	1.513	1.732	1.980	2.261	2.579	2.937	3.342	3.797
15	1.161	1.346	1.558	1.801	2.079	2.397	2.759	3.172	3.642	4.177

$$FV_n = PV(1 + i)^n \tag{6}$$
$$\$774 = \$300(1 + .09)^n$$
$$2.58 = (1 + .09)^n$$

Thus we are looking for a value of 2.58 in the $FVIF_{i,n}$ tables, and we know it must be in the 9% column. Looking down the 9% column for the value closest to 2.58, we find that it occurs in the $n = 11$ row. Thus, it will take 11 years for an initial investment of $300 to grow to $774 if it is invested at 9% compounded annually.

At what rate must $100 be compounded annually for it to grow to $179.10 in 10 years? In this case we know the initial investment, $PV = \$100$; the future value of this investment at the end of n years, $FV_n = \$179.10$; and the number of years that the initial investment will compound for, $n = 10$ years. Substituting into equation (6), we get

$$FV_n = PV(1 + i)^n \tag{6}$$
$$\$179.10 = \$100(1 + i)^{10}$$
$$1.791 = (1 + i)^{10}$$

We know we are looking in the $n = 10$ row of the $FVIF_{i,n}$ table for a value of 1.791, and we find this in the $i = 6\%$ column. Thus, if we want our initial investment of $100 to accrue to $179.10 in 10 years, we must invest it at 6%.

COMPOUND INTEREST WITH NONANNUAL PERIODS

Until now we have assumed that the compounding period is always annual; however, it need not be, as evidenced by savings and loan associations and commercial banks that compound on a quarterly, daily, and in some cases continuous basis. Fortunately, this adjustment of the compounding period follows the same format as that used for annual compounding. If we invest our money for five years at 8% interest compounded semiannually, we are really investing our money for 10 six-month periods during which we receive 4% interest each period. If it is compounded quarterly, we receive 2% interest per period for 20 three-month periods. This process can easily be generalized, giving us the following formula for finding the future value of an investment for which interest is compounded in nonannual periods:

$$FV_n = PV\left(1+\frac{i}{m}\right)^{mn} \tag{7}$$

where
FV_n = the future value of the investment at the end of n years
n = the number of years during which the compounding occurs
i = annual interest (or discount) rate
PV = the present value or original amount invested at the beginning of the first year
m = the number of times compounding occurs during the year

In the case of continuous compounding, the value of m in equation (7) is allowed to approach infinity. In effect, with continuous compounding, interest begins to earn interest immediately. As this happens, the value of $[1 + (i/m)]^{mn}$ approaches e^{in}, with e being defined as follows and having a value of approximately 2.71828:

$$e = \lim_{m\to\infty}\left(1+\frac{1}{m}\right)^{m} \tag{8}$$

where ∞ indicates infinity. Thus the future value of an investment compounded continuously for n years can be determined from the following formula:

$$FV_n = PV \times e^{in} \tag{9}$$

where
FV_n = the future value of the investment at the end of n years
e = 2.71828
n = the number of years during which the compounding occurs
i = the annual interest (or discount) rate
PV = the present value or original amount invested at the beginning of the first year

Continuous compounding may appear complicated, but it is used frequently and is a valuable theoretical concept. Continuous compounding is important because it allows interest to be earned on interest more frequently than any other compounding method does. We can see the value of intrayear compounding by examining Figure 19-4. Since interest is earned on interest more frequently as the length of the compounding period declines, there is an inverse relationship between the length of the compounding period and the effective annual interest rate.

For example, if we place $100 in a savings account that yields 12% compounded quarterly, what will our investment grow to at the end of five years? Substituting $n = 5$, $m = 4$, $i = 12\%$, and $PV = \$100$ into equation (7), we find

FIGURE 19-4   The Value of $100 Compounded at Various Intervals

For One Year at *i* Percent

i =	2%	5%	10%	15%
Compounded annually	$102.00	$105.00	$110.00	$115.00
Compounded semiannually	102.01	105.06	110.25	115.56
Compounded quarterly	102.02	105.09	110.38	115.87
Compounded monthly	102.02	105.12	110.47	116.08
Compounded weekly(52)	102.02	105.12	110.51	116.16
Compounded daily(365)	102.02	105.13	110.52	116.18
Compounded continuously	102.02	105.13	110.52	116.18

For Ten years at *i* Percent

i =	2%	5%	10%	15%
Compounded annually	$121.90	$162.89	$259.37	$404.56
Compounded semiannually	122.02	163.86	265.33	424.79
Compounded quarterly	122.08	164.36	268.51	436.04
Compounded monthly	122.12	164.70	270.70	444.02
Compounded weekly (52)	122.14	164.83	271.57	447.20
Compounded daily (365)	122.14	164.87	271.79	448.03
Compounded continuously	122.14	164.87	271.83	448.17

$$FV_5 = \$100 \left(1 + \frac{.12}{4}\right)^{4 \cdot 5}$$

$$= \$100(1 + .03)^{20}$$
$$= \$100(1.806)$$
$$= \$180.60$$

Thus, we will have $180.60 at the end of five years. Notice that a calculator solution is slightly different because of rounding errors in the tables, as explained in the previous section, and that it also takes on a negative value.

As another example, how much money will we have at the end of 20 years if we deposit $1,000 in a savings account yielding 10% interest continuously compounded? Substituting $n = 20$, $i = 10\%$, and $PV = \$1000$ into equation (9) yields

$$FV_{10} = \$1,000(2.71828)^{.10 \cdot 20}$$
$$= \$1,000(2.71828)^2$$
$$= \$1,000(7.38905)$$
$$= \$7,389.05$$

Thus, we will have $7,389.05 at the end of 20 years.

PRESENT VALUE

Up until this point we have been moving money forward in time; that is, we know how much we have to begin with and are trying to determine how much that sum will grow in a certain number of years when compounded at a specific rate. We are now going to look at the reverse question: What is the value in today's dollars of a sum of money to be received in the future? The answer to this question will help us determine the desirability of investment projects. In this case we are moving future money back to the present. We will be determining the **present value** of a lump sum, which in simple terms is the current value of a future payment. What we will be doing is, in fact, nothing other than inverse compounding. The differences in these techniques come about merely from the investor's point of view. In compounding we talked about the compound interest rate and the initial investment; in determining the present value we will talk about the discount rate and present value. Determination of the discount rate can be defined as the rate of return available on an investment of equal risk to what is being discounted. Other than that, the technique and the terminology remain the same, and the mathematics are simply reversed. In equation (6) we were attempting to determine the future value of an initial investment. We now want to determine the initial investment or present value. By dividing both sides of equation (6) by $(1 + i)^n$, we get

$$PV = FV_n \left[\frac{1}{(1+i)^n} \right]$$

(10)

where
FV_n = the future value of the investment at the end of n years
n = the number of years until the payment will be received
i = the annual discount (or interest) rate
PV = the present value of the future sum of money

Because the mathematical procedure for determining the present value is exactly the inverse of determining the future value, we also find that the relationships among n, i, and PV are just the opposite of those we observed in future value. The present value of a future sum of money is inversely related to both the number of years until the payment will be received and the discount rate. Graphically, this relationship can be seen in Figure 19-5.

For example, what is the present value of $500 to be received 10 years from today if our discount rate is 6%? Substituting FV_{10} = $500, n = 10, and i = 6% into equation (10), we find

$$PV = \$500 \left[\frac{1}{(1+.06)^{10}} \right]$$

$$= \$500 \left(\frac{1}{1.791} \right)$$

$$= \$500 \, (.558)$$

$$= \$279$$

Thus, the present value of the $500 to be received in 10 years is $279.

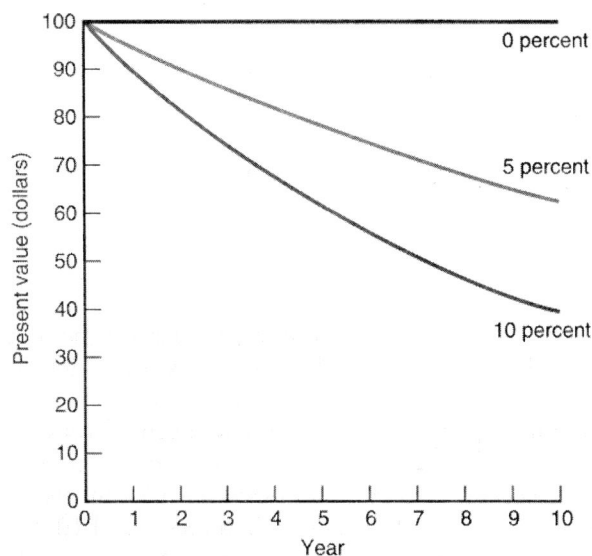

FIGURE 19-5
Present Value of $100 to Be Received at a Future Date and Discounted Back to the Present at 0, 5, and 10%

To aid in the computation of present values, the **present-value interest factor** for i and n ($PVIF_{i,n}$) defined as $[1/(1+i)^n]$, has been compiled for various combinations of i and n and appears in Appendix C. An abbreviated version of Appendix C appears in Figure 19-6. A close examination shows that the values in Figure 19-6 are merely the inverse of those found in Figure 19-3 and Appendix B. This, of course, is as it should be, as the values in Appendix B are $(1+i)^n$ and those in Appendix C are

FIGURE 19-6 $PVIF_{i,n}$ or the Present Value of $1

n	1%	2%	3%	4%	5%	6%	7%	8%	9%	10%
1	.990	.980	.971	.962	.952	.943	.935	.926	.917	.909
2	.980	.961	.943	.925	.907	.890	.873	.857	.842	.826
3	.971	.942	.915	.889	.864	.840	.816	.794	.772	.751
4	.961	.924	.888	.855	.823	.792	.763	.735	.708	.683
5	.951	.906	.863	.822	.784	.747	.713	.681	.650	.621
6	.942	.888	.837	.790	.746	.705	.666	.630	.596	.564
7	.933	.871	.813	.760	.711	.655	.623	.583	.547	.513
8	.923	.853	.789	.731	.677	.627	.582	.540	.502	.467
9	.914	.837	.766	.703	.645	.592	.544	.500	.460	.424
10	.905	.820	.744	.676	.614	.558	.508	.463	.422	.386
11	.896	.804	.722	.650	.585	.527	.475	.429	.388	.350
12	.887	.789	.701	.625	.557	.497	.444	.397	.356	.319
13	.879	.773	.681	.601	.530	.469	.415	.368	.326	.290
14	.870	.758	.661	.577	.505	.442	.388	.340	.299	.263
15	.861	.743	.642	.555	.481	.417	.362	.315	.275	.239

$[1/(1 + i)^n]$. Now, to determine the present value of a sum of money to be received at some future date, we need only determine the value of the appropriate $PVIF_{i,n}$, either by using a calculator or consulting the tables, and multiply it by the future value. In effect we can use our new notation and rewrite equation (10) as follows:

$$PV = FV_n(PVIF_{i,n})$$

(10a)

For instance, what is the present value of $1,500 to be received at the end of 10 years if our discount rate is 8%? By looking at the $n = 10$ row and $i = 8\%$ column of Figure 19-6, we find the $PVIF_{8\%, 10\,yr}$ is .463. Substituting this value into equation (10), we find

$$PV = \$1,500(.463)$$
$$= \$694.50$$

Thus, the present value of this $1,500 payment is $694.50.

Again, we only have one present-value—future-value equation; that is, equations (6) and (10) are identical. We have introduced them as separate equations to simplify our calculations; in one case we are determining the value in future dollars and in the other case the value in today's dollars. In either case the reason is the same: To compare values on alternative investments and to recognize that the value of a dollar received today is not the same as that of a dollar received at some future date. We must measure the dollar values in dollars of the same time period. Because all present values are comparable (they are all measured in dollars of the same time period), we can add and subtract the present value of inflows and outflows to determine the net present value of an investment.

As another example, what is the present value of an investment that yields $500 to be received in five years and $1,000 to be received in 10 years if the discount rate is 4%? Substituting the values of $n = 5$, $i = 4\%$, and $FV_5 = \$500$; and $n = 10$, $i = 4\%$, and $FV_{10} = \$1000$ into equation (10) and adding these values together, we find

$$PV = \$500 \left[\frac{1}{(1+.04)^5}\right] + \$1,000 \left[\frac{1}{(1+.04)^{10}}\right]$$

$$= \$500\,(PVIF_{4\%, 5\,yr}) + \$1,000\,(PVIF_{4\%, 10\,yr})$$
$$= \$500(.822) + \$1,000(.676)$$
$$= \$411 + \$676$$
$$= \$1,087$$

Again, present values are comparable because they are measured in the same time period's dollars.

ANNUITIES

An **annuity** is a series of equal dollar payments for a specified number of years. Because annuities occur frequently in finance—for example, as bond interest payments—we will treat them specially. Although compounding and determining the present value of an annuity can be dealt with using the methods we have just described, these processes can be time consuming, especially for larger annuities. Thus, we have modified the formulas to deal directly with annuities.

Compound Annuities

A **compound annuity** involves depositing or investing an equal sum of money at the end of each year for a certain number of years and allowing it to grow. Perhaps we are saving money for education, a new car, or a vacation home. In any case we want to know how much our savings will have grown by some point in the future.

Actually, we can find the answer by using equation (6), our compounding equation, and compounding each of the individual deposits to its future value. For example, if to provide for a college education we are going to deposit $500 at the end of each year for the next five years in a bank where it will earn 6% interest, how much will we have at the end of five years? Compounding each of these values using equation (6), we find that we will have $2,818.50 at the end of five years.

$$
\begin{aligned}
FV_5 &= \$500(1 + .06)^4 + \$500(1 + .06)^3 + \$500(1 + .06)^2 + \$500(1 + .06) + \$500 \\
&= \$500(1.262) + \$500(1.191) + \$500(1.124) + \$500(1.060) + \$500 \\
&= \$631.00 + \$595.50 + \$562.00 + \$530.00 + \$500.00 \\
&= \$2818.50
\end{aligned}
$$

From examining the mathematics involved and the graph of the movement of money through time in Figure 19-7, we can see that this procedure can be generalized to

$$
FV_n = PMT \left[\sum_{t=0}^{n-1} (1+i)^t \right] \tag{11}
$$

where FV_n = the future value of the annuity at the end of the nth year
   PMT = the annuity payment deposited or received at the end of each year
   i = the annual interest (or discount) rate
   n = the number of years for which the annuity will last

Year	0	1	2	3	4	5
Dollar deposits at end of year		500	500	500	500	500
						$ 500.00
						530.00
						562.00
						595.50
						631.00
Future value of the annuity						$2,818.50

FIGURE 19-7
Illustration of a Five-Year $500 Annuity Compounded at 6%

To aid in compounding annuities, the **future-value interest factor for an annuity** for i and n ($FVIFA_{i,n}$) defined as $\left| \sum_{t=0}^{n-1} (1+i)^t \right|$ is provided in Appendix D for various combinations of n and i; an abbreviated version is shown in Figure 19-8.[1]

Using this new notation, we can rewrite equation (11) as follows:

$$FV_n = PMT(FVIFA_{i,n}) \tag{11a}$$

Reexamining the previous example, in which we determined the value after five years of $500 deposited at the end of each of the next five years in the bank at 6%, we would look in the $i = 6\%$ column and $n = 5$ year row and find the value of the $FVIFA_{6\%, 5\,yr}$ to be 5.637. Substituting this value into equation (11a), we get

$$
\begin{aligned}
FV_5 &= \$500(5.637) \\
&= \$2{,}818.50
\end{aligned}
$$

This is the same answer we obtained earlier using equation (6).

Rather than asking how much we will accumulate if we deposit an equal sum in a savings account each year, a more common question is how much we must deposit each year to accumulate a certain amount of savings. This problem frequently occurs with respect to saving for large expenditures and pension funding obligations.

For example, we may know that we need $10,000 for education in eight years; how much must we deposit in the bank at the end of each year at 6% interest to have the college money ready? In this case we know the values of n, i, and FV_n in equation (11); what we do not know is the value of PMT. Substituting these example values in equation (11), we find

$$\$10{,}000 = PMT \left| \sum_{t=0}^{8-1} (1+.06)^t \right|$$

$$
\begin{aligned}
\$10{,}000 &= PMT(FVIFA_{6\%, 8\,yr}) \\
\$10{,}000 &= PMT(9.897) \\
\frac{\$10{,}000}{9.897} &= PMT \\
PMT &= \$1{,}010.41
\end{aligned}
$$

Thus, we must deposit $1,010.41 in the bank at the end of each year for eight years at 6% interest to accumulate $10,000 at the end of eight years.

How much must we deposit in an 8% savings account at the end of each year to accumulate $5,000 at the end of ten years? Substituting the values $FV_{10} = \$5{,}000$, $n = 10$, and $i = 8\%$ into equation (11), we find

$$\$5{,}000 = PMT \left| \sum_{t=0}^{10-1} (1+.08)^t \right| = PMT\left(FVIFA_{8\%, 10\,yr}\right)$$

---

[1] Another useful analytical relationship for FV_n is $FV_n = PMT\,[(1+i)^n - 1]/i$.

FIGURE 19-8 $FVIFA_{i,n}$ or the Sum of an Annuity of $1 for n Years

n	1%	2%	3%	4%	5%	6%	7%	8%	9%	10%
1	1.000	1.000	1.000	1.000	1.000	1.000	1.000	1.000	1.000	1.000
2	2.010	2.020	2.030	2.040	2.050	2.060	2.070	2.080	2.090	2.100
3	3.030	3.060	3.091	3.122	3.152	3.184	3.215	3.246	3.278	3.310
4	4.060	4.122	4.184	4.246	4.310	4.375	4.440	4.506	4.573	4.641
5	5.101	5.204	5.309	5.416	5.526	5.637	5.751	5.867	5.985	6.105
6	6.152	6.308	6.468	6.633	6.802	6.975	7.153	7.336	7.523	7.716
7	7.214	7.434	7.662	7.898	8.142	8.394	8.654	8.923	9.200	9.487
8	8.286	8.583	8.892	9.214	9.549	9.897	10.260	10.637	11.028	11.436
9	9.368	9.755	10.159	10.583	11.027	11.491	11.978	12.488	13.021	13.579
10	10.462	10.950	11.464	12.006	12.578	13.181	13.816	14.487	15.193	15.937
11	11.567	12.169	12.808	13.486	14.207	14.972	15.784	16.645	17.560	18.531
12	12.682	13.412	14.192	15.026	15.917	16.870	17.888	18.977	20.141	21.384
13	13.809	14.680	15.618	16.627	17.713	18.882	20.141	21.495	22.953	24.523
14	14.947	15.974	17.086	18.292	19.598	21.015	22.550	24.215	26.019	27.975
15	16.097	17.293	18.599	20.023	21.578	23.276	25.129	27.152	29.361	31.772

$$\$5,000 = PMT(14.487)$$

$$\frac{\$5,000}{14.487} = PMT$$

$$PMT = \$345.14$$

Thus, we must deposit $345.14 per year for 10 years at 8% to accumulate $5,000.

Present Value of an Annuity

Pension funds, insurance obligations, and interest received from bonds all involve annuities. To compare them, we need to know the present value of each. While we can find this by using the present-value table in Appendix C, this can be time consuming, particularly when the annuity lasts for several years. For example, if we wish to know what $500 received at the end of the next five years is worth to us given the appropriate discount rate of 6%, we can simply substitute the appropriate values into equation (10), such that

$$PV = \$500\left[\frac{1}{(1+.06)}\right] + \$500\left[\frac{1}{(1+.06)^2}\right] + \$500\left[\frac{1}{(1+.06)^3}\right] + \$500\left[\frac{1}{(1+.06)^4}\right] + \$500\left[\frac{1}{(1+.06)^5}\right]$$

$$= \$500(.943) + \$500(.890) + \$500(.840) + \$500(.792) + \$500(.747)$$

$$= \$2106$$

Thus, the present value of this annuity is $2,106.00. From examining the mathematics involved and the graph of the movement of these funds through time in Figure 19-9, we see that this procedure can be generalized to

Year	0	1	2	3	4	5
Dollars received at the end of year		500	500	500	500	500

$ 471.50 ←
445.00 ←
420.00 ←
396.00 ←
373.50 ←

Present value of the annuity $2,106.00

FIGURE 19-9

Illustration of a Five-Year $500 Annuity Discounted to the Present at 6%

$$PV = PMT \left| \sum_{t=0}^{n} \frac{1}{(1+i)^t} \right|$$

where
PMT = the annuity payment deposited or received at the end of each year
i = the annual discount (or interest) rate
PV = the present value of the future annuity
n = the number of years for which the annuity will last

To simplify the process of determining the present value of an annuity, the **present-value interest factor for an annuity** for i and n (**$PVIFA_{i,n}$**), defined as $\left| \sum_{t=1}^{n} \frac{1}{(1+i)^t} \right|$ has been compiled for various combinations of i and n in Appendix E with an abbreviated version provided in Figure 19-10.[2]

Using this new notation we can rewrite equation (12) as follows:

$$PV = PMT(PVIFA_{i,n}) \tag{12a}$$

Solving the previous example to find the present value of $500 received at the end of each of the next five years discounted back to the present at 6%, we look in the $i = 6\%$ column and $n = 5$ year row and find the $PVIFA_{6\%, 5\,yr}$ to be 4.212. Substituting the appropriate values into equation (12a), we find

$$PV = \$500(4.212)$$
$$= \$2,106$$

This, of course, is the same answer we calculated when we individually discounted each cash flow to the present. The reason is that we really only have *one* table; the Figure 19-10 value for an n-year annuity for any discount rate i is merely the sum of the first n values in Figure 19-6. We can see this by comparing the value in the present-value-of-an-annuity table (Figure 19-10) for $i = 8\%$ and $n = 6$ years, which is 4.623, with the sum of the values in the $i = 8\%$ column and $n = 1, \ldots, 6$ rows of the present-value table (Figure 19-6), which is equal to 4.623, as shown in Figure 19-11.

---

[2]Another useful analytical relationship for PV is $PV = PMT[1 - 1/(1 + i)^n]/i$.

FIGURE 19-10 *PVIFA*$_{i,n}$ or the Present Value of an Annuity of $1

n	1%	2%	3%	4%	5%	6%	7%	8%	9%	10%
1	0.990	0.980	0.971	0.962	0.952	0.943	0.935	0.926	0.917	0.909
2	1.970	1.942	1.913	1.886	1.859	1.833	1.808	1.783	1.759	1.736
3	2.941	2.884	2.829	2.775	2.723	2.673	2.624	2.577	2.531	2.487
4	3.902	3.808	3.717	3.630	3.546	3.465	3.387	3.312	3.240	3.170
5	4.853	4.713	4.580	4.452	4.329	4.212	4.100	3.993	3.890	3.791
6	5.795	5.601	5.417	5.242	5.076	4.917	4.767	4.623	4.486	4.355
7	6.728	6.472	6.230	6.002	5.786	5.582	5.389	5.206	5.033	4.868
8	7.652	7.326	7.020	6.733	6.463	6.210	5.971	5.747	5.535	5.335
9	8.566	8.162	7.786	7.435	7.108	6.802	6.515	6.247	5.995	5.759
10	9.471	8.983	8.530	8.111	7.722	7.360	7.024	6.710	6.418	6.145
11	10.368	9.787	9.253	8.760	8.306	7.887	7.499	7.139	6.805	6.495
12	11.255	10.575	9.954	9.385	8.863	8.384	7.943	7.536	7.161	6.814
13	12.134	11.348	10.635	9.986	9.394	8.853	8.358	7.904	7.487	7.103
14	13.004	12.106	11.296	10.563	9.899	9.295	8.746	8.244	7.786	7.367
15	13.865	12.849	11.938	11.118	10.380	9.712	9.108	8.560	8.061	7.606

For example, what is the present value of a 10-year $1,000 annuity discounted back to the present at 5%? Substituting $n = 10$ years, $i = 5\%$, and $PMT = \$1,000$ into equation (12), we find

$$PV = \$1,000 \left[\sum_{t=1}^{10} \frac{1}{(1+.05)^t} \right] = \$1,000 \left(PVIFA_{5\%, 10\,yr} \right)$$

Determining the value for the $PVIFA_{5\%, 10\,yr}$ from Figure 19-10, row $n = 10$, column $i = 5\%$, and substituting it in, we get

$$PV = \$1,000(7.722)$$
$$= \$7,722$$

Thus, the present value of this annuity is $7,722.

As with our other compounding and present-value tables, given any three of the four unknowns in equation (12), we can solve for the fourth. In the case of the present-

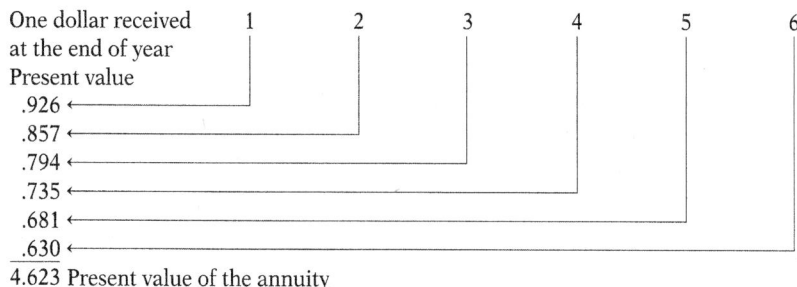

One dollar received at the end of year	1	2	3	4	5	6
Present value						

.926 ←
.857 ←
.794 ←
.735 ←
.681 ←
.630 ←
4.623 Present value of the annuity

FIGURE 19-11
Present Value of a Six-Year Annuity Discounted at 8%

value-of-an-annuity table we may be interested in solving for PMT, if we know i, n, and PV. The financial interpretation of this action would be: How much can be withdrawn, perhaps as a pension or to make loan payments, from account that earns i percent compounded annually for each of the next n years if we wish to have nothing left at the end of n years? For example, if we have $5,000 in an account earning 8% interest, how large an annuity can we draw out each year if we want nothing left at the end of five years? In this case the present value, PV, of the annuity is $5,000, n = 5 years, i = 8%, and PMT is unknown. Substituting this into equation (12), we find

$$\$5,000 = PMT\,(3.993)$$
$$\$1,252.19 = PMT$$

Thus, this account will fall to zero at the end of five years if we withdraw $1,252.19 at the end of each year.

AMORTIZED LOANS

This procedure of solving for PMT, the annuity payment value when i, n, and PV are known, is also used to determine what payments are associated with paying off a loan in equal installments over time. Loans that are paid off this way, in equal periodic payments, are called *amortized loans.* For example, suppose a firm wants to purchase a piece of machinery. To do this, it borrows $6,000 to be repaid in four equal payments at the end of each of the next four years, and the interest rate that is paid to the lender is 15% on the outstanding portion of the loan. To determine what the annual payments associated with the repayment of this debt will be, we simply use equation (12) and solve for the value of PMT, the annual annuity. Again we know three of the four values in that equation, PV, i, and n. PV, the present value of the future annuity, is $6,000; i, the annual interest rate, is 15%; and n, the number of years for which the annuity will last, is four years. PMT, the annuity payment received (by the lender and paid by the firm) at the end of each year, is unknown. Substituting these values into equation (12), we find

$$\$6,000 = PMT\left[\sum_{t=1}^{4} \frac{1}{\left(1+.15\right)^t}\right]$$
$$\$6,000 = PMT(PVIFA_{15\%,\ 4\ yr})$$
$$\$6,000 = PMT(2.855)$$
$$\$2,101.58 = PMT$$

To repay the principal and interest on the outstanding loan in four years the annual payments would be $2,101.58. The breakdown of interest and principal payments is given in the *loan amortization schedule* in Figure 19-12, with very minor rounding error. As you can see, the interest payment declines each year as the loan outstanding declines.

PRESENT VALUE OF AN UNEVEN STREAM

While some projects will involve a single cash flow and some annuities, many projects will involve uneven cash flows over several years. There we will be comparing not

FIGURE 19-12 Loan Amortization Schedule Involving a $6,000 Loan at 15% to Be Repaid in Four Years

Year	Annuity	Interest Portion of the Annuity[a]	Repayments of the Principal Portion of the Annuity[b]	Outstanding Loan Balance after the Annuity Payment
1	$2,101.58	$900.00	$1,201.58	$4,798.42
2	2,101.58	719.76	1,381.82	3,416.60
3	2,101.58	512.49	1,589.09	1,827.51
4	2,101.58	274.07	1,827.51	

[a]The interest portion of the annuity is calculated by multiplying the outstanding loan balance at the beginning of the year by the interest rate of 15% Thus, for year 1 it was $6,000.00 × .15 = $900.00, for year 2 it was $4,798.42 × .15 = $719.76. and so on.

[b]Repayment of the principal portion of the annuity was calculated by subtracting the interest portion of the annuity (column 2) from the annuity (column 1).

only the present value of cash flows between projects but also the cash inflows and outflows within a particular project, trying to determine that project's present value. However, this will not be difficult because the present value of any cash flow is measured in today's dollars and thus can be compared, through addition for inflows and subtraction for outflows, to the present value of any other cash flow also measured in today's dollars. For example, if we wished to find the present value of the following cash flows given a 6% discount rate, we would merely discount the flows back to the present and total them by adding in the positive flows and subtracting the negative ones. However, this problem is complicated by the annuity of $500 that runs from years 4 through 10. To accommodate this, we can first discount the annuity back to the beginning of period 4 (or end of period 3) by multiplying it by the value of $PVIFA_{6\%, 7\ yr}$ and get its present value at that point in time. We then multiply this value times the $PVIF_{6\%, 3\ yr}$ in order to bring this single cash flow (which is the present value of the 7-year annuity) back to the present. In effect we discount twice, first back to the end of period 3, then back to the present. This is shown graphically in Figure 19-13 and numerically in Figure 19-14. Thus, the present value of this uneven stream of cash flows is $2,657.94.

Year	Cash Flow	Year	Cash Flow
1	$500	6	500
2	200	7	500
3	−400	8	500
4	500	9	500
5	500	10	500

What, then, is the present value of an investment involving $200 received at the end of years 1 through 5, a $300 cash outflow at the end of year 6, and $500 received at the end of years 7 through 10, given a 5% discount rate? Here we have two annuities, one that can be discounted directly back to the present by multiplying it by the value of the $PVIFA_{5\%, 5\ yr}$ and one that must be discounted twice to bring it back to the

Year	0	1	2	3	4	5	6	7	8	9	10
Dollars received at end of year		500	200	–400	500	500	500	500	500	500	500

$471.50 ←
178.00 ←
– 336.00 ←
$2,791 ←
2,344.44 ←

Total present value $2,657.94

FIGURE 19-13

Illustration of an Example of Present Value of an Uneven Stream Involving One Annuity Discounted to Present at 6%

present. This second annuity, which is a four-year annuity, must first be discounted back to the beginning of period 7 (or end of period 6) by multiplying it by the value of the $PVIFA_{5\%, 4\,yr}$ Then the present value of this annuity at the end of period 6 (which can be viewed as a single cash flow) must be discounted back to the present by multiplying it by the value of the $PVIF_{5\%, 6\,yr}$

To arrive at the total present value of this investment, we subtract the present value of the $300 cash outflow at the end of year 6 from the sum of the present value of the two annuities. Figure 19-15 shows this graphically; Figure 19-16 gives the calculations. Thus, the present value of this series of cash flows is $1,964.66.

PERPETUITIES

A **perpetuity** is an annuity that continues forever; that is, every year from its establishment this investment pays the same dollar amount. An example of a perpetuity is preferred stock that pays a constant dollar dividend infinitely. Determining the present value of a perpetuity is delightfully simple; we merely need to divide the constant flow by the discount rate. For example, the present value of a $100 perpetuity discounted back to the present at 5% is $100/.05 = $2,000. Thus, the equation representing the present value of a perpetuity is

FIGURE 19-14 Determination of Present Value of an Example with Uneven Stream Involving One Annuity Discounted to Present at 6%

1. Present value of $500 received at the end of one year = $500(.943) = $ 471.50
2. Present value of $200 received at the end of two years = $200(.890) =   178.00
3. Present value of a $400 outflow at the end of three years = –400(.840) =   –336.00
4. (a) Value at the end of year 3 of a $500 annuity, years 4 through 10 =
   $500(5.582) = $2,791.00
   (b) Present value of $2,791.00 received at the end of year 3 =
   $2,791 (.840) =   2,344.44
5. Total present value =   **$2,657.94**

Year	0	1	2	3	4	5	6	7	8	9	10
Dollars received at end of year		200	200	200	200	200	−300	500	500	500	500

$ 865.80 ←

−223.80 ←

$1,773←

1,322.66 ←

Total present value $ 1,964.66

FIGURE 19-15
Illustration of an Example of Present Value of an Uneven Stream Involving Two Annuities Discounted to Present at 5%.

$$PV = \frac{PP}{i} \tag{13}$$

where
PV = the present value of the perpetuity
PP = the constant dollar amount provided by the perpetuity
i = the annual interest (or discount) rate

What is the present value of a $500 perpetuity discounted back to the present at 8%? Substituting PP = $500 and i = .08 into equation (13), we find

$$PV = \frac{\$500}{.08} = \$6,250$$

Thus, the present value of this perpetuity is $6,250.

SUMMARY

To make decisions, financial managers must compare the costs and benefits of alternatives that do not occur during the same time period. Whether to make profitable investments or to take advantage of favorable interest rates, financial decision making requires an understanding of the time value of money. Managers who use the time value of money in all of their financial calculations assure themselves of more logical decisions. The time value process first makes all dollar values comparable; because money has a time value, it moves all dollar flows either back to the present

FIGURE 19-16 Determination of Present Value of an Example with Uneven Stream Involving Two Annuities Discounted to Present at 5%

1. Present value of first annuity, years 1 through 5 = $200(4.329) $ 865.80
2. Present value of $300 cash outflow = −$300(.746) =   −223.80
3. (a) Value at end of year 6 of second annuity, years 7 through 10 =
       $500(3.546) = $1,773.00
   (b) Present value of $1,773.00 received at the end of year 6 = $1,773.00(.746) =   1,322.66
4. Total present value =   **$1,964.66**

FIGURE 19-17 Summary of Time Value of Money Equations*

Calculation	Equation
Future value of a single payment	$FV_n = PV(1 + i)^n = PV(FVIF_{i,n})$
Future value of a single payment with nonannual compounding	$FV_n = PV\left(1 + \dfrac{i}{m}\right)^{mn}$
Present value of a single payment	$PV = FV_n\left[\dfrac{1}{(1 + i)^n}\right] = FV_n\left(PVIF_{i,n}\right)$
Future value of an annuity	$FV_n = PMT\left[\sum\limits_{t=0}^{n-1}(1 + i)^t\right] = PMT\left(FVIFA_{i,n}\right)$
Present value of an annuity	$PV = PMT\left[\sum\limits_{t=1}^{n}\dfrac{1}{(1 + i)^t}\right] = PMT\left(PVIFA_{i,n}\right)$
Present value of a perpetuity	$PV = \dfrac{PP}{i}$

Notation:		
FV_n	=	the future value of the investment at the end of n years
n	=	the number of years until payment will be received or during which compounding occurs
i	=	the annual interest or discount rate
PV	=	the present value of the future sum of money
m	=	the number of times compounding occurs during the year
PMT	=	the annuity payment deposited or received at the end of each year
PP	=	the constant dollar amount provided by the perpetuity

*Related tables appear in Appendices B–E.

---

or out to a common future date. All time value formulas presented in this chapter actually stem from the single compounding formula $FV_n = PV(1 + i)^n$. The formulas are used to deal simply with common financial situations, for example, discounting single flows, compounding annuities, and discounting annuities. Figure 19-17 provides a summary of these calculations.

SELF-CORRECTION PROBLEMS

1. You place $25,000 in a savings account paying annual compound interest of 8% for three years and then move it into a savings account that pays 10% interest compounded annually. How much will your money have grown at the end of six years?

2. You purchase a boat for $35,000 and pay $5,000 down and agree to pay the rest over the next 10 years in 10 equal annual end of year payments that include principal payments plus 13% compound interest on the unpaid balance. What will be the amount of each payment?

3. For an investment to grow eightfold in nine years, at what rate would it have to grow?

SOLUTIONS TO SELF-CORRECTION PROBLEMS

1. This is a compound interest problem in which you must first find the future value of $25,000 growing at 8% compounded annually for 3 years and then allow that future value to grow for an additional three years at 10%. First, the value of the $25,000 after three years growing at 8% is

$$FV_3 = PV(1 + i)^n$$
$$FV_3 = \$25{,}000(1 + .08)^3$$
$$FV_3 = \$25{,}000(1.260)$$
$$FV_3 = \$31{,}500$$

Thus, after three years you have $31,500. Now this amount is allowed to grow for three years at 10%. Plugging this into equation (6), with $PV = \$31{,}500$, $i = 10\%$, $n = 3$ years, we solve for FV_3:

$$FV_3 = \$31{,}500(1 + .10)^3$$
$$FV_3 = \$31{,}500(1.331)$$
$$FV_3 = \$41{,}926.50$$

Thus, after six years the $25,000 will have grown to $41,926.50.

2. This loan amortization problem is actually just a present-value-of-an-annuity problem in which we know the values of i, n, and PV and are solving for PMT. In this case the value of i is 13%, n is 10 years, and PV is $30,000. Substituting these values into equation (12) we find

$$\$30{,}000 = PMT \left[\sum_{t=1}^{10} \frac{1}{(1 + .13)^t} \right]$$
$$\$30{,}000 = PMT(5.426)$$
$$\$5528.93 = PMT$$

3. This is a simple compound interest problem in which FV_9 is eight times larger than PV. Here again three of the four variables are known: $n = 9$ years, $FV_9 = 8$, and $PV = 1$, and we are solving for i. Substituting these values into equation (6) we find

$$FV_9 = PV(1 + i)^n$$
$$FV_9 = PV(FVIF_{i,n})$$
$$8 = 1 (FVIF_{i,\,9\,yr})$$
$$8.00 = FVIF_{i,\,9\,yr}$$

Thus we are looking for an $FVIF_{i,\ 9\ yr}$ with a value of 8 in Appendix B, which occurs in the 9-year row. If we look in the 9-year row for a value of 8.00, we find it in the 26% column (8.004). Thus, the answer is 26%.

QUESTIONS

1. What is the time value of money? Why is it so important?
2. The processes of discounting and compounding are related. Explain this relationship.
3. How would an increase in the interest rate (i) or a decrease in the holding period (n) affect the future value (FV_n) of a sum of money? Explain why.
4. Suppose you were considering depositing your savings in one of three banks, all of which pay 5% interest; bank A compounds annually, bank B compounds semi-annually, and bank C compounds continuously. Which bank would you choose? Why?
5. What is the relationship between the $PVIF_{i,n}$ (Figure 19-6) and the $PVIFA_{i,n}$ (Figure 19-10)? What is the $PVIFA_{10\%,\ 10\ yr}$? Add up the values of the $PVIF_{10\%,\ n}$ for $n = 1, \ldots, 10$. What is this value? Why do these values have the relationship they do?
6. What is an annuity? Give some examples of annuities. Distinguish between an annuity and a perpetuity.
7. What does continuous compounding mean?

PROBLEMS

1. **Compound Interest.**   To what amount will the following investments accumulate?

   a. $5,000 invested for 10 years at 10% compounded annually
   b. $8,000 invested for 7 years at 8% compounded annually
   c. $775 invested for 12 years at 12% compounded annually
   d. $21,000 invested for 5 Years at 5% compounded annually

2. **Compound Value Solving for n.**   How many years will the following take?

   a. $500 to grow to $1,039.50 if invested at 5% compounded annually
   b. $35 to grow to $53.87 if invested at 9% compounded annually
   c. $100 to grow to $298.60 if invested at 20% compounded annually
   d. $53 to grow to $78.76 if invested at 2% compounded annually

3. **Compound Value Solving for i.**   At what annual rate would the following have to be invested?

   a. $500 to grow to $1,948.00 in 12 years
   b. $300 to grow to $422.10 in 7 years
   c. $50 to grow to $280.20 in 20 years
   d. $200 to grow to $497.60 in 5 years

4. **Present Value.** What is the present value of the following future amounts?

   a. $800 to be received 10 years from now discounted back to present at 10%
   b. $300 to be received 5 years from now discounted back to present at 5%
   c. $1,000 to be received 8 years from now discounted back to present at 3%
   d. $1,000 to be received 8 years from now discounted back to present at 20%

5. **Compound Annuity.** What is the accumulated sum of each of the following streams of payments?

   a. $500 a year for 10 years compounded annually at 5%
   b. $100 a year for 5 years compounded annually at 10%
   c. $35 a year for 7 years compounded annually at 7%
   d. $25 a year for 3 years compounded annually at 2%

6. **Present Value of an Annuity.** What is the present value of the following annuities?

   a. $2,500 a year for 10 years discounted back to the present at 7%
   b. $70 a year for 3 years discounted back to the present at 3%
   c. $280 a year for 7 years discounted back to the present at 6%
   d. $500 a year for 10 years discounted back to the present at 10%

CHAPTER 20

Introduction to Capital Budgeting

Managers often must make important strategic decisions. For example:

- Should Roosevelt High School purchase new laboratory equipment?
- Should partners of Stone, Goldberg, and Gomez (a law firm) buy personal computers for the staff?
- Should Boeing begin production of a proposed new airplane?
- Should Kellogg's introduce a new breakfast cereal?

Such decisions, which have significant financial effects beyond the current year, are called **capital-budgeting decisions.** Capital-budgeting decisions are faced by managers in all types of organizations including religious, medical, and government enterprises.

Capital budgeting has three phases: (1) identifying potential investments, (2) selecting the investments to undertake (including the gathering of data to aid the decision), and (3) follow-up monitoring, or "postaudit," of investments. Accountants usually are not involved in the first phase, but they play important roles in phases 2 and 3.

Managers use many different capital-budgeting models in *selecting* investments. Each model summarizes facts and forecasts about an investment in a way that provides information for a decision maker. In this chapter we compare the uses and limitations of various capital-budgeting models, with particular attention to relevant-cost analysis.

FOCUS ON PROGRAMS OR PROJECTS

In planning and controlling operations, managers typically focus on reports covering a particular time period. For example, the chief administrator of a university will be concerned with all activities for a given academic year. But the administrator will also be concerned with individual *programs* or *projects* that have a longer-range focus. Examples are new programs in educational administration or health care education, joint law-management programs, new athletic facilities, new trucks, or new parking lots. In fact, many organizations may be perceived as a collection of individual investment projects.

This chapter concentrates on the planning and controlling of those programs or projects that affect more than one year's financial results. Such decisions require investments of resources that are often called *capital outlays*. Hence the term *capital budgeting* has arisen to describe the long-term planning for making and financing such outlays.

All capital outlays involve risk. The organization must commit funds to the project or program but cannot be sure what—if any—returns this investment will yield later. Many factors affecting future returns are unknowable, but well-managed organizations try to gather and quantify as many knowable or predictable factors as possible before making a decision. Capital-budgeting models facilitate this process.

Most large organizations use more than one capital-budgeting model. Why? Because each model summarizes information in a different way and reveals various useful perspectives on investments. There are three general types of capital-budgeting models: discounted-cash-flow models, payback models, and rate-of-return models. We look at each of these model types in turn in this chapter.

DISCOUNTED-CASH-FLOW MODELS

Discounted-cash-flow (DCF) models focus on a project's cash inflows and outflows and explicitly and systematically incorporate the time value of money. To evaluate investment proposals, we must first set guidelines by which we measure the value of each proposal.

Use Cash Flows Rather than Accounting Profits

We will use cash flows, not accounting profits, as our measurement tool. The firm receives and is able to reinvest cash flows, whereas accounting profits are shown when they are earned rather than when the money is actually in hand. Unfortunately, a firm's accounting profits and cash flows may not be timed to occur together. For example, capital expenses, such as vehicles and plant and equipment, are depreciated over several years, with their annual depreciation subtracted from profit. Cash flows correctly reflect the timing of benefits and costs, that is, when the money is received, when it can be reinvested, and when it must be paid out.

Think Incrementally

Unfortunately, calculating cash fiords from a project may not be enough. Decision makers must ask: What new cash flows will the company as a whole receive if the company takes on a given project? What if the company does not take on the project? Interestingly, we may find that not all cash flows a firm expects from an investment proposal are incremental in nature. In measuring cash flows, however, the trick is to *think* incrementally. In doing so, we will see that only *incremental after-tax cash flows* matter. As such, our guiding rule in deciding if a cash flow is incremental will be to look at the company with, versus without, the new product. As you will see in the upcoming sections, this may be easier said than done.

Beware of Cash Flows Diverted from Existing Products

Assume for a moment that we are managers of a firm considering a new product line that might compete with one of our existing products and possibly reduce its sales. In determining the cash flows associated with the proposed project, we should consider only the incremental sales brought to the company as a whole. New-product sales achieved at the cost of losing sales of other products in our line are not considered a benefit of adopting the new product. For example, when General Foods' Post Cereal Division introduced its Dino Pebbles in 1991, the product competed directly with the company's Fruity Pebbles. (In fact, the two were the same product with an addition to the former of dinosaur-shaped marshmallows.) Post meant to target the market niche held by Kellogg's Marshmallow Krispies, but there was no question that sales recorded by Dino Pebbles bit into—literally cannibalized—Post's existing product line.

Remember that we are only interested in the sales dollars to the firm if this project is accepted, as opposed to what the sales dollars would be if the project is rejected. Just moving sales from one product line to a new product line does not bring anything new into the company, but if sales are captured from our competitors or if sales that would have been lost to new competing products are retained, then these are relevant incremental cash flows. In each case these are the incremental cash flows to the firm—looking at the firm as a whole with the new product versus without the new product.

Look for Incidental or Synergistic Effects

Although in some cases a new project may take sales away from a firm's current projects, in other cases a new effort may actually bring new sales to the existing line. For example, in September 1991 USAir introduced service to Sioux City, Iowa. The new routes connecting this addition to the USAir system not only brought about new ticket sales on those routes, but also fed passengers to connecting routes. If managers were to look at only the revenue from ticket sales on the Sioux City routes, they would miss the incremental cash flow to USAir as a whole that results from taking on the new route. This is called a *synergistic* effect. The cash flow comes from *any* USAir flight that would not have occurred if service to Sioux City had not been available. The bottom line: Any cash flow to any part of the company that may result from the decision at hand must be considered when making that decision.

Work in Working Capital Requirements

Many times a new project will involve additional investment in working capital. This may take the form of new inventory to stock a sales outlet, additional investment in accounts receivable resulting from additional credit sales, or increased investment in cash to operate cash registers, and more. Working capital requirements are considered a cash flow even though they do not leave the company. How can investment in inventory be considered a cash outflow when the goods are still in the store? Because the firm does not have access to the inventory's cash value, the firm cannot use the money for other investments. Generally, working capital requirements are tied up over the life of the project. When the project terminates there is usually an offsetting cash inflow as the working capital is recovered.

Consider Incremental Expenses

Just as cash inflows from a new project are measured on an incremental basis, expenses should also be measured on an incremental basis. For example, if introducing a new product line necessitates training the sales staff, the after-tax cash flow associated with the training program must be considered a cash outflow and charged against the project. If accepting a new project dictates that a production facility be reengineered, the after-tax cash flows associated with that capital investment should be charged against the project. Again, any incremental after-tax cash flow affecting the company as a whole is a relevant cash flow, whether it is flowing in or flowing out.

Remember That Sunk Costs Are Not Incremental Cash Flows

Only cash flows that are affected by the decision making at the moment are relevant in capital budgeting. The manager asks two questions: (1) Will this cash flow occur if the project is accepted? (2) Will this cash flow occur if the project is rejected? *Yes* to the first question and *no* to the second equals an incremental cash flow. For example, let's assume you are considering introducing a new taste treat called Puddin' in a Shoe. You would like to do some test marketing before production. If you are considering the decision to test market and have not yet done so, the costs associated with the test marketing are relevant cash flows. Conversely, if you have already test marketed, the cash flows involved in test marketing are no longer relevant in project evaluation. It's a matter of timing. Regardless of what you might decide about future production, the cash flows allocated to marketing have already occurred. Cash flows that have already taken place are often referred to as "sunk costs" because they have been sunk into the project and cannot be undone. As a rule, any cash flows that are not affected by the accept-reject decision should not be included in capital-budgeting analysis.

Account for Opportunity Costs

Now we will focus on the cash flows that are lost because a given project consumes scarce resources that would have produced cash flows if that project had been rejected. This is the opportunity cost of doing business. For example, a product may use valuable floor space in a production facility. Although the cash flow is not obvious, the real question remains: What else could be done with this space? The space could have been rented out, or another product could have been stored there. The key point is that opportunity-cost cash flows should reflect net cash flows that would have been received if the project under consideration were rejected. Again, we are analyzing the cash flows to the company as a whole, with or without the project.

Decide If Overhead Costs Are Truly Incremental Cash Flows

Although we certainly want to include any incremental cash flows resulting in changes from overhead expenses such as utilities and salaries, we also want to make sure that these are truly incremental cash flows. Many times, overhead expenses—heat, light, rent—would occur whether a given project were accepted or rejected. There is often not a single specific project to which these expenses can be allocated. Thus, the question is not whether the project benefits from overhead items but whether the overhead costs are incremental cash flows associated with the project—and relevant to capital budgeting.

Ignore Interest Payments and Financing Flows

In evaluating new projects and determining cash flows, we must separate the investment decision from the financing decision. Interest payments and other financing cash flows that might result from raising funds to finance a project should not be considered incremental cash flows. If accepting a project means we have to raise new funds by issuing bonds, the interest charges associated with raising funds are not a relevant cash outflow. When we discount the incremental cash flows back to the present at the required rate of return, we are implicitly accounting for the cost of raising funds to finance the new project. In essence, the required rate of return reflects the cost of the funds needed to support the project. Managers first determine the desirability of the project and then determine how best to finance it.

MEASURING A PROJECT'S BENEFITS AND COSTS

In measuring cash flows, we will be interested only in the **incremental,** or differential, **after-tax cash flows** that can be attributed to the proposal being evaluated. That is, we will focus our attention on the difference in the firm's after-tax cash flows *with* versus *without* the project. The worth of our decision depends on the accuracy of our cash flow estimates. For this reason we first examined the question of what cash flows are relevant. Now we will see that, in general, a project's cash flows will fall into one of three categories: (1) the initial outlay, (2) the differential flows over the project's life, and (3) the terminal cash flow.

Initial Outlay

The **initial outlay** involves the immediate cash outflow necessary to purchase the asset and put it in operating order. This amount includes the cost of installing the asset (the asset's purchase price plus any expenses associated with shipping or in-

---

FIGURE 20-1   Summary of Calculation of Initial Outlay Incremental After-Tax Cash Flow

---

1. Installed cost of asset
2. Additional nonexpense outlays incurred (for example, working capital investments)
3. Additional expenses on an after-tax basis (for example, training expenses)
4. In a replacement decision, the *after-tax* cash flow associated with the sale of the old machine

---

stallation) and any nonexpense cash outlays, such as increased working capital requirements. If we are considering a new sales outlet, there might be additional cash flows associated with investment in working capital in the form of increased inventory and cash necessary to operate the sales outlet. Although these cash flows are not included in the cost of the asset or even expensed on the books, they must be included in our analysis. The after-tax cost of expense items incurred as a result of new investment must also be included as cash outflows—for example, any training expenses or special engineering expenses that would not have been incurred otherwise.

Finally, if the investment decision is a replacement decision, the cash inflow associated with the selling price of the old asset, in addition to any tax effects resulting from its sale, must be included.

Determining the initial outlay is a complex matter. Figure 20-1 summarizes some of the more common calculations involved in determining the initial outlay. This list is by no means exhaustive, but it should help simplify the calculations involved in the example that follows.

Tax Effects—Sale of Old Machine

Potentially one of the most confusing initial outlay calculations is for a replacement project involving the incremental tax payment associated with the sale of an old machine. There are three possible tax situations dealing with the sale of an old asset:

1. The old asset is sold for a price above the depreciated value. Here the difference between the old machine's selling price and its depreciated value is considered a taxable gain and taxed at the marginal corporate tax rate. If, for example, the old machine was originally purchased for $15,000, had a book value of $10,000, and was sold for $17,000, assuming the firm's marginal corporate tax rate is 34%, the taxes due from the gain would be ($17,000 – $10,000) × (.34), or $2,380.
2. The old asset is sold for its depreciated value. In this case no taxes result, as there is neither a gain nor a loss in the asset's sale.
3. The old asset is sold for less than its depreciated value. In this case the difference between the depreciated book value and the salvage value of the asset is a taxable loss and may be used to offset ordinary income and thus results in tax savings. For example, if the depreciated book value of the asset is $10,000 and it is sold for $7,000 we have a $3,000 loss. Assuming the firm's marginal corporate tax rate is 34%, the cash inflow from tax savings is ($10,000 – $7,000) × (.34), or $1,020.

To clarify the calculation of the initial outlay, consider an example of a company in the 34% marginal tax bracket. This company is considering the purchase of a new

---

FIGURE 20-2   Calculation of Initial Outlay for Example Problem

Outflows:

Purchase price	$30,000	
Shipping fee	2,000	
Installation fee	3,000	
Installed cost of machine		$35,000
Increased taxes from sale of old machine		
($15,000 – $10,000)(.34)		1,700
Increased investment in inventory		5,000
Total outflows		$41,700
Inflows:		
Salvage value of old machine		15,000
Net initial outlay		**$26,700**

---

machine for $30,000 to be used in manufacturing. It has a five-year life (according to IRS guidelines) and will be depreciated using the *simplified straight-line method.* The useful life of this new machine is also five years. The new machine will replace an existing machine, originally purchased for $30,000 10 years ago, which currently has five more years of expected useful life. The existing machine will generate $2,000 of depreciation expenses for each of the next five years, at which time the book value will be equal to zero. To put the new machine in running order, it is necessary to pay shipping charges of $2,000 and installation charges of $3,000. Because the new machine will work faster than the old one, it will require an increase in goods-in-process inventory of $5,000. Finally, the old machine can be sold to a scrap dealer for $15,000.

The installed cost of the new machine would be the $30,000 cost plus $2,000 shipping and $3,000 installation fees, for a total of $35,000. Additional outflows are associated with taxes incurred on the sale of the old machine and with increased investment in inventory. Although the old machine has a book value of $10,000, it could be sold for $15,000. The increased taxes from gain on the sale will be equal to the selling price of the old machine less its depreciated book value times the firm's marginal tax rate, or ($15,000 – $10,000) × (.34), or $1,700. The increase in goods-in-process inventory of $5,000 must also be considered part of the initial outlay, with an offsetting inflow of $5,000 corresponding to the recapture of this inventory occurring at the termination of the project. In effect, the firm invests $5,000 in inventory now, resulting in an initial cash outlay, and liquidates this inventory in five years, resulting in a cash inflow at the end of the project. The total outlays associated with the new machine are $35,000 for its installed cost, $1,700 in increased taxes, and $5,000 in investment in inventory, for a total of $41,700. This is somewhat offset by the sale of the old machine for $15,000. Thus, the net initial outlay associated with this project is $26,700. These calculations are summarized in Figure 20-2.

Differential Flows over Project's Life

The differential cash flows over the project's life involve the incremental after-tax cash flows resulting from increased revenues, plus labor or material savings and reductions in selling expenses. Overhead items, such as utilities, heat, light, and ex-

---

FIGURE 20-3   Summary of Calculation of Differential Cash Flows on After-Tax Basis

1. Added revenue offset by increased expenses
2. Labor and material savings
3. Increases in overhead incurred
4. Tax savings from an increase in depreciation expense if the new project is accepted.
5. Do *not* include interest expenses if the project is financed by issuing debt, as this is accounted for in the required rate of return

---

ecutive salaries, are generally not affected. However, any resultant change in any of these categories must be included. Any increase in interest payments incurred as a result of issuing bonds to finance the project should *not* be included, as the costs of funds needed to support the project are implicitly accounted for by discounting the project back to the present using the required rate of return. Finally, an adjustment for the incremental change in taxes should be made, including any increase in taxes that might result from increased profits or any tax savings from an increase in depreciation expenses. Increased depreciation expenses affect tax-related cash flows by reducing taxable income and thus lowering taxes. Figure 20-3 lists some of the factors that might be involved in determining a project's differential cash flows. However, before looking at an example, we will briefly examine the calculation of depreciation.

Depreciation, the Tax Reform Act of 1986, and the Revenue Reconciliation Act of 1993

The Revenue Reconciliation Act of 1993 largely left in tact the modified version of the Accelerated Cost Recovery System introduced in the Tax Reform Act of 1986. This modified version of the old Accelerated Cost Recovery System (ACRS) is used for most tangible depreciable property placed in service beginning in 1987. Under this method, the life of the asset is determined according to the asset's class life, which is assigned by the IRS; for example, most computer equipment has a five-year asset life. It also allows for only a half year's deduction in the first year and a half year's deduction in the year after the recovery period. The asset is then depreciated using the 200% declining balance method or an optional straight-line method.

Depreciation Calculation—Simplified Straight-Line Depreciation Method

Depreciation is calculated using a simplified straight-line method. This simplified process ignores the half-year convention that allows only a half-year's deduction in the year the project is placed in service and a half-year's deduction in the first year after the recovery period. By ignoring the half-year convention and assuming a zero salvage value we are able to calculate annual depreciation by taking the project's initial depreciable value and dividing by its depreciable life as follows:

$$\frac{\text{annual depreciation using}}{\text{the simplified straight-line method}} = \frac{\text{initial depreciable value}}{\text{depreciable life}}$$

The initial depreciable value is equal to the cost of the asset plus any expenses necessary to get the new asset into operating order.

This is not how depreciation would actually be calculated. The reason we have simplified the calculation is to allow you to focus directly on what should and should not be included in the cash flow calculations. Moreover, because the tax laws change rather frequently, we are more interested in recognizing the tax implications of depreciation than in understanding the specific depreciation provisions of the current tax laws.

Our concern with depreciation is to highlight its importance in generating cash flow estimates and to indicate that the financial manager must be aware of the current tax provisions when evaluating capital-budgeting proposals.

Differential Flows over Project's Life

Extending the earlier example, which illustrated the calculations of the initial outlay, suppose that purchasing the machine is expected to reduce salaries by $10,000 per year and fringe benefits by $1,000 annually, because it will take only one part-time person to operate, whereas the old machine requires two part-time operators. In addition, the cost of defects will fall from $8,000 per year to $3,000. However, maintenance expenses will increase by $4,000 annually. The annual depreciation on this new machine is $7,000 per year, whereas the depreciation expense lost with the sale of the old machine is $2,000 for each of the next five years. Annual depreciation on the new machine is calculated using the simplified straight-line method just described—that is, taking the cost of the new machine plus any expenses necessary to put it in operating order and dividing by its depreciable life. For the new machine these calculations are reflected in Figure 20-4.

Because the depreciation on the old machine is $2,000 per year, the increased depreciation will be from $2,000 per year to $7,000 per year, or an increase of $5,000 per year. Although this increase in depreciation expenses is not a cash flow item, it does affect cash flows by reducing book profits, which in turn reduces taxes.

To determine the annual net cash flows resulting from the acceptance of this project, the net savings *before* taxes using both book profit and cash flows must be found. The additional taxes are then calculated based on the before-tax book profit. For this example, Figure 20-5 shows the determination of the differential cash flows on an after-tax basis. Thus, the differential cash flows over the project's life are $9,620.

FIGURE 20-4 **Calculation of Depreciation for Example Problem Using Simplified Straight-Line Method**

New machine purchase price	$30,000
Shipping fee	2,000
Installation fee	3,000
Total depreciable value	$35,000
Divided by depreciable life	$35,000/5
Equals: Annual depreciation	$7,000

FIGURE 20-5   Calculation of Differential Cash Flows for Example Problem

		Book Profit		Cash Flow
Savings:	Reduced salary	$10,000		$10,000
	Reduced fringe benefits	1,000		1,000
	Reduced defects ($8,000 – $3,000)	5,000		5,000
Costs:	Increased maintenance expense	–4,000		–4,000
	Increased depreciation expense			
	($7,000 – $2,000)	–5,000		_____
Net savings before taxes		$ 7,000		$12,000
Taxes (34%)		–2,380	→	–2,380
Net cash flow after taxes				**$ 9,620**

Terminal Cash Flow

The calculation of the terminal cash flow is in general quite a bit simpler than the preceding two calculations. Flows associated with the project's termination generally include the salvage value of the project plus or minus any taxable gains or losses associated with its sales.

Under the current tax laws, in most cases there will be tax payments associated with the salvage value at termination. This is because the current laws allow all projects to be depreciated to zero, and if a project has a book value of zero at termination and a positive salvage value, then that salvage value will be taxed. The tax effects associated with the salvage value of the project at termination are determined exactly like the tax effects on the sale of the old machine associated with the initial outlay. The salvage value proceeds are compared with the depreciated value, in this case zero, to determine the tax.

In addition to the salvage value, there may be a cash outlay associated with the project termination. For example, at the close of a stripmining operation, the mine must be refilled in an ecologically acceptable manner. Finally, any working capital outlay required at the initiation of the project—for example, increased inventory needed for the operation of a new plant—will be recaptured at the termination of the project. In effect the increased inventory required by the project can be liquidated when the project expires. Figure 20-6 provides a sample list of some of the factors that might affect a project's terminal cash flow.

Extending the example to termination, the depreciated book value and salvage value of the machine at the termination date will be equal to zero. However, there will be a cash flow associated with the recapture of the initial outlay of work-in-

---

FIGURE 20-6   Summary of Calculation of Terminal Cash Flow on After-Tax Basis

1. The after-tax salvage value of the project
2. Cash outlays associated with the project's termination
3. Recapture of nonexpense outlays that occurred at the project's initiation (for example, working capital investments)

---

process inventory of $5,000. This flow is generated from the liquidation of the $5,000 investment in work-in-process inventory. Therefore, the expected total terminal cash flow equals $5,000.

If we were to construct a cash flow diagram from this example (Figure 20-7), it would have an initial outlay of $26,700, differential cash flows during years 1 through 5 of $9,620, and an additional terminal cash flow at the end of year 5 of $5,000. The cash flow occurring in year 5 is $14,620, the sum of the differential cash flow in year 5 of $9,620, and the terminal cash flow of $5,000.

Cash flow diagrams similar to Figure 20-7 will be used through the remainder of this chapter with arrows above the time line indicating cash inflows and arrows below the time line denoting outflows.

Throughout the rest of this section, we use the following example to illustrate the major concepts: A buildings and grounds manager at the University of Minnesota is contemplating the purchase of some lawn maintenance equipment that is expected to increase efficiency and produce cash-operating savings of $2,000 per year. The useful life of the equipment is 4 years, after which it will have a net disposal value of zero. The equipment will cost $6,075 now, and the minimum desired rate of return is 10% per year.

Net Present Value (NPV)

The **net-present-value (NPV) method** is a DCF approach to capital budgeting that discounts all expected future cash flows to the present using a minimum desired rate of return. To apply the NPV method to a proposed investment project, a manager first determines some minimum desired rate of return. The rate depends on the risk of a proposed project—the higher the risk, the higher the minimum desired rate of return. The minimum rate is based on the *cost of capital*—what the firm pays to acquire more capital—and it is also called the **required rate of return, hurdle rate,** or **discount rate.** Managers then determine the present values of all expected cash flows from the project, using this minimum desired rate. If the sum of the present values of the cash flows is positive, the project is desirable. If the sum is negative, it is undesirable. Why? A positive NPV means that accepting the project will increase the value of the firm because the present value of the project's cash inflows exceeds the present value of its cash outflows. (If by some chance, the NPV is exactly zero, a decision maker would be indifferent between accepting and rejecting the project.) When choos-

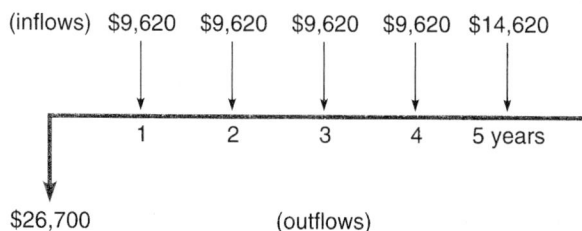

FIGURE 20-7
Example Cash Flow Diagram

ing among several investments, the one with the greatest net present value is the most desirable.

Applying the NPV method. The NPV method is applied in the following three steps, which are shown in Figure 20-8:

1. *Prepare a diagram of relevant expected cash inflows outflows:* The right-hand side of Figure 20-8 shows how these cash flows are sketched. Outflows are in parentheses. Be sure to include the outflow at time zero, the date of acquisition. Although a sketch is not essential, it clarifies thought.
2. *Find the present value of each expected cash inflow or outflow:* Examine Appendix C. Find the present value (PV) factor from the correct row and column of the table. Multiply each expected cash inflow or outflow by the appropriate present value factor. For example, the $2,000 cash savings that will occur 2 years hence is worth $2,000 × .8264 = $1,653 today.
3. *Sum the individual present values:* The sum is the project's NPV. Accept a project whose NPV is positive, and reject a project whose NPV is negative.

Figure 20-8 shows a positive net present value of $265, so the investment is desirable. The value today (i.e., at time zero) of the four $2,000 cash inflows is $6,340. The manager pays only $6,075 to obtain these cash inflows. Thus a favorable difference can be achieved at time zero: $6,340 − $6,075 = $265.

Choice of the correct table. Figure 20-8 also shows another way to calculate the NPV, shown here as approach 2. The basic steps are the same as for approach 1. The only difference is that approach 2 uses Appendix E instead of Appendix C. Appendix E is an annuity table that provides a shortcut to reduce hand calculations. It gives discount factors for computing the present value of a *series of equal* cash flows at equal intervals. Because the four cash flows in our example are all equal, you can use Appendix E to make one present-value computation instead of four individual computations. Appendix E is merely a summation of the pertinent present-value factors of Appendix C. Therefore the annuity factor for 4 years at 10% is:

$$.9091 + .8264 + .7513 + .6830 = 3.1698$$

In this example, Appendix E accomplishes in one computation what Appendix C accomplishes in four multiplications and one summation.[1]

Beware of using the wrong table. Appendix C should be used for discounting individual amounts, Appendix E for a *series* of equal amounts. Of course, Appendix C is the fundamental table. If shortcuts are not desired, Appendix C can be used for all present-value calculations.

The use of Appendices C and E can be avoided entirely by those with a present value function on their hand-held calculator or those who use the present value function on a spreadsheet program on their personal computer. However, we encourage you to use the tables when learning the NPV method. Using the tables leads to an understanding of the process that does not come if calculators or computers are used

---

[1]Rounding error causes a .0001 difference between the Appendix E factor and the summation of Appendix C factors.

FIGURE 20-8   Net-Present-Value Technique

Original investment, $6,075. Useful life, 4 years. Annual cash inflow from operations, $2,000. Minimum desired rate of return, 10%. Cash outflows are in parentheses; cash inflows are not. Total present values are rounded to the nearest dollar.

| | Present Value of $1, Discounted at 10% | Total Present Value | Sketch of Cash Flows at End of Year | | | | |
			0	1	2	3	4
Approach 1: Discounting Each Year's Cash Inflow Separately*							
Cash flows							
Annual savings	.9091	$1,818		←------ $2,000			
	.8264	1,653		←----------------- $2,000		
	.7513	1,503		←--------------------------- $2,000	
	.6830	1,366		←------------------------------------ $2,000
Present value of future inflows		$6,340					
Initial outlay	1.0000	(6,075)	$(6,075)				
Net present value		$ 265					
Approach 2: Using Annuity Table[†]							
Annual savings	3.1699	$6,340		←---- $2,000	$2,000	$2,000	$2,000
Initial outlay	1.0000	(6,075)	$(6,075)				
Net present value		$ 265					

*Present values from Appendix C.
[†]Present values of annuity from Appendix E. (Incidentally, calculators or computers may give slightly different answers than tables because of rounding differences.)

exclusively. Once you are comfortable with the method, you can take advantage of the speed and convenience of calculators and computers.

Effect of minimum rate.   The minimum desired rate of return can have a large effect on NPVs. The higher the minimum desired rate of return, the lower the present value of each future cash inflow and thus the lower the NPV of the project. At a rate of 16%, the NPV of the project in Figure 20-8 would be –$479 (i.e., $2,000 × 2.7982 = $5,596, which is $479 less than the required investment of $6,075), instead of the +$265 computed with a 10% rate. (Present-value factor 2.7982 is taken from Appendix E.) When the desired rate of return is 16% rather than 10%, the project is undesirable at a price of $6,075.

Internal Rate of Return (IRR)

Another way to decide whether to make a capital outlay is to calculate a project's **internal rate of return (IRR),** the discount rate that makes the NPV of the project equal to zero, as Figure 20-9 shows. Expressed another way, the IRR is the discount rate that makes the present value of a project's expected cash inflows equal to the present value of the expected cash outflows, including the investment in the project.

Applying the IRR Method.   The following three steps in calculating IRR are shown in Figure 20-9.

1. *Prepare a diagram of the expected cash inflows and outflows:* Follow this step exactly as you did in calculating the NPV (see Figure 20-8).
2. *Find an interest rate that equates the present value of the cash inflows to the present value of the cash outflows:* In other words, find an interest rate that produces an NPV of zero. Approach 1 uses Appendix B and can be used with any set of cash flows. However, if one outflow is followed by a series of equal inflows, you can use approach 2 and the following equation:

$$\text{initial investment} = \text{annual cash inflow} \times \text{annuity PV factor (F)}$$

$$\$6,075 = \$2,000 \times F$$

$$F = \frac{\$6,075}{\$2,000} = 3.0375$$

In Appendix E, scan the row that represents the relevant life of the project, row 4 in our example. Select the column with an entry closest to the annuity PV factor that was calculated. The factor closest to 3.0375 is 3.0373 in the 12% column. Because these factors are extremely close, the IRR is almost exactly 12%. Approach 2, like approach 1, shows that an interest rate of 12% indeed produces an NPV of zero.

3. *Compare the IRR with the minimum desired rate of return:* If the IRR is greater than the minimum desired rate, the project should be accepted. Otherwise it should be rejected.

Interpolation and trial and error.   Not all IRR calculations work out this neatly. Suppose the expected cash inflow in step 1 were $1,800 instead of $2,000. The equation in step 2 would produce

FIGURE 20-9 Two Proofs of Internal Rate of Return

Original investment, $6,075. Useful life, 4 years. Annual cash inflow from operations, $2,000. Internal rate of return (selected by trial-and-error methods), 12%. Total present values are rounded to the nearest dollar.

	Present Value of $1, Discounted at 12%	Total Present Value	Sketch of Cash Flows at End of Year
			0 1 2 3 4

Approach 1: Discounting Each Year's Cash Inflow Separately*

Cash flows

Annual savings	.8929	$1,786	$2,000
	.7972	1,594	$2,000
	.7118	1,424	$2,000
	.6355	1,271	$2,000
Present value of future inflows		$6,075	
Initial outlay	1.0000	(6,075)	$(6,075)
Net present value (the zero difference proves that the rate of return is 12%)		$ 0	

Approach 2: Using Annuity Table†

Annual savings	3.0373	$6,075	$2,000 $2,000 $2,000 $2,000
Initial outlay	1.0000	(6,075)	$(6,075)
Net present value		$ 0	

*Present values from Appendix C.
†Present values of annuity from Appendix E.

$$\$6,075 = \$1,800 \times F$$

$$F = \frac{\$6,075}{\$1,800} = 3.3750$$

On the period 4 line of Appendix E, the column closest to 3.3750 is 7%, which may be close enough for most purposes. To obtain a more accurate rate, you must interpolate. The factor 3.3750 is between the 7% factor (3.3872) and the 8% factor (3.3121):

	Present-Value Factors	
7%	3.3872	3.3872
Approximate rate		3.3750
8%	3.3121	
Difference	.0751	.0122

Thus,

$$\text{approximate rate} = 7\% + \left(\frac{.0122}{.0751} \times 1\%\right) = 7.16\%$$

These hand computations become even more complex when the cash inflows and outflows are not uniform. Then trial-and-error methods are needed. See Addendum 20 for examples. Of course, in practice, managers today use computer programs and spreadsheets to greatly simplify trial-and-error procedures.

Meaning of internal rate of return. Figure 20-9 shows that the present value of four annual cash inflows of $2,000 each is $6,075, assuming a rate of return of 12%. That is, 12% is the rate that equates the amount invested ($6,075) with the present value of the cash inflows ($2,000 per year for 4 years). Figure 20-10 shows that, if money were obtained at an effective interest rate of 12%, the cash inflow produced by the project would exactly repay the principal plus the interest over the 4 years. If money is available at less than 12%, the organization will have cash left over after repaying the principal and interest.

Figure 20-10 also highlights how the IRR is computed on the basis of the investment tied up in the project from period to period instead of solely on the initial investment. The internal rate is 12% of the capital invested during each year. The $2,000 inflow is composed of two parts, as analyzed in columns 3 and 4. Consider year 1. Column 3 shows the interest on the $6,075 invested capital as .12 × $6,075 – $729. Column 4 shows that the amount of investment recovered at the end of the year is $2,000 – $729 = $1,271. By the end of year 4, the series of four cash inflows exactly recovers the initial investment plus annual interest at a rate of 12% on the as yet unrecovered capital.

Figure 20-10 can be interpreted from either the borrower's or the lender's vantage point. Suppose the university borrowed $6,075 from a bank at an interest rate of 12% per annum, invested in the project, and repaid the loan with the $2,000 saved each year. Each $2,000 payment would represent interest of 12% plus a reduction of the loan balance. At a rate of 12%, the borrower would end up with an accumulated wealth of zero. Obviously, if the borrower could borrow at 12%, and the project could

FIGURE 20-10 Rationale Underlying Internal-Rate-of-Return Model (Same data as in Figure 20-9) Original investment, $6,075. Useful life, 4 years. Annual cash savings from operations, $2,000. Internal rate of return, 12%. Amounts are rounded to the nearest dollar.

Year	1) Unrecovered Investment at Beginning of Year	(2) Annual Cash Savings	(3) Interest at 12% per Year (1) × 12%	(4) Amount of Investment Recovered at End of Year (2) – (3)	(5) Unrecovered Investment at End of Year (1) – (4)
1	$6,075	$2,000	$729	$1,271	$4,804
2	4,804	2,000	576	1,424	3,380
3	3,380	2,000	406	1,594	1,786
4	1,786	2,000	214	1,786	0

Assumptions: Unrecovered investment at beginning of each year earns interest for whole year. Annual cash inflows are received at the end of each year. For simplicity in the use of tables, all operating cash inflows are assumed to occur at the end of the years in question. This is unrealistic because such cash flows ordinarily occur uniformly throughout the given year, rather than in lump sums at the end of the year. Compound interest tables especially tailored for these more stringent conditions are available, but we shall not consider them here.

generate cash at more than the 12% rate (i.e., in excess of $2,000 annually), the borrower would be able to keep some cash—and the internal rate of return, *by definition*, would exceed 12%. Again the internal rate of return is the discount rate that would provide a net present value of zero (no more, no less).

Assumptions of DCF Models

Although both DCF models are good, neither is perfect. Two major assumptions underlie DCF models. First, we assume a world of certainty. That is, we act as if the predicted cash inflows and outflows are certain to occur at the times specified. Second, we assume perfect capital markets. That is, if we have extra cash at any time, we can borrow or lend money at the same interest rate. This rate is our minimum desired rate of return for the NPV model and the internal rate of return for the IRR model. If these assumptions are met, no model could possibly be better than a DCF model.

Unfortunately, our world has neither certainty nor perfect capital markets. Nevertheless, the DCF models are usually preferred to other models. The assumptions of most other models are even less realistic. The DCF models are not perfect, but they generally meet our cost-benefit criterion. The payoff from better decisions is greater than the cost of applying one of the DCF models. More sophisticated models often do not improve decisions enough to be worth their cost.

USE OF DCF MODELS

In using DCF models of both types, managers must keep in mind the limitations of these models. Using such models is also complicated by the difficulties of determining a desired rate of return.

Choice of the Minimum Desired Rate

There are two key aspects of capital budgeting: investment decisions and financing decisions. *Investment decisions* focus on whether to acquire an asset, a project, a company, a product line, and so on. *Financing decisions* focus on whether to raise the required funds via some form of debt or equity or both.

Depending on a project's risk (i.e., the probability that the expected cash inflows will not be achieved) and what alternative investments are available, investors usually have some notion of a minimum rate of return that would make various projects desirable investments. The problem of choosing this required rate of return is complex and is really more a problem of finance than of accounting. In general, the higher the risk, the higher the required rate of return. In this book we assume that the minimum acceptable rate of return is given to the accountant by management. It represents the rate that can be earned by the best alternative investments of similar risk.

Note too that the minimum desired rate is not affected by whether the *specific project* is financed by all debt, all ownership capital, or some of each. Thus the cost of capital is not "interest expense" on borrowed money as the accountant ordinarily conceives it. For example, a mortgage-free home still has a cost of capital—the maximum amount that could be earned with the proceeds if the home were sold.

Depreciation and DCF

Accounting students are sometimes mystified by the apparent exclusion of depreciation from DCF computations. A common homework error is to deduct depreciation from cash inflows. This is a misunderstanding of one of the basic ideas involved in the concept of the discounting. Because the DCF approach is fundamentally based on inflows and outflows of *cash* and not on the accounting concepts of revenues and expenses, no adjustments should be made to the cash flows for depreciation expense (which is not a cash flow).[2] In the DCF approach, the entire cost of an asset is typically a *lump-sum* outflow of cash at time zero. Therefore it is wrong to also deduct depreciation from operating cash inflows. To deduct periodic depreciation would be a double-counting of a cost that has already been considered as a lump-sum outflow.

Use of DCF Models by Nonprofit Organizations

Religious, educational, health care, government, and other nonprofit organizations face a variety of capital-budgeting decisions. Examples include investments in buildings, equipment, national defense systems, and research programs. Thus, even when no revenue is involved, organizations try to choose projects with the least cost for any given set of objectives.

The unsettled question of the appropriate discount rate plagues all types of organizations, profit-seeking and nonprofit. One point is certain: As all cash-strapped

---

[2]Our examples often assume that cash inflows are equivalent to revenues and that cash outflows are equivalent to expenses (except for depreciation). Of course, if the revenues and expenses are accounted for on the accrual basis of accounting, there will be leads and lags of cash inflows and cash outflows that a precise DCF model must recognize. For example, a $10,000 sale on credit may be recorded as revenue in one period, but the related cash inflow would not be recognized in a DCF model until collected, which may be in a second period. Such refinements are not made in this chapter.

organizations soon discover, capital is not cost-free. A discussion of the appropriate required rate of return is beyond the scope of this book. Often departments of the federal government use 10%. It represents a crude approximation of the opportunity cost to the economy of having investments made by public agencies instead of by private organizations.

Progress in management practices and in the use of sophisticated techniques has generally tended to be faster in profit-seeking organizations. Although DCF is used by many federal departments, it is less frequently used at state and local levels of government. Thus, in general, managers have more opportunities in nonprofit than in profit-seeking organizations to contribute to improved decision making by introducing newer management decision models such as DCF.[3]

Review of Decision Rules

Before proceeding, take time to review the basic ideas of discounted cash flow. The decision maker in our example cannot readily compare an immediate outflow of $6,075 with a series of future inflows of $2,000 each because the outflows and inflows do not occur simultaneously. The NPV model expresses all amounts in equivalent terms; that is, in today's monetary units (e.g., dollars, francs, marks, yen) at time zero. An interest rate measures the cost of using money. At a rate of 12%, the comparison would be:

Outflow in today's dollars	$(6,075)
Inflow equivalent in today's dollars @ 12%	6,075
Net present value	$ 0

Therefore, at a required rate of return of 12%, the decision maker is indifferent between having $6,075 now or having a stream of four annual inflows of $2,000 each. If the interest rate were 16%, the decision maker would find the project unattractive because the net present value would be negative:

Outflow	$(6,075)
Inflow equivalent in today's dollars @ 16% =	
$2,000 × 2.7982 (from Table 2) =	5,596
Net present value	$ (479)

At 10%, the NPV is positive, and the project is desirable:

Outflow	$(6,075)
Inflow equivalent in today's dollars @ 10% =	
$2,000 × 3.1699 from Table 2 =	6,340
Net present value	$ 265

[3]An extensive study by the General Accounting Office cited the U.S. Postal Service as being the best of the federal agencies regarding capital budgeting. The Postal Service uses discounted cash flow, sensitivity analysis, and postaudits.

We can summarize the decision rules offered by these two models as follows:

Net-Present-Value (NPV) **Model**	**Internal Rate-of-Return (IRR)** **Model**
1. Calculate the NPV, using the minimum desired rate of return as the discount rate.	1. Compute the IRR by trial and error (e.g., by using present-value tables).
2. If the NPV is positive, accept the project; if negative, reject the project.	2. If this rate exceeds the minimum desired rate of return, accept the project; if not, reject the project.

A report in *Business Week* provided an example of using an NPV model:

> Like many of the amounts being paid in big acquisitions of the last year, the $350 million that Eaton Corp. will have paid this January to acquire Cutler-Hammer, Inc., appears to be a stiff price. . . . Eaton is justifying the price in large part by using an old but increasingly popular financial tool: discounted-cash-flow analysis (DCF). To set the price, Eaton projected the future cash flows it expects from Cutler over the next 5 to lo years and then discounted them, using a rate that reflects the risks involved in the investment and the time value of the money used. Eaton figures that, based on DCF, Cutler will return at least 12% on its $350 million outlay.

SENSITIVITY ANALYSIS AND ASSESSMENT OF RISK IN DCF MODELS

Capital investments entail risk. Why? Because the actual cash inflows may differ from what was expected or predicted. When considering a capital-budgeting project, a manager should first determine the riskiness of the investment. Then the inputs to the capital-budgeting model should be adjusted to reflect the risk.

There are three common ways to recognize risk. They can be used singly or in combination:

1. Increase the minimum desired rate of return for riskier projects.
2. Reduce individual expected cash inflows or increase expected cash outflows by an amount that depends on their riskiness.
3. Reduce the expected life of riskier projects.

In the examples in this book we assume that an appropriate risk adjustment is included in the minimum desired rate of return.

One method that helps identify the riskiness of a project is to compare the results of different capital-budgeting models. For example, a manager can compare the NPV and IRR results with those of simpler measures such as the payback period and accounting rate of return (discussed later in this chapter).

Another approach is the use of sensitivity analysis, which shows the financial consequences that would occur if actual cash inflows and outflows differed from those expected. It can be usefully applied whenever a decision requires predictions. It answers such "what-if" questions as: What will happen to my NPV or IRR if my predictions of useful life or cash flows are inaccurate? Spreadsheet software is ideally suited for this type of analysis.

There are two major types of sensitivity analysis: (1) comparing the optimistic, pessimistic, and most likely predictions and (2) determining the amount of deviation from expected values before a decision is changed. These analyses produce results such as the following:

1. Suppose the forecasts of annual cash inflows in Figure 20-8 could range from a low of $1,700 to a high of $2,300. The pessimistic, most likely, and optimistic NPV predictions are

   Pessimistic: ($1,700 × 3.1699) − $6,075 = $5,389 − $6,075 = −$686
   Most likely: ($2,000 × 3.1699) − $6,075 = $6,340 − $6,075 = $265
   Optimistic: ($2,300 × 3.1699) − $6,075 = $7,291 − $6,075 = $1,216

   Although the expected NPV is $265, the actual NPV might turn out to be as low as −$686 or, as high as $1,216.

2. A manager would reject a project if its expected NPV were negative. How far below $2,000 must the annual cash inflow drop before the NPV becomes negative? The cash inflow at the point where NPV = 0 is the "break-even" cash flow:

   $$NPV = 0$$
   $$(3.1699 \times \text{cash flow}) - \$6{,}075 = 0$$
   $$\text{cash flow} = \$6{,}075 \div 3.1699$$
   $$= \$1{,}916$$

   If the annual cash inflow is less than $1,916, the project should be rejected. Therefore annual cash inflows can drop only $2,000 − $1,916 = $84, or 4%, before the manager would change the decision. Thus managers must decide whether a given margin of error is acceptable or whether undertaking a project represents too great a risk.

Sensitivity analysis can also be performed on predictions of the useful life of capital equipment. Suppose 3 years is a pessimistic prediction, and 5 years is optimistic. Using present-value factors from the third, fourth, and fifth rows of the 10% column of Appendix E, the NPVs are as follows:

   Pessimistic: (2.4869 × $2,000) − $6,075 = −$1,101
   Most likely: (3.1699 × $2,000) − $6,075 = $265
   Optimistic: (3.7908 × $2,000) − $6,075 = $1,507

If the useful life is even 1 year less than predicted, the investment will be undesirable.

Sensitivity analysis provides an immediate financial measure of the consequences of possible errors in forecasting. Why is this useful? It helps to identify decisions that may be readily affected by prediction errors. After managers identify such decisions, they can gather additional information to help them better predict cash flows or useful life before making their decisions.

THE NPV COMPARISON OF TWO PROJECTS

Seldom are managers asked to perform analyses on a single option. More often, managers want to compare several alternatives.

Total Project Versus Differential Approach

Two common methods for comparing alternatives are (1) the *total project approach* and (2) the *differential approach.*

The **total project approach** compares two or more alternatives by computing the total impact on cash flows for each alternative and then converting these total cash flows to their present values. It is the most popular approach and can be used for any number of alternatives. The alternative with the largest NPV of total cash flows is preferred.

The **differential approach** compares two alternatives by computing the *differences* in cash flows between alternatives and then converting these differences in cash flows to their present values. Its use is restricted to cases in which only two alternatives are being examined. (There are always at least two alternatives. One is the status quo—that is, doing nothing.)

To compare these approaches, suppose a company owns a packaging machine that it purchased 3 years ago for $56,000. The machine has a remaining useful life of 5 years but will require a major overhaul at the end of 2 more years at a cost of $10,000. Its disposal value now is $20,000. In 5 years its disposal value is expected to be $8,000, assuming that the $10,000 major overhaul will be done on schedule. The cash-operating costs of this machine are expected to be $40,000 annually. A sales representative has offered a substitute machine for $51,000, or for $31,000 plus the old machine. The new machine will reduce annual cash-operating costs by $10,000, will not require any overhauls, will have a useful life of 5 years, and will have a disposal value of $3,000. If the minimum desired rate of return is 14%, what should the company do to minimize long run costs? (Try to solve this problem yourself before examining the solution that follows.)

A difficult part of long-range decision making is the structuring of the data. We want to see the effects of each alternative on future cash inflows and outflows. To apply either the total project or the differential approach, the first step is to arrange the relevant cash flows by project. Figure 20-11 shows how the cash flows for each alternative are sketched. The next step depends on the approach used:

Total Project Approach: Determine the net present value of the cash flows for each individual project. Choose the project with the largest positive present value (i.e., largest benefit) or smallest negative present value (i.e., smallest cost).

Differential Approach: Compute the differential cash flows; that is, subtract the cash flows for project B from the cash flows from project A for each year. Calculate the present value of the differential cash flows. If this present value is positive, choose project A; if it is negative, choose project B.

Figure 20-11 illustrates both the total project approach and the differential approach. Which approach you use when there are only two alternatives is a matter of preference. (The total project approach is necessary when analyzing three or more alternatives simultaneously.) However, to develop confidence in this area, you should work with both at the start. One approach can serve as proof of the accuracy of the other. In this example, the $8,429 net difference in favor of replacement is the result under either approach.

FIGURE 20-11 Total Project Versus Differential Approach to Net Present Value

	Present Value Discount Factor, at 14%	Total Present Value	Sketch of After-Tax Cash Flows at End of Year					
			0	1	2	3	4	5
I. Total Project Approach								
A. Replace								
Recurring cash operating costs, using an annuity table*	3.4331	$(102,993)		($30,000)	($30,000)	($30,000)	($30,000)	($30,000)
Disposal value, end of year 5	.5194	1,558						$3,000
Initial required investment	1.0000	(31,000)	($31,000)					
Present value of net cash outflows		$(132,435)						
B. Keep								
Recurring cash operating costs, using an annuity table*	3.4331	$(137,324)		($40,000)	($40,000)	($40,000)	($40,000)	($40,000)
Overhaul, end of year 2	.7695	(7,695)			($10,000)			
Disposal value, end of year 5	.5194	4,155						$8,000
Present value of net cash outflows		$(140,864)						
Difference in favor of replacement		$ 8,429						
II. Differential Approach								
A-B. Analysis Confined to Differences								
Recurring cash operating savings, using an annuity table*	3.4331	$ 34,331		$10,000	$10,000	$10,000	$10,000	$10,000
Overhaul avoided, end of year 2	.7695	7,695			$10,000			
Difference in disposal values, end of year 5	.5194	(2,597)						$(5,000)
Incremental initial investment	1.0000	(31,000)	($31,000)					
Net present value of replacement		$ 8,429						

*Appendix E.

Analysis of Typical Items Under DCF

When you array the relevant cash flows, be sure to consider four types of inflows and outflows: (1) initial cash inflows and outflows at time zero, (2) investments in receivables and inventories, (3) future disposal values, and (4) operating cash flows.

Initial cash inflows and outflows at time zero.   These cash flows include both outflows for the purchases and installation of equipment and other items required by the new project, and either inflows or outflows from disposal of any items that are replaced. In Figure 20-11 the $20,000 received from selling the old machine was offset against the $51,000 purchase price of the new machine, resulting in a net cash outflow of $31,000. If the old machine could not be sold, any cost incurred to dismantle and discard it would have been *added* to the purchase price of the new machine.

Investments in receivables and inventories.   Investments in receivables, inventories, and intangible assets are basically no different from investments in plant and equipment. In the DCF model, the initial outlays are entered in the sketch of cash flows at time zero. At the end of the useful life of the project, the original outlays for machines may not be recouped at all or may be partially recouped in the amount of the salvage values. In contrast, the entire original investments in receivables and inventories are usually recouped when the project ends. Therefore all initial investments are typically regarded as outflows at time zero, and their terminal disposal values, if any, are regarded as inflows at the end of the project's useful life.

The example in Figure 20-11 required no additional investment in inventory or receivables. However, the expansion of a retail store, for example, entails an additional investment in a building and fixtures *plus* inventories. Such investments would be shown in the format of Figure 20-11 as follows:

Sketch of Cash Flows				
End of year	0	1	2 . . . 19	20
Investment in building				
and fixtures	(10)			1
Investment in working				
capital (inventories)	(6)			6

As the sketch shows, the residual value of the building and fixtures might be small. However, the entire investment in inventories would ordinarily be recouped when the venture is terminated.

The difference between the initial outlay for working capital (mostly receivables and inventories) and the present value of its recovery is the present value of the cost of using working capital in the project. Working capital is constantly revolving in a cycle from cash to inventories to receivables and back to cash throughout the life of the project. But to be sustained, the project requires that money be tied up in the cycle until the project ends.

Future disposal values.   The disposal value at the date of termination of a project is an increase in the cash inflow in the year of disposal. Errors in forecasting terminal disposal values are usually not crucial because the present value is usually small.

Operating cash flows.   The major purpose of most investments is to affect revenues or costs (or both). The cash inflows and outflows associated with most of these effects may be difficult to measure, and three points deserve special mention.

First, in relevant-cost analysis, the only pertinent overhead costs are those that will differ among alternatives. Fixed overhead under the available alternatives needs careful study. In practice, this is an extremely difficult phase of cost analysis, because it is difficult to relate the individual costs to any single project.

Second, depreciation and book values should be ignored. The cost of assets is recognized by the initial outlay, not by depreciation as computed under accrual accounting.

Third, a reduction in a cash outflow is treated the same as a cash inflow. Both signify increases in value.

Cash Flows for Investments in Technology

Many capital-budgeting decisions compare a possible investment with a continuation of the status quo. One such decision is investment in a highly automated production system to replace a traditional system. Suppose a manufacturing company is considering investment in a computer integrated manufacturing (CIM) system. One of the most difficult parts of the decision is predicting relevant cash flows. It is easy to overlook some benefits of such a system and thereby underestimate its desirability.

Cash flows predicted for the CIM system should be compared with those *predicted for continuation of the present system into the future.* The latter are not necessarily the cash flows currently being experienced. Why? Because the competitive environment is changing. If others invest in CIM systems, failure to invest may cause a decline in market share and therefore lower revenues. Competitors may use their CIM systems to increase quality, change product designs more readily, and be more responsive to customer demands. Instead of predicting a future similar to the present situation, the future without a CIM might be a continual decline in revenues and a noncompetitive cost structure.

A CIM system can also lead to unanticipated cost savings. Certainly some savings, such as lower inventory levels, reduced machine downtime, and shorter cycle times, can be predicted and the savings quantified. However, others, such as flexibility to change product mix easily, ability to implement design changes quickly and cheaply, and general reduction of non-value-added activities, may be difficult to predict and especially difficult to measure.

There are two ways to deal with difficult-to-predict revenue and cost effects. First, they can be quantified as best as possible and included in an NPV analysis. Second, they can be recognized subjectively. For example, investment in a CIM may have a *negative* NPV of $500,000 without considering subjective effects. A manager must then decide whether the potential losses in contribution margin from a decline in competitiveness—plus possible nonquantified cost savings—exceed $500,000. If so, the CIM is a desirable investment, despite its negative NPV.

Complications

The foregoing material has been an *introduction* to the area of capital budgeting. In practice, a variety of factors complicate the analysis, including

1. *Income taxes:* Comparison between alternatives is best made after considering tax effects, because the tax impact may alter the picture.
2. *Inflation:* Predictions of cash flows and discount rates should be based on consistent inflation assumptions.
3. *Mutually exclusive projects:* When the projects are mutually exclusive, so that the acceptance of one automatically entails the rejection of the other (e.g., buying Toyota or Ford trucks), the project that has the largest net present value should be undertaken.
4. *Unequal lives:* If alternative projects have unequal lives, comparisons may be made over the useful life of either the longer-lived project or the shorter-lived one. For our purposes, we will use the life of the longer-lived project. To provide comparability, we assume reinvestment in the shorter-lived project at the end of its life and give it credit for any residual value at the time the longer-lived project ends. The important consideration is what would be done in the time interval between the termination dates of the shorter- and longer-lived projects.

OTHER MODELS FOR ANALYZING LONG-RANGE DECISIONS

Although the use of DCF models for business decisions has increased steadily over the past four decades, simpler models are also used. Often managers use them in *addition* to DCF analyses.

These models, which we are about to explain, are conceptually inferior to DCF approaches. Then why do we bother studying them? First, because the simpler models might provide some useful information to supplement the DCF analysis. Second, because changes in business practice occur slowly. Many businesses still use the simpler models. Finally, because when simpler models are in use, they should be used properly, even if better models are available.

Of course, as always, the accountant and manager face a cost-and-value-of-information decision when they choose a decision model. Reluctance to use DCF models may be justified if the more familiar payback model or other simple models lead to the same investment decisions.

One existing technique may be called the emergency-persuasion method. No formal planning is used. Fixed assets are operated until they crumble, product lines are carried until they are obliterated by competition, and requests by managers for authorization of capital outlays are judged on the basis of their ability to convince top management that the investment is necessary. These approaches to capital budgeting are examples of the unscientific management that often leads to bankruptcy.

In contrast, both the payback and the accounting rate-of-return models, although flawed, are attempts to approach capital budgeting systematically.

Payback Model

Payback time or **payback period** is the measure of the time it will take to recoup, in the form of cash inflows from operations, the initial dollars of outlay. Assume that

$12,000 is spent for a machine with an estimated useful life of 8 years. Annual savings of $4,000 in cash outflows are expected from operations. Depreciation is ignored. The payback period is 3 years, calculated as follows:

$$\text{payback time} = \frac{\text{initial incremental amount invested}}{\text{equal annual incremental cash inflow from operations}}$$

$$P = \frac{I}{O} = \frac{\$12,000}{\$4,000} = 3\,\text{years}$$

The payback model merely measures how quickly investment dollars may be recouped—it does not measure profitability. This is its major weakness. A project with a shorter payback time is not necessarily preferable to one with a longer payback time. On the other hand, the payback model can provide a rough estimate of riskiness, especially in decisions involving areas of rapid technological change.

Assume that an alternative to the $12,000 machine is a $10,000 machine whose operation will also result in a reduction of $4,000 annually in cash outflow. Then the payback periods are:

$$P_1 = \frac{\$12,000}{\$4,000} = 3.0\,\text{years}$$

$$P_2 = \frac{\$10,000}{\$4,000} = 2.5\,\text{years}$$

The $10,000 machine has a shorter payback time, and therefore it may appear more desirable. However, one fact about the $10,000 machine has been purposely withheld. What if its useful life is only 2.5 years? Ignoring the impact of compound interest for the moment, the $10,000 machine results in zero benefit, whereas the $12,000 machine (useful life 8 years) generates cash inflows for 5 years beyond its payback period.

The main objective in investing is profit, not the recapturing of the initial outlay. If a company wants to recover its outlay fast, it need not spend in the first place. Then no waiting time is necessary, because the payback time is zero. When a wealthy investor was assured by the promoter of a risky oil venture that he would have his money back within 2 years, the investor replied, "I already have my money."

The formula for payback time given above can be used with assurance only when there are equal annual cash inflows from operations. When annual cash inflows are not equal, the payback computation must take a cumulative form—that is, each year's net cash flows are accumulated until the initial investment is recouped.

Assume a cash flow pattern as follows:

End of Year	0	1	2	3
Investment	($31,000)			
Cash inflows		$10,000	$20,000	$10,000

The calculation of the payback period is:

| | | Net Cash Inflows | |
Year	Initial Investment	Each Year	Accumulated
0	$31,000	—	—
1	—	$10,000	$10,000
2	—	20,000	30,000
2.1	—	1,000	31,000

In this case, the payback time is slightly beyond the second year. Interpolation within the third year reveals that the final $1,000 needed to recoup the investment would be forthcoming in 2.1 years:

$$2 \text{ years} + \left(\frac{\$1,000}{\$10,000} \times 1 \text{ year} \right) = 2.1 \text{ years}$$

Accounting Rate-of-Return Model

Another non-DCF capital-budgeting model is the **accounting rate-of-return (ARR) model:**

$$\text{accounting rate–of–return} = \frac{\text{increase in expected average annual operating income}}{\text{initial increase in required investment}}$$

$$\text{ARR} = \frac{O - D}{I}$$

where ARR is the average annual accounting rate of return on initial additional investment, O is the average annual incremental cash inflow from operations, D is the incremental average annual depreciation, and I is the initial incremental amount invested. The accounting rate-of-return model is also known as the *accrual accounting rate-of-return model* (a more accurate description), the *unadjusted rate-of-return model*, and the *book-value model*. Its computations dovetail most closely with conventional accounting models of calculating income and required investment, and they show the effect of an investment on an organization's financial statements.

Assume the same facts as in Figure 20-8: Investment is $6,075, useful life is 4 years, estimated disposal value is zero, and expected annual cash inflow from operations is $2,000. Annual depreciation would be $6,075 ÷ 4 = $1,518.75, rounded to $1,519. Substitute these values in the accounting rate-of-return equation:

$$\text{ARR} = \frac{\$2,000 - \$1,519}{\$6,075} = 7.9\%$$

Some companies use the "average" investment (often assumed for equipment as being the average book value over the useful life) instead of original investment in the denominator. Therefore, the denominator becomes $6,075 ÷ 2 = $3,037.5, and the rate doubles:[4]

$$ARR = \frac{\$2,000 - \$1,519}{\$3,037.50} = 15.8\%$$

With the original investment in the denominator, the ARR is usually less than the IRR. When the "average" investment is used, the ARR generally exceeds the IRR.

Defects of Accounting Rate-of-Return Model

The accounting rate-of-return model is based on the familiar financial statements prepared under accrual accounting. Unlike the payback model, the accounting model at least has profitability as an objective. Nevertheless, it has a major drawback. The accounting model ignores the time value of money. Expected future dollars are erroneously regarded as equal to present dollars. The DCF model explicitly allows for the force of interest and the timing of cash flows. In contrast, the accounting model is based on *annual averages*.

The accounting model uses concepts of investment and income that were originally designed for the quite different purpose of accounting for periodic income and financial position. The resulting *accounting* rate of return may differ greatly from the project's *internal* rate of return.

To illustrate, consider a petroleum company with three potential projects to choose from: an expansion of an existing gasoline station, an investment in an oil well, and the purchase of a new gasoline station. To simplify the calculations, assume a 3-year life for each project. Figure 20-12 summarizes the comparisons. The projects differ only in the timing of the cash inflows. Note that the accounting rate of return indicates that all three projects are equally desirable. In contrast, the internal rate of return properly discriminates in favor of earlier cash inflows.

PERFORMANCE EVALUATION

Potential Conflict

Many managers are reluctant to accept DCF models as the best way to make capital-budgeting decisions. Their reluctance stems from the wide usage of accounting income for evaluating performance. That is, managers become frustrated if they are instructed to use a DCF model for making decisions that are evaluated later by a non-DCF model, such as the typical accounting rate-of-return model, which is based on accounting income instead of cash flows.

To illustrate, consider the potential conflict that might arise in the example of Figure 20-8. Recall that the internal rate of return was 12%, based on an outlay of

---

[4]The measure of the investment recovered in the preceding example is $1,519 per year, the amount of the annual depreciation. Consequently, the average investment committed to the project would decline at a rate of $1,519 per year from $6,075 to zero; hence the average investment would be the beginning balance plus the ending balance ($6,075 + 0) divided by 2, or $3,037.50. Note that when the ending balance is not zero, the average investment will *not* be half the initial investment.

FIGURE 20-12 Comparison of Accounting Rates of Return and Internal Rates of Return

	Expansion of Existing Gasoline Station	Investment in an Oil Well	Purchase of New Gasoline Station
Initial investment	$ 90,000	$ 90,000	$ 90,000
Cash inflows from operations			
Year 1	$ 40,000	$ 80,000	$ 20,000
Year 2	40,000	30,000	40,000
Year 3	40,000	10,000	60,000
Totals	$120,000	$120,000	$120,000
Average annual cash inflow	$40,000	$40,000	$40,000
Less: average annual depreciation ($90,000 ÷ 3)	30,000	30,000	30,000
Increase in average annual net income	$ 10,000	$ 10,000	$ 10,000
Accounting rate of return on initial investment	11.1%	11.1%	11.1%
Internal rate of return, using discounted-cash-flow techniques	16.0%*	23.3%*	13.4%*

*Computed by trial-and-error approaches using Appendices C and E. See Addendum 20 for a detailed explanation.

$6,075 that would generate cash savings of $2,000 for each of 4 years and no terminal disposal value. Using accounting income computed with straight-line depreciation, the evaluation of performance for years one through four would be:

	Year 1	Year 2	Year 3	Year 4
Cash-operating savings	$2,000	$2,000	$2,000	$2,000
Straight-line depreciation, $6,075 ÷ 4	1,519	1,519	1,519	1,519*
Effect on operating income	481	481	481	481
Book value at beginning of year	6,075	4,556	3,037	1,518
Accounting rate of return	7.9%	10.6%	15.8%	31.7%

*Total depreciation of 4 × $1,519 = $6,076 differs from $6,075 because of rounding error.

Many managers would be reluctant to replace equipment, despite the internal rate of 12%, if their performance were evaluated by accounting income. They might be especially reluctant if they are likely to be transferred to new positions every year or two. Why? This accrual accounting system understates the return in early years, and a manager might not be around to reap the benefits of the later overstatement of returns.

As indicated, managerial reluctance to replace is reinforced if a heavy book loss on old equipment would appear in year 1's income statement—even though such a loss would be irrelevant in a properly constructed decision model. Thus performance evaluation based on typical accounting measures can cause the rejection of major, long-term projects such as investments in technologically advanced production systems. This pattern may help explain why many U.S. firms seem to be excessively short-term oriented.

Reconciliation of Conflict

How can the foregoing conflict be reconciled? Many organizations use the typical accounting model both for making capital-budgeting decisions *and* for evaluating performance and do not use DCF models at all. Yet, as we noted earlier, DCF models remain the best tool for capital-budgeting decisions, so this is not often a good solution.

Another obvious solution would be to use DCF for both capital-budgeting decisions and performance evaluation. A recent survey showed that most large companies (approximately 76%) conduct a follow-up evaluation of at least some capital-budgeting decisions, often called a **postaudit.** The purposes of postaudits include

1. Seeing that investment expenditures are proceeding on time and within budget
2. Comparing actual cash flows with those originally predicted, in order to motivate careful and honest predictions
3. Providing information for improving future predictions of cash flows
4. Evaluating the continuation of the project

By focusing the postaudit on actual versus predicted *cash flows,* the evaluation is consistent with the decision process.

However, postauditing of all capital-budgeting decisions is costly. Most accounting systems are designed to evaluate operating performances of products, departments, divisions, territories, and so on, *year by year.* In contrast, capital-budgeting decisions frequently deal with individual *projects,* not the collection of projects that are usually being managed simultaneously by divisional or department managers. Therefore, usually only selected capital-budgeting decisions are audited.

The conflicts between the longstanding, pervasive accrual accounting model and various formal decision models represent one of the most serious unsolved problems in the design of management control systems. Top management cannot expect goal congruence if it favors the use of one type of model for decisions and the use of another type for performance evaluation.

SUMMARY

Specifically, we examine the measurement of incremental cash flows associated with a firm's investment proposals and the evaluation of those proposals. In measuring cash flows we focus on the **incremental** or differential **after-tax cash flows** attributed to the investment proposal. In general, a project's cash flows fall into one of three categories: (1) the initial outlay, (2) the differential flows over the project's life, (3) the terminal cash flow. A summary of the typical entries in each of these categories appears in Figure 20-13.

Capital budgeting is long-term planning for proposed capital outlays and their financing. Because the DCF model explicitly and automatically weighs the time value of money, it is the best method to use for long-range decisions. The overriding goal is maximum long-run net cash inflows.

The DCF model has two variations: IRR and NPV. Both models consider the timing of cash flows and are thus superior to other models. Common errors in DCF analysis include deducting depreciation from operating cash inflows, using the wrong

---

FIGURE 20-13 Summary of Calculation of Incremental After-Tax Cash Flows

A. Initial Outlay
   1. Installed cost of asset
   2. Additional nonexpense outlays incurred (for example, working-capital investments)
   3. Additional expenses, on an after-tax basis (for example, training expenses)
   4. In a replacement decision, the after-tax flow associated with the sale of the old machine
B. Differential Cash Flows over the Project's Life
   1. Added revenue offset by increased expenses
   2. Labor and material savings
   3. Increases in overhead incurred
   4. Tax savings from an increase in depreciation if the new project is accepted.
   5. Do not include interest expenses if the project is financed by issuing debt, as this is accounted for in the required rate of return
C. Terminal Cash Flow
   1. The after-tax salvage value of the project
   2. Cash outlays associated with the project's termination
   3. Recapture of nonexpense outlays that occurred at the project's initiation (for example, working capital investments)

---

present-value table, ignoring disposal values on old equipment or future disposal values on new equipment, and incorrectly analyzing investments in working capital (e.g., inventories).

Risk is present in almost all capital investments. Sensitivity analysis helps to assess the riskiness of a project.

The payback model is a popular approach to capital-spending decisions. It is simple and easily understood, but it neglects profitability.

The accounting rate-of-return model is also widely used in capital budgeting, although it is conceptually inferior to DCF models. It fails to recognize explicitly the time value of money. Instead, the accounting model depends on averaging techniques that may yield inaccurate answers, particularly when cash flows are not uniform through the life of a project.

Performance evaluation using accounting income can conflict with the DCF analyses used for decisions. Frequently, the optimal decisions under discounted cash flow will not produce good accounting income in the early years. For example, heavy depreciation charges and the expensing rather than capitalizing of initial development costs will hurt reported income for the first year. Postaudits help to limit the effect of this conflict.

SELF-CORRECTION PROBLEM

1. Review the problem and solution shown in Figure 20-11. Conduct a sensitivity analysis as indicated below. Consider each requirement as independent of other requirements.

   a. Compute the NPV if the minimum desired rate of return were 20%.

   b. Compute the NPV if predicted cash-operating costs were $35,000 instead of $30,000, using the 14% discount rate.

c. By how much may the cash operating savings fall short of the $30,000 predicted before reaching the point of indifference, the point where the NPV of the project is zero, using the original discount rate of 14%?

SOLUTION TO SELF-CORRECTION PROBLEM

1. a. Either the total project approach or the differential approach could be used. The differential approach would show:

	Total Present Value
Recurring cash operating savings, using an annuity table (Appendix E):	
2.9906 × $10,000 =	$29,906
Overhaul avoided: .6944 × $10,000=	6,944
Difference in disposal values:	
.4019 × $5,000 =	(2,010)
Incremental initial investment	(31,000)
NPV of replacement	$ 3,840
b. NPV value in Figure 20-11	$ 8,429
Present value of additional $5,000 annual operating costs	
3.4331 × $5,000	(17,166)
New NPV	$ (8,737)

c. Let X = annual cash operating savings and find the value of X such that NPV = 0. Then

$$0 = 3.4331(X) + \$7,695 - \$2,597 - \$31,000$$
$$3.4331X = \$25,902$$
$$X = \$7,545$$

(Note that the $7,695, $2,597, and $31,000 are at the bottom of Figure 20-11.)

If the annual savings fall from $10,000 to $7,545, a decrease of $2,455 or almost 25%, the point of indifference will be reached.

An alternative way to obtain the same answer would be to divide the NPV of $8,429 (see bottom of Figure 20-11) by 3.4331, obtaining $2,455, the amount of the annual difference in savings that will eliminate the $8,429 of NPV.

QUESTIONS

1. Capital budgeting has three phases: (1) identification of potential investments, (2) selection of investments, and (3) postaudit of investments. What is the accountant's role in each phase?
2. Why is discounted cash flow a superior method for capital budgeting?

3. Distinguish between simple interest and compound interest.
4. Can NPV ever be negative? Why?
5. Distinguish among the models DCF, NPV, and IRR.
6. "The higher the minimum desired rate of return, the higher the price that a company will be willing to pay for cost-saving equipment." Do you agree? Explain.
7. "The DCF model assumes certainty and perfect capital markets. Thus it is impractical to use it in most real-world situations." Do you agree? Explain.
8. "Double-counting of costs occurs if depreciation is separately considered in DCF analysis." Do you agree? Explain.
9. "Nonprofit organizations do not use DCF because their cost of capital is zero." Do you agree? Explain.
10. "We can't use sensitivity analysis because our cash-flow predictions are too inaccurate." Comment.
11. Name three common ways to recognize risk in capital budgeting.
12. Why should the differential approach to alternatives always lead to the same decision as the total project approach?
13. "The higher the interest rate, the less I worry about errors in predicting terminal values." Do you agree? Explain.
14. "The NPV model should not be used for investment decisions about advanced technology such as computer-integrated manufacturing systems." Do you agree? Explain.
15. "DCF approaches will not work if the competing projects have unequal lives." Do you agree? Explain.
16. "It is important that a firm use one and only one capital-budgeting model. Using multiple models may cause confusion." Do you agree? Explain.
17. "If DCF approaches are superior to the payback and the accounting rate-of-return methods, why should we bother to learn the others? All it does is confuse things." Answer this contention.
18. What is the basic flaw in the payback model?
19. Compare the accounting rate-of-return approach and the DCF approach with reference to the time value of money.
20. Explain how a conflict can arise between capital-budgeting decision models and performance evaluation methods.

PROBLEMS

1. **Comparison of capital-budgeting techniques.**   St. Luke's Hospital is considering the purchase of a new exercise machine at a cost of $20,000. It should save $4,000 in cash operating costs per year. Its estimated useful life is 8 years, and it will have zero disposal value.

   a. What is the payback time?
   b. Compute the net present value if the minimum rate of return desired is 10%. Should the company buy? Why?
   c. Compute the internal rate of return.
   d. Using the accounting rate-of-return model, compute the rate of return on the initial investment.

2. **Sensitivity analysis.** Hewitt Dental Group is considering the replacement of an old billing system with new software that should save $5,000 per year in net cash operating costs. The old system has zero disposal value, but it could be used for the next 12 years. The estimated useful life of the new software is 12 years and it will cost $25,000.

   a. What is the payback period?
   b. Compute the internal rate of return.
   c. Management is unsure about the useful life. What would be the internal rate of return if the useful life were (1) 6 years instead of 12 or (2) 20 years instead of 12?
   d. Suppose the life will be 12 years, but the savings will be $3,000 per year instead of $5,000. What would be the internal rate of return?
   e. Suppose the annual savings will be $4,000 for 8 years. What would be the internal rate of return?

3. **Exercises in compound interest.** Use the appropriate table to compute the following:

   a. You have always dreamed of taking an African safari. What lump sum do you have to invest today to have the $12,000 needed for the safari in 3 years? Assume that you can invest the money at

      (1) 5%, compounded annually
      (2) 10%, compounded annually
      (3) 16%, compounded annually

   b. You are considering partial retirement. To do so you need to use part of your savings to supplement your income for the next 5 years. Suppose you need an extra $15,000 per year. What lump sum do you have to invest now to supplement your income for 5 years? Assume that your minimum desired rate of return is

      (1) 5%, compounded annually
      (2) 10%, compounded annually
      (3) 16%, compounded annually

   c. You just won a lump sum of $400,000 in a local lottery. You have decided to invest the winnings and withdraw an equal amount each year for 10 years. How much can you withdraw each year and have a zero balance left at the end of 10 years if you invest at

      (1) 6%, compounded annually
      (2) 12%, compounded annually

   d. A professional athlete is offered the choice of two 4-year salary contracts, contract A for $1.4 million and contract B for $1.3 million:

	Contract A	Contract B
End of year 1	$ 200,000	$ 450,000
End of year 2	300,000	350,000
End of year 3	400,000	300,000
End of year 4	500,000	200,000
Total	$1,400,000	$1,300,000

Which contract has the higher present value at 14% compounded annually? Show computations to support your answer.

4. **NPV, IRR, ARR, and payback.**   Sally's Subs is considering a proposal to invest in a speaker system that would allow its employees to service drive-through customers. The cost of the system (including installation of special windows and driveway modifications) is $60,000. Sally Holding, manager of Sally's Subs, expects the drive-through operations to increase annual sales by $50,000, with a 40% contribution margin ratio. Assume that the system has an economic life of 6 years, at which time it will have no disposal value. The required rate of return is 14%.

   a. Compute the payback period. Is this a good measure of profitability?
   b. Compute the NPV. Should Holding accept the proposal? Why or why not?
   c. Compute the IRR. How should the IRR be used to decide whether to accept or reject the proposal?
   d. Using the accounting rate of return model, compute the rate of return on the initial investment.

5. **NPV and sensitivity analysis.**   Kittitas County Jail currently has its laundry done by a local cleaners at an annual cost of $36,000. It is considering a purchase of washers, dryers, and presses at a total installed cost of $50,000 so that inmates can do the laundry. The county expects savings of $15,000 per year, and the machines are expected to last 5 years. The desired rate of return is 10%.

   Answer each part separately.

   a. Compute the NPV of the investment in laundry facilities.

   b. (1) Suppose the machines last only 4 years. Compute the NPV.
      (2) Suppose the machines last 7 years. Compute the NPV.

   c. (1) Suppose the annual savings are only $12,000. Compute the NPV.
      (2) Suppose the annual savings are $18,000. Compute the NPV.

   d. (1) Compute the most optimistic estimate of NPV, combining the best out comes in parts b and c.
      (2) Compute the most pessimistic estimate of NPV, combining the worst outcomes in parts b and c.

   e. Accept the expected life estimate of 5 years. What is the minimum annual savings that would justify the investment in the laundry facilities?

ADDENDUM 20: CALCULATIONS OF INTERNAL RATES OF RETURN

This addendum shows how to compute internal rates of return. It uses data from Figure 20-12.

Expansion of Existing Gasoline Station

The IRR formula can be used in evaluating the expansion of the existing gas station:

$90,000 = present value of annuity of $40,000 at X percent for 3 years, or what factor F in the table of the present values of an annuity will satisfy the following equation

$90,000 = $40,000 × F

  F = $90,000 ÷ $40,000 = 2.2500

Now, on the year 3 line of Appendix E find the column that is closest to 2.2500. You will find that 2.2500 is extremely close to a rate of return of 16%—so close that interpolation between 14% and 16% is unnecessary. Therefore the internal rate of return is approximately 16%.

Investment in an Oil Well

Trial-and-error methods must be used to calculate the rate of return that will equate the future cash flows with the $90,000 initial investment for the investment in an oil well. Why? Because cash inflows vary from year to year. As a start, note that the 16% rate was applicable to a uniform annual cash inflow. But now use Appendix C and try a higher rate, 22%, because you know that the cash inflows are coming in more quickly than under the uniform inflow:

		Trial at 22%		Trial at 24%	
Year	Cash Inflows	Present-Value Factor	Total Present Value	Present-Value Factor	Total Present Value
1	$80,000	.8197	$65,576	.8065	$64,520
2	30,000	.6719	20,157	.6504	19,512
3	10,000	.5507	5,507	.5245	5,245
			$91,240		**$89,277**

Because $91,240 is greater than $90,000, the true rate must be greater than 22%. Try 24%. Now $89,277 is less than $90,000 so the true rate lies somewhere between 22% and 24%. It can be approximated by interpolation:

Interpolation		Total Present Values
at 22%	$91,240	$91,240
at True rate		90,000
at 24%	89 277	
Difference	$ 1,963	$ 1,240

$$\text{approximate rate} = 22\% + \left(\frac{1,240}{1,963} \times 2\%\right)$$

$$= 22\% + 1.3\% = 23.3\%$$

Purchase of a New Gasoline Station

In contrast to the oil-well project, a new gasoline station will have slowly increasing cash inflows. Thus the trial rate should be *lower* than the 16% rate applicable to the expansion project. Let us try 12%:

Year	Cash Inflows	Trial at 12% Present-Value Factor	Trial at 12% Total Present Value	Trial at 14% Present-Value Factor	Trial at 14% Total Present Value
1	$20,000	.8929	$17,858	.8772	$17,544
2	40,000	.7972	31,888	.7695	30,780
3	60,000	.7118	42,708	.6750	40,500
			$92,454		$88,824

Because $92,454 is greater than $90,000, try 14%. Then interpolate a rate between 12% and 14%:

Interpolation		Total Present Values
at 12%	$92,454	$92,454
at True rate		$90,000
at 14%	88,824	
Difference	$ 3,630	$ 2,454

$$\text{approximate rate} = 12\% + \left(\frac{2,454}{3,630} \times 2\%\right)$$

$$= 12\% + 1.4\% = 13.4\%$$

CHAPTER 21

Capital Budgeting Decisions and Depreciation

Capital budgeting, as we learned in Chapter 20, requires making decisions that will have significant financial impacts beyond the current year. This chapter examines how two major factors, taxes and inflation, affect capital budgeting decisions.

Nearly all economic decisions affect taxes. Companies certainly recognize this truth as they write large tax checks to the government. Annual tax bills for some major U.S. corporations exceed $1 billion. To avoid paying more taxes than are required, companies need to consider the tax effects when making capital-budgeting decisions. This chapter introduces tax considerations. However, the tax law is exceedingly complex, so qualified counsel should be sought when the slightest doubt exists.

Inflation is nearly as pervasive as taxes. **Inflation** is the decline in the general purchasing power of the monetary unit. For example, a dollar today will buy only half as much as it did in the late 1970s. Although inflation in the U.S. is well below the double-digit level of a decade or so ago, it still persists. Even a 5% annual rate results in a rise of more than 60% in average prices over 10 years. In countries such as Brazil and Argentina, triple-digit annual inflation rates (i.e., average prices more than doubling each year) are common-place. Therefore, inflation can greatly influence the cash flow predictions used in capital-budgeting decisions.

INCOME TAXES AND CAPITAL BUDGETING

Income taxes are cash disbursements. Income taxes can influence the *amount* and the *timing* of cash flows. Their basic role in capital budgeting is no different from that of any other cash disbursement. However, taxes tend to narrow the cash differences between projects. Cash savings in operations will cause an increase in taxable income and thus a partially offsetting increase in tax outlays. For example, a 40% income tax rate would reduce the net attractiveness of $1 million in cash operating savings to $600,000, because $400,000 of the $1 million would be paid in taxes.

The U.S. federal government and most states raise money through corporate income taxes. State income tax rates differ considerably from state to state. Therefore, overall corporate income tax rates can vary widely.

U.S. federal income tax rates also depend on the amount of pretax income. Larger income is taxed at higher rates. In capital budgeting, the relevant rate is the **marginal income tax rate,** that is, the tax rate paid on additional amounts of pretax income. Suppose corporations pay income taxes of 15% on the first $50,000 of pretax income and 30% on pretax income over $50,000. What is the *marginal income tax rate* of a company with $75,000 of pretax income? It is 30%, because 30% of any *additional* income will be paid in taxes. In contrast, the company's *average income tax rate* is only 20% (i.e., 15% × $50,000 + 30% × $25,000 = $15,000 of taxes on $75,000 of pretax income). When we assess tax effects of capital-budgeting decisions, we will always use the *marginal* tax rate because that is the rate applied to the additional cash flows generated by a proposed project.

Effects of Depreciation Deductions

Organizations that pay income taxes generally keep two sets of books—one for reporting to the public and one for reporting to the tax authorities. In the United States this practice is not illegal or immoral—in fact, it is necessary. Tax reporting must follow detailed rules designed to achieve certain social goals. These rules do not lead to financial statements that best measure an organization's financial results and position, so it is more informative to financial statement users if a separate set of rules is used for financial reporting. In this chapter we are concerned with measuring cash payments for taxes. Therefore we focus on the *tax reporting* rules, not those for public financial reporting.

One item that often differs between tax reporting and public reporting is depreciation. Recall that depreciation spreads the cost of an asset over its useful life. Income tax laws and regulations have increasingly permitted the cost to be spread over *depreciable lives* that are shorter than the assets' useful lives. In addition, for tax purposes, *accelerated depreciation* is often allowed, which charges a larger proportion of an asset's cost to the earlier years and less to later years. In contrast, an asset's depreciation for public reporting purposes is usually the same each year, called straight-line depreciation. For example, a $10,000 asset depreciated over a 5-year useful life would result in straight-line depreciation of $10,000 ÷ 5 = $2,000 each year and accelerated depreciation of more than $2,000 per year in the early years and less than $2,000 in the later years.

Figure 21-1 shows the interrelationship of income before taxes, income taxes, and depreciation for Martin's Printing. Please examine this key exhibit carefully before reading on. Assume that the company has a single fixed asset, a printing press, which was purchased for $125,000 cash. The number of years over which an asset is depreciated for tax purposes is called the **recovery period.** The press has a 5-year recovery period for tax purposes. It is used to produce annual sales revenue of $130,000 and expenses (excluding depreciation) of $70,000. The purchase cost of the press is tax deductible in the form of yearly depreciation. Depreciation deductions (and similar

---

FIGURE 21-1   Martin's Printing
Basic Analysis of Income Statement, Income Taxes, and Cash Flows

---

Traditional Annual Income Statement

(S)	Sales	$130,000
(E)	Less: Expenses, excluding depreciation	$ 70,000
(D)	Depreciation (straight-line)	25,000
	Total expenses	$ 95,000
	Income before taxes	$ 35,000
(T)	Income taxes @ 40%	14,000
(I)	Net income	**$ 21,000**

Total after-tax effect on cash is
    either S − E − T = $130,000 − $70,000 − $14,000 = $46,000
    or I + D = $21,000 + $25,000 = $46,000

Analysis of the Same Facts for Capital Budgeting

	Cash effects of operations:	
(S–E)	Cash inflow from operations: $130,000 − $70,000	$ 60,000
	Income tax outflow @ 40%	24,000
	After-tax inflow from operations	
	(excluding depreciation)	$ 36,000
	Cash effects of depreciation:	
(D)	Straight-line depreciation:	
	$125,000 ÷ 5 = $25,000	
	Income tax savings @ 40%	10,000
	Total after-tax effect on cash	**$ 46,000**

---

deductions that are noncash expenses when deducted) have been called **tax shields** because they protect that amount of income from taxation. However, all allowable expenses, both cash and noncash items, could be called tax shields because they reduce taxable income and thereby reduce income taxes.

Depreciating a fixed asset such as the press creates future tax deductions. In this case, these deductions will total $125,000. The present value of this deduction depends directly on its specific yearly effects on future income tax payments. Therefore the present value is influenced by the recovery period, the depreciation method selected, the tax rates, and the discount rate.

Figure 21-2 shows two methods for analyzing the data for capital budgeting, assuming straight-line depreciation. Both lead to the same final answer, a net present value of $40,821 for the investment in this asset. The choice of analytical method is a matter of personal preference. However, we will use method 2 in this chapter because it highlights the impact of the alternative depreciation methods on present values.

The $125,000 investment really buys two streams of cash: (1) net inflows from operations plus (2) savings of income tax outflows (which have the same effect in capital budgeting as additions to cash inflows) because the depreciation is deductible in computing taxable income. The choice of depreciation method will not affect the cash inflows from operations. But different depreciation methods will affect the cash outflows for income taxes. That is, a straight-line method will produce one present

FIGURE 21-2 Impact of Income Taxes on Capital-Budgeting Analysis

Assume: original cost of equipment, $125,000; 5-year life; zero terminal disposal value; pretax annual cash inflow from operations, $60,000; income tax rate, 40%; required after-tax rate of return, 12%. All items are in dollars except discount factors. The after-tax cash flows are from Figure 21-1.

	12% Discount Factor, from Appropriate Tables	Total Present Value at 12%	Sketch of After-Tax Cash Flows at End of Year					
			0	1	2	3	4	5
Method 1 (Discount the total annual effects together)								
Total after-tax effect on cash (see Figure 21-1)	3.6048	$165,821		46,000	46,000	46,000	46,000	46,000
Investment	1.0000	(125,000)	(125,000)					
Net present value of the investment		$ 40,821						
Method 2 (Discount two annual effects separately)								
Cash effects of operations excluding depreciation	3.6048	$129,773		36,000	36,000	36,000	36,000	36,000
Cash effects of straight-line depreciation: savings of income taxes	3.6048	36,048		10,000	10,000	10,000	10,000	10,000
Total after-tax effect on cash		165,821						
Investment	1.0000	(125,000)	(125,000)					
Net present value of the investment		$ 40,821						

value of tax savings, and an accelerated method will produce a different present value. It is easier to pinpoint such differences by using method 2.

Tax Deductions, Cash Effects, and Timing

Before proceeding, review the basic relationships just portrayed:

Line	(A) Items Used in Computing Taxable Income	(B) Current Pretax Cash Effect	(C) Effect on Income Tax Cash Outflows at 40%	(B) – (C) Net After-Tax Cash Effect
1. Sales	$130,000	$130,000	$52,000	$78,000
2. Expenses, excluding depreciation	70,000	70,000	28,000	42,000
3. Cash effect of operations	$ 60,000	$ 60,000	$24,000	$36,000
4. Depreciation	25,000	0	(10,000)	10,000
5. Net cash effects	_____	$ 60,000	$14,000	$46,000
6. Income before income taxes	$ 35,000			
7. Income taxes	14,000			
8. Net income	$ 21,000			

This tabulation highlights why the net cash effects of operations (the items on lines 1 to 3) are computed by multiplying the pretax amounts by 1 – the tax rate, or 1 – .40 = .60. The total effect is the cash flow itself less the tax effect. Each additional $1 of sales also adds $.40 of taxes, leaving a net cash inflow of $.60. Therefore, the after-tax cash inflow from sales is $130,000 × .6 = $78,000. Each additional $1 of cash expense reduces taxes by $.40, leaving a net cash outflow of $.60. Thus the after-tax effect of the $70,000 of *cash* expenses (line 2) is a cash outflow of $70,000 × .60 = $42,000. The net effect is a cash inflow of $78,000 – $42,000 = $36,000, or $60,000 × .6 = $36,000.

In contrast, the after-tax effects of the *noncash* expenses (depreciation on line 4) are computed by multiplying the tax deduction of $25,000 by the tax rate itself, or $25,000 × .40 = $10,000. Note that this is a cash *inflow* because it is a decrease in the tax payment. The total cash effect of a noncash expense is *only* the tax-savings effect.

Throughout the illustrations in this chapter, we assume that all income tax flows occur simultaneously with the related pretax cash flows. For example, we assume that both the net $60,000 pretax cash inflow and the related $24,000 tax payment occurred in year 1 and that no part of the tax payment was delayed until year 2.

This assumption of no lags in income tax effects is also largely in accordance with the facts in the real world. Why? Because both individual and corporate taxpayers generally "pay-as-you-go." That is, estimated tax payments are made in installments at least quarterly, not in one lump sum in the subsequent year.

Another assumption throughout this chapter is that the companies in question are profitable. That is, the companies will have enough taxable income from all sources to use all income tax benefits in the situations described.

Accelerated Depreciation

Governments have frequently enacted income tax laws that permit accelerated depreciation instead of straight-line depreciation. **Accelerated depreciation** is any pattern of depreciation that writes off depreciable assets more quickly than does ordinary straight-line depreciation. These laws are aimed at encouraging investments in long-lived assets.

An extreme example clearly demonstrates why accelerated depreciation is attractive to investors. Reconsider the facts in Figure 21-2. Suppose, as is the case in some countries, that the entire initial investment can be written off immediately for income tax reporting. Using method 2 we see that net present value will rise from $40,821 to 54,773:

	Present Values	
	As in Figure 21-2	Complete Write-Off Immediately
Cash effects of operations	$129,773	$129,773
Cash effects of depreciation	36,048	50,000*
Total after-tax effect on cash	165,821	179,773
Investment	(125,000)	(125,000)
Net present value	$ 40,821	$ 54,773

*Assumes that the tax effect occurs simultaneously with the investment at time zero: $125,000 × .40 = $50,000.

In summary, the earlier you can take the depreciation, the greater the *present value* of the income tax savings. The *total* tax savings will be the same regardless of the depreciation method. In the example, the tax savings from the depreciation deduction is either .40 × $125,000 = $50,000 immediately or .40 × $25,000 = $10,000 per year for 5 years, a total of $50,000. However, the time value of money makes the immediate savings worth more than future savings. The mottoes in income tax planning are: "When there is a legal choice, take the *deduction sooner* rather than later," and "Recognize *taxable income later* rather than sooner."

Managers have an obligation to stockholders to minimize and delay taxes to the extent permitted by law. This is called tax avoidance. Astute tax planning can have large financial payoffs. In contrast, tax evasion, which is *illegally* reducing taxes by recording fictitious deductions or failing to recognize income, is not to be condoned.

Double-Declining-Balance Depreciation

A popular accelerated depreciation schedule uses the *double-declining-balance* (DDB) method. This method is the basis for most depreciation or cost recovery schedules in U.S. tax law. See Addendum 21A for details.

The DDB method divides 100% by the number of years over which an asset is to be depreciated, then doubles the resulting rate. For example, the DDB rate for 5-year assets is (100% ÷ 5) × 2 = 40%. This percentage is applied to the *undepreciated amount* each year to compute the annual depreciation. A 5-year DDB schedule has depreciation of 40% × 100% = 40% of the original investment in the first year, 40% × (100% −

40%) = 24% of the original investment in the second, 40% × (100% − 40% − 24%) = 14.4% of the original investment in the third, and so on.

A DDB schedule includes a switch to straight-line depreciation for the remaining undepreciated amount at the time when straight-line depreciation over the remaining recovery period provides more depreciation for the next year than would continuation of DDB. For a 5-year asset the switch comes in the fourth year, as the following DDB schedule for a $1,000 asset shows:

Year	Beginning Undepreciated Amount (1)	DDB Rate (2)	Depreciation (3) = (1) × (2)	Ending Undepreciated Amount (4) = (1) − (3)	Depreciation as a Percentage of Initial Investment (5) = (3) ÷ $1,000
1	$1,000	.40	$400	$600	40.0%
2	600	.40	240	360	24.0%
3	360	.40	144	216	14.4%
4	216	*	108	108	10.8%
5	108	*	108	0	10.8%

*Switch to straight line with 2 years remaining. Depreciation for years 4 and 5 is $216 ÷ 2 = $108. Continuation of DDB would have provided fourth-year depreciation of .40 × $216 = $86.40, which is less than the $108 straight-line amount.

Figure 21-3 presents DDB depreciation schedules for recovery periods of 3 through 10 years. DDB depreciation can be applied to the example in Figure 21-2 as follows:

Year	Tax Rate (1)	PV Factor @ 12% (2)	Depreciation (3)	Present Value of Tax Savings (1) × (2) × (3)
1	.40	.8929	$125,000 × .400 = $50,000	$17,858
2	.40	.7972	125,000 × .240 = 30,000	9,566
3	.40	.7118	125,000 × .144 = 18,000	5,125
4	.40	.6355	125,000 × .108 = 13,500	3,432
5	.40	.5674	125,000 × .108 = 13,500	3,064
				$39,045

How much was gained by using DDB instead of straight-line depreciation? The $39,045 present value of tax savings is $2,997 higher with DDB than the $36,048 achieved with straight-line depreciation (see Figure 21-2, Method 2).

Present Value of DDB Depreciation

In capital-budgeting decisions managers often want to know the present value of the tax savings from depreciation tax shields. Figure 21-8 in Addendum 21B provides present values for $1 to be depreciated over double-declining-balance schedules for 3-, 5-, 7-, and 10-year recovery periods. You can find the present value of tax savings in three steps:

1. Find the factor from Figure 21-8 for the appropriate recovery period and required rate of return.

FIGURE 21-3   Selected Double-Declining-Balance Depreciation Schedules

Depreciation in Year	Recovery Period							
	3 Years	4 Years	5 Years	6 Years	7 Years	8 Years	9 Years	10 Years
1	66.7%	50.0%	40.0%	33.3%	28.6%	25.0%	22.2%	20.0%
2	22.2%	25.0%	24.0%	22.2%	20.4%	18.8%	17.3%	16.0%
3	11.1%	12.5%	14.4%	14.8%	14.6%	14.1%	13.4%	12.8%
4		12.5%	10.8%	9.9%	10.4%	10.5%	10.5%	10.2%
5			10.8%	9.9%	8.7%	7.9%	8.1%	8.2%
6				9.9%	8.7%	7.9%	7.1%	6.6%
7					8.6%*	7.9%	7.1%	6.6%
8						7.9%	7.1%	6.6%
9							7.2%*	6.5%*
10								6.5%*

*Rounded to make the total 100%.

2. Multiply the factor by the tax rate to find the tax savings per dollar of investment.
3. Multiply the result by the amount of the investment to find the total tax savings.

For example, consider our investment of $125,000 in equipment with a 5-year DDB depreciation schedule. A 12% after-tax required rate of return and a 40% tax rate produce a tax savings with a present value of .7809 × .40 × $125,000 = $39,045.

Gains or Losses on Disposal

The disposal of equipment for cash can also affect income taxes. Suppose the press purchased for $125,000 is sold. Consider three different assumptions about cash proceeds and when the sale occurs. For simplicity, straight-line depreciation is assumed:

	Press Sold at End of Year		
	5	3	3
(a) Cash proceeds of sale	$10,000	$70,000	$ 20,000
Book value: zero and [$125,000 − 3 ($25,000)]	0	50,000	50,000
Gain (loss)	$10,000	$20,000	$(30,000)
Effect on income taxes at 40%:			
(b) Tax saving, an inflow effect: .40 × loss			$ 12,000
(c) Tax paid, an outflow: .40 × gain	$ (4,000)	$ (8,000)	
Net cash inflow from sale:			
(a) plus (b)			$ 32,000
(a) minus (c)	$ 6,000	$62,000	

Ponder these calculations. Note especially the third column, which shows that the total cash inflow effect of a disposal at a loss is the cash proceeds *plus* the income tax savings ($20,000 + $12,000 = $32,000).

The often-heard expression "What the heck, it's deductible" sometimes warps perspective. Even though losses bring income tax savings and gains bring additional income taxes, gains are still more desirable than losses. In the foregoing tabulation, the $30,000 loss in the last column produces income tax savings of $12,000.[1] Each $1,000 of additional proceeds would reduce the tax savings by $400, but it would still result in $600 more cash. Suppose proceeds equal to book value ($50,000) were received. The total cash inflow would be $50,000 instead of $32,000; no tax effect would occur.

Income Tax Complications

It may come as a shock, but in the foregoing illustrations we deliberately avoided many possible income tax complications. Income taxes are affected by many intricacies including progressive tax rates, loss carrybacks and carryforwards, state income taxes, short- and long-term gains, distinctions between capital assets and other assets, offsets of losses against related gains, exchanges of property of like kind, exempt income, and so forth.[2]

Now keep in mind that miscellaneous changes in the tax law occur each year. An example is the *investment tax credit*, which provided lump-sum tax reductions to companies making qualified investments. The credit was equal to a specified percentage of the investment. It was first available in the United States in 1962, and since then it has been suspended and reinstated, and the allowable percentage has been changed several times. Most recently it was again suspended. Always check the current tax law before calculating the tax consequences of a decision.

CONFUSION ABOUT DEPRECIATION

The meanings of *depreciation* and *book value* are widely misunderstood. Pause and consider their role in decisions. Suppose a bank is considering the replacement of some old copying equipment with a book value of $30,000, an expected terminal disposal value of zero, a current disposal value of $12,000, and a remaining useful life of three years. For simplicity, assume that the bank will take straight-line depreciation of $10,000 yearly. The tax rate is 40%.

These data should be examined in perspective, as Figure 21-4 indicates. In particular, note that the inputs to the decision model are the predicted income tax effects on cash. Book values and depreciation may be necessary for making *predictions*. By themselves, however, they are not inputs to DCF decision models.

---

[1]In this case, the old equipment was sold outright. Where there is a trade-in of old equipment for new equipment of like kind, special income tax rules result in the gain or loss being added to, or deducted from, the capitalized value of the new equipment. The gain or loss is not recognized in the year of disposal; instead, it is spread over the life of the new asset as an adjustment of the new depreciation charges.

[2]For book-length coverage of these and other complications, see *Federal Tax Course* (Upper Saddle River, NJ: Prentice Hall), published annually.

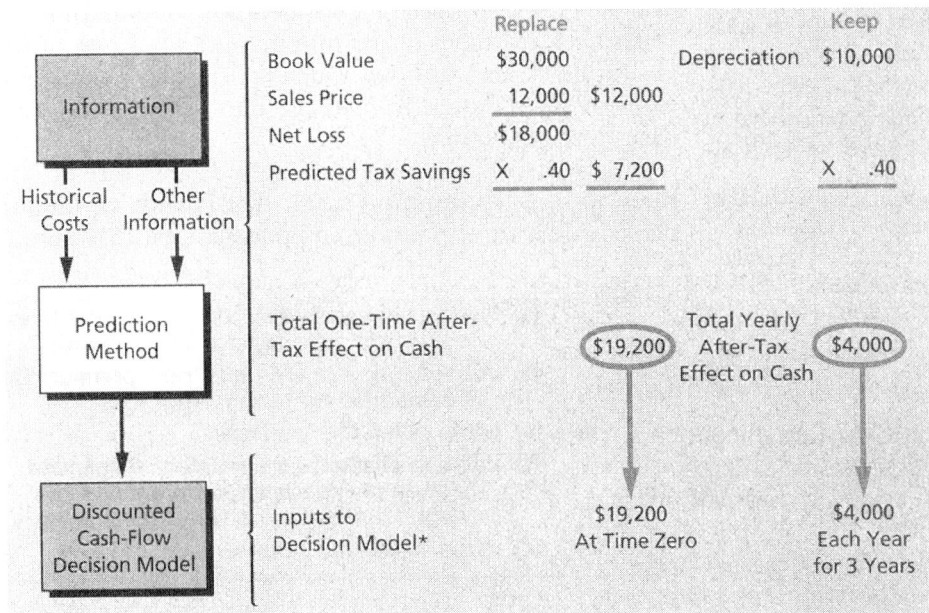

	Replace			Keep	
Book Value	$30,000		Depreciation	$10,000	
Sales Price	12,000	$12,000			
Net Loss	$18,000				
Predicted Tax Savings	X .40	$ 7,200		X .40	

Information

Historical Costs   Other Information

Prediction Method

Total One-Time After-Tax Effect on Cash $19,200

Total Yearly After-Tax Effect on Cash $4,000

Discounted Cash-Flow Decision Model

Inputs to Decision Model*

$19,200 At Time Zero

$4,000 Each Year for 3 Years

*There can, of course, be other related inputs to this decision model, for example, future annual cash flows from operations.

FIGURE 21-4
Perspective on Book Value and Depreciation

The following points summarize the role of depreciation regarding the replacement of equipment:

1. *Initial investment.* The amount paid for (and hence depreciation on) old equipment is irrelevant except for its effect on tax cash flows. In contrast, the amount paid for new equipment is relevant because it is an expected future cost that will not be incurred if replacement is rejected.
2. *Do not double-count.* The investment in equipment is a one-time outlay at time zero, so it should not be double-counted as an outlay in the form of depreciation. Depreciation by itself is irrelevant; it is not a cash outlay. However, depreciation must be considered when *predicting income tax cash outflows.*
3. *Relation to income tax cash flows.* Relevant quantities are expected future data that will differ among alternatives. Thus book values and past depreciation are irrelevant in all capital-budgeting decision models. The relevant item is the *income tax cash effect,* not the book value or the depreciation. Using the approach in Figure 21-4, the book value and depreciation are essential data for the *prediction method,* but the expected future income tax cash disbursements are the relevant data for the DCF decision model.

Role of Depreciation

Critics of income tax laws emphasize that capital investment is discouraged by not allowing the adjusting of depreciation deductions for inflationary effects. For instance, the net present value would be larger if depreciation were not confined to the $40,000 amount per year. The latter generates a $16,000 saving in 19X1 dollars, then $16,000 in 19X2 dollars, and so forth. Defenders of existing U.S. tax laws assert that capital investment is encouraged in many other ways. The most prominent example is provision for accelerated depreciation over lives that are much shorter than the economic lives of the assets.

Improvement of Predictions with Feedback

The ability to forecast and cope with changing prices is a valuable management skill, especially when inflation is significant. Auditing and feedback should help evaluate management's predictive skills.

The adjustment of the operating cash flows uses a *general-price-level* rate of 10%. However, where feasible managers should use *specific* rates or tailor-made predictions for price changes in materials, labor, and other items. These predictions may have different percentage changes from year to year.

SUMMARY

Income taxes can have a significant effect on the desirability of an investment. An outlay for a depreciable asset results in two streams of cash: (1) inflows from operations plus (2) savings in income tax outflows that may be analyzed as additions to cash inflows. The after-tax impact of operating cash inflows is obtained by multiplying the inflows by 1 minus the tax rate. In contrast, the impact of depreciation on cash flows is obtained by multiplying the depreciation by the tax rate itself.

Accelerated depreciation and short recovery periods increase net present values of depreciation tax shields. They have been heavily used by the U.S. government to encourage investments. When income tax rates and required rates of return are high, the attractiveness of immediate deductions heightens. Generally, depreciation deductions should be taken as early as legally possible. Managers have an obligation to minimize and delay income tax payments to the extent allowed by law. This is called tax avoidance. Tax evasion, the use of illegal means, is not to be condoned.

SELF-CORRECTION PROBLEMS

1. Consider the investment opportunity presented in Figure 21-2: original cost of equipment, $125,000; 5-year economic life; zero terminal salvage value; pretax annual cash inflow from operations, $60,000; income tax rate, 40%; required after-tax rate of return, 12%. Assume that the equipment is depreciated on a 5-year DDB schedule for tax purposes. The net present value (NPV) is:

Present Values (PV)	
Cash effects of operations,*	
$60,000 × (1 −.40) × 3.6048	$129,773
Cash effects of depreciation on income	
tax savings using DDB	
$125,000 × .40 × 7809†	39,045
Total after-tax effect on cash	$168,818
Investment	125,000
Net present value	$ 43,818

*See Figure 21-2 for details.
†Factor .7809 is from Figure 21-8.

Consider each question independently.

a. Suppose the equipment was expected to be sold for $20,000 cash immediately after the end of year 5. Compute the net present value of the investment.

b. Ignore the assumption in part a. Return to the original data. Suppose the economic life of the equipment was 8 years rather than 5 years. However, DDB depreciation over 5 years is still allowed for tax purposes. Compute the net present value of the investment.

2. Examine the DDB depreciation schedule above. Assume an anticipated inflation rate of 12%. How would you change the present values of depreciation to accommodate the inflation rate?

SOLUTIONS TO SELF-CORRECTION PROBLEMS

1. a. Net present value as given $43,818
   Cash proceeds of sale — $ 20,000
   Book value — 0
   Gain — $ 20,000
   Income taxes at 40% — 8,000
   Total after-tax effect on cash — $ 12,000
   PV of $12,000 to be received in
   5 years at 12%, $12,000 × .5674 — 6,809
   NPV of investment — $50,627

   b. Net present value as given $43,818
   Add the present value of $36,000 per year
   for 8 years
   Discount factor of 4.9676 × $36,000 = $178,834
   Deduct the present value of $36,000 per year
   for 5 years 129,773
   Increase in present value 49,061
   Net present value $92,879

The investment would be very attractive. Note especially that the depreciation period for tax purposes and the economic useful life of the asset need not be equal. The tax law specifies lives (or recovery periods) for various types of depreciable assets. The tax life is unaffected by the economic useful lives of the assets. Thus a longer useful life for an asset increases operating cash flows without decreasing the present value of the tax savings.

2. The computations would not be changed. The tax effects of depreciation are unaffected by inflation. U.S. income tax laws permit a deduction based on the original dollars invested, nothing more.

QUESTIONS

1. Distinguish between average and marginal tax rates.
2. "Congress should pass a law forbidding corporations to keep two sets of books." Do you agree? Explain.
3. Tax laws generally provide two types of acceleration of depreciation. Identify them.
4. "An investment in equipment really buys two streams of cash." Do you agree? Explain.
5. Why should tax deductions be taken sooner rather than later?
6. What are the major influences on the present value of a tax deduction?
7. "If income tax rates do not change through the years, my total tax payments will be the same under every depreciation method. Therefore I really do not care what depreciation schedule is permitted." Do you agree? Explain.
8. Distinguish between tax avoidance and tax evasion.
9. "Tax planning is unimportant because the total income tax bill will be the same in the long run, regardless of short-run maneuvering." Do you agree? Explain.
10. Explain why accelerated depreciation methods are superior to straight-line methods for income tax purposes.
11. How much depreciation is taken in the first year if a $10,000 asset is depreciated on a double-declining-balance schedule with a 4-year recovery period? How much in the second year?
12. "Immediate disposal of equipment, rather than its continued use, results in a full tax deduction of the undepreciated cost now—rather than having such a deduction spread over future years in the form of annual depreciation." Do you agree? Explain, using the $30,000 book value of old equipment in Figure 21-4, as a basis for your discussion.
13. "When there are income taxes, depreciation is a cash outlay." Do you agree? Explain.
14. What are the three components of market (nominal) interest rates?
15. Describe how internal consistency is achieved when considering inflation in a capital-budgeting model.
16. "Capital investments are always more profitable in inflationary times because the cash inflows from operations generally increase with inflation." Comment on this statement.

17. Explain how U.S. tax laws fail to adjust for inflation.
18. "The MACRS half-year convention causes assets to be depreciated beyond the lives specified in the MACRS recovery schedules." Do you agree? Explain.
19. Give the MACRS class for each of the following assets: automobiles, office furniture, farm buildings, and residential rental property.

PROBLEMS

Special note: Throughout this assignment material, *unless directed otherwise,* assume that (1) all income tax cash flows occur simultaneously with the pretax cash flows, and (2) the companies in question will have enough taxable income from other sources to use all income tax benefits from the situations described.

1. **Straight-line depreciation and present values.**   A manager of Lotus is contemplating acquiring 60 computers used for designing software. The computers will cost $300,000 cash and will have zero terminal salvage value. The recovery period and useful life are both 3 years. Annual pretax cash savings from operations will be $150,000. The income tax rate is 40%, and the required after-tax rate of return is 16%.

   a. Compute the net present value, assuming straight-line depreciation of $100,000 yearly for tax purposes. Should Lotus acquire the computers? Explain.
   b. Suppose the computers will be fully depreciated at the end of year 3 but can be sold for $40,000 cash. Compute the net present value. Should Lotus acquire the computers? Explain.
   c. Ignore part b. Suppose the required after-tax rate of return is 12% instead of 16%. Should the computers be acquired? Show computations.

2. **DDB and present values.**   The president of Southern States Power Company is considering whether to buy some equipment for its White River plant. The equipment will cost $1.5 million cash and will have a 10-year useful life and zero terminal salvage value. Annual pretax cash savings from operations will be $360,000. The income tax rate is 40%, and the required after-tax rate of return is 16%.

   a. Compute the net present value, using a 7-year recovery period and DDB depreciation for tax purposes. Should the equipment be acquired?
   b. Suppose the economic life of the equipment is 15 years, which means that there will be $360,000 additional annual cash savings from operations in years 11 to 15. Assume that a 7-year recovery period is used. Should the equipment be acquired? Show computations.

3. **Gains or losses on disposal.**   An asset with a book value of $50,000 was sold for cash on January 1, 19X6.
   Assume two selling prices: $65,000 and $30,000. For each selling price, prepare a tabulation of the gain or loss, the effect on income taxes, and the total after-tax effect on cash. The applicable income tax rate is 40%.

4. **Straight-line depreciation and present values.**   The president of a company specializing in the production of peripheral equipment for personal computers

is considering the purchase of some equipment used for research and development. The cost is $400,000, the recovery period is 5 years, and there is no terminal disposal value. Annual pretax cash inflows from operations would increase by $140,000, the income tax rate is 40%, and the required after-tax rate of return is 14%.

    a. Compute the net present value, assuming straight-line depreciation of $80,000 yearly for tax purposes. Should the equipment be acquired?

    b. Suppose the asset will be fully depreciated at the end of year 5 but is sold for $20,000 cash. Should the equipment be acquired? Show computations.

    c. Ignore question b. Suppose the required after-tax rate of return is 10% instead of 14%. Should the equipment be acquired? Show computations.

5. **DDB and present values.**   The general manager of a cruise ship company has a chance to purchase a new navigation device for all its vessels at a total cost of $250,000. The recovery period is 5 years. Additional annual pretax cash inflow from operations is $84,000, the economic life of the equipment is 5 years, there is no salvage value, the income tax rate is 35%, and the after-tax required rate of return is 16%.

    a. Compute the net present value, assuming double-declining-balance depreciation for tax purposes. Should the equipment be acquired?

    b. Suppose the economic life of the equipment is 6 years, which means that there will be an $84,000 cash inflow from operations in the sixth year. The recovery period is still 5 years. Should the equipment be acquired? Show computations.

6. **Income taxes and disposal of assets.**   Assume that income tax rates are 30%.

    a. The book value of an old machine is $20,000. It is to be sold for $8,000 cash. What is the effect of this decision on cash flows, after taxes?

    b. The book value of an old machine is $20,000. It is to be sold for $30,000 cash. What is the effect on cash flows, after taxes, of this decision?

ADDENDUM 21A: MODIFIED ACCELERATED COST RECOVERY SYSTEM (MACRS)

Under U.S. income tax laws, most assets purchased since 1987 are depreciated using the Modified Accelerated Cost Recovery System (MACRS). Under MACRS, each asset is placed in one of the eight classes shown in Figure 21-5.

MACRS Schedules

MACRS depreciation schedules for 3-, 5-, 7-, and 10-year assets are based on the double-declining-balance (DDB) method described in the body of the chapter.[3] How-

[3]MACRS schedules for 15- and 20-year assets are based on the 150% declining-balance method, and schedules for 27.5- and 31.5-year assets are based on straight-line depreciation. Details about these schedules are beyond the scope of this text.

FIGURE 21-5   Examples of Assets in Modified Accelerated Cost Recovery System (MACRS) Classes

3-year	Special tools for several specific industries; tractor units for over-the-road.
5-year	Automobiles; trucks; research equipment; computers; machinery and equipment in selected industries.
7-year	Office furniture; railroad tracks; machinery and equipment in a majority of industries.
10-year	Water transportation equipment; machinery and equipment in selected industries.
15-year	Most land improvements; machinery and equipment in selected industries.
20-year	Farm buildings; electricity generation and distribution equipment.
27.5-year	Residential rental property.
31.5-year	Nonresidential real property.

ever, MACRS requires application of the **half-year convention,** which treats all assets as if they had been placed in service at the midpoint of the tax year. One-half year of depreciation is taken for tax purposes in the year an asset is acquired, regardless of whether it is purchased in January, July, or December. The DDB rate is then applied to the remaining undepreciated amount each year, until a switch to straight line is advantageous. The tax depreciation schedule for a 5-year asset is shown in Part A of Figure 21-6. Note that a half-year's depreciation is carried over to the sixth year. Schedules for 3-, 5-, 7-, and 10-year assets are shown in Figure 21-7.

To compute the tax depreciation that applies to each year of an asset's life, you must recognize that each year of an asset's life does not match perfectly with a tax year. For example, suppose a 5-year asset is purchased on July 1, 19X0. The first year of the asset's life overlaps two tax years, 19X0 and 19X1, as shown below:

Part B of Figure 21-6 shows how to use the 5-year MACRS schedule to determine the tax depreciation for each of the 5 years of the asset's life.

Suppose a manufacturing company purchased a $125,000 machine on July 1, 19X0, and expected it to provide pretax cash inflows from operations of $60,000 annually for 10 years. Despite the 10-year *useful* life of the machine, it qualifies as a 5-year property for MACRS purposes. The tax rate is 40%, and the required after-tax rate of return is 12%.

The annual after-tax cash inflows from operations, excluding the tax effects of depreciation, are $60,000 × .60 = $36,000. Their present value is 5.6502 × $36,000 = $203,407. (The 5.6502 factor comes from the 12% column and 10-year row, Appendix E.)

The present value of the tax savings from depreciation depends on the method of depreciation and the recovery period used. The tax savings can be computed independently of the cash effects of operations.

Suppose for a moment that the company used straight-line depreciation over the useful life of 10 years to compute tax depreciation. Annual tax savings would be ($125,000 ÷ 10) × .40 = $5,000. Using the 12% column and 10-year row of Appendix E, we find the present value of the tax savings to be 5.6502 × $5,000 = $28,251.

But suppose the company's management, following the motto "Take the deduction sooner rather than later," decides to depreciate the machine over 5 years (as allowed by MACRS), rather than 10 years. If the company would continue to use straight-line depreciation, the annual tax savings would be ($125,000 ÷ 5) × .40 = $10,000. The present value is 3.6048 × $10,000 = $36,048. The company would gain $36,048 − $28,251 = $7,797 in present value by taking the same total $125,000 depreciation over 5 rather than 10 years, using the straight-line method.

Finally, suppose management also realizes that accelerated depreciation is better than straight line for tax purposes. Therefore they decide to use the MACRS tax depreciation rates shown in the last column of Part B of Figure 21-6:

FIGURE 21-6   Five-Year MACRS Schedule for $10,000 Asset Purchased at Midpoint of Tax Year

Part A: Computation of Depreciation on Tax Statements				Part B: Computation of Depreciation for Each Year of an Asset's Life		
Tax Year	DDB Rate	Undepreciated Amount	Depreciation	Asset Year*	Depreciation Amount	Depreciation Rate
1	.40 ÷ 2 = .20†	$10,000	$2,000			
				1	2,000 + [(1/2) × 3,200] = $3,600	36.00%
2	.40	8,000	3,200			
				2	[(1/2) × 3,200] + [(1/2) × 1,920] = 2,560	25.60%
3	.40	4,800	1,920			
				3	[(1/2) × 1,920] + [(1/2) × 1,152] = 1,536	15.36%
4	.40	2,880	1,152			
				4	[(1/2) × 1,152] + [(1/2) × 1,152] = 1,152	11.52%
5	‡	1,728	1,152			
				5	[(1/2) × 1,152] + 576 = 1,152	11.52%
6	‡	576	576			

*Assumes the asset is acquired at the midpoint of the year. Therefore the first tax year plus half of the second tax year comprise the first year of the asset's life, and so on.
†Half-year convention applied.
‡Switch to straight-line with 1 1/2 years remaining. Fifth-year depreciation is (2/3) × $1,728 = $1,152; sixth-year depreciation is (1/3) × $1,728 = $576.

Asset Year	Tax Rate (1)	PV Factor @ 12% (2)	Depreciation (3)	Present Value of Tax Savings (4) = (1) × (2) × (3)
1	.40	.8929	$125,000 × .3600 = $45,000	$16,072
2	.40	.7972	125,000 × .2560 = 32,000	10,204
3	.40	.7118	125,000 × .1536 = 19,200	5,467
4	.40	.6355	125,000 × .1152 = 14,400	3,660
5	.40	.5674	125,000 × .1152 = 14,400	3,268
		Total present value of tax savings		$38,671

Accelerated depreciation adds $38,671 − $36,048 = $2,623 to the present value of the tax savings. By using the MACRS 5-year recovery period instead of 10 years and accelerated (DDB) depreciation rather than straight line, the company gained $7,797 + $2,623 = $10,420 in present value. That is, the present value of the MACRS tax savings (which uses DDB depreciation over 5 years) exceeds the present value of the tax savings from straight-line depreciation for 10 years by $38,671 − $28,251 = $10,420.

Income Tax Rates

The U.S. federal government and most states levy corporate income taxes. The current federal tax rate on ordinary corporate taxable income below $50,000 is 15%. Rates then increase until companies with taxable income over $335,000 pay between 34% and 38% on additional income. These rates are sometimes subject to additional surcharges that may vary from year to year. Congress also makes frequent changes in the rates. Therefore, it is important to consult the most current schedules when analyzing tax effects.

State income tax rates vary considerably. Consequently, different companies may have widely different total income tax rates, depending on the states in which they operate as well as their overall level of taxable income.

FIGURE 21-7   Selected MACRS Depreciation Schedules

Tax Year	3-Year Property	5-Year Property	7-Year Property	10-Year Property
1	33.33%	20.00%	14.29%	10.00%
2	44.45	32.00	24.49	18.00
3	14.81	19.20	17.49	14.40
4	7.41	11.52	12.49	11.52
5		11.52	8.93	9.22
6		5.76	8.92	7.37
7			8.93	6.55
8			4.46	6.55
9				6.56
10				6.55
11				3.28

ADDENDUM 21B: PRESENT VALUE OF DOUBLE-DECLINING-BALANCE DEPRECIATION

Investment in a depreciable asset results in a tax savings because each dollar of depreciation is deductible in computing income taxes. Most investments are depreciated by accelerated methods for tax purposes. Figure 21-8 provides the present value of double-declining-balance depreciation on a $1.00 investment over 3-, 5-, 7-, and 10-year recovery periods for several different interest rates. For instance, for a 5-year asset and a 10% desired rate of return, the present value is (assuming depreciation is at the end of each year[4]) as follows:

Year	(1) Depreciation	(2) PV Factor @ 10%	(1) × (2) Present Value of Depreciation
1	$0.40	0.9091	$0.3636
2	0.24	0.8264	0.1983
3	0.144	0.7513	0.1082
4	0.108	0.6830	0.0738
5	0.108	0.6209	0.0671
Total depreciation	**$1.000**		
Present value of $1 of depreciation, shown in Figure 21-8			**$0.8110**

FIGURE 21-8 Present Value of $1 of Double-Declining-Balance Depreciation

Discount Rate	3-Year	5-Year	7-Year	10-Year
3%	.9584	.9355	.9138	.8827
4%	.9453	.9156	.8879	.8487
5%	.9325	.8965	.8633	.8170
6%	.9200	.8781	.8399	.7872
7%	.9079	.8604	.8175	.7593
8%	.8960	.8433	.7963	.7331
9%	.8845	.8269	.7760	.7085
10%	.8732	.8110	.7566	.6853
12%	.8515	.7809	.7203	.6429
14%	.8308	.7528	.6872	.6050
15%	.8208	.7394	.6716	.5876
16%	.8111	.7265	.6567	.5711
18%	.7922	.7019	.6286	.5406
20%	.7742	.6788	.6027	.5130
22%	.7570	.6571	.5788	.4879
24%	.7405	.6367	.5566	.4651
25%	.7325	.6270	.5461	.4545
26%	.7247	.6175	.5359	.4443
28%	.7095	.5993	.5167	.4252
30%	.6950	.5821	.4987	.4077
40%	.6301	.5088	.4245	.3378

[4]The year refers to a year of the asset's life. This may not correspond to a calendar (or tax) year. See Figure 21-6.

To find the present value of the *tax savings* from $1.00 of investment, multiply the present value of $1 of depreciation (from Figure 21-8) by the income tax rate. If the tax rate is 40%, the present value of the tax savings for the example is $0.40 \times \$0.8110 = \$0.3244$, or 32.44% of the acquisition cost of the asset.

Capital Structure, Leasing, and Debt Financing

CHAPTER 22

Introduction to Cost of Capital

A firm's cost of capital is simply a weighted average of the rates of return required by investors in the firm's securities. Thus, the cost of capital serves as the linkage between a firm's investment and financing decisions. In this chapter we take an in-depth look at the cost of capital or hurdle rate for new investments. Specifically, we will discuss the following topics:

1. The cost-of-capital concept
2. The factors that determine investor-required rates of return
3. The assumptions underlying the measurement of a firm's cost of capital
4. The calculation of the weighted average cost of capital
5. An empirical study of large firms' estimates of their cost of capital

THE COST-OF-CAPITAL CONCEPT

The cost of capital is the opportunity cost of using funds to invest in new projects. This is appropriate because the cost of capital is that rate of return on the firm's total investment which earns the required rates of return of all the sources of financing. Furthermore, if the firm earns the required rates of return on all its sources of financing, including that of the common shareholders, then the value of its common stock will not be changed by the investment. By the same reasoning, if the firm earns a rate of return higher than the cost of capital, then the excess return will lead to an increase in the value of the firm's common stock and, consequently, an increase in shareholder wealth. Thus, the logic of using the cost of capital as the hurdle rate for new capital investment can be summarized as follows:

INVESTMENT RATE OF RETURN	SHAREHOLDER WEALTH
Internal Rate of Return < Cost of Capital	Decrease
Internal Rate of Return = Cost of Capital	No Change
Internal Rate of Return > Cost of Capital	Increase

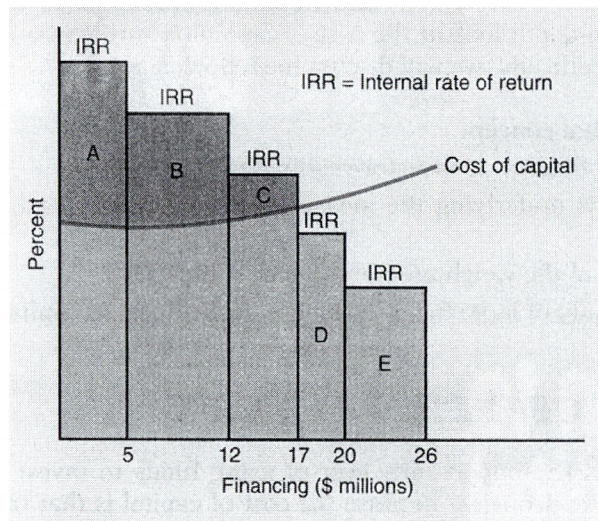

FIGURE 22-1
Investment and Financing Schedules

Figure 22-1 provides an illustration of the use of the cost of capital to determine a firm's capital budget. The internal rates of return on projects A, B, and C exceed the firm's cost of capital and should be accepted, whereas projects D and E should be rejected. The result is a capital budget equal to $17 million.

We have made two important assumptions in our analysis thus far, and these should be stated explicitly:

1. We have assumed that all five of the projects in Figure 22-1 are of equivalent risk. That is, the opportunity cost of capital is the same for all five investments. Obviously, we would not have the same opportunity cost of capital for an investment in short-term Treasury bills and for an investment involving drilling for oil in a politically unstable part of the world.
2. We have assumed that the mix of financing sources remains constant for all investments. The reason for this assumption will become clear when we discuss the calculation of the cost of capital.

To illustrate the calculation of the cost of capital, consider the capital structure of the Salinas Corporation found in Figure 22-2. The company has three sources of capital: debt, preferred stock, and common stock. Management is considering a $200,000 investment opportunity with an expected internal rate of return of 14%. The current cost of the firm's capital (i.e., its required rates of return) for each source of financing is as follows:

Cost of debt capital	10%
Cost of preferred stock	12
Cost of common stock	16

FIGURE 22-2 Salinas Corporation Capital Structure

	Amount	Percentage of Capital Structure
Bonds	$ 600,000	30%
Preferred stock	200,000	10
Common stock	1,200,000	60
Total liabilities and equity	$2,000,000	100%

Given this information, should the firm make the investment? The creditors and preferred stockholders would probably encourage us to undertake the project. However, because the 14% internal rate of return on the investment is less than the common stockholders' required rate of return, shareholders might argue that the investment should be forgone. What is the right choice?

To answer this question, we must first determine what percentage of the $200,000 is to be provided by each type of investor. If we intend to maintain the same capital structure mix as reflected in Figure 22-2 (30% debt, 10% preferred stock, and 60% common stock), we could compute a **weighted cost of capital,** where the weights equal the percentage of capital to be financed by each source. For our example, the weighted cost of the individual sources of capital as computed in Figure 22-3 is 13.8%. From this calculation we would conclude that an investment offering at least a 13.8% return would be acceptable to the company's investors. The investment should be undertaken, because the 14% rate of return more than satisfies all investors, as indicated by a 13.8% weighted cost of capital. Again, the **weighted cost of capital** is equal to the cost of each source of financing (debt, preferred stock, and common stock) multiplied by the percentage of the financing provided by that source.

In summary, two basic elements are necessary to calculate the cost of capital:

1. Estimates of the required rates of return for each of the firm's sources of capital
2. The proportions of each source of capital used by the firm

In this chapter we will concern ourselves with the determination of the first of these elements and take the second as given.

FIGURE 22-3 Salinas Corporation Weighted Cost of Capital

	Weights (Percentage of Financing)	Cost of Individual Sources	Weighted Cost
Debt	30%	10%	3.0%
Preferred stock	10	12	1.2
Common stock	60	16	9.6
	100%	Weighted cost of capital:	13.8%

But What If?

The weighted cost of capital may be fine in theory, but what if a company could borrow the entire amount needed for an investment in a new product line? Is it really necessary to use the weighted cost of capital, or would it be all right to make the decision based simply on the cost of the debt which is providing the funding?

Consider the Poling Corporation. Management believes it could earn 14% from purchasing $500,000 in new equipment, which would allow it to expand the business. Although the firm works to maintain a capital structure with equal amounts of debt and equity, the bank is willing to loan the firm the entire $500,000 at an interest rate of 12%. Without our even having to compute it, we know the firm's earnings per share would increase if the firm earned a rate exceeding the cost of the financing, in this case 12%.

Poling's financial officer has also estimated the firm's cost of equity (common stock) at 18%. Because the firm can finance the purchase fully by debt, however, management has decided to make the investment and finance it by borrowing the money from the bank at 12%. The investment is made, and all seems well.

The following year, management finds another investment opportunity costing $500,000 but with an expected internal rate of return this time of 17%—better than the previous year's 14%. But when management approaches the bankers for financing, they find them unwilling to lend any more money to Poling. In the words of one banker, "Poling has used up all of its debt capacity." The firm must now issue new common stock before the bank will be agreeable to fund any more loans. However, because the investment does not earn the cost of equity of 18%, management sees no option other than to reject the investment.

What is the moral of this story? Intuitively, we can see that Poling's management has made a mistake. Making the investment in the first year has denied the firm the opportunity to make a better decision in the second year.

As a more general statement, we can conclude that a firm should never use a single cost of financing as the hurdle rate (discount rate) for making capital-budgeting decisions. Particularly when we use debt, we have implicitly used up some of our *debt capacity* for future investments, and not until we complement the use of debt with equity will we be able to continue to use more debt in the future. Thus, we ought always to use the weighted cost of capital, and not an individual cost of funds, as our discount rate for investment decisions. So, let's look more carefully at the weighted cost of capital.

FACTORS DETERMINING THE COSTS-OF-CAPITAL SOURCES

What are the elements in the business environment that cause a company's weighted cost of capital to be high or low? Figure 22-4 identifies four primary factors: general economic conditions, the marketability of the firm's securities (market conditions), operating and financing conditions within the company, and the amount of financing needed for new investments.

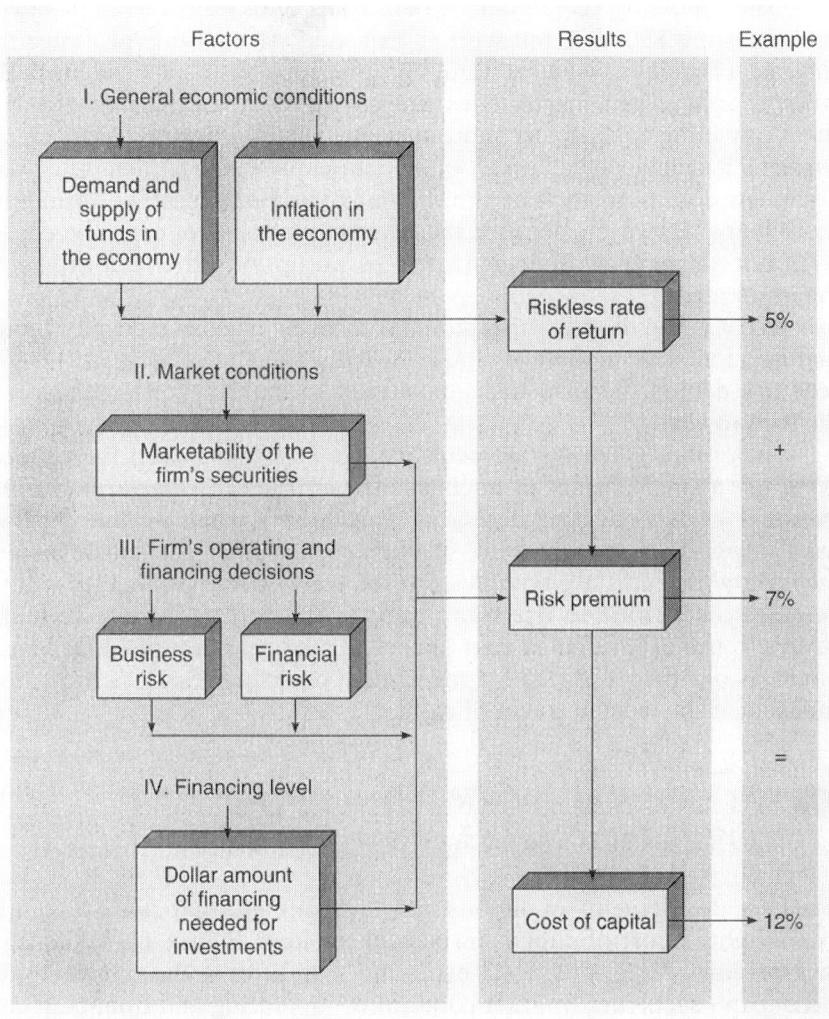

FIGURE 22-4
Primary Factors Influencing the Cost of Particular Sources of Capital

Factor 1: General Economic Conditions

General economic conditions determine the demand for and supply of capital within the economy, as well as the level of expected inflation. This economic variable is reflected in the riskless rate of return. This rate represents the rate of return on risk-free investments, such as the interest rate on short-term U.S. government securities. In principle, as the demand for money in the economy changes relative to the supply, investors alter their required rate of return. For example, if the demand for money increases without an equivalent increase in the supply, lenders will raise their required interest rate. At the same time, if inflation is expected to deteriorate the purchasing power of the dollar, investors require a higher rate of return to compensate for this anticipated loss.[1]

Factor 2: Market Conditions

When an investor purchases a security with a significant investment risk, an opportunity for additional returns is necessary to make the investment attractive. Essentially, as risk increases, the investor requires a higher rate of return. This increase is called a **risk premium.** When investors increase their required rate of return, the cost of capital rises simultaneously. Remember we have defined risk as the potential variability of returns. If the security is not readily marketable when the investor wants to sell, or even if a continuous demand for the security exists but the price varies significantly, an investor will require a relatively high rate of return. Conversely, if a security is readily marketable and its price is reasonably stable, the investor will require a lower rate of return and the company's cost of capital will be lower.

Factor 3: Operating and Financing Decisions

Risk, or the variability of returns, also results from decisions made within the company. Risk resulting from these decisions is generally divided into two types: business risk and financial risk. **Business risk** is the variability in returns on assets and is affected by the company's investment decisions. **Financial risk** is the increased variability in returns to common stockholders as a result of financing with debt or preferred stock. As business risk and financial risk increase or decrease, the investor's required rate of return (and the cost of capital) will move in the same direction.

Factor 4: Amount of Financing

The last factor determining the corporation's cost of funds is the level of financing that the firm requires. As the financing requirements of the firm become larger, the weighted cost of capital increases for several reasons. For instance, as more securities are issued, additional **flotation costs,** or the cost incurred by the firm from issuing securities, will affect the percentage cost of the funds to the firm. Also, as management approaches the market for large amounts of capital relative to the firm's size, the investors' required rate of return may rise. Suppliers of capital become hesitant to grant relatively large sums without evidence of management's capability to absorb this capital into the business. This is typically "too much too soon." Also, as the size of the issue increases, there is greater difficulty in placing it in the market without reducing the price of the security, which also increases the firm's cost of capital.

---

[1]This relationship is frequently referred to as the Fisher Effect.

A Summary Illustration

To summarize, the important variables influencing a corporation's cost of capital include the following:

1. **General economic conditions.** This factor determines the risk-free rate or riskless rate of return.
2. **Marketability of a company's securities.** As the marketability of a security increases, investors' required rates of return decrease, lowering the corporation's cost of capital.
3. **Operating and financial decisions made by management.** If management accepts investments with high levels of risk or if it uses debt or preferred stock extensively, the firm's risk increases. Investors then require a higher rate of return, which causes a higher cost of capital to the company.
4. **Amount of financing needed.** Requests for larger amounts of capital increase the firm's cost of capital.

The right-hand margin of Figure 22-4 presents an illustration of the cost of capital for a particular source. The risk-free rate, determined by the general economic conditions, is 5%. However, owing to the additional risks associated with the security, the firm has to earn an additional 7% to satisfy the investors' required rate of return of 12%.

ASSUMPTIONS OF THE WEIGHTED COST-OF-CAPITAL MODEL

In a complex business world, difficulties quickly arise in computing a corporation's cost of capital. For this reason, we make several simplifying assumptions.

Constant Business Risk

Business risk is defined as the potential variability of returns on an investment, and the level of business risk within a firm is determined by management's investment policies. An investor's required rate of return for a company's securities—and therefore the firm's cost of capital—is a function of the firm's current business risk. If this risk level is altered, the corporation's investors will naturally change their required rates of return, which in turn will modify the cost of capital. However, the amount of change in the cost of capital resulting from a given increase or decrease in business risk is difficult to assess. For this reason, the cost of capital calculation assumes that any investment under consideration will not significantly change the firm's business risk. In other words, *the corporation's cost of capital is an appropriate investment criterion only for an investment having a business risk level similar to that of existing assets.*

Constant Financial Risk

Financial risk has been defined as the increased variability in returns on common stock resulting from the increased use of debt and preferred stock financing. Also, financial risk relates to the threat of bankruptcy. As the percentage of debt in the capital structure increases, the possibility that the firm will be unable to pay interest and the principal balance is also increased. As a result, the level of financial risk in a company has an impact on the investors' required rate of return. As the amount of debt rises, the common stockholders will increase their required rate of return. *In other words, the costs of individual sources of capital are a function of the current financial structure.* For this reason, the data used in computing the cost of capital are appropriate only if management continues to use the same financial mix. If the present capital structure consists of 40% debt, 10% preferred stock, and 50% common stock, this capital structure is assumed to be maintained in the financing of future investments.

Constant Dividend Policy

A third assumption required in estimating the cost of capital relates to the corporation's dividend policy. For ease of computation, we generally assume that a firm's dividends are increasing at a constant annual growth rate. Also, we assume this growth to be a function of the firm's earning capabilities and not merely the result of paying out a larger percentage of the company's earnings. Thus, it is implicitly assumed that the dividend payout ratio (dividends/net income) is constant.

The aforementioned assumptions of the weighted cost of capital model are quite restrictive. In a practical investment analysis, the financial executive may need a range of possible cost of capital values rather than a single-point estimate. For example, it may be more appropriate to talk in terms of a 10% to 12% range as an estimate of the firm's cost of capital, rather than assuming that a precise number can be determined. In this chapter, however, our principal concern will be with calculating a single cost of capital figure.

COMPUTING THE WEIGHTED COST OF CAPITAL

A firm's weighted cost of capital is a composite of the individual costs of financing, weighted by the percentage of financing provided by each source. Therefore, a firm's weighted cost of capital is a function of (1) the individual costs of capital and (2) the makeup of the capital structure—the percentage of funds provided by debt, preferred stock, and common stock. Also, as we noted earlier, the amount of funds needed affects the cost of capital. We will discuss this last consideration, the level of financing, later.

As we explain the procedures for computing a company's cost of capital, it is helpful to remember three basic steps outlined in Figure 22-5.

The computations are not difficult if we understand our purpose: We want to calculate the firm's weighted cost of capital. For a simple exercise, calculate the average age of students in a course where 40% are 19 years old, 50% are 20 years old, and 10% are 21 years old. We can easily find the average age to be 19.7 years by weighting each age by the percentage in each age category [(40%) (19) + (50%) (20) + (10%) (21)]. In a similar way, the weighted cost of capital is estimated by weighting the cost of each individual source by the percentage of financing it provides. If we finance an investment by 40% debt at a 10% cost and 60% common equity at a cost of 18%, the weighted cost of capital is 14.8% (.40 × 10% + .60 × 18% = 14.8%).

FIGURE 22-5   Computing the Weighted Cost of Capital: Basic Steps

---

Remember: To compute a firm's weighted cost of capital requires us to do three things:

1. Compute the cost of capital for each and every source of financing (i.e., each source of debt, preferred stock, and common stock).
2. Determine the percentage of debt, preferred stock, and common stock to be used in the financing of future investments.
3. Calculate the firm's weighted average cost of capital using the percentage of financing as the weights.

Thus, although the details become somewhat involved, the basic approach, which is summarized in Figure 22-5, is relatively simple.

Determining Individual Costs of Capital

Companies attempting to attract new investors have created a large variety of financing instruments. However, we will examine only three basic types of securities: debt, preferred stock, and common stock. In calculating their respective costs, the objective is to determine *the rate of return* the company must earn on its investments to satisfy investors' required rates of return after allowing *for any flotation costs incurred in raising new funds*. Also, because the cash flows used in capital-budgeting analysis (net present value, profitability index, and internal rate of return) are on an after-tax basis, the required rates of return should also be expressed on an after-tax basis.

Cost of Debt

The cost of debt may be defined as the rate that must be received from an investment *to achieve the required rate of return for the creditors*. The required rate of return for debt capital may be found by a trial-and-error process or with the use of a financial calculator, where we solve for R_d in the following equation:

$$P_0 = \sum_{t=1}^{n} \frac{\$I_t}{(1 + \text{bondholder's required rate of return})^t} + \frac{\$M}{(1 + \text{bondholder's required rate of return})^n} \tag{1}$$

where

P_0 = the market price of the debt
$\$I_t$ = the annual dollar interest paid to the investor
$\$M$ = the maturity value of the debt
n = the number of years to maturity

If we use the interest factors in the present value tables, the equation would be restated as follows:

$$P_0 = \$I_t (PVIFA_{\text{required return, } n}) + \$M (PVIF_{\text{required return, } n})$$

Assume that an investor is willing to pay $908.32 for a bond. The security has a $1,000 par value, pays 8% in annual interest, and matures in 20 years. Using either a calculator or table values, the investor's required rate of return is found to be 9%, which is the rate that sets the present value of the future interest payments and the maturity value equal to the price of the bond, or

$$\$908.32 = \sum_{t=1}^{20} \frac{\$80}{(1+.09)^t} + \frac{\$1,000}{(1+.09)^{20}}$$

$$\$908.32 = \$908.32$$

However, if brokerage commissions and legal and accounting fees are incurred in issuing the security, the company will not receive the full $908.32 market price. As a result, the effective cost of these funds to the firm is larger than the investor's 9% required rate of return. To adjust for this difference, we would simply use the *net price* after flotation costs in place of the market price in equation (1). Thus, the equation becomes

$$NP_0 = \sum_{t=1}^{n} \frac{\$I_t}{(1+k_d)^t} + \frac{\$M}{(1+k_d)^n} \qquad (2)$$

where NP_0 represents the net amount received by the company from issuing the debt, k_d equals the *before-tax* cost of debt, and the remaining variables retain their meaning from equation (1). If in the present example the company nets $850 after issuance costs, the equation should read

$$\$850 = \sum_{t=1}^{20} \frac{\$80}{(1+k_d)^t} + \frac{\$1,000}{(1+k_d)^{20}}$$

$$= \$80\left(PVIFA_{k_d, 20}\right) + \left(PVIF_{k_d, 20}\right)$$

Solving for k_d in equation (2) may be achieved by trial and error using the present value tables. We know that the rate is above 9% because a 9% rate had already given us a $908.32 value. We need the discount rate that gives us an $850 value. If *10%* is selected as a trial discount rate, a present value of $830.12 results. With this information, we may conclude that the before-tax cost of the debt capital is between 9% and 10%; therefore, we may approximate it by interpolating between these two rates. The computation is shown as follows:

Rate	Value	Differences in Values	
9%	$908.32		
k_d	850.00 net proceeds	58.32	$78.20
10%	830.12		

Solving for k_d by interpolation,

$$k_d = .09 + \left(\frac{\$58.32}{\$78.20}\right)(.10-.09) = .0975 = 9.75\%$$

The same answer may be found by using a financial calculator. Thus, the company's cost of debt, before recognizing the tax deductibility of interest expense, is 9.75%.[2]

We want to know the *after-tax* cost of the debt, however, not the before-tax cost. Because interest is a tax-deductible expense, for every $1 we pay in interest, we lower the firm's tax liability by $1 times the tax rate. If our company has an effective tax rate, including all federal and state taxes, of 40%, then a dollar in interest means that we save $.40 in taxes. That is, the after-tax cost is only $.60, or $1(1 − .40 tax rate). Applying the same logic to our cost of debt, we may correctly conclude that the after-tax cost of debt is found by multiplying the before tax interest rate by (1 − tax rate). If t is the company's marginal tax rate and k_d is the before-tax cost of debt, the after-tax cost of new debt financing is found as follows:

$$\text{after-tax cost of debt} = k_d(1 - t) \tag{3}$$

If in the present example the corporation's tax rate is 40%, then the after-tax cost of debt is 5.84%:

$$9.75\% \, (1 - .40) = 5.84\%$$

In summary, the firm must earn 5.84% on its borrowed capital *after the payment of taxes.* In doing so, the investors will earn a 9% rate of return (their required rate) on their $908.32 investment (market price of the bond), and the firm will earn a 9.75% before-tax return on the $850 bond proceeds.

Cost of Preferred Stock

Determining the cost of preferred stock follows the same logic as the cost of debt computations. *The objective is to find the rate of return that must be earned on money raised through the sale of preferred stock to satisfy their required rate of return.*

The value of a preferred stock, P_0, that is nonmaturing and promised a constant dividend per year was defined as follows:

$$P_0 = \frac{\text{dividend}}{\text{required rate of return for a preferred stockholder}} \tag{4}$$

From this equation, the required rate of return, R_p, is defined as

$$\text{required rate of return} = \frac{\text{dividend}}{\text{market price} \, (P_0)} \tag{5}$$

If, for example, a preferred stock pays $1.50 in annual dividends and sells for $15, the investors' required rate of return is 10%:

$$\text{required rate of return} = \frac{\$1.50}{\$15.00} = 10\%$$

---

[2]For simplicity, we have ignored the fact that flotation costs may be amortized as a tax deductible expense over the life of the bond. The difference in the answer is relatively small.

Yet even if these preferred stockholders have a 10% required rate of return, the effective cost of this capital will be greater owing to the flotation costs incurred in issuing the security. If a firm were to net $13.50 per share after issuance costs, rather than the full $15 market price, the cost of preferred stock, k_p, should be calculated using the net price received by the company. Therefore

$$k_p = \frac{\text{dividend}}{\text{net price}} = \frac{D}{NP_0} \tag{6}$$

For the preceding example, the cost would be

$$k_p = \frac{\$1.50}{\$13.50} = .1111 \text{ or } 11.11\%$$

No adjustment for taxes is required, since preferred stock dividends are not tax deductible. Thus, the firm must earn the cost of preferred capital after taxes have been paid, which for the preceding example was 11.11%.

Cost of Common Stock

Although debt and preferred stock must be issued to receive any new money from these sources, common stockholders can provide additional capital in one of two ways. First, new common stock may be issued. Second, the earnings available to common stockholders can be retained, in whole or in part, within the company and used to finance future investments. Retained earnings represent the largest source of capital for most U.S. corporations. On average, as much as 70% of a company's financing in any year comes from the profits retained within the business. To distinguish between these two sources, we will use the term **internal common equity** to designate the profits retained within the business for investment purposes, and **external common equity** to represent a new issue of common stock.

Cost of internal common equity.   When managers are considering the retention of earnings as a means for financing an investment, they are serving in a *fiduciary* capacity. That is, the stockholders have entrusted the company assets to management. If the company's objective is to maximize the wealth of its common stockholders, management should retain the profits *only if* the company's investments within the firm are at least as attractive as the stockholders' next best investment opportunity.[3] Otherwise the profits should be paid out in dividends, permitting the investor to invest more profitably elsewhere.

How can management know the stockholders' alternative investment opportunities? Certainly identifying those specific investments is not feasible. However, the investors' required rate of return should be a function of competing investment opportunities. If the only other investment alternative of similar risk has a 12% return, one would expect a rational investor to set a minimum acceptable return on investment at 12%. In other words, *the investors' required rate of return should be equal to the*

[3]Other factors may justify management's not adhering completely to this principle.

expected rate of the best competing investment available. Thus, if the common stockholders' required rate of return is used as a minimum return for investments financed by common stock investors, management may be assured that its investment policies are acceptable to the common stockholder.

To measure the common stockholders' required rate of return, we will suggest three alternative approaches: (1) the dividend-growth model, (2) the capital asset pricing model, and (3) the risk-premium approach.

Dividend-growth model.   The value of a common stock was defined as equal to the present value of the expected future dividends, discounted at the common stockholders' *required rate of return.* Because the stock has no maturity date, these dividends extend to infinity. Thus, the value of a common stock, P_0, promising dividends of D_t in year t would be

$$P_0 = \frac{\text{Dividend}_1}{\left(1 + \text{required return}\right)^1}$$

(7)

$$+ \frac{\text{Dividend}_2}{\left(1 + \text{required return}\right)^1} + \ldots + \frac{\text{Dividend}_\infty}{\left(1 + \text{required return}\right)^\infty}$$

Because the market price of the security, P_0, is known, the required rate of return of an investor purchasing the security at this price can be determined by estimating future dividends, D_t, and solving for it using equation (7). Furthermore, if the dividends are increasing at a constant annual rate of growth (g), that is, less than the investor's required rate of return, then the required rate of return can be measured as follows:

$$\begin{array}{c}\text{investors} \\ \text{required rate} \\ \text{of return}\end{array} = \left(\frac{\text{dividend in 1 year}}{\text{market place}}\right) + \left(\begin{array}{c}\text{annual growth rate} \\ \text{in dividends}\end{array}\right)$$

(8)

$$= \frac{D_1}{P_0} + g$$

To convert from the common investor's required rate of return in equation (8) to the cost of internal common funds, no adjustment is required for taxes. Dividends paid to the firm's common stockholders are not tax deductible; therefore, the cost is already on an after-tax basis. Also, flotation costs are not involved in computing the cost of internal common equity, because the funds are already within the business. Thus, the investor's required rate of return is the same as the cost of internal common equity, k_c.

To demonstrate the computation, the Talbot Corporation's common stockholders recently received a $2 dividend per share, and they expect dividends to grow at an annual rate of 10%. If the market price of the security is $50, the investor's required rate of return is

$$k_c = \frac{D_1}{P_0} + g \qquad (8)$$

$$= \frac{\$2(1 + .10)}{\$50} + .10$$

$$= \frac{\$2.20}{\$50} + .10 = .144$$

$$= 14.4\%$$

Note that the forthcoming dividend, D_1, is estimated by taking the past dividend, $2, and increasing it by 10%, the expected growth rate. That is, $D_1 = D_0 (1.10) = \$2 (1.10) = \$2.20$.

The dividend-growth model has been a relatively popular approach for calculating the cost of equity. The primary difficulty, as you might expect, is estimating the expected growth rate in future dividends. One possible source of such expectations are investment advisory services such as Merrill Lynch and Value Line. There are even services that collect and publish the forecasts of a large number of analysts. For instance, Institutional Broker's Estimate System (IBES) publishes earnings per share forecasts made by about 2,000 analysts on a like number of stocks. Although these forecasts are helpful in reducing the problems of the dividend-growth model, they cannot be considered completely accurate. Growth estimates are generally available only for about five years, and not for the indefinite future, as required by the constant growth model. Also, analysts usually state their forecasts in terms of earnings rather than dividends, which does not meet the strict requirements of the dividend-growth model. Even so, the earnings information is helpful, because dividend growth in the long run is dependent on earnings. Also, the analysts' forecasts are helpful because they provide direct measures of the expectations that determine prices in the market.

The use of analysts' forecasts in conjunction with the dividend growth model to compute required rates of return for the Standard and Poor's 500 stocks has been studied by Harris.[4] Computing an average of the analysts' forecasts of five-year growth rates in EPS, Harris used this average as a proxy for the growth rate in dividends. Then, using the dividend-growth model (equation 8), he estimated an average cost of equity for the S&P 500 stocks. He next compared these required rates with the yields on U.S. Treasury bonds to see how much risk premium common stockholders were expecting. The analysis was conducted for each quarter from 1982 through 1984. Results of the Harris study are presented in Figure 22-6. The findings suggest that common stockholders have required a return of between 17.26% and 20.08% on average for 1982 through 1984. For the three-year period, the average required rate of return was 18.41%. The average risk premiums of common stockholders each year, which are shown in the last column of Figure 22-6, ranged from 4.78% to 7.16%, for an average of 6.16%. However, we should remember that these returns apply only for equity investments of average riskiness. As we well know, the risk of individual securities will differ from the average, as will the stockholders' required returns.

---

[4] Robert Harris, "Using Analysts' Forecasts to Estimate Shareholder Required Returns," *Financial Management* (Spring 1986), pp. 510–67.

FIGURE 22-6   Required Rates of Return and Risk Premiums

| | Government Bond Yield | S&P 500 | |
		Required Return	Risk Premium
1982			
Quarter 1	14.27	20.81	6.54
Quarter 2	13.74	20.68	6.94
Quarter 3	12.94	20.23	7.29
Quarter 4	10.72	18.58	7.86
Average	12.92	20.08	7.16
1983			
Quarter 1	10.87	18.07	7.20
Quarter 2	10.80	17.76	6.96
Quarter 3	11.79	17.90	6.11
Quarter 4	11.90	17.81	5.91
Average	11.34	17.88	6.54
1984			
Quarter 1	12.09	17.22	5.13
Quarter 2	13.21	17.42	4.21
Quarter 3	12.83	17.34	4.51
Quarter 4	11.78	17.05	5.27
Average	12.48	17.26	4.78
Average 1982–1984	12.25	18.41	6.16

Source: Robert Harris, "Using Analysts' Forecasts to Estimate Shareholder Required Returns," *Financial Management* (Spring 1986), p. 62. Used by permission.

Although the results in Figure 22-6 look reasonable, the same computations for individual stocks may not be as plausible, largely because of measurement errors that occur when only one or a few stocks are analyzed. Moreover, the constant growth assumption of the model may be inconsistent with reality.

The CAPM approach.   We can estimate the cost of equity using the capital asset pricing model (CAPM). Remember that investors should require a rate of return that at least equals the risk-free rate plus a risk premium appropriate for the level of systematic risk associated with the particular security. Using the CAPM, we may represent the equity-required rate of return (cost of internal equity) as follows:

$$k_c = k_{rf} + \beta(k_m - k_{rf}) \tag{9}$$

where k_c = the required rate of return of the equity shareholders, and also the cost of internal equity capital since there are no transactions costs incurred in retaining earnings

k_{rf} = the risk-free rate

β = beta, or the measure of a stock's systematic risk

k_m = the expected rate of return for the market as a whole—that is, the expected return for the "average security"

For example, assume the risk-free rate is 7%, the expected return in the market is 16%, and the beta for Talbot Corporation's common stock is .82. Then the cost of internal equity would be estimated as follows:

$$k_c = k_{rf} + \beta(k_m - k_{rf})$$

$$= 7\% + .82\,(16\% - 7\%)$$

$$= 14.4\%$$

Although using the CAPM appears relatively easy, its application is not entirely straightforward, particularly in the corporate setting. In estimating the risk-free rate, the market rate, and the security's beta, our goal is to describe the expectations in the minds of the investors, because it is these expectations that determine how assets are valued. Such a task is difficult. However, financial service companies now help provide limited information about investor expectations.

Risk-premium approach.   Because we know that common stockholders will demand a return premium above the bondholder's required rate of return, we may state the cost of equity as follows:

$$k_c = k_d + RP_c \tag{10}$$

where, as before, K_c and K_d represent the cost of common equity and debt, respectively. RP_c is the additional return premium common stockholders expect for assuming greater risk than bondholders. Because we can compute the cost of debt with some degree of confidence, the key to estimating the cost of equity is in knowing RP_c, the risk premium.

We again are in some difficulty, because we have no direct means of computing RP_c. We can only draw from our experience, which tells us that the risk premium of a firm's common stocks relative to its own bonds has for the most part been between 3% and 5%. In times when interest rates are historically high, the premium is usually low. In years when interest rates are at historical lows, the premium has been higher. Using an average premium of 4%, we would approximate the cost of equity capital as follows:

$$k_c = k_d + 4\%$$

For a firm with Aaa-rated bonds that have a cost of 9%, the cost of equity would be estimated to be 13% (9% cost of debt plus the 4% average premium); a more risky company, with bonds that are rated Baa with a 13% cost, could expect its cost of equity to approximate 17% (13% + 4%).

The risk-premium approach is somewhat similar in concept to CAPM in that both recognize that common stockholders require a risk premium. The differences between the two approaches come from using different beginning points (CAPM uses the risk-free rate and the risk-premium approach uses the firm's cost of debt) and in how the risk premium is estimated. Both estimates of the risk premium involve subjectivity; however, CAPM has a more developed conceptual basis. Even so, the risk premium approach is at times the best we can do, especially when the dividend-growth model and the CAPM give unreasonable estimates. Even if the dividend-growth and CAPM approaches are thought to fit the situation, the risk-premium technique gives us a good way to verify the reasonableness of our results.

Cost of new common stock.   If internal common equity does not provide all the equity capital needed for new investments, the firm may need to issue new common stock. Again, this capital should not be acquired from the investors unless the expected returns on the prospective investments exceed a rate sufficient to satisfy the stockholders' required rate of return. Returning to the dividend-growth model equation (8), the only adjustment necessary is to consider the potential flotation costs incurred from issuing the stock. The effect of the flotation costs on the cost of common stock may be found by reducing the market price of the stock by the amount of these costs.[5] Thus, the cost of new common stock, k_{nc}, is

$$k_{nc} = \frac{D_1}{NP_0} + g \tag{11}$$

where NP_0 equals the net proceeds per share received by the company. If, in the preceding example, flotation costs are 15% of the market price, the cost of capital for the new common stock, or external common, would be 15.18%, calculated as follows:

$$k_{nc} = \frac{\$2.20}{\$50 - .15(\$50)} + .10$$

$$= \frac{\$2.20}{\$42.50} + .10 = .1518$$

$$= 15.18\%$$

In this example, if management achieves a 15.18% return on the net capital received from common stockholders, it will satisfy the investors' required rate of return of 14.4%, as determined earlier by equation (8).

Selection of Capital Structure Weights

The individual costs of capital will be different for each source of capital in the firm's capital structure. To use these costs of capital in our investment analyses, we must compute a composite or overall cost of capital.

   The weights for computing this overall cost should reflect the corporation's financing mix. For instance, if creditors are expected to finance 30% of the new investments and common stockholders are to provide the remaining 70%, the weighted cost should reflect this mix.

   Several choices for selecting the financing weights for a composite cost of capital are available. Theoretically, the actual mix to be used in financing the proposed investments should be used as the weights. This approach, however, presents a problem. The costs of capital for individual sources depend on the firm's financial risk, which in turn is affected by its financial mix. If management alters the present financial structure, the individual costs will change, making it more difficult to compute

---

[5]For another approach to adjusting for flotation costs, see John R. Ezzell and R. Burr Porter, "Flotation Costs and the Weighted Average Cost of Capital," *Journal of Financial and Quantitative Analysis, 11* (September 1976), pp. 403–13.

FIGURE 22-7 Ash, Inc., Capital Structure

Investor Group	Amount of Funds Raised ($)	Percentage of Total
Bonds	$1,750,000	35%
Preferred stock	250,000	5
Common stock	3,000,000	60
Total new financing	$5,000,000	100%

---

the cost of capital. Thus, we will assume that the company's financial mix is relatively stable and that these weights will closely approximate future financing. Although this assumption may not be strictly met in any particular year, firms frequently have a **target capital structure** (desired debt—equity mix), which is maintained over the long term. The target financing mix provides the appropriate weights to be used in calculating the firm's weighted cost of capital. Consider the following:

The Ash Company's current financing mix is contained in Figure 22-7. The firm's chief financial officer, Tony Ash, does not want to alter the firm's financial risk. Instead, he chooses to maintain the same relative mix of capital in financing future investments. Thus, given our assumption of a constant financial mix, we will use these percentages as the weights in computing Ash's weighted cost of capital.

Computing the Weighted Cost of Capital

Let's now compute the weighted cost of capital for a firm, which is simply the weighted average of the individual costs, given the firm's financial mix. This calculation is best demonstrated with an example. So let's continue with Ash, Inc. In Figure 22-7, we estimated Ash's financial mix for the purpose of computing the firm's weighted or overall cost of capital. Let's further assume that management has computed the individual costs of capital for the firm, shown in Figure 22-8. For the time being, we will restrict equity financing to the retained earnings available for reinvestment, or internally generated common equity. We are assuming Ash will not issue any new common stock. Therefore, the cost of new common stock is not relevant. Figure 22-9 combines the weights from Figure 22-7 and the individual cost for each security from

---

FIGURE 22-8 Component Costs of Capital for Ash, Inc.

Investor Group	Component Costs
Bonds (after-tax cost)	7%
Preferred stock	13
Common stock (internal only)	16

FIGURE 22-9   Weighted Cost of Capital for Ash, Inc., If Only Internal Common Is Used

(1) Investor Group	(2) Weights[a]	(3) Individual Costs[b]	(4) Weighted Costs (2×3)
Bonds	35%	7%	2.45%
Preferred stock	5	13	0.65
Common stock (internal only)	60	16	9.60
		Weighted cost of capital (k_o):	12.70%

[a]Taken from the desired financing mix presented in Figure 22-7.
[b]Taken from Figure 22-8.

Figure 22-8 into a single weighted cost of capital, k_o. Given that the assumptions of the weighted cost of capital concept are met and that common equity requirements can be satisfied internally, the company's weighted cost of capital is 12.7%. This rate is the firm's minimum acceptable rate of return for new investments. It therefore is the appropriate discount rate for capital budgeting analysis for Ash, Inc., and a key number used in the calculation of the net present value of prospective capital investments.

We have now observed the process for measuring a company's weighted cost of capital. We cannot overstate the importance of this calculation; so much of what we do depends on our measuring the firm's weighted cost of capital with some degree of accuracy. Again, however, we must take care not to place too much confidence in our measurement techniques. We cannot say with any real conviction that we can precisely measure a firm's cost of capital. Remember the limiting effects of our assumptions, especially about constant business and financial risk. At best, we will only have an approximation of the firm's weighted cost of capital, but an approximation certainly beats assigning an arbitrary rate. Nevertheless, given the difficulties in measuring the cost, we must test the sensitivity of our results, that is, the value of the net present value, according to a reasonable range of values for the cost of capital rather than using a single-point estimate.

We now need to consider the effects of the level of financing on the firm's cost of capital. That is, as the firm continues to raise more capital for investment purposes, how is the cost of capital affected?

Level of Financing and the Weighted Cost of Capital

Impact of a new common stock issue. In the previous illustration, we assumed that no new common stock was to be issued. If new common stock is issued, the firm's weighted cost of capital will increase, because external equity capital has a higher cost than internal equity owing to flotation costs.

Generally the firm should use its cheapest sources of funds first while maintaining its desired debt-equity mix. In other words, because internally generated common equity costs less than issuing common stock, it should be blended with debt until fully exhausted. Beyond this point, the weighted cost of capital increases, be-

---

FIGURE 22-10 Crisp Corporation's Investment Opportunities

	Investment Cost	Expected Internal Rate of Return
Geological equipment	$1,500,000	14%
Water flooding equipment	2,000,000	18
Drilling equipment	2,500,000	11

---

cause the firm has to rely on new common stock for its equity financing. This basic concept is best explained through an example.[6]

The Crisp Corporation, an independent oil company, is contemplating three major capital investments in 1995. The first proposal is the acquisition of equipment used to examine geological formations. This new equipment should improve the success ratio in discovering productive oil and gas reserves. The second proposal is investing in water flooding equipment. This process would involve injecting large amounts of water into underground oil reserves, which permits a more efficient recovery of the minerals. Third, new and advanced drilling equipment appears to offer significant cost savings in drilling for oil and gas. The costs and expected returns for these three possible investments are shown in Figure 22-10. Management must decide which of these projects should be accepted.

If any of the proposed projects are accepted, the financing will consist of 50% debt and 50% common. Based on the anticipated profits during 1995, the company should have $1,500,000 in profits available for reinvestment (internal common). The costs of capital for each source of financing have been computed and are presented in Figure 22-11.

The weighted cost of capital, k_0, would be calculated as follows:

$$k_0 = \left[\left(\begin{array}{c} \text{percentage of} \\ \text{debt financing} \end{array} \right) \times \left(\begin{array}{c} \text{cost of} \\ \text{debt} \end{array} \right) \right] \tag{12}$$
$$+ \left[\left(\begin{array}{c} \text{percentage of} \\ \text{common financing} \end{array} \right) \times \left(\begin{array}{c} \text{cost of} \\ \text{common} \end{array} \right) \right]$$

If only internally generated common is utilized, the weighted cost of capital is 10%:

$$k_0 = [50\% \times 6\%] + [50\% \times 14\%] = 10\%$$

When new common stock is used rather than internally generated common, however, the weighted cost of capital is 12%:

$$k_0 = [50\% \times 6\%] + [50\% \times 18\%] = 12\%$$

Which weighted cost of capital should be used in evaluating the three investments?

---

[6]Although we assume a constant debt equity mix, we have no reason or need to assume a constant mix between internally generated equity and new common stock. Rather, we assume that we first use internal equity funds until exhausted, and then, if more equity is needed, we issue common stock.

FIGURE 22-11 Crisp Corporation's Individual Costs of Capital

Source	Cost
Debt (after-tax cost)	6%
Internally generated common ($1,500,000)	14
New common stock	18

To answer this question, we must first rank the projects in descending order by their respective internal rates of return. Second, we must calculate the level of *total* financing at which point our internal equity is expended. In the Crisp Corporation illustration, $3 million in total new investments may be financed with internal common and debt, without having to change the current financial mix of 50% debt and 50% common, and without having to issue common stock. The $3 million is determined by solving the following equation:

$$\begin{array}{c}\text{internally generated}\\\text{common financing}\\\text{available}\end{array} = \left(\begin{array}{c}\text{percentage of}\\\text{common financing}\end{array}\right) \times \left(\begin{array}{c}\text{total financing}\\\text{from all sources}\end{array}\right) \qquad (13)$$

For the Crisp Corporation,

$$\$1,500,000 = (50\%) \times (\text{total financing})$$

which indicates that if Crisp has $1,500,000 in internally generated common and management maintains a 50% debt ratio, it will be able to finance $3 million of total investments without issuing new common stock. Equation (13) may be changed to solve directly for the amount of total financing; this is

$$\begin{array}{c}\text{total financing}\\\text{from all sources}\end{array} = \frac{\text{internally generated common}}{\text{percentage of common financing}}$$

$$= \frac{\$1,500,000}{.50} \qquad (14)$$

$$= \$3,000,000$$

Therefore, for a total investment level of $3 million or less, the firm's weighted cost of capital is expected to be 10%. Beyond this level of total financing our internal common is totally exhausted, and the weighted cost of capital increases to 12%. This reflects the increased cost of new common beyond the $3 million in total financing from both debt and common.

The relationship between the weighted costs of capital and the amount of financing being sought is portrayed graphically by Figure 22-12. The graph depicts the firm's **weighted marginal cost of capital.** The term *marginal* is used because the computed cost of capital shows the weighted cost of each additional dollar of financing. This marginal cost of capital represents the appropriate criterion for making investment decisions. Thus, the firm should continue to invest up to the point where the marginal rate of return earned on a new investment (IRR) equals the marginal cost of

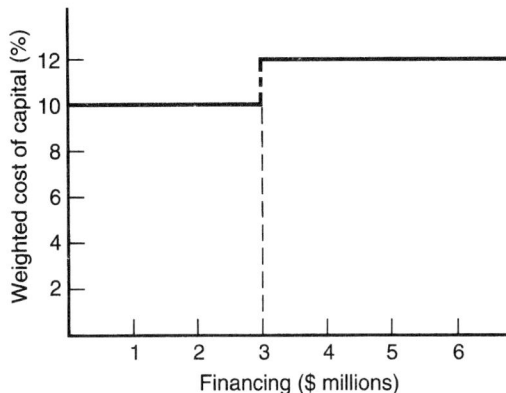

FIGURE 22-12
Crisp Corporation's Weighted Marginal Cost of Capital

new capital. This comparison is reflected in Figure 22-13, where the firm's optimal capital budget is found to be $3,500,000. The company should invest in water flooding machinery and the geological equipment. However, because the weighted marginal cost of capital is greater than the expected internal rate of return of the drilling equipment, this investment should be rejected.

General Effect of New Financing on the Marginal Cost of Capital

Thus far, we have considered only the effect of increases in the cost of common stock on the firm's weighted marginal cost of capital. Similar effects will occur as the cost

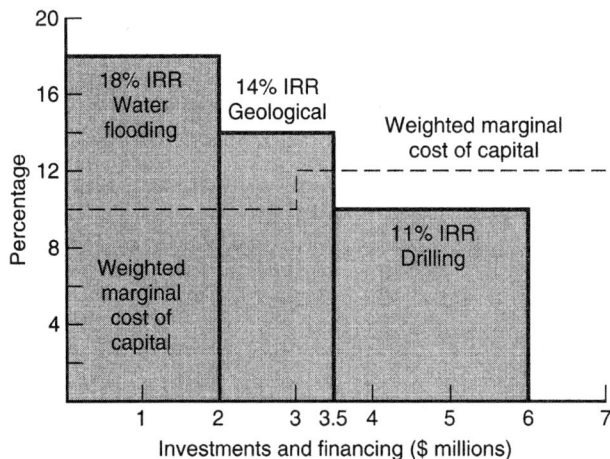

FIGURE 22-13
Crisp Corporation: Comparison of Investment Returns and the Weighted Marginal Cost of Capital

of any source of financing increases. If the 6% cost of debt capital for Crisp Corporation increased to 8% after the firm issued $2 million in bonds, an increase in the weighted marginal cost of capital would have occurred at the $4 million financing level from all sources. This **break** in the marginal cost of capital curve is determined as

$$\frac{\text{total financing}}{\text{from all sources}} = \frac{\text{maximum amount of lower–cost debt}}{\text{percentage of debt financing}} \tag{15}$$

$$= \frac{\$2,000,000}{.50}$$

$$= \$4,000,000$$

As a general rule, *changes in the weighted marginal cost of capital will occur when the cost of an individual source increases.* The break in the marginal cost of capital curve will occur at the dollar financing level where

$$\frac{\text{total financing}}{\text{from all sources}} = \frac{\begin{array}{c}\text{maximum amount of a}\\ \text{lower–cost source of capital}\end{array}}{\begin{array}{c}\text{percentage financing}\\ \text{provided by the source}\end{array}} \tag{16}$$

Summary of Computations

The steps that have been described in calculating a firm's weighted *marginal* cost of capital may be summarized as follows:

1. Determine the percentage of financing to be used from each source of capital (debt, preferred stock, and common equity).
2. Compute the points on the marginal cost of capital curve where the weighted cost will increase.
3. Calculate the costs of each individual source of capital.
4. Compute the weighted cost of capital for the company, which will be different as the amount of financing increases.
5. Construct a graph that compares the internal rates of return for prospective investment opportunities with the weighted cost of capital, which will indicate which investments should be accepted.

MARGINAL COST OF CAPITAL: A COMPREHENSIVE EXAMPLE

To help bring together the principles for computing a firm's weighted cost of capital, consider J. M. Williams, Inc., a manufacturer of medical and surgical instruments. The firm's desired financing mix is presented in Figure 22-14. Management attempts to maintain a relatively constant capital structure mix from year to year.

FIGURE 22-14 J. M. Williams, Inc., December 31, 1994

Total Liabilities and Equity	Financial Structure Equity Mix (%)
Bonds	30.0%
Preferred stock	7.5
Common stock	62.5
Total liabilities and equity	**100.0%**

The most recent earnings per share (1994) was $8, which was twice the earnings per share in 1988, and this represents a growth rate of about 12%.[7] Dividends and the market price of the firm's common stock have grown at the same rate. The dividend payout ratio, which equals the ratio of common dividends to earnings available to common, has been 50%, and J. McDonald Williams, president, intends to hold to this dividend policy in the future. Five investments are being examined by the company for 1995. The costs and the expected internal rates of return for these projects are provided in Figure 22-15. To finance these investments, Williams expects to have $500,000 from 1995 retained earnings available for reinvestment, and new security issues can be sold. The firm's current financing mix will be maintained and the firm's business risk should not change. The following information is available regarding the individual costs of capital:

1. **Bonds.** An amount not exceeding $240,000 could be issued in new bonds. The issue, after considering the effect of flotation costs, would have an effective before-tax cost of 13%. If additional debt is required, the effective yield would have to be increased to 16%. The firm's marginal tax rate is 34%.
2. **Preferred stock.** New preferred stock could be issued by Williams with a par value of $50, paying $6 in annual dividends. The market price of the security is $45, but $1.80 per share in flotation costs would be incurred for an issue size of $105,000 or less. Additional preferred stock could be sold at $45; however, the flotation costs would be $3.33 per share.
3. **Common stock.** Common stock can be sold at the existing $75 market price. If the issue size is not greater than $375,000, a 15% flotation cost would result. For any additional common stock, the flotation costs would increase to 20% of the market price. As already noted, last year's dividend per share was $4 and dividends are expected to grow at 12% per year.

With the foregoing information and by using the following five steps, we can construct a weighted marginal cost of capital curve as follows:

Step 1: *Determine the financial mix.* In Figure 22-14, the desired financial mix for Williams was shown to be 30% in debt, 7.5% in preferred stocks, and 62.5% in

---

[7]This growth rate is computed by dividing the 1994 earnings per share by the 1988 earnings per share, $8/$4 = 2, which represents the compound interest factor for 6 years at 12%. That is, [EPS 1988 $(1 + g)^6$ = EPS 1994], or $4 $(1 + g)^6$ = $8; thus, $(1 + g)^6$ = $8/$4 = 2. Looking up a compound interest factor of two for six years in Appendix B, we find it corresponds to a growth rate of about 12%. The same solution could be found by using the present value equation.

FIGURE 22-15 J. M. Williams, Inc., 1995 Investment Opportunities

Investment	Estimated Cost	Projected Internal Rates of Return
A	$ 450,000	22%
B	500,000	19
C	300,000	17
D	250,000	14
E	500,000	12
Total proposed budget	**$2,000,000**	

---

common equity. For Step 1, we assume that future financing will be made in the same proportions.

Step 2: *Compute when costs will increase.* With the preceding weights and knowing the amount of capital available at each cost, we can compute the points at which breaks in the marginal cost curve will occur. Remember that an increase in the weighted cost of capital occurs when one of the individual costs increases. For example, if the cost of debt rises, the weighted cost must also be higher. We need to know where these increases in the weighted cost will occur. For Williams, Inc., we know that the cost of the bonds increases if we issue more than $240,000 in new bonds. If debt represents 30% of all sources, how much in total financing will be possible before this increase in debt financing (bonds) affects the weighted marginal cost of capital? Using equation (16), we see that the weighted cost will increase when $800,000 in total capital has been raised, which is computed as follows:

$$\frac{\text{total financing available}}{\text{with the lower-cost debt}} = \frac{\substack{\text{total debt available at} \\ \text{a lower cost}}}{\text{percentage of debt financing}}$$

$$= \frac{\$240,000}{.30}$$

$$= \$800,000$$

In other words, when we raise $800,000 in total financing and 30% is from debt, we will have used $240,000 in bonds (30% of $800,000). This same procedure must be followed for increases in the cost of preferred stock and for common equity, both for internally generated common and new common stock. These calculations are shown in Figure 22-16, and the results indicate two breaks in the curve. Increases in the marginal cost of capital occur as the amount of total financing reaches (1) $800,000 (cost of debt and common equity simultaneously increase), and (2) $1,400,000 (cost of preferred stock increases and cost of common equity increases). This result is presented in Figure 22-17.

Step 3: *Calculate the cost of individual sources.* The next step requires computing the individual costs of capital, which is presented in Figure 22-18, where the

---

FIGURE 22-16 J. M. Williams, Inc., Dollar Breaks in Marginal Cost of Capital Curve

I. Debt

$$\frac{\text{total financing available with}}{\text{the lower-cost debt}} = \frac{\text{total debt available at lower cost}}{\text{percentage of debt financing}}$$

$$= \frac{\$240,000}{.30}$$

$$= \$800,000$$

II. Preferred Stock

$$\frac{\text{total financing available with}}{\text{cheaper preferred stock}} = \frac{\text{total preferred stock available at lower cost}}{\text{percentage of preferred stock financing}}$$

$$= \frac{\$105,000}{.075}$$

$$= \$1,400,000$$

III. Common Stock

$$\frac{\text{total financing available with}}{\text{internal common}} = \frac{\text{total internal common available}}{\text{percentage of common financing}}$$

$$= \frac{\$500,000}{.625}$$

$$= \$800,000$$

$$\frac{\begin{array}{c}\text{total financing available with}\\ \text{both internal common and}\\ \text{with cheaper new common}\\ \text{stock}\end{array}}{} = \frac{\begin{array}{c}\text{total internal common plus new}\\ \text{common stock at lower cost}\end{array}}{\text{percentage of common financing}}$$

$$= \frac{\$500,000 + \$375,000}{.625}$$

$$= \$1,400,000$$

---

amount of capital and the costs for these funds are provided. For debt the costs need only to be adjusted by Williams' marginal income tax rate. For a 34% income tax rate, the 13% and 16% costs of debt have an effective after-tax cost of 8.6% and 10.6%, respectively. The cost of preferred stock, which equals the dollar dividend relative to the net price per share received by the company, equals 13.9% for the first $105,000 and 14.4% for any greater amounts. The cost of internally generated common equals the dividend yield (the forthcoming dividend per share/price) plus the expected growth in dividends. The dividend yield is 6% ($4.48/$75). An annual compound growth rate of 12% is estimated from the past growth in earnings per share. The dividend

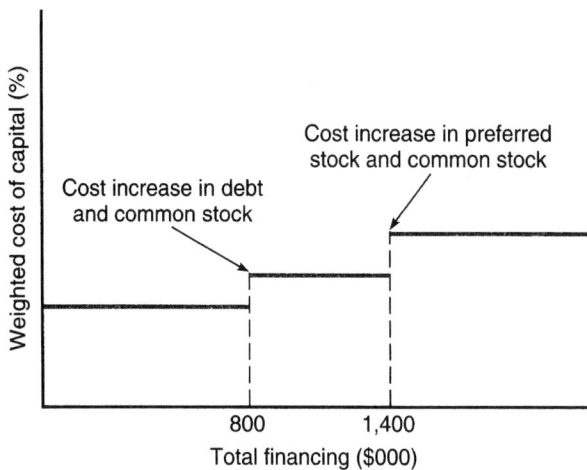

FIGURE 22-17
J. M. Williams, Inc., Breaks in the Weighted Cost of Capital

yield of 6% plus the 12% growth rate produces an 18% cost of internally generated common. The costs of new common stock are easily determined by adjusting the required rate of return of the common stockholders by the flotation costs in issuing the stock. These calculations yield a cost of new common of 19% up to $375,000 and 19.5% for an amount exceeding $375,000.

Step 4: *Solve for the weighted marginal cost of capital.* With the preceding information, the weighted marginal costs of capital relative to the funds raised may be determined. Because the weighted cost of capital does not change for the first $800,000 in total financing, the weighted marginal cost of capital is determined by using the lowest costs of the individual sources. The weighted costs of financing up to $800,000 are calculated in Figure 22-19. The percentage of capital that would be provided by each source is presented in column 2, and the cost of each individual source of capital appears in column 3 (taken from Figure 22-18). Multiplying the weights (column 2) times the individual costs (column 3) and summing the results produce a weighted cost of 14.87%. This cost applies to any amount of financing (including debt, preferred stock, and common equity) up to but not exceeding $800,000.

After the first $800,000 has been used to finance new investments, the costs of debt and common equity will increase. The costs increase because we will have exceeded $240,000 in debt and $500,000 in common equity. Taking the increased costs from Figure 22-18 for these two sources (preferred stock cost has not changed), we calculate a weighted marginal cost of capital for an amount greater than $800,000 but not exceeding $1,400,000. This weighted cost is now 16.10% and is given in Figure 22-20, where the new costs for debt and common equity are shown in the boxes. Otherwise the calculation is no different from the weighted cost of capital for less than $800,000.

Should the firm finance over $ 1,400,000, the weighted marginal cost of capital will rise again. Because we now need over $105,000 in preferred stock and

FIGURE 22-18 J. M. Williams, Inc., Amount and Costs of Individual Sources

Source	Amount Available	Costs Calculations
I. Debt		(after-tax cost of bonds) = (before-tax cost) (1 − tax rate)
	(a) $0 – 240,000	$k_d(1 - t) = 13\% \ (1 - .34) = 8.6\%$
	(b) Over 240,000	$k_d(1 - t) = 16\% \ (1 - .34) = 10.6\%$
II. Preferred stock		$(\text{cost of preferred}) = \left(\dfrac{\text{dividend per share}}{\text{market price less flotation costs}} \right)$
	(a) $0 – 105,000	$k_p = \left(\dfrac{\$6}{\$45 - \$1.80} \right) = .139 \text{ or } 13.9\%$
	(b) Over $105,000	$k_p = \left(\dfrac{\$6}{\$45 - \$3.33} \right) = .144 \text{ or } 14.4\%$
III. Common financing		
A. Internal common		$\left(\begin{array}{c} \text{cost of} \\ \text{internal common} \end{array} \right) = \left(\dfrac{\text{dividend in year one}}{\text{market price}} \right) + \text{growth}$
	(a) $0 – $500,000	$k_c = \left(\dfrac{\$4 \ (1 + .12)}{\$75} \right) + .12 = .18 \text{ or } 18.0\%$
B. New common stock		$\left(\begin{array}{c} \text{cost of new} \\ \text{common stock} \end{array} \right) = \left(\dfrac{\text{dividend in year one}}{\text{market price less flotation costs}} \right) + \text{growth}$
	(a) $0 – $375,000	$k_{nc} = \dfrac{\$4 \ (1 + .12)}{\$75 - \$11.25} + .12 = .19 \text{ or } 19.0\%$
	(b) Over $375,000	$k_{nc} = \dfrac{\$4 \ (1 + .12)}{\$75 - \$15} + .12 = .195 \text{ or } 19.5\%$

$875,000 in common equity to raise more than $1,400,000 in total financing, the costs of preferred stock and common equity will increase. These new costs are presented in Figure 22-21. They result in a final weighted cost of capital of 16.45%.

In summary, the weighted cost of capital for J. M. Williams, Inc., increases as the amount of money needed becomes larger, with the costs being as follows:

Total Financing	Weighted Cost
$0 – $800,000	14.87%
$800,001 – $1,400,000	16.10%
Over $1,400,000	16.45%

Step 5: *Compare investment returns with weighted costs.* The weighted marginal costs
of capital are to be used in determining whether to accept any or all of the
investment prospects being reviewed by Williams. A ranking of the projects,
taken from Figure 22-15, and a comparison of the returns against the weighted
costs of capital are given in Figure 22-22. As is evident from the figure, Williams' optimal capital budget for 1995 is $1,250,000. The particular invest-
ments that should be included in the budget are projects A, B, and C, with
the returns for projects D and E falling short of the weighted cost of capital
hurdle rate.

FIGURE 22-19 J. M. Williams Inc.,
         Weighted Marginal Cost of Capital for $0 – $800,000 Funds Raised

(1)	*(2)*	*(3)*	*(4)*
			Weighted Cost
		Cost of	*of Capital*
Source	*Proportions*	*Capital*	*(2 × 3)*
Bonds	30.0%	8.6%	2.58%
Preferred stock	7.5	13.9	1.04
Common equity	62.5	18.0	11.25
	100.0%	Weighted cost of capital:	**14.87%**

FIGURE 22-20 J. M. Williams Inc.,
         Weighted Marginal Cost of Capital for $800,001 – $1,400,000 Funds Raised

(1)	*(2)*	*(3)*	*(4)*
			Weighted Cost
		Cost of	*of Capital*
Source	*Proportions*	*Capital*	*(2 × 3)*
Bonds	30.0%	10.6%	3.18%
Preferred stock	7.5	13.9	1.04
Common equity	62.5	19.0	11.88
	100.0%	Weighted cost of capital:	**16.10%**

FIGURE 22-21 J. M. Williams Inc.,
         Weighted Marginal Cost of Capital for More Than $1,400,000 Funds Raised

(2)	*(2)*	*(2)*	*(4)*
			Weighted Cost
		Cost of	*of Capital*
Source	*Proportions*	*Capital*	*(2 × 3)*
Bonds	30.0%	10.6%	3.18%
Preferred stock	7.5	14.4	1.08
Common equity	62.5	19.5	12.19
	100.0%	Weighted cost of capital:	**16.45%**

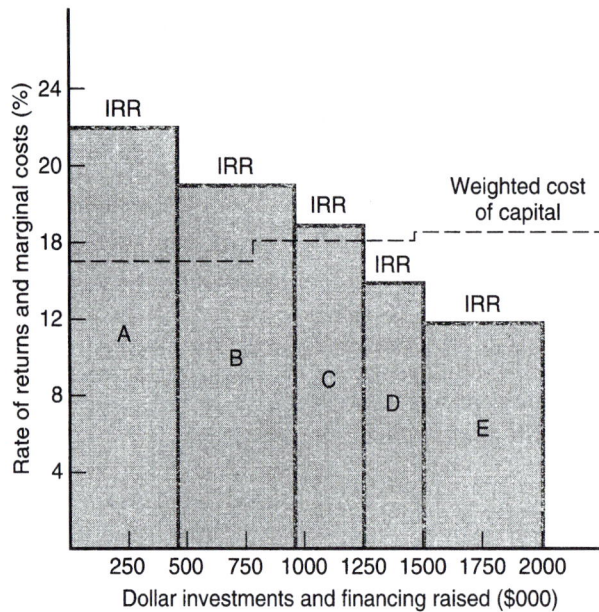

FIGURE 22-22
Investment Returns and Weighted Cost of Capital for J. M. Williams, Inc.

A FIRM'S COST OF CAPITAL: RECENT EVIDENCE

An interesting survey of the 100 largest corporations listed on the New York Stock Exchange was conducted by Blume, Friend, and Westerfield. In this survey, managers were asked to indicate various costs of capital figures.[8] The results are reported in Figure 22-23.

Of the 30 companies that responded to the survey, 10 were public utilities and 20 were nonfinancial corporations from a variety of industries. From the results, we can see that higher costs of capital prevailed when public utilities were excluded, which implies that public utilities are less risky. Even more significantly, the results suggest that new common stock is slightly more expensive than internal common (retained earnings) and that internal common is four to five percentage points more costly than the *before-tax* cost of debt. We should also note that the weighted cost of capital, which falls around 12% to 13%, is at the bottom range of the cutoff or hurdle rate used to evaluate investments in plant and equipment. Thus, either new investments were considered more risky than existing investments or management was imposing capital rationing.

In addition to the results summarized in Figure 22-23, the authors found that

---

[8]Marshall E. Blume, Irwin Friend, and Randolph Westerfield, "Impediments to Capital Formation: Summary Report of a Survey of Nonfinancial Corporations," Working Paper (Philadelphia: Wharton School, University of Pennsylvania, 1980), p. 6.

FIGURE 22-23 Average Costs of Capital and Investment: Cutoff Rates for Plant and Equipment

| Industries | Before-Tax Cost-of-Debt (%) | After-Tax Cost (%) | | | | After-Tax Cutoff Rate for Plant and Equipment Investments | |
		New Common Equity	Retained Earnings	Debt	Weighted Cost	Least Risky	Most Risky
All industries	12.5%	17.2%	16.6%	6.4%	12.4%	12.9%	19.6%
All industries except public utilities	12.5	17.3	17.0	6.3	13.1	13.1	20.3

Source: Marshall E. Blume, Irwin Friend, and Randolph Westerfield, "Impediments to Capital Formation: Summary Report of a Survey of Nonfinancial Corporations," Working Paper (Philadelphia: Wharton School, University of Pennsylvania, 1980), p. 6.

1. The dividend-growth model was the most frequently used method for estimating the cost of equity. However, the CAPM is also used.
2. If management perceives the cost of a particular source to be excessive, it will rely more heavily on other sources. That is, how a firm finances its investments is affected by management's perception of the relative costs of each source of capital.

SUMMARY

Cost of capital is an important concept within financial management. In making an investment, the cost of capital is the rate of return that must be achieved on the company's projects in order to satisfy all the investors' required rates of return. If the rate of return from the corporation's investments equals the cost of capital, the price of the stock should remain unchanged. In other words, the firm's cost of capital may be defined as the rate of return from an investment that will leave the company's stock price unchanged. Therefore, the cost of capital, if certain assumptions are met, represents the minimum acceptable rate of return for new corporate investments.

The factors that affect a firm's cost of capital consist of four components. First, general economic conditions (as reflected in the demand and supply of funds in the economy), as well as inflationary pressures, affect the general level of interest rates. Second, the marketability of the firm's securities has an impact on the cost of capital. Any change in the marketability of a firm's stock will affect investors' required rate of return. These changes directly influence the firm's cost of capital. Third, the firm's operating and financial risks are reflected in its cost of capital. Finally, a relationship exists between a firm's cost of capital and the dollar amount of financing needed for future investments.

Cost of Individual Sources of Financing

The cost of debt is equal to the effective interest rate on new debt adjusted for the tax deductibility of the interest expense. The cost of preferred stock is equal to the effective dividend yield on new preferred stock. In making this computation, we should use the net price received by the company from the new issue. Thus,

$$\text{cost of preferred stock} = \frac{\text{annual dividend}}{\text{net price of preferred stock}}$$

In calculating the cost of common equity, we distinguish between the costs of internally generated funds and the costs of new common stock. If historical data reasonably reflect the expectations of investors, the cost of internally generated capital is equal to the dividend yield on the common stock plus the anticipated percentage increase in dividends (and in the price of the stock) during the forthcoming year. If, however, the common equity is to be acquired by issuing new common stock, the cost of common should recognize the effect of flotation costs. This alteration results in the following equation for the cost of new common stock:

$$\left(\begin{array}{c} \text{cost of new} \\ \text{common} \end{array} \right) = \left(\frac{\text{dividend in year 1}}{\text{market price} - \text{flotation cost}} \right)$$
$$+ \left(\begin{array}{c} \text{annual growth rate} \\ \text{in dividends} \end{array} \right)$$

where (market price – flotation cost) is equivalent to the net market price.

We may also compute the cost of equity by using the CAPM or the risk-premium technique.

Weighted Cost of Capital

A firm's weighted cost of capital is a composite of the individual costs of financing, weighted by the percentage of financing provided by each source. In this chapter we assume that the firm is to finance future investments in the same manner as past investments. Hence, the existing capital structure was used for developing the weighting scheme.

Marginal Cost of Capital

Because the amount of financing has an effect on the firm's weighted cost of capital, the expected return from an investment must be compared with the marginal cost of financing the project. If the cost of capital rises as the level of financing increases, we should use the marginal cost of capital, and not the average cost of all funds raised. Following the basic economic principle of marginal analysis, investments should be made to the point where marginal revenue (internal rate of return) equals the marginal cost of capital.

SELF-CORRECTION PROBLEMS

1. Compute the cost for the following sources of financing:

   a. A $1,000 par value bond with a market price of $970 and a coupon interest rate of 10%. Flotation costs for a new issue would be approximately 5%. The bonds mature in 10 years and the corporate tax rate is 34%.

   b. A preferred stock selling for $100 with an annual dividend payment of $8. If the company sells a new issue, the flotation cost will be $9 per share. The company's marginal tax rate is 30%.

   c. Internally generated common totaling $4.8 million. The price of the common stock is $75 per share, and the dividend per share was $9.80 last year. The dividend is not expected to increase.

   d. New common stock where the most recent dividend was $2.80. The company's dividends per share should continue to increase at an 8% growth rate into the indefinite future. The market price of the stock is currently $53; however, flotation costs of $6 per share are expected if the new stock is issued.

2. The Argue Company has the following capital structure mix:

Debt	30%
Preferred stock	15
Common stock	55
	100%

   Assuming that management intends to maintain the above financial structure, what amount of total investments may be financed if the firm uses (a) $100,000 of debt, (b) $150,000 of debt, (c) $40,000 of preferred stock, (d) $90,000 of preferred stock, (e) $200,000 of internally generated common equity, (f) $200,000 of internally generated common equity plus $300,000 in new common stock?

3. The Zenor Corporation is considering three investments. The costs and expected returns of these projects are shown below:

Investment	Investment Cost	Internal Rate of Return
A	$165,000	17%
B	200,000	13
C	125,000	12

   The firm would finance the projects by 40% debt and 60% common equity. The after-tax cost of debt is 7% for the first $120,000, after which the cost will be 11%. Internally generated common totaling $180,000 is available, and the common stockholders' required rate of return is 19%. If new stock is issued, the cost will be 22%.

a. Construct a weighted marginal cost of capital curve.

b. Which projects should be accepted?

4. Todd Owens is the new vice-president-finance for Brister, Inc. He is preparing his recommendations for the firm's capital budget. With the information provided below, prepare a graph comparing the company's weighted cost of capital and the prospective investment returns. Which investments should be made?

Investment	Investment Cost	Internal Rate of Return
A	$200,000	18%
B	125,000	16
C	150,000	12
D	275,000	10

The firm's capital structure consists of $2 million in debt, $500,000 in preferred stock, and $2.5 million in common equity. This capital mix is to be maintained for future investments. The cost of debt (before-tax) is 12% for the first $120,000; thereafter, the cost will be 15%. The company's preferred stock sells for $95 and pays a 14% dividend rate on a par value of $100. A new offering of this stock would entail underwriting costs and a price discount of 8% of the current market price. If the issue exceeded $50,000, the flotation costs would increase to 11%. The common equity portion of the investments will be financed first by profits retained within the company of $150,000. If additional common financing is needed, new common stock can be issued at the $30 current price less flotation costs of $3 per share. Management expects to pay a dividend at the end of this year of $2.50, and dividends should increase at an annual rate of 9% thereafter. The firm's marginal tax rate is 34%.

SOLUTIONS TO SELF-CORRECTION PROBLEMS

1. a. $$\$921.50 = \sum_{t=1}^{10} \frac{\$100}{\left(1+k_d\right)^t} + \frac{\$1,000}{\left(1+k_d\right)^{10}}$$

Rate	Value		
11%	$940.90		
k_d%	$921.50	$19.40	$53.90
12%	$887.00		

$$k_d = 0.11 + \left(\frac{\$19.40}{\$53.90}\right) 0.01 = .1136 \text{ or } 11.36\%$$

$$k_{d(1-t)} = 11.36\% (1 - 0.34) = 7.50\%$$

b. $k_p = \dfrac{D}{NP_0}$

$k_p = \dfrac{\$8}{\$100 - \$9} = .0879 \text{ or } 8.79\%$

c. $k_c = \dfrac{D_1}{P_0} + g$

$k_c = \dfrac{\$9.80}{\$75} + 0\% = .1307 \text{ or } 13.07\%$

d. $k_{nc} = \dfrac{D_1}{NP_0} + g$

$k_{nc} = \dfrac{\$2.80\,(1 + 0.08)}{\$53 - \$6} + 0.08 = .1443 \text{ or } 14.43\%$

2. $\text{dollar breaks} = \dfrac{\text{amount of financing at a given cost}}{\text{percentage of funds provided by the specific source}}$

a. $\dfrac{\$100,000}{0.30} = \$333,333.33$ b. $\dfrac{\$150,000}{0.30} = \$500,000$

c. $\dfrac{\$40,000}{0.15} = \$266,666.67$ d. $\dfrac{\$90,000}{0.15} = \$600,000$

e. $\dfrac{\$200,000}{0.55} = \$363,636.36$ f. $\dfrac{\$500,000}{0.55} = \$909,090.91$

3. a. Increases (breaks) in the weighted marginal cost of capital curve will occur as follows:

Increase from the cost of debt:

$$\dfrac{\$120,000}{.40} = \$300,000$$

Increase from the cost of common:

$$\dfrac{\$180,000}{.60} = \$300,000$$

$0 – $300,000 Total Financing				Over $300,000 Total Financing			
	Weights	**Costs**	**Weighted Costs**		**Weights**	**Costs**	**Weighted Costs**
Debt	40%	7%	2.80%	Debt	40%	11%	4.4%
Common stock	60	19	11.40	Common stock	60	22	13.2
			k_o = **14.20%**				k_o = **17.6%**

b. Only project A should be accepted.

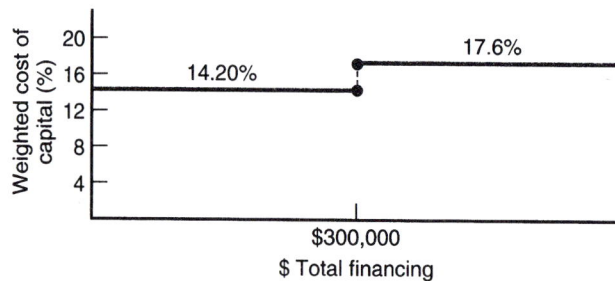

4. a. Compute weights

	Capital Structure	Capital Mix (Weights)
Debt	$2,000,000	40%
Preferred stock	500,000	10
Common stock	2,500,000	50
	$5,000,000	**100%**

b. Compute individual costs

Debt

$0 – $120,000: 12% (1 – .34) = 7.92%
over $120,000: 15% (1 – .34) = 9.90%

Preferred stock

$0–$50,000: $\dfrac{\$14}{\$95(1-.08) = \$87.40} = \dfrac{\$14}{} = .1602$ or 16.02%

over $50,000: $\dfrac{\$14}{\$95(1-.11) = \$84.55} = \dfrac{\$14}{} = .1656$ or 16.56%

Common stock

$0–$150,000: $\left(\dfrac{\$2.50}{\$30}\right) + .09 = .1733$ or 17.33%

over $150,000: $\left(\dfrac{\$2.50}{\$27}\right) + .09 = .1826$ or 18.26%

c. Calculate increases (breaks) in the weighted marginal cost of capital curve caused by increases in the cost of

Debt	Preferred Stock	Common Stock
$\dfrac{\$120,000}{.40} = \$300,000$	$\dfrac{\$50,000}{.10} = \$500,000$	$\dfrac{\$150,000}{.50} = \$300,000$

d. Construct the weighted cost of capital curve

$0 – $300,000 Total Financing

	Weights	Individual Costs	Weighted Costs
Debt	40%	7.92%	3.17
Preferred stock	10	16.02	1.60
Common stock	50	17.33	8.67
			$k_0 = 13.44\%$

At Least $300,001 But Not More Than $500,000

	Weights	Individual Costs	Weighted Costs
Debt	40%	9.90%	3.96
Preferred stock	10	16.02	1.60
Common stock	50	18.26	9.13
			$k_0 = 14.69\%$

Over $500,000

	Weights	Individual Costs	Weighted Costs
Debt	40%	9.90%	3.96
Preferred stock	10	16.56	1.66
Common stock	50	18.26	9.13
			$k_0 = 14.75\%$

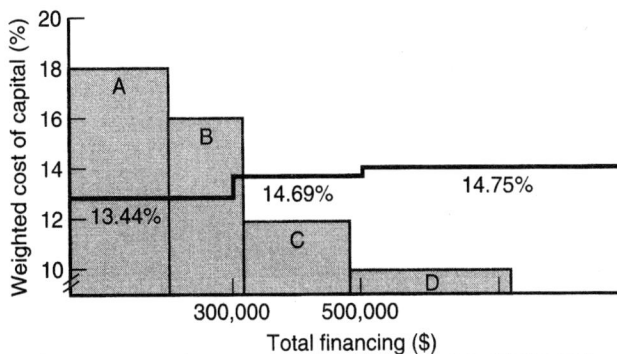

Total financing ($)
Accept investments A and B for a total of $325,000

QUESTIONS

1. Define the term *cost of capital.*
2. Why do we calculate a firm's cost of capital?
3. In computing the cost of capital, which sources of capital do we consider?
4. In general, what factors determine a firm's cost of capital? In answering this question, identify the factors that are within management's control and those that are not.
5. What limitations exist in using the firm's cost of capital as an investment hurdle rate?
6. How does a firm's tax rate affect its cost of capital? What is the effect of the flotation costs associated with a new security issue?
7. a. Distinguish between internal common equity and new common stock.
   b. Why is a cost associated with internal common equity?
   c. Compare approaches that could be used in computing the cost of common equity.
8. Define the expression *marginal cost of capital.* Why is the marginal cost of capital an appropriate investment criterion?
9. How may we avoid the limitation of the weighted cost of capital approach when it requires that we assume business risk is constant?
10. What might we expect to see in practice in the relative costs of different sources of capital?

PROBLEMS

1. **Individual or Component Costs of Capital.**   Compute the cost for the following sources of financing:

   a. A bond that has a $1,000 par value (face value) and a contract or coupon interest rate of 11%. A new issue would have a flotation cost of 5% of the $1,125 market value. The bonds mature in 10 years. The firm's average tax rate is 30% and its marginal tax rate is 34%.

   b. A new common stock issue that paid a $1.80 dividend last year. The par value of the stock is $15, and earnings per share have grown at a rate of 7% per year. This growth rate is expected to continue into the foreseeable future. The company maintains a constant dividend/earnings ratio of 30%. The price of this stock is now $27.50, but 5% flotation costs are anticipated.

   c. Internal common equity where the current market price of the common stock is $43. The expected dividend this coming year should be $3.50, increasing thereafter at a 7% annual growth rate. The corporation's tax rate is 34%.

   d. A preferred stock paying a 9% dividend on a $150 par value. If a new issue is offered, flotation costs will be 12% of the current price of $175.

   e. A bond selling to yield 12% after flotation costs, but prior to adjusting for the marginal corporate tax rate of 34%. In other words, 12% is the rate that equates the net proceeds from the bond with the present value of the future cash flows (principal and interest).

2. **Level of Financing.** The Mathews Company has the following capital structure mix:

Debt	$525,000
Preferred stock	225,000
Common stock	450,000

Using that capital structure mix, compute the total investment amount if the company uses

a. $700,000 of debt

b. $67,500 of preferred stock

c. $300,000 of retained earnings only, or

d. $100,000 of retained earnings plus $600,000 of new common stock

CHAPTER 23

Term Loans and Leasing Financing

The principal characteristic of short-term loans is that they are self-liquidating in less than a year. Frequently, they finance seasonal or temporary funds requirements. Term financing, on the other hand, finances more permanent funds requirements, such as those for fixed assets and underlying buildups in receivables and inventories. The loan is usually paid with the generation of cash flows over a period of years. As a result, most of these loans are paid in regular, periodic installments. We regard term financing as involving final maturities between 1 and 10 years. Although the 1-year boundary is rather commonly accepted, the 10-year upper limit is somewhat arbitrary. In this chapter we examine various types of term debt as well as lease financing.

TERM LOANS

Commercial banks are a primary source of term financing. Two features of a bank **term loan** distinguish it from other types of business loans. First, a term loan has a final maturity of more than 1 year. Second, it most often represents credit extended under a formal loan agreement For the most part, these loans are repayable in periodic installments—quarterly, semiannual, or annual—that cover both interest and principal. The payment schedule of the loan is usually geared to the borrower's cash-flow ability to service the debt. Typically, the repayment schedule calls for equal periodic installments, but it may specify irregular amounts or repayment in one lump sum at final maturity. Sometimes the loan is *amortized* (gradually extinguished) in equal periodic installments except for a final *balloon payment* (a payment much larger than any of the others). Most bank term loans are written with original maturities in the 3- to 5-year range.

Costs and Benefits

Generally, the interest rate on a term loan is higher than the rate on a short-term loan to the same borrower. If a firm could borrow at the prime rate on a short-term basis, it might pay .25% to .50% more on a term loan. The higher interest rate helps to compensate for the more prolonged risk exposure of the lender. The interest rate on a term loan is generally set in two ways: (1) a fixed rate established at the outset that remains effective over the life of the loan or (2) a variable rate adjusted in keeping with changes in market rates. Sometimes a floor or a ceiling rate is established, limiting the range within which a variable rate may fluctuate.

In addition to interest costs, the borrower is required to pay the legal expenses that the bank incurs in drawing up the loan agreement. Also, a **commitment fee** may be charged for the time during the commitment period when the loan is not "taken down." For an ordinary term loan, these additional costs are usually rather small in relation to the total interest cost of the loan. Typically fees on the unused portion of a commitment range between .25% and .75%. Suppose, for example, that the commitment fee was .50% on a commitment of $1 million and a company took down all of the loan 3 months after the commitment. The firm would owe the bank a ($1 million) $\times$ (.005) $\times$ (3 months/12 months) = **$1,250** commitment fee.

The principal advantage of an ordinary bank term loan is flexibility. The borrower deals directly with the lender, and the loan can be tailored to the borrower's needs through direct negotiation. The bank usually has had previous experience with the borrower, so it is familiar with the company's situation. Should the firm's requirements change, the terms and conditions of the loan may be revised. In many instances, bank term loans are made to small businesses that do not have access to the capital markets and cannot readily float a public issue. The ability to float a public issue varies over time in keeping with the tone of the capital markets, whereas access to term loan financing is more dependable. Even large companies that are able to go to the public market may occasionally find it more convenient to seek a bank term loan than to float a public issue.

Revolving Credit Agreements

A *revolving credit agreement* is a formal commitment by a bank to lend up to a certain amount of money to a company over a specified period of time. The actual notes evidencing debt are short term, usually 90 days, but the company may renew them or borrow additionally, up to the specified maximum, throughout the duration of the commitment. Many revolving credit commitments are for three years, although it is possible for a firm to obtain a shorter commitment. As with an ordinary term loan, the interest rate is usually .25 to .50% higher than the rate at which the firm could borrow on a short-term basis under a line of credit. When a bank makes a revolving credit commitment, it is legally bound under the loan agreement to have funds available whenever the company wants to borrow. The borrower usually must pay for this availability in the form of a commitment fee, perhaps .50% per annum, on the difference between the amount borrowed and the specified maximum.

This borrowing arrangement is particularly useful at times when the firm is uncertain about its funds requirements. The borrower has flexible access to funds over a period of uncertainty and can make more definite credit arrangements when the uncertainty is resolved. Revolving credit agreements can be set up so that at the maturity of the commitment, borrowings then owing can be converted into a term loan at the option of the borrower. Suppose that the company you work for is introducing a new product and is facing a period of uncertainty over the next several years. To provide maximum financial flexibility, you might arrange a three-year revolving credit agreement that is convertible into a five-year term loan at the expiration of the revolving credit commitment. At the end of three years, the company should know its funds requirements better. If these requirements are permanent, or nearly so, the firm might wish to exercise its option and take down the term loan.

Insurance Company Term Loans

In addition to banks, life insurance companies and certain other institutional investors lend money on a term basis but with differences in the maturity of the loan extended and in the interest rate charged. In general, life insurance companies are interested in term loans with final maturities in excess of seven years. Because these companies do not have the benefit of compensating balances or other business from the borrower and because their loans usually have a longer maturity than bank term loans, the rate of interest is typically higher than a bank would charge. To the insurance company, the term loan represents an investment and must yield a return commensurate with the costs involved in making the loan, as well as the risk and the maturity of the loan and the prevailing yields on alternative investments. Because an insurance company is interested in keeping its funds employed without interruption, it normally has a prepayment penalty, whereas the bank usually does not. Insurance company term loans are generally not competitive with bank term loans. Indeed, they are complementary, for they serve different maturity ranges.

PROVISIONS OF LOAN AGREEMENTS

When a lender makes a term loan or revolving credit commitment, it provides the borrower with available funds for an extended period. Much can happen to the financial condition of the borrower during that period. To safeguard itself, the lender requires the borrower to maintain its financial condition and, in particular, its current position at a level at least as favorable as when the commitment was made. The provisions for protection contained in a loan agreement are known as protective **covenants.**

The **loan agreement** itself simply gives the lender legal authority to step in should the borrower default under any of the loan provisions. Otherwise, the lender would be locked into a commitment and would have to wait until maturity before being able to take corrective actions. The borrower who suffers losses or other adverse developments will default under a well-written loan agreement. The lender will then be able to act. The action usually takes the form of working with the company to straighten out its problems. Seldom will a lender demand immediate repayment, despite the legal right to do so in cases of default. More typically, the condition under which the borrower defaults is waived, or the loan agreement is amended. The point is that the lender has the authority to act, even though negotiation with the borrower may be instituted to resolve the problem.

Formulation of Provisions

The formulation of the different restrictive provisions should be tailored to the specific loan situation. The lender fashions these provisions for the overall protection of the loan. No one provision is able by itself to provide the necessary safeguard. Collectively, however, these provisions act to ensure the firm's overall liquidity and ability to repay a loan. The important protective covenants of a loan agreement may be classified as follows: (1) general provisions used in most loan agreements, which are usually variable to fit the situation; (2) routine provisions used in most agreements, which are usually not variable; and (3) specific provisions that are used according to the situation.

General provisions.   The *working capital requirement* is probably the most commonly used and most comprehensive provision in a loan agreement. Its purpose is to preserve the company's current position and ability to repay the loan. Frequently, a straight dollar amount, such as $6 million, is set as the minimum working capital the company must maintain during the duration of the commitment. When the lender feels that it is desirable for a specific company to build working capital, it may increase the minimum working capital requirement throughout the duration of the loan. The establishment of a working capital minimum is normally based on the amount of present working capital and projected working capital, allowing for seasonal fluctuations. The requirement should not unduly restrict the company in the ordinary generation of profit. Should the borrower incur sharp losses or spend too much for fixed assets, common stock repurchases, dividends, redemption of long-term debt, and so forth, it would probably breach the working capital requirement.

The *cash dividend and repurchase of common stock restriction* is another major provision in this category. Its purpose is to limit cash going outside the business, thus preserving the liquidity of the company. Most often, cash dividends and repurchases of common stock are limited to a percentage of net profits on a cumulative basis after a certain base date, frequently the last fiscal year end prior to the date of the term loan agreement. A less flexible method is to restrict dividends and repurchases of common stock to an absolute dollar amount each year. In most cases the prospective borrower must be willing to restrict cash dividends and repurchases of common stock. If tied to earnings, this restriction will still allow adequate dividends as long as the company is able to generate satisfactory profits.

The *capital expenditures limitation* is third in the category of general provisions. Capital expenditures may be limited to a yearly fixed dollar amount or, more commonly, either to an amount equal to current depreciation charges or to a certain percentage of current depreciation charges. The capital expenditures limitation is another tool the lender uses to ensure the maintenance of the borrower's current position. By directly limiting capital expenditures, the bank can be more sure that it will not have to look to liquidation of fixed assets for repayment of its loan. Again, the provision should not be so restrictive that it prevents adequate maintenance and improvement of facilities.

A *limitation on other indebtedness* is the last general provision. This limitation may take a number of forms, depending on the circumstances. Frequently, a loan agreement will prohibit a company from incurring any other long-term debt. This provision protects the lender, inasmuch as it prevents future lenders from obtaining a prior claim on the borrower's assets. Usually a company is permitted to borrow within reasonable limits for seasonal and other short-term purposes arising in the ordinary course of business.

Routine provisions.   The second category of restrictions includes routine, usually inflexible, provisions found in most loan agreements. Ordinarily, the loan agreement requires the borrower to furnish the bank with financial statements and to maintain adequate insurance. Additionally, the borrower normally must not sell a significant portion of its assets and must pay, when due, all taxes and other liabilities, except those it contests in good faith. A provision forbidding the future pledging or mortgaging of any of the borrower's assets is almost always included in a loan agreement. This important provision is known as a **negative pledge clause.**

Ordinarily, the company is required not to discount or sell its receivables. Moreover, the borrower generally is prohibited from entering into any leasing arrangement of property, except up to a certain dollar amount of annual rental. The purpose of this provision is to prevent the borrower from taking on a substantial lease liability, which might endanger its ability to repay the loan. A lease restriction also prevents the firm from leasing property instead of purchasing it and thereby getting around the limitations on capital expenditures and debt. Usually, too, there is a restriction on other contingent liabilities. The provisions in this category appear as a matter of routine in most loan agreements. Although somewhat mechanical, they close many loopholes and provide a tight, comprehensive loan agreement.

Special provisions.   In specific loan agreements, the lender uses special provisions to achieve a desired protection of its loan. A loan agreement may contain a definite understanding regarding the use of the loan proceeds, so that there will be no diversion of funds to purposes other than those contemplated when the loan was negotiated. A provision for limiting loans and advances is often found in a term loan agreement. Closely allied to this restriction is a limitation on investments, which is used to safeguard liquidity by preventing certain nonliquid investments.

If one or more key executives are essential to a firm's effective operation, a lender may insist that the company carry life insurance on them. Proceeds of the insurance may be payable to the company or directly to the lender, to be applied to the loan. An agreement may also contain a management clause, under which certain key individuals must remain actively employed in the company during the time the loan is outstanding. Aggregate executive salaries and bonuses are sometimes limited in the loan agreement to prevent excessive compensation of executives, which might reduce profits. This provision also closes another loophole. It prevents large shareholders who are officers of the company from increasing their own salaries in lieu of paying higher dividends, which are limited under the agreement.

Negotiation of Restrictions

The provisions just described represent the most frequently used protective covenants in a loan agreement. From the standpoint of the lender, the aggregate impact of these provisions should be to safeguard the financial position of the borrower and its ability to repay the loan. Under a well-written agreement, a borrower cannot get into serious financial difficulty without defaulting under an agreement, thereby giving the lender legal authority to take action. Although the lender is instrumental in establishing the restrictions, the restrictiveness of protective covenants is subject to negotiation between borrower and lender. The final result will depend on the bargaining power of each of the parties involved.

EQUIPMENT FINANCING

Equipment represents another asset of the firm that may be pledged to secure a loan. If the firm either has equipment that is marketable or is purchasing such equipment, it is usually able to obtain some sort of secured financing. Because the terms of such loans are usually more than a year, we take them up in this chapter rather than under short-term secured loans. As with other secured loans, the lender evaluates the marketability of the collateral and will advance a percentage of the market value, depending on the quality of the equipment. Frequently, the repayment schedule for the loan is set in keeping with the economic depreciation schedule of the equipment. In setting the repayment schedule, the lender wants to be sure that the market value of the equipment always exceeds the balance of the loan.

The excess of the expected market value of the equipment over the amount of the loan is the margin of safety, which will vary according to the specific situation. For example, the rolling stock of a trucking company is movable collateral and reasonably marketable. As a result, the advance may be as high as 80%. Less marketable equipment, such as that with a limited use, will not command as high an advance. A certain type of lathe may have a thin market, and a lender might not be willing to advance more than 50% of its reported market value. Some equipment is so specialized that it has no value as collateral.

Sources and Types of Equipment Financing

Commercial banks, finance companies, and the sellers of equipment are among the sources of equipment financing. Because the interest charged by a finance company on an equipment loan is usually higher than that charged by a commercial bank, a firm will turn to a finance company only if it is unable to obtain the loan from a bank. The seller of the equipment may finance the purchase either by holding a secured note itself or by selling the note to its captive finance subsidiary or some third party. The interest charge will depend on the extent to which the seller uses financing as a sales tool. The seller who uses financing extensively may charge only a moderate interest rate but may make up for part of the cost of carrying the notes by charging higher prices for the equipment. The borrower must consider this possibility in judging the true cost of financing. Equipment loans may be secured by either a chattel mortgage or by a conditional sales contract arrangement.

Chattel mortgage. A *chattel mortgage* is a **lien** on property other than real estate. The borrower signs a security agreement that gives the lender a lien on the equipment specified in the agreement. To *perfect* (make legally valid) the lien, the lender files a copy of the security agreement or a financing statement with a public office of the state in which the equipment is located. Given a valid lien, the lender can sell the equipment if the borrower defaults in the payment of principal or interest on the loan.

Conditional sales contract.   With a **conditional sales contract** arrangement, the seller of the equipment retains the title to it until the purchaser has satisfied all the terms of the contract. The buyer signs a conditional sales contract security agreement to make periodic installment payments to the seller over a specified period of time. These payments are usually monthly or quarterly. Until the terms of the contract are completely satisfied, the seller retains title to the equipment. Thus, the seller receives a down payment and a **promissory note** for the balance of the purchase price upon the sale of the equipment. The note is secured by the contract, which gives the seller the authority to repossess the equipment if the buyer does not meet all of the terms of the contract.

The seller may either hold the contract or sell it, simply by endorsing it, to a commercial bank or finance company. The bank or finance company then becomes the lender and assumes the security interest in the equipment. If the buyer should default under the terms of the contract, the bank or finance company could repossess the equipment and sell it in satisfaction of its loan. Often, the vendor will sell the contract to a bank or finance company *with recourse.* Under this arrangement, the lender has the additional protection of recourse to the seller in case the buyer defaults and the lender realizes less than the loan balance from the sale of the equipment.

LEASE FINANCING

A **lease** is a contract. By its terms the owner of an asset (the lessor) gives another party (the lessee) the exclusive right to use the asset, usually for a specified period of time, in return for the payment of rent. Most of us are familiar with leases of houses, apartments, offices, or automobiles. Recent decades have seen an enormous growth in the leasing of business assets such as cars and trucks, computers, machinery, and even manufacturing plants. An obvious advantage to the lessee is the use of an asset without having to buy it. For this advantage, the lessee incurs several obligations. First and foremost is the obligation to make periodic lease payments, usually monthly or quarterly. Also, the lease contract specifies who is to maintain the asset. Under a *full-service* (or *maintenance*) *lease,* the lessor pays for maintenance, repairs, taxes, and insurance. Under a **net lease,** the lessee pays these costs.

The lease may be cancellable or noncancellable. When cancellable, there sometimes is a penalty. An **operating lease** for office space, for example, is relatively short term and is often cancellable at the option of the lessee with proper notice. The term of this type of lease is shorter than the asset's economic life. In other words, the lessor does not recover its investment during the first lease period. It is only in leasing the space over and over, either to the same party or to others, that the lessor recovers its costs. Other examples of operating leases include the leasing of copying machines, certain computer hardware, word processors, and automobiles. In contrast, a **financial lease** is longer term in nature and is noncancellable. The lessee is obligated to make lease payments until the lease's expiration, which generally corresponds to the useful life of the asset. These payments not only amortize the cost of the asset but provide the lessor an interest return. Our focus in this chapter is on financial as opposed to operating leases since it is this longer term arrangement that is employed when a lease is used as a source of intermediate- to long-term financing.

Finally, the lease contract typically specifies one or more options to the lessee at expiration. One option is to simply return the leased asset to the lessor. Another option may involve renewal, where the lessee has the right to renew the lease for another lease period, either at the same rent or at a different, usually lower, rent. A final option would be to purchase the asset at expiration. For tax reasons, the asset's purchase price must not be significantly lower than its **fair market value.** If the lessee does not exercise its option, the lessor takes possession of the asset and is entitled to any **residual value** associated with it.

Forms of Lease Financing

Virtually all financial lease arrangements fall into one of three main types of lease financing: a sale and leaseback arrangement, direct leasing, and leveraged leasing. In this section we briefly describe these categories. In the subsequent section we present a framework for the analysis of lease financing.

Sale and leaseback.   Under a **sale and leaseback** arrangement a firm sells an asset to another party, and this party leases it back to the firm. Usually the asset is sold at approximately its market value. The firm receives the sales price in cash and the economic use of the asset during the basic lease period. In turn, it contracts to make periodic lease payments and give up title to the asset. As a result, the lessor realizes any residual value the asset might have at the end of the lease period, whereas before, this value would have been realized by the firm. The firm may realize an income tax advantage if the asset involves a building on owned land. Land is not depreciable if owned outright. However, since lease payments are tax deductible, the lessee is able to indirectly "depreciate" (or expense) the cost of the land. Lessors engaged in sale and leaseback arrangements include insurance companies, other institutional investors, finance companies, and independent leasing companies.

Direct leasing.   Under *direct leasing,* a company acquires the use of an asset it did not own previously. A firm may lease an asset from the manufacturer. IBM leases computers. Xerox Corporation leases copiers. Indeed, capital goods are abundantly available today on a lease-financed basis. A wide variety of direct leasing arrangements meet various needs of firms. The major types of lessors are manufacturers, finance companies, banks, independent leasing companies, special-purpose leasing companies, and partnerships. For leasing arrangements involving all but manufacturers, the vendor sells the asset to the lessor who, in turn, leases it to the lessee. As in any lease arrangement, the lessee has use of the asset, along with a contractual obligation to make lease payments to the lessor.

Leveraged leasing.   A special form of leasing has become popular in the financing of big-ticket assets such as aircraft, oil rigs, and railway equipment. This device is known as **leveraged leasing.** In contrast to the two parties involved in a sale and leaseback or direct leasing, there are three parties involved in leveraged leasing: (1) the lessee, (2) the lessor (or equity participant), and (3) the lender. We examine each in turn.

From the standpoint of the lessee, there is no difference between a leveraged lease and any other type of lease. The lessee contracts to make periodic payments over the basic lease period and, in return, is entitled to the use of the asset over that period of time. The role of the lessor, however, is changed. The lessor acquires the asset in keeping with the terms of the lease arrangement and finances the acquisition in part by an equity investment of, say, 20% (hence the term "equity participant"). The remaining 80% of the financing is provided by a long-term lender or lenders. Usually the loan is secured by a mortgage on the asset, as well as by the assignment of the lease and lease payments. The lessor, then, is itself a borrower.

As owner of the asset, the lessor is entitled to deduct all depreciation charges associated with the asset. The cash-flow pattern for the lessor typically involves (1) a cash outflow at the time the asset is acquired, which represents the lessor's equity participation; (2) a period of cash inflows represented by lease payments and tax benefits, less payments on the debt (interest and principal); and (3) a period of net cash outflows during which, because of declining tax benefits, the sum of lease payments and tax benefits falls below the debt payments due. If there is any *residual value* at the end of the lease period, this of course represents a cash inflow to the lessor. Although the leveraged lease may seem the most complicated of the three forms of lease financing we have described, it reduces to certain basic concepts. From the standpoint of the lessee, which is our stance, the leveraged lease can be analyzed in the same manner as any other lease. Therefore, we will not treat it separately in the rest of this chapter.

Accounting Treatment

Accounting for leases has changed dramatically over time. A number of years ago lease financing was attractive to some because the lease obligation did not appear on the company's financial statements. As a result, leasing was regarded as a "hidden" or "off- balance-sheet" method of financing. However, accounting requirements have changed so that now many long-term leases must be shown on the balance sheet as a "capitalized" asset with an associated liability being shown as well. For these leases, the reporting of earnings is affected. Other leases must be fully disclosed in footnotes to the financial statements. As the accounting treatment of leases is involved, we discuss it separately in the Addendum to this chapter in order to maintain the chapter's continuity. The main point is that it is no longer possible for a firm to "fool" informed investors and creditors by using a lease as opposed to debt financing. The full impact of the lease obligation is apparent to any supplier of capital who makes the effort to read the financial statements.

Tax Treatment

For tax purposes, the lessee can deduct the full amount of the lease payment in a properly structured lease. The Internal Revenue Service (IRS) wants to be sure that the lease contract truly represents a lease and not an installment purchase of the asset. To assure itself that a "true" lease is in fact involved, it may check on whether there is a meaningful *residual value* at the end of the lease term. Usually this is construed to mean that the term of the lease cannot exceed 90% of the useful life of the asset. In addition to this criterion, the lessee must not be given an option to purchase the asset or to release it at a nominal price at the end of the lease period. Any purchase option must be based on the asset's *fair market value* at the lease's expiration, such as would occur with an outside offer. The lease payments must be reasonable in that they provide the lessor not only a return of principal but a reasonable interest return as well. In addition, the lease term must be for less than 30 years; otherwise it will be construed as an installment purchase of the asset.

The IRS wants to assure itself that the lease contract is not, in effect, a purchase of the asset, for which the lease payments are much more rapid than would be allowed with depreciation under an outright purchase. As lease payments are deductible for tax purposes, such a contract would allow the lessor to effectively "depreciate" the asset more quickly than allowed under a straight purchase. If the lease contract meets the conditions described, the full lease payment is deductible for tax purposes.

With leasing, the cost of any land is amortized in the lease payments. By deducting the lease payments as an expense for federal income tax purposes, the lessee is able to effectively write off the original cost of the land. If, instead, the land is purchased, the firm cannot depreciate it for tax purposes. When the value of land represents a significant portion of the asset acquired, lease financing can offer a tax advantage to the firm. Offsetting this tax advantage is the likely residual value of land at the end of the basic lease period. The firm may also gain certain tax advantages in a sale and leaseback arrangement when the assets are sold for less than their depreciated value.

Economic Rationale for Leasing

The principal reason for the existence of leasing is that companies, financial institutions, and individuals derive different tax benefits from owning assets. The marginally profitable company may not be able to reap the full benefit of accelerated depreciation, whereas the high-income taxable corporation or individual is able to realize such. The former may be able to obtain a greater portion of the overall tax benefits by leasing the asset from the latter party as opposed to buying it. Because of competition among lessors, part of the tax benefits may be passed on to the lessee in the form of lower lease payments than would otherwise be the case.

Another tax disparity has to do with the **alternative minimum tax (AMT).** For a company subject to the AMT, accelerated depreciation is a "tax preference item," whereas a lease payment is not. Such a company may prefer to lease, particularly from another party that pays taxes at a higher effective rate. The greater the divergence in abilities of various parties to realize the tax benefits associated with owning an asset, the greater the attraction of lease financing overall. It is not the existence of taxes per se that gives rise to leasing but divergences in the abilities of various parties to realize the tax benefits.

Another consideration, albeit a minor one, is that lessors enjoy a somewhat superior position in bankruptcy proceedings over what would be the case if they were secured lenders. The riskier the firm that seeks financing, the greater the incentive for the supplier of capital to make the arrangement a lease rather than a loan.

In addition to these reasons, there may be others that explain the existence of lease financing. For one thing, the lessor may enjoy economies of scale in the purchase of assets that are not available to individual lessees. This is particularly true for the purchase of autos and trucks. Also, the lessor may have a different estimate of the life of the asset, its salvage value, or the opportunity cost of funds. Finally, the lessor may be able to provide expertise to its customers in equipment selection and maintenance. While all of these factors may give rise to leasing, we would not expect them to be nearly as important as the tax reason.

EVALUATING LEASE FINANCING IN RELATION TO DEBT FINANCING

To evaluate whether or not a proposal for lease financing makes economic sense, one should compare the proposal with financing the asset with debt. Whether leasing or borrowing is best will depend on the patterns of cash flows for each financing method and on the opportunity cost of funds. To illustrate a method of analysis, we compare lease financing with debt financing, using a hypothetical example. We assume that the investment worthiness of the project is evaluated separately from the specific method of financing to be employed. We also assume that the firm has determined an appropriate capital structure and has decided to finance the project with a fixed-cost type of instrument—either debt or lease financing. We turn now to examining the two alternatives.

Suppose that McNabb Electronics, Inc., has decided to acquire a piece of equipment costing $148,000 to be used in the fabrication of microprocessors. If it finances the equipment with a lease, the manufacturer will provide such financing over seven years. The terms of the lease call for an annual payment of $27,500. The lease payments are made in advance; that is, at the beginning of each of the seven years. The lessee is responsible for maintenance of the equipment, insurance, and taxes; in short, it is a *net lease.*

Embodied in the lease payments is an implied interest return to the lessor. If we ignore possible residual value, the before-tax return to the lessor can be found by solving the following for R:

$$\$148{,}000 = \sum_{t=0}^{6} \frac{\$27{,}500}{(1+R)^t} \tag{1}$$

$$= \$27{,}500 + \$27{,}500 \, (PVIFA_{R,\,6}) \tag{2}$$

Because these lease payments are made in advance, we solve for the internal rate of return, R, that equates the cost of the asset with one lease payment at time 0, plus the present value of an annuity consisting of six lease payments at the end of each of the next six years. When we solve for R, we find it to be 9.79%. If, instead of this return, the lessor wishes a before-tax return of 11%, it would need to obtain annual lease payments of X in the following equation:

$$\$148{,}000 = \sum_{t=0}^{6} \frac{X}{(1+.11)^t}$$

$$\$148{,}000 = X + X \, (PVIFA_{11\%,\,6})$$
$$\$148{,}000 = X + X \, (4.231) \tag{3}$$
$$\$148{,}000 = X \, (5.231)$$
$$X = \$148{,}000/5.231$$
$$X = \mathbf{\$28{,}293}$$

In equation (3), 4.231 is the present value interest factor of an annuity at 11% for six years. Therefore, the annual lease payment would be $28,293.

If the asset is purchased, McNabb Electronics would finance it with a seven-year term loan at 12%. The company is in a 40% tax bracket. The asset falls in the five-year property class for modified accelerated cost recovery (depreciation) purposes. Accordingly, the depreciation schedule discussed earlier is used:

	YEAR					
	1	**2**	**3**	**4**	**5**	**6**
Depreciation	20.00%	32.00%	19.20%	11.52%	11.52%	5.76%

The cost of the asset is then depreciated at these rates, so that first-year depreciation is .20 × $148,000 = **$29,600** and so forth. At the end of the seven years, the equipment is expected to have a salvage value of $15,000. McNabb Electronics is entitled to this residual value, as it would be the owner of the asset under the purchase alternative.

Present Value for Lease Alternative

By comparing the present values of cash outflows for leasing and borrowing, we are able to tell which method of financing should be used. It is simply the one with the *lowest* present value of cash outflows less inflows. Remember that the company will make annual lease payments of $27,500 if the asset is leased. Because these payments are an expense, they are deductible for tax purposes, but only in the year for which the payment applies. The $27,500 payment at the end of year 0 represents a prepaid expense and is not deductible for tax purposes until the end of year 1. Similarly, the other six payments are not deductible until the end of the following year.

As leasing is analogous to borrowing, an appropriate discount rate for discounting the after-tax cash flows might be the after-tax cost of borrowing. For our example, the after-tax cost of borrowing is 12% times (1 − .40), or 7.2%. The reason for using this rate as our discount rate is that the difference in cash flows between lease financing and debt financing involves little risk. Therefore, it is not appropriate to use the company's overall cost of capital, which embodies a risk premium for the firm as a whole, as the discount rate.

FIGURE 23-1   Schedule of Cash Flows for the Leasing Alternative

End of Year	(a) Lease Payment	(b) Tax-Shield Benefits $(a)_{t-1} \times (.40)$	(c) Cash Outflow after Taxes (a) − (b)	(d) Present Value of Cash Outflows (at 7.2%)
0	$27,500	—	$27,500	$27,500
1–6	27,500	$11,000	16,500	78,165*
7	—	11,000	(11,000)	(6,761)
				$98,904

*Total for years 1–6.

FIGURE 23-2   Schedule of Debt Payments

End of Year	(a) Loan Payment	(b) Principal Amount Owing at End of Year $(b)_{t-1} - (a) + (c)$	(c) Annual Interest $(b)_{t-1} \times (.12)$
0	$28,955	$119,045	$ 0
1	28,955	104,375	14,285
2	28,955	87,945	12,525
3	28,955	69,543	10,553
4	28,955	48,933	8,345
5	28,955	25,850	5,872
6	28,952	0	3,102

Given the foregoing information, we are able to compute the present value of cash flows. The computed figures are shown in the last column of Figure 23-1. We see that the present value of the total cash flows under the leasing alternative is *$98,904*. This figure must then be compared with the present value of cash flows under the borrowing alternative.

Present Value for Borrowing Alternative

If the asset is purchased, McNabb Electronics is assumed to finance it entirely with a 12% unsecured term loan with a payment schedule being of the same general configuration as the lease payment schedule. In other words, loan payments are assumed to be payable at the beginning, not the end, of each year. This assumption places the loan on a basis roughly equivalent with the lease in terms of the time pattern of cash flows. A loan of $148,000 is taken out at time 0 and is payable over seven years with annual payments of $28,955 at the beginning of each year.[1] The proportion of interest in each payment depends on the unpaid principal amount owing during the year. The principal amount owing during the first year is $148,000 minus the payment at the very start of the year of $28,955, or **$119,045.** The annual interest for the first year is $119,045 × .12 = **$14,285.**[2] As subsequent payments are made, the interest component decreases. Figure 23-2 shows these components over time.

To compute the cash outflows after taxes for the debt alternative, we must determine the tax effect.[3] This requires knowing the amounts of annual interest and annual depreciation. Using the modified accelerated cost recovery schedule for the five-year property class listed earlier, we show the annual depreciation charges in

[1]This amount is computed in the same manner as in equation (3), using 12% instead of 11%. However, rather than relying on Appendix E for $(PVIFA_{12\%, 6})$ we chose to use the *PVIFA* formula in order to get a figure that was accurate to more significant digits.

[2]For ease of illustration, we round to the nearest dollar throughout. This results in the final debt payment in Figure 23-2 being slightly less than would otherwise be the case.

[3]We assume for ease of illustration that the firm's regularly determined tax is higher than its AMT. Therefore, the tax-shield benefits of depreciation (a "tax preference item") are not lost (or lowered) through a debt-financed purchase.

FIGURE 23-3 Schedule of Cash Flows for the Debt Alternative

	(a)	(b)	(c)	(d)	(e)	(f)
						Present
				Tax-Shield	Cash Outflows	Value of
End of	Loan	Annual	Annual	Benefits	after Taxes	Cash Outflows
Year	Payment	Interest	Depreciation	[(b) + (c)] × (.40)	(a) − (d)	(at 7.2%)
0	$ 28,955	$ 0	$ 0	$ 0	$28,955	$28,955
1	28,955	14,285	29,600	17,554	11,401	10,635
2	28,955	12,525	47,360	23,954	5,001	4,352
3	28,955	10,553	28,416	15,588	13,367	10,851
4	28,955	8,345	17,050	10,158	18,797	14,233
5	28,955	5,872	17,050	9,169	19,786	13,976
6	28,952	3,102	8,524	4,650	24,303	16,013
7	(15,000)*	0	0	(6,000)**	(9,000)	(5,532)
			$148,000			$93,484

*Salvage value.
**Tax due to recapture of depreciation, $15,000 × .40 = $6,000.

column (c) of Figure 23-3. Because both depreciation and interest are deductible expenses for tax purposes, they provide tax-shield benefits equal to their sum times the assumed tax rate of 40%. This is shown in column (d) of the table. When these benefits are deducted from the debt payment, we obtain the cash outflow after taxes at the end of each year, shown in column (e). At the end of the seventh year, the asset is expected to have a salvage value of $15,000. This *recapture of depreciation* is subject to the corporate tax rate of 40% for the company, which leaves an expected after-tax cash inflow of $9,000. Finally we compute the present value of all of these cash flows at a 7.2% discount rate and find that they total $93,484.

This present value of cash outflow for the debt alternative, $93,484, is less than that for the lease alternative, which is $98,904. Therefore, the analysis suggests that the company use debt as opposed to lease financing in acquiring the use of the asset. This conclusion arises despite the fact that the implicit interest rate embodied in the lease payments, 9.79%, is less than the explicit cost of debt financing, 12%. However, if the asset is bought, the company is able to avail itself of modified accelerated cost recovery depreciation, and this helps the situation from a present value standpoint. Moreover, the residual value at the end of the project is a favorable factor, whereas this value goes to the lessor with lease financing.

Another factor that favors the debt alternative is the deductibility of interest payments for tax purposes. Because the amount of interest embodied in a "mortgage-type" debt payment is higher at first and declines with successive payments, the tax benefits associated with these payments follow the same pattern over time. From a present value standpoint, this pattern benefits the firm relative to the pattern of lease payments, which are typically constant over time. These advantages of a debt financed purchase more than offset the implied interest-rate advantage to lease financing. The lease payment terms are simply not attractive enough to give up the tax and other benefits associated with ownership.

Other Considerations

The decision to borrow rests on the relative timing and magnitude of cash flows under the two financing alternatives, as well as on the discount rate employed. We have assumed that the cash flows are known with certainty. While this is reasonable for the most part, there is some uncertainty that, on occasion, can be important. The estimated salvage (residual) value of an asset is usually subject to considerable uncertainty, for example.

As we can see, deciding between leasing and borrowing can involve some rather extensive calculations. Each situation requires a separate analysis. The analysis is complicated if the two alternatives involve different amounts of financing. If we finance less than the total cost of the asset by borrowing but finance 100% of the cost by leasing, we must consider the difference in the amount of financing, both from the standpoint of explicit as well as implicit costs. These considerations and the others mentioned throughout this chapter can make the evaluation of lease financing rather detailed.

The Importance of the Tax Rate

Lease-versus-borrow analyses are very sensitive to the tax rate of the potential lessee. If the effective tax rate is 20% instead of the 40% in our previous example, the present value comparison changes. The tax-shield benefits are lower and the discount rate—the after-tax cost of borrowing—higher, i.e., 12% (1 − .20) = **9.6%.** By reworking the figures in Figures 23-1 and 23-3, we can determine that these two changes result in the present value of cash outflows for the lease alternative being $121,554 and for the debt alternative $118,577. The debt alternative still dominates but by a lesser margin than before. At a zero tax rate and using the full 12% as the discount rate, the present value of cash outflows for the lease alternative is $140,564 versus $141,215 for the debt alternative. The lease alternative now dominates by a slight margin.

The important lesson of these examples is that the tax rate of the lessee matters a lot. In general, as the effective tax rate declines, the relative advantage of debt versus lease financing declines and may actually reverse, depending on the circumstances. This explains why lease financing usually is attractive only to those in low or zero tax brackets who are unable to enjoy the full tax benefits associated with owning an asset. By leasing from a party in a high tax bracket, the lessee may be able to get part of the tax benefits of ownership because lease payments are lower than they otherwise would be. How much lower depends on the supply and demand conditions in the leasing industry. The exact sharing of the tax benefits is negotiable, and it depends on the competitive situation at the time.

For all practical purposes, the leasing industry in the United States is an artifact of the tax laws. As these laws change, the industry is impacted, often in dramatic ways. Parties that financed via the leasing route may no longer do so, while others may find it attractive. Previous lessors may step out of the business, while others may be able to serve this role to advantage. The greater the change in laws affecting asset write-offs, tax rates, and alternative minimum taxes, the greater the disequilibrium, and the longer the equilibration process as parties exit or enter the market as either lessors or lessees. One thing is clear: Taxes have a dominant influence on the leasing industry.

SUMMARY

- A *term loan* represents debt originally scheduled for repayment in more than 1 year but generally in less than 10 years.
- Commercial banks, insurance companies, and other institutional investors make term loans to business firms. Banks also provide financing under a *revolving credit agreement,* which represents a formal commitment on the part of the bank to lend up to a certain amount of money over a specified period of time.
- Lenders who offer unsecured credit usually impose restrictions on the borrower. These restrictions are called protective *covenants* and are contained in a *loan agreement.* If the borrower defaults under any of the provisions of the loan agreement, the lender may initiate immediate corrective measures.
- On a secured basis, firms can obtain intermediate-term financing by pledging equipment that they own or are purchasing. Banks, finance companies, and sellers of the equipment are active in providing this type of secured financing.
- In lease financing, the lessee (the renter) agrees to pay the lessor (the owner), periodically, for economic use of the lessor's asset. Because of this contractual obligation, leasing is regarded as a method of financing similar to borrowing.
- An *operating lease* is a short-term lease that is often cancellable, while a *financial lease* is a long-term lease that is not cancellable.
- A financial lease can involve the acquisition of an asset under a *direct lease*, a *sale and leaseback* arrangement, or a *leveraged lease.*
- One of the principal economic reasons for leasing is the inability of a firm to utilize all the tax benefits associated with the ownership of an asset. This can arise because of (1) unprofitable operations, (2) the provisions of the alternative minimum tax (AMT), or (3) insufficient earnings to effectively utilize all of the possible tax benefits.
- A common means used for analyzing lease financing in relation to debt financing is to discount to present value the after-tax net cash flows under each alternative, using the after-tax cost of borrowing as the discount rate. The preferred financing alternative is the one that provides the lower present value of cash outflows.

SELF-CORRECTION PROBLEMS

1. Burger Rex is expanding its chain of fast-food outlets. This program will require a capital expenditure of $3 million, which must be financed. The company has settled on a three-year revolving credit of $3 million, which may be converted into a three-year term loan at the expiration of the revolving credit commitment. The commitment fee for both credit arrangements is .5% of the unused portions. The bank has quoted Burger Rex an interest rate of 1% over prime for the revolving credit and 1.5% over prime for the term loan, if that option is taken. The company expects to borrow $1.4 million at the outset and another $1.6 million at the very end of the first year. At the expiration of the revolving credit, the company expects to take down the full-term loan. At the end of each of the fourth, fifth, and sixth years, it expects to make principal payments of $1 million.

    a. For each of the next six years, what is the expected commitment fee in dollars?

    b. What is the expected dollar interest cost above the prime rate?

2. Assuming that annual lease payments are made in advance (an annuity due) and that there is no residual value, solve for the unknown in each of the following situations:

    a. For a purchase price of $46,000, an implicit interest rate of 11%, and a six-year lease period, solve for the annual lease payment.

    b. For a purchase price of $210,000, a five-year lease period, and annual lease payments of $47,030, solve for the implied interest rate.

    c. For an implied interest rate of 8%, a seven-year lease period, and annual lease payments of $16,000, solve for the purchase price.

    d. For a purchase price of $165,000, an implied interest rate of 10%, and annual lease payments of $24,412, solve for the lease period.

3. U.S. Blivet wishes to acquire a $100,000 blivet-degreasing machine, which has a useful life of eight years. At the end of this time, the machine's scrap value will be $8,000. The asset falls into the five-year property class for cost recovery (depreciation) purposes. The company can use either lease or debt financing. Lease payments of $16,000 at the beginning of each of the eight years would be required. If debt financed, the interest rate would be 14%, and debt payments would be due at the beginning of each of the eight years. (Interest would be amortized as a mortgage-type of debt instrument.) The company is in a 40% tax bracket. Which method of financing has the lower present value of cash outflows?

SOLUTIONS TO SELF-CORRECTION PROBLEMS

1. a. b. (in thousands)

	Year					
	Revolving Credit			Term Loan		
	1	2	3	4	5	6
Amount borrowed during year	$1,400	$3,000	$3,000	$3,000	$2,000	$1,000
Unused portion	1,600	0	0	0	1,000	2,000
Commitment fee (.005)	8	0	0	0	5	10
Interest cost above prime (1% first 3 years and 1.5% in last 3)	14	30	30	45	30	15

2. A generalized version of equation (2) as the formula is used throughout.

    a.

$$\$46,000 = X + X \left(PVIFA_{11\%, 5} \right)$$
$$\$46,000 = X + X \left(3.696 \right) = X \left(4.696 \right)$$
$$X = \$46,000/4.696 = \mathbf{\$9,796}$$

    b.

$$\$210,000 = \$47,030 / \left(1 + PVIFA_{X, 5} \right)$$
$$\$210,000/\$47,030 = \left(1 + PVIFA_{X, 5} \right) = 4.465$$

Subtracting 1 from this gives $PVIFA_{X,5} = 3.465$. Looking in Appendix E, across the *4-period row*, we find that 3.465 is the figure reported for 6%. Therefore, the implied interest rate, X, is *6%*.

c.
$$X = \$16,000 (1 + PVIFA_{8\%, 6})$$
$$X = \$16,000 (1 + 4.623) = \mathbf{\$89,968}$$

d.
$$\$165,000 = \$24,412 (1 + PVIFA_{10\%, X})$$
$$\$165,000/\$24,412 = (1 + PVIFA_{10\%, X}) = 6.759$$

Subtracting 1 from this gives 5.759. Looking in Appendix E in the *10% column*, we find that 5.759 corresponds to the *9-period row*. Therefore, the lease period is 9 + 1, or *10 years*.

3. Schedule of cash flows for the leasing alternative

End of Year	(a) Lease Payment	(b) Tax-Shield Benefits $(a)_{t-1} \times (.40)$	(c) CashOutflow after Taxes (a) – (b)	(d) Present Value of Cash Outflows (at 8.4%)
0	$16,000	—	$16,000	$16,000
1–7	16,000	$6,400	9,600	49,305*
8	—	6,400	(6,400)	(3,357)
				$61,948

*Total for years 1–7

The discount rate is the before-tax cost of borrowing times 1 minus the tax rate, or (14%) (1 – .40) = 8.4%.

Annual debt payment:

$$\$100,000 = X (1 + PVIFA_{14\%, 7})$$
$$\$100,000 = X (1 + 4.288) = X (5.288)$$
$$X = \$100,000/5.288 = \$18,910$$

Schedule of debt payments

End of Year	(a) Loan Payment	(b) Principal Amount Owing at End of Year $(b)_{t-1} - (a) + (c)$	(c) Annual Interest $(b)_{t-1} \times (.14)$
0	$18,910	$81,090	$ 0
1	18,910	73,533	11,353
2	18,910	64,917	10,295
3	18,910	55,096	9,088
4	18,910	43,899	7,713
5	18,910	31,135	6,146
6	18,910	16,584	4,359
7	18,906*	0	2,322

*The last payment is slightly lower due to rounding throughout.

Schedule of cash flows for the debt alternative

	(a)	(b)	(c)	(d)	(e) After-Tax	(f)
End of Year	Debt Payment	Annual Interest	Annual Depreciation	Tax-Shield Benefits (b + c) .40	Cash Flow (a) – (d)	PV of Cash Flows (at 8.4%)
0	$18,910	$ 0	$ 0	$ 0	$18,910	$18,910
1	18,910	11,353	20,000	12,541	6,369	5,875
2	18,910	10,295	32,000	16,918	1,992	1,695
3	18,910	9,088	19,200	11,315	7,693	5,962
4	18,910	7,713	11,520	7,693	11,217	8,124
5	18,910	6,146	11,520	7,066	11,844	7,913
6	18,910	4,359	5,760	4,048	14,862	9,160
7	18,906	2,322		929	17,977	10,222
8	(8,000)*			(3,200)**	(4,800)	(2,518)
			$100,000			$65,344

*Salvage value.
**Tax due to recapture of depreciation, ($8,000) (.40) = $3,200.

As the lease alternative has the lower present value of cash outflows, it is preferred.

QUESTIONS

1. What is the purpose of protective covenants in a term loan agreement?
2. How does a *revolving credit agreement* differ from a *line of credit?*
3. How should a lender go about setting (a) the working capital protective covenant in a loan agreement? (b) the capital expenditure covenant in a loan agreement?
4. As a borrower, how would you approach negotiating the working capital and capital expenditure restrictions a lender wished to impose?
5. What are the key financial institutions that provide intermediate-term financing to business firms?
6. How does a *chattel mortgage* differ from a *conditional sales contract* when it comes to financing equipment?
7. How does a *financial lease* differ from an *operating lease?* How does a *full-service* (or *maintenance*) *lease* differ from a *net lease?*
8. Contrast a *sale and leaseback* with *direct leasing.*
9. In general, how is lease financing treated from an accounting standpoint versus debt financing?
10. Discuss the probable impact that a sale and leaseback arrangement will have on the following:
    a. Liquidity ratios
    b. Return on investment
    c. Return on equity
    d. The risk class of the corporation's common stock
    e. The price of the corporation's common stock

11. Some business people consider that the risk of obsolescence and inflexibility is being transferred from the lessee to the lessor. How is the lessor induced to accept higher risk and greater inflexibility?

12. In your opinion, would the following factors tend to favor borrowing or leasing as a financing alternative? Why?
    a. Increased corporate tax rate
    b. Faster accelerated depreciation
    c. Rising price level
    d. Increased residual value of the leased asset
    e. An increase in the risk-free interest rate

PROBLEMS

1. Eva Forlines Fashions Corporation wishes to borrow $600,000 on a five-year term basis. Cattleperson's National Bank is willing to make such a loan at a 14% rate, provided the loan is completely amortized over the five-year period. Payments are due at the end of each of the five years. Set up an amortization schedule of equal annual loan payments that will satisfy these conditions. Be sure to show both the principal and interest components of each of the overall payments.

2. On January 1, Acme Aglet Corporation is contemplating a four-year, $3 million term loan from the Fidelity First National Bank. The loan is payable at the end of the fourth year and would involve a loan agreement that would contain a number of protective covenants. Among these restrictions are that the company must maintain net working capital (current assets minus current liabilities) of at least $3 million at all times, that it cannot take on any more long-term debt, that its total liabilities cannot be more than .6 of its total assets, and that capital expenditures in any year are limited to depreciation plus $3 million. The company's balance sheet at December 31, before the term loan, is as follows (in millions):

Current assets	$7	Current liabilities	$3
Net fixed assets	10	Long-term debt	
		(due in 8 years)	5
		Shareholders' equity	9
Total	$17	Total	$17

The proceeds of the term loan will be used to increase Acme Aglet's investment in inventories and accounts receivables in response to introducing a new "fit-to-be-tied" metal aglet. The company anticipates a subsequent need to grow at a rate of 24% a year, equally divided between current assets and net fixed assets. Profits after taxes of $1.5 million are expected this year, and these profits are expected to grow by $250,000 per year over the subsequent three years. The company pays no cash dividends and does not intend to pay any over the next four years. Depreciation in the past year was $2.5 million, and this is predicted to grow over the next four years at the same rate as the increase in net fixed assets.

Under the loan agreement, will the company be able to achieve its growth objective? Explain numerically.

3. Given the following information, compute the annual lease payment (paid in advance) that a lessor will require:

   a. Purchase price of $260,000, interest rate of 13%, five-year lease period, and no residual value
   b. Purchase price of $138,000, interest rate of 6%, nine-year lease period, and a near-certain residual value of $20,000
   c. Purchase price of $773,000, interest rate of 9%, ten-year lease period, and no residual value

4. Volt Electronics Company is considering leasing one of its products in addition to selling it outright to customers. The product, the Volt Tester, sells for $18,600 and has an economic life of eight years.

   a. To earn 12% interest, what annual lease payment must Volt require as lessor? (Assume that lease payments are payable in advance.)
   b. If the product has a salvage value (known with certainty) of $4,000 at the end of eight years, what annual lease payment will be required?

5. Fez Fabulous Fabrics wishes to acquire a $100,000 multifacet cutting machine. The machine has a useful life of eight years, after which there is no expected salvage value. If Fez were to finance the cutting machine by signing an eight-year lease contract, annual lease payments of $16,000 would be required, payable in advance. The company could also finance the purchase of the machine with a 12% term loan having a payment schedule of the same general configuration as the lease payment schedule. The asset falls in the five-year property class for cost recovery (depreciation) purposes, and the company has a 35% tax rate. What is the present value of cash outflows for each of these alternatives, using the after-tax cost of debt as the discount rate? Which alternative is preferred?

6. Valequez Ranches, Inc., wishes to acquire a mechanized feed spreader that costs $80,000. The ranch company intends to operate the equipment for five years, at which time it will need to be replaced. However, it is expected to have a salvage value of $10,000 at the end of the fifth year. The asset will be depreciated on a straight-line basis ($16,000 per year) over the five years, and Valequez Ranches is in a 30% tax bracket. Two means for financing the feed spreader are available. A lease arrangement calls for annual lease payments of $19,000, payable in advance. A debt alternative carries an interest cost of 10%. Debt payments will be made at the start of each of the five years using mortgage-type of debt amortization. Using the present value method, determine the best financing alternative.

7. The Locke Corporation has just leased a metal-bending machine that calls for annual lease payments of $30,000 payable in advance. The lease period is six years, and the lease is classified as a capital lease for accounting purposes. The company's incremental borrowing rate is 11%, whereas the lessor's implicit interest rate is 12%. Amortization of the lease in the first year amounts to $16,332. On the basis of this information, compute the following:

   a. The accounting lease liability that will be shown on the balance sheet immediately after the first lease payment.

b. The annual lease expense (amortization plus interest) in the first year as it will appear on the accounting income statement. (The interest expense is based on the accounting value determined in Part a.)

c. The annual lease expense for tax purposes.

ADDENDUM 23: ACCOUNTING TREATMENT OF LEASES

The accounting treatment of leases has undergone sweeping change over the past three decades. At one time leases were not disclosed in financial statements at all. Gradually lease disclosure was required and appeared first in the footnotes to the financial statements. With only minimal disclosure, leasing was attractive to certain firms as an "off-balance-sheet" method of financing. There is, however, no evidence that such financing had a favorable effect on company valuation, all other things the same. Nevertheless, many companies proceeded on the assumption that "off-balance-sheet" financing was a good thing. Then came the Financial Accounting Standards Board Statement No. 13 (called **FASB 13**) in 1976 with an explicit ruling which called for the capitalization on the balance sheet of certain types of leases.[4] In essence, this statement says that if the lessee acquires essentially all of the economic benefits and risks of the leased property, then the value of the asset along with the corresponding lease liability must be shown on the lessee's balance sheet.

Capital and Operating Leases

Leases that conform in principle to this definition are called *capital leases.* More specifically, a lease is regarded as a capital lease if it meets one or more of the following conditions:

1. The lease transfers ownership of the asset to the lessee by the end of the lease period.
2. The lease contains an option to purchase the asset at a bargain price.
3. The lease period equals 75% or more of the estimated economic life of the asset.
4. At the beginning of the lease, the present value of the minimum lease payments equals 90% or more of the fair market value of the leased asset.

If any of these conditions is met, the lessee is said to have acquired most of the economic benefits and risks associated with the leased property. Therefore, a capital lease is involved. If a lease does not meet any of these conditions, it is classified (for accounting purposes) as an *operating lease.*[5] Essentially, operating leases give the lessee the right to use the leased property over a period of time, but they do not give the lessee all of the benefits and risks that are associated with the asset.

---

[4]*Statement of Financial Accounting Standards No. 13, Accounting for Leases* (Stamford, CT: Financial Accounting Standards Board, November 1976).
[5]Earlier in this chapter, we used the term *operating lease* to describe a short-term lease. Accountants, however, would also apply this term to any (long-term) financial lease that did not technically qualify to be considered a capital lease.

Recording the value of a capital lease. With a capital lease, the lessee must report the value of the leased property on the asset side of the balance sheet. The amount reflected is the present value of the minimum lease payments over the lease period. If executory costs, such as insurance, maintenance, and taxes, are a part of the total lease payment, these are deducted, and only the remainder is used for purposes of calculating the present value. As required by the accounting rules, the discount rate employed is the lower of (1) the lessee's incremental borrowing rate or (2) the rate of interest implicit in the lease if, in fact, that rate can be determined.

The present value of the lease payments should be recorded as an asset on the lessee's balance sheet. (If the fair market value of the leased property is lower than the present value of the minimum lease payments, then the fair market value would be shown.) A corresponding liability is also recorded on the balance sheet, with the present value of payments due within one year being reflected as current liabilities and the present value of payments due after one year being shown as noncurrent liabilities. Information on leased property may be combined with similar information on assets that are owned, but there must be a disclosure in a footnote with respect to the value of the leased property and its amortization. The capital-lease-related portions of a hypothetical balance sheet might look like the following:

Assets		Liabilities	
Gross fixed assets[a]	$3,000,000	Current	
Less: accumulated		Obligations under	
depreciation end		capital leases	$90,000
amortization	1,000,000	Noncurrent	
Net fixed assets	$2,000,000	Obligations under	
		capital leases	$270,000

[a]Gross fixed assets include leased property of $500,000. Accumulated depreciation and amortization includes $140,000 in amortization associated with such property

Here we see in the footnote to the balance sheet information that the capitalized value of leases of the company is $500,000 less $140,000 in amortization, or $360,000 in total. The liability is split between $90,000 in current liabilities and $270,000 due beyond one year. In addition to this information, more details are required in footnotes. Relevant information here includes the gross amounts of leased property by major property categories (these can be combined with categories of owned assets); the total future minimum lease payments; a schedule, by years, of future lease payments required over the next five years; the total minimum sublease rentals to be received; the existence and terms of purchase or renewal options and escalation clauses; rentals that are contingent on some factor other than the passage of time; and any restrictions imposed in the lease agreements.

Disclosure of operating leases. For operating leases, as for capital leases, some of the same disclosure is required, but it can be in footnotes. For noncancellable leases having remaining terms in excess of one year, the lessee must disclose total future minimum lease payments; a schedule, by year, for the next five years plus a total figure for all years thereafter; the total sublease rentals to be received; the basis for contingent rental payments; the existence and terms of purchase and renewal options and escalation clauses; and any lease agreement restrictions. The last two categories are included in a general description of the leasing arrangement.

Amortizing the Capital Lease and Reducing the Obligation

A capital lease must be amortized and the liability reduced over the lease period. The method of amortization can be the lessee's usual depreciation method for assets that are owned. It should be pointed out that the period of amortization is always the lease term even if the economic life of the asset is longer. If the economic life is longer, the asset would have an expected residual value, which would go to the lessor. FASB 13 also requires that the capital lease obligation be reduced and expensed over the lease period by the "interest method." Under this method, each lease payment is separated into two components—the payment of principal and the payment of interest. The obligation is reduced by just the amount of the principal payment.

Reporting earnings.   For income reporting purposes, FASB 13 requires that both the amortization of the leased property and the annual interest embodied in the capital lease payment be treated as an expense. This expense is then deducted in the same way that any expense is to obtain net income. As you can appreciate, the accounting for leases can become quite complicated.

SELECTED REFERENCES

Arnold, Jasper H., III. "How to Negotiate a Term Loan." *Harvard Business Review* 60 (March–April, 1982), 131–38.

Bower, Richard S. "Issues in Lease Financing." *Financial Management* 2 (Winter 1973), 25–34.

_____, and George S. Oldfield, Jr. "Of Lessees, Lessors, and Discount Rates and Whether Pigs Have Wings." *Journal of Business Research* 9 (March 1981), 29–38.

Bower, Richard S., Frank C. Herringer, and J. Peter Williamson. "Lease Evaluation." *Accounting Review* 41 (April 1966), 257–65.

GE Capital: Guiding You Through the "Leasing Maze." Stamford, CT: General Electric Capital Corporation, 1992.

Gill, Richard C. "Term Loan Agreements." *Journal of Commercial Bank Lending* 62 (February 1980), 22–27.

Hull, John C. "The Bargaining Positions of the Parties to a Lease Agreement." *Financial Management* 11 (Autumn 1982), 71–79.

Lease, Ronald C., John J. McConnell, and James S. Shallheim. "Realized Returns and the Default and Prepayment Experience of Financial Leasing Contracts." *Financial Management* 19 (Summer 1990), 11–20.

Lewellen, Wilbur G., and Douglas R. Emery. "On the Matter of Parity Among Financial Obligations." *Journal of Finance* 36 (March 1981), 97–111.

Lewellen, Wilbur G., Michael S. Long, and John J. McConnell. "Asset Leasing in Competitive Capital Markets." *Journal of Finance* 31 (June 1976), 787–98.

Lummer, Scott L., and John J. McConnell. "Further Evidence on the Bank Lending Process and the Capital-Market Response to Bank Loan Agreements." *Journal of Financial Economics* 25 (November 1989), 99–122.

McConnell, John J., and James S. Schallheim. "Valuation of Asset Leasing Contracts." *Journal of Financial Economics* 12 (August 1983), 237–61.

McDaniel, Morey W. "Are Negative Pledge Clauses in Public Debt Issues Obsolete?" *Business Lawyer* 38 (May 1983), 867–81.

Miller, Merton H., and Charles W. Upton. "Leasing, Buying, and the Cost of Capital Services." *Journal of Finance* 31 (June 1976), 787–98.

Myers, Stewart C., David A. Dill, and Alberto J. Bautista. "Valuation of Financial Lease Contracts." *Journal of Finance* 31 (June 1976), 799–820.

Slovin, Myron B., Marie E. Sushka, and John A. Polonchek. "Corporate Sale-and-Leasebacks and Shareholder Wealth." *Journal of Finance* 45 (March 1990), 289–99.

Van Horne, James. "A Linear-Programming Approach to Evaluating Restrictions under a Bond Indenture or Loan Agreement." *Journal of Financial and Quantitative Analysis* 1 (June 1966), 68–83.

_____. "The Cost of Leasing with Capital Market Imperfections." *Engineering Economist* 23 (Fall 1977), 1–12.

Weingartner, H. Martin. "Leasing, Asset Lives and Uncertainty: Guides to Decision Making." *Financial Management* 16 (Summer 1987), 5–12.

CHAPTER 24

Valuing
Long-Term Debt

What determines the value or price of an asset, such as a bond or stock or land? Why does the value of an asset change so radically at times? For example, why did IBM common stock sell for about $100 in 1992 but for only $50 in early 1993? Knowing the fair value or price of an asset is no easy matter. The *Maxims* of the French writer La Rouchefoucauld, written over three centuries ago, still speak to us: "The greatest of all gifts is the power to estimate things at their true worth."

In this chapter we examine the concepts of and procedures for valuing an asset and apply these ideas to valuing bonds, one form of a company's long-term debt.

Understanding how to value financial securities is essential if managers are to meet the objective of maximizing the value of the firm. If they are to maximize the investor's value, they must know what drives the value of an asset. Specifically, they need to understand how bonds and stocks are valued in the marketplace; otherwise, they cannot act in the best interest of the firm's investors.

In this chapter, we will undertake to do the following:

1. Examine a variety of definitions given for the term value, including book value, liquidation value, market value, and intrinsic value.
2. Explain the basic process for valuing an asset.
3. Develop an understanding of the characteristics of bonds.
4. Describe the different types of bonds.
5. Learn how to value bonds.
6. Examine the concept of the bondholder's *expected* rate of return.
7. Explain three important relationships that exist in bond valuation.

DEFINITIONS OF VALUE

The term *value* is often used in different contexts, depending on its application. Examples of different uses of this term include the following:

Book value is the value of an asset as shown on a firm's balance sheet. It represents the historical cost of the asset rather than its current worth. For instance, the book value of a company's preferred stock is the amount the investors originally paid for the stock and therefore the amount the firm received when the stock was issued.

Liquidation value is the dollar sum that could be realized if an asset were sold individually and not as part of a going concern. For example, if a firm's operations were discontinued and its assets were divided up and sold, the sales price would represent the asset's liquidation value.

Market value of an asset is the observed value for the asset in the marketplace. This value is determined by supply and demand forces working together in the marketplace, where buyers and sellers negotiate a mutually acceptable price for the asset. For instance, the market price for Ford common stock on March 22, 1993, was $52. This price was reached by a large number of buyers and sellers working through the New York Stock Exchange. In theory, a market price exists for all assets. However, many assets have no readily observable market price because trading seldom occurs. For instance, the market price for the common stock of Blanks Engraving, a Dallas-based family-owned firm, would be more difficult to establish than the market value of J. C. Penney's common stock.

The intrinsic or economic value of an asset can be defined as the present value of the asset's expected future cash flows. This value is the amount the investor considers to be a **fair value**, given the amount, timing, and riskiness of future cash flows. Once the investor has estimated the intrinsic value of a security, this value could be compared with its market value when available. If the intrinsic value is greater than the market value, then the security is undervalued in the eyes of the investor. Should the market value exceed the investor's intrinsic value, then the security is overvalued.

We hasten to add that if the securities market is working efficiently, the market value and the intrinsic value of a security will be equal. Whenever a security's intrinsic value differs from its current market price, the competition among investors seeking opportunities to make a profit will quickly drive the market price back to its intrinsic value. Thus, we may define an **efficient market** as one in which the values of all securities at any instant fully reflect all available public information, which results in the market value and the intrinsic value being the same. If the markets are efficient, it is extremely difficult for an investor to make extra profits from an ability to predict prices.

The idea of market efficiency has been the backdrop for and battle between professional investors and university professors. The academic community has contended that someone throwing darts at the list of securities in *The Wall Street Journal* could do as well as a professional money manager. Market professionals retort that academicians are grossly mistaken in this view. The war has been intense but also one that the student of finance should find intriguing, and it can be followed each month in *The Wall Street Journal*, where the investment performance of dart throwers and different professional investors are compared. Through March 1993, there had been 34 contests between these rivals. The score: Nineteen for the professional managers and 15 for the dart throwers.

VALUATION: AN OVERVIEW

For our purposes, *the value of an asset is its intrinsic value or the present value of its expected future cash flows,* where these cash flows are discounted back to the present using the investor's required rate of return. This statement is true for valuing all assets and serves as the basis of almost all that we do in finance. Thus, value is affected by three elements:

1. The amount and timing of the asset's expected cash flows
2. The riskiness of these cash flows
3. The investor's required rate of return for undertaking the investment

The first two factors are characteristics of the asset; the third one, the required rate of return, is the minimum rate of return necessary to attract an investor to purchase or hold a security. This rate must be high enough to compensate the investor for the risk perceived in the asset's future cash flows.

Figure 24-1 depicts the basic factors involved in valuation. As the figure shows, finding the value of an asset involves:

1. Assessing the asset's characteristics, which include the amount and timing of the expected cash flows and the riskiness of these cash flows;

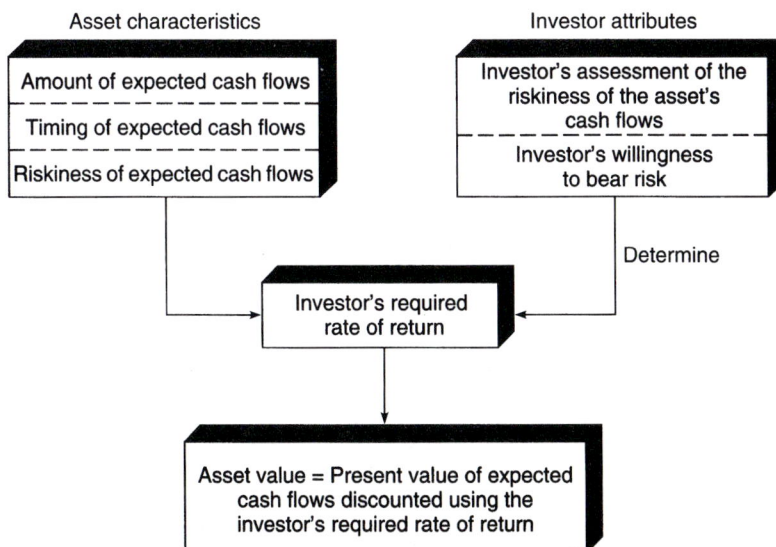

FIGURE 24-1
Basic Factors Determining an Asset's Value

2. Determining the investor's required rate of return, which embodies the investor's attitude about assuming risk and perception of the riskiness of the asset; and
3. Discounting the expected cash flows back to the present, using the investor's required rate of return as the discount rate.

VALUATION: THE BASIC PROCESS

The valuation process can be described as follows: It is assigning value to an asset by calculating the present value of its expected future cash flows using the investor's required rate of return as the discount rate. The investor's required rate of return, k, is determined by the level of the risk-free rate of interest and the risk premium that the investor feels is necessary to compensate for the risks assumed in owning the asset. Therefore, a basic security valuation model can be defined mathematically as follows:

$$V = \frac{C_1}{(1+k)^1} + \frac{C_2}{(1+k)^2} + \ldots + \frac{C_n}{(1+k)^n} \qquad (1)$$

or

$$V = \sum_{t=1}^{n} \frac{C_t}{(1+k)^t}$$

where C_t = cash flow to be received at time t.
   V = the intrinsic value or present value of an asset producing expected future cash flows, C_t, in years 1 through n.
   k = the investor's required rate of return.

Using equation (1), there are three basic steps in the valuation process:

Step 1: Estimate the C_t in equation (1), which is the amount and timing of the future cash flows the security is expected to provide.
Step 2: Determine k, the investor's required rate of return.
Step 3: Calculate the intrinsic value, V, as the present value of expected future cash flows discounted at the investor's required rate of return.

Equation (1), which measures the present value of future cash flows, is the basis of the valuation process. If we understand equation (1), all the valuation work we do, and a host of other topics as well, will be much clearer in our minds. With the foregoing brief but important principles of valuation as our foundation, let's now look at the nature of bonds and how they are valued.

TERMINOLOGY AND CHARACTERISTICS OF BONDS

Before applying our valuation expertise to valuing bonds, we first need to understand the terminology related to bonds. Also, we should be apprised of the different types of bonds that exist. Then we will be better prepared to determine the value of a bond.

When a firm or nonprofit institution needs financing, one source is **bonds.** This type of financing instrument is simply a long-term promissory note, issued by the borrower, promising to pay its holder a predetermined and fixed amount of interest each year. Some of the more important terms and characteristics that you might hear about bonds are as follows:

- Claims on assets and income
- Par value
- Coupon interest rate
- Maturity
- Indenture
- Current yield
- Bond ratings

Let's consider each in turn.

Claims on Assets and Income

In the case of insolvency, claims of debt in general, including bonds, are honored before those of both common stock and preferred stock. However, different types of debt may also have a hierarchy among themselves as to the order of their claim on assets.

Bonds also have a claim on income that comes ahead of common and preferred stock. In general, if interest on bonds is not paid, the bond trustees can classify the firm insolvent and force it into bankruptcy. Thus, the bondholder's claim on income is more likely to be honored than that of common and preferred stockholders, whose dividends are paid at the discretion of the firm's management.

Par Value

The **par value** of a bond is its face value that is returned to the bondholder at maturity. In general, corporate bonds are issued in denominations of $1,000, although there are some exceptions to this rule. Also, when bond prices are quoted, either by financial managers or in the financial press, prices are generally expressed as a percentage of the bond's par value. For example, a Detroit Edison bond that pays $90 per year interest and matures in 1999 was recently quoted in *The Wall Street Journal* as selling for 95 1/8. That does not mean you can buy the bond for $95.125. It means that this bond is selling for 95 1/8% of its par value of $1,000. Hence, the market price of this bond is actually $951.25. At maturity in 1999, the bondholder will receive the $1,000.

Coupon Interest Rate

The *coupon interest rate* on a bond indicates the percentage of the par value of the bond that will be paid out annually in the form of interest. Thus, regardless of what happens to the price of a bond with an 8% coupon interest rate and a $1,000 par value, it will pay out $80 annually in interest until maturity (.08 × $1,000 = $80).

Maturity

The **maturity** of a bond indicates the length of time until the bond issuer returns the par value to the bondholder and terminates or redeems the bond.

Indenture

An **indenture** is the legal agreement between the firm issuing the bonds and the bond trustee who represents the bondholders. The indenture provides the specific terms of the loan agreement, including a description of the bonds, the rights of the bondholders, the rights of the issuing firm, and the responsibilities of the trustee. This legal document may run 100 pages or more in length, with the majority of it devoted to defining protective provisions for the bondholder. The bond trustee, usually a banking institution or trust company, is then assigned the task of overseeing the relationship between the bondholder and the issuing firm, protecting the bondholder, and seeing that the terms of the indenture are carried out.

Typically, the restrictive provisions included in the indenture attempt to protect the bondholder's financial position relative to that of other outstanding securities. Common provisions involve (1) prohibitions on the sale of accounts receivable, (2) constraints on the issuance of common stock dividends, (3) restrictions on the purchase or sale of fixed assets, and (4) constraints on additional borrowing. Prohibitions on the sale of accounts receivable are specified because such sales would benefit the firm's short-run liquidity position at the expense of its future liquidity position. Constraints on common stock dividends generally mean limiting their issuance when working capital falls below a specified level, or simply limiting the maximum dividend payout to some fraction, say 50% or 60% of earnings under any circumstance. Fixed-asset restrictions generally require lender permission before the liquidation of any fixed asset or prohibit the use of any existing fixed asset as collateral on new loans. Constraints on additional borrowing are usually in the form of restrictions or limitations on the amount and type of additional long-term debt that can be issued. All these restrictions have one thing in common: They attempt to prohibit action that would improve the status of other securities at the expense of bonds and to protect the status of bonds from being weakened by any managerial action.

Current Yield

The **current yield** on a bond refers to the ratio of the annual interest payment to the bond's current market price. If, for example, we have a bond with an 8% coupon interest rate, a par value of $1,000, and a market price of $700, it would have a current yield of

$$\text{current yield} = \frac{\text{annual interest payments}}{\text{market price of the bond}} \tag{2}$$

$$= \frac{.08 \times \$1,000}{\$700} = \frac{\$80}{\$700} = 0.114 = 11.4\%$$

Bond Ratings

John Moody first began to rate bonds in 1909; since that time three rating agencies—Moody's, Standard and Poor's, and Fitch Investor Services—have provided ratings on corporate bonds. These ratings involve a judgment about the future risk potential of the bond. Although they deal with expectations, several historical factors seem to play a significant role in their determination.[1] Bond ratings are favorably affected by (1) a greater reliance on equity then debt in financing the firm, (2) profitable operations, (3) a low variability in past earnings, (4) large firm size, and (5) little use of subordinated debt. (Subordinated debt will be described shortly.) In turn, the rating a bond receives affects the rate of return demanded on the bond by the investors. The poorer the bond rating, the higher the rate of return demanded in the capital markets. Figure 24-2 provides an example and description of these ratings. Thus, for the financial manager, bond ratings are extremely important. They provide an indicator of default risk that in turn affects the rate of return that must be paid on borrowed funds.

Having an understanding of the basic terms and characteristics of bonds in general, we can now consider the different types of bonds that companies use in funding their debt needs.

TYPES OF BONDS

Whereas the term *bond* may be defined simply as long-term debt, there are a variety of such creatures. Just to mention a few, we have

- debentures
- subordinated debentures
- mortgage bonds
- Eurobonds
- zero and very low coupon bonds
- junk bonds

We will briefly explain each of these types of bonds.

Debentures

The term **debenture** applies to any unsecured long-term debt. Because these bonds are unsecured, the earning ability of the issuing corporation is of great concern to the bondholder. They are also viewed as being more risky than secured bonds and as a result must provide investors with a higher yield than secured bonds provide. Often the issuing firm attempts to provide some protection to the holder through the prohibition of any additional encumbrance of assets. This prohibits the future issuance of secured long-term debt that would further tie up the firm's assets and leave the

---

[1]See Thomas F. Pogue and Robert M. Soldofsky "What's in a Bond Rating?" *Journal of Financial and Quantitative Analysis,* 4 (June 1969), pp. 201–28; and George E. Pinches and Kent A. Mingo, "A Multivariate Analysis of Industrial Bond Ratings," *Journal of Finance,* 28 (March 1973), pp. 1–18.

FIGURE 24-2   Standard and Poor's Corporate Bond Ratings

AAA   This is the highest rating assigned by Standard and Poor's for debt obligation and indicates an extremely strong capacity to pay principal and interest.

AA   Bonds rated AA also qualify as high-quality debt obligations. Their capacity to pay principal and interest is very strong, and in the majority of instances they differ from AAA issues only in small degree.

A   Bonds rated A have a strong capacity to pay principal and interest, although they are somewhat more susceptible to the adverse effects of changes in circumstances and economic conditions.

BBB   Bonds rated BBB are regarded as having an adequate capacity to pay principal and interest. Whereas they normally exhibit adequate protection parameters, adverse economic conditions or changing circumstances are more likely to lead to a weakened capacity to pay principal and interest for bonds in this category than for bonds in the A category.

BB
B   Bonds rated BB, B, CCC, and CC are regarded, on balance, as predominantly speculative with
CCC   respect to the issuer's capacity to pay interest and repay principal in accordance with the terms
CC   of the obligation. BB indicates the lowest degree of speculation and CC the highest. While such bonds will likely have some quality and protective characteristics, these are outweighed by large uncertainties or major risk exposures to adverse conditions.

C   The rating C is reserved for income bonds on which no interest is being paid.

D   Bonds rated D are in default, and payment of principal and/or interest is in arrears.

Plus (+) or Minus (−): To provide more detailed indications of credit quality, the ratings from "AA" to "BB" may be modified by the addition of a plus or minus sign to show relative standing within the major rating categories.

Source: *Standard and Poor's Fixed Income Investor*, Vol. 8 (1980). Reprinted by permission.

bondholders less protected. To the issuing firm, the major advantage of debentures is that no property has to be secured by them. This allows the firm to issue debt and still preserve some future borrowing power.

Subordinated Debentures

Many firms have more than one issue of debentures outstanding. In this case a hierarchy may be specified, in which some debentures are given subordinated standing in case of insolvency. The claims of the **subordinated debentures** are honored only after the claims of secured debt and unsubordinated debentures have been satisfied.

Mortgage Bonds

A **mortgage bond** is a bond secured by a lien on real property. Typically, the value of the real property is greater than that of the mortgage bonds issued. This provides the mortgage bondholders with a margin of safety in the event the market value of the secured property declines. In the case of foreclosure, the trustees have the power to sell the secured property and use the proceeds to pay the bondholders. In the event that the proceeds from this sale do not cover the bonds, the bondholders become general creditors, similar to debenture bondholders, for the unpaid portion of the debt.

Eurobonds

Eurobonds are not so much a different type of security as they are securities, in this case bonds, issued in a country different from the one in whose currency the bond is denominated. For example, a bond that is issued in Europe or in Asia by an American company and that pays interest and principal to the lender in U.S. dollars would be considered a Eurobond. Thus, even if the bond is not issued in Europe, it merely needs to be sold in a country different from the one in whose currency it is denominated to be considered a Eurobond. The Eurobond market actually had its roots in the 1950s and 1960s as the U.S. dollar became increasingly popular because of its role as the primary international reserve. In recent years, as the U.S. dollar has gained a reputation for being one of the most stable currencies, demand for Eurobonds has increased. The primary attractions to borrowers, aside from favorable rates, in the Eurobonds market are the relative lack of regulation (Eurobonds are not registered with the Securities and Exchange Commission, or SEC), less rigorous disclosure requirements than those of the SEC, and the speed with which they can be issued. Interestingly, not only are Eurobonds not registered with the SEC, but U.S. citizens and residents may not be offered them during their initial distribution.

Zero and Very Low Coupon Bonds

Zero and **very low coupon bonds** allow the issuing firm to issue bonds at a substantial discount from their $1,000 face value with a zero or very low coupon rate. The investor receives a large part (or all on the zero coupon bond) of the return from the appreciation of the bond. For example, in April 1983 Homestead Savings issued $60 million of debt maturing in 1995 with a zero coupon rate. These bonds were sold at a 75% discount from their par value; that is, investors only paid $250 for a bond with a $1,000 par value. Investors who purchased these bonds for $250 and hold them until they mature in 1995 will receive a 12.25% yield to maturity, with all of this yield coming from appreciation of the bond. Homestead Savings, on the other hand, will have no cash outflows until these bonds mature; however, at that time it will have to pay back $60 million even though it only received $15 million when the bonds were first issued.

As with any form of financing, there are both advantages and disadvantages of issuing zero or very low coupon bonds. The disadvantages are, first (as already mentioned), when the bonds mature Homestead Savings will face an extremely large cash outflow, much greater than the cash inflow it experienced when the bonds were first issued. Second, discount bonds are not callable and can only be retired at maturity. Thus, if interest rates fall, Homestead Savings cannot benefit by requiring the investors to sell their bonds back to the company. The advantages of zero and low coupon bonds are, first, that annual cash outflows associated with interest payments do not occur with zero coupon bonds and are at a relatively low level with low coupon bonds. Second, because there is relatively strong investor demand for this type of debt, prices tend to be bid up and yields tend to be bid down. That is to say, Homestead Savings was able to issue zero coupon bonds at about half a percent less than it would have been if they had been traditional coupon bonds. Finally, Homestead Savings is able to deduct the annual amortization of the discount from taxable income, which will provide a positive annual cash flow to Homestead.

Junk Bonds

Junk or **low-rated bonds** are bonds rated BB or below. Originally, the term was used to describe bonds issued by "fallen angels"; that is, firms with sound financial histories that were facing severe financial problems and suffering from poor credit ratings. Today, **junk bonds** refers to any bond with a low rating. The major participants in this market are new firms that do not have an established record of performance, although junk bonds have been issued to finance corporate buyouts. Still, the backbone of the junk bond market involves young firms without established records of performance. Before the mid-1970s these new firms simply did not have access to the capital markets because of the reluctance of investors to accept speculative grade bonds. However, by the late 1980s, junk bonds grew to the point that they represented between 10% and 20% of the total public bond issuances by U.S. corporations. As the economy slowed in the late 1980s and early 1990s, junk bonds were issued less frequently. This growth is illustrated in Figure 24-3, which shows the proliferation of new issues of junk bonds. Today, with the leveraged buyout movement of the late 1980s over, junk bonds play a smaller role in corporate finance than they had. The bankruptcy of Drexel, Burnham, Lambert; the jailing of the "king of junk bonds,"

FIGURE 24-3	New Issues of Junk Bonds (Billions of Dollars)					
Year	(1) Newly Issued Public Straight Junk Bonds[a]	(2) Exchange Offers and Private Issues Going Public[b]	(3) Total Junk Bond Issuance (1) + (2)	(4) Total Public Bond Issues by U.S. Corporations[b]	(5) (1) as % of (4)	(6) (3) as % of (4)
1987	28.9	n.a.	n.a.	219.1	13.2	n.a.
1986	34.3	11.3	45.6	232.5	14.8	19.6
1985	15.4	4.4	19.8	119.6	12.9	16.6
1984	14.8	0.9	15.7	73.6	20.1	21.3
1983	8.0	0.5	8.5	47.6	16.8	17.9
1982	2.7	0.5	3.2	44.3	6.1	7.2
1981	1.4	0.3	1.7	38.1	3.7	4.5
1980	1.4	0.7	2.1	41.6	3.4	5.0
1979	1.4	0.3	1.7	25.8	5.4	6.6
1978	1.5	0.7	2.2	19.8	7.6	11.1
1977	0.6	0.5	1.1	24.1	2.5	4.6

[a]From Drexel, Burnham, Lambert (1987). The 1987 figure from *Investment Dealer's Digest*.
[b]From *Federal Reserve Bulletin*.

Source: Kevin J. Perry and Robert A. Taggart, Jr., "The Growing Role of Junk Bonds," *Journal of Applied Corporate Finance*, 1 (Spring 1988), p. 38.

(A) Cash Flow Information

Periodic interest payments
For example, $65 per year

Principal amount or par value
For example, $1000

(B) Term to Maturity

For example, 12 years

(C) Investor's Required Rate of Return

For example, 8 percent

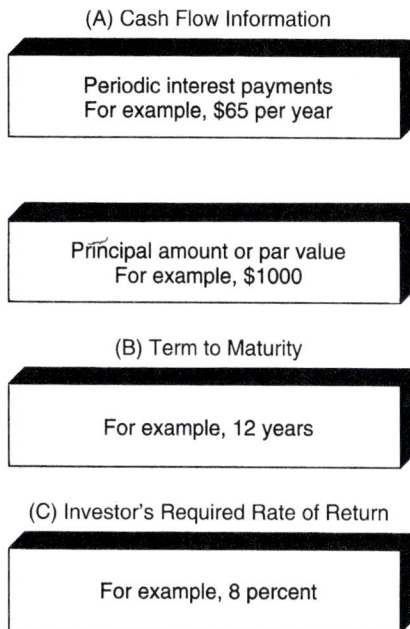

FIGURE 24-4
Data Requirements for Bond Valuation

Michael Milken; and the realization that high leverage is dangerous have all contributed to a shrinkage of this market. However, as we look forward to the mid- and late-1990s and the century ahead it appears that although the role of junk bonds may be reduced, they will continue to play an important role for new firms raising capital for the first time.

Because junk bonds are of speculative grade, they carry a coupon interest rate of between 3% to 5% more than AAA grade long-term debt.

Having an understanding of the basic characteristics of bonds, we will now turn our attention to valuing a bond.

BOND VALUATION

The valuation process for a bond, as depicted in Figure 24-4, requires knowledge of three essential elements: (1) the amount of the cash flows to be received by the investor, (2) the maturity date of the loan, and (3) the investor's required rate of return. The amount of cash flows is dictated by the periodic interest to be received and by the par value to be paid at maturity. Given these elements, we can compute the value of the bond, or the present value.

Consider a bond issued by Alaska Airlines in 1984 with a maturity date of 2014 and a stated coupon rate of 6.875%.[2] In late 1992, with 22 years left to maturity, investors owning the bonds were requiring an 8.5% rate of return. We can calculate the value of the bonds to these investors using the following three-step valuation procedure:

[2]Alaska Airlines remits the interest to its bondholders on a semiannual basis on January 15 and July 15. However, for the moment assume the interest is to be received annually. The effect of semiannual payments will be examined later.

Step 1:   Estimate the amount and timing of the expected future cash flows. Two types of cash flows are received by the bondholder:

a.   Annual interest payments equal to the coupon rate of interest times the face value of the bond. In this example the interest payments equal $68.75 = .06875 × $1,000. Assuming that 1992 interest payments have already been made, these cash flows will be received by the bondholder in each of the 22 years before the bond matures (1993 through 2014 = 22 years).

b.   The face value of the bond of $1,000 to be received in 2014. To summarize, the cash flows received by the bondholder are as follows:

Years	1	2	3	4	...	21	22
	$68.75	$68.75	$68.75	$68.75	...	$68.75	$68.75 +$1,000.00 $1,068.75

Step 2:   Determine the investor's required rate of return by evaluating the riskiness of the bond's future cash flows. An 8.5% required rate of return for the bondholders is given. The investor's required rate of return is equal to a rate earned on a risk-free security plus a risk premium for assuming risk.

Step 3:   Calculate the intrinsic value of the bond as the present value of the expected future interest and principal payments discounted at the investor's required rate of return.

The present value of Alaska Airline's bonds is found as follows:

$$\text{bond value} = V_b = \frac{\$ \text{ interest in year 1}}{\left(1 + \text{required rate of return}\right)^1}$$

$$+ \frac{\$ \text{ interest in year 2}}{\left(1 + \text{required rate of return}\right)^2}$$

$$+ \ldots + \frac{\$ \text{ interest in year 22}}{\left(1 + \text{required rate of return}\right)^{22}}$$

$$+ \frac{\$ \text{ par value of bond}}{\left(1 + \text{required rate of return}\right)^{22}}$$

or, summing over the interest payments,

$$V_b = \sum_{t=1}^{22} \underbrace{\frac{\$ \text{ interest in year } t}{\left(1 + \text{required rate of return}\right)^t}}_{\text{present value of interest}} + \underbrace{\frac{\$ \text{ par value of bond}}{\left(1 + \text{required rate of return}\right)^{22}}}_{\text{present value of par value}}$$

Using I_t to represent the interest payment in year t, M to represent the bond's maturity (or par) value, and k_b to equal the bondholder's required rate of return, we may express the value of a bond maturing in year n as follows:

$$V_b = \sum_{t=1}^{n} \frac{\$I_t}{(1+k_b)^t} + \frac{\$M}{(1+k_b)^n} \tag{3a}$$

Finding the value of the Alaska Airlines bonds may be represented graphically as follows:

Year	0	1	2	3	4	5	6	...	22
Dollars received at end of year		$68.75	$68.75	$68.75	$68.75	$68.75	$68.75	...	$68.75 $1,000.00 $1,068.75
Present Value	$840.59								

Thus, if investors consider 8.5% to be an appropriate required rate of return in view of the risk level associated with Alaska Airline's bonds, paying a price of $840.59 would satisfy their return requirement.

Semiannual Interest Payments

In the preceding illustration, the interest payments were assumed to be paid annually. However, companies typically pay interest to bondholders semiannually. For example, rather than disbursing $68.75 in interest at the conclusion of each year, Alaska Airlines pays $34.375 (half of $68.75) on January 15 and July 15.

Several steps are involved in adapting equation (3a) for semiannual interest payments. First, thinking in terms of *periods* instead of years, a bond with a life of n years paying interest semiannually has a life of $2n$ periods. In other words, a five-year bond ($n = 5$) that remits its interest on a semiannual basis actually makes 10 payments. Yet although the number of periods has doubled, the *dollar* amount of interest being sent to the investors for each period and the bondholders' required rate of return are half of the equivalent annual figures. I_t becomes $I_t/2$ and k_b is changed to $k_b/2$; thus, for semiannual compounding, equation (3a) becomes

$$V_b = \sum_{t=1}^{2n} \frac{\$I_t/2}{\left(1 + \dfrac{k_b}{2}\right)^t} + \frac{\$M}{\left(1 + \dfrac{k_b}{2}\right)^{2n}} \tag{3b}$$

BONDHOLDERS' EXPECTED RATES OF RETURN (YIELD TO MATURITY)

Theoretically, each investor could have a different required rate of return for a particular security. However, the financial manager is only interested in the required rate of return that is implied by the market prices of the firm's securities. In other words, the consensus of a firm's investors about the expected rate of return is reflected in the current market price of the stock.

To measure the bondholder's expected rate of return $\hat{k}_b$, we would find the discount rate that equates the present value of the future cash flows (interest and maturity value) with the current market price of the bond.[3] The expected rate of return for a bond is also the rate of return the investor will earn if the bond is held to maturity, or the **yield to maturity.** Thus, when referring to bonds, the terms *expected rate of return* and *yield to maturity* are often used interchangeably.

To illustrate this concept, consider the Brister Corporation's bonds, which are selling for $1,100. The bonds carry a coupon interest rate of 9% and mature in 10 years. (Remember the coupon rate determines the interest payment—coupon rate × par value.)

In determining the **expected rate of return** ($\hat{k}_b$), implicit in the current market price, we need to find the rate that discounts the anticipated cash flows back to a present value of $1,100, the existing market price (P_0) for the bond.

Finding the expected rate of return for a bond using the present value tables is done by trial and error. We have to keep trying new rates until we find the discount rate that results in the present value of the future interest and maturity value of the bond just equaling the current market value of the bond. If the expected rate is somewhere between rates in the present value tables, we then must interpolate between the rates.

For our example, if we try 7%, the bond's present value is $1,140.16. Since the present value of $1,140. 16 is greater than the market price of $1,100, we should next try a higher rate. Increasing the discount rate, say, to 8% gives a present value of $1,066.90. (These computations are shown below.) Now the present value is less than the market price; thus, we know that the investor's expected rate of return is between 7% and 8%.

		7%		8%	
Years	Cash Flow	Present Value Factors	Present Value	Present Value Factors	Present Value
1–10	$ 90 per year	7.024	$ 632.16	6.710	$ 603.90
10	$1,000 in year 10	0.508	508.00	0.463	463.00
		Present value at 7%:	**$1,140.16**	Present value at 8%:	**$1,066.90**

Because we now know the rate is between 7% and 8%, we may interpolate to find the expected return. The process is as follows:

Rate	Value	Differences in Value	
7%	$1,140.16		
		$40.16	
$\hat{k}_b$	1,100.00		$73.26
8%	1,066.90		

---

[3]When we speak of computing an expected rate of return, we are not describing the situation very accurately. Expected rates of return are ex ante (before the fact) and are based on "expected and unobservable future cash flows" and, therefore, can only be "estimated."

Solving for $\hat{k}_b$ by interpolation, we have:

$$\hat{k}_b = 7\% + \left(\frac{\$40.16}{\$73.26}\right)(8\% - 7\%) = 7.55\%$$

Thus, the expected rate of return on the Brister Corporation's bonds for an investor who purchases the bonds for $1,100 is approximately 7.55%.

BOND VALUATION: THREE IMPORTANT RELATIONSHIPS

We have now learned to find the value of a bond (V_b), given (1) the amount of interest payments (I_t), (2) the maturity value (M), (3) the length of time to maturity (n years), and (4) the investor's required rate of return, k_b. We also know how to compute the expected rate of return ($\hat{k}_b$), which also happens to be the current interest rate on the bond, given (1) the current market value (P_0), (2) the amount of interest payments (I_t), (3) the maturity value (M), and (4) the length of time to maturity (n years). We now have the basics. But let's go further in our understanding of bond valuation by studying several important relationships.

First Relationship

The value of a bond is inversely related to changes in the investor's present required rate of return (the current interest rate). In other words, as interest rates increase (decrease), the value of the bond decreases (increases).

To illustrate, assume that an investor's required rate of return for a given bond is 12%. The bond has a par value of $1,000 and annual interest payments of $120, indicating a 12% coupon interest rate ($120 ÷ $1,000 = 12%). Assuming a five-year maturity date, the bond would be worth $1,000, computed as follows:

$$V_b = \frac{I_1}{\left(1 + k_b\right)^1} + \ldots + \frac{I_n}{\left(1 + k_b\right)^n} + \frac{M}{\left(1 + k_b\right)^n} \tag{3a}$$

$$= \sum_{t=1}^{n} \frac{I_t}{\left(1 + k_b\right)^t} + \frac{M}{\left(1 + k_b\right)^n}$$

$$= \sum_{t=1}^{5} \frac{\$120}{\left(1 + .12\right)^t} + \frac{\$1,000}{\left(1 + .12\right)^5}$$

Using present value tables we have:

$$V_b = \$120 \, (PVIFA_{12\%, \, 5\,yr}) + \$1,000 \, (PVIF_{12\%, \, 5\,yr})$$
$$V_b = \$120 \, (3.605) + \$1,000 \, (.567)$$
$$= \$432.60 + \$567.00$$
$$= \$999.60 \cong \$1,000,00$$

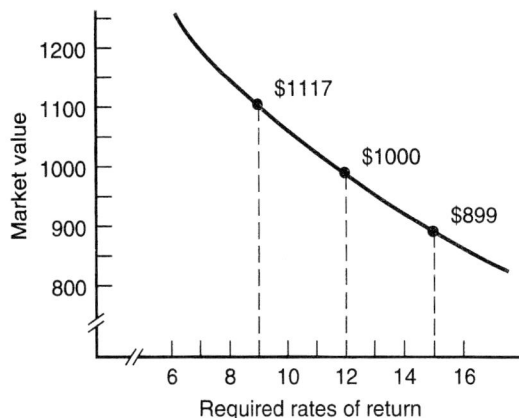

FIGURE 24-5
Value and Required Rates for a 5-Year Bond at 12% Coupon Rate

If, however, the investor's required rate of return increases from 12% to 15%, the value of the bond would decrease to $899.24, computed as follows:

$$V_b = \$120 \ (PVIFA_{15\%, \ 5 \ yr}) + \$1,000 \ (PVIF_{15\%, \ 5 \ yr})$$
$$V_b = \$120 \ (3.352) + \$1,000 \ (.497)$$
$$= \$402.24 + \$497.00$$
$$= \$899.24$$

On the other hand, if the investor's required rate of return decreases to 9%, the bond would increase in value to $1,116.80:

$$V_b = \$120 \ (PVIFA_{9\%, \ 5 \ yr}) + \$1,000 \ (PVIF_{9\%, \ 5 \ yr})$$
$$V_b = \$120 \ (3.890) + \$1,000 \ (.650)$$
$$= \$466.80 + \$650.00$$
$$= \$1,116.80$$

This inverse relationship between the investor's required rate of return and the value of a bond is presented in Figure 24-5. Clearly, as an investor demands a higher rate of return, the value of the bond decreases. The higher rate of return the investor desires can be achieved only by paying less for the bond. Conversely, a lower required rate of return yields a higher market value for the bond.

Changes in bond prices represent an element of uncertainty for the bond investor. If the current interest rate (required rate of return) changes, the price of the bond also fluctuates. An increase in interest rates causes the bondholder to incur a loss in market value. Since future interest rates and the resulting bond value cannot be predicted with certainty, a bond investor is exposed to the risk of changing values as interest rates vary. This risk has come to be known as **interest-rate risk.**

Second Relationship

The market value of a bond will be less than the par value if the investor's required rate is above the coupon interest rate; but it will be valued above par value if the investor's required rate of return is below the coupon interest rate.

Using the previous example, we observed that:

1. The bond has a *market* value of $1,000, equal to the par or maturity value, when the investor's required rate of return equals the 12% coupon interest rate. In other words, if

$$\text{required rate} = \text{coupon rate, then } \textit{market value} = \textit{par value}$$
$$12\% \quad = \quad 12\% \text{ , then} \quad \$1,000 \quad = \$1,000$$

2. When the required rate is 15%, which exceeds the 12% coupon rate, the market value falls below par value to $899.24; that is, if

$$\text{required rate} > \text{coupon rate, then } \textit{market value} < \textit{par value}$$
$$15\% \quad > \quad 12\% \text{ , then} \quad \$899.24 \quad < \$1,000$$

In this case the bond sells at a discount below par value; thus it is called a **discount bond.**

3. When the required rate is 9%, or less than the 12% coupon rate, the market value, $1,116.80, exceeds the bond's par value. In this instance, if

$$\text{required rate} < \text{coupon rate, then } \textit{market value} > \textit{par value}$$
$$9\% \quad < \quad 12\% \text{ , then} \quad \$1,116.80 \quad > \$1,000$$

The bond is now selling at a premium above par value; thus, it is a **premium bond.**

Third Relationship

Long-term bonds have greater interest-rate risk than do short-term bonds.

As already noted, a change in current interest rates (required rate of return) causes an inverse change in the market value of a bond. However, the impact on value is greater for long-term bonds than it is for short-term bonds.

In Figure 24-5 we observed the effect of interest rate changes on a five-year bond paying a 12% coupon interest rate. What if the bond did not mature until 10 years from today instead of 5 years? Would the changes in market value be the same? Absolutely not. The changes in value would be more significant for the 10-year bond. For example, if we vary the current interest rates (the bondholder's required rate of return) from 9% to 12% and then to 15%, as we did earlier with the 5-year bond, the values for both the 5-year and the 10-year bonds would be as shown below.

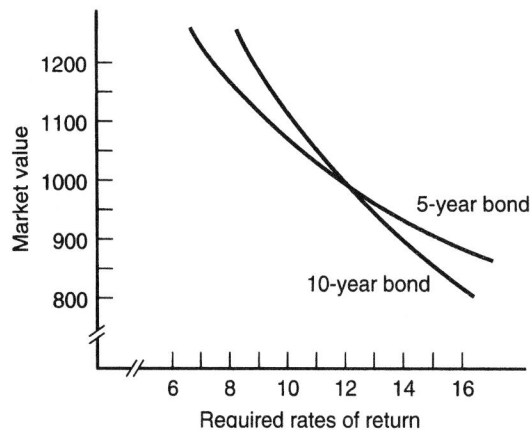

FIGURE 24-6
Market Values of a 5-Year and a 10-Year Bond at Different Required Rates

| Required Rate | Market Value for a 12% Coupon-Rate Bond Maturing in | |
	5 Years	10 Years
9%	$1,116.80	$1,192.16
12	1,000.00	1,000.00
15	899.24	849.28

Using these values and the required rates, we can graph the changes in values for the two bonds relative to different interest rates. These comparisons are provided in Figure 24-6. The figure clearly illustrates that the price of a long-term bond (say, 10 years) is more responsive or sensitive to interest rate changes than the price of a short-term bond (say, 5 years).

The reason long-term bond prices fluctuate more than short-term bond prices in response to interest rate changes is simple. Assume an investor bought a 10-year bond yielding a 12% interest rate. If the current interest rate for bonds of similar risk increased to 15%, the investor would be locked into the lower rate for 10 years. If, on the other hand, a shorter-term bond had been purchased, say one maturing in 2 years, the investor would have to accept the lower return for only 2 years and not the full 10 years. At the end of year 2, the investor would receive the maturity value of $1,000 and could buy a bond offering the higher 15% rate for the remaining 8 years. Thus, interest-rate risk is determined, at least in part, by the length of time an investor is required to commit to an investment. However, the holder of a long-term bond may take some comfort from the fact that long-term interest rates are usually not as volatile as short-term rates. If the short-term rate changed one percentage point, for example, it would not be unusual for the long-term rate to change only .3 percentage points.

SUMMARY

Valuation is an important issue if we are to manage the company effectively. An understanding of the concepts and how to compute the value of a security underlie much that we do in finance and in making correct decisions for the firm as a whole. Only if we know what matters to our investors can we maximize the firm's value.

For our purposes, *value is the present value of future cash flows expected to be received from an investment discounted at the investor's required rate of return.* In this context, the value of a security is a function of (1) the *expected cash inflows* from the asset, (2) the *riskiness* of the investment, and (3) the investor's *required rate of return.*

Valuing an asset with a finite stream of cash flows involves computing the present value of the individual cash receipts for each period. A bond that matures on a designated date is an example of such an asset. Here we find both the present value of the interest payments and the present value of the maturity or par value.

The *expected rate of return* on a bond is the required rate of return of the bondholders who are willing to pay the present market price for the bond, but no more. This rate is reached at the point where the present value of future cash flows to be received by the bondholder is just equal to the present market price of the bond. This rate of return is important to the financial manager because it equals the required rate of return of the firm's investors.

Certain key relationships exist in bond valuation, three of these being:

1. A decrease in interest rates (required rates of return) will cause the value of a bond to increase; an interest rate increase will cause a decrease in value. The change in value caused by changing interest rates is called *interest-rate risk.*
2. If the bondholder's required rate of return (current interest rate):
   a. Equals the coupon interest rate, the bond will sell at par, or maturity value.
   b. Exceeds the bond's coupon rate, the bond will sell below par value, or at a *discount.*
   c. Is less than the bond's coupon rate, the bond will sell above par value, or at a *premium.*
3. A bondholder owning a long-term bond is exposed to greater interest-rate risk than one owning a short-term bond.

SELF-CORRECTION PROBLEMS

1. Trico bonds have a coupon rate of 8%, a par value of $1,000, and will mature in 20 years. If you require a return of 7%, what price would you be willing to pay for the bond? What happens if you pay *more* for the bond? What happens if you pay *less* for the bond?

2. Sunn Co.'s bonds, maturing in seven years, pay 8% interest on a $1,000 face value. However, interest is paid semiannually. If your required rate of return is 10%, what is the value of the bond? How would your answer change if the interest were paid annually?

3. Sharp Co. bonds are selling in the market for $1,045. These 15-year bonds pay 7% interest annually on a $1,000 par value. If they are purchased at the market price, what is the expected rate of return?

SOLUTIONS TO SELF-CORRECTION PROBLEMS

1. $\text{Value}\left(V_b\right) = \sum_{t=1}^{20} \dfrac{\$80}{\left(1.07\right)^t} + \dfrac{\$1,000}{\left(1.07\right)^{20}}$

Thus,

Present value of interest:	$80 (10.594) =	$ 847.52
Present value of par value:	$1,000 (0.258) =	258.00
	Value (V$_b$) =	**$1,105.52**

If you pay more for the bond, your required rate of return will not be satisfied. In other words, by paying an amount for the bond that exceeds $1,105.52, the expected rate of return for the bond is less than the required rate of return. If you have the opportunity to pay less for the bond, the expected rate of return exceeds the 7% required rate of return.

2. If interest is paid semiannually:

$\text{Value}\left(V_b\right) = \sum_{t=1}^{14} \dfrac{\$40}{\left(1+0.05\right)^t} + \dfrac{\$1,000}{\left(1+0.05\right)^{14}}$

Thus,

$40 (9.899)	=	$395.96
$1,000 (0.505)	=	505.00
Value (V$_b$)	=	**$900.96**

If interest is paid annually:

$\text{Value}\left(V_b\right) = \sum_{t=1}^{7} \dfrac{\$80}{\left(1.10\right)^t} + \dfrac{\$1,000}{\left(1.10\right)^{7}}$

$V_b = \$80 (4.868) + \$1,000 (0.513)$

$V_b = \$902.44$

3. $\$1,045 = \sum_{t=1}^{15} \dfrac{\$70}{\left(1+\hat{k}_b\right)^t} + \dfrac{\$1,000}{\left(1+\hat{k}_b\right)^{15}}$

At 6%: $70 (9.712) + $1,000 (0.417) = $1,096.84

At 7%:   Value must equal $1,000.

Interpolation:

Expected rate of return: $\hat{k}_b = 6\% + \dfrac{\$51.84}{\$96.84} \ (1\%) = 6.54\%$

QUESTIONS

1. What are the basic differences between book value, liquidation value, market value, and intrinsic value?
2. What is a general definition of the intrinsic value of a security?
3. Explain the three factors that determine the intrinsic or economic value of an asset.
4. Explain the relationship between an investor's required rate of return and the value of a security.
5. a. How does a bond's par value differ from its market value?
   b. Explain the difference between a bond's coupon interest rate, the current yield, and a bondholder's required rate of return.
6. Describe the bondholder's claim on the firm's assets and income.
7. What factors determine a bond's rating? Why is the rating important to the firm's manager?
8. Distinguish between debentures and mortgage bonds.
9. Define (a) Eurobonds, (b) zero coupon bonds, and (c) junk bonds.
10. Define the bondholder's expected rate of return.

PROBLEMS

1. **Bond Valuation.**   Calculate the value of a bond that expects to mature in 12 years and has a $1,000 face value. The coupon interest rate is 8% and the investors' required rate of return is 12%.

2. **Bond Valuation.**   Enterprise, Inc., bonds have a 9% coupon rate. The interest is paid semiannually and the bonds mature in eight years. Their par value is $1,000. If your required rate of return is 8%, what is the value of the bond? What is its value if the interest is paid annually?

3. **Bondholder's Expected Rate of Return.**   The market price is $900 for a 10-year bond ($1,000 par value) that pays 8% interest (4% semiannually). What is the bond's expected rate of return?

4. **Bond Valuation.**   Exxon 20-year bonds pay 9% interest annually on a $1,000 par value. If bonds sell at $945, what is the bond's expected rate of return?

5. **Bondholder's Expected Rate of Return.**   Zenith Co.'s bonds mature in 12 years and pay 7% interest annually. If you purchase the bonds for $1,150, what is your expected rate of return?

6. **Bond Valuation.**   National Steel 15-year, $1,000 par value bonds pay 8% interest annually. The market price of the bonds is $1,085, and your required rate of return is 10%.

   a. Compute the bond's expected rate of return.
   b. Determine the value of the bond to you, given your required rate of return.
   c. Should you purchase the bond?

7. **Bond Valuation.**   You own a bond that pays $100 in annual interest, with a $1,000 par value. It matures in 15 years. Your required rate of return is 12%.

   a. Calculate the value of the bond.
   b. How does the value change if your required rate of return (i) increases to 15% or (ii) decreases to 8%?
   c. Explain the implications of your answers in part (b) as they relate to interest rate risk, premium bonds, and discount bonds.
   d. Assume that the bond matures in 5 years instead of 15 years. Recompute your answers in part (b).
   e. Explain the implications of your answers in part (d) as they relate to interest rate risk, premium bonds, and discount bonds.

8. **Bond Valuation.**   Arizona Public Utilities issued a bond that pays $80 in annual interest, with a $1,000 par value. It matures in 20 years. Your required rate of return is 7%.

   a. Calculate the value of the bond.
   b. How does the value change if your required rate of return (i) increases to 10% or (ii) decreases to 6%?
   c. Explain the implications of your answers in part (b) as they relate to interest rate risk, premium bonds, and discount bonds.
   d. Assume that the bond matures in 10 years instead of 20 years. Recompute your answers in part (b).
   e. Explain the implications of your answers in part (d) as they relate to interest rate risk, premium bonds, and discount bonds.

Equity Financing and Business Restructuring

CHAPTER 25

Valuing Preferred and Common Stock

Previously, we developed a general concept about valuation, where economic value was defined as the present value of the expected future cash flows generated by the asset. We then applied that concept to valuing bonds, one form of a company's long-term debt.

In this chapter we continue our study of valuation, but our attention is now given to valuing stocks, both preferred stock and common stock. As already noted at the outset of our study of finance, and on several occasions since, the financial manager's objective should be that of maximizing the value of the firm's common stock. Thus, we need to understand what determines stock value. Also, only with an understanding of valuation can we compute the firm's cost of capital, a concept essential to making effective capital investment decisions.

What we especially seek to accomplish in this chapter is the following:

1. Identify the basic characteristics and features of preferred stock and common stock.
2. Learn how to determine the economic value of preferred stock and common stock.
3. Examine the concept of the *investor's expected rate of return, as it relates to preferred stock and common stock.*[1]

PREFERRED STOCK

Preferred stock is often referred to as a hybrid security because it has many characteristics of both common stock and bonds. Preferred stock is similar to common stock in that it has no fixed maturity date, the nonpayment of dividends does not bring on

---

[1]We have already learned how to measure the expected rate of return on a bond. As we will see, the logic for measuring the expected rate of return for stocks is the same as for bonds; only the procedure is somewhat different.

bankruptcy, and dividends are not deductible for tax purposes. On the other hand, preferred stock is similar to bonds in that dividends are limited in amount.

The size of the preferred stock dividend is generally fixed either as a dollar amount or as a percentage of the par value. For example, Texas Power and Light has issued $4 preferred stock, while Toledo Edison has some 4.25% preferred stock outstanding. The par value on the Toledo Edison preferred stock is $100; hence, each share pays 4.25% × $100, or $4.25 in dividends annually. Because these dividends are fixed, preferred stockholders do not share in the residual earnings of the firm but are limited to their stated annual dividend.

In examining preferred stock we will first discuss several features common to almost all preferred stock. Next we will investigate features less frequently included and take a brief look at methods of retiring preferred stock. We will close by learning how to value preferred stock.

Features of Preferred Stock

Although each issue of preferred stock is unique, a number of characteristics are common to almost all issues. Some of these more frequent traits include:

- Multiple classes of preferred stock
- Preferred stock's claim on assets and income
- Cumulative dividends
- Protective provisions
- Convertibility

Other features that are less common include:

- Adjustable rates
- Participation
- PIK preferred

In addition, there are provisions frequently used to retire an issue of preferred stock, including the ability of the firm to call its preferred stock or to use a sinking-fund provision. All these features are presented in the discussion that follows.

Multiple classes.   If a company desires, it can issue more than one series or class of preferred stock, and each class can have different characteristics. In fact, it is quite common for firms that issue preferred stock to issue more than one series. For example, Philadelphia Electric has 13 different issues of preferred stock outstanding. These issues can be further differentiated in that some are convertible into common stock and others are not, and they have varying priority status regarding assets in the event of bankruptcy.

Claim on assets and income.   Preferred stock has priority over common stock with regard to claims on assets in the case of bankruptcy. The preferred stock claim is honored after that of bonds and before that of common stock. Multiple issues of preferred stock may be given an order of priority. Preferred stock also has a claim on income prior to common stock. That is, the firm must pay its preferred stock dividends before it pays common stock dividends. Thus, in terms of risk, preferred stock is safer than common stock because it has a prior claim on assets and income. However, it is riskier than long-term debt because its claims on assets and income come after those of bonds.

Cumulative feature.   Most preferred stocks carry a **cumulative feature** that requires all past unpaid preferred stock dividends be paid before any common stock dividends are declared. The purpose is to provide some degree of protection for the preferred shareholder. Without a cumulative feature there would be no reason why preferred stock dividends would not be omitted or passed when common stock dividends were passed. Because preferred stock does not have the dividend enforcement power of interest from bonds, the cumulative feature is necessary to protect the rights of preferred stockholders.

Protective provisions.   In addition to the cumulative feature, protective provisions are common to preferred stock. These protective provisions generally allow for voting rights in the event of nonpayment of dividends, or they restrict the payment of common stock dividends if sinking-fund payments are not met or if the firm is in financial difficulty. In effect, the protective features included with preferred stock are similar to the restrictive provisions included with long-term debt.

To examine typical protective provisions, consider Tenneco Corporation and Reynolds Metals preferred stocks. The Tenneco preferred stock has a protective provision that provides preferred stockholders with voting rights whenever six quarterly dividends are in arrears. At that point the preferred shareholders are given the power to elect a majority of the board of directors. The Reynolds Metals preferred stock includes a protective provision that precludes the payment of common stock dividends during any period in which the preferred stock sinking fund is in default. Both provisions, which yield protection beyond that provided by the cumulative provision and thereby reduce shareholder risk, are desirable. Given these protective provisions for the investor they reduce the cost of preferred stock to the issuing firm.

Convertibility.   Much of the preferred stock that is issued today is **convertible** at the discretion of the holder into a predetermined number of shares of common stock. In fact, today about one-third of all preferred stock issued has a convertibility feature. The convertibility feature is, of course, desirable to the investor and thus reduces the cost of the preferred stock to the issuer.

Adjustable rate preferred stock.   In the early 1980s, another new financing alternative was developed aimed at providing investors with some protection against wide swings in principal that occur when interest rates move up and down. This financing vehicle is called **adjustable rate preferred stock.** With adjustable rate preferred stock, quarterly dividends fluctuate with interest rates under a formula that ties the dividend payment at either a premium or discount to the highest of (1) the three-month Treasury bill rate, (2) the 10-year Treasury bond rate, or (3) the 20-year Treasury bond rate. Although adjustable rate preferred stock allows dividend rates to be tied to the rates on Treasury securities, it also provides a maximum and a minimum level to which they can climb or fall, called the *dividend rate band.* The purpose of allowing the interest rate on this preferred stock to fluctuate is, of course, to minimize the fluctuation in the value of the preferred stock. In times of high and fluctuating interest rates, this is a very appealing feature indeed. In Figure 25-1 several issues of adjustable rate preferred stock are identified.

In the late 1980s **auction rate preferred stock** began to appear. Auction rate preferred stock is actually variable rate preferred stock in which the dividend rate is set by an auction process. In the case of auction rate preferred, the dividend rate is set every 49 days. At each auction, buyers and sellers place bids for shares, specifying the yield they are willing to accept for the next seven-week period. The yield is then set at the lowest level necessary to match buyers and sellers. As a result, the yield offered on auction rate preferred stock accurately reflects current interest rates, while keeping the market price of these securities at par.

Participation.   Although participating features are infrequent in preferred stock, their inclusion can greatly affect its desirability and cost. The **participation feature** allows the preferred stockholder to participate in earnings beyond the payment of the stated dividend. This is usually done in accordance with some set formula. For example, Borden Series A preferred stock currently provides for a dividend of *no less than* 60 cents per share, to be determined by the board of directors. Preferred stock of this sort actually resembles common stock as much as it does normal preferred stock. Although a participating feature is certainly desirable from the point of view of the investor, it is infrequently included in preferred stock.

PIK preferred.   One by-product of the acquisition boom of the late 1980s was the creation of pay-in-kind (PIK) preferred stock. With **PIK preferred,** investors receive

FIGURE 25-1   Adjustable Rate Preferred Stock

Issuer	Amount of Offering ($000)	Dividend Rate at Offering	Dividend Rate Thereafter (Applicable Rate)[a]	Dividend Rate Band	Call Protection
Bank America Corp.	$400,000	9.25%	Adjusted quarterly to 4.00% below the applicable rate	6%–12%	No call allowed for the first 5 years.
J.P. Morgan & Co., Inc.	250,000	9.25	Adjusted quarterly to 4.875% below the applicable rate	5%–11 1/2%	No call allowed for the first 5 years.
Integrated Resources, Inc.	100,000	12.50	Adjusted quarterly to 0.75% higher than the applicable rate	8%–15%	No call allowed for the first 5 years.
Liberty National Corp.	25,000	11.00	Adjusted quarterly to the applicable rate	6 1/2%–13%	No call allowed for the first 5 years.
Reading & Bates Corp.	37,500	13.00	Adjusted quarterly to 0.75% higher than the applicable rate	7%–14%	No call allowed for the first 5 years.
Gulf States Utilities Corp.	30,000	11.50	Adjusted quarterly to 0.65% higher than the applicable rate	7%–13%	No call allowed for the first 5 years.

[a]In all cases the "applicable rate" refers to the highest of (1) the 3-month Treasury bill rate, (2) the 10-year Treasury bond rate, or (3) the 20-year Treasury bond rate.

no dividends initially; they merely get more preferred stock, which in turn pays dividends in even more preferred stock. Eventually, usually after five or six years if all goes well for the issuing company, cash dividends should replace the preferred stock dividends. Needless to say, the issuing firm has to offer hefty dividends, generally ranging from 12% to 18%, to entice investors to purchase PIK preferred.

Retirement features.   Although preferred stock does not have a set maturity associated with it, issuing firms generally provide for some method of retirement. If preferred stock could not be retired, issuing firms could not take advantage of falling interest rates.

Callable preferred.   Most preferred stock has some type of call provision associated with it. In fact, the Securities and Exchange Commission discourages the issuance of preferred stock without some call provision. The SEC has taken this stance on the grounds that if a method of retirement is not provided, the issuing firm will not be able to replace its preferred stock if interest rates fall.

The call feature on preferred stock usually involves an initial premium above the value or issuing price of the preferred of approximately 10%. Then, over time, the call premium generally falls. For example, Quaker Oats in 1976 issued $9.56 cumulative preferred stock with no par value for $100 per share. This issue was not callable until 1980 and then was callable at $109.56. After that the call price gradually drops to $100 in the year 2000, as shown in Figure 25-2.

By setting the initial call price above the initial issue price and allowing it to decline slowly over time, the firm protects the investor from an early call that carries no premium. A call provision also allows the issuing firm to plan the retirement of its preferred stock at predetermined prices.

Sinking-fund provisions.   A **sinking-fund** provision requires the firm periodically to set aside an amount of money for the retirement of its preferred stock. This money is then used to purchase the preferred stock in the open market or through the use of the call provision, whichever method is cheaper. Although preferred stock does not have a maturity date associated with it, the use of a call provision in addition to a sinking fund can effectively create a maturity date. For example, the Quaker Oats issue we just examined has associated with it an annual sinking fund, operating between the years 1981 and 2005, which requires the annual elimination of a minimum of 20,000 shares and a maximum of 40,000 shares. The minimum payments are designed so that the entire issue will be retired by the year 2005. If any sinking-fund payments are made above the minimum amount, the issue will be retired prior to

FIGURE 25-2   Call Provision of Quaker Oats $9.56 Cumulative Preferred

	Date	Call Price
Date of issue	until 7/19/80	Not callable
7/20/80	until 7/19/85	$109.56
7/20/85	until 7/19/90	107.17
7/20/90	until 7/19/95	104.78
7/20/95	until 7/19/00	102.39
After 7/19/00		100.00

2005. Thus, the Quaker Oats issue of preferred stock has a maximum life of 30 years, and the size of the issue outstanding decreases each year after 1981.

Valuing Preferred Stock

As already explained, the owner of preferred stock generally receives a *constant income* from the investment in each period. However, the return from preferred stock comes in the form of *dividends* rather than *interest*. In addition, while bonds generally have a specific maturity date, most preferred stocks are perpetuities (nonmaturing). In this instance, finding the value (present value) of preferred stock, V_{ps}, with a level cash flow stream continuing indefinitely, may best be explained by an example.

Consider AT&T's preferred stock issue. We will use a three-step valuation procedure.

Step 1: Estimate the amount and timing of the receipt of the future cash flows the preferred stock is expected to provide. AT&T's preferred stock pays an annual dividend of $3.64. The shares do not have a maturity date; that is, they go to perpetuity.

Step 2: Evaluate the riskiness of the preferred stock's future dividends and determine the investor's required rate of return. The investor's required rate of return is assumed to equal 7.28%.[2]

Step 3: Calculate the economic or intrinsic value of the share of preferred stock, which is the present value of the expected dividends discounted at the investor's required rate of return. The valuation model for a share of preferred stock, V_{ps}, is therefore defined as follows:

$$V_{ps} = \frac{\text{dividend in year 1}}{(1 + \text{required rate of return})^1} \tag{1}$$

$$+ \frac{\text{dividend in year 2}}{(1 + \text{required rate of return})^2}$$

$$+ \ldots + \frac{\text{dividend in infinity}}{(1 + \text{required rate of return})^\infty}$$

$$= \frac{D_1}{(1 + k_{ps})^1} + \frac{D_2}{(1 + k_{ps})^2} + \ldots + \frac{D_\infty}{(1 + k_{ps})^\infty}$$

$$V_{ps} = \sum_{t=1}^{\infty} \frac{D_t}{(1 + k_{ps})^t}$$

Because the dividends in each period are equal for preferred stock, equation (1) can be reduced to the following relationship:[3]

$$V_{ps} = \frac{\text{annual dividend}}{\text{required rate of return}} = \frac{D}{k_{ps}} \tag{2}$$

[2]For now the required rate of return is given.
[3]To verify this result, consider the following equation: *(continued on next page)*

Equation (2) represents the present value of an infinite stream of cash flows, where the cash flows are the same each year. We can determine the value of the AT&T preferred stock, using equation (2), as follows:

$$V_{ps} = \frac{D}{k_{ps}} = \frac{\$3.64}{.0728} = \$50$$

COMMON STOCK

Common stock involves ownership in the corporation. In effect, bondholders and preferred stockholders can be viewed as creditors, whereas the common stockholders are the true owners of the firm. Common stock does not have a maturity date, but exists as long as the firm does. Nor does common stock have an upper limit on its dividend payments. Dividend payments must be declared by the firm's board of directors before they are issued. In the event of bankruptcy the common stockholders, as owners of the corporation, cannot exercise claims on assets until the firm's creditors, including the bondholders and preferred shareholders, have been satisfied.

In examining common stock, we will look first at several of its features or characteristics. Then we will focus on valuing common stock.

Features or Characteristics of Common Stock

We now examine common stock's claim on income and assets, stockholder voting rights, preemptive rights, and the meaning and importance of its limited-liability feature.

Claim on income.   As the owners of the corporation, the common shareholders have the right to the residual income after bondholders and preferred stockholders have

---

[3](continued)

(i) $$\frac{D_1}{V_{ps}} = \frac{D_2}{\left(1 + k_{ps}\right)^1} + \frac{D_n}{\left(1 + k_{ps}\right)^2} + \dots + \frac{}{\left(1 + k_{ps}\right)^n}$$

If we multiply both sides of this equation by $(1 + k_{ps})$, we have

(ii) $$V_{ps}(1 + k_{ps}) = D_1 \frac{D_2}{\left(1 + k_{ps}\right)^1} + \dots + \frac{D_n}{\left(1 + k_{ps}\right)^{n-1}}$$

Subtracting (i) from (ii) yields

$$V_{ps}(1 + k_{ps} - 1) = D_1 \frac{D_n}{\left(1 + k_{ps}\right)^n}$$

As n approaches infinity, $D_n / \left(1 + k_{ps}\right)$ approaches zero. Consequently,

$$V_{ps}k_{ps} = D_1 \text{ and } V_{ps} = \frac{D_1}{k_{ps}}$$

Since $D_1 = D_2 = \dots = D_n$, we need not designate the year. Therefore

(iii) $$V_{ps} = \frac{D}{k_{ps}}$$

been paid. This income may be paid directly to the shareholders in the form of dividends or retained and reinvested by the firm. Although it is obvious the shareholder benefits immediately from the distribution of income in the form of dividends, the reinvestment of earnings also benefits the shareholder. Plowing back earnings into the firm results in an increase in the value of the firm, in its earning power, and in its future dividends. This action in turn results in an increase in the value of the stock. In effect, residual income is distributed directly to shareholders in the form of dividends or indirectly in the form of capital gains on their common stock.

The right to residual income has both advantages and disadvantages for the common stockholder. The advantage is that the potential return is limitless. Once the claims of the most senior securities (bonds and preferred stock) have been satisfied, the remaining income flows to the common stockholders in the form of dividends or capital gains. The disadvantage: If the bond and preferred stock claims on income totally absorb earnings, common shareholders receive nothing. In years when earnings fall, it is the common shareholder who suffers first.

Claim on assets.   Just as common stock has a residual claim on income, it also has a residual claim on assets in the case of liquidation. Only after the claims of debt holders and preferred stockholders have been satisfied do the claims of common shareholders receive attention. Unfortunately, when bankruptcy does occur, the claims of the common shareholders generally go unsatisfied. This residual claim on assets adds to the risk of common stock. Thus, while common stock has historically provided a large return, averaging 10% annually since the late 1920s, it also has large risks associated with it.

Voting rights.   The common stock shareholders are entitled to elect the board of directors and are in general the only security holders given a vote. Early in this century it was not uncommon for a firm to issue two classes of common stock, which were identical except that only one carried voting rights. For example, both the Parker Pen Co. and the Great Atlantic and Pacific Tea Co. (A&P) had two such classes of common stock. This practice was virtually eliminated by (1) the Public Utility Holding Company Act of 1935, which gave the Securities and Exchange Commission the power to require that newly issued common stock carry voting rights, (2) the New York Stock Exchange's refusal to list common stock without voting privileges, and (3) investor demand for the inclusion of voting rights. However, with the merger boom of the eighties, dual classes of common stock with different voting rights again emerged, this time as a defensive tactic used to prevent takeovers.

Common shareholders not only have the right to elect the board of directors, they also must approve any change in the corporate charter. A typical charter change might involve the authorization to issue new stock or perhaps a merger proposal.

Voting for directors and charter changes occurs at the corporation's annual meeting. While shareholders may vote in person, the majority generally vote by proxy. A **proxy** gives a designated party the temporary power of attorney to vote for the signee at the corporation's annual meeting. The firm's management generally solicits proxy votes and, if the shareholders are satisfied with its performance, has little problem securing them. However, in times of financial distress or when management takeovers are threatened, **proxy fights**—battles between rival groups for proxy votes—occur.

While each share of stock carries the same number of votes, the voting procedure is not always the same from company to company. The two procedures commonly used are majority and cumulative voting. Under **majority voting,** each share of stock allows the shareholder one vote, and each position on the board of directors is voted on separately. Because each member of the board of directors is elected by a simple majority, a majority of shares has the power to elect the entire board of directors.

With **cumulative voting,** each share of stock allows the shareholder a number of votes equal to the number of directors being elected. The shareholder can then cast all of his or her votes for a single candidate or split them among the various candidates. The advantage of a cumulative voting procedure is that it gives minority shareholders the power to elect a director.

Preemptive rights.   The **preemptive right** entitles the common shareholder to maintain a proportionate share of ownership in the firm. When new shares are issued, common shareholders have the first right of refusal. If a shareholder owns 25% of the corporation's stock, then he or she is entitled to purchase 25% of the new shares. Certificates issued to the shareholders giving them an option to purchase a stated number of new shares of stock at a specified price during a 2- to 10-week period are called **rights.** These rights can be exercised, generally at a price set by management below the common stock's current market price, can be allowed to expire, or can be sold in the open market.

Limited liability.   Although the common shareholders are the actual owners of the corporation, their liability in the case of bankruptcy is limited to the amount of their investment. The advantage is that investors who might not otherwise invest their funds in the firm become willing to do so. This limited-liability feature aids the firm in raising funds.

Valuing Common Stock

Like both bonds and preferred stock, a common stock's value is equal to the present value of all future cash flows expected to be received by the stockholder. However, in contrast to bonds, common stock does not promise its owners interest income or a maturity payment at some specified time in the future. Nor does common stock entitle the holder to a predetermined constant dividend, as does preferred stock. For common stock, the dividend is based on the profitability of the firm and on management's decision to pay dividends or to retain the profits for reinvestment purposes. As a consequence, dividend streams tend to increase with the growth in corporate earnings. Thus, the growth of future dividends is a prime distinguishing feature of common stock.

The Growth Factor in Valuing Common Stock

What is meant by the term *growth* when used in the context of valuing common stock? A company can grow in a variety of ways. It can become larger by borrowing money to invest in new projects. Likewise, it can issue new stock for expansion. Management could also acquire another company to merge with the existing firm, which would increase the firm's assets. In all these cases, the firm is growing through the use of new financing, by issuing debt or common stock. Although management could accurately say that the firm has grown, the original stockholders may or may not participate in this growth. Growth is realized through the infusion of new capital.

The firm size has clearly increased, but unless the original investors increase their investment in the firm, they will own a smaller portion of the expanded business.

Another means of growing is internal growth, which requires that management retain some or all of the firm's profits for reinvestment in the firm, resulting in the growth of future earnings and hopefully the value of the common stock. This process underlies the essence of potential growth for the firm's current stockholders and what we can call *the only relevant growth, for our purposes in valuing a firm's common shares.*[4]

To illustrate the nature of internal growth, assume that the return on equity for PepsiCo is 16%.[5] If PepsiCo's management decides to pay all the profits out in dividends to its stockholders, the firm will experience no growth internally. It might become larger by borrowing more money or issuing new stock, but internal growth will come only through the retention of profits. If, on the other hand, PepsiCo retained all the profits, the stockholders' investment in the firm would grow by the amount of profits retained, or by 16%. If, however, management kept only 50% of the profits for reinvestment, the common shareholders' investment would increase only by half of the 16% return on equity, or by 8%. Generalizing this relationship, we have

$$g = ROE \times r, \tag{3}$$

where $\quad g \ = \quad$ the growth rate of future earnings and the growth in the common stockholders' investment in the firm.

$\qquad ROE \ = \quad$ the return on equity (net income/common book value).

$\qquad \quad r \ = \quad$ the company's percentage of profits retained, called the profit-retention rate.[6]

Therefore, if only 25% of the profits were retained by PepsiCo, we would expect the common stockholders' investment in the firm and the value of the stock price to increase or grow by 4%; that is,

$$g = 16\% \times .25 = 4\%$$

In summary, common stockholders frequently rely on an increase in the stock price as a source of return. If the company is retaining a portion of its earnings for reinvestment, future profits and dividends should grow. This growth should be reflected in an increased market price of the common stock in future periods, provided that the return on the funds reinvested exceeds the investor's required rate of return. Therefore, both types of return (dividends and price appreciation) are necessary in the development of a valuation model for common stock.

To explain this process, let us begin by examining how an investor might value a common stock that is to be held for only one year.

---

[4]We are not arguing that the existing common stockholders never benefit from the use of external financing; however, such benefit is more evasive when dealing with efficient capital markets.

[5]The return on equity is the percentage return on the common shareholder's investment in the company and is computed as follows:

$$\text{return on equity} = \frac{\text{net income}}{(\text{part value} + \text{paid in capital} + \text{retained earnings})}$$

[6]The retention rate is also equal to (1 − the percentage of profits paid out in dividends). The percentage of profits paid out in dividends is often called the **dividend-payout ratio**.

Common Stock Valuation—Single Holding Period

For an investor holding a common stock for only one year, the value of the stock should equal the present value of both the expected dividend to be received in one year, D_1, and the anticipated market price of the share at year end, P_1. If k_{cs} represents a common stockholder's required rate of return, the value of the security, V_{cs}, would be

$$V_{cs} = \text{present value of dividend in one year } (D_1)$$
$$+ \text{present value of market price in one year } (P_1)$$

$$= \frac{D_1}{\left(1 + k_{cs}\right)} + \frac{P_1}{\left(1 + k_{cs}\right)}$$

Suppose an investor is contemplating the purchase of RMI common stock at the beginning of this year. The dividend at year end is expected to be $1.64, and the market price by the end of the year is projected to be $22. If the investor's required rate of return is 18%, the value of the security would be

$$V_{cs} = \frac{\$1.64}{1 + .18} + \frac{\$22}{1 + .18}$$

$$= \$1.39 + \$18.64$$

$$= \$20.03$$

Once again we see that valuation is a three-step process. First, we estimate the expected future cash flows from common stock ownership (a $1.64 dividend and a $22 end-of-year expected share price). Second, we estimate the investor's required rate of return after assessing the riskiness of the expected cash flows (assumed to be 18%). Finally, we discount the expected dividend and end-of-year share price back to the present at the investor's required rate of return.

Common Stock Valuation—Multiple Holding Periods

Since common stock has no maturity date and is frequently held for many years, a **multiple-holding-period valuation model** is needed. The general common stock valuation model can be defined as follows:

$$V_{cs} = \frac{D_1}{\left(1 + k_{cs}\right)^1} + \frac{D_2}{\left(1 + k_{cs}\right)^2} + \ldots + \frac{D_n}{\left(1 + k_{cs}\right)^n} + \ldots + \frac{D_\infty}{\left(1 + k_{cs}\right)^\infty} \tag{4}$$

Equation (4) indicates that we are discounting the dividend at the end of the first year, D_1, back one year; the dividend in the second year, D_2, back two years; the dividend in the nth year back n years; and the dividend in infinity back an infinite number of years. The required rate of return is k_{cs}. In using equation (4), note that the value of the stock is established at the beginning of the year, say January 1, 1994. The most recent past dividend, D_0, would have been paid the previous day, December 31, 1993. Thus, if we purchased the stock on January 1, the first dividend would be received in 12 months, on December 31, 1994, which is represented by D_1.

Fortunately, equation (4) can be reduced to a much more manageable form if dividends grow each year at a constant rate, g. The constant growth common stock valuation equation may be presented as follows[7]:

$$\text{common stock value} = \frac{\text{dividend in year 1}}{\text{required rate of return} - \text{growth rate}} \qquad (7)$$

$$V_{cs} = \frac{D_1}{k_{cs} - g}$$

Consequently, the intrinsic value (present value) of a share of common stock whose dividends grow at a constant annual rate can be calculated using equation (7). Although the interpretation of this equation may not be intuitively obvious, simply remember that it solves for the present value of the future dividend stream growing at a rate, g, to infinity, assuming that k_{cs} is greater than g.

Consider the valuation of a share of common stock that paid a $2 dividend at the end of the last year and is expected to pay a cash dividend every year from now to infinity. Each year the dividends are expected to grow at a rate of 10%. Based on an assessment of the riskiness of the common stock, the investor's required rate of return is 15%. Using this information, we would compute the value of the common stock as follows:

1. Since the $2 dividend was paid last year (actually yesterday), we must compute the next dividend to be received, that is, D_1, where

---

[7]Where common stock dividends grow at a constant rate of g every year, we can express the dividend in any year in terms of the dividend paid at the end of the previous year, D_0. For example, the expected dividend one year hence is simply $D_0(1 + g)$. Likewise, the dividend at the end of t years is $D_0(1 + g)^t$. Using this notation, the common stock valuation equation in (4) can be rewritten as follows:

$$V_{cs} = \frac{D_0(1+g)^1}{(1+k_{cs})^1} + \frac{D_0(1+g)^2}{(1+k_{cs})^2} + \ldots + \frac{D_0(1+g)^n}{(1+k_{cs})^n} + \ldots + \frac{D_0(1+g)^\infty}{(1+k_{cs})^\infty} \qquad (5)$$

If both sides of equation (5) are multiplied by $(1 + k_{cs})/(1 + g)$ and then equation (4) is subtracted from the product, the result is

$$\frac{V_{cs}(1+k_{cs})}{1+g} - V_{cs} = D_0 - \frac{D_0(1+g)^\infty}{(1+k_{cs})^\infty} \qquad (6)$$

If $k_{cs} > g$, which normally should hold, $[D_0(1 + g)^\infty/(1 + k_{cs})^\infty]$ approaches zero. As a result,

$$\frac{V_{cs}(1+k_{cs})}{1+g} - V_{cs} = D_0$$

$$V_{cs}\left(\frac{1+k_{cs}}{1+g}\right) - V_{cs}\left(\frac{1+g}{1+g}\right) = D_0$$

$$V_{cs}\left[\frac{(1+k_{cs}) - (1+g)}{1+g}\right] = D_0$$

$$V_{cs}(k_{cs} - g) = D_0(1+g)$$

$$V_{cs} = \frac{D_1}{k_{cs} - g} \qquad (7)$$

$$
\begin{aligned}
D_1 &= D_0 (1 + g) \\
&= \$2 (1 + .10) \\
&= \$2.20
\end{aligned}
$$

2. Now, using equation (7),

$$
\begin{aligned}
V_{cs} &= \frac{D_1}{k_{cs} - g} \\
&= \frac{\$2.20}{.15 - .10} \\
&= \$44
\end{aligned}
$$

We have argued that the value of a common stock is equal to the present value of all future dividends, which is without question a fundamental premise of finance. In practice, however, managers, along with many security analysts, often talk about the relationship between stock value and earnings, rather than dividends. We would encourage you to be very cautious in using earnings to value a stock. Even though it may be a popular practice, the evidence available suggests that investors look to the cash flows generated by the firm, not the earnings, for value. A firm's value truly is the present value of the cash flows it produces.

We now turn to our last issue in stock valuation, that of the stockholder's expected returns, a matter of key importance to the financial manager.

STOCKHOLDER'S EXPECTED RATE OF RETURN

The expected rate of return on a bond is the return the bondholder expects to receive on the investment by paying the existing market price for the security. This rate of return is of interest to the financial manager because it tells the manager about the investor's expectations. The same can be said for the financial manager needing to know the expected rate of return of the firm's stockholders, which is the topic of this section.

The Preferred Stockholder's Expected Rate of Return

In computing the preferred stockholder's expected rate of return, we use the valuation equation for preferred stock. Earlier, equation (2) specified the value of a preferred stock, V_{ps}, as

$$
V_{ps} = \frac{\text{annual dividend}}{\text{required rate of return}} = \frac{D}{k_{ps}} \tag{2}
$$

Solving equation (2) for k_{ps}, we have:

$$
k_{ps} = \frac{\text{annual dividend}}{\text{value}} = \frac{D}{V_{ps}} \tag{8}
$$

That is, preferred stockholder's *required* rate of return simply equals the stock's annual dividend divided by the intrinsic value. We may also restate equation (8) to solve for a preferred stock's *expected* rate of return, $\hat{k}_{ps}$ (pronounced "k-hjat"), as follows[8]:

$$\hat{k}_{ps} = \frac{\text{annual dividend}}{\text{market price}} = \frac{D}{P_0} \tag{9}$$

Note that we have merely substituted the current market price P_0, for the intrinsic value, V_{ps}. The expected rate of return, $\hat{k}_{ps}$, therefore equals the annual dividend relative to the price the stock is presently selling for, P_0. Thus, the expected rate of return, $\hat{k}_{ps}$, is the rate of return the investor can expect to earn from the investment if bought at the current market price. For example, if the present market price of preferred stock is $50 and it pays a $3.64 annual dividend, the expected rate of return implicit in the present market price is

$$\hat{k}_{ps} = \frac{D}{P_0} = \frac{\$3.64}{\$50} = 7.28\%$$

Therefore, investors at the margin (who pay $50 per share for a preferred security that is paying $3.64 in annual dividends) are expecting a 7.28% rate of return.

The Common Stockholder's Expected Rate of Return

The valuation equation for common stock was defined earlier in equation (4) as

$$\text{value} = \frac{\text{dividend in year 1}}{(1 + \text{required rate of return})^1}$$

$$+ \frac{\text{dividend in year 2}}{(1 + \text{required rate of return})^2} \tag{4}$$

$$+ \ldots + \frac{\text{dividend in year infinity}}{(1 + \text{required rate of return})^\infty}$$

$$V_{cs} = \frac{D_1}{(1 + k_{cs})^1} + \frac{D_2}{(1 + k_{cs})^2} + \ldots + \frac{D_\infty}{(1 + k_{cs})^\infty}$$

$$V_{cs} = \sum_{t=1}^{\infty} \frac{D_t}{(1 + k_{cs})^t}$$

Owing to the difficulty of discounting to infinity, we made the key assumption that the dividends, D_t, increase at a constant annual compound growth rate of g. If this assumption is valid, equation (4) was shown to be equivalent to

---

[8]We will use $\hat{k}$ ("k-hjat") to represent a security's expected rates of return versus k for the investor's required rate of return.

$$\text{value} = \frac{\text{dividend in year 1}}{\text{required rate of return} - \text{growth rate}} \qquad (7)$$

$$V_{cs} = \frac{D_1}{k_{cs} - g}$$

Thus, V_{cs} represents the maximum value that an investor having a required rate of return of k_{cs} would pay for a security having an anticipated dividend in year 1 of D_1 that is expected to grow in future years at rate g. Solving equation (7) for k_{cs}, we can compute the common stockholder's required rate of return as follows[9]:

$$k_{cs} = \left(\frac{D_1}{V_{cs}}\right) + g \qquad (10)$$

$$\uparrow \qquad \uparrow$$

dividend annual
yield   growth
rate

From this equation, the common stockholder's required rate of return is equal to the dividend yield plus a growth factor. Although the growth rate, g, applies to the growth in the company's dividends, given our assumptions the stock's value may also be expected to increase at the same rate. For this reason, g represents the annual percentage growth in the stock value. In other words, the investors' required rate of return is satisfied by receiving dividends and capital gains, as reflected by the expected percentage growth rate in the stock price.

As was done for preferred stock earlier, we may revise equation (10) to measure a common stock's *expected* rate of return, $\hat{k}_{cs}$. Replacing the intrinsic value, V_{cs}, in equation (10) with the stock's current market price, P_0, we may express the stock's expected rate of return as follows:

$$\hat{k}_{cs} = \frac{\text{dividend in year 1}}{\text{market price}} + \text{growth} = \frac{D_1}{P_0} + g \qquad (11)$$

Example.   As an example of computing the expected rate of return for a common stock where dividends are anticipated to grow at a constant rate to infinity, assume that a firm's common stock has a current market price of $44. If the expected dividend at the conclusion of this year is $2.20 and dividends and earnings are growing at a 10% annual rate (last year's dividend was $2), the expected rate of return implicit in the $44 stock price is as follows:

$$k_{cs} = \frac{\$2.20}{\$44} + 10\% = 15\%$$

As a final note, we should understand that the *expected* rate of return implied by a given market price equals the *required* rate of return for investors at the margin. For these investors, the expected rate of return is just equal to their required rate of re-

---

[9]At times the expected dividend at year end (D_1) is not given. Instead we might only know the most recent dividend (paid yesterday), that is, D_0. If so, equation (7) must be restated as follows:

$$V_{cs} = \frac{D_1}{(k_{cs} - g)} = \frac{D_0(1 + g)}{(k_{cs} - g)}$$

turn, and therefore they are willing to pay the current market price for the security. These investors' required rate of return is of particular significance to the financial manager, because it represents the cost of new financing to the firm.

SUMMARY

Valuation is an important process in financial management. An understanding of the concepts and computational procedures in valuing a security underlies sound decision making. Valuation supports the financial officer's objective of maximizing the value of the firm's common stock.

For our purposes, *value is the present value of future cash flows expected to be received from an investment discounted at the investor's required rate of return.* In this context, the value of a security is a function of (1) the *expected cash inflows* from the asset, (2) the *riskiness* of the investment, and (3) the investor's *required rate of return.* In a world of uncertainty returns are measured in terms of the *expected cash flows* anticipated from the security; a derivation of expected value takes into account possible future events and their probability.

Although the valuation of any security entails the same basic principles, the procedures used in each situation vary. For example, valuing a finite stream of cash flows involves computing the present value of the individual cash receipts for each period. An example of this type of valuation problem would be a bond that is scheduled to mature on a designated date. A second category of cash flow patterns involves an *infinite* cash flow stream, such as those from preferred stock and common stock. Although the underlying premise of valuation does not change—that is, value equals the present value of future cash flows—valuing such an asset requires a modification in the procedure. For securities with cash flows that are constant in each year, such as preferred stock, the present value equals the dollar amount of the annual dividend divided by the investor's required rate of return. Furthermore, for common stock where the future dividends are expected to increase at a constant growth rate, value may be given by the following equation:

$$\text{value} = \frac{\text{dividend in year one}}{\text{required rate of return} - \text{growth rate}} \tag{7}$$

The *expected rate of return* on a security is the required rate of return of investors who are willing to pay the present market price for the security, but no higher price. This rate of return is important to the financial manager because it equals the required rate of return of the firm's investors. This rate is reached at the point where the present value of future cash flows to be received by the investor is just equal to the present market price of the security.

SELF-CORRECTION PROBLEMS

1. What is the value of a preferred stock where the dividend rate is 16% on a $100 par value? The appropriate discount rate for a stock of this risk level is 12%.

2. You own 250 shares of Dalton Resources' preferred stock, which currently sells for $38.50 per share and pays annual dividends of $3.25 per share.

   a. What is your expected return?
   b. If you require an 8% return, given the current price, should you sell or buy more stock?

3. The preferred stock of Armlo pays a $2.75 dividend. What is the value of the stock if your required return is 9%?

4. Crosby Corporation's common stock paid $1.32 in dividends last year and is expected to grow indefinitely at an annual 7% rate. What is the value of the stock if you require an 11% return?

5. Blackburn & Smith's common stock currently sells for $23 per share. The company's executives anticipate a constant growth rate of 10.5% and an end-of-year dividend of $2.50.

   a. What is your expected rate of return?
   b. If you require a 17% return, should you purchase the stock?

SOLUTIONS TO SELF-CORRECTION PROBLEMS

1.

$$\text{Value}\left(V_{ps}\right) = \frac{.16 \times \$100}{.12}$$

$$= \frac{\$16}{12}$$

$$= \$133.33$$

2. a. $\text{Expected return} = \dfrac{\text{Dividend}}{\text{Market Price}} = \dfrac{\$3.25}{\$38.50} = 0.0844 = 8.44\%$

   b. Given your 8% required rate of return, the stock is worth $40.62 to you:

   $$\text{Value} = \frac{\text{Dividend}}{\text{Required Rate of Return}} = \frac{\$3.25}{0.08} = \$40.62$$

   Because the expected rate of return (8.44%) is greater than your required rate of return (8%) or because the current market price ($38.50) is less than $40.62, the stock is undervalued and you should buy.

3. $\text{Value } (V_{ps}) = \dfrac{\text{dividend}}{\text{required rate of return}} = \dfrac{\$2.75}{0.09} = \$30.56$

4.

$$\text{Value } (V_{cs}) = \left(\frac{\text{last year dividend } (1 + \text{growth rate})}{\text{required rate of return} - \text{growth rate}} \right)$$

$$= \frac{\$1.32 \,(1.07)}{0.11 - 0.07}$$

$$= \$35.31$$

5. a. $\underset{\text{of return}}{\text{Expected rate}} \ (\hat{k}_{cs}) = \frac{\text{Dividend in Year 1}}{\text{Market Price}} + \underset{\text{rate}}{\text{growth}}$

$$k_{cs} = \frac{\$2.50}{\$23.00} + 0.105 = .2137$$

$$k_{cs} = 21.37\%$$

b. $\qquad V_{cs} = \dfrac{\$2.50}{.17 - .105} = \$38.46$

The expected rate of return exceeds your required rate of return, which means that the value of the security to you is greater than the current market price. Thus, you should buy the stock.

QUESTIONS

1. Why is preferred stock referred to as a hybrid security? It is often said to combine the worst features of common stock and bonds. What is meant by this statement?
2. Inasmuch as preferred stock dividends in arrears must be paid before common stock dividends, should they be considered a liability and appear on the right-hand side of the balance sheet?
3. Why would a preferred stockholder want the stock to have a cumulative dividend feature and protective provisions?
4. Distinguish between fixed rate preferred stock and adjustable rate preferred stock. What is the rationale for a firm issuing adjustable rate preferred stock?
5. What is PIK preferred stock?
6. Why is preferred stock frequently convertible? Why would it be callable?
7. Compare valuing preferred stock and common stock.
8. Define the investor's *expected* rate of return.
9. State how the investor's required rate of return is computed.
10. The common stockholders receive two types of return from their investment. What are they?

PROBLEMS

1. **Preferred Stock Valuation.** What is the value of a preferred stock where the dividend rate is 14% on a $100 par value? The appropriate discount rate for a stock of this risk level is 12%.

2. **Preferred Stockholder Expected Return.** Solitron's preferred stock is selling for $42.16 and pays $1.95 in dividends. What is your expected rate of return if you purchase the security at the market price?

3. **Preferred Stockholder Expected Return.** You own 200 shares of Somner Resources' preferred stock, which currently sells for $40 per share and pays annual dividends of $3.40 per share.

   a. What is your expected return?

   b. If you require an 8% return, given the current price should you sell or buy more stock?

4. **Common Stock Valuation.** You intend to purchase Marigo common stock at $50 per share, hold it one year, and sell after a dividend of $6 is paid. How much will the stock price have to appreciate for you to satisfy your required rate of return of 15%?

5. **Common Stockholder Expected Return.** Made-It's common stock currently sells for $22.50 per share. The company's executives anticipate a constant growth rate of 10% and an end-of-year dividend of $2.

   a. What is your expected rate of return if you buy the stock for $22.50?

   b. If you require a 17% return, should you purchase the stock?

6. **Common Stock Valuation.** Header Motor, Inc., paid a $3.50 dividend last year. At a constant growth rate of 5%, what is the value of the common stock if the investors require a 20% rate of return?

7. **Measuring Growth.** Given that a firm's return on equity is 18% and management plans to retain 40% of earnings for investment purposes, what will be the firm's growth rate?

8. **Common Stockholder Expected Return.** The common stock of Zaldi Co. is selling for $32.84. The stock recently paid dividends of $2.94 per share and has a projected constant growth rate of 9.5%. If you purchase the stock at the market price, what is your expected rate of return?

9. **Common Stock Valuation.** Honeywag common stock is expected to pay $1.85 in dividends next year, and the market price is projected to be $42.50 by year end. If the investor's required rate of return is 11%, what is the current value of the stock?

10. **Common Stockholder Expected Return.** The market price for Hobart common stock is $43. The price at the end of one year is expected to be $48, and dividends for next year should be $2.84. What is the expected rate of return?

11. **Preferred Stock Valuation.** Pioneer's preferred stock is selling for $33 in the market and pays a $3.60 annual dividend.

    a. What is the expected rate of return on the stock?

    b. If an investor's required rate of return is 10%, what is the value of the stock for that investor?

    c. Should the investor acquire the stock?

12. **Common Stock Valuation.** The common stock of NCP paid $1.32 in dividends last year. Dividends are expected to grow at an 8% annual rate for an indefinite number of years.

    a. If NCP's current market price is $23.50, what is the stock's expected rate of return?

    b. If your required rate of return is 10.5%, what is the value of the stock for you?

    c. Should you make the investment?

13. **A Comprehensive Problem in Valuing Securities.** You are considering three investments. The first is a bond that is selling in the market at $1,100. The bond has a $1,000 par value, pays interest at 13%, and is scheduled to mature in 15 years. For bonds of this risk class you believe that a 14% rate of return should be required. The second investment that you are analyzing is a preferred stock ($100 par value) that sells for $90 and pays an annual dividend of $13. Your required rate of return for this stock is 15%. The last investment is a common stock ($25 par value) that recently paid a $2 dividend. The firm's earnings per share has increased from $3 to $6 in 10 years, which also reflects the expected growth in dividends per share for the indefinite future. The stock is selling for $20, and you think a reasonable required rate of return for the stock is 20%.

    a. Calculate the value of each security based on your required rate of return.

    b. Which investment(s) should you accept? Why?

    c. (1) If your required rates of return changed to 12% for the bond, 14% for the preferred stock, and 18% for the common stock, how would your answers change to parts (a) and (b)?

       (2) Assuming again that your required rate of return for the common stock is 20%, but the anticipated constant growth rate changes to 12%, how would your answers to parts (a) and (b) change?

CHAPTER 26

Business Restructuring and Failure

INTRODUCTION

On the whole, mergers and acquisitions during the 1980s were motivated by change. Specifically, this period saw some of the largest corporate giants taken private through leveraged buyouts, then dismembered and sold off piecemeal. What emerged from the process was a leaner and far more profitable corporation. Investors and the investment bankers that served them applauded these reformations, while bondholders and employees frequently decried what they saw as unwarranted attempts by shareholders to capture a larger portion of the firm's value. Shareholders, on the other hand, simply said they were reclaiming what was theirs all along.

A breed of specialists has been created to remake staid old corporations and return them to financial health. One such individual is Albert J. Dunlap, who now heads Scott Paper Company's efforts to restructure itself.[1] Mr. Dunlap developed his reputation for turning around poor performing companies working for Sir James Goldsmith (a British takeover specialist), where he turned around Crown Zellerbach and Diamond International. So what does Mr. Dunlap (known by some as "Rambo in Stripes" and to others simply as "Chainsaw") have in mind to reengineer Scott paper? The answer is quite simple. Learn to do more with less (cut the labor force by one third or lay off 10,500 workers) and focus on the firm's core businesses. Sounds simple. So why was it necessary to bring in Mr. Dunlap to accomplish the task? The answer is that the job of downsizing a firm is not a pleasant task, and few have the stomach for the trauma that it creates within an organization. Some, like Mr. Dunlap, do and they become turnaround specialists.

[1]Based on Glenn Collins, "Tough Leader Wields the Ax at Scott," *New York Times* (August 15, 1944): C1, C6.

WHY MERGERS MIGHT CREATE WEALTH

Clearly, for a merger to create wealth, it would have to provide shareholders with something they could not get by merely holding the individual shares of the two firms.

Economies of Scale

Wealth can be created in a merger through economies of scale. For example, administrative expenses including accounting, data processing, or simply top-management costs, may fall as a percentage of total sales as a result of sharing these resources.

Restating the question: What benefits are there to shareholders from holding the stock of a new, single firm that has been created through a merger as opposed to holding stock in the two individual firms prior to their merger? Let's consider some of these benefits.

Tax Benefits

If a merger were to result in a reduction of taxes that is not otherwise possible, then wealth is created by the merger. This can be the case with a firm that has lost money and thus generated tax credits but does not currently have a level of earnings sufficient to use those tax credits. Operating losses can be carried back three years and forward a total of fifteen years. As a result, tax credits that cannot be used and have no value to one firm can take on value when that firm is acquired by another firm that has earnings sufficient enough to employ the tax credits. In addition, a merger allows for previously depreciated assets to be revalued; wealth is created from the tax benefits arising from the increased depreciation associated with this revaluation of assets.

The sharing of resources can also lead to an increase in the firm's productivity. For example, if two firms sharing the same distribution channels merge, distributors carrying one product may now be willing to carry the other, thereby increasing the sales outlets for the products.

Unused Debt Potential

Some firms simply do not exhaust their debt capacity. If a firm with unused debt capacity is acquired, the new management can then increase debt financing, and reap the tax benefits associated with the increased leverage.

Complementarity in Financial Stack

When cash-rich bidders and cash-poor targets are combined, wealth may be created. This is particularly true where the cash-poor firm is a small business with limited access to capital markets. In effect, the merger allows positive NPV projects to be accepted that would have been rejected if the merger had not occurred.

Removal of Ineffective Management

A merger can result in the replacement of inefficient operations, whether in production or management. If a firm with ineffective management can be acquired, it may be possible to replace the current management with a more efficient management team, and thereby create wealth. This may be the case with firms that have grown from solely production into production and distribution companies, or R & D firms that have expanded into production and distribution; the managers simply may not know enough about the new aspects of the firm to manage it effectively.

Increased Market Power

The merger of two firms can result in an increase in market or monopoly power. Although this can result in increased wealth, it may also be illegal. The Clayton Act, as amended by the Celler-Kefauver Amendment of 1950, makes any merger illegal that results in a monopoly or substantially reduces competition. The Justice Department and the Federal Trade Commission monitor all mergers to ensure that they do not result in a reduction of competition.

Reduction in Bankruptcy Costs

There is no question that diversification can reduce the chance of financial failure and bankruptcy. Furthermore, there is a cost associated with bankruptcy. First, if a firm fails, its assets frequently cannot be sold for their true economic value. Moreover, the amount of money actually available for distribution to stockholders is further reduced by costs and legal fees that must be paid. Finally, the opportunity cost associated with the delays related to the legal process further reduces the funds available to the shareholder. Therefore, because costs are associated with bankruptcy, reduction of the chance of bankruptcy adds value.

The risk of bankruptcy also entails indirect costs associated with changes in the firm's debt capacity and the cost of debt. As the firm's cash flow patterns stabilize, the risk of default will decline, giving the firm an increased debt capacity and possibly reducing the cost of its debt. Because interest payments are tax deductible, they provide valuable tax savings. Thus monetary benefits are associated with an increased debt capacity. These indirect costs of bankruptcy also spread out into other areas of the firm, affecting things like production and the quality and efficiency of management. Firms with higher probabilities of bankruptcy may have a more difficult time recruiting and retaining quality managers and employees because jobs with that firm are viewed as less secure. This in turn may result in less productivity for these firms. In addition, firms with higher probabilities of bankruptcy may have a more difficult time marketing their product because of customer concern over future availability of the product. In short, there are real costs to bankruptcy. If a merger reduces this possibility of bankruptcy, it creates wealth.

"Chop-Shop" Approach—Buying Below Replacement Cost

The "chop-shop" approach, which will be discussed more fully later, suggests that the sum of the individual parts of a firm may be worth more than the current value of the whole. In the 1980s, many corporate raiders were driven by the fact that it was less expensive to purchase assets through an acquisition than it was to obtain those assets in any other way. This was particularly true of both conglomerates and oil companies. For conglomerates, corporate raiders found that they often sold for less than the sum of the market value of their parts. Much of the merger and acquisition activity associated with oil companies was driven by the fact that it was cheaper to acquire new oil reserves by purchasing a rival oil company than it was through exploration. If assets are mispriced, as this approach seems to suggest, then identifying those assets and revealing this information about the undervalued assets to an investor may result in the creation of wealth.

It should be noted that the free cash flow theory could explain this creation of wealth as easily as a mispricing theory. In particular, the oil industry was characterized in the late 1970s and early 1980s by overexploration and drilling activity in the face of reduced consumption while oil price increases created large cash flows. During this period, managers attempted to increase reserves to protect them from possible future market fluctuations. As mergers and restructuring raged through the oil industry, wealth was created. Again, this creation of wealth did not necessarily come about through any correction of mispricing. It may have been the elimination of wasteful exploration expenditures that created the wealth.

DETERMINATION OF A FIRM'S VALUE

One of the first problems in analyzing a potential merger involves placing a value on the acquired firm. This task is not easy. The value of a firm depends not only on its cash flow generation capabilities, but also upon the operating and financial characteristics of the acquiring firm. As a result, no single dollar value exists for a company. Instead, a range of values is determined that would be economically justifiable to the prospective acquirer. The final price is then negotiated by the two managements within this range.

To determine an acceptable price for a corporation, several factors are carefully evaluated. We know that the objective of the acquiring firm should be maximization of the stockholders' wealth (stock price). However, quantifying the relevant variables for this purpose is difficult at best. For instance, the primary reason for a merger might be to acquire managerial talent, or to complement a strong sales staff with an excellent production department. These *synergistic effects* are difficult to measure using the historical data of the companies involved. Even so, several quantitative variables are frequently used in an effort to estimate a firm's value. These factors include (1) book value, (2) appraisal value, (3) market price of the firm's common stock, and (4) expected cash flows.

Book Value

The **book value** of a firm's net worth is the balance sheet amount of the assets less its outstanding liabilities or the owners' equity. For example, if a firm's historical cost less accumulated depreciation is $10 million and the firm's debt totals $4 million, the aggregate book value is $6 million. Furthermore, if 100,000 shares of common stock are outstanding, the book value per share is $60 ($6 million ÷ 100,000 shares).

Book value does not measure the market value of a company's net worth because it is based on the historical cost of the firm's assets. Seldom do such costs bear a relationship to the value of the organization or its ability to produce earnings.

Although the book value of an enterprise is clearly not the most important factor, it should not be overlooked. It can be used as a starting point to be compared with other analyses. Also, a study of the firm's working capital is particularly important to acquisitions involving a business consisting primarily of liquid assets like financial institutions. Furthermore, in industries where the ability to generate earnings requires large investments in such items as steel, cement, and petroleum, the book value could be a critical factor, especially where plant and equipment are relatively new.

Appraisal Value

An **appraisal value** of a company may be acquired from an independent appraisal firm. The techniques used by appraisers vary widely; however, this value is often closely tied to replacement cost. This method of analysis is not adequate by itself, since the value of individual assets may have little relation to the firm's overall ability to generate earnings, and thus the going-concern value of the firm. However, the appraised value of an enterprise may be beneficial when used in conjunction with other valuation methods. Also, the appraised value may be an important factor in special situations, such as in financial companies, natural resource enterprises, or organizations that have been operating at a loss.[2]

The use of appraisal values does yield several additional advantages. The value according to independent appraisers may permit the reduction of a counting goodwill by increasing the recognized worth of specific assets. *Goodwill* results when the purchase price of a firm exceeds the book value of the assets. Consider a company having a book value of $60,000 that is purchased for $100,000 (the 540,000 difference is goodwill). The $60,000 book value consists of $20,000 in working capital and $40,000 in fixed assets. However, an appraisal might suggest that the current values of these assets are $25,000 and $55,000, respectively. The $15,000 increase ($55,000 – $40,000) in fixed assets permits the acquiring firm to record a larger depreciation expense than would otherwise be possible, thereby reducing taxes. A second reason for an appraisal is to provide a test of the reasonableness of results obtained through methods based upon the going-concern concept. Third, the appraiser may uncover strengths and weaknesses that otherwise might not be recognized, such as in the valuation of patents, secret processes, and partially completed R & D expenditures.

---

[2]The assets of a financial company and a natural resources firm largely consist of securities and natural reserves, respectively. The value of these individual assets has a direct bearing on the fimrm's earning capacity. Also, a company operating at a loss may only be worth its liquidation value, which would approximate the appraisal value.

Thus the appraisal is generally worthwhile if performed with additional evaluation processes. In specific instances, it may be an important instrument for valuing a corporation.

Stock Market Value

The **stock market value,** as expressed by stock market quotations, is another approach to estimating the net worth of a business. If the stock is listed on a major securities exchange, such as the New York Stock Exchange, and is widely traded, an approximate value can be established on the basis of the market value. The justification is based on the fact that the market quotations indicate the consensus of investors as to a firm's cash flow potential and the corresponding risk.

The market-value approach is the one most frequently used in valuing large corporations. However, this value can change abruptly. Analytical factors compete with purely speculative influences and are subject to people's sentiments and personal decisions. Thus the market is not a weighing machine, on which the value of each issue is recorded by an exact and impersonal mechanism, in accordance with the specific qualities. Rather, should we say, the market is a voting machine, whereon countless individuals register choices which are the product partly of reason and partly of emotion.[3]

In short, the market-value approach is probably the one most widely used for determining the worth of a firm; a 10% to 20% premium above the market price is often required as an inducement for the current owners to sell their stock. Even so, executives who place their entire reliance upon this are subject to an inherent danger of market psychology.

"Chop-Shop" Value

The "chop-shop" approach to valuation was first proposed by Dean Lebaron and Lawrence Speidell of Batterymarch Financial Management. Specifically, it attempts to identify multi-industry companies that are undervalued and would be worth more if separated into their parts. This approach conceptualizes the practice of attempting to buy assets below their replacement cost.

Any time we confront a technique that suggests that stocks may be inefficiently priced, we must be a bit skeptical. In the case of a multi-industry firm, inefficiency in pricing may be brought on by the high cost of obtaining information. Alternatively, these firms may be worth more if split up because of agency problems. Shareholders of multi-industry companies may feel they have less control of the firm's managers, since additional layers of management may have developed with multi-industry firms. These agency costs may take the form of increased expenditures necessary to monitor the managers, costs associated with organizational change, and opportunity costs associated with poor decisions made as a result of the manager acting in his or her own best interest rather than the best interest of the shareholders.

The "chop-shop" approach attempts to value companies by their various business segments. As it is implemented by Batterymarch, it first attempts to find "pure-

[3]Benjamin Graham, David L. Dodd, and Sidney Cottle, *Security Analysis,* 4th ed. (New York: McGraw-Hill, 1962), 42.

play" companies—that is, companies in a single industry from which it computes average "valuation ratios." The ratios frequently used compare total capitalization (debt plus equity) to total sales, to assets, and to income. In effect, these ratios represent the average value of a dollar of sales, a dollar of assets, and a dollar of income for a particular industry based on the average of all pure-play companies in that industry. Assuming that these ratios hold for the various business segments of a multi-industry firm, the firm can then be valued by its parts.

For the chop-shop valuation technique to be feasible, we must naturally have information about the various business segments within the firm. This requirement is fulfilled, at least in part, by the reporting rules set forth in *Statement 14* of the Financial Accounting Standards Board (the public accountants governing group). This standard requires that firms provide detailed accounting statements along the various lines of business or what is called Standard Industrial Codes (SIC). Of course, we know that not all firms in the same industry are in fact the same—some have more growth potential or earning ability than others. As such, this methodology should be viewed cautiously. However, it is in use by financial managers, and we should understand it.

The "chop-shop" approach is actually a three-step process.

Step 1: Identify the firm's various business segments and calculate the average capitalization ratios for firms in those industries.
Step 2: Calculate a "theoretical" market value based upon each of the average capitalization ratios.
Step 3: Average the "theoretical" market values to determine the "chop-shop" value of the firm.

To illustrate the chop-shop approach, consider Cavos, Inc., with common stock currently trading at a total market price of $13 million. For Cavos, the accounting data set forth four business segments: industrial specialties, basic chemicals, consumer specialties, and basic plastics. Data for these four segments are as follows:

Business Segment	Segment		
	Sales ($000)	Assets ($000)	Income ($000)
Industrial specialties	$ 2.765	$2.206	$186
Basic chemicals	5.237	4.762	165
Consumer specialties	2.029	1.645	226
Basic plastics	1.506	1.079	60
Total	$11.537	$9.692	$637

The three steps for valuing Cavos would be

Step 1: We first identify "pure" companies, that being firms that operate solely in one of the above industries; we then calculate the average capitalization ratios for those firms. This could easily be done using a computer data base, such as the Compustat tapes, which provide detailed financial information on most publicly traded firms. The average capitalization ratios for Cavos's four business segments have been determined and are as shown in Figure 26-1.

Step 2:   Once we have calculated the average market capitalization ratios for the various market segments, we need only multiply Cavos's segment values (that is, segment sales, segment assets, and segment income) times the corresponding capitalization ratios to determine the theoretical market values. This is done in Figure 26-2.

Step 3:   Finally, the theoretical values must be averaged to calculate the "chop-shop" value of the firm. The average of the three theoretical values in Figure 26-3 is $18,923,000, computed as follows:

$$\frac{\text{value based on sales} + \text{value based on assets} + \text{value based on income}}{3}$$

or

$$\frac{(\$23,518,500 + \$21,087,700 + \$12,132,800)}{3}$$

$$= \$18,913.00$$

Hence Cavos, Inc. is selling for significantly less than its chop-shop value—$13 million compared with $18.9 million.

The major limitation of a valuation model such as the chop-shop approach is that it is not derived from any theoretical basis. What it does is assume that average industry capitalization relationships—in this case, ratios of capitalization to sales, assets, and operating income—hold for all firms or conglomerate subsidiaries in that particular industry. Of course, this is frequently not the case. It is easy to identify specific companies that simply produce superior products and whose future earnings growth is, as a result, brighter. These companies, because of their expected future growth, should have their sales, assets, and operating income valued higher.

Given this limitation of the chop-shop valuation approach, why have we dealt with it in such detail? The reason is that it reflects a view among some investors and corporate raiders that the replacement value of a firm's assets may exceed the value placed on the firm as a whole in the market. The chop-shop method attempts to value the multi-industry firm by its parts. Moreover, as we will see when we explore the cash flow approach to valuation, there simply is no way to estimate the value of a takeover candidate with complete confidence. Thus, this method provides the decision maker with additional information.

FIGURE 26-1   Average Capitalization Ratios for Industries in Which Cavos, Inc., Is Active

Business Segment	Capitalization Sales	Capitalization Assets	Capitalization Operating Income
Industrial specialties	0.61	1.07	21.49
Basic chemicals	2.29	2.43	17.45
Consumer specialties	3.58	2.92	19.26
Basic plastics	1.71	2.18	15.06

FIGURE 26-2   Calculation of the "Theoretical Values" for Cavos, Inc.,
              Using Market Capitalization Ratios

| | Value Based on Market Capitalization/Sales | | |
Business Segment	(A) Market Capitalization Sales	(B) Segment Sales	(A) × (B) Theoretical Market Value
Industrial specialties	0.61	$2,765	$1,686.7
Basic chemicals	2.29	5,237	11,992.7
Consumer specialties	3.58	2,029	7,263.8
Basic plastics	1.71	1,506	2,575.3
Total			$23,518.5

| | Value Based on Market Capitalization/Sales | | |
Business Segment	(A) Market Capitalization Assets	(B) Segment Assets	(A) × (B) Theoretical Market Value
Industrial specialties	1.07	$2,206	$2,360.4
Basic chemicals	2.43	4,762	11,571.7
Consumer specialties	2.92	1,645	4,803.4
Basic plastics	2.18	1,079	2,352.2
Total			$21,087.7

| | Value Based on Market Capitalization/Sales | | |
Business Segment	(A) Market Capitalization Income	(B) Segment Income	(A) × (B) Theoretical Market Value
Industrial specialties	21.49	$186	$3,997.1
Basic chemicals	17.45	165	2,879.3
Consumer specialties	19.26	226	4,352.8
Basic plastics	15.06	60	903.6
Total			$12,132.8

The Cash Flow Value

Our last look at valuation models should be familiar to us, given our prior work in finding the present value of cash flows, when we studied capital budgeting. Using the cash flow approach to merger valuation requires that we estimate the incremental net cash flows available to the bidding firms as a result of the merger or acquisition. The present value of these cash flows then will be determined, and this will be the maximum amount that should be paid for the target firm. The initial outlay then can be subtracted out to calculate the net present value from the merger. Although this is very similar to a capital-budgeting problem, there are differences, particularly in estimating the initial outlay.

Finding the present value of the cash flows for a merger involves a five-step process:

Step 1: Estimate the incremental after-tax cash flows available from the target firm. This includes all synergistic cash flows (including those to both the bidding and target firms) created as a result of the acquisition. It should also be noted that interest expenses are not included in these cash flows, as they are accounted for in the required rate of return.

Step 2: Estimate the after-tax risk-adjusted discount rate associated with cash flows from the target firm. The target firm's, not the bidding firm's, required rate of return is appropriate here. If there is any anticipated change in financing associated with the target firm as a result of the acquisition, this change should also be considered.

Step 3: Calculate the present value of the incremental cash flows from the target firm.

Step 4: Estimate the initial outlay associated with the acquisition. The initial outlay is defined here as the market value of all securities and cash paid out plus the market value of all liabilities assumed.

Step 5: Calculate the net present value of the acquisition by subtracting the initial outlay from the present value of the incremental cash flows from the target firm.

Estimation of the incremental after-tax cash flows resulting from an acquisition can be extremely difficult. A certain lack of precision is inherent in these calculations because of the problem of estimating the synergistic gains from combining the two firms. For example, it is very difficult to estimate the gains that might be expected from any reduction in bankruptcy costs, increased market power, or reduction in agency costs that might occur. Still, it is imperative to estimate these gains if we are to place a value on the target firm. Once the required rate of return is determined, the present value of the incremental cash flows from acquiring the target firm can then be calculated. The final step then becomes the calculation of the initial outlay associated with the acquisition.

Let's look at the example of Tabbypaw Pie, Inc., which is being considered as a possible takeover target by ALF, Inc. Currently, Tabbypaw Pie uses 30% debt in its capital structure, but ALF plans on increasing the debt ratio to 40% (we will assume that only debt and equity are used) once the acquisition is completed. The after-tax cost of debt capital for Tabbypaw Pie is estimated to be 7%, and we will assume that this rate does not change as Tabbypaw's capital structure changes. The cost of equity after the acquisition is expected to be 20.8%. The current market Value of Tabbypaw's debt outstanding is $110 million, all of which will be assumed by ALF. Also, let's assume that ALF intends to pay $260 million in cash and common stock for all of Tabbypaw Pie's stock in addition to assuming all of Tabbypaw's debt. Currently, the market price of Tabbypaw Pie's common stock is $210 million.

Step 1: Estimate the incremental cash flows from the target firm, including the synergistic flows, such as any possible flows from tax credits. This estimation for Tabbypaw is provided in Figure 26-3. Here we are assuming that any cash flows after 1999 will be constant at $75 million. Also, we subtract any funds that must be reinvested in the firm in the form of capital expenditures that are required to support the firm's increasing profits.

Step 2: Determine an appropriate risk-adjusted discount rate for evaluating Tabbypaw. Here we will use the weighted cost of capital (k_0) for Tabbypaw as our discount rate, where the weighted cost of capital is calculated as

$$k_0 = W_d K_d + W_c K_c$$

where W_d, W_c = the percentage of funds provided by debt and common, . respectively

K_d,K_c = the cost of debt and common, respectively

For Tabbypaw,

$$K_0 = (.40)(.07) + (.60)(.208) = .1528, \text{ or } 15.28\%$$

Step 3: Next we must calculate the present value of the incremental cash flows expected from the target firm. Assuming that cash flows do not change after 1999, but continue at the 1999 level in perpetuity, and discounting these cash flows at the 15.28%, we get

$$\begin{pmatrix} \text{present value} \\ \text{of all cash flows} \end{pmatrix} = \begin{pmatrix} \text{present value} \\ \text{of 1995--1998} \\ \text{cash flows} \end{pmatrix} = \begin{pmatrix} \text{present value} \\ \text{of cash flows} \\ \text{after 1998} \end{pmatrix}$$

where the present value of cash flows for 1995 through 1998 would be $190.772 million, determined as follows:

$$\frac{\$63}{(1+.1528)} + \frac{\$66}{(1+.1528)^2} + \frac{\$70}{(1+.1528)^3} + \frac{\$72}{(1+.1528)^4}$$

FIGURE 26-3   Estimated Incremental Cash Flows from Tabbypaw Pie, Inc. ($ millions)

	1995	1996	1997	1998	1999 and Thereafter
Net sales	$496	$536	$606	$670	$731
Cost of goods sold	354	385	444	500	551
Administrative and selling expenses	28	30	32	35	38
Earnings before depreciation and interest	114	121	130	135	142
Depreciation	39	40	41	42	43
Earnings before interest and taxes	75	81	89	93	99
Taxes (incremental)	27	30	34	36	39
Net income	48	51	55	57	60
Net income	48	51	55	57	60
+Depreciation	39	40	41	42	43
−Capital expenditures	24	25	26	27	28
Net after-tax cash flow (before interest)	$ 63	$ 66	$ 70	$ 72	$ 75

and the present value of the $75 million cash flow stream, beginning in 1999, is computed to be $277.921 million.[4]

$$\frac{\dfrac{\$75}{.1528}}{(1+.1528)^4} = \$277.921$$

Thus the present value of the cash inflows associated with the acquisition of Tabbypaw Pie by ALF is $468.693 million, or $468,693,000; that is, the sum of $190.772 million and $277.921 million.

Step 4: Next, we estimate the initial outlay associated with the acquisition. As already noted, the initial outlay is defined as the market value of all securities and cash paid out plus the market value of all debt liabilities assumed. In this case, the market value of the assumed debt obligations is $110 million. This amount, along with the acquisition price of $260 million, comprise the initial outlay of $370 million.

Step 5: Finally, the net present value of the acquisition is calculated by subtracting the initial outlay (calculated in step 4) from the present value of the incremental cash flows from the target firm (calculated in step 3):

NPV acquisition   = PV inflows − initial outlay
                = $468,693,000 − $370,000,000
                = $98,693,000

Thus the acquisition should be undertaken because it has a positive net present value. In fact, ALF could pay up to $468.693 million for Tabbypaw Pie.

FINANCING AND CORPORATE RESTRUCTURING[5]

In recent years, we have seen significant changes in the financing practices of U.S. firms, in part the result of the restructuring of corporate America. The outstanding debt of many companies increased as they borrowed heavily to finance restructuring activity. As part of this restructuring, three popular types of highly leveraged transactions have developed: MBO, LBO, and the leveraged Employee Stock Ownership Plan (ESOP). How significant are these financing techniques? The use of LBOs increased from less than $5 billion in 1983 to more than $60 billion in 1989. These three financing approaches are described subsequently.[6] Following a discussion of these techniques, we will look at the use of a bond that drew great attention during the 1980s—the junk bond.

---

[4]Remember that we can find the present value of an infinite stream of cash flows, where the amount is constant, in each year, as follows:

$$\text{value} = \frac{\text{annual cash flow}}{\text{required rate of return}}$$

Because the cash flows do not begin until the fifth year, our equation is finding the value at the end of the fourth year; thus we must discount the value back for four years.

[5]The ideas in this section come largely from Leland Crabbe, Margaret Pickering, and Stephen Prowse, "Recent Developments in Corporate Finance," *Federal Reserve Bulletin* (August 1990): 595–603.

[6]Taken from John D. Martin and John W. Kensinger, Exploring the Controversy Over Corporate Restructuring (Morristown, NJ: Financial Executive Institute Research Foundation, 1990), 46.

MBOs

An **MBO** occurs when a group of investors forms a shell corporation to acquire the target firm or buy the target firm directly. The distinguishing features of an MBO are (1) the group of investors includes members of the management of the target company; (2) following the acquisition the newly formed company goes private; and (3) the acquisition is financed primarily by debt, so the resulting firm is much more highly leveraged than most publicly traded companies.

LBOs

An **LBO** is a more general type of restructuring device that can be distinguished from an MBO in that the new owners do not necessarily have to include members of the original management team, and the firm is not necessarily taken private following the acquisition. Most LBOs are also MBOs, and the term LBO is more generally used in describing high-leverage acquisitions and restructurings. Figure 26-4 illustrates the process of an LBO, using the events surrounding the RJR Nabisco LBO as an example.

Leveraged ESOPs

In a leveraged **ESOP,** the rank-and-file employees participate with management in the purchase of stock in their corporation. In these arrangements, a special trust is formed to borrow money to purchase the firm's stock. The loan is then repaid from the employees' retirement funds, and the shares are credited to the employees' retirement account. The employer corporation typically guarantees the loan. The stock is held in trust until the participating employee retires or terminates employment. There are three distinct tax advantages with an ESOP: (1) Dividends paid by the company to stock owned by an ESOP are tax deductible; (2) the institution lending the money to create the ESOP has to pay income tax on only half of the interest received from the ESOP, and thus the plan allows borrowing at low interest rates; and (3) the employer corporation is allowed to make tax-deductible contributions of cash or stock to the ESOP

Junk Bonds

Junk bonds, which have been described in several earlier chapters, have been closely linked to the large, and at times unsuccessful, mergers of the 1980s. The use of these bonds has been viewed as a common element in some of the country's worst financial disasters in the late 1980s. Examples include the failure of the Campeau retailing empire and the bankruptcy of Drexel, Burnham, Lambert.

Some critics blame many of the market ills on junk bonds. According to these critics, junk bonds fueled the merger mania of the 1980s, caused the excessive use of debt, and created instability in the financial markets. Although these opinions are certainly understandable, the evidence does not support these extreme charges against

FIGURE 26-4   An LBO: The Case of RJR Nabisco Corp.

First indication	October 21, 1988. F. Ross Johnson, CEO of RJR, announced a proposed MBO for $75 per share.
Completion date	December 1, 1988. KKR won a bidding war for RJR for $109 per share.
Major events	
10/21/88	RJR announced a proposed MBO.
10/27/88	KKR began a $20.8 billion tender offer for RJR.
11/8/88	RJR management was joined by Shearson Lehman Hutton and Salomon on a buyout offer of $21.16 billion ($92 per share). RJR opened the bidding process for sealed bids.
11/30/88	KKR appeared to have won the bidding contest for RJR with a bid of $23.7 billion ($103 per share).
12/1/88	KKR officially named the winner of the bidding war with a bid of $109 per share, or $25 billion.
2/7/89	Swiss Bank and J. P. Morgan (Switzerland) demanded that RJR call its Swiss Franc Bonds at face value because of losses incurred by bondholders due to the LBO financing.
2/10/89	KKR completed the takeover.
3/23/89	Swiss court issues temporary order to stop the completion of the RJR takeover. The order is on behalf of Swiss bondholders who have seen the value of their RJR bonds decrease due to the buyout.
4/6/89	RJR plans to sell $5.5 to $6 billion in assets. RJR also files prospectus for $4 billion bond issue. These bonds are to be used to pay interest on current debt.
4/28/89	Shareholders vote final approval of RJR buyout.
5/12/89	$4 billion bridge loan refinanced.
6/1/89	Federal judge rejects Metropolitan Life's claims that RJR had violated an unwritten requirement to treat bondholders fairly.
6/7/89	RJR sells five of its European food businesses for $2.5 billion.
6/12/89	Federal judge rules that RJR can sell off assets to help pay debt incurred by LBO. Met Life files suit to protect bondholders' rights.
6/21/89	Chung King sold for $52 million.
7/28/89	Scandinavian food unit sold for $20.4 million.
8/1/89	Several corporate apartments and houses sold for $8.6 million.
9/7/89	Del Monte Tropical Fruit sold for $875 million. Negotiations underway for the sale of Del Monte Foods canned food unit for $1.5 billion.

Source: John D. Martin and John W. Kensinger, *Exploring the Controversy over Corporate Restructuring* (Morristown, NJ: Financial Executive Institute Research Foundation, 1990), 11.

junk bonds.[7] Junk bonds align with our expectations in terms of risk and expected returns. They are not inherently different from other securities—they have greater risk but also greater expected return. Also, the junk bond market, although significant, was too small to have caused the 1980s' merger boom, nor was it large enough to account directly for the growth in corporate debt.

Junk bonds in fact accounted for only 14% of the growth in corporate debt during the 1980s. Nevertheless, the financing that had been available through the junk bond market essentially evaporated at the conclusion of the 1980s. Merger activity accordingly declined noticeably during the first part of 1990 as a consequence of the

[7]These ideas come from Sean Beckett, "The Truth About Junk Bonds." Federal Reserve Bank of Kansas City, *Economic Review* (July–August 1990): 45–54.

virtual unavailability of new financing in the low-grade bond market. Also, the more cautious attitude of commercial banks and the weakening in the market for asset sales contributed to the decline. Nevertheless, well-structured acquisition proposals, especially those aimed at enhancing a firm's competitive position within its own lines of business, continue today.

TENDER OFFER

As an alternative approach in purchasing another firm, the acquiring corporation may consider using a **tender offer.** A tender offer involves a bid by an interested party of controlling interest in another corporation. The prospective purchaser approaches the stockholders of the firm, rather than the management, to encourage them to sell their shares, typically at a premium over the current market price. For instance, in late 1990, AT&T made a $6.1 billion tender offer for NCR, or $90 per share. NCR's management quickly responded by telling the stockholders they should refuse the offer because the stock was worth $125, even though it had only been selling for $48 per share before AT&T's tender offer. After a real dog fight, the final agreement was for $110 per share.

Because the tender offer is a direct appeal to the stockholders, prior approval is not required by the management of the target firm. However, the acquiring firm may choose to approach the management of the target firm. If the two managements are unsuccessful in negotiating the terms, a tender offer may then be attempted. Alternatively, a firm's management that is interested in acquiring control of a second corporation may try a surprise takeover without contacting the management of the latter company. T. Boone Pickens of Mesa Petroleum is a prime example of someone who has used the tender offer in his efforts to acquire such firms as Cities Service and Gulf.

RESISTANCE TO MERGERS

In response to unfriendly merger attempts, especially tender offers, the management of the firm under attack will frequently strike back. Several defense tactics are used to counter tender offers. These defensive maneuvers include white knights, shark repellents, poison pills, and golden parachutes. Let us examine these more closely.

A *white knight* is a company that comes to the rescue of a corporation that is being targeted for a takeover. For example, when Pennzoil made a tender offer for Getty Oil, the Getty management opposed the Pennzoil attempt. To prevent the takeover, Texaco, at the encouragement of Getty's management, made its own tender offer for Getty at a higher price. Texaco was the white knight for Getty. However, Pennzoil later received a $10 billion judgment against Texaco for its action in the Getty acquisition.

PacMan, the name taken from the video game, is another defensive tactic to tender offers, where the firm under attack becomes the attacker. For instance, Bendix Corporation tried to take control of Martin-Marietta by a tender offer. When the takeover effort failed, Martin-Marietta counterattacked by buying Bendix stock in an attempt to take control of Bendix. Martin-Marietta became the PacMan. To recounter, Bendix successfully courted Allied Corporation to come to its rescue. Allied bought

Bendix so that Martin-Marietta could not buy enough for control. Allied was a white knight.

Shark repellents are policy changes or legal manipulations that can be used to discourage unfriendly takeovers. As an example, a firm may revise its bylaws to stagger the terms of directors so that only a few come up for election in any one year. A firm making a tender offer would have to wait at least two years before gaining a majority of board members. Another ploy is to reincorporate in a state with rules that favor existing management. Gulf Oil was incorporated in Pennsylvania, where minority stockholders could use cumulative voting to gain a voice on the board of directors. When T. Boone Pickens began buying major blocks of Gulf stock, Gulf reincorporated in Delaware, where cumulative voting could not be used, making it more difficult for Pickens to have any impact on the management of Gulf.

Another tactic is the **poison pill,** an action initiated automatically if an unfriendly party tries to acquire a firm. For instance, management might devise a plan whereby all the firm's debt becomes due if the management is removed. Still another tactic is the *golden parachute,* which stipulates that the acquiring company must pay the executives of the acquired firm a substantial sum of money to "let them down easy" as new management is brought into the company.

The disadvantages of the unfriendly takeover are readily apparent from the preceding examples. If the target firm's management attempts to block it, the costs of executing the offer may increase significantly. Also, the purchasing company may fail to acquire a sufficient number of shares to meet the objective of controlling the firm. Conversely, if the offer is not strongly contested, it may possibly be less expensive than the normal route for acquiring a company, in that it permits control by purchasing a smaller portion of the firm. Also, the tender offer has proven somewhat less susceptible to judicial inquiries regarding the fairness of the purchase price, because each stockholder individually decides the fairness of the price.

DIVESTITURES

Although the merger-and-acquisition phenomenon has been a major influence in restructuring the corporate sector, divestitures, or what we might call "reverse mergers," may have become an equally important factor. In fact, preliminary research to date would suggest that we may be witnessing a "new era" in the making—one where the public corporation has become a more efficient vehicle for increasing and maintaining stockholder wealth.[8] Whereas corporate management once seemed to behave as if 2 + 2 were equal to 5, especially during the conglomerate heyday of the '60s, the wave of reverse mergers seems based on the counter proposition that 5 – 1 is 5. And the market's consistently positive response to such deals seems to be providing broad confirmation of the "new math."[9]

A successful divestiture allows the firm's assets to be used more efficiently and therefore to be assigned a higher value by the market forces. It essentially eliminates a division or subsidiary that does not fit strategically with the rest of the company;

---

[8]See Robert Comment and Gregg A. Jarrell, 1995, "Corporate focus and stock returns." *Journal of Financial Economics* 37:67–87; and Kose John and Eli Ofek, 1995, "Asset sales and increase in focus." *Journal of Financial Economics* 37:105–126.

[9]Joel M. Stern, and Donald H. Chew, Jr. (eds.), *The Revolution in Corporate Finance* (New York: Basis Blackwell, 1986), 416.

that is, it removes an operation that does not contribute to the company's basic purposes.

The different types of divestitures may be summarized as follows:

1. **Selloff.** A selloff is the sale of a subsidiary, division, or product line by one company to another. For example, Radio Corporation of America (RCA) sold its finance company and General Electric sold its metallurgical coal business.
2. **Spinoff.** A spinoff involves the separation of a subsidiary from its parent, with no change in the equity ownership. The management of the parent company gives up operating control of the subsidiary, but the shareholders retain the same percentage ownership in both firms. New shares representing ownership in the diverted assets are issued to the original shareholders on a pro-rata basis.
3. **Liquidation.** A liquidation in this context is not a decision to shut down or abandon an asset. Rather, the assets are sold to another company, and the proceeds distributed to the stockholders.
4. **Going private.** A company goes private when its stock that has traded publicly is purchased by a small group of investors, and the stock is no longer bought and sold on a public exchange. The ownership of the company is transferred from a diverse group of outside stockholders to a small group of private investors, usually including the firm's management. The leveraged buyout is a special case of going private. As noted earlier in the chapter, the existing shareholders sell their shares to a small group of investors. The purchasers of the stock use the firm's unused debt capacity to borrow the funds to pay for the stock. Thus the new investors acquire the firm with little, if any, personal investment. However, the firm's debt ratio may increase by as much as tenfold.

SUMMARY

Business combinations historically have represented a major influence in the growth of firms in the United States. This avenue for growth has been particularly important during select periods, such as in the 1980s.

Value Creation through Merging

The assertion that merger activity creates wealth for the shareholder cannot be maintained with certainty. Only if the merger provides something that the investor cannot do on his or her own can a merger or acquisition be of financial benefit.

Valuing a Firm

Determining the value of a firm is a difficult task. In addition to projecting the firm's future profitability, which is a cornerstone in valuation, the acquirer must consider the effects of joining two businesses into a single operation. What may represent a good investment may not be a good merger.

In estimating a firm's worth, several factors are frequently considered, including (1) the firm's book value, (2) its appraisal value, (3) the stock market value of a firm's common shares, (4) its chop-shop value, and (5) the present value of future free cash flows.

Financing the Merger

Financial innovation frequently has come in conjunction with corporate restructuring; most notable examples include MBOs, LBOs, and leveraged ESOPs. Certainly these concepts are not new, but the extent of their application has increased significantly. In more recent years, we have seen a marked increase in the use of debt. Before the takeovers of the 1980s, managers strove to maintain a targeted capital structure mix. In the 1980s, the use of an LBO sometimes meant that an acquired firm's debt might be increased tenfold; the intent was not to maintain that high level of debt but rather to bring it down to more acceptable norms as soon as possible. As the 1990s began, the failure of some large firms to meet their large debt obligations brought on by mergers has recently led to the use of equity as a favored way to finance a merger.

Tender Offers

Normally, the purchaser approaches the management of the firm to be acquired. Alternatively, the purchasing firm can directly approach the stockholders of the firm under consideration. This bid for ownership, called a tender offer, has been used with increasing frequency. This approach may be cheaper, but often the managers of the target firm attempt to block it.

Divestitures

A divestiture represents a variety of ways to let go of a portion of the firm's assets. It has become an important vehicle in restructuring the corporation into a more efficient operation.

Resisting a Hostile Takeover Attempt

Some of the most interesting and colorful language of finance has arisen out of the attempts of target firms to resist an unwanted takeover. For example, when firm A is under attack from hostile takeover firm B, it may seek out a more friendly arrangement by seeking out a third bidder who will come in and purchase the firm. In the jargon of the merger literature, the third firm is called a white knight (for obvious reasons). Another popular tactic, the poison pill, comes right out of the spy novel tradition. In this instance, the target firm puts in place a set of conditions that are triggered only in the event that the firm is taken over by an unfriendly suitor. For example, the firm might arrange for the issuance of new common stock to be distributed to everyone other than the hostile takeover firm, or the firm's debt might be made due and payable immediately should the firm fall victim to an unwanted take-over. The list goes on, and the techniques that might be devised to resist an unwanted takeover are limited only by the imagination of the management of the firm and the boundaries set by state and local law.

SELF-CORRECTION PROBLEM

Using the chop-shop approach, assign a value for the Calvert Corporation, where its common stock is currently trading at a total market price of $5 million. For Calvert, the accounting data set forth two business segments: auto sales and auto specialties. Data for the firm's two segments are as follows:

Business Segment	Segment Sales ($000)	Segment Assets ($000)	Segment Income ($000)
Auto sales	$3,000	$1,000	$150
Auto specialties	2,500	3,000	500
Total	$5,500	$4,000	$650

Industry data for "pure-play" firms have been compiled and are summarized as follows:

Business Segment	Capitalization Sales	Capitalization Assets	Capitalization Operating Income
Auto sales	1.40	3.20	18.00
Auto specialties	.80	.90	8.00

SOLUTION TO SELF-CORRECTION PROBLEM

	Capital-to-Sales	Segment Sales	Theoretical Values
Auto sales	1.40	$3,000	$4,200
Auto specialties	0.80	$2,500	2,000
			$6,200

	Capital-to-Assets	Segment Assets	Theoretical Values
Auto sales	3.20	$1,000	$3,200
Auto specialties	0.90	3,000	2,700
			$5,900

	Capital-to-Income	Segment Income	Theoretical Values
Auto sales	18.00	$150	$2,700
Auto specialties	8.00	500	4,000
			$6,700

Theoretical based on	
Sales	$6,200
Assets	$5,900
Income	6,700
Average value	$6,267

QUESTIONS

1. Why might merger activities create wealth?
2. Why is book value alone an imperfect measure of the worth of a company?
3. What advantages are provided by the use of an appraisal value in valuing a firm?
4. What is the concept of the chop-shop valuation procedure?
5. Compare the NPV approach used in valuing a merger with the same approach in capital budgeting.
6. Describe an MBO, LBO, and leveraged ESOP.
7. What are the disadvantages of the tender offer?
8. Explain the different types of divestitures.

PROBLEMS

1. **Chop-Shop Valuation.**   Using the chop-shop approach, assign a value for Dabney, Inc., whose common stock is currently trading at a total market price of $7 million. For Dabney, the accounting data sets forth three business segments:

consumer wholesaling, specialty services, and retirement center's. Data for the firm's three segments are as follows:

Business Segment	Segment Sales ($000)	Segment Assets ($000)	Segment Income ($000))
Industrial specialties	$2,765	$2,206	$186
Basic chemicals	5,237	4,762	165
Consumer specialties	2,029	1,645	226
Basic plastics	1,506	1,079	60
Total	$11,537	$9,692	$637

Industry data for "pure-play" firms have been compiled and are summarized as follows:

Business Segment	Capitalization Sales	Capitalization Assets	Capitalization Operating Income
Consumer wholesaling	0.80	.70	12.00
Specialty services	1.20	1.00	6.00
Retirement centers	1.20	.70	7.00

2. **Chop-Shop Valuation.** Using the chop-shop method, determine a value for Aramus, Inc., whose common stock is trading at a total market price of $15 million. For Aramus, the accounting data are divided into three business segments: sunglasses distribution, reading glasses distribution, and technical products. Data for the firm's three segments are as follows:

Business Segment	Segment Sales ($000)	Segment Assets ($000)	Segment Income ($000)
Sunglasses distribution	$ 3,500	$ 1,000	$ 350
Reading glasses distribution	2,000	1,500	250
Technical products	6,500	8,500	1,200
Total	$12,000	$11,000	$1,800

Industry data for "pure-play" firms have been computed and are summarized as follows:

Business Segment	Capitalization Sales	Capitalization Assets	Capitalization Operating Income
Sunglasses distubution	1.0	.8	8.0
Reading glasses distribution	.9	.8	10.0
Technical products	1.2	1.0	7.0

3. **Free Cash Flow Valuation.** The Argo Corporation is viewed as a possible takeover target by Hilary, Inc. Currently, Argo uses 20% debt in its capital structure, but Hilary plans to increase the debt ratio to 30% if the acquisition is consum-

mated. The after-tax cost of debt capital for Argo is estimated to be 8%, with either 20 or 30% debt financing. The cost of equity after the acquisition is expected to be 18%. The current market value of Argo's outstanding debt is $40 million, all of which will be assumed by Hilary. Hilary intends to pay $250 million in cash and common stock for all of Argo's stock in addition to assuming all of Argo's debt. Currently, the market pace of Argo's common stock is $200 million. Selected items from Argo's financial data are as follows:

	1995	1996	1997	1998	Thereafter
		(Millions)			
Net sales	$200	$225	$240	$250	$275
Administrative and					
selling expenses	15	20	27	28	30
Depreciation	10	15	17	20	24
Capital expenditures	12	13	15	17	20

In addition, the cost of goods sold runs 60% of sales and the marginal tax rate is 34%. Compute the net present value of the acquisition.

4. **Free Cash Flow Valuation.**   The Prime Corporation is viewed as a possible takeover target by Big Boy, Inc. Currently, Prime uses 25% debt in its capital structure, but Big Boy plans to increase the debt ratio to 40% if the acquisition is expected to be 20%. The current market value of Prime's debt outstanding is $30 million, all of which will be assumed by Big Boy. Big Boy intends to pay $150 million in cash and common stock for all of Prime's stock in addition to assuming all of its debt. Currently, the market price of Prime's common stock is $125 million. Selected items from Prime's financial data are as follows:

	1995	1996	1997	1998	Thereafter
		(Millions)			
Net sales	$300	$330	$375	$400	$425
Admininstrative and					
selling expenses	40	50	58	62	65
Depreciation	25	30	35	38	40
Capital expenditures	30	37	45	48	50

In addition, the cost of goods sold runs 60% of sales, and the marginal tax rate is 34%. Compute the NPV of the acquisition.

APPENDICES

USING A CALCULATOR

A Tutorial on the Hewlett-Packard HP 17BII

As you prepare for a career in business, the ability to use a financial calculator is essential, whether you are in the finance division or the marketing department. For most positions, it will be assumed that you can use a calculator in making computations that at one time were simply not possible without extensive time and effort. The following examples let us see what is possible, but they represent only the beginning of using the calculator in finance.

In demonstrating how calculators may make our work easier, we must first decide which calculator to use. The options are numerous and largely depend on personal preference. We have chosen to demonstrate the Hewlett-Packard HP 17BII.

I. Introductory Comments

In the examples that follow, you are told (1) which keystrokes to use, (2) the resulting appearance of the calculator display, and (3) a supporting explanation. The keystrokes column tells you which keys to press. The keystrokes shown in an unshaded box tell you to use one of the calculator's dedicated or "hard" keys. For example if $\boxed{+/-}$ is shown in the keystrokes instruction column, press that key on the keyboard of the calculator. To use a function printed in gold lettering above a dedicated key, always press the gold key $\boxed{}$ first, then the function key. For example, keying in 2 and pressing $\boxed{}$ $\boxed{+/-}$ calculates the square root of 2.

When the calculator is on, a set of labels appears across the bottom of the display. This is called a *menu*, because it presents you with the choices of what you can do next. Press the key directly beneath the menu label to access that function. Menu keys are represented with a shaded box in the keystrokes column. For example, $\boxed{\text{TIME}}$ displays the current date and time, and the other $\boxed{\text{TIME}}$ menu options.

II. An Important Starting Point

Purpose: Before each new calculation, clear the variables, and if need be, change the number of digits displayed, the number of payments per period, and the beginning or end mode.

Example: You want to display four numbers to the right of the decimal.

Keystrokes	Display	Explanation
$\boxed{\text{DSP}}$	Select display format.	Sets display to show four numbers to the right of the decimal
$\boxed{\text{FIX}}$ 4 $\boxed{\text{INPUT}}$	0.0000	
$\boxed{\text{CLR}}$	0.0000	Clears display

Example: You can display two payments per year to be paid at the end of each period.

Keystrokes	Display	Explanation
FIN TVM OTHER 2 P/YR END EXIT	 2 P/YR END MODE	Sets number of payments per year at 2 and timing of payment at the end of each period

III. Calculating Table Values for:
A. The compound sum of $1 (Appendix B)

Purpose: Compute the table values for Appendix B, the future value of $1.

Method: Solve for the future value of $1: $FVIF_{i,n} = \$1(1 + i)^n$

Example: What is the table value for the compound sum of $1 for 5 years at a 12% annual interest rate:

Keystrokes	Display	Explanation
FIN TVM		Displays TVM menu
OTHER 1 P/YR END EXIT		Sets 1 payment per year; END mode
▯ CLEAR DATA	1 P/YR	Clears TVM variables
1 +/− PV	PV = −1.0000	Stores initial $1 as a negative present value. Otherwise the answer will appear as a negative
5 N	N = 5.0000	Stores number of periods
12 I% YR	I%YR = 12.0000	Stores interest rate
FV	FV= 1.7623	Table value

B. The present value of $1 (Appendix C)

Purpose: Compute the table values for Appendix C, the present value of $1.

Method: Solve for the present value of $1: $PVIF_{i,n} = \dfrac{\$1}{(1 + i)^n}$

Example: What is the table value for the present value of $1 for 8 years at a 10% annual interest rate?

Keystrokes	Display	Explanation
FIN TVM CLEAR DATA		Clears TVM variable; verifies the correct number of payments per year and the BEG or END mode
1 +/− FV	FV = −1.0000	Stores future amount as negative value
8 N	N = 8.0000	Stores number of periods
12 I% YR	I%YR = 10 0000	Stores interest rate
FV	PV = 0.4665	Table value

C. The sum of an annuity of $1 for n periods (Appendix D)

Purpose: Compute the table values for Appendix D, the sum of an annuity of $1.

Method: Solve for the future value of an annuity of $1:

$$FVIFA_{i,n} = \$1 \sum_{t=0}^{n-1} (1+i)^t$$

which may also be solved as $FVIFA_{i,n} = \dfrac{(1+i)^n - 1}{i}$

Example: What is the table value for the compound sum of an annuity of $1 for 6 years at a 14% annual interest rate?

Keystrokes	Display	Explanation
FIN TVM CLEAR DATA		Clears TVM variable, verifies the correct number of payments per year and the BEG or END mode
1 +/− PMT	PMT = −1.000	Stores annual payment (annuity) as a negative number. Otherwise the answer will appear as a negative
6 N	N = 6.0000	Stores number of periods
14 I% YR	I%YR = 14.0000	Stores interest rate
FV	FV= 8.5355	Table value

D. The present value of an annuity of $1 for n periods (Appendix E)

Purpose: Compute the table values for Appendix E, the present value of an annuity of $1.

Method: Solve for the present value of an annuity of $1:

$$PVIFA_{i,n} = \$1 \sum_{i=1}^{n} \frac{\$1}{(1+i)^t}$$

which may also be solved as $PVIFA_{i,n} = \dfrac{1 - \left[1/(1+i)^n \right]}{i}$

Example: What is the table for the present value of an annuity of $1 for 12 years at a 9% annual interest rate?

Keystrokes	Display	Explanation
FIN TVM CLEAR DATA		Clears TVM variable, and verifies the correct number of payments per year and the BEG or END mode
1 +/− PMT	PMT = −1.0000	Stores annual payment (annuity) as a negative number. Otherwise the answer will appear as a negative.
12 N	N = 12.0000	Stores number of periods
9 I% YR	I%YR = 9.0000	Stores interest rate
PV	PV = 7.1607	Table value

APPENDIX B

COMPOUND SUM OF $1

n	1%	2%	3%	4%	5%	6%	7%	8%	9%	10%
1	1.010	1.020	1.030	1.040	1.050	1.060	1.070	1.080	1.090	1.100
2	1.020	1.040	1.061	1.082	1.102	1.124	1.145	1.166	1.188	1.210
3	1.030	1.061	1.093	1.125	1.158	1.191	1.225	1.260	1.295	1.331
4	1.041	1.082	1.126	1.170	1.216	1.262	1.311	1.360	1.412	1.464
5	1.051	1.104	1.159	1.217	1.276	1.338	1.403	1.469	1.539	1.611
6	1.062	1.126	1.194	1.265	1.340	1.419	1.501	1.587	1.677	1.772
7	1.072	1.149	1.230	1.316	1.407	1.504	1.606	1.714	1.828	1.949
8	1.083	1.172	1.267	1.369	1.477	1.594	1.718	1.851	1.993	2.144
9	1.094	1.195	1.305	1.423	1.551	1.689	1.838	1.999	2.172	2.358
10	1.105	1.219	1.344	1.480	1.629	1.791	1.967	2.159	2.367	2.594
11	1.116	1.243	1.384	1.539	1.710	1.898	2.105	2.332	2.580	2.853
12	1.127	1.268	1.426	1.601	1.796	2.012	2.252	2.518	2.813	3.138
13	1.138	1.294	1.469	1.665	1.886	2.133	2.410	2.720	3.066	3.452
14	1.149	1.319	1.513	1.732	1.980	2.261	2.579	2.937	3.342	3.797
15	1.161	1.346	1.558	1.801	2.079	2.397	2.759	3.172	3.642	4.177
16	1.173	1.373	1.605	1.873	2.183	2.540	2.952	3.426	3.970	4.595
17	1.184	1.400	1.653	1.948	2.292	2.693	3.159	3.700	4.328	5.054
18	1.196	1.428	1.702	2.026	2.407	2.854	3.380	3.996	4.717	5.560
19	1.208	1.457	1.753	2.107	2.527	3.026	3.616	4.316	5.142	6.116
20	1.220	1.486	1.806	2.191	2.653	3.207	3.870	4.661	5.604	6.727
21	1.232	1.516	1.860	2.279	2.786	3.399	4.140	5.034	6.109	7.400
22	1.245	1.546	1.916	2.370	2.925	3.603	4.430	5.436	6.658	8.140
23	1.257	1.577	1.974	2.465	3.071	3.820	4.740	5.871	7.258	8.954
24	1.270	1.608	2.033	2.563	3.225	4.049	5.072	6.341	7.911	9.850
25	1.282	1.641	2.094	2.666	3.386	4.292	5.427	6.848	8.623	10.834
30	1.348	1.811	2.427	3.243	4.322	5.743	7.612	10.062	13.267	17.449
40	1.489	2.208	3.262	4.801	7.040	10.285	14.974	21.724	31.408	45.258
50	1.645	2.691	4.384	7.106	11.467	18.419	29.456	46.900	74.354	117.386

n	11%	12%	13%	14%	15%	16%	17%	18%	19%	20%
1	1.110	1.120	1.130	1.140	1.150	1.160	1.170	1.180	1.190	1.200
2	1.232	1.254	1.277	1.300	1.322	1.346	1.369	1.392	1.416	1.440
3	1.368	1.405	1.443	1.482	1.521	1.561	1.602	1.643	1.685	1.728
4	1.518	1.574	1.630	1.689	1.749	1.811	1.874	1.939	2.005	2.074
5	1.685	1.762	1.842	1.925	2.011	2.100	2.192	2.288	2.386	2.488
6	1.870	1.974	2.082	2.195	2.313	2.436	2.565	2.700	2.840	2.986
7	2.076	2.211	2.353	2.502	2.660	2.826	3.001	3.185	3.379	3.583
8	2.305	2.476	2.658	2.853	3.059	3.278	3.511	3.759	4.021	4.300
9	2.558	2.773	3.004	3.252	3.518	3.803	4.108	4.435	4.785	5.160
10	2.839	3.106	3.395	3.707	4.046	4.411	4.807	5.234	5.695	6.192
11	3.152	3.479	3.836	4.226	4.652	5.117	5.624	6.176	6.777	7.430
12	3.498	3.896	4.334	4.818	5.350	5.936	6.580	7.288	8.064	8.916
13	3.883	4.363	4.898	5.492	6.153	6.886	7.699	8.599	9.596	10.699
14	4.310	4.887	5.535	6.261	7.076	7.987	9.007	10.147	11.420	12.839
15	4.785	5.474	6.254	7.138	8.137	9.265	10.539	11.974	13.589	15.407
16	5.311	6.130	7.067	8.137	9.358	10.748	12.330	14.129	16.171	18.488
17	5.895	6.866	7.986	9.276	10.761	12.468	14.426	16.672	19.244	22.186
18	6.543	7.690	9.024	10.575	12.375	14.462	16.879	19.673	22.900	26.623
19	7.263	8.613	10.197	12.055	14.232	16.776	19.748	23.214	27.251	31.948
20	8.062	9.646	11.523	13.743	16.366	19.461	23.105	27.393	32.429	38.337
21	8.949	10.804	13.021	15.667	18.821	22.574	27.033	32.323	38.591	46.005
22	9.933	12.100	14.713	17.861	21.644	26.186	31.629	38.141	45.923	55.205
23	11.026	13.552	16.626	20.361	24.891	30.376	37.005	45.007	54.648	66.247
24	12.239	15.178	18.788	23.212	28.625	35.236	43.296	53.108	65.031	79.496
25	13.585	17.000	21.230	26.461	32.918	40.874	50.656	62.667	77.387	95.395
30	22.892	29.960	39.115	50.949	66.210	85.849	111.061	143.367	184.672	237.373
40	64.999	93.049	132.776	188.876	267.856	378.715	533.846	750.353	1051.642	1469.740
50	184.559	288.996	450.711	700.197	1083.619	1670.669	2566.080	3927.189	5988.730	9100.191

Compound Sum of $1 (continued)

n	21%	22%	23%	24%	25%	26%	27%	28%	29%	30%
1	1.210	1.220	1.230	1.240	1.250	1.260	1.270	1.280	1.290	1.300
2	1.464	1.488	1.513	1.538	1.562	1.588	1.613	1.638	1.664	1.690
3	1.772	1.816	1.861	1.907	1.953	2.000	2.048	2.097	2.147	2.197
4	2.144	2.215	2.289	2.364	2.441	2.520	2.601	2.684	2.769	2.856
5	2.594	2.703	2.815	2.932	3.052	3.176	3.304	3.436	3.572	3.713
6	3.138	3.297	3.463	3.635	3.815	4.001	4.196	4.398	4.608	4.827
7	3.797	4.023	4.259	4.508	4.768	5.042	5.329	5.629	5.945	6.275
8	4.595	4.908	5.239	5.589	5.960	6.353	6.767	7.206	7.669	8.157
9	5.560	5.987	6.444	6.931	7.451	8.004	8.595	9.223	9.893	10.604
10	6.727	7.305	7.926	8.594	9.313	10.086	10.915	11.806	12.761	13.786
11	8.140	8.912	9.749	10.657	11.642	12.708	13.862	15.112	16.462	17.921
12	9.850	10.872	11.991	13.215	14.552	16.012	17.605	19.343	21.236	23.298
13	11.918	13.264	14.749	16.386	18.190	20.175	22.359	24.759	27.395	30.287
14	14.421	16.182	18.141	20.319	22.737	25.420	28.395	31.691	35.339	39.373
15	17.449	19.742	22.314	25.195	28.422	32.030	36.062	40.565	45.587	51.185
16	21.113	24.085	27.446	31.242	35.527	40.357	45.799	51.923	58.808	66.541
17	25.547	29.384	33.758	38.740	44.409	50.850	58.165	66.461	75.862	86.503
18	30.912	35.848	41.523	48.038	55.511	64.071	73.869	85.070	97.862	112.454
19	37.404	43.735	51.073	59.567	69.389	80.730	93.813	108.890	126.242	146.190
20	45.258	53.357	62.820	73.863	86.736	101.720	119.143	139.379	162.852	190.047
21	54.762	65.095	77.268	91.591	108.420	128.167	151.312	178.405	210.079	247.061
22	66.262	79.416	95.040	113.572	135.525	161.490	192.165	228.358	271.002	321.178
23	80.178	96.887	116.899	140.829	169.407	203.477	244.050	292.298	349.592	417.531
24	97.015	118.203	143.786	174.628	211.758	256.381	309.943	374.141	450.974	542.791
25	117.388	144.207	176.857	216.539	264.698	323.040	393.628	478.901	581.756	705.627
30	304.471	389.748	497.904	634.810	807.793	1025.904	1300.477	1645.488	2078.208	2619.936
40	2048.309	2846.941	3946.340	5455.797	7523.156	10346.879	14195.051	19426.418	26520.723	36117.754
50	13779.844	20795.680	31278.301	46889.207	70064.812	104354.562	154942.687	229345.875	338440.000	497910.125

n	31%	32%	33%	34%	35%	36%	37%	38%	39%	40%
1	1.310	1.320	1.330	1.340	1.350	1.360	1.370	1.380	1.390	1.400
2	1.716	1.742	1.769	1.796	1.822	1.850	1.877	1.904	1.932	1.960
3	2.248	2.300	2.353	2.406	2.460	2.515	2.571	2.628	2.686	2.744
4	2.945	3.036	3.129	3.224	3.321	3.421	3.523	3.627	3.733	3.842
5	3.858	4.007	4.162	4.320	4.484	4.653	4.826	5.005	5.189	5.378
6	5.054	5.290	5.535	5.789	6.053	6.328	6.612	6.907	7.213	7.530
7	6.621	6.983	7.361	7.758	8.172	8.605	9.058	9.531	10.025	10.541
8	8.673	9.217	9.791	10.395	11.032	11.703	12.410	13.153	13.935	14.758
9	11.362	12.166	13.022	13.930	14.894	15.917	17.001	18.151	19.370	20.661
10	14.884	16.060	17.319	18.666	20.106	21.646	23.292	25.049	26.924	28.925
11	19.498	21.199	23.034	25.012	27.144	29.439	31.910	34.567	37.425	40.495
12	25.542	27.982	30.635	33.516	36.644	40.037	43.716	47.703	52.020	56.694
13	33.460	36.937	40.745	44.912	49.469	54.451	59.892	65.830	72.308	79.371
14	43.832	49.756	54.190	60.181	66.784	74.053	82.051	90.845	100.509	111.19
15	57.420	64.358	72.073	80.643	90.158	100.712	112.410	125.366	139.707	155.567
16	75.220	84.953	95.857	108.061	121.713	136.968	154.002	173.005	194.192	217.793
17	98.539	112.138	127.490	144.802	164.312	186.277	210.983	238.747	269.927	304.911
18	129.086	148.022	169.561	194.035	221.822	253.337	289.046	329.471	375.198	426.875
19	169.102	195.389	225.517	260.006	299.459	344.537	395.993	454.669	521.525	597.625
20	221.523	257.913	299.937	348.408	404.270	468.571	542.511	627.443	724.919	836.674
21	290.196	340.446	398.916	466.867	545.764	637.256	743.240	865.871	1007.637	1171.343
22	380.156	449.388	530.558	625.601	736.781	865.668	1018.238	1194.900	1400.615	1639.878
23	498.004	593.192	705.642	838.305	994.653	1178.668	1394.986	1648.961	1946.854	2295.829
24	652.385	783.013	938.504	1123.328	1342.781	1602.988	1911.129	2275.564	2706.125	3214.158
25	854.623	1033.577	1248.210	1505.258	1812.754	2180.063	2618.245	3140.275	3761.511	4499.816
30	3297.081	4142.008	5194.516	6503.285	8128.426	10142.914	12636.086	15716.703	19517.969	24201.043
40	49072.621	66519.313	89962.188	121388.437	163433.875	219558.625	294317.937	393684.687	525508.312	700022.688

APPENDIX C

PRESENT VALUE OF $1

% of return *Present value* *(PVIF)*

n	1%	2%	3%	4%	5%	6%	7%	8%	9%	10%
1	.990	.980	.971	.962	.952	.943	.935	.926	.917	.909
2	.980	.961	.943	.925	.907	.890	.873	.857	.842	.826
3	.971	.942	.915	.889	.864	.840	.816	.794	.772	.751
4	.961	.924	.888	.855	.823	.792	.763	.735	.708	.683
5	.951	.906	.863	.822	.784	.747	.713	.681	.650	.621
6	.942	.888	.837	.790	.746	.705	.666	.630	.596	.564
7	.933	.871	.813	.760	.711	.665	.623	.583	.547	.513
8	.923	.853	.789	.731	.677	.627	.582	.540	.502	.467
9	.914	.837	.766	.703	.645	.592	.544	.500	.460	.424
10	.905	.820	.744	.676	.614	.558	.508	.463	.422	.386
11	.896	.804	.722	.650	.585	.527	.475	.429	.388	.350
12	.887	.789	.701	.625	.557	.497	.444	.397	.356	.319
13	.879	.773	.681	.601	.530	.469	.415	.368	.326	.290
14	.870	.758	.661	.577	.505	.442	.388	.340	.299	.263
15	.861	.743	.642	.555	.481	.417	.362	.315	.275	.239
16	.853	.728	.623	.534	.458	.394	.339	.292	.252	.218
17	.844	.714	.605	.513	.436	.371	.317	.270	.231	.198
18	.836	.700	.587	.494	.416	.350	.296	.250	.212	.180
19	.828	.686	.570	.475	.396	.331	.277	.232	.194	.164
20	.820	.673	.554	.456	.377	.312	.258	.215	.178	.149
21	.811	.660	.538	.439	.359	.294	.242	.199	.164	.135
22	.803	.647	.522	.422	.342	.278	.226	.184	.150	.123
23	.795	.634	.507	.406	.326	.262	.211	.170	.138	.112
24	.788	.622	.492	.390	.310	.247	.197	.158	.126	.102
25	.780	.610	.478	.375	.295	.233	.184	.146	.116	.092
30	.742	.552	.412	.308	.231	.174	.131	.099	.075	.057
40	.672	.453	.307	.208	.142	.097	.067	.046	.032	.022
50	.608	.372	.228	.141	.087	.054	.034	.021	.013	.009

n	11%	12%	13%	14%	15%	16%	17%	18%	19%	20%
1	.901	.893	.885	.877	.870	.862	.855	.847	.840	.833
2	.812	.797	.783	.769	.756	.743	.731	.718	.706	.694
3	.731	.712	.693	.675	.658	.641	.624	.609	.593	.579
4	.659	.636	.613	.592	.572	.552	.534	.516	.499	.482
5	.593	.567	.543	.519	.497	.476	.456	.437	.419	.402
6	.535	.507	.480	.456	.432	.410	.390	.370	.352	.335
7	.482	.452	.425	.400	.376	.354	.333	.314	.296	.279
8	.434	.404	.376	.351	.327	.305	.285	.266	.249	.233
9	.391	.361	.333	.308	.284	.263	.243	.225	.209	.194
10	.352	.322	.295	.270	.247	.227	.208	.191	.176	.162
11	.317	.287	.261	.237	.215	.195	.178	.162	.148	.135
12	.286	.257	.231	.208	.187	.168	.152	.137	.124	.112
13	.258	.229	.204	.182	.163	.145	.130	.116	.104	.093
14	.232	.205	.181	.160	.141	.125	.111	.099	.088	.078
15	.209	.183	.160	.140	.123	.108	.095	.084	.074	.065
16	.188	.163	.141	.123	.107	.093	.081	.071	.062	.054
17	.170	.146	.125	.108	.093	.080	.069	.060	.052	.045
18	.153	.130	.111	.095	.081	.069	.059	.051	.044	.038
19	.138	.116	.098	.083	.070	.060	.051	.043	.037	.031
20	.124	.104	.087	.073	.061	.051	.043	.037	.031	.026
21	.112	.093	.077	.064	.053	.044	.037	.031	.026	.022
22	.101	.083	.068	.056	.046	.038	.032	.026	.022	.018
23	.091	.074	.060	.049	.040	.033	.027	.022	.018	.015
24	.082	.066	.053	.043	.035	.028	.023	.019	.015	.013
25	.074	.059	.047	.038	.030	.024	.020	.016	.013	.010
30	.044	.033	.026	.020	.015	.012	.009	.007	.005	.004
40	.015	.011	.008	.005	.004	.003	.002	.001	.001	.001
50	.005	.003	.002	.001	.001	.001	.000	.000	.000	.000

Present Value of $1 (continued)

n	21%	22%	23%	24%	25%	26%	27%	28%	29%	30%
1	.826	.820	.813	.806	.800	.794	.787	.781	.775	.769
2	.683	.672	.661	.650	.640	.630	.620	.610	.601	.592
3	.564	.551	.537	.524	.512	.500	.488	.477	.466	.455
4	.467	.451	.437	.423	.410	.397	.384	.373	.361	.350
5	.386	.370	.355	.341	.328	.315	.303	.291	.280	.269
6	.319	.303	.289	.275	.262	.250	.238	.227	.217	.207
7	.263	.249	.235	.222	.210	.198	.188	.178	.168	.159
8	.218	.204	.191	.179	.168	.157	.148	.139	.130	.123
9	.180	.167	.155	.144	.134	.125	.116	.108	.101	.094
10	.149	.137	.126	.116	.107	.099	.092	.085	.078	.073
11	.123	.112	.103	.094	.086	.079	.072	.066	.061	.056
12	.102	.092	.083	.076	.069	.062	.057	.052	.047	.043
13	.084	.075	.068	.061	.055	.050	.045	.040	.037	.033
14	.069	.062	.055	.049	.044	.039	.035	.032	.028	.025
15	.057	.051	.045	.040	.035	.031	.028	.025	.022	.020
16	.047	.042	.036	.032	.028	.025	.022	.019	.017	.015
17	.039	.034	.030	.026	.023	.020	.017	.015	.013	.012
18	.032	.028	.024	.021	.018	.016	.014	.012	.010	.009
19	.027	.023	.020	.017	.014	.012	.011	.009	.008	.007
20	.022	.019	.016	.014	.012	.010	.008	.007	.006	.005
21	.018	.015	.013	.011	.009	.008	.007	.006	.005	.004
22	.015	.013	.011	.009	.007	.006	.005	.004	.004	.003
23	.012	.010	.009	.007	.006	.005	.004	.003	.003	.002
24	.010	.008	.007	.006	.005	.004	.003	.003	.002	.002
25	.009	.007	.006	.005	.004	.003	.003	.002	.002	.001
30	.003	.003	.002	.002	.001	.001	.001	.001	.000	.000
40	.000	.000	.000	.000	.000	.000	.000	.000	.000	.000
50	.000	.000	.000	.000	.000	.000	.000	.000	.000	.000

n	31%	32%	33%	34%	35%	36%	37%	38%	39%	40%
1	.763	.758	.752	.746	.741	.735	.730	.725	.719	.714
2	.583	.574	.565	.557	.549	.541	.533	.525	.518	.510
3	.445	.435	.425	.416	.406	.398	.389	.381	.372	.364
4	.340	.329	.320	.310	.301	.292	.284	.276	.268	.260
5	.259	.250	.240	.231	.223	.215	.207	.200	.193	.186
6	.198	.189	.181	.173	.165	.158	.151	.145	.139	.133
7	.151	.143	.136	.129	.122	.116	.110	.105	.100	.095
8	.115	.108	.102	.096	.091	.085	.081	.076	.072	.068
9	.088	.082	.077	.072	.067	.063	.059	.055	.052	.048
10	.067	.062	.058	.054	.050	.046	.043	.040	.037	.035
11	.051	.047	.043	.040	.037	.034	.031	.029	.027	.025
12	.039	.036	.033	.030	.027	.025	.023	.021	.019	.018
13	.030	.027	.025	.022	.020	.018	.017	.015	.014	.013
14	.023	.021	.018	.017	.015	.014	.012	.011	.010	.009
15	.017	.016	.014	.012	.011	.010	.009	.008	.007	.006
16	.013	.012	.010	.009	.008	.007	.006	.006	.005	.005
17	.010	.009	.008	.007	.006	.005	.005	.004	.004	.003
18	.008	.007	.006	.005	.005	.004	.003	.003	.003	.002
19	.006	.005	.004	.004	.003	.003	.003	.002	.002	.002
20	.005	.004	.003	.003	.002	.002	.002	.002	.001	.001
21	.003	.003	.003	.002	.002	.002	.001	.001	.001	.001
22	.003	.002	.002	.002	.001	.001	.001	.001	.001	.001
23	.002	.002	.001	.001	.001	.001	.001	.001	.001	.000
24	.002	.001	.001	.001	.001	.001	.001	.000	.000	.000
25	.001	.001	.001	.001	.001	.000	.000	.000	.000	.000
30	.000	.000	.000	.000	.000	.000	.000	.000	.000	.000
40	.000	.000	.000	.000	.000	.000	.000	.000	.000	.000

Future Value Annuity

SUM OF AN ANNUITY OF $1 FOR _n_ PERIODS

n	1%	2%	3%	4%	5%	6%	7%	8%	9%	10%
1	1.000	1.000	1.000	1.000	1.000	1.000	1.000	1.000	1.000	1.000
2	2.010	2.020	2.030	2.040	2.050	2.060	2.070	2.080	2.090	2.100
3	3.030	3.060	3.091	3.122	3.152	3.184	3.215	3.246	3.278	3.310
4	4.060	4.122	4.184	4.246	4.310	4.375	4.440	4.506	4.573	4.641
5	5.101	5.204	5.309	5.416	5.526	5.637	5.751	5.867	5.985	6.105
6	6.152	6.308	6.468	6.633	6.802	6.975	7.153	7.336	7.523	7.716
7	7.214	7.434	7.662	7.898	8.142	8.394	8.654	8.923	9.200	9.487
8	8.286	8.583	8.892	9.214	9.549	9.897	10.260	10.637	11.028	11.436
9	9.368	9.755	10.159	10.583	11.027	11.491	11.978	12.488	13.021	13.579
10	10.462	10.950	11.464	12.006	12.578	13.181	13.816	14.487	15.193	15.937
11	11.567	12.169	12.808	13.486	14.207	14.972	15.784	16.645	17.560	18.531
12	12.682	13.412	14.192	15.026	15.917	16.870	17.888	18.977	20.141	21.384
13	13.809	14.680	15.618	16.627	17.713	18.882	20.141	21.495	22.953	24.523
14	14.947	15.974	17.086	18.292	19.598	21.015	22.550	24.215	26.019	27.975
15	16.097	17.293	18.599	20.023	21.578	23.276	25.129	27.152	29.361	31.772
16	17.258	18.639	20.157	21.824	23.657	25.672	27.888	30.324	33.003	35.949
17	18.430	20.012	21.761	23.697	25.840	28.213	30.840	33.750	36.973	40.544
18	19.614	21.412	23.414	25.645	28.132	30.905	33.999	37.450	41.301	45.599
19	20.811	22.840	25.117	27.671	30.539	33.760	37.379	41.446	46.018	51.158
20	22.019	24.297	26.870	29.778	33.066	36.785	40.995	45.762	51.159	57.274
21	23.239	25.783	28.676	31.969	35.719	39.992	44.865	50.422	56.764	64.002
22	24.471	27.299	30.536	34.248	38.505	43.392	49.005	55.456	62.872	71.402
23	25.716	28.845	32.452	36.618	41.430	46.995	53.435	60.893	69.531	79.542
24	26.973	30.421	34.426	39.082	44.501	50.815	58.176	66.764	76.789	88.496
25	28.243	32.030	36.459	41.645	47.726	54.864	63.248	73.105	84.699	98.346
30	34.784	40.567	47.575	56.084	66.438	79.057	94.459	113.282	136.305	164.491
40	48.885	60.401	75.400	95.024	120.797	154.758	199.630	295.052	337.872	442.580
50	64.461	84.577	112.794	152.664	209.341	290.325	406.516	573.756	815.051	1163.865

n	11%	12%	13%	14%	15%	16%	17%	18%	19%	20%
1	1.000	1.000	1.000	1.000	1.000	1.000	1.000	1.000	1.000	1.000
2	2.110	2.120	2.130	2.140	2.150	2.160	2.170	2.180	2.190	2.200
3	3.342	3.374	3.407	3.440	3.472	3.506	3.539	3.572	3.606	3.640
4	4.710	4.779	4.850	4.921	4.993	5.066	5.141	5.215	5.291	5.368
5	6.228	6.353	6.480	6.610	6.742	6.877	7.014	7.154	7.297	7.442
6	7.913	8.115	8.323	8.535	8.754	8.977	9.207	9.442	9.683	9.930
7	9.783	10.089	10.405	10.730	11.067	11.414	11.772	12.141	12.523	12.916
8	11.859	12.300	12.757	13.233	13.727	14.240	14.773	15.327	15.902	16.499
9	14.164	14.776	15.416	16.085	16.786	17.518	18.285	19.086	19.923	20.799
10	16.722	17.549	18.420	19.337	20.304	21.321	22.393	23.521	24.709	25.959
11	19.561	20.655	21.814	23.044	24.349	25.733	27.200	28.755	30.403	32.150
12	22.713	24.133	25.650	27.271	29.001	30.850	32.824	34.931	37.180	39.580
13	26.211	28.029	29.984	32.088	34.352	36.786	39.404	42.218	45.244	48.496
14	30.095	32.392	34.882	37.581	40.504	43.672	47.102	50.818	54.841	59.196
15	34.405	37.280	40.417	43.842	47.580	51.659	56.109	60.965	66.260	72.035
16	39.190	42.753	46.671	50.980	55.717	60.925	66.648	72.938	79.850	87.442
17	44.500	48.883	53.738	59.117	65.075	71.673	78.978	87.067	96.021	105.930
18	50.396	55.749	61.724	68.393	75.836	84.140	93.404	103.739	115.265	128.116
19	56.939	63.439	70.748	78.968	88.211	98.603	110.283	123.412	138.165	154.739
20	64.202	72.052	80.946	91.024	102.443	115.379	130.031	146.626	165.417	186.687
21	72.264	81.698	92.468	104.767	118.809	134.840	153.136	174.019	197.846	225.024
22	81.213	92.502	105.489	120.434	137.630	157.414	180.169	206.342	236.436	271.028
23	91.147	104.602	120.203	138.295	159.274	183.600	211.798	244.483	282.359	326.234
24	102.173	118.154	136.829	158.656	184.166	213.976	248.803	289.490	337.007	392.480
25	114.412	133.333	155.616	181.867	212.790	249.212	292.099	342.598	402.038	471.976
30	199.018	241.330	293.192	356.778	434.738	530.306	647.423	790.932	966.698	1181.865
40	581.812	767.080	1013.667	1341.979	1779.048	2360.724	3134.412	4163.094	5529.711	7343.715
50	1668.723	2399.975	3459.344	4994.301	7217.488	10435.449	15088.805	21812.273	31514.492	45496.094

Sum of an Annuity of $1 for *n* Periods (continued)

n	21%	22%	23%	24%	25%	26%	27%	28%	29%	30%
1	1.000	1.000	1.000	1.000	1.000	1.000	1.000	1.000	1.000	1.000
2	2.210	2.220	2.230	2.240	2.250	2.260	2.270	2.280	2.290	2.300
3	3.674	3.708	3.743	3.778	3.813	3.848	3.883	3.918	3.954	3.990
4	5.446	5.524	5.604	5.684	5.766	5.848	5.931	6.016	6.101	6.187
5	7.589	7.740	7.893	8.048	8.207	8.368	8.533	8.700	8.870	9.043
6	10.183	10.442	10.708	10.980	11.259	11.544	11.837	12.136	12.442	12.756
7	13.321	13.740	14.171	14.615	15.073	15.546	16.032	16.534	17.051	17.583
8	17.119	17.762	18.430	19.123	19.842	20.588	21.361	22.163	22.995	23.858
9	21.714	22.670	23.669	24.712	25.802	26.940	28.129	29.369	30.664	32.015
10	27.274	28.657	20.113	31.643	33.253	34.945	36.723	38.592	40.556	42.619
11	34.001	35.962	38.039	40.238	42.566	45.030	47.639	50.398	53.318	56.405
12	42.141	44.873	47.787	50.895	54.208	57.738	61.501	65.510	69.780	74.326
13	51.991	55.745	59.778	64.109	68.760	73.750	79.106	84.853	91.016	97.624
14	63.909	69.009	74.528	80.496	86.949	93.925	101.465	109.611	118.411	127.912
15	78.330	85.191	92.669	100.815	109.687	119.346	129.860	141.302	153.750	167.285
16	95.779	104.933	114.983	126.010	138.109	151.375	165.922	181.867	199.337	218.470
17	116.892	129.019	142.428	157.252	173.636	191.733	211.721	233.790	258.145	285.011
18	142.439	158.403	176.187	195.993	218.045	242.583	269.885	300.250	334.006	371.514
19	173.351	194.251	217.710	244.031	273.556	306.654	343.754	385.321	431.868	483.968
20	210.755	237.986	268.783	303.598	342.945	387.384	437.568	494.210	558.110	630.157
21	256.013	291.343	331.603	377.461	429.681	489.104	556.710	633.589	720.962	820.204
22	310.775	356.438	408.871	469.052	538.101	617.270	708.022	811.993	931.040	1067.265
23	377.038	435.854	503.911	582.624	673.626	778.760	990.187	1040.351	1202.042	1388.443
24	457.215	532.741	620.810	723.453	843.032	982.237	1144.237	1332.649	1551.634	1805.975
25	554.230	650.944	764.596	898.082	1054.791	1238.617	1454.180	1706.790	2002.608	2348.765
30	1445.111	1767.044	2160.459	2640.881	3227.172	3941.953	4812.891	5873.172	7162.785	8729.805
40	9749.141	12936.141	17153.691	22728.367	30088.621	39791.957	52570.707	69376.562	91447.375	120389.375

n	31%	32%	33%	34%	35%	36%	37%	38%	39%	40%
1	1.000	1.000	1.000	1.000	1.000	1.000	1.000	1.000	1.000	1.000
2	2.310	2.320	2.330	2.340	2.350	2.360	2.370	2.380	2.390	2.400
3	4.026	4.062	4.099	4.136	4.172	4.210	4.247	4.284	4.322	4.360
4	6.274	6.362	6.452	6.542	6.633	6.725	6.818	6.912	7.008	7.104
5	9.219	9.398	9.581	9.766	9.954	10.146	10.341	10.539	10.741	10.946
6	13.077	13.406	13.742	14.086	14.438	14.799	15.167	15.544	15.930	16.324
7	18.131	18.696	19.277	19.876	20.492	21.126	21.779	22.451	23.142	23.853
8	24.752	25.678	26.638	27.633	28.664	29.732	30.837	31.982	33.167	34.395
9	33.425	34.895	36.429	38.028	39.696	41.435	43.247	45.135	47.103	49.152
10	44.786	47.062	49.451	51.958	54.590	57.351	60.248	63.287	66.473	69.813
11	59.670	63.121	66.769	70.624	74.696	78.998	83.540	88.335	93.397	98.739
12	79.167	84.320	89.803	95.636	101.840	108.437	115.450	122.903	130.822	139.234
13	104.709	112.302	120.438	129.152	138.484	148.474	159.166	170.606	182.842	195.928
14	138.169	149.239	161.183	174.063	187.953	202.925	219.058	236.435	255.151	275.299
15	182.001	197.996	215.373	234.245	254.737	276.978	301.109	327.281	355.659	386.418
16	239.421	262.354	287.446	314.888	344.895	377.690	413.520	452.647	495.366	541.985
17	314.642	347.307	383.303	422.949	466.608	514.658	567.521	625.652	689.558	759.778
18	413.180	459.445	510.792	567.751	630.920	700.935	778.504	864.399	959.485	1064.689
19	542.266	607.467	680.354	761.786	852.741	954.271	1067.551	1193.870	1334.683	1491.563
20	711.368	802.856	905.870	1021.792	1152.200	1298.809	1463.544	1648.539	1856.208	2089.188
21	932.891	1060.769	1205.807	1370.201	1556.470	1767.380	2006.055	2275.982	2581.128	2925.862
22	1223.087	1401.215	1604.724	1837.068	2102.234	2404.636	2749.294	3141.852	3588.765	4097.203
23	1603.243	1850.603	2135.282	2462.669	2839.014	3271.304	3767.532	4336.750	4989.379	5737.078
24	2101.247	2443.795	2840.924	3300.974	3833.667	4449.969	5162.516	5985.711	6936.230	8032.906
25	2753.631	3226.808	3779.428	4424.301	5176.445	6052.957	7073.645	8261.273	9642.352	11247.062
30	10632.543	12940.672	15737.945	19124.434	23221.258	28172.016	34148.906	41357.227	50043.625	60500.207

NPV = PV − PV − FV

IRR $\emptyset$ = PMT X PVIFA$_{i,n}$ −

Borrowing money

PRESENT VALUE OF AN ANNUITY OF $1 FOR *n* PERIODS

%

PVIFA

n	1%	2%	3%	4%	5%	6%	7%	8%	9%	10%
1	.990	.980	.971	.962	.952	.943	.935	.926	.917	.909
2	1.970	1.942	1.913	1.886	1.859	1.833	1.808	1.3783	1.759	1.736
3	2.941	2.884	2.829	2.775	2.723	2.673	2.624	2.577	2.531	2.487
4	3.902	3.808	3.717	3.630	3.546	3.465	3.387	3.312	3.240	3.170
5	4.853	4.713	4.580	4.452	4.329	4.212	4.100	3.993	3.890	3.791
6	5.795	5.601	5.417	5.242	5.076	4.917	4.767	4.623	4.486	4.355
7	6.728	6.472	6.230	6.002	5.786	5.582	5.389	5.206	5.033	4.868
8	7.652	7.326	7.020	6.733	6.463	6.210	5.971	5.747	5.535	5.335
9	8.566	8.162	7.786	7.435	7.108	6.802	6.515	6.247	5.995	5.759
10	9.471	8.983	8.530	8.111	7.722	7.360	7.024	6.710	6.418	6.145
11	10.368	9.787	9.253	8.760	8.306	7.887	7.499	7.139	6.805	6.495
12	11.255	10.575	9.954	9.385	8.863	8.384	7.943	7.536	7.161	6.814
13	12.134	11.348	10.635	9.986	9.394	8.853	8.358	7.904	7.487	7.103
14	13.004	12.106	11.296	10.563	9.899	9.295	8.746	8.244	7.786	7.367
15	13.865	12.849	11.938	11.118	10.380	9.712	9.108	8.560	8.061	7.606
16	14.718	13.578	12.561	11.652	10.838	10.106	9.447	8.851	8.313	7.824
17	15.562	14.292	13.166	12.166	11.274	10.477	9.763	9.122	8.544	8.022
18	16.398	14.992	13.754	12.659	11.690	10.828	10.059	9.372	8.756	8.201
19	17.226	15.679	14.324	13.134	12.085	11.158	10.336	9.604	8.950	8.365
20	18.046	16.352	14.878	13.590	12.462	11.470	10.594	9.818	9.129	8.514
21	18.857	17.011	15.415	14.029	12.821	11.764	10.836	10.017	9.292	8.649
22	19.661	17.658	15.937	14.451	13.163	12.042	11.061	10.201	9.442	8.772
23	20.456	18.292	16.444	14.857	13.489	12.303	11.272	10.371	9.580	8.883
24	21.244	18.914	16.936	15.247	13.799	12.550	11.469	10.529	9.707	8.985
25	22.023	19.524	17.413	15.622	14.094	12.783	11.654	10.675	9.823	9.077
30	25.808	22.397	19.601	17.292	15.373	13.765	12.409	11.258	10.274	9.427
40	32.835	27.356	23.115	19.793	17.159	15.046	13.332	11.925	10.757	9.779
50	39.197	31.424	25.730	21.482	18.256	15.762	13.801	12.234	10.962	9.915

n	11%	12%	13%	14%	15%	16%	17%	18%	19%	20%
1	.901	.893	.885	.877	.870	.862	.855	.847	.840	.833
2	1.713	1.690	1.668	1.647	1.626	1.605	1.585	1.566	1.547	1.528
3	2.444	2.402	2.361	2.322	2.283	2.246	2.210	2.174	2.140	2.106
4	3.102	3.037	2.974	2.914	2.855	2.798	2.743	2.690	2.639	2.589
5	3.696	3.605	3.517	3.433	3.352	3.274	3.199	3.127	3.058	2.991
6	4.231	4.111	3.998	3.889	3.784	3.685	3.589	3.498	3.410	3.326
7	4.712	4.564	4.423	4.288	4.160	4.039	3.922	3.812	3.706	3.605
8	5.146	4.968	4.799	4.639	4.487	4.344	4.207	4.078	3.954	3.837
9	5.537	5.328	5.132	4.946	4.772	4.607	4.451	4.303	4.163	4.031
10	5.889	5.650	5.246	5.216	5.019	4.833	4.659	4.494	4.339	4.192
11	6.207	5.938	5.687	5.453	5.234	5.029	4.836	4.656	4.487	4.327
12	6.492	6.194	5.918	5.660	5.421	5.197	4.988	4.793	4.611	4.439
13	6.750	6.424	6.122	5.842	5.583	5.342	5.118	4.910	4.715	4.533
14	6.982	6.628	6.303	6.002	5.724	5.468	5.229	5.008	4.802	4.611
15	7.191	6.811	6.462	6.142	5.847	5.575	5.324	5.092	4.876	4.675
16	7.379	6.974	6.604	6.265	5.954	5.669	5.405	5.162	4.938	4.730
17	7.549	7.120	6.729	6.373	6.047	5.749	5.475	5.222	4.990	4.775
18	7.702	7.250	6.840	6.467	6.128	5.818	5.534	5.273	5.033	4.812
19	7.839	7.366	6.938	6.550	6.198	5.877	5.585	5.316	5.070	4.843
20	7.963	7.469	7.025	6.623	6.259	5.929	5.628	5.353	5.101	4.870
21	8.075	7.562	7.102	6.687	6.312	5.973	5.665	5.384	5.127	4.891
22	8.176	7.645	7.170	6.743	6.359	6.011	5.696	5.410	5.149	4.909
23	8.266	7.718	7.230	6.792	6.399	6.044	5.723	5.432	5.167	4.925
24	8.348	7.784	7.283	6.835	6.434	6.073	5.747	5.451	5.182	4.937
25	8.422	7.843	7.330	6.873	6.464	6.097	5.766	5.467	5.195	4.948
30	8.694	8.055	7.496	7.003	6.566	6.177	5.829	5.517	5.235	4.979
40	8.951	8.244	7.634	7.105	6.642	6.233	5.871	5.548	5.258	4.997
50	9.042	8.305	7.675	7.133	6.661	6.246	5.880	5.554	5.262	4.999

YMS

Present Value of an Annuity of $1 for *n* Periods (continued)

n	21%	22%	23%	24%	25%	26%	27%	28%	29%	30%
1	.826	.820	.813	.806	.800	.794	.787	.781	.775	.769
2	1.509	1.492	1.474	1.457	1.440	1.424	1.407	1.392	1.376	1.361
3	2.074	2.042	2.011	1.981	1.952	1.923	1.896	1.868	1.842	1.816
4	2.540	2.494	2.448	2.404	2.362	2.320	2.280	2.241	2.203	2.166
5	2.926	2.864	2.803	2.745	2.689	2.635	2.583	2.532	2.483	2.436
6	3.245	3.167	3.092	3.020	2.951	2.885	2.821	2.759	2.700	2.643
7	3.508	3.416	3.327	3.242	3.161	3.083	3.009	2.937	2.868	2.802
8	3.726	3.619	3.518	3.421	3.329	3.241	3.156	3.076	2.999	2.925
9	3.905	3.786	3.673	3.566	3.463	3.366	3.273	3.184	3.100	3.019
10	4.054	3.923	3.799	3.682	3.570	3.465	3.364	3.269	3.178	3.092
11	4.177	4.035	3.902	3.776	3.656	3.544	3.437	3.335	3.329	3.147
12	4.278	4.127	3.985	3.851	3.725	3.606	3.493	3.387	3.286	3.190
13	4.362	4.203	4.053	3.912	3.780	3.656	3.538	3.427	3.322	3.223
14	4.432	4.265	4.108	3.962	3.824	3.695	3.573	3.459	3.351	3.249
15	4.489	4.315	4.153	4.001	3.859	3.726	3.601	3.483	3.373	3.268
16	4.536	4.357	4.189	4.003	3.887	3.751	3.623	3.503	3.390	3.283
17	4.576	4.391	4.219	4.059	3.910	3.771	3.640	3.518	3.403	3.295
18	4.608	4.419	4.243	4.080	3.928	3.786	3.654	3.529	3.413	3.304
19	4.635	4.442	4.263	4.097	3.942	3.799	3.664	3.539	3.421	3.311
20	4.657	4.460	4.279	4.110	3.954	3.808	3.673	3.546	3.427	3.316
21	4.675	4.476	4.292	4.121	3.963	3.816	3.679	3.551	3.432	3.320
22	4.690	4.488	4.302	4.130	3.970	3.822	3.684	3.556	3.436	3.323
23	4.703	4.499	4.311	4.137	3.976	3.827	3.689	3.559	3.438	3.325
24	4.713	4.507	4.318	4.143	3.981	3.831	3.692	3.562	3.441	3.327
25	4.721	4.514	4.323	4.147	3.985	3.834	3.694	3.564	3.442	3.329
30	4.746	4.534	4.339	4.160	3.995	3.842	3.701	3.569	3.447	3.332
40	4.760	4.544	4.347	4.166	3.999	3.846	3.703	3.571	3.448	3.333
50	4.762	4.545	4.348	4.167	4.000	3.846	3.704	3.571	3.448	3.333

n	31%	32%	33%	34%	35%	36%	37%	38%	39%	40%
1	.763	.758	.752	.746	.741	.735	.730	.725	.719	.714
2	1.346	1.331	1.317	1.303	1.289	1.276	1.263	1.250	1.237	1.224
3	1.791	1.766	1.742	1.719	1.696	1.673	1.652	1.630	1.609	1.589
4	2.130	2.096	2.062	2.029	1.997	1.966	1.935	1.906	1.877	1.849
5	2.390	2.345	2.302	2.260	2.220	2.181	2.143	2.106	2.070	2.035
6	2.588	2.534	2.483	2.433	2.385	2.339	2.294	2.251	2.209	2.168
7	2.739	2.677	2.619	2.562	2.508	2.455	2.404	2.355	2.308	2.263
8	2.854	2.786	2.721	2.658	2.598	2.540	2.485	2.432	2.380	2.331
9	2.942	2.868	2.798	2.730	2.665	2.603	2.544	2.487	2.432	2.379
10	3.009	2.930	2.855	2.784	2.715	2.649	2.587	2.527	2.469	2.414
11	3.060	2.978	2.899	2.824	2.752	2.683	2.618	2.555	2.496	2.438
12	3.100	3.013	2.931	2.853	2.779	2.708	2.641	2.576	2.515	2.456
13	3.129	3.040	2.956	2.876	2.799	2.727	2.658	2.592	2.529	2.469
14	3.152	3.061	2.974	2.892	2.814	2.740	2.670	2.603	2.539	2.477
15	3.170	3.076	2.988	2.905	2.825	2.750	2.679	2.611	2.546	2.484
16	3.183	3.088	2.999	2.914	2.834	2.757	2.685	2.616	2.551	2.489
17	3.193	3.097	3.007	2.921	2.840	2.763	2.690	2.621	2.555	2.492
18	3.201	3.104	3.012	2.926	2.844	2.767	2.693	2.624	2.557	2.494
19	3.207	3.109	3.017	2.930	2.848	2.770	2.696	2.626	2.559	2.496
20	3.211	3.113	3.020	2.933	2.850	2.772	2.698	2.627	2.561	2.497
21	3.215	3.116	3.023	2.935	2.852	2.773	2.699	2.629	2.562	2.498
22	3.217	3.118	3.025	2.936	2.853	2.775	2.700	2.629	2.562	2.498
23	3.219	3.120	3.026	2.938	2.854	2.775	2.701	2.630	2.563	2.499
24	3.221	3.121	3.027	2.939	2.855	2.776	2.701	2.630	2.563	2.499
25	3.222	3.122	3.028	2.939	2.856	2.776	2.702	2.631	2.563	2.499
30	3.225	2.124	3.030	2.941	2.857	2.777	2.702	2.631	2.564	2.500
40	3.226	2.125	3.030	2.941	2.857	2.778	2.703	2.632	2.564	2.500
50	3.226	2.125	3.030	2.941	2.857	2.778	2.703	2.632	2.564	2.500

Accounting Glossary

absorption approach A costing approach that considers all factory overhead (both variable and fixed) to be product (inventoriable) costs that become an expense in the form of manufacturing cost of goods sold only as sales occur.

accelerated depreciation Any pattern of depreciation that writes off depreciable assets more quickly than does ordinary straight-line depreciation.

account Each item in a financial statement.

account analysis Selecting a volume-related cost driver and classifying each account as a variable cost or as a fixed cost.

accounting rate-of-return (ARR) model A non-DCF capital-budgeting model expressed as the increase in expected average annual operating income divided by the initial increase in required investment.

accounting system A formal mechanism for gathering, organizing, and communicating information about an organization's activities.

accounts payable Amounts owed on open accounts whereby the buyer pays cash some time after the date of sale.

accounts receivable Amounts owed to a company by customers who buy on open account.

accrual basis A process of accounting that recognizes the impact of transactions on the financial statements in the time periods when revenues and expenses occur instead of when cash is received or disbursed.

accrue To accumulate a receivable or payable during a given period even though no explicit transaction occurs.

activity analysis The process of identifying appropriate cost drivers and their effects on the costs of making a product or providing a service.

activity-based accounting (ABA) A system that first accumulates overhead costs for each of the activities of an organization, and then assigns the costs of activities to the products, services, or other cost objects that caused that activity.

activity-based costing (ABC) *See* activity-based accounting.

activity-level variances The differences between the master budget amounts and the amounts in the flexible budget.

adjustments Recording of implicit transactions, in contrast to the explicit transactions that trigger nearly all day-to-day routine entries.

agency theory A theory used to describe the formal choices of performance measures and rewards.

assets Economic resources that are expected to benefit future activities.

attention directing Reporting and interpreting information that helps managers to focus on operating problems, imperfections, inefficiencies, and opportunities.

audit An examination or in-depth inspection that is made in accordance with generally accepted auditing standards. It culminates with the accountant's testimony that management's financial statements are in conformity with generally accepted accounting principles.

avoidable costs Costs that will not continue if an ongoing operation is changed or deleted.

backflush costing An accounting system that applies costs to products only when the production is complete.

balance sheet A snapshot of financial status at an instant of time.

balanced scorecard A performance measurement system that strikes a balance between financial and operating measures, links performance to rewards, and gives explicit recognition to the diversity of stakeholder interests.

behavioral implications   The accounting system's effect on the behavior (decisions) of managers.

bench marks   General rules of thumb specifying appropriate levels for financial ratios.

book value   The original cost of equipment less accumulated depreciation, which is the summation of depreciation charged to past periods.

break-even point   The level of sales at which revenue equals expenses and net income is zero.

budget   A quantitative expression of a plan of action, and an aid to coordinating and implementing the plan.

budgeted factory-overhead rate   The budgeted total overhead divided by the budgeted cost driver activity.

by-product   A product that, like a joint product, is not individually identifiable until manufacturing reaches a split-off point, but has relatively insignificant total sales value.

capacity costs   The fixed costs of being able to achieve a desired level of production or to provide a desired level of service while maintaining product or service attributes, such as quality.

capital budget   A budget that details the planned expenditures for facilities, equipment, new products, and other long-term investments.

capital turnover   Revenue divided by invested capital.

capital-budgeting decisions   Decisions that have significant financial effects beyond the current year.

cash basis   A process of accounting where revenue and expense recognition would occur when cash is received and disbursed.

cash budget   A statement of planned cash receipts and disbursements.

cash equivalents   Short-term investments that can easily be converted into cash with little delay.

cash flow   Usually refers to the net cash flow from operating activities.

cash flows from operating activities   The first major section in the statement of cash flows.

cellular manufacturing   A production system where machines are organized in cells according to the specific requirements of a product family.

Certified Management Accountant (CMA)   The management accountant's counterpart to the CPA.

Certified Public Accountant (CPA)   In the United States, an accountant earns this designation by a combination of education, qualifying experience, and the passing of a two-day written national examination.

coefficient of determination (R²)   A measurement of how much of the fluctuation of a cost is explained by changes in the cost driver.

committed fixed costs   Costs arising from the possession of facilities, equipment, and a basic organization: large, indivisible chunks of cost that the organization is obligated to incur or usually would not consider avoiding.

common costs   Those costs of facilities and services that are shared by users.

common stock   Stock that has no predetermined rate of dividends and is the last to obtain a share in the assets when the corporation is dissolved. It usually has voting power in the management of the corporation.

common-size statements   Financial statements expressed in component percentages.

component percentages   Analysis and presentation of financial statements in percentage form to aid comparability, frequently used when companies differ in size.

computer-integrated manufacturing (CIM) systems   Systems that use computer-aided design and computer-aided manufacturing, together with robots and computer- controlled machines.

conservatism convention   Selecting the method of measurement that yields the gloomiest immediate results.

consolidated financial statements   Financial statements that combine the financial statements of the parent company with those of various subsidiaries, as if they were a single entity.

constant dollars   Nominal dollars that are restated in terms of current purchasing power.

continuity convention   The assumption that in all ordinary situations an entity persists indefinitely.

continuous budget   A common form of master budget that adds a month in the future as the month just ended is dropped.

contribution approach   A method of internal (management accounting) reporting that emphasizes the distinction between variable and fixed costs for the purpose of better decision making.

contribution margin   The sales price minus the variable cost per unit.

controllable cost   Any cost that is influenced by a manager's decisions and actions.

controller/comptroller   The top accounting officer of an organization. The term comptroller is used primarily in government organizations.

conversion costs   Direct labor costs plus factory overhead costs.

corporation   A business organized as a separate legal entity and owned by its stockholders.

cost   A sacrifice or giving up of resources for a particular purpose, frequently measured by the monetary units that must be paid for goods and services.

cost accounting   That part of the accounting system that measures costs for the purposes of management decision making and financial reporting.

cost accounting systems   The techniques used to determine the cost of a product, service, or other cost objective by collecting and classifying costs and assigning them to cost objects.

cost accumulation   Collecting costs by some natural classification such as materials or labor.

cost allocation   Tracing and reassigning costs to one or more cost objectives such as departments, customers, or products.

cost allocation base   A cost driver when it is used for allocating costs.

cost application   The allocation of total departmental costs to the revenue-producing products or services.

cost behavior   How the activities of an organization affect its costs.

cost center   A responsibility center for which costs are accumulated.

cost drivers   Activities that affect costs.

cost function   An algebraic equation used by managers to describe the relationship between a cost and its cost driver(s).

cost measurement   The first step in estimating or predicting costs as a function of appropriate cost drivers.

cost method   The method of accounting for investments whereby the initial investment is recorded at cost and dividends are recognized as income when they are received.

cost object   *See* cost objective.

cost objective   Any activity or resource for which a separate measurement of costs is desired. Examples include departments, products, and territories.

cost of capital   What a firm must pay to acquire more capital, whether or not it actually has to acquire more capital to take on a project.

cost of goods sold   The cost of the merchandise that is acquired or manufactured and resold.

cost of quality report   A report that displays the financial impact of quality.

cost pool   A group of individual costs that is allocated to cost objectives using a single cost driver.

cost prediction   The application of cost measures to expected future activity levels to forecast future costs.

cost recovery   A concept in which assets such as inventories, prepayments, and equipment are carried forward as assets because their costs are expected to be recovered in the form of cash inflows (or reduced cash outflows) in future periods.

cost-allocation base   A cost driver when it is used for allocating costs.

cost-benefit balance   Weighing estimated costs against probable benefits, the primary consideration in choosing among accounting systems and methods.

cost-benefit criterion   An approach that implicitly underlies the decisions about the design of accounting systems. As a system is changed, its potential benefits should exceed its additional costs.

cost-management system   Identifies how management's decisions affect costs, by first measuring the resources used in performing the organization's activities and then assessing the effects on costs of changes in those activities.

cost-volume-profit (CVP) analysis   The study of the effects of output volume on revenue (sales), expenses (costs), and net income (net profit).

credit   An entry on the right side of an account.

cross-sectional comparisons   Comparisons of a company's financial ratios with ratios of other companies or with industry averages for the same period.

current assets   Cash and all other assets that are reasonably expected to be converted to cash or sold or consumed during the normal operating cycle.

current cost   The cost to replace an asset, as opposed to its historical cost.

current liabilities   An organization's debts that fall due within the coming year or within the normal operating cycle if longer than a year.

current-cost method   The measurement method that uses current costs and nominal dollars.

currently attainable standards   Levels of performance that can be achieved by realistic levels of effort.

cycle time   The time taken to complete a product or service, or any of the components of a product or service.

debentures   Formal certificates of indebtedness that are accompanied by a promise to pay interest at a specified annual rate.

debit   An entry on the left side of an account.

decentralization   The delegation of freedom to make decisions. The lower in the organization that this freedom exists, the greater the decentralization.

decision making   The purposeful choice from among a set of alternative courses of action designed to achieve some objective.

decision model   Any method for making a choice, sometimes requiring elaborate quantitative procedures.

deferred revenue   *See* unearned revenue.

depreciation   The periodic cost of equipment which is spread over (or charged to) the future periods in which the equipment is expected to be used.

differential approach   An approach that compares two alternatives by computing the differences in cash flows between alternatives and then converting these differences in cash flows to their present values.

differential cost   The difference in total cost between two alternatives.

direct costs   Costs that can be identified specifically and exclusively with a given cost objective in an economically feasible way.

direct method   A method for allocating service department costs that ignores other service departments when any given service department's costs are allocated to the revenue-producing (operating) departments.

direct-labor costs   The wages of all labor that can be traced specifically and exclusively to the manufactured goods in an economically feasible way.

direct-material costs   The acquisition costs of all materials that are physically identified as a part of the manufactured goods and that may be traced to the manufactured goods in an economically feasible way.

discount rate   *See* required rate of return.

discounted-cash-flow (DCF) models   A type of capital-budgeting model that focuses on cash inflows and outflows and explicitly and systematically incorporates the time value of money.

discretionary fixed costs   Costs determined by management as part of the periodic planning process in order to meet the organization's goals.

discriminatory pricing   Charging different prices to different customers for the same product or service.

dividends   Distributions of assets to stockholders that reduce retained income.

double-entry system   A method of record keeping in which at least two accounts are affected by each transaction.

dysfunctional behavior   Any action taken in conflict with organizational goals.

earnings   *See* profits.

earnings per share   Net income divided by the average number of common shares outstanding during the year.

effectiveness   The degree to which a goal, objective, or target is met.

efficiency   The degree to which inputs are used in relation to a given level of outputs.

efficiency variance   *See* usage variance.

efficient capital market   A market in which market prices fully reflect all information available to the public.

engineering analysis   The systematic review of materials, supplies, labor, support services, and facilities needed for products and services: measuring cost behavior according to what costs should be, not by what costs have been.

equities   The claims against, or interests in, an organization's assets.

equity method   Accounts for the investment at the acquisition cost adjusted for the investor's share of dividends and earnings or losses of the investee after the date of investment.

equivalent units   The number of completed units that could have been produced from the inputs applied.

expected cost   The cost most likely to be attained.

expenses   Gross decreases in assets from delivering goods or services.

factory burden   *See* factory-overhead costs.

factory-overhead costs   All costs other than direct material or direct labor that are associated with the manufacturing process.

favorable expense variable   A variance that occurs when actual expenses are less than budgeted expenses.

Financial Accounting Standards Board (FASB)   The primary regulatory body over accounting principles and practices. Consisting of seven full-time members, it is an independent creation of the private sector.

financial accounting   The field of accounting that develops information for external decision makers such as stockholders, suppliers, banks, and government regulatory agencies.

financial budget   The part of a master budget that focuses on the effects that the operating budget and other plans (such as capital budgets and repayments of debt) will have on cash.

financial capital maintenance   The concept that income emerges after financial resources are recovered.

financial planning models   Mathematical models of the master budget that can react to any set of assumptions about sales, costs, or product mix.

first-in, first-out (FIFO)   An inventory method that assumes that the stock acquired earliest is sold (used up) first.

first-in, first-out (FIFO) process-costing method   A process-costing method that sharply distinguishes the current work done from the previous work done on the beginning inventory of work in process.

fixed assets   Physical items that can be seen and touched, such as property, plant, and equipment.

fixed cost   A cost that is not immediately affected by changes in the cost driver.

fixed overhead rate   The amount of fixed manufacturing overhead applied to each unit of production. It is determined by dividing the budgeted fixed overhead by the expected volume of production for the budget period.

flexible budget   A budget that adjusts for changes in sales volume and other cost-driver activities.

flexible-budget variances   The variances between the flexible budget and the actual results.

Foreign Corrupt Practices Act   U.S. law forbidding bribery and other corrupt practices, and requiring that accounting records be maintained in reasonable detail and accuracy, and that an appropriate system of internal accounting controls be maintained.

full cost   The total of all manufacturing costs plus the total of all selling and administrative costs.

fully allocated cost   *See* full cost.

general ledger   A collection of the group of accounts that supports the items shown in the major financial statements.

general price index   A comparison of the average price of a group of goods and services at one date with the average price of a similar group at another date.

generally accepted accounting principles (GAAP)   Broad concepts or guidelines and detailed practices, including all conventions, rules, and procedures that together make up accepted accounting practice at a given time.

goal congruence   A condition where employees, working in their own personal interests make decisions that help meet the overall goals of the organization.

going concern convention   *See* continuity convention.

goodwill   The excess of the cost of an acquired company over the sum of the fair market values of its identifiable individual assets less its liabilities.

gross book value   The original cost of an asset before deducting accumulated depreciation.

gross margin   The excess of sales over the total cost of goods sold.

gross profit   *See* gross margin.

half-year convention   A requirement of the modified accelerated cost recovery system that treats all assets as if they were placed in service at the midpoint of the tax year.

high-low method   A simple method for measuring a linear cost function from past cost data, focusing on the highest-activity and lowest-activity points and fitting a line through these two points.

historical cost   The amount originally paid to acquire an asset.

holding gains (or losses)   Increases (or decreases) in the replacement costs of the assets held during the current period.

hurdle rate   *See* required rate of return.

hybrid-costing system   An accounting system that is a blend of ideas from both job costing and process costing.

ideal standards   *See* perfection standards.

idle time   An indirect labor cost consisting of wages paid for unproductive time caused by machine breakdowns, material shortages, and sloppy scheduling.

imperfect competition   A market in which a firm's price will influence the quantity it sells.

incentives   Those formal and informal performance-based rewards that enhance managerial effort toward organizational goals.

income   *See* profits.

income percentage of revenue   Income divided by revenue.

income statement   A statement that measures the performance of an organization by matching its accomplishments (revenue from customers, which is usually called sales) and its efforts (cost of goods sold and other expenses).

incremental cost   *See* differential cost.

incremental effect   The change in total results (such as revenue, expenses, or income) under a new condition in comparison with some given or known condition.

indirect costs   Costs that cannot be identified specifically and exclusively with a given cost objective in an economically feasible way.

indirect labor   All factory labor wages, other than those for direct labor and manager salaries.

indirect method   In a statement of cash flows, the method that reconciles net income to the net cash provided by operating activities.

inflation   A general decline in the purchasing power of the monetary unit.

Institute of Management Accountants (IMA)   The largest U.S. professional organization of accountants whose major interest is management accounting.

intangible assets   Long-lived assets that are not physical in nature. Examples are goodwill, franchises, patents, trademarks, and copyrights.

internal control system   Methods and procedures to prevent errors and irregularities, detect errors and irregularities, and promote operating efficiency.

internal rate of return (IRR)   The discount rate that makes the net present value of the project equal to zero.

inventory turnover   The number of times the average inventory is sold per year.

investment center   A responsibility center whose success is measured not only by its income but also by relating that income to its invested capital, as in a ratio of income to the value of the capital employed.

investments in affiliates   Investments in equity securities that represent 20% to 50% ownership. They are usually accounted for under the equity method.

investments in associates   *See* investments in affiliates.

job costing   *See* job-order costing.

job order   *See* job-cost record.

job-cost record   A document that shows all costs for a particular product, service, or batch of products.

job-cost sheet   *See* job-cost record.

job-order costing   The method of allocating costs to products that are readily identified by individual units or batches, each of which requires varying degrees of attention and skill.

joint costs   The costs of manufacturing joint products prior to the split-off point.

joint products   Two or more manufactured products that (1) have relatively significant sales values and (2) are not separately identifiable as individual products until their split-off point.

just-in-time (JIT) philosophy   A philosophy to eliminate waste by reducing the time products spend in the production process and eliminating the time products spend on activities that do not add value.

just-in-time (JIT) production system   A system in which an organization purchases materials and parts and produces components just when they are needed in the production process, the goal being to have zero inventory, because holding inventory is a non-value-added activity.

labor time tickets   The record of the time a particular direct laborer spends on each job.

last-in, first-out (LIFO)   An inventory method that assumes that the stock acquired most recently is sold (used up) first.

least-squares regression   Measuring a cost function objectively by using statistics to fit a cost function to all the data.

ledger accounts   A method of keeping track of how multitudes of transactions affect each particular asset, liability, revenue, and expense.

legal value   *See* par value.

liabilities   The entity's economic obligations to nonowners.

LIFO layers   Separately identifiable additional layers of LIFO inventory.

LIFO increments   *See* LIFO layers.

limited liability   Creditors cannot seek payment from shareholders as individuals if the corporation itself cannot pay its debts.

limiting factor   The item that restricts or constrains the production or sale of a product or service.

line authority   Authority exerted downward over subordinates.

linear-cost behavior   Activity that can be graphed with a straight line when a cost changes proportionately with changes in a cost driver.

liquidation   Converting assets to cash and using the cash to pay off outside claims.

long-range planning   Producing forecasted financial statements for five- or ten-year periods.

long term liabilities   *See* noncurrent liabilities.

lower-of-cost-or-market (LCM)   An inventory method in which the current market price of inventory is compared with its cost (derived by specific identification, FIFO, LIFO, or weighted average) and the lower of the two is selected as the basis for the valuation of goods at a specific inventory date.

management accounting   The process of identifying, measuring, accumulating, analyzing, preparing, interpreting, and communicating information that helps managers fulfill organizational objectives.

management audit   A review to determine whether the policies and procedures specified by top management have been implemented.

management by exception   Concentrating on areas that deviate from the plan and ignoring areas that are presumed to be running smoothly.

management by objectives (MBO)   The joint formulation by a manager and his or her superior of a set of goals and plans for achieving the goals for a forthcoming period.

management control system   A logical integration of management accounting tools to gather and report data and to evaluate performance.

managerial effort   Exertion toward a goal or objective including all conscious actions (such as supervising, planning, and thinking) that result in more efficiency and effectiveness.

manufacturing overhead   *See* factory-overhead costs.

margin of safety   Equal to the planned unit sales less the break-even unit sales; it shows how far sales can fall below the planned level before losses occur.

marginal cost   The additional cost resulting from producing and selling one additional unit.

marginal income   *See* contribution margin.

marginal income tax rate   The tax rate paid on additional amounts of pretax income.

marginal revenue   The additional revenue resulting from the sale of an additional unit.

markup   The amount by which price exceeds cost.

master budget   A budget that summarizes the planned activities of all subunits of an organization.

master budget variance   The variance of actual results from the master budget.

matching   The relating of accomplishments or revenues (as measured by the selling prices of goods and services delivered) and efforts or expenses (as measured by the cost of goods and services used) to a particular period for which a measurement of income is desired.

materiality   The accounting convention that justifies the omission of insignificant information when its omission or misstatement would not mislead a user of the financial statements.

materials requisitions   Records of materials issued to particular jobs.

measurement of cost behavior   Understanding and quantifying how activities of an organization affect levels of costs.

minority interests   An account that shows the outside stockholders' interest, as opposed to the parent's interest, in a subsidiary corporation.

mixed costs   Costs that contain elements of both fixed and variable-cost behavior.

motivation   The drive for some selected goal that creates effort and action toward that goal.

net book value   The original cost of an asset less any accumulated depreciation. *See* book value.

net income   The popular "bottom line"—the residual after deducting from revenues all expenses, including income taxes.

net worth   A synonym for owner's equity.

net-present-value (NPV) method   A discounted-cash-flow approach to capital budgeting that discounts all expected future cash flows to the present using a minimum desired rate of return.

nominal dollars   Dollar measurements that are not restated for fluctuations in the general purchasing power of the monetary unit.

nominal rate   Quoted market interest rate that includes an inflation element.

non-value-added costs   Costs that can be eliminated without affecting a product's value to the customer.

noncurrent liabilities   An organization's debts that fall due beyond one year.

normal costing   A cost system that applies actual direct materials and actual direct-labor costs to products or services but uses standards for applying overhead.

normal costing system   The cost system in which overhead is applied on an average or normalized basis, in order to get representative or normal inventory valuations.

objectivity   Accuracy supported by a high extent of consensus among independent measures of an item.

operating budget   A major part of a master budget that focuses on the income statement and its supporting schedules.

operating cycle   The time span during which cash is spent to acquire goods and services that are used to produce the organization's output, which in turn is sold to customers, who in turn pay for their purchases with cash.

operating leverage   A firm's ratio of fixed to variable costs.

operation   A hybrid-costing system often used in the batch or group manufacturing of goods that have some common characteristics plus some individual characteristics.

opportunity cost   The maximum available contribution to profit forgone (or passed up) by using limited resources for a particular purpose.

outlay cost   A cost that requires a cash disbursement.

overapplied overhead   The excess of overhead applied to products over actual overhead incurred.

overtime premium   An indirect labor cost, consisting of wages paid to all factory workers in excess of their straight-time wage rates.

owners' equity   The excess of the assets over the liabilities.

paid-in capital   The ownership claim against, or interest in, the total assets arising from any paid-in investment.

par value   The value that is printed on the face of the certificate.

parent company   A company owning more than 50% of another business's stock.

participative budgeting Budgets formulated with the active participation of all affected employees.

partnership An organization that joins two or more individuals together as co-owners.

payback period *See* payback time.

payback time The measure of the time it will take to recoup, in the form of cash inflows from operations, the initial dollars of outlay.

payroll fringe costs Employer contributions to employee benefits such as social security, life insurance, health insurance, and pensions.

perfect competition A market in which a firm can sell as much of a product as it can produce, all at a single market price.

perfection standards Expressions of the most efficient performance possible under the best conceivable conditions, using existing specifications and equipment.

performance reports Feedback provided by comparing results with plans and by highlighting variances.

period costs Costs that are deducted as expenses during the current period without going through an inventory stage.

physical capital maintenance The concept that income emerges only after recovering an amount that allows physical operating capability to be maintained.

postaudit A follow-up evaluation of capital budgeting decisions.

practical capacity Maximum or full capacity.

predatory pricing Establishing prices so low that competitors are driven out of the market so that the predatory pricer then has no significant competition and can raise prices dramatically.

preferred stock Stock that typically has some priority over other shares regarding dividends or the distribution of assets upon liquidation.

price elasticity The effect of price changes on sales volumes.

price variance The difference between actual input prices and expected input prices multiplied by the actual quantity of inputs used.

prime costs Direct labor costs plus direct materials costs.

pro forma statement *See* master budget.

problem solving Aspect of accounting that quantifies the likely results of possible courses of action and often recommends the best course of action to follow.

process costing The method of allocating costs to products by averaging costs over large numbers of nearly identical products.

product costs Costs identified with goods produced or purchased for resale.

product life cycle The various stages through which a product passes, from conception and development through introduction into the market through maturation and, finally, withdrawal from the market.

production cycle time The time from initiating production to delivering the goods to the customer.

production-volume variance A variance that appears whenever actual production deviates from the expected volume of production used in computing the fixed overhead rate. It is calculated as (actual volume – expected volume) × fixed-overhead rate.

productivity A measure of outputs divided by inputs.

profit centers A responsibility center for controlling revenues as well as costs (or expenses)—that is, profitability.

profit plan *See* operating budget.

profits The excess of revenues over expenses.

prorate To assign underapplied overhead or overapplied overhead in proportion to the sizes of the ending account balances.

prorating the variance Assigning the variances to the inventories and cost of goods sold related to the production during the period the variances arose.

quality control The effort to ensure that products and services perform to customer requirements.

quality-control chart The statistical plot of measures of various product dimensions or attributes.

quantity variance *See* usage variance.

recovery period The number of years over which an asset is depreciated for tax purposes.

regression analysis *See* least-squares regression.

relevant information The predicted future costs and revenues that will differ among alternative courses of action.

relevant range The limit of cost-driver activity within which a specific relationship between costs and the cost driver is valid.

required rate of return The minimum desired rate of return, based on the firm's cost of capital.

residual income Net income less "imputed" interest.

residual value The predicted sales value of a long-lived asset at the end of its useful life.

responsibility accounting Identifying what parts of the organization have primary responsibility for each objective, developing measures of achievement of objectives, and creating reports of these measures by organization subunit or responsibility center.

responsibility center   A set of activities assigned to a manager, a group of managers, or other employees.

retained earnings   *See* retained income.

retained income   The ownership claim arising as a result of profitable operations.

return on investment (ROI)   A measure of income or profit divided by the investment required to obtain that income or profit.

return on sales   *See* income percentage of revenue.

revaluation equity   A portion of stockholders' equity that shows all accumulated holding gains.

revenue   A gross increase in assets from delivering goods or services.

rolling budget   *See* continuous budget.

sales budget   The result of decisions to create conditions that will generate a desired level of sales.

sales forecast   A prediction of sales under a given set of conditions.

sales mix   The relative proportions or combinations of quantities of products that constitute total sales.

sales-activity variances   Variances that measure how effective managers have been in meeting the planned sales objective, calculated as actual unit sales less master budget unit sales times the budgeted unit contribution margin.

scarce resource   *See* limiting factor.

scorekeeping   The accumulation and classification of data.

Securities and Exchange Commission (SEC)   By federal law, the agency with the ultimate responsibility for specifying the generally accepted accounting principles for U.S. companies whose stock is held by the general investing public.

segment autonomy   The delegation of decision-making power to managers of segments of an organization.

segments   Responsibility centers for which a separate measure of revenues and costs is obtained.

sensitivity analysis   The systematic varying of budget data input to determine the effects of each change on the budget.

separable costs   Any cost beyond the split-off point.

service departments   Units that exist only to support other departments.

sole proprietorship   A business entity with a single owner.

source documents   Explicit evidence of any transactions that occur in the entity's operation, for example, sales slips and purchase invoices.

specific identification   An inventory method that recognizes the actual cost paid for the specific item sold.

specific price index   An index used to approximate the current costs of particular assets or types of assets.

split-off point   The juncture of manufacturing where the joint products become individually identifiable.

staff authority   Authority to advise but not command. It may be exerted downward, laterally, or upward.

standard cost   A carefully determined cost per unit that should be attained.

standard cost systems   Accounting systems that value products according to standard costs only.

Standards of Ethical Conduct for Management Accountants   Codes of conduct developed by the Institute of Management Accountants, which include competence, confidentiality, integrity, and objectivity.

stated value   *See* par value.

statement of cash flows   A statement that reports the cash receipts and cash payments of an organization during a particular period.

statement of financial condition   *See* balance sheet.

statement of financial position   *See* balance sheet.

statement of retained earnings   A financial statement that analyzes changes in the retained earnings or retained income account for a given period.

statement of retained income   *See* statement of retained earnings.

static budget variance   *See* master budget variance.

step costs   Costs that change abruptly at intervals of activity because the resources and their costs come in indivisible chunks.

step-down method   A method for allocating service department costs that recognizes that some service departments support the activities in other service departments as well as those in production departments.

stockholders' equity   The excess of assets over liabilities of a corporation.

strategic plan   A plan that sets the overall goals and objectives of the organization.

subordinated   A creditor claim that is junior to the other creditors in exercising claims against assets.

subsidiary   A company owned by a parent company that owns more than 50% of its stock.

sunk cost   A cost that has already been incurred and, therefore, is irrelevant to the decision making process. Synonyms are historical cost or past cost.

tangible assets   *See* fixed assets.

target costing   A strategy in which companies first determine the price at which they can sell a new product or service and then design a product or service that can be produced at a low enough cost to provide an adequate profit margin.

tax shields   Depreciation deductions and similar deductions that protect that amount of income from taxation. All allowable expenses, both cash and noncash items, could be called tax shields because they reduce income and thereby reduce income taxes.

time cards   *See* labor time tickets.

time-series comparisons   Comparison of a company's financial ratios with its own historical ratios.

total project approach   An approach that compares two or more alternatives by computing the total impact on cash flows for each alternative and then converting these total cash flows to their present values.

total quality management (TQM)   The application of quality principles to all of the organization's endeavors to satisfy customers.

transaction   Any event that affects the financial position of an organization and requires recording.

transaction-based costing   Activity-based costing.

transfer price   The amount charged by one segment of an organization for a product or service that it supplies to another segment of the same organization.

transferred-in costs   In process costing, costs incurred in a previous department for items that have been received by a subsequent department.

treasury stock   A corporation's own stock that has been issued and subsequently repurchased by the company and is being held for a specific purpose.

unavoidable costs   Costs that continue even if an operation is halted.

uncontrollable cost   Any cost that cannot be affected by the management of a responsibility center within a given time span.

underapplied overhead   The excess of actual overhead over the overhead applied to products.

unearned revenue   Collections from customers received and recorded before they are earned.

unexpired cost   Any asset that ordinarily becomes an expense in future periods, for example, inventory and prepaid rent.

unfavorable expense variance   A variance that occurs when actual expenses are more than budgeted expenses.

usage variance   The difference between the quantity of inputs actually used and the quantity of inputs that should have been used to achieve the actual quantity of output multiplied by the expected price of input.

value chain   The sequence of functions that adds value to the company's products or services.

value-added cost   The necessary cost of an activity that cannot be eliminated without affecting a product's value to the customer.

variable budget   *See* flexible budget.

variable cost   A cost that changes in direct proportion to changes in the cost driver.

variable-cost percentage   *See* variable-cost ratio.

variable-cost ratio   All variable costs divided by sales.

variable-overhead efficiency variance   When actual cost-driver activity differs from the standard amount allowed for the actual output achieved.

variable-overhead spending variance   The difference between the actual variable overhead and the amount of variable overhead budgeted for the actual level of cost-driver activity.

variances   Deviations from plans.

verfiability   *See* objectivity.

visual-fit method   A method in which the cost analyst visually fits a straight line through a plot of all the available data, not just between the high point and the low point, making it more reliable than the high-low method.

Finance Glossary

A-B-C system An *ad hoc* technique of monitoring inventory. *A*-items are high value, *C*-items are low value, and *B*-items fall between.

accounting profit Earnings amount derived from accrual accounting practices that correspond with generally accepted accounting principles.

accounting rate of return Nondiscounted profitability measure that divides accounting earnings by average investment.

accounts receivable turnover ratio Method of monitoring trends in customer payments; higher turnover is considered positive.

add-on interest Interest calculated on the amount of funds to be lent and added to loaned amount to determine loan's face value.

adjustable-rate preferred stock (ARPS) A capital market security that periodically adjusts the dividend amount in the direction of interest rate movements.

adjusted present value (APV) A value derived by evaluating financing cash flows separate from operating cash flows.

agent A person who performs activities for another person, called a *principal*. Managers are agents of the firm.

aging schedule Process of classifying accounts by the amount of time they have been outstanding. The schedule usually displays the percentage of receivables that are one month old, two months old, and so on.

American depository receipt (ADR) Receipt issued by bank; represents ownership of foreign company's common stock. The shares of the foreign companies are held in trust.

amortizing term loan A loan with serial payments for principal and interest.

annual clean-up period Period of time the bank wants the borrower to be free of bank credit or to have the balance below some agreed amount. The purpose is to show the bank that the firm does not need the loan as a source of permanent financing.

annual operating cash flows The cash outflows incurred for material, labor, and overhead; excludes all financing costs.

annual percentage rate (APR) The rate per period times the number of periods per year.

annual report The formal financial statement issued yearly by a corporation. The annual report shows assets, liabilities, income, and how the company stood at the close of the business year. It usually also includes other information of interest to shareholders.

annualized cost of a missed discount (ACD) The cost of foregoing cash discounts and paying at some date beyond the discount period.

annuity due A series of equal cash payments occurring at the beginning of each period with equal amounts of time between each payment.

asked price The lowest price at which a dealer offers to sell securities—the sell side of the bid-asked spread.

average collection period (ACP) The amount of time accounts receivable are outstanding; used to evaluate the quality of the investment in accounts receivable.

balance proportions An accounts receivable monitoring technique that relates the outstanding balance to the sale that generated the receivable.

balance sheet Statement of a firm's financial position on a given date. Shows what the firm owns (its assets), what it owes (its liabilities), and the residual or equity of the owners (the net worth).

bank discount rate method Interest calculated on the face amount of the loan. Lender deducts the interest in advance.

bankruptcy   A legal proceeding to decide whether to liquidate or reorganize a company and the administration thereof.

bar chart   A graph of a period's high, low, and closing price. The price range is a vertical bar. The close is a short horizontal bar.

bass point   One hundredth of a percentage point. Used to express changes in interest rates.

Baumol EOQ model   A mathematical model for calculating the optimal cash order size. The model minimizes the total ordering and holding costs.

bearer bond   A bond issued without a record of the owner's name. Payment is made to whomever holds the bond.

beta   A measure of a security's nondiversifiable risk; shows the relationship between an individual security's performance and the performance of a market index.

bid price   The price at which a dealer offers to buy a security.

bill (T-bill)   Short-term (one year or less) security issued by the U.S. Treasury. T-bill is issued at a discount and pays no coupon.

bond   Long-term (over ten years) security which pays a specified sum (called the principal) either at a future date or periodically over the length of a loan, during which time a fixed rate of interest may be paid on certain dates.

bond market   Financial market for trading long-term debt instruments issued by firms and governments; bonds represent promises to repay specified amounts at a future time.

book value of assets   Historical value of the assets adjusted for depreciation of fixed assets and other asset writedowns.

business organization   An institution that buys material and labor and organizes them to produce and sell goods and services.

business risk   The risk associated with the returns generated by a firm's assets as if the firm were financed entirely by equity. Risk associated with debt financing is ignored.

business sector   Part of the economy that consists of units that produce and provide goods and services to households and other businesses.

buy-and-hold strategy   Investment strategy of buying securities and holding them for a period of time. Opposite of trading in an attempt to sell at each market high and buy at each market low.

buyout specialists   Organizations that use borrowed funds to buy public firms and privatize them.

call provision   A feature of the trust indenture of a bond that allows the issuer to repurchase outstanding bonds at a given price from the holders after a given date.

callable preferred stock   Preferential stock that can be retired by the issuer; unlike equity security, may not have infinite life.

capital budgeting   Process of identifying, evaluating, and implementing approved capital expenditures.

capital gain   Increase in value of a security over its original cost.

capital gains tax   Tax on the excess of proceeds over cost from the sale of capital asset as defined by the Internal Revenue Code. The Tax Reform Act of 1986 made the capital gains tax rate the same as the tax on other income.

capital investments   Expenditures of a firm for assets, such as plant and equipment.

capital loss   Decrease in value of a security from its original cost.

capital market line (CML)   The relationship between risk and return in well-diversified portfolios.

capital market   A market for securities with maturities beyond one year.

capital rationing   A situation in which new investments are limited to less than those economically justifiable.

capitalizing cash flow   The process of dividing future cash flow amounts by an interest rate representing the minimum return the cash flows should earn; for example, if future cash flow is $10 per year in perpetuity and the interest rate is 4%, the cash flows have a capitalized (economic) value of $10 − 0.04 = $250.

cash budget   A schedule of expected cash receipts and disbursements and the borrowing requirements for a given period of time.

cash conversion cycle   The operating cycle less the accounts payable and accrued liabilities deferral period.

cash dividend   Cash payment from the firm to its shareholders.

cash inadequacy   Insufficient cash to meet current obligations.

causal model   Assumes that the factor to be forecast exhibits a cause-and-effect relationship with a number of other factors.

certainty equivalent (CE)   A technique used to adjust uncertain cash flows downward to a level that the decision maker is indifferent between the risky unadjusted cash flows and the certain adjusted cash flows.

collateral trust bond   A *bond* secured by pledges of stocks and bonds.

common-size analysis Accounting statements expressed as a percentage of net sales or total assets to aid comparison.

compensating balance A bank's requirement that the borrower maintain a minimum noninterest-bearing average balance; used to compensate banks for services; borrower pays interest on these balances.

compound interest Interest computed on both the principal sum and the interest earned by the principal sum as of a given date.

compounding Process by which a given amount is adjusted to yield a future value. Compounding is the opposite of *discounting*.

concentration bank A bank to which a company transfers all excess cash balances daily.

contribution margin proportion The proportion of each sales dollar left after paying *variable costs;* ratio of (sales − variable costs) ÷ sales.

convertible bond A bond that pays fixed interest payments and has a specified maturity, just like an ordinary bond, but differs in that it can be exchanged for a specified number of shares of common stock.

correlation Measure of the degree to which two variables move together.

cost of capital Minimum market rate of return on new investments required to maintain the value of the firm.

cost of debt *Yield to maturity* of the instrument.

cost of equity Market rate of return required by investors to hold the company's common stock.

cost of preferred stock Preferred stock dividend divided by the market price of the stock.

covariance A statistical term used to reflect the extent to which two variables move together. A positive value means that on average, they move in the same direction. The covariance depends not only on the correlation between the two variables but also the *standard deviations* of each variable.

covenants Restrictions placed on the borrower requiring specific standards be met, as verified by the trustee.

credit Arrangement that allows a customer to take goods or services and delay paying for them.

credit standards Criteria used to determine which customers receive credit. Usually encompasses an examination of the customer's credit rating, credit references, outstanding debt, and financial statements.

credit terms The payment provisions that are part of a credit arrangement.

cumulative voting A voting system in which a shareholder may cast votes equal to the number of shares owned times the number of directors to be elected. The votes may be cast for only one director but in any combination.

currency risk The risk that fluctuating exchange rates will adversely affect the investment.

current assets Assets that will turn into cash within the normal business cycle.

current liabilities Liabilities that are payable within the firm's business cycle.

current ratio A measure of liquidity, defined as current assets divided by current liabilities.

debenture A debt obligation not secured by specific property but backed by the general credit of the issuing company.

debt security Agreement to pay a specified sum (called the principal) either at a future date or over the course of a loan, during which time interest may be paid on certain dates.

declaration date The date the firm's directors issue a statement declaring a dividend. The dividend becomes a legally binding obligation of the corporation.

default (credit) risk The chance that interest or principal on a debt security will not be paid on a payment date and in the promised amount.

default risk premium The premium on a loan charged in case the borrower fails to make a contracted payment.

defensive interval ratio A measurement of the number of days of normal cash expenditures covered by quick assets.

deficit (borrowing) units Net borrowers, who spend more than they save. The business sector is considered a net deficit unit.

degree of financial leverage (DFL) The percentage change in net income for a given change in earnings before interest and taxes.

degree of operating leverage (DOL) The percentage change in earnings before interest and taxes for a given change in sales.

degree of total leverage (DTL) The percentage change in net income for a given change in sales.

dependency The degree of association, or *correlation,* between two variables. Dependency is low for small levels of correlation and high for high levels of correlation.

depository transfer check (DTC) An instrument used to transfer funds between bank accounts of the same firm. No signature is required. The DTC clears through the normal channels, similar to a check.

direct send   The check clearing process bypasses at least part of the normal Federal Reserve collection system in an effort to accelerate collection of funds.

discount   The amount by which a bond (or preferred stock) sells below its par value. The security trades at a discount when the coupon rate is lower than the market rate of interest.

discount factor   Present value of $1 received at a stated future date.

discount rate   Interest rate charged to member banks on their loans from the *Federal Reserve Banks*. It is so called because the interest on a loan is discounted when the loan is made, rather than collected when the loan is repaid.

discounted cash flow analysis   The process of converting future cash flows to their present values. This process is the opposite of *future value analysis.*

discounted payback period   A discounted cash flow technique that calculates the time it takes to recover the original investment.

discounting   Process by which a given amount is adjusted at interest to yield a present value. Discounting is the opposite of *compounding.*

diversifiable risk   The amount of risk that can be eliminated through proper *diversification.*

diversification   Investing in more than one asset to reduce risk.

dividend payout ratio   The proportion of earnings paid out in dividends.

Dow Jones Industrial Average   A price index of 30 listed stocks. The price of the stocks is added and divided by a number that adjusts for *stock splits*. An example of a stock split is when a share selling for $90 is split into two shares selling for $45 each.

duration   A number which summarizes the various factors that affect a bond's price sensitivity to changes in interest rates.

Dutch auction   A process where investors submit bids for securities. The issuer ranks the bids from high to low and sequentially selects those bids that are most advantageous to the issuer.

earnings available to common shareholders   Net income less dividends paid to preferred shareholders.

EBIT indifference level   The level of earnings before interest and taxes to which management is indifferent between financing alternatives.

economic returns   Payments to a firm in excess of the economic costs, including normal profit.

economic system   Relationship between the components of an economy (such as its households, firms, and government) and the institutional framework of laws and customs within which these components operate.

economic value of assets   The expected value of an asset derived by capitalizing future cash flows at an appropriate interest rate. See *capitalizing cash flows.*

economic value of cash   The expected return that a firm gives up when it invests in cash rather than in a risk-free security.

effective annual rate (EAR)   The true interest rate that is paid on a loan.

efficiency ratios   Measures that portray how quickly assets or liabilities are used. The higher an efficiency ratio, the more efficient management is perceived in utilizing the resources committed to the measured activity.

efficient financial market   Prices for traded securities embody all currently available relevant information. Characteristics of efficient markets include low transaction costs, freely accessible information, many investors, and quick price corrections.

efficient frontier   The frontier is the boundary line marking off the best risk-and-return combinations available to the investor.

efficient investment   An investment offering the best expected return for a given risk, or the lowest risk for a given expected return.

efficient market   Market condition in which prices always fully reflect all available information. Adjustment to new information is virtually instantaneous.

efficient market hypothesis (EMH)   The concept that competition in the financial markets alerts investors to information so that prices adjust almost instantaneously to new information.

electronic depository transfer check (EDTC)   An electronic version of the DTC. Funds are transferred by wire.

electronic wire transfer   A means of effecting the immediate transfer of funds from one bank account to an account at another bank.

EOQ model   A mathematical model for calculating the optimal inventory order size; it minimizes the total ordering and holding costs.

equilibrium price   Price of a commodity or service determined in the market by the intersection of supply and demand; the price at which the market clears.

equipment trust certificate (ETC)   A bond issued to pay for new equipment; secured by a lien on the purchased equipment.

equity security Security which provides ownership in the firm issuing it. The security has no maturity date.

equivalent annual annuity (EAA) An even cash flow that yields the same present value amount as the project's net present value.

Eurobond An international debt instrument denominated in a currency different from the currency of the country in which it is sold.

Eurocapital market An international market for debt and equity securities.

Eurocurrency loans Loans by commercial banks denominated in currencies other than the currency of the country in which the bank resides.

Eurodollar market A market for dollar-denominated deposits outside the United States.

Euroequity An ownership financial instrument denominated in a currency different from the currency of the country in which it is sold.

excess profits Returns in excess of profits required to satisfy the investor for the amount of risk involved.

excess reserves Quantity of a bank's legal reserves over and above its required reserves. Excess reserves are the key to a bank's lending power.

ex-dividend date Date when ownership of the security is without the right to a dividend about to be paid by a firm.

expected inflation premium The premium investors require to compensate them for the expected eroding effect of inflation on the value of money.

expected portfolio return The weighted arithmetic average of all possible outcomes for the *portfolio*, where the weights are the probabilities that each outcome will occur.

expected return The weighted average of all possible outcomes, where the weights are the probabilities that each outcome will occur. It is the expected value or mean of a probability distribution.

expected return-risk principle Given the risk exposure, securities are priced to provide investors with a return that compensates for the risk.

external financing requirement (EFR) The amount of funds that must be supplied by creditors or investors to satisfy financing needs.

factor A company in the business of buying accounts receivable from other businesses at a discount to their face value.

factoring Selling accounts receivable at a discount to a financial institution. The *factor* usually bears the risk of collection.

favorable financial leverage Positive effects of debt financing on shareholders' claims on earnings.

federal funds rate Interest rate at which banks borrow excess reserves from other banks' accounts at the Fed, usually overnight, to keep required reserves from falling below the legal level. In general, the lower the volume of excess reserves, the higher the federal funds rate. Therefore, the federal funds rate is an important indicator that the Fed watches to decide whether to add to banks' reserves or take away from them.

Federal Reserve Bank (Fed) One of the 12 banks (and branches) which make up the Federal Reserve System. Each serves as a "banker's bank" for the member banks in its district by acting as a source of credit and a depository of resources.

finance The study and practice of making money-denominated decisions. As a discipline, finance can be classified into three areas: managerial, investments, and markets and institutions.

finance subsidiary A separate legal entity owned by the parent corporation that specializes in financing the company's sales.

financial assets Financial instruments with claims on real *assets.*

financial (capital) lease A long-term, noncancelable *lease* that has many characteristics of debt. The lease obligation is shown directly on the balance sheet.

financial intermediaries Financial institutions that serve as middlemen between lenders and borrowers. They create and issue financial claims against themselves in order to acquire financial claims against others. Examples: banks, savings and loans associations, and pension funds.

financial intermediation The process of wholesaling or retailing funds between lenders and borrowers by *financial intermediaries.*

financial leverage The effects of debt financing on shareholders' claims on earnings.

financial leverage ratios Measures that show how the use of debt affects the firm's ability to repay the obligations.

financial markets One of the three areas of finance. Markets of the economy in which both short-term and long-term securities are exchanged.

financial risk Variability in the earnings stream of a company that results from the use of debt.

financial system The channel through which the savings of surplus sectors flow to the deficit sectors that wish to borrow.

first-in, first-out (FIFO)   A method of inventory accounting in which the oldest item in inventory is assumed to be sold first.

fiscal policy   Deliberate exercise of government's power to tax and spend in order to achieve price stability, help dampen the swings of business cycles, and bring the nation's output and employment to desired levels.

five C's of credit   An *ad hoc* approach for evaluating credit applicants that looks at the customer's character, capacity, capital, collateral, and conditions.

fixed-charge coverage ratio   A risk ratio to measure the level of earnings available per dollar of interest, fixed charges, and principal payments. Does not reflect the true cash flows available to meet the obligations.

fixed cost   A cost that remains relatively constant regardless of the volume of operations. Examples: rent, depreciation, and property taxes.

fixed income securities   Debt and preferred stock securities which make fixed dollar payments to investors over their lives.

float   Checks in the process of collection.

floating-rate preferred   A preferential security whose dividend adjusts periodically to track changing interest rates.

forward exchange rate   Foreign exchange bought (or sold) at a given time and at a stipulated current or "spot" price, but payable at a future date. By buying or selling forward exchange, importers and exporters can protect themselves against the risks of fluctuations in the current exchange market.

forward rates   Future interest rates implied by currently available spot interest rates.

fourth market   Direct trading of securities between institutions without the service of dealers or brokers.

fractional reserve banking system   The practice of keeping only a fraction of the deposits of depository institutions as cash reserves.

free reserves   Excess banking reserves minus reserves borrowed from the Federal Reserve by depository institutions.

funding constraint   A fixed amount of money available for investments aggregating in excess of the amount.

funds   Any means of payment.

future value analysis   The determination of the future worth of a series of cash flows. This process is the opposite of discounted cash flow analysis.

future value formula   The value of $(1 + r)^n$, where r is the interest rate and n is the number of time periods.

future value of an annuity due   The value at a known future date of a series of constant cash flows for a known number of periods, with the cash flows occurring at the beginning of each period.

future value annuity factor (FVIFA)   The sum of the future value of $1 amounts, using the future value formula, which occurs in periods $1, 2, \ldots, n$.

general obligation bond (GO)   A municipal bond for which the coupon and maturity payments are backed by the "full faith and credit" of the issuing municipality.

geometric average   The nth root of the product of n observations.

goodwill   The excess of the purchase price over the assessed value of the *tangible assets* acquired.

hedge   To take an action to remove or reduce an exposure or a position.

hedging strategy   The matching of asset and liability cash flows.

holder-of-record date   The date as of which all shareholders listed in a company's records are noted to receive the declared cash or stock dividend when it is paid.

holding-period rate of return   Rate of return earned from holding an asset during a given time period.

horizontal analysis   Common-size analysis that compares the same accounts from year to year.

household sector   Part of the economy that consists of units that consume and provide funds and labor to business sector. Households purchase goods and services from business sector.

imperfect competition   A market type in which a large number of firms compete with one another by making similar but slightly different products; there is *asymmetrical information*—not all firms know what other firms are doing.

income   Revenues for the period minus the costs for the period.

income statement   Financial statement of a firm showing its revenues, costs, and profit during a given period. Also known as a profit-and-loss statement.

incremental expense cash flow   Additional cash outflows for expenses that result from accepting a *capital budgeting* project.

incremental investment   The additional investment the firm will encounter as a result of implementing a new credit policy.

incremental operating cash costs   The additional cash operating costs that result from the acceptance of a *capital budgeting* project.

incremental sales The additional sales that result from the acceptance of a *capital budgeting* project.

indenture A contract specifying the legal requirements between the bond issuer and the bond holders.

independence No association, or *correlation,* exists between two variables.

inflation Rise in the general price level of all goods and services—or equivalently, a decline in the purchasing power of a unit of money (such as the dollar).

informational signaling An increase in the dividend signals positive information; a decrease signals negative information.

insider trading Process of trading in a company's stock to profit from information that is not available to the public.

installed cash cost Cash expenditure to buy, install, and make operative the item proposed by the *capital budgeting* proposal.

interest coverage ratio Measures the amount of earnings before interest and taxes available to pay interest. Its shortcoming is that earnings are not cash flow.

interest rate The price paid for borrowing money. It is the rate of exchange of present consumption for future consumption, or the price of current dollars in terms of future dollars.

interest rate parity An economic principle that holds that the differential in interest rates between countries is the only determinant of the difference between the spot and forward currency rates.

interim loan A bridge loan until permanent financing is arranged.

internal rate of return (IRR) A time value of money technique that finds the interest rate that equates the present value of cash inflows with the present value of cash outflows.

intraperiod interest rate The annual interest rate divided by the number of compounding periods within one year.

intrinsic value The "real" value that a stock "should" have, based on fundamental factors affecting value.

inventory turnover A ratio used to evaluate the number of times average inventory has been sold during the period.

investment banker A financial organization that specializes in selling newly issued securities. Investment bankers also advise clients on financial matters, negotiate mergers and takeovers, and sell previously issued securities.

investment decisions Decisions pertaining to the selection and diversification of the purchase of assets.

investment goods Additions to the economy's real capital stock) that is, all final purchases of capital equipment (machinery, tools), all construction, both residential and nonresidential, and changes in inventory.

investment grade rating Bond ratings *BBB* (by S&P) or *Baa* (by Moody's) or above.

investment opportunity schedule A graph of the firm's investment projects ranked in order of their rates of return.

investment tax credit (ITC) A tax deduction, approved by the federal income tax statutes, allowed corporations investing in equipment. Politicians approve it and repeal it depending on what they think is good for the economy.

investment turnover The amount of sales that each $1 of investment generates.

investment-type cash flows An initial cash outflow followed by positive cash inflows in future periods.

investments One of the three areas of finance. It deals with the commitment of funds toward the purchase of securities or assets issued by firms, governments, or individuals.

irrelevant cash flow Cash flow that does not change as a result of some specific action.

judgmental forecast A nonstatistical technique that relies on the forecaster's experience or best estimate.

junk bonds Bonds rated below investment grade—rated *BB* (by S&P) or *Ba* (by Moody's) or below.

just-in-time (JIT) inventory system A production and management system in which inventory is cut down to a minimum through adjustments to the time and physical distance between the various production operations.

last-in, first-out (LIFO) A method of inventory accounting in which the newest item in inventory is assumed to be sold first.

lease A contractual agreement between the owner of an asset (lessor) and the user of the asset (lessee), which calls for the lessee to pay the lessor an established lease payment.

line of credit Prearranged agreement with a lender for short-term borrowings on demand under prespecified terms. There is no legal commitment on the part of the lender to provide the stated credit.

liquidation The termination of the firm. Assets are sold and the proceeds are paid to creditors. Any monies remaining after paying creditors is distributed to shareholders.

liquidity A characteristic of a security that refers to its risk, both credit risk and *market risk,* and its marketability. High liquidity requires low risk and high marketability.

liquidity effect   The fall (rise) in the rate of interest caused by an increase (decrease) in the supply of money balances.

loan-type cash flows   An initial cash inflow followed by cash outflows in future periods.

lock box   A post office box address to which credit customers mail payments.

long-term value index (LVI)   The proportion of the stock price that is based on cash flows expected to be received after the first five years.

majority voting   A voting system in which the number of votes a shareholder may cast for any director may not exceed the number of shares owned.

managerial finance   One of the three areas of finance. It deals with management decisions relating to obtaining funds and assets for the firm, controlling costs, and managing the firm's cash flows.

margin of safety   The amount long-term financing exceeds permanent asset investment in current and fixed assets.

market anomalies   Situations in which the *efficient market hypothesis* is not supported.

market portfolio   An imaginary *portfolio* that includes all risky assets in proportion to their market value.

market risk   The risk inherent in the ownership of any security because the market fluctuates. This risk cannot be eliminated.

market structure indicators   Factors that measure actions of the market in terms of highs and lows, breadth, volume, and strength.

market timing   Strategy of varying the proportion of certain types of securities in a portfolio depending on where the investor views the market to be at a particular time.

market value of assets   The value exchanged in an arm's-length transaction between a willing buyer and a willing seller.

materials requirement planning (MRP)   A computerized system for determining inventory requirements and when to place orders.

maximize shareholders' wealth   The theoretical objective management should follow to increase the long-term value of the company's common stock.

Miller-Orr model   A cash management control limit model that allows irregular cash patterns in order to minimize costs of investing in cash.

mini-muni   Municipal bond with a par value of less than $1000.

monetary indicators   Factors that signal monetary changes in the economy which influence stock prices.

monetary policy   Deliberate exercise of a country's monetary authority's (for example, Federal Reserve's) power to induce expansions or contractions in the money supply in order to help dampen the swings of business cycles and bring the nation's output and employment to desired levels.

money market   A market for securities with less than one year to maturity. Typical securities are Treasury bills, repurchase agreements, negotiable certificates of deposit, and bankers' acceptances.

money market preferred stock (MMPS)   *Preferred stock* with a short life that trades in the money market.

money supply   Money is a medium of exchange. The money supply measures the amount of the exchange medium available.

mortgage bond   A bond secured with a lien on real property.

multinational firm   A business with investments and operating facilities in more than one country.

mutual fund   An investment company that issues redeemable shares (sometimes called units) to the public and invests the proceeds in a portfolio of securities.

mutually exclusive   Either-or decision; take one project or the other.

net advantage to leasing   The difference between the cost to purchase the asset and the present value of lease payments.

net cash flow from financing (NCFFF)   Shown in the Statement of Cash Flows as cash generated or reduced from the sales or repurchase of securities used to finance the business or the payment of dividends.

net cash flow from investing (NCFLI)   Shown in the Statement of Cash Flows as cash generated or reduced from the sales or purchases of investment in long-term securities or plant and equipment.

net cash flow from operations (NCFFO)   Shown in the Statement of Cash Flows as cash generated or consumed by the productive activities of a firm over a period of time; represents cash profits.

net present value (NPV)   A time value of money technique that nets the present value of cash inflows against the present value of cash outflows.

net working capital   The excess of current assets over current liabilities. Alternatively, the excess of equity and long-term debt over fixed and other noncurrent assets. As it applies to capital expenditures, it is defined as current assets less noninterest bearing current liabilities that change as a result of a capital budgeting decision.

net worth The ownership interests of common and, perhaps, preferred shareholders in a company; on a balance sheet, equity equals total assets less all liabilities.

neutral financial leverage The effect of debt financing has no effect on shareholders' claims on earnings.

New York Stock Exchange Composite Index Value-weighted price index based on all stocks traded on the New York Stock Exchange. *Value-weighted* means the market value of the firm's equity, relative to the aggregate equity market value of all firms traded on the exchange.

no-growth firm Firm whose investment opportunities simply earn the required market rate.

nominal interest rate The observed rate of interest, uncorrected for inflation. *Nominal* means in name only, and thus is likely not the effective rate of interest.

nonspontaneous financing Financing that has either an explicit or an implicit cost associated with it.

note Medium-term (one to ten years) security. Note holder receives coupon payments.

odd lot The quantity of securities that is less than the established unit for trading.

open market operations Purchases and sales of government securities by the Federal Reserve System. Purchases of securities are expansionary because they add to commercial banks' reserves; sales of securities are contractionary because they reduce commercial banks' reserves.

open market purchase Purchase of shares on the exchanges or in the over-the-counter market without any public announcement.

operating breakeven sales level The point at which the firm's operating revenues equal its operating costs. To compute the breakeven point, costs are divided into fixed and variable components.

operating costs Expenses incurred in operating a business, excluding all financing expenses.

operating cycle The period of time between the acquisition of material, labor, and overhead inputs for production and the collection of sales receipts.

operating lease A lease in which the present value of the lease payments is less than 90% of the initial cost of the asset; the life of the lease is less than 75% of the economic life of the asset; no bargain purchase option exists in the lease; and no transfer of ownership of the lease asset to the user exists.

operating leverage The effect of fixed operating costs on earnings when sales revenue changes.

operating loan Bank credit used to finance a temporary need for working capital funds.

operating return on assets A measure of the productivity of assets on a before tax basis; defined as EBIT ÷ assets.

ordinary annuity A stream of cash flows of equal amount occurring at the end of each period for a specified number of periods.

over-the-counter-market (OTC) Secondary markets conducted by dealers who supply buy-sell quotes on the securities in which they deal. If the securities are listed on an organized exchange, the market is called the *third market.*

payback period A nondiscounted cash flow technique that determines the estimated time it takes to recover the original investment.

payment date Date company actually mails out dividend checks to stockholders.

perfect competition A theoretical state that occurs in markets in which a large number of firms sell an identical product; there are many buyers; there are no restrictions on entry; firms have no advantage over potential new entrants; and all firms and buyers are fully informed about the prices of each and every firm.

perpetuity An investment offering a level stream of cash flows with no maturity date.

point and figure chart A charting device that records every price change of a certain minimum amount, rather than every price change.

points An up-front fee where one point is 1% of the value of the loan.

portfolio A combination of multiple securities that attempt to obtain the best balance between risk and return.

portfolio beta An index representing the undiversifiable risk of a group of stocks formed into a *portfolio.*

portfolio risk The variability associated with a collection of securities grouped into a *portfolio.*

preemptive right A provision in the corporate charter or in state law that allows the existing stockholders to purchase additional shares of stock before they are offered for sale to the public. This allows existing stockholders to maintain their proportionate ownership in the firm.

preferred stock Shares of stock that receive priority over common stock at a fixed rate in the distribution of dividends, or in the distribution of assets if the company is liquidated.

premium The amount by which a bond (or preferred stock) sells above its par value. The security trades at a premium when the coupon rate is above the market rate of interest.

present value annuity factor (PVIFA)　The sum of the present value of $1 amounts, using the *present value formula,* which occurs in periods 1, 2, . . . , n.

present value formula　A formula showing how the current price of an asset is related to its expected future cash flows, through the use of a rate of interest. The formula is $1/(1 + r)^n$ where r is an interest rate and n is time periods.

present value of an annuity due　The value today of a series of constant cash flows for a known number of periods, with the cash flows occurring at the beginning of each period.

present value of growth opportunities (PVGO)　Projects available to a firm that have an expected return in excess of the firm's required market return.

primary market　The market in which the initial sale of securities occur.

principal　An individual who establishes a compensation scheme to motivate an agent to choose activities advantageous to the principal. Shareholders are *principals* of the firm.

principal　The face (or par) value of a bond that must be repaid at maturity.

principal-agent problem　The possibility that an agent will act in her or his own self-interest to the detriment of the principal for whom she or he is acting.

private placement　A securities issue offering made to institutional investors. The securities are not registered with the Securities and Exchange Commission.

production opportunities　The diversion of some present wealth into activities which result in increased future wealth.

profitability index　A discounted cash flow technique that compares the present value of future cash flows to the initial cash outflow.

prospectus　A legal document provided to potential investors in a new securities issue detailing all pertinent facts concerning the securities to be offered.

proxy　A document that a stockholder gives to another party for the purpose of voting the shares.

purchasing power parity　A principle stating that comparable goods should sell for equivalent prices regardless of the currency used to price the goods.

purchasing power risk　The risk that an investment's principal and income will lose their purchasing power because of *inflation.*

pure time value of money　Theoretical interest rate on a long-term, riskless loan, where the interest payments are made solely for the use of someone else's money. In practice, this rate is often approximated by the interest rate on long-term negotiable government bonds.

quick ratio (acid test ratio)　A measure of liquidity, defined as cash, marketable securities, and accounts receivable divided by current liabilities.

range　A crude measure of dispersion defined as the difference between the highest value and the lowest value in a data set.

rate of return　In a financial framework, it is the interest rate that equates the present value of cash returns on an investment with the present value of the cash expenditures relating to the investment.

ratio projection method　The historical proportion of cash to sales to estimate the amount of cash that should be held.

real assets　Land, buildings, plant and equipment, inventories, and consumer durable goods.

real interest rate　The observable *(nominal)* rate of interest minus the rate of *inflation.*

recaptured depreciation　The difference between the selling price of a depreciable asset and its net book value, up to the original cost of the asset.

registered bond　A bond issued with a record name of the owner. Payment is made directly to the registered owner of the bond.

reinvestment (interest rate) risk　Uncertainty about the rate of return that will be earned by future cash flows from an investment.

relevant cash flow　Cash flow that changes as a result of some specific action.

reorganization　A legal process in which all financial claims against the company are settled to reflect the firm's intrinsic value. The firm continues its operations.

reserve requirements　Minimum amount of legal reserves that a bank is required by law to keep behind its deposit liabilities.

return on assets　An accounting based ratio showing the profitability of the book value of assets.

return on beginning equity　An accounting profitability measure, which divides profits by beginning equity shown on the balance sheet.

return on equity　An accounting based ratio showing the return on the book value of equity.

return on sales　A measure of the proportion of each sales dollar that is left after meeting all expenses.

revenue bond　A municipal bond for which the coupon and maturity payments are paid from revenues from a specific revenue-generating project, such as a toll road.

revolving loan　Legally assured *line of credit* with a bank. Interest charged at one rate for the amount used and at a lower rate for the amount not used.

risk   Quantitative measurement of an outcome, such as a gain or loss; the chance of an outcome.

risk aversions   It is a dislike for risk. Higher risk requires higher expected return.

risk-free rate   The interest rate for an asset that is virtually riskless. For example, debt issued by the government maturing in one year has a precisely predictable rate of return for one year.

risk premium   The actual return on a security minus the risk-free rate of return.

round lot   A unit of trading of a security.

S&P 500 Index   A value-weighted price index made up of 500 large companies traded on the New York Stock Exchange. *Value-weighted* means the market value of the firm's equity, relative to the aggregate equity market value of all firms traded on the exchange.

salvage value   The resale value of an asset.

salvage value tax adjustment   The calculation of income taxes on an asset that is sold for either more or less than its depreciated book value.

secondary market   Securities markets that handle transactions in existing securities. Often contrasted with *primary market*.

secured loan   Financing that is backed by the pledge of some asset. In liquidation, the secured creditor receives the cash from the sale of the pledged asset to the extent of the loan value.

securitization of accounts receivable   Substitution of tradable financial securities for privately negotiated accounts receivable.

security interest   A legal term meaning a lender has a secured interest in an asset. Unsecured lenders cannot look to the secured asset for repayment.

semistrong-form efficiency   Market condition in which current prices not only reflect all informational content of historical prices but also reflect all publicly available knowledge about the firm under study.

sentiment indicators   Factors that attempt to measure the buying and selling psychology of investors.

shelf registration   Securities and Exchange Commission Rule 415, which allows companies to register all securities they plan to issue over the following two years. The companies then file short statements when they wish to sell any part of these securities during the period.

sample discount   The difference between the future value and present value when simple interest is used.

simple interest   Interest computed by multiplying the original principal by the percent of interest by the time period involved. It is paid when the loan matures.

specialist   Broker to the brokers.

sponsored ADR   ADR issued by a single depository institution.

spontaneous asset   An asset that increases or decreases as sales increase or decrease.

spontaneous financing   Those liabilities such as accounts payable and accrued wages that arise automatically, without negotiation, in the course of doing business.

spontaneous liability   A liability that increases or decreases as sales increase or decrease.

spot exchange rate   The rate at which one currency can be converted into another, or the price of one currency in terms of another. For example, if the price of the German mark were $0.25 per mark, it would require $0.25 to purchase one mark or four marks to purchase $1.

spread   In *underwriting,* the difference between the price that the underwriter pays the company for the new securities and the price at which the securities are sold to the public or are privately placed.

stakeholders   Claimants on cash flows of the firm.

standard deviation   A statistic used to measure dispersion about an expected value. A high (low) standard deviation is associated with high (low) risk. It is the square root of the variance.

standby credit   A *term loan* that matures at the expiration date of the loan. It cannot be paid down and reused again without being renegotiated.

statement of cash flows   An accounting statement that traces the sources and uses of cash as a result of organizational activity.

stock dividend   A dividend paid in securities rather than cash.

stock exchange   A physical location where securities trade like at an auction. Securities are always bought by the highest bidders and sold by the lowest offerers.

stock market   The financial market for trading claims (shares) of a firm.

stock split   The division of a corporation's outstanding shares into a larger number of shares.

straight bond value   That component of a callable bond that acts like an ordinary bond.

strategic decisions   The set of decisions resulting in the formulation and implementation of strategies, or plans, designed to achieve the objectives of the organization.

stretching accounts payable   Failing to pay within the prescribed trade credit period.

strong-form efficiency   Market condition in which no information that is available, be it public or private, can be used to earn superior investment returns consistently.

sunk costs   Cash flow expended in the past.

surplus (saving) units   Net savers, who save more than they spend. The *household sector* is considered a net surplus sector.

sustainable growth   Growth the firm can maintain over time given its dividend policy, financing policy, asset management performance, and profitability of sales.

tactical decisions   The set of decisions designed to carry out daily activities so as to meet strategic objectives.

tangible assets   Physical assets such as plant and equipment.

tax-loss carryovers   Taxable losses carried forward into future years to offset tax liability of those years.

tender offer   A publicly announced offer to buy the stock of a firm directly from its shareholders.

term loan   A loan with a maturity greater than one year.

term structure of interest rates   The relationship between yield and time to maturity of a debt security.

terminal nonoperating cash flows   Cash flow occurring at the end of the investment's life; included are *salvage value,* taxes on sale of asset, and liquidation of all net working capital associated with the investment.

terminal value   The value of cash flows compounded forward to some later time at an appropriate interest rate.

third market   Over-the-counter trading of securities that are listed on organized exchanges.

time deposit   Bank accounts and other deposits that earn a higher interest than savings accounts but which must be left on deposit for a specified period of time (their maturity).

time preference rate   Human desire for a good in the present as opposed to the future. The rate is reflected by the price people are willing to pay for immediate possession of the good, as opposed to the price they are willing to pay for future possession.

time value of money   A principle stating that dollars at different points in time can only be directly compared when they are first adjusted by the interest rate representing the opportunity cost of money.

timeliness   Indicator used by Value Lines Investment Services to signify the potential price changes in stocks.

total debt-to-equity ratio   A measure of financial leverage risk, defined as total debt divided by shareholders' equity.

total risk   Diversifiable risk + nondiversifiable risk.

trades on the equity   The use of debt to increase the expected return on equity.

trading   The buying and selling of securities to take advantage of price swings.

trading post   Place on the exchange floor where a company's stock trades.

treasury stock   Common stock that has been repurchased by the company that originally issued it.

trend analysis   A variable of interest is analyzed against time.

Treynor index   A measure of reward per unit of risk. It indicates the rate of return on the market index required to make the expected rate of return on a portfolio equal to the risk-free rate.

underwriting   A guarantee by investment banking firms to an issuing corporation that a definable sum of money will be paid on a specified date for the issue of stocks or bonds.

unfavorable financial leverage   Negative effects of debt financing on shareholders' claims on earnings.

unlevered firm   A firm financed entirely with equity financing.

unsecured loan   Financing that requires no assets as collateral but allows the lender a general claim against the borrower, rather than a lien against specific assets.

unsponsored ADR   *ADR* issued by more than one depository institution.

valuation   The worth of an economic asset.

value of unlevered firm   Value of a firm that is financed entirely with equity.

variable cost   A cost that moves directly with a firm's output, rising as output increases over a full range of production. Examples: Raw materials and sales commissions.

variance   A statistic that measures dispersion about the expected value. A high (low) variance is associated with high (low) risk. It is the *standard deviation* squared.

vertical analysis   Common-size analysis that compares accounts in the income statement to net sales and amounts in the balance sheet to total assets.

weak-form efficiency   Market condition in which current prices reflect all information that is contained in the historical sequence of prices.

weighted average cost of capital   The minimum rate of return that is acceptable on new nonrisk changing investments in order to maintain the value of the firm.

window dressing   Making financial statements appear more favorable than they really are.

Yankee bond   A foreign bond denominated in U.S. dollars.

yield curve   A pictorial representation of the *term structure of interest rates.*

yield to maturity (YTM)   Percentage figure reflecting the effective yield on a bond, based on the difference between its purchase and redemption prices, and any returns received by the bondholder in the interim.

zero balance account (ZBA)   A demand deposit account that has a zero balance at the end of the day. Checks presented against the account are covered by funds transferred from another account.

zero coupon security   A note or bond that earns no annual interest payments. The difference between the purchase price and the par value at maturity represents interest to the holder.

Topic Index

Company Index